THE RAINBOW'S END

THE RAINBOW'S END

The National Library of Poetry

Diana Zeiger, Editor

The Rainbow's End

Library of Congress
Cataloging in Publication Data

ISBN 1-57553-005-8

Manufactured in The United States of America by
Watermark Press
11419 Cronridge Dr., Suite 10
Owings Mills, MD 21117

Editor's Note

It has been said many times, in many ways, "There is nothing new under the sun." Many scholars have advanced the notion that there are only seven or so basic literary themes, and that all poems, novels, and short stories are based upon these prototypes.

Yet a man named Thomas Berger has been quoted as saying, "Why do writers write? Because it isn't there." And of course, reams of new written material are produced each and every day.

Where does the truth lie? Each observation has at least a grain of truth; surely there must be some happy medium. The search for that middle ground has provoked many a lively debate, and no doubt will continue to do so.

Perhaps the best way to begin the discussion is to define "good" or "successful" writing — for the purposes of this particular anthology, *The Rainbow's End*, "good" or "successful" poetry. Aside from such obvious criteria as following the parameters of a particular poetic form (should the poet choose to express his or her ideas in a standardized form), a successful poem communicates an idea from the artist to the reader. The easiest way to do this is to take some notion, experience, or situation, that is likely to be common — even universal — so that the reader can relate to it and have some frame of reference.

But if this subject is universal, one might ask, is it not a cliché? I say that the talent of the artist in question is what keeps a work from becoming trite. The poet's ability to find a fresh phrase, a new simile, a comparison that has not been thought of before (but is nevertheless totally apt) is what marks the difference between the hackneyed and the unique.

Christina Padilla's "Reunion: Abuelita Padilla Y Tia Dominga" ("Abuelita" is an affectionate diminutive of "Grandmother"; "Tia" means "Aunt") takes an idea with which many of us are familiar—the comparison of human lives with the cycle of seasons — and looks at it with a slightly different perspective. "Reunion: Abuelita Padilla Y Tia Dominga," which is the Grand Prize-winning poem in the contest connected with *The Rainbow's End*, is set at a family gathering. Two old women (Abuelita Padilla and Tia Dominga) have made what is most likely their first trip from Spain to America, where they meet their many descendants. The old women speak no English, and the narrator of the poem speculates as to what they are thinking while they are "bound in Spanish silence." Ms. Padilla describes the women as "the winter of our family": they are "like two / bare, knarled trees, stark against a pale / snowy sky"; they are also as silent as winter.

Perhaps, Ms. Padilla suggests, they are recalling their earlier days, "when their faces were / petal-fresh and hope ripened in their / spring hearts." Or maybe they are thinking of the bounty of those years when, as the olives and grapes ripened in the Spanish summer, so too were their lives the fullest.

Like the seasons, however, the cycle of life moved on. "[T]hings began detaching / themselves" from these two matriarchal trees, whether through death or by emigration to America, as leaves scatter in the autumn.

Finally, we are brought back to the present, where from their vantage point of youth, the children at the reunion regard the old women from a distance as far as that of April from December. Across the huge gap of age and language, the young ones

look on the winter mothers like
impossibilities —
nothing could be so old.

Ms. Padilla's poem has taken ideas which are likely to be familiar to us all, but through the careful choice of words and images, has made her extended metaphor both graceful and fresh.

Another poem in this anthology which uses familiar themes to new effect is Christina Aldridge's "The 1982nd Serpent." (p. 138) This poem is about the loss of innocence (through, it is suggested in the poem, sexual abuse); throughout the poem, images are used of the archetypal loss of innocence: Adam and Eve in the Garden of Eden. Both the topic and the images Ms. Aldridge uses are disturbing, even shocking, but the skill with which she uses this literary conceit marks "The 1982nd Serpent" as a truly successful work.

The reader is immediately introduced to the innocence of the persona as well as the Biblical allusions:

He gave us apple juice to drink,
in baby bottles,
and told us to suck out every last drop, until it was finished.

Like the Serpent in the Garden of Eden, the evil presence in this poem tempts the persona (traditional interpretations suggest that the Serpent tempted Eve with an apple); like Adam and Eve, the narrator of this poem is truly innocent. Although, in this case, partaking of the fruit itself is not the instrument of the Fall, it is a prelude to it.

The abuser is given many of the attributes of the Serpent — the pain he inflicts is compared to that of fangs, and the image of "his sandpaper tongue rasping / in the air high above my head" is evocative of a snake. In addition, he possesses some of the omnipotence of God. The narrator tries to hide after the sin is committed (though it is not truly her sin), in the same way that Adam and Eve tried to hide after their own. But the abuser "spie[s] our naked heads" and follows behind, to mete out further punishment. In the guise of a caring guardian, he tucks them into bed, using this as an excuse "to make sure we'd changed." This phrase carries sinister implications, hinting that the abuser is ensuring that not only have garments been changed, but so has the narrator's body.

With "The 1982nd Serpent," Christina Aldridge has crafted a searingly intense poem that uses familiar images to illuminate the details of a particularly loathsome experience. Thus, though the reader may not have endured similar situations, he or she is still able to empathize.

Empathy is the key to understanding other poems in this collection, such as Rosemary Waikuny's "Images Of Mother Past"(p. 266), Katherine Avinger's "Grape Juice Tears" (p. 367), and Christiana Muntzel's "Skinny" (p. 129). The first two are the reflections of the poems' respective personas, and each uses familiar images of childhood and its pain and pleasure to embody the personas' thoughts. "Skinny," on the other hand, conjures up the pain an adolescent girl feels as she leaves her childhood behind.

In "Grape Juice Tears," the narrator describes feelings of inadequacy, and compares these feelings to those of a child who has committed some grave (in the context of childhood) error. These emotions must be kept in check, in order to avoid displeasing others: she begs, as children have begged since time immemorial,

> *Please Don't Be Mad.*
>
> *I clench my teeth, grip tightly to my truth,*
> *try to balance it quietly in both hands the way they taught me*
> *to hold the juice cups in preschool.*

At the moment, though, the persona is not having much success at controlling these wayward emotions. Ultimately, like the child who has made a mistake, she must "'fess up;" she finds, also like that child, that the reaction is not so bad as she had feared:

> *...I spill myself out to you,*
> *All Over You...*
> *and you Thank me.*

"Images Of Mother Past" is a tribute lovingly paid. The narrator recalls scenes from her childhood, as well as the succor that was given her by her mother — her mother's reassuring presence when she was ill ("When my eardrum bangs inside my head your strong arms cradle me press / me against your lilac-scented body"), and the times her mother played with her when she was rejected by other children. To the narrator, her mother was the ultimate comforting presence, and though she is now grown up and there may be surface differences, she has followed her mother's example: "I feel my spine is just like yours."

Christiana Muntzel's "Skinny" explores the mind of a girl who suffers from anorexia. This girl is trying to deny her own reality and mortality; she starves herself as a part of this denial:

> *she watches her wiry shadow dance*
> *and fancies herself a fairy's child,*
> > *exempt from mortal rituals*
> > *like meals and menstruation;*
> > *strong and somehow magical,*
> > *transformed by deprivation.*

Although she wishes that she could remain in this state forever, deep down she knows this cannot be:

> *she laments that it cannot last;*
> *standing on a scale every day, she despairs*
> *for the skinnier days of the past...*

Unless one has experienced an illness such as anorexia oneself, it is practically impossible to understand the sufferer's mental processes. However, by presenting the character's thoughts of and wishes for magic, as well as the fear of growing up — things most of us have thought of, wished for, or feared at some time or another — Ms. Muntzel has given us, as readers, something within this girl's mind with which we can relate.

Other poems of note within this anthology are "Through A Single Speculum" (p. 182), by Jill Holtz; "The Blue Eye Of The Universe" (p. 445), by Joseph Jesuit; "Janis Joplin Have You Ever Been To Reno?" (p. 344), by Mark G. Koetting; "Devour Me Divine" (p. 306), by Magdalena Rose Kohanna; "The Message The Mongoose Never Delivered" (p. 79), by Jessica Riley, and "Parent's Parent's Place" (p. 284), by Rainee S. Shelton. I urge you to seek out all these poems and read them with special attention.

There are scores of poems in *The Rainbow's End* which deserve to be commended. I wish that time and space allowed me to present a detailed examination of every poem included in this anthology, but as they do not, I would simply like to salute everyone who contributed to this volume.

I would also like to thank the Staff at the National Library of Poetry. *The Rainbow's End* is the culmination of the efforts of numerous individuals whose contributions were vital to the production of this publication. Many, many thanks to all the editors, judges, graphic and layout artists, customer service representatives, and office administrators who participated in the production of this anthology.

Congratulations to all those featured in *The Rainbow's End*. I hope you will enjoy reading it as much as I have enjoyed editing it.

Diana Zeiger, Editor

Cover Art: Tim Kelly

Grand Prize Winner

Christina Padilla/Mount Pleasant, MI

Second Prize

Christina Aldridge/Seattle, WA
Katherine Avinger/Apex, NC
Jill Holtz/Pittsburgh, PA
Joseph Jesuit/East Moline, IL
Mark Koetting/San Francisco, CA

Magdalena Kohanna/Warner Robins, GA
Christiana Muntzel/Bethesda, MD
Jessica Riley/Saratoga Springs, NY
Rainee Shelton/Hillsboro, OH
Rosemary Waikuny/Jackson Heights, NY

Third Prize

Lauren Anderson/Hartsville, SC
Jules Brandell/Shorewood, WI
Michael Brandt/San Diego, CA
Scott Buster/Austin, TX
William Cain/Alpharetta, GA
P. Chandler/Santa Rosa, CA
Troy Davis/Ripon, CA
J. Michael Deerfield/Dallas, TX
Katherine Edwards/Charlotte, NC
Adam Finley/Auburn, IA
Teresha Freckleton/Gainesville, FL
Earl Gillanders/Oxford, OH
D. C. Goedel/Pleasanton, CA
Christine Heurkins/Burbank, CA
Sandra Hudgins/Oklahoma City, OK
William Johnson/San Diego, CA
Nyuka Laurent/Bondville, VT
Jeremy Lee/Florence, AZ
Mildred Lightfoot/Prince George, VA
Nell Lindenmeyer/Farmington, NM
Wayne Lockwood/Decatur, IL
Scott Mackenzie/Suisun, CA
Cindy Mercurio/Hoboken, NJ
Wojtek Migdalski/Manchester, MA
Brian Morrow/Richardson, TX
K. A. Mossey/Sterling, VA
Treva Myatt/Toledo, OH
Eric Nelson/Concord, CA
Meghan Nuding/Hoboken, NJ
Maiko Ochi/Lynwood, WA

Sheenagh O'Rourke/New York, NY
Renuka Pant/Austin, TX
Sherry Philpott/Winter Park, FL
Charles Potts/Mitchellville, MD
Sabrina Ramet/Seattle, WA
Barbara Reid/Cottonport, LA
Cindy Rivers/Byron, GA
Shawn Roberson/Loretto, PA
Justin Rouse/Indianapolis, IN
Zoe Savitsky/San Francisco, CA
Vincent Sheehan/Phoenix, AZ
Laura Spalding/Highland Park, IL
Kevin Still/El Dorado, AR
Robin Stone/Houston, TX
Kim Susedik/Spokane, WA
Margaret Swoager/Jacksonville, FL
Shane Tanzymore/Lansdowne, PA
Lori Tout/Three Rivers, MI
Alan Wayne/Jamesville, NY
Sylvia Weinberg/Louisville, KY
Michal Weiser/Towson, MD
Linda Welch/Odessa, TX
K. Haley Whipple/Richmond, VA
Elyse Whitmore/Montclair, NJ
Linda Williams-Avila/Hercules, CA
Thomas Wolf/Bangor, PA
MH Wylde/Santa Maria, CA
Judith Yaker/Bloomfield Hills, MI
Charles Ziavras/Lowell, MA

Congratulations also to our Editor's Choice Winners!

Grand Prize Winner

Reunion: Abuelita Padilla Y Tia Dominga
They are the winter of our family,
the old women bound in Spanish silence, like two
bare, gnarled trees, stark against a pale
snowy sky. They watch us, unspeaking,
from behind thick glasses, their eyes distorted and

huge, maybe remembering when their faces were
petal-fresh and hope ripened in their
spring hearts, before the coming of summer
when their bodies matured with the olives
and the grapes and their dreams were born into

their joyous midst, before the autumn began
and their raven hair went silver with the
golding leaves, before things began detaching
themselves, like dying husbands or children scattering
to the winds, before coming to America and

meeting these hundreds of great-grandchildren
whose language is unintelligible
and who look on the winter mothers like
impossibilities—
nothing could be so old.
                    —Christina Padilla

Ode To My Toad

You are the strangest cat I've ever known,
Your presence simulates a "cat cyclone."
Your piercing voice is always far too loud,
But you keep on meowing-acting oh-so proud.
Your vision is lacking...so is all your luck,
If it can fit...your head is getting stuck!
Your basic need - canned food six times a day,
Is this just so you can trip me on the way?
You crave attention, demand it day and night,
But if I pet...you turn around and bite!
I confess there have been times I didn't know,
Just exactly where I wanted you to go.
But you stick to me like glue, you never nap,
Can't your love for me at least include a lap?
Your devotion was quite clear right from the start,
But just how do you expect to win my heart?
You fight and spray - tail twitching all the time,
It's the Miles Meigs way of saying that "you're mine."
Sometimes I cuss the reasons that you're here,
And then you kiss me and I have to call you dear.

Cindy Meigs

Find Me Not

You will never know me - not the way you desire.
Your hands will never reach the center of my fire.
Your eyes will always read the outside of my book.
But through my rough edged pages your mind will never look.
And when you want to touch me - my skin you'll always find,
But you will never feel my heart beating inside.
You will always recognize the sound of my voice,
But never will you comprehend the meaning it brings forth.
And if your lips should ever meet mine,
And we engage in a passionate kiss for a time,
Understand, it's my nectar that you won't find.
And if our bodies do become one -
Realize it was lust that pushed me my love-
You have not won.

Cynthia Leigh Chadwick

I Remember

I think of you and remember,
Your face appears in my mind and without my wanting to,
   I remember...
The memories come flooding back, and I remember...
Your smile filters through my dreams,
Your eyes I can just recall; and then I remember...
Your voice I hear calling; your presence I feel,
   and then I remember...
I remember... that I'll never see your face again,
Never watch your eyes light up when you smile;
Your voice will never again call my name.
And then I remember,
You'll never truly be gone; cause I know, I will always remember.

Amanda Ray

Make Your Mark

I don't know but I've been told
You have let your love for life grow cold
If I were you I'd live life for what it's worth
And somehow make a mark on the earth
Do what you need to do and say what you have to say
And when you feel confused don't forget to pray
Please don't take life for granted and remember you're the one
Who can make it boring or you can make it fun
Remember to be the nicest you can be
And then you can say "I made a mark" in life and it's "me"

Cindy Platt

Pain Killer

I am facing you— you, with you cold eyes,
Your cruel words, and empty heart.
I see you and think
I can live without you.
I can live without you.

You, who beat me, and drug me down.
You, who forced me to love you,
Then made me pay for my devotion.
I can live without you.
I can live without you.

I believed the books of lies.
I cried the rivers of tears.
I let myself die a thousand deaths.
I can live without you.
I can live without you.

So I say goodbye.
Your words mean nothing now,
For I belong to me, and not you.
I can live without you.
I can live without you.

Emily Jorgensen

"And"

And how the warm summer sunbeams stroke
your cool brown hair
And your complexion is so deep
And your eyes sparkle like a field of diamonds,
And are as brown as a wild stallion.
And your smile is like a warm embrace.
The way you look at me with your soft,
kind eyes makes me realize how much
I love you.

Your hands are soft yet rough,
And they have such a tender touch,
they make me warm all over,
will you be my lover?

Your secure arms hold me so tight
and keep me warm all throughout the night.
And you soft sweet voice calls out my name
And I know I'll be with you always.

Christina Rieber

The Future

If you look out into the misty sea,
You will not believe what your eyes will find:
Bewildering shadows, a mystery,
Sights of terror— a wish to be blind.

For on those dark and dangerous waters
Great monsters search for the unsuspecting.
Hiding behind enduring rock towers—
Waiting for the confused and trembling.

Those who wander past are forever caught.
And to the web of futility they go;
Never to overcome the battles fought—
New victims to life's overwhelming flow.

Daggers and swords cannot slay these dragons.
Only a courageous heart will survive.
So look beyond the mist, past the demons—
And behold, at the end you will arrive.

Deborah Vogel

Mother Martha

You are magnificent in every way,
you were with me through everyday.
You clothed me with happiness that I can't describe,
you taught me of God, whom will lift us on high.
You gave me a family, I thank you for that,
you gave me good schooling, and that is a fact.
But there is only one thing which I am truly thankful for,
you may not have been the one who brought me into this world,
but when I met you,
you reopened the door.

Amanda Koeller

How Often?

How often did we sit and think about what we had going?
You say,
"If only I had played my card straight."
And
How often did we sit and reminisce about the past?
You cry,
"If only time would allow us the moment again."
And,
How often did we share our joys,
   Our dreams,
Our laughter,
   Our love,
Our pains.
How often did we?
   How often?
And I say,
"If only it would have been that way."

Charmaine Jennings

My Love

You're like a little buttercup,
you keep my love soaring up and up.
If I could win you as I would like to do,
I would feel like a millionaire, even when I despair.

It is my heart's greatest appeal,
To have you know just how I feel,
I yearn someday, to take you away,
To the land of flowers,
That would then be ours.

Will you not answer my little prayer
And say that you will soon be there?
In our first little meeting place,
Where love first dawned upon my face,
It is only then that I could say,
My happiness will live from day to day.

Carl H. Clawson

The Presence Of Love

With every sentence you can feel the love. If it is there
you hear it in the voice, you can feel it in the touch.
No one has ever been loved so much. It's too big to contain,
without your presence I can not remain.
My life is a shambles if from you I refrain. Seems the pain
Is so deep the tears fall like rain. Stay close beside me
So my life won't be all pain.
Sometimes the darkness engulfs me so I know not the way.
But without a light we might all fall by the way. You can
Lead me your way or send me away, but with you my heart
Will always stay, for I love you darling more each day.

Frances S. Wiles

Unwanted Love

You can wash away rain,
You can wash away tears,
But you can't wash away the emotion he fears.
The feeling that sticks deep down inside,
The emotion of "Love" that cost him his pride.
All those good-byes and everlasting lies,
Love is what caused all those breakdowns and cries.

Half-hearted love is the worst kind of all,
When your spouse don't care about nothing at all.
He thought it would last,
He thought he would win,
But love is so powerful it puts you through sin!

Cheryl Calderone

Memories

You truly are a gift from God as is your brother John.
You both have blessed your Dad and me as years have come and gone.

But now the spotlight is on you, your coming wedding day.
So let us walk down mem'ry lane and reminisce, okay?

Remember games "Come here" and such that you and I would play?
We had some fun, but more than that, they taught you to obey.

A frosty igloo made of snow we built in winter's cold.
You worked so hard and long to make a haunted house unfold.

I'll ne'er forget the flowers wild you brought to me with pride.
But best of all I fondly 'call the stereo surprise.

Now life moves on and there will be new mountains you will climb
But true success comes from the Lord who gave you gifts and time.

No matter what the day may bring stand tall with head held high.
Good times and bad together bring the strength that must arise.

The future holds so many hopes for you and your new bride
As you seek wisdom from above for truly He will guide.

Hold on, my son, to memories that stand the test of time
For one day you and your new bride will build memories sublime.

I hope that you can plainly see these words are meant to say
I'm proud to be your Mom today, and plan to stay that way.

Christine A. Corcoran

Ode To My Lord

You are in the wind that whispers my name,
You are in the sun that shines in fame,
You are in the sky of blue,
from this we know your love is true.
You are my one and only true Lord,
you keep us from evil, you are our sword.
You are watching me as I write
This is because we are always in your sight
You are in every mothers womb,
You are in every flowers bloom,
You are the beauty of day,
And for all this we say,
   We love you Lord.

Brianne Miskie

The Reflection

   I see myself standing here,
Without a thought, without a fear,
I see my reflection as bright as day,
Whispering words I'd like to say,
Nothing I can say or do,
Will make this darkened day, blue,
If I had one chance to be,
I would be walking along the deep blue sea,
Being alone and free.

April Buckley

4

Untitled

To this dark threshold all roads have led,
Yet I fear to part the seal.
What will be lost as the portal is crossed,
Knowledge, love, anger, shame and fear?
Will I still witness the horrors I've seen
On the bloody sands of the South China Sea?
Could joy with pain and hatred be lost,
like teardrops shed in a dreary rain?
Memories are mine, or are they me?
Have I truly seen what I perceived?
Will there be a silence where I once went?
Will any reflect how our paths once crossed?
The knocking is near, and the past is barred,
So concede time must to life's demand,
And pass through this frame for another path.
A Comrade yet waits I've not yet seen.
He has tarried long at the grand gateway,
So thoughts and feelings lost or along
Are set aside as I take a last breath.
Open, for I put the slug-horn to my lips.

Claud Edward Jones

Untitled

Love and Hate both mean something different,
Yet, go together by fate
Love means Peace
Hate means war
Why is Hate on the Earth for
Love is to Win
Hate is to Sin
When you say you hate
Think before you make that human mistake
Because if and when you have gone to the kingdom of our Lord
And Love is how you lived your earth life before
Then you have just won a greater gift then Hate and War
You have just won what Jesus Christ died for

Danielle Harris

Dreams

Dreams are forever in your heart
Yet for me they always seem to part

For dreams are like a drug;
An addiction but like all drugs;
Dreams do not last.
I know this for all my dreams are in the past.

Still I ask forgiveness for what I've done
For this dream has just begun!

Christina Garcia

A Middle Kid's Message

If the truth be told,
Would it be believed?

If tears be shed in its behalf,
Whether they be out of love, pity,
Or the mere fact that the fantasy's been all shot to hell,
Do it while my back is turned.
It's better not knowing the reason.

Use it
As a reminder to those that hear;
A lesson for those who follow.

Remember me
As the laughing child,
And loving woman at your side...

I lie somewhere in between.

Dana A. Hamilton

Transiency

Standing beneath the sky
worshiping the Sacred Ground
calling upon the feathered sun
to heal my nightly wounds
I see myself
a thousand years ago
drinking the echo of your voice inside my throat
Blood pounding in my head
floating through my veins
I run
brandishing the truth, my truth
Wounded forehead, the name
My name
travels through the possibility of your soul
and the vastness of a drum call
Life after life, the pain
and the weight of our tribal past awaiting in
the clouds
The circle dance completes the you, the I
Ancient arrows flying from our hands...

Agnes T. Ruiz-Lòpez

Kid

Be true to yourself, don't worry 'bout me,
Work hard, play hard, be all you can be.

Don't ever give up whenever you're down,
Pick yourself up, go another round.

Life's not easy when people are cruel,
Learn to shrug your shoulders, try to keep your cool.

Do what you can and be happy you tried,
Don't set the world on fire, just keep a flame inside.

May God be your God, love be your guide,
Desiderata your credo, a mate by your side.

The wind at your back, the sun in the sky,
Ducks within range, a springer standing by.

What more can I say, what more can there be?
Strive to be happy, then you'll plainly see.

Be true to yourself, that's really the key,
Work hard, play hard, be all you can be.

Bill Hammer

Footsteps

Steps,
words unspoken,
time spun in perilous waste.
Love's lost emotion.
Rivers run dry from overflowing sand
which flows freely from my hands,
Falling softly to the ocean below.
Seagulls cry in the desert,
echoing my love's lost words
in the folds of endless time.
Those first perilous steps of emotion t'wards the sun...
rising,
setting,
Conquering.

Aimee Prisbrey

Sound And Light

No one knows the consequences
When sound is darkened by silence
No one knows if they're fighting right
If dark is louder than the light
And no one knows if they're homeward bound
If the air is lower than the ground.

Andrea Wells

Minutes

Sometimes minutes step with
Wooden legs, their swishing knees
Clumsily clanging the seconds together.

Other times, minutes march in perfect
Formation, swelling their precision
Chests with pride.

Only yesterday, I watched the mad medley
Of furious minutes dashing wildly toward
The destination of an hour.

Barbara R. Reid

To My Parents

I am product of you
without you I am nothing
Because of you I am something
You inspire me
You make me cry
With you I laugh

Because of you I will go
Somewhere that is good
You taught me all that I should know
and all that I should fear

Because of you I know of love
I feel the joy
the sorrow
the anger

You created me when you could have destroyed me
You loved when you could have hated
You taught when you could have ignored

I make you proud
You make me strong
My protectors, my parents, my friends

Elizabeth Kalfayan

The Red Parka

Yesterday my daughter left for the first time
   without holding my hand or tearfully turning back
for one last kiss or irrepressible hug, walking the path
   to the school, alone. I tracked her journey up Laurel Hill,
moving soundlessly, until our parallel paths parted at the ridge
   where eyes could not go. The heart as seeker stretched
toward her, elastic in its trust and fear, as she bounded
   to the top of the hill, with arms raised, straining
for balance and attention, soaring, rapt, toward the glistening
   hawthorne fields, the bumper blackberries she'd snatch
with pure spirit along the way, as cows watched, mothers
   and newborns, serene sentinels in reverent gaze at her face,
petal-bright rose, bent sunlit on its bowed stem, angling with
   theirs. How often had we passed this scene before, but now
amazed, she bent over them, like a kind of holiness, whispering,
   "Welcome to the world!" I waited on the road to meet her -
how the sky beamed, as if suddenly opening its eyes.

Mornings feel strangely different - unanchored, perilously
   limp in this unyielding change, since the red parka vanished
from my sight, crossing the main road and the threshold of home.

Beatrice Lazarus

Love

With little words for a strong meaning
With a light touch of sweet melodies.
With strong meanings to meet thy heart
With sweet soft words to comfort
I come forward to enter my thoughts and to bring joy
I bring a gift to show my kindness
I bring a special gift of my true love

Felicia Hawkins

Just Us

Criminal justice is exactly that
...within the system, it serves and protects
Just who it defends is based on the fact
that shrouded intents exploit wrong effects
Its judicial arms embrace criminals
by sanctioning rights free men never get
Though in for murder, assault, or scandals,
these individuals seldom regret
Instead they're rewarded at our expense
with lawyers, doctors...(how can we compete?)
Even if punished, oh what a sentence...
before you know it, they're back on the street!
If they're caught again...so what, "Justice" works...
they'll find protection within the system
With all that it offers in premier perks,
lucky for them they're not the poor victim
Take it from us who have been victimized
...my wife, my daughter, and I sought justice
But when they failed us, we then realized
there never was support...oh no, just us

Bob G. Martinez

"The Land Of Enchantment"

I walk along the desert trails,
With rolling hills and cottontails.
I marvel at the things I see,
The yucca, the sagebrush, the mesquite tree.

Rattlesnakes and scorpions abound,
Watch your step as you amble around!
Gila monsters and lizards bask in the sun,
While jackrabbits and horned toads scamper in fun.

And when the day is almost done,
The sky's on fire from the setting sun.
Such magnificent colors to behold,
Yellow, orange, red, and gold.

It's not a dull and lifeless place,
As you might first believe.
For if you take a closer look,
A wondrous land you will perceive.

Brian Morris

Call To Freedom

Confinement to super structured buildings
With mortar and plexiglass windows, floors of shiny mosaic tile,
Holding schedules passed down from the top;
These grinding restrictions stifled my soul
I silently shouted, FREE ME A WHILE!
So my psyche tripped out, over gates hung on concrete fences
To devour a wished-for world,
Where friendly clouds met expectation,
The thickets on curved country paths
Rustled briskly in my passing
That led to a field of wild-flowers, blossoming
Fast food chain for butterflies and bees;
This brought me to a budding forest
That drink from a mountain-fed creek
Where a myriad of fish dodged boulders
Embedded in a smooth gravel bottom
A plush greening pasture came in view
Readying to hail coming of unborn cattle;
Through invisible shutters mind escaped the city,
O, that self could not have gone too is such a pity.

Charles H. Henderson

Conversation With Jesus!

I've been laying on my bed
With all kinds of thoughts running through my head.
I just can't seem to get to sleep,
Memories keep coming from way down deep.
My age will soon be sixty-five
And I guess I'm lucky to be alive.
I think of some of the things I've shared
And lost of folks that I knew who cared.
I've met lots of people over the years,
We've shared laughter and sunshine and a lot of tears.
I've got a lot to be thankful for and, dear Lord, I know it,
So, when folks needed help, I tried to bestow it.
There were times when I didn't know if I could survive,
But, here I am, Jesus, you've kept me alive.
I've come a long way since the days of my youth,
Your loving spirit has taught me the truth.
When I'd think I was lost and had no one to care,
You'd send me a friend who my burden would share.
So I send you my thanks and all of my love,
For watching over me from heaven above.

Ethel M. Pocius

Waterfall

She rushed down the mountain hitting the rocks
with a loud crash.

Her splash danced, leaving the mist of a rain cloud.

The trees were enhanced by her spray.

Cooling driblets blanketed, a refreshing,
tingling feeling soothed.

The rocks on the edge, heaven's rocks,
were the clouds.

Jagged edges became a soft, mellow, and tranquil glow.

Sunlight twinkled. Crisp water shimmered and sparkled,
radiating delight.

She slapped the rocks, making her presence known.
They turned her life.

She rushed down to peacefulness, and suddenly stopped.
The sun took control and whispered softly.

He could not be with her forever.
He would warm her now.

Perhaps again tomorrow. She basked in the now.

She softly said hello, and watched him set.

Majestic colors of goodbye warmed. She continued on her journey.

Barbara L. Blair

Cody

Sometimes he will stand and look at me and then our eyes will meet
   with a few quick steps and to my surprise he's walking on my feet.
Those big brown eyes will disarm you or maybe a faint subtle frown
   which just widens to a smile and he's just a little clown.

How can I describe him? What can I say?
   about this little fellow who steals my day away.
He's just a little con man, he really knows his stuff
   he'll pout and smile and dance about, a diamond in the rough.
But there's that tender moment when he feels so all alone
   a whisper of a cry, a tear that soon is gone.
And in his sleep I see a smile, then suddenly a sigh
   and what he dreams I'll never know, boy, what a great little guy.
It's said that we will live again, I'm so inclined to agree
   that many, many aeons from now I'll have him at my knee.
And once again I'll hear his voice and see that smile so sweet
   he'll dance a little and run to me and walk across my feet.

Charles Atkins

Heartbeat

I am like a predator in the wilderness, late at night in the dead of winter. Everything else is silent to me, but that bump, bump.... bump, bump. Blood rushing back and forth. Blood rushing up and down. Blood rushing in and out. Blood rushing straight and around. I do more than hear it, I listen to it. As the beating gets stronger, my desire for it gets louder. I know it's your heart. Please... stop running. The faster you run, the faster I run. The beating throws me in a frenzy. Stop hiding... look into my face. Find the answers to your questions. I know you have been hunted before and injured, nearly killed. Your body still shakes from the slightest touch, you cringe at the faintest sound. But everybody has a heartbeat. Hearts jump into the hands of one to the next, from this one to that one everyday. Each jump lands the heart into a different palm, producing this phenomenal heartbeat. Its new joy becomes old joy, its old joy becomes new pain. Constantly repeating, so always heard. After giving a patient smile, I look at your beauty as you sit high on a cold, icy mountaintop. Things change. One day the sun will creep up from behind you, melt that cold, icy covering, and make you slide down. I'll be there for the catch, good hunters always are.

Christopher D. Hill

Dream Child Dream

Round and round the carousel goes
Will it stop? Maybe so
Little children, waving at others
Good-bye or hello to their fathers and mothers
Unsuspecting, innocent waves
How to know what's in the future days
Hold on tight, little one, as the carousel turns.
What knowledge unknown, you should one day yearn.

Round and round the carousel goes
Will it stop? Only you know.
Little child, look up from your dream.
Life holds more than it seems.
The world around you is bigger than this.
Blink once more and blow it a kiss
You'll never have it unless you reach.
Put your head back down and chase your dream.

Carla Taylor

A Bit Of Sun

He woke one morn and to his right, he found his
wife had died that night. He blinked his eyes,
he called to her; yet still she lay, she did not stir...

A year did pass, her memory gone. Her spirit cried,
she was alone. No heaven called, no hell-bound soul;
there was just her stone, her cold dark hole.

A child, one day, he found this place. He saw the grave; he
made a face. The site was cold! The ground was bare!
He plucked a rose, and laid it there.

An angel saw this kindly deed. He spoke to God, and then,
with speed, he found her soul, he held her tight. She'd be
no more alone at night...the child grew old, and when he
died, there sat an angel at his side. The spirit there - who was
that wife - she led the way to eternal life.

The moral is? A simple rhyme: A memory shouldn't fade with time.
But if it does, and you're aware, then find some love and place
it there.

Caroline Owens

War Of Words

Sometimes I wonder if I'll ever find
  Why words whirl and worry through my head
  Lovely, luring, and longing to be said
The subtle, softly, silent and sublime
Do jest and jeer both gentle and unkind
  Thinking falsely that the phrases now are dead
  Annoying, gnawing; I lie awake in bed
Wondering why these words rush through my mind.

Aroused, arriving as they ought
  Agonizingly forced into rhyme
Almost are spoken-but then are caught

  Finally to face the crime
The war of words has now been fought
  Remaining rigid, trapped in time.

Crystal Armes Wagner

Love Gone By

Things you said come easily to mind.
Why, oh why are they so easy to find?

They continue to cause me pain.
They keep adding to the strain.

The lump in my chest is getting larger.
The tears start falling harder and harder.

All because you said you had to go away.
Had to go away because you had to play.

True you had to play.
But not the normal way.

In the game you play the rules are not fair.
The winner wins all, the loser walks away in despair.

You hurt me badly.
And to think I was in love with you madly.

It hurts me to realize I was so blind.
It hurts me to realize at first you were so kind.

There's nothing left to say.
Because you left me and your love has gone
astray.

Amy Porter

Endless Race

Run faster, do not delay.
Why is it that the one I love agitates herself?
Is it because I neglect you?

My love for you is like the dew drop in the morning,
Like the crystalline water rushing down the stream,
Like the moon coming out of its nuptial chamber.

My palate has become dry, like a waterless desert,
Do not hesitate my dearest one to mitigate my thirst
Because I have pronounced you the one to whom I have
  entrusted my love.

Run in truth and justice, and the seal of perfection becomes
  like a diadem around your head.
Run and do not stop.
Keep on pressing and do not look back,
Like a whirling storm rushing forward and never backward.

My loved one,
I do know that it is painful to run without stopping,
But at the end of the race, I will be there waiting for you -
  to nurture you and support you.
And from there on, we will continue running to the end of time.

Bienvenido Jorgensen

"Who?"

Who I can turn to, when you've gone away
Who's gonna to be there, to brighten my day
Who's gonna make me smile
when I just want to cry, who's gonna love me Mama
when you die?

Who's gonna give me strength, to
carry my heavy load
Who's gonna take the time to
put me on the right road
Who's gonna make me smile
When I just want to cry
Who's gonna love me Mama,
when you die?

Who's gonna dry my tears and
give me a helping hand
Who's gonna tell me everything is all right
and that they understand.
Who's gonna make me smile
when I just want to cry
Who's gonna love me Mama, when you die?

Bonnie Jean Gower

A Tale Of Two Students

Bully, chase, intimidate. The unanswered question
"Who you with?" punctuated with bullets.
One under the eye, four in the arms, one in each leg.
No smiles upon his return, makes crude remarks in class
Jungle survival, Invincible.

R.O.T.C. cadet, poet, hearts over the i's
'Life is precious, also very gracious.'
Scrawled in the margin, sincerely,
'Thanks for a good creative time.
This poem came from the heart.'
Call to his mom, "I'll be a bit late."
A shot rang out, wrong place, wrong time
His heart's poem is blood. Funeral.

Why does one live, the other die?

I know you work in mysterious ways.
Did you do it for dramatic effect,
as if we're characters in a novel?
Or is this a lesson too harsh for my learning,
like a final exam never studied for?
I just don't understand. Do You?

Daniel T. Shere

Phraseology

There once lived a sagacious? lady
who possessed a highly expanded vocabulary.

All were impressed by her twelve-letter words;
yet her speech was bombastic, and very obscure.

For circumlocution was a game she would play,
trapping Folly's disciples in circular way.

Verisimilitude was a word she would use,
but as for the meaning, she had not a clue.

And with tautological soliloquies
her pretention seemed ambiguous-
near predilection-
yet not quite capricious!

But look my fine friends, and you will see
that these last few lines are mere verbosity!

A sample of
her charlatan calls-
for one of these stanzas
says nothing at all!

Daphne Khoury

An Ode To A Black Man

I am the product of many.
Who lived and died before me.
There are none like those - not any;
Black man of honor - I will never forget you.

I am the daughter of one,
Who lived and loved me dearly.
No one else can ever take his place.
I can remember his face so clearly.
Black man, my father, I still love you.

I was the wife of one.
Who lived and died at the hands of a brother.
At times, I have wondered dear God,
If I'd ever be a black man's mother.
Black man, my husband, I still miss you.

I am the beginning of a few.
Who lives in a world of violence.
I am so afraid of what lies ahead.
My cries are heard in silence.
Black man, my child, I pray for you.

Flora Banks

"My Dad"

To My dad from your son
Who helped me to walk,
And taught me to run,
Who played with me in the yard,
And told me to study very hard,
He came and watched all my games,
Win or lose I was still the same,
He showed me how to fix my car,
And warned me about drinking in the bars,
Never drive when you drink,
Don't open your mouth until you think,
And though he yelled when I was wrong,
Still he was gentle, yet he was strong,
He always loved me for who I was,
And not who I tried to be,
No matter what I did in my life,
He said it's okay I was just being me,
And even though I talk to much,
These words I've never said,
I love you and I'm proud you're my dad!

Bill Hayston

Without You

Soft, soothing sunsets leading through endless, diamond skies
    Whispering winds of happiness drift silently past my concerned eyes
Abandoned beaches drenched in golden sunlight is where an empty
heart has turned
    All these cherished places is where my love for you has burned
We are agonizing miles apart in body
    Yet inseparable inches away in soul
As soon as I looked into your loving eyes I knew my life was complete
    and whole
    If I could live my entire life with someone so trusting and true
I would not take one moment to think of living it without you

Erin Michelle Zoellick

Where The Angels Walk

Where the angels walk, birds sing, flowers bloom
Where the angels walk, there is no hurt, or gloom
Where the angels walk, the sun is forever shining
Where the angels walk, there are endless rainbows
Where the angels walk, there is eternal life
Where the angels walk, God is always there
leading the way.

Amanda Adkins

Sounds Of A Country Night

Shh, listen to the chirp of a small cricket.
...which soon becomes a chorus of crickets.
...the screech of a barn owl getting ready to hunt its prey.
...the song of a nightingale.
Shh, listen to the gentle rustle of leaves blowing in the breeze.
...a squirrel nestling down in his hole.
...the howl of a lone coyote.
...joined by the echoing call of other coyotes in the distant hills.
Shh, listen to the croaking of the bullfrogs down by the pond.
...the gurgling of the little creek down in the pasture.
...the mooing of a cow as she settles down for the night.
...the neighing of a horse as he is put in the stable.
Shh, listen to the quacking of the ducks as they call their little
    ones to them for safety in the night.
...the honking of geese as they lay down for the night.
...the clucking of chickens as they snuggle down in their nests.
...the last crow of the rooster as he tells everyone that it is bedtime.
Shh, listen to the thumps of a dog's tail as he gets comfortable in
    his dog house.
...the quiet padding of a cat curling up on the end of a bed.
Shh, listen to the good nights of children being tucked in their beds.
Shh, listen to the quiet of a country night.

Debra L. Buchanan

The United States Of Vulgarica

Oh to have reached a state—how wonderful—
Where yellow goes with green
Where four-letter words
Compete with the birds
To say what doesn't mean!
And oh what clothes!
You share your toes with passersby
Or enclose your toes with rubber-white
That leads to denim blue.
And then the glorious
Shirt of T
That new and wonderful mode
That shows one what to say and think.
I mean, what the FOO, man!
You got all the luck, man!
You know what I mean?
You know what I mean?
You know what I mean?

Franklin William Storti

Black

He knows of a place in his mind
where, if searched deeply, he can find
goodness and sanity in Decay
He calls it Black and goes on to say:

"Black is Night, Black is Soul
Evil lies behind self-control
Lose it once and you will see
What it is like to be me.

Black is the brink of Insanity and Death
Feel the chill of Their cold breath
Depression is a state of mind
tell me to snap out of it, but I'm not your kind.

Black is seen in a well-lit room
flowers Wilt while still in Bloom
Loss of mind, loss of life
only Savior is a gleaming knife.

Black imprisons, no escape
Its dark walls my fingers scrape
No way out-be one with it forever
Eternal ties with Blackness I can't sever."

Cindy Mercurio

Castle In The Sky

Oh, my castle is in the sky
where dreams of life merely wing nigh,
and it will be the end of me
when, if ever, I touch reality.

Reality if naught but pain
bears grief and sorrows again and again.
The wounds of my heart just cannot heal,
so I must escape from what is real.

In my castle in the sky
a healthy steed is standing by.
Upon his back, the knight in white satin
avows, "Ego amo te," I love you in Latin.

They beckon to me, I cannot turn back.
This world is turning my soul to black.
I must go to HIM for surcease from sorrow.
Maybe I will return upon the morrow.

Betty J. Derryberry-Sullivan

War's Survivor

The cap lies there all stiff in crown
Where blood has oozed upon the ground...

The shadows of the soldiers play
Where once they shot and fought for gain...

The bones they leave will soon decay
Returning man from whence he came...

The clothes will rot, the snaps will rust
Then back to earth will go their dust...

But still the cap lies on the ground...
A non-decaying, plastic crown.

Faye Howard Harris

Victory

Durst, hast pity on thou love.
Whence greater soul art thou.
From love whence tears I cry lonely doves.
Thou art prithee of thine and thine love to come now.
And turmoil shall hast on thine.
To cast all evil o'er I it shall be and above.
Fluency o'er my life has no meaning if love isn't kind.
And, bear I will, being shot by the arrow of love.
Yet life becomes a obstacle of thou not being mine.
Confused my spirit always represents grace indeed.
Loving am I, loving am I, as I put fourth passion so fine.
Quarrels of love, thou proceed.
Thy need nor learn, no introduction to love.
Thou eyes shall see glory through the seed grown above.
Creator of love I become. Inserting a will of nature to all.
Yet ye doesn't put fourth a crumb.
Powerful I will still stand tall.
Thou modern ye life becomes.
Thy shall not be defeated.
I've won I did not give in too lust I have not cheated.

Franco Anderson

Summer Dream

With the rustling of the leaves and the rolling of the waves
We sit in our lawn chairs perched on the old warped dock.
As time flies by, we remember that special summer,
The summer when the moon was high and the water was calm.
And with those two special days in 1994,
Many life long wishes and dreams came true.

Aaron Thorpe

Tears From Heaven

When there are rain drops
When the sun is shining
God is smiling, with happy tears

When he is angry for the corrupt, sick and lame
You will see and feel his pain
He will weep and moan with hail and thunderstorm.

It is frightening
When he hurls his thoughts
Like a bolt of lightning.

For the corrupt, filth and sin,
He will send tornado and howling winds.

To purify the air we breathe
He will send snow and freezing temperature,
That will destroy the disease.

The morning after the ordeal,
The air is fresh, sun is shining.
Children will play, birds will sing,
And God in heaven will smile once again.

Annie M. McCants

Untitled

There is a time
when I was, lived and breathed
Strength

That lifetime taught great pain and
in turn an enormous joy

I would gaze at
the golden moon and cry
for my people who were hungry
and I fed them

This lifetime and
this golden moon finds we still seeing people
who are hungry, homeless

and I cry tears within and without but
they don't burn not like before

This lifetime
I have no power to change hunger or cold

...perhaps only because
I have not remembered seeing
the moon before, far away, and
I forgot how powerful I am

Evelyn McAllister

Daydreams

When daylight seems so far away, and nightmares plague my sleep,
When I get scared when curtains sway, and I begin to weep,
I close my eyes and dream of nights when I won't be so scared;
When someone says "the bed bugs bite" and I laugh at things I feared.
When nighttime seems to drag along, when the clocks ticking slows,
I write a poem, or sing a song, or follow where my daydreams go...
  The stars are shining brightly as we walk along the street.
  I hold your hand so tightly, our love is oh-so-sweet.
  We stop beneath a street light and gaze up at the sky.
  It's such a lovely summer night, I softly start to cry.
  You understand my tears, and you understand my pain,
  You understand my fears, still, you say we've much to gain.
  So maybe you are right, and maybe scars will heal,
  And maybe on some other night, this daydream will be real...
But now the sun is rising, as night starts its retreat,
I softly sigh, I close my eyes, it's time to get some sleep.

Barbara M. Ellis

Sweet Bird Of Youth

My mind recalls the distant past
When I was just a child at play
Time went by so slow - and yet so fast
The Sweet Bird of Youth seemed here to stay.

Then I became a restless lad
And traveled far and wide
Went through times both good and bad
The Sweet Bird of Youth was at my side.

Life was at times an uphill pull
But I seldom had much fear
For I knew my cup was truly full
While The Sweet Bird of Youth was near.

As time went by and I grew older
I had much to cheer and much to grieve
The summers seemed hotter and the winters colder
The Sweet Bird of Youth was about to leave ...

As I approach the autumn of my years,
It saddens me to say
After all the laughter and all the tears
The Sweet Bird of Youth has flown away!

Alfred Langer

Marathon Celebration

It was a humid 4th of July
When I stumbled and fell into
That crack in the floor at the super-duper
Warehouse store.
As the world paraded past, I cried,
"Help, help! I'm too young to die."
Shopping cart wheels and a zillion feet
Passed above my eyes.

I was wedged in tight
My knees and feet dangled out of sight
While the procession passed in greenish light.

The janitor saw my plight
He drug over a jack: introduced himself as Max
Squeezed apart the crack, and told me to relax.

Together we wandered away from the store
Towards a distant quay to watch the sky lore:
Those purplish, crimson, yellow-green starbursts of light
That make the sky aglow for our delight.

Coleen M. Ede

I Cry Real Tears

I cry real tears when a baby is born,
When I behold the sunrise on a summer morn.
For that beautiful butterfly fluttering by the tree,
I cry for the chrysalis it will no more be.

On lazy Sundays my heart yearns,
For Sundays gone years ago that will never return.
My tears are real they come from inside,
Spilling over relieving passion I try to hide.

I cry real tears for a broken heart,
For loved ones destined to be apart.
When I think of all the hatred in this world,
I cry with the innocence of a little boy or girl.

I cry real tears on a moonlit night,
Looking up at the firmament so heavenly and bright.
With my tears I cushion any unkind word ever said,
They roll and fall, like shattered dreams and hopes now dead.

I cry for happiness, I cry when I am sad,
I cry when good people sometimes act bad.
From my precious flowing tears you will surmise,
The empathy I feel through these tearful eyes.

Cheril D. Weir

Living Water

Springs of Living Water well up within my soul
When I ask of Jesus, please come and make me whole.
I know that I'm not worthy, perfect I'll never be
But God doesn't ask perfection from such a one as me.
His precious Living Water is a gift forever free
I know he'll do for others what he has always done for me.
Just let him know you love him and want to do your best,
Tell him that you're ready and he'll help you do the rest.
From that time on you'll never thirst,
You'll have that Living Water because you put him first.
He'll fill your cup with blessings like you've never seen before
And meet your needs so fully, you'll never be wanting more.
How can anyone deny him or fail to heed his call
When you know that he was willing, for us, to give his all?
From us he asks so little but for us he does so much,
He's always there to fill your need with a kind and gentle touch.
So ask today with a fervent prayer with obedience as your goal
And his precious Living Water will flow in and save your soul.

Elizabeth Thornton Watkins

No Longer Daddy's Girl

There comes a time each dad's life
when his daughter's no longer daddy's girl.
She grows up in such short time it seems,
the years go by in just a whirl.

When she arrived on God's great earth but a few short years ago.
I could not imagine this day would come,
when a man would come, and she would go.

She seemed so fragile in my arms the day that we first met.
She was so small and beautiful me feelings of love I'll ne'er forget.

God blessed us then, her mom and I
by making our union as man and wife
a fruitful relationship of care and love
entrusting us with this gift of life.

We now give this woman, our only child
to this man under God's watchful eye.
We know that he will honor and love her as much as her mother and I.

God Bless you daughter and son-in-law
May your live be filled with peace and love
As you travel down life's winding pathways
you will have continued guidance from above.

Bruce A. Haury

I Am A Distant Voice

What have I done
What will I do
No one knows
I am a distant voice

I am always dreaming but never sleeping
Fearing the future; tired of the past
Crying out my vision but they are unheard
I am a distant voice

Fame in the future, I doubt
Glory in the past, none
My past is gone
My future going
Never slowing for me
I'm caught in the middle of life
A distant voice like so many
Fading out of time
Never being heard
Never being known
A distant voice

Fred Garris Jr.

Life

Sometimes I wonder
what the use of it is
It seems I only exist, but not live
A body without a soul
waiting for someone, something
to make me happy
But all I get is sadness,
anger and loneliness
Feeling unwanted, unloved, unneeded
Just to feel the responsibility
Being torn between love and hate
I look for an answer, but it's not there
I feel insecure of what might happen
waiting for something to happen that won't
Don't know what's out there waiting for me
Don't know my future
Don't know if today is my last,
or if fate will be the answer to all my questions.

Colleen Bond

Pensive

And you there, for what reason do you strike me down?
What? Surely I am not different.
Count my fingers: I have ten.
Look at my eyes: I have two.
And on my head, do I not have hair?
When I am cut, do I not bleed red?
What then makes me different?
The color of my skin?
The difference of my speech?
Are we not all His children?
And so what if He is called by different names.
Is it because my eyes are not blue?
See here, don't they look blue to you?
And my hair, is it the wrong color as well?
Is it my fault it is not the color of light?
Should I not wear this star with pride?
Why do you make His symbol that of hatred?
Come now my brethren, free us from bondage
From this place of death I must flee
It is my family that my heart seeks

Brennan Anderson

Baseball, U.S.A.

Write a theme about your country
What it means to you, the U.S.A.
An elementary school dilemma, one sees
Something more than jingoism this day

Yesterday we sat on hard steeled bleachers
We watched the best athletes compete
How does one apply this sobriquet for teachers
The sun reddened our faces, enthusiasm replete

The intellectuals said baseball, inane
The seventh inning ritual stretch
In closeted heart, they envied freedom of game
Remembering childhood throw and fetch

And so go the game and the United States
Free to run, win and yell aloud
To all there is, some way, an open gate
Bases loaded, what next, the crowd

Umpires rhubarb as do politicos
We gulp down hot dogs and sparkling drinks
And this is the way America goes
And so, baseball, with another chance, when sun sinks.

Antoinette Adelquist Bell

Bargaining With The One

I know there is no time for sequels right?
What am I saying?
I don't know if this is the last chapter of her life
That you are writing!

Perhaps though, before this book goes to print
I was wondering if you had some time
For an epilogue
Or even a postscript.

Anything will do....

You see...I'm a fan of her life's story....
I ought to be. She is my beloved mother.

Angella A. Focas

Needs

Again I try to understand
What a woman needs in a man

She needs the love he has to give
Each woman needs that to live

She needs to know the trust is there
That he loves her and really cares

She needs the strength to help her grow
To help her with things she does not know

She needs a kiss upon her cheek
Instead of the tears that she weeps

She needs the arms that hold her tight
That holds and cuddles her through the night

Again I try to understand
Where God put this perfect man

Debbie Barclay

"Waiting Room"

If you ask me what I'm doing,
well, waiting's all it is
my actions don't mean that much
and I don't think like this

it grows late now, dawn will
soon be here. Sleep comes not
too easily to me, but it's
not the dreams I fear

waiting is all I do, because
waiting's all there is
I'll be awake forever, sitting
just like this.

So don't ask me what I'm doing
you know you've done it too
and when this waiting room is full, I'll leave
and find a future without you.

Ame Beard

New Words

I am so bored and without knowledge, I will make a new word.
Well, how about two, or three, here it is; querd.

This new word means kind and caring, unlike jime;
This demonstrates a person who is late, and never on time.

This is sort of fun, I could be doing scraday
But that's okay, I hate school work anyway.

I have two reasons for making up words like tzyme
For fun, and to get these dumb poems to rhyme.

Christina Mancl

"A Note To Mother"

"Please, dear Mother, don't shed your tears,
We won't be apart forever.
Yes I know you are there, and I am here,
But someday we'll be together"

"I know you think of me,
As I wonder about you.
Heaven is where I have to be,
And someday you'll be here too!"

"I am an angel now, earning my wings,
I'm hoping I'll get them soon.
I would have loved to hear you sing,
But the Lord choose me to leave your womb"

"Just look up at a twinkling star
And you'll see my love.
Don't worry, dear Mother, I'm not far
I'm just watching you all from above"

April Daigle

Rigidity

For fear of the unknown, we stay in one place.
We wait, one place in time, never wanting to grow.
Never finding a new plateau, or climbing to a new high;
Thus, having no room for others at different road tolls.

The forces of our lives propel us to new destinies;
Yet, when the heart is set in permanent bond
To an ancient spot in time, no power on earth
Can soften a resolve or loosen a will for other molds.

Rigidity is to be feared for it can be a force of evil
That isolates a mind for the may future years,
And hinders the co-existence of one who loves us
By blinding our senses to life's many evolving folds.

Whether it be father or lover, we allow their iron wills
To shelter and stop the growth of us as companions.
We let them rule our thoughts and processes of living;
Thus, ever anchoring us to another's praise and scolds.

Becky J. Richardson

Today We Become One

Today we become one, we spread our wings and fly
We take the world on together
And search the endless sky

God placed us hand in hand and
bound us with his love, now He sends us on our way
And keeps watch from above

He gave us times of good and
bad and feelings we didn't
Understand, but that was
to grow me as a woman and you as a man

The Lord is our shepherd and
He shall guide our way and
give us the grace and strength
to handle what comes our way

I will always stand beside you
And go where God may lead, for
He brought us together, He planted the seed

Today, I give you my heart
for all eternity, to share
With our Lord Jesus, who died for you and me.

Tonya Lofton

The Lord Our Shepherd (Psalm 23:1-6)

The Lord is our good shepherd
We shall not want or despair.
In pastures green, He maketh us
To lie down in his care.

Beside still waters He leadeath us.
To calmly there partake.
Restoring our souls and leading us.
In righteousness for His namesake.

Yea though we walk in the shadow of death,
We know that thou art there,
We fear no evil for thy rod and thy staff
Shall comfort us with thy care.

In the presence of our enemies,
A table thou preparest before us.
The oil of thy salvation,
Thou freely poureth over us.

Surely, goodness and mercy shall follow us.
For he shall leave us never.
And we will swell in the house of the Lord.
Forever and ever and ever.

Psalm 23:1-6
(verse submitted by Carlotta Seagraves, The Gifted Pen II)

Untitled

Wrapped in madness
We rise,
All that love Truth
All that can see through the haze of words
Beasts encased,
Under the un-living society
The metal and zombies rule and
the selfish ends they pursue
Lead
the blindly obedient
walking the wire, not creating their inner - fire
Which wants to erupt, and merge with each into reality
Awaiting it stirs
Inside the battle in your mind to unionize
And bring about the "self" - the purest from of existence.
The writer then becomes his own author
And is free to create anything.
The power is with-in awaiting to be tapped.
See past the veiled reality - makers who are only put cake makers
Break free fly aimlessly, until you find your stairway
to the self which will in turn direct each to their call
Salvation, Immortality, Celestine!

Christina A. Nuta

Late Love

And now our days of loving have grown shorter
We knew the end was somewhere down the line
But "here" is slowly changing to "hereafter"
and through the change you always will be mine

I close my eyes and hold you to me tightly
Your hand has always held mine to your heart
But time has been our enemy forever
And now through death we really have to part

I'll stay with you till there are no more heartbeats
And kiss your eyes and know that they are still
And mourn your gentle passing from my lifetime
I love you now and know I always will.

Frances Regan

Unbreakable Connection

We are two of a kind
We have the same likes and dislikes
We share our loves and hatreds
Their have been tough times
But, we always have stayed close
Being able to tell each other everything
Laughing, crying, fighting,
Knowing what was on the other's mind
Not needing words to understand each other
Going out, staying home, or talking on the phone
sharing secrets and desires
Feeling that we are connected body and soul
A closeness so strong that
We feel each other's pain and sorrow
But, knowing whatever happens
We will not face it alone
Because we have an
Unbreakable connection

Dana Capaccio

Misery

I have been thinking of a way to say good-bye
We have shared some good and bad times
But they have all come to an end.
Together we are never going to make it
Apart we may have a chance to last.
Once, you said you loved me,
But now I realize you loved the danger of our love.

Today, I discovered that I don't need you in my life
I need to learn how to love myself.
Before I can commit to us, I commit to me
Maybe we can find each other or maybe not.

Please don't try to change my mind
It was decided a long time ago
The day I said good-bye to the devil.
You and I are dangerous duo.
We part our ways at the crossroads.

I want you to know that I am fine.
Pain doesn't live here anymore.
I ran the race of my life and came out a winner.
Maybe one day you will see that misery is not a friend.

Angela Powell

Days Of Thanksgiving

As we gather with family on Thanksgiving Day
We feast on our bounty and thoughtfully pray.

We're thankful for living in a land of great wealth
And ask that we continue to enjoy good health.

Many of us donate to someone in need
Hoping to find hungry mouths to feed.

Our hearts seem much bigger this time of the year
As we approach December and the month of good cheer.

If only these feelings would last all year through
And not just for this season or two...

If only we made it our practice each day
To ask God's direction and humbly pray...

Then each day would be like Thanksgiving you see-
For His work would be done through you and me!

Carol Masters

3 Words

As these days seem to fly by,
We ask ourselves where they went and why.
So many hours come and go,
How many seeds for God did we sow?
Only human, are we all, in the end,
We must prepare for his coming again.
No hands be raised meaning to inflict pain,
There is always a better solution with more to gain.
Raising our kids with attitudes of "go hit them back",
Is showing my point of how much we lack.
We all are looking for a better life,
Without the daily problems of money and strife.
This world has too much greed, anger and hate,
Can't we stop now before it's too late?
Love Thy Neighbor and Peace On Earth,
Nothing we have could compare in worth.
With these 2 little phrases with 3 words each,
Imagine how rich our souls could reach.

Alma Kristine Briscoe-Leon

Divine Power

God our Father, Jesus His Son.
  Was born on this earth, for His will to be done.
He was born in Bethlehem, with animals so near.
  People who knew, rejoiced with a tear.

The star in the sky, brought people to see.
  What marvelous birth, had just come to be.
He grew very tall and when His work was done.
  He learned about God, to tell every one.

He prayed all the time to His Father up above.
  To give Him strength, wisdom, and love.
He died on the cross with His hands and feet nailed.
  Knowing in His heart, He had not failed.

All you have to do is believe in Him.
  He'll forgive you forever of all your sins.
So pray to Jesus to show you the way.
  He'll save you now on this very day.

Charlene Ann Guffey

"July"

July is a month filled with vacationing.
Warm nights and hot days.
Bikinis, sand castles, young lads and lasses.
Moonlight swims, back yard barbecues.
Carnivals, fair and county square dancing.
But lets not forget fireworks and sparklers.
People get out more and enjoy the sun with volley ball and tennis.
It's just a whole lot of fun.
Now the night breezes as begun.

Twilight skies, filled full of stars, most every night.
Sitting around an open campfire.
Toasting marshmallows and telling tall tales,
Of ghostly delights.
A night full of p.g. adventures.
Dogs on the prowl.
Cats snarl.
Beyond the light shadows change.
It makes you feel that your on a stage.
Family and friends socially in twine.
Making July come alive.

Frances Kelly

"Now You Are Free"

The echoes of sweetness is all that you hear,
wandering the night and counting the fear.
Singing the sadness and watching the glory
following rivers into a strong story,
touching the coldness as the sky showers,
feeling the loneliness, seeing the flowers.
Pushed into darkness, about to confess,
feeding the mind, taught to be kind,
needing the softness, not wanting less.
Stringing a puppet, running to be met
facing an answer, the words never slur,
being named a clown, being forced down.
Now what can they do?
They see they've killed you.
Running away they cannot escape,
not even under a dark blue cape.
They say they are sorry and now you are free.

Brittany Patterson

Stained Glass Soliloquy

A temple raised! A hole in a wall, few feet wide, stood so many tall.
Vision of a silent architect talented maker of windows great or small.
I, the sea sand common and clear, was hammered, heated and mixed
With varied hues, cooled cut puzzle-fitted together and forever fixed.

Sand am I finely thus dressed to suit the artist's self-chosen mission
Fire burned! Cutter hurt! Hot lead holds the curious inspired vision.
Mute architect admires, only a moment, then is gone without a trace.
He is driven by the emptiness within to meet a need in another place.

Finished! Polished! Crucified parti-colored glass with leaded seams.
By whom? For what? Who knows wither went the maker of dreams?
Behold, the sunrise! Glorious marker of Father Time greet the day.
I come alive in the eyes of those soul-touched inside by your display.

Nightfall! Miracle in reverse! Passersby stop to admire it, transfixed.
Chorus of loving light pouring through colored panes artfully mixed.
Daylight, stored in souls like fireflies, returns a just measure
And through silent sand radiate into darkness their glowing treasure.

Knowing no more, nor happier than life lived as the simplest sea dust.
I, like all atoms am condemned to ceaseless change. Evolve so I must.
Visible, yet invisible 'twixt this and that, alone yet not alone I stand.
By Master Mind made man-like but still at heart just a grain of sand.

Charles E. Potts

Our God Is Here

Why do we suffer when things around
  us seem so bright?
Why do we hope when our hopes are
  turned to despair?
Look at us, we who trod the road of agony
We are the children of the higher being.
We are not forgotten,
We will never be forgotten,
We are the masterpiece of the creator.
We cannot be forgotten.
We are hope, we are love He will hear our cries,
How can He not hear for He is God.
Why cry "O my soul" my God will lead the way.
The morn brings another day.
The evening ushers it out.
Our God smiles at our cry and says
  tomorrow will be your day.
Why do we fear? Our God is here.

Christine Knight

Grandpa

I could always tell when Grandpa came
Upstairs to his bedroom:
The stairs always squeaked!

He was a good size man, in this fertile,
Rich harvest land: six feet, three inches, 240 pounds.

Plus add to that his Sears and Roebuck coveralls
And size fourteen boots. Fo' more than anybody could
Remember, he put 'em to very good use.

When I was 'bout six, the climb was steady and quick.
But when I was twenty-three, the climb was much
Slower and he was hardly able to see!

Then by twenty-five, Grandpa was no longer alive!
His long life was done: Thy kingdom come.

  For as much as many have taken in hand
  to set forth in order a declaration of
  those things which are most surely
  believed among us.

The Gospel According To Luke
David R. Lewis

To Want, To Need, To Desire

To want, to need, to desire
  unselfishly everything.
To want, to need, to desire
  the sweetest rays of light.
To want, to need, to desire
  an even state of peace of mind.
To crave for, to long for, to die for
  fruitful bearing, a soft pitter-patter
  of tiny feet, a growing warmth from within.
To search for, to pursue, to chase
  the open gates of Eldorado.
To fight, to control, to overcome
  guilt, fear, rage.
To wish for, to yearn for, to cry for
  a soft voice at night, a gentle approach,
  a gentle touch.
To want, to need, to desire
  an end to all that is real.
To have, to hold, to exist
  darkness.

Brandi Sullivan

Dakota Creek

Spawned in a prairie, "no count" riverlet
unattended, left to roam alone, bereft.
A nameless muddy creek in no hurry
much different than the wide Missouri.
You creep like a salamander around stones
slither like a garter snake without bones.
You wander unashamedly around tin cans
feeling your way as with outstretched hands.
Timid, lazy, backwards, not always true!
Time spent in repose, until spring storms
when you become a gluttonous snake
and like a boa swallow all you can
to do a flying cannonball off the dam.
The quiet townfolk hang over the bridge
wide-eyed for a better view
of this wild, tempestuous side of you.

Anne Swan-Johnson

Offerings

In a wastebasket lay
two long-stemmed carnations
still fresh, not dry
I wondered about them
how they had been tended
to be cut
to be chosen
to be a source of joy, perhaps
for someone and now
having served for that fleeting moment
lay in a gray, metal trash can
with lipstick-imprinted, half-smoked cigarettes
torn paper
ashes...

Charles Martinez

"Harvard"

Two little boys late one night,
Tried to get Harvard on the end of a kite.
The kite string broke
And down they fell.
Instead of going to Harvard
They went to....
Now don't get excited
And don't get pale.
Instead of going to Harvard,
They went to Yale.

Christina Locke

Deceptions

Dark eyes inviting and tentative
Trembling hands grasp the unknown
Gentle light conceals simmering anger
Mistaken for passion by familiar arms.

Tension-filled limbs awaiting release
Fleeting moments of joy create peace
Empty phrases whispered to oblivious ears
Echo the silence of agonizing sorrow.

Familiar flesh intertwined and unconnected
Enduring nights pursue unfulfilled promises
Tears of sadness usher the daylight
Bright with the glare of reality.

An intrepid venture without direction
Performed by an unbidden guest,
An intimate resident within my core
Effecting such torment and isolation.

Christie A. Gooch

The Pecan And The Pecan Man

While you were sitting on the bench under my
tree, I became a tag by a friendly little Bee
As the rains came and the winds blew
the days became months and I hardly grew.
Your thoughts were so many and the long
nights seemed chilly.
All of a sudden my coat turned brown with a
tug and a thump, I finally hit the ground.
You picked me up and tucked me in, my shell
you cracked and didn't once grin.
I didn't mind going in the pint bag, with a little
teasing and a whole lot of nag.
All the work wasn't pleasant and funny, until
in comes Loris and Linda with a handful of
money.

Dorothy W. Mullins

The Battle Of Little Bighorn

In the trying days of the Indian wars,
Treaties were broken with little cause.

From those days the West was born,
Thus came the story of Little Bighorn.

General Custer knew the land,
He was not prepared to make a stand.

The Indians massed for the attack,
Then thundered on to close the gap.

Custer knew they forced his hand.

He formed a ring, his men held the line,
The help they needed did not come in time.

Sitting Bull refused to yield,
He sent his best into the field.

That ring of fire withered down,
History was written from what was found.

It's over now, those days are gone.
It all happened at the Battle of
Little Bighorn.

Charles W. Murdock

The Golden Hawk

The day was almost over, I was happy, hoping, as I drove
Traffic congested, people busy, all going places
Me, I knew where I was going, perhaps to realize a dream.

Yes, I had thought about it, worked, wanted it to come true
At times, almost gave up, could not see over that mountain
Yet, I did keep looking forward, yes, beyond my youth.

To own my own Studebaker, one perhaps my dad,
He could have helped build this very one, by trade
Yes, a 1957 Golden Hawk Studebaker, gold in color, the car for most

As I turned from the highway, my head ached, my heart skipped a beat
My wife reached to touch my hand, to smile, to assure me
Soon upon the hill, I could see the 1957 Golden Hawk, oh! My

My whole body shaking, as I took the grand site in, excitement, joy
I want this car, yes, I do, and I paid the man, thank you, started it
  up, surprised
We have a way to go I know, it's so old, 30 years, rust and
deterioration, unseen

Sweating and back breaking, cutting away years of old, we became friends
Replacing worn. Almost impossible with new, getting more beautiful
  by day
Now I enjoy it, go to car shows, won 1st place, crowing it the best,
  my Golden Hawk

Elizabeth Boldt

Retirement

Migrating with the clever birds, cloud - borne.
To warmth and blossoms of such flaming hues,
To citrus fruits that offer gifts of health,
For skies for all to view, both day and night;
To watch the growth of living things sans stress,
To plant and nurture these beyond my door,
Then praying for the rain from heaven, wind;
No evil thought besmirches hours or days.
The green of verdure rests the eye and brain.
No need for clocks, no weather testing,
No fancy clothes to vie with woman kind.
Cosmetics long forgotten, I need not,
As happiness is mine, is my new home.

Florence K. Wiener

16

"Loneliness And Hope"

Roaming through the continental skies
Towards a destination far, far away.
This has been a dark day.

From the holy city of angels,
To the region of Cape Cod,
My heart fell apart during the way

With the feeling of hope
That happiness would be on its way,
For not loneliness I prayed.

Wishing somehow I'll find again the way
To the warm breezes of Newport and Orange Fields.
All I feel is guilt.
For have left thy love out there.

Though my heart has gone cold,
I'll feel your warmth every night
As my soul meets yours in a dream.
Hopefully happiness will shine on me like a light beam.

I can do no more from 3,000 miles away
Than ask you to wait,
I promise I'll find a way.

Bill Bacellar

Once Upon A Midnight

Once upon a midnight,
Too many years ago,
An owl was in midflight —
Someone shot him with a stone.

The owl tumbled downward,
Silent where he fell.
A sparrow woke and found him—
He had something to tell...

The owl spoke his last words
Of love and hope and friends.
He told how they were living
In a world that never ends.

And in his last breathing moment,
The owl gave a sigh.
He had taught that friends will never part—
He was ready now to die.

Anne Hendler

Untitled

Too much stuff is happening,
Too dangerous for you to be out there;
Guns, drugs, alcohol, violence,
Makes it all even harder
For all of us to deal with.

The people are changing,
The world is changing,
It's too dangerous out there,
Teenagers are dying,
Before they even reach the age of 20.
And so many of us are changing the world,
With our own hands,

We don't even realize
That what we're doing,
Is totally wrong.
Parents hurting kids,
Kids hurting parents
It's all a guffy mess,
In a world of disaster.

Anamaria Miclea

The Anatomy Of A Friend

You opened your mind in attempt to comprehend my ideals;
    to understand.
With your eyes you looked around seeing things as I portrayed them.
On your ears fell rantings, rage, declarations of injustice.
From your mouth came utterances of advice when needed,
    words of comfort in troubled times; amusing anecdotes during
    sorrowful times.
Your shoulders absorbed many tears and helped carry the
    weight of what seemed like unbearable burdens.
Your arms wrapped around me to shield away further pain
    or to share blessed joys.
With your feet you strode the rugged paths beside me,
    though weariness threatened to overtake you.

But the dearest and greatest gift was the gift of your heart.
A heart that exuded love and understanding, a love that lessened
    loneliness and tried to understand; whatever the situation.
A heart that helps make you unique and special.
The heart that beats as that of a FRIEND.

Elaine F. Satchell

Country Boy On Stoney Creek

A barefoot country boy stop by a garden gate a while,
To smell the honeysuckle in bloom with a smile,
Carrying a wooden tackle box and a fishing pole,
Ma-ma said son, don't go down to Stoney Creek hole.

A boy's voice calls old Shep from the back steps he'd say,
Shep wag his tail with affection, darting along the sod,
Casey look so discouraged, to stay home and play,
So they hurry to a roaring sounds on Stoney Creek.

Casey curls up under the shade of a sycamore tree,
There where the catfish are biting like bees,
With a drop line hooked to his toe and ol' cane pole,
To sink a hook into Dad's ol' fishin' hole.

Casey return home with a string of catfish in his hand,
A crawfish floppin' around in a bucket of sand.

And there Casey learned to bathe in Stoney Creek,
And hunt rabbits in a blanket of clover with joy,
I'm thankful for God that I'm a country boy,
Exploring the beauty of nature on Stoney Creek.

Carroll Sears

Waiting, Waiting For The Tide

We all sit, side by side, waiting, waiting for the tide
to roll its wondrous waves to shore
Only this, and nothing more.
With quiet eyes of admiration, pounding deep anticipation
Crying out beyond the thick, dark sky
to this and nothing else I wonder why.
Sensing only pain's release, I fit the puzzle piece by piece
Next to my life so neatly on the shelf;
No end in sight I know to find myself.
Anxiously reach out our hands
Our minds are meshed in far off lands
Without our bodies present in this place,
Simply, sadly of this dying race.
A race of colors mixed to hues
of blacks and whites and reds and blues
To laugh and sing so carelessly; dangers gone out to an open sea.
And so to make a lifelong friend, I pray the day may see an end
Of hatred built upon years past,
Extinguish evil deeds at last.
We all sit, side by side, waiting, waiting for the tide
to roll its wondrous waves to shore,
Only this, and nothing more.

Andrea R. Coggan

17

Devoted Love

I promise to you my darling to be your special one,
To not measure our love by moments of time but in
   timeless moments.
To give you that special love as silently and undemanding
   as in the past,
To honor the memories of our past, and the love in our future,
   not questioning the future that fate holds,
Cherishing the joy of your smile, the warmth of your body,
   the strength of your arms, the tenderness of your kiss,
Thinking of you often as the day is gone.

Fran C. Vaughan

Highway Cowboy

Click, click, click my diesel motor is on. I look to my left and
to my right, then I check my mirrors. I got to roll out before the night.

I notice the yellow and white line that does not wait, so I travel
day and night.

Here I am on the road, destination unknown. Enjoying my favorite
song, looking at the drivers who move along, looking at the beautiful
scenery and listening to these damn wheels screaming.

Over the mountains and through the plains with a bird's eye view, I cruise.

I'm the lonely cowboy who rides the concrete and asphalt roads
shifting these gears, stop and go, yield I guess, I'm going up this
hill. First gear, second gear I find, third gear I grind. I hope
I make it on time.

On this long endless road, I am towing this heavy load. The only
friend, I know are the ones on the radio. These are my true amigos.
I pull off for a bite, I hope this food won't keep me up all night.

The white line never seems to end. Through rain, thunder, snow
and sun these eighteen wheels must run!

Benjamin Olivares

No Less, No More

As the sun christens the dawning of a new day,
to my knees I fall and my God I pray

To grant me the strength and courage to be,
the believer that lyes inside of me

And in this prayer I ask him for,
Guidance and willingness,
no less, no more

Dennis O'Meara

"Soldier"

As I stand tall and proud I salute
to loyalty, to honor, to heritage. I stand
proud my head held high I salute to freedom,
to courage, to blood, I know I have to be
strong and I have to fight for those who
are weak. I respect the fact that I am
to influence, lead, and guide others to
show confidence, to never let you guard
down, and so leads me to believe I'm a
real American soldier.

Claine Rosado

Only A Breath Away

The lights are not dimmed softly
The violins are not played sweetly
Words of good-bye are not rehearsed repeatedly
The scenes are not changed hurriedly
But it happens.....as sure as life; death!
Only.....a.....breath.....away

Cynthia McQueen

The First Hall Of Famer

You have to be a Detroit fan
To like or even respect this man.

Other towns don't like him much
'Cause he's a hitter in a clutch.

Hits the ball so hard on a fly
That's a fact you can't deny.

Alone in his dugout he sharpens his spikes
'Cause every third baseman he intensely dislikes.

Some call him dirty, but he doesn't care.
He'll play his own game, so crybabies beware.

As the first Hall of Famer, he stands out from the mob.
If you haven't guessed by now, his name is Ty Cobb.

Brick Mengel Spurio

Charity

They say we need reform, new laws
To lift America out of menopause
Country's fading, on a fast downward spiral
World media has put America on trial

Yet when trouble comes in far off places
We grab the reins, kick over the traces
Lift others up from the muck and mire
They've created from their greed and desire

Their jealousy, their greed, their envy and lust
But it's our sons and daughters buried in the dust
From fighting wars of other nations
And we are sick of their conflagrations

So we are putting the world on notice
When you choose to war, don't look to us
To ride to the rescue, your tails to save
The rest of the world must learn to behave
For charity begins at home
Ours

Annie Darlene Moss

My Last

My last breath I have saved
To kiss your lips one last time

My last glance I gave to see you
One last time

My last thought shall be of you
For these last times I give them all to you.

My last words shall speak your name
My last touch will be to hold your hand
My last wish will be that you don't cry
As I say my last good-bye

Amy Ballowe

New Beginnings

I watched the sun rise this morning.
Through the mist of grays fading silently
from the grassy lowland, I watched.
As the miracle of new beginnings reenacted
its breathtaking transformations, I watched.
In the stillness of recreated moments
applause from my soul swelled
to a thunderous ovation of thanksgiving
...and I listened.

Charles Vernon Hicks

Thoughts On Fence Crossing

Throughout our lives our efforts commence,
To gain turf on the other side of the fence,
We work, slave, sweat and toil,
As we envy tenants on that other soil.

We climb, scratch, push and pull climbing that hill,
Though oft we find our efforts for nil,
While on the opposite side their successes appear,
To give them prosperity they endear.

Deciding we must cross that proverbial wall,
For to succeed...we must leave,
Only to find our move a surprise to all,
Yet, we do not perceive.

Our lives become quite pathetic,
But for all the envy, and zest we endeavored,
To find our new environment quite synthetic,
For the grass is cold, lifeless and green...forever.

Nothing is as it seems... we now know.
The perpetually green turf was only...Astro!

Dale Bates

My Mountain Experience

Upon the mountain high I awake in early morn
To drink in the splendor of a world reborn
The soothing melody of the rushing stream
The precious peace the feel of a mystic dream
I was no longer alone eyes watched from near
From across the water approached a small deer
I sensed the presence of my maker in this wondrous place
And marveled that someday I would see his face
Diving into a deep hole I startled a trout
Which certainly wondered what I was all about

From lofty overlook I saw beauty afar
Rolling mountains with green attire
The vast expanse of a brilliant blue sky
To think in all of this God would notice I
I came upon prickly mother porcupine
With her precious baby not far behind
As I descended I beheld the raw beauty of a waterfall
I love this wonder perhaps best of all
The peace I have soaked up as the mountains I roam
I wish with all my heart to take home

Charlotte Powers

Time

There isn't time, there isn't time,
To do the things I want to do
With all the mountains and hills to climb,
And all the forest to wander through
With all the rivers and lakes to see,
And everywhere else there is to go
All I want to do is be free,
To be able to hear the wind gently blow
I ask myself where the time goes by,
As I sit here thinking and wondering why.

Ellen Mazzara

Call Of The Wild

The birds and bugs and animals call out to me
to come and see, what's right for me.
I do not come, but still they call, and in a
certain kind of way, they guide me through each night and day.
They say, "Do what's right, and not what's
wrong." But I don't listen to their song.
So they stop calling, and I wish, that they,
could have been more like me, and not listened.

Abbie Mullaney

One Drink

One drink is all it takes
To cause havoc in this life.

One drink is all it takes
To start a chain reaction of
Drinkers and those who live with drinkers
For generations to come.

One drink is all it takes
To become two, three, or more drinks!

One drink is all it takes
For loved ones to suffer,
As well as our bodies suffer,
From the poison.

One drink is all it takes
For days to become mixed up and lives to become screwed up.

Don't take that one drink!
Take one day at a time!

Christine Devorsky

The Gold Digger

She pounces like a cat from above
To catch the unsuspecting family off guard

She brings nourishment to the bereaved
At the death of mother and spouse

She circles her prey patiently
and never wavers from her goal

They accept her and welcome her in
until it is too late to stop her

They realize her passion,
To marry, not for love or compassion

She robs the children of lifelong dreams
as they watch their world fall apart

Father is lost as he turns against them
Innocence is screamed through evil hisses

Heirlooms disappear in front of their eyes
As Father fades, passes and dies

The will is read, the sentence given
She licks her lips like a well-fed kitten

Elaine B. Fryar

The Crying Lakes And Beaches

Once we were pure, free, and uncontaminated you see. Oh, how we loved
to caress the chubby legs of infants, to tickle toes, to nourish
living things, and to be a place for fun and relaxation to all people.

Oh, how we love to splish, splash! We are beginning to get
contaminated you see. Things are riding on top of us—cans, bottles,
papers, oils, and all kinds of debris. Why are these things
hindering us? We are suppose to flow free. Oh, how we love to be
free! Splish, splash! Splish, splash!

Today, we are crying you see. People—men, women, and children—are
in and all around us. They see, use, and then litter us. We do not
need the big environmental groups. Just common people—men, women,
and children—like yourselves to be and flow free. We are the crying
lakes and beaches you see. Oh, how we love to be free. Splish,
splash! Splish, splash!

We have no lawyer, no trial, and no jury. We are fighting a
war without weapons. Please let us remain forever to flow
free. Be our voice, we do not want to die you see. We are
your crying lakes and beaches that you see. Oh, how we love
to be and flow free. Splish, splash! Splish, splash!

Ceola Washington

Shackled

Here I am hoping, longing
To be freed from the chains of frustration
To be unshackled and set free
From the bondage cast upon me
Being totally useless
Unable to ride off into the sunset
Or to even greet the sunrise with sweet anticipation
Knowing that another day will go by untoiled
Trudging through mother nature's inferno
Reaping nothing, but instead wallowing in rejection
Trying desperately to free myself from the shackles that bind me
Hoping somewhere out there a key will be found
And I'll be set free once again
Free to roam the streets and sidewalks
Knowing that someone really cares about me
Cares enough to help me find that key
That key that will unshackle the chains that bind me.

Anthony Melville

Basking In Love

Bask: to lie in warmth
To be exposed
Or to expose to a comfortable warmth.

No urgency. No pretense
Sincerity and interest
Marking a slow, steady exchange of
thoughts, happenings and dreams.

Thoughtful listening
caring concern.
Friendship growing, building slowly
a bond to last through time and troubles

Some jesting
A few chuckles
Delightful awareness of a joining of
minds and hearts sharing the joy of life.

Audrey Neiffer

A Hero's Glory

The creator breathes the breath of life
  to be born,
To train for the life of a warrior.
To leave his memories of his fondest home,
To make his name a name of fame
  known throughout the world,
To find his place in battle,
To reach his ultimate goal and earn
  his rewards,
To meet his maker, for this is a
  hero's story.

Erik Herber

Friends

Friends are people who never let you down.
They're always there to lift you up.
They don't say mean things
To make you look like a clown.

Friends are always there to care and share.
All the comfort you can bear.
Friends are people you can't live without
Or it would be lonely without a doubt.

To have a friend be a friend, that's no mystery.
To have a friend be a friend, that's the secret you see.

Brina Nicole Johnston

My Days In The Sun

My days in the sun,
  to bark and wag my tail and run.

To snap at flies, and terrorize cats
  and squirrels and butterflies.

To run astray, and return in just one day
  and still have time to eat and play.

For lots of love a member of
I've even been a victim of a robbery
  and a rescue too
  and that's what makes me such a part of you.

And then one day I turn old and gray,
  and you no longer have to tell me stay.

For in my eyes you realize how very close we are
  in each others eyes.

And when I die I know you'll cry,
  because you will finally say
  he (she) was a really good guy.

Annette L. Sparks

Dreadful Realities

Why, why must they the cherubs, toddlers,
  tiny tots, preschoolers,
Die for the sins of greed.
Why, Serbia, Why?
Mothers and Fathers, your hearts cry for them.
These cherubs, toddlers, tiny tots,
  and preschoolers - killed.
Why, Serbia, Why?

Grandmothers and Grandfathers - show us
  your bravery, your courage, valor, heroism,
  virility - you with your experience.
Help us see why our cherubs, toddlers
  tiny tots, preschoolers - died
Why, Serbia, Why?

Don't cry for us, who die -
Alas, we, the cherubs, toddlers,
  tiny tots, preschoolers
Will never hear or see another bullet,
Another blast, another sleepless night.
Why, Serbia, Why?

Angie Pascua

"Southern"

They perform for their elders,
Though they are children, too, in a way.
They speak of their hospitality,
You wouldn't know of it if they didn't,
For it is not shown.

Criticize faults in others,
The same faults that lie in them.
Anger, of an event 130 years past,
Is shown by their flag.

This land is a private club,
One to which I don't know the password.
Keep my feelings inside, if I want to fit,
And make the best of it.

I do not speak of all,
But truly kind, "real" souls are few.
My home waits for me,
That is all the comfort I need.

Brian T. O'Connell

Those Glimpses And Dreams

Never forget, always remember
Those places in your past,
Those people whom you love the most,
Those memories you cannot forget,
Those dreams you wanted to come true,
Those morals you were raised on,
Those goals you strived for,
Those ideals you wanted to achieve.

For in your striving and venturing,
You love lost and your goals achieved,
Your memories forgotten, and your pinnacles reached,
There will always be something bigger,
There will always be someone higher.

We on this earth are just passing through
From the richest to the poorest.
For life is just a glimpsing moment in time,
Here one minute and vanishing the next.

Barbara L. Younker

"My Mother's Hands Were Made Of Gold"

My mother's hands were made of gold,
This is a story to be told.
A professional seamstress, as you can see,
With three daughters, busy as a bee.
Silks and satins and velvets, too,
Buttons and bows, to name a few.
She'd cut the material and quick as a wink,
The sewing machine followed, right on the brink,
Her work was impeccable, without a doubt,
We could wear our dresses, inside out.
I'm sure up above, the angels are dressed,
With her gossamer gowns, that are surely blessed.
Can I ever forget, to this very day,
Her wonderful sewing, whenever I pray.

Frances Coco

Demons

They stood in the dark, casting no shadows.
They stood in the dark, gleaming blood red.
They stood in the shadows with evil intentions running through minds
    warped with the dark.

One stepped away, and gestured.
One stepped away, and clicked a jaw.
One stepped up and circled around you while running talons on your
    throat then pulled away.

Fear coursed through you, as they circled 'round.
Fear coursed through you, as they touched you.
Fear coursed hotly as they licked jaws red with glistening saliva and
    looked at you.

You fight back, as they close in.
You fight back, when teeth catch your skin.
You fight desperately and wrench from their clenching hold and give
    right back.

They cower in fear, as you growl.
They cower in fear, as you crouch.
They cower and quiver as you vent your anger in heaving rips and
vulgarly kill what you fear.

Emily Nichols

Dangling

Like a dictator, your words control me,
They push, pull, form, and mold me.
From a thread I hang fragile and weak
Waiting for the wind from the words you speak.
At times I feel stability from the sway,
But your smallest act sends me on way:
Spinning and twirling, my vision is hazed,
Caught in this whirlpool, confused and dazed.
Making something of nothing, more of less.
My heart inflates with a smile or caress.
But if you don't notice when walk in the room,
An apathetic glance can pop my balloon.
My emotions I no longer command,
They are lifted and lowered by the force of your hand.
I am trapped in this maze with no way out,
Stranded on an island of questions and doubt.
Hung on your rope, I continue to swing,
Someone give me scissors to cut the string.

Alyssa Anne Peterson

The Ledge

I'm holding on as best I can. I'm holding on, I am.
They may push me to the edge. But I'm holding on, I am.
And every time they shove me, I trip towards the edge...
Somehow steadying my footing, before I leave that final ledge.
He's telling me he hates her, she tells me she hates him.
I am the mediator, I speak of tales grim.
So greedy and so anxious, vengeful visions are all they see.
Not remembering that the love they shared,
Is how I came to be.
Their last link of loathing, how can they not see?
That their anger will destroy
the mediator...Me.

Deena A. Rashedi

Flowers

The flowers that lie on the floor tonight...
They brought me so much joy and delight,
But now they mean nothing lying there...
Sometimes I wish that he were still here.
The memories we had I will always hold...
But they aren't as happy, they are so cold.
They all say not to worry, there are others just right,
But why do I lie here so lonely tonight?
Maybe I'll find someone to love soon...
So then in my heart new flowers will bloom!

Angela Meier

The Storm

I lie here alone, tangled in my sheets; my emotions.
The sky rages; the jagged beauty of the storm
    frightens me, encompasses me, consumes me.
To catch a piece, one solitary bolt, is my dream.
But I can't catch the lightning in a jar - so to speak.
With tears streaming down my face, I run
    outside and let the fury of the storm
    cleanse my senses.
The clouds twist and turn in a wrathful dance;
I imitate them with my voice.
Loud and strong I sing my apology...
Soft and pure I plead for forgiveness...
In my exhaustion I collapse and let the
    rain comfort me as I sleep for the
    first time in centuries.

Deborah J. Logan

Vignettes

One cannot own a cat!
There's nothing wrong with that.
We bought "Gizmo" food, litter and a mouse
Before he deigned to rule our house.

Loving you in their world
Is like getting on the exit ramp
To go north
On the southbound freeway.

I read the reviews every day
In the paper where they hold sway.
I find this writer to be weak,
One who envies, thus must critique.

Steel-tipped claws
To velvet paws
Gizmo's gift.

For years I assumed God was "He",
But now some say he's "she".
I balk a bit asserting "it".
Could it perhaps be "We"?

Eve Lewis-Chase

Whiter Than Snow

Have you ever been out in a new fallen snow?
There's nothing so white in this whole world below
So shining, so glistening, so pure and so clean
The most beautiful white man has ever seen.
But there is a white that is whiter than snow
Our God has proclaimed it, and I know it's so.
Though your sins be as scarlet, a bright crimson red
They'll be whiter than snow, when washed in the Blood Jesus shed.
Whiter than snow, whiter than snow
Jesus Blood washes sins whiter than snow.

If your garments are sin stained, soiled and unclean.
Won't you come to Jesus, oh come be redeemed?
Repent of your sins, lay them all at his feet.
He'll cleanse you, redeem you, make your life complete.
For there is a white that is whiter than snow
Our God has proclaimed it and I know it's so.
Though your sins be as scarlet, a bright crimson red
They'll be whiter than snow, when washed in the Blood Jesus shed
Whiter than snow, whiter than snow
Jesus Blood washes sins whiter than snow.

Freda B. Still

Happy Birthday Lighthouse

You say the leaf doesn't fall far from the tree
There's a strong connection between you and me
You are like my lighthouse in so many ways
You give me strength and direction to start each new day
You are like my personal shining tower
I would settle for a husband like you, if only for a few hours
In times of pain, I'll cry with you
When you are happy, there's tears of happiness too
When you left the nest, the memories did flood
Of childhood, then teens, then father hood
I didn't lose a son, I am happy to say
But I gained a daughter that I love in every way
So on this day I think of you most
If we are apart, I'll drink a toast
To the wonderful man, who came from me
A part of you is mine, I hope that you see
No matter where ever you are on this day.
I wish you love and happiness in every possible way

This light house is my Dan.

Cova Moore Coppler

Willie

It's not cold anymore
there is sunshine
on my face warming my soul

I hear the splash
of a beckoning fish calling my name
the snap of a twig
heralds the approach
of a magnificent stag

I can ride the wind
across the valley of
my heaven as the power of the steed
beneath me fills my heart

I don't sleep, for now I am really alive
so don't look for me and don't cry for me

I will just go ahead of you and make the
camp fires ready under the stars
God created

I will patiently wait
until you join me
For today I am truly where I belong.

Dani McNeil

Waiting

Somewhere out in the distance
There is someone waiting
Waiting for the right moment
A moment to rise into the light
Waiting, watching, listening
Wondering when to begin
Wanting to be noticed but not knowing how
Speaking but not being heard
Trying to exist in a society with strong opinions
Trying to find herself
Trying to show her true self to a world of disbelievers
Wanting to fit in but being outcast
Wanting to understand something that can not be understood
Wishing, hoping, wanting
Her dream to come true
Still she sits ... waiting
Hoping for a friend
A friend that will stay beside her, guide her, follow and protect
Then she stops waiting and starts doing
And her friend is there beside her every step of the way

Dana M. Schwaller

The House on the Hill

What's in the old house on the hill?
There is a glass ballerina on the window sill.
Its long, pink, flowing dress is torn on the side,
Where is the rest?
It sits on the sill, in the house on the hill.

Way back when, in the good old days,
it was a mighty fine house, if I might say.
Lying on the brand new porch, in the sun very hot,
Now a days the porch, ready to rot.
Ready to rot, in the sun very hot.

The beautiful pink dress, with the tear on the side.
The tear isn't small, it is quite big, quite wide.
Where is the fabric to fill the tear?
Maybe it's here, maybe it's there.
We must fill the hole from the tear on the side.

Hey, look! What's that over there?
By the books, behind the chair.
It looks like a piece of fabric that's pink.
Now we have found the missing link,
For the glass ballerina on the window sill.

Erin Sarah Babcock

Like A...

Like a cheap surprise staring me in the face,
then leaving without a trace.
Like an ardent desire burning in my mind,
mostly being left behind.
Like a kind of warfare eating at me,
tempting my eyes only to see.
Like another sleepless night,
and next not knowing wrong from right.
Like a fool telling me where to go,
next ending up on losers row.
Like a moist victual charming,
but to my waist harming.
Like a peace that passes all comprehension,
leaving no tension.
Like a world that is perfect,
not a world wrecked.
Like a bored girl with nothing to do in sight,
so she thinks of comparisons to write.

Courtney Rycroft

Craving

If you hate me
Then hate me with all your heart
Since hate and love are so closely linked
An emotion as strong as hate can only come from the heart
Hate me with blinding rage
Not hiding behind smiles and tentative hellos
Cruel, sarcastic jokes are fine
But don't patronize me with false affection
Let your hate drip from every word
Like a blood soaked knife
My last request is that you hate me
With the essence of your being
Give me genuine, pure hate
Let it radiate from your eyes
Like a lighthouse aglow during a tempestuous night
And let it pour from your lips
In an endless stream of sardonic laughter
I relish in it
I will devour every bit of it and beg for more

Erika Thomas

Pan's Flute

Roller-blades scrape across the pavement. Harsh Atlantic waves toss
themselves on the scorching sand. Children whine in the wilting heat.
Laughter, raucous, comes from the cheap, boardwalk, bar. Girls giggle
as they allow plastic-faced boys to grease their sleek, well-fed,
barely covered, bodies. The South American street musicians prepare
to play and stand with their cases open in the hopes of gaining U.S.
dollars. I watch. They begin to slowly play, and I am pulled closer.
His, the flutist's, long, blue-black, hair gently lifts with the
steamy breeze. His lips form and puff at each tube. His copper
fingers contrast with the stark white, half-moons in his nails and
with the pale wooden flute. Satin lashes close to mask the ancient
soul peering from behind his liquid amber eyes. Soon he possesses my
spirit and he carries me with him, spiraling upward over snow-capped
mountains and then downward through mist enshrouded forests which hide
the ruins of temples of Gods he resurrects. Again, we fly above
winding mountain trails traversed by weary Alpacas and stoop
shouldered old men. They weave their way into an impoverished city
polluted by North American factories. We climb higher and lazily
drift on gentle air currents. Suddenly, we are forced to return to
the present. The music stops. My blue eyes meet his. We look away.
Our embrace ends with his song, and I want another, but the roller
blades, the waves, and the decaying boardwalk swim into unwelcome focus.

Cristiana Ritchie-Carter

"Fishing For Friends"

Pixies and elves are beautiful folk
Their features sharp and delicate
Their bodies are smaller and trimmer than most
Their sense of humor is definite

They flash their smiles wear innocent looks
Their eyes spark twinkles of mirth
They lure you in with subliminal hooks
And pull you in to their berths

Don't fear that your life will be taken my friend
They only want a companion
Their friendship is valued and true to the end
You just can't turn that down now can you

This is one final valuable point
From it you just can't deviate
These pixies and elves they can invade your heart
So don't let love intermediate

Christopher Wayne Pritchard

Erotic Sorceress

Submerged into the opaqueness of solicitude
The young female, more an object rather than human being,
    entered exile
Forced to flaunt as opposed to conserve
Innocence stolen by the barbaric vandal, categorized only by
    her kind - women of the night - as criminal
The erotic sorceress had finally been violated in her
    escapade,
She had lost control.

Angel Grooms

"Change"

Years ago when we were young,
The word "equal" hadn't come,
When blacks were slaves and us their masters
They were whipped and worked in pastures.

Unfair is the word I'd use,
Some were beaten and abused,
Others were treated very fairly,
But still I worked all day and wanted to be free.

Martin Luther King once said,
"Not to worry all shall soon come to an end"
And that it did not long ago,
When blacks were freed the rest you know.

Then "equal" came in to play,
Now we raise our heads and say,
Blacks may all be free to roam,
And shall live in a decent home.

Cortney Kendall

"Solitude"

As I sit here in the shade, I see beauty all around;
The way the lateral lines are laid, and the way they have
cared for the ground.

Surely kings and queens must rest here, under the gardeners
tool, for this is no place for the common man, the beggar, or
the fool.

But just because the monuments gleam, does that make it a
holy place?
For even though they have joined their maker, they shall
never see his face.

David Mills

The Ocean

The ocean floor is green and blue,
The waves they ripple through and through,
The sun that shines so nice and bright, gives off
colors lovely lights, and when it reflects upon the floor
I think and think and think some more, then the
the daytime that once was turns to shining stars above, I
watch until the tide comes in... the ocean, stars and
moon so bright, will always be there day or night.

Christine Geanuracos

You're Everything To Me

You're the breath of my life
The vision in my soul
The heart that beats within me
And you'll always be everything to me

Kids grow up and go their way
So till then I'll hold you very close to me
I dread the day you go away
For yesterday never again can ever be

And as you grow through all your childish ways
I'll live through all that's within you
And perhaps inspire something
That's already inside of you

When you hurt I feel the pain
When you cry, tears I shed, but not in vain
In year to come the sweet memories
Will live on in my heart very melancholy

All past heartaches I've cast aside
All frustrations I've swept to the sea
You're my joy, my life, my pride
'Cause you're everything, yes everything you're everything to me

Evelyn Woodward

One More to Hades

From a blackened, lonely heart
  the tears of blood red hate
    Seethe through veins
    and finally escape
      To the ducts
        of glassy staring eyes
          A salty sea
          growing deep
          and cold
            Two final drops
            slowly make
            a silent waltz
              down a lifeless face
                Before this life, slipped away
                a voice
                  cold as ice
                    sold his soul
                      to the king of lies...
                      his heart
                        turned to coal

Catherine Marooney

Old Timber

The forest of old trees silently reminded me to pray.
The sounds of the forest creatures reminded to me
listen to what God had to say.
The beauty of the woodland flowers reminded me of
Gods many blessings.
The fragrance of the forest that floated on the
soft breeze breathed peace and energy into my soul.
It is good to be with trees that are about one-hundred years old.

Alyce M. Nielson

Laura Sings

She stands at the window
the sun admires her hair of young strawberries
her skin of smooth white porcelain.

Lips softly forced
the small bird escapes
first lingering then rising
coloring the air with breaths of loving and vision.
Arias of loneliness and forgiving
Hymnodies to soft rain and dried petals in small tin boxes.

Wings then stilled
for the graceful descent
to perch on tiny coral lips.

Such sadness in leaving this glorious day
but to pierce the veins of this tender child and drink the sweet fluid
is the strength behind the flight.

One look back
wings gently folded
the bird is lovingly swallowed.

Elyse J. Whitmore

Untitled

The night was cobalt blue and sultry
The stars were our companions
The day is dawning yellow
My blue-eyed cat is half-asleep
This is a beautiful day!
The brown sparrows are chirping
Any bread today?
Green weeds grow tall like wheat
In red clay pots on the black tar roof
The redbrick wall has chinks in its armor
Mortar is needed
Inside the ceiling has sinuous cracks
Like the map of Yugoslavia
City people need green in their lives but
The subways are grey and dirty
As I drink my black coffee, grey headlines say
Bosnia is grey and dirty with grey men
In steel helmets and tanks, grey, grey, grey
Where is the Olympic Sarajevo?
What happened to the beautiful day?

Claire Perrone

I'll Still Be Waiting

Just as echoes in a tunnel,
the sound of my voice perceives.
Just as moments of glory,
my heart still feels the needs.
Just as long enduring heartaches,
I can still feel the pain.
Even though you may not be listening or understand,
Or even if you don't share the same feeling.
I'll be the one waiting with all the voice, needs, and pain.
And when you know the way I feel about you,
And realize you need someone who will be your friend,
And can understand the love I share for you,
Just come to me and I'll be there.

Casey Allen Martin

Emotions

The passion in the kiss was a likeness to my death,
The drama in the moment was a grasping at my last breath,
I screamed into the night my sinful soul you had released,
My corrupted thoughts had thoughtfully been ceased,
My sinful thought soon became more than a secret from within,
They became my reality in this deadly sin.

Crystal Main

"Soundings"

The view of a quiet lake at sunrise.
The sound of a trickling brook and
The birds chirping in the trees.
Ocean waves breaking
And the splash of a sailboat on a breezy day.
The quietness of a plane way up high
Then, a wet tongue licking my face
It's my dog Bingo.
She wants to go someplace
These are the sounds that fill my life.

Antony C. Galdi

Updraft

I am torn between the lone trail and the sunrise which is you
The solitude of nighttime and the softness of the dew

From the morning when I waken to the evening's fingered light
I have struggled with the raging of my soul to see the night.

Can I weep for all that might have been and truly say goodby?
When only but a glance from you will thunder up the sky.

Do you drive me from you hurried cause you fair can see my plight?
Do you fear to join me separate and go chasing up the night?

Can we really keep our solitudes yet never say goodby?
Or ever cling or never cling until we too shall die?

Must I choose my soul which cries for peace, my heart which cries for you?
Is there really not a way to choose except between the two?

Must I "take the road less travelled by" and say farewell to you?
Or in your care will you be there and take the same trail too?

Fred Yonkman

Wonders

Have you ever wondered about
the sky, or the moon? Or the rain,
or the hail, or the snow that may lay there?
Have you ever felt like you were
flying through the sky, or walking through
the ground and wondering why?
Have you ever wondered what it's
like to die, or go to heaven?
Do you ever wonder what it
would be like in someone else life?
Do you ever look around at the trees
and clouds, or look up at the starry sky at night?
Do you ever wonder how all the
beautiful nature was put here?
Have you ever wondered of
mysteries of life like these?
Wonders.

Crystal Schoch

The Leftovers

Many times I have seen them in
the shadows, silently watching and hoping,
that somebody cares.
The Leftovers.

Under the couch hidden forever.
Working their ways late at night.
When the house is quite.
The Leftovers wait.

On a hidden shelf in a hidden library.
Dust covers the rotting bindings,
mildew creeps between the pages.
The Leftovers.

In the hidden recesses of my mind.
In the dark corners of my well being.
The Leftovers wait.

Brian Greenough

The Child Died

A child died, in my embrace last night.
The silver moon was the child's last sight.
I cried silver tears, that streamed down my face.
Tiny sobs heard, the child cried in my embrace.
I held on tight not wanting to let it go.
The grieving process is one that is always painful and slow.
I kicked and cried and screamed, I fought against the Lord.
Who took the child from me, on silver wings it soared.
I pressed my face to the earth, as I sank down to my knees
With visions of the child, sailing over silver seas.
Now I must stand strong, for the child who had died.
Was the one inside of me, the one who never lied.
The one who had the innocence, and hope inside her heart.
But now the innocence and the knowledge will forever be apart.
The child inside of me, I embraced last night.
The events of my life, sent it upon its flight.
Now I am left to reflect, on the tears upon my face.
And remember the tiny sobs I heard, and the child who died in my embrace.

Amber Christopherson

Shadows Of The Mind

While watching sunlight through the trees,
The shadows start to fade
Another day has slipped away,
No life's decisions made.
Tonight I'll come to you again
In dreams I'll see your face
With outstretched arms I'll reach for you,
We'll kiss in an embrace
We'll hold each other once again
Our hearts both young and free
Forgetting for the moment,
That our love cannot be
When daybreak comes, I'll leave again
To walk my path alone
The memory of last night's dream,
To you will be unknown.
I dare not think of you today,
For you must stay behind
In darkness you must wait for me
In the shadows of my mind.

Bonnie Atkinson Charles

Life Of A Rose Bush

February,
The seed of our relationship is planted in the nutrient rich soil of
our hearts. The seed is soon sprinkled with love and caring, and
starts to grow.
March,
A downpour of love and newly found affection causes the seed to sprout
into a seedling. Buds begin to form, and beautiful green leaves of
trust and honesty grow rapidly along the stems.
April,
The newly formed buds bloom, and the rose, in all its glory, is
displayed. Not yet a mature plant, the rose bush grows, and for every
roses that appears, several thorns join it. These thorns hurt and give
pain unfelt before...but these thorns are quickly put aside as more
love and caring are mixed into the soil. This added love causes the
roots to grow strong, and they hold fast into the soil, giving the
rose everything they need to grow and survive.
May,
The rose bush, with ever increasing love, caring, and affection
watering it, grows more beautiful than ever. And with careful
trimming and pruning the bush is finally ready to take on any
challenges that it might encounter.
June,
The rose bush is fully mature now, and new complexities await its
future, but the roses will always be in bloom, no matter what happens
to them. For the water they receive, along with a strong foundation
of roots that grow deep into the soil of our hearts, will never allow
anything to destroy the plant we've worked so hard to grow, together.

Brian Streich

Ode To Fifty

Sadly I gazed at the moon,
The same old moon—
    How many dreams,
    How many tears,
    How many heartaches,
    How many years?
And I looked down the street,
The same old street—
    How many skipping, jumping feet,
    How many trudging, dragging feet,
    How many laughing girls and boys,
    How many years?
And I stood on the banks of the little brook,
The same little brook—
    Rushing, tumbling, under the bridge,
    Frozen, trickling under the bridge.
    How many heartaches,
    How many years,
    How many moons,
    How many tears?

Ardelle D. Crommett

"Half Mast"

As I watch T.V. to see if Sadat is dead,
the radio plays "Imagine there's no heaven."
A flood of memories come drifting pass,
A riderless horse; the Presidential
hearse; flags flown at half mast.
For all to share he had a dream,
that all men were equal, that God did care.
Again the widow cries, when shots
ring out during California's
celebration . . . .
and the young Senator dies.
Upon our hearts the scars remain,
of near assassinations on
our own leader, a religious one afar.
Bullets flying everywhere on
blood stained streets,
Still, the parade passes by.
As I watch T.V.
the radio plays "the world will
be as one".

Debbie Johnston

Reunion: Abuelita Padilla Y Tia Dominga

They are the winter of our family,
the old women bound in Spanish silence, like two
bare, gnarled trees, stark against a pale
snowy sky. They watch us, unspeaking,
from behind thick glasses, their eyes distorted and

huge, maybe remembering when their faces were
petal-fresh and hope ripened in their
spring hearts, before the coming of summer
when their bodies matured with the olives
and the grapes and their dreams were born into

their joyous midst, before the autumn began
and their raven hair went silver with the
golding leaves, before things began detaching
themselves, like dying husbands or children scattering
to the winds, before coming to America and

meeting these hundreds of great-grandchildren
whose language is unintelligible
and who look on the winter mothers like
impossibilities—
nothing could be so old.

Christina Padilla

Night Sun

As darkness sluggishly falls over the sweet day air.
The night sun comes out of its forbidden cave.
It rises above the rest and seems to engulf the still darkness.
As it moves it seems to be traveling on a path around the earth's aura.
When after his time is up, he must go back to that forbidden cave
to live alone.
When the day moon does not rise it seems to be an omen of sadness
and misfortune.
When after it rises, peace returns.

Dana Rinkle

What Is Black

Black is a raven or a crow flying across the sky
The night sky on a cloudy night
A witch's dress or a magician's hat
A black cat may give you bad luck
The coal in the fire's strong smell
Black is ashamed of something it did
it hides in the darkness
it holds an important role in the color family
for it is the great grandfather of all the colors
with white as its wife

Annie Bolotin

My Sorrows

The night and the people aren't the same.
The night is nice but, the people are ashamed.
Why in the day the people change?
Is it because they fear life is going away.
What does it take to see the sorrow in my eyes?
Is it me or could it be you in a life of endless lies.

Why does it have to be me in a world of defenseless fights.
Why does it have to be me when the warriors are in
unnecessary battles, and that the innocent are taken
from their destinies in life.

But don't they know that life itself is crying
every second of the day.
Why don't they take it seriously instead of thinking it's a game?

The people don't know and neither do I that life
is a big surprise.
But can't you just see the tears in my eyes.
Can't you see my sorrows grow deeper and deeper, and
that my heart grows sadder and sadder.
So now you know how I feel about life and what in it.
But still my life had always and will be my sorrows.

Anita Perez

Blue Sherbet Skies

Miracles and magic, fantasies and dreams
The mystique of a child's imagination
Is the reason for his schemes.
Childish observations that are made every day
Are perceived by little minds in a most unusual way.
Giant sugar-coated mountains tickling blue sherbet skies
With cotton candy clouds quickly floating by
Is the way it is seen through a child's eye.

Curious young people who ask questions galore
Thirsting for answers, craving to learn more.
The miracle of childhood goes by very fast
For a short time, it is the present
Soon after, it is the past.
All the fantasies and dreams that played important parts
Become cherished memories tucked inside our hearts.
If we can feel the magic of blue sherbet skies,
We will remember our childhood with stars in our eyes.

Carolyn Kessler

A Hint

You are the one I long for in my dreams,
The most special person in the world to me.
The love I see in your smile's gleam,
Is the answer I seek to my lover's plea.

Someday I know you will be with me.
Someday in another time or place,
As soon as I find the misplaced key,
True love will be yours and mine.

Our lives would be filled with pleasures so deep,
When I unlock the way to your heart.
You and I together - nothing could be sweeter.
I can't imagine us ever apart.

And so I pledge to you my love,
A life of new joys everlasting.
We will fit together like hand and glove,
So let your heart answer what I am asking.

Austin B. Carpenter

Night And Day Dreams

The sun is warm in tender loving care.
The moon is cold it chills the air
The stars are guardians of the moon
at night they block out the sun
light up the sky, they give you sweet dreams
and nasty nightmares.
Indians believe in the dream catcher
for sweet dreams all night.
The sun comes, it fades away the nasty nightmares
it is a new day.
Now we the people live this new day,
wear it down and fade it away.
We sleep of sweet dreams; no nightmares,
under the chilly moon and guardian stars.
We wake up all over again—sweet dreams

Corrie L. Parr

Untitled

I don't know why I can't say good-bye,
The memories are just too far deep inside.
The tears I've shed have rolled down my cheek
Into an empty pit that's dark and bleak.
The pain and anger I've felt inside,
Is just too hard for me to let it slip by.
Not knowing why I had let him die,
Because a friend let a friend drink and drive.

Abbie L. Watson

Positive Love

A positive love is around, now it's a world of knowing
the love that feels the world with attitude to go
toward a new start.

Keeping your love in touch with yourself to know there
is no one better than yourself.

There's a positive outlook to everyone you meet and how
you start, it feels good and good comes out of it.

It now time to start by keep telling yourself
Stand by that positive love don't let no one
take it from you.

Christine Slominski

Rain Drops

A sudden summer rain,
The landscape starts to slowly change,
Small muddy puddles for frogs to play,
Bubbles form, then burst with spray,
On a rainy summer day.
Birds sit patiently in the trees,
waiting for a gentle breeze,
To drive the dark clouds away,
And bring up dinner from the clay,
worms wiggle softly, on damp earth,
The birds watch silently from their perch,
wings flutter, and from earth's bounty
They take home nourishment for their family.
This will always be the way,
of the end of a rain on a summer's day.

Brenda Chavis

Michael

I listen to the clock tick and stare at
the kitchen table.
You sit there, quietly reading a book.
I stand against the counter,
Picking at the chipped formica with a
Jaggedly bitten fingernail,
Feeling words of anger drop from my tongue.
A tongue once healing to your soul.
Now my soul is all I have.
Your eyes turn you away from me to
Peer out the window of security.
I cannot open my mouth and say nothing.
I cannot save what is dead.
I can only stand here and allow you to leave
My mind.
I can only release you and pray that you find
Your way home.
"I don't know you anymore," I whisper.
You blink
And I know that you have already left.

Cessy Adamczyk

The Silent Words

With the moments that all the hours possess,
The joys, the fears, and sadness every day-
The times when one should speak I must confess
Are moments I've mishandled every way.
The fool speaks up when words will smart and sting...
I speak of times when words might most console,
Those moments... silence would be last to bring
Some comfort to a friend or needy soul.
When thinking of those words one might have said -
In their reflections... when those moments passed
I cursed myself... for such a heart of lead
And stilted tongue, the bond their silence cast!
Oh, how un-Christian! Thoughtless! How unfair
Were all those words I failed to speak right there!

Allen Grant

Untitled

A baby blessing,
ten little fingers,
ten little toes,
a sweet little smile,
a cute little nose!
A gift was sent from Heaven above,
for Mom, and Dad, and every one to love.

Emily Volz

My Legacy

I leave the mountains green and tall
The honeysuckle on the garden wall
The weeping, weeping willow trees
That sorrow for the things that cannot be.

I leave sweeping fields of corn
To sustain generations yet unborn
The weeping, weeping willow trees
That sorrow for the things that cannot be.

I leave the children's laughter at play
The little falls and hurts along the way
The weeping, weeping willow trees
That sorrow for things that cannot be.

I leave strains of a melody
Its memories of tragicomedy
The weeping, weeping willow trees
That sorrow for things that cannot be.

I leave no material wealth
Just love of God with whom I've dealt
The weeping, weeping willow trees
That sorrow for things that cannot be.

Frances H. Sacks

A Twist Of Fate

There's a young man and a dark haired girl, walking hand in hand up
  the hill
Headed for that special place to declare a love so real
They climbed upon the rock one day with love and joy deep in their hearts
He gazed into her soft brown eyes and said, I know we'll never part
The names written on the rock that day, were to seal their love forever
For little did they know, that soon they would not be together

A twist of fate, a few mistakes, would separate these two lovers
But in their hearts, a love remained, that they only felt for each other
Years past by, one by one, keeping them miles apart
But miles were only numbers, for they were always as close as the heart

A twist of fate, a few mistakes, separated these two lovers
But now a simple phone call, brought them back together
Tears of joy and happiness, were shed upon that day
Years and miles had kept them apart, but they were only a heartbeat away

There's a young man and a dark haired girl, walking hand in hand up
  the hill
Headed for that special place, to declare a love so real
The names that were written long ago, on the rock still remained
A little faded, a little worn, but to them, looked the same
This time they added a new name, and carved it upon the rock
Of a baby girl with soft brown curls, from a love that will never stop

Barbara Riley Harless

The Dice Game

One up, one down,
The dice go round.
Turn about, different route,
New shooter coming out.

In and out, a brand new rumble,
Across the table, dice do tumble.
Some will win, some will loose,
The numbers we get, we do not choose.

And whether we guess, or whether we pray,
Each of us has chosen to play.
Life is a game we may not win,
But if were lucky, we get to roll the dice again.

Adam Brodofsky

A Sublime Summer Day

The leaves are a magnificent green;
The grass is a tinted brown.
It is such a beautiful scene,
As if time itself was rewound.

There is a gentle rustle in the brush;
Deer in the shade, alarmed, swivel their ears.
Through the meadow there is a distinctive hush;
Then it relaxes, it's only a child and his peers.

In the brilliance of the summer days,
Everything lives in serenity.
Over her babies the mother bird lays
With no presence of town or city.

No presence of overcrowding or miseries;
No violence or hatred,
No pollution or disease;
Or people who are hungry and underfed.

It is a place of happiness and peace;
It almost couldn't happen, you know.
But think of it when your frustration needs to ease:
A peaceful little meadow.

Casey Taylor

My Friend The Wind

To the mountains, rivers and winds ridges and cascading hills
The flat bottomed valley floors
that dwell in the land where I was born
Resisting the strong teeth or the sand and the
murmuring breeze in the musical woods.

To the silence and rich aroma of the dark African nights.
Lit by the bright dancing moon and stars
dangling from the skies above, watching the stillness of the night.
Pierced only by the gentle whispers of my friend the wind

To the rich sands and soils carpeting the rich earth below,
Ready to womb seeds in due season.
Feels and gives virgin sensations,
when freshly turned on cultivation
gin the first welcome of spring.

To the ululations and heart rendering cries of the mothers of my land,
Filling the air with glory and hope.
The choral voices of African birds,
lifting me in an unwilled expectation,
Floating miles away into my temple,
courtesy of my friend the wind.

Bwosinde Hophine

Lovers

Of all the grand old places
The farm most dear to me
Where Mom and Dad sit hand in hand
Under the old shade tree.

They sit there like two young lovers
Talking of times gone by.
Of the fun they had together
Of my brothers, my sister, and I

They talk of their joys and sorrows
Of the turmoil this old world's in
They pray to God together
To keep their children from sin.

Then the moon comes up over the mountain
The stars guide them from above
They kiss and thank God for that wonderful gift
Of teaching them how to love

Ellen Gilfoyle Andrew

A Storm Far Away

Freedom, but for a price of mine.
The Eagle is strong, but only for thine.
We must belong, yet we long.
Nobody is closer, yet we are all alone.

Sounds of thunder loom so long,
They last forever, then they are gone.
Lost in the moment, then back again.
As loud as the boom, and then it began.

Moving into the storm where all is wild.
To young to know, some were still but a child.
Dark all around, yet the sky is mild.
Dark inside where emotions are piled.

Lost in youth and we were naive.
Only He knows of our desperate deeds.
Wanting to be there, wanting to do more.
Wandering alone, if we would soon be poor.

A price forever will be, it will last forever in thee.
Winds and Eagles are strong, but for a price of mine.
No country, or person, or king shall be.
Freedom, but for a price of mine.

Andrew E. Reibly

Growing Up

As I grew older day by day, I'd put one thing of a child away.
The dolls, the memories, no time to play,
No more little voices coming my way.

As I grew older and older still, no more daydreams by the window sill.
A little less fun, a little less zeal,
No more time to 'the apple off the peel'.

As I grew older more and more, a little less I'd knock on grandma's door.
No more stories or sitting on the floor,
A little less adventure in my laugh once more.

But when I grown, there was a change in my tone.
No dolls, no daydreams, no never alone,
Never making a wish on a wish bone.

Now that I'm older and older still, I wish to daydream by the window sill.
I want the adventure in my laugh once more,
To read stories and to sit on the floor.

I can do that, yes I can, for now another takes my hand,
Wants to hear stories and play in the sand.
Oh! To dream of being young, and to live your life before day is done.

Anne E. Harper

Heartache

My pillow holds so many tears, how could it be, in all these years?
The days gone by, held so much joy, and now my heart is like a toy.
It's been abused and tossed around, to say it's broken, should not astound.
How big a heart can show no pain, when love does not return again?
How long must I just wait and cry, and never know the reason why?
My love for you, you do not feel, but yet you know, that it was real.
So now you've taken bit by bit, my love and heart, and broken it.
Why do you like to see me blue, when you know that my love was true?
If tears could mend this broken heart, then we would never be apart.
But all my tears have been in vain, for I've not found my love, again.
But though I suffer, lone and blue, someday it may reverse to you.
And if you ever shed a tear remember, once you had me near.
And if your heart should start to break, you'll know just how my
  heart did ache.
And if you pray that it will mend, just don't forget, my love did end.

Anna H. White

"Springtime"

Springtime is here - and you will surely find.
The days getting warmer - the sun's fiery gem shines.
The buds on the trees begin their fragrant display,
With blossoms of beauty - signaling the month of May.

Little homes constructed of twigs and such things,
Cradle tiny colorful eggs that in a short time bring
Fuzzy little birds sweetly singing out their songs:
"Feed us!! We are hungry!" all the day long.

The warning ponds hold a world of their own,
Tiny tails swishing quickly - soon to be grown
Into frogs who croak out the glories of summer,
Sometimes so loudly - you just listen in wonder!

Tight little bundles enclosed in silken rooms
Hold sleeping caterpillars who are changing and groomed
With summers banners so boldly displayed,
Bright, beautiful butterflies proudly flitting away!

The meadows are a palette of colors galore -
Resplendent with such beauty - carpeting all of earth's floor.
The perfect combination of yellows, pinks and greens
Is there anything more beautiful that your eyes have ever seen?

Cindy L. Allen

Untitled

I want to live near the edge of tomorrow
The dawn of a new day brightening the sky

No dusty yesterdays to cloud the vision
And obscure the view of that which will be

The regrets of yesterdays brushed aside
By the breeze of an early morning

I'd like to begin as if all were new
As a butterfly leaves its cocoon
  breathes the warm fresh air
    tests its wings
And flies free

Carla Kassaw

Lost

As I sit among the big, wide, open world,
The cool breezes chill my body down to the bone.
The feeling of being trapped in a frigid, hollowed hole in the ground,
Covered in the darkness of evil lurking about.
The darkness slowly starts covering the world.
Making it untransparent for me to see. I am lost.

Carrie Hutson

The Competition

It's the feel of ice running under your blade.
The cool breeze hitting your face as you
spin and as you jump up in the air and
you land on your blade.
The feeling you get as you feel the glory
of winning a beautiful gold medal that
you've worked so hard for.
The hours of practice.
The people who have helped!
The coaching you go through.
All the work, but it's worth it.
You've made so many people proud.
Mom, dad, family, friends, your coach.
But most of all have lots of fun.
Because in the end winning isn't everything.

Elizabeth Rocco

The Cardinal's Song

The pounding in my brain and chest calms only when you're near.
The clumsiness and cloudy thoughts then, also, disappear.
The hunger and longing, the needing and the pain
Are stilled by just your tender touch like gently falling rain.

The cardinal gave approval through the window as we lay
In bed that one bright morning in each other's arms at play.
The laughter and the loving, the gentle looks and smiles
Were serenaded by the birds, ceasing internal trials.

I'll share my life and love with you through all we're to endure.
We've shared together once before and that love, too, was pure.
We hold our future in our hands to mold and shape and form.
We'll conquer all we must to reach our shelter from the storm.

And when we've reached our destiny and all is calm and clear,
We'll hold each other every day to drive away the fear.
My love for you is in my soul; my soul will never die.
My love for you is in my eyes; my eyes will never lie.

Debra A. Gray

Leading Him On

The squeak of her skin pressed against
the clean, white toilet mingled
with "Just relax and enjoy it" in her
pierced ears, just before
they were shut off.

His long fingers wrapped around her
knees as they were opened, shaking, then
her skin became separate.

She tasted the salty tears in her mouth
mixed by his tongue, and
"No" escaped right before
her lips froze.

Her eyes could not stay open, exhausted
from pleading.
Her body limp, every one of her senses begged to be somewhere else.
They woke to the creak of an opened door,
the pale light on the cold tiles,
and her underpants at her ankles.

Catherine Rotchford

The Summertime Bugs

Bugs, bugs, so many bugs
The bugs come out and fly all about
Then they land on my hand
And then they bite and take flight again

Bugs, bugs, so many bugs
The bugs come out and fly all about
They're all around my little town
They're here and there and everywhere

Bugs, bugs, so many bugs
The bugs come out and fly all about
To pest us all
Just to have a ball

Bugs, bugs, so many bugs
The bugs come out and fly all about
Ow, one bit me here, one bit me there
I could swear there's a billion out there

Andrea Liddick

Destiny's Song

The sun rides low as I approach
The brooding cliffs and rugged slopes
To lay to rest my silent hopes
Beneath their reddened glow.

Then labor I in mist that chills
From roaring surge that river spills
On somber ground a grave to build
For bygone pride, therein resides, the song I'll never know.

Now night descends as ravens slip
Through ghostly pine tree finger tips
Whose grasp, like mine, has failed to find
Its Destiny to hold.

So seize, my grief, the sickle moon
Then reap the shadows from her tomb
I've dreamed too long to wake so soon
A broken trance, a twist of chance and finally fades the light of home.

But chained to fate I'll blindly cast
To go the way my future passed
Down long and empty roads at last
A fevered race to cross the gates that time and death draw closed.

Alex Rodriguez

Words In The Wind

Come children listen to this pledge for you destruction, rise in
the breeze, the drugs smile angelically at you and the weapons
beckon for your prints upon it.
Listen children to whispers of changes for your morality been
shut off, voices of the rappers unfold and claim from all of you,
your decency that you should own only comes as words in the wind.
Quietly my eyes see the children lost for the streets have
conquered their very souls.
Hearken to the words of the wind, wake up and take control of your
destiny, fate awaits us, all it rests around the corner beyond
the next bend.
Blowing and swaying tenderly calling a halt into the wild of
childhood memories to clear your mind a new born spring
rising from the ground.

Bessie Cochran

Storms

As night falls, a strong wind blows from the South and takes
the bite of winter out of the air. As the storm approaches
my heart and mind open. I am afraid. I have been here
alone many times before.

As the full moon breaks through the stormy clouds, my heart
races. Maybe I'm not alone, maybe there is hope. As the
emotions start to flow, I close my eyes. I feel that someone
is here, holding me. I feel the comfort, the love and passion.
The deep pain in my heart is gone.

Suddenly a clap of thunder, I reach out to that someone.
No one is there. I open my eyes and everything is dark.
Then I realize I am alone. As my heart starts to ache, I fight
back the tears, nobody comforts me now. Like so many
storms in my life.

If only my heart can make it till morning the storm will be
gone. Though my heart will still ache. There will be many
people that will walk with me in the light and a few that might
venture into the night, but I need someone to stand by and
lead me through the storms.

Darryl Smith

"Another World And Another Time"

Day was departing
The beauty of dusk lay over the land
Its fading pinks and somber grays
Cast a glow over the oncoming darkness.

At the foot of the path he was waiting
He took my hand, just as eerie darkness
Fell like a pall about us.

We travelled far that night through forests
And forgotten paths of long ago.
Somehow, we lost our way among the tangled
Weeds and twisted pines;

I searched, but I could not find you
Or the hand that held mine so lovingly;

Perhaps, some day, in another world
And another time, I will find you again,
Among the tangled weeds and the twisted pines.

Emeline (Caretti) Shannon

Untitled

God made the flowers, birds, and trees
The beautiful sunset, oceans, and seas

Then he made man to rule the earth
To produce food, clothing and all our needs

To cherish each other and enjoy our blessings
To help the poor and all those in need

God's angels watch over us
The angels protect us from Satan

Some day we will see Jesus
Who died for us and all will be worth while

The earth will pass away
But in Heaven we will be

No more tears or sorrow
How heaven that will be!

Evelyn Stuart

The Changing Of Time

On this nice and sweet sunny day
The air is chilled, but the robins still play,
A cool breeze now and then, to let us know of winters end.
Bringing to mind on this joyous day,
The reasons we sing, serve, and pray.
People everywhere should make amends.
First with yourself, then others and friends.
How soon will we realize, How soon will we begin
To notice the changing of seasons and the direction of the wind.
It all displays, like an open book
The changing of seasons where ever you look.
People have to change, get back on the road
We all have the same, I mean the same goal.
The time is changing as the seasons unfold.
GOD is the reason and HEAVEN is our goal.

Billy J. Todd Sr.

Dreams

Sing me a lullaby,
tell me a fairy tale
I don't want to know about the real world.
I can imagine better things than I can see,
If only you could give this to me.
To know a better life than I could live
The world is filled with hatred and dread.
To look forward to a day with no murders, no crime,
That is a dream of mine.

Amanda Scott

Grasp A Positive Attitude

A positive attitude is positive thinking.
That's what it's all about; this world
May seem dark and dim but a positive
Attitude is what we need.

Thinking is a fact of life.
Put it together with a positive attitude
You can climb the tallest mountain,
You can over come obstacles,
But a positive attitude is what we need.

We live by faith and not by sight.
Put this together with a positive attitude
And not altitude.
You will survive, with the fate of life behind you.
A positive attitude is what it's all about.

What is this thing called positive attitude?
It's putting everything in the hands of the one who made us.
Smiling when all around us may seem dark.
Walking Tall because you know who hold your hand.
Loving when no one seems to care.
Put these together and a positive attitude is what it is all about.

Beulah Odum

Judy Rose

Judy Rose, do you suppose
That you are in love with me
Cause, if you do, I love you too
That you can plainly see.

Judy Rose with your turned up nose
And your lips so tenderly
When you're alone and your heart you own
Is there a place for me.

Judy Rose with all your buttons and bows
Could you ever be true
If there's a way, then I can say
Judy Rose, I love you.

Bradley LaBrosse

The Day I Fell

A day not so far ago, not far ago at all
That was the day, the day that I would fall
I painted a smile on my face, as so many often do
I looked in the mirror and wondered if it's true

That a smile meant so much, that it took away the fear
no one could ever hurt you, but for me no one could come near

The look on my heart wasn't real, in my reflection I saw that lie
But there was nothing beneath me, I could have died inside

I held at my wrist a device parallel
my thoughts were no where, thought I was in hell
Screaming from all sides of me, I took life in mind
I wanted my life to be there so bad, I left myself behind

I couldn't quite figure out who was I to blame
everything I ever did and put it on my name?

I want to close my eyes and see the dawn again
I hadn't planned that far, what would I do then?

An angel once said to me, I'll never let you down
I'm drowning deep inside, I've already drowned

I hope you remember me - someone you knew well
as someone who lived and tried - on the day I fell

Coe Terronez

Music Is The Language Of The Soul

Music is the language of the soul
That opens hearts to enter in the fold.
The wooing of the Spirit can be heard
In joyful psalms and singing of His word.

Music is the language of the soul;
It strengthens as we strive to reach our goal.
It makes the countenance bright and adds a spark
To fill the night with peace and light the dark.

And it can be the glue, the tie that binds,
The refreshing and renewing of our minds.
Its healing power can make the body whole,
'Cause music is the language of the soul.

Misuse of music through demonic strain
Can cause enormous anguish, grief, and pain.
Satanic use exacts a heavy toll,
For music is the language of the soul.

But the seven-fold doxology shall be
Upon our lips in glorious harmony
When with the rapture, we His face behold,
For music is the language of the soul!

Estelle Gifford Jackson

"I Love You" Means Forever

"I love you" means that I accept you for the person that you are, and
that I don't wish to change you into someone else. It means that I do
not expect perfection from you, just as you don't expect it from me...

"I love you" means that I will love you and stand by you even
through the worst of times. It means loving you when you're in a bad
mood or too tired to do the things I want to do. It means loving you
when you're down, not just when you're fun to be with.

"I love you" means that I know your deepest secrets and do not
judge you for them, asking in return only that you do not judge me
for mine. It means that I care enough to fight for what we have
and that I love you enough not to let you go. It means thinking of
you, dreaming of you, wanting and needing you constantly, and hoping
you feel the same way for me. "I love you" means forever.

Crystal Powell

In Heaven's Shadow

Not once, but twice it seems to be
That Heaven above is calling me;
Through many years of love and care
My first beloved joined Him, up there.
I mourned my loss for several years,
Our favorite songs brought on more tears.
At last I found someone to share
My life, to start again, and care,
But alas, again, after many years
He took away my final tears.

Albert J. Flintzer

Red?

The red glimmer in a zebra's eye
  Takes a glimpse at the red cobweb pie,
Crisp leaves the color of wine
  Dance and sing in the wild sunshine,
The ruby red sadness of an elephant's frown
  Stabs my heart way deep down,
The dank red smell of a vulture's breath
  Tragically reminds me of an antelope's
  Death,
The bitter red taste of the whispering wind
  Makes me wonder whose shadow
  Is around the bend.

Anisa Marie Perez

A Sane Man

As he looked at the body, he could see
That he had made a terrible mistake.
But him, and only him, would pay the fee
Of killing this woman by the calm lake.

He wondered if he could accomplish this;
This plan conceived for his drastic mission
Of torturing her, for he could not miss
This opportunity, his great vision.

He had asked her politely to marry,
But she scoffed at him for even trying.
What did he have to offer? Not very
Much she had decided. She was lying.

So his wonderful plan went down the drain,
And how he's considered not at all sane.

Deborah Klein

If Love Were

If love were for sale it wouldn't come cheap, an object
that everyone would be sure to keep.
If love were water I would give you the sea, but would
you give it back to prove you love me.
If love were stars I would give you the midnight sky
and if love were truth I would never lie.
If love were color I would give you a rainbow, and
the way I feel about you would surely show.
If love were life I would give you mine and if you
ever need me give me a sign.
If love were time I would give you the past and
just enough time for our love to last.
If love were the world I would give you the Universe
and if love were pain I would be your nurse.

Carrie Sever

That Uncertain Smile

I have no faith in it; that half shed smile
That crawls across the contour of your chin
And briefly rests beneath your nose a while
And won't let joy or amusement in.

It brings no pleasure, and it doesn't quite enhance
The stubborn shadow of your solitude
And the sharp obliqueness of your downward glance
Where lips and teeth remain precise and nude.

I have no need of it; that grim advance
Of shallow feeling from the cave of sound
Which holds back passion on the happenstance
That the soul reveal itself if it's around

I would prefer that you not smile at me
As grant me that sparse and poor facsimile.

Alison Wyrley Birch

Tell Me

Tell me you're on a walk.
Tell me you're searching for the sunset.
But don't tell me I've lost you yet.

Tell me you're cutting grass, tell me anything.
But don't tell me you've passed.

Tell me I'll hug you again.
Tell me I'll hear your laugh.
My heart has finally realized you've passed.

Tell me you're finished.
Tell me good-bye dear friend.
I know you loved me to the end.

David S. Shelton

Within Each Pearl

Some men say -
  that a woman is most beautiful
  when only clothed with a strand of pearls
  about her throat...
    and so I too wear pearls.

  But each one that dangles from my neck
  also holds a memory that I cherish.
  For every time I encounter
  something new,
  my fingers grasp this as a rosary
  caressing one, precious, bead at a time
  until my prayers
    are answered...

And I often wonder -
  what excites a man
  to see a woman standing nude before him
  with her life falling...
    towards the swell of her breast.

Darla Parsons

Freedom

Seagulls in flight, wings gently floating in graceful motion
Swooping down on the caverns of the beach's mustard sands
Serenity surrounding their eloquent trimmed bodies
In total peaceful resistance to the fluffy currents of air.

To be free like that seagull, in total ecstasy with nature
Reigning over the land like a king over his subjects
Royal in stature with the confidence of his queen by his side
Seeing the beauty in the stillness of it all.

Knowing the secrets of the wilderness
The brief moments of shared pleasures
Total abandonment of self for the divine
Your freedom is eternal when you see
Him in all things, the birds in flight
The flowers in summer, the children in the meadow.

Perched above the boardwalk lights
Peering down on their view of humanity
Seeing from their lofty heights
A closer view of God.

Estelle Isbitski

Maybe I'm Dead

Jumper cables attached to my face
sulfuric sparks running through me.
I need some drugs to kill what's inside you
only to find the darkness is in me.
I jump from the top onto the salt covered grass.
Sinking clouds and blowing winds
the anesthesia's wearing off.
I think my head's exploding
brains in the bathtub.
I'm washing my hair inside out
with the sub-conscious mind of tomorrow.
The walls are crumbling, my fate is tumbling
maybe my problem is I have no blood
running through my veins.
I guess all that's there is your embalming fluid...

Chris Martin

"Unplanned"

Single mother, working full-time
Struggling to make ends meet
Emotionally prepared, but not financially
One paycheck away from being homeless
Making too much salary for government aid
But not enough to make ends meet
Living in an unheated apartment
Unable to pay the phone bill
Second-hand furniture and hand-me-down clothes
Sleepless nights and medical bills
Standing in line at the local food bank
Embarrassed and sad
Wondering if it's all worth it
Looks into her baby's toothless smile and trusting face
...and knows that it is.

Anne McInerney

"Someone Else Cares"

When times are rough and your
Struggling to go on living.
  You have too big of a heart that's full
Of love you keep giving.
  The pain is sometimes hard to hide
But you kept your chin up and swallowed
  your pride.
Dreams are shattered, hearts are broken
  These words are true that I have
Spoken.
  So many people wanting love and
Affection are asking
  But that's one of the problems in
This world that's lacking
  And there's so much in this world
That one bares.
  I just want you to know that
Someone else cares.

Emily Fay Foat

Bar Wave Bang

Loco-charged thunder drives me ahead,
Straight, toward grinding machinations
And repetitive movement.

I follow, over again, forward
Against all resistive
Break in powered trance
Of edified run, now, as heart-headed
Symmetry of psyche changes
This ethereal disc of transported moonbeam.

Where time goes, does passion,
In squeaky-clear rhythms
Of transitive gelling delight;
Sensual nonsense
Of layered piece packets
Spiral out in motive waves,
Spinning blindly,
In dark, surreal, transcendence.

Fred Funk

Wife

A wife — someone who cares
Stands behind you and never fails you
A friend, an ear, a shoulder to share
The bearer of your pride, and children
A beautiful relationship. Love can be
So fragile and frail, it has to be held gently
Cherish and care and soon you shall see
The side of life only a wife can give

Charles L. Funkhouser Jr.

Night Dance

Reflecting on a time when the sun
started bedding for the night. I would sit
on the porch steps catching a cool breeze.
The breeze drifted twinkling bright lights.

Watching them appear on a humid
summer night. I imagined they were
fairies dancing in the dark of night.

Fumigating my lungs to a slow poison
this night. I catch a breeze now to chase
away my tension. Again the fireflies
twinkling their bright lights.

Watching the fireflies my twenty-third
year tonight. I wonder where is that little
girl who danced with fairies.

Maybe if I believed hard enough there
will be fairies tonight. And maybe that
girl can dance with the fairies tonight.

Cassie Lynn Wilkerson

My Old Best Friend

The beautiful, calm sea was my best friend
Splashing and swimming would never end.

I loved it when it trickled over my feet
And made the night air smell so sweet.

Until one day my feelings ceased
When the sea became a wretched beast.

My dearest friend had swept away
A beloved young boy that sad, sad day.

Ever since then people mourn
And my heart became so bitterly torn.

Now as I look out into the sea
Being its friend is just a memory
For my old, best friend is now my enemy.

Catherine Elizabeth Cannon

The Old Bridge Of Destiny

Standing on my bridge, so called Destiny
Spanning from Rye Ridge corralled 'gainst the sea
Sought an ark on hopes to flee infernal deluge
Rotten bark on ropes 'low me insure no refuge

The island of my youth falling down in flames
Motherland oh mine you're calling out my name
Dare pursue a fate when been repressed
Dare rescue a maiden in distress

I won't cry, won't make that last goodbye
Oh don't die, don't take that last sad sigh
Pastor in the sky dispatch the inner gloom
Catcher in the Rye please catch me in your womb

Its fury flames Love's pyre—dying in roar 'n flame
This Hurricane of Fire—so Time is your name
Numbed I watch her innocence he just raped
From this monster's violence I must 'scape

Death in me traced your spell to abyss miles deep
Destiny brace yourself through this mist I'll leap
My soiled face wet by the molten tears, kisses of fear
My child days set, now adult in years...I disappear

Daniel Romero Morales Jr.

The Tranquil Adornings Of Midsummer's Eve

The soft cooing of a mourning dove blends in with the
sound of the gentle waves lapping against the grainy sand, as
cattails sway in the cool summer breeze. The small dock feels
cold against my warm feet as I walk to the edge and sit down,
skimming my toes across the warm water.

The setting sun casts pink and auburn reflections across
the lake, and feeling quite tranquil, I sip my hot tea. In
the distance, over the foothills, I hear the waves of Lake
Michigan, crashing up against the dunes and jetty.

My herbal tea, seasoned with Rosehips, warms me as it
travels down my esophagus. For a moment I can see my breath,
as I let out a contented sigh. The sun has now set and a Mead
moon is radiating with magical honey-tinted light, casting
the Goddess's power over me, and the world, making me so
blissful, as I bask in the essence of it all.

Claire Sandberg-Bernard

I Remember

I remember running my fingers through his hair
Sometimes I still feel his hair between my fingers
I remember the softness of his hands when they touched mine.
I remember his touch - so gentle
I remember the way it felt when his arms were wrapped around me.
I remember the looks he gave me - once he winked
I remember the games he played - the flirting back and forth
I miss him - I wish I could see him again
I remember the sound of his voice
Every minute without him is a minute closer to my death.
I remember the way he smells - perfect
I remember the way he dresses
I know so little about him, but remember so much
I remember his caring - being sad - he comforted me
I remember the way he looks when frustrated or upset
I remember the way he walks
I remember having my arms around him
I remember that "close encounter"
I remember the touch of his lips - they way they felt touching mine
I remember his smile - his teeth - the way they felt.

Amber Butz

"Silent Love"

Close your eyes darling, your lips speak not a word
Something's sound better if gone unheard
Cling to my arms darling, I'll forever be near
For I love you my darling, I love you my dear
Come lay beside me, forever be mine
I promise to love you until the end of time
I'll always be with you, I promise this my love
To cherish you forever by the stars above
There will never be another to love me like you do
I'll hold you in my arms and forever love you.
The silence between us, the love that goes unheard
I know in my heart you love me, though you speak not a word
The sweet gentle way you hold me, that no eyes can see
The secret I hold oh so dear, that no one knows but me
So close your eyes darling, your lips speak not a word
This love I have for you, will forever go unheard.

Cathy Lucas

Tears

How do you say "good-bye" to your love?
Someone you thought came from above?
The one you called your only one?
The one who knew your heart he won?
The one you planned the future as forever?
The one who said "Us part - yeah, whatever!"?
The one you'd give all forever to stay?
The one you'd give up all for his way?
I can't find any answers for my mind,
Nor answers for my heart to find.
It's so hard to realize I can't anymore have him,
He's got a new future - mine is so dim.
I will do anything for him to come back to me,
But I know it's "rose colored glasses" I see.
If anyone has someone very special near,
Do all to keep them or like me, you'll have tears!

Darlene Samples

Maternal Stranger

A crowd on the corner, a person on the street; perhaps she's
someone I'm soon to meet.

A shadow in the dark, a reflection in a lake; I may never meet her,
that's a chance I take.

A whisper on the wind, a teardrop in the rain; there's someone
out there whom I look the same.

An image in a dream, a thought in my mind; I pray every day
it is she that I find.

A smile from a stranger, a hug from a friend; I want her to know
it's my love I send.

A chance of a lifetime, a chance like no other; maybe someday
I'll find her, that woman... my mother.

Barbara J. Sarraf

"Apprentices Of Ti Chi"

Every morning they gather.
Some alone
some in pairs
some in groups
Yet, all of them possess one objective.

Some of them vigilante warriors
arms flying invincible weapons
flawless and precise leg extensions
forever warding off the elements of darkness
that constantly breed the temptations of evil.

Some dance to an intricately choreographed ballet
to a sonnet only they can hear
graceful, elegant so much like butterflies or feathers
suspended on the breeze of an early summer's morn.

Yet others assume the stance
reflecting into a panoramic ethereal world
as repose envelopes their being.

All customizing their own paraphrase
of a lost art
conceived in an ancient dimension all - but forgotten.

Annette H. Baldao

Freedom

As gentle as a slow moving stream,
so it seems upon this gliding dream.
Swiftly flying over the thoroughfare,
although it doesn't go anywhere.
Wildly curving and bending,
the gracefulness never ending.
The freedom is flowing,
gently gets you to glowing.
Wind whistling through your hair,
as you skim up a hill and into the sun's glare.
When the wind dies, so ends your fun,
and you glide into town on your
Harley Davidson.

Cindy VanReed

The Human Race

I would like to find a cool, green grassy knoll,
so I may sit and watch as the people run their race.
People running here and there, those that are here running there,
and those that are there running here.
Each time they get to where they think they should be,
they find this not where they need to be.
So as they run their futile race never ending, only stopping
at days end to rest and start again.
I will watch the human race run here and there,
and then I will leave my quiet place, so cool and green, so still
and calm, and return to the race, still not knowing why I join the
human race.

Delores McCall

The Mirror

Yesterday, I spoke to the voice inside...so simple,
so honest, so pure.
It knew my destiny.....so clear, so logical.

The fountain of strength derived from the voice inside,
dreams so real.....within grasp....the aroma so sweet,
drops of manna trickle down my lips.

Today, I was awakened by reality...life's simplest tasks, so
complicated by mistrust, greed, jealousy, intrigues...

I ask the voice inside, "why?"......and it replied...
"Today is the mirror of tomorrow, yet not shattered, having
learned to see beyond the shadows of uncertainty.... and
thus reflecting this knowledge of yesterdays to face another day."

Bobby L. Barnhill Jr.

God's Masterpiece

The artist of creation with a warm and loving heart,
smiled as He created a masterpiece of art.

For the skies above us, from His palette, He chose blue;
for the distant sunrise, a glorious golden hue.

The high majestic mountains He wrapped in purple cloaks,
and on their peaks, placed snow-white caps, with gentle, loving strokes.

The mighty oak, the stalwart elm, in forests evergreen
grew strong and tall and heaven-bound beside a silver stream.

In the fields and the meadows, the wildflowers danced;
upon a stage ablaze with color, to and fro they pranced.

A hummingbird, a butterfly, He dabbled here and there,
with the brilliance of a rainbow color burst forth everywhere.

At last, His treasured work of art complete, He said "I'll call it Earth,"
and hung it proudly on the wall of His vast universe.

Ann E. Nickels

Untitled

A man sat quietly on a stone
  slowly, quietly he became the stone.
He played in the memory of the stone
  was thoroughly awed by the visions of
  things that had taken place in view of the stone.

He drifted back further in the memory
  to a place where there were no
  images but only feelings, upward feelings,
    feelings of an impending new form
      a feeling that there was
      something more than darkness
      and being touched on all
      sides by other stones.
A feeling of waiting for something exciting to happen.

The man now having reached a depth
at which he was excited yet comfortable
but beyond which he did not desire
to go, like a diver, began to
drift up, until, slowly he became
a man sitting quietly on a stone.

      David Murphy

"Dreams"

I dream of having a little country house,
Sitting on a hill with tall oak trees giving shade.
Rocking on the front porch.
Sipping ice-cold lemonade.
Listening to the birds sing.
Don't take my dreams away.
That's part of life
Having dreams, whether or not they ever happen.
Looking back, I've lived this dream.
It was my childhood.

      Evelyn H. Allen

A Wasted Life

She sits
Silently staring darkness in the face
Nothing to do
Nowhere to go
Her time on Earth almost expired
Regrets of what she didn't do roll through her mind
Sorry for the things she did do
She cries in apology to those she hurt
Another life lived
Another life wasted
Abandoned by her own soul at 19 years old
Her limp, lifeless body is all that is left
Soon to be diminished along with her young heart
A pill bottle falls to the ground spilling its contents
As she recites her last words ever to be heard
"I only took a few of them. I wouldn't have done it.
If only I had known."
Her eyes slowly close as she collapses to the ground
Silence fills the room
As yet another life is wasted

      Aubree Bergtholdt

Summer Dreams

  My life is complete on Friday nights singing at Hampton West with
Richie Summer Nights. He's sweet sincere and handsome as can be I
fall head over heels when he has his arms around me.
  I love Richie with all of my heart if he was mine we'd never part.
We are friends right now that's ok by me if he would give me a chance
I could show him what LOVE can be

      Elise Lagueux

She Cries

Earth cries out in a wrenching pain,
Showered only by acid rain.

Air is polluted the light hurts my eyes,
The ozone is dying I can hear her cries.

We have stripped her forest bare to the soil,
Mined her well and taken her oil.

We have pouched, pillared, ravaged, and raped,
And in the end have we sadly sealed our own fate?

Volcanos erupt in a fiery devastating wrath,
Destroying everything that comes in her path.

Acre by acre of rain forest demolished each day,
We don't want to see so we turn away.

Her cries sound like that of hurt child,
Once so submissive, now she's gone wild.

For the cries cannot be muffled or silenced any longer,
With each passing day she grows violently stronger.

What will the price be that we must pay?
No place to hide, we can't run away.

What will we say to our children when it's all gone,
Sorry we tried, but we just did it all wrong!

      Beva Smith

A Greater Love

In a dream she came to me, one night
shimmering in the most radiant of all light.
Her eyes were like the brightest of all stars in the sky.
And her skin was like cream, pure without dye.

Her medium brown hair as thick as rope.
And her words like a song as she spoke:
"I watch and protect you, you have not to fear.
I have come in my Son's peace and to me you are dear"

I dearly love the blessed lady all dressed in blue.
She is not a fake, but all holy and true.
Without a sin, in the world she weeps
And hate is at fault.
To love and share is the
  greatest love of all.

      Allison Marie Keene

Deadly Love

Endless nights. Dreary days.
Sheltered with a purple haze.

I close my eyes. I call your name.
I could have sworn, I thought you came.

The lights are out. The room is black.
I smile and know you won't be back.

Your long brown hair, your deep green eyes,
your sexy body; full of lies.

I start the car. I turn the key.
I drive to your house, and what do I see?

Long blonde hair, eyes of blue,
Long thin legs, and she's with you.

I open the door. I step inside.
I hold the gun down by my side.

I look around. Can anyone see?
Too bad, what's this? You're begging me.

Two shots go off. My ears start to ring.
I look at my work. I just want to sing.

I look at your bodies. I know that you're dead.
Two little shots. Two little heads.

      Beth Oliver

Passage

You cast off the cloak of my motherhood like the snake
shedding its too small skin.
You rise to the self that waits on the dawning of your maturity.
My arms ache, my heart is bruised as you break each cord of
childhood.
My lullabies have been silenced, my tongue stilled
I can no longer conduct the rhythms of your existence.
You have moved beyond the need of my parenting.
Adulthood looms on your horizon and you eagerly grasp its threads
Spinning, weaving the tapestry of your life
designing the fabric of your dreams.

Elizabeth J. Coleman

"When The Rain Began To Fall"

The rain reminds me of the tears I once
shed. The waves crashing on the shore reminds
me of my heart reaching out for you when my
love for you began, and from their, where it has led.
The thunder rolls, the clouds gather together
as they cry out heavy clear tears, known
as rain. As the raindrops hit their oceans waves,
and as the waves crash upon the beach, the
sound reminds me of the hurt, the sorrow, the pain.
As the rain falls in the forest, the
wolves look for shelter where it is dry. I, too, run
during the rain, searching for you to hold me, I sit,
and wonder why.
Why have I yet to find you? Why must
I hurt so? I know we are apart, yet I still
wish I was forever with you, and forever more.

Debbie Sutherland

My Mother

I used to have someone to lean on,
She was my mother.
Though I still have a father,
My mother was like no other.

Her favorite flowers were roses,
Her favorite cat was named Moses.
Life goes by much too fast,
I learned to live each day as it were my last.

On February 25 she died of cancer,
Though there really was no answer.
As each day slowly passed by.
I can't help but wonder why.

She lifted me up when I was down,
But all I can do now is nothing but frown.
She somehow always made me smile,
I wish she could have stayed for a longer while.

I'm telling this to you, on this gloomy night,
I hope you don't have to go through, this dreadful fright.
My mother is gone, and so is the sun,
When I was with her, I had nothing but fun.

Eric Arciszewski

Set Free

Set free from the confines of a body gone awry.
Set free from the pain that made my loved ones cry.

Set free to walk, to run, to smile.
Set free to leave you for just awhile.

Set free to take my Savior's hand.
Set free to abide in His promised land.

Set free with your love.
Set free by His love.
Set free, at last, I am set free!

Ann A. Palmer

Temple Door

She slipped her finger through the ring.
She turned it slowly.
It was hard and smooth.
She always knew it was there.
She knew it was gold, a precious metal.
She liked silver better.
She couldn't help turning the ring all the time.
Maybe it was just something to do.
She didn't really think about it a lot.
The ring didn't mean she was attached or anything like that.
Not really.
Maybe it meant she belonged to someone at the time, but that
didn't necessarily mean the ring was a permanent fixture.
But still, she knew it was there.
She could feel it all the time.
She couldn't decide if it hurt sometimes or not.
Maybe just an irritation.
Just a few mixed emotions.
Emotions she might not have.
Had she not been pierced.

Al Desrochers

Death

As he holds her in his arms,
She begs for his forgiveness.
He says with sensitivity, "Why so my love?"
She answers him with a cry
"I've been with another!"
He is shocked and cannot reply.
She is crying, begging him to forgive her,
Yet he hears nothing,
He is in the non-living world,
For he is so deeply crushed by this unwanted news.
Then he slowly wilts away like a flower,
A slow and painful death.

Emmy G. Brown

Untitled

Greatness invented upon his birth
Shakespeare, a man of undeniable worth
Earned so much respect by
Selling his dreams afar

Many joke and mock
Yet, hypocritically to his plays they flock
Laugh and criticize others, they may
But each one knows, they too, enjoyed his play

Authors intensely show the need
For his success, and instead grow greed
Because no one's as great, no one's as neat
As Shakespeare's works represent

Greed leads to dislike and tales
Of invented yarns of dirty trails
Left behind his unknown life, true it's scattered
Yet, his dreams and plays are left unshattered

Mock and criticize
Go ahead you may
But be sure to introduce yourself
To one of his plays

April DaShaune King

Guidance

This Country is full of beauty and love
Sent to us from our dear Lord above

We also have our share of woe and care
But with God's help we can stand and bear

We should pray for our leaders night and day
And ask that God will show them the way

Let us seek help from the Holy Book
Remember, it is to Him we must look

God in His goodness will always provide
If we turn to Him and ask and confide

May everyone in this land learn the way
To receive salvation and praise Him each day

Erline E. Shubin

The First Look

'Tis Bliss when thou weary eyes pass,
Seen afar as if sleepy,
Yet, in essence, misty
Like some subtle enchantment flickering,
About the face.
So the Heart gives in with turning fear,
Glancing incessantly with a broken stare.
What of it, I say?
Surely nothing like the usual happiness,
But a Lewis's bliss that's just out of reach.

Chen Wang

Day By Day

Day by day things keep changing.
Seems like not so long ago I was a baby
Seems as though my life is getting tougher.
Things just aren't the same.
The lessons of life are so much more harder.
People keep changing, they never stay the same.
Making friends is so much tougher. You're always being judged.
Day by day everyone and everything changes. Nothing ever stays the same.
Day by day we grow closer.
Day by day we make it through.
Day by day you hope you'll stay strong.
Day by day is a constant battle to stay alive.
Day by day we'll never change cause day by day will always become easier and better.
For day by day we are brought closer to each other because of life's journey.

Amber Grace Lewin

Subconscious Heart

Lonely sighs, on bended knees,
Seeking His presence, within the stream.

Forest Glen, dark and cool,
Gentle breeze, moss and dew.

Footsteps of time, a drifting life,
Intermingled dreams, vision bright.

Daydreams enhanced, the shimmering sun,
Gazing deep, sensing the one.

Shadowed reflections, snare Her emotions,
Appearance of, unspoken devotion.

Subconscious Heart, await from the stars,
Outcast arms beckon, infertile desire.

Drifting clouds, floating by,
Away from beatific, step at a time.

Nature's breath mingle's, within the stream,
Subconscious Heart, Seasons and Dreams.

Cheryl E. Ralph

Sensing the Storm

Look out the window.
See the darkening sky.
See the wind thrash the trees.
See the sky split in two.
See the lightning slice through the night.

Open the window.
Hear the roaring of the wind.
Hear the electricity crackle in the air.
Hear the crashes of thunder that shake the earth.
Hear the pounding of the rain as it falls upon the roof.

Climb out the window.
Feel the wind try to bend you like the trees.
Feel the rain beat upon your body.
Feel the heat and the thickness of the air.
Feel the awesome power of the storm.

Carol Hurlbut

In Time

When I am older than I am today I hope to
see children around me, and a husband that
believes in me. When I am old and gray I
will look back upon today and say time
just slipped away.

Alydia Edwards

My Feeling...Yours?

My heart is pounding and my feet are numb
Seconds pass with each emotion
A wonderful premise of the future
Stress from usual livelihood
Knowing...strength...perseverance
These qualities exist...tomorrow awaits the hard work of today
No promises...self esteem...
DON'T GIVE UP...EVER!
Tears...there a part of nature, like misty rain on a sunny day
Feelings...no need to expand
Will we ever really understand?
Each day provides new of these...feelings that is...
Each mind holds the key to unlock the unanswered
We must find the dream, the goal...just one?
No...but the early emotions will be known
Trust yourself and time will answer...feelings will never die

Christina J. Ferretti

"The Love Inside"

This thing they call love, they
say it's in the mind,
They say it has to be understood.
Well, if love must be understood,
then true love,
The kind that comes from the
heart, knows no understanding.
This thing called love is confusing,
beautiful and for all to share peacefully.
And, yet, there are those who are
so deep in love of others that they kill
and are killed by those who are loved most.
The lovers are afraid to love with
their hearts, therefore, they hate with
their minds and form a dark cloud
over their hearts and souls.
Although this is true for most
people, I, your lover, could never know of
this hate, all I know of is love, anger
and passion.

Brenna Lyne Oliveira

The Orator With Muse

Stick around; see me go
Say a poem, I'd like to know

You've come to see a distinct expectation
Or maybe just an inebriation

A heart so bold as the one who stands
A heart to travel so many waste lands

My mind has wondered:
Into deeper depths the ones un pondered

Have you felt the sunshine upon leaving the pines?
Have you a book to interpret life's many signs?

And if so who wrote it?
And by what authority could you quote it?

A dreamer knows all, amazing
A dreamer laughs while gazing

Sit down, enjoy
These writings I'll employ

I am around to speak
I am the resident freak

An animal is sinless
And life's game to me seems win less.

Allen Trepp

Musical Friends

A centaur, dragon, griffin, and a unicorn,
Sat as the latter made music on silver horns.
An elf, fairy, faun, and a nymph clapped to the beat,
And the earth gave slightly under their prancing feet.
Mermaids and tritons watch and listen from their lakes,
Singing in harmony with no mistakes.
An ogre, giant, goblin, and a troll (all very strong)
Sat and listened to the song.
A roc and harpy listen from above,
And soon they're joined by a dove.
Creatures gather from all around,
Talking to friends, newly found.

April Kahgee

Two Little Children And A Bee

Two little children happy and gay
Run outside to go and play.
Then they come back in crying and loud
From a little bee that was flying around
Then they go back, back outside
To run and play and seek-n-hide
Now here they come again,
Oh no for the little bee is on the go.
Now the children
Have come back in,
Knowing the bee is not their friend.
For on a small hand
On the littlest finger
There you will find
The little bee's stinger.

Erin M. Miller

Transitions

Friends and acquaintances pass through life
Past indiscretions, pain and strife.
Forgiveness asked, none received.
Stark realization of wishes perceived.
Words humbly given, at long last.
Goodbye my friend
Time to bury the past.

Debra L. Jensch

Where Is My Love?

Why does love pass me by
Run further away the harder I try
It dances around and teases a bit
then slips always, falls into a pit
I don't know why it happens to me
My love is somewhere locked up with no key
I wonder and wish and think about him
Is his name Robert, Ronald, or Tim?
My love is hiding, no where to be found
Tiny tears fall - with out making a sound
I am still looking, I can't give up hope
But love's killing me softly with a red silky rope

Chivon M. Baker

Cove Waters

Betwixt between twin Ozark hills of green
Rippling cove waters sparkle a shimmering gleam
Lapping stories of long lost lore
Against rocky shore of times before, before
Massive dam entrapped tumbling streams
Hard built by meddling minds so full of dreams
To ease the spring time flooded plain
In days of ceaseless falling rain
Tales of Indians camped at river's edge
And settlers sheep fold on outcropping ledge
Re-enacted drama in Shepherd of the Hills play
For curious tourist leisure play filled day
Now cove water anglers lines entice and lure
Where Indian arrows made camp secure
Our present dreams enfold and mingle
On moon beamed waters where spirits tingle
And lapping sounds murmur soft and low
Your time to lost memories too will ago.

Dolores Hinde

A Wish Can Come True

I thought of a wish tonight,
Right after I turned out the light.
I lay still in bed where I lead myself into a dream.
Right then, I seek a land full of laughter.
But could it be, oh yes, I see this was my wish.
A wish that took place in a land full of wonder.
And like that, whenever I said the name,
I had anything.
But how could it be, would they let such a
wonderful land sit without a soul knowing about it?
But of course, now I see, this was my dream,
I could be a beauty queen.
Anything I want will be mine, oh so fine.
But could you do whatever I ask of you?
Some place nice just like sugar and spice.

Amanda Nicole Tsoumakas

Going Home

Teardrops like the dew on a rose
Rest on her cheek in sweet repose,
So silently they slipped past her lips
   pursed with care as she hovered near
   that pure white hair,
Holding the hands that once held hers
   telling stories — it all is such a blur
So long ago - oh tell me please - why
   do we wait to set our hearts at ease?

"If only's" come and go and "wish I did",
But here now, it's her time so put your
   heart at rest,
Think of how she must be blessed.
She's gone through all the trials
   and most likely passed the test.

Ann A. Ryen

Birds Of Flight Come To Sight

Did you see a white night bird?
Riding blowing wind without flapping
Straightly making his way through
Circling screeching hawk, who are watching
Atop the shifting landscape.
[Cracking wings against the buckling sky.]

Did you see the shadow race?
Wing and tail outlined on the
lighted, leafy, side of mountain
Shadowed although no eclipser
Was there upon looking up
[Sloping mountain splattered with sunshine]

Did you hear air the grouse shook?
Shaking wings, escaping
Surprisingly quiet rock walkers
And floating too far in coverings
Of thicket and sharpened thorn
for rock walkers like ourselves.
[Fluttering wings come from the green pine]

Burgess Tomlinson

Thoughts

Our lives we create from the substance of our minds.
Rich or poor, happy or sad we fashion over time.
Our thoughts and our emotions can control our very life.
For happiness is a common goal of every man and wife.

Thoughts are things as real and solid as the mountains and the shores.
Control your thoughts for they're the only thing that's truly yours.
Tell me someone's prevailing thoughts and I'll tell you where he'll be.
Fate has nothing to do with it, we control our destiny.

We are the living embodiment of every thought we've had.
And our minds obey, they don't distinguish whether good or bad.
So look in the mirror and ask yourself "Where do I want to be?"
Then take control of your greatest asset, Your mind will set you free.

Alan G. Uliasz

Tears

The emerald strands that bound the evil serpent, closely
resembling her loved-ones tears.
Tears that follow her spirit through the rich soil to the
darkness below.
Blending into the River Styx, brimming and overlapping the
edges, soaking the dirt, smothering it with sorrow. A sorrow
that only the ones that have loved can feel.
An unsteady emptiness awaits her, a chill alone set out to
torture good and evil, a partner to death.
Her husband's tears splash the cold sides of the boat, along with
ten thousand others, pleading the return of his wife.
After a first failing attempt, he ask again. Crying on the bank
not standing to live without her, he melts into the water;
love-filled tears.

Elizabeth Tomei

Please Don't Let Your Child Go Astray

Children feel the need to belong
Regardless whether the decision be right or wrong.
So with a strong enticement they easily sway
Please don't let your child go astray.
There may be times when they seem demanding
When all they're seeking is a little understanding.
Just try to realize what they're trying to say
Please don't let your child go astray.
Parents sometimes fail to see in children a certain liability
Therefore not being there to fulfill that special availability.
Do your best to be there to assure them everything's going to be okay
Please don't let your child go astray.

Frederick B. Catlin

The Idea That Would End Big Wars

Two Russian Veterans and I...many years ago,
Reasoned out some good ideas...that many wish would grow.
Ideas that would stop "Big Wars", you see
Of regions, religions...and nationality.

If wars are the results of..."Failed Diplomacy",
Let diplomats engage in war...instead of you and me.
If they couldn't agree..no matter what the cause,
In isolated regions, they could fight these vicious wars.
If "World Leaders" had to fight these wars,
And suffer the wars consequences,
They would spend less time in "Planning War"...
And more time "Mending Fences"!!

So, let the diplomats fight...let them all agree...
On the size of the fight...and the type of "Weaponry"..
"Remote regions battlefields" would be littered...this I know..
With "Ping..Pong" balls and "Tennis" balls...embedded in the snow!!

Andrew Henry Steenbergen

"Winds So Quiet Reality Passes Me"

Winds so quiet
Reality passes by me;
Suns blinding light;
Earths mighty axis;
Oceans swift deceit.

"As we all some day discover Ignorance.
For millions of years we all lived like the animals.
Assume our imaginations no longer exist.
We would not have the communication
bearer some of us seem to possess within our
tiny minds, because if we even had a clue to love
instead of destroy our imaginations
Peace would be a reality—"

David M. Bailey

Poet, Poet

The meaningless words of a poet
Rambling on and on,
Maybe he's drinking Moet
Until his brain is gone

Poet, poet wasting your mind away
Show the world defiance,
You choose the darkness that you stay
Forget the world, your body and soul need an alliance

Death, you laugh at
Oh poet, burn your evil pen,
In center ring you sat
In the middle of the lions den

Poet, poet where are your words from?
Do you see them down the barrel of a gun?

Christopher Tracy Chuck

Sonnet: A Child To Me Is Like A Tree

In a quiet garden corner,
  Protected and hidden from view,
Firmly rooted in fertile earth,
  A sapling burst to life and grew.
Always bending—never breaking—
  Throughout seasons of storm and change,
Giving radiance or shelter,
  Outward its branches spread the range.
Coiling with inner rings of strength,
  Growing sturdy year after year,
To be—to endure in our midst.
  Let no harm come, no final fear.
That by careless means we destroy
  A future source of life and joy.

Annie King Phillips

Butterflies Speak Without A Sound

Harmless little butterflies, vigorously flying by.
Promises each bring to skies, loudly I ask them why.

Why they are so perfect in design? Why do they fly so lively?
Why they can't be only mine? And why, I ask, are they so lovely?

And every time I ask these things, they only fly on in their life.
Each one gently, swiftly, dancing, on in peace and strife.

Although they never answer me, I know just what they'd say.
To fly on and view the beauty, and fill and love my life each day.

They'd say to see things differently, and enjoy what life will bring.
And fly in life so pleasantly, so I delight and savor everything.

The butterflies speak without a sound, they tell us what to do.
And when they begin to come around, their beauty fills earth too.

Annette Shelton

Young Delinquents

In raw, deceiving, incontestable darkness they lived
Product of their own stubborn, passionate, ignorant whims
They felt and cried tears of denial

Long summers, years, egotistical days
They struggled for nothing
Gained pain from their minds
In a lonely state they refrained from the truth
Trying to portray a wisdom only the ancients know of

And all along intense, lively, permeable light
Shone through soft, unspeakable, brown spheres
All along someone knew the conditions of their hearts
Its fears, carelessness, longings
All along the world was open, and its magical sights,
Unbelievable dreams, challenging thoughts, were only one poem away
And they awoke

Full blooms of inspiration, admiration
Their aspiration
So young, so ideological yet so free
With the spirit much swifter than the mind

Adriana Mourad

The Tear In My Heart

Food for the Hungry,
proclaims a sign on the shopping bag
from which you offer sandwiches indiscriminately.

I watch you from a nearby street bench,
my eyes hidden behind darkened glass,
and wonder whether you are surprised, offended,
at how many merely pass you by

even those whose layered garb, gritty stubble
and ropey hair
announce a lack of condescension
to pieces of bread and what they uphold.

As you offer others food, I am glad
you have found your sustenance.
But do you know how it feels
to remain hungry after a meal?

I don't know about the others,
but this is why I must reply,
"No, thank you."

Eileen Tabios

Spoken Rain

Piercing its victims with the strike of their disturbing
presence, relentlessly driving downward with an anger and
determination that divides its prey, which trembles in a
tormenting dismay.

Then as quickly as this unexpected villain appear, it melts
magically, into an easing and calm moment, a fragment of a
much missed time when the drops cleansed each drooping
blade of hazy green grass and instantly dresses every
individual leaf in a pristine, emerald-like armor.

The heart is allowed to free its soul from an aching drought
of shameless dancing and rejoicing. The simplicity, yet
impact of each of these heaven sent tear drops rejuvenate an
almost lost dreamer, gives a renewed vision of an unjaded
tomorrow.

Christy Vorkink

Take God With You

As you enter your room your rest to seek,
Pray to Him who watches o'er sleep.
And as you wake to morning bright,
Thank Him for watching o'er the night.
And as we tread life's path each day, ask Him to guide you
    along the way.
For God is with you each step you take, when you asleep, and
    when your awake.
His loving arms are open wide, all you need do is step inside.
He'll guide and guard you each step of the way.
So take Him into your heart today.

Evelyn M. Karlberg

An Angel

You've been called an angel. An angel that's
praised. An angel that one day will be raised to
heaven. An angel that they want to follow.
Because your pride you swallow. Your heart
is not hollow. It's filled solid with love.
You know you got a glow. A glow that shows.
All of your love will grow, grow, and grow.
A love that snows upon your peers.
A snow of love that'll wash away their tears
from fears. A love that snows upon us all.
Oh we love you mother dear.

Anthony Ray Baxter

Rain Dance Of December

The beating of the sun drains me,
    powerless,
as I dance naked in its shower,
and jump through its misty clouds,
when others stare at me I never feel
thoughtless,
falling to the ground with joy,
    legs in the air,
    I pose of a toy.

Then arising with arms out,
    a gift is given to my eye like the knife of
    a surgeon.

Around they bleed,
    the dirt screams,
        yawns,
    and awakens from its sleepy summer.

Colorful blooms are now,
    then later never, as I continue,
    the rhythm is greater.

It stops, I fall weak, and again sunshine to, all.

Adam W. Randolph

Poverty

Poverty is needing,
Poverty is wanting,
It is barely getting what you need,
Getting what you want is a dream,
A tale,
Impossible.

Poverty is sadness,
Poverty is filth,
Poverty is looking ahead for nothing,
No future.

Poverty is pain,
Poverty is shame,
It is being glanced at with pity,
But no one lends a helping hand.

Poverty doesn't just happen in other places,
It is here all around you.

Poverty is watching hope slip through your fingers,
Poverty is needing life.

Allison Lenhard

"The Great Unknown"

　Fear sets in, an unsettled moan, as most
ponder, the great unknown;
　Tales passed on, no proof is shown,
but death's a certainty, we cannot postpone;
　angelic figures, celestial tones,
beckon souls, into the great unknown;
　Be it heaven, that spiritual zone,
the eternal peace, for which our faith is honed;
　Or be it hell, Satan's home, that flaming
agony, where sinners roam;
　Only time's wisdom, the foreclosure on our
mortal loan, shall reveal the secret, of the
great unknown.

David Tancredi

"Disillusion Of The Soul"

Just about had it,
Plunging down
　to the abyss...
A game, a fools game
all lost who play.
A hope, a flicker, a glimmer of light
The abyss consumes all.
　Hold back the flood gate
the water is rising, it fills the sights.
The heart is aching.
What is true? What is false?
False hopes,
A serpent bite.
To grieve once more.
Need to be repeated, love lost, yet never had.
Melancholy, torment, destruction-wrath and rage
Inner self-finds the game of abyss.
To see and touch the heavens-an end without a beginning.

Debbie Lynn

Raindrops

Raindrops falling ever softly on the windowpane
Pitter-patter down my rooftops and the tree alike
These droplets form diamonds on the wild daisies
Making them alive and refresh again

These delicate drops from above
Playfully dances on my pot
Rusted and worn from the passage of time
Forms beads on its surface

What a wonder it is?
That these raindrops bring
Suddenly appearing and then disappearing
Just to refresh the land everywhere

How beautifully they fall?
Caressing the mountain's side
Covering the valley with its haze
They form little streams below

These little raindrops
Are so precious and few
Giving life with its gentle touch
As it caresses my face in the rain

Debby Kaulili

Lost Love

Deep within your eyes I fret,
Piercing thine heart, my tears are wet.
My hunger grows, the thoughts I crave,
Your love I have, but lust is grave.
Don't lose sight in me, you embrace my soul,
Our love together is only on hold.
You've captured my heart, which now I lack,
I'm in too deep, there's no turning back.
Not being in your arms makes me drown,
Please forgive me for grasping you down.
It's your move, I await your call,
But the wall between us has yet to fall.
Until then, only time will tell,
Whether we fly in heaven, or live in hell.
But always shall you be in my dreams,
Because we might never be, it seems.
So please think of me always, of the warmth in my hug,
The happiness in my eyes, and a touch of love.

Cecilia Bentulan

Wishing

People wish, and people pray.
People hope everyday.
People wish for things to come true.
But they have to face reality...
Things do what they do.

People wish for fortune and money.
Others wish for their hearing or sight.
People wish for a turtle and bunny.
Others wish not to get in a gang fight.

People wish for a new dress and ice cream.
Others wish for clothes or food.
People wish for parties and a big house.
Others wish for a family or shelter.

Fortunate people wish for romance, good friends
　and a sunny day.
Less fortune people wish for love, peace
　or happiness.

Alison T. D'Amato

The Moon Is My Friend

The moon is my friend
People ask me why
Smiling I reply
The moon never changes; yet it changes everyday
The moon is constant; but it moves across the sky

The stars are my friends
People ask me why
Smiling I reply
The stars are always there; but some are dying out
The stars are like fireflies, yet I know are not

The sun is my friend
People ask me why
Smiling I reply
The sun is always shining; yet sometimes it's dark
The sun gives me life; but it takes someone else

The sky is my friend
People ask me why
Frowning I say
Haven't you been listening to me?
I'm a dreamer, and a dreamer's friends are the moon, stars and sun.

Dana Robinette

The Three Of Us

The three of us went walking,
   Peeking in each store window.
We took the longer way around,
   To get to the grocery store.
But coming back, home the shorter way,
   We did alright, until we crossed the street
To get up on the curb from the street,
   Too high to step, we knew.
Try as we did, Mary's foot slipped,
   So down onto the street she slid.
Of course it wasn't enough that she went,
   She took me along for the slide.
As we both went down, then couldn't get up,
   Finally, with a lot of struggle, I got up.
Then Estelle and I finally got Mary up,
   No one was hurt so we trotted off home.

Catherine M. Karpiak

What Would You Give

What would you give if you could be,
   Peaceful and happy and fancy free.

What in your life would you let go,
   To free your heart from pain and heal your woe.

Your pain and your joy are both the same,
   For from the depth of your soul they both came.

Would you give one day of love from the love you lost?
   To free you from death's pain what would be your cost?

You would have not felt pain nor anger so,
   Had the one you loved not been called to go .

They are gone it's true, them no longer you can hold,
   But they're forever in your heart, a wealth beyond man's gold.

So be patient please, love's not left you alone,
   Think about your heart, before to you, your lost love was known.

They will help you heal, if you'll let them try,
   Close your eyes and relax, there's no need to cry.

You see life's lost days and sorrows on earth, are but for us,
      A few grains of sand,

Our love together in time ever after, is eternity's beach and
            God's paradise for man.

Darlene J. Guy

Here I Am

Here I am in a world surrounded by so much hatred;
Painful and confusing situation, but not a tear is shed.
The cry for help kept deep inside,
For there are laws by which we all abide.
But, is there really justice for all,
Where rich men flourish, and poor men fall?
Judgement by shade of skin or origin, is that fair?
To choose your friend by the color he may wear.
A smile from any man's face is the same.
Is there any need to play this game?
A game of death, which we all shall learn,
Unless, everyone is given the chance to earn.
Earn the respect they deserve and will need,
To live their lives to the fullest, indeed!

Christina Roder

Proud To Say

   I am proud to say, as I looked
out my window today.
   A sign in my neighbors window,
"It's a boy."
   My eyes filled with tears of joy,
to think it's a boy.
   I've lived here most of my life.
I've raised two boys, and I know what it
is like. The parents will be showing off
the new teeth, no other baby could beat.
   Then he walks and talk's and is going
to school, for he will be learning the
Golden rule.
   Playing baseball and learning to swim
so many things I wouldn't know where
to begin. Any ways, congratulation go
out to my neighbor.
   For starting a new baby boy generation.

Betty Jane Selhoust-Leanen

Our Child Gone Forever

Our child a precious memory
Our child a precious lost

I once had a son, I once had a daughter
I once had a child, who called me mother

I gave him understanding and plenty of love
I would kiss and hug her when she was sad

I once had a child
Who called me dad

He made me his best friend, I was her pal forever
I once had a child, who called me mother

He would hold up his arm to show me his muscles
She would jump up and down to show new dress she had

I once had a child
Who called me dad

He gave us his memory to never forget
She gave us her memory to never forget

We once had a child
We will never forget

Our child a precious memory
Our child a precious lost

Elnora S. Moore

43

Love Makes The World Go 'Round

I suppose in everyone's life love is needed.

Love is the one thing that is a necessity
other than water.

But, with love there must also be something,
someone, or some idea to make love
possible.

Although that thing or idea may be one
single memory, one last grain of sand,

it is someone's love, someone's heart,
someone's world.

So I have come to the conclusion that, that
old phrase is indeed true,

and that is,

Love Makes The World go 'round!!!

Angela Daniels

In God's Eyes

What is man that God is mindful of him
Or that in God's image he is made,
He is but a passing vapor
On life's thoroughfare being portrayed.

Man was put on earth for a purpose
To do what God had planned,
Working diligently day by day
Toiling laboriously with his hands.

Why has man become so sinful
Full of deceit, trouble and strife?
It's because he has failed the plan of God
Doing as he pleases all his life.

God is not pleased with lifestyle of mankind
Nor will he forever hold his anger,
It's because of His grace and mercy
That we are not in more imminent danger.

Consider the graciousness of God
His kindness and goodness always realize,
Being made a little lower than angels
We all are precious in God's eyes.

Alice Webb

Dreams

Wild as an exotic rose
Or subtle as an ocean breeze,
Dreams are mysterious and confusingly wonderful.

Bump! Crash!
What was that awful noise?
Dreams can be scary and horrifying.

You feel like a butterfly drifting higher and higher into the clouds.
The clouds into which the Savior rose
Cushion your head as your dreams lift you.

The ideas in a dream are bright pictures
Of a fictional life coming forth,
Causing much happiness for you to endure.

When you finally awake from this chimera,
You realize that it was only a genuine dream
Because your thoughts have returned to reality.

Casey Jones

My Independence

I'll know I'm independent when I don't need my parents for food or money.

I'll know I'm independent when I can make healthy choices for
myself... when I'm proud of my decisions.

I'll know I'm independent when I can be happy with me. When I no
longer need outside things to make me feel good.

I'll know I'm independent when my needs come before someone
else's wants.

I'll know I'm independent when my biggest supporter is me.

Ellen Bohnstengel

"Reality"

If people would allow for human natures
open or biased opinions, the world would be more peaceful.

You cannot expect or demand perfection,
in an imperfect world since,
everyone's thoughts and actions are their own.

If you accept people for who or what they are,
Instead of what you think they should be,
you would be a happier person.

People cannot be anything more than what they are,
mortals, made of flesh and blood and bones, God's imperfect creations.

Strike me and I may bruise or break,
cut me verbally or physically and I may bleed,
starve me of knowledge and experiences and I may wither away and die.

We as individuals or as a whole are not flawless,
we will make our mistakes and we will accept and learn from them also.

I, as a person will set my own goals, some I will obtain-others
were not meant to be at this time, but they were all mine.

With all the imperfects drawing strength from one another,
they will eventually establish a feeling of perfection,
while accepting each other for themselves.

Cynthia L. Kallinen

Mind Binge

All the nonsense from your mind and soul I will purge.
Only until death do us part, and I will sing your dirge.
I cannot let you go so easily from me,
Did you care so much, my true feelings you could not see?
You only wanted to see false light and not understand my psychosis,
Or see any dark, even if it meant many a times false bliss.
A mind that enraged me so has made me see his wraith,
that presence, so putrid and demoniac, away I will cleanse and bathe,
with only ones blood that is pure and a mind not twisted.
Only one presence summoned upon me has insisted,
to do away with you and another spirit not needed.
Ashes to ashes, dust to dust, frightfully my warning was never yet heeded.
There is a time that can come so late, that time has arrived.
So sad is the fact, but to you from me many chances were never deprived.

Dani Carpenter

Hostages Released

Two hostages captured,
One in Bosnia, one in a bank holdup.
Each feels the same fear and terror.

Time ticks away slowly,
Full of menace. Tension builds.
Life seems exceedingly precious.
Both cry and pray.

Suddenly - release.
Each feels the joy of freedom, the wonder of a new life.
One lives.
One dies.

Carolyn Shafer

Planets

That I could steal one kiss,
one precious moment of her time;
would be a grateful pleasure
   you could bestow upon me.

One touch of her hand;
upon my cheek, stroking tenderly,
lovingly, would be the last request
given by me as I set sail into the night.

Two worlds, revolving within sight of
their common sun - love.
That which keeps them together
   and apart.

While one revolves faster,
to catch the other's pace;
one slows down,
to meet the other behind.

Whence the two meet,
an explosion of love
shall endure to rival
   the heat of their sun...

     Curt T. Walker III

From The Heart

One must face a challenge from the start,
One must take the task to their heart.
One must look forward to what lay ahead.
One must wake early and leave their bed.
One must do all of this,
   If they are willing to take the risk.
If they will risk failing and falling down,
If they can change their face when it holds a frown.
If they can ignore life's daggers and spears,
If they can hold out to their many fears.
   When one can take the thorns and find a rose,
When one can accept the result of what they chose.
When one can take an enemy and make him a friend,
When one is ready to quit, yet stays 'til the end.
   Then they can love everyone just as they are,
Then they will radiate beauty even from afar.
Then they will accept each night and day,
Then when night falls, they will find time to pray.
Then after all of the joy and pain,
Within their heart will peace forever reign.

     Cynthia L. Hardy

Goodnight Sweet Light

I hold this gun in my hand.
One day it will have its trigger pulled.
The small metal object will protrude from its shaft and enter my
   skull,
And life will end,
From the darkness comes light,
But I see no light in this darkness,
Only black,
Endless black,
Forever black,
There is no light at the end of this tunnel,
Only a hole,
A dark, black, endless, forever hole,
"So why not pull the trigger?" questions the laughing clown,
"Then my misery would end, and I'd have nothing,"
So as I pull the trigger,
I smile at the clown,
As he laughs at me,
Never
Forever gone, now.

     Eric William Jones

"Sail Away"

You always voiced your desire to "sail away"...
One day...

And your "baby" always suggested it would someday
Come true...
One day...

You gave all you ever could time after time...
For you always knew that day would finally arrive;
Then you could close your heart and ultimately just...
"Sail away"...
One day...

All the broken promises, all the faded dreams;
They haven't been so bad...
Because you know they won't mar the fruits of your day...
One day...

And when the dust settles in the end...
O, what a time you will spend...
As you release your wings and "sail away"...
One day...

     Anthony Newcombe

Wine...

Life is like fine wine.

Smooth, sweet and relaxing.
Once you have had a glass you just want more.

Life is like sour grapes.

When you're tasting them they taste bitter
and hard to deal with.
Once they are swallowed and you take a
sip of fine wine you don't taste them as much!

A LIFE TIP TO GO BY...

WHEN TASTING SOUR GRAPES ALWAYS TRY TO FIND
   A FINE WINE CHASER TO GO WITH THEM...

     Chandra Michelle Lauber

One Last Look

Once you were here but now you are gone
Once full of cheer but now there is none
We all know you are standing in Heaven
Looking down at us on this sad occasion
We all knew you were sick and prayed every night
You would get better and receive all your might
You were a wonderful woman to one and all
Everyone loved you, even the baby, who's small
You would get a bit better then sick again
We certainly never wanted your life to end
We all know God takes everyone away
But no one wanted you to go that way
One day when you told your sons "you know I'm going to go"
And the doctor says "Just a few days that I know"
We really wanted to try
To help you get better as the days went by
Then the Lord called you for your time
And each knew you were in Heaven Divine
You will always be missed since God cleared you with his book
As everyone gathered to take one last look

     Deanna Campbell

The Lost Poets

Where have all the poets gone?

It seems as though they've vanished, like the morning dew that once blanketed my soul.

When will they return?

Now that we are all left to wander through the endless forests of our minds.

Have they forgotten how to write?

Maybe there exists for the poets a sense of abandonment, for a once familiar world.

Can we believe this?

The return of the poets is necessary, for life return to its splendor.

Shall we wait together?

Our restoration of faith in mankind will be needed, in order for our lost poets to find their way back home.

Daniel Manganiello

Eavesdropping

I feel that have Eavesdropped
On the sighs of two scandalous lovers
Through my window pane.

Tonight, I hear the breeze, and the passionate rustling
Sighs of the Aspen Tree.

I think of you as I hear their union.
The breeze, she straddles her Aspen tree
Like I mount you my love, and she rides him like the wind.

The echoes of her passion
Brush my naked body,
Like the heat of an August night, and
I feel gusts of passion penetrate me, and the pores
Of my imagination until they reach my cavity of
Pleasure and life.

I toss and turn like the breeze searching for
Her lover and I am transformed to a river in search of
The mouth of the sea, but you are not here
My love, and I am left with drops of dew in the early morning hours,
Listening to the breeze and her Aspen.
With erotic thoughts... remembering you.

Deborah Quintana-Job

In Discovery Of Marriage

When my eyes met yours I knew your heart was mine.
On the day we married we journeyed through our time.
We laughed, we loved, we-together, shared our minds.
Our hearts became one, bodies one, our souls entwined.
We struggled, we cried, we grew and life became joyful for us two!
Whenever, I placed my hands upon you my soul crept into yours.
As, I lay in the stillness of self, quietly, I desired you even more.
I craved the touch and the taste of you my dearest love.
It is your soul that slides into mine as one perfect glove.
I remembered at thirty-six how I laughed at what I never knew.
In discovery of marriage my life was to be shared with you.
From this day forward and always we will dwell inside each others' souls.
Love makes us immortal an eternity unfolds.
I love you, my love, to the depths and breaths of my souls desire.
The winds and the rains of fire; unceasingly beats without retire.
Though the many sands of our seasons.
During the rhythm and rhyme of life without reasons.
It is not the quantity of life that brings us fulfillment; rather, the
quality of fulfillment that brings us everlasting life.
It is in loving you, my dearest love, that we have grown to live.
Though marrying you that I have chosen to give.

Elaine Dunstatter

...Until Today

I see your reflection in my mind,
Your touch is so gentle,
Your words are so kind.
When you pass,
Your smile brings sunshine to me,
Like petals of rose bud, a beauty to see.
If only for a moment, Our lips could meet,
So soft and delicate, warm and sweet.
I love you more than you will ever know,
More than I could ever show.
Never before have I felt this way,
Never before... until today.

Lindsay Woodward

My Old Piano

Your keys are worn, your tone is flat;
Your top is marred, where glasses sat.
Your bench is gone, I don't know where,
And you don't fit here, or over there.

The songs you sing are out of date,
These "Bee-Gee" songs you say you hate?
Well, you can't play "Bop" or "Jazz" or "Swing",
But I think your "Waltz-time" is just the thing.

And anyway, you're here old dear
I hope you'll stay, for many a year
For we love you, just as you are
In spite of many a scratch and scar.

Our mother's hands did love you too,
She gave me you, when she was through.
Now, little hands are coming soon
To learn the scale, and "Lorna Doone".

So, Old Piano, stay right here
Move you again? I wouldn't dare.
For surely you would fall apart.
And there is no glue to mend my heart.

Marge Kelley

Another Chance

You begged me for another chance
Your sweet lies put me into a trance
At the time I was too blind to be
That we were never meant to be
I thought you were a sweet guy
I thought you were willing to try
At the time I didn't have a clue
I thought I could believe in you
I finally figured it out
Now I see what you're all about
You play your little game
I think it's pretty lame
You try to act sweet to all the new girls you meet
You do what you can
to get what you want again and again
I told you I didn't want to play
You said you didn't want to anyway
When you broke up with me
I slowly started to see, I feel out of your trance
Now they'll never be another chance

Kelly Peckham

The Forest Floor Bequeath

Pine needles like palm fronds cover the grassy forest floor,
your search for more is sky and clouds overhead,
in hand a book you've read,
lean back and enjoy the sunlit more,
Jesus would approve your respite.
Spin world, Spin
A niche you've found,
among the ground,
the smoke and mist of morning dew, have cleared,
and thoughts transparency divine.
Like once frosted glass of wine, to sip as darkness falls,
you drank Christ's blood the forest well,
and await starlit moon and star bright sky,
and you may ask the question "Why?"
but spin world, spin, and now again,
your circle is complete, round you go and whirly rows,
with hugs and kiss and golden times, your life filled replete.
You ask for more, on forest floor,
beneath evergreen so tall, and for a circle grow,
and you to know, that life is birth and awe.

Kurt H. Pedersen

Grandpa Graffiti

You were born in Vista, sometime after noon,
Your name Paige Johanna—the date, 14 June.
If you also must know the particular year,
It's one-nine-nine-five, but you need not fear
There are fancy machines that keep track of it all,
And spit it back out when you need to recall.
Such as when you reach teens, that's two thousand seven,
Or when you will drive, that's twenty eleven.
But do not despair that there's nothing to do,
There are plenty more things that are left up to you.
Such as when to use potty, or take off and walk,
Or eat solid food, or start grown-up talk.
But those things can wait, we won't scare you now,
There's plenty of time and we'll show you how.
Let's concentrate first on the very next thing,
So you can cope with whatever each new day will bring.
You must decide now, though it may sound dumb,
Should you use a pacifier, or just shove in a thumb?
After that you can lie back and do what you do,
Until two-oh-six-oh when your FICA comes through.

Joe Plassmeyer

"Only In The Night"

Your whisper is the wind through the trees at night
Your laughter is the clear cool stream in the wood,
Your heart is the sun, the source of my light
And your beauty is the nature of all that is good.

Your eyes...the stars gleam
Your voice...the bird sings
Your face...the Gods dream
Your touch...the hope it brings

I woke up dreaming of your embrace
My fading vision was of your face,
Smiling an innocence and sighing so sweet
I tried to sleep again so that we could meet.

I see you only in the night.

Your sigh...breeze of the ocean
Your lips...honey of the bee
Your body...mystery of the motion
Your words...only for me.
...only for me.

Michael Panza

The Way I Look At Things Between Us

Your mouth speaks lies,
    your eyes tell the truth.

Just one look can say so much
    of what you may feel deep down inside.

I notice the way you look at me
    I look at you the same.

Why can't you tell me how you feel
    I am tired of these games.

So I am asking you
    Let's be more than friends.

If I am wrong about all of this
    you need not know who I am.

If I am right then you know
So why bother to sign my name.

Loredana N. Palma Tascione

Chris

You can tell you were loved by the tears in the hall
You'll be missed by your friends, you'll be missed by all

Through good times and bad, you helped us stay glad
By showing us to be happy for the things that we had

God was calling you that one sad, spring day,
the way he does often in his own mysterious way

Don't worry or fear,
for a better place you will near

We all have a mission in life, so they say,
You must have fulfilled it in your own special way

In our heart you will stay,
We'll mourn our own way

But not for your death, but the life that you lived
For a child to die is God's call and his cry,
one we must follow, both you and I.

Jillian Murphy

Goodbye

You made me laugh when I was sad, you made me smile if I were mad.
You were like the childhood friend I never had,
And now that you're gone it makes me sad.
I never got a change to say goodbye,
Or to say to you just one last hi.
When I heard of this tragedy, I wanted to cry,
But surrounded by my peers, I had to try.
My eyes watered up, and I clenched my fists tight,
And alas I knew that this thing was not right.
My throat began to hurt as my soul dropped low,
I can't stand to think of it, tell me it's not so.
The thing that hurts the most and makes me cry,
Is that I never got to say that last goodbye.
Although you are gone, you are still here,
So please my friend don't shed a tear.
You've left now, but you've played your apart,
Yes, my friend, you're still in my heart.
In complete darkness, we're all the same,
It's only our knowledge and wisdom that separates us,
Don't let your eyes deceive you....

Matthew Charles McCary

Remembering

It's been so long since you left us all behind.
You traveled to the destination of all importance.
Knowing you'd be missed to such a great extent.
I can still remember the last time we talked.
The conversation is so vivid and I still hear your voice.
Each night I lay here and wonder why?
Why you had to die;
Why we had to lose you;
I just don't understand the way things turned out.
Why we got dealt a bad hand.
None of this makes any sense to me.
First I was confused, then I was upset, then I was mad, and now it
   just hurts.
We still think about you all the time
And we'll always love you.
The only thing that's changed is you're gone.
With this I close, wishing I could have said good-bye.

Jennifer Kennedy

Freedom

I talk of freedom
you talk of slavery
I talked of kindness
you talk of hatred
if I could tell you
this is what I'd say
I've left my hell I've left you there
the me that you knew is now dead
in fact he was never really alive
he was just an android
programmed by your lies and deceptions
now I'm alive, now I'm me
now I'm in control
you no longer have power to make me feel like dirt
you've lost everything, I've gained everything
I found the real utopia
I'm miracle-bound
so don't try and bring me down
take your toys and go home to play
and don't even think of coming another day

Marcus Wolfe

Dream People

Exploited and blinded they plug you in.
You take what they slip you and fly a
false grin.
They keep you confused, it's easier that way.

Thinking of thoughts believed of your own.
But pumped propaganda has found its way
home.

You live of their life.
You strive for their mark.

You're lost and don't know it, your
heads in the dark.

Except for the Dream people, it's our minds
that they prey.

Believe in the Dream People, our lives
let yours stay.

John B. Adcock Jr.

Why Things Change

Changes are God's way of saying,
You should be kneeling,
You should be praying!
Sometimes they're happy,
Sometimes they're sad.
Sometimes they're good,
Sometimes they're bad!
But He always knows what He's doing,
   Even if you think He's wrong!
And sometimes we think loved-ones are here,
   Even when we know their gone!
Why must things change,
   Why must people die!
Why must people try to hide their feelings,
   Why must people lie?
We often ask why,
   But He doesn't say!
Then we ask again,
   And all He says is: Live day by day and please don't go astray!

Laura Hughes

My Last Wish

I wish for you
You seem to never show
Without seeing you
The love for you will never grow
I wish, I could walk the Earth
Go in complete circles if I must
One moment with you
Why won't you trust
I wish I could fly the world
But, from the sky your beauty would be so dull
So I will stay on the ground
And look at you in awe
I wish, there was no time
As it seems to fly right by
Now the only thing left to do
Is just fade away and die

Jason Zaremba

Untitled

You never really know who you are
You search all of your life to find the real you
Just to find a new aspect of yourself around every turn
Never knowing what to expect
Just feeling that you aren't up to your full capabilities
Knowing that you must be more than what you see in the mirror
You search in vain
With every thing that you learn
You become somebody new
So you never really find all of you
But the best aspects of yourself will come to the surface
Without really trying to bring them you.

Gail Halstead

Child

...Of mine. Born on a cold March day.
you brought sunshine, tears of joy and
thanksgiving. You grew with God's Grace,
(despite my mistakes!) to a loving and caring
young man. And now, there is a

Child

...Of my child. born on a cold February
day, he brought sunshine, tears of joy and
thanksgiving. And he'll grow with God's Grace,
(despite your mistakes!) to a loving and caring
young man.

Kathy Rothrock

Down The Path

As you travel down the path so twisted worn and torn.
You sadly wish at last, you had not lost your past.

And it scares you so, the things you do not know,
What the future holds, and where it is that you shall go.

For deep inside, you wish you could retreat and hide,
back to the safety of your past, where all your dreams and memories
forever last.
But you know you can't turn back, and you know you cannot stay,
For time goes by, it won't let you stay, it gently pushes you
on your way.

What is it you should do, Where is it you should go?
How are you to act, how are you to know?

To you life brings so many things,
And as you travel down this path, so twisted worn and torn,

You have to leave the past behind,
Maybe you'll lose some dreams, and I know how hard that seems.

But as time goes on, you'll find all your past is not gone.
more dreams will come, and be fulfilled for some dreams can't be killed.
And from your past what meant so much, will not be forever lost,
For some things in your heart forever stay, and can't be lost no
matter what the cost.

Lori Shoup

Barney Beagle Burns

There once was a family of four.
You probably never met before.
They have gone through everything,
As though it was nothing.

One eerie Saturday morning.
Something struck without warning.
The sad news came sadly...slowly.
Poor helpless animal,
Wagging happily on the table without even knowing.
They said their farewells,
And hugged and kissed as well.
They went out sadly knowing they would never see him again.

Now as the dark brown pile sits in its own style.
Trying to get along well with another.

As it starts all over again.

Jennifer Burns

God's Love

When I'm feeling lost and alone,
You are closer than the nearest phone.

Sometimes I drop down to my knees,
Other times I cry out, Lord help me please.

You are there to offer comfort and love,
As you watch over me from above.

You give me strength, you dry my tear stained face,
Yes Lord you hold my hand while I run this race,

Just like the footprints in the sand,
Sometimes you carry me, not only holding my hand.

Although I'm not always as I should be,
The utmost thanks Lord I give to thee.

Gina D. Myles

"You"

As I think of you, I grow old.
You paralyzed my mind from thinking of anything but you.
I am buried with lost affection, so much of it because of your ways.
You never bothered to acknowledge the fact.
Our eyes would meet and I wanted to stare into them as I stare into
the stars, wondering what lies beyond.
To me, you were real, not a fantasy, like the others.
I searched and found a sense of loneliness, a disposition of blankness
yearning for someone.
The sense of unknown made me crave for more knowledge.
Your brown eyes were so deceiving, what lurked behind I desperately
wanted to know.
You don't know how I feel when I look at you, knowing that you don't
have a clue of who I am or how I feel towards you. To you, nothing
has changed. My mind is fragile, tangled up in the web of depression
you unknowingly created.
I am over you now. I feel freedom, yet somehow I miss you.
You could have been the one, but now that is gone.
I feel as if you'll never understand.
You can't change the way I feel nor the way I am.
Before I close the door, look into my eyes one last time and say
goodbye, a goodbye that doesn't follow a hello or even a conversation,
for we have never spoken.
The door will shut and our everlasting eternity together will be
locked out, keeping you company.

Laura Ragsdale

Frankie's Jeans

Today I found a pair of your old blue jeans.
You must have worn them when you were three or four.
A pair of Bristol Blues, they are ragged on the cuffs,
Thin on the seat, and threadbare on the knees.

I hold them in my hands, and I remember
You running here and there as if you were
A little being of the woods, perhaps a tiny frog, hopping,
A swift deer, running, or a frisky pony, galloping.

Then I place them against my heart,
And once again I can feel you
As I used to when I carried you —
  Holding me tightly in a loving mood,
    Laying your tired head wearily on my shoulder,
      Sometimes struggling fiercely to be freed.

Finally I touch them against my face,
And tears well up in my eyes,
So I say a prayer to our Mighty Savior,
  Thanking Him for the little boy you were,
    Asking him to guard the teen you are becoming,
      And praying that He will guide the man you will be.

Joe Segura

Man Oh Man

Blood red heart
you make it pump with the juice of love/life
mighty feeling
high hard steady sometimes calm
always wanting more.. of you...
your smile laugh playful attitude
that look from your eyes
straight into my soul   genuine.

Busy, you make time for me
we're all there is...
Poet of the 90's
man of the millennium
soft hard thinking concerned.
The breath of your love is like life cement
blowing a warm spring wind
through the cracks in my wintered soul

Linda Honeysett

Untitled

The Dream of You is what I want to believe.
You in my arms, you in my kiss.
You being held is the moment that the clocks fear,
  the moment when they will never work again.
Clocks and watches and sundials, they come to me
And show me their contracts for possessing you.
They try to surround.
But you in a big bed and a smile have erased the ticking.
You in a hand on my face have closed my eyes to Hell.
Where I touch your hair lightly, that is the place.
If I trace your lips with my finger, am I touching love?
The Dream of Love is what I want to believe.

Nick Viggiano

Grandbaby - First Born

Grandbaby, grandbaby, so quick to learn, cherish the love
you have earned.
Grandbaby, grandbaby, so divine, so sweet, so cuddly,
I'm glad you're mine.
How proud your parents must be to have such a joy, so swift,
so carefree.
So proud too, I am to be your grandma, oh little one,
how I love thee, your sweet little smile I can see.
Your little voice I can hear, you are always in my prayers.
So far away you might seem in my heart you are near always.
Grandbaby good dreams I hope you have, success in life,
happiness and a good laugh.
Your Mommy's my daughter I'm proud to say.
Respect your parents, love them each day with a kind word.
In good graces you will always stay.

Muriel McCoy

Sweet Lover

I see you coming near and my soul dances.
You eyes are hypnotic and piercing.
Your eyes start aflame within me.

My heart begins to hasten as you slowly move
Toward me. A moment of silence and my heart
Cries, touch me! Looking into your eyes, I
Search for tenderness. I have lost all reason.

The warmth of your bronze body caresses mine.
Sweet lover surrender to my heart. Sweet lover
Thy breath is like a honeysuckle bloom. With
Each passionate kiss, thy mouth is warm. Thy mouth
Is sweet like honey flowing from the comb.

Your warm body covers mine like a blanket of
Rose petals, I slowly close my eyes like a
Child in bliss. Tenderly, I touch you ever
So gently. Sweet lover of my mind.

Jo Smith

Love

Sometimes you put your heart out on your sleeve.
You expect it to be sheltered by someone else.
Then turn comes to turn,
You see that no one can protect your heart, but you.
Do me wrong once,
Shame on you.
Do me wrong twice,
Shame on me.
Don't do me wrong again.
I don't want to be blinded by the truth.
Please don't hurt me again.

Jeanna Kay Broyles

The Final Lesson

Dedicated to Sylvia T. Gallo
Dear Mom,
You asked me to pray: You claimed your words lacked eloquence.
You asked me to sing: You said you had no angelic voice.
You asked me to smile: You thought your face reflected less
  serenity.

Then I watched Death take you from me.
And in return...

You taught me to pray, for the Kingdom of God you saw.
You taught me to sing, for you praised the Lord.
You taught me to read, for you revealed the Word.
You taught me to smile, for you found peace.

Goodbye, Mom. I love you.

Mary Antoinette Gallo Sunyoger

"Our Special Cowboy"

Today J.C., you're One Year Old,
You are more precious to us than gold.
We've watched you grow and start to talk,
And oh, so sweet, when you were learning to walk.

Sometimes you were happy, and sometimes sad,
But you were never, ever really bad!
That happy face, that sparkling smile,
For you we would walk many a mile.

Your Daddy and Mama are so proud of you,
They think you are perfect, everything that you do.
Slow down J.C., you're growing too fast,
We want these wonderful moments to last!

This year with you has brought such joy,
You are our Special Little Cowboy.

Margaret J. Winchester

Of Love And Life

My precious son, how I love you so.
You are God's gift to me don't you know.

All of my life I always knew,
That God would bless me with a little guy like you.

He told me to watch and see how you grow,
He said before you know it the little man in him would show.

He said to watch this little guy as he learns to walk,
Listen to his words as he learns to talk.

Help him to understand the ways of a man,
Teach him to be the best that he can.

He said show him the difference between right and wrong,
Answer his questions, teach him to be strong.

He said he depends upon me to do these things,
He wanted me to prepare you for what life brings.

That is the happiness with the laughter, the sadness with the tears,
The pains of growing older, and the courage to face your fears.

Son all of these things and more, from me you will learn,
Then when you are older, God will give you your turn.

He will bless you with a little guy like he did with me,
That is how life goes on and on don't you see.

Geronimo C. Bridgewater

The Yoke

I see us as a team
Yoked together on life's field,
Turning up the rocks of minor crises
Along with deep, rich mother-earth.
You do not step in front
To cast me in your shade,
Nor do I lean to bear
More than I should.
Step by step we share the load between us.
Sometimes the path arcs right...
Your side. You lead the way
Because your sight is clear
And I must pull without the current vision.
But then the furrow sweeps left.
You nudge me to the fore
And support my lead unselfishly.
We are both enriched:
The burden is halved
While the joy is doubled.

Judith McGrath

Just A Man

He's just a man, a man in every way.
Yes, He's a good man ... what more can I say,
but that he works from dawn 'til dusk,
because he's a poor man and he must.

So if you're looking for fortune and fame,
he's the wrong man but who can you blame,
because you know he's just a man, a poor man,
though he works as hard as he can.

No, there would be no silver and no gold,
only a strong hand for you to hold.
There would be no fortune and no fame,
but he's a good man just the same.

He's a man who's earned everything he owns,
but a man who is tired of being alone.
Though there isn't much he can give,
his whole life for you he'd live.

Mary Ann Carswell

Draggin' Dragon

Draggin' dragon's spittin' fire,
Yellow stripes, wings in flight.

Draggin' dragon's seekin' friends,
Wantin' fun but folks all run.

Draggin' Dragon's chasin' after,
Beggin' them to stay and play.

Fearin' they'd become her victuals,
Folks all scatter and sprint faster.

Draggin' dragon's all alone,
Looks for fun, and folks all run.

Draggin' dragon sighs and cries
'Til salty tears stream down her face.

Draggin' dragon's tears come faster,
Sprinklin' salt 'til the fire's gone out.

Then the folks move closer, closer;
Now they feel safe and now wish to stay.

Draggin' dragon's not alone now;
All join hands and dance and play.

Kathryn M. Braeman

My Favorite Hobby

Ever since I was in the 11th grade, I've loved to
write poetry;

For, to me, it's a good way to relax and is
important to me.

I had a wonderful English teacher in 11th grade
and she made me want to write

Various forms of poetry and the timing seemed to
be just right!

I'll never forget her, Mary Wilson, and what she
means to me;

And since that year, 1962, a poet I've wanted
to be.

I like all subjects of poetry and hope to continue
writing a long time,

Because this is my favorite hobby, the most enjoyable
one I've ever found!

Joyce Greuel

Reality

A place I can stay out of the rain
would be better than here.
Although I am wet, I can feel the cold hearts
of the people as they pass
worrying about time and money
as though only they mattered.
Reaching out to grab hold of
that ruthless, selfish world I'd like to belong to
I find myself crying and wishing I wasn't here.

Curled up in a ball, dreaming selfish dreams
as I would like to be.
Where I could talk and people would listen
instead of ignoring my whimpering cry for money.
I want to belong to that selfish world full of greed
and find myself passing the bums on the street
and watch them cry and whimper and moan
as I laugh in their faces.
And then the sky gets dark
and I close my sore eyes
and try to sleep on the cold, hard cement.

Julie McBride

Not A Dandy-Lion

Starting from the bottom
working slowly my way up.
I've faltered here and wavered there,
but I've always kept on going.
I've fallen over once or twice, withered you might say.
But fear not my little one, no lasting harm was done
I picked myself back up again
and always kept on going.
The climb itself was pretty steep
with thorns all along the way.
I was pricked and poked and pecked at
but I always kept on going.
When I finally reached the top
it 'twas the grandest sight to see,
endless waves of soft red petals
rippling at my feet.
Looking back, the journey seemed so tough
but now that I am here
among the blossoming, rippling waves
I'm glad I kept on going.

Kristen DiStassio

"The Liquid Sky"

As he looks up through a liquid sky, he stares at the stars and wonders "Why"?
"Why?" He wonders, to answers he cannot find. "Why?" He wonders,
  "Are the nice left behind?"
Try as he may to succeed. He is always pushed back because good is
  his deed. He cries aloud, with his fist in the air.
  "God," he demands, "Show yourself if you dare!"
But there is no answer that he can hear, and for a brief moment, he
fights back a tear.
He doesn't really hold God to blame. He just wishes to stop the pain.
The pain that is with him night and day. Pain which is the price he
feels he must pay.
But deep in his heart there is always hope, and without that he could
never cope.
  "Prepare for the worst, and hope for the best."
And with out that saying, he would surely be like the rest.
So once again he pulls himself together, and holds tight to that
imaginary tether.
Making his way again, with hope held high. Making his way,
  under a Liquid Sky.

John W. Stamp

I Care

A teenage girl who likes to help people.
Wondering why people hate other people because they're different.
Hearing desperate cries of homeless children.
Seeing enemies becoming friends.
Wanting to help the needy.
A teenage girl who likes to help people.

Pretending that this is a carefree world.
Feeling sorry toward these people.
Touching the hands of people who were once healthy.
Worrying about the future.
Crying for all the people who have to suffer.
A teenage girl who likes to help people.

Understanding that I cannot help everybody.
Saying, "Do not have hatred towards anyone".
Dreaming for the day that all this will happen.
Trying to be a very understanding person.
Hoping for my dreams to come true.
A teenage girl who like to help people.

Mirah Lucas

This Troubled Heart

Within these cries you can hear the pain
Within these cries you can see the rain
  flooding this heart so it cannot soar
This troubled heart cries for more

Those who are lost, those who can't sleep
Ones who are so lonely, ones who are too weak
  to believe in me and keep me new
This troubled heart aches for you

Familiar friends and sacred places
You watched me grow...knew all my faces
You've left me now, I'm so very cold
This troubled heart misses the old

So 'let down' and not of worth
Will I ever find a place on earth
  with love trust for promises made
This troubled heart feels betrayed

From inside out transform in time
So sure, so true and be not blind
If not this spirit will be sealed
For this troubled heart needs to be healed

Kathleen Vanderbeck

Prelude

Everywhere life blooms and abounds in delightful designs
Within the bowl of the sky. Spiraling cedars and pines
Thrust from the foreheads of hills, patient sentinels of change.
While somewhere buzzards glide in slow concentric rings,
Blanketing the air with their feathery darkened wings.

Yet, I stand among blank, brooding men who deliberate
Over new methods of postponing Nature's reign. The weight
Of their pallid white coats casts a slow, painful
Quality to their movements. Like burdened clouds they creep,
Blotting out the light- denying the sweet comfort of sleep.

And it's unsettling to admit my closest friend is dying.
He says the pain resembles a hammer, pounding
Him in the chest, until nothing else but the pain seems real.
I'm sure Death has reserved for him a soft painless place
To Rest, but sadly he's too drugged to welcome Death's coming face.

Glorious hand-shaped leaves of majestic maples may surpass
Other scenes of beauty, but they too must wither and amass
Lifelessly at our feet. As joyous as the lark's melodies are,
Silence will one day prevail- stealing his song in mid-breath.
So we must never deny one profound fact- life is simply a prelude
  to Death.

Mark McDonnell

Untitled

Clouds pass me by, like a life time slowly passing away
With you for the first, I felt safe
With you, I felt alive
With you, I felt

Is it all gone
Did you take what you needed and leave
Was there anything there at all
Or was I just imagining
Was I just dreaming
Was I, hoping

Things are unclear now
I know where I stand, but not where I fell
It's almost insane, the way I felt
But it was real,
My feelings that is

I'm unsure of many things,
But mostly,
I'm unsure of myself,
Are these tears,
Or is it raining

Jeffrey Storm

In Search Of A Dream

I came to Florida to start a new life,
With two thousand dollars, some clothes and my wife.
She has a sister with an American spouse,
Happily abiding in a three bedroom house.
After two weeks vacation we were invited to return,
Such an opportunity was not to be spurned.
Six months later we said, 'farewell, the U.K.,'
And aimed for Orlando where our relatives stay.
Our welcome was a warm one in more ways than one,
Smiles, hugs, and handshakes, and a really zealous sun.
The few friends we'd made came round on the night,
To celebrate our arrival, till dawn's early light.
The following week we legalized our stay,
But this process is a long one, not done in a day.
Meanwhile time is idled away, staying cool,
Enjoying country music, swimming, playing pool.
It's one long vacation till officialdom is through,
Then we can find work, and really start life anew,
Once that is achieved, to our future it's the key,
We can prosper contented in the land of the free.

Ken Linnecor

War

The Revolutionary War was really cool
With treason, trickery, and a duel.
The colonists wanted a war,
'Cause the British were mean and they wanted to even the score.
The British first thought this would be easy,
But after a few years they felt a little queasy.
Britain tried and tried but they couldn't destroy
George Washington and his clever ploy.
The Redcoats had tons of supplies, but not the American troops,
Heck practically the only thing they had was day-old soup!
After a while the French jumped in,
They wanted to help the Americans win.
The Spanish soon followed France's lead,
They too wanted to crush Great Britain's greed.
The fight at Saratoga was really a battle,
John Burgoyne agreed to surrender and skedaddle.
Benedict Arnold was really a traitor;
A minute on one side, on the other a minute later.
Well, the British family quit and laid down their arms,
And promised never to set foot on America's farms.

Joshua Eikenberry

Thoughts

Bringing to mind the passages through time,
With things to think of with a curious mind.

Memories of times we wish we were dead,
And knowing that we are not yet in that mortal bed.

With thoughts of love lost and with love kept,
And memories of lovers we wish we had never met.

Never once do thoughts of hope and of faith
Enter my mind with unbearable strength.

Mary Mendis

Tales Of Trees

Oh the tales these trees have seen
With thick brown trunk and leaves of green
Born of seedling a century ago
Lifetimes later continuing to grow·
Originally farm land, pure and vast
Across the horizon, from east to west
Along with the maple the community grew
Now the trees are far and few
Though between the dwellings some still stand
Simpler was the day when plentiful was land

Nancy Ryan

"A Moment With My Granddaughter"

A little girl sat one day behind a door
With tears rolling down her little face,
She cried because she was hurt inside,
She felt laughed at and misplaced.
    She told with broken words and thought
    She felt very strongly about her plight.
    She was serious about the events so far
    And she needed someone to enlighten.
I told her they didn't mean to hurt her;
They weren't really making fun you see.
Sometimes people make funny faces and things
Because they want to make you happy.
    I dried her tears and wiped her face
    And she stood to leave the room.
    I slowly removed myself from the floor
    As the little girl jogged away with a zoom.
It felt good to see her smile again
And later she laughed as she said good-night,
And wouldn't it be nice if from behind a door
I could always make her life just right.

Kenneth Haynes

The Unspoken Word

The infatuating phrase, the unspoken word,
With so much in life still left to be learned.
It whispers in the flurry of a warm Spring eve,
Calling gently to us, but yet to believe.
Lingering on my lips, forever chanting your name,
Friends grown to lovers, we still remain the same.
Night fades away as the sun kisses the earth,
We walk hand-in-hand along the crashing surf.
It blinds us again, capturing the dream,
Shining ignorantly to us, for all else to be seen.
It shouts loudly to us but still can't be heard,
The enchanting embrace of the unspoken word.

Melissa Brinkly

"One Life"

One life, such a minute part of the universe, yet filled
with promise!

So vast it touches the heart of God
Each life well lived contributes
Unlimited good to many
Though fleeting, it is eternal.

The importance of a life
Can be measured by the love and
Kindness Shown to mankind!

Life will end, but
Love given freely and
Unselfishly will go on
Forever.

Live to give, love the unlovable
Reach out to the hurting masses
In this way one life is not one,
But many.

June Conant-Rusch

"Day Awakened"

I awaken slowly from out of the night
With outstretched arms I can feel the light
The beams now brighten to my delight
As life itself scatters from sight
They are the darkness creatures we are told
Yet one stays steady as if to behold
The wonder and beauty that light does hold
I will always be grateful in my growing old
Just to awaken each day and be able to say
My what a sight to behold today
The leaves above move tightly controlled
Yet far below the bark gathers mold
Brighter and brighter the rays become
As louder and louder we hear the hum
Of all the creatures there is a sum
May only survive being bathed by the sun
Light as we know brightens our day
And it's shown many times dear since you went away
I pray that on this day maybe you to will awaken
And say my what a sight to behold today.

Leroy Ratzlaff

A Train Runs Through Every Community

A train runs through every community.
You can hear it in the depth of night,
if you listen,
if you know how to listen.
You can see it in the breadth of daylight,
or, maybe not;
but it is there, it is there.
A train runs through every community.

John Felton

True Blue

All alone in a world of strangers
With nobody to call my friend,
When suddenly you confronted me,
And put my unhappiness to an end.
You made me feel like I belonged,
And you gave me someone to turn to.
I know I never would have made it if it weren't for you.
You took a chance with me, a quiet
girl who knew no one.
You accepted me for me and showed me
how to have fun.
You'll never know just how
grateful I am that you had a hand to lend.
And you never could see just
how thankful I am that I finally have found you,
My true blue best friend!

Michele A. DiLissio

The Gift

My children are angels, when their in beds
With little halos, upon their heads
I sneak in their room, and feel their breath
To make sure they're breathing, and not in death
Of this gift, I have been bestowed
Those angelic faces, they just glowed
The moon from above, just shining in
These sweet little children, could never sin
I cover them up, and make sure they're warm
Two little bodies, on a bed they do form
I tiptoe around, and give them a kiss
I remember the day, they were born, it was bliss
I am their mother, and I am so proud
I'll protect them alone, or within a crowd
It is my duty, as you can see
My children have no one, no one but me

Lynn Whitesel

Eternal Decay

A space of time must live and die,
  with every world I save;
But still I find, death of time,
  can steal life away;
Can't live in search of what has died
  to overcome pain;
When hunting death, the future dies,
  yet tragedies remain;
Then chaos feeds, on life that's caught,
  between times uncertain space;
Until greeting death, pleads tragic life,
  to relieve chaos from embrace;
Stripped of life, without a fight,
  death consumes its prey;
Now a conquered mind, will join the
  blind, in herds of eternal decay.

Michael P. Nielsen

Penelope's Lament

This loom has become my savior
With a house full of men
And the only one I need across the sea.
The yarn with which I weave is wearing thin
It won't be long before this charade ends.
Twenty long years have gone by
As I've sat in tortured concentration
The shouts of the suitors ring in my ears.
As my fingers work to unwind
The modest cloth that keeps me alive.
...And they will call him brave.

Kate Leahy

Reflection

Where have you gone, my lovely little lass
  With dandelions in your hand,
Skipping lightly o'er the green, green grass
  Or playing in the sand?

Where have you gone, my sturdy little lad,
  A' sailing your kite so high,
Or pulling your wagon? Oh, what fun we had,
  You and your pup and I!

The years have flown like a blown autumn leaves
  And yet, it seems to me,
I think I hear you laughing, down beside the brook
  But when I take a look
There are other children, playing in my yard,
  Who look and who sound like you.

The generations circle swiftly on.
  I know they're my children, too.
  I love my grandchildren too.

Margaret Mills Muntz

A Monday Morning

The Sun slowly rises on a Monday morn;
With creeping light, the day is born.
A clock set for six o'clock...
Goes tick-tock, tick tock, RINGGGGG!
Let the trumpets sound, the father has risen with a frown.
The Provider, the father of three, the King of the Castle is cranky.
The Queen follows the King,
The mother is a beauty (as I have seen)
Next come the kids one, two, three
Justin, Karen, and little Lee, who really needs to go pee!
We shall now skip the beautifying procedures,
Because what some do, could give people seizures.
We are now at the time of the morning meal,
And scents and smells are of veal.
Eggs and bacon are made with care,
For an intact egg is very rare.
The family finishes eating,
And soon they all leave;
Forgetting a briefcase, backpacks, and one forgotten purse.

Michael Chiang

Snow Dance

It was a hot chocolate kind of a day
with a thick grey sky snuggling down against the earth
squeezing out all sound
creating a dense, silent cocoon
of snow and cloud filtered sunlight
such that even the trees seemed to bend against its weight

And I realized all at once
what I should perhaps have always known

That if you close your eyes
and hold your breath
you can hear the snowflakes whispering
their giggling merriment to each other
as they whirl and romp through
their one and only dance
to earth

Michael Brandt

While I'm Sleeping

Sometimes I wonder when I close my eyes;
Will I awake with the morning rise;
Or will I did before the night.
And while I'm sleeping will others weep?
Or will they rejoice that I'm with my King?
Then I awake with a certain pride;
Because I will live before I die.

Kimberly A. Rossini

Reflections In Sand And Time

I looked across the lake then onto the sand,
wishing I was still standing there
holding your small hand.

Sandcastles, buckets and shovels
flashed into my mind,
as I remember all those precious
memories you left there, behind.

Tiny footprints took me
years back in time,
but of those I looked at,
yours I couldn't find.

But as I stood there
going so far back in the sand,
I could almost feel you
firmly holding my hand.

Linda M. Trimmer

"The Passing Of Summer"

Since summer is now gone,
Winter is finally coming along.
Snow, rain, and windy weather,
No birds in the sky,
Not even a feather.
Summer is gone and I'm a bit sad,
But so far winter is not that bad.
Maybe it's because school has just started,
But summer and me just can't be parted.
I loved the weather that was so rad,
But then again winter isn't that bad!

Leyna Marie Zagiel

Love

What is love?
Wings of a dove flying over mountains of May.
What is love?
The smell of a rose perfect in every way.
Love is the wind blowing,
the glory of knowing what is love,
the sound of the sea when it sways.
There are so many ways...
What is love?

Katie Swagler

Imagine That....

A unicorn is standing on a hill, the
wind whips around him yet he gets
no chill,

Far below the hill lies the great blue
sea, where the mermaids swim and sing
so merrily

Behind the hill a dragon breathes, his
burning fire comes out with ease,

In front of the hill mountains arise,
where the winged snow leopards make
their cries,

Then up! up! up! right up to space, aliens
are having a dune buggy race,

Fantasy, fantasy that's for me, where
I can always set my mind free.

Meghan Manion

Life Today

Listening to the wind chimes and watching the
    wind blown trees,
I know that our life together was ended as fast
    as a gusty breeze,
For one long year I've been alone, but the
    memories we made are dear,
Each day we should live as though it is our last
    for our days are numbered here.

Tell someone each day you love them and offer
    a helping hand,
Our tomorrows are no more reality than the grains
    of the blowing sand.
Don't put off what is important to you, as time
    certainly can slip away,
And once you've lost your mate to death, the material
    things are still here to stay.
You work hard to make life easier and perhaps you
    accomplish a lot,
    but when one is taken before you fulfill your plans
    what have you really got?

Louise Mynster

Faith

I once met a man with a heart like Grand Canyon,
Wide open to all, and beautiful to behold,
Kind words, kind ways, always smiling and helping,
Those who are burdened and feel all alone.

Charlie is strong, his spirit soars,
To a power higher than himself, where he gets
    his strength,
Then he gives away everything he receives from above,
Peace and Joy—Unconditional Love.

His faith is unshakable, his goodness endures,
The world is a sad place, but Charlie is sure—
That each day can get better.

There is a prayer I've often heard him say,
In every kind of weather,
"Lord, help me to remember,
    nothing is going to happen today,
That you and I can't handle together."

Jeanne M. Smith

Aladdin's Lamp

They say the world spins so fast that we don't even notice it moving;
Why then, does it seem to be dragging on forever?

Day after day it's the same endless nightmare - my entire existence is
bottled up in Aladdin's Lamp just waiting for you to rub it the right
way- releasing my soul, freeing it forever!

Are you afraid of what might be yours to own for eternity?

Afraid because you don't know what lies inside this unique design and
gleaming surface.

Afraid because you don't want to be foolishly betrayed when you find
out what you have finally won!

You poor fool!

Don't you know that riches were never found, kingdoms were never built
and battles never won by those who played it safe.

Go on - take a chance!

Julie A. Morss-Thomas

55

"Why?"

Have you ever asked yourself why?
Why do the waves crash down like thunder?
Why does the wind roar through the trees?
Why does a baby cry for its mother?
Why does a ship sail on the sea?
Why do we not know where we are going?
Why is life's path so rocky and steep?
Why does the sun beat down on the desert?
Why can't I fall asleep?
Why do the stars shine so brightly?
Why do the birds flutter and tweet?
Why do I question the motives I seek?

Mercy Chipman

Acknowledgement

I know you saw that my light was on.
Why didn't you acknowledge it?
Was my light so different,
    that you were scared of it?
Was it because my light shined so bright
    or was it not the brightness,
        but its color and size?
Many people have done the same as you,
Why don't they acknowledge me as one of them?

Jennifer Adams

As Fire Moves Through The Forest

You watch as the fire moves through the forest.
Why Anastasia? I don't understand.
What are your reasons for choosing to act without a conscience?
Do you have any clue?
You must have sufficient reason, I know it exists.
What motivates you to spread rumors that you know are untrue?
Don't you see the fire moving through the forest?
Can you see the pain that you provoke in people?
Is it refreshing to see them in pain?
I would tell you to open your eyes, but I can't.
It wouldn't be right if they were opened by force.
It's all up to you.
Extinguish the fire before there is no forest left.
If you were to ask me for help I would sincerely answer,
Yes, Anastasia.

Maria-Cristina Pallares

"A Child's Innocence"

A child's innocence, a mother's pain
who's to venture, who's to gain

Truth be honest, truth be told
a liars fury do behold

When all you want is to clear the air
harsh words and lies cause a child's despair

A loving mother tho not by birth
I love Janell and all she's worth

I want to take this child of illusion
and give her a life a reality not delusion

Maybe half her age, but full of fight
I love this child, this child for life

God hear my prayer it will not change
Give me this child I will not estrange

Good days and bad days and all of the above
but promising whether the reason she'll always know love
So I pray for your wisdom I pray for your peace
give me this child and our love will release!

Kathe Tomaro-Chapman

"We Love You Pop"

Not everyone gets a chance to see,
who their children, grand children and great grandchildren will be.

To enjoy their laughter and watch them learn,
how to talk ...and walk ...and turn.

Eighty-four years on this earth is a very long time from birth.
But to have over fifty with the woman you love,
was surely the greatest gift from above.
"We love you pop!" we said that night. "Now go to sleep, and do sleep tight."

Without a complaint, you did what you were asked.
Even when...it was a very hard task.

To tend to his garden, the Lord needs you now. You won't need your cane, or even a plow.
So till we meet once again, in that wonderful place, we all know you'll keep that big smile on your face.

Mary J. Tolbert

Gimp

This is the story of a young man called Gimp.
Who often moved about with a slight limp.
And a gleam in his eye like that of an imp.
He was fond of adventure and not a wimp.

He hunted gators, hogs, and even snakes.
The things he did gave strong men the shakes.
Often tested, he always had "what it takes."
When the hunted got away, he said, "that's the breaks".

At times, he had to work for his living.
For creditors aren't people who are giving.
Since it was out of doors for which he was pining,
He sought jobs where the sun was shining.

The place he lived, he called it a "farm".
It was small, but there was plenty of charm.
Many creatures greeted visitors with voices of alarm.
However, they were usually gentle and caused no harm.

There was more to this young man called Gimp.
His good nature was ruled by a heart the size of a blimp.
In kindness to children and animals he would never scrimp.
As time goes by, you will eventually hear of "Old man Gimp".

Jene M. Holland

Serenity

Who knows the true meaning of serenity?
    Who knows the liquidious repose?
The place where a lull is a century
    As above the waves open and close.

Yea, even a king is a mute,
    For the element is not his own.
Neither his pages, his lyre, or lute
    Can produce even a whispering tone.

The state is luxuriously quiet.
    The hubbub's been left far behind.
For there is luxury even in reticence
    And among the rarities known to mankind.

Hawk Freeman

Untitled

When I looked at you and you looked at me,
We both knew that it was meant to be.
As time slowly passed, we quickly fell apart
Somewhere down the road, you broke my lonely heart.
Although the words, "I'm sorry" cannot remend my heart
I know you'll always love me... 'til death do us part.

Glenece Williams

"Who Touched Me?"

"Who touched me?" asked the Saviour on that day long ago.
"Who is it needs my favor? Someone touched me I know."

Slowly a woman with humble head silently moved from the crowd.
"Only to touch His hem," she said. "No need to be noticed or loud."

Walking along with head now high.
Lifting eyes of adoration
To the land, to the sky—
"I'm healed!" she cried in exultation.

Going about from day to day,
She bowed in humbleness only,
Kissing the children hurt at play,
Comforting the sad, loving the lonely.

"Who touched me?" asks the Saviour
Still lovingly today,
When we ask for healing, guidance
And wisdom as we pray.

Feeling better from day to day—
Comforting the sad, loving the lonely,
Kissing the children hurt at play,
Touched - not in body only!
Mildred S. Magouirk

To My Friend

How like a hov'ring angel is my friend,
who from celestial bidding takes her task!
I cannot doubt that only God could send
her prowess to my needs before I ask.
By mortal measurement she seems unreal:
so far her scope exceeds most standards set
for quality in woman that will deal
her goods to needy and forgive a debt.
Yet walks she never proudly in the throng
but wears ethereal stature modestly
while her transcendent air breathes silent song
in witness of a heav'nly Majesty.
That such a being can exist today
revives ideals and tests what words can say.
Marcia Mankin

Untitled

Now comes apartheid type scholars
Who don't want to share any powers
They devise a bell curve
To give bigots the nerve
To say, this land is theirs and not ours

How can a same man abide
Only he has the Lord on his side
That his race has a gene
That makes him supreme
But the Asians can share in his pride

So here comes the scholars, like Schockley
Who's thesis of genes is a mockery
Of intelligent men
With pretty-hued skin
Scholars should be amazed they're not cocky

Most men who say they're superior
Are really afraid they're inferior
They'll discount environment
And go to retirement
Hoping no one will see their interior
Jesse P. Faithful

Phoenix

He is the one,
Who burns to dust,
Which scatters in the wind,
But he rises again.

Ashes are where he sleeps.
He rises with the new day,
To fly to symbolize utter immortality,
So that others may watch with joy and scorn.

His wings glow like rubies in the sunlight,
As he flies through the still air.
At night he burns like the hottest of fires,
To become ashes so that he might rise again.
Joseph Slowik

A Stranger?

The stranger at birth that made funny faces
Who bought me dresses with bows and laces
A person who came every time I cried
Who taught me to be me and not to be shy
A man that did not mind my interest in sports
And the first to complain that my clothes were too short
The one that was there through the good and the bad
The one that I am now proud to call Dad
Kimberly M. Payne

Grandma's House

The signs of happiness are everywhere, those
who are present attempt to care.
The pictures of the children upon the walls,
show people who have called, her Grandma.
The chairs show sign of wear, for our Grandma
almost always rest upon there.
The sewing room is filled with clothes, the girl's
tied with a special bow.
Her bedroom is somewhat decorated as a child,
for she herself thinks of them quite awhile.
The kitchen is filled with wonderful smells,
everything shining like a golden bell.
Grandma's house is very special, for you see
she has helped many people there, especially me.

If you have time, always stop by Grandma's house.
Nicole Dehnert

The Garden

I walk in the garden at twilight,
While the blossoms still give their fresh scent
Ahead lies a path of stone.
Behind, the burning sand waits for others.
The birds sing their closing songs.
And a cool breeze floats in on breath of heaven.
The cool stones refresh my feet as I walk to the fountain.
I wade in a sea of tulips,
And roses climb the walls.
An oak tree provides shade,
And an apple tree provides food.
This journey through daffodils and lilacs and cockleshells
Ends at a beautiful fountain with sunflowers rising up behind it
I take a drink and quench my thirst.
This is the end of the journey
And this is where I'll stay.
Katie Roe

Friendship

We only have so many friends
Which we can count upon.
They're very few and in between
And friendship is lifelong.
And when we find friends like these
It's very hard you see,
Because usually we have to let them go eventually.
But friendship will always last between
The teardrops and the woes.
The sadness in this life
Of the things we can't let go.
And when we're in the next life,
That is where we will rejoice,
Because there will we meet again
And hear each other's voice.

Michelle M. Charnesky

The River

The river springs up from somewhere,
which seems like nowhere in particular.
It cuts and gouges its way through the ground,
anywhere it can take course.
Sometimes violently swift, sometimes gentler.
Whirlpools and undercurrents take time
out to play their little games,
then flow back into the mainstream,
rushing ever onward with the rest of the river.

Winding in and out, up and down and around.
Resting at intervals in quiet pools,
as if to gather up speed to continue on,
to God only knows where.
Defiantly taking possession of its path.
Giving to and taking nurture from
man, animal and plant alike.

Onward it goes, as far as its force takes it.
Sometimes to the oceans, sometimes just plays out.
Yet never makes apology or accepts thanks
for its presence. It just is.

Lucille H. Faubus

Happy Birthday To A Dear Niece

Here's to your birthday
which always comes anyway,
I remember the moment after you were born,
what a pretty baby and how well formed
for I was there at the very first time
when the Dr. paddled your behind,
you were the cutest thing, I had
    seen in I don't know when.
Look! At that dimple in her chin.
See! She is the image of her Dad.
Boy! Will she charm everyone mad.
How many years have gone by
and you are still as sweet as pie.

Jewell B. Dedeaux

Pray For Peace

Life in this world what a fragile thing,
where wars rage and birds sing.
Humanity has created our shriveling demise,
with all our wisdom and all our lies.
We cry out for peace but death screams back,
with suffering and pain for which there's no lack.
What will it take for us to comprehend,
the frailty of life to the bitter end?

Gene R. Scovell

"The Big Oak Tree"

I sit beneath this big oak tree,
where I made houses and lanes; and fields,
filled with horses and cows of glass,
all wrapped around with a fence,
made of stick posts and wire of twine.
Love, I can feel it here,
Love, blowing gently through the trees.

I sat in the rocking chair,
on the porch of the old house there,
and in mama's silence, she took me everywhere,
through soundless theories that have left their proof.
And underneath that tranquil roof,
where my life was sweet and happy,
now in quietude, I dwell with mama and daddy.

Here I sit and weep for them,
and, I weep for me,
but, in them, I also rejoice!

Jean Mobley Herndon

Consider This

Shattered glass surrounds the empty space
    where hope once thought to find a home

Anxious whispers
Shocked and disgraced
    that you would fall apart while not alone
    "but, consider this," she said
As she slowly waved a determined goodbye
"Too afraid to admit my pain and loneliness, rejection awaits
    why should I die with no one by my side
    with no one to wonder to why?"

Shattered glass
Reflections of the past
    seem to lead her back to a time and place
Where hope once lost can now be found
    she shyly turns and walks away

Was that a smile that dressed her face?
A warm embrace we failed to share
    "consider this," we heard her say
    "in search of love; an open door
    never more afraid, I'm on my way."

Marcella D. Usher

Beyond The Moon

There lies a place beyond the moon where memories no longer exist.
Where earthly possessions and mortal obsessions.
Are lost in the dense of the mist.

Time stands still beyond the moon, the mind can pause in peace.
Our lee side desires and wind crippled dires.
Are obscured when we search our beliefs.

Silence abounds beyond the moon, attentions can focus within.
Our earthborn concerns and deep mortal years,
Are drowned in the undetectable din.

Vision is clearest beyond the moon yet no light traverses the sky.
We can revel in solitude, there's nothingness in plenitude.
And all unfolds in the mind's eye.

Souls are found beyond the moon, those lost and those never known.
Peace calms the spirit and silence is a lyric,
And we know we truly have grown.

Peace is found beyond the moon, our world can slow and rest.
Bodies loose tension, minds move to ascension.
And there we are at our best.

Go there
with Godspeed.

Koni Huddleston

Field Of Dreams

There is a place, I'd rather be;
Where dreams come true, you're soon to see.
A place to have joy, A place to have fun;
You'll never get tired because all work's done.
You need not look hard you need not look long;
Just open your ears it's all in a song.
All about joy and love and peace;
All about happiness never to cease.
Where is this place you had to have thought;
Just open your mind that's all to be sought.
It's all in your heart it happens at night;
It comes in a vision it comes in a sight.
Just open your eyes and open your soul;
Just open your heart there is no toll.
And you'll find yourself in that field of dreams;
Where we're on all sides no reason for teams.
We all go together and never apart;
It's like we will all live inside of one heart.
All sewn together bound at the seams;
Together forever in the field of dreams.

Jessica Weld

Advice For The Hurting

Tears and pain seem to help a bit
When you can cry and not get whipped
Your frustrations inside need to come out
Instead you sit in silence, cry, and pout.
I know how that feels the hurt and abuse
To run from your problems and feel there's no use
Advice I can not yet give to thee
Except the advice that was given to me.
Try to show love-the kind sent from above
Try to help out-don't sit and pout
And try to tell others about how you feel
Otherwise the pain inside may never heal!

Jessica Leatherman

Untitled

Jealousy and rage burn in my soul,
when will this torment end?
My tears are hot, they burn my eyes.
My heart pounds heavily in my hollow chest.
Each beat screaming your name.
I try to forget you,
   your touch,
   your face,
   your eyes,
Yet they STILL haunt me!
Leave me!
Be with her, enraptured in lust.
Forgetting me, and leaving love behind.
Let me be!
Do not say you still love me
You are nothing but a crude mass of lies.
You stole from me, my heart lies at your feet.
Heal me! Leave me!

Melissa A. Miller

Leukemia

I get up to walk but can't even stand. I
was fine yesterday, Lord. What's wrong with
me? How can this be? I've always been healthy?
I'm rushed to the hospital not knowing why, the needles,
IV's, what's happening.
All that's going through my head is am I dying?
No...! can't be.

Karensa Riley

Remember When

The Younger folk are prone to scoff and frown
When we recall "the good old days" in town
Reminding us of what we lacked back then
But I remember how we walked alone
On country lanes so many miles from home
To pick wild flowers or berries - or to dream
Beside an unpolluted bubbling stream.
Our doors and windows were unlocked and still
Our homes were safe from those who rob and kill.
Our children played unharmed and worry-free
And childhood was what it was meant to be.
The daily paper's news was mostly good
(And ink stayed on the paper as it should);
We bought our food without the slightest thought
Of all the "no-no's" in the treats we sought.
Our children went to school without a care -
No drugs or guns or danger lurking there.
Reflecting on these facts makes one ask "WHY?"
Did "progress" cause our love of living HIGH? Did "creature comforts"
warp our mind and soul? Did we lose sight of our Eternal Goal?

Mary Roselle

There May Never Be A Day

There may never be a day
When the whole world will accept
Your true thoughts and true feelings
And will cease to object.

There may never be a day
You can let it all be known
Without fear of rejection
Or being left all alone.

There may never be a day
You can walk down the street
Without noticing smirks or rude comments
With each person you greet.

There may never be a day
The world will be rid of disease
A day where every person can be happy
And live life as they please.

There may never be a day
When you won't be hiding behind a lie
If our friendship was the only strong thing that could protect you
I promise you'd never have to cry.

Lorena Lupinacci

The Ode

An ode was heard
  when the grounds of the earth
  were new and fresh
   created in the birth of nature
   the first dawn rose
    in a brilliance of light
    glistening on the river
     in the ripples of the water
     life was born to a world
      filled with new life
      an ode was heard once more
       singing its song
        for the beauty of the earth
        as two love birds moved closer
        in the new spring

Maureen Emily Orr

I Remember The Old Days

I remember the old days,
when the bees buzz over the roses
the zephyr rush under the leaves,
making music, all over the trees.

I remember the old days,
when the lovers hand in hand
quietly, walked over the sand,
while the waves splash on the seashore,
leaving the foam to disappear, at their feet.

I remember the old days,
when in the meadow, where the flowers
and the fern, used to grow,
the rays of the sun, breaking in wondrous
colors, at a touch, on the waterfall
and it seems to evolve,
the butterflies, in it.

I remember the old days,
long passed now;
when life was, oh!! Sooo gentle!!
and sooo nice!!

  Josefina T. Dudek

"The Unicorn In My Dream"

One night I had a dream, that I was sitting in the grass,
When something white ran passed me, going very fast.
It finally stopped near a tree, and turned its head around,
And it looked deep into my eyes, as it laid upon the ground.
It was a beautiful unicorn, with hair of silky white,
And I couldn't believe my very eyes on this wonderful, magical, night.
It had a spiral golden horn, on its head, that pointed to the sky,
And it had flowers around its neck, and blue within its eyes.
Then the unicorn stood up, and came to me with grace,
And I felt its golden horn, and touched its loving face.
Its eyes were full of kindness, and its heart was full of love,
For I knew that this was a creature, who was sent from Heaven above.
So I'll never forget that dream I had, a dream of fantasy,
In which I met a unicorn, that walked over to me.

  Lisa Ann Florio

"It Shall Be"

The summer's begun, but that is not on my mind;
  When it will end is what I'm trying to find.

The one I love is away from me,
  But only as far as the eye can't see.

He will be in my heart until the end of time.
  I want to be with him, for he is always on my mind.

I long for the day when he will be so near,
  When I can have him alone to hold so dear.

Please grant that I may have, this one wish I long for,
  To simply be secure in knowing,
He is mine, forevermore.

  Melissa Kelly Sasser

My Mom

My mom is so bright
When it turns gloomy
She lights up the world with all her might.
She loves us all equally
Everyday is another loving sequel.

She loses her patience
But she still understands
The needs of a child
And their everyday plans.

  Kristin Price

Memories

Will the memories stay,
  when I'm dead and gone?
Will they remember me,
  when I've past on?
Will they think of the quotes that I once said,
  when my children have grown-up,
  and I am dead?
Will the people say when they're at my grave,
  here lies a man who was really brave?
Will they fulfill my wish,
  which is by the way,
  for my memories, to always stay?

  Jeremy Surprenant

My Point Of Destiny

When I looked at you, I saw...
When I spoke to you, I heard...
When I touched you, I felt...
I knew that you were my point of destiny.

Meeting you made me stop, take my
Destiny by the hand and look at it.

I liked what I saw, and now my
Love, I show it to you.

  Kathy Shelton

The Sea Of Tranquility

A calm and peace wash over me,
when I see a tranquil sea.

The soft waves lap upon the sand,
and change formations of the land.

Tides will rise and tides will fall,
like life's routine stirs us all.

Orange glows when the day turns night,
and the sea turns to gold so bold and bright.

As the sun falls into the sea,
it turns dark and lonely.

A calm sets in and fills our heart,
because we know it is just a start.

Tomorrow will come for all to see,
you will find peace and tranquility.

  Laura M. Atkins

How Much You Love Me

When I open my eyes, I see love in the air.
When I open my ears, I hear love sounds.
When I open my heart, I feel loved, so I just ask...

How much you love me? Oh, I said, how much you love me?
Love is special and love is kind, so I ask..how much you love me?

When I wrote this song, I felt down. When I sing this song,
I feel down. But, you can make me happy by telling me...

How much you love me. Oh, I said, how much you love me?
Love is special and love is kind, so I ask..how much you love me?

Now that you told me that you love me, I can say that...
I know that you love me and I know that I love you.
Love is special and love is kind, so I want you to know
  I LOVE YOU!!!

  Jeanele Bolder

A Raindrop's Lament

Last night I was sleeping, listening to rain,
When I began dreaming of a far away place.
I drifted from world of sorrow and pain,
And welcomed the water falling soft on my face.

If I was a raindrop where would I be?
Most likely fleeing from the troubled sky,
Or creating a rainbow, a glory to see -
Oh, raindrops are so much more carefree than I!

But then I paused for a second glance
At the paths from which a raindrop must choose,
And it seemed that though all life is a chance,
As a raindrop I'd be more apt to lose.

For if I was a raindrop, where would I be?
Plummeting hard toward the merciless earth,
Or worse yet, free-falling to be drowned at sea.
Ceasing to exist before discovering my worth.

So this morning I awoke in bright sunshine,
My raindrops gone - stolen by saffron light.
I reflected on life - both a raindrop's and mine -
And grieved for those tragically lost in the night.

Gina Pirrello

'Tis The Season

Once again 'tis Christmas season
When everybody has a reason
To be merry, happy, jolly
While hanging Christmas wreaths and holly.
And children too can laugh with glee
As they decorate the tree.
Everyone is in a hurry
All caught up in shopping flurry.
Now I know, as well as you,
There are many things to do—
Gifts to wrap, cards to write
Keep us busy day and night.
There's baking, cooking, special treats
Amongst the luscious Christmas eats.
Diets? Not for Christmas dinner.
We've all next year to grow thinner!
The many things that must be done
Mean extra work but also fun.
That Christmas comes each year is nice,
But we're truly glad it's once—not twice!

Mary Lou Lassen

Bank's Lake's Steamboat Rock

How long, I ask, has this old monstrous "steamer" sat in dry dock?
When did it lay a-wash in Columbia's original course?
Time has dripped the chartreuse lichen from off its dusty decks,
And parasitic rust has splotched its hull with ruddy scars.
Much flotsam has accrued on slant, piled against the aged hulk,
And plant-like barnacles suction hold on the rubbish climb;
Porthole caves now face man's lake where once the river flowed—
The grounded boat pits strength against the storms and heat and time!

Did this grand ship once sail submerged on that old river bed,
Or with its decks emerged, was it berthed with engines dead?
In any case, the mighty Columbia rushed round about that rock,
And was its sea— till blocked away— which left the ship in shock!

I've no answers to the riddles about steamboat rock today;
And God, who beached the derelict, may never, every say!

Lauraine Lee

Life's Staircase

Going up the staircase of life, wandering
what's ahead; how you should act, what should be said.

Keeping the memories of what you left behind;
with you as you embark upon new times.

Scared and timid you are as you climb the
winding stairs; keeping your head held high
through all the smiles and glares.

When you make it to the top and look at all you
did; you realize you couldn't of made it
without everyone who helped you as a kid.

Mary Murphey

I Sometimes Wonder

I sometimes wonder about life after death;
Whatever happens to us when we take our last breath?
Do our spirits rise to the heavens above;
To live in serenity and float like a dove?
Are our spirits reborn to live life anew
Here on this earth again; Will I ever meet you?

I sometimes wonder; did I roam this land before?
Was I woman or man? Did I have a farm or a store?
Does the Lord send us down to give us a second chance;
to improve ourselves? Let's take another glance.

I sometimes wonder what era I lived;
Was I poor, was my roof like a sieve?
Maybe I was rich, living in high society.
Doesn't it make your mind wonder with curiosity?

I sometimes wonder was I a good person or bad?
Did I have a family, was I happy or sad?

I sometimes wonder will I meet my love once more?
In this life, maybe we've had each other before.
So before we get frightened by the dark of death,
Stop and think...just maybe: We'll have another breath.

Joni Dilts

Untitled

I've always lived by the doubts.
What was real,
right, and good?
Even when I thought I knew,
I followed my doubts.
They always seemed stronger than the truth.
I always made sure
the doubts became true,
because I feared the real truth.
I can stop the doubts now,
just by looking at you.
When you are near
there is no place for all the doubts.
The truth is too real.

Lorie Rubenser

Realization

Everything is just an illusion, nobody means
what they say.
I'm left sitting numb with confusion, walking
blindly all over this day.
My mouth is left with the taste from my tears,
pouring out of my empty eyes.
I weep for myself looking back to the years,
was I a childish fool to see blue in the skies.
When I was young everything was so pure,
now deceit makes me think it's not true.
With all the pain and hatred I endure, I rue
the day I will do harm to you.

Melissa M. Massie

Looking Ahead

As I face each new morning I sometimes wonder...even ponder
What it holds...Rain Sunshine Clouds Snow...Who knows?
When I see a bright sunrise I can't be glad
For some of my worse days have been sunny.
If I see rain I can't be sad
For some of my best days have been rainy!

So how can I anticipate the future when I only know the past?
The unsteady awful wonderful past!
Sometimes I deny the past hoping it will go away.
Sometimes I cling to the past as though it were the answer to my future.
So misleading! Not revealing! Actually tampering! Even hampering!
My ability to anticipate my future.

So I make a decision to relinquish the past
Use this new morning to begin my future
How can I do this?
Then I hear the Still Small Voice saying...
I knew you when...I loved you then
I know you now...my love I vow.

Leave your future to Me
I can see farther from up here!

Mercile Duggan

"Window Wonder"

A child is sitting by a window.
What is she looking at?
Is she looking at a rainbow?
Could she see a butterfly floating in the breeze?
Maybe she is waiting for a friend, her mother or her brother.
As she is sitting by the window staring blankly. It makes me wonder.
How she can sit so still so peaceful.
Still she is sitting there. Her face shows nothing but childhood
innocence, and the sweet angelic smile that graces her face.
Wait, you have yet to look into her eyes and see and feel that sense
of purity.
Soon this little angel that graces this window sill shall soon grow to
be someone's
love, but for now she is still sitting by that window.

Michael Baker

Shop Till You Drop

My Lord doesn't run a bargain basement;
What He offers is perfect and guaranteed.
No two for one sales to get to Glory;
We must each go to Him on bended knee.
There's no half price for our redemption;
Christ paid in full on Calvary.
You can't use vouchers or sweepstakes coupons;
The price is the same as the years roll by.
You need not bargain to gain entrance to Heaven;
There's no better price than free to all.
If you've reached the age of accountability,
His "red light special" may not last very long.
His sale has been on since the crucifixion;
It won't be extended when He returns for His own.
If we accept His lifetime offer,
That means on earth and through eternity.
Have you considered buying into Jesus?
Your life will be brighter, your burdens lighter,
When you go shopping at Jesus Mall.

Mary Helen Biggers

The Marten Song

Beautiful Martens tell me true,
What do you do when the night sky turns blue?
What do you do when you know that your friends are heading for doom?
And your soul is twisting with blooms of gloom.
Do you listen to a tune,
do you listen to the loons or do you sing the Marten song
to the gloomy grey moon?
What do you do when you are stuck and confused?
Do you turn to a friend to help you
or maybe you should sing the Marten song to the gloomy grey moon.

Lydia Ramsey

True Love

My husband is the true love of mine
We've been through thick and thin
With him I've enjoyed endless times
Now where shall I begin?

In the church nursery we did meet
To cry and play together
We formed friendship that is so complete
That ties could never sever

We dated in our high school days
Our love did bloom and grow
We shared much laughter and some tears
'Cause forever we'd stay I know

We married at the age of twenty-one
Our love continued to soar
We've had so much happiness and fun
The future can only hold more

I give my thanks to God above
To me a wonderful husband he gave
We have such a true and pure love
That will last to the end of our days

Linda Myers

The Flow Of Self Esteem

Remembering things, when I was seven,
Were things that were, so close to heaven.
IT WAS THEN, MY DAD, CAUSED ME MY FATE.
THE FEELING, HE CAUSED, WOULD NOT ABATE.

Remembering how, the car was hot,
Was remembering things, when just a tot.
IT WAS THEN, MY DAD, OPENED UP THE GATE,
ALLOWING SELF ESTEEM, TO BECOME MY MATE.

Remembering how dad, had stopped the car.
The next bathroom, was just too far.
IF WE HADN'T STOPPED, IT WOULD BE TOO LATE.
I WOULD BE WET, MY TEETH WOULD GRATE.

Remembering me, standing by the road,
Feet in the sand, to relieve the load,
PROPELLING THE FLOW, UNABLE TO WAIT.
WAY WAY OUT, WAY PAST THE GATE.

Remembering my dad saying, how far I could pee.
Hearing him say, a champion pee-er, to be.
THE FEELING HE GAVE ME, PERSISTS TO THIS DATE.
KNOWING, WITHOUT A DOUBT, A POEM I COULD WRATE.

Gerald E. Mowery

Thoughts And Memories

Last night my thoughts in dark of night
Went back to memories just out of sight
The year just passed like wings in flight

Did I do some good, did I stand tall
When some one in need did I hear their call
To see the good in others no matter how small

In dark of night I knew it seemed
I failed to live the things I dreamed
The year was gone then like a miracle the answer came

I met a stranger I held out my hand
To give her friendship in a lonely land
Just to pass the love from God to man

And thoughts about this year just spent
I've received back more than I ever sent
I got a miracle - I made a friend

Larry Hieb

"Forever Sorry!"

As we took the steps of life in stride,
We loved one another and really tried,
To tell each other how we felt,
To make our hearts really melt, into one, forever.

There were times, so many times,
When we had our schemes!
There were times, so many times,
When we had our dreams!

But somewhere along the way,
Our dreams began to stray.
So, now we are not as one
And will never see the setting sun...as one.

"I'll be forever sorry,
For what I did to you!"
"I'll be forever sorry,
For what I put you through."
"And, if it takes forever,
somehow, I'll make it up to you!"

Jesse M. Oliver III

And You Came...

Wide as life can be, joyful and expectant, as a table set for a
wedding, or hopeful and expectant, as the table set for a pauper can
be, the presence of your absent presence filled my serene emptiness.

I inhaled your aroma, tasted your womanhood, caressed your subtle,
almost transparent forms of an absent lover, glancing at me,
with the smile of your distant and nearly imperceptible presence.

I longed for you, with every breath and fiber of my famished mind.
My thoughts became the house where my dreams danced and shared with
you all those things that the distance won't dare to vanish or forbid.

Then my dreams began to feel the pains of labor, and your crowned
head, with the smile of a newborn, the serenity of a queen, the
firmness of a truth, said to me: long no longer, dream no more...
here I am, I've become!

And then you rose...solid as an anchor in the middle of a crystal
rock, real as the sunshine of the morning sun over the eyelids of my
dreams. Jealous as the Master of the Dream's wife, unwilling to share
the table with the dream starving souls trying to rejoice and pretend...

And today when you ask me, with a real voice of a real lover born of
a real dream, What are you dreaming on, my loved one? I answer with
afar silence: Be quiet, don't you see? I'm dreaming on you!

Mario Swing

Oklahoma, Oklahoma

Oklahoma City, the world moans with you,
We know that you are in sorrow and we are too.
Just keep looking up to the skies,
There is a God up there who will wipe away all of
The tears from your eyes.
He knows of all your troubles, he is always near,
Whenever you pray day or night, he hears your prayer.
Just keep looking up to heaven, God is looking down on you,
He knows your heavy burden, heart ache, and pain,
And will see you through.

Oklahoma, oklahoma your hurt is still there,
I can still see you moaning, I can still see your tear,
But God won't allow you through anymore than you can bear.
So cheer up, cheer up, and try to forget that awful day,
When the bombing took place and swept your love ones away.
Just thank God for tomorrow, the future is ahead,
Your loved ones are just sleeping, they are not dead.

Lue Pitts

As Time Goes By

As time goes by and seasons change,
We go from Winter through Fall and Spring.
Through hot summer months so hot and dry,
We laugh a little as well as cry.

If we could slow the pace of time,
Slow down our bodies and rest our minds.
Take time to think of things we do,
To smell the flowers with the morning dew.

As time goes by and we speed along,
There's a lot we miss as life goes on.
Like the beautiful Butterflies and Bees,
And the gentle rustling of the leaves.

The rippling waters of the creek,
A place where once we cooled our feet.
The rising sun that shines so bright,
And that big old moon that lights the night.

As time goes by the pace gets faster,
There's even little time for laughter,
All this God gave us to enjoy,
but as time goes by, we only destroy.

Jo Lynn Nichols

Our Dying World

As the sun ripples down on the soft shore line
We wait to see the coming rime
The day goes fast, the time flies by
We all are hoping for it all but to die
We have no time, no life of plea
We only hope that someday we will see
The sculptures of our life's world today
The kind we see, with no need to pay
But yet we plead so much for this time to come
Not understanding it has already been done
So we take for granted our world's life beauty
And plaster on a fake new duty
To make our world better and great
But all we do is add to the hate

Kristie M. Ribal

"Memories Of Our Days"

Remembering those days of our great and wonderful times, wishing that
We can do them again.
That we know they will always stick in the corner of our mind never to
Be forgotten.
Recalling things like our childhood or other happy times makes us feel
Happy and joyful, joyful to live our lives.
Our happiness is so great that we accomplish more things
That it is all, like a cycle of love, happiness, harmony...
And that in the end we have more ever-lasting memories of our days...

Gregory Burkman

The Hidden Place

Safe, warm, secure, in the knowledge
we can always hide within ourselves
the brave front we all put out for others to see
    I felt a sadness of a soul
one that's been beaten, abused and used.
yet I felt the strength of what was deep inside
searching still for the wholeness of
what was missed in childhood
they say men don't cry nay!
They scream in silence
    Begging for the touch and knowledge
of another that knows and has felt
the inner torture.
    Look out and trust if you can
there is a hand, a heart that's been
there and understands.
    It's hard to open our hearts to
trust when that door's slammed,
still try we must do or we curl up
and blow away as easy as the dust on which we stand.

Judy Brown

The Day You Left Me

The day you left me is the day I died, You left me on the street
watching the people walk by. I can't understand what I did to deserve
this, I want you back and that's my only wish. I love you too much to
let our love walk away, Come back love me and please won't you stay.
I was looking through the window reminiscing on our love, I know you
were my God sent from the heaven above. Why did you leave me here
with nothing to do? Don't you know how life is without you? I was
your candle and you were my flower, The two of us will come together
and create a bonding power. I was the bird and you were my wings, You
made me feel higher than words will ever bring. We use to huddle and
cuddle never ever go astray, But here I am lonely and scared no one to
love today. I look in the mirror and I see a sad girl, Remembering
how her love was her one and only world. I tried to avoid the tears
that wanted to be shed, But just thinking of you brings memories to my
head. I tried to get away from all the pressure I got today. So I go
on a mountain looking down on our love of fountain. In five seconds a
new baby would be born, and in the dusk of dawn I realize I was gone.

Monique McClean

A Subtle Five Dollars

The best five dollars I ever spent
    was something quite priceless to me—
You could never guess what the $5 bought
    but it was a reasonable fee.
Five bucks doesn't sound like a heck of a lot
    particularly in this day and age—
But back when I spent it, a long time ago
    it was more than a full day's wage.
So what did I get for the five buck charge
    a necklace with diamonds and jade?
Not at all my friend far better than that—
    it was when the preacher got paid.

Joe B. Anderson

To My Beloved Mother

You are the earth I came from,
    warm, good and always there.
Unchanging through time,
    independent of place.
You are love, protecting, yet bolstering,
    helping and guiding,
    unchanging through storms or naught.
You are strength, who helped in weakness
    and straightened bowing backs and minds.

Thanks for your being,
Thanks for your smiles,
Thanks for the doors You opened.

You are God's Goodness
    You are a Mother -
    my Mother.

Now - You do not dwell among us - anymore -
    yet You are still with me.

Marta Broido

"I'm Now Yours Forever"

I was once so lonely and sad! Till I placed a personal ad! I
wanted to find my true love, Heaven heard me from up above.

Then my ad brought us together. Everything is getting better.
Feelings have grown since that first call, You have brought down that
painful wall.

Heart beats faster each time we talk, You're with me wherever I walk.
Since that first letter, I've found love, I'm ready to make that big move.

You have captured my lonely heart, Can't stand for us to be apart.
Since placing that ad awhile back, I've fallen in love, that's a fact.

My love grows stronger by the day. Can't wait to be with you, I say.
Want to be in your loving arms, And take in all your loving charm.

My heart sure aches to be with you! Real love is so much over due!
I can't wait to stand beside you, just like husband and wife.

Can't wait to share my life with you. I'll surely chase away your
blues, because I'm now yours forever. The way we met sure was clever!

Can't wait until we're man and wife. You'll have lots of T.L.C. in
your life. My love for you is forever, because I'm now yours forever!

Marsha Anne Hoffman

"Soul Protector"

Lonely nights,
Wandering the streets,
Sitting on a curb,
Trying not to weep.
Then a light shines in my eyes.
A vision from paradise;
Being told not to worry,
And go on with my life.
Why does it have to be this way,
I have to ask?
It's a problem I have to deal with, from my past.
Next thing I know, I am in my home,
in my bed, still all alone.
Yet, I feel a presence beside me,
a special spirit, to love,
and guide me.

Melissa Michelle Pearlman

The New Way

Words on the wind circle haunting souls
wandering in time seeking truth
life blood flowing slowly

Values linger as ghosts
forgotten and still
spirits broken catch a glance

Little ones confused who is my family?
Fathers, mothers, friends
broken roots bleed for life

Everything is green, greed and power
a blight is upon our land
freely stomping on our minds soaring we tune in
missing the beauty of gardens never sown

Values, morals misunderstood
until the heart misses a beat
the new way begins seeking the old path
over grown with neglect one finds the way
marking each step while the world slithers into the night

Walk in harmony with nature and man
strong, yet humble that we not stumble on our deeds.

Joyce Turner

"Deception"

He is but a wolf in a lamb's cloak
Waiting to vault on his next blameless victim
For no apparent reason he takes them in
With his fraudulent outer appearance
Only to tell them that he isn't what he seems to be
He is a snake hiding in a paradise full of
Naive children of whom want to play his game
Their parents have warned them of the snake's cunning ways but
They must find out for themselves
That their curiosity will pull them in but
They will come away bleeding
From the razor sharp claws of the beast.
The beast seeks to taste their innocence
Is it out of anguish and pain that he preys on them
Or is it just a hobby for him
I hear the loneliness of his call
But is that what I'm hearing
Or is it the charm of a rattler with no fear
Will I take my chances like the rest
Or will I shrink back and wait for the lamb to be sheared

Jammie Knox

Heaven's Reach

Fate buried in the clouds,
Waiting on winds to blow,
A motion for an answer just,
So one may know what one must,
That which awaits the anxious crowds,
Then to gauge what life allows,
Captive dimensions to the field one plows.

But some choose not
This tilling plot,
Instead to trod on dangerous trail,
Gripping life on narrow ledge,
Heaven quest by fingernail.

Greg Spain

Love Is A Many Splendored Thing

People say love is a many splendored thing.
Waiting for that moment when you get that ring.
That should mean only wonderful things to come.
Babies, weddings and then some.

Jennifer Ford

Step-Father

I was very young when we met, I was forever confused and always upset.

We went through some very rough times as I began to grow, we rarely got along and arguing was all we had to show.

You must have realized that it wasn't you that I was unhappy about, but the only way that I could express my pain was to constantly scream and shout.

I know I judged you unfairly when you were only tying to teach me, but at the time clouds of darkness filled my head and resentment was all that I could see.

Many years and many tears later I began to see you in a different light, you were no longer the enemy so why should we fight?

What you then became was a father and a hero to me, you were a God-send, the savior of our little family.

Lishele Cellini

Farewell Poverty

Poverty, you pitiless beast! You have encroached
Upon my life for such a lonesome time.
You have sent many good people
To their graves before their time.
Your dreadful bite knows no age nor race.
When you cling to a soul, you tear it
Into absolute misery for death to salvage the rest.
Your poisonous grip turn a goodman into nothingness
And cause him to hate his fellow beings;
And when he does overcome you with riches,
He's greedy so as to stay away from you.
Oh! you mischievous brat; today is your last chance
To bite me as your mouth can swallow, for you
Shall never get this opportunity again in my life time.

Gabriel O. Dokun

Gonna Catch A Dragonfly And Ride Upon His Back

Gonna catch a dragonfly and ride
upon his back
Rain drops can't touch me
Butterflies can't catch me
Gonna catch a dragonfly and ride
upon his back
Bull frogs can't jump so high
Fireflies can't dance
In the nigh
Gonna catch a dragonfly
and ride upon his back

Ginger B. Maldeney

Nature Saddened

The hills are trying to push themselves
up between the concrete and steel,
appearing like tawny suede
on the belly of a raging bull we call society.
We look up...
to a sky black and blue,
the melting sun humming sweet sorrow
to the slaves of life
and their dimly lit accomplishments.

Melinda Huisingh

65

Untitled

Newfound love I can't change you
  Unless you want to change for me

You cannot change me
  Unless I want to change for you.

Overcoming barriers of our love will
  come when we divide for each other and wait.

My feelings change when I am loved
  I must know that love.

If I listen to my heart and soul
  And spirit, you may reach out to me.

Though I prefer to be an angel, I am
  mortal. Sin knocks at my door.

My prayers are that of a child and my
  words construe misleading thoughts.

Overcoming life alone is only capable
  for us that wait.
Your love will lengthen my life and
  change me into a symbol of love and peace
  Peace that I have so long hungered for.
Peace that comes from deep within my soul.

  Nancy C. Rosch

Dancer Of The Night

I dance amid the dew-kissed grass,
Twirl lightly upon the sun-warmed ground.
My arms move in the cold-crisp air,
My feet will follow without a sound.

The moon above me glows softly,
Bathing me in its eternal light.
Around the moon the stars glisten,
Surrounded by the darkness of night.

Yet the darkness does not frighten,
Night becomes one of my confidantes.
And with it I release my fears,
And in my dance I express my wants.

I want this night to never end,
So I'll dance until the dawn grows near.
As the sky brightness, I must go,
And so, with the moon, I disappear.

  Nicholas Kosmicki

A Blessing From God

   The first time they laid you in my arms you
turned on the charms. And from that moment on
I knew I had to fight to keep you from harm.
   The first time I gazed into your eyes, I
experienced God's greatest miracle, that of a
sweet little child. And through this creation
the greatest love of all.
   Much to my surprise, the first time I saw you
smile I experienced the true meaning of joy.
   The first time you squeezed my fingers with
your little hands I knew you had the right to
become yourself.
   The first time I heard your voice the angels
sang with the strongest and truest harmony of
faith and hope, love and joy.
   And from that moment on I knew I was blessed
with the most beautiful girl and boy. And
experienced the warmth and beauty of being a
mother...

  Linda Andreasen

The Maze

The path is portrayed as clear,
Trudged by other feet.

The sides may be what they be,
But never the same.

It can be long and short,
Never-ending as one might seem.

The path may seem rough, slippery and smooth,
All at the same time.

Some parts are even uninhibited and unclear,
But do not be mistaken-
The maze is ever-changing.
  Natalie D. Hardin

Best Friends Forever

Through thick and thin you have always been there.
Troubles that we have, are troubles that we share.
Sometimes we'll laugh and sometimes we'll fight,
But the friendship shall always remain tight.
Our friendship means so much to me,
Best friends we shall always be.
You've lent me your shoulder so I could cry,
And you stayed with me until my tears were dry.
We've laughed together throughout the years,
And admitted to each other our smallest fears.
A friend like you is hard to find,
One who is loyal, sweet and kind.
I love you as if you were my own kin.
For us not to be friends—it would be a sin.
Our friendship is something I'll always treasure.
We are and always will be, best friends forever.
  Jamie Kurihara

A Single Raindrop

The skies cried today, and a single raindrop clung to the branch.
Trembling in the pause of flight sliding, hugging, begging "Hold me,
for I fear the fall."
And the moisture of many rains of before slid down and
hugged the raindrop, and jointed it at the branch sliding,
hugging, begging, "Fear not," we are together.
And the raindrops of many rains poured down from the branch giving
life to a single daffodil.
Sliding, hugging, begging, giving life to a single fearful daffodil.
Sliding, hugging, begging, each petal seeking nourishment.
And the sun's rays peeked down and saw the daffodil, and made it rise
in glory.
And the raindrop dried its tears sliding, hugging, begging to be
returned to heaven once more.
And the rainbow streaked a promise across the sky, and the raindrop
rode into Heaven.
Joyful amid the crimson hues sliding, hugging, begging, to return to
the daffodil once more.
  Linda Kovacik

Eventide

When the spider of age
Traces its web across your countenance
When the splendor of youth becomes a distant sun
When the fire of passion
Becomes
The cool stream of devotion
There is no greater love

In the depths of our forever
The messages I carried are half of what you are
I smile in my heart
And know the mystery
  Les McGowan

The Child

the folly of the past, I escape unscathed... or so I believed until today
I looked into a child's eyes, and saw the past I left behind
and now it's virtue I declare, to weep in silence, I cannot bear

as I look into her gaze,
her Eyes, her Feet, her Hands, her face
I pray, I cry, I Repent, I weep
but what I've lost is out of reach

"Child so young, so fresh, so pure
it's not too late for you to detour
for I've seen death, and I've seen pain
I've seen hatred come torture and slain"

she looks at me unshaken, unchanged
she tells me that things will be ok
but I know this path I know its ways
I know what danger stands in her way

"I'll be careful, I'll be safe, just let me go I'll be ok"
with soft kiss pressed upon my check,
she runs into darkness...she runs to the beast

Who is this child my heart embrace?
her name is innocence... come know her grace

John Mancino

Dreaming

To think while you sleep
To wander in the deep,
subconscious peeking through
Thoughts and hopes mixed like witches brew.

Dreams are hopes.
Dreams are goals.
Generalized hope, continue to sleep,
when broken, begins to weep, and
reality beckons like the sea.

Dreams are storybook lands.
Escape to and be free.
Dreams are like birds, flying, soaring,
longing to be as free, to fly, fly, fly.

Dreams are happy thoughts.
Thoughts of a better life,
of a far away time,
of a not yet reachable goal.

Day dreams and night dreams
Wrong dreams and right dreams
Keep on dream, dream, dreaming.

Kara Lea Reimler

"Yearning"

I came to this beach, to walk on its sands,
To touch it shells gently, with my hands,
The tides too strong, my spirit still trapped,
My shells pulled to sea, their lives unmapped.

The beaches beyond, may still feel my walk,
The tides and my spirit, they yearn to talk,
The moon will change with me, my spirit will grow,
The sands more firm, my shells they stay, my spirit to know.

Marilyn Dickson

Cacophonies

So, as to those innocent promises made to unworthy images of unknown torture,
    to those phantoms whose misery manages to encompass
    the portholes of a sandman's forgotten moments, and
    to those arrows whose poisoned tips have severed the gentle folds
    of a tender soul.

Let it be known that the mellow half notes of a saxophone can make
    lilacs bloom and irises bloom, and
    the hues of light which tiptoe down the skyline can whisper
    melodies so pure that they are comparable to the crystal drops
    that dance off a diving dolphin's fin.

Then, shall the twinkle glow brightly,
    the rose blossom slightly, and
    through luscious sounds all will know clearly that phantoms and
    saxophones are in fact flexible and even egos have survived
    tornadoes and spilled milk many a time more than we will ever
    know.

Michal Weiser

A Thank You For Christmas Gift

All dressed up to go
To the theater for brunch and show
Pictures were taken before we went in
What we saw were tables
With all white cloth napkins
Crystal that gleamed from candlelight
The food was great
And served on white plates
The dessert was all chocolatey
And I enjoyed every bite
The show came on with dancers and song and;
I sat on the edge of my seat
Wishing I had dancing feet at 90 years
Old, but;
I'm still on the go
And hope to be going to many more shows
It is plan to see, I have kids that care and;
Grandma won't sit out her days in a rocking chair

Josephine Campbell

Trust

Trust is the key that unlocks the door
To the innermost soul of man;
It bridges the space from heaven to earth
'Tis a beautiful, golden strand.

Trust lets us be "like a little child"
God said we must all become,
If we would enter His Kingdom
And hear Him say, "well done!"

Trust help us to "love our neighbor"
In spite of the things He's done,
For we know not the load He carries
Nor the long, hard race He's run.

Trust is a bridge so fragile
Like a spider's web, so thin,
Yet strong enough, if it's anchored well
To carry us safely in.

Lila B. White

Mechanical Marvel

From my rosy childhood I grew
to the age in which I could attain
A stiff piece of forma, certified driving paper.

With this burden I then went to buy
a fume-excreting mechanical marvel of the times.

Accompanied by this albatross I quickly learned the perils
of life and highway frustrations.

Linda Marie Golian

Golden Gifts

Lady luck I'm calling upon you
to take my hand and lead me through
the path of life, be it happy or sad
and the changes of time, whether they make me dispirited or glad.
Father Time, I'm asking you
to keep me young in the things I do
raising children, singing life's songs
staying in step with each day as it moves along.
Passion of Prayer, hold me near
and keep the things I pray for always dear
a stronger heart for the troubles I find
a stronger soul for the toughest of times.
Beggar of Truth, listen heartily
to the things I ask you to give to me
an easy mind, an honest truth
a strength to do things that life says I must do.
Through the years as I travel along
I hope to find my steps are sturdy and strong
Using the gifts I am given, I will forge my way
with the assurance of a new sunset and a better day.

Kimberli Bolinger Joyce

Birthdays

To some people birthdays mean slumber parties.
To some people birthdays mean presents galore.
To some people birthdays mean cake and ice cream.
To some people birthdays means seeing friends and family
To me birthdays mean all this and much, much, more.

Derrick Dawson

A Road To Nowhere Until They Fought Back

Back when Hitler was a God
to some people, and to others he
was their worst nightmare.
There once lived my family the Marschalls
well that is our name now.
Back in it Italy was a trashed disgusted
world of horror and troubles.
My family for a long time lived under
depression and lots of filth, putting
up with what I think, is Hitler's trash.
Finally my great great
great great grandparents escaped
and hid in New York where,
for them, it was safe. They rented
an apartment and changed their
names to fun Marschall. Now,
it's the Great Marschall.
Ever since that day there's never been a minute
where someone's not laughing or smiling.
Fun Marschall is definitely still living within us all.

Mandy Marschall

Untitled

For many years I felt it wrong
to share with you, my heart's sad song
In you I saw a deep despair
to add my pain seemed quite unfair
I had a job, to guard and protect
to carry the load, to feel no affect
and when the load grew too heavy to bear
with you and the rest, I still would not share
When the anger inside had grown, oh so much
My family was guarded, for I took the punch
I know that life has been painful for you
And I'm proud of you Mom, for making it through
Although many years have since gone past
I found my strong Mother, Finally, at last
Now I can talk without any fear
with my Mother who I, have always held dear
"HAPPY MOTHERS'S DAY"

Leslie K. Groner

Live For Today And Die For Tomorrow

Live for today and die for tomorrow
To see the starving and the homeless
and all the sorrow
People are dying and the lost are all crying
The dreams that they dream are lost
in souls of the lying
The darkness is near for the ones who live in fear
The terror inside, you cannot hide
So live for today and die for tomorrow
For yet fear in one is the fear in all
For the pain and suffering is short
Do not let the soul of a man die in pain
But bring happiness to all and live for today
and die for tomorrow.

Gary W. Keeton

Then The Rain Came

The sky above was a vibrant breathtaking blue
To see so many birds where they once briskly flew
Pretending that I could be a part of it too!

And the fluffy white clouds with patterns so many
As a child once, one's imagination was quite funny
I was carried atop just one to be brought where the light so sunny.

To feel the rays heat upon my face
Filling my eyes with such wondrous grace,
Yet leaving me with so little space.

But before me the vibrant blue changed to a dull gray,
only to feel the fall of a light spray
The fluffy white clouds were no longer
while a part of me was feeling much stronger.

I was being brought back still desperately
wanting to stay only to realize it couldn't always be the same
Then the rain came.

Gigi Pastore

Good Bye

My body aches for your touch. I love you so much. But I'm
tired of playing the fool. Bored of waiting around for you.
My heart won't play this game. I'll do anything to stop the
pain. What do I do? And where do I go, when I'm too scared
to be alone. Still I am strong. Too strong to let you lead
me wrong. There is so much I can do. With or without you.
Even though I must go, I want you to know: As long as there
are stars in the sky, we will never truly say good-bye.

Kelly Landt

"Two Little Bugs"

There were two little bugs who climbed up a big tree
To see how far their eyes could see
To look for the horizon if it was there to see
Look and look they did
But the horizon they could not see
That the horizon was not
Confined and limited
But far-reaching and
To the end of time
So down went the two little bugs
Destined to live
In their own little world
Limited by their lack
Of vision and imagination
To a life here and now
Never to know that
The future lies beyond
Their myopic view of the horizon
And cannot be limited to our
Lack of vision but only time...

Gilbert Paradis

Songs From Billy Joel

The piano man did all he can,
to please them in the bar.

Captain Jack, hid his sack
of Marijuana in the car.

The entertainer was a complainer,
he never stuck around.

While the food in the Italian restaurant,
Was laying on the ground.

Ole Billy Joel, was all about soul
When he wrote that song.

Then he went to, the Great Wall of China
and hit a great big gong.

Good night my Angel time to close your eyes
Dream about the fluffy clouds in the sky.

And he took a bath, in the River of Dreams
For that is the closing seems.

Jeremy Erickson

We're Really Too Old

We're really too old to drive a fast speed
To plant spruce trees or exotic grass seed.
We're really too old when the snow whirls about
To fill a wood box or take ashes out.
We're really too old to feed cows grain
To handle big bales without intense pain,
We're really too old to go fish with grand kids
To play hopscotch or remove stubborn jar lids.
We're really too old to hunt with the dog
To ear tag a calf or pull a sheep from the bog.
We're really too old to drive a long way
Or weed a garden a whole full day.
We're really too old to frolic or dance
Even too old for much of romance!
All these things we try, that I told,
But really my dear, we are too darned old!

Martha J. Patterson

Tranquil Minds

Over hills of mysterious proportions
To plains of stormy weaving grasses
Across seas and oceans of the mind to its tranquil stores.

The caves of darkness are nightmares of life,
Dreams ruined or nightly visitors unwanted.
Our souls crying from remorse some plain hidden from the light of day.

Dreams of what's to come, to arise over the horizon.
The hopes for happiness, or safety form bubbles so easily destroyed.
Yet, when visioned are so appealing.

Sensations of love, hate, despair all demons in just one like,
Never ceasing, always turning full circles.
Always spiraling, always burning.
Hotter than some, a flame red and bright.
Some a full waste of time.

Over hills of mysterious proportions
To rolling plains of wildly weaving grasses.
Across seas and oceans of the mind to its tranquil stores.

Martha Findley

Leaving Me In The Dark

You are the flame in the candle that sits on the table next
to my bed where I sleep at night.
You remain bright and strong no matter what emotion
blows over me.
You keep me warm at night when the brisk wind enters
my dreams.
You are always there for me when I need you.
I could mold you into anything that I wanted,
but instead I leave it up to you to take your own shape.
I trust that you will always remain beautiful.
Whenever I am feeling down I turn to you and you speak
to me in soft whispers.
You make me realize that I too, am also as beautiful and
special as you are.
But I know that no matter how much love and trust we
have in each other your bright flame will turn into a dim
flicker and die.
Leaving Me in the Dark.

Melissa L. Matney

Once We've Been Labeled

Why is it that someone who has been known
to make rain before is always, regretfully
thought of when there's rain?

And why then, when the rain stops do we so
wholeheartedly, thank the sun, and not the rainmaker?

After all, he produced the rain which in turn gives us
such great relief when we finally see the sun.

If it weren't for the rain, would we still appreciate the sun?

Therefore, the rainmaker can also be thanked for the beauty of the sun.
They are neither as powerful alone, and could be classified as one
and the same.

Kimberly Barber

A Cry For Help

They cry for help in the middle of the night,
Their tears flood our hearts with sympathy and compassion.
These are the poor and their plight,
The homeless and the suffering.

They dwell in the cities for refuge against the seasons,
Their enemy is the bitter coldness of winter.
These are God's children.
Their fate is in our hands.

Kimberly Ann Solinsky

The First Year

The first year with you, I have learned so much,
To love and be loved by someone,
with such a tender caring touch.
The first year with you, has filled my heart,
No matter how distant, we are never apart.
The first year with you I hold wonderful
Memories that are forever burned in my mind,
Always there to remind me, someone
like you I will never again find.
And with this years passing, we begin
a new,
where every year will be like the first year,
that I spent with you.

Joseph Kmetz Jr.

The Bogs Of Ireland

In the cold damp bogs of Ireland, I go to dig the turf.
To keep the fires of Ireland burning
and to warm our cold cold earth.
Our air is cool and smells so sweet
like Primroses on the vine.
And the morning dew gives my clothes
a fresh smell so I hang them on the line
so if you should get a chance visit, our dear old Erin's Isle.
Then you will know just what I mean
and you'll turn to me and smile.
The country side is beautiful and the air is fresh and sweet
and the people there are friendly
and to you they'll come to greet.

Mary D. Meier

My True Friend

No words can express how grateful I am
To have a friend like you;
For real friends are hard to find.
(You've found that to be true.)

Years come and years go, and you are always there;
You listen and understand how much I've had to bear.
Now, you are the one who is tempted and tried,
And I'd like to show I care.

But, you're the one who's still offering to help
in ways I could not dare.

So, what can I say but, "God bless you, my dear!"
As kind as you are, you should have nothing to fear.
My prayers are that God will see you through
These trying times, 'til gray skies turn to blue.

Laura E. Gunby

God's Gifts

Sometimes we don't really give much thought
To everything that God has brought.

He's brought us the vast, open sky,
To gaze at by and by.

And He's brought us trees and nature,
For us to admire their great feature.

He has also brought ones to love us,
Who'd stay with us through the largest fuss.

But do we think of this day by day?
No, we throw it all away.

Mandy R. Dean

Street Encounters

I'll know when you slip me your greasy eye
to go uptown and get nameless faces
on your petition.
But I'll understand why when you shift past by
that you don't need me
only my submission.

Your penetrating screams
are but pulsating whispers in my ear.
And your careful thoughts
are nothing I need to hear.

I'll know when I see your face plastered in front of me
that your smile is vacant
and my mind is free.
And I'll understand why I still feel your dampness
that your touch was lasting
though I dried myself clean.

Your transparent screams
are but dying whispers in my ear
And your softening thoughts
are nothing I will hear.

Meghan A. Nuding

Break Time For My Soul

I went for a walk the other night.
To give my soul a break.
And came upon some diamonds bright.
Swimming in the lake.

The moon, just up for her night out.
Was putting on the show.
It made me want to sing and shout.
And let the whole world know.

That it's there for free, when the moon does shine.
So take your soul for a break.
Take some time to rest your mind.
Just relax, and contemplate.

God gave us these bright little scenes.
To heal our troubled hearts.
So let's take the time to gaze and dream.
Before we fall apart.

Naomi Lowry Wood

The Light Bulb

Raindrops falling from clouds of darkness,
   To form puddles of brilliant light,
      Giving revelation to insight,
         And revealing secrets otherwise hidden.

It is to us,
   Like a soft yellow blanket is,
      To a child.
         And it is to us,
            A shower of truth
               That some may drown.

It is not merely a source of light,
   It is the electrical centerpiece of our intelligence,
      Illuminating not only our eyes,
         But our minds.

With a click,
   There is eureka,
      With a click,
         There is.

Linda Patton

Model Of Inspiration

Inspiration, what a wonderful pathway
    To follow throughout the years
Feeding appetites with interest every day
    Brightening the hours to disallow fears.

Inspiration, given by someone well known
    Who unconsciously exudes a radiance
That is so gracious and pleasantly shown
    To friends and every acquaintance.

Thus, many a road has been smoothed
    For those traveling a rocky trail
Weary hearts and minds having been soothed
    Letting inspiration and hope prevail.

Bettering the lot of many around
    Erasing many heights of despair
Letting clear thoughts be found
    Of life and its ability to care.

To pattern ones life so many little ways
    After someone who faced problems standing tall
Brings strength and understanding every day
    To face the future bravely, and never fall.

Laura Poceta

You

I sit here....... unresponsive. Waiting, wondering
To figure out just what happened to us.

We were so in love, at least I was!
How can I just sit here and let you slip away,
You told me you loved and cared for me, which now I know is a lie.

I must have been muddled with reality because,
I can't seem to watch you go
As our relationship falls apart,
You can hear the breaking of my heart.

I want to hold you just once more, but it's much too painful
So before you go just lend me your ear
And let me tell you, "I love you so very much"!

I know that it don't hurt you a bit to walk out of my life,
Besides, you don't even care now.
I thought this would pass and we'd make it through.
I never thought it would end like this

And that is..............me without you!!!

And always remember in the back of your mind,
You're my one and only true love.

Mary Ann Starr

"Just A Moment Of Your Time"

We'd like to take a moment
To express our thoughts to you.
Not meaning to complain or whine,
But vent's what we must do.
We helplessly observed as you began to devastate
The only home we've known with your industrialized waste.
The water was our sanctuary, a haven, our safe space,
But Death, Disease, and Detriment came to claim their destined place.
When the day is done, not one of us goes home to kids or wife.
But why concern yourselves about the plight of Marine Life!
We now exist in a world filled with darkness and decay.
We're forced to observed each other as we slowly waste away.
Our lives to be extinguished,
In this matter we have no voice.
No polls or surveys taken
With which to offer us a choice.
So, as the old comedian sang
To troops found overseas,
We've got one wish to extend to you,
It's Thanks for the memories!

Marcia Leslie

Fairies

When night falls, fairies come out,
To dance and play and frolic in the mist,
Their silvery wings are iridescent,
Under the moon's light.
Like little fireflies,
They glow and shimmer, flying about,
Their tiny footprints, glistening of pixie dust,
Grace the forest floor.
When daylight pierces the canopy of trees,
Kissing the moss covered floor.
Their voices disappear until darkness,
When a new game begins.

Monique Small

Father, Make Me A Willing Vessel

Father, make me a willing vessel
To conform to your will
Teach me to listen and hear your voice
To be still
I want so much to please you
To let you have your way
To walk in your love
Day by day
Help me to trust that you are God
Even when I don't understand your ways
For you are he who numbers the grains of sand
And plans our days

Lord, I sense your strong hand upon my life
But I am not afraid
For I know you are the potter
And I am the clay.
Father, make me a willing vessel
This is my prayer, I pray
Your eternal purposes fulfilled
In your holy way.

Lisa Jo Fanelli

Begin Again

Where disappointment crowds the mind,
'tis best to leave the past behind.
No longer shall you find disgrace;
let the future put a smile upon your face.

Believe in miracles to bring you 'round.
Step lightly, lifting off the ground.
The sky shall ruffle your feathers again;
And free at last...your heart will spin...
to sing the songs...
of love...
and hope...
and sympathy.

Break away to brighter paths...
let nothing set your bounds.
Breathe free - feel hope-
and...
walk firmly
on new ground.

Gayle Barrett Abe

Nature's Beauty

Take time to enjoy the beauty in life,
The small things that we often take for granted
The flowers and the trees that blossom in the spring.
The birds and the squirrels up in the trees.
The running water in a small creek.
The laughter and the hollering of children running wild.
The beautiful rainbow after a rain shower.
The moon and the stars on a clear night.

Olga R. Reta

See Psalm 42:1

I am a doe
Timid, big brown eyes, darting, prancing down to the river
Never, NO NEVER standing IN the rushing waters
Always on the bank, edge

I glance to the left, then the right, OK looks safe
Lowering my head, I take a sip of water
Cold, cool, thirst quenching. The water of life

I glance up, a "flash" of light
What's that? I jerk my head up
Where? Over there. Bright ORANGE and
an ever so slow upward movement

On edge, nostrils open, I sniff the air
Man? Gun? Danger, Danger! I BOLT
to the woods, safe hidden, covered

Frowning, head down, he steps out from his cover
The "flash" of light swings down in front of his chest
harmless. A camera.
Remember? Remember the doe
She
is her only foe.

Nancy E. Carmichael

Ethics

Endangered, like the grand and powerful pachyderm,
Timeless, as beauty or life itself,
Hard driving, demanding to be heard, ethics must
struggle for its existence.
Impossible odds, like a crap shoot on a Saturday
night, but the game continues.
Courage, compassion intertwined with culture and
criticism, ethics eludes extinction once again.
Will the capricious character continue to survive,
despite man's willful attempts to destroy it?
Will it become extinct as did the powerful and
dynamic dinosaur; one can only ponder, and pray.

Judy Locke

A Working Mother's Aching Heart

There's the sound, it's here again.
Time to get up, get ready and go in.

Another full day there on the job.
Sometimes I sigh; sometimes I sob.

I could teach them to cook, garden, and clean.
Are they eating enough? They look so lean.

I could teach them new songs and how to pray—
the love of learning. Oh, I miss them today.

Work is busy and I'm very involved.
Will this guilty pang ever be resolved?

I drive right home anxious to see
my two little boys, running straight to me.

If only I could be home and be with them each day.
The guilt would be gone, and we could laugh, love, and play.

My Lord has a reason for me to serve
out in the workplace, so I must not swerve.

To miss His plan and be out of His will
would be even worse than these feelings I feel.

I know He loves me and understands this pain.
The importance of life is a perspective I've gained.

Karen L. Axley

The Quiet Storm

Gray clouds gather unnoticed by the clan
Thunder rumbles the body and quickens the hand
Verbal lightning and eyes that rain
The shrew is free and cannot be tamed

Year by year the winds grew power
contemplating the time and hour
Passive clouds once ruled the sky
Until the day the tornado discovered its eye

The winds swept and split the path
Dividing the rubble half and half
The storm fell quiet once it made its peace
The shrew went west and the boar went east

Mona Lisa Bass

One Memory I Would Never Erase

My love for you burns like a wild fire.
Through this love I search for a strange desire.
You don't know I exist
But it's you I can't resist.
My eyes fall upon you,
Like someone telling me this love is true.
I wish I said something but I was to shy.
God made me this way, I don't know why.
The one thing that will always stick with me.
Is that love is so hard to find
And you will always be on my mind.
There will always be a place for you in my heart.
Even though were so far apart.
This is one memory that I would never erase

Jeff Taylor

Daughter Of A Sailor

As he served in the navy for twenty years.
Through the days we had many fears.
A fear of disaster, a fear the days wouldn't
go by any faster.

But by calling and sending us each a letter.
He let us know everything was looking better.
So as we waited and waited for the day,
that there would be no leaving and he would stay.
No more ships or trips to take him away.
Ohh how we longed for that day.
Now the day has come and we don't know what to say.
Our dad is retiring and is home to stay!

Jessica Rider

Defense

My body trembling
Thoughts of defense racing
Yet my lips remain sealed

Words tearing into me
Bruising my soul
The holes in my heart beginning to bleed
I must remain strong

It's only anger
Harsh words, not actions
Don't let them hurt

This will pass, although it feels like eternity
Grit your teeth, grit your teeth
Breath
Don't forget to breath...

Joy Ellen Eickhoff

Eternal

I am looking forward to ridding myself of
this mortal body and its constant limitations.
I am anxious to be free, to have no bounds on
my mind — my real being.
Nothing could hold me back — my mind and soul
free to soar.

I lived before my birth and I shall continue
to live long after my death. My mortal existence is
a mere minuscule of time in my endlessness. Death is
not frightening — it is anything but [that].
Although, I am curious as to what will become of me
once I am dispelled from this body I know that, finally,
I will be free and my human fate determined. Humanity is
weakness and in death I am Eternal...

Jessica A. Miller

When I Look Into The Mirror, What Do I See?

When I looked into the mirror
This morning, what did I see?
That white-haired lady with her
Head bending low was someone I felt
I did not know.

Surely that woman could not be me
So shriveled and wrinkled
Scarcely able to see. She was not,
She is not, she cannot be me.

Then I looked again. What did I see:
Eyes filled with warmth and caring,
Lips that could kiss with love
And sharing, shriveled arms
That could hug with delight,
An encouraging smile which made me know
Youth may be gone, but love does not go.
It has ever been so. The lady I know!

Martha E. Sena

"My Gift To You"

"My child" He said, "Here is my gift to you."
"This gift I give you is more precious than any other."
He said to me one day "I want you to love this gift for as
long as you are on earth."
"And always remember" he said, "Try not to raise a hand or a
belt to this gift I am giving. For, I want him to grow with
love in his heart."
"This Gift" he said, "will have many thoughts to teach you and
always try to learn from him, every detail you can."
"This gift that I am giving you which is so precious to me,
should be as precious to you."
With that I was handed the most wonderful gift God could
have given me "A CHILD."

Lisa Paul

Such Sweet Sorrow

Such sweet sorrow coming in,
  This didn't just start to begin.
Hatred, sadness, violence, too,
  I don't know what I should do.
One bullet and everyone is sad,
  But not me, I'm mad.
Tears fall down, more than a few,
  Babies hardly ever coo.
Sadness fills all the air,
  Why can't everyone be fair?
I close my eyes and wish it away,
  But when I open them, I have to get on my knees and pray.
Such sweet sorrow coming in,
  This didn't just start to begin.

Jennifer Cornell

Remember The Butterflies

When you look at a butterfly,
Think of an old one.
When you see a caterpillar,
Think of an infant.

Just as a caterpillar morphoses -
Changes into a more lovely butterfly,
A child will change into a wise old one.
Not always there, in more respects than one.
The butterfly remembers its time as a caterpillar,
And an old one remembers when it was young.
Listen to the butterflies
For they have stories to tell.

Old and new, Young and old.
They are different,
Yet so alike.
When you see an old one,
Think about their wisdom.
Remember their stories.
Listen to their tales.
REMEMBER THE BUTTERFLIES.

Karsten P. Huneycutt

My Wife, My Life To My Wife Fran

From the day you promised to cherish and love,
Things have changed,
She is now in charge of all of the above,
She gets you up and out to your job,
Takes care of the house and the kids,
And you when you return at the end of the day.
One messy blob, she lets you think that
you are in charge, and doing all right,
And when you and your neighbor had words,
She even said that you had won the fight.
She becomes the doctor when you and the kids
are sick, runs to the store, laundry, the bakery,
And still gets home quick.
You say these things are not all true,
Because you don't want to world to see through.
But if the truth were really told,
Without this lady you call your wife,
Like a man on an island, you would be a lost soul!

Lewis Greene

Sand Castles

If all the little Children were all of the world —
they would teach each other to build a Sand Castle and
let Time wash it away...

They would hold their hands out to one another in
Friendship, instead of greed.

A Child is Forgiving of hurt and anger.

A child is the Beautiful Self that is tucked away -
deep in the Hearts of everyone and Forgotten; because
Time did not wash away the Sand Castles.....

Its passing changed our Reflection and disguised
the Child's Innocence.

In each of us there is a Mirror that still Reveals
the Child...

Lisa Lynne Vangsness

A Child Is A Human Being

A child is like a breath of fresh air
They go through out the day without a care
They always find things very amusing
Sometimes though they can be very confusing
Never try to understand a mind of a child
Because they have imaginations that run wild
Before you scold a child, remember back when you were little
Please don't spank them, for their bones are very brittle
Take time with them and teach time things they should know
And in return for your efforts you will see a face glow.
Remember a child is a human being
Often though we treat them like machines
A child has feelings just like you and me
So encourage them to become who they want to be.

Neta Williams

Untitled

To you I write these tender words;
they, from me, you have never heard.
Why, I'm not sure, you've touched my heart.
And in there, you will always hold a special part.
Tender looks and words and touches,
sometimes they scare me very much.
But I promise, this won't make me run,
because the time I spend with you is fun.
Your voice, your looks, your soft caress,
from a man like you, I would expect no less.
You may never know what you've done for me.
It's kind of like new blossoms on a tree.
I may open up and bloom one day,
and in the wind my branches will sway,
and cover you with leaves in fall.
And maybe, just maybe, we can have it all.

Laurie M. Cogswell

Butterflies And Wildflowers

The Butterflies and Wildflowers,
They can be yours, mine and ours.
They just seem to go together,
In all of the beautiful weather.

The nectar from the Wildflowers is so sweet.
The Butterflies seem to gather all they can eat.
What a beautiful array of color,
Red, green, blue, orange, pink and yellow.

Only God can create such a sight.
That's why it all looks and seems so right.
Forget your worries and woes of the day.
Let the Butterflies and Wildflowers get in your way.

They are only here to enjoy for just so long.
Then they all disappear and are gone.
But the great show that they did put on,
Makes me thank the Lord for the day I was born.

I will always remember how radiantly they did look
And record as many as I can in my memory book.
So until next year, at this same time,
I'll just wait to write about them with another rhyme.

Leigh Silver

Choose To Be The Victor

Traveling life's pathway, be it short or long,
The heart will carry hurt from another's wrong.
The initial pain is a knife in the chest.
Choosing to invite "Bitterness" as a guest,
Chases away the desired friends, "Health" and "Peace".
Embrace "Forgiveness" and dump "Anger", the beast.
Already a victim by the inflictor,
Reunite with "Health" and "Peace"...be the victor!

Karen Quick

Yesterday's Heroes

Let's run up the flag for yesterday's heroes
They came and they conquered
They fought and they won
They earned all their medals
By playing so bravely
But just can't imagine that yesterday's done.

Let's all give three cheers for yesterday's heroes
They taught us the value of hard work and play
In all of their efforts we basked in their glory
And never looked on to a new hero's day.

Let's all say a prayer for yesterday's heroes
And hope that they know that a new games begun
'Cause love doesn't die at the end of the cheering
It grows 'cause it knows that there's worlds to be won.

Margaret Kritikos

"Violence???"

Gangs, Rape, Drugs, Suicide.
These are the Violence that we Face. These are the Rages that we
   look through
Our very eyes.
Abuse, Murder, Lies, Adultery.
These are the Violence that We Do. These are the Compulsion that
   we have on
Our innocent conscience.
These are the Duress that the Ten Commandments want us to Avoid.
Prejudice, Prostitution, Temptation, Kidnappings.
These are the THINGS that we Experience.
These are the Rages that OUR God does not want us to experience.
VIOLENCE??? Why does Violence spread from City to City? Why does
Violence effect our very lives?? Why does Violence Happen in our
neighborhoods, in our lives, in our Countries, and to our best Friends????
It all started when some people disobeyed the one person in all
of our lives, God. It started when some of our own people disobeyed
the Number One commandment, "Love one another, as we Love ourselves".
We owe it to ourselves to prevent and to remove Violence from our
neighborhoods, cities, and eventually our Country, America.

Matthew S. Cabrera

Sharon

I look in the mirror, but it's hard for me
There's something there I just don't see.
You were so smart.
But something was wrong deep in your heart
This life had nothing more to offer you
You decided you had had enough; you were through.
So now you won't hear the crash of the
   waves against the shore
You won't see sunrises anymore
When you came into this world your parents
   thought they were in heaven
But after 18 years, you decided it wasn't
   and left by a .357
No note, no last words, no goodbyes...
Leaving the word "why" the loudest of
   our cries.

Gina M. Pawlewicz

Silent Echoes

Reflection on the pond a-miss,
   the fish has surfaced for some air;

The circle widen bigger still,
   wreaths reaching t'ward an unknown shore;

The fish has claimed a breath, will live,
   and the circle knows it must change;

It widens further and smooths out,
   silent echoes remain, un-scene.

Nora A. Loch

How Do You Know?

How do I put it?
There's just so much to it.
A kiss and a touch,
How much is too much?
How do you know when you're in love?
Do you hear a voice from up above?
I wish I could find the words to say,
How much I hope this feeling will stay.
The way you make me feel,
Seems too good to be real.
You've helped me get through a lot,
By giving me all that you've got.
I'm glad we can talk about the past,
Things we would change, or glad didn't last.
Together we're growing,
Without even knowing,
What the world will bring.
Trust in God and we'll make it through,
The best for me, and the best for you.

Jill Root

A New Life

You have begun a new life with new hopes and dreams.
There will be many, many changes now, it seems.
You'll have sunshine on your face throughout the days.
There will be no more days of sorrow, only praise.
You left us behind for a better world.
Why you left, we will never know!
But we are strong and are willing to let go.
The mourning, the cries, the sighs of grief
Are heard by all as signs of relief.
You are better off now, we all know.
But we want you back, "Why did you go?"
My life's big events you won't see because we're apart,
But you will always be there forever in my heart.
Memories will last forever, until the end of eternity.
Your love, I know will always and forever be with me.
Since all these changes are occurring,
There's one thing that's not even stirring,
It's the fact that you are my Babcia, FOREVER!

Nadine N. Sokolik

"From This Day On"

I used to not believe in much of anything
There was disappointment in even Santa Claus
Sometimes we just need someone to believe in us
As I believe in you

On a squelching summer day
I felt a cool reassuring breeze
Touching me from inside to outside
Gently turning my attention

As my head stretch upward
Our eyes need no introduction
For they are familiar
Meeting long ago

We conversed in perfect harmony
Pausing only to catch a breath
You spoke eloquently
Possessing a sense of style new to me

Without the slightest bit of doubt
My decisions were instantaneous
Knowing I must give thanks to God
For the return of a true soul

Michelle A. Williams

Lonely Dolls

All day long and all of the night.
There they sit, scared with fright.
"Will she come?" they say.
The old ones sigh, "Not today."
"I guess she's too busy or getting too old."
"I'll bet she doesn't care anymore."
It's sad to think they used to be her whole world.
She's growing up, she's not a little girl.
Soon the dust is beginning to fall.
And I guess Barbie and Ken weren't so great after all.
Now youth is gone, and teenhood has set in.
What's so wrong? Growing up is not a sin.
But still, those dolls are all worried and scared.
No one to dress them or brush their hair.
"What will we do without her around?"
"It seems to me that we're not important now."

Kendra Benson

The Power Of Positive Feedback

In every stranger's furtive glance
there lies a sense of fear;
Only a victim of circumstance,
he knows no one here.

Yet no one reassures him
with a pleasant word or two;
To help him on his lonely quest
to acclimate anew.

And will no one step forward to counteract
the ultimate destiny that we are sharing?
To be ignored and forsaken with so much left to give?
To be deemed burdensome by eyes young and uncaring?

Each new face renders us a chance
to invigorate, to praise, or to heal.
Yet so many prefer to "constructively" criticize,
all kind words and thoughts to conceal.

When we consider the words that leave our hearts,
we might well ponder this;
No one is so fortunate that they can afford
a kind deed, word, or smile to miss.

Missy Sue Mastel

"The Wild Rose"

A breeze flows through the garden
There are whispers throughout the flower colony
They describe how they are against the wild rose
She is the class act
Yet she socializes with weeds
She deserves butterflies
Yet she only allows honey bees to take her nectar
Her entire family is white
She is red and has a pink bud
She will wilt and her buds will follow her ways
So the wild rose shall live on forever

Lynn Steinbrunner

Child Of Mother Earth

The trees are the bars that surround my crib,
the sky is a fleecy blanket that Mother Earth wraps me in.
The clouds are my sisters huddled close to me.
The wind is my hair that blows freely.
The moon is my night-light,
the sun is my eyes,
my teddy bear is the wild wolf that howls out his cry.
My mother is the sky that looks down with a loving smile,
I am a child of Mother Earth.

Lisa Gregersen

Watching The World Go By

I love to sit by my window, and watch the world go by,
There are smiling happy faces, and others about to cry.
Some look worried, some frightened, some are burdened with care,
others hold their heads up high, to them! No one else is there.

Sometimes there's a gay young couple, love in their eye shining bright,
whispering soft sweet nothings, they never dream of night.
Now and then there is a Braggart, or a Loafer, just wasting time,
or maybe I see a Drunkard, who is always wanting a dime.

Then there's the neighborhood gossip, who is always on the go.
She needs no morning paper, she'll find out all there is to know.
There goes the thoughtless fellow, he wants only money and fame.
True friendship to him means nothing, his friends must have money and
    a name.

Now and then I see a Dreamer, dreaming of things yet to be,
Looking through rose colored glasses, seeing only what he wants to see.
None of us are faultless, we all make mistakes I know.
I wonder how I look to others, as along life's highway I go?

On this a while I ponder, and I bow my head in shame,
When I think what others may think of me, or how they speak my name.
And as I sit and recollect, some memories make me cry,
But I still love to sit by my window, and watch the world go by.

Theora P. Baughman

The Trial

I am an angel fallen from grace
There are bruises and scars on my face
My once green eyes are now dark black
From that last brutal attack.
Why would you tell someone, "I Love You"
When scream and hit is all you do
You take your anger out on me
You have a plan, you know my destiny.
I know in my heart I am going to die
And you will weep and ask why
But you will know down deep
And I will come and haunt your sleep.
Because what goes around comes around
And one day, you too, will be placed in the ground.

Jessica Gartman

Your Love

A hazy rainbow covers the sky
Then slowly it gets darker
Darker.
Out you come my friend.
Through sorrow and joy
During disappointment and success
You followed me
Chasing after the car on long journeys home.
Smiling at me when I felt no one cared
When I walk you light up the way
Beautifying the ocean and the sky.
Making romance possible
Helping dreams come true.
You stand alone, yet you care for everyone.
I wish you were mine alone.
But I know, my friend,
You have too much love for only me.

Judy Moody

Something Think About

To be an animal would be a dream.
Then life wouldn't need to be so extreme.
I'd let my mind wander free
Like a cat's nonstop curiosity.

If I were a bird I'd glide through the sky,
and never worry if the time flies by.
A rabbit can pounce through uncut grass,
and not care if the next day will pass.

A bumble bee can buzz through blossoms,
and live with nature just like possums.
If a caterpillar starves, he will cry
because he won't live to be a butterfly.

So, if you're stressed out just take the time
to read this poem and let your mind climb.

Michelle Moore

Life

Life came and was kindled in the mother's womb,
then burst into bloom. A child was born.
To live and yet to die some far off by and by.
Until time has run across its mighty span.
Destiny fulfilled, life's breath stilled.
Its growth like a tree cast upon a turbulent sea
will sink and rise again after each wave has reached
its crest.
It will reach that far off shore, uncertainties
overcome, and though weathered by the storm.
Its majesty like some, will have placed its
eternal mark where others have placed none.
Life ends, the flame goes out.
The flower wilts. Yet it blooms in some
far off unknown land where others before it have
gone to be planted in the sand.
We live and we die.

Michael P. Yearout

Why Do I?

Why do I sit here,
their words bouncing square off my face?
Sometimes I fear the walls around-
I fear them to be more attentive than I.
But how can I pay attention
in a world that has no happiness?
Despair, destruction, and war are nothing to me-
What happened to all of the good things?
What happened to childhood ignorance?
The sweet summer days,
The lazy, nothing to do days,
The days of no worries or cares;
Where did these go?
New thoughts and ideas thrust upon me daily-
Why? Why? Why?
Why must I grow up-
throwing away the part,
looking towards the horizon,
leaving the only world I have ever known,
behind.

Matthew Lopez

Fuzzy

My fuzzy, small monster is so quiet. She is smaller
than a mouse but lives in my house. She is so kind to me.
My cat tried to eat her but fuzzy ate my cat instead. She
lives in my doll house but sleeps in my bed. Oh, what am I
going to do with my fuzzy little friend!!

Mindi Laurent

"The Monster Within"

I am not scared of most monsters
Their slimy claws and huge fangs do not frighten me
However, one always seems to get me
The monster
The creature
Lives deep down
Inside my heart
In the dungeons of my soul
It criticizes
It degrades
It hurts me
I try to find it
I try to stop it
The evil voice I hear in my head
That criticizes
And degrades
And hurts me
I search and search but never see
The monster
That is really me.

Meredith Levine

My Two Sons

There is no one else I'd rather be with, than my two sons—
Their eyes sparkle with dreams, their smiles are full of hope,
Their cheeks are full of laughter, my two sons—

Each brand new day they bring me joy, in the future as men, now
As little boys—my love is shared between the two, words cannot
Express my ecstasy for my two sons—

My heart and soul is of them, every day my breath is of them,
My love is unconditional for my two sons—
Whatever life may bring them, whatever God's plan is for them,
I know He will take care of my two sons—

For when my time on earth is through, I won't be sad because I
will have loved my two sons.

Micki Red Eagle

Music Unembraced

Once, an orchestra of stars would play at night; with the moon as
their conductor the strains of music would serenade the clear
darkness with light. Falling showers of gold mingling, in the open
air. Once, the stars heard applause in the souls of those who
gathered to listen close and
Thirstily catch the falling notes; clasping them close to heal,
And cleanse, and bring solace.

But slowly, other sounds began to scribble across the night sky, and
Listening is forgotten as noise comes louder and faster.
Crashing and colliding.
The moon hides, ashamed of her tarnished face.
The notes fall—no one catches them, and
The next morning the ground is littered with the corpses of notes;
Unnoticed.

Tonight, only a few will gather together in stillness and quiet,
Protected from the crushing sounds that fall away.
About to suffocate, they listen as
Strains of music begin to serenade the clear darkness with light,
Only accompanied by the sound of breathing.

Nicole Dawn Haskell

"Barren Tree"

She stands alone, youth and beauty gone.
The years have taken their toll,
Leaving her barren and old.
Her limbs are twisted and bare,
From age and lack of care.
Birds no longer nest among her leaves;
But pass her by for younger more fruitful trees.

Often travelers found comfort in her shade
And there many children ran and played.
She conformed to seasons as they came and went
Adjusting to each as it was sent

Now she is too weak to stand tall,
Yet it is not her time to fall.
Soon her decaying trunk and twisted limbs,
Will give way and fall to earth,
Back to the mother of her birth.

Kathleen Tutor

"Time To Do Your Part"

Death came to do his part,
The woman, Anne, showed strength
deep within her heart.
In the hour of shock and grief,
Her tears were put aside - locked in.
But now, it's time to do your part.
Unlock those doors - not one by one
but unanimously.
Shed the tears for eternity.
Tell our God one thousand thank-yous
For answering the prayer that was most true.
Eliminate the burden of unshed tears,
Cleanse the heart of unhappy fears.
It's time to do your part.

Martha L. Weeks

Untitled

The young boy sins
The wise man grins
Then their trip begins

There's a ship made of silver
And it's filled with gold, pictures, scriptures, and scrolls
Of myths and legends that were never told
The young boy watches forgotten history
As the pages unfold

It never fails, they ditch the holy grails
And raise the leather sails, leaving no trails
For the greedy males, and billions of killer whales.

They did not seek clarity, they did not need charity.

The seas were their home, and on the lands they would not roam
They lived happily on their own, and their destiny was never known

The young boy grew bold
The wise man grew old
And what they learned was never told....

There's a ship made of silver and it's filled with gold,
Picture, scriptures, and scrolls of myths and legends that were never told.

Joe Hufford

Explaining Autumn Leaves To A Child

The frost came and it turned them red.
The wind it came and the leaves were dead,
so it tumbled them from the trees
and floated them away on the breeze.
It scattered them over the countryside
in a hustling, rustling, bustling tide,
'til all were gone, to the very last
and the trees stood bare in the wintry blast.

But the Lord looked down on the shivering trees,
(It seemed they prayed for protection, please.)
And then God thought: "It's cruel that they suffer so.
I'll send them down a blanket of snow
to cover each twig with downy white
and keep them snug through the wintry night
until it is time for the next budding spring
and the new green garments that it will bring."

Mae Smith

Beached Whale

The air is alive with gulls screaming at each other.
The wind is moaning through the stunted trees.
A school of flashing herring turn,
rushing along with the tidal sea's hiss.
The great whale lies alone on the abandoned beach,
wanting, wanting, to be free as a gull.
The sleek body, so powerful that it can capsize a ship,
is yet so helpless to save its own life.
The giant tail will not lift again,
to splash through calm coastal waters.
The eyes, gazing blankly over the misty horizon,
slowly close, never to open again, except to welcome death.
You cannot regret walking through your own thick grief,
when you know the weight of its great collapsing heart.
Lay your hands on the pulse still of life,
and join hands with the soul now knowing nothing but light.
Think of a new language,
to whisper gentleness to lighten some of the sadness.
Can you take a breath as deep as hope?
Keep it until the world is broken.

Maiko Ochi

THE CHRISTMAS TREE

Darling, will you smile at him tonight,
The way you smiled at me?
And will you put your arms around him,
THERE BESIDE THE CHRISTMAS TREE?

Will you open up his presents,
By the early evening light?
And will he hold you in his arms,
WHEN THE BELLS OF CHRISTMAS TOLL TONIGHT?

Will you share the joys of Christmas,
And wear your coat of Christmas White?
Will you whisper words of love to him,
AND LET YOUR KISSES SAY GOOD-NIGHT?

Now are you really in love with him,
The way you once loved me?
OR, IS HE JUST ANOTHER ORNAMENT,
TO DECORATE YOUR TREE?

Jack Dominy

Lost Man

The eyes of the sea await me as the captain stands alone
The waves are full of treasures, mine per chance to own.
My mind is a lonely wanderer as I watch the moonlit sky.
The ship goes slowly farther as I gather my thoughts tonight.
Another knot I watch go by...
Another dolphin kisses the sky...
The sea is but a lonely place... just she and I.
I feel the wind against my neck, its breath beckons me on.
I feel the call of the wanderer, me all alone.
The captain shouts "AHOY."
My dream is but awoken. My land is but at stake.
I wrench at my chest to catch a breath, as I have found my home.
The trees are but a part that sway against my face.
For I will not be here long, I know there is another place.
A tear brings on a sudden rain. The captain shouts again.
The sails in the sky are Giant in a pirate's eye.
The sea once again draws me in.
Will I ever be home again? No, 'tis "I" who live my life by sea.
My lady is there waiting for me,
but this is the life I lead... the sea and me

Karla a. Kuliga (Pen name - "Kid")

Everything In Its Time

The wave, which pushes me further
The water, which soaks my sorrow
The mist, which hides my emotion
The strength I need for all my tomorrows.

The sky, where my hopes shall fly
The night, where my dreams may live
The truth, to conquer all the evil
This is all I ask of you to give.

The word, which expresses a single thought
The song, which relives a feeling
The look, which deceives our souls
You and me...with all of our meaning.

Jena Lynn Landberg

"My Rib"

Smelling
The warmth of your body escaping from your breasts
is it really Christmas? The blood flowing

It drifts to the curb, a waterfall in search
of sticky oceans merging in the gutter

Saddened, at the end of sweet deceit
remembering laughter as pain
your lust hitting me like a hangover

Curious, I wanted to know what it felt like
to rip you open like a rag doll

What a strange sound...What was that?

Hearing, the dog down the alley
licking your blood off a Coke can

My inevitable hunger forced me to your flesh.
A black hole light does not escape

Anticipating
The union of c***ingly c***ful contusioning confusion
Excited Emancipated Ejaculated
Why, because you are woman
I want my rib back.

Jose Antonio Rivera

A New Love

I don't love you like I used to,
the vigor of the newness;
the excitement from the wonderment;
the freshness of a new love.
Pondering questions, shyness;
the enchantment of a new frontier.
Embarrassment, untruths, spontaneity;
mystery no longer envelopes the relationship.

I don't love you like I used to;
the yearning, the passion, the adoration...

I don't love you I used to,
the stability of a constant love.
It will always be there?
Nothing is taboo, there are no secrets;
the metamorphosis of the unknown to a certainty.
Brashness, sincerity,
steadfast feelings, emotions.
A ripened, hardened kinship unfolds.

I don't love you like I used to;
...a more settled feeling.

John E. Terpko

Higher Realm

Visions so enchanting they can not be possible.
The unnamed one walks into my life.
We soar into the realms of passion.
We discover ourselves in each other and wear each others masks.
Our souls combine - we dance as one.
Flower petals fall as raindrops.
Liquid gold rays reflect off our bare skin as we stand naked in a
field of hope.
Motes of fate float through the air and land on our entwined fingers.
Words flow out of your mouth with a musical quality.
I sing along - our music drifts through the air and reaches others
lonely ears.
We lay upon these hopes - they elevate us.
Secured in mid - air by rope made from the silky strands of our dreams
Up we climb - as one - that third person "we" creates.
Up the rope of dreams we climb.
The end of the climb is our destination - our destiny.
The third person separates and allows us to be individuals.
Side by side we walk upon the fragile web of love until we reach the
higher realm.

Jennifer Thomas

Nana's Farm

I remember Nana's farm with memories so warm.
The times we walked the tree lined road and played inside the barn.
The water there was cold and pure and berries did abound,
why everywhere we looked or went new wonders soon were found.
The times down at the swimming hole were always so much fun and on
the way back to the house we always had to run, what energy we had
back then when we were very young. Sometimes I think that I can hear,
once more the songs we'd sung.
    Out on the porch at eventide, we'd watch the deer at play. And
when at night we went to bed, thanked God for that day.
I'm so glad we have the ability to recall, for these were carefree,
happy days when I was very small.

Karla Ihrie

The Message The Mongoose Never Delivered

Tomorrow I dreamt I was standing here with you now.
The tidal wave swept my body over the stone wall
until I swallowed my heart in a gulp of salt water.
I saw the yellow Schwinn three speed I fell off when I was ten,
the huge wheels of your pride rolled over my body like pavement.
My tears filled a fish tank full of stones
and I asked myself why you never came by anymore.
You answered me lonely after I told you happy was the way to be.
I swam your world 400 meters like a butterfly over and over.
The water my nose held powered my strength— I continued on.
the moon dark of my eyes expressed no light of compassion
Yet I stumbled over to your nest and collapsed on your strong hands.
Smiling, your tired body, I want to hold you—
my wings your guide—and fly crooked into that tidal wave.
I would have sent the mongoose
but the cage fell out of the plane and landed on the moon.
So here I am half happy, half lonely.
Let the flames smolder inside
hold me close Mr. Majesty like you used to
and I will tell you someday about my trip to the moon

Jessica Riley

Family Loses!

Why did he have to die?
The thought of him just makes me cry.
It must be the way God wanted it to be.
Sometimes this is something I just can't see.
Late at night I try to see his face.
But it's just an empty space.
Words, they can't explain.
My pain is in the extreme.
You left me with all these questions and each one has no answer.
Then she got cancer.
The pain just grows stronger and stronger.
I don't know if I can take this much longer.
Next, the car didn't protect him.
I remember that again and again.
Life goes on they say.
Now it's the thirteenth of May.
I wish time would go back.
All I do now is slack.
Will I survive,
Just to keep their souls alive?

Jessica Raymond

Even As Woman

The mountain weeps.
The tears of years
Have stained her face.
While far below
Through summer's rain and winter's snow
The mosses grow.

Her trials and fears are ages old
And yet, when soft gray arms of mist enfold
She hides her head
Behind a cloud
And comforted
The mountain sleeps.

Martha S. Lawrence

Nation Nation Listen Now

Nation Nation — listen now
The taps of bugles sound afar
Let it be sounds of joy — and not of war
For oh nation you must not forget
Your countless soldiers who marched to war
The flag-draped coffins coming home
The sobs of those who cried
The rows of crosses of our brave
Who now remain in foreign lands
The many soldiers that were lost
No marked graves - no hope - no coming home

Nation nation - listen now
To the bouncing triumphant martial sound
Of bugles and resounding drums
That thunder with precision rhythm march
In parades of joy and happy times
In my peaceful nation - in my hometown
Nation nation - listen now.

Maria Grace Ramirez

Those Were The Days

And I remember way back when,
The sun did break the formless masses,
The sky was clear, those were the days.

Responsibility was limited, carelessness was abundant,
Those were the days.

You were innocent, I was tranquil,
As the wind blew across the dawn, spontaneity was the law,
For rigidness breeds apathy, those were the days.

As the sun found its way among the clouds,
So the words emulated through your depths
To unknown boundaries did we explore.
Passing on heaven's door step.
Never coming down, joined in bonds of ecstasy rather than complacency
Those were the days.

So the sun touched the auburn sky,
And in turn we had our traces,
Now conformity rules, and uniqueness is held prisoner,
Until once again the sun explodes,
Brilliance upon the sky,
That'll be the day.

Michael N. Mercurio

Passion

The words come unbidden to my mind,
The strange cry of passion.
Passion. Passion. What is passion?
It cries out to me as it seeks an outlet for its powerful strength.
From within, the passion struggles to find its release.
I feel it as it pulses and moves,
Like a tree, limbs waving in a storm.
I am powerless to suppress this force that blows within;
Nor do I desire to end the life of this passion.
I would rather see it grow and spread over the whole of my being
To give it a shimmering, colorful hue.
I only wait for the fullness of time.
Oh, let this time pass quickly, and when it has passed,
Let this passion burst forth to light the world.
Passion for the mind and for the body. Passion for the soul.
Passion for love and for hate. Passion for life.
Passion for all that is and will be.
Passion.
The power of it can create a world.

Malinda Jane Davis

This, In Remembrance

Winter has come, and now I am alone.
The stars in the wind-swept sky
No longer shine so bright, and the sun seems dimmed.
How I hate you for dying! Couldn't you wait for me?
We shared our youth in unbelievable ways
And watched too many dreams fade to dust.
Yet through it all, always, we had each other.

At age fourteen we met and began our journey together.
Us against them - remember? We had so little then.
Hand-down clothes, charitable church baskets of food,
Always on the outer edge of life.
No ribbons for our hair, no pretty things to bring us comfort.
And still, we hoped and dreamed and shared our sweet small triumphs.
Our poverty was never that of the soul.
Now you too are gone, preceded in death by both our husbands.
I grieve for you - my friend, my spirit sister, my confidant who never judged,
Stay in my memory; help me find pity for those less fortunate than we.
Be my Lady of the Lake;
Guide my frail boat to safety in that Avalon
Where once again, we all will be together.

Mona Robertson Raby

Autumn

As I imagined
the sound of a violin so real,
but fiction to my ears.
The smooth out cry was near.
In the overshadow through the transom,
I could see a fawn, next to a large oak,
with tiny acorns aglow.
Fall all in my soul and spirit was all I could feel.
Like abstract art a vision was near,
a large tree with crimson leaves.
The lullaby in my mind filled all the days
and all the nights forever gone.
The sky with all of its gray and white
color momentarily captured all the sunny
days worn out.
The scenery was fainting
just like a canvas painting.
Summer is gone and fall is near.

Jeanie Lou Campbell

silence

can you not hear
the soft whisper of my heart
as we lie close together
silent in the dark?

listen hard dear loved one
to the silence of the night
there's so much to hear
after the sun's last light

"i love you" says so little
there's much more I need to say.
so, instead not a word I'll utter
'til you hear my silence at the end of the day.

Jessica Roberts

A Line At A Time

A line at a time
That's the way life is
We live each day, not knowing what it comprises.
We wake with a smile and perhaps go to bed wondering why our actions
    were so far wrong or perhaps unexpectedly wondrously right.
A line at a time is what we write in diaries, letters and poems.
It's what we feel and means so much, people's influences and great times,
We have to put it on paper to see if others feel the same and
    help us see what the past and our relatives would want us to proclaim.

Gloria Unger

"Football"

Football is a collision sport,
The smell of turf in your face,
The loud crack of the helmets,
The smell of new pads as you put them on.

The adrenaline rush when you walk onto the field,
The power you feel when you hit someone of the opposing team,
The kindness, generosity, or courtesy you never give in to on
    the football field.

Football is pure and primitive, and that's how we like it!

Joey N. Cook

Of Time

Like the vague mist from a citrus peel as the fruit is unveiled,
the smell of the rain in the air before the first drop falls,
the heat felt before bodies meet
are the Times
Right Before.

When I was young,
it was the taste of fruit,
the wetness of rain,
the touching of bodies
that meant so much.

For youth means Now,
But age means Time.

So, of late, it is upon the Times
Right Before that I reflect.

The smell of spring before flowers bloom,
the breath drawn before words are uttered,
the flash of red behind closed lids
before opening one's eyes on a sunlit morning!

Of late, the Times Right Before
sometimes mean more.

Melodie Lynn Clark Thompson

Home For The Holidays

I love to come home for the holidays
the smell of pine in the air
everyone's so happy just to be there
no one fighting and fussing no one shedding a tear
for this is everyone's favorite time of the year
turkey, stuffing, cornbread, mom's homemade rolls
the smell draws you near the pots cooking on the stove
"get your hand out that pot "mom would always say
you'll spoil your dinner tasting all day
as the grace is said
we remember the people who went away
and it brings us closer as a family
on this and every day

Gina R. Cappaninee

A Silent Plea

The thunder rolled,
The lightning struck,
But all I could see was the hurt in your eyes.
You gave me a look that said innocence and betrayal,
But I didn't know what the look or the words could mean.
The thunder rolled,
The lightning struck,
But all I could hear was your soul crying out to me.
But I couldn't understand what it was saying.
The thunder rolled,
The lightning struck,
And all I could do was cry.

Jennifer Frey

The Battle

The dragon's tail whips around
The shining scales rub the ground
His mighty throat lets out a roar
For he shall have the final score.

The daring knight rose his mighty blade
His armor bright and unscathed
His steed's coat is luminous
Thundering hooves sing in chorus.

Both of their blood warms and races
Both make circles in large full paces
Each one's blade's sharp for the kill
Each one has such perfect skill.

The malevolent foes charged with frightful speed
Eagerly intent on completing the deed
The clash echoed through the misty air
Causing the townfolk to stop and stare.

Never before had they seen a sight so gory
This is the end of our story
Who won the battle - the man or beast?
Well, the dragon had a bone and human blood feast.

Lynn Rest

Forgotten Love

The wind whispers a silent name.
The shadows feed a silent flame.
Silhouettes dancing in the moonlight.
Trees swaying to the music of the night.

The young woman watches in wonder.
Night storms that do not thunder.
Much like her heart of silence and anger.
For he left her, alone, a stranger.

He's forgotten her, gone on with his life.
She remembers, it cuts like a knife.
His gentle touch and carefree laugh.
His passionate eyes, and walks down a wooded path.

She may be forgotten now, but not forever.
Someday another will come, one who will not sever,
Sever a relationship so fair.
For he will be the one that cares.

Jodi Bonner

My Father's Strength

He was the one who cradled his baby girl in one massive hand.
The same hand that brushed my waist-length hair in later years.
He was the one who carried me on his shoulders...
And ran many miles behind me on the giant blue bike.
He put his only child on motorcycles and horses and trusted
    enough to let me go...
Because he taught me and taught me well.
He was the teacher and I his only student.
Our classroom was a pond, his pick-up, the woods, or under
The nearest tree. Wherever we were together.
Time has passed...we have both grown and aged.
I look at him now and feel anger and bitterness at the illness
That robbed me of my super-Dad.
In a sense, I have become his strength and his muscle.
The little girl grew up and learned he is only human.
But in a grown woman's eyes, he is still the super-Dad...
    Still the teacher...
    And always my hero.

Gina Garver

"Getting What I Deserve"

Mother's calling, but I haven't got the time.
The river's white water rushes,
Inviting me to take part in the friendly competition
we've always shared.

Today I turn my back on both.
I have toiled hard all day,
And although both have given me bliss in the past,
Surely my reward will make me happier than anything.

Most people work to receive their reward,
And it comes as some sort of pay back, and makes them happy.
I work just to see my reward,
And do anything for her, my reward, to make her happy.
It seems ironic this reversal of roles

And then, like the stupid fool I am,
I toil for my reward, and she won't have me.
Can you believe the nerve?
I turned my back on my friend the river,
And this is how she treats me.

Well, I guess this is my reward,
But I sure as hell don't think I deserve it.

Gray Stream

"Waning Beauty"

The light of love brightens the soul allowing growth of new emotions.
The rain of passion fulfills our every aching desire
and the soil we have derived feeds every quivering compulsion.
Alas for the gift of maturity, a true success.
Young colors of the physical nature express an array of our attire.
All in all, somehow unexpectedly the storms of a gloomy season
separate our seeds into lost places.
Life begins elsewhere for sadly enough, undoubted reasons.
The love we knew is now deeply buried and the surfaces
are scarred by destruction of the only known happiness.
The rain of passion is long over taken control by a drought of fear.
Now painfully scorched by heat of anger that dries the joy only known
of him near.
The flower of love finally reveals her inner bleeding
as she gasps for air, but is far from succeeding.
And that beauty I had a hold of once deep in my soul
has left me sad and alone forevermore.

Jennifer Nevins

Nuclear Family

Drowning in purple, the King settles on his throne.
The Queen resting on hers
  with a distorted view of the crown upon her head.
Ever heard of a corrupt monarchy?

Rest easy
  restless country,
Your King shall roam.
A traditional nuclear attack to the situation at hand.
The King roars through the jungle
entrapped between four walls.
The Queen shuttering inside
  and will not respond yet desponds to the attack.
Distill you growing power unto me
Fly off the mounted pedestal
Oh free me sweet Queen!

Now back in the woods,
  a nuclear structure, in a valley, on a hill—
There stands the King
There rests the Queen
There the Royal children play by the nuclear power plant.

Jill O'Quin

A Comfort To The Loneliness

The gentle pattering of the rain,
The peaceful whistle of the far away train,
The lonely sounds of the night,
I wonder if you're lonely tonight?

I'm watching the rushing waterfall,
Amazed at the beauty of it all.
As I take in the beauty of this joyous land,
I long for the joyous touch of your hand.

I go for a walk, it's a beautiful day!
You walk beside me all the way.
I have a million things I'd like to say,
But, why do you seem so far away?

The day is glorious, but I still feel rain,
I'm searching for love and finding pain.
All through the day, all through the week,
An end to my loneliness I continually seek.
I'm searching out to find comfort with you,
And keep wondering to myself, are you lonely too?

Jill T. Ardary

Untitled

The sight of her in my heart and soul made me lose control.
The overwhelming desire to be near her could never be replaced.
The natural beauty I see inside her makes me love her even more.
And when I see her cry, the pain inside of me is hell on earth.
When I see her I want to thank God for have creating such a
beautiful creature.
Her eyes I peer into are the eyes of one with no soul.
She loves me the way no other person could love.
She holds me with such a gentle touch only an angel could bring,
When the light hits her face, the beauty appears and the wrong
words I said brings her in tears.
I wish God would strike me dead for making her feel this way.

Mandiee Harbin

Our Book

My family is like an old torn book. All ripped to shreds.

My brother Jason is like the cover of the book, all hard on
the outside not wanting to know what's inside.

My step-sister Shannon is like the binding of the book,
trying as hard as possible to keep our book together.

My step-mother Peg is like the table of contents of the
book, always knowing everything about "Our Book."

My mother Laurie is like the index of the book, trying in
every way she can to help us.

My father Steve is like the glossary of the book, wanting to
be a big part of the book but always coming last.

For me I am the pages of the book, all torn and ripped just
wanting to be a part of everyone's life.

Kacee Sanders

Nirvana

The brightest light casts the darkest shadows.
The greatest gift can be the heaviest weight;
Kurt Cobain's gift was his affliction
His nirvana was his hell.

His music touched the hearts of thousands
Yet couldn't save one soul.
He surrendered to the darkness in search of light.

I hope he's found his place in the sun
A safe place where there are no apologies.
The brightest light casts the darkest shadows
And the greatest gift is within.

Lindsay Legé

Tapestry

I walked into a dimly lit room,
the only furnishings a table, and a loom
and on this loom I saw the most magnificent tapestry,
obviously the work of unequalled mastery.
For in every warp and woof of flaxen fabric
a picture shimmered with life and magic.
A closer look, I gasped astonished!
Was I being admonished?
In every picture the past events of life depicted,
But each scene changed so fast, my future predicted,
unable to change the past, the course of destiny I could effect.
If only I take time to deeply reflect.
A miraculous gift this tapestry of life,
A bittersweet mixture of triumph and strife,
inextricably interwoven with threads of chance.
Color, texture, pattern dance
as the tapestry's mystery is revealed
nothing is concealed.
I am my life, the power is mine,
the energy within me, the source divine.

Katherine E. Wilson

Bones

Silent, stalking, quiet and serene,
The most beautiful of cats, moves unseen.

The greed of man, robs us all forever more,
Our children will not know, except through lore.

So sad, not to know the beauty and grace,
for too long, we've endured the selfishness of the human race.

Do something now, for we are on the brink,
It's too late, to just sit and think.

We'll talk and discuss - Oh what should we do?
Pass a law, declare it wrong, fill up a zoo?

We'll say "it's a shame", "It can't be allowed",
"They won't let it happen, not such a dark cloud",

To stop the carnage, we must all gather round,
How many will stand together, to hold our ground!

It's up to us to stop it all,
To save what's left, we can no longer stall.

They use the bones, how awful is that?
for naught but vanity, forever - kill a cat.

How do we explain to the Lord above.
How we let go - the Tigers we Love.

Lisa Washington

I Am A Seed

I am a seed.
The Lord will take me,
and plant me in my designated spot.
I will grow from the light the Lord will send,
I will prosper with his love—
   sent from above!
I am a seed,
Mother Nature is my friend.
She's around me like the wind through my leaves.
The Lord is my teacher—
   preparing me for life's unknown.
The Sunlight is my father,
The Rain is my mother—
   they raise me form birth to death!
They never leave their seed—
   and never hurt their seed—
they love their seed and raise it right.
I am a seed—
   Now I am a flower!

Khristie Hulse

Storms Can't Hold Back The Dawn

The storm clouds rolled across the sky and painted gray the earth.
   The lightening flashed, the thunder rolled.
      Wind howled with savage mirth.

Subduing all beneath its power with awesome strength and might,
   The fury of the storm did rage
      through the seeming endless night.

When all seemed lost, the earth was bruised,
   The lark had lost his song;
The sun brought forth a strip of gold...
   Storms can't hold back the dawn...

And so, the winds of life had blown and painted gray my world,
   The storm clouds rolled within my mind
      as wicked darts were hurled.

The fury came with strength and might, my heart was dark and cold;
   I hid my light beneath my tears,
      I fell beneath the load.

When all seemed lost, my life was bruised,
   And my soul had lost its song,
The Son brought forth His light of love...
   Storms can't hold back the dawn.

Linda C. James

The Last Two

We'll probably be,
the last two on earth.

After the last husband
neglects the last wife for business' sake,
After the last wife
rejects the last husband
for his lack of understanding.

After the last neighbor declares war
on the person next door,
'cause he doesn't want to step
in dog's mess anymore.

After the last lover rejects his mate,
she can't have her friends anymore
and she can be herself no more.

After the last friend sleeps
with her best friend's mate,
and the last mate sleeps
with his boss's wife.

There will be two shadows
left cast on this earth,
yours and mine
standing side by side,
because of the unconditional
friendship we share.

Margery Tauriainen

Journey Home

Travelling by night on my way back home.
The foothills roll like waves
Increasing in intensity
To mountains and valleys.
Distant lights beckon
From desolate mountain peaks
Like lonely hearts crying out for love.
The air is fresh and sky clear.
I am overwhelmed by the number of stars every time.
Years go by, but nothing really changes.
I know every turn of the road
On my way back home.

Lori Kanestrin

When It's Done

The old man lies in his bed,
the last page of his life's been read
He listens to the falling sand,
as he waits for the reaper's hand. (It's so sad)

What thoughts fill his head,
things he's done or things he's said.
Precious youth faded away,
only memories of yesterday. (They've gone away)

A body full of fragile bones
Sing a song of lonely moans
A feeble hand raised to the sky,
No tears just a silent sigh

Why does it have to end this way,
to have your mind just fade away.
Where's my pride and dignity,
lost inside senility (I've gone away)

Fade to gray and into the black,
can't stop the clock there's no turning back.
Hear the sound of the falling sand.
Reach out and touch the reapers hand. (Take his hand)

John Rivera

"A Voice Of The Land"

A voice rings out across the land,
the land of hatred, the land of man.
Where love was a part of yesterday, forgotten somewhere
there is only today. Where the cries of children are heard,
but not helped because all we can think of is only ourselves.
A voice rings out so loud, so clear, but
no one can hear through the silence of tears.
A land where judgement is what we've
learned to do and in the end through our eyes, the winner is you.
Where crime and violence have blinded
us all and we stand in the darkness, just waiting to fall.
A voice rings out but weaker its sound
for the people of the land cannot swim only drown.
Where the time to be brave when we look
in the mirror has now been replaced by
the innocence of fear.
Where man's Hate has now prevailed and
Love's last attempt has forever failed.
A voice is now silent across the land.
The land of hatred, the land of man.

Laura Nilles

The Glorious Fourth

Sing a song of long ago
The glorious fourth, to remember.
The splendor of such magnificent light
And voices sang out, singing low.
Each glad heart was ever filled,
Of the red, white and blue in sight
That made our childish heart so thrilled;
Of the good old fourth of long ago.

Cherry blossoms and apple buds, lotus all in bloom.
A fragrant smell of blossoms in the summer breeze,
And hearts palpitated with such glee!
The childish voices sang out with joy
And all was in such harmony.
The good old fourth of long ago, that made us feel so free.

It was the good old fourth of long ago,
The sky was bright, all aglow, and so, up the winding path, and then-
Some tangled grass in fields of ferns, and so,
Old times fade and land falls to waste;
The old times pass, and beyond, it parts,
Of the childlike songs in our hearts
Of the good old fourth July of long ago.

Gloria A. Miller

Ghost

How long is forever?
The ghost that you left in my life
says that's how long he'll stay.

His mission is to become brighter,
while making his competition fade.
His success humiliates me,
for I give him the power
which will lead me to doom.

His finest asset is that he only
reminds me of his beauty and charm,
while his more tarnished side had faded away
with each change of the tide and set of the sun.

I am left with beautiful ghost
whose tarnish has turned into dust,
He is gleaming in his perfection.
He says he'll stay with me forever.
Why can't a ghost exist?

Jill Woodward

"What's In Your Hand?"

Look into your hands, what do you see?
The future of our children, is held by you and me!
Did I say something you didn't understand, why do you look at me so?
There is obviously a lot you really don't know.
In this country, yes the Good Ol' USA, children are abused, uneducated
and starving everyday!
How can that be you ask?
It's understandable, when you consider all those who are either
unknowing or uncaring to the helping task.
There is so much that can and must be done.
There are so many question, but really the answer is only one.
All the questions of food, shelter, help for the abused and abuser,
money, and teaching can all be solved with LOVE.
As with any need, first we must ask help from our Father above,
Then with all the love in our hearts do ALL we can
To help all the children of this land!
Believe it or not their future is in mine and your hands!!

Lora Renee Yarber

The Proposal

Old father time has sounded his call,
The future is waiting for two becoming as one.
A special given place for a special decision
The joining of two hands against the world.
The figment once imagined is real.
To the depths of the sea and to the
Sky with the birds,
Let it be known I need your hand in mine.
Sound trumpets and bring down the walls,
Let all know you were chosen from above.
The grasps of death can not catch us.
Through darkness you lead me by my hand.
You can show me all the goodness in life
The magic words, I love you,
Can be heard on the wind in the heather.
All you must do is close your eyes,
I will watch and protect you at all times.
I need you baby, you need me.
Let's he tie the knot officially, here's the question:
Will you marry me?

Jason Leon

"Behind Every Strong Man"

The walls are covered with panelling
the floor smooth with Chinese silk rugs
the desk polished to a high gloss
the wall behind the desk proves his credentials

The shadow on the wall is tall and slender
the voice is soft and determined
business is done on the phone in the front office
agreements prepared in that office but not signed

It has been going on for centuries
it has been known as the shadow in this world
even hours spend
an acceptance of the roles

The glass walls are dividing the offices
the glass ceiling is keeping a lid on the confidential work done here
strings are being pulled
the power is on the name tag on the door

She is standing behind him
a strong hand on his shoulder
the deal has been prepared
soon he will add another plaque to his credentials

Marianna Linder-Madsen

These Dreams Of Mine

How beautiful the angels are that I see
The eyes of blue staring into me
Big and wide like the sea
there are three that appear to me

Each night that I sleep and dream of these
I ask for comfort and love, which they give with ease
For each passing day may not be a breeze
I love to sleep and dream of these

I ask how's my brother, nephew and dad
They say fine and definitely not sad
Thank goodness for these three friends of mine I have
Without them I would feel very very bad

As I awake by morning's light
I hold my dreams so much in sight
Because of my angels I won't be in fright
So each new day will bring a glorious night!

Melissa J. Burke

Battlefields

Our most painful wars are fought on the battlefields in our mind,
the enemy lurks within, invisible and undefined,
negative feelings of doubt and aggression,
leave us with a sense of anxiety and depression.

Loneliness causes us suffering, anguish and pain,
there's so little to lose and so much to gain,
by striving to leave the problems behind
as we work toward true peace of mind.

The future is molded by the events of the past,
every experience from the first to the last,
all that has gone before linger within,
quietly gathering from the moment life begins.

Memories are triggered by events and faces,
glimpses of the past viewed in strange places,
emotions pour into us as if by command,
provoking reactions we do not understand.

Our feelings of love and contentment cannot last,
unless we reconcile ourselves with remembrances of the past,
for no matter what we become as the years march on,
we're shaped somehow by times long gone.

Georgia A. Ecker

"The Shining Beauty" (Ode To A Falling Star)

Her dress seems to glow as she shoots through the night.
The dust of her tail glistens like hair, all shiny and bright.
Over the clouds and between the stars,
Her weary feet have traveled so far.
She has lived thousands of years
Before her burning disappears.
How old is she, God only knows.
For He created that which glows.
Across the heavens, as black as coal,
She rushes along to meet her goal.
She is amazing and grand,
And envied by man.
Like a fox, one must be keen and sly
For she disappears in the blink of an eye.
Like ashes to ashes, and dust to dust,
The shining beauty has lost its thrust.
My mom always said, "You are lucky to see
A sight so wondrous as she
For as she nears and passes by
Your wishes are granted and the witches die."

Julie Shute

"The Stream Flows By Slowly"

The stream flows by slowly and all
the dreams in it still not at ease.
Still linger for life for I will not let them leave.

Like a mirror shattered by the hands of a child.
My life breaks with harshness too.
Everything I ever had is quickly broke into.

Never knowing where things will turn up next.
Locked up inside myself,
A silent scream only heard by other silent bystanders.
Slowly all life begins to drain out of me and no one knows how
or why, but me, myself.

I know that someday the sun will come shining through.
All hopes and dreams will not die.
And until then...the ones which still linger and
hold on for life will leave from within.

But until then I gasp for air and reach upward, toward the
sky for fear I will go under.
I hold to everything within my grasp as to not be lonely.
And to make warmth between my hands, I hold to someone caring.
Still the stream flows by slowly.

Kelli Green

"Divine Paint Brush"

He painted the sky a pastel blue
The delicately colored rainbow too.
The stately mountains and clouds above.
He sprinkled the hill sides trees with love.
He spread the whispering winds along the beach and sands.
Never missing a stroke of His loving hands.
The proud eagle of this great land,
Who flies so high,
So freedom no man can deny.
Painted man, woman and child with grace in all race.
So they may live in harmony at their own pace.
Is it any wonder the sun, moon
and stars are so bright
In this great world of day and night.

Mary M. Clay

Can You Feel Your Knees

Can you feel your knees
the day you realize you're mortal?
When you fall to the ground
in helpless fright
Does anyone hear?
Can anyone feel?
The loneliness you feel that night.

Can you feel your knees
when your loved ones
tell you not to worry?
When you walk about in helpless fright
Does anyone understand?
Can anyone feel?
The quietness you feel that night.

Can you feel your knees when your doctor calls?
"Your test came back positive."
When your heart falls to the ground in helpless fright?
What can you do? Where can you run?
Is this the end to all my fun?

Please God, please give me strength as I lie down to sleep tonight.
Michelle Henderson-Breen

The Heel Of Achilles

Today I Need:-
The confidence of Lucy - The wisdom of Minerva
The patience of Job - The honor of a Boy Scout
The humor of a court jester - The trust of a baby
The serenity of a nun - The security of a blanket
The stamina of a marathon runner - The strength of an Amazon
The energy of the sun - The glow of the moon
The body of Venus - (attached to the arms of Morpheus)
The smile of Mona Lisa - The compassion of an Angel
The selflessness of Florence Nightingale - The mind of a computer
The exultation of a lark - The loyalty of a puppy
The softness of a kitten - The gentleness of a bunny
The determination of a two year old - The force of an avalanche
The twinkle of a star - The calm in the eye of a storm
The freedom of a butterfly - The abandon of a harlot
The roar of a lion - The faith of a flower child
The love of humanity and the hope of eternity.
Today I Have:
The Heel of Achilles
Martha Howett

The Secret Places

Take me away to the secret places
The childhood secret places where no one else can know
Where no one else can enter
Where no one else can go.

Take me away to the secret places
Where daffodils line the path
Far from the polluted things of man
Let me drown in their soothing bath.

Take me away to the wooded stairs
Where imaginations run free
Where one can grow and laugh
And be all one wants to be.

Take me away to the quiet places
To a chapel set staunch on a hill
Absorbed by the faith grown wisdom
Of those Spirits walking still.

Take me back to the secret places
And let no one take them away
Where sanity and peace and sweet release
Are only a memory away.
Marcia K. Dunnavant

Family

All is quiet now, an unsettling peace falls upon the house.
The children, gone, one by one, have left their nest to make it
    on their own.

They no longer demand to use the telephone, we now longer ask,
    "when will you be home."

No need wait up at night, wondering of they're alright.

The day we dreamed of has finally come, we only wish time would
    back up some.

To hear the laughter, to hear a cry, to see them wave their first bye-bye.

To mend their arms and knees too, to teach them the meaning of
    "I love you."

We hope they know the extent of our love, how it surpasses the unknown
    regions above.

Our hearts are bound by three children dear, we only wish they could be near.

Strange as this may sound, our freedom is new found.

Time for us and our needs, time for us sow different kinds of seeds.

as we once did, not so long ago, now closer together we can grow.

We can now pursue our dreams, for we know what true happiness means.

A family that's priceless, our family full of love.
Kendra Jeanne Girod

Fiancé

We sat on the backyard swing snuggling together under
the bright golden moon and a soft antique quilt. The amore
was so thick it could have been cut with a knife and served
like a delicious ice cream cake. It was a night to drink hot
tea and talk about cares, wishes and sentiments. But as the
conversation ended, the silence grew and the feeling for closeness
increased. Our faces gazed and touched and all hands
grip-locked. Our fingers sweated as an invisible glue drew
us together. Our lips explored together a passion so intense
it was difficult to say no. The furtherance of physical contact
needed to wait for a future moment. The feelings crescendoed
as the words "I love you" floated and my chest heaved
from the knowledge that we would enjoy each other in the
fullest at a later date. This evening was the most romantic
love we never made.
Karen C. Humphreys

My Heart

There is something just inside me
That's imbedded firm and deep
It governs all emotions
Makes me laugh, sigh and weep

It never ceases beating
Whether heavy or light
It keeps working continually
Morning, noon and night

Today it beats so steady
Tomorrow it may be still
But at any rate, its object
Is to obey God's will

It's a safety vault for all secrets
That you do not wish to impart
Now, of this wonderful machine I've been talking
It's a miracle machine, my heart.
Oneida Daniel

My Mother, The Flower

There's flowers that's blooming everywhere,
That's gorgeous on hill and dale,
But the sweetest flower in all the world,
To us will never fail.

Because that flower is Mother dear,
Whom we all love so well,
The way she adores her children here,
No human tongue can tell.

Her hair is white, with work worn hands,
Her voice is sweet and mild,
We know that we are still all loved,
Each one her wayward child.

We wish her all the very best,
That this old world can yield,
With love of Jesus in her heart,
She's one flower never gone afield.

Lucille C. McCarthy

Not What They Seemed

Every night I have this wonderful dream
That you love me as I do you
But when I awaken things aren't what they seemed
And the reality comes out through and through
The reality of you and me,
Of being two best friends and that's all
I try to be the best I can be,
But when I'm with you, in love I fall
I'm in love with the person that you are
My feelings have grown in many ways,
But they're strongest now by far
Growing still stronger everyday,
But I'll try to hold them within
And continue to lie
And hope one day soon they will end
So our friendship won't have to pass us by...

Katie Marie Lozon

Our Bible

Our Bible is our wish book,
   that we may be like men of old
To Christians here, there, and everywhere
   it's the sweetest story ever told

The Bible is our rule book,
   it gives instructions and a guide
It tells you what will happen
   when, with Jesus you side

Our Bible is our comfort book,
   it tells us where to look
When we become discouraged
   remember, our sins to the cross he took

The Bible is a history book,
   it tells how nations rise and fall
How in our obedience to Him
   we grow wise, and strong, and tall

Our Bible is a promise book,
   if we its contents obey
We'll one day go to live with Him
   where we'll forever stay, and for others pray.

Lillian Clay

"My Grandfather's Legacy"

This little rock came from a stone,
That was once on the land of my grandfather's home,
He lived there quite a few years back,
And the house still stands as a matter of fact!

Your parents took a trip to the past,
And brought you these remembrances-I hope they will last!
To pass on to your children when they are grown,
So they will know of their original home!
SANDHULT, EBBERARD, SWEDEN

Martha Hultin Ekdahl

Paint Me A Picture

Paint me a picture so vividly clear,
That the eyes of my soul can discern,
The minute details of the beauty within.

Let me drink in the splendor,
Of the beautiful creations of Heaven,
The likes of which no mortal can exact.

Fill my eyes which gaze at the firmament,
With the understanding of the vastness of eternity,
And perhaps a glimpse into tomorrow.

As an artist puts forth his brush,
And lovingly strokes the canvas,
Splash the sky with the beautiful colors to form the rainbow.

The beauty of creation cannot be totally seen,
Nor appreciated by mortal eyes,
Paint me a picture spiritually and my soul shall rejoice.

Judith F. Holt

River

Whose tiny little bubbles flow down the wild river?
That streaming blue water flows over the rocks,
Yet in a unique way it begins to talk,
Telling us a story of why they go so slow.

Rivers have so many jobs, doesn't anyone see?
How dear these precious waters are to me?
They teach a lesson that no one seems to see,
No one, that is, but me.

I have learned to watch over nature,
Learned to plant a tree.
Learned to help all creations grow,
All this the river taught me.

I know the life of nature,
Rivers go slow to do their work,
Looking over nature, planting trees,
Helping all creations grow,
Whatever you do don't take the river away!

Nicole Rubisch

"Smiling Face"

Don't be sad and full of gloom
take your broom, sweep it out of the room
don't be mad or even bad
put a smile on and let's be glad
if your heart feels heavy and full of tears
grab a box of tissues and blow
away those fears
the dark clouds will certainly fade
when you open the curtains and
pull up the shades
try and be happy as long as you can
chase the bad out the window
and the good in again
everyone will see what a difference it makes;
to change a frown into a smiling face.

Lora D. Hughes

Reality

Their eyes no longer sparkle and the glow of happiness
that may have been once there no longer exists.
They have become a part of the daily life of living,
the part that most of us don't want to remember...to know.
Our mothers,
Our fathers,
Our brothers,
Our sisters,
Our grandparents,
Our friends,
Everyone,
Ourselves.
The street is the only home they now know.
A bed of concrete,
A pillow of stone.
The forgotten man.

Gina Barton

Impressions

It's not just inspiration or the memories we keep,
That makes this life on earth a loving one.
It's the pathway that we each must walk
When we take that final leap.
Can we truly say "I've done my best, I've won?"
We reminisce on younger days and deep within our hearts.
Perhaps regrets, perhaps with pride we think,
Have I given everything I could? Does it matter where I start?
We're here, we live at times right on the brink.
It isn't what we own that counts.
It's what we've done in life.
The help we've given others that we've met.
Are the feelings deep inside us filled with love or filled
With strife.
Was it worth the toil, worth the work and sweat?
Our life is but a roadway, we each must trod its path,
It's up to us to choose which way is right.
When the final curtain has been drawn and life on earth has passed,
Will those remaining see our trail of light?

Norma Fuhrmann

Part Of Me

You were once a part of me,
That I never did understand.

I see you everyday, but nothing changes,
When your over there and I'm over here,
I remember about the fun we used to have.
Then I remember it was just my imagination.

When I see two people walking, talking, and laughing,
I sit here and wonder - will we ever be like that?
  Didn't think so.
You're over there and I'm over here.

Every morning, I see the sun blooming over
What seems to be tiny ants.
A new day, but the same old us.
You're over there and I'm over here.

I sit here waiting, the clock ticking.
Which seems to the beating of my heart.
Together, as one thing, soon it gets uneven.
Then it stops.
You're over there and I'm over here.

Kelly Olson

Tears Of Fear

Why is it
that I live in tears of fear,
clouds of darkness,
and where the grass is always greener on the other side?

Why, did I do something wrong in a past life
to deserve this sort of punishment?
Or is it my passion
for sweet revenge on those that oppress?

My seas are always murky,
My doors are always closed,
No one ever knocks on my door,
No one ever knows.

My depression is everlasting,
I can't find my own self esteem,
Sadness has taken over my body,
Happiness will never be redeemed.

But wait, I see a ray of light,
Someone is reaching out!
I now have to leave my tears of fear,
and no longer will I pout.

Marie-Reine Velez

In My Dreams

Here you are standing next to me silhouetted by the pale sunlight
that hits you, I stare at you and you stare back at me as if I were
looking at my own reflection, our eyes are locked by each other's
strong gaze, the world has frozen - Not a sound do I hear
No rivers running, no birds chirping, no leaves rustling, no wind
blowing, nothing, then I hear it a heartbeat - But I only hear one
"Why can't I hear your heartbeat?" I asked, but no words came out -
Just silence, our gaze has become even more intense
As I look into your eyes I see all that we had done together
Our first date at Tony's Restaurant, You kissing me goodnight
Us walking in the park and you holding my hand tightly, You and I
at the movies, Us together enjoying a romantic candlelight dinner,
You bent down on one knee
I see you mouth the words, "I love you Rachel, Will you marry me?"
I answer, "Yes, Raymond", then I see myself in front of your grave
"WHY, WHY?" I screamed! Then it all goes blank,
I begin to feel dizzy Red, Purple, Yellow, Green
All the colors spinning around, like a top, inside my head
I fall back, back into your arms and I hear you say, "I love you"
Then it all goes blank as I wake up back in my bed... Alone

Gianna N. Zunino

Untitled

Strong is the man who is not afraid to admit
That he is falling helplessly and that he desperately needs
The support of another

Strong is the man who feels no shame
In shedding a tear for a hurt friend
Or in a beautiful moment

Strong is the man who is not afraid
To commend another for a job well done
Or admit he was wrong to a friend

Strong is the man who needs to be held
And reassured
That he is a beautiful and important being

For strength lives in the heart and in the mind
In those places invisible to the eye
Strength cannot be measured
And knows no inequality

Strength is the integrity of deciding who you are
And holding steadfastly to this ideal self
And never letting anyone take more
Than you are willing to give

Jennifer Lee Morrow

88

Two Seasons

There's something about winter
   that dares to call a midday sun its own.
With bold, cold strokes does winter paint the landscape white,
   to leave in muted glow the night.
This icy reign of terror, that blankets the shivering field,
   now rests in silent beauty, its raging fully spent,
   till weakening, dying, to spring does finally yield.

O blessed spring, her song now sing,
   a hymn of tender promise in pregnant fields of green.
A world forlorn is born anew,
   fresh and glistening as sweet morning dew.
This season of glad winter thaw, enshrined in lenten rite,
   beholds the wakening earth in awe,
   and heralds the rising of summer bright.

Laurie Gaskell Nelson

Paul

What could there be to give more joy?
Than for me to have you - my ten-year-old boy!
When I look at your face I see
A mystical blend of your Daddy and me.
When I gaze into your smile
I see the promise of a man from a child.

If I could, I'd keep you like you are in a bubble.
Always as now - just fun and no trouble.

But I know our days are numbered,
Soon you'll grow to be a man,
Someday into those teeth you'll grow,
Your cow-lick will lay down - I just know,
You'll be taller than me and think of things other than play.
When puberty raises its ugly head and leads you away.

But I know when I get to glory once again I'll see
My ten-year-old boy smiling at me.
Down the endless ski slope we'll go
Sailing together to and fro.

Having you for a son is so much fun!
You're my personal toy - my ten-year-old boy.

Nancy Gregory

Untitled

The shoes are the same from the perennial penny loafer to the favorite
tennis shoe (yes I've even kept the ones that glow in the dark...)
I'm still most at home in my 501(s)...the faded ones that fit like
an old friend though you'll find several of my old stand-by Khakis in
the closet...the ones that have weathered the years...the ones even
an iron can't seem to make respectable; I still wear t-shirts of all
kind...and I've been known to embarrass someone now and then with the
sayings, but I seem to gravitate more these days to my favorite blue
denim or that corduroy shirt that feels so soft to the skin. And the
streaks of grey that are beginning to shine through in my hair...for
now I like the look...they seem to add credibility to thoughts
leftover from my youth...

There is a process to aging that I am seeing gradually and that parts
of me are humored by...I glance in the mirror with my high-top cons,
t-shirt and those incredibly irrelevant jeans with holes in them and I
am somewhat confused...because according to all charts I am halfway
through the life process and I don't even feel old enough to enter the
race yet...

...And then I look at my hands...there is a intricate webbing of lines
beginning..creating a pattern only an abstract artist could understand
delicate weavings of skin wrapped over baby blue veins...like a water
color of my life...pictures I only remember on the hands of old women
hands that betray a lifetime lived when the soul refuses to tell

This is me at 35...

Nell Lindenmeyer

Change

Why are you telling me where I ought to be
Telling me I am equal telling me I am free
Keeping me in chains, putting me on ships
Taking me from my families from across the sea
Forbidding me to adequately learn to read and write
Condoning the raping of women and female children at night
I have a conscious and I have a dream can't you see?
Yes, this is different from what you have planed for me
This country belongs to you and to me
Does this country deserve to be great
You bet it does, time will out live this evil, that is my fate
What is the American conscious and the American dream?
Is our memory equal, imagination dull, equality the same?
Art of life is the art of avoiding pain
Why are you telling me where I ought to be
Your favorite chore is to Take and Take
Trying to make me feel guilty because I want a piece of the stake.
Can't you see the formula created for you and for me
Will be changed.
I will not procrastinate.
Knowledge is Power make no mistake.

Lettie Wright Echols

"Baby Blue"

Baby blue, as the clouded Kingdom which walks the sky,
Swimming deeper than the under water world of Atlantis drowning
out the pain in every tear he cries.
Baby blue, as colorful as pastel one which possesses the talents
Through the hands of creativity, divine, to every stroke in which
brushes upon the medium painting a picture of supremacy
Baby blue, as the ink which compliments the writings in which
my pen seeks nothing but the page, writing until my own tears
stain the paper and wash the ink away
Baby blue, as a stain Glass window that delivers the house of God,
strengthened by the crossing of his son, eighteen inches from
the heart.
Baby blue, as a newly dyed rose which only smells as beautiful
as you are, or only travels as far, as a wish on a shooting star.
Baby blue, as the garment worn by a promising fair lady torn
between a king and a knight, knowing not which way to turn,
until the victor of the fight
Baby blue, as the eyes of a new born child being brought
into this world, cause it will be daddy's little bundle
of joy. Whether it be "Baby blue" or Girl.

Kevin Brian Wright

Dogwood Spring

The dogwood and the redbud dot the hillsides in Kentucky.
Swaying, they herald yet another spring.
I've missed so many springs in Kentucky
I don't want to miss them anymore.
This year, I was there—in May
But I missed it, anyway. May was messy.
It was the same the May we buried Mother.
Just like Daddy, she was "asleep in Christ" when we found her.
Now I can see Mother and Daddy cradling my Mary Ann
Called home on the morning of her birth
Thirty-one years ago—in May.
The poet tells us that April is the cruelest month
And poets tell the truth or they wouldn't have the name.
But most likely T.S. (Eliot)
Had not been to Kentucky—in May.
One day all the past and future springs will be as one
And the dogwood/redbud will bloom again
Blue/green/white/pink
And we will rise again, will love again
In the great beyond of Kentucky—in May.

Laura Beth Hunt Spalding

Memories Of Vermont

Green mountains
Stonewalls
Covered Bridges
Maple trees in sugar orchards
Sunlit meadows filled with strawberries
Cemeteries flag-filled
Lilacs by the armful, every hue
Narrow country roads,
Ponds of shimmering water
Silver Birches, both white and yellow
Blackberries and Raspberries in wild patches
Church spires, pointing upward,
Family reunions
Holiday gatherings at Grandparents's farm
Church camp in Summer, picnics by the wayside
Christmas carolling in Winter
Choir practice on Saturday nights
School programs, special times
Good books, particularly the Book
Snowy winter sports, Summer camps, meeting old friends, making new
Happy events throughout the years
Blessings that have brought us to this special place.

Merrilyn Williams Towne

Battle Scars

Within the fleshly conflict, of the modern man;
stands a tattered soldier, sword gripped in his hand.
Though his companions have all deserted him,
he stands fearless, awaiting command.

For he knows if he lays to rest
he faces his worst oppression;
not peril or pain, but Satan himself
in his most cunning form, temptation.

After many years of battle,
for his mortal soul,
when anguish and death surround him
his eyes hold fast their goal.

Then through the smoke of the battle
he sees a brilliant light.
He lifts his hands in praise.
At last! The end of the fight.

Though others have failed before him,
we now find the strength of this man,
the symbol of his life long war,
the saviours nail-scarred hand.

Gina VanSickle Kelly

Rest In Peace

If only you were here, I would have less fear,
Standing alone with a tear in my eyes telling you "I love you"
while glancing up at the sky! I now only have memories
of you, that doesn't seem like enough, sometimes I think back
to when you were here and it is so tough!!
I want to hug you one last time and let you know your
thoughts are with me all the time.
I could never forget you, how
would it be possible when your
Memories come into my mind, they
become unstoppable.
For God took you home, so as
now you lay alone, we
will join again,
sometime,
but until then I'll
Always have your memories in my mind!!

Geli Nicole Redman

Captain Blue

I saw his eyes and they smiled at me
Sparkling like the sea
Compelled me to go along with him to the land that may never be

His ship was huge, its sails, vast
I feared to step on board
But he beckoned me and so I came
For his eyes held some reward

Once on board his magical ship my spirit longed to be free
To roam the hills, the valleys past, the mountains;... till eternity

I asked his name for I knew not how
He could ever be
A person of the common land whom I had never seen

He said his name was Captain Blue, freedom was his wife
Sailing about the soul in and out
Was the story of his life

I knew right then I had been deceived by the twinkle in his eye
He laughed, I cried, then realized
That my Captain Blue and his world just died.

Lee Ann Chedrick

"You Are My Mother Poem"

These words are my words to express my love. To my mother
on a special day like this. A card would not do, so I
choose to tell my own wishes to you.
   You are my Mother, no matter what you do
   You are my Mother, that makes wishes and dreams
come true.
   You are my Mother, who gave me life.
Life is full of loving, caring, giving and sharing. Life is
Understanding, mentally, physically and emotionally scaring.
Unless you have the good Lords faith and courage to
over look all evil.
   You are my Mother, who know what to do
at all times through and through. I'll always have
extra love in my heart for you. I couldn't wish
for anything better or for worse. I wouldn't dare
divorce you to be frank and true, you're my Mother
and that's true.
   You are my Mother, and mothers knows
best cause I'm a Mother just like you.

Ella Parson

Food Food Food

   Give my sandwich a slice of cheese,
Oh don't forget the hamburger please,
   A little pickle on the side,
some ketchup lettuce a bun and, I'd
Also like a lot of fries,
   A milk shake and one of those little pies.
   A scoop of ice-cream on the side.
After all I ate then I cried,
Maybe I should watch my weight,
After all the food I ate.

I do hope you have it ready
Because I'd really like spaghetti.
A steak with mushrooms if you please,
A salad with some creamy cheese.
Oh, some of that great garlic bread,
And a tasty Sunday with sauce I said.
After all I ate, then I cried,
Maybe I should watch my weight, after all the food I ate.

Why does it have to taste so good.
I'd not eat it if I could.

Beverly Hodgson

My Valentine

You've fulfilled a dream of mine.
You're much more than a Valentine.
It isn't hard for me to say,
I love you, Sweetheart on this day.
I'll always love you, all my life.
You see, my Valentine's my wife

William V. Rush

Chills

Your voice,
Your smile,
Your face,
All send chills
from head to toe,
And I know
That you are
The one that makes
Me feel so
Alive and free
And I only hope
That you feel the same
For me.

Rusty Jay Wilson

Mary's View

I see You bearing Your cross.
Your pain is my pain, too.
My heart aches, my eyes must watch.
There is nothing I can do.

My firstborn, flesh of my flesh,
Your skin by thorns pierced through:
Flowing blood causing weakness;
There is nothing I can do.

You turn to say, "Weep not for me."
Your Word is ever true,
But now my tears cannot cease.
There is nothing I can do.

Jesus, Son of the Most High,
What men have done to You!
Your will to be crucified,
There is nothing I can do.

I cannot bear what is to be!
What other way? I wish I knew.
Do not take my son! Please take me!
But there is nothing I can do.

Phyllis M. Hubbell

The Way

The kindest love, that I have known
Your gentle hands have built.
In all the years, that I have grown
You've helped me through the guilt.

You make the sun, ashamed to shine
The rivers stop to flow.
Poems no longer find a rhyme
While the moon, forgets to glow.

You've taken away insecurities
That always had me down.
I let go of those anxieties
Which used to have me bound.

My greatest gift from up above
God's will, it shall be done
This heart has found its way
  through love.
That only you have won.

Sheila Hayes

Think About It

Even before I knew you, I felt
you with me
All my life you've been there,
waiting
When we first met, we had
met before.
When we first kissed, we had
Kissed before,
When we first loved, we had
loved before,
When we first lived....?

Shelia Gilbreath

Forever In Love

Even though we're far apart
You will always be here
Within my heart.
Even though I made you blue
Somehow I wish that we could
Start anew.
Even though my wish may
Never come true
Remember this I'll Always Love You.

Rose Emanuel

"Best Friends Are Not Always Forever"

When I met you
you were just like me,
we would talk for hours.
Since we'd gotten to know
one another, we began to
spend more time together!
We were starting to think
about high school and
and hoped that we would
never depart, until one
day we did.
We went our separate ways
in high school.
Meeting new friends
was hard to do,
for I was getting
over losing my
best friend.

Sara Renzenbrink

The Sacrificial Lamb

Oh Christ, the sacrificial Lamb,
You knew me even before I am.
Sweet Jesus, precious Son,
the battle rages, but the war is won.
For my sins you were cruelly killed,
and rose in glory, death's joy stilled.
You walked paths I may never see;
You overcame what confounds me.
Lord, You are the way that's true;
gladly, Lord, I follow You.
Precious Jesus, Lord and savior,
Your way is right, the goal is sure.
Humble Son, Glorified King,
Your praise I love to sing.
Your Word was written by God's command.
It shall be my Rock on which I stand.

William C. James

Days

In your room
you remember of days gone by

A special friend
a loving touch or
a first kiss

Those days are gone
and you long for them

You know
they can never come back

That is what makes your childhood
SPECIAL

Everyone has one thing
they like from their childhood

Do you want to know mine
Here it is

I liked it when people
liked me for who I was
They didn't go on gossip

Those are the days
I really miss

Rachel Mehlberg

"Letting Go"

You made me laugh
You made me laugh

We walked together the longest mile

We were friends and lovers too
Yes, hard times us struggled through

A perfect pair you and me
I think our children would agree

I will always love you deep inside
Although your love for me has died

You are the only life I've known
And now I will live my life alone.

Valerie A. Bobenrieth

Dear Lord Almighty

You've been my rock through all my pain.

My strength, my sunshine, in the rain.

And when my world began to crumble
  you held me so I wouldn't stumble.

You came to me with open arms
  you filled my soul to make me strong.

It's still so hard to let him go
  to sit and wait time goes so slow.

I know your love will set him free
  and in your kingdom he will be.

My father's life on earth was touched
  by everyone he loved so much.

Good-bye my dear father, until
  I see you again.

Shirley Carver

Once In A Lifetime Moment

Far across the waters
you have gone to a desert land
days and days of labor
in the burning sands
sleepless nights aching feet
Charlie horses in the legs
fatigue - unplanned meals
and blisters on your hands
imagination plays a part
in helping me to see
all of the things you do
each day - out there in the heat
I see your smiling face
beautiful eyes
and dimples appear as you smile
to think of me
but, there will be a
once in a lifetime moment
when you come back home to me.

Ruth A. Myers

The Scars Within...

Like a reoccurring dream
You can't stop dreaming
Like a memory
You can't stop remembering
Like a traumatic experience
You can't stop experiencing
An endless pain
You can't stop feeling
The scars within will never let you go.
The scars within will ruin your soul.

Rosa Maria Santiago

An Easter Poem

You are my best friend,
You are the light in my life.
I hope God takes away
All of your strife.

He that gives new life
Has given you a chance to
Put all of your worries aside
And become renewed!

As spring flowers start to appear
And their fragrances linger in the air
Know that you're a rose
Soft, smooth and fair.

The time has come
For you to bloom.
So wash away your worries,
And your gloom.

Remember I'll always be there.
I will always be by your side.
Take what you need from me,
And become beautiful inside.

Valerie Bolen

Summer

Sunny days, blue skies,
White flowers, bird cries,
Green grasses swaying there,
A day like this is very rare!

Crystal waters shimmer and shine,
Buzzing bees flutter and whine,
The yellow sun in a glow,
Summer breezes lazily flow.

Sayeh Nikpay

A Memory

A memory is what
you are just another
whisper in the wind.

A memory is what you
are just another toy
I outgrew.

A memory is what you
are just another ship
that didn't make it
through the storm.

A memory is what you
are and what you'll always be.

Stephanie Tison

Shadow

Standing alone,
Yet I am not.
The shadow stands beside me.
The picture full of black -
Only to be seen like that.
The naked eye cannot make out
figures or features.
The shadow moves in my direction,
but does not feel.
The shadow doesn't know love
from hate.
As dull as it may be -
I'd rather be the shadow,
than be me.

Robyn Krasko

Gone

Why? Why did he have to go?
Yes, he did let me know.
He went, went away, me praying
to God that he'll come back today
he left but shall return than my
heart shall no longer burn.
Gone, to God knows where I'm
wondering will he take me there?
I don't want to believe that he's
gone, for I try not to feel so alone
He's gone, bye-bye, and now all I
can do is cry
He's gone, and not too far,
but he'll always be my shining star.
He's my guy all I want to know
is why did he have to go?

Quintina Craven

Dreams

Late at night I fall asleep,
without a sound, not even a peep,
I dream of you and soundly sleep.
Oh how I wish you were here with me.

Your body close, your mind asleep,
that's when you look so much at peace.

I'm hoping that you dream of me,
even in your somberest sleep.

Your touch, your smell,
your warm embrace,
the picture of you I can't erase.
The love I feel so very deep,
will never, ever, ever sleep...

Valerie Carr

Justice

In this world of
wrong and right, right
at times seems all so
wrong and wrong at
times seems all so
right so how does
Justice really work.
Let the wrong go
home lock the right
up tight. It's confusing
to me for I cannot
see what's right what's
wrong, guess we got to
be strong so maybe
someday the harder
we pray we'll all see
the light of justice.

Tameka Wells

The Camp No One Came Out Of...

You could see the fear
Wound with confusion
Children crying people dying
Bodies falling limp
Lined up for miles
They all knew what laid ahead
Nowhere to run nowhere to hide
The fear was building deep inside
Their hearts began to race as they
came to the door.
Memories of time that's past
And this the most horrid would
be their last.
Stepping inside a darkened room
Feeling nothing but sorrow
Because for them there's no tomorrow

Shannon Bidinger

Favorite Things

Light colored bonnet
worn with wear,
once covered someone's
long, soft hair.

Patches sewn together with utmost care,
stitched to the time of a fiddle,
stitched to the time of a fiddle.

Hook once busy making rugs
pulling fabric through the canvas
with a tug, tug, tug.

Embroidery hoop tan and smooth,
through which busy fingers did move.
Pretty stitches and colorful threads,
made into pictures, verses and rhymes.
Treasures, soft and worn with time.
All things old are beautiful,
if they are precious to you,
if they are precious to you.

Rachel Elizabeth Grewe

Life

Moments passed
we watched
Clocking time untouched
longing for each to last
Printing pictures left unfinished

Patricia K. Hudson

The Beauty Of Love

There's a beauty of love, and it lies
within the heart and you don't know
when it happens, or where it gets its start.

But that beauty of love will always
become greater when you reach for his
arms like a big alligator

He will tell you he loves you and you
will say 'I know' you wrap
your arms around him just like snow.

You look deep into his eyes, what do you
see? You say 'You're cheating on me'
You slap him on the face, he says
'It's not true!' But do you believe
him? — you always do!

Tammy Antonucci

In Praise Of The Mother

She sits in her chair
With you in her arms.
Do you know her now?
Why cause her harm.

Mine is still needed,
She's like a best friend.
When times start to fall,
On her I depend.

And I hope she knows
My love is always there.
I don't say much
But I do care.

And as you sit
Alone in that chair
Think of her for once
Cause she did her share.

Yours may not be mine,
But her love is true.
Nothing can ever beat
What a mother can do.

William Hasan

Don't Let Me Hurt Your Tender Heart

Don't let me hurt your tender heart
With words I do not mean
The light of love that's in your eyes
Is easy to be seen
Promises I've made to you
Are only fleeting dreams
Made by a man in autumn years
To a young girl in her teens

The love I had for many years
Was taken away from me
And left me a life of loneliness
An empty memories

Then you appeared and gave back to me
My youth and all its dreams
It young delights and starlit nights
And all the romantic schemes

But the light of dawn has wakened me
To the fact that we must part
For I don't wish to make you dream
And hurt your tender heart.

Philip E. Cvach

Uncolored Eyes

He was born to the earth
With uncolored eyes
He could say "I love all"
Without telling lies.
For you see he'd not noticed
The difference of skin
The thin outer shell
That we're hiding within.
He made no distinction
Between white and black,
Or yellow or red
All stood back to back.
Some gave him their sorrow
They thought it was sad
That an uncolored world
Must be driving him mad.
But he shocked all of them
Was ahead at the end
Because each one he met
Was truly his friend!

Teri Seeger

Words Of Cheer

Write down a word or two
With thoughts turned in on you.
The things going on inside
We always try to hide.
But a word going to a friend,
May cause his heart to unbend.
It may help someone sad,
May cause him to be glad.
We never know when a word of cheer
May be what he longs to hear.
A smile, a word, can be pure gold
Could be worth treasure untold.
So don't shut yourself away
Go out and help someone today.

Reta McLain

Suddenly Strangers

I watched you
With the eyes of a stranger,
One suddenly alienated
From a friend.

I felt the distance
As you kept on walking,
Until you were out of touch,
Out of reach, out of view.

I called your name silently
And willed you to return.
But you could not hear
And I wasn't sure I cared, anymore.

Sandra Dinnall

Where Go Dreams

Where go dreams - there go I
    With gladsome cry.
Pass the rainbow pie.

Where go dreams - there go I
    Sneaking out on the sly,
Leaving my tears to dry.

Where go dreams - there go I
    In the meadow of your mind to lie
    Amid the wild flowers, sigh.

Poet Pierritz

Courthouse On The Square

I like a courthouse on the square
With columns here and turrets there.
It lends a charm that is complete
To each small town with county seat.
Of sturdy brick or hand hewn stone,
Its dominance is clearly shown.
The wealth of history found therein
Records the deeds of fearless men;
Of strong and rugged pioneer
Who willed to us a land so dear.
This is a place of beauty rare,
A county courthouse on the square.

Virginia Blakemore Moody

Will You Be Mine?

I think about you all the time
Wishing you could be mine
And I swear, I will be there
I know I like you very much
So please keep in touch
O darlin' you look so fine
You are just my kind
I know it's that time of year
For a lot of people to fear
But if you say yes, it will be fate
And you will be my perfect mate
Roses are red, violets are blue
O please say yes
To this question I am going to ask you
Please baby be mine
Please, O please, be my valentine?

Robert J. Bialk

My Special Friend

One day after spring.
Why did the telephone let out a ring?
The life had come to an end.
The life of my special friend.

I ran out the door.
To try to ignore.
That my friend's life ended
Only because a car bended.

As I cried and cried
One question come to mind
Why not me?
Why couldn't I have died?

Ursula A. Johnson

"The Pow'r Of God"

O'Lord the great and awesome God,
Whose mighty pow'r to save;
you give us life - that we may live;
To serve you and be brave.

Though trials and disaster be,
An aching heart and tragedy;
If we believe - we will receive;
What-e'er we ask of thee.

The fight is fierce the battle long,
But victory will prevail;
You give us strength - to carry on;
And so we cannot fail.
My heart is fixed for heaven bound,
All obstacles removed;
Cause Jesus Christ - my savior;
Has made my life improved.

Roald Constantine Fraites

Ancient Of Days

Where then hides the childish sprite
Whose laughter warmed my winter nights?
Come back again and sing for me
    Of summertime
        Of being free.

My eyes are tired, my fingers numb
The wrath of age has stilled my tongue
And yet within my heart I yearn
To dance again amidst the fern.

Where then hides the childish sprite
Whose laughter warmed my winter nights?
Who taught this blind man how to see
    and how to love
        and how to be?

Susan Imbs-Brewer

The Dying Soul

You
Who are you
Fantasy reality terror
Punishing destroying
Stay buried!
You knew but never told
What did you say?
What are you that lives - that kills
Thoughts of endless darkness
Words stained of flesh and blood
I do not know - and - can not
And stand less to know -
Again

Patricia L. Hinojosa

"Searching For Tomorrow"

I've been searching for tomorrow
  While today just slips away;
And I find myself looking back
  on my yesterdays

I've seen dewdrop frothing fountains
  in each drop, there lived a dream;
I've scaled the highest mountains
  but have forgotten where I've been

I've walked a hundred miles alone
  each step, a story untold;
I've ridden breakers to the shores
  in search of pirate's gold

I've sung a range so broad and loud
  each note just set me free;
I've read the myths of life and love
  but the truth was hard to see

I'll stop running towards tomorrow
  It'll come soon enough, and then;
I'll remind myself the place to look
  for happiness — is within

Sheryl Smith

What Could Have Been There

As the world turns gray
  When he awakes.
We just sit there
  And watch the hate,
We can't do anything
  But stare and
Think about,
  What could have been there.

Terra Rushing

Feelings

Tears rolling down my eyes
While thinking of you leaving.
Trying to be strong for you
Which was ever so deceiving

Staring blankly across the room
Not knowing how to start
Picking up the pieces
That once made up my heart

You appear to me in a dream
As I close my eyes to sleep
I realize you're not really here
So once again I weep

Thinking of that final time
When we can come together
And you promise me with all your heart
That you will stay forever

Trinicia Strickland

Out Beyond The Blue Horizon

Out beyond the blue horizon
Where I wandered as a boy
Sweet dreams followed me
As I roamed all day in joy.

Seeking for beauty in the wood land
Where birds sang so joyously,
I listened in wonder all the day
As I dreamed of days to come.

When I would wander from home
To roam in places far away
To seek the spot where I'd live
Out beyond the blue Horizon.

Wm. Carl Smith

I Know It's There

I've been to a place
  where I can roam about.
Just be myself
  inside and out.

This place is magical
  that I can see.
I know it's there
  but how can that be?

I need no map
  I do not care.
I know it by heart
  I know it's there.

This place has wonders
  all its own.
I do not know them
  but I'm not alone.

This is a place
  that no one else will see.
But I do not care
  it's inside of me.

Yvonne Amiott

Untitled

Life is a game
That costs $2.98
  plus tax.
. . . The instructions
  are extra.

Yvonne DeLaine-Vermillion

Transformation

For reasons inexplicable,
Whenever I'm with you,
There is a transformation
Of everything in view.

A softening veil of loveliness
Envelops all I see
And imperfections are obscured
Because you are with me.

They say this is a transient state
Engendered by the heart,
Susceptible to changing whim,
No stronger than each part.

But if it should evaporate
With cruel reality,
I'll readjust my French beret
And soothe my soul with "C'est la Vie."

Virginia W. Loehlein

From My Eyes

Let me be your voice
When you can't talk.
Let me be your legs,
When you can't walk.

I will be there to help you
With everything you say and do.
There is nothing in this world
I love more than you.

For my life without you
Would be full of sorrow.
There would be no
Meaning for my tomorrow.

In sickness and in health
Are the vows we said,
Because "Together"
We have a long life ahead.

You are going through a difficult time
Together we can make it through
Just remember-with all my heart
I'll always love you.

Terri S. Carter

Who Knows!

Lord!
When I die,
Where I'll go?
Oh!
Who knows!
What you'll do,
In remaining years?

Socorro Dias Do Rosario

Savior

  There once was a time...
when I debated the question of life.
  Could I?
Would I?
  Should I?
But then like a bright beam...
  of sunlight you entered my life.
Securing my existence....
  giving me a reason to live,
Thank you.

Tiffany Lynn Aldridge

"Dreams"

I slowly wait for close of day
When dreams will carry me away
From the world so dark and bleak
All is fine when I'm asleep
I wake up to find despair
Problems mounting everywhere
My pillow is A mass of tears
A product of my wasted years
In my dreams I am a king
I'm not afraid of anything
I feel the joy of holding close
All the things I've wanted most
Suddenly at break of day
My precious dreams fade away
I'm forced to face reality
Your not really here with me
When we meet you walk on by
A million times each day I die
Your unaware your mine to keep
In my dreams while I'm asleep

Vernie Elizabeth Hoskins

Question

I ask myself these questions,
What will life be like?
I ask myself these questions,
In the middle of the night.

I ask these questions
To the one inside.
I ask these questions
Against the flowing tide.

I ask questions
Of the one who knows.
I ask questions
to reason out the lows.

I question
time itself.
I question
inside myself.

Question
things
Question.

Tiare Greene

Just A Little Poem For You

Words really can't describe
what I really want to say, but
some things just stand in my way.

When I look into your eyes all
I see is tomorrow and I would
do anything to spend tomorrow with you.

I realize in my heart that tomorrow
is meant for you and only you.

Only if we didn't go our own
ways. Only if things didn't
block the way tomorrow would
have been just me and you.

Tina Scott

Truth And Life

I tell the truth
what he needs to
hear, I tell him
the truth but it
is a lie

If I only knew
what to do or
say. If I
tell the truth, he
wants the lie

Truth and a lie,
love and a hatred
what to do and
what not to do
truth or lie?

Shannon Thomas

Untitled

Time washes over me
Wearing away
Rough edges
Bits and pieces
In the out with the tide
Making me smoother
The rest to drift off
Forgotten.....

Susan Falo

Passages

Through a passage of the night,
We see them.
All bandaged up,
So captive,
Yet so free.
They speak a different language,
Yet we don't notice,
How savage they can be.
They are going on a voyage,
Don't worry they will manage.
They are very creative,
Yet they dare not show.
Their knowledge might be negative,
But we don't notice,
How wrong we are.
We give them little justice,
And they give us no trouble.
They are lost souls,
Just passing through the night.

Renee Lynn Schneider

Forever Friends

We joke
We poke
And we make fun of our folks.

During rainy showers
or by sunny flowers
we will be forever friends.

We talk on the phone
and listen to each other
moan and groan.

We talk about boys
clothing and toys.

Through thick and thin
there till the very end
forever friends
You and Me - Best friends forever

Tiffany Hilliard

Texas Timex

The holy dew of morning
washes away the longing
and sleepless nights
And blends into the blaze
of daily living.
The encyclopedia of sweat shirts
declare their views and opinions
as they march and dart
Through the maze of humanity
and the hum of traffic as it
winds into the distance,
bearing the angry, unknown faces
That peer blankly back
from speeding vehicles.
The Texas Timexes worn on
waving wrists keep violent time
to the rise and fall
of the volume and commentary,
As radio-listening drivers
talk back to Rush Limbaugh.

Ruby Q-Petersen

Wee Baby Girl

A wee baby girl with a small brown curl,
Was born to these arms one night
When I looked down on her
There was no other sight.

She was pink and oh so warm
With beautiful brown eyes
When I held her close to me
She gave small sighs.

Now she is grown and I am so proud
Whenever I can, I boast on her loud
Her achievements are great, her life's
walk so true.
This from your mother, says "I love you"

R. Charlene Pooley

The Night Does Fall

How silently the night does fall
upon the light of day,
The moist darkness secures the earth
the forenoon parts away.

The wind it whispers a melody
a frail and breathless tune,
The evening's only life is sorrow
its only comfort gloom.

The charcoal pavements glisten
from the street light's single glow,
Broken paths of the day lie hidden
within the mist below.

Yet still there is much beauty
in what the blackness holds,
Mere secrets of a new day beginning
until the eve unfolds.

How silently the night does fall
upon the light of day,
The earth it brings forth the dawn
the darkness drifts away.

Roesther Preston

Untitled

The moon shone palely
upon the glistening snow
as the eagle wept.

The sunset quivered
as the sea silently slipped
into blissful sleep.

The wind laughingly
tore through the silent valley
as the people cringed.

Majestic mountains
sprawled along the shore flowing
into the pounding sea.

The red dragon crouched
silent above the valley
and the people slept.

Raissa M. Hall

A View Of Life

The morning dew was heavy,
Upon the fresh mown hay;
The birds were singing a gay song,
In the trees beside the way.

There came a lad along the path,
With a fresh cut fishing pole;
He was walking happily along,
Down to the old fishing hole.

'Twas a cheerful, carefree day,
Everything was delightful and bright;
The cares and troubles of life,
Were nowhere in sight.

Yet life in all reality isn't so free,
For along the path there are sorrows;
Their presence troubles us every day,
And robs us of the joys of the tomorrows.

Still our Lord watches from above,
Ready to share His loving care;
He keeps giving us grace in abundance,
Along life's pathway everywhere.

Will H. Havens

War

A bird flies in the sky
unseen by human eyes.
It watches
the destruction
on earth.
Soldiers fighting
children crying
people dying.
For what reason?
War.
Bombs exploding,
guns loading,
firing at the enemy.
Why?
Must it be this way?
No.
We chose it to be this way.
And now we must fix it.

Rachel Karpf

The Library

A safe place...
Unhurried and inviting
Away from chaos...
Ordered and beautiful,
Welcomed always.

A warm place ...
Abounding with books;
Books to...
Kindle a mind,
Spark an interest,
Ignite the imagination.
There for the offering.
Fuel a fantasy...
Ablaze with reading...

A powerful place...
Resourceful yet reminiscent,
Nourishing and now.
Enter and enjoy.
The first steps,
To a BETTER LIFE.

E. Anne Crow

God's Art

The majestic mountains
 towering high,
Snow-capper peaks
 touching the sky,
Lush green forests
 below timberline,
Pines standing tall
 on steep inclines.

In the mountains,
 lakes abound,
The coldest, clearest water
 ever to be found.
The rough and tumbling rivers rush;
Over the great rocks they gush.

The beauty of the flowers so fair,
Their fragrance so overpowering and rare,
The air so sweet and pure,
Heaven is near; that's for sure.

Ronnie Rae Davis

Little One, Where Have You Gone?

Little one, where have you gone?
 Tousled head, bright eyes
Chubby arms, held me tight
 Early morn, in the night
Saying, mum, that's my mum!

Childhood play, grade school days
 Sturdy legs, running free.
Boyish grin, impish heart
 Having fun, teasing me.
Little one, where have you gone?

Sister's chum, high school fun
 Patience test, teachers pest
Looking up, scolding you
 Wishing now that you were two.
Little one, where have you gone?

My heart falls, service calls
 Tearful eyes, silent cries
School clothes shed, empty bed
 Silent room, letters soon
Overseas, prayers please little one, where
have you gone?

Velma Bailey Nealy

Death Of A Newborn Soul

A blood curdling scream of death,
Took her first and last breath.
Taken straight from her mothers womb,
Far away to a cold dark tomb.
It was destined from the start,
That it would break her heart.
A chill ran through her blood,
And she was left in a puddle of mud.
Buried six feet under the ground,
All her family gathered around,
To gaze with wondrous teary eyes,
At the dark and grim skies.
The clouds roared, and the rains fell,
With only a sad story to tell,
Of a little baby that died,
Because her mother took liqueur inside.

Pamela S. Oslund

Run Back

Run back to Jesus,
 to the shelter
Of His arms.
 It is not He
Who has abandoned us...
 It is we
Who have abandoned Him.
 Run back! Run back!

Priscilla Davenport

The Pot Belly Sub

You want a pot bellied pig
To sit on a rug by the fire.
But to get something like that
You may have to wish on a star.

So this spotted Pudgy Piglet
Comes to take its place.
He waddles and oinks and his nose
Moves making a cute little face.

He won't upset the bag of trash,
Or bother your rabbit or dog.
He will always stay little and cute
And won't grow up to be a hog.

He can sit on a rug by the fire,
Or on your lap if you please.
And he is always available
To receive a hug or a squeeze.

And if someday you get lucky
And get a live pot bellied pig,
Please don't forget little Pudgy or
The hole he filled so it wasn't so big.

Roberta Van Note

If You Could Only See

If you could only see
This pain inside of me
I hurt so bad, but I can't get mad
I trusted you once again
With everything within
My mistake, I shouldn't have given in
If you could only see
You are my everything
It took so long
My denial so strong
I finally believe we are meant to be
Now and forever...until eternity

Tara J. Cox

Smile

A thought for you
To ponder this eve
A thought I hope
A smile will leave
Your inside world
Is so very confused
With so much to see
And so much to do
If you look for happiness
In small simple things
An answer you'll find
And a smile it'll bring
For you dear friend
I hope this is true
For a frowning face
It just isn't you

Peter Judkins

Life

To look inside the eyes of fear,
    To dance within the flame.
We all know the end is near,
    Though we don't know its name.

To live life to the fullest
    Is not dwelling on the past,
But looking to the future,
    On every question that is asked.

To dream of peace on earth,
    Is a comfort we all know,
But you have to come to reality,
    That's the place that we all go.

Life has many ups and downs,
    Many places to explore,
But there is always something better,
    Just beyond the farthest door.

Shelby Mitchem

No More Tears

Did you ever look into the light
    through your tears?

The glistening of gold
    and crystal streams glowing.

One day as I cried,
    I looked up to Heaven.

God showed me the place
    where no more tears will be.

As I stood there, tears streaming,
    my face began gleaming.

I could see through my tears
    the place I will be:

The gold and the glitter,
    where nothing will wither,
And peace will overcome me.

Now I don't need to cry,
    as I say my goodbyes,
For my God has comforted me.

Wanda Cooper

Wild Horses

Gallops free
through the sunset
out to the sea.

Beautiful tail and mane
flowing through the air
with no rein.
Wild young mare
running with the stallions,
running by the thousands.
Why isn't there anymore?
What are they running for?
Running with all the glory.
That is the end of this story.

Robin Douglas

Rose-Colored Glasses

I look at the world
Through rose-colored glasses;
I don't see skin color
Or social classes.

We all have a purpose
We're all in the plan,
The need to be loved
Is the spirit of man.

I won't judge you
So don't judge me;
I love what you are
And all you can be.

Believe in yourself
And trust in the masses,
Look at the world
Through rose-colored glasses.

Susan M. Zaborsky

What Have I Left To Give?

What have I left to give?
Thou you have taken it all.
My Love, My Heart, My Soul.

What have I left to give?
Though my mind is empty.
No more fears, No more pain,
No more sorrow. For those
who long the affection.

What have I left to give?
Though you have now taken
my eyes. No more sights of
beauty, no more sight of hate,
No more sights of you. No more
tears to cry.

What have I left to give?
Will thou find me? I'm wondering
around in this field of confusion.
Tell me, and I will listen.
What have I left to give?

Tera Scott

The Test

Of all the things that
Remain to be seen?
Only one thing remains
The most pure still
Of all that be,
What is it?

Johnny Blackpool

Another Land

It's evil and it's waiting
This burden to us all
With its tiresome pounding
To the skull and to its walls
It burns with pain
This pounding to the brain
And it goes on
Like the night moves on
Into the next day
With its certain glance
And gaping stare
That makes you stop
And wish you weren't there

In another land
In another place
It wouldn't matter how you felt
But take a look at what you missed
When you were looking over your shoulder
At another lands disenchanted disorder

Timothy Taylor

Peace On Earth And God Bless America

Times are rather different and strange.
Things are not the same.
In all may we not change.

In past times we used to read the bible
and pray in our schools.
We use to talk of God's blessings
and thank him every day.

Lets get back to more peace
on earth and God bless America.
It's what our land needs today.
Men sit and ponder, discuss
and try to find solutions.

But what we need is more
peace on earth and more
God bless America.

As I watch my children sleep
I wonder what their future
will be. So I will pray for
more peace on earth and
more God bless America.

Sharon S. Dolan

Fairies

Fairies love to dance and sing
    they bring smiles to our faces.
They're with everyone and everything
    in all the earth's places.
They're in the flowers and the trees
    they're in the leaves and stone.
They're with the butterflies and bees
    and us when we are alone.
They love to hide in a hollow log
    and under the mushroom, too.
They can ride on a frog
    they love to misplace your shoe.
Around the fire they sit at night
    they want us to know their ways.
So our lives can be happy and light
    with peace and happiness to fill our days.

Sandra K. Skidmore

"In Winter"

These are the dreary days.
These are the weary days.
February, why are you so long,
While being so short?

Did I hear a robin chirp?
Or is my longing soul over-eager
To hear what is not there?
Do I see buds where there are none,
Or green grass under the ice and snow?

Oh spring, you are so sweet,
you take so long.
Let me be patient for just a little
while yet.
Winter, you are charming with
your first snow,
But why must you over-stay your
welcome?
Please go!

Ruth C. Wagener

Through The Eyes Of An Eagle

Through the eyes of an Eagle
there's the look of despair.
For what once was his domain
now he must share.

Man has moved in on him
and left him with less.
He now woefully searches
for a place for his nest.

As he soars through the sky
aimlessly searching below,
through the eyes of an Eagle
there's nowhere to go.

So we must remember
When we're building our towns,
Not to take over
his sacred grounds.

And maybe, just maybe
if we do our best,
Through the eyes of an Eagle
he'll do the rest.

William C. McDaniel

"My Love"

The one I love is very fine.
There's no doubt that he's my valentine.

The way he looks into my eyes,
Makes me get all tongue-tied.

When we go out and have some fun,
We call each other honeybun.

Oh, I love him with all my heart.
And I'll make sure we'll never part.

Thuy Nguyen

Peace

Peace is not within the rocks,
The winds, the waters or city blocks.

The birds nor fish nor even mountains,
Can have the peace that's found in
fountains.

Of living waters from God on high
who puts all the peace within you
and I.

Ryan Grusecki

Color Is Only Skin Deep

With the depth of my heart
There's a passion burning inside
To stop all this fighting, and hate
So together we can stand side by side

Don't just sit there in your chair
Wishing this problem will go away
For if we do nothing
The color lines are here to stay

Your skin may be white
Mine may be brown
But that gives you no reason
For you to put me down

We're all brothers and sisters
Though you may not seem to care
But I would risk my life for you
Would you even take that dare?

Whether you're white, black, brown or blue
I don't care about the color of your skin
Because we all need to look amidst the person
  we see
And search for the person within

Shereen C. Rabara

Shirley May

First, Daddy's girl,
Then wife and mother,
No time for any other.
Who can know then,
Upon the morrow
When days of laughter
Turn to sorrow,
That God above
Still sends his love
In ways unknown.

Who can see
the anguished heart
Or feel the hurt within,
But one who knows
The one that's prayed
for healing to begin.
When upon my knees,
To God I went
'Twas Shirley May,
Whom God hath sent.

Robert W. Murphy

The Moon Is Silver

The Moon is Silver,
The Sun is Gold,
And Dewdrops are Diamonds,
Or so I've been told.

The sky above is sapphire blue,
And violets have an amethyst hue,
Floating clouds bear a pearly sheen,
While grassy slopes show emerald green.

And here the rose wears ruby red,
Near tiger lily's orange head.
The buttercup, a topaz shade,
Nods in the breeze the wind has made.

Bend down low,
Or look up high,
There's a gladsome world,
Beneath the sky!

Sigrid Purer

The Crooked Mile

The mysteries of life are many
The ways are never clear
And I find myself on a lonely
Road, wishing you were near.

My heart cries out "I am no island"
I want you here to hold.
My head retorts "you can be strong,
You can be brave, be bold!"

Our lives have become entangled
And I cannot surely say why
But I know, for me, it feels right
And of this I would not lie.

So on the road of life
We'll take a short reprieve
And I'll be yours and you'll be mine
Until it's time to leave.

And when we've gone our separate way's
I'll think of you with a smile
And remember how you helped me
Walk, that lonely crooked mile.

Suzanne D. Kaczor

Dreaming

Floating along in the land of dreams,
  The things of yesterday
Come drifting through my mind and seem
  So real in every way.

Dreaming of days when life was gay
  And everything was bright,
And all our cares were driven away —
  That's what brings delight.

Oh! to relieve those happy hours
  That once were mine to enjoy,
But now are just my thoughts in power,
  Which no one can destroy.

Vivian Keene

The Silence Of Lonely

Have you felt
The sting of a belt
A hand of a slave
A lock of hair from a brave
Or the silence of the lonely

Have you tasted
The things that you wasted
A rotten apple pie
A dirty lie
Or the silence of the lonely

Have you smelt
The leather of your daddy's belt
A stinky sock
A rusty old lock
Or the silence of the lonely

Have you been
The evil person who did the sin
A nightmare in real life
A shiny sharp knife
Or the silence of the lonely

Suzi Hodovanic

Sudden Chill

The wind caresses my face;
the static of a million souls
brushes my hair and taps the inner
boundaries of my mind

Strong as that of the seven seas
a rush of excitement runs down my spine
It tightens and bends
yet freely accepts in full
all energy

It explodes!

My entire body grabs for
portions of a rage
that moves thoughts
I have in my head
I question them for a moment
then realize...

God is with me and I am in love

Stephen Daum

The Sea

The sea can be calm
The sea can be rough
The more I go on,
The more I learn
   the tide always changes
The waves crash against
   the sides of the boat
The dark of the storm
   keeps light at bay.
But I must go on
The silence drives me insane
The voices comfort and cheer me
The more I go on,
   the more I learn.

Wendy Vetter

Rainy Daze

Every once in awhile, I feel
   the real need for a rainy day
Time to be blue - melancholy too,
   time to be grateful it's gray.

Dark days, I find, are good ones
   for turning and tuning out;
For world watching through a window
   wondering what it's all about!

As time flows in rivers of hours
   with each wavelet I'll feel better.
I'll heal my hurts in a teacup
   and wrap my woes in a sweater.

I have used a day that is stormy
   to quiet down and be all alone;
To march to no other's drum beat
   but set to a pace of my own.

I've relished rain rich moments
   spent packing my burdens away
Freeing up room for the rainbows
   and space for the sunshine next day.

Renee M. Miller

Storm At My Window

This morning when I awoke
The rain was crying at my window,
While the wind shook the house in scorn.
Awake awake it seemed to cry,
The storm is a thing of beauty
Come watch the wave tops fly.
Catch the breath of the gale
Dance with me on the beach
Hide behind a dune
I will search every cranny,
Scour your mind thought free.
Stay till I vent my fury
And hurry off to the east,
Next time you hear me calling
Or rattling your window pane,
Be quick to answer my summons
And I will come again and again.

Robert Slayter

on either aisle

on either aisle of
the political spectrum,
politics takes thinking.
every issue that comes
forth reason must prevail.

reason with measured thought;
what is the best for
all concerned. unselfishness
must start with the heart
down deep inside, no matter

what side of the aisle we're on.
politics takes thinking—
though voices raise
and shouts are heard, it's
reason that still must prevail.

reason with goodness,
for all the world,
reason and freedom to be
understood on either
side of the aisle

e. p. frasure

"Snowfall"

Hush and hear the silence;
The peaceful solitude.
So many drifting flakes;
The Earth cannot elude.

They quickly come down upon us;
We at times are not aware.
For heaven opens up its doors;
They flutter through the air.

Consuming each branch and tree limb;
A scene of angelic white.
The world we knew outside our door;
Will be blanketed tonight.

The reverence of its beauty;
Cannot from my lips be known.
For words could do no justice;
Through eyes it must be shown.

As you watch out your window;
And the stately event unfolds.
Hush and hear the silence;
A silence that is so bold.

Wanda Mizner

Of Wind And Rain

The wind plays the song,
The only one who knows it,
Plays it.
The leaf, the branch, twig and trunk
Are all twined
With an elusive spirit
With which the wind plays
The rain, the sun, the sky
Play along with the wind's sweet harp
The sun's Rasta drum.
The Koto of the sky
The bittersweet voice of the rain.
If you listen at smoky dawn
You may hear their music like fireworks
Flashing flowers
And fountains
If you listen closely at twilight,
You will hear the pulsing,
The heart beat of the wind.

Zoe Savitsky

Untitled

The sky is shiny.
The ocean gleams,
No one speaks,
But watches the whale disappear.
Down deep he goes,
No one knows where,
With grace and beauty, it swiftly
goes deep into the ocean.
His family waits he tells of us,
And up he comes for all of us to see,
The Beauty and grace of all the family.

Serena Shaw

The Watching Owl

  In the still of
the night the owl hoots.
It's a mysterious hoot to me,
but still it sends a
special message to the
other wild life owls.
For it's a warning to hide quickly.
So every owl family
goes into their tree trunk
home and waits until they're
sure the coast is clear,
but it's not yet, for now
the watching owl has been
caught by the hunters.
And again he gives a long hoot
to say goodbye to friends
and to his family, that's
the last any wild life
creature will see him.

Rachel Gregory

"Best Friend"

I have a best friend,
She's really cool.
We have lots of things in common,
For one we hate school.
We do things together,
We're there for each other.
We like the same stars,
Keanu Reeves is ours.
And our friendship will never end,
She will always be my friend.

Michelle Marie Deveraux

Nature's Beauty

Out in the county where I live.
The music of nature you
can always hear.
The hum of the bees
The wind in the trees
and the rippling waters
flow by,
And late at night when
all is still, you can hear
the call of the whippoorwill,
the grass is so green, the
sky is so blue, even when
it's raining it refreshes you
when the sun is shining
its rays.
You can see nature's beauty
in them too.

Ruby M. White

The Soddie

American Fever!
The lure of the West,
a soddie,
hard work,
a test for the best.

Indians -
weather -
and many a bug,
Small Pox,
Cholera -
many graves were dug.

Tough and bitter,
Rugged and rough,
Yet the Pioneers faith was enough....
To brave the storms,
in a Soddie.

Patry Denton

An Angel's Promise

Now I lay me down to sleep,
The Lord He took my soul to keep.
I went so sudden, yet not afraid,
For all my sins the Lord had paid.
Way beyond the sky so blue,
My eyes watch over each of you.
In your heart I'll always be,
Someday soon you're sure to see.
Heaven knows not the nights so dark.
The trees and flowers never grow stark.
I stand by the gates of pearl so tall,
And patiently wait for one and all.
While at my Savior's feet I stay,
Trust in Him to guide your way.
So as the skies one day will part,
Your journey upward you shall start.
And here we'll stay with wings on high,
Never again to say good-bye.

Susan Allen-Otterness

Still

It's been years, yet your memories
    still here
It fills my heart
Where there should be a place
for a new start

Vera Midgette

"Our Friend"

Give us love and laughter,
The kind that friendship brings;
Someone to share our happy times,
And the silly, daily things.

Someone we can care for,
And worry they're okay;
And pray for them each night we sleep,
And laugh with them each day.

Give us the kind of friend,
Who feels comfort in our home;
To share the joy our daughter brings,
And relax when we're alone.

One who doesn't mind,
Our "messy little dream",
And things like rolling in the yard,
And obnoxious little screams.

We're happy she returns again,
For a rollicking good time;
Our friend's a little "worse for wear",
But her smile is always fine.

Veronica Lynn Lee

Past To The Future

On a beautiful night in June,
    The jukebox was playing a tune.
The club was filled to the brim,
    When I sat down next to him.
We talked and laughed a lot
    Till time almost came to a stop.
We danced and reveled all night,
    And the future looked oh so bright.
The next day we played in the sun,
    Listened to tapes and had fun.
When night rolled around again
    I knew I had met my best friend.
That friendship turned into love,
    Which I felt was blessed from above.
The road has been rocky and long,
    But my love will always be strong.
To the four winds he did roam,
    Now I wait for his return home.

Patricia A. Marchesi

Untitled

   As her soft gentle hands slip across
the glossy white keys of the new grand
piano she begins to think, to think of
what life would mean without the fear
of DEATH. DEATH the word we all fear.
No one can escape it, it becomes us it
over comes us. The shadow of DEATH is
always lurking near watching, waiting,
for the one moment when he can take it
all away. Away your happiness, away
your joy, away your passion to live.
   What would life mean without the
Fear of DEATH...

Shannon Biely

Ebony And Ivory

Ebony and Ivory were friends until
the end. They were only three or
four and their world had just begun.
But they would soon begin to see
his skin is not like mine.
My hair is in a kinky puff, but
his is straight and fine.
They tease my ways and call me
names, but he can't get a job.
I wish we were back in the days
when we could run and play.
Now you see me in the street
and try to look away.

Sara Williams

My Father's Flag

Her colors have now faded some,
The edges frayed and worn.
Then, She was His, but now she's Mine
To an azure view adorn.

She still flies on special days
And does so very well.
One cannot help have pride in Nation,
My Dad, and those who fell.

During conflicts past and present,
And, most likely those to be!
Those Mandated by our consciences
To keep us and others free.

As She flies above on Holidays
With younger Flags around,
They wave to Her and She waves back
In salutation-so profound!

HIS FLAG: She flutters, flaps, and waves,
Now unfurled and raised by Me.
Still, She represents My DAD, OUR LAND,
And flies with DIGNITY...

Richard Rush

Waters Of The Heart

Melted from the snow atop the crest
The drop begins the journey
Expectations of the best
Are altered in the learning

Clear waters and unblemished trees
Greet it at the start
But unforeseen tendencies
Play havoc with the heart

Discarded waste, a wilted leaf
Are gathered on the way
Unguarded haste eventually
Leads the heart astray

Ripples of life, currents below
And obstructions, eddies impart
But Love will smooth the flow
In the waters of the heart

Peter K. Burgess

Dreams

Fantastic, vital
Laughing, dancing, flying
The mind's desires fulfilled
Frightening, jolting, ominous
Trapping, paralyzing
Nightmares

Sybil Diekmann

His Tiny Big World

The beach becomes a sweeping sandbox
the damp sand becomes his clay.
A quilt becomes rolling farmland
with his crops of corn and hay.
The kitchen chairs become a train
that chug-chug around the table.
A blanket becomes a hero's cape.
The garage his horses' stable.
A jungle now is our backyard.
With wild beasts a-crouchin'.
A turkey baster, known as his sword,
fights the savage beasts a-pouncin'.
Our carpet is the broad blue sea.
The recliner - a cabin cruiser.
His bed's a giant trampoline.
Our hamper a huge bulldozer.
Life's an adventure to him who's three
chock-full of fun and mystery.
The type that only we can see,
from memories of past imaginability.

Sarah P. Dolbow

In Mind's Eye

The beach, the breeze, a summer dirge,
the clear air stills, our senses merge.
And as we sit, our minds they ponder
about these feelings, ever stronger.

Unconscious beauty drifting, clear,
emerging softly, terms endear.
Upon her breath, the fragrance lingers,
and fills the air with votive fingers.

The light her eyes directs so free,
the wonders that I hope to see,
and melancholy, 'gainst the blue,
from lofty heights, our minds preview.

Perfection's spirit, perceived as art,
the values sensed, the peace of heart.
It comes in silence, within, above,
these inclines of the soul, called love

William Robert Johnson

Fun In The Rain

The sky so dark
The air so still
Nothing is moving
A storm must be brewing

Strike of lightning lights the sky
Distant thunder replies
The rain falls to earth
Giving hope to a new birth

Sun rays shining on wet leaves
Dancing pellets sway with the breeze
Then falling to the earth below
Where children running to and fro.

Catching the falling leaves
Playing with them in the stream
Look at mine go; one child screams
Another child, that was my dream.

Phyllis Leavitt

Acceptance

It's been a while since her child died
The aches inside are duller now,
She holds in view many memories.
And sometimes prays;
"I wish he were in my arms again."

But as she watches
    Money changing hands
    In the shadows of the town:
As she hears
    Sirens hour after hour;
As the gunshots
    Ring out from the school next door;
She prays again:
"Thank you Lord for taking him."

Rachel S. Widgren

Mickey

There's a little boy at our house
    that'll make you very gay
Because he laughs and smiles and goes
    at everything you'll say
His eyes are big, his eyes are blue
    his face a million dimples
His laugh is true, his troubles few
    because he makes life simple
He's two foot long and just as wide
    his bulk a mass of wrinkles
And when his mommy's at his side
    his eyes light up in twinkles
He's just a little tot you know
    but he spreads sunshine to and fro
And wait and see as he will grow
    from his little lips always laughter will flow
Now I could go on for a million years
    but people today won't believe their ears
And so I say through all of the years
    we love little Mickey and will guard him
    from fears.

William M. Dixon

Brown Cardboard Boxes

When you looked at me
that way
You seemed to pull
me into the blueness
extracting all that is
        painful
        ugly
        intriguing
        sincere and
        beautiful
All of those secret, sentimental
    abstractions
hidden in the brown cardboard
boxes in the attic of my soul
(that I just couldn't throw away)
You haven't yet opened
    me—completely
But your eyes invited yourself
through the attic door. Honestly,
I appreciate the company.

Sara June Knudson

Praise To The Priest

Carry thy thine light,
That thy may lead me,
Through this the darkness of the night,
Like a shepherd lead me.
A minister of thy flock,
Art thy of the souls,
Entrusted unto thee,
Thou the guardian of the church,
Great praise be unto thee.

Stanley Clarke Wyllie

Mr. E

It's now nine years I have known
that man called Mr. E.
And when I hear that lavish tone
it evokes a vision for me.
No math professor Mr. E knew
for he dwelt with artistic minds,
his musical talent constantly grew
as did his father - like bind.
You may spy this poet at work
erect beside the stand
flowing and pulsing his hands about
with a baton clutched in his hand.
The palpitation of the son
endorsed him to falter to and fro,
as he beckoned the sound that longed
so mellow, tender and low.
Some maintain that to this day
he is the henchman of Sousa,
but he laughs and grins, at what they say
and sings a solitary song.

Sarah Sorge

Secret Love

I have a secret love
that I hold deep inside,
It's a love only for you
And sometimes it's hard to hide.

If you looked in my eyes
then maybe you would know.
All those nights you held me
I never wanted to let you go.

Maybe it's too soon for me
to feel this way,
But this love I hold inside
Is in my heart to stay!

Tammy Neely

Memories

Memories are the windows
that hold the past in view,
Through them we can see
again each joy we have ever known.
Of all the happy times
so special to recall,
the times we shared together
were the nicest ones of all.
Today brings back the memories
that we've gathered though the years.
We will treasure them within
our hearts like precious
souvenirs.

Susan Wolfe

The Little Man

There's a little man
That goes running 'bout the house,
Quicker than a shadow
And quiet as a mouse.

He strews about the clothes
That mother's put away;
And lets others take the blame
When he leaves the house astray.

He tracks some mud across the floor
With other people's shoes;
And laughs when mother asks who it was,
And everyone looks confused.

He spills the crumbs at supper time
And doesn't seem to care,
'Cause when it's time to lay the blame
You'll never see him there!

For many have tried to catch him
And have retreated without a clue;
But, oh, how happy I will be
When someone catches him, won't you?

Rachel Redden

A Gift

Distance is the sound
    that falls upon deaf ears

Fog upon blue waters
    doesn't seem what it appears

A rising mist lingers
    upon dawns new early light

While wind as still as silence
    begins to take on flight

White gulls swoop upon the waters
    to feed without a care

To hear them talk, to hear them sing
    would be a gift to share

As shells lay at my feet
    and grace the shoreline ground

The beauty is in seeing
    much more than hearing sound

Waves crash upon the sandy earth
    retreating caps of foam

A taste of salt upon my lips
    I walk the beach—silent—all alone.

Paula B. Carder

"A Star Has Fallen" (Fallen From Grace)

A star has fallen-how can it be
That a star so brightly-shined for me
A star has fallen-this very night
A lonely star-fallen from sight

A star is fallen-out of its place
Shattered pieces- "fallen from grace"

A star has fallen-as the night goes dim
A star has fallen-fallen again

A star has fallen-from its space
Scattered pieces-"fallen from grace"

A star has fallen-and left no trace
A lonely star-"Fallen from grace"

Clark

The Glorious Sea

Beauty....that touches the heart!
Sunshine, bathing the sea
with its brilliance;
Translucent, dancing water!
Beneath, the happy sea dwellers
celebrating,
Waltzing their way in their
graceful movement.
Nature, unbelievably beautiful!
O'er head, seagulls fly mingling
with the other birds;
Singing their songs in the air.
Yes..., today the sea brings
forth peace and tranquility.
Tomorrow?
Tomorrow is another day!

Ramon G. Palanca

Californis Poppies In A Vase

Each one is separate
sun, slicing through
layers of haze to the
blazing of my thirteenth
summer.

Astride a palomino I
won an imaginary race
across a plateau aglow
with cadmium petals and
cut imaginary calves in
and out of the arroyo
above the bungalow
where my aunt's lungs
had become like cactus.

As I evoked the day for
her, blue eyes already
fading into gray, turned
black with memory as
she whispered "Go for it,
—and never look back!"

Ruth Middleton

"School Is Cool"

Be cool
Stay in school
Have fun
Get done
Being in school
Is cool
Doing your work
No home work
Play all day
In the sun
So you can have fun

Terra Hawkins

Untitled

Life is like a rainbow
Starts off big and bright
All your hopes and dreams
Fading in the light
Keep that rainbow burning
Let the light stay bright
For life is like a rainbow
Fading in the night

Sarah Bayliss

Untitled

Two mountains
    Standing apart
    Shifting winds
    Casting their shadows
        To touch

Two mountains
    Bearing aloft
    To heaven
    Reaching the summit
        Of time

Two mountains
    Crumble apart
    Together
    Casting their shadows
        To touch

Thomas John Adams

Dawning

O'er the heavens, deeply clouded,
Sprang the flush of morning breaking
First the depth of jeweled indigo
Changed to tones of rarest violet,
Followed by the flush of crimson,
Then the all pervading rose tints,
Cast across the sweeping heavens.
Finally in golden glory
Rose in majesty the sun God,
Bringing unto all the people
Promise of eternal blessings.
Life and health, and all things needed,
By the ones who can accept it.
Peace unto their souls forever,
When they join this great at-one-ness,
Then they know their souls immortal.

Ruth Edwards Wilcox

Angels

A halo sits on their heads
Some people say,
They never get lost
For God leads the way,
Hair made of silk
A twinkle in their eye,
Never are they sad for
They live in the sweet by-n-by,
A heavenly body
Not a flaw at all,
Wings tipped with gold
Never do they fall,
Pure in spirit
Made by God's hand,
They were created
To guard us and
Defend the promise land.

Tonya H. Taylor

The Tree

I a majestic mountain
silently sleep under snow
that sifts like the sands
of time.
    I
        alone
        await
            erosions
            end.

Sarah Anne Pike

"Saying Goodbye"

Gentle were your hands.
Soft as a morning breeze,
Across the beach sands,
Ever blowing through the trees.

Soft as a silk bow,
for their marks of time
were left to show
my loss is a crime.

Your heart soft as it was,
And also very caring.
I know this because
for our love you were daring.

My life you did touch
And I will forget you never.
I love you very much
And this is forever.

What happened was wrong
but on my way
I promise to be strong
Each and every day.

Tammy Hanley

Bedtime

Nine o'clock came
so very fast
Time for bed
we were always harassed

Go to bed now!
mother would say
Get under the covers
there you will stay

Until morning
when you open your eyes
To see the bright sun
and the beautiful blue skies

Tomorrow you can play
out in the front lawn
All day long
until you yawn

Then that means
it is bedtime
So close your eyes
and remember this rhyme

Seth Goodell

Just A Kid

She's just a kid,
so now you've spoken.
She's just a kid,
her heart you've broken.
She's just kid,
she hears y   ı say.
She's just a kid,
she'll be back one day.
She's just a kid,
ask any other guy,
there's more to a kid
than meets the eye.

Talia Rotter

To My Children

I have to leave
So please don't cry
The hardest part
Is saying goodbye

I know you'll know
As time goes by
My love for you
Will show you why

You don't know
What's come about
Sometimes I know
You want to shout

Some things are scary
Without a light
But my love to you
Is a starry night

Your time is now
May you understand
My love for you
Is in your hand

Richard Fries

Somewhere

Somewhere, in the distant past
So long, so long ago
Hide memories of wanton days
And nights of loving prose
Held back, in check, until the time
Etched in ethereal space
For emotion to blend with arching back
In hearts that quickly race
To enter the mind so eerily
Not from what's been said
But by the act, entwining love,
When soul and body wed
And spirits leave their proper place
A-swirl in passioned light
And join together in haunting grace
To create enlightened life
The past, the present, the future merge
Bathed in moonlight hues
And stir the old with the new
In release of loving truth

William C. Gray

To The One I Love

You are the one of my dreams,
So I will try everyday.
To open your heart to me,
And send your love my way.

You may not yet no this,
But my feelings for you are true.
I hope you do believe me,
When I tell you I love you.

I will search this world entirely,
But I know that I'll never find.
A guy who is as great as you,
Darling, you're the perfect kind.

So you know my feelings for you,
Now I will just wait and see.
If you will ever open your heart.
And tell me that you love me.

Tracey Seiler

Sad

You held me once
So close to you
Your every inch
by heart I knew
You loved me back
At least I thought
But emptiness
This life has brought
I love you still
These things I know
And I can never
Let you go
You hate me now
And treat me bad
Because of this
My life is sad.

Patricia Barrus

Tomorrow

Like the disappearing candle
Slowly eaten by its flame,
So our tomorrows disappear:
Never to be planned again.

The time once called tomorrow
Now has a different name:
A different tomorrow has taken place;
It too will enter times burning flame.

No more to be called tomorrow,
For tomorrow is yet to be.
Only hopes and dreams can dwell
In the tomorrows before reality.

Who can live in not yet time?
Who can breath, or touch or see
The void of time not yet arrived?
Who can offer future guarantee?

The consuming flame of today
Draws tomorrow rapidly near,
Ever changing future tomorrow day
Into now, yesterday, and yesteryear.

Vernice L. Darland

Night

Dark, peaceful
sleeping, dreaming, resting
stars, moon, sun, clouds
running, playing, jumping
light, fun
day

Paul Cerny

My Brothers

My days are long and lonely
Since you have gone away,
It seems like only yesterday
That we were children at play.
God must have had a plan for you
To take you from our sight,
And we will never comprehend
His Why, His Where or Might.
There was not time to hold you near
Or tell you how much we would miss you,
For He took you from us
And left us with our sorrow
But gave us the hope
To see you in the Great Tomorrow.

Rosemary P. Gardner

Our Angel

You've been a part of us
Since the day you were conceived
An angel sent from above
Asking only for our love

A seed planted by the Master
Inside of me to look after
A part of your Daddy and of me
Our darling baby you would be

Our love for you grew stronger
As on you we would ponder
We longed for your arrival
And prayed for your survival

You stole our hearts that day
When to us you came to stay
You were given to us alone
To make our house a home

We cherish our little girl
All dressed up in lace and frill
She's a blessing from the Father
And we thank Him alone for her

L. A. Spurlock

"Happy And Sad"

Happiness and sadness are very
similar
Yet so different
Most people think sadness is
darkness
And happiness is brightness
You can feel sad for a lonely
child
But happy that they're getting
help
When you think about it
happiness can turn into sadness
And sadness can turn into
happiness
Sadness and happiness
Happiness and sadness
What a combination they are!

Stephanie Marlowe

One World, One Disgrace

The howling of Lords,
shouting evil words,
the cries of the people,
and the falling of a steeple.
The clashing of metal,
what is the use of a pebble?
Parents are crying,
as their children are dying.
Fire from dragons,
dead bodies in wagons.
A war of the Gods,
the kings are like dogs.
The children are playing,
while the soldiers are slaying.
A land that once held peace,
now cries in the agony of defeat.
One world,
with one disgrace
that of which,
is the human race.

Trevor Lee Kennett

Your Love

Like the tide beating against the
shore washing away the footprints
left from the past. So your love
washes away the pain from
my past.

Like the hot sun burning an
inferno of gas giving life to the
planet that gives life to us. So
your love burns in me a passion
for the life we will share.

Like the rain falling helplessly from
the clouds caressing the wind and
penetrating the earth. So your love
caresses my heart and penetrates
my soul.

Like a man stranded in the desert,
delirious from the heat, crawling
desperately, aimlessly in search for
water. So I would be without
your love.

Shirley J. Haynes

Her Bleeding Heart

Over mountains, over valleys
She flies
She searches through the dark
She cries
She knows not what she's looking for
Nor if it can be found
She'll never give up trying
Till she wears the crown
She's lost now in the darkness
And yet she's not alone
Shadows now encircle
And distant shrieking moans
When the princess couldn't bear it
When she thought she'd die of fright
Along rides her hero
A strong and gallant knight
He takes her in his arms
And on his mighty steed
They ride off in the sunset
Her heart no longer bleeds

Sydney Laird

My Mother

Special in every way
She appears to be
A woman with an endless
Amount of love to share.

Patient as she always is
With a smile on her face
She rises to each new challenge
Never lacking in courage or strength.

She let's you know she's there
For a good laugh or cry.
Ready with encouraging words
Or sympathy of some kind.

A friend you'll never lose
She'll stay through thick and thin.
Years of memories she'll tuck
Away, for a rainy day.

All this she will do for you
Knowing her only reward for
Loving and caring for you
Is what you give back to her.

Traci J. Tekulve

I Want To Grow Up

I want to grow up and be
Seventeen. But I'm only nine but
I'm on a swimteam. When I grow
up I'm going to be...Gee, it's
all up to me! I could be a news
reporter, a doctor, a singer or maybe
a clown! But a clown with a frown
and shoes really tight just doesn't
seem right! I know I'll be a bird,
a bird with bright feathers, but
what about the weather! And worms
for breakfast! Na, I'll move to Texas.
I'll be a cowgirl and I'll ride my
horse Lance. Na no chance, I'll move
to France! But wait! I can't
finance. I got it! I be an elf
but better yet I'll just be myself!

Sarah Picard

Untitled

Fall leaves on a Winter day,
Seasons blend into harmony,
Time divided-
Though remain as one.

Wendy Staples

Gotcha!

A fair face beauty.
Saw to her seduction duty.
My boyfriend who looked like a sheik,
Overcome by this sexy sneak.
There I stood like a dope,
Letting her insult get my goat.
My mind screamed out - I hate her!
Other girls saw her as an invader.
Casting her popularity bait,
fair beauty found another date.
Monday morning at high school.
Her latest prince laid down this rule:
"You've got the right one honey.
Don't do anything funny,
just remember dear."
Clyde told her with a sneer.
"I have your frighten confidence,
I want no disobedience."

Sonya L. Evins

Relent

Again me again
Relentlessly expressing
Relentless relentlessness
Again over and over again
The illness in me they see
They touch they recoil
In fear and disgust
I understand
God understand me
Their backs I see
Running from me
In fear and disgust
God
All I've got
Can you too be
Lost and distant from me
In the clouds
My illness
Relentlessly expressing
Relentless relentlessness

Stephen Riggs

"The Flame"

Once there were two people,
Really lovers at heart,
When they were first criticized,
They were faced apart.
But as in reality, it is not so,
Because they would just ignore it
And on the relationship would go.

They went to parties, went to balls,
and even went to a dance
and still with all the criticism around,
it wouldn't ruin their kind of romance

Was it a difference in likeness,
or a difference in looks
That made these two people the same.
Because no ones for sure,
and God only knows
what makes two sparks, turn into a flame.

Timothy A. Michonski

Shoreline Shines Metal

Flowing past experiences
pumping repetitiously

Protectors lie motionless
punishing only when struck.

Body is covered rapidly
as well as the contractor

Lacerations are consistent
with speed.

Aggressiveness depths below
will contribute to

Lessons in proper behavior
as revealing myths surface.

rejected teachings from ones
who have felt superior for

Centuries will be the only
communication needed for

Support of their own
destruction.

Patrick Morgan

A Little Tiny Heart

Little tiny hands
puffy, pink and splotchy
so soft, so smooth
stretching, reaching, grasping

A little tiny mouth
open, moist and awesome
so shapely, so perfect
cooing, smiling, demanding

Little tiny feet
chubby, cute and curly
so powerful, so plump
wriggling, kicking, pushing

Little tiny eyes
glassy, dark and wide
so present, so alive
searching, panning, exploring

A little tiny heart
eager, warm and gentle
so trusting, so forgiving
filled with unconditional love.

Sherry L. Falk

Mother's Day Poem

My ringlets fell over my shoulders
protecting me
a false barrier
the true armor
was you.
Your hand adjoined
to mine.
It still is.

Rachael S. Neal

Dear Lord

Dear Lord,
Please stop the fighting,
Bring us peace and prosperity,
Instead of hate and anger.
Make the noises go away,
And fill my ears with love,
So I'll know that you're there.
Spread your arms of love
So they may touch my house,
And with your will
Create love and peace between my
Mother and Father.

Tony Mello

Upon My Knees

Our Father who are in heaven,
please hear these words I pray.
Protect my woman and guide her Lord,
especially while I'm away.
All the wrong I've done in vain,
today dear Lord I see.
But this is for the sake of love,
because she means everything to me.
You said you wouldn't forsake us Lord,
just call and you'll be there.
Well this is a time I need you most,
to tell how much I care.
I pray with all my heart dear Lord,
and with it, I do say please.
For you are the Father of us all,
and I thank you on bended knees.

Ramero R. Edwards

Untitled

Distance, became less
Passion, turned hot
It melts away
my fear remains

The touch of your hand
it reaches my heart

The sound of your voice
creates tranquility
safe in your arms
gentle and strong
You ask me my feelings
I'll write you my song

Questions, no words answer
Just look in my eyes
it's yours to see
They'll tell you no lies

You'll come and you'll go
from this moment in my life
But you've taught me
that I can love again

Paeca M. Hallett

Charlie And Me

No lemonade in the ice box
Papa San, he wears no socks
We're happy as can be
Just Charlie and me
Fighting in South Vietnam.

Soon we'll be in a firefight
We'll shoot at each other just for fun
If I get killed by a bullet
The VA will raise my sons.

If I get crippled by shrapnel
A booby trap or mine
I can ride around in a wheelchair
Before I blow out my mind.

When the B-52's start their bomb runs
The NVA will be gone in a flash
I think they know when they're comin'
The U.S. is wasting a lot of cash.

Richard Perry Larson

Relinquishment

We cannot go back to live
Our yesterdays again.
The bridge behind is burned;
Ashes scattered to the wind.

Though our hearts remember,
Not a thing can change....
The way it was is the way it is!
It can't be rearranged.

Let be! There's hope! Be still!
Cease to dwell on hurtful things.
God's arms are reaching out...
Embrace the love He brings!

Ruthellen Shelton

Daddy Went To Heaven

We stand together
our hearts grow together.
He held his hand out to me
When he helped me climb
his rock
I took it
It felt warm and strong
and I had the funny feeling
That as long as I held
onto his hand
I would never fall.

Shirley Foster

Questions

Are they really out there
  -Or is it our mind?
Is there an advanced civilization
  -Are we that far behind?
We think it's just us
  -Is that really true?
Or is there more than we think
  -More than just me, and you?
Is there more life
  -Out beyond the stars?
Are there more living planets
  -Other than ours?

Sarah Winter

Your Love Is All I Need

Sometimes I question you
Only because I cannot see
How perfect is your will
And how much you care for me

You know my deepest feelings
You are my help when in need
Oh, Lord you are so great
Unto you will I plead.

When I am left alone,
Drowning in my tears
You come and rescue me
Quieting all my fears

Lord I have learned
Only your love is true
You love me patiently
No matter what I do.

Sometimes I question you
But now I can see
No matter what happens
Your love is all I need.

Stephanie C. Inks

Question

If thou could ask thee
  one question,

what would it be?

Aye, if thou could ask thee
  one question,

  it would be:

"If thy has once found love,
  given so freely and graciously
  by thee,

so beautiful,
  so true
  so free,

would that

  Love

  ever
  fly
  away
  like
  a
    dove?"

Thao Ngoc Nguyen

Nobody Notices

As many people starve
One person laughs.
While many children work
Few children play.
When one man kills himself
Several people are born.
While many live on the brink of poverty
One man swims in his undeserved wealth.
Many people are abused
A few people are loved.
Many people die
Nobody notices.

Scott Wilson

The Gift

There is a gift
One here to stay
A gift to celebrate
Everyday

This gift brings happiness
This gift brings cheer
It's the kind of gift
That stays all year

This gift reminds me
Of a singing dove
Can you guess what it is?
This gift is love.

Raven Vassallo

To A Special Person...

To a special person
One full of love
When I choose a, b, or c
I choose all of the above.

You're one of kindness
Tenderness in one touch
The comfort I get from you
Makes me love you very much.

When I look into your eyes
I see the love you have for me
And it has always said
I love you as far as I can see

And each time I see
A painful tear in your eye
I feel the pain
As each day goes by.

To a special person
I send all of my love
With a little help
From the heavens up above.

Shannon Funkhouser

Untitled

Candle light, moon light, sitting here
on a lonely night are all I see.

Listening to the sounds of nature and
dreaming that your thinking of me.

The wind has a mysterious cool sense
as it flickers the candle slowly to fade.

I desire to see your smiling face and
feel the touch of your warm embrace
coming out of the shadows and shade.

My life may be only one big fantasy
full of love and romance.

All I need is for you to be here
with me so we can take that chance.

Where are you tonight, as I sit by
moonlight, watching the precious
stars fall.

Thinking of you and beginning to
fear, maybe you don't care at all.

Trish Randolph

The Little Sun Ray

While sitting in the quiet
On a late winter's day,
I watched in magical wonderment
The dance of a little sun ray.

She danced her way through the curtains
Swaying and swirling about,
She danced all around each fiber
Weaving in and out.

She was like a ballerina
So lovely to behold,
This little ray of sunlight
So shy, and yet so bold.

She sparkled and shimmered
As she twirled round and round.
She floated without effort
And without a sound.

As the evening shadows quickened
And twilight gathered near,
She danced ever so slowly
Then quickly disappeared.

Pegeen Palczak

Divorced

Why did this happen?
Oh, I don't know.
How did I get here?
I still don't know.

Am I to blame?
Or is it he?
I still don't know.
Go ahead, blame me.

"Weather the storm"
He said to me.
Can't believe this
Happened to me.

No cover for
The storm raging inside,
Inner tears cried...
My marriage had died.

Until death do us part
We both did say.
This still hurts...
Even today_____DIVORCED.

S. L. Anthony

Waiting

My eyes are filling with tears
My chest is tight and aching
I want to cry because
What we have is disappearing
You keep living in the past
I need you in the present
We have both made mistakes
Neither one of us is perfect
We have had a few good times
And a few bad
But we are still together
I want you in my life forever
Unconditionally
I am waiting with open arms and
I am here when you want me
But be quick about it
I won't wait forever
Just an eternity

Stacey Ossowski

Mentor

It is Yu Huan,
  of whom I'm most fond,
for now his wondrous spirit
  swirls around me
like wind around chimes.

  His words spoken
like strings of violins playing a sweet
  and pure melody of wisdom and heart.

A painting I see
  of balance and harmony.
A sight of order and thought,
  A strong tree with roots deep
in solid ground,
  A road travelled by few
he has found.

  I do not tire
from this view
  for I discover many
a new,
  Shapes of color and hue.

Rebecca Brust

A Proposal Of Marriage

In this Agony
of Seems and Be,
the little stillness
of Self glimmers
awhile, then fades.

There remains only
that Reflection
of a dying ember
to mark our Beauty
on the film of Time.

Let us flare brightly
at least, and bend
the fire-edged swords
of our Souls together

To carve a palace
of Light and Alabaster.

P. Chandler

Butterfly Child

Conceived in a warm cocoon,
nurturing warm loving care.
Singing you my special song,
my soul I wish to share.

Growing more and more,
just a blink of an eye.
Born into this world,
how your colors beautify.

Seasons pass by,
the colors of your wings changed.
Mature and independent,
Childhoods views rearranged.

Guidance and patience,
unconditional love of a mother's hand.
Wings slowly opening,
on two sturdy legs you will stand.

Era of letting go,
magnificent colors glorify.
It's time my butterfly child,
to spread your wings and fly.

Robyn R. Johnson

Untitled

I thought you truly loved me
Now I know why
I was only being used
to occupy your time
I thought you truly cared
how could I be so wrong
I only tried to deny it
I knew someone else would come along
You even called me sunshine
'cause I brightened up your day
whoever would've known
you wouldn't think to stay
I thought it was real love
but it was all a big lie
just to satisfy your loneliness
for a small period of time
you really broke my heart
I didn't even get mad
I can't believe you're gone
I'll be forever sad

Sheryl Warnock-Root

My Love

We have spun our own golden web
Not to even a spider can weave,
We get along remarkably well
It's really hard to believe,

I love you within my soul
And deep within my heart,
Our lives have mended together
So therefore we cannot fall apart,

Since the first day I met you
I've had this feeling within me,
I know I'll love you forever
So I know I'll always be free,

If things get a little bit tough
You can bet our love I'll stay,
No matter how tough it can get
It would be too hard to walk away,

I truly and honestly love you
Like a river it will smoothly flow,
Also like the heavenly light above
It will forever stay aglow.

Pamela Landreneau

Time

Time, is like a crime.
No one is safe,
It steals you blind.

Time, passes by.
What's the meaning,
I wonder why.

What a shame, it does not last,
What was now, is now the past.
What is time, it's like a wheel,
A state of mind, or is it real.

It moves so fast, it never slows,
It does not stop, Time just goes.
Time, is where you will find,
The inner truth, the reasons why.

So now and then,
Where times begins.
Is where it starts,
And where it ends.

Robert D. Hedrick

Twenty Lines

There is a story
No more than twenty lines
I would like to tell you
I hope they rhyme
I have dine and I have been kind
But, in my mind I cannot find
The words to fill this poem of mine
It's all about twenty lines
In my thoughts I have search and search
All through the time
and it's only nine
I have grown tired and I am sleepy
Hopeful I be for a sign
So I can finish
All about twenty lines.

Rebecca Ridley

Untitled

The wonder of the darken
night the haunting dreams
at a past life. If only I could
see inside my soul, to
prepare me for the morning's light.

Violet Craven

You are the moon
  Mysterious and enchanting
You are the air
  Sweet and fresh
You are children
  Full of life and care-free
You are the storm
  Powerful and tempestuous
You are the wolf
  Silent predator
You are the sea
  Calming and patient
You are the flesh
  Soft and warm
You are my love
  Mind and body.

JWCCarbonell

My Skateboard

Now that I've learned to ride,
My skateboard,
You are many things to me.

I am a cowboy
Busting a bronco,
Taming it, riding free
Over hill and dale
And beside the rumpled sea.

Now, I am a test pilot
Doing loop-the-loops in the sky,
Performing every stunt
Way, way up high.

Next, I am a circus star
Swinging on the trapeze,
Gliding far above the crowds
Stirring up a special breeze.

Finally, I am me,
A boy who matches skills
With other kids
And even takes some spills!

Ruth E. Fisher

My Poem

My poem is big but not so small.
My poem is large but not so tall.
It's big and fat but not so chubby.
My poem is perfect, that's all.

Rebecca Armbruster

You'll Never Know.....

I don't know what to do,
My love for you will always be true,
The beating of my heart, so strong
My river for you will always run blue.
I'll try my best to get along
But I know I'll never belong
I'll never be able to part
Let me be alone to sing our song.

The aching in my heart
It's like you hit me with a dart.
I wish you didn't have to go
For I cannot stand to be apart.
I'll never be so low,
To hate you, although,
The love I hold you'll never know,
The love I hold you'll never know.

Tomi Jo Kelly

Untitled

Today I lost another love
  my life is flashing past.
A special one who took my hand
  and loved me to the last.
He taught me how to ride my bike
  and took me to the zoo.
He showed me how to fly a kite
  and roller skating too.
We walked along the beach and watched
  the waves roll out to sea.
We talked about the world to come
  and what my life should be.
He told me I could be the best
  in anything I tried.
And told me always to be true
  to what I feel inside.
This wonderful man, to me had never lied,
  without a goodbye,
    in the still of night,
    he died.

Sharon Newton-Fox

Precious Gift

My youth,
My life,
My sorrow,
My happiness
My shelter
My friend
My courage,
My strength,
My wisdom,
My heartbeat,
My existence,
My love,
My husband,
God's precious gift of love.

Shirley Bendawald

Tired Dreams

In the bed
  my laziness sink
    and I spit nightmares
I squeeze tired dreams
  like oranges in the morning
I cover with sheets the rubbish of dawn
I pinch my eyelids
  for the day to go away
I just want a cup of tea

Yvonne Mattar

Looking Up

Looking up, my goal I keep,
my journey on course.

Looking up, my mansion I see,
as the covenant I keep.

Looking up, my source reveals
the answers to life's questions.

Looking up, my faith is sustained
as a rainbow, a promise remembered.

Life emanates from above
and blessings are bestowed below.

Looking up, my thanks I give
as I point the way to everlasting life
and hope others will follow the
path of righteousness.

Rogelio Stone

If They But Knew

I tossed a coin to choose my love
My heart — it didn't matter.
It turned up tall and nice and dark
With coin I could scatter.

Now I've been married five long years,
My friends all envy me.
Alas, if they but knew how long
Five loveless years can be.

Wilda N. Whitescarver

Grandma

As I watched a tree slowly die
  my heart became cold and lifeless...
    for it was a part of me.
It was not just any tree; it was one of
  my greatest friends,
    a tree which held all of my
      deepest secrets.

And now it is gone...

The wind blows.
  I walk on.
    And as I look back,
      I catch a small reflection,
      and remember.

Sara J. VandeGriend-Olsen

The Soul

The beauty of the soul is
It transcends the exterior
That one displays, and
Secrets the inner sanction
If innocence we manifest
So it shall never be exempt.

Shannon Berg

Islands In The Sky

Bright islands in the sky,
my eyes can scarce explore
the glory of your distant shores.

Done sailing the azure sea,
Bold pirate sun buries in thee
His treasure all rosen gold.

Lying on a bed of green,
Wondering if other eyes have seen,
And lustily plundered your rich store,

I watch, until bereft,
Grey and still you fade, and I am left
To follow telltale diamonds strewn
  To show me the way home.

E. M. Edmisson

Secret Garden

There's a secret garden in
my dreams
One with birds and a flower
that gleams
That gleaming flower is a
single red rose
One that glistens shimmers and
glows
I love this single red rose
It loves me too, a part of
me knows
This gleaming rose is my
favorite flower
It gives that part of me a
mighty power
I look at this rose and a
part of me beams
For this secret garden in
my precious dreams

Tia Lane

Untitled

On a solitary hike
my brother found a lily,
shortly he returned for me.
As important for him to show his find
as it was for me to see.

You've heard of that conundrum,
if no one is around
and a tree falls in the forest
does it really make a sound?

If you carry an idea too close
is it really there?
How do you count your joy accrued
unless your treasure is shared?

Gloria Olson

Untitled

You didn't tell me you were leaving
most of the time you do,
If only to go to the store
or down the road a mile or two.

You didn't tell me you were leaving
and I know not where you are at
I sit and watch, and stare and wonder
waiting for you to come back.

Phyllis Kent

Evening Walk

This night of peace, I cherish dearly.
Memories are the thorns in my side.
Hope is my inspiration;
And love keeps my spirit alive.
Dreams add the spice,
To the pasta of life.
Every noodle is a piece
of happiness or strife.
Each day is a new adventure
And a challenge to face.
I must remember
To keep up the pace.
Some music plays inside me.
The melodic tune
Is a violin's sigh
By the light of the moon.
Quietly the crickets hum.
They're brushing a gentle wing.
From the shadows, I will come.
But through the evening, I will sing!

Patricia Holland

Reflections

Listening to rhyme,
Measuring meter—
Words as art
Express the soul.

Man yearns to create,
As did his Creator,
Reflections of poetry
Long since foretold.

Rita Berry

Most Important

You were always there to pick
  me up when I would fall
And you would always come
  running when I would call.

You were always there no
  matter what trouble I'd find
And you'd stand beside me
  time after time.

We moved away and we
  moved far apart
But you were always kept
  close to me within my heart.

I'm not the same girl that
  left many years ago
But my love for you shall
  always grow.

No matter how many men should come and go
There's one thing that I want you to know.

No matter if he's mister wrong or mister right
You'll always be the most important man in
  my life.

Susan Brill

Throes Of Passion

Upon love's threshold,
Lingering, we viewed
The wonders of droplets
And natures mood.
Each glistening bead
Clung, as dew
Her tears of joy
For love's debut.

Sandra Ruscin De Vonish

Does Anyone Care

The land being destroyed,
Many people being annoyed;
Seeing protests everywhere,
More pollution filling the air;
Trees being cut down one by one,
If his keeps up there will be one;
What has happened to our earth?
Seems like more death instead of birth;
People thinking at a different pace,
Prejudice hurting all kinds of race;
Gangs invading all our streets,
More abuse instead of treats;
It's our home but does anyone care?
When damage is done people just sit and stare;
Animals dying for a dumb reason,
for them less homes every season;
Our earth needs help everywhere,
It's our home and I do care.

Teri Lanterman

Prayer

Jesus heal my evil heart
Make me pure like thee
Thus we two shall never part
Throughout eternity.

Jesus guard me through the night
Where demons seek my soul
Shepherd may the morning light
Find me safe in fold

Jesus guide me through my death
Make fear and shadows flee
Grant Lord that my dying breath
Shall speed my soul to thee.

Robert Baldridge

"Passion"

Oh! Passion what are you that
  love should keep you bound?
A sensual disk? A torrid breeze?
  perhaps a broken sound?
You touch a life, you mist its eye,
  then pass on, so it will cry,
Oh! Passion where are you?
Oh! Passion where are you,
  that I should be aware?
Emotions coiled into a smile
  that life sees everywhere?
Are you just love, that's
  ravished hot?
Sometimes held close-
  sometimes not?
You nip a life, but don't remain,
  then man cries out,
Oh! Passion come again!

Sylvia N. Grimes

Summer Song

My heart is with the daffodils
Lining the grassy rolling hills.
My soul rests in a robin's nest
Sequestered among the leaves of
  a sturdy oak tree.

The woes I carried were swept away
By the breezes as they played
Among the towers of trees and flowers
  in fields of new mown
    hay.

Wanda L. Strickland

Love Is....

Love is hurt,
Love is sorrow,
I wonder if love,
Will be there tomorrow.

I wonder if love will be
here today,
'Cause I've never seen love
that way.

I guess Love is fun,
Give Love to everyone,
If you Love then you'll
hurt and sorrow like I,
That special love will be
in your heart till the day
you die.

I love, love and love is fun,
So give love to everyone,
Some people don't get it,
And they forget it.
So Please Give Love!

Tiffany Nolton

Love

Love is real
Love is sincere
Love casts out fear
Love is care
Love is grace and mercy
Love is giving a drink
When one is thirsty
Love is not revenge
Love is not sin
Love is lending a hand
So just LOVE everyone if you can.

Tammy Jackson

A Welcome Sight

I thought they had been killed off
Long ago,
The pesticides getting them, for sure.
But no! Last eve I saw their tiny glow.

Leaning on the window sill,
I watched in thrilled delight.
I wondered if they knew
The beauty of their flight.

How often we as children
Watched them as they gleamed,
And asked the timeless question,
"What makes them beam?"

I'm sure the answers varied,
As answers sometimes do.
But God made fireflies
To do what they do.

Susan Abendroth

I Need...

I don't want a dad.
I want a Father.
  I don't want a man.
  I want a friend.
I don't want a critic.
I want a rock.
  I don't want a prophet.
  I want a godly parent.
I don't need a dad.
I need a Father.

Samantha M. Velazquez

"Living In The Street"

Hey! Sister and brother,
living in tent.
Living in fear.
Living in a world, that didn't
really care.
The ground is hard with,
rock and stones.
Sticking in my back, but
who give a care.
Do you give a care.
I give a care.
Do you give a care.
I give a care.
Do you give a care.
I give a care.
So get out the rut now!
And keep on, strutting now!
God bless you soul, sister and brother.

Patricia A. Yarbrough

The Snake

A slithering, slimy snake,
Lives under my four post bed.
It's there when I wake,
And sometimes I wish it were dead.

When I'm snoozing,
Up my leg he ascends.
I wish I weren't losing,
My very dear friend.

But now he is sick,
And I fear the worst.
He gave me a lick,
Since worrying makes my head burst!

The vet says he'll pull through,
Cheers came from me.
Y-a-h-o-o!
He soon was well, and I set him free.

Sara Strecker

Secrets Of The Heart

The Heart believes in simple things
Like moonlight, magic and love.
It finds a star and makes a wish
It clings to the light above.

It longs to know the secrets
Locked deep within its core.
The blinding force that forges lives
For now and evermore.

Then once revealed, it struggles free
And soars above the sky.
It leaps beyond impediments
To dreams too long denied.

But tell me, does it strive in vain?
Will any dream come true?
It only knows one path to take,
The path that leads to you.

Rosanne Masone

"Essence Of Life"

Youth has no handle
Like a vapor it's gone—
In ignorance you abuse it
As life goes along.

The young wish to be older,
The old envy the young-
What a sad combination,
Time- waits for no one.

Don't rush youth-o-children,
Life tends to be tough,
Live in innocence longer- then
GOD willing- you'll be old soon enough...

Virginia Muncy

Rainbow Ride

It's a magic thing
Like a fresh day in Spring
An amazing light
The colors so bright
They fall from the sky
And catch your eye
When you see the glow
You will know
It's sent from above
With plenty of love
Remember to pray
Each and every day
That when it's your time
The light will shine
And you step inside
For your rainbow ride

Sandra Gleason

Oklahoma Pain

A tragedy in our home town
Left fear and heartache much abound.
The people there were oh-so-sure
That all was safe and good and pure.
The evil-hearted tried to take
Our peace of mind and chaos make.
Kindness, love and helping hands,
So many came from other lands.
To show the evil murderous ones;
We stood our ground and did not run.
The children's voices silent, still.
Their place in Heaven God has filled.
Taken when they were so young
A precious life had just begun.
Though emptiness and sadness stay,
With prayer this too will go away.
To have them taken seems unfair,
I can't forget, because I care.
We'll miss these tiny precious dears,
They're safe with God, shed no more tears.

Toni Sue Lusk

Untitled

Sometimes I feel like
keeping to myself
This world is so dependent
on fortune and wealth
It seems like a ratrace
that I've been trapped in
And to play their game
is the only way to win.

Tara Meadows

My Baby Bunny

My baby bunny is so cute,
Just look at her little face.
Poking around the daisies,
Running at a quickened pace.

Baby likes to look around,
And takes a tiny hop
How hungry little Baby is,
To see a juicy carrot top!

Baby loves me,
As I love her,
Especially when I,
Stroke her fur.

Off to dreamland baby goes,
Where she dreams of joy and sorrow.
Nothing moves, just Baby's nose,
We shall have fun tomorrow!

Valerie Schrader

To My Love

Love is kind
just like mine.
Love is sweet
just like treats.
Love is everything
you ever need.

Love is gentle
just like grandparents.
Love is soft
just like feathers.
Love is quiet
just like the night.
Love is family and friends.

Love is in the heart
that is why you are so smart.
Love is being near
to give us a cheer.
That is why you are so dear!

Sandra Franklin

Shattered Dream

There are no memories
Just curious thoughts
A dream of mine shattered
But no one's fault

As I look in the sky
A vision appears
Of the child that was not
And all of our tears

Our pain and our anguish
Are all kept inside
Which we cannot control
Nor can we hide

As the days pass us by
And the wind blows at night
I can't help but wonder
"Is what they did right?"

We all make mistakes
That we cannot forgive
But oh what a joy
If that baby could live

Stephanie Jamien Butts

Oldster

For 90 years
I've been around.
I've lived on farms
And in the town.
Army life I've known that too.
Three years I spent
In World War Two.
I've rode the rails
And been to sea.
And even climbed
A cherry tree.
How long I'll last
I do not know.
But I'm not ready yet to go.

M. Edward Nielson

"Nuclear War"

The pain,
It's there,
But do we care?
We kill to win,
But that's not fair.
Innocent people die,
As bombs explode.
If you look,
With your heart,
You will know.
The pain,
It's there,
It's everywhere.
But do we care?
Do we care?

Sarah Hobbs

Love

Love is a two way thing,
It's like a duet in which
two people sing.
Love has its ups and downs,
Depending on which moods
you'll see smiles or frowns.
There are many types of love,
Some people say the
symbol for love is a beautiful dove.
Sometimes for love people
sacrifice many things,
Like most important their
independence because, they
decide to present each other
with engagement rings.
The love you and your
lover have all depends,
On if it last long or
always ends up coming
to sudden ends.

Patricia Fye

The Tree Of Life

The tree of life
Its branches fruit heavy;
Some of the fruit is good;
Some is bad;
Some ripe with age;
Some newly forming;
But only the right fruit is picked
by the Master's Hands

Wesley Burden

Afraid To Cry

Your heart is breaking
it's aching
You're afraid to cry
You don't want people
to see
what you feel
on the inside

You cry silently
from within
trying not to reveal
the pain that you feel

You walk around
smiling
hoping that you
wouldn't cry

Afraid to cry
so you keep it
all bottled up
hoping that it
wouldn't erupt

Regina Woods

Feelings

There's a feeling inside me
it's a lot like rain
It's crying, I'm crying
I feel the pain

My mind is trying to find inner peace
My heart is searching for laughter
Yet I still haven't found
   what I'm after

Peace of mind
is hard to find
Laughter in a heart
when it's torn apart

There's a feeling inside me
it's a lot like rain
It's crying, I'm crying
I'm drowning in pain

Shana Kandilian

About

A time ago I wondered how
it would be to go out on my own.
I was certain I was capable
of handling any situation.

But time would tell
what was to be.
It has a way of making you realize
Why you are the way you are.

Occasionally I thought I had it going
and life and the world were mine.
Yet I always felt in my heart
that I was losing my direction.

Unless I stop myself and ponder
about why and what I'm doing,
I'd surely lose sight of reality
And wander off too far.

To think He gave His life for me
And promised never to leave or forsake.
I can never forget to think on these things
to know my direction in life.

Tom Beamesderfer

Just A Kiss

When you were young,
it wasn't like this.
I could make it better,
with just a kiss.

But now, every hour,
I ponder my part.
And sadly, my darling,
I don't have the power,
to ease the pain in your heart.

I never taught you to express,
the anger within.
Because, I too, always,
kept mine bottled in.

If I could change any of this,
I'd hold you in my arms,
not a heartbeat would I miss.
I'd make it all better,
with just a kiss.....

Peggy Vineyard

Absence Of Color

I closed my eyes and I could see
It was just as clear as it could be
The people focused in my sight
Were neither black, nor were they white

The people that my mind was seeing
Were not men or women, just human beings
Yellow, brown, black or white
They have no color in my sight

The heart and soul are all I se
Is that so very wrong of me?
If I were deaf or I were blind
What color people would I find

We're all the same inside our skin
Just open up, let love flow in
If you were here inside my mind
Would you be pleased with what you find

Life's too short and precious too
To throw the stones that will hurt you
So stop and think, and try to see
How very simple it should be!!!

Sherry L. Jones

When No One Cared

I set and think about the way
it used to be, there's a lot of people
who said and done cruel things
to me.
   When I found you, you gave me
some light to make me see,
   Between all the worlds madness
and all the sadness, you brought
out only the gladness
   I've gotten close to you in
the days we've shared, I never
thought anyone cared

Through all the laughter and all
the tears you took away most
of my biggest fears,
I hope it will last a million years,
   Just when I thought
my world was going to end
I finally found someone I
can call a friend

Toni Simpson

The Little Things That Mean So Much!

I like the way you smile,
It seems to go for miles.
The way you're always there,
Really shows me you care.
I often try to think how things would be,
If it wasn't you and me.
It would be so hard to remain,
If there was lots of sorrow and pain.
But there's not, and it's plain to see,
That you're full of love just for me!

Tonya Clother

Gone

Where is the world?
  it is gone
    gone with the wind
    far across the plains
the willows will soon bend,
  not in search
  but in pain
gone is the light,
  of happiness and joy
only to be replaced,
  by grief and dismay
gone is the love,
now is the pain
  gone
    gone
      all gone

Peicha Chang

The Still Of The Night

In the still of the night
It is dark and quiet;
  Not a sound, not even a whisper.
In the still of the night,
  The flamboyant moonlight shines
Over the crystal seas.

  Suddenly, the break of dawn!
Reluctantly, the moon fades away;
  Day is on the way!
As the sky births light,
  The ambivalent sun eventually rises.
The still of the night is gone!

Tara Smith

The Mustang

  He gallops 'cross the meadows green.
It is a vision I have seen.
  Oh how I long to be astride,
That graceful back, so strong and wide.
His movements are of pure ballet,
He leaps a hedge with a tour jeté
One glance, then he's gone.
And suddenly, I'm all alone.
But just as night begins to fall,
I hear his distant bugle call.

Stephanie Pepka

Untitled

Having seen the carnage,
I perceive no mercy
in the eyes of your mother
nature.

K. Barnett Gramckow

It's Hard To Let Go

  You sit and wonder why
it had to happen to you
That your children were killed
by someone close and near

But you can't forget the loving
moments that you had together
You know that they won't only
be loved by you but by God too.
You know that you can't ever
have them back but you always
have the love that they gave you

Your children will be forever
in your heart but you can't
forget their beautiful faces
and their shining smiles
that warmed so many hearts

Reyna Gleason

Heart

It all happened so fast.
It didn't even hurt until now.
I knew our cutting and clawing
had gotten out of hand,
but I am shocked to see
you standing there,
a red river flowing
between your fingers,
and, there, in your hand.
Still beating,
and swelling in pain,
sits my heart.

Rachel Beyer

Demise Vision

I felt drawn toward the placid sight
It caught my eye, the eerie light
A shimmering star, intertwined
Among a twisted state of mind
Reality struck, an uncommon scene
Thrown upon rays of luminous beam
A spectrum of color served as my street
Paradise stood upon my feet
Clean sense of calm shone from the fate
Disappearing ghastly life and hate
A sudden jerk, brought back to now
It all had been a dream, somehow

Susan Meeink

Untitled

Being an exchange student
Is a journey, few take
An adventure, few dare.
A lesson, few learn
And a life, few live.

An exchange student
Is someone understanding.
Someone courageous.
Someone wise,
And someone special.

Keep your experience
In your heart for eternity,
For it is an achievement
so rare.

Stephanie Hall

Yawn

Lily pad green wax
Inhabitant song
Nightly mosquito choreography
Windy uncurtained stage
Angel infested balcony
Pitter-pat ovation

Balls of star dew
Dotting soft petals
Girthly motivation
Roll to blend pond
Quiet waves float east
To shake the sun awake

A. Norbert Hoofnagle

"Sitting Here"

Sitting here
In this comfortable chair,
Drink within reach
But cupboard bare.
Too soon to see what I'll become,
But something,
Something, must be done.
For each day passes
And I'm to blame,
For everything that
Stays the same.

Sharon M. Weller

Listening

We often talk to the Lord
In the way we say our Prayers
We Praise Him for his Divine grace
For we know he is always there.

But what we often fail to do
Is to listen to the many ways
In which he talks to us
Every hour of every day

When we see the beautiful rainbow
He tells us the storm has gone by.
He tells us that the night is near
By the golden sunset in the sky.

The multicolored leaves of autumn
Tells us that the summer has passed
and when the snow covers the ground.
He tells us that winter is here at lost.

Yes, he talks to us in many ways.
As sure as the dew-drops glisten
If only we would take the time
To look around and listen!!

J. Price

Just Another Day

I am slowly treading water
in the third corner,
the low one,
of the forever triangle,
which is tediously filling
on a drip drop basis
from my tears.
Nevertheless I must act
as if it's
another joyful day
at the beach;
never mind the shark
feeding on my heart.

J. F. Smith Sr.

End Of A Fragile Balance

Noises, stomps, screams
in the open field of contest,
rise like deep dust
in a morbid crib of lust
long interrupted dreams.

The battle starts like a feast
dwells in a rage
ends in the ground
with no sounds.

Valeria Lanza Clarke

The Dreams To Be Dreamt

Angels call to me
 in the deepness of sleep.
In me they awaken
 the dreams to be dreamt.

Forever they keep in
 the hearts of many.
The angels that sing
 the dreams to be dreamt.

As we lie,
 in the final sleep,
The angels will sing for eternity,
 the dreams to be dreamt.

Rachael Marie Gorey

Lost Child

I am a survivor of my youth.
In the dark was kept my eyes
From seeing the real truth
Of intimate family ties.

Anger is my Teddy's name,
His fur is worn with fear.
Though it hurts me just the same,
I hold him very near.

Now that I am fully grown,
I cry for that lost child.

In a corner of my room
There is a special place.
Safe as a mother's womb,
I ask for God's grace.

I am a survivor of my youth.
In the light I keep my eyes.
To know the real truth,
Brings intimate, loving ties.

Theresa J. Topham

In The Shadows

In the jungle, eyes are watching
In the closet, ears are listening
In the night, things are waiting
In the shadows something's lurking
Something creepy, something crawly.
Something howling, what a fright
Something glowing a ghostly white
Something with claws nd horrible fangs
What could it be and why should it be?
It is coming, my heart is racing
Here it comes one step closer.
It keeps coming make it stop.
One step, steadily, after the other
There it is within my reach
Here I am, within its reach
What should I do, what could I do?
Should I run? Or wait it out.
I know, I think I'll...

Sarah Van Hoosen

Unfounded Evil

The demons
In my soul,
You have not seen them,
But they have seen you.
They hide behind;
A sweet smile, and a freckled face
Waiting for the right moment,
For you to disturb them,
Then they will arise,
And eat at your conscience,
Forever.

Renee Futch

Memory

It was an evening
in May,
the courtyard barely visible
in the starlight.

The warm night air
carried your scent of cigarettes
and cologne so softly
touching my skin.

We talked,
we laughed,
we kissed;
you were me and I was you.

My thoughts carry me back
there sometimes
in the early morning hours
and I won't sleep.

But the day comes soon
which only means I grow
further away from
the reality of you.

Rebecca Phillips

Elvis Stojko

The most exciting new star
In ice skating is Elvis Stojko
But he took a hard fall
This young Olympic winner
Gold Medalist in Norway
Now must work at healing his foot.
His jumps were perfect
He did two triple jumps
He overcame his injured foot
He land the first set of marks so far
He won a true champion!
His third Gold Medal!

Virginia Anderson

Love's Tear

We made love that night
If only in our minds

The passion and desire
Of what we once were

My thoughts reached out to you
In return, yours to mine

And although we could not give
What we desired to give

I left with the knowledge that
We made love that night

Randall Scott Wineriter

Two Spanish Students

We go to Spanish Class each week
In hopes that we can learn
To understand our Spanish friends
And answer, in return.
Our teacher is a lady
She's as patient as can be
Sometimes I really wonder
How she puts up with me.

But all she does is tell us,
"You're really doing fine.
You've learned to read and write it,
The speech will came in time."
And so each week we struggle
With tenses and with words,
We also must remember
How to conjugate the verbs.

We may not ever reach our goal
That is, 'Of speaking Spanish'
But we enjoy our lessons
And our hopes will never vanish.

Sally Kirby

Gray Kingdom

Under the burning stars,
In between the dark and light,
A castle stands immured in gloom,
Guarded all of the endless night,
From those who would bring it doom:
Those with the power of sight.
The King and Queen are gray.
Their soldiers are all lined in rows.
The Reaper patiently waits,
For soon the blood must flow.
Instead of light, the sky pours rain.
Opaque sheets that cloud the mind,
Create an ocean of thought restrained;
Everyone is running blind.
Navigating the neverending gray,
They search for a place to hide,
A safe-haven from God and man,
Where no one is forced to choose sides.
Under the burning stars,
In between the dark and light,
Lies a bloody kingdom,
Where there is no wrong or right.

Tracy Chambliss

The Voice

A silence, it echoes here
In a place alive, it calls
An eerie cry deaf to passers-by
A tear drop left alone to dry
Without a few well chosen words,
some feeling left unspoken
To evoke such emotion, a heart
so cold still frozen
Often told so many ways
A touch, a look, some caring
The needed warmth to melt it down
Allowing a silent heart to hear
the sounds
Of loving there is much to say
I've heard the voice of silence,
whispered to its heart
In its corridors I have heard
the sound
A voice within my heart
Love, it echoes here

Paul G. Ruhl

She Shouts, But They Don't Hear

Just as life is enslaved by time,
Imprisoned is she
With her many problems.

She struggles to express them.
With words. With actions.
Yet, they remain unseen, unheard.
Invisible.

How strong she must be
To handle the pain,
As it slowly
Steals her life away,
Until she is no longer—there.

So hard she tries.
She shouts, but they don't hear.

Sara Ann Deringer

Creation

Skills of the hand create,
Images drawn to scale,
Oil paintings of passion
An authors aspects of tall tales.
One hand holding another's
Hand caressing their lovers.
Lips aching for romance
Eyes looking into another's.
Bodies becoming one
Thoughts; emotions joining
Moments of lust and desire,
Bring forth
a new life,
  creation.

Tara Sears

I Have Lost My Way

I have lost my way.
I'm used, but not wanted.
I serve, but am not appreciated.
I love, but am not recompensed.
I wait, but am not rewarded.
I live, but only for the future.
I drink, out of frustration.
I pray, for better things.
I spend, superficially.
I cope, with my family.
I survive, barely.
I think I have a mind.
I hope, things will change.
I grasp, at straws.
I play, the Lotto.
I know I am desperate.
I need, a Greater Power.
I hope, He will hear.
I hope, all is not lost.

Shirley J. Deyo

Prisoner Of Reality

  Darkness put its chains on me,
I'm shackled by my destiny,
I can't escape I must concede,
I'm a prisoner of reality,
  I walk the earth so aimlessly,
In search of truth I find deceit,
Perplexed by all I feel and see,
I'm beckoned by insanity,
  I tried to run but can't retreat,
I stood to fight and met defeat,
There's no way out I can't break free,
I'm a prisoner of reality.

Walter M. Zimmerle

Nylon Insecurities

Today is Thursday and
I'm going to take my umbrella.
The weather reports a high
in the eighties, sixty percent chance
of rain and a tanning index of 4.

But, I might keep the rain away
if I take my umbrella.
I can carry it.
I can go back when
I leave it in the
restaurant after lunch.
Or, I can shield the
seventy year old
from the sun... or rain,
while she waits at the bus stop —
maybe I'll leave it
behind the twelve shoe boxes
in the back of closet.

Nylon covered spokes
wrapped around a single stick.

Peggy Hoover

The Word

When two or more can breathe a word
I'll spare a breath or two.
But when you've found my hidden name
I'll give my breath to you.

Quentin Martin

"The Sneeze"

Consider a sneeze
If you please
With the force of a freight train
Germs spread like fleas.

Oh, why does this happen?
And why through my nose?
Secretly revitalizing
That's how it goes.

But the worst of all
Is not the one that rattles your gums...
It seductively teases you
And never quite comes.

Richard Mullvain

Let There Be Peace

On the wings of the wind
I whispered a prayer.
That peace may cover this world.
I hear the call of the doves.
As they sing a morning song.
I see the beauty of the earth.
God's gift to man.
I dream of little children
May they never be hungry again.

Stand up "Oh Lion and Pray"
Let the weapons of war, be no more.
Help them to see the folly of it all.
And come to gather again and pray
May they see they are brothers.

"Oh wind spread your wings
Take this plea to the heart of God.
As I breath this prayer for peace.
"Let it begin in me."

Thelma Barnes

Life Without Love

My people never loved me
I was a child of the streets
I had no dreams to guide me
than to find a way to eat.

As I grew a little older
I got wise to ways of crime
And I never did get caught
Because I learned to bide my time.

But I never learned to love
You could be killed if you weren't tough.
And while others shook in fright
I'd never admit I had enough.

I'd come from rags to riches
And I never did back down,
There'd been no one to push me
Who wasn't rotting underground

Now as the days grow colder
And there's a shortness in my breath,
I look back upon those wasted years
And realize there's nothing left.

Phil Richey

I Never Did Tell You

Before we first met,
I was a bit unsure,
Your smile, your words,
Did I ever tell you, how much I admire?

When we first held hands,
I started to wonder,
Your thoughts, your mind,
Did I ever tell you, how much I care?

When we first kissed,
I began to hope,
Your interest, your concern,
Did I ever tell you, how much I'd give?

When we first lay together,
I started to believe,
Your emotions, your happiness,
Did I ever tell you, any of my dreams?

When we first disagreed,
I felt us grow,
Your honesty, your understanding,
I never did tell you Kendra, how much I love you!

Keith Gissel

I'm Choking

Flip back the calendar
I want to go back
Or imagine I have
I didn't mean to tear you
I've torn myself
Regrets not dissolving
A taste of self destruction
Surrounds my being
Take me back
Not for me in that second
But for what I'll be
There's no artificial love
Only the shadow of mistake
That constantly hovers.

Sarah Wojner

Remember Me

Remember me on this joyous day.
  I want to be normal.
  I want to be loved.
  I want to play.

Remember me in a loving way.
  I loved my family.
  I loved my friends
  I want to play.

Remember me for this, I say:
  I had heart.
  I had courage.
  I want to play.

I'll remember all of you today.
  You gave me life.
  You gave me love.
Excuse me now, for I'm in a place where
  I can play.

Richard G. Downer

Tears Of Autumn

Then comes one day, you must go
I walk you to the end of the road
With your arms, you embrace me
A gentle kiss, you then leave me

Looking out the window everyday
I sit as time slips away
But I keep your words alive inside
That you'll be back and by my side

I miss you, my husband at war
Fighting somewhere far away
Nights I walk down the same old road
In hope to see your returning shadow

Leaves grow old and once again fall
I stand against the opened door
I close my eyes so I can dream
That you are here and come walking in

But that's the worst thing I can do
Hold on to a dream that won't come true
I dry my tears as I hear the distant thunder
Sounding the fall of another soldier

T. T. Le

My Mistake

As I lay here this morning
I think about last night
What got into me I wonder
Guess I just lost sight

It all happened so quickly
I didn't have time to think
I didn't want it to go that far
It wouldn't have; but I had that drink

He is waking up now
He rolls over to give me a kiss
All I can think about is last night
It started just like this

I know I don't love him
He says he loves me
That I'm really special
And we were meant to be

I'm sorry that it happened
I wish I had said no
All I can do is pray
That he'll just let me go

Sarah Mynheir

The World Now

I look up
I see dark clouds towering over me
I hear the trees start to rustle
I feel the wind blowing against me
Harder, Harder
I see my dreams being blown away
The dark clouds laughing over me
My life being controlled by nature
My future being flushed down a drain
Clones, clones is all I see
I feel myself being transformed into one
Now besides the wind all I hear is
  "No Life"
  "No Life"
  "No Life"

Allison Chadwick

I Promise

If you give me your hand,
I promise to take it.
If you give me your heart,
I promise not to break it.
If you give me your arms,
I promise to embrace you,
If you give me your lips,
I promise to taste you.
If you give me your love,
I promise to accept it,
If you give me your soul,
I promise to protect it.

Sharon E. Sherry

Happiness

Happiness is a state of mind
I pray to God I will find

Searching and seeking it out each day
Hoping it will soon hurry my way

I found it today within my own heart
And I'm hanging on so it doesn't part

Happiness is the greatest treasure
That no one can ever measure

Thomas J. Keylon

Love's Farewell

Behold you standing with such grace
I ponder momentarily
Flawlessly outlined in lace
Wantonly I seek out thee
Your scent's sweet whisper calling me
Anticipations overtake
If only we were two not three
Just a pair I wish to make
Oh sweet one I bid farewell
For nothing more will come of we
Eyes close tight as teardrops swell
Another love not meant to be...

Philip Pickard

The Divorce

He said he never loved you,
He only married you for sex.
He wasn't worth 20 years of loyalty.
Aren't you glad he's now your ex!

Ruth Wise

Reflection III

Just like this feeble poem
I offer with my pen -
So is all my righteousness
That is but wrapped in sin.

Just like Paul Apostle
Wrote in his book, so true -
That I would do, I do not;
That I wouldn't, is what I do.

Lord, I seek you in the morning,
I need you ev'ry hour;
I cannot break from chains of sin
Without your grace and pow'r.

Dear Lord, I am not worthy
Of the grace you've shown to me -
But I pray you'd give me more,
For of more I am in need.

Timothy Munger

The Scent

I purchased a new perfume today;
I now must wear a mask.
Changes have to be made sometime
Concerning present and past.

Thoughts of dark-lined lips
and toned up hips
Come to the surface of the scene;

Red finger nails and soft black veils
Hang flowingly to the knee.

Mellow tunes in other rooms,
Verdi on the bench;
Flowers in bloom,
Brides and grooms,
Dinner in the tent-

Can I trust that all this stuff
Is contained within the scent?

D. Dragon Moon

I Need A Friend

I need a friend to love and care
I need a friend who's always there.
I need a friend when I am down—
to wipe away that saddening frown

I need a friend when I am glad—
to share the good times that we each had.

I need a friend to warm
my heart and be the
best right from the start.

Sarah Hotchkiss

No One

No one knows how I feel.
I am all alone in a world of my own.
No one knows just how I hurt,
No one feels the pain I feel.
Argument upon argument
fight upon fight
every moment nothing is right.
As the tears stream down on my plush
pale cheeks as I morn, wonder,
and weep, how someone I have
loved could hurt me so much.

Shannon Trammell

How Do I Miss You

Let me count the ways.
I miss you at six
When I wake.
I miss you at seven
And then at eight.
I miss you at nine
When it's coffee time.
I miss you at ten
And at eleven; again.
It's twelve now
It has not changed.
It's now one and I feel the same.
Now it's two, three, four,
Then five, now six.
Twelve hours gone
So now I wait for the phone.
Seven, eight, nine, and now ten.
Eleven rings; I hear your voice,
I feel so great, then it's over.
Back to missing you again.

Pattie Nichols

Just For Me........

I like the way,
I live each day,
just for me.......

I try my best,
to be better than all the rest,
just for me.......
Work is hard,
but so am I,
just for me.......

There will be a day,
where life is never gray,
just for me.......
Life is sometimes painful and hard,
but many times gainful and starred,
just for me.......

Ronald Malabed

The Spirit Of A Poet

As my youth approached
I knew from the start,
There were words for One
That sprang from my heart.

Like a newborn fawn
With legs overwhelming
The first steps unsure
Yet the Light slowly dawning.

Soothing are the thoughts that come,
Like music from my pen, they run.
Things expressed not from my lips,
But from my heart to one's fingertips.

Oh how I love to feel the flow
Of words unknown to thy tongue,
Yet as they come the Source I know
Sweet songs in wait to be sung.

Let nothing but good spring forth this day
From these poetic rivers;
Given by One who knows the way,
In Whom I will trust to deliver.

Susan G. Margraf

Loss Love

When my love left
I felt so all alone.
The times we spent together were
the most happiest moments
to spend my life with this one special
person were my plans.
Until one day when he had gone I
was and felt heartbroken.
But then I remembered he
will think of me.
For we were both so madly
in love.
The way I lost him I
will remember.
But my love for him
will stay in my heart
FOREVER!

Roxanne Ortiz

How To Pray

I'm just a lonely prisoner Lord
I don't know how to pray
I've read about you in a book
that someone threw away.

This book says you are Jesus
and you love even me
so I began to wonder Lord
How could all this be?

I know you love me very much
But you have no reason to
I've been a real bad sinner Lord
That's why I've turned to you

Now Lord if you'll stay by me
And help me day by day
I know this lonely prisoner
will soon learn how to pray.

Ron Cady

Quinnehtukqut...Connecticut...Saiagiad...

Always in dreams
I cry for a peace
And the family that will not know me...
And then it snows...

  Who cries behind your eyes
  I know...
  Who is father to the rain...
  Walk on...wakan...

  Creators...creations...
  Children us all of
  Who's art in heaven...
  Where is your light when sleeping?

...Keep walking...walk on...wakan...
...Quinnehtukqut...Saiagiad...ho!

Virginia Redden Boland

Happiness

Tears of joy fall down my face,
Happiness surrounds my very being,
As if no anger could ever enter,
The bright beautiful colors glare at me,
Hitting my warm soul,
It lifts me up,
An angel is looking down at me,
Smiling at what she sees,
I can never fall

Vickie Bryant

Pin Oak

I am a pin oak tree.
I can feel
the summer
breeze,
and feel
the nice
intense
sun on me!
And when
the sun
goes down,
and the
moon hangs
From the starry sky, my leaves fall
asleep! I am a pin oak tree.

Rachael Marie Lambeau

Love's Desire

I do not know how to show you
I am worthy of your trust.
Time will have to show you
I am truer than the rest.

You need not have to worry
For I will never stray.
From now until you leave my side
It will be this way.

I what to share my life, my love,
My fears and joys with you.
So if you let me in your heart
I'll show you I am true.

I realize that scars of past
Will always be in mind,
But I know that you can love me
If just given ample time.

Tricia Travers

Dad

Thanks for the love,
I always felt it reach high above.
I treasure your gifts,
That have guided me through mists.
I have grown up strong,
I feel I can't go wrong.
But, it's so great to know,
That you're not far now!
All the time, when I through a fit.
I remember, "don't you quit!"
So many phrases, quotes or stories,
I hold onto in my memories.
And when the time comes to retrieve,
I can find it and believe,
That you guided me with love,
To the lady I am now, flying like a dove!

Veronica J. Vasquez

The World Is So Sweet

If the world was chocolate
how tasty it would be
Swimming pools would be soda
Oceans would be tea
Clouds would be cookies

Y U M M Y!

Although this would be tasty
and quite a sight to see
I like the world as it is
I guess it's fine with me

Tara Keith

Faces

Count the faces that I wear
How many do you see?
They change like seasons of the year
Which one is really me.

The smile upon a happy face
Contrived to hide the pain
Like snow upon the frozen earth
Beneath it's not the same.

The cold facade of anger
A smile as yet tears flow
Each mask provides protection
For this heart I alone must know.

No one knows this mask I wear
Which face I let them see
Assuming there's joy in laughter
Blind and yet they see.

But you see through these masks I wear
What others see only in part
My masks with you are useless
You see me with your heart.

Rudy McNeill

Untitled

A child growing up in a
household with no love
The child just a little
person which has no meaning
A child is a human-being
but a baby not born will
Never become a child

Why must people do this,
You have a human-being
Inside you but yet you
Can't take actions for your doings
This child unborn has done
Nothing wrong but yet you
Demand to have it killed

The baby needs a chance
to learn and grow and love
The baby is not fake
but yet it is real
Real as Real as you
and me, so why must you kill yourself?
KILL YOURSELF?

H. Holmes

It Is Always There

Faith is the substance of things
Hoped for
It is not seen or felt
But yet it is there
It may dwindle or grow
But it is always there
Faith endures all things in life
It is tested
And sometimes broken
But yet enough remains to grow again
It is always there

Robert Poyner Jr.

The Search

Lover can you show the way,
Hold my heart while we play.
Heaven's gift a fleeting chance,
Tell me that we can romance.
Broken rule's have spoiled the fun,
Now the real game has begun.
Hateful words we use to win,
Tell me, have you never sinned.
Strive for freedom with all your might,
Unseen terror has changed your life.
Run away for all your worth,
You'll only gain peace on earth.
Ugly things we use and say,
To rip our hearts and turn to clay.
When will kindness reign again,
When fighting in the world of men.
Love is such a special glimpse,
Of adoration's burning kiss.
Love needs only two hearts to play,
Tell me can you show the way.

Sandra Whitley

"Our Lord"

He watches us from the valley
He's watching from the plains,
He's on top of every mountain
He brings the lovely rain.

He sees our every move we make
He knows your heart and mine,
He's our precious Lord in heaven
His love is pure divine.

As we go through our daily travels
Our Lord is always there,
He's our shelter in times of danger
He will soothe your worst nightmare.

He's the strength we tend to lean on
The almighty power from above,
No matter where we wander or stray
We always have his love.

Let's always thank him for what we have
And what we've been able to be,
For without our wonderful savior
There may not have been a we.

Phyllis Johnson Massey

St. Patrick's Day 1924

Those ancient times now seem so near
Her voice so gentle to my ear
Her arms around me soft and warm
She cared not the cause of my storms

She brushed the hair away from my eyes
She cared enough for little white lies
Nothing too good to comfort her baby
My friend, my mom, and fine young lady

Her death it came in life's very prime
For a mother's death there is no time
She gave me everything from my start
She gave me myself, she gave me my heart

For all of this I have nothing to give
I can't have my wish for her to live
If I could only see her now above
I'd thank her for teaching me to love.

M. A. Little

Untitled

I listened as she gently wept,
Her secrets so intently kept
Let me in, I began to cry
Please child, before I die.
What troubled my baby so
How was I to ever know?
I failed to hear, to understand
Her troubled soul dropped through my hands.
She chose life's darker path,
Our love gone, an aftermath.
If the chance should rise again,
I'll not stop, 'til I get in.

Susan Taylor

The Lily

There she sits
her pale, haunting beauty.
Leaning to see
her own reflection,
In a pool.

In time her beauty fades,
each falling petal
takes some beauty,
To the pool.

There she lies
trying not to see,
her beautiful reflection fade.
With the drop of each petal,
giving her beauty to the pool.

As she watches her beauty die.
She hears a cry,
that of the pool
her cry of pleasure.
For she will envy
the lily no more.

Stephanie Palmer

Jayne

I watched her walk away from me,
Her living beauty in each side.
Her eternity danced on her arms
With bright and laughing eyes.

The sun shines upon her now where
She rests, as it did that day.
Though her voice is silenced evermore,
She still has much to say.

She's alive inside my soul right now.
The gift she gave me lives.
Knowing her was a cherished blessing.
Loving her still is.

Sherry Rodenborn

Untitled

Spiritual gift I behold
Heir of my body
Conceived with love
Time honored through act
Of guidance
Expressible admittance
Recognizing an understanding
One's own way
Unity of time
Put in remembrance
Flower of age and
Beauty
Living for ever
My child

Revina Mihalek

Nobody's Fool

His family just moved into town;
He lives in a modest old home.
He has a dog named Jake,
His sister loves *David the Gnome*.

He lives on the "good" side of town,
And rides the bus to school.
It seems like a normal life,
But he's nobody's fool.

He hears what they say behind his back,
How different he is to them.
They call him names and steal his stuff,
It's the way it's always been.

So they move from town to town,
Searching for a change.
But wherever they end up,
It'll always be the same.

He'll always be a target,
As well as his kids and kin.
And he'll cry his tears and scream his rage,
'Cause of the color of his skin.

Tara D. Clark

With No Strings Attached

Costume dressed to please the crowd
he does whatever he's allowed
dangling arms will swing and sway
going this and that a way
dancing feet go Flippity Flop
bouncing with a hippity hop
with his own distinctive style
he wears a happy painted smile
jerking up and down he springs
thanks to those connecting strings
from a clinging hand atop
he either stands or goes aplop
all moving parts are aptly strung
here and there and in among
but if somehow he comes united
those parts of him will not abide
performing as a jumbled mess
he'll be a puppet in distress
his smile will turn into a frown
when sadly he hangs up side down

Robert J. Pool

Innocence's Rhyme

The stories of life
have grown through time
the years have said, "good bye."

So now they turn to empty cradles
finding their children gone.
Swept away from their innocence
leaving the cradle empty and robbed.

Your children are gone,
your children are gone away!
Buried in the sand
their childhoods lie

Lost and gone from time;
no more innocence,
no more love
broken the child's rhyme!

Tim Smith

Untitled

Last in the shadows
Haunted by my past
Ready I have learned
Nothing real will last
The golden setting sun
Must fade into blackened night
As consciousness falls bleak
Swollen eyes which fear more tears
A shrieking heart
It soon disappears
What part of me is there left to give?
Nothing is responsive
Rendered unattractive
Giving up the will to fight
Fade in the shadows
Until once again I am lost

Teri Ambre

Numb

Numb,
has my soul
from what life has done to me
or what I have done myself

Numb
has my soul
from wrong doing of others
or those of mine

Numb
has my soul
safe and hidden
behind a wall of ice

Numb
has my soul
never to be
Touched again.

Numb
has my soul
forever.

Rosemarie Gallo

Remembering Ann

The sun has dimmed; the moon
  has lost its glow
The stars no longer shine and
  nights are long
Our days are far too slow.

Our hearts are heavy since
  you have gone
You spread such cheer - your
  smile so dear cannot return
You are not here.

We must not mourn - you are with God
  you're free from pain
We must not grieve, your loss
  we must sustain;
Your love surrounds us - HE MAKES
  YOU WHOLE AGAIN.

Ruth Davis

A Terrible Dream

In a terrible dream, I heard a great
gray wolf howl at a silver moon
upon a rocky ridge I heard an owl
calling from an old oak tree
  I heard a dove mourning in
the gray, quiet down.
  I heard an old black cat crying
on my neighbor's dying lawn.
  I heard people screaming as the
planes flew overhead,
I heard the bombs explode, then I
heard no more
  In my terrible dream, all the
earth was dead

Versa Kohut

Age Of Aging

Most of our youth is spent reaching
Grasping for riches and dreams.
Adulthood comes too soon for most
At least to the aged it seems.

The midyears are filled with
The ups and downs
Our lives are our children and selves
We become giants and clowns.

When the house becomes empty
Just the two of you left.
All your plans for the future
Leave your delusions bereft.
Then the age of the aging
Settles down in a gloom.
All your thoughts are remembrances
Of a past gone too soon.

William F. Schmid

Rose Of Love

Sweet, pale rose of love,
Give me your fragrant blossoms
That you all sorrows may remove
And fulfill life's cherished dreams.
Give comfort, peace as petals fly,
Upward swirling to the sky,
And fall in masses at my feet
Lovely, beautiful, complete.
No rose could charm away the light
Except the rose you hold tonight.
No rose, so red or white or pink
Could catch love's glory in a wink
As roses, fresh with morning dew,
Proclaiming lover's dreams come true.

Phyllis Capen

Untitled

I thought of you today
You're so wonderful
And you treat me so well
You are the kindest person
That I have ever met
I think of you and
I care about you so much
If you were not in my life
I would feel empty
I need you near me
I need you in my life
I hope you will always
Be here for me because
I love you.

Nancy L. Woolson

Memories Sung Through Time

Sing secret songs, sing the songs before time began
Of nothingness, of empty space
But time speeds ahead at a rapid pace
The first notes are soon to sound

Sing secret songs, sing the songs of yesteryear
Eternal notes lodged in the brain
Recalled with ease upon face and name
The beginning of a flowing tune

Sing secret songs, sing the songs of the present day
The images depict time and space
An ominous opening to a wondrous place
The tune grows in rhythm and strength

Sing secret songs, sing the songs of future years
Filled with goals achieved and rewarded
For each goal reached you are awarded
The final notes echo through eternity...

Aimee Sinclair

Blood

   Seeping out of my mist as all the dreams drain out
of my sow. Rolling down my arm to drop to the floor
like a cold tear running down my face to only lose
ground once it falls off my quivering chin. Shattering,
as the sun rose to shine light over my beloved darkness.

   Torture must be waited for ever so longingly. I
won't be able to see my pain until twilight is
gone and darkness fills me with passion once
again. Chaos will be able to run through my
mind freely. Suffering will be within my punished
heart. The legacy of the screams and shadows will
awaken the betrayed spirituals, and then I'll be
able to escape into hell for its reassurances.
covered with wood and fool of agony, I will be
welcomed for eternity!

Autumn Tomasi

From The Time Of Remembering

From the time of remembering, I have heard
of Jesus and His precious word.
I heard, that's true, but that's all that I did
as a child of darkness, I ran and hid.

From the time of remembering, I have seen
the results of accepting and a heart made clean.
I've seen, that's true, but nothing more,
my heart was cold and black to the core.

From the time of remembering, I also felt
the longing, the searching, the need for help.
I felt, that's true, but that is all
I heeded not the warning or the call.

From the time of remembering, my senses learned true
it takes the Master to give real freedom to you.
So one night in great sorrow and deep despair
in faith, opened my heart, and He was there.

I'm saved, I'm saved, I have seen His face
I now know His love, His peace, His grace.
I now must study and pray and grow
and tell others of blessings that they can know.

Bessie C. Steele

My Reason For Living

What do you think about when you see the bloom
   of fresh spring flowers?
When you feel the first drop of new rain?
When you feel warmth from a ray of sunshine?
When you hear the cry of a newborn baby?
Or when you hear the words "I love you" from
   someone closer than a friend?
I think about life;
I think about how it feels having you
   to make me feel strong again,
   to make me feel worth and value again.
For me you are the sunshine
   the fresh flower
   the new drop of rain
   the freshness of a newborn baby's cry...
You are the first breath of life
That lets me know everything has a reason;
That everything is going to be all right
Because of who we are for each other.

Debbie Morder

"Thank You Lord, For These Golden Years"

From these golden years, I can now look back,
O'er the hills and the valleys, where I left my tracks,
And it's a mighty long journey, from there to here,
As I'm now experiencing, these golden years.

Many times I stumbled, and many times I fell.
But I made it through, and now I'm here to tell,
About those times when I laughed, and the times I shed tears,
Oh, thank you Lord, for these golden years.

Tho the color of my hair, is now silver lined,
Joy and contentment, I still can find,
So, again I say thanks, for my being here,
Enjoying these days, of my golden years.

Now, I know where I'm headed, as I live these golden years,
For there's a place called heaven, and I know that it's near,
But I'm happy that I can say, before I leave here,
Thank you Lord, for these golden years!!

Clyde L. Heathcock Sr.

Quota Of Biota

Outdoors I sit, with Planter's Punch my brew,
Observing quadrupeds; i.e., the ruminants.
They're even-cloven-hoofed, their cud they chew.
Some formic strays have fallen in my drink;
They're swimming crazily and do not sink.
Behavior caused by rum in ants, I think.

Oh, here's a fact that is sublime!
The footprints of some ancient lizards
Were found by geologic wizards
Upon the sands of time.

Said Poe, "The raven's always in a hungry mood;
Forevermore, it's ravenous for food.
It always gulps the largest where it sits.
Indeed, my crow will eat no micro bits.

We saw the cat fall off the roof.
It was unscathed, its blood unshed.
Incredible! It seemed a proof
It had nine lives. It could be said
Just eight are left to see it through.

Alan Wayne

119

Infatuation

Its imitation is filled with delusions
Numbed by the arrow of another.
For now boiling over with
Ardent kisses and quickening pulses.
Tethered responses without deeper
Understanding that weave shackles.
And after it evaporates, because it does,
Transcending love still waits
In spirit and soul mate passion, while the
Odyssey continues to the one like
No other.

Bree Gale

Your World

When I stepped into your world, I didn't know what to except.
Now that I am here, I can't wait to see what's next.
The time we share is special and I am never bored.
My mind once said run, but my heart was truly floored.

Every time I see you the easier it seems.
Every time I'm with you it feels just like a dream.
The way you say you love me, the expressions on your face,
The way you touch and hug me, damn, I love this place.

If you left tomorrow, I know I'd surely die.
A world of tears and sorrows would be my last demise.
I truly love you; more than words can say,
And I really want to show you I'm just waiting for that day.

These words are part of me, feeling I can't control,
Just like the passion I have for you that sometimes overflows.
I hope you understand and can read between these lines,
Searching through these words, there's a love for you to find.

David R. Freeman

Then And Now-The Seasons Of Love

Then we shyly chose the rings that we would wear,
Now strands of gray, like diamonds sparkle in your hair.
  Then the wedding was in May,
  Now it seems like yesterday,
And we knew the love we shared was truly rare.

Then those summer days that trailed the path of spring,
Now shape the essence of our memories and dreams.
  Then as each bird in seasons sings,
  Now cool breaths from angel's wings
Chill this autumn of our lives, or so it seems.

Then with vision not yet honed by eyes of time,
Now behold this flowered love of yours and mine.
  Then as a seed sown in each heart,
  Now as two vines that never part,
Entwined, shall wither with the snow - the winter's sign.

Alice Louise Jones Goode

To God

There is nothing like my baby's breath
No smell on God's earth like my baby's breath
There is no smooth breeze from God's heaven trees
That feel like my baby's breath
There is no sunbeams from God's angels
That makes me shine like my baby's breath
So why God did you take my baby's breath

And God said
Babies breath are angels breeze
They blow across your heart and your soul
When all is well baby's breath are heaven breeze

Cle Fedak

The Last Customer

All alone, at the end of the bar
Nothing left, but a drink in my hand.
Not a lover beside me, nor a friend beside me
No one, to ever try to understand.

When out of the shadows, came a tall slender man!
He sat down beside me, I slowly took his hand

As he spoke I listened, his intentions so clear.
I have watched you drink whiskey,
And I have watched you drink wine,
And I have noticed each time you were here!

We arose from a table, and we walked hand in hand.
He said, I'll take you somewhere! And I think you will understand.

I listened quite closely,
To the stories he told, about how I drank my life away
And how I have grown old as we walked along, and I began to see!
How I had wandered form the path. That he intended for me!
I saw the road beneath me, my life about to unfold!
The road it was gold, and my heart was of stone.
He said do not worry, you are not alone
My name is Jesus, and I have come to take you home!!

Barbara D. Guy

Between Life And A Dream

Here I sit all alone
Not knowing what to feel
I can hear myself moan
I can see myself kill
Then I wake up
I'm sweating, I'm scared
Who is it? Is it me? Is somebody there?
I saw my life pass in front of my eyes
Was it me? Was it me? Was I in disguise?
My family, my friends were all in it too
Oh no, oh no, what should I do
I'm trapped between life and a dream.

Here I sit and all alone
Not knowing what to feel
I can hear myself moan
I can see myself kill
I can't make up!
I'm trying, I'm trying!
Please help, I'm dying
I'm trapped between life and a dream.

Clarissa Henry

What I Had I Did Not Know

What I had I did not know
Nor, till it gone, would it I miss;
Some say loss will help you grow,
But I'd trade all to feel her kiss.

How I ache for one more chance,
Her body close, my arms surround;
To hear our song ... to dance our dance,
That special bond 'tween hearts that pound.

It's not my choice, this life alone,
You know my sort ... traditional man;
Without me close, my children grown,
I've failed my God and his grand plan.

Alone in bed, no one to share
The ups and downs of all that's life;
Someone to Love and just be there,
To cherish, hold and be my Wife!

The fire is out, my heart no glow,
My lesson learned ... a lesson sad;
For Love had gone with wind that blow
And now I know just what I had.

D. H. Nuske

A Candle

I never meant to be a torch held high,
Nor a beacon brightening the way.
I only meant to be a candle,
Softly glowing, sometimes flickering.
Guiding, ever encouraging you,
My children, to find your way through the dark.

Alberta S. Lynch

Eyes

They're mystifying,
No telling where they have been
You may look deeply into them
But you will never know what they have seen.

You don't know if they reveal
Horror, happiness, or confusion
But they laugh and dance
As if to mock you

They don't match her face
Wonderful smile and perfect dimples
When you look into them you see something
Each person sees something different
Because you know that the eyes,
Are the gateway to the soul

When you look into them you see something of someone
You see your most inner thoughts, and your future
You look into someone else's eyes and see yourself
What you see may scare or amuse you
But don't underestimate what you see because the eyes never lie

Andrea Koch

Waiting

A teenage girl sits alone, tears trickling down her face.
No one is able to console her,
No one even knows that she is feeling this way.
The unknown frightens her, haunts her, and makes her heart race.
To her, everything now seems a blur.
Time passes slowly as she awaits her test day.

She weeps and she weeps.
She feels so afraid and so terribly alone.

In the darkness of night, she stares up at the ceiling.
Her head completely full of question.
She questions the darkness but receives no answer.
She doesn't want to talk about the way she's feeling.
No one would understand her. No one!
But, she does pray, "God, please, don't let me have cancer."

Finally she sleeps.
This is the scariest feeling she's ever known.

Amiee Renee Doan

The Panther

The panther is sly and cunning. It catches its prey at
nightfall. The only sound you hear is the wind blowing through
the willows. The panther's green eyes glow in the darkness. Its
claws so sharp you think they could penetrate through glass. Its
teeth glow white in the moonlight. Its fur black and silky moves
gracefully with every step. The panther waits for signs of life
then it POUNCES!

Amanda Tamez

Mosquitoes

The humid air pressed close like a moist cloud as
nightfall lingered.

A whining in your left ear and a soft buzzing
in your right, you swat thoughtlessly at the disturbance.

The dry, brittle crab grass chafes your skin, an
irritation and the droning hum returns.

"Ignore it," you tell yourself reassuringly. Relax and
bathe in the moonlight.

Glances are exchanged and an exposed surface is
chosen in calculating randomness, a perfect accident.

A tickling sensation and hairs brush against hairs
without meaning.

With a sharp sting an exchange takes place, and
blood is greedily drawn.

Watching helplessly, thoughts coupled with feelings
assert themselves, each answer asking a question.

Rather than extinguish the waning light you become
prey and progress.

"Was it?" you ask yourself dolefully. Summer and
its solitary memory.

Ben Keene

Beginnings

Shadows gave into light.
Night gave into the day.
Dawn emerged from the darkness,
and beginnings were found.

The beginning of love, of joy and happiness.
The beginning of the world.
The beginning of our lives.

But beginnings must end, as everything does.
Early hues to dawn, subside to the colors of day,
Night's shadows become the darkness of twilight.
And hark to the sound of the nightingale's sweet song,
for that too must someday end.

But beginnings happen more than once,
a new day emerges from the old.
Dusk approaches once again,
and dawn's sweet light fills us with spirit once again.

As beginnings end, and beginnings start,
we all become more.
Better within ourselves at each coming day.
Shadows give into light.

Chenxi Jiao

Limbo

Nothing
Nothing above me
Nothing below me
Nothing around me
Emptiness
Loneliness
A total void
I am nowhere
I am everywhere
I move but will never reach a destination
Fore there is none to reach
There is no one around
Nothing to hear
There is no heaven
No hell
No life or death
Fore Limbo is where I dwell

Christina Wright

121

Never To Return

I shall go out into dark oblivion,
　　Never to return

To see distant ports and far away horizons
their storms sudden fiery brings forth havoc and demises
Upon persons, properties
With everyone hoping it'll,
　　Never to return

Sailors remembering old forgotten wives tales
Fathers folklore
Singing drunken bar songs
About the women they entail

Grant us to master in the middle o' night
Weigh our anchor and set course true
For our sails to take flight,
　　Never to return

Many port of all port calls,
Can only answer my prayers
I shall keep my vow —
　　Never to return.

　　Arthur Thomas

A Precious Thing To Say

　The only way to describe it isn't ordinary
never one word to say about it, but what we
can say about it is that we all take it for
granted, wanting but never giving

　It can't go on forever for it just won't
always be there for us. For we all know
the future will soon be the past waiting
to haunt us once more

　My way to say about our costly problem
is that life is everything, and so then everything
will always be life, forever.

　　Catherine Ketner

To Lovers ...

Who care and strive for the happiness the other can offer. Who will
never leave and betray.

To lovers who are willing to give up the world to be with each other.
Who are never to be apart for more than a minute, and each minute is
one too long.

To lovers who would rather see inside the soul of their mate than the
outside wall. Who will share the deepest part of their heart with.

To lovers who can say I love you without having to hesitate. Who are
joined together by the endless bounds of God, and who will never
ever say good bye.

　　Amanda Arrington

Your Store-House

What do you store in your store-house is it mostly silver and gold
Never helping those in need because it's yours to have and to hold

Is jealousy growing because of what they did to you
Are all your thoughts painted with a grim color of blue

Do you store hatred and anger and a chance to get even some day
Or to murder with tongue to ruin a name just to get back some way

Turn from this living begin by giving what God has given to you
To God and man-kind be honest be faithful and true

God will store without measures to your store-house above
So open up your heart and start sharing your love

Light the lamp of love cause love has no bounds
And in turn God will give you a heavenly crown.

　　Cecil G. Bosley

"Living Behind The Trigger"

Living behind the trigger, always on the run,
Never go anyplace without my gun.
I'm on a rampage and it's time to have some fun.
A young brother got shot 'cause he didn't do his part.
If he had played it cool and kept his smarts,
he wouldn't be dead.
From the start I think about all the people that didn't like
me, and I wonder how long it will be before I'll be laying
on a slab like my friends.
But, wouldn't you figure that's what you get when you are
living behind the trigger?
I can't cry now because this is the life I chose.
Now, I want to have fun, but the gun won't let me.
I got caught up in living behind the trigger.
I think about dying and doing time in the State Pen, but
I have to live with it now 'cause I'm on the run,
and life has lost all its fun...
with me living behind the trigger.

　　Anthony L. Grant

"When You Think Of Me"

If I were to die today. There are so many things that I still
need to say, I love you all so very much don't let your pain get
in the way. And know you'll feel better some far away day.
Because you all mean the world to me. Having everyone sad isn't
the way I would want it to be. I want you to smile when you
think of me. Because that's what I'll do, when I look down from
Heaven at you. We need to be strong and comfort each other, we
need to be happy and love one another So it will be hard for
some of you I know, but it was just my time to go. I didn't
want to I'm sure you all know but when God calls you, you cant
say no, so please be happy when you think of me. Have a party
or plant a tree because that's how I want you all to be I know
your all hurting right now this is true but try to Remember how
much I loved you. I'm very sorry I'm causing such sorrow, but I
know you'll feel better on Some Tomorrow.....

　　Danielle S. Hand

Bridges Of Life

The bridges of life are many,
　'N life goes on, with us or without.
Love is the strongest bridge of all,
　As our hearts will never doubt.

The bridges of life are all one direction,
　For there's no turning around.
We must forge ahead together,
　Always seeking familiar ground.

The bridges of life lead to friends,
　'N some become the very best.
As communicating amongst us,
　While friendships take the test.

The bridges of life carry memories,
　For all to remember or regret.
Some are happy ones 'N some are sad,
　But, forgiveness is the greatest bet.

　　Elmer A. Rasmussen II (Bud)

"My Wife"

My wife is more than a wife to me.
My wife is much more, much more than anyone else could ever be.
My wife is my friend, my friend who listens to my every plea.
My wife is like a mother who cares,
She lifts my pain and sorrows and they alone she bears.
My wife is a wife who listens and understand,
She sacrifices her precious time to write to me so she will know how
   I stand.
My wife is like a father who guides and directs my every move,
She has patience and concern and wants me to be soothed.
My wife is like a daughter who showers me with Love,
My wife is so tender, gentle, and warm, as if she is an
   angel from up above.
My wife is more than many things anyone could ever be.
My wife is very, very special to me.
My Darling Wife, there's one thing I want you to know,
Please never leave me, for I love you so.

Burton Fariss

"Confused"

Writing; my most wonderful love,
  My signature below with my words above.
Coming from the heart, the pen flows with ease,
  Words with rhythm, to the mind they please.

We love your work, write for us,
  We want your work, pay for thus.
We'll give you money, to write a subject on this,
  Here's your bill, pay-don't miss.

So confused, but I love the print,
  I don't want to deprive anyone, my words of mint.
I love to share, it makes me feel good,
  If I could gain in my mind, I always would.

But , like all in this world, we do have a price,
  No matter how sugar coated, or painted so nice.
To have your work lined, you get so amused,
  But the offers, and deals, I am so confused.

Albert J. Adams Jr.

Untitled

As I lay in a field of sweet Chamomile,
My lordship hands me a quaint, antique, little vial.

"What for?", Ask I,
But no reply,
Just a nod and a faint little sigh.

With all my trust,
To whom I've shared my lust,
I slowly take a sip.

With a taste that of wine,
And my body feeling fine,
I whisper a faint, "I love you".

But who ever knew,
What my Lordship would do,
To his one and everlasting love.

Chava N. Litwin

The Quality Of Understanding

Time has granted us the peace that we need to be easy...
Like Sunday mornings...lazy days....and cloudy afternoons....
Except for the truth...there is nothing else....
Some people love romance novels....
And on the other hand....everyone wants to be happy...
What can be more peaceful than a calming sea?...
Resting atop an endless valley of passionate openness...
In deed....I know that still waters do run deep.

Adib Abdullah Rasheed

Baby, I Love You

Baby, I want to share with you,
my hopes and dreams I've tried.

Baby, I want to hold you close
and see our future inside.

Baby, I know there's a life for us somewhere,
I just don't know how.
I want to give that life to you,
but baby I can't right now.

The pain you will hurt, I will hurt too,
'cause baby no one loves you as much as I do.

Please don't be angry and please don't be sad,
baby, I've given you all that I had.

Dallas Donna Ellis

Tracks Of My Dreams

With every thought, at every beat,
my heart seems to explode.
Is it a longing, a need to care?
Am I on the right road?

Who knows what way our life should go?
What life we have to lead.
At times a path we seem to take,
Sometimes we do not heed

Many times we take a chance,
A lot of times we fail
There's grief and sadness, laughter and fun.
We take chances to no avail.

I'll never regret the lives I've touched;
The one's I've love before.
Still I have a lot to give;
And I'll give my best and more.

One day that person will come my way.
One day they will fulfill.
I'll be ready, I know I'm ready,
Cause I've lots of love in me still.

Frederick R. Marshall

Catching A Baseball In The Eye

My eyes were closed to light and joy about me,
My heart and mind were full of fear;
Then faith and prayer brought Jesus to the rescue,
I felt His presence then so very near.

The time of crisis comes to us as Christians,
The way of faith is hard to see;
He gives us light to guide us on our pathway,
I'll follow Him through all eternity.

How wonderful the light that Christ doth give me,
How marvelous that He can set me free;
I'll never turn my eyes from Him who healed me,
I'll love Him through eternity.

Dean E. Burton

Untitled

The soft milk tide upon linen strands a bundle.
Listen to the delicate chorus of song birds-asleep.
Close misty lids of Silver satin-
and let the hidden story teller tell his tale.
The tale of rider's night-
and unexpected adventures afloat.
Think of heart's words-
whispered as lips brush upon an ear.
Imagine the gentle caress of soft hands,
Lain away from worry-
and hope dawn's rise comes quickly.

David Hughes

Memories Of My Father

I grew up in a world that's tough
My father taught me still to trust

Life is but a show you see
Always keep your faith like me

Do your work and you'll be fine
Remember, that honesty is not a crime.

Loyalty is important too
Remember this for you'll be married soon.

Days will come when you feel alone
Hope and faith will bring you home.

Words of wisdom
From my fathers lips
Was the most decent man
That ever exist.

Carmen Torres

The Beauty Of A Rose

A rose slowly drifts over
my face, its bright and vivid pink
petals feel like silken velvet

Its proud head held high,
looking toward the glowing orange-red
rays of the gracious sun

Red, pink, and orange dew slips
from the strong, yet graceful head to the thick,
bright green stem

The dew is caught on a fine-edged thorn, and
soon falls among the luscious
grass

A girl whose thoughts are
filled with passion and love
picks the rose, and tenderly removes
the satin-like petals trying
to find love

The soft petals gently flow with
the wind toward the pink and blue heavens.

Bridget De Lau

Sleepless Nights

Tossing, turning, I can not sleep
My eyes get wet, then I weep.

I'm up I'm down the whole night through
All my thoughts are centered on you.

Why can't I get you off my mind?
It's not as if you were that kind.

After all you played with my heart
Stomped on it and left only a part.

But the part that remains aches worse at night
I dream and I pray for morning light.

For with the light comes chores and work
Fooling myself - it didn't really hurt.

This pain - could it have been that real?
I know - I'll make myself a deal.

Tonight when I enter that lonely bed
I'll put all thoughts of you from my head.

But then I see the fading of the light
And know I face another sleepless night.

Cindi Cope

One Afternoon

Reclining, pensively, with no one there
My body caressed by the rays of the sun;
Just a gentle breeze playing with my hair
As though a new friendship had just begun.
I'm looking upwards - way beyond the clouds
Into the vast blue yonder;
A realm sublime and void of doubts,
A place so full of wonder.
And I feel drawn-up by the infinite sky
Like I wanted to penetrate the blue;
Higher and higher I'd like to fly
Far beyond the earth and its moon.
But what am I searching for way out there,
In the utter vastness of outer space?
Answers to questions? The words to a prayer?
The origins of the human race?
Am I longing to be touched by a power divine
Or to behold in awe the eternal light?
Just then a shiver runs down my spine,
And - reluctantly - I go inside.

Erna Kaluza

The Hidden Truth

Since I know past, present and future exist now
My belief in a static karma vanished anyhow.
A near omnipotent feeling of exemption
Waves through my entire self in extension.
All that which I truly believe
Cause the limits I can not leave,
Till I discover my hidden ideas about life
I feel at the mercy of destiny's knife.
This knowledge from the simple truth
Is evoked deep in my heart so smooth,
It released all the helpless fears
Altered still into powerful gears.
With my free will I choose to focus where
Hence I am about my thoughts aware,
The following emotions energize them straight
And so my joyful world I will create.
If there is within my life a clouded point
Makes me feel as if this creation is out of joint.
So I look to find my belief inside of me
Resolving it into what I want it to be.

Claudia Elam

(One January In Northridge)

I hate you for what you've done to me,
My baby only cries

When you made the earth dance violently,
You took the apple of my eye

Awaken by pleading screams for mercy,
You took me for a ride

When you dropped your gavel on my house,
You left my wife inside

You selfish, manipulating, murdering witch,
I've done my best to keep you blue and green

If you had the nerve to show yourself,
I'd repay you for your greed

Nobody can hide forever,
Not even a mothering fraud

I hope you remembered all things must end,
We all must answer to God.

Braden Andreas

Tears

In the lonely reaches of the night
my aching heart weeps——

Soon un-spent tears of yesteryear
course down my cheeks——

They scald and sear as painful memories
once more appear.

The salty tears do leave a trace
My fingers try their etchings to erase——

A futile gesture I must say
O'heavy heart they're here to stay——

Tho blessed dark my tears conceal
The coming daylight will reveal

I cried again last night——

Anne A. Knable

Restoration

For time to proceed, the future
must be breached.
Two souls are needed from an unknown time.
One must be a dove, and the other an eagle.
These souls were misplaced by God.
"What God?" They sometimes questioned.
"What was life really worth?"
"Nothing" they answered,
but at the same time — everything.
Love — what is it? He was
her guardian, her protector.
She was his obsession; and his master.
The height of their love was known only to soulmates,
and soulmates only existed in a long forgotten time.
With a kiss of pure passion that began
the merging of minds, a Castle appeared.
The age of knights and ladies,
of true love, and wrongs to be made right
shined bright in its new life with the
marriage of an eagle and a dove.

Amy Bixler

Mother's Day For Mom

What is Mother's Day to You?
Moms work and work for little or no pay.
They take care of the important things in life -
Our home, our money and most of all, our children.

Mother's Day to me - a day of rest for Mommy
No duties for Mommy and lots of love and kisses!
She does it all - everyday without complaint.
Never even once asking for any money.

She is a pillar - putting up with all our cries -
Day to Day, Night after Night love flows in lullabies -
Mommies are the greatest of all GOD has made.
One Mommy bore our LORD JESUS, years ago.

Love flows from Mommies day after day -
As the sun flows with ray after ray.
God is good to all of us -
The love He shares through Mommies to us.

This day is yours MOM, with all our love.
We will always look for to care -
You deserve the best today - you will show
That you have a very, very special glow.

Daniel E. Meché

You're My Friend

O Lord of all Lords...
Mold me
Shape me with your perfect hands
Name me with your lips
Breath air into this empty shell of a soul
Tease my spirit with your fingertips
O King of all Kings...
Create in me a new spirit
Let me know thy word
Let me live without sin
I stand now Lord-I stand to be heard
O Father of all Fathers...
Strengthen me
Let not my soul fall prey to the enemy
For I am your humble servant
And I shall be for eternity
For you're my Father, my Lord, my God, my Saviour,
My Sun, my Moon, My Stars, my Maker,
You are! The whisper in the wind,
You're my friend.

Daryl E. Horton Jr.

Return From Als

Watching rain-drenched people
Mingle among the lighted fortunes of men,
Voices fade with the rain.
I journey into the hazy dark horizon
Remembering the island of the blue maiden.
Knowing that I had found my life there,
The irrational world jealously awaited my return.

Now eternal rains have come to flood my emptiness.
Oh! Bewitching one, Enigma of my young life,
My being survives only to die a slow death.
Threatening my freedom, she stimulates the soul
And unknowing condemns me to Eternity.

David L. Cronic

Unhidden Memories

Memories long, never lost
Memories she knew would be at cost

Memories are not always pleasant and bright
She awaits the day to conquer this fight

This memory battle she must face alone
Her strength at pace is not by-gone.
Alas! this memory decides to surrender-

(L)earning to fight
(O)only for what's right
(V)ictory not accomplished over night
(E)ver and ever this memory in sight

Memories are long, never lost. This memory
is always youthful and tender-
Yes! "Love" will guide this memory aid
never could she hide this memory our creator made.

Bernita Addison

Everlasting

You are like the forest, Your spirit is all around,
In your arms I feel comfort,
In your eyes I see love,
Throughout the world you are forever living
A strong spirit you'll always be
Like a forest eternity.

Carla Lattimer

Look Up And See The Moon

Games, first love
Memories from above
Look up and see the moon
Do you see the moon

College, first job, marriage, first child, first home
Events setting the tone
Look up and see the moon
Do you see the moon

Culture, community, relaxation
The differences in the sensations
Look up and see the moon
Do you see the moon

Grandchildren, special birthdays, special anniversaries, retirements
The scents
Look up and see the moon
Do you see the moon
Yes, I see the moon

Candace Willrich-Scott

Pollution

Mr. Factory with your machines so green. Why are you so cruel and mean? Look at what you are doing to our gulfs and streams.

Am I cruel? No, I'm not. I just give you what you want. I give life to new industry.

NO! Mr. Factory can't you see? You are causing an intrusion and that can't be. You are upsetting our ecology!

Stop and take a look around. The trees were green and the air was clean.

Look at the smog and stream, and look at what you have done to our natural green. The birds in the air will soon disappear...and the fish in the ponds will all be gone.

Do you want the people of this land not be? Can't you clean the air so we can see?

No! Man polluted the land in which he lives. He started this before he invented me. Man is responsible for what happens to thee. For I am a machine and you made me.

For you put me here, and here I shall stay till the end of man and the end of day. I cannot change the will of man. I am a machine can't you see? I have no way of helping thee. But there is a chance, if man can see.

For man changed the world once when he invented me and he can change the world again if he wish it to be.

If man doesn't want the world he has, then he might as well get started and do whatever he can. That is all I can do, if man doesn't heave he'll soon turn blue.

Maybe just maybe someone will lend a hand and help preserve this land, for I cannot, can you? For it will take many to clean this land and have it fit and grand.

Blanca Estella Gonzalez

The Jungle

I like to go to the jungle when the skies
just turn blue,
Because the leaves are still covered with dew.
I like to watch the monkeys jump around,
Sometimes they miss and fall to the ground.
The lion awakes and lets out a roar,
Nobody's asleep anymore.
They all wake up singing,
Just like church bells ringing.
The whole jungle is alive.

Brien Russell

Good Morning Lord!

As I humbly come before Thee and You see me, Gracious Lord,
May You fill me with Your Spirit; help me understand Your Word.
Guide my thought, my word, my action, every moment - every day.
May I feel Your loving presence every step along life's way.
Use me, mold me, build me up. You know all I can be.
Fill me so completely that everyone may see...
See how marvelous, forgiving, ever-present that You are.
May everyone want closeness, not to know You from afar.
If I may be Your instrument, your servant tried and true,
I'll possess life's greatest blessing through this unity with You.
Thank You so much, dear Jesus, for everything You give.
In every lesson, every day, I'm learning how to live.
Send me on my way now to those ears that long to hear,
"God loves you. God forgives you. He always wants you near."
Wrap Your blessing all around me. With Your strength I will not sway.
I will know Your loving presence every minute of this day.
Your promise I'll hold on to until this day is through.
Whatever today may bring me, may I turn it all to You.

Erika Tipton

Northland

The wind blown snow has fallen,
Masking all in a covering of white.
And smoke rises from the chimney,
So free, billowy and light.
Below crowds rush to and fro,
They're so busy, yet really have,
No place to go.
They scurry back and forth, up and down, in and out,
No one knowing or remembering,
What it is all about.
And I? I set, high, up in the Northland.
Watching!

Ben Benner

The Human Race

The human race, the human race,
Marooned all together on an Island in Space;
And for all we know, there's no other place
For the Human Race.

So let's stop killing and saving face,
And try to join hands with a friendly grace.
As we move towards a future we can all embrace,
And a decent life for the human race.

A saving grace? A better place?
No. The rule today is to kill apace;
To murder, to maim, for religion and race;
To dehumanize the Human Race.

Can we move towards a future we can all embrace?
The decision is up to the Human Race.

Caroline S. Service

Kali

Saying goodbye is real hard to do
Just know little Kali that we all love you -
Our Papa is waiting in Heaven to hear
Your bark, as you run - white clouds will appear!
He'll be on the big one, waiting, you'll see -
A book in his hand - some cookies and Sees -

Take care of each other up high in the sky
Just know you'll be sitting right there by his side.
Healthy and happy our Yorkie will be
God's promise fulfilled - brown eyes that can see.
We'll never forget the love that you gave -
Tough little girl who was always so brave.

Beverly C. Hannan

126

Remembering Classmates

Remembering school years, thinking back
Many, many have long since passed, forty-three to be exact.
No car of your own, no bussing,
Just up early, dress, eat and no fussing.
Out of the house, up the road,
Walk two miles or more.
Talking and laughing, finally the open school door.

No mischief, please,
Get to the books, off to the gym,
later to homemaking class, for some taste bud appease.

Graduation soon to be, caps and gowns neat.
Class reunions we will again meet.
Now our children are all grown,
With children of their own.

Many classmate memories, mostly good.
With God's help, lived best we could.

Elvera Story

Tears, Fears And Everything Inside!

When the rain comes from the sky
Makes it good for a man to cry

It hides his tears
And all the fears
That he may have inside

When the sun is here and the sky is clear
He hides his tears
And all his fears
That he may have inside

Hope for rain and not the sun
Just until your tears are done.

The sun is good it makes it hot
But sometimes rain is all you got
To hide your tears
And all your fears
And everything you may have inside!

Bernie Reilly

Love Me

Love me unconditionally
Love me completely
Love me forever
Love me for me

You say you love me generally
   But do you love me genuinely
   And love me generously

Love me when I'm happy
Love me when I'm sad
Love me for always
Love me for me

Love me for my heart; for there's room for you inside
Love me from your soul
Love me more than anything

Don't love me selfishly
Don't love me for my body
Don't even for my smile

Love me because I love you
I love you endlessly because your you.

Denice Thimm

Two Hearts, Two Lives

Love is the bond that endures all.
Love is truth, mutual respect, trust,
Faithfulness, appreciation, tenderness,
And believing in one another.

Love is passionate, gentle, happy;
It will not submit to defeat, and knows
No boundaries. Love is patient, understanding,
Unselfish, and would rather give than receive.

Love is having a best friend, a friend you
Can share your most intimate thoughts.
Love will not perish without cause, but
Must be nourished in order to survive.

Love binds two hearts, two lives.
Marriage is the commitment to that love,
And serves to bless and sanctity your
Desire to walk life's path together.

Darryl J. Bechthold

"Love"

Love is a gift from within the heart,
   Love is a gift from the start.
No words can explain what love does to the heart,
   But without it life will fall a part.

All His love came from within,
   He bled and He died to forgive our sins.
This man was an example of pure love,
   Peaceful He was, just like a dove.
Jesus died because He loved us so,
   He'll never turn away, He'll never say no,
Just pray, He'll listen.
   Just pray, He'll listen.
Because of His love we shall eternally live,
   And that's why He died,
   To forgive our sins.

Cary Fisher

Untitled

If you've ever been in love, you'll know what I'm saying.
Love hurts every one of us.
When you're in love, you get blinded without a clue,
You constantly long for your other to say I love you.

If you've ever been in love, or are as we speak,
You probably think you'll never love another and tell me when you do.
You'll learn that only words say I love you.

If you've ever been in love, you know that love's a feeling.
It can not be described in words, it comes straight from the heart.
I know you probably say it too, but no word can express the fact
that I love you.

If you've ever been in love, I hope you've learned by now,
that all the kisses in the world mean nothing to the sender.
It's only things, little things they do,
that smack you in the forehead and prove that they mean, I love you.

If you've ever been in love, please listen to me now.
The person you live and die for, the one that you long for,
Probably fits you like a glove,
But the one that you don't love at all is the one that gives you love.

Barbara J. Grimm

127

Keepless

Suffocation from this empty hole
lost everything from this what was stolen?
  How do you go on with lost control?
Gypsy traveler have my possessions,
wondering now!
But the draining rain keeps me down.
chained and restless caused by myself fear.
  How do you go on with such tears?
Their headed up there gold mine mirage
leaving behind others pain,
living off fluid minds, that they gain.
  Is their a reason for liras to be sold
for fortune?
At the end we all stand naked, bargaining
for a piece of solution to salvage
it all back from the destruction of other.
Simple minds that have no Dominating Power.
  Except to sponger over other lawful
  claims that isn't theirs.

Astra J. Beck

Experience The River

Despite earlier weather, the night was clear and warm.
Looking into the heavens you could be entertained by the
twinkling stars striving to equal the powerful glow of the
full moon. The campfire flamed brightly, casting out a radiant
light; causing shadows to dance on the wall of the forest,
and behind you was dead air, but to the front you could
feel the coal's warm, radiant energy upon you, a pleasing
sensation. And to the side was the river. Gushing, sloshing,
neverending churning, until the rocks which it lay upon
were as smooth and round as hailstones. Listening to it
could hypnotize you, as was I, but the shrill cry of a
whippoorwill broke the trance, then he sounded again, then
once more, and I counted twenty before he ceased.

Bryan Swartzlander

Misplaced

It's twilight now at the edge of the pond
Looking in, there's reflection of sun going down,
Not a sound can be heard anywhere around
Just a twig creaking from my weight on the ground

Ice formed on the water makes a prism appear
And the colors of sunset shine in and smear,
The clouds are thick and sink down so low
They seem to be bulging from the weight of the snow

The silence is broken by the sound of a knock
It's beating a rhythm like the tick of a clock,
A single woodpecker reminds me of TIME
And I know I should leave, I am running behind

The branches are barren, so lonely it stands
This magnificent oak with its outstretched hand
In its desolation surrounded in night
Enhancing the magnitude of this awesome sight

I so long to linger, mesmerized by the scene
As the pond sprays silver, emphasized by moonbeams,
But spotted owl scolds, "you're not part of this place"
I reluctantly turn back to the civilized rat race

Carol A. McLester

Winter's Majesty

The speckled geese huddle together,
long necks coiled into their wings
for protection against the stinging cold.
Glittering snow dances about on the wind
before ceasing the eager movement.
Quiet calm shrouds the scene.
Fat flakes float down with dizzying slowness
in a lazy, muted world.
Tiny puffs of foggy air
wisp about the pinkened face
of a lone walker scurrying for shelter.
Deepening dusk mingles with the snow,
casting an eerie spot-light of blackness
to accent the listless twirling.
Deep infinity looms
before, behind, above, and beyond
for ages.

Charlotte Gray

Silence

The silence envelops me, surrounds me with time,
Listen so carefully, thoughts will unwind.
Touch the silence so tenderly, with mind and with soul,
Releasing energy into time is the goal.
Silence comforts me, holds me so close,
Hugs me and whispers to me, "Stop, smell the rose."

I stop, see the silence, and know in my heart,
That peacefulness lies here, with me it won't part.
I taste the silence, the air it is sweet,
Such food for me, will make this complete.
Silence comforts me, holds me so close,
Touches me lovingly, takes away all my woes.

I wait, let the silence clothe me tonight,
Knowing He will be there at my side on this night.
I feel the silence, emotions running high,
But then, let the silence, my feelings will abide.
Silence comforts me, holds me so close,
It will be with me always, no matter where I go.

Cathy Nunez

It's Okay

When life just doesn't add up...
Listen carefully
The Master's voice will whisper
"It's Okay!" "I'm in control!" "It's okay!"

The Master's Voice whispers
"It's Okay!"
When life seems stressed
Beyond human endurance.

The Master whispers gently
"It's Okay!"
Midst the emotional ups and downs
of daily living.

The Master speaks lovingly
"It's Okay!"
As loneliness and despair blurs
hopes and dreams

When life just doesn't add up...
Listen carefully
The Master's voice will whisper
"It's Okay!" "I'm in control!" "It's okay!"

Elizabeth Gail Sewell

Am I Dreaming

Am I dreaming? I never thought that someone
like you, could love someone like me. You
hold on, yet you lift me up. You show me
a new direction to spread my wings in. You
tell me to fly, but I don't dare fly where you
are not. Am I flying? I feel the way I want to
to feel. I look the way I want to look. Are you
the one? The one to hold me and to love me?
Are you the one who will stay forever? If
I am dreaming, let me sleep. Please God,
I don't want the wind beneath my wings
to ever go away. If this is not the one,
please God, let me live the memories
of a fairy tale, alone. Forever.

Crystal Cordell

Locked-Up

In a bottle are where my feelings are kept
like under a carpet away they are swept
for no-one knows what goes on inside
from my friends and foes I'll watch and hide
I sit alone and stare at the wall
for they don't know I'm about to fall
I sit and wonder what life is all about
but all there is nothing, I start to shout
but I cannot shout and I cannot scream
oh why can't I wake up from the horrible dream
I crawl around just wanting to die
is this really happening to me I ask why?
Finally I wake up and stare blankly at the sky
and then but only then I realize life is just a lie.

Christine Jones

Before You Know It

Before you know it, everything before your eyes changes.
Like there's someone reading a book about your life,
and they just keep turning the pages.
Before you know it, things don't seem easy anymore.
All these things you now learn, but
you don't know what you'll use them for.
Before you know it, you are out in this world all on your own.
Everything seems dark and hopeless, you feel like you're all alone.
Before you know it, people make things seem like they just can't wait.
Your parents and friends think it's about time you find the perfect mate.
Before you know it, you realize that you can't jump into things.
That you have to let God take you at your own pace.
He'll guide you, let you fly on his wings.
Before you know it, you have your life in your own hands.
You must have ideas, thoughts, and your own plans.
Well, before you know it, your life story is over.
You have done your deed on earth,
but your love will be spread forever.

Debbie Miller

In The Beginning

In the beginning all was darkness; when He proclaimed, "Let there be light."
Brought intercession of the seasons, the measured good of day and night.
The He created man from dust; it was with faith and love He placed
A fertile woman, by man's ardor sought, demurred with subtle grace.
There came defilement of the spirit, changing Paradise to strife.
Creation by desires wiles, proscribes man's destiny in life.
Mute beast, winged fowl, seed time and harvest gleaned-and man thou
   callest thine,
A law innate that God endowed, "All life engenders kind."
The sun, the moon, the stars that guide from faithful orbits never fall.
His vigilance perceives mankind - for God is just: He knoweth all.

Florence Vahey Williams

Skinny

Running, her bony knees protrude
like some predator, hungry, in the wild;
she watches her wiry shadow dance
and fancies herself a fairy's child,
   exempt from mortal rituals
   like meals and menstruation;
   strong and somehow magical,
   transformed by deprivation.
Holding herself aloof, she laughs
and calls her hunger discipline;
She lives on tea and carrot sticks
but never quite feels thin.

Secretly reassured by worried stares,
she laments that it cannot last;
standing on a scale every day, she despairs
for the skinnier days of the past
   when once she danced, elflike,
   a willowy sprite
   defying the earth
   like the tail of a kite.

Christiana Muntzel

My Sweet Love

Last night I gazed into his sad, brown eyes
Like a young, lost animal in quicksand.
If only he'd notice the love I have.
Thinking of him by day, dreaming by night,
Awake now with a disappointed soul
He doesn't realize how much I care,
And how much I need his complete true love.
Tomorrow seems like an eternity.
He doesn't know the truth, he moves past me
Looking at another, a stranger to him.
My wish to love together for all time,
For time stands still when one loves another.
Now I sit alone, waiting anxiously
For my sweet love just once to glance my way.

Jessica Kuhn

The Lonely Tree

Lonely is the tree that stands alone,
   like a person coming to a new school.
The whistling of the leaves as they pass through the breeze,
   like a person hearing far off voices in the hall.
The dark, hollow trunk of the tree,
   like the person's heart.
The hard, coarse outer part,
   like the person's shell they've built around themselves.
The tree full of leaves,
   like the person's memories from their last home.
The occasional falling of rain drops,
   like the tears from the person
The breaking off of branches,
   like the person tearing away from the past.
The forming limbs,
   like the person's new friends.
The distance from this home to their last,
   like the person's far away look in their eyes.
Lonely is the tree that stands alone,
   like the sadness in her heart some days.

Audrey Reeves

Formidable Adversary

My strength lies in vast reserves of bitterness cultivated from
lifelong experience, and is reinforced by innate rebellion,
finely honed apathy, and natural defensiveness;
my heart's blood has the flow and consistency of ice water

I can no longer be hurt, but can incapacitate opponents,
striking the first blow and inflicting phenomenal emotional anguish...
then disappearing, sight unseen, long before one can recover or reciprocate

I as a woman, sweet and guileless, can wound as a man;
I am cognizant of how the male mind functions,
and can outmaneuver it as it only begins to contemplate retaliation

I don't care enough to ever cry, and can quite easily remain
indifferent, with little empathy or remorse for the foolhardy,
unwitting offender...
and though I may occasionally bend, I cannot be broken

My armor is impenetrable, deflecting arrow, spear, and innuendo...
I can compete with, subdue, and conquer the mightiest warrior
while blindfolded, with hands tied behind my back.

Elana D. Tyson

No Place To Hang Your Hat

Amidst gutter trashed allies and ticket stub subways
lies a lifetime of mime. Speechless pale faces
hoping to survive through the coming days
always spent in most abominable places.
A hat more ragged from misery and wear
than from a head keeping the little heat it owns.
By day it asks for your change to spare
until dusk when cold, gusty winds whisper and moan.

Thin clothing bundled in a cardboard box-hidden
are the eyes of the shattered lives scattered
like trash; thrown
from the lives they were living;
a man out of work or a housewife battered
to nothing but empty hats, covering empty bodies and frail bones.

Bethany E. Hall

Red, White, Blue, And Yellow

Gunshots ricocheted over boundaries of open sea.
Landing in a downpour of racism and bigotry.
Uncle Sam cried treason of yellow skin and slanted eyes.
Treason of citizens, of little boys and of fishermen.
Evicted from their homes, empty handed and empty hearted,
Holding on only to their history in their frightened hands,
Replacing their citizenship with fences and guard towers.
A prison of yellow skin filled with anger and sand and stone.
Locked away from their livelihood,
Condemned to sail a fruitless sea of war and solitude.
They hopelessly went on,
Their destination blurred and unknown,
On the cruise of Manzanar.
One day the bullets stopped and the wind began to blow,
Blowing down the fences, freeing the innocent prisoners,
But closing the door as they tried to enter their country.
Leaving them stranded, unwelcome in their own country,
Or Japan, a land they did not know.

Buffy Shaheen

The Pain

I relax, I meditate, but mostly I pray.
It comes, it goes, but mostly it stays.
I use heat, ice, but mostly pills.
It comes, it goes, but mostly it kills.
I ignore it, I laugh at it, but mostly I cry.
OH! DEAR GOD, PLEASE TELL ME WHY.

Betty Turner

A Vision Of Hope

Standing on the threshold of tomorrow,
knowing only today that tomorrow is only a dream.

There's a place somewhere, meanwhile we wait
on the promise of hope; dreading yet another
day of pain, fear, sorrow, and tears.

Children dying, babies crying, mother's
praying and father's nowhere around.

Yet, stood I on the threshold of time looking
wondering where hope can be found.

Then, stood I looking out on yonder field
when visions of hope appeared. Then I knew
that love is the only conqueror of all my fears.

Ethel M. Bowman

The Child

As a mother carries her first unborn child;
knowing it will be so weak and so mild.
Waiting for their first touch and to hear its first cry;
she knows she won't be the best, oh but how she will surely try.
The love she already feels deep inside,
will be worth every cost and can't be bought at no price.

Then the child is born and begins to grow;
the mother shall give it all, even her soul.
It takes everything the mother can possibly do;
to lead and guide the child hoping she can make it through.

Then it comes for the ties to be broken;
and the love they share doesn't have to be spoken.
and the child realizes the one whom she can always depend,
is not only her mother but her best friend.
And after the mother has given all she can give,
she realizes without this child, she would have never learned to live.

Angela M. Smith

Untitled

Knock, knock at your door.
Knock, knock at your heart.

Do you open it, do you let them in.

Which would be safer?, Which would cause less despair?

Which would be easier?, Which would be fair?

Let the door shut,
and risk not knowing what lurks on the other side.

Let your heart stay shut,
risk the emotions you will never feel.

Which is the safer?, Which is the wiser?

Let the door fly wide open,
let it come inside.

Let it lift your mind and feelings,
let it lift your life.

Let your heart come open,
let the tears of life come alive.

Feel the emotions within you, feel the gleam of light.

Experience with each door, experience with your heart.

Do not stay shut, do not stay closed.
Let your life become a part.

Angela E. Paul

Ashtray

Stand alone you're no one else
just wait for them to give the orders
majestic pinball isn't always
played alone - they've got you in
this closest - tied you up in wire
hangers - form you in an ashtray
I hope you rot real slowly
I can smell your decay - it's
been there for too - long - I hope you've
seen the ground from here - I've got
you in an intestinal view - finder -
she's grown up a seductive bison -
lay her over this desk - cluttered with
straight A essays - get to work with
these ball point pens - cause I've
stolen all your erasers - spawn
your ignorant daisy larva all
over this town - back into the
strawberry sewers down into hell back again

Adam Finley

"Work"

Work, who wants to work, not me, I tell you I
just love to sleep,

Around the clock for nearly a whole week.
And bum around the country in my sleep.

Work, who wants to work, not me.
My thumb can take me where I want to go.

In sunshine, rain, or snow.
You really don't have to have the dough.

A whole mess of clothes, who needs them just the wealthy,

Shoes they pinch your feet, Mister, they're not even healthy.

Eat! I love to eat!
What I find, I store in my little brown satchel.

If I'm lucky, I'll treat myself to the White Castle.

So take it from me, don't live in a hurry.
Sit back and relax, don't let yourself worry.

Hey! listen my friend, don't keep yourself too busy,

Worrying about money, can sure make you dizzy,

You say work? Who me?
No sir! My friend! Not me!

Charlotte L. De Marco

Forever/San

Jesus loves me, San
Just know I love you no matter what I say
  You're Blind, Deaf, you're Dumb
Please help me, San
My eyes, my eyes are sometimes stained
But my ears center my brain
I once heard the prettiest scene
Not even my eyes could show you what it means
My head, well I have yet to figure out
I will someday, I have no doubt,
  You're Blind, Deaf, you're Dumb
Thank you, San, we become one
Walk with me, show me how you dance
I love you, give me one more chance
Touch me, teach me how to hug
Kiss me, turn me on some
Talk with me, sing me a song
Smile for me, think of me when I'm gone
If you can't, somehow I will know
You twist my mind, body and soul... Goodnight Buffalo

Brett Zwettler

Hard Times

Your hate is trapped in your inside,
just because there is nowhere else to hide.
Your heart has broken into two,
and there isn't a thing anyone can do.
All of this is driving you insane,
and you don't know how to deal with all of this pain.
The way this is all trapped inside your heart,
your life has been falling apart.
You wish there could be any other way.
You life is getting worse day by day.
Every time you try to work it out,
you end up with some kind of doubt.
If you could make someone see.
It is too hard to let life be.

Amanda Joder

Animals

Insects fly here and there
Joy and laughter fill the air
Kittens are catnip-crazy
Lizards are VERY lazy
There is a prickly porky-pine
With pins and needles on his spine
There's lots of quail
There's even a squirrel with a swishy-tail
Now we exit off and away
That's enough for us today!

Aprile McGilvray

God Is Love

Space hung like a dark drape of endlessness.
Its presence resembled a statute's stance of stillness.

Scenery of space in depth, in height, in length, in width, and in
  weight registered sameness.
Silence ruled its volume of vastness.

Our Creator majestically moved upon this expansiveness.
Then the everlasting God of eternity etched myriad of variety in all
  this spaciousness.

The Almighty God's divine wisdom willed a world into existence.
God's faithful fingers worked a week accomplishing everything
  requiring beginning to ending through His omnipotence.

His holiness graciously granted the finest of the best for His creatures
  of every habitation.
This heavenly Father produced, provided, and proclaimed man's
  authority with humanity to rule His priceless earthly creation.

As Lord of Lords, He lighted a spark of love in each human creature.
And King of Kings, He kindled kindness within each man's nature.

Ethel Marie Chisholm

My Looking Glass

My looking glass is tall, I can see outside of it
It is my transportation to the other side
of this side world of loneliness.
People come to see me and my looking glass to the other world.
I use it all the time and still think of everything else around.
My looking glass is all sorts of colors.
Through it I see all sorts of things are different,
But this is the best; my loving glass is a world
beyond my lonely cell. I think of freedom
And then look back through my looking glass.
My looking glass stands tall, and I not so tall.
It is my freedom from this world.
And yet I cannot expect to escape, but I try to do it anyway.
I am trapped in this chair forever.

Christina Brenner

My Loss

So many feelings I have to hold
It's okay to have them, so I'm told.

Robbed of something that I hold dear
No longer will I have her to hold near.

Memories are all I have left,
No insurance for this kind of theft!

Straining so hard not to cry.
As she rises to her place way up high.

Many nights I've stayed up wondering why,
But, in vain, I give up and sigh.

A doubt in faith will soon be regained
A moment in time that will forever be stained.

The emptiness in my heart will never be filled.
Unlike a glass that overflows and spills.

But her spirit is there, watching with care
Special memories I have, I will never share.

April R. Elvira

Who Is Perfect?

You say that I need to change
It's not news to me that I have many faults
Who is Perfect?

If I changed everything that you wanted me to
Will I ever be what you want me to be or
What else can you find to change?

I am who I am
Take it or leave it
Some things I can change
Some things I need to change

Accept me for what I am
Inside and out
I want your acceptance

Our interests are different
And we don't always listen to each other
We need a lot of work together
After all, Who is Perfect?

Dayle Susan Gloege

"A Drifting Family"

It's a shame when families drift apart!
  It's hard to make a fresh new start.
We should stay friendly in good times and bad,
  Because when you lose one, that's really sad!
Learn to love and respect each other,
  For some day you may be without one another.
Let's be as close as we can be
  And allow our children to play in harmony.
Can't we visit with each other once more?
  Every time I come, you won't answer the door.
In the past year when we've gathered together
  You could see that things still were no better.
Feelings were so cold and words so brief
  We had to leave, just to get relief!
Let's please try again and this time not inter fear
  We can be friends again that live very near.
So let's start again today, to be a friend
  Let's not let this family come to an end!

Eileen Thompson

Inquiry Into Iniquity

(Move by Miami Holocaust Memorial)
The huge outstretched hand seems to be reaching;
Its gesture upward is so surely beseeching—
All to no avail.

The number A13898 is tattooed on the wrist.
Did this number, this person, ever exist?
The question must prevail.

Many people are climbing and clinging to the forearm,
Reflecting the hopelessness of their alarm.
At the base, others trail.

Two people at opposite sides hand up a child,
Even then to these young deaths unreconciled;
Faces expressing their travail.

An elderly couple, each with shaved head,
Clasp arms in Farewell, aware they'll soon be dead,
Still studying the loved features' detail.

We study that beautifully ugly reaching hand,
Unable, unwilling, after years, to understand
Why it was— all to no avail!

Anita Kippelman

The Hawk Swoops Down From Overhead

Its hypnotic gaze staring through the branches
Its eyes spying a prey nearby
It swoops down from overhead
Making little noise as it flies.
It snatches the victim with its claws
And brings it to her nest
Providing supper for her young ones
As the wind flows through her crest.
Her young ones chirping loudly
Awaiting their daily feast
They begin to rip apart the little mouse
And devour it piece by piece.
Soon their hunger is satisfied
As their meal is done
That is, of course, until the sun rises
And another day has begun
When a mouse comes scurrying idly by
Searching for something to eat
When the hawk swoops down from overhead
To satisfy her young ones' need for meat.

Alexander Flipse

The One That Took The Children

There is violence all around out there
It's everywhere, but "they" don't care.
What can we say, what can we do?
This kind of violence is all brand new.
Innocent people getting killed or not,
Why ever did God come up with this plot?
Can't we all get along; or at least try
Then maybe the U.S. will not cry.
Everyone should do what they may,
Maybe then we'll have peace some day.
Terrorists came to attack, can we not send them back?
We refer to "it" as the one; that took the children away.
Did we the people do something so terrible?
It was such a big price to pay.
Why did all this horror start?
What can we do to forget this day?
I suppose that some people's happiness
Is a whole country's terror.
Why did Oklahoma City have to fall, to a bomb's terrible fate?
I guess it all comes down to "those people's hate".

Elizabeth Eitel

A Walk

Her path of life leads to unconditional love,
it's a love she shares with so many.
   Children lost in a world of pain seek
shelter in her arms of gold.
   She smiles, hugs and makes everything feel true.
   And occasional "thank you" may echo in her ears,
which isn't enough in my eyes.
   Her strength is felt with every motion
down her path.
   She is made of truth and inspiration.
Whether it be home or work, to me she's a hero.
   With all she has inside, she is to me
a champion that deserves a medal everyday.
   This is a path I hope to someday follow.
I love you, Mom!

   Amie Robb

For The Children

What is that mournful sound I hear?
It's a baby crying - perhaps quite near.
Do you hear that child sobbing in the night?
Do you hear a child crying out in fright?
How can someone abandon, leave it all alone,
And how can someone abuse their very own?

What is that sorrowful sound I hear?
It's a teenager hiding her shame and fear.
She cries alone so no one will know.
Who can she turn to and where can she go?
The pain she has is deep inside -
How much more can this child abide?

What is that tuneless whistle I hear?
It's a young boy whistling to hide his fear.
He's walking bravely down a familiar street,
Wishing - hoping - no gangs will he meet.
Too late. Too late. He's surrounded by them.
A gun - a shot - no more whistling for him.

What is that mournful sound so near?
It's God weeping for His Children. Can you hear?

   Evelyn M. Howell

Amongst The Stars

I missed the bus again today
It was on its way to Pluto
I even had my suitcase
I would of loved just to go

I just want to get away from here
It doesn't really matter where I go
Any place where there are no fears
and the salty tears do not flow

Yeah Mars is really hot
But any things better than being on earth
The galaxy is the best place to get lost
Away from all this pain and hurt

Next week I'm definitely goin' to the sun
What I would do just to touch one flame
It's gonna be cool, do you wanna come
Or would you rather stay here and just wish you came

I just want to sit amongst the stars
Away from the noise and away from the aching
Just any place, nowhere's to far.
Where no one can hear my heart breaking.

   Adrienne Ford

Am I Losing My Mind?

I wrote a poem today. Who cares what it said
It was mental gymnastics, much better than staying in bed.
It stirred my emotions. Shed a tear. Cracked a smile.
Brought up some memories. I relived life for awhile.

A strange new experience. A bit overwhelming.
My life's been family, causes, action.
So unaware a rhyme I could make.
Now it's a comfort, a great satisfaction.

Writing poetry? You're losing your mind.
Losing it maybe. It is loose and flowing.
An easy feeling - I sorta like it.
As long as it lasts I'll keep going.

At night my slumber, my sleep is broken.
A thought so sudden - so sublime.
Ignore it I can't. My sleep won't return
'Til out of bed, I write it on a line.

It's a joy just getting it together.
Keeps my soul, myself, my mind intact.
Guess I'll keep on writing
As dreams and thinking awake me at night.

   Elizabeth Tolle

Brighten Up My Life

There you were, when I first saw you.
It seemed strange, almost unreal
that someone like you would
suddenly appear into my life.

Can you tell me who you are?
Salvation or just an image?
If you were an image, I wouldn't be able to touch you
And.....that would make my eyes eternal tears.

Ease my pain, be my salvation.
I never thought I'd reach your soul,
But now that we are here, I know I'll never let you go.

If you leave my heart would sink
Just as a sunken ship goes down
Down so deep and so heavy with shivers
It can never come up again.

Take me completely.
Make me float as the Sun floats on the sea,
Knowing it will always come up again to brighten up our new days.
And, together with Him,
You'll brighten up my life.

   Andrea Dieterich

One Single Rose

To you from me
It means so much
This one single rose,
Shows how much I love you.

My love is like the rose
The more it grows
The more I love you.

My love for you is stronger than its scent
Although the rose may soon die
My love will never die.
This one single rose
Shows how much,
   I LOVE YOU

   Adina D. Dixon

Color-Coded Generation

What is this war around me?
It is staring me in the face.
Everyone has a color,
but no one has a face.
We always overlook the sky
or the green grass of the field;
the only color we seem to see is the color of our shields.

Children fighting children -
who has taught us what's right?
People getting killed,
because they're too dark or too light.

I wish the world was blinded
or that we had no skin.
Then maybe this fighting would stop,
and into each others' hearts
we would be welcomed in.

I don't want to leave the world
all this complication.
It's sad but our children will see us
as the color-coded generation.

Angel Hutson

America, We Love You

Bind up your bleeding wounds.
It is not your fault, but ours,
That blows have fallen to cause you shame.
There is no land better than you.
Your idealism still holds hope for us.
Your wounds will heal.
We, your people will learn.

Hold your head high, America.
You are the land of the brave.
Your scars will make your freedom
  bells more mellow
And to ring louder and clearer for all.
America, we, your people love you.

Alice Lorraine Hill

A Kiss Of Death

You catch a glimpse of her as she comes over
It is almost as if she could fly
Your eyes catch sight of those ruby lips
They are almost like blood
As you stare into her eyes you get lost
Suddenly everything goes dark
Now it is just the two of you, alone
Your faces move closer to each other
The kiss is warm and like no other
Suddenly a strange felling comes over you
It seems like you are falling
All you can do is wait
Suddenly you land with a loud thud
This place is new to you
Never have you seen it
On a big door you see the word "Death"
It all becomes clear, you are dead
But how did it happen, was it the kiss
You are in your eternal resting spot
Never again to see the light of day

Angie Stone

"Love Is Part Of The Game"

As a reporter I have a scoop.
It is about a lively group.
They're on the courts most every day
and Tennis is the game they play.

They hit the ball above the net.
If it don't clear, they have regret.
It's quite an interesting thing.
So come on out and have your fling!

They play out in the nice fresh air.
About the game, they really care.
With a little guidance from above,
you'll learn the meaning of "Forty... Love."

Frank Grom

Jesus Anchors Me

Jesus anchors me when the storms come and go.
It is a daily blessing we know.
Oh, what would I do without Him to still my raging heart.
To really let me know He's will never depart.
It is a comfort to know He's standing near to anchor my soul.
In the storm I pray and to Him I unfold.
Thank You sweet Jesus for what you are to me.
From all bondage I am set free.
Only Jesus can help us when we're going through...
So accept His love so true.
Accept His love to make us steadfast and strong,
God will help us to do no wrong.
God will help us to stand the test.
We only have to do our best.
When the storms blow so hard,
Only wait a while for our reward.
From God it will come
Listen to the Holy One.
Jesus anchors me day by day.
I only have to wait and pray.

Clarice James Robinson

Flowers

We planted a seed to create a flower
it grew and it grew each day by the hour.

And when the time came for us to be one,
we carried her home nothing left to be done.

She grows on her own with such strength
and pride.

A real joy to us both we certainly
can not deny.

We'll love and cherish our flower more than
the world.

For you see our flower is our little girl.

Catherine Filcek

"What's In A Word"

What is the crime, to speak what's on one's mind
is it the sound, that turns meaning around,
inside out, and upside down.
A single word, is just formed of letters,
when scribed upon a page;
Yet, when spoken, a word, becomes a maze.
I've heard that words, are a creative art,
tone, and expression, play their part.
In a mere word, what can it hold;
within it; lies a meaning, I am told.
From where is this meaning,
formed and created;
could it simply be, from imagination.

Barbara Lepper

My Special Place

I have a place I always go, it doesn't hail,
it doesn't snow. It doesn't flood, there is no
rain, I feel safe and warm and there is no pain.
I come here often when I'm alone, a place to go
and never leave home. I found this place one
rainy day, I couldn't go out, it was too cold of
a day. So I stayed home where I was dry and
warm, and my daughter and I were safe from harm.
Her daddy's at work, and she's fast asleep, an
idea just came to me that was quiet and neat.
I sat on my couch just watching the rain,
all by myself - I was going insane. When I look down
on the floor, I saw paper and pen, I just picked them
both up and began to begin. Words and ideas I could
just throw together! I wrote about my daughter and
about the bad weather. I worked on some poems about
pain and on love, some were fiction, some were true.
I'm glad I found my special place, where I can go
when I need peace. You should try it when you're at
home, go there anytime when you're alone.

Dawna Holmes Fletcher

"We're In The Same Boat"

You may be black, white, yellow or brown,
It doesn't matter, under one God, were we found.
We've all been placed in the same neighborhood
It's up to us to do what's right and good.

Some prefer the North, South, others East, or West
When will we learn? We all must give our best.
Let's join together before it's too late.
For while we're looking up - down might be our fate.

If I help you - won't you succeed
If I hold back - I'll be in need

We're in the same boat brother, and it's about time
that we've made up our mind to end Apartheid.
We're in the same boat sister, remember your roots,
For you were the first to take of the fruit.

Let it row, let it row, and yet it will
Reach the great land of Peace - be still.
So don't let the cares of the world cause you to choke
Sail on! Sail on! we're in the same boat.

Charles Stovall

Like The Candle's Flame

There's a candle on our window sill
It burns both night and day
In memory of our loved one, still
Whose life so suddenly was taken away.

For twenty-six years you were our son
A blessing bestowed on your dad and me
Until our days on earth are done
We will be together again with thee.

For twenty-one years you were Craig's brother
A leader, a pal, a friend
For Craig there will never be another
Until in time his life comes to end.

For five short years you were Amber's father
A responsibility filled with lots of love and care
You left behind a precious daughter
Blond, blue-eyed, and fair.

All these things you were and more
And just like the candle's flame
You will never be forgotten
Because our love for you remains.

Brenda J. Becker

My Private Room

My private room
is where I spend
my spare time.
That is where I
tell my very private
secrets that will never
be told. That is My Private Room.

When I sit by the window,
looking at the sky and birds,
wondering seeing myself
as a teen, married or what.
But all those secrets will
always be there and never be told.
That's why it will always be My Private Room.

Elizabeth Rodriguez

The Church

The desire to lay down and rest in unrest
is now a thing not possible.
To sit quietly in your anger; no chance
right when you have come up with a rhyme to
best describe your neighbor, 'round the corner
comes another to say, "You are right"! No!
I'm half left you say,
when the ugly monster of anger and malice
wants to gently sit along side of you and
point the finger and laugh, some wild
one rebukes him, binds him, and commands
him - depart, so now there is only one ugly
monster sitting there, and it's you, and when
you want to say... "I can't help that I am
a monster", someone says the most simple word
with such brevity so as to stick you
in the heart with a sword that has
two sharp edges, twists it and says "I love you",
and means it, Church is a great place.

Chris Occhilto

Truth's Song

A man, who's fully a man,
Is free to be whomever he can
He chooses to fear...or chooses to love
He roots himself, then does what he does.

A woman, who's grown on her own,
Is free to make her way all alone.
She chooses to fear or chooses to love
She roots herself, then does what she does.

A child, whose self is not made,
Looks to his elders for guidance and shade.
If treated with love, he'll grow fine and tall
If nurtured with wisdom, then he'll have it all.

The Earthly World begins with these three
Men, women, and children create what will be.
The choices are...to fear or to love
Which will it be...the snake or the dove?

Erin O'Connor

King On The Mountain

In the pre-evening sun,
In the still winter air,
In a field setting the sun,
In a field of the setting sun;
It's a game of king on the mountain:
Where a herd of cattle are milling around,
Playfully butting heads on a knoll in that field,
Stirring up dust against the descending sun.

Brent Unruh

"The Pirate In My Mind"

The pirate in my mind,
Is a thief for sure.
He makes me want no other,
He has become Captain of my thoughts.
He has the most bedazzling eyes,
The color of emeralds they are.
They truly are expensive,
For they cost me my entire heart.
His beauty is hard to explain,
His face is of flawless perfection.
His appearance far surpasses winsome,
He is as ethereal as any angel.
His hair is waves of ebony,
With ripples moving like an ocean in a breeze.
How could I cast away this pirate,
When he dominates my thoughts so well?
He is the ruler of my dreams,
He has taken harbor in my mind forever,
My pirate, thief of my soul.

Christina M. Terry

My Sanctum

The single bronze interruption of darkened oak's face
Invitingly embraces your hand
And lingeringly withdraws
To reveal subtle scents and inclination.

The gentle slope of polished cedar, arrested
By the flourish of whirling, woven tails,
Floats over perched paws, gently gripping the thread
Of clouds over exotic, sand-spread places.

A tall, sultry blonde in burnished gold reaches
Out from the corner, shedding light,
Exploring the facets of ancient scenes
Impressed in the feel of varnished walls' cut.

An opulent bureau lounges along the wall in golden reflection,
   glimmering,
Covered in a sheet of silken paper, light and liquid script with
   flowing strokes.
Aside lies a limp and life-less reed, somnolent and anticipating,
Inviting the tender pressure of pen on paper by my patient fingers.

Chris Ogilvie

Had Enough

Through life and love's long
intertwining course I have...
Climbed the highest peaks
been washed down flash-flooded arroyos
into quiet sunlit meadows
picked up by a gentle breeze
floated across unconditional terrain
dropped deep into a tumbling unforgiving sea
thrashed repeatedly over rocks
tossed high into the air to soar over and
under and over and under until I

HAD ENOUGH I

reached out and gripped with one hand with two with one foot with two

Until I could stand and
the wind
blew around me and
the water
was content to lap at my feet.

Debi McClure

Towards Nothing

Through the maze of brilliance
Inside a psychedelic rainbow
Across what multitudes of craziness
Inside what is not understood
Without comprehension or control
Toward the center of nothingness
By the means of the psycho roller coaster
of life.
Throughout a searcher's time, his soul searches
For nirvana
Of which most cannot find
Amid the static nature of chaos.
Despite the meaning of his life
By the time he's reached his peace
Against the will of man he is cold
And without light.

Dawne Howard

Freeway On A Rainy Day

We creep along the slippery streets
   in traffic

Like clumsy elephants marching
   in a circus ring

Holding truck to tail—hoping,
   as they must,

The one in front doesn't stop
   too quickly.

Move slowly, stay in line, watch the signals.

And when the show is over, our destination
   Safely accomplished,

We say a prayer of thanks that we have been
   able to perform well
   one more time.

Evelyn Vela

Psychopathic

Insane, personified, living in this hell
In this crazy state of mind, nothings going well.

Set up for murder in the first degree
no thoughts of what I've done
Will I regain my sanity, living under the gun.

Thinking of strange and evil things
for the people I love to hurt.
You never know what hell I bring
you may be raped or burned.

A shot in the dark, the endless dream,
I've got you on my mind.
You've met the perfect killing machine
and it's only a matter of time.

My reign of terror has just begun,
the horror never ends,
looking in the mist you'll see the evil I send!!

Craig Gallagher

"Another Day"

I stood facing the treasure;
I have long awaited for this day;
I have finally found it.
I must follow the simple rules or death would be upon me;
It seems easy from sights, but it's not.
This summer day would be remembered and cherished forever;
For I have won the battle of dark waters;
I have cleaned my room.

David Blake Davis

The Light

Morning comes fast as the sun rises
　in the east
And the morning dew
Evaporates from around our feet
As the rays of the sun warm the air
　and our rosy cheeks
Another day has come upon us so to speak
But it is not long
For the sun starts to go down in the west
And evening is upon us
And it is time to rest
Now it is night-time
But there is still rays of light
From the twinkling stars
And the Brilliant moon light
But even in the darkest hour
There is still a ray of light
For it is God
He is the way and the Light

Emmanuel Clary

The Space Race

The race for space began in October 1957.
In November the Russians launched artificial
satellite Sputnik under the Heavens.

The Russians told the United States we will conquer
space, so look out boys now you're in for a race.

The United States told the Russians don't brag too soon,
because we are going to put a man on the moon.

February 20, 1962 the United States
told the Russians we are ahead of you.

We are telling you boys we are not in a hurry.
We are going to launch Friendship 7, Project Mercury.

Astronaut John Glenn and the astronaut crew
boarded that ship knowing what to do.
John Glenn sent that space craft off into space,
leaving the Soviets behind in the race.

Astronaut John Glenn blasted that space craft off on time,
leaving planet Earth far behind.

John Glenn landed on the moon with a thought in mind,
As he stepped of the ship he said one step for me
and one giant step for mankind.

Daisy B. Martin

"It's True"

I'm very simple minded
In my material needs it's true

But when it comes to thinking
I dive so very deep it's true

If you do not pay attention
I might lose you half way through

But remember that it is you who is losing me
and not me who's losing you

Cause when it comes down to it
We both know that it's true

Barbara J. Tipton

A Lost Love

I know that we never meet again
In my heart I feel it is true
Our love was promised to last forever
I feel the same, but do you?

The times that we spent together
Will linger with me though you are away
I cherished each lasting moment
With your love a symbol of joy.

I will never awake to happiness
As moments flee you refuse to call
To know that we will never kiss or love again
Are the saddest times of all

Someday I hope that we will meet again
Come back to me my love, I miss you so
I need your arms and your kisses
I will be waiting don't ever let me go.

I know that I will never feel the same
My heart will perish without your love
So please come back and restore the fireless flame
Let's hope some day we will meet again.

Emma Bernice Wilson

War

What is the definition of war?
In my eyes a squabble that drips blood, wounds, death,
　souls and the very lives of innocent people,
When people fight in wars they are supposedly being patriotic
　but some leader who probably did no fighting collects
　the glory.
There is no use looking at the past when we should be
　looking toward the future and a better world, not
　for my generation but for all and everyone and everything
　living now and in the future.
Stop talking about peace and put effort forward to bring
　it close to us.
Keep the peace!

Elizabeth Louth

Paraphrasis

Though sea of snow may mark the dazzled eye,
In every fold not every sheep shows white,
And never wheeling flock but joins the eye
With soaring fancy mimicking its flight.
No more can suitor blinded of his love
See maid's true nature darkened in its ray
Then can he, focused on the sun above,
See starry truth deep-shadowed by its day.
Neutral is nature; neutral man is not:
Truth images man-fancied beg in vain.
Question proposed determines answer wrought,
Light light-beguiled beshadowed must remain.
By wicked lamp's caprice are blackened sheep,
Love's labor's lost and lost is lover's sleep.

Eric Nelson

Untitled

Whatever I do seems to be wrong.
I seem to be weak, but maybe I'm strong.
If all these things I could rise above.
Maybe I'd earn some more of your love.
I look around and what do I see?
But some far worse off than me.
I'm happy with things right now you see,
and wait for what's ahead in life for me.
If life was all easy and fun now see-
there'd by no reason for what's yet to be.

Frances Ledford

137

The 1982nd Serpent

He gave us apple juice to drink,
in baby bottles,
and told us to suck out every last drop, until it was finished.

When he sat on his trampoline, barring the doorway,
his vine covered snake slithered
out of hiding, and he said the price of passage into the garden
was to stroke its bobbing body.

We crawled up the staircase, but couldn't make the top before
he spied our naked heads, and stalked behind, to tuck
us in our beds, and to make sure we'd changed.

He opened my clothes, as I cried gently under my breath,
and his touch slid down past my stomach; a slow searing
of fangs, the poison inching into my festering skin.

Scratching his body to mine, his sandpaper tongue rasping
in the air high above my head, he scaled my dying skin and curled
up in the coldness of my shaking mind.

Christina Aldridge

An Ode To Elwin

It's fitting to write some praise, and this is Heaven sent for I know,
in all my days, I never met a nicer gent! He loved his family, and
all who he met-and showed them kindness and love and we know that he
is surely all set, in those Pearly Gates above!

Dogs and cats, any animals and birds-he couldn't see them hurt. If he
knew anyone that needed help, he'd even give you his shirt. You'd
never see Elwin in his old blue van, without the three dogs by his
side. He'd say "I'm not out to get a tan, the poor things just love a ride!"

And then there were two-just Lady and Sassy, as they'd lay and sleep
by his chair and you know, they all looked pretty classy, as he petted
and stroked their hair. For Aunt Hazel he'd help me make little things
we crafted and made out of wood she probably enjoyed them better than
rings-he always said it made her feel good!

Last year he helped me with the recipe "irons", I think we made twenty
six I said "If we don't finish in time, we'll surely be in a fix." He
loved to sing, and loved the old hymns, and it certainly did inspire
us all to see his loyalty and love, he just loved the Grantham choir.

We miss you Elwin, and it hurts a lot, as we look at your empty seat
but we can hear you singing along-sounds great-you didn't skip a beat.
As with all things, the time has come, to bring this note to an end
keep singing with us-maybe even hum, we shall ALWAYS miss you, dear
Friend!

Frank J. Fremgen

Winter Queen

Winter is a Queen
In a dress of Snowy White.
She sleeps under a silver moon;
She loves to nap under the light.

The meadows have no color now
With a song so sweet;
They have little ponds turned into ice—
She is very petite.

She loves the little white trees.
They are light green and dark green, too.
The snow flakes come down swiftly;
The carpet is white and blue.

Alisa Ann Miller

Help Me

Do you believe
in
Hate. For so many have this Power. Especially Her.
in
Emotion. For so many hide it well. Especially Her.
in
Love. For so many never learned. Especially Her..
in
Pain. For so many have this gift. Especially Her.
in
Mercy. For so many don't understand. Especially Her.
in
Ending. For so many are just beginning. Especially Me.

Amy Cormier

Visions

I am nearest God when I am:
Imagining myself in a flowering mountain meadow... wild and free as
the wind that caresses my hair and tickles my senses...

Meditating in a great silent forest, engrossed by the captivating
harmonies of Earth's nature symphony...

Basking in the warm sand and sun... of a secluded cove... lulled by
the whisper of gentle waves nuzzling the shoreline.

Intrigued by rocky shores... the mournful horns crying out in the
misty night... saluting the bell buoys that toll a knell for fog
blinded ships... and shrieking gulls that SOS mariners who
venture dangerously close to land fall

Enraptured by the melodic enchantment of the "Boston Pops" or lost in
the simple, soulful, flowing breath of a Native American flute...
its echoes resounding throughout the vast Southwest canyons

Delighting in the joy life brings... making the most of HIS mercy and
limitless love...

Or... just trying to live as we were meant to be... sharing love and
friendship amongst all peoples... without bias... without hatred..
without greed or jealousy!

Bernadette M. Bland

I'm Sick

I'm sick of crying myself to sleep at night,
I'm sick of trying to fight,
The urge I feel to die,
My whole life is just a lie,

Nothing is ever fair,
And the world doesn't seem to care,
Sometimes it is almost more than I can bare

I don't know how much more I can take,
Because from inside is where I ache,

I wish I could make it stop,
But I don't know where to start,
Because the ache,
Is in my heart

Alaina Davio

The Fear Within

I will not let him see the fear in my eyes,
Hoping that he will realize,

I love him so much, I can't let him go,
This I pray he will someday know.

Wanting to be with him all of the time.
Thoughts of him constantly go through my mind.

With him there may never be permanent ties.
I will not let him see the fear in my eyes.

Claire Schmitz

"Revelation"

Whenever you are near
  I'm in heaven all the while,
And I tingle when you look at me
  With that cute, bewitching smile.

When you speak to me so sweetly
  I just wilt at every word.
For your line is the grandest
  That I have ever heard.

Just the mere touch of your hand
  Sends thrills up and down my spine.
And, dear, when you caress me
  The sensation is sublime.

I can't resist your ardent kisses
  Which leave me speechless from the start
Can't you guess how you affect me
  By the pounding of my heart?

Oh, don't look so astonished
  At these things I dare to say.
They could be true any other time,
  But it's April first today?

  Frances E. Antijunti

Untitled

I've finally come to my senses, I've finally woken up.
I'm done crying, I'm done regretting, I've finally had enough.
At first it hurt that you had gone leaving no explanation.
And yes, there was a time when I would have taken you back
without any hesitation.
But like the clouds are pushed along with no resistance by
the wind, not sure where they're being sent,
Time has carried me to a place where I can start over again.
When I see you on the street I'm suddenly aware,
That though we used to share so much, the feelings are no
longer there.
An awkward silence fills the space that smiles used to occupy,
But all's well that ends well, so I'll wipe this final tear
from my eye.
The great times that we had, they will always be in my heart,
But I'll push the memories to the back of my mind, and I'll
begin to make a new start.

  Aimee Goodenough

"The Desert"

The voice of "The Desert" is calling
I'm bewitched by its haunting refrain
And its promise to be my salvation
From a life fraught with trouble and pain.

Other voices have joined in the chorus
Enhancing the beckoning croon
As I eagerly follow a moonlit trail
To the shore of a peaceful lagoon.

At last, I am free of the burdens
Created by fortune and fame
The magical spell of "The Desert"
Has staked another claim.

  Elinor K. Keller

What I've Learned In These Ten Years

What I've learned in these ten years is that you can't
hide broccoli in a glass of milk.
I've learned that my favorite toy is only one third the
size it is on television.
And most importantly,
I've learned that quack grass doesn't get its name
because it quacks in the middle of the night.

  Erika Steckmeyer

My Blue Rose

Was my son from head to toes,
  I'll always love that rose, only
the Lord really knows
  He was just a tot, when I lost
him on the spot.
  Life I go on living, love I try
to go on giving.
  I'm waiting for the day he'll
come back and say mommy I have loved you as I lived above you
  Together now we can be, you are
freed, you have no more needs,
  That's the day I'll see my
Blue rose and me walking hand
in hand through the Lord's
heavenly sands.

  Cathy Blaylock

For Jenny

If I were to create a world for you
If your breath would give birth to the air
I would paint the sky the blue of your eyes
And the grass would be soft as your hair.
All over the land would be lilies and
Roses of soft, blushy tints
From the pink of your cheeks; and the breath from you reeks
Would perfume the soft-blowing winds.
The sun all the day would shine in a way
Only your smile could ever compare;
The sun always will show for the clouds surely know
To appear they must never dare
Rich the land would be, abounding with trees
Ablossom in fragrance and grace;
The same I detect, the scent from your neck,
And the beauty from only thine face.
A world built for you from my love so true
But I profess I cannot take you there;
For the blossoms red dye, the sun and the sky
Before you would grow dim in compare.

  Charles Frederick Becker

Gone Fishing

Often when I was but a child,
  If the ocean was very, very mild,
Grandpa and I would make it a day -
  We'd board a boat docked in the bay.
Windswept with mist we'd anxiously await
  For the anchor to drop and be given some bait.
Grandpa always used a rod and a reel,
  But with a dropline, on a bench I would kneel.
The sun was warm and the ocean was blue -
  The mackerel were running - I hooked a few!
With scraps for the sea gulls swooping near,
  The fish were filleted as we returned to pier.
Still debating who hooked the biggest one,
  We set out for home - our day was done.
On rubbery sea legs and our faces aglow,
  We arrived at the door, our catch in tow.
Nana beamed and applauded our bucket of fish -
  For supper that night, I had one on my dish.
These are fond memories of our days at sea
  When I was young and Grandpa was with me.

  Dawn Ingham

139

To Mother Blue

Dear Grandma,
If it delivers any comfort to your ailing heart,
I'd like to tell you that I love you, and Happy Birthday.

If it means anything to you, now that you're gone,
I'd like to tell you that you are a major part of me.
My smile, my wit, my charm and more

If for a second, I could embrace your giving soul,
I'd tell you more than once in many ways,
How dear you are to me and all.
If by some powerful force, I could touch your hand
I'd take with me your scent, and only you and I will understand.
Dear grandma, I miss you more than I miss the moon
that shone so brightly and said so much to me last night.
I miss you more than that.
Dear Grandma, let me know that you heard my cry
by placing a beautiful star in the sky!
Happy Birthday, Grandma!

Celeste D. Ragland

"My Thoughts"

I'd be the world's greatest author, yes, for real!
If I'd sit down and write just how I feel
About my lovely daughter, Paula Rae,
And I wish every mother could feel this way.
She's everything I ever wanted for me,
Thoughtful, kind, loving, and always free
To help someone out whatever the task,
She's just always willing you never need ask.
I keep telling myself and friends galore
Of my special daughter whom I adore.
It's never too late to express how one feels
About that special someone before God steals us back home to stay
With love not expressed and buried away!
So, instead of being an author I openly reveal,
Because there's far too much love for any book to conceal!

Bertha J. Absec

Untitled

Long ago when I was 24 I thought I'd really lived!
I'd been a nurse, I'd been to War,
I'd fallen in love, could there be more?
That's what I asked at 24.

Then looking back at 44 I realized there was so much more.
For I'd been married 25 years or so by then
Had children, 2 boys, 2 girls that equals four-at 44.

By 54 I'd come to know the gift of a grandchild
With a promise of more to grow!
Illness, surgery, the death of dear ones
But the children were married, who needed more?
That's what I thought at 54!

Now as I look forward to the age of 74
I laugh as I look back and remember I thought I had it all at 24!

But life has been good to me, I wouldn't change it for a minute.
God has blest me wondrously
And I've had lots of Precious Moments in it!

I would not trade the pain and tears with anyone I know,
And when I face life's closing door
I'll thank my God for letting me live past 24!

Eileen D. Wilson

Changes

I used to think
I'd be seven years old forever
But now here I am
Almost a high school graduate.
People always tell you
that friends are forever,
but the truth of the matter is
people lose touch, therefore ,
    lose each other.
I don't mind changes,
But I just wish there weren't so many.
    I love nature
and the beautiful things God gave us,
but here we are destroying it with "technology".
    all that I wish for...
are less changes!
You try being seven years old again,
write an old friend or lost love,
save God's wonderful creations,
just, please, lessen the changes in this scary world

Cassie Denise Dalton

I Dare To Discover Space

I dare to discover the planets and stars,
I would like to go them but they are so far
To look at their bright shine, I wish they were mine
They soar so high in the sky, why they are there, I wonder why
They are filled with dust, like they appeared with a gust
Then there are great planets, as they spin in their orbits

Made of rock and gas, so heavy with mass
I wish to go and walk on the moon, I hope I can very soon
As planets spin, and the moon grins
We look in the sky, as they soar so high
As the galaxy will change, ideas will exchange
Who knows, what out there grows
Maybe a kind of life, a planet and new animal life
As astronomers work, they will find what lurks
As facts pour in, we still don't know what lies within
Remember this, planets and stars are too good to miss

Carrie Selski

I Am A Short Person That Loves Animals

I am a short person that loves animals.
I wonder what I will be like in the future.
I hear the cry of hungry children.
I see all the violence around the world.
I want to help all of those in need.
I am a short person that loves animals.

I pretend that there is peace and happiness.
I feel that I can do anything.
I worry what will be of me tomorrow.
I cry at all the children that get killed each year.
I am a short person that loves animals.

I understand that we are all the same.
I say that we are all different.
I dream that I will be a veterinarian some day.
I try to be all the me I can be.
I hope that all the violence will stop.
I am a short person that loves animals.

Celeste Lindell

I Wish

I wish for lavender and lace
I wish for rainbows and unicorns
I want to see pictures pasted on walls
And I am going to cry

I wish for rainbows and stamp collections
I wish for penguins and pink flamingoes
I want to hug you again
And I am going to cry

I wish for blue jeans and sweaters
I wish for gum wrappers and braces
I want to say I love you once more
And I am going to cry

I wish for dance recitals and costumes
I wish for camping and swimming
I want to back up in time
And I am going to cry

I wish for dollhouses and cabbage patch dolls
I wish for long hair and french braids
I say goodbye for now sweet sixteen niece
And I am crying

Anne L. Welch

A Physical Soul

Physically, everybody will die.
I will die, physically.
You will die, physically.
Nobody's soul will die.
My soul will live forever.
Your soul will live forever.
If you give your soul to Jesus,
before you die, physically,
your soul will live forever with happiness.
If you don't give your soul to Jesus,
before you die, physically, your
soul will be happy, until you die,
physically, then you will live on
forever in torture.

Andrea Waters

David

On June 29, 1983, twelve years ago
I wasn't sure and I sure didn't know,
Whether or not, you would make it through,
But then with love and hope, it's really you.

You will always be my pride and joy
All because you are my only little boy,
You know I love you, with all my heart
And I hope that nothing will pull us apart.

For on this day, I wish you the best
Because the years to come will be a test,
To know that we will always love each other
Because after all, I am your MOTHER.

Beverly Young

The Bird And The Feather

I AM the bird that flies in the sky
I AM the bird that flies above the clouds
I AM the bird that flies real high
   I AM the feather on the bird
I AM the feather that flies with the bird
I AM the feather and I'm smooth as silk
I AM the bird I AM the feather
   and we love to FLY.

Eric Parent

Destiny's Acrid Humor

My nervous heart kept my eyes gleaning the empty ground,
I wanted to express my awkward affections, I only dared lift my head,
Toward your sweet presence.

A brisk walk out of necessity, all that we took,
A few words of convenience, all that we shared,
A second's worth of glances, all that I dared.

Separated by circumstances, we are fated,
To cross paths only at a dying star's command.
If God's souls do will to love and search,
Our star-crossed paths will meet again.

In the while, wind blows my passing time hither and thither—
I long to traverse the road less traveled, looking back,
I see a glimpse of birth and death, all that is in-between, through,
within, and without, I've lived with a pain gilded regret.

Like the empty ground under a careless tree, I await Fall and Wind,
Conditions of happenstance, longing for the embraces of certain leaves,
And looking for compassionate stars.

When all my moments alone with other souls are mere pretenses,
Why do I look for Substance? Why do I hope for Nobility?
When my true longing is for a tumble weed existence.

Danny H. Wang

Expecting ... With The Unexpected

I can't believe it happened ... does it really start this quick?
I wake up in the morning feeling nervous-tired and sick.

How could it be that yesterday I was responsible for just myself...
And suddenly I have a lifetime commitment nurturing someone else.

Where will I find that kind of strength to help me be the one?
To give everything in my heart and soul to a daughter or a son.

Maybe if I close my eyes, it won't be quite so real...
But ...oops...just in time...a kick for me to feel.

Well-Imagine that... it must be a boy, to have made me lose Control...
Why I bet with a bit of practice - I could ultimately reach my Goal.

To teach and love and encourage this child to be whatever he wants to be.
And to never give up when the going gets tough...
I didn't...and you're the best thing that's happened to me!!

Dani VanSickle

The Country Lane

Walking down a country lane, in summer was a joy.
I use to do it many times when I was just a boy.

Those carefree days, in many ways, I wish could be again.
But now with me, half century, I can but just pretend.

My thoughts return to bad sunburns and muddy swimming holes.
To B.B. guns and neighbors sons and home made fishing poles.

I can recall the summers all and all the fun I had.
Target practice in a field and baseball with my dad.

When winter came, the country lane became a paradise.
Down hill sliding, bob-sled gliding, skating on the ice.

Spring time crept as winter slept, the lane was in full bloom.
My secret pond where tad poles spawn. The whole world was my room.

Then summer came and back again, I'd walk the lane with joy.
I use to do it many times, when I was just a boy.

Dave A. Thomas

Old Friend

She smiles as I gently rub her back,
I touch her cheek, the skin so slack,
It's hard for me to see her pain,
Frailness of body is very plain,
I finish her care then say goodnight,
Walk to the door and turn out the light,
A tear rolls silently down my cheek,
Illness has robbed her and made her weak,
"Life's been good," she'd always say,
"Just make the best of each new day,"
I fear the end is drawing near,
It's just not fair for one so dear,
I come to work early to see her next day,
"She died in her sleep," the nurses say,
I walk to her room to say good-bye,
Turn to the window and softly cry.

Ellen Jacoby

"Early Morning Wonderings"

Who was it that called my name before the break of day?
I searched through the darkness but no one dared to say........
It sounded so familiar, warm and clear ....
Could it be a loved one drawing me near?
I pulled the covers up close and waited for its refrain,
But quiet only filled the room and I never heard it again.
Could it be that I imagined this incident as real?
Or does this always happen when it's quiet and still..........?
No one shall ever know of this visitor from beyond,
For in the early morning, we shared a special bond.
Did it see, hear or touch my wildest dreams?
Or did it make its presence known to tell me what they mean?
I have no way of knowing when it will return again.............
Until it does I'll wait, lie still, and wonder about the early
morning journeys of my.................

Secret......................
     Mysterious..................
          Friend!

Alice F. Powers

Meeting You

Meeting you on a fine morning I thought, "Who is he?"
I searched all the pages in my memory
No, I have never seen you before.

But, the nature, the stature, the impression
You made on me that's familiar
It could never ever be a confusion.

As a kid I've admired my mother saw the entire world in her
Then I admired my dad: Like any child at that.

It was then my teacher, my sister
Later it was some friends and other
I grew from a kid to a man,
Like some and dislike many others.

Turning the pages, I figured;
What was so familiar and similar-
You have given me a part of each page I turned.

Love, affection, life, fun, joy,
Responsibility, direction, wisdom, knowledge and realization;
Fond remembrances, bliss and tears...
Tears of happiness and eternal joy.

There'll never be a new page without you on its face.

Anil Telikepalli

My Guardian Angel

Late at night when I lay awake,
I say a prayer and hope it will take,
Me to slumber land and a sea of dreams,
Where my guardian angel waits for me.

With a boat made of copper,
And oars made of brass,
The air is like crystal,
The water like glass.

We float down a long narrow river of thoughts,
Of hopes, dreams, can and cannots,
I think of the cans and hope they come true,
For they are the things I hope some day to do.

We stop at a port,
And she lets me on shore,
And I know that the dream won't go on anymore,
But I know anytime, anyplace, any day, anywhere, my guardian angel is
watching me up in the air.

Christine Kobus

My Ship

Tall, white sails with stalwart masts,
I remember the ships of my past.
Lull of the ocean, smell of the sea,
the wind in my hair, the salt in my tea.
Stretching forever, the sky shone azure,
the bottlenose jumping, the humpbacks demure.

The chain of the anchor, CLANG! CLANG! On the rocks,
the bustle of people upon foreign docks.
My destination came soon with no haste,
and I stepped onto land, no time could I waste
to wave to my ship as it pulled out to sea,
leaving lonesome and lovesick, on the shore, me.

Never again did I feel that same gust,
on the deck of a ship, stark and robust.
A poor lonely ghost ship is what it is now,
the mast on the rocks, water beating at the prow.

Erin M. Nelson

Stay With Me

I need you to stay with me tonight
I need you to stay and hold me tight
To show me that I still have a heart
To tell me that we never have to part
To show me that I'm still alive

Stay with me and share my life
Help me through the struggles and strife
Stay with me so we can be shown
A love for each other neither has known
I know we can do it if we give it a try

Hold close my heart and do it no harm
Let me feel your soft skin and charm
Just hold me close and never let go
Show me a love that without you I'd never know
Together we can love and grow old

Stay with me and let me show
A love for you that will forever grow
Let me give you all the love from my heart
Just stay with me and let's make a start
A love for each other that will never die

Ernest O. Lynn

The Joy Of John

The Joy of John came when I realized that he identifies with me.
I met him once so long ago, a quiet boy with a mysterious soul.
When low in spirit and soul is dry, I call on John and he'll identify.
He reminds me to take pleasure in the small insignificant things
like a streaming cup of coffee or a night of gentle rain.
Perception, a major view to surviving human living,
John puts into focus by his gracious listening.
Through my precious friend I see the world in a softer light.
Fortunately for me, he touched my life.
I recognize his soul's sacrifice,
His gentle tone and tender giving.
He brings joy into everyday living.
So my passing through this hardening world
Much easier I have found
that thinking on the Joy of John my life is quite profound.

Catherine R. Newmyer

Beyond

Oh to close my eyes and as they open again,
I look up into the heavens and soar to
the depths of space and eternity.
No feelings of pain nor sorrow,
Laughter and joy just a vague memory.
No breath of life in me you'll find,
Yet alive I know I am.
Only existing.
Existing in the vastness of space, in the presence of God.
No thoughts or fears of tomorrow because tomorrow is surely today.
Protected in God's greatness,
Sheltered in his love.
No disappointing lows or unexpected highs,
To know God's presence and feel his touch,
Peace and tranquility in me you'll find.
To reach beyond this flesh, beyond the breath of life,
Beyond the mind's comprehension of time and space.
A plane of existence that no man can see,
Only God's greatness and His vast eternity.

Bill Rymer

To Question

To the constant rushing of the ocean
I lay the guilt of calmness to its rest.
Beyond the silence,
Within the shadows of the moon
The strength of sunlight is put to test.

Will the unlimited universe
Choose solely to allow
What one cannot see to exist?
Passion plays a part in every man's living script.
What does happen when the page is turned?

The sun it rises in the east
The stars beat heavy on its crest of dawn.
A new beginning.

Carolyn Grooms

Night Sounds

Last night as I lay my head on my pillow, soft and white,
I heard the distant thunder in the stillness of the night.

I also heard the music of a lonely whip-poor-will,
And somewhere in the far off, a mocking birds voice so shrill.

As the night grew longer, toward the midnight hour,
I heard two voices chanting, 'twas two owls hooting over power.

And as the owls were fussing, I heard another scream-
'Twas my little bantam rooster crowing-morning can be seen.

Colleen Kitch

A Knock

While lying down a taking a nap
I heard a knock, it's getting louder now
When I got to the door no one was there
So I went back in and laid back down.

The knock came again, it was louder than ever.
When I got to the door, no one was there.
Then the strangest thing started to take hold.
I was guided back in by a beautiful Angel.

She told me things that was going to happen
And showed me sights to see in Heaven.
I want you to do a job, God has assigned for you.
Go tell the people of these things that you've seen.

Tell them about the love that He freely gives.
About your feelings that are real.
About Angels singing and rejoicing in Heaven.
While their homes are being made
As God's son has promised.

The knock at the door was me just to tell you
That you've got a job to do
So tell about Heaven.

Ava Yocum

A Tribute To My Guardian Angel

Oh my dear angel and my guide
I have you always by my side
You've taught me how to learn and speak
You suffered with me when I would weep
When I'm in doubt you come to me
You tell me just how things should be
You remind me of my prayers each day.
And never, never go away
You sooth me when I cannot sleep
It's a safe watch that you keep.
I know when God assigned you to me
My heart was opened with a spirit key.
As time runs out - we'll be face to face
And everlastingly embrace.
You'll have done your job - a job well done
I'll strive to see that goal is won
The good and bad deeds - you will tell
To the Master who rules over heaven and hell.
I know in my life time you will see
That I have the spirit of God in me.

Charlotte M. Lake

Take Time To Dream

I am as invincible as the Greek Gods,
I have the power to read a mind.
I can the seasons,
I can speed up, slow down or stop time.
I can push away dark clouds,
And bring out the sun.
I can make the whole happy,
My work is never done.
I can make love's hand
Touch even the coldest heart.
I can capture and bring forth faith and love,
That you must admit is a useful art.
I can cause the wars to cease,
I alone can bring unto you Universal Peace.
You can do all of these things too.
It's not as hard as it may seem.
All you really have to do,
Is take a little time to dream...

Debra Snyder

To Sweet Pea's Daddy

I can remember when I was a little girl,
I had long dark hair with natural curl.
I was an angel to the dark-haired man.
He was my daddy, I was the last of the clan.
One sister, two brothers - I was the last of his four.
A dad full of love whom we all did adore.
He stood like a giant to a child so small,
"Sweet Pea" was what he called me since the day I could crawl.
And now I am grown and have been married five years,
I still call my daddy with a lot of my fears.
With faith in the scriptures and in God up above,
He silenced my fears with nothing but love.
His support has encouraged me to do what I can,
Now I am here to thank him for all that I am.
So thank you Daddy for all that you have done,
Now think of your children and the hearts that you've won.

Deborah Ann Williams

A Black Male

I have been spat at, I have been beaten up, I have been stared at. Why?
I guess it's because I'm a Black Male.

In stores I have to watch how I move, how I walk, what I touch. Why?
Because if an officer believes that I have stolen something, I could
    end up in juvenile hall, or if I'm old enough - prison.

Many have perspectives of the black male. They think he shoots whom
    he pleases. They think he steals. They think he deals drugs. But
    that isn't how I act.

But once they see my black skin, my African hair, they believe that I am
    all of those things.

Who really is the Black Male? A rapper that makes fun of women?
    A man who leaves his illegitimate children with his girlfriend?
    A gangster? A jailbird? A drug dealer?

NO!

The real Black Male, is the educated Black Male.

Brandon L. Schaffers

"Hope"

When you were brought to day's light
I gave to you my hope
a hope that has carried me from land to land

Hold these hopes and grow bright
but never grow without this hope
because it is hope that will allow you to dream in midnight's sand

Follow these hopes and you will see beyond your sight
Though it will be hard to cope
You will soon understand.

Hopes are a kite
They are free explorers who encompass an imaginable scope
That can be held in one's hand to command

My hope is given to you with intentions
that it will help you find your strand
in life and not that it is to please me

When my time comes for redemption
of my joys with you, do not be sad but hold my hopes in your hand
and remember, you can be all that you want to be.

Andrew L. Hong

Flying High

To fly about the trees, so high
I feel like I can touch the sky
Down to earth, I turn and look to see
All that unfolds in front of me

The ragged mountains standing so tall
I look at the life that covers them all
Clear blue water in the lakes and streams
This is the fulfillment of all my dreams

I spread my wings out wide, as I sore
And look at the life that I adore
I float in the air so easy and free
Hoping that all will just let me be

The wind is so soft upon my face
As I fly around from place to place
The sun comes out to really shine
And lights up this path of mine

I fly through clouds, so fluffy and white
And flap my wings with all my might
To break free of all that life has given
And make my way on up to heaven

Flossie Barnett

Do You Believe?

Do you believe there other life forms out there in the galaxy? Well I do!
Sometimes it is just the knowing - that keeps me going!
Living on this planet is daily measure
of trying to hold on to those "things" that we treasure!
All the violence, hate, wars, and strife! - Seems to consume my whole life!
This planet is so full of confusion!
Often makes me feel very disillusioned!
Those times when I smile and with a cheerful "good morning!"
and their response is a blank stare! - just as if I wasn't even there!
No matter how hard I try to act formal!-
something inside tells me this is not normal!
Why do I feel that being in this "human" state!
is the reason why - I can't relate?
No matter how much I try to persevere! I always feel the end is near!
Again I ask you - do you believe there are other life forms
out there in the galaxy? Well I do!
And when I say "beam me up Scotty!" I damn sure hope!
That he is not on the potty!

Dorris Hameditoloui

"Pain"

The pain was deep inside and would not let me go;
I couldn't sleep, I didn't eat, it tormented me so.
I wanted to feel normal, I wanted to smile again,
The world was a desolate place, for I had lost my best friend.
You didn't up and leave me; it was your heart that went astray.
The pain cut so deep and would not go away.
Sadness so deep, pain so sharp, it tossed me all about.
At times I wanted to cry aloud, and this is what I'd shout:
I can't give in I must go on, to travel this
    emotion laden path is something I must do.
Will I be traveling all alone, or can I
    count on you?

Deborah Marie Fritz

Magic Mushrooms

Radiating red with addictive fumes;
Growing in a box on the basement floor
is my yearly crop of magic mushrooms
that will never be sold in any store.

My parents didn't know of my little patch,
But one day they found my box encasement.
I thought they were mad, but they liked my batch,
so now they dwell in our moldy basement.

Candy Bouquet

144

His Smile

Whispers in the darkness, his body close to mine,
I close my ears to silence, my heart I close to time.

The hurt I felt has vanished though I know it will return,
I want so much to hold him, it's for his love I yearn.

I don't know how he feels, does he feel as much as me,
Is his heart a seasoned vessel or a ship that's lost at sea?

Does he want to love me, or just to be my friend,
What is his desire, does he have a pain to mend?

Right now I really need him, I wonder does he know,
Just how much he means to me, I can't tell if it shows.

He lives so far away from me but in my mind he's near,
I want to see his smile, smiles can ease away my tears.

Becky Raymond

I Cannot No More

I cannot see or hear them any more.
I cannot hear my name anymore, when
  in need of hug and kiss.
I cannot hear and tell me, I'm sorry.
I cannot have them to eat with any more.
I cannot have the time with my loved one
  to play with no more.
I cannot have birthday and holidays no more,
I cannot have the best three little words
  I often hear, I love you, I Love you.
All I got left is memories, and that's
  not enough, any more.
I did not want this memory,
I just wanted my love one forever more.
I know my love one is with Jesus forever more.

Beverly Crego

Change Of Life

"LORD, speak to me in my secret heart
I am THY child, but, dumbly, stand apart.

I feel a growing heat and fire
to work my chosen field, my hearts desire,

Given to me from THY great Bounty.
It's time to act, to make fiction fact.

I am a repository of empathetic love
for all persons, here...there.. and above

No matter what they may be
Race, creed or nationality.

  And so,
I am a single glowing coal
from the furnace of Gods
Eternal, endless, infinitely loving Soul."

Charles Rowley

The Perfect Boy

I know one day I will find the perfect boy.
I do not know when or where,
But I know I will someday.

He may live near,
He may live far,
Or may live beyond a star.

I know the time will be right,
Sometime in my life.
And when I find him,
It will make me feel like a burning firecracker,
Spreading lots of light.

Carlye S. Burns

Tears

These tears I cry are because of you
I am so lonely I am so blue.
You took my innocence, I don't know why,
My only way out is to cry.
These tears on my pillow have been there for years
and may never dry up... that is my fear.
These tears I cry are because of you
I am so lonely I am so blue.
I sit and wonder and sometimes stare, how can
one memory make me feel as if I don't care,
I try to hide these feelings inside,
I used to feel so alive.
These tears I cry are because of you
I feel so lonely I am so blue.

Cynthia Santiago-Williams

Truth

I am written over, slandered.
I am buried. Meandered,
Into something else.

I hold no prejudices, no pretenses,
(And I wish no deceptions or boundaries.)
Yet limited to exclusive appearances.

Spoken so often in a whisper,
A sword of double edges plays
The most useful tool.

Claimed by everyone. Realized by few.
I am their faceless candidate
I am the shadow in the mirror

You thought you knew.
I am truth. I am alone.
Harder than you.

Anthony Ryba

Our World Today

Racial problems of today,
Hurt us reach and every way,
It brings guns and violence to our streets,.
And leaves dead ones families to weep.

This problem has gone on for quite a while,
In fact, since my great grandmother was just a child,
Black on white, white on black,
Why can't our country get on track?

If we don't do something really soon,
Our world is gonna burst like a balloon,
Gunshots here, gunshots there,
Racism itself should just disappear.

Then we would all have better lives,
And we would never have any guns or knives,
We wouldn't care about the color of our skin,
We would only care about the love within.

Annessa C. Oufnac

Who Am I?

I am every blade of
grass, every unfolding leaf,
every planet and sun, I
am the troubled waters of the sea
the rolling thunder and flashing lightning
I am the bird who sang, the winds that
scatter upon you and me.
I am the beasts that roam the plain
the moon that walks its silvery path
which are visible expressions of
my power, wisdom and love.

Crystal May

145

My Mother's Table

Many tables I have seen my Mother set,
how pretty each would be.
With loving hands and laughing eyes,
she was setting her table for me.

She would cheerfully put each piece in its place
on a freshly ironed cloth:
china cups - a touch of lace.

As my thoughts wander back to those special times
I cannot restrain the tears in my eyes.

Now I will use those very same cloths,
freshly ironed with love learned from her.
I pray I can have those same laughing eyes
as I now set each place for my own.
For I realize now just how much I was taught
at my Mother's table where such love was shown.

Bettie Lee Moore

Lonely Unwanted Humans

As the days go by, I often wonder,
How people can ignore the needs of another.

Their daily wants are greater than some,
They wander for shelter from the setting sun.

And at nightfall they are buried in leaves,
Newspapers as pillows, filthy air to breathe.

When the sun rises they are off on their journey,
Working for food trying to make a days earning.

I don't understand how their lives are taken away,
They walk around wondering if they will survive another day.

I feel so bad knowing these people are alone,
They will never fit in or have a place to call home.

Freda C. Fistzgiles

New Moons

How many moons have we shared together?
How many times looked into the sky?
Pearly luminescence shining upon us
Light so white that we can't hide
From that which seems so clear between us
Brightens with courage, we face and see
Force of Nature, undaunted, victorious
And yet we wait for what will be.

For soon the new moon which is much gentler
Its inky blackness setting us free
To softly reach out, touch each other
Enshrouded quiet, the stars and me
And you and us, the future looks brighter
This semidarkness where emotions lie
Enough in the present to light and guide us
As the full moon grows in hearts with time.

Carol Anne Bundy

Untitled

Love grows as the old tree we sit under.
For many seasons my arms and mind hold you.
Love we take for granted at times
Driving steel words into our hearts
Filling our planted bed with blood
The passions of anger - hate
Pass! Thank God!
Then we merge together.
Giving our lives a love
That catches the sun like
The leaves of the old oak tree.

Dan Ferguson

Home

To have your first home, and to furnish it, too;
   How excited you two must be.
Wanting everything to be perfect;
   Choosing what you will need, and where things will be.

For they say a man's home is his castle,
   And also a woman's, it's true,
So may your home be a reflection,
   Of what you've found in him, and he's found in you.

I hope things will go well for you,
   That you'll have love, and laughter, too.
That you'll talk over misunderstandings,
   And keep your love strong, whatever you do.

May you have enough rain to love rainbows,
   Enough clouds to appreciate sun;
May each of your tastes come together,
   To make a feeling of Home, when you're done.

Charlotte A. Fife

Angels In The Sky

Fly high, high past the skies limits into a world of love,
Hope, joy and happiness.

The angels soft skin, her voice represents the power of the angels.
Her hair soft and silky, the sound of her harp twinkling, echoing
through the clouds, people wonder to themselves "How does it feel to
be an angel?"

They look in the sky and watch sparks of gold shining upon there
faces "try to touch the sun".

At night people look up at the sky and see one star shine and
they think "If God is watching...."

They fall asleep and dream....

Dream of angels flying upon the highest clouds and watch them
shimmer as they dance, and in a land of evergreen grass, beautiful
blue skies, and white doves flying across the sky.

Sometimes you dream of yourself dancing and singing to yourself
"God is with me, he'll protect me. In a land of trees and water falls
shimmering and...an angel."

Cynthia Macias

Haunted Memories

As the night's warm winds blew in her ear,
His sweet voice she swore she could hear,
Oh, how she wished she could hold him near.

As she slowly drifted off to sleep,
She soon awoke and began to weep.
She got up to walk but fell in a heap.

Why wouldn't the memories of that tragic day,
just leave her alone and go away?
But inside she knew they were here to stay.

So she took the gun from her drawer,
By now there is blood on the floor,
and the memories haunt her no more.

Christina R. Lloyd

Grace

   These ridiculous billboards stand motionless. Discarded
food exudes similar colors in the aisles of garishly dressed
spectators. The ball hit out of the stadium is love. Lifting
their arms to the sky, the screaming crowd tries desperately
to catch it, crying like a collective infant.

Albert Frenzel

This Man I Loved

His eyes were swollen from a decade of pain
His smile stolen from endless shame
His touch of peace was now of fear
His aching heart, its ending near
This man I loved, I did not know
For his stories were buried low,
Beneath the grass, beneath the snow
Tried to find them in his eyes
But lost them in his aching cries
To want to know him was a gift
Not to know him was his death
His pride was stolen long ago
So I feel, this I know to grow old and die alone
Breaks my heart this pain unknown
To contest, it's now too late
For his spirit has left the gate
This man I loved and did not know
I thank him with a loving soul
Just to have sweet memories
Leaves my mind with gentle ease

Ericca Wallet

Loving Chambermaid

She was quick to remember why she left him.
His one way pants.
Nine to five or six or eight, supper-finished meal.
Five, hot
Six, warm
Eight, late.
Children never knew. Him. Always him.
Her lost apron, Harriet dreams.
White pickets jab hard.
Edge of the lawn, edge of her life.
Blind ambition, nine months at a time.
Foul carbon rising from her mind-clouded.
And with a fierce interior whisper;
"Take the clouds by the rains."
A cold shower always helped him thought gather
Never enough.

Lacking memory of her sad, failed acts of love.
He never knew her name or really who she was.

Brandon Russ

Goodbye

Her chin is lifted and her lips are pursed
Her eyes gaze toward the heavens
There's pain in her expression; bittersweet
Quiet solitude

Her heart is crying and her soul is grieved
Her spirit pleads with heaven
There's desperation on her face; yearning
Silent isolation

Her arms are raised and her hands are reaching
She longs to be in heaven
There's reminiscence in her mind; anguish
Penetrating sorrow

He shoulders are sagging and her strength is spent
She turns away from heaven.

A voice is sounding in her ears; assurance
Gentle resolution

Her chin is lifted and her lips are smiling
Her eyes gaze toward the heavens
There's peace in her expression; bittersweet
Quiet consolation

Amy Tetlow Canada

My Mom Is Special To Me

My mom is very special to me
her care and love I can see.

She risked her life to give me birth
that I may live upon this earth.

When I'm sick and feeling bad
my mom is all I've ever had.

She wipes my tears and makes me glad
she is my mom and my dad.

She buys me toys and lots of good things
she treats me really neat and like a king.

She bakes me cookies and brownies too
my mom sure knows what to do.

Because she calls me her gift from God above
and treats me with lots of care and love.

That's why my mom is so special to me
her care and love even you can see.

Brandon M. Sazon

No Place To Hide

They took away her pride, gave
her a hurt inside and then they
said she lied. A little girl of three
with no place to hide.
They said, remember which side
your bread is buttered on. As if a
little girl of three could ever forget
such a thing as that, with no place to hide.
The strong winds blow and the Lord
he knows and the rain came to wash
the dirt from the sky and our little
ones need to know we are on their side.

Cora Hoxtell

Downfall

The August leaves majestically overlooked Alien ground,
held secure by the successful branches.
Each received its nourishment
and withstood the threatening rains.
They were able to go to the ends of the tree,
potential thus manifested.
But the cold, rebellious winds of September and October
began to infiltrate the placid, organized foliage.
Then finally came the traumatic shock.
The wind seized a clear shot at the tree
and pulled its trigger.
Ripe rulership expired.
The leaves, lacking their provider, fluttered in their descent,
brought down to earth.
It was the end of a stately, glorified Era.
The leaves stared up helplessly at their deprived stronghold.
Knowing only Red lay ahead.

Dan Wagner

"Infectious Wound"

There's an infectious wound in our mother land
Healing never came because scabs were pricked by our own hand
Slavery was enforced by the slothful ambitious rich
Turning from the American dream; life became a bitch
Then came the civil War - leaving our land with an hideous scar
Family ties split - Brother against brother;
   no true identity of who you are
Shortly afterward; Wars through nations began to progress
Americans striving for peace - our boys had no rest
Today we're facing a new War - the after math is gloom
Prejudice and hatred - we continue life with our infectious wound

Dennis Anders

Tex Ritter

Tex Ritter is a brave handsome man
He was born out west near the Rio Grande.
With nice red hair, he's full of hot air
He's cute! And he acts like a man
He fell in love with Juanita,
A lovely dark eyed Senorita,
Their love lasted long.
While he sand her love songs
While making love to his Juanita
One day she sent him a letter
Saying don't be broken hearted
I'm going to Mexico
I'm going to study some more
But I'll always think of you Tex Ritter.
Oh you're crying for your Juanita
Your lovely dark eyes Senorita
She's gone to Mexico
She won't come back no more
But you always can have me Tex Ritter.

Antoinette Licari Tranchina

Across The Sea

I remember, when my son came to me one day.
He told me, he was going far away.
I can still remember the smile he wore. And how his eye shown with pride. His voice was full of excitement, as he told me every word. And as he spoke, a tear tell from my eye.
I wanted to tell him no, but; I had to ask him why.
He took my hand so gently; and placed it between his; and began to whisper these words to me. "Mom, I'm leaving for awhile. I'm going across the sea. Don't cry Mom; please, I'm going there , for you, for her, and for me. I don't have to tell you who she is. I think you know. She's this great country God gave us; long ago.
Oh, it's not all that bad, I'll back in awhile! Anyway, I'm a man now Oh don't you see? I've got to go, for you, for her, and for me."
But; that was many years ago, since he went across the sea.
I'm old and tired now; and lonely as can be.
And I wake up, calling his name through the night. And I ask God to help me, to remember; that he was right. And at times, I can see him as a little boy again; running to me. But it's only a dream, that was long ago. I have nothing, now, except my memories. For both my men left me, and went, and stayed across the sea.

Barbara Heidelberg

Vision Of Peace

The Lord observed my troubled soul, then decided what he must show.
He put me into a kind of sleep, one not too light, one not too deep.
The Lord saw I was finally ready, my mind rested, my body steady. He now opened the eyes to my worried soul, and allowed the vision to unravel, unfurl, unfold.

Out of nowhere, the sky appeared directly above, saturated with beauty, filled with a glorious love. It seemed so peaceful, warm, a soft bright, lifting me out from the darkness and into the heavenly light. Then out of the blue a white bird appeared, and seconds later another joined it there. They stroked the wind in harmonic unison with wings stretched wide with each gentle glide. How silent, how peaceful the atmosphere abound as the white pair took to the air without a sound. They flew with such grace and an even pace, just high enough that I may witness the GLORY, the LOVE, the BEAUTY, the BLISS that such a vision could behold as this.

This vision of peace, what a wonderful blessing a gift of love, a spiritual lesson.

Bernadine Coggins

Gift Of True Life

Do you know who an organ donor is?
He is a caretaker.
She is a provider of life.
They are givers of health.
Your heart transports oxygen to all extremities of his body.
    The heart giver of color
My lungs aid her breathing.
    These lungs providers of the colored giving oxygen
Our pancreas delivers the insulin needed to break down her uncontrolled sweetness.
    A pancreas controller of sugars
His kidneys cleanse my son's body of poisonous toxin.
    Two kidneys destroyers of poison
Her liver decomposes the infant's impurities.
    One liver gobbler of pollutants
See one will say — Donors are givers of life.
Ponce De Leon searched for the Fountain of Youth
I seek the Fountain of organ giving life.
And you, you are my life.
Ms. Organ Donor not only are you a person that gives life; you are the water of my fountain.
Look at me; I see through your eyes.
In my soul and body, you are very much alive.
Be the waters of many streams — give life.

Anna Marie Sanchez

One Man Journey

If a child lives today
He has choices of his own

To be brought up
in a world alone

But with help of people
Close far and near

There is hope for him
With a Good heart and ear

He listen wisely to all sort of things
Things that make sense, things that seem mean

For he grows up, up in this world
Facing choices, choices of this world

For he tries all his might
Upon day until night

The boy grows into a young man
Family upon him at hand

He treats them right as good as can be
But life is too harsh for his family

He is an old man now happy and proud
He has done his deed it is done now

Austin R. Wells

I Love You

I love you and that's never
Gonna change.
When it's either sunny or when
it rains,
My love for you is so very strong
it would break my heart if we
wouldn't get along.
I bet I was put on this earth for one thing,
to stay with you whether it's fall or spring,
I hope you love me as much as I love you.
It would really make me happy if you do,
I love you so much and I won't ever let you go.
So I decided to write you this poem to let you know.

Cathy Ledoux

148

"Who Is There?"

Has someone kissed your forehead, yet.... no one was there?
Have you felt two arms around you, but still the room was bare?
Has someone sat upon your bed, in the dark of night?
Did you ask, "Who is there?" but no one was in sight?

Have you heard a quiet murmur, yet.... you couldn't understand?
Or felt the slightest pressure, like something touched your hand?
Have you heard muffled footsteps, or the creaking of a stair?
Or seen an empty chair rock, then called out, "Who is there?"

Have you smelled a fragrance worn by someone who's now gone?
Have you felt love surround you when you heard a special song?
Have you ever had a dream where you traveled "out" somewhere,
Then woke up with a start and cried out, "Who is there?"

Have you felt unseen protection while walking in the park?
Or found a light on in a room you know that you left dark?
Have you seen a moving shadow or felt a coolness in the air?
Has your pet acted strangely and you've wondered, "Who is there?"

If you really want to know if someone has been there with you,
Go to a restful silent place, then ask, "Please, tell me who?"
Soon a knowing will be felt, and your mind's eye will see so clear
The loved one who's been visiting, to let you know, "I AM HERE!"

Bev Planck

Magic

Have you ever chased a rainbow, or tried to find a pot of gold?
Have you ever followed all those colors, to the treasure, so it's told?
Did you see a leprechaun with a four leaf clover?
Did he play tricks on you, and fool you over and over?

Have you ever seen a goblin, lurking in the shadowy night?
Among the other ghosts and devils who vanish in daylight.
Was he staring at you with his bright yellow eyes?
Did he come to attack you, or simply pass you by?

Have you ever been to fairyland, where the sun forever shines?
Seen the lilies and buttercups; visited giant waterfalls and gold mines?
Where all living creatures, fluttered in the sky.
And none of them would ever die.

If you've never seen these things, I tell you they're all true.
But the only places you can find them, are the places deep inside of you.

Andrea Baier

The Life Within Your Soul

The life within your soul
has a life all its own.
For the day we have begun
is another song to be sung.
Fill your soul with life and dares of great power,
for only these things do indeed matter.
Therefore we must let go of the scared and slothful soul,
for it is out to get us.
But only God will know what we have done
that is neither worthwhile nor fun.
The only time we have is life on earth,
not the aftermath, the aftermath of a life wasted.
There is nothing worse than that.
Not even what is bad.
Fill your soul with life,
and live life to its fullest.
But you must achieve these goals
and the song that must be sung
because today hasn't started
until we believe yesterday is done.

Celeste M. Provencher

"Games"

Society contemplates our fate,
hanging by a string the future lingers
Then society takes its manipulative hands and molds
the clay, that is we, looking at what it has
created it scoffs at our mistakes, mocks
our choices.
Dare we challenge it back, it will wrench its
ugly head in horror and disgust.
To differ from the 'norm' is unexpectable,
what would everyone think? Asking not what
you yourself feel.
In time we know one another better than we
do ourselves.
Still the rise and stand above the rest is
encouraged. When you succeed at it, finding its
lonely away from the rest-society, king of
hypocrites, beckons us back into its mechanical lair.
Double standards seem to be every card in the deck
of the game that society plays.
Refuse to play, defy the rules and you have won the game.

Eve Marie Cerny

I Saw Clearly My Love Growing

I saw clearly my love growing
Growing faster and stronger than I knew what to do.
I saw how it just hit me -
How you don't look for love,
It looks for you!

I found the one I can turn to,
The one I know I can trust -
The one who knows me inside and out -
And knows I do what I must!

Love growing deep - far and wide
Standing tall - making sure not to hide
Growing stronger, with more pride

Clearly that great image appeared to me,
Like some pure white pearl from the sea.
And as it grew - I surely knew -
He was the one for me.

Adrianna Gardner

Bald Cypress Tree (Age 3,500 Years)

Old tree why stand so long
Gripping Florida sandy sod
Visiting people stand in awe
At a giant so great and tall
You've stood to see
Nations discovered — slaves set free

Man on the moon — the space age
Are you immortal or waiting for some event
Like Christ coming your intent
You've weathered hurricane winds
Lightning ripped your side
Storms you outride

Head held high for the eagle's nest
Your everlasting wood stood the test
Birth goes back to David's time
Shepherd of sheep harp and rhyme
You wait for the artist sketch
Of scarred trunk's skyward stretch

Bertha (Byrum) Robinson

Soul Suicide

In a house made of candy, a life bittersweet.
Good days as rare as rainbows, confusion in repeat.
Tears in heaven for the lost, times gone to the worst.
A protector unknown, as if lives were reversed.
An invisible shield keeping me from feeling any pain.
But how can I be sure that I'm not alone with nothing to gain?
I ask this same question, with every passing day.
No one to listen or to answer.
They all seem to like it that way.
I have, been lying in the crossroads,
Waiting to see drastic changes of the time after to unfold.
Only now there is no more emotion left in me,
Just the patience holding me, until the story's told.
Before it was a nightmare, I find few to blame.
But it never really mattered, because those few just count
Daisies, and forget about the rain.
One can hold still and live with misery they want to share.
Because, since time began, it's always worse to love
What was never was really there....

Angel Howard

Critic's Exposition

Each thought brings up a thousand more
going back even farther than good pirate lore.
'Tis trite to say, "I don't really care,"
when your voice turns out like a great grizzly bear.
Those thoughts in your mind they might seem
to come rumbling forth: my requiem.
Though reality out there should send no alarm
there never seems any safety from my peril or harm.
Jokes they might sound, slurs in my speech.
No, you were mistaken, I never shall preach.
The campfire we share sends smoke up in coils
all you can think of is how the blood boils.
Don't give me that look, leaven no blame;
it's hardly my fault, and 'twas no shame.
Please give up that frown, maybe to smile.
Unless you wish to leave your dreams disheveled in a pile.
So leave me now, smiling, and say a prayer,
for the days such as these: gentle and fair.

David Edward Durovy

"Clay Prints"

They told me my baby was still born,
God what a horrible fright!
I swear as long as I live,
I'll never forget that night.
I knew I'd be holding him one last time,
Dark hair and a pink precious face,
Salty tears I was forced to taste.
We decided to name him Kyle,
We had that name picked out for a while.
They gave me pictures and clay hand prints,
I swear it was such a sin.
Oh why O Lord why him!
We'll celebrate his birth and death each year,
by sending balloons up to heaven.
I know as long as I live,
there will always be one more tear,
for the baby we loved for nine months.
For the son we hold so near.
They'll be no explanations, no expectations.
KYLE DOUGLAS is gone and we must move on.

Barbara Craig Panzeter

Night And Day

I fly on my winged white horse with rubies glistening brightly as I
glide through the silver clouds.
Dew gathers on my skin for it is early dawn, and I am on my way to
you, for you are night - I am day.
I must bring you back with me to my paradise of warmth and golden
sunshine;
where perfumed flowers grow surrounded by a pure and purple ecstasy
of love and life.
I'll take you away from your cold and dread life of darkness;
to make you happy and fill each hour with memories never thought of,
never forgotten.
I'll make life surround you in her utmost kindness, and I'll have
clouds shower you in all their sweetness.
I'll take your moon, and with my sun I'll make a union-
a union of one heaven above all earth where you and I shall live forever.
For you there will be an understanding like there never was before.
For you there will be a love that you thought had died into the night.
So, you are night - I am day.
I am here to comfort you and heal you of your sorrowful tears of woe.
Never regret my coming to you...
For day leads into night, and night leads into day.
Together they will lead each other.

Charla Ludwig

The Admirer

Marc is like a lurid path with light
    gleaming through the trees,
Natural beauty of the woods is discovered as his
    inner self gradually leaves the darkness behind.
His whisper brings a chill to the body,
    which reminds one of a cool breeze,
His soothing touch reminds one of the innocence of nature.
The admirer notices his mysteriousness
    and his uniqueness as the road winds.
The admirer looks beyond the darkness
    and sees the beauty of the path.
Curiously observing the road,
    the admirer follows into the darkness
    and hopes to enlighten the way.
I, the admirer, believe...
that this untraveled path may seem,
to be an everlasting dream,
but, I, the admirer,
have faith that it will one day be,
....an everlasting reality.

Dana Lewis

Diogenes

That lantern set against the noonday sun
Gleamed brighter yet when measured by intent,
An ancient search begun by him so bent
With wonder that the ideal form lacked men.
A simple quest that dreams of gold did shun,
But sought a finer gift as yet unspent.
Thus did he raise that lantern high and sent
Its light to find a man — a pure one.
No answer did he hope to hear
To his flickering question burning stark,
No single flame, nor could a thousand suns
Illume the darkness that he knew was there.
Yet did his mocking probe give spark
To the pyre of truth, a symbol of the aeons.

Charles E. Ziavras

150

Pass Me By

Oh Love, of you I have tried,
Giving my heart to a field of lies.
Flowering words blooming of deceit,
Gave to me a bouquet of consuming grief.

Where were those promised sunlit days;
Full of lovers as they happily played?
My eyes seeking light, saw only darkness;
Our song of love, was sung larkless.

Oh Love, nevermore approach my door.
Pass me by, seek another to adore.
The pain of passion has so bruised my breast;
From the lies of Love, I embrace my rest.

Elaine J. Jones

To Dream

To dream of changing things in my life,
gives hope in the mist of the turbulent storms...
To dream of a beautiful rose garden in full
bloom, the sky so perfectly blue, the clouds
and the big yellow moon too, gives hope of
a new and brighter day...
To dream of a better tomorrow than I saw
yesterday, gives me to thank God, my Creator
for his love, mercy and wonderful grace...
To dream of a family surrounded by love,
happiness, joy, laughter and peace helps me
smile for I understand the importance of God
truly loving man...
To dream of justice and equality for every
man, no matter the color of the skin, means
that our ancestors didn't die in vain...

Darlene "Samihah" Thompson

Circles Of Fire

Auburn glowing embers, perpetually burning
Gaze of fire, gaze of flame
Gift of prometheus encased
Radiating insane rationale
Never blinking, ever thinking
Scorches the soul
Heat seeking, heat speaking
Beautiful trial by fire
Orbs ablaze pierce the dark
Transfixing with glow
Silence, but everything is said
Fire igniting, spheres exciting
Slow burn of desire
Unlike fire of the fallen
No brimstone, no fire lake
But forging and fusing
Forever glowing, yet never showing
Concealment of the flames

Andrew Turse

Angel's Tears

Rain is Angel's tears falling from the sky,
for something has happened, and they don't know why!!
The light in a child's eyes has gone out!!
No more hope, no more desire, no more dreams,
Just a frightened child.
LIGHTING and THUNDER are there warning,
to those how do the harm to the young and the defenseless!!
They best be warned,
for the harm they do today, will come back tomorrow
IN THE EYES OF A FRIGHTENED CHILD!!!!!

Ann Rene Hanlin

Today

This morning I saw a robin red breast,
gathering straw to build her nest,
she seemed so happy as she hopped along,
as from a nearby branch her mate, chanted a song.
Farther down the lane I could see,
Pink blossoms on a green cherry tree,
The fragrance floated me on the wind,
as pure as the truest words, lovers can send.
The grass so green is cool to the touch,
and dotted with flowers of pink, and yellow, and such.
Today the world seems so fresh and new,
I'm very glad to be part of it too,
Here beauty blooms as sweet as a rose, in June,
And the days are played out like a fine instrument, in tune.
Today is like the day of one's birth,
When the warm sunshine touches the earth.

Betty Lou Bates

Coping

Out from behind the cold dark grate, all was black and grey.
Gaping mouths with wide opened eyes were trying hard to say,
"Don't leave me here, don't turn your backs, I didn't ask to lose my grip."
"Can't you take a minute to try to understand?"

No sound was heard by many, only a few really cared.
The wrenching fear is only felt by those who know it's there.
A hand is stretched across to those who feel the pain.
Then it is yanked right back again, their faces photographed in your eyes.

The long walk back is made with the others you have come to know
who made that journey back again, wanting to lead you home.
They help you see yourself is who you thought you were,
As in sanity, you help yourself — so do you now and don't even know.

This side is so much better, I finally have control.
Wait, listen, look there, Oh here we go,
Your ears start gathering sorrows; your eyes see all this pain,
Which side of sanity am I really on? Can I really do this all again?

Caroline Louise Cowen

Time

She stood beside me very young
full of life and filled with joy
and me an awkward soldier boy
just home from the war.

Time, you march on so unforgiving,
relentless in your run.
Don't you know we can't keep up,
We have barely seen the sun.

We need space to walk sandy beaches
or hike mountain trails by morning's glow,
or stand by the mighty Ohio
and watch its rushing waters flow.

Time, you have been here forever,
What's your hurry, anyway?
Eternity is yours, Mr. Time,
we only have today.

Carl Head

"Virgin Angels"

Virgin angels in white satin
floating majestically across the pale blue sky
staring down at me with the brightest eyes,
stirringly and softly,
they tell me,
painfully, goodbye.

Bonnie S. Bailey

Understand Me

So it may seem I'm not like other folk,
Full of games and in others' lives they poke.
No, I don't appear to be concerned with the thoughts of mankind,
Keeping solely to myself, selfishly that which I feel is mine.
Holding on to my thoughts, my emotions and my dreams,
Fearing man doesn't exist just to know what to me this means.
They see me as hiding, hoping the emotions will pass,
While deep inside I pray and know, they will always last.
Understand! I need only to love the heart of a being,
And in doing so, my life has a true and honest meaning.
To wander in the minds of men or the mind of I,
Would cause me such confusion, I would surely die.
For in every heart there is a will to do good,
But with our puny minds we say, "only if I could".

Deborah N. Hudson

My Father

He squirms from the taste left in his mouth
  from the whiskey he drank.
He sits on the steps of his prison
  and thinks of tomorrow.
He questions why he's here
  and doesn't know who to thank.
He wonders when he'll part forever
  from his' sorrows.
  But, in his face, no emotions are reflected,
  Like a statue, as a monument erected,
  and all he can do is wait.
He stands, and walks into the sun's burning heat as he's
done many times before, hoping that today is one less day.
  I sit and see him disappear into the golden fields,
and inside, I give him praise:
His hands are made of marble showing the punishment of time.
His hair reflects the wealth of others, rich with silver.
In his smile the love of a king,
In his eyes the hate of a prisoner.
God and Satan poured into one body; a man, my father.

Carlos A. Sanchez

Connections

I am connected. Lines go straight
From me to Eleanor of Aquitaine
Along the leaves of family trees
Of marriages and births and deaths
Of women, all their long lives strong
Surviving and sustaining through great wrong.

I am connected. Lines go straight
From me to Civil War with tales of women
Carrying water from the spring
In oaken buckets slopping, glistening
With harried haste and posture
As hostile muskets imperiously gesture.

I am connected. I go straight
From heart to nurture up and down
In all the now connections,
Soothing fast - past grandchild wiles - to get to
Mothers, others, those who need, below, above,
The hand-held transfer of connecting love.

Catherine Fitch Druitt

Languages

Languages languages everywhere languages
Familiar and foreign
German and Spanish
Odd and Understandable
Ancient and Modern
But still, languages are spoken through the mouths of humans

Cipriano Rivera

Why?

Sometimes we are weak and we go astray
From God the Father's Holy Way.
Then our hearts are lonely and sad
Cause we've found it hurts when we are bad.
Why, oh why, do we leave His love
When we know there's peace from up above?
Why can't we be faithful and do our part,
Let Jesus Christ reign in our hearts.
He's good, He's kind, He's a just God, too.
So let us to Him try to be true.
It hurts Him so when we disobey
For He wants us to live for Him each day.
Let's pray that we might be given grace
To meet the Master face to face
With humble hearts that are full of love
For our fellow man and our God above.

Carol Wilson George

Life

When we are young, life seems to go on
forever, and as we get older we wonder
where the time has gone by so quickly.
The past is gone and we can't change it,
we have only to live for today and the
hope for tomorrow. Don't worry, Life is like
a breeze, as it blows first one way and
then it blows the other way and then it's gone.
When we are young we are like a limb on
a tree able to bend with the wind, but when
we are older we are like a bowl of cereal,
snap, crackle and pop!

Fred Witthuhn

Africa

Your inhumanity has disturbed my rest
Forcing me to get out of bed to protest
Have you forgotten the reason for Creation?
In my opinion it was God's love for man and nation.
As I look at the broken bodies through the years
The wicked ones have caused me to shed many tears
Wondering when this human carnage will stop
Probably not before everyone is wiped off the map.
Do you ever reflect on the "Colonial era"
Which you inadvertently thought was terror
Well, try to honestly compare it with now
And see if you deserve a welcome bow.
Human beings are God's gifts to earth
Stop treating them like un-recycled garbage and dirt.

Andre L. Procope

Life

Don't feel that life has passed you by—
For you have your moments to recall, to cherish, to relive.
Moments some would give all, just to have had a single one.
Life doesn't pass anyone, it's always there—
  for the seekers, the lovers, the 'in' people.
The seekers find the happiness to fulfill their desires.
The lovers possess that special feeling for the world
  and those in it.
The 'in' people can find living in all they do.
Then there are the few that are definitely the elite and say—
  "I'm in love—in love with life."
If you desire life, strive for it,
  for life is awaiting your arrival!

Elaine S. Shugar

Saying Goodbye

She bowed her head as the dirt was replaced,
For there lied a very dear friend.
Her sorrow would last for many days,
It seemed her heart would never mend.
She knew in her mind she had to move on,
But her heart just wouldn't let her.
She had known her friend would soon be gone,
When her condition had never grown better.
She would have liked just one more day,
To spend with her dear old friend.
But now respects she did pay,
And blessings she did send.
But through all her sadness and sorrow,
There was one good thing she knew.
She was happy to have known her friend,
Because true friends for her were few.
Eventually she did move on,
And although she and her friend did part,
A small smile curved her saddened lips.
Because a great memory lived on in her heart.

Cathleen Micklo

Inspirations

Many people may be inspirations
for others such as you and me.
Take Martin L. King, Neil Armstrong, and John F. Kennedy
to name merely three.

The outcome of their efforts
shows what hard work can do.
No one can say the final result was easy
especially if the burden's on you.

Wisdom, determination, and endurance
are some qualities needed we see.
But let us not forget prayer
because without God it will never be.

Once we conquer our own problems,
we may be an inspiration too.
Just think there are many little ones
requiring some guidance from you.

We need this world to be a better place;
many problems are to be solved.
And with our past and present inspirations
we may further get involved.

Brian Bimaj Johnson

Is This Real

Don't hold me too tight
For I might break
Heart of glass
Mind of steel
My love please don't steal
Is this real
Or just what I need
At this point in time.
Is there a path
That we will walk
Or a side to fall
Love is like a leaf
Comes and goes
But the tree is always there
Like the tree I will be here when it's spring.

Bryan Williams I

Mikell's Legacy

Shameless was her favorite song, she wanted so badly
for him to love her that way...it was playing the day
they ran away, the third time, from all the things that wouldn't let go,
he handed her a rose through the window
with a smile that made you wonder if he knew where they were going...

Daddy says, a police officer came today —
and the words slowly make their way to your brain
he's shot himself, he's dead,
and you live with the tornado in your head,
because you hated him, and loved him too - and you still do
and you have a note for his son instead of a father
because of one choice, one gun
that looked like a toy in the hand of the man
that was your hero
that will never again touch your face, to show love or hate
and you can't fix it now, it's just above the edge of the clouds
and your heart aches to see his face, or hear his voice
if only in a dream
and you know you'll never know that kind of love again
but you can't be sure that it's a bad thing

Chelsea Treverton

America The Glory

Oh beautiful for stars and stripes that wave above the earth.
For every man to linger on, the land of Glory's birth.
America, America! The land of the Free!
Shelter us from hardship and despair, from sin and poverty.

Oh beautiful for children's feet, running without care.
A home in cardboard on the street, their bodies cold and bare.
America, America! What has become of Thee?
When children use dirty flags for clothes, and die upon our streets.

Oh beautiful for patriot dreams, the dream of success and fame.
The flag waves through polluted air, Americans view the shame.
America, America! A burnt flag falls to the ground.
Blackness of a corrupted world leaves Glory's Majesty in
Frown.

Amy Lynne McGee

Thank You Lord

My heart is full of thanks to thee dear Lord
For all you have done for me
For health and strength in time of need
For all the benefits thou has given me
The good green earth beneath my feet
The air I breathe the food I eat
For clouds and rain and gentle breeze
Oh Lord I give thee thanks
I hope and pray that I may be
The person you want me to be
And when my earthly life is through
That I may be worthy of a place with thee
Oh Lord God my grateful thanks to thee

Annie Mae Hobes

Far Away

Far away to another place is where I want to go;
Far away to another place where many things grow.

Far away to another place where many things rest;
Far away to another place where many things are blest.

Far away to another place where large fields roam;
And all these things that are far away, I call home.

Angela Kaye Freeman

153

To Those Whose Lives He Touched In Loving Memory Of
Jacob Wine

A child is now at rest
For a safer place remains
A world of goodness and beauty
A world without worry or pain.

No fear will he encounter
For a better place he'll be
A place where the sick are healed
And where blinded eyes can see.

Our world has forever changed
Our lives are not the same
But close within our hearts
His precious face remains.

We give to him our tears
And our prayers we send above
We cherish all the memories
Filled with happiness and love.

This battle is faced head on
Many obstacles to overcome
But in the end together,
This battle will be won.

Elisabeth Crockett

Thoughts

I'm in a flying saucer,
Flying way out into space,
Looking for the peace folks want,
Almost every place.

Now, that's not the way to find it,
That I soon found out,
So I'm back to earth again,
For I know what it's about.

To have a friend, you have to be one,
Be kind, be honest, be true;
And if folks need a helping hand,
Well then, you help them, too.

Now if you're going to be fishers of men,
Then bait your hook with love, not sin.
Never let them get away.
If there's love they'll always stay.

The world is dying for love, they say,
So do your best and start today.
Also don't forget to pray;
God will help you in a special way.

Edith Elma Hill

Welcome The New Day

They come from the soft Atlantic seashores
flying in from the kingdom of glassy skies
appearing on the winds of change
   they fly by night not to be detected
to take what is left of the morning,
and blow it into a sweet whisper of hope
As day breaks the edible green quakes
anticipating the warmth cascade of sunshine
   that will soon be upon them
The heavens and their snowflake brilliance welcomes a new day
A carnival in the sky my circus of friends
   we'll all be back together again
The tree line is cut so define, as though the sea gulls
screams can be soaked up into it
The rainbow disappears into the mist, with a sweet whisper
saying...love
welcome the new day
saying...peace

Deborah S. Toepfer

The Butterfly

I wish I were a butterfly
Fluttering in the sky
So pretty, soft, and carefree
Then I wouldn't have to be me.
The pain, the loneliness of a lost love
Depending on no one—only God above
To get me through each day
And to make this hurt go away.
It seems there's nothing left unsaid
Wondering if I'm in hell and am I dead?
Someone wake me—make me get up
Put some happiness and love in my empty cup.
No one can—I know that
I guess that's why I'm where I'm at
It's all up to me and God up above
For it's with him that we find love.
Love is the greatest of all things
So butterfly spread your beautiful wings
Fly and flutter for me to see
And remind me always—it's ok to be me!

Betty Mills

Laguna Niguel

Laguna Niguel keeps calling me home, where all the beautiful
flowers are grown.

Sunny, cheerful, busy and calm, this is the place where I call home.

A dream of mine for five years at least, finally came true, now
I feel at peace.

No trip away is too long to travel, as long as I can come back
home to unravel.

The ocean breeze is only minutes away, Dana Point Harbor I go
almost everyday.

To relax, meditate, soak in the ocean air, here I find calm,
tranquil moods that are rare.

Inner peace, religious experiences to heal mind, body and soul
Laguna Niguel, a piece of the whole.

Eleanor Hope

The Stranger

   As I sit here in this room,
filled with dark thoughts of madness and doom.
   Outside it's nice, very bright,
warm and sunny filled with light.
   In this room it's cold and dark,
like a black sea with a great white shark.
   In walks a stranger, tall and thin,
as he smiles at me with a nasty grin.
   Maybe he was friend and maybe he was foe
I couldn't tell and I'll never know.
   As I run, down the hall,
behind me, the stranger, thin and tall.
   Dark brown hair and light blue eyes,
no one here to hear my cries.
   I wish I was somewhere, anywhere but here,
for the stranger is following, following I fear.
   Faster, faster, he's closing in,
that tall thin stranger with that nasty grin.

Bess Grosskopf

The Gift

Poetry from the soul. The heart. The mind.
Feelings buried deep all knotted and entwined.
Emotions and memories you so desperately seek.
At last surfaces with a longing to speak.
Thoughts pour out as you search for the right words.
Relieved for they are no longer caged as gilded birds.
Call it a smile, a glow, a newfound release.
At last you've found inner peace.
In writing, your healing, your letting go...
For pain and grief can weigh heavy and take a toll.
So when your sad and feeling blue;
Pick up a pen and a paper or two.
Jot a few lines and soon you'll see..
Poetry is a gift for all to read.

DeAnna Lynne Abatie

God

"Oh God!" I cried, "How could this be?"
Feeling his warmth beside me. So very
far yet oh so near. So very tender, so very
dear. The nicest man I have ever met, and
even better yet. He made the
sun, he made the moon, and he made
you and me very soon. He is the almighty,
my everything. He is the wind beneath
my wings. He is the one who did
it all. The one who will lift they that
fall. He wants to be the path you follow along
because he will never say "So long!"

Erin Michael Benz

Untitled

Let my skin crumble with meaning of time
feel the love and the meaning of rhyme
The clouds in the sky with meaning of blue
calls to me now with wanting of new
I feel your pain and desire for truth
with all of your blessings please share now the proof
The sun in the clouds with crystal clear thought
brings down the warmth to share with the lot
But the sadness I feel with bellowing white
blocks all the messages close to the light
Please send the messages more in the air
to get past my heart and feeling of care
I want you to lift me and float me away
to see in the land where all of you stay
Maybe in time I'll learn all of the truth
to share with the rest I must have some proof
Be kind when I ask "for you lift me away"
for you know in my heart I must now not stay
I just want to feel the warmth of the sun
the love in my heart and the meaning of one

Frances Dea Coolidge

Untitled

The sun sets and leaves the earth in a dreary darkness.
Dark trees are like evil giants that come to life after the sun sets.
They creep, slowly, softly, up to my window
And watch me in my slow state of slumber
Then whisper softly to one another as the moon sets.
The giants creep back to their spots as they sense a new day coming
upon the world. The sun rises. A new day has begun.

Cheryl Kilhefner

Question

Where are you from I wonder out loud?
   Far away in the distance.
Smothered by the burning crowd.
   Far away in the distance.
I hear the horrible screams let out.
   Far away in the distance.
So maybe I hear myself shout.
   Far away in the distance.
It's closer, it's closer, it's almost near.
   Far away in the distance.
So close to me I feel its tears.
   Far away in the distance.
Its ear-piercing sound makes me go hazy.
   Far away in the distance.
Loud enough to send a man crazy...
   Far away in the distance.

Carmelissa Edwards

Who's That Standing in the Corner?

Who's that standing in the corner, smiling, peering out of humorless
eyes, observing life's ritualistic dance, with a bemused dispassion,
reserved for martyrs, fools and kings?

Who's that standing in the corner, sighing, hearing truths that
turn to lies, witnessing events precariously linked to chance,
the new now old in fashion, and who dreams of brightly colored things?

Who's that standing in the corner, crying, daring not to break the
ties, longing yet for a lost romance, and who seems to have failed
the lesson, that sleeping wounds will yawn with spring?

Who's that standing in the corner, trembling, fearing still to remove
the disguise, harboring doubts that man will advance, beyond the rage
that censors reason, and forges masks that cannot sing?

Who's that standing in the corner, dying, nearing the light in
heavenly skies, that place the mind in a timeless trance, wondering
now if life's fruit of passion, becomes the final sighting of the brass ring?

Bruce R. Adrian

Breasts

Oh so beautiful, full and round,
exquisite in its shape.
Blessed with two, one on each side,
balanced, happy bouncing breasts.

The day of infamy, cancer, malignant,
— operation, chemo, radiation, all so heavy,
all so hard... why oh why.....you beautiful breast.

What is your message of us. —
Woman-Man you are not immortal.
Pay attention to the rest—

Guide yourself with care —
Take care of yourself with love —
Life is strange, life is unpredictable
Life just is...

Learn to love and learn to bless
Day by day the gifts given — and the gifts
not taken away.

The awareness of what we have —
Oh how slight our understanding
The fullness of our cup, and the emptiness of our gratitude.

Elliott Derek Politi

Life

Life is nothing but a dream.
Everyone have to love, have to hate.
Sometimes happy for a moment, sad the next.
I often dream of a happy life,
Without problems, without sorrow, and without loneliness.
But then.... I realized, this is reality.
That could only happen in a world of fantasy.
There's always problems, sorrow, and loneliness.
Day after day my life gets more difficult.
Someone always have to cause me pain.
Sometimes I think life isn't worth living.
But then.... this is my life.

Carole Tran

Hangover

Emotions all tangled -
every tear falls harder, every laugh calls louder.

My head reels.
I can't see straight as I dial the phone.

But wait —
I cannot call you,
I can call no one.

Even as I stagger out the door - fumbling with the knob -
I have no voice.

Certain things come to bear significance only to me,
pain only to me.

It's hard to understand
a drunkard's hurt pride,
a drunkard's loss of himself.

But I understand - I am as he -
although my disease is not in a bottle.

Tears and laughter mix cynically; I grow harder and colder...
only pain reaches me.

Vestiges only remain, emotions amplified to deafening decibels
as I live — Drunk on Anger.

Anita Jo Hackney

Ever Present

A silent presence to watch over you,
Ever present,
Always true.

An invisible hand to support and guide,
You through life,
Remaining forever by your side.

A memory strong and dear,
That brings a smile to your face,
And joy to your heart that is always near.

A life time of love,
Shared and treasured,
Now shining down on you from above...car 1995

Carie Runyon

My Love For You

Just the thought of losing you brings tears into my eyes.
Even through all the pain and suffering that my heart denies.

I'll go through this because I care and love you oh so much.
It doesn't matter if I hurt as long as I have your touch.

I never knew I could love this much but now I know it's true.
I'll never be in love again like I'm in love with you.

Allisha Clendenin

Train Ride

I love to ride on trains -
Especially on Amtrak,
Looking out the window as it rains,
While the train races along the track.

I enjoy looking out the window
As I wait for the call to dinner,
Getting hungry and eager to go,
While listening to the train wheels whir.

I love to sleep on the train
In my roomy, comfortable compartment,
A good night's sleep I hope to gain
As I slowly drift off in deep contentment.

I love the early morning sound
Of the steward's call for breakfast,
Another great day has rolled around
As I hurry to get up and dressed.

I pass the rest of the train ride
In great joy and anticipation,
For while I'm enjoying the country side,
I know my love is waiting at the station.

Catherine F. Seidel

An Angel

I once saw an angel, life she breathed in me;
emotions wrought within my heart, none since have I seen.
I once saw an angel, love she stirred within;
a raging storm within my soul, I waited to begin.
I once saw an angel, her love did I seek;
a love to hold within my grasp, love of which I'd keep.
I once saw an angel, a love so intense;
my body, heart, mind and soul: alas I lost all sense.
I once saw an angel, beauty beyond compare;
but all my love and giving self, oh she did not care.
I once saw an angel, a foolishness of my mind;
lying beneath the outer skin deceit I'd surely find.
I once saw an angel, emotions she took from me;
a stealing thief within the night, that I did not see.
I once saw an angel, my eyes searched the skies;
lying within the outer shell, alas.....a devil in disguise.

Annette L. Hostetter

Emotions Written Down

Emotions bundled up inside.
Emotions that I hide.
Sometimes I'm fighting,
When I feel like crying

Then the person who gave birth to me,
gave me a gift for only me to see

She provided an answer for my problems,
an answer for me to release my bundled emotions.

She gave me a gift that should be,
a secret between her and me.

She gave me a chance to express my feelings,
and a chance for me to start healing,
She gave me a book for all year round,
a book, a journal, that allows my emotions written down.

A thank you is not enough,
my gratitude can only cover so much.
But maybe some simple words will do.
Mother,
I love you!

Christina Cook

Three Little Kittens

Three little kittens, kittens to me
Eight years old, one is three
  The one that's three
  Stirs and frolics
  Around the room
  Then up the stairs
  Cooing her guttural song.

One eight year old, male and content
  Watches wide-eyed
  Her antics.

Another eight year old, female and slight
  Princess of my home
  Jumps with frenzied leaps
  At my plecostomus
  Feverishly eating algae.

My home spells peace
My home spells joy
  A peacefulness and joy brought about by
  Three little kittens
Now slumbering.

Anna Lu Leta

Anguish

Dusk condenses the pale rays of light.
Echo of awakening elaborates the extinct site.
The pigment of immorality goes by.
Indelible umbers sigh and cry.

Romantic ode has the highest depth.
Gleamy and obscure days have met.
Impressive soar stays on hold.
Old story ends, newer is untold.

Cold faces, hard hearts, feelings like stone;
magnitude dooms crowd from the throne.
Gulping the misery, using the trade;
strode on the shoreline, where breeze is made.

Yearning to see the color of seven skies.
Roaming wondrously without fears and cries.
Growing more animated, wishing to subdue.
Cold fury goes deep, deep as virtue.

The spiral wind wails and blasts.
Rainbow peaks through and casts.
Bitter reproach, secret remorse, and a little test;
wringing with anguish, dying for some rest.

Ellie Kamran Belfiglio

My Prayer

I get teardrops on my pillow
Each night I pray to the Lord above
To watch over the ones I love.
Then I ask him to help me meet, and beat,
The challenge he gave to me to complete.
Then I begin to wonder why.
This is when I begin to cry,
Lying alone to await
The company of my lifelong mate.
This is when I get teardrops on my pillow.

Eleanor V. McKinney

Untitled

Sprawling!
Drifting!
Falling fast,
Visions of life's light rushing...

The molecular structure quickly disintegrates,
And then reassembles to face its terrible fate.

Swiftly!
Directly!
Consumed by the fire,
Time's ceremonial master burns the funeral...

The new configuration could only regurgitate,
Painfully small, portions of its previous state.

Turning!
Toward!
A far distant past,
This familiar endeavor will not be the...

Now, all the houses still look quite the same,
The colors have changed but the spirit remains,
As, the sun beats down blindly on memory lane.

Alex DuFault

My Views On Religion

I kinda have an understanding with the "Man" upstairs.
Don't practice much religion but "He" knows I care.
Most folks probably figure I'll end up in hell.
It that's the way "He" sees it, then very well.

Don't go to church, though I know I should.
If everyone practiced what they preach, I suppose I would.
But too many folk will do you six days a week.
And then on Sunday, forgiveness they seek.

I never dealt much with the middle man.
Go right to the top every time I can.
Try not to bother "Him" with petty stuff.
Save my requests for when things are really rough.

Oh, we'll visit from time to time.
Maybe talk weather, or why I can't make a dime.
But I run my life as I see fit.
And right or wrong, "He" goes along with it.

My church will always be the great outdoors.
From the mountain peaks to the valley floors.
And when the time comes to tally up my sins.
We'll see how "He" votes, will "He" let me in?

Ford Frederick

"My Friend"

I'll always be here for whatever you need,
Don't ever forget that I will.
We've been through so much, no one can touch
The place in my heart that you fill.

Please don't ever worry about being alone,
Don't let anything stand in your way.
If you need to cry, my shoulder's dry,
And with me, you're welcome to stay.

If you have a thought, a dream or a wish,
I hope I'm the first to hear.
So put on that smile, and I'll listen awhile,
Soon you'll see, there's nothing to fear.

For a lifetime we'll treasure the closeness we've found,
Nothing can ruin what we share.
No matter what comes our way, tomorrow or today,
Rest assured, I'll always care.
My friend.

Debra A. Lipczynski

"Heart's Plea"

Where does this heartache come from?
  Does it hurt everyone, or just some?
Out of nowhere,
  And it doesn't care,
It causes lumps in my throat,
  And there seems to be no anecdote,
My nerves in my stomach start to twist,
  I try to look into the mirror,
It's like a haze through my gaze,
  Or trying to find my way through a maze,
This great depression,
  And the feeling of aggression.
What has it come for?
  Doesn't it know I can't give anymore?
Soon everything in me will collapse,
  Or, maybe, just perhaps...
I will fade away,
  Out of this world, into a different dimension, if I may?

Carrie E. Burgess

"What I'm Not Saying"

When you look into my eyes what do you see?
Do you see my well known mask or do you see me?
I have went through life scared of letting anyone to close.
Constantly rejecting a hug, the thing I needed most.

I have been hurt and was afraid of being hurt again.
Tell me is this attitude really such a sin?
I was extremely scared of being let down.
So I went through life with a fake smile instead of a frown.

During all of the hurt I have built around me a wall.
But kindness and love could make this wall fall.
I learned early in life love has a heart breaking fee.
So I ask again do you know my mask or do you know me?

If you look closely you can see the real me trying to come out.
It's sad, but even when you give me your heart I still have
severe doubt.
With all my insecurity it is me that must be paying.
So please try to hear what I'm not saying.

Amy D. Phillips

Tranquility

Is Life really just a bowl of cherries?
Do we live in a marshmallow world with no worries?

The good times are here and prosperity is booming.
Only one dark cloud over us is looming.

The kids are great and doing well in school.
Chat with them and you will find they are nobody's fool.

The music is fast and loud and everybody can sing.
We have the line dance, two-step and they are still doing the swing.

There is one thing that has filled our hearts with sorrow.
Think about it today, don't wait until tomorrow.

Our precious high morals of which we were so proud,
During all the pomp and glory lost in the crowd.

With faith, pride and patriotism we can tell the whole world
America will always be number one when our flag is unfurled.

Alta Good Dill

Light Night

Seeming darkness...feeling lightness. (Bedroom night)
  Digital clock...rosy red light.
    'Round midnight.

Wall switch glow...orange oval light.
  Go for cooled water, a mite. (Kitchen night)
    Fridge light...white-white, bright-bright.

Amble into (living room night).
  Answering machine...glowing green light.
    Cable box...ample amber light.

Oh, yes what a sight!...VCR recording tonight.
  Blazing broad band of backlit light.
    Trailing along...bold blue light.

In a while...night-light to day-light...re-light.
  Watch with delight for more enlight.
    Alright!

Eli Dimeff

"Choices Of The River"

The River flows freely, always moving past the sunlight, through the
deep blue night and into the early morning dawn.
Sometimes I stand there all alone and I wonder of all the places that
River has been and if we are not in some way connected.
Maybe that River grows weary of traveling the same way each day.
I question that if the River was to flow into the ocean if it would
not get lost and drown within itself.
Those are the chances that River must take.
Within itself it must decide if it would rather die brave and
insightful or if it would routinely go on and finally wither away old
and tired and secure.
The River of Life streams by every day, sometimes taking new courses,
winding and twisting.
Inevitably, one day, that River will run dry, but there will always be
that mark, that tiny drop of water, that tells the world you were
there and that part of you will never say goodbye.

Abbie Lynn LeBlanc

What Am I?

I'm small in size but lovable in a big way. Some people think I'm so
cute they pet me all day. They touch me; they hang on me; their hands
are always in my hair. They can't seem to resist, because I'm always
there. Such affection doesn't go unnoticed, for that would be rare,
but I wonder quite often what would they think? Should I dare? If I
were a dog and I could think like you, would I just ignore the
innocence of what you do? But I'm not a dog, a cat, or anything from
the zoo, and I hope that I am more considered than you. So let me
take a minute to lovingly enlighten you. Would you allow it or would
you want to say something, too? I say this with love, for you are
special to be, but please!! I'm not your pet, but just li'l ole me,
just 5 feet tall, with emotions, feelings and thoughts, the same as
all of you. Sometimes I get aggravated, and show it too, but stop and
think it over, if you were in my place, could I do this to you? Would
you understand? I hope that you would. So this rhyme is from me to
you. Consider who I am and set me free!! Your hands are for you and
mine are for me. I am not a prejudiced person, whether race, color or
personality. For all have been guilty.
Family-Friends-Students-and Faculty!

Beverly LaSalle

Depression

Feeling as if you are trapped in a cage. Screaming and
crying and fighting with rage. Inside you are struggling to get
out but on the outside you look normal without a doubt.

You feel as if no one understands the pain that is lying
with your hands, You try to ignore it and leave it behind but it
just keeps on crawling back into your mind.

You feel very sick with aches and pains and even when it's
sunny you feel like there is rain. You try to act like nothing is
wrong. You have even started to fool your Dad and your Mom.

But then one morning you wake up to see the sun shining
in your window and you're as happy as can be! Finally your depression
has gone away and you start your life over on this brand new day!

You are smiling and laughing and jumping with joy. You
feel like a child with a brand new toy!

As you can see things never stay the same, these feelings
leave just as fast as they came!

Life will always have its ups and downs, laughs and tears,
smiles and frowns!

But there is one thing that I want you to know. Life is
like a river so just let it flow!

Carly Kraft

Crumbled White Paper

Here I stand a black letter on a
crumbled white piece of paper, that's
what it's like living in the Western World.
So many letters lived and died
speaking truth, when will the white
paper unfurl.

Every wrinkle represents infinite,
but not useless tears.
Death with hell close behind are
apparent by the wrinkled letters
that appear.

The red, yellow and black letters
are not legible, because of the visible creases.
Hopefully the big letter "G", will
straighten out these creases.

The red I, yellow J and black A
must appear on the white paper legible
to keep the big G, whose plan
is to destroy, from throwing the
white paper into a receptacle.

Alonzo W. Hill

A Million Years

I've tried for a million years
Covered your tracks, hid all the fears
Lost the world to a thousand cheers
Stood outside covering windows with smears

The past and present has made me strong
Tomorrow or never will be too long
Fantasy too real to be right or wrong
Only with you feeling where I belong

Understand or not at all
The mind rejects what's over its wall
Terribly sorry for such a great fall
Open your heart to hear my faint call

Nearer still is not good-bye
Make up the rest until we die
A million years or so I did try
To see a truth come from a lie.

Amy Lutz Rump

Realizations

I closed my eyes, shut them firm;
Covered my ears and barred my room.
More so than any, I sweated
My term, which never ended
I snubbed the caresses,
Fortified my core;
Envied hearts hard be torn.
Seldom, ah, the joys of pleasure I tasted——
But finally,
Love I opted——
But came too late.
When I opened my eyes,
I found myself so desolate.

Eneil Ryan P. De La Peña

Teen-Age Pregnancy

Who is to blame for teen-age pregnancy?
Could it be fathers who don't teach decency?
I've thought and wondered about replies.
Most of them are nothing but lies.
One thing stand out as plain as can be...
Hold on a moment and then you too will see.
Our society dictates when we should show how we feel.
From one to ten it is okay for fathers to show daughters that love is real.
At ten - daddy's girl is too big to sit and on his lap and kiss.
If daddy's do - then sexual abuse is amiss.
Some fathers are not even there...
To teach a girl that a man can care.
Now we have a child too big to show affection to...
But too young to find love through sex and what have you.
What is a young girl left to do?
But run into the arms of a young boy who says his love is true.
Our fathers should be able to express themselves.
Not put their emotions on shelves.
Our fathers need to love their daughters while in their teens.
Society please don't let our daughter's confuse sex with love as
other means.

Blondell Chisolm Robinson

Moments

There are moments in my life, I wish I
could freeze in time.
Precious, dear moments, so sweet, so sublime.

Like the birth of my children, was it so
long ago?
How does time go by so fast? I just
don't know.

It seems like yesterday, they were babes
at my breast.
Their sweet warm breath, so innocent
so blessed.

And moments with my husband, my lover,
my friend.
Just the two of us sharing, life's ever
changing blend.

And now, the very dearest of all.
Spending time with my parents, no
matter how small.

Because I realize, one day I'll miss them so.
Their bittersweet memory, will be all that I know.

Deborah L. Taylor

Clouds

Wind blown water fountains, snow covered hills
Cotton soft canyons, funny shaped wheels
Silhouette portraits of you and me
A kitten, a ball, an elephant in a tree
All of these pictures in the clouds in the sky
How does it happen mommy and please tell me why

A wintry white fire truck
The moon and a kite
A big scary monster who gives you a fright
Pictures and illusions you see in the clouds
A church and its people in a small country town

An angel from heaven blowing its horn
A crying little babe in a crib, that's new born
Your mother, your daddy,
A swing in a tree
But nothing more beautiful
Than you are to me

Barbara Jean Meeks

Mortally Immortal

Seasons change and the wold spins, burdened with the
confusion and chaotic ways of human existence.
These ways that make one want to be a part of it, but
in the same fragment of a thought make one vile towards
man who can be selfish and unfeeling.
The heart sometimes yearns to be loved by this world
and the mind sighs and echoes... Why?
For what the mind considers a burden, the heart considers a necessity.
Why this is, no mortal may know for if this were
so, then the color of life would be tainted.
Some things are better represented as mysteries, as a
wise man once said, and whose wise thoughts put to
words still echo in my head.
Life is vast to the mortal, yet it has its limits.
Only the soul knows of the vast existence of the
immortal world. The soul knows no boundaries.
Some things are better represented as mysteries, yes,
some things such as the mortal and immortal.
The world spins, the suns rises, and the sun sets as
the mortal and immortal struggle to connect.

Adrienne N. Hill

Losing You

The thought of you wanting to leave me behind
Confuses me and boggles my mind

You say you've lost interest in me
I don't understand, how can this be?

Where did I go wrong with you?
I try so hard not to be blue

I cry myself to sleep at night
Only wishing to turn back time, so I can hold you tight

I've tried to show you that I care
I've only loved you and you alone to be fair

I'd throw myself in dangers path, just to save you
I'm trying to say believe in me and if you only knew

I Love You and miss you, oh, so much
I don't know how much longer I can live without your touch

Betty Jo Knutson

Untitled

Stormy grey dawn,
come sprinkle her porcelain body
With tiny glittering drops of rain...
come trace her skin with your
   breezy fingers...
This gentle morn she is no longer a child.
   And yet,
Where is your serenity?
Shadows drenched with solitude
   from the previous sleepless night
cling to her throat and chest
   With sharp, black claws -
she waits at the window
   at the break of day
for the lullaby of the August storm
   to stop the bleeding.

Alysia Lea Polito

In Your Arms

Sometimes the wind and rain of life
Come crashing all around me,
And just to hear You speak calms the storm.

Sometimes I feel alone with not a friend in the world,
But then Your love surrounds me,
Your presence fills my heart.

Sometimes I feel desperate and afraid,
And I long to see Your face, and for You to hold me tight,
Yet, I know, that I am constantly, safely in Your arms.

Aimee R. Adams

Honeysuckle

Honeysuckle on a vine
Climbing up the barn divine
Tell me what you hear?
Humming birds whisper sweet nothings in my ear
Buzzing bees around my leaves
Butterflies flutter like sheets of color
In the breeze
In the wind
Flocking to a hint of sweet honey scent

Brad Murray

Night In The City

Golden light off the concrete rivers running the city around
Circles of light like shining halos, lifting our world off the ground
And millions of lights twinkle at night, stars in a dim, dark place
Neon in darkness, sparkles like rainbows, lighting the maze of the race
Turn to the left, climb the ladder, step on whoever you need
Grab a window, the corner office, whatever it takes to succeed
And in this world of work and self, where caring is a crime
Where the trampled stand on the street, "Buddy can you spare a dime?"
Drugs and gangs rule the schools, guns the kids have held
Killers escape through legal loopholes, homeowners now are jailed
And politics, they have never changed, they saw all this and cried
All have claimed they would fix it, we all know that they lied
Police are hiding. Teachers quit. Kids can't even read
Crime and corruption laugh and sing, on society they will feed
But in this dark and dreary world, a golden light abounds
Calling out, "Come inside" to all the hearts around
The lights they gather, huddled close, preparing now to fight
Islands formed of heart and hope, bastions of the light
And as the war peaks to its height, the sun begins to rise
Staying till tomorrow the gruesome war, when another child dies.

David Nation

If Rivers Could Talk

I'm a river that rages in fury. Against those who would change my course.
You've levied my banks and dammed me up. To retrain me from
    mouth to source.

And it seems to work for a while. I run at your beckoned call.
Progress overtakes nature, but is this progress at all?

Every now and again though, I must remind those who take me in stride.
I push back your levees and tear down your dams and roar
    with ferocious pride.

When I run calm, you adore me. The Great River becomes my new name.
You pollute me, strip my resources, and all for prosperity and gain?

When I run rapid and swollen, you may search for a way to confine.
I'll rise up in protest and break through your walls to take
    back the land that was mine.

Build by my banks if you will, but keep distance between you and me
For when rains cry down upon me, I am sure to run wild and free.

Debra Gagnon

The Pollen Grain

It flies through the air on a still gentle breeze,
Causing every allergenic to sniff and to sneeze,

It comes in all colors of many a shade,
With its own little job, but no need to get paid,

Its size is so small, you can't hardly see it,
But if you lived near a garden, you wouldn't believe it.

You can smell it so true, without any trouble,
if you have asthma, you may need to live in a bubble,

Much can be said, about this thing fallen,
But go look for yourself, it's a small grain of pollen.

Adam Morganthaler

A Meaning Of Love

Selfishness versus selflessness
caused by cruising alone;
seeing reality, ideals and modes of
existence differently;

Descending down a stairway of
too many differences, creating a hell here between our souls;
not touching our minds one
to the other or trying to disagree
peacefully and respectfully; knowing

That what started out as love was
only superficial desire and understanding.
When change in values and goals
came which changed our own selves we were not prepared.

Thus our spirits put time
and space between them in the way of
anger; and our covering up of the pain
helped them to start to die——

Until we discovered on our own what
love is—forgiving, respecting and seeing
our deepest selves; allowing for change.

Barbara Hayden

Alcohol And Drugs

Alcohol and drugs the troublesome pair
cause grief to those who are unaware
that they cloud the mind that once was clear
and fill the soul with anger and fear

At first the feelings they bring seem nice
but later these habits demand a price
when they control lives they always win
over their victims who yield to sin

Arlene V. McMorris

Life Goes On

Wait for me, wait for me
Cause your the one I want to see,
Your one, I'm one, that makes two,
We're humans on the go.

We travel slow we travel fast
We're going to the future, we've been through the past.
The road we're on is going somewhere,
I have no idea, what we will do when we get there.

But we must go on we cannot try
We have a lot that we must carry
The world is on a spin,
We're going out, we're going in.

We're seeing the glory of liberty
As we live our lives ever free
We go on down the road, you and me
Stopping for everything, we see.

Charles Barbour

Lone Wolf

I know what's hidden beneath your skin
    'Cause I'm on the outside looking in;
And on the outside there is pain
    For on the outside I remain.

I'm the lone wolf cryin' in the night,
    Driven out by malice and by spite;
Driven out 'cause I didn't fit in,
    The lonely wolf who has no kin.

My sin that I was different,
    Their's, that they weren't more tolerant;
Of my pain they remain ignorant,
    So of their ways I remain defiant.

Still the lone wolf howls from the hill;
    The packs expectations, I could not fulfill
Long I have cried, and longer I will,
    Until the wolf pack decides to kill.

Candace McBride

No Longer

In the early morning shadows,
    cast by a pale moonlight,
    a man sits and writes these words.

No longer am I a lover to the one I adore,
    but more so a friend.
Where walls have crumbled and
    cities have sunk-
    where trees grow and flowers bloom-
    the soil is fertile for friends.
That land is mine just as it is yours
    and upon that land we shall stake our
    claim.

Once you were my lover, but now-
    as you always were-
    you're a friend.

David Preston Vickers

161

The Lament Of Darby Hicks

Now I've been here...Like three score and ten...and I
Can't remember when...things have been so screwed
Up...my cup...runneth over and I've had enough...too
Much bulls**t prevails....overcrowded jails...mixed
Messages that confuse...what's suppose to be funny
Doesn't amuse..."Big Mac" and "Crack" consumed by the
Masses...dumb asses!...more for the greedy...and f**k
The needy...I got mine you get yours...the homeless
Down on all fours...a lotta "ego trippin" takin'
Place...and just in case...you haven't heard...the
"Ego" is a jealous God that must be served...now I
Know the man upstairs is pissed off with the flock...
So if I'm walkin' down a block....and pass a house
Owned by a cat named noah! ... I'm walkin' slower...to
See if he's buildin' a boat in the back...and Jack!...
If he is...I'm signin' up square biz...'cause if that
Hole in the ozone gets any bigger... be you sp**k...
G**k...h**ky or n****r...I figger....no need to worry
'Bout them and they...Hey! ...not the have not or the
Have's...'Cause everybody's ass will be up for grabs.

Bob Washington

Untitled

Lovers entwined in a ghostly dance
Can you hear the strain of the music?
Someone banging on the door
The couple rises and falls to the sound of their heartbeat
Whirling faster and faster across the floor
Her hair fans out into the night

Tears fall silently to the floor
Blurring the stars, impassive and bright
There is no moon; it has fled
With the shattering of the music, so sweet to its soul

Running down the corridor
Neverending, it seems to shimmer
Undulating and twisting like a serpent in the sun
All light is extinguished
Blind are my senses, empty is my soul

Pain seers through my mind like quicksilver,
Will the silence end, with the echoes of my scream
The night knows
Carrying the shattered remnants of my soul
Broken by the music

Ashley Baggett

Blame

To blame our actions on our childhood abuse.
  Can no longer be our excuse.

If we rape another,
  just blame it on mother.

When we beat our wife,
  father was not in our life.

Stealing from our neighbor,
  we're not paid enough for our labor.

We discriminate against a race,
  just because he's in our space.

If another person we abuse,
  just blame it on our own abuse.

Take another life,
  then excuse it because of our life.
Blame is our own excuse.

Connie Parfitt

Sweet Memories

Oh way down south
By the ocean seas,
There is docked a little row-boat, and sweet memories.

Of moonlit nights, and sunny days.
Of love and friendship,
Shown in special ways.

Of rows across the lake
On warm days in July,
Picnic lunches while floating adrift,
And lemon meringue pie.

Of romantic evenings for two
To hear the crickets sing.
While tucked away in a pocket,
There shines a little ring.

And two words spoken that night
Will make their dreams come true.
The little row-boat heard them say,
Those two small words: "I do."

And though its paint is faded now, and it has a leak or two,
The little row-boat sits there still and waits for the days it knew.

Amber McClung

The Stranger Within

If you measure man by his kindness to others,
By his gentle nature and love of all God's meeker creatures;
If you accept others, not for their outward presence,
But for that inner beauty we all possess;
If you see the injustices of the world, and in knowing
You alone can not make them right,
Still care enough to hurt;
And if you can be forgiving of the shortcomings of others,
Whether intentional or through ignorance;
Truly then, you have achieved total success!

For success is more learning to live with ourselves
Than what we acquire during the quest.
For "as we judge others, so shall we be judged"
And the reward is in experiencing a far greater place on earth
Than most even dream exist in heaven.
It is that mystical insight into our true being;
A meeting with the stranger within;
That most of us fear.
This is our soul. The final measure of our humanity.

Debbie Schwartz

To My Sister

Dear sister, how I love you on this your wedding day!
You've always meant so much to me - far more than words can say.
Wherever life may lead us, wherever we may roam,
Whenever we're together, it's just like coming home.
May all the years ahead of you be filled with love each day
As you and Teke walk hand in hand along life's long pathway.
There'll never be a bride more fair, nor one to me more dear,
Don't mind if coming down the aisle you see me shed a tear.
It's just because I love you and wish the best for you,
A whole world filled with happiness and with a love that's true.
So whether we are far apart, or whether we are near
On this and all the days to come no one could be more dear
Than you, my only sister; may God bless you every day,
And remember that I love you more than words can ever say.

Shirley F. Bancroft

Gliders

Zip,
  Zam,
    Zoom,
through the air go flyers,
paper gliders fly higher and higher,
down the hall
and with a CRASH!
They hit the wall.
The fun is done for Grover,
crumple them into a ball,
then start all over.

Kelin J. Mead

"Grandmother"

When I'm sad or full of fear,
  you're there to make my smile appear.
Because I'll just pick up the phone,
  no longer am I left alone.

If I'm sick and it is late,
  I surely will not hesitate.
Because Mom and Dad may not be there,
  I'll call Grandma, she won't care!
In dancing shows or a sports event,
  Almost nothing would prevent,
  my grandmother from seeing the show.
How she managed I'll never know!

Not everyone may know,
  what lives in grandma's heart.
She loves us unconditionally,
  right from the very start.

No matter if you're near or far,
  whether I see you by plane or car,
  it won't change what I say or do,
  especially how much I LOVE YOU!!

Kimberly J. Baker

Tower Of Tabor

What an awesome sight,
You're a landmark of beauty
Within your own right.

Tower of Tabor,
What a story you've told
You've baptized the young
And buried the old.

Your lofty spire
Has a story to tell
Of the faith, of many,
Plus you're the home of our bell.

A bell that's called many
To the house of the Lord,
To sing his praises
And to hear His Word.

Oh, I've seen steeples higher
And bigger in size,
But, Tabor, your tower
Is number one in my eyes!

Luverne Enquist

Dragon

Flying to the ivory moon,
with a ball of fire in his mouth,
his raging fire lighting the sky
against the dying of the night.

Joe Erno

The Pack

Your words were great indeed.
Your mind has seen the greed.
You have been bought.
You have been sold.
You are no longer even whole
Your mind is warp.
Your body is stain.
With the blood of your friends that died in vain.
You are no longer human you're no longer a man.
Your just animal with blood on your hands.
Tell me my friend how does it feel.
To take the venom that makes you steal.
You said you would live longer than the rest.
At last you are dying with every last.
breath.
Your body is shrivel your mind is gone.
Soon you will be singing the devil song.

John Jason Deveau

Lover Of The Universe

Wings for a bird to fly
Young pictures at eleven
Aching for a lovers touch
When he's died and gone to heaven

I saw you walk in the moonlight
Felt your feet melt in the sand
Touched your love growing inside me
as of earth, as of man

Once a lover of the universe
Twice the man of my dreams
Three times Freedom of the sky
Oh God, why was it his time to die?

'Tis not an answer for you to know
each person has their chance to go
each being has their chance to be
Innocent steps, blind before you see

Neli Morrison

Hope

Keep on trying,
  You'll soon be flying.
Reach for your star
  In life you'll go far.
Be willing to fight
  For what you believe is right.
Challenge you fear,
  Wipe away that tear...
Don't be afraid to move on,
  Light will come and with it dawn.
Always keep hope alive
  Challenge and you will survive.

Melissa Lefebvre

Ode To Mom

You taught me to read
You taught me to write
You came when I cried in
the middle of the night.

You taught me manners
You taught me to behave
You told me no matter
what always be brave.

So when I grow up (If I
ever do!) I will tell my kids
what I learned from you.
MOM

Jeff Hirth

Rock My World

You told me you'd rock my world
You'd turn me inside out
It took some time to convince me
Now I have no doubt

You loved me with a passion
We took a moonstruck chance
We laughed in our enchanting dreams
And danced the devil's dance

I love you still, inside my head
I cannot let you know
For passion felt this dangerously
Is chaos with nowhere to go

Someday I'll awake to silence
That only you will hear
My heart is cold and vacant
Realize my fear

Anxiety and death
Visit those who dwell in pain
Being dead while gently hypnotized
Drove me hopelessly insane

Lynn Ellyn Sheldon

"Your Charm"

You always had the charm
You were always on alarm
You had that special something
That no one but me could see.
Everything's so perfect
Nothing's ever changed
All my world is exciting
With nothing left to blame.
We never went through misery
We never had a shame
No ever blamed us
For the problems that remain.
We will always be together
I'll be forever in your arms
I really don't want to lose you
Or your sweet, loving, charm.

Jodi Baque

Self-Preservation

You bleed a liquid called deceit
You think you've accomplished quite
  a feat because
You can cry plastic tears
But I can see your hidden fears
Your eyes are empty, the color of haze
I cannot stand to meet your gaze
I turn around and shrink away
I could never stay; no, I could
  never stay

Kelly McCarty

Wishes

Life is sweet,
Yet life can also be mean.
When you have a friend
That will not be there to understand,
You realize that you've made a mistake,
And only wishes can go back
And correct it.
Yet when you're all out of wishes,
And all out of friends,
There is nothing you can do,
But wish, to wish again!

Jessica Snyder

163

His Eyes

Looking through his eyes
  You see the world begin
His cheerful smile, his wonderment
  That all of these are his
His eyes light up as leaves blow
  As lights come on at night
As fishes swim, as doggies play
  you sit and watch with him
You can't go back in time they say
  But this just isn't true
He's six months old
  We're going strong
Discovering all that's new.

Lois Phelps

To Be A Real Dad

You need to be willing;
You need to be smart,
You need to be firm;
But still have a heart.

You need to be patient.
You need to be kind.
You need to be stern
Without losing your mind

A real Dad myself
I know what this means
Thank God for you Dad
You taught me these things

Kim M. Osborne

"My Empty Love"

My love... is for you
You make me high through and through
And I know my love is true
For I can't let go... let go of you!

I can't go on living this way
To you I dedicate my everyday
You're the only way I know to cope
You fill my thoughts and give me hope

My empty love, I can't control
You steal my mind, you steal my soul
My empty love why can't you see?
My empty love...please set me free.

Your chains bind my fragile hands.
It's so hard to understand
I can't break free, from the pain
You're torment is driving me insane

My empty love I wish to lose
My empty love I'm so confused
My empty love, can't fight the pain
My empty love has won the game.

Gayle Bartholomew

Untitled

I want to teach you to
With the red, white and blue.
Even though you may be
Stubborn; I will show you
The right to be buttoned.
More and more your promise
Is to be broken;
Let me show you my appreciation
With a token.

Jason B. Steen

Before The Bloom

Before the bloom
You have already dried up
Your stem bent low
Your leaves dried with a faded yellow.
A faint crimson red
could be seen shriveled on top
The bud which gave up hope
On the harsh autumn day.

Before the bloom
You have already dried
Like a child un-awakening
On the day of its birth.
A faint crimson red
could be seen shriveled on top
The bud which gave up hope
On the harsh autumn day.

Jenny Y. Kim

"Pilgrims"

I am.
You are.
We live!
Entwined and yet apart.
Distinct though individual,
Connected by the heart.

Our minds on different plains,
Even so our thoughts the same.
Is this life reality or some crazy game?

What is the purpose of life?
What are we here for?
Where lies the answer?
Is it behind a hidden door?

But the door is not hidden.
It's there for all to see!
Only the truly pure in heart,
Have access to the key.
So journey on and find,
The key to peace of mind.

Joan Y. Washington

A Simple Request

I stand amidst a crowd,
Yet not one sees my pain,
The discussion not allowed;
The words on down the lane.

If just one would turn my way,
To ask my inmost thought,
There's so much I wish to say,
If only it was sought.

There I stand, alone,
Turn and you will see;
My life shall then be shown,
For just a silent fee.

Kristina D. Rutledge

"A Valentine For Friends"

Hello my friend
With this message
  I do send
Hoping our friendship
  We'll never end
So be my valentine forever
So it's best I say I love you now
  then never

Mark K. Horvath

By Myself

I walk amongst friends,
Yet I am By Myself.
When will this road end,
Will I still be By Myself.

I live amongst love ones,
Yet I am By Myself.
They are all grown ups,
So I am By Myself.

My love holds me,
Yet I am By Myself
Our love will always be,
Still I am By Myself.

How I long to share,
Yet I keep to Myself.
You do not know I care,
Still I stay By Myself.

I want to be with you,
Yet I can only be with Myself.
All these things I want to do,
Yet I want to stay By Myself.

Maria-Elena Montoya

In Love Again...

I swore to myself it
wouldn't happen again.

I vowed to myself that
this was the end.

The end of this longing
this yearning so strong.

I said I was over you
but oh was I wrong.

Now here it is quite
a while later.

And now my love for
you is now even greater.

Margaret Russo

Searching

Wandering lost and alone
without any direction.
Looking for someone
that will help me navigate
through the difficulties of life.
Looking in all the wrong places.
Trying to find that help
in the bottom of a glass
or the touch of a stranger's hand.
Finally learning
the only one able to navigate
this vessel through life is me.
I must go on alone.
I can't rely on a stranger
or find hope in a bottle.

Melodie J. Beavers

Untitled

The sky above surrounds me,
with its tender arm.
Protecting me from the world,
and all its evil charm.

I'm amazed by its magnificence
seduced by its touch,
how can I both love it still
yet fear it all so much?

Lisa Clark

The Love Of Joey

A talent lay
Within my soul,
An unused, unmarked,
Burning hole.

All my efforts
To pursue,
Very often,
Ran askew.

Then a bit of life,
All twenty pounds,
Brought out the gift,
In leaps and bounds.

The love of Joey,
My grandson,
Has helped me see
The battle won.

Joan Kelly

"God's Wonders"

Stop and smell the roses
with your turned up noses.
Stop and smell the flowers
have fun for hours and hours.

Stop and feel the rain
it will wash away your pain.
Stop and feel the sun
while you're at the beach having fun.

Stop and look at the trees
swaying slowly in the breeze.
Stop and watch the birds flying high
flying against the bright blue sky.

Stop and watch the little kids
making castles in the sand.
Stop and watch the lovers
strolling along the beach hand in hand.

Stop and watch the waves splashing on the beach
just out of my outstretched reach.
Stop and look at the sea shells on the shore
stop and enjoy God's wonders once more.

Karen Atwood

An Old Polaroid

An old Polaroid
with yellow marigolds.
Two pairs of eyes,
staring.
Polyester pants,
now tattered, knit sweaters.
Too young. Sisters
looking,
faces so naive.
Hearts, that want to believe.
Two paths, extreme,
knowing
not what lie ahead,
nor, what lie in the past,
but the moment.
Surviving.

Juli Henshaw

Life's Bays

On the ocean at midnight
with the black moon overhead,
the nightingale sings.
And from above the cliffs,
the rain falls hard upon
the ships adrift.
The sky rips open and I
see the Hand of God and
feel the movement of the
waves drifting on.
As the sand passes through
the hour glass, I hope I'll
be ready for that which I
must be shown
And wonder if I might have known.

Monica Hanson

Goodbye

As you lied down
with nothing more to say,
  You closed your eyes
and said good-bye.

  Your face got pale
and I filled with tears,
  But I've got memories
that'll live through out the years.

  I had a dream where you
spoke to me, and it felt so real,
  You said not to let no one hit me
'cause the pain will never heal.

  I often still wonder
what it could have meant,
  I try not to think about it
but I just can't.

Norma Dina Ramirez

Passage Of Time

You give them your life
  With love and devotion
They grow and they flourish
  With your love and devotion
You teach them values and traditions
  You pray that they learn
Then you let them go their way
  With your love and devotion
  Oh, you feel so much pride.

But life becomes very lonely and barren
  When the house is so quiet
You don't let them know and
  You try to keep showing
  Your love and devotion.

Linda K. Clelland

Woman And Man

She's soft and pretty
  with a gentle little kiss
He's strong and handsome
  with his firm grip
For this is the difference
  between woman and man
If this were not so
  nothing would be on land
There must be a tie
  between these two
A love that is concealed
  and so very, very true

Lesia M. Anderson

A Song

I live my life, it's no surprise
With long last looks, and sad good-byes.
On and on these games repeating
All the while my heart keeps beating.

They ask me why I sing the blues
As I hook the buckle on my shoes
Of brown and white patent leather.
I just hope this night gets better.

But he refuses me a dance.
While I know it's our last chance,
To latch both our hearts together
Because I may lose him forever.

He insists it isn't me,
So I sit waiting patiently,
To find out what makes him so sad,
And wait until his heart is glad.

As I sit and sing the blues,
He taps the buckle on my shoes
Of brown and white and takes my hand.
This so-so night turned into grand.

Leigth Mitcheltree

The Light Of A New Day

The rising sun suddenly appears
  with greetings from a bluebird
The soothing light calms my fears
  with songs of hope to be heard

The new day has begun
  with dreams and burning desires
The Lord's will shall be done
  with the strength to fight the fires

The sunlight will slowly fade
  with colors of the rainbow
The Lord's judgment will be made
  with the salvation to save my soul

The night may overwhelm me
  with darkness shadowing the light
The Lord's guidance sets me free
  with the wisdom to do what's right

Margaret Ann Rodkey

How I Feel

I loved you
with all my heart
and in my heart I still do

But you could never love me
So to me you were untrue
You stole my very soul
and broke my will in two

And then you left
just went away
My spirit left with you

Now you're back to let me know
you've found a love that's true
but sometimes she can hurt you
she makes you feel a fool

You know inside she's not the one
yet you're stuck to her like glue
Now you know how it was for me
How I feel for you

Maria J. Burgos

Despair

Doors closed
Windows shut tight
Sunlight diminished
Replaced by the night
Tears flow
There is no glow
No stars to glisten in the sky
The rose has wilted
All hope is jilted
Emptiness invades the soul
Alas, there is no goal
The twinkle of an eye gone dull
The whimpering cry of alone sea gull
Please God, my heart repair
For these are the voices of
Quiet despair

Gillian Carruthers Hoffman

You

Why should it matter to me?
Why should they?
The world blackens a few oppressors,
When my soul should be stronger!
Should it not?
If it weren't for the caring and love.
You.
Why should I let it tear me
Up inside me is a lock
How can I allow it
To ruin it,
For you,
For anyone else.
I have to stop saying
It's my fault
If the world should come to a halt
There would still be
You
There would still be
me.

Jessica Marie Houston

Moon

Man in the moon,
   why are you weeping?
The rest of the world,
   has long been sleeping.
The birds and the elephants,
   wolves howling at night.
The fish and flamingoes
   such a beautiful sight.
The plants and the flowers,
   the fields full of cattle...

The fighting and hatred,
   we're losing the battle
There's barely a moment.
   when I just hear silence,
Because our whole world,
   is filled with violence,
Man in the moon..
   I know now why you're crying,
Because our whole world,
   is practically dying.

Kim Coffin

The Ship Sunk

Sadness is an ocean
Whose waves leap and weep

Sailing over it
I heard the water cry

The whales of the ocean
Sang a song of sorrow

Suddenly, the boat began to leak

As the ship sank
so did I
As it touched the bottom of the
Ocean's floor
So did I

Becoming one of the whales
I began to sing the song

Some whales die and others live
Waiting to be rescued
From this ocean made of tears

I wait with them hoping that
Someone
Will hear the lonely song

Melissa C. Montgomery

My Love

You are the harp
whose tender strings
play out my dreams
of today and yesteryear.

With delicate musings
they captivate my soul.
Their melody drifts on
their song - a life replete.

Lois Montgomery

Sarah Smiled

(Dedicated to Sarah Plankington)
She was a tiny little gal.
Who was very ill.
Yet, Sarah smiled.

She couldn't play as
the other children could.
Yet, Sarah smiled.

She knew lots of doctors
who fed her with tubes.
Yet, Sarah smiled.

She had a willful spirit
but her body was weak.
Yet, Sarah smiled.

Her little life cut short
by no fault of her own.
Yet, Sarah smiled.

God came and took her
and now there's no pain.
Yes, Sarah's smiling.

Jessica Pospisil

Grandmother's Plea

I have a little granddaughter
Who is sweet, as she can be
But when it comes to mealtime
Her sweetness turns to misery.

Drink your milk, I plead with her
It will make you healthy and strong
But I rather have junk food
Teasing me along

Eat your veggies, I add with a smile
But I do not like them is her reply
Drink your milk again, I repeat
If I do, will I get a treat

The game is on one, two, three
The milk is gone
I clap my hands
And say, well done.

Lucy Durant

Life Goes On

Life goes on,
While you're miles away.
Time moves on,
as a night steals a day.
Keep the candle burning,
as long as the world is turning.
If you only knew how much I miss you.
Some day I'll be with you.

Jennifer Coy-Moultrup

A Two way Street

A two way street
Which way do I go?
How far will it take me?
Does anybody know?
And if I get lost
Will you be there?
To guide me to safety
And show me you care?
And if I decide
To turn back around
Will you be there
In case I fall down?
And if I keep going
For all eternity
Who will be there
To stop and meet me?

Kimberly Jansen

Lie On Love

Why should I believe you
when you look into my eyes
you tell me that you love me
but all you do is lie.

I should of known from the start
that it was a game to you,
you wanted me to fall in love
but love was not for you.

I didn't pay attention
the truth would not come out,
you always had to have your way.
If not, you would always part.

So now I'm standing up
and saying we are done,
I'm never going through this again
cause to you, this was all fun.

Jessica Tucker

166

The River

The river is rain
which floods the ground
one desperate rainy eve.

I could never hear
the call at hand,
'cause the words are hard
to perceive;
but, thoughts are words
that come to mind
words only I
can hear.

How cleaver
is the weather man
who projects
both thought and fear.

More cleaver yet,
is the pen in hand
that writes the words
so DEAR.

Julie Weidner

Leaders

I follow my parents' path,
wherever the end may be.
Though hard sometimes to believe,
they want the best for me.
I trust their eyes and judgement,
I walk with them to become free.

Kerry A. Bute

Outside

Outside a world of wonder
Where you can hear a roll of thunder
Where the animals roam
Trying to find a new home

Outside a world of hope
Animals tugging on a rope
To find the end of this struggle
Hoping to stop this on going smuggle

Outside a world of dreams
Clean rivers and streams.
People trying to stop pollution
Everyone looking for a solution

Outside a world of despair
People destroying our air
If they only took pride
In what we were given outside.

Lisa Voit

"Heaven"

"I believe in a place,
Where the clouds are our bed.
It is so peaceful there,
You have nothing to dread.
You can fly on unicorns
And soar through the sky.
Say hello to our loved-ones,
It's so hard to say goodbye".

Noele Kasper

The Old House

In this old house where dust lay,
Where I used to live,
where I used to play,
There lies an old doll,
There lies an old bat,
There lies my favorite dress up hat,
I come back now so much older,
These things mean so much less,
My doll is torn,
My hat is worn,
But this old house is still blessed.

Meghan R. Lewis

But Yet A Dream... And Nothing More

I once ventured to a place
Where I stood outside the gates,
To ponder upon a heavenly face
Of gold and pearl implore.
...But yet a dream and nothing more.

Traveled a foot again I rise
With sorrows broken,
Flamed surprise
Souls crying I knew not nor.
...But yet a dream and nothing more.

I land again full of scorn
Where bottles change moods,
To hate with thorns
What a pity for the house of four.
...But yet a dream and nothing more.

The first place Heaven
The second Hell,
But of the third I dare not tell
Yet childlike hope and love is sure.
...For 'twas all a dream and nothing more.

Nicholas Carpenter

Dreamland

An enchanted land
Where fairies fly
And dragons still exist
Where animals talk
And unicorns sharpen
Their magic horns
A single word
From an enchantress
Can make a forest grow
A world where
One wish
Upon a star
Can make your dream
Come true
And all you have to do
To get there is
Go to sleep.

Kayla Davis

"Dreamers"

Angels spread star dust
to put all to sleep.
Oh no! The angels missed one,
he can see everything that
goes on during the night,
which is a secret.
Maybe he will fall asleep
soon or maybe he's dreaming.

Kira Moseley

The Blind Mind

In the mind of the weak is
where darkness lies,
Eating at the brain at the
terrible insane,
In the padded room where you can
do no harm,
Thoughts of death inter seed into
your head,
Poisonous venom injected to stop
the hurt,
Daily allowances there are none,
One step away from all the rest,
but miles away from all humanity.

Kevin D. Robinson

Loneliness

Life is hard when you're all alone
When your parents leave you home.
Life is hard when you're all alone
And no one can hear you moan.

You call out for someone to save you.
You call out for someone to hold.
You call out for someone who cares.
No one's there.

When they leave home I feel so lonely
Sometimes I just want to cry.
When they leave home I feel so lonely.
Sometimes I wish I could die.

And when these feelings come over me
I wish I could say good bye
To all the loneliness in my life.
Good bye to the loneliness in my life.

They don't know how much it hurts me.
They don't know how hard I cry
Every time I have to say good-bye,
Good-bye.....

Jenney Eager

Yesterday

I fell asleep this evening
when the sun began to set
thinking about last night
and the eyes I can't forget
I stood so close
I saw them shining in the light
but they looked out far above me
somewhere in the night
and I prayed to the night
to carry me fast and far away
and set me down by your side
to recapture yesterday

Lisa Ann Liso

Relationships

I am me,
Thou art thee.
Thee, me -
Separate entities.
Together,
We are One
You see.
For heart to heart
And mind to mind,
Thou art me,
I am thee.

Olivia Jean Box

Saying Goodbye

Saying goodbye is very hard to do,
When someone is cared for
As much as for you.

Each day it gets harder
To hold back this emotion,
I feel like a fool
For some silly notion.

Saying goodbye
So confused and blue,
With millions of thoughts
of being with you.
It's not what I expect
or want to do,
I've come to one conclusion,
I feel love for you.

Now before you get sick
And start rolling your eyes,
I want you to know,
I never want to say goodbye!

Jim Spear

The Hereafter

Why is death so greatly feared?
When love of life is looked on so dear
Many will ask, when it is time
Will I walk through the tunnel
To the light which shines

To have faith in our God
Is all you need
Our loving father
Will create new seeds

When these seeds
Return to earth
Will this by chance
Be our rebirth

How I want
To believe it so
Only in the hereafter
We will know.

Marshall Dorn Brinkman

Thinking, Wondering, Crying

That's what I do
when I think of you.

Thinking about all the times
we shared
Wondering if you ever
cared
Crying because I know the truth.

You treated me with respect
But soon broke my heart

Why can't we be together?
I want to be with you forever

Kim O'Byrne

These Hands...

These hands I hold
These hands I kiss
And when they're grown
These hands I'll miss

I've loved these hands
Right from the start
For with these hands
You've touched my heart

Michael J. Demers

You Left Me! There's An Ending

True love. I looked, and it was gone.
When I looked into your eyes
It came as no surprise to me.
I can't believe the pain that I'm
Feeling inside of me.
You left me! There's an ending
To the song that we were sharing.
I feel that I can't go on anymore.
I feel my life is ending.
I can't foresee another beginning
Of life for me.
Life is a time span that goes on
Without any meaning in it for me.

Kelly Anderson

Untitled

When I am hopeless and cannot go on
When I am desperate and cannot hang on
I reach for you...

When the fight is too much to dare
When the pain is too much to bare
I reach for you..

It is a very long way
It is a lonely, cold stay
I try my best to get through each day

I cannot give up
I will not be stuck
In this unforgiving world of mine

So here I endure
Until I am strong
Until I am heard
I reach and I beseech for eternal life with you
God.

Margot Valle

Forever

It was July 9, 1993; the day had come
When all of my dreams would come true,
It was the day I had always known
would come; the day we said "I do."

We have shared a lot of laughs, and we
have even cried some tears,
We have helped each other to grow and
to face our deepest fears.

He had already been my best friend, the
one with whom I always could confide.
This wonderful man is now my
husband - always to be side by side

Together in our new home we will share
and spend the rest of our life
Until death do us part - we will be
forever husband and wife.

Jennifer (Reddig) Newman

Mothers

Mothers go a long, long way.
They have to work every day.

Mothers drive you all those places.
Mothers have such different faces.

Mothers cook you all those dinners
They should be number 1 Winners

Mothers have a special touch
That's why I love my Mother so much!

Jennifer Millecam

Peace And Love

War,
what for?

Pray to the
Lord above for world
peace, love, and harmony.

Have fun,
talk peacefully - don't argue
please don't use a gun.

Life is to dear,
to live in fear.

Together we must live,
give and forgive.

Together we
have to share,
and care.

Around the world
let the bells chime,
put a end
to war and crime.

Karen Dobson

Untitled

Friend of my heart's Desires
   what did we fail to say,
Such hypnotic fire
   is not easy to convey.

Kindred spirits ignited
   in self-consuming flame,
I could not find your open gate
   and you are not to blame.

Intellectual fences
   impossible to part,
Emotional sensitivities,
   piercing poisoned darts

I will not easily forget you
   though I hardly knew you well
But that I knew you least of all
   only time will tell.

And should you chance to think of me
While passing through the years
   remember I saw my reflection
When your soul was the mirror.

Lorna Laird

I Know What Death Is

I'm still real young, but I know
What death is.
I remember the dream when
Grandmommy died.
And the tears when
Uncle Wayne passed on.
And the tears Mike cried,
When His dad was gone.
And all the cries when
Uncle Curtis went to Heaven.
And now that I'm eleven
I recall all of this,
But mostly I recall the tears I cried
When you had died.
I'm writing this poem
to talk to you
It's the only way I can get through.
I love you Heath.
Yes, I love you.

Maisie Danekas

A Country Road

A country road,
weathered and rocky.
Plenty days ago,
wagons rode.

To places yet untold.

But now let free!
Spirits now come!
Battered soldiers torn and gone,
their spirits now roam.

The silver moonlight falls upon a cloak.
Of a traveler long gone.
Their thoughts left behind.

A country road,
weathered and rocky.
Plenty days ago,
wagons rode.

To places yet untold.

Margaret Russo

Justice

New world order comes to town
we must fight to stay up,
or we will surely go down.
Grab your guns for there will
be a fight, a fight that
will end all, tonight.
Children and adults alike will
be slain. For there is no prejudice
in a bullet, only pain.
It does not matter what your
wealth or color for
you will die the same.
There is no justice in the gun
only pain.

Jordan Lane

My Tree House

My old tree house used to be
Way up high in a cottonwood tree.
A spiraling staircase gracefully wound
The huge gnarled trunk from the ground
To the house some twenty feet above,
Nestled in branches like a dove.
My tree house was a fine retreat
To get away from the summers heat,
Or to set enjoying nights breeze.
The beautiful view was sure to please
Most anyone who sat up where
My castle stood high in the air
Many an hour I did spend
As leaves rustled in the wind
Reading or dreaming little boy's dreams.
Now, when it's hot and anger steams,
I recall memories that were good
And always think of the cottonwood
With my house nestled in her hair.
I wonder if they're both still there.

George Lehnhard

City Girl

Underneath the umbrella,
Watching a raindrop
Catch her nose.
I am warm and dry,
Protected by my safety net.
She is wet.
She is cold.
I am rich of money.
She is rich of raindrops,
Laughing at her funny clothes,
Her funny ways of being rich.
Who can be rich from raindrops?
"Nobody!" I reply.
But it seems as though
It is not I who wears the smile.

Mary Karsten

The Uncalled For Bombing

The Oklahoma City bombing
wasn't the very least bit
charming, but unfortunate
was very harming.
It left the federal
building in ruins, I'd like
To know what they thought
They were doing.
All the people that
have died have left many
who have cried
Are they satisfied?
Probably not, but they
sure are on the spot,
But maybe when, they're
about to get fried, they'll think
about all those who haven't
survived.

Lisa Molinare

My Dad

My knight in shining armor
Was a guy in overalls.
His soft words of love
Might sound like muted cattle calls.
He's up with the sun
Cleaning his plate—
His whole world is out there
And he knows it won't wait.
He's in tune with Mother Nature
Her whims and her quirks.
The outcome of it all
He's never quite sure —
He just digs in, and
Works and works and works.

Genevieve Fredelake

Split

One mind split
Twenty separate parts,
confusion - fear - apprehension,
pain - sadness, hope, and love
we will remain many inside.
Conflict black, red, evil.
We try to forget the past.
hope, white, yellow, snow, sky.
Want pureness and innocence back.
We will never give up that
goodness will triumph over evil.
Happiness can still come for us.

Jeanne Kanera

Footsteps

Child in search of knowing —
Walk-free to explore
Moves with eager footsteps
Loosed at last from bondage
Of a mother's grasp
Laughing with the victory —
All at once runs back.

Youth in search of Manhood —
Diploma-free of school
Drives with reckless urging,
Tired of parents' rule
Grown-up, first-home taking —
Never once looks back.

Man in search of Comfort —
Age-free of chore and child
Moves with stiff-kneed aching,
Lifetime near run out.
Freed of work and doing —
Tear stained, dreams it back.

Jessie Hearle

To Be A Friend

One day a light was shining
Upon my window sill
Glowing bright and peaceful
With love so warm and real

I thought I did not need it
I'd save it for another day
I tried and tried to cage it
The light would not stay

Finally out of anger
I did not want to play
I closed my shade on it
I wanted it my way

One day I was sad and lonely
My shade, I opened wide
My little light had left
I sat alone and cried.

Lonza R. Pagans

Wind And Rain

The wind and the rain
up in the moonlit sky.
Whisper softly to me
of people and places I've known.
They remind me of the past
and how I thought it would last.
But like lightning in the sky
time comes and passes you by.
Things you thought would be forever
the bonds of time always sever.
Leaves you distant memories of the past
memories fading all too fast.
Hopes and dreams you once had
all of the good and the bad.
Move like the sands of time
with a rhythm and a rhyme.
From the last to the first
visions all to well versed.
To bring you one last play
of each and every day.

Gregory Lusby

169

My Best Friend - In Memory Of Naomi

It's amazing how much a friend can mean
Until they are no more
And how many things you miss
That you should have done before

The times you spent just talking
With no cares in the world
And the secrets with them you shared
That nobody else ever heard

More than the things you did
It's how on them you could depend
To always make you feel better
And let you know they'd be your friend

With the Lord my friend now walks
Upon the streets of gold
Still my friend is with me
In all the memories I still hold

When I go to meet the Lord
And the pearly gates open wide
My best friend will be standing there
Right by His side

Kathy Thomas

Untitled

The Story
Under the endless sky
Beneath a million stars
With in the course of a
lifetime
How very young we are
As I stumble on this
journey
Along a road to what is real
These eyes deceive the words
I speak
Don't tell the story beneath

Kami Conner

Inspirational Destitute

The blackness of my soul is
Incomparable to
The sadness of my heart.

The bitterness of my mind is
Pity compared to
The sourness of my feelings.

The ugliness of my hatred is
Beautiful compared to
The sight of my love.

The sight of my life is
Blinded by
The glow of my insanity.

The darkness of my loneliness is
Understated by
My happy-appearance.

Mandi Rae Thompson

The Beginning

The wind and the sea.
The tree and the leaves.
The river and the stream.
The woman and the man.
The child in their hand.
The sun and the sky.
The nature and the high.

John Rooney

Morning Brewed

I doze off, pondering
   Toss and turn, wondering
Wake with a start, quivering
   Brew some coffee, thirsting
Climb in my cup, hiding

   It's warm in here, swimming
In the brown liquid, plunging
   Sun's arisin', climbing
"I'm sane," I say, frowning
   "Look-I'm not hot enough to drink!"

Nicholas R. Kloka

Imagine This Child

An angel who snuck into my heart
Took a piece of my soul
A joy and a pleasure
Worth more than gold.

She sings and dances
So sweet and cute
She claps and laughs
So brave and bold.

She throws kisses, gives hugs
And snuggles with a grin;
A wonderful treasure
So precious and dear.

Listen - someone is whispering;
But it's not the wind.
Someone keeps her safe
And kisses her ear.

It's my Guardian Angel
Who whispers from above -
About memories, sweet dreams —
And - LOVE!!!

Gloria-Marie Norman

Confusion?

Too young to love.
Too young to cry.
Too young to hate,
   Why?
Do emotions come with age?
Or does it decrease?
   What?
Does everyone fall in love?
Do we all chase our past?
   When?
Do you have a caretaker?
Does he/she shed tears?
   Who?
Does everyone have a future?
Do you want to turn back time?
   Where?
Questions, decisions, it's not clear.
Why? What? When? Who? Where?

Mandy Jankowicz

"Dreams"

Dreams.
The truth comes out.
A steady heartbeat; a hand held out.
Blurry visions from up above;
Reminders of family, romance, and love.
At times you almost start to cry,
as a brush with death passes you by.

Marianne Sperry

To My Daughters

I have shown you the roads
   to wisdom - to contentment.
It is through knowledge of science,
   of the universe,
through the words of the poets
   and through the music
   of the masters.
Travel these roads
   again, again and again.
Until they become your very existence.
Then travel them again
and build new roads
So others may also grow in wisdom
   and in contentment.

Mignon Taylor

Inside Thoughts

I wish I had the answer
to why God put me in this
place. As I lay on my back
I get scared. So I just
look up at the ceiling then I
know you're watching over.
I start to feel like there is
a ghost inside of me. And then
I close my eyes I see a pretty
place - Free of drugs, violence,
and broken homes. When I open
my eyes I hear "it's all right"
whispered softly in my ear.

Melissa Wilson

Blood

I know how it Feels
to touch the face of God-
To leap gracefully,
-beautifully-, to bound
like an Angel,
-on silver gilded wings-
to reach out a hand,
and gently brush Him
with swollen fingers-

I feel His Power, His Grace,
His Healing, I emanate,
brighter than the Sun, -His Son-

My Mind, Soul, and Body
find Peace, Love, -Contentment-

I know how it Feels
-after touching My God-
to hit the ground
-the Solid, Impassive
Earth- to then look down
and see Myself in the palm of My hand.

Michael Craig Bonafede

"The Tale"

A story is spoken
to the world all around.
But the meaning
is never...truly found.
Only those
who write the thought,
can tell you of
the adventures fought.
And even then
you'll never see.
You were not there
and never be.

Melanie Rexroth

Competition

You've got something
   to say I guess
You've felt pain
   and loneliness

Where I've been
   you've been before
You've been there
   and suffered more

I'll say this
   in your defense
Your feelings sure
   are more intense

These are your thoughts
   to the letter
What I said
   You said better

     Kathy Watts

Untitled

What must I do
To prove it to you?
That my love is real,
And not easy to lose.

Love is forever,
Friendship just so long.
I don't want to be friends,
Not that it's wrong,

But my love is real
And much too strong
To be ignored and condemned
By you for this long

My plans for our future
Went up in smoke
When you broke my heart
For words that I spoke.

So, just remember,
When the world seems cold,
My love for you
Will never grow old.

     Lindsay Commissaris

It

Fairy tales aren't what's real
to our world today.
More like O.J., rape, and murder
sneaking closer in every way.

It's slashing its way through,
Banging with its fists.
It's crossing off accomplishments
on its never ending list.

Wars, killings, suicides
Just keep on coming.
It's on a steady pace
With a rhythmic humming.

HIV, pollution, stealing,
all feeling their way through.
Watch out, because it's coming,
and its next stop may be you.

     Jennifer McCormick

Heavenly Hope

I know a place to rest my head.
To live like the wind
Where the lost are led.
My heart lies there beating as a drum.
Waiting for the moment
When my soul will come.
Life on earth is just a test
To see who will live
Their very best.
Searching for my purpose here.
Ever so far
Yet, ever so near.
My hope, my love, my peacefulness
Can be found
In my quest.
Clouds of dust are swept away
With every step
Of the way.
Tomorrow will be another day
To live my life with what comes my way.

     Jessica Beth Cheser

The Kiss

As I sit here alone with you I want
to kiss you.
I want to see love real love.
I want a promising kiss from you
to me.
I want you to press your sweet lips
to mine.
I have been longing for a real kiss.
Sure I have had many kisses before,
and a little more, but they were not real.
For I don't like my father's idea
of a kiss.

     Jessy Sewell

Hourglass

To grasp the essence of a moment,
To hold time in our hand.
As we gaze through the hourglass,
Slowly drifts the sand.

For what reason do we exist?
Are we a part of some ploy?
To the supreme master mind,
Are we, but merely a toy?

Peace, happiness, love and hurt,
Emotions so hard to grasp.
For is the reason for life,
The question, should we even ask?

As we journey down a lonely road,
Each of us to travel, has our own.
Though our paths may cross many times,
To each, the journey is never known.

     Marcus H. Zander

Dust

Boulders, rocks, stones, pebbles, sand
The water of time washes over all
Pebbles, gravel, sand
Dust
When our time has come to an end
Boulders to rocks
Stones to pebbles
Sand to dust
Only the breath of the wind
Moves the dust

     Linda Jane Carpenter

Legacy

The future seems to be blank pages
to fill with toil for meager wages
The children's laughter is our pay
And books that take us far away
Of late our only conversation
Is that of home and procreation
The future holds a dim salvation
With work and home and family
We cherish hours when we are free
To ride a book on moonlit sea
So on we toil, incessant earning
Nose to grindstone, ever turning
Then home again with muscles burning
Where through the veil of unshed tears
A little freckled face appears
Erasing foolish, selfish fears
This one inheritance we'll leave
when over our grave offspring grieve
These books to them that we did read
And taught them to believe in dreams

     Lynn McLochlin

Hooked

Cruel barbed hook, shaped to impale,
to capture.
Open trusting eye, coming too close,
seeing too little.
You desire to hurt, for sport.
I desire to feed, for life.
I am hooked.

What remains? To be reeled in —
Finished with a merciful blow?
But no —
You let me pull against the hook,
Thrash from side to side,
Struggle.

Panic — a small dot, growing larger,
Obscuring all else.
At last the beautiful rainbow colors fade.
I am gray — a dull, muddy gray.

     Naomi W. Caldwell

"Fate Said Only You"

On fate won't let me sing these words,
   To anyone but you,
If I may sing to someone else,
   My dream will not come true.

These are the words Fate sang to me,
   To sing to only you,
"Dear Love me now for evermore,"
   Make every dream come true.

There is no other love for me,
   My heart could ever give,
My love is made for you only,
   Just as long as I live

You're locked in this heart of mine,
   Until my life is through,
No other one could enter in,
   For Fate said only you.

     Joseph H. Young

The Basics Of Love

To all who came before me,
To all who fell behind,
Watch your step very carefully,
Cause love will make you blind.
Never take a short cut,
Never run the mile,
Always stay in between, the papers
in love's files.
Keep your distance from the start,
And try to stay away from the end,
And watch out for the saying,
"I just want to be your friend."
For not all love is good,
And not all love is bad,
Just hope you'll never look back on,
The love that you once had.

Megan J Stillwell

Untold Love

I wish you knew how I felt about you
Though myself, I cannot say
You look at me, and hold me
As if you feel the same way
I could never tear myself away
When I look into your eyes
Being away from you
Brings out tears from cries

I can't truly say
That I've never felt this way
  about anyone other than you
If only I
Can show you what's inside
I'd hope you'd feel the same way too

But my lips are not able to say
"I love you," and for this my heart aches
For the thought of losing you as a friend
  is a chance I don't want to take

Mirlandre Beauvais

The Loving Edge

Human person all unique
Though his traits are sometimes weak.
Granted rule of all he surveys,
With soul imbued to guide his ways,
He travels on life's risky path,
Trying to avoid God's wrath.

And there's help to do the right
In life's everlasting fight.
Of the spirit crowning jewel,
Love can conquer in the duel.
It rises from the human soul,
Thwarting evil's wicked role.

Of all God's many creatures,
There is not one that features
This capacity for loving,
Except man who should be proving
That this great gift, when used as meant,
Could save a world, ruin bent.

Mary Louise Boyle-Durgin

The Old Folks Home

Listing gray vessels
rusty bolts rattling around, rudderless.
We are all veterans
of life's struggles.

Julie Benson

Untitled

Beach, blue music, stones and foam
This ... you use it, far from home.
Sorrow of shadows dagger down-
your smile will stagger to a frown
God you hurt me deep inside
Into darkness I creep to hide.
Tears so slow and hesitant
tell where you go... where you went.
Like water screams, like nowhere flies
you drag your dreams through your eyes.
Teach you to choose it death to bone
Beach, blue music, stones and foam.

Laura Stelljes

Dragon

My physiology is a curious thing
This outside seems rough
Should blood streams run thin

The reason escapes me
For having these shapes
A neck full of corners
Wild tail, seldom straight

My muscles are strong
Huge feet, long and flat
What might be worse
Put a hang nail on that

I have come to the wind-up
Dragons have it, lad
Ragged scales slightly ugly
Teeth that look bad

This is not a downer
Oh no, never that
It is just that, by matter
These are the facts

Linda Sue Gallagher

A Mother's Plea

Oh, Father, do incline your ear;
This mother's prayer, I beg You hear -
Be with my boy where'er he walks,
Direct his mouth whene'er he talks.

Open his ears to hear Your Word
For it's the sweetest ever heard;
Open his eyes to see Your Light -
May it guide him through the night.

And bless his heart to make it kind
For it's the gateway to his mind;
These things I ask for my dear boy
That they may give him purest joy.

Mary L. Shelton

They Are But A Thought Away

They are but a thought away.

Though the touch is hollow,
the sound is silent,
still they live.

A few steps ahead.

They have passed
through earth's darkened doors
and received the everlasting light.

So far and yet so near,
only a thought away,
close in your heart to stay.

JoAnn Wright Noyce

Broken Hearts Fused Together

Together, alone again
This love could never end.

High atop
The grassy hill
All is quiet, all is still.

Sitting under the lonely old tree
I'll hold you tight
And keep away the cold breeze.

Night has fallen
And the moon is full
Sit on my lap as I sit upon my throne,
We'll always rule.

The stars burn feverishly
Just to appear white
Our wings catch wind
We take flight.

I'll drop you off at your house
You should've been there a couple hours ago
When we finally say "goodbye"
I'll wish I never let you go.

John Hess

"Little Girl Gone"

I watch her as she sits and plays
This little replica of me
And when into my memory, I retreat
Another little girl, is what I see

Sitting out underneath an old oak tree
With every dolly bathed and dressed
She talks to each one separately
And each one is separately addressed

Everyone is carefully dressed and sent
To school or out to play
As "mommy" watches over them
To make sure, that safe they stay

I think back again, to how very sad
When this little girl in dismay
Put all her precious dollies in a box
And carefully packed them all away

For tomorrow, has finally come
And her dollies she's out grown
And all the dreams that she has dreamed
Must now, become full blown

Lora Emery

My Closet

In my closet there are
Things for all
Like a broken hula-hoop
And a ripped up ball

Shoes and skates,
A box and a crate
Fishes and dishes
And all kinds of bait

If I had one wish-
To wish for more,
I'd wish for thick walls-
And a sturdier door.

Leslie Holmes

Saying Good-Bye

I love you there's no doubt
There's nothing I wouldn't do
That's what loves about

I hope it will never end
I want it to last forever
All your needs I will tend to
but, you are clever

You lie about some other girl
You say she's just a friend
The blonde with just one curl
Why does she have your ring on her hand?

So I guess this is good-bye
I'll always love you
No other can take your place
You'll always be in my heart

I'll never forget your face
but, I'll never forget why we had to part
You broke my heart in two
but, I will always love you
Good-bye

Lacy Buford

Poetry Is Silent

Poetry is silent;
there is no light within
my soul;
no river of music flowing
through me.
Dance, dance in the shadows
for the music is in darkness.
You must feel it,
never hearing,
till the end
of the song.

Karen M. Weece

A Couch Potato

In every home,
There is at least one of these.
Who sits on the couch,
With nothing but ease.
Eating the junk food,
And consuming the fat.
Drinking the beer,
And wearing a hat.
Flipping through channels,
With a remote in the hand.
Not going out,
To play in the sand.
With their feet on a footstool,
And pillows stacked high,
It could be days,
Before they see the sky.
And these we call couch potatoes.
Do you wonder why?

Kathryn S. Wiese

A Life In The Day Of

Scream and you'll see
The joy that I feel
When I watch
A thousand lives
Play themselves out
On my walls
Daily

Kevin LaVoy

God

I doubt in the Universe
There could exist
An ultimate authority
So infinitely wise
To predetermine one's fate
Influence events
And with consummate power
Interpose in human lives

Or is the truth that I seek
heart burdened with doubt
That such a wisdom prevails
In permitting we mortals
Freedom of choice
To raise our voice
Select our path
Ascend the heights
Or fall and fail.

Graham H. Stewart

The Wedding Camel

Utterly so, I heard a ring
The wedding camel doth bring
The bells of marriage
The natives sing
Gift given, receiving
Another to pass, and to begot
Seeking, and then sought
Not enough, and yet too much
Kinsmen irked at the lot
Contemplation will breed sin
Then, and only then
Negotiation will begin
Before long, the will of one
Will turn to the will of many
And then through homestead-
Gate will pass
The wedding ox at last

John Frederic Baker

My Friend

Your eyes sparkle,
The voice gravelly.
"Whadda you want?"
Your hand shakes slightly
As you hand me the gift.
A box of little yellow flowers.
Your walk a shuffle now.
"My feet hurt."
Ah, but I can see what
Used to be.
Strength, determination,
Humor, and goodness.
A hero long years ago.
A man who once commanded respect.
Needing recognition now.

Maryland Short

The Dolphins

Soul Mates -
  Swimming
from sea to sea,
  Being together
    through all weather,
Jumping the waves,
  Basking in the sun,
Oh, yes ... and having fun!

Margaret Horner

Slow Music Of Snow

The frost
  The twilight
    Slow music of snow
The puffs of whiteness
  The frozen smoke
Against
  The depth of bleached blue sky
Over
  My wooden cabin
    All aglow
Amid
  The forest

The fireplace is softly telling lies
Do gently open the door to my hope
Teach me the magic
Don't think twice!

Taste the champagne of fresh cool air
The frost....the twilight...not my despair.
I wish you share the delight of the show:
Slow music of snow...slow music of snow...

Guennadi Slasten

Shooting Stars

A shaft of light pierces
the still moonlit sky
bursting the bubble
that is night

sparks streak across the heavens
in one furious blaze
then
are lost to the eye
forevermore

a loving heart, however
knows not
the meaning of
gone

such things neatly filed
in the recesses of one's soul
take on new life
on many a moonless night
when solitude
is one's only companion

Maria Tanya Karina A. Lat

The Rose

Its petals the color of blood
The smell so sweet
Its head hung low as if ashamed
Petals around the vase; dead
No sunshine, no moonlight, no rain
All it needs is a tear
The baby's breath holding its own
Still alive as with no fear
Its love life is falling through
The redness of romance dying out
The significance of Valentine's Day
  is over
A petal lost everyday
Everyday my heart aches
My heart aches and a tear falls
The rose is alive again

Marissa Smith

Untitled

Encircling me
The room is round
no door to be found
A razor in the corner
the only way out
the same old thing
day in, day out
cut my hair, pierce my ear
desperate for change
screaming out
they pretend to hear
they try
Encircling me,
voices - voices ...

Kelsey Neal

If

If the mountains crumble to the sea
The rivers dried and ceased to be
If the sun began to fade away
Darkness would fill each lonely day.

If roses somehow forgot to bloom
All the sweetness would turn to gloom
If the rainbows suddenly left the sky
We'd be upset and wonder why.

If the stars above lost all their light
There'd be no beauty to fill the night
If fun and joy all went away
There'd be only sadness day by day.

If I had a wealth of silver and gold
I'd trade it all for you to hold
If all the life on earth was through
My love would still belong to you.

Joyce Race

Point Of No Return

When my life takes me to
The point of no return;
And death kisses my lips;
And God seals my forehead
And the devil passes me
The bill.

Don't cry for me;
Remember me in a beautiful
Sunset and in a child's
Innocent sight

Nelson Balmaceda

Devil's Twilight

For his last dance in the innocence of
The night was a curse

And no one's eyes saw that these were
his last breaths

The air on which his lungs did feast,
Proved to be the last supper.

As the wind that swept beneath his
feet was the horse his soul rode into
eternal darkness.

The music has stopped, and the floor
left empty ... as empty as my heart.

And I can only still wonder - if I'd
been the one to stop the music, would
he still have danced death's dance-
into the night, and out of my life.

Melanie L. Smith

Open Field

An open field
the nature's shield
protects the wild
like an unborn child
the feeling of being free
bare wooded trees
wild growing flowers
long fantasy hours
warm sunny rays
mist of rainy days
a feeling of change
that now even the mind can rearrange.

Maronda Moore

Untitled

The stars are shining bright tonight,
  The moon a white crescent
    against the star-studded night.
There is a light breeze,
  stirring the leaves lightly
A blanket of darkness
  falls over nightly,
    Everything is still...
      Suddenly blood curdling
        screams broke the silence
One shot, no two shots shurking
  ring out like a cannon...
She falls into the deadly
  grip of her broken heart
For today was a good day
  for her to die.
Why so high a price to pay
  for a love so true?
Why such violence
  to someone you thought you knew?

Kari Harrison

A Single Rose

A single rose among
The many thorns,
holds itself high,
Ignoring the laughs and scorns.

It's the last of its kind,
All the rest gave in
To the wickedness of the thorns,
and gave their beauty up to sin.

Every now and then,
When no one else can see
A single tear, a single petal.
Drops in a silent plea.

A single rose once was red,
now has faded to pink.
Each day another petal falls,
Another tear, another link.

A single rose among thorns
Has died
Its last petal has fallen,
Its last tear was cried.

Melissa Croad

Contradiction

The comedic tragedy,
The horror of laughter,
The guilt of the innocent,
Remains forever after.

The hilarity of death,
The joyfulness of sorrow,
The tragic human life,
The waiting for tomorrow.

The sinfulness of purity,
The beggar's wealth,
The life of a dead man,
The feeble man's health.

The ridicule of logic,
The senses gone awry,
The senselessness of violence,
Make happy people cry.

Nicole Miles

"Peace On Earth"

Peace on earth' peace on earth'
The heavens shout loud and clear'
But peace on earth we'll never share
Until all beings learn to love and care.
The wars all fought for greed and hate
Must be overcome,
There'll never be peace on earth,
'Til all can live as one.

Joan Reego Gully

'Rocky Mountain Sunrise'

Slowly,
  the gilded clouds warm,
The aspen trees
burn.
With a radiant
  crimson glow.
The snow,
  sullen in its bed,
Awakens to become
  celestial
  diamonds.
The birth of a
  rocky mountain sunrise
has
  begun.

Joscelyn Beahm

Still Vision

In stillness,
The eye gleams like crystal,
Seeing
the sparkling surface
of the pool,
Seeing
the mud swirl
when disturbed,
Seeing
the bottom
when clear;
Seeing depth within depth,
Absorbing all
as experience
through rod and cone,
Sending the wisdom of the moment,
that which is real.

Breathe in stillness,
And watch like crystal.

Mark T. Larsen

Untitled

Outside, the rain falls softly
The day dark, dreary
It seems as if God has forgotten me.
So many things gone wrong
At a time when I'm not very strong.
A lost child, a broken heart,
How could our lives have come apart?
We never knew
What this kind of pain could do.
You reach deep inside,
Searching...trying to hide.
Someone, something always reminds,
Even though they try to be kind.
The pain you feel is O' so real!
As the days begin to pass,
The heart begins to heal.
I look around...and without a sound,
I face the reality...my hopes, my dreams for
    this child
Are now with God.

Karen Helmick

Abandoned, Wife's On Jury

Gee another day,
the clouds outside are here to stay.
The sun isn't shining,
but I'll do no whining
cause I'm alive and free,
who knows what will be,
my wife left for court to see.
A verdict maybe reached,
no confidence will be breached.
More evidence will be given,
the defendant wants forgiven.
Yet the plaintiff persists,
he's hurt everything but his wrist.
Golly-gee is it more, he sees,
wonder how the jury believes?
Go for a decision today,
or again on Thursday, you'll stay.
Well whatever will be,
just let my wife come home to me.

Larry V. Brooksher

Your Eyes

In your eyes all life is dark.
The clouds are filled with rain.
The lights is dim, there is no end,
To life's eternal pain.
In your eyes there is no hope.
Your life remains a lie.
Nothing matters, no one cares.
The children live to die.
In your eyes you see that blood.
As wars rage without end.
The people kill, buildings burn.
No one is your friend.
In your eyes the world is dead.
Its people raped and gone.
No one loves, no one cares.
Just where do you belong?
In your eyes you feel the hate.
It eats away your mind.
Numb, you sit there all alone.
From the world you're left behind.

Jennifer L. Musto

"The Playhouse"

The sky has opened up this morn,
The clouds are all unfurled,
They move to let the sun-shine through,
To warm our cold, cold world.

Oh what great gifts God gave to us,
The sun, the moon, the rain,
The stars, the wind, the snow, all free
They perform again and again.

For the world is one big play house,
The earth is just the stage -
And we are all the actors,
But it's God who turns the page.

For it's He who writes the story,
And teaches us all to sing,
And when the play is over,
He'll be waiting in the wing.

Joy Chappell

Branches of Life

Seeds are gently dispersed from
the branches of life. They soon
reach earth and nestle themselves
in the rich soil and fall
into a deep slumber. The seedlings
sleep until the following morning,
which brings sunshine and warmth.
A seedling gently pokes its head
through the blanket of earth. Growing
towards the sun, outreaching, spreading life.

Megan Cassella

Once We Were...

Once we were friends,
the best I might say.
Your cheerful hello
brightened every day.
"We will be friends forever"
I always thought.
We had so much fun
and we never fought.
You made each day
so worthwhile,
And you were always there
with a big, bright smile.
It's different between us now,
our friendship has taken a dive.
There's no more happiness,
we now live separate lives.
I could never hurt you,
and I'm sorry it ended this way.
I'll remember the times we had,
and maybe we will talk again ... someday.

Julie Lindly

Autumn

Slowly the sun is moving down.
The air is crisp and cool.
The leaves are changing color and
are falling to the ground.

Jennifer Woodley

Each Time Your Angel Sings

There is a happiness in you
    that's near to having wings.
And I'm convinced it's sure to be
    each time your angel sings.

Her song may come to you
    in many different forms.
It may be the laughter of a child,
    or the beauty of a storm.

She sings and watches over you
    each and every day.
To celebrate the joy of love
    in each and every way.

If the angel you know brings
    you a smile so fair.
Her song of love is working
    with joy beyond compare.

So watch and listen
    for that familiar ring.
That bring happiness in you
    each time your angel sings.

Linda Henry

Untitled

Is creativity the thought
that sprouts between the rock
and that very hard place of battle
where right and wrong
scream their songs of allegiance?

Can the artist live
outside the edge
where are born the questions
to the answers alleged?

We will survive the feast
wherein the fast we found
the very need to question?

Is to be not to see
but with faith want to be

A maker?

Marley Porter

Child Soul

Lord, protect my child soul
that speaks not with a bitter tongue
like those old and grown
who've seen the world
and jaded have become;

Who justify those acts of men
(that vanish not) with a shrug or nod,
(as if to wave a magic wand),
who blame it all on God.

This babe soul needs to dwell on light.
Lord, turn my eyes towards these;
Your gifts of love and life and hope
and the innate good in me.

Laura Marie Brown

My Magic Box

I have a magic box
that only I can open.
My little magic box
is what I wish and hope in.
In my magic box
I'd put the day in camp,
walking through the redwoods
drafty, dark, and damp.
I loved to watch the ocean
in the cool spring breeze,
watching all the harbor seals
jump into the sea.
It was fun to watch the tide-pools,
looking at the crabs,
watching all the sculpins
I wish I could have grabbed.
Why did I have to leave.
I wish it didn't end.
What made it all so special
was being with my friends.

Lorna Elizabeth Port

Silent Tears

A baby's tears
that never were.
A mother's heart filled
with pain and hurt,
she sometimes feels in her heart
and in her mind.
That sometimes God can be
so very unkind.
So she holds her tears inside,
for the baby whose
tears were never cried.

Micki Morgan-Ramsey

"Pure Poetry"

Your love is like pure poetry
that lifts my spirits high
Your heart is like a butterfly
that softly flutters by.
Your touch is like a cool spring breeze
that rustles through the trees
Your kiss is like the honeycomb
that caters to the bees.
Your eyes are like a sunny day;
as bright as bright can be
Your words are like the sweetest wine
that makes my soul feel free.
Your spirit's like a little lamb
that sleeps upon the grass
Your tears are like a gentle rain
that softly taps the glass.
So now we'll speak our poetry
and softly flutter by
Someday we'll have to stop and rest
Someday we'll have to die.

Jesica Miller

Wilt

As the last hour falls hanging low
Stained-brow bleeds a steady flow

Eyes glazed over, searching black sky
Arms pinned down, breath shrivels dry

My life embraced, His own denied
This wood holds more than a man who died

Through His pain forgiveness sails
As I watch I question, "Was I the nails?"

Kevin A. Still

What Is This Thing?

What is this thing called poetry
That itches me inside?
I'll tell you this in secrecy
And then let you decide.

It's the song the bluebirds sing;
The noise of flowers that grow;
The flutter of butterfly wing;
The sound of new fallen snow.

It's brightness of a new sunbeam;
The twinkling eyes of a child;
The music of a mountain stream;
A little fawn running wild.

It's voiceless wind a whispering;
The laughter of summer rain;
Good friends intermingling;
A blue sky with clouds in lain.

What is this thing called poetry
That itches me inside?
To me it's still a mystery
So I'll let you decide.

Martha Brock

The Day The Dam Broke

Today is the day
that all men shall say
we hope and we pray
that the wall will stay

Today is the day
when the wind is tough
and we can't all stop
the waves so rough

Today is the day
the hard shell has cracked
three hundred houses
will all be smacked

Today is the day
that the dam has broke
Today is the last day
that the villagers will never know

John Rhem

A Whispering Pond

Reflecting on my sorrow
tears whispering to my soul
persuading change
Sometimes forced, Sometimes not
We forfeit control
from the time we were born,
yet unable to understand
until we are faced
with its grasp on our meek hold
Looking ahead and beyond
paints a picture so vague,
and rightly so,
For as we have learned...
These forces of change
will surely wash over us
again and again.

Laura Jones

Little Brothers

Little brothers are the
sweetest things when they're tiny
and can be sane. They can be
pesty at sometimes or they can
help you out of binds. I don't know
why little brothers are like this,
Why they tease you or try to
impress you. They can make
you look like fools or they can
make you look pretty cool. When
your friend comes over, your
brother may try to be a push over.
But sometimes or another he
can be more a friend than a brother.
Where he gets the last of the fudge
bars and you start to argue.
You guys may try to make a
bargain. I guess the reason they
do the things they do is because
they really love you.

Lauren Martin

Sharks

The sharks of old,
Swam, swam, swam
Into boats they round
Breathless, so I'm told

368 species of sharks
Large, seven inches small,
Not that they are tall
Studying, I am, their marks.

The man went around the reef,
His friend went with him two,
He saw him top the water too,
But he swam on, like a leaf.

Suddenly he realized what,
His friend was trying to say,
There was a shark in May!
The shark turned, as he spat

Mary McFeely

The Breaking Of Shell

There is a shell,
Surrounding my heart;
Like the egg yolk,
Protected by the rounded wall,
Hidden in it a potential life.

Sometimes my heart itches,
When I see gray light,
Trying to penetrate the shell,
Touching the tender seed,
Giving the shell a cracking line.

What if the shell breaks?
Where shall the tender self hide behind?
Can I close my eyes not to see,
as long as I'm awake?

The gray light touches the shell,
Breaking through the wall from the cracked line,
Gushing out the yolk of white,
Illuminating the space with golden light.
As if a flash of lightning,
In the darkness of a glooming night.

Kim Hong Yeoh

Stories Of The Air

Leaves coat my drive,
Sunset colors
Stories of ages past,
Songs of birds
Of wind and waves,
Things living and not,
Songs of mothers,
Stories they told,
All turned colors,
Brilliant Colors.
The summers days
Sunshine, rain
Cushioning footballs,
The fall of rain.
Leaves tell stories
In the ways they fall.
Tell stories,
Made of everything
And of nothing.

Laura Mommsen

My Love Is The Ocean

My love is the ocean,
Struggling beneath in seaweed,
Are his arms around me
Crashing into rocks.
Dehydrating by the sun,
A sand crab needing water,
But burned by the heart.
Suffocating tentacle of an octopus,
Dying in his poisoned love.
Flowing into the waves, is my love,
For now, all I have is a breeze.

Kristine K. McCreery

He Whispered To Say

His arms in pain
Stretched out to its length

The pierce he gave
Trickles down his beautiful face

From the crown of bristle thorns
They made him wear in disgrace

This saint divine
Hung with liars and thieves

His mother stands there idly
With sorrow, she grieves

The worst death by man
to hang on the cross

For three days did he linger
His life whisper to say

I died for your life
Never throw it away

Ne'Keisha Alexander

Beginnings

Don't deny the inner voice,
Speaking softly in your mind.
It's your life, you have a choice,
Of all the millions, oh, so blind.
Seize your desires and live your dreams,
Take a step and make your start.
It's not as frightening as it seems,
Just listen close and trust your heart.

Julie Beck

Inside Passage

The sedated torso
stretched lengthwise
along the flat bed,
sterile staples racing
back and forth
like railroad ties.

Stopping.

The first leg
of the journey was over.

Starting.

Switching tracks
approaching the
end of the line.

The knife that carved
along this route
traveled this line before.

Another trip
down memory lane.

Judith G. Yaker

It's Simple

The world
Strange to many
Yet simple

Our lives
Many seem stressful
Still simple

Ones love
To us a confusing daze
Simplest of all

Clear to fact
No one is the same
But simple as the
Others differences

Why waste time on
The hard efforts
Pleasure is found
In the simplest ways

Jennifer McGuire

Memories Of A Great-Grandmother

Stories of when she was little,
Stories before unheard,
Come from an old, wrinkled form
To a young girl's answering heart.

Stories about school long ago,
Stories just about her home,
Days long gone,
  History, her story
    Almost forgotten.

Wonderful things, endless marvels,
Left to the young imagination,
One generation to the next.
Our best inheritance.

Jennifer Justice

A Thousand Miles To Go

Long into the journey
Stopping, looking, reflecting
All is well, not well
My morning glory eludes me.
Turning to continue
I bumped into the front gate.

Martin D. Kelly

Snowflakes

Fragile and silvery
Stars made of ice.
Delicate, intricate,
Dear beyond price.

Nature's own handiwork
Feathery, soft.
Spun by the angels,
Dropped from aloft.

Brushing your nose and face
Falling with timely grace
Covering all;
Trees, hills and rooftops
Like winter's dewdrops
Silent and small.

Joyce VandenBerg

"Memories"

I can still see the old house
  standing so graceful and tall
The faded wall paper and old
  pictures on the wall
The old lace curtains tattered
  and torn with age
As memories go back, like an
  old book, with torn page
The floors are all rotted
  ready to fall.
Yet, I seem to hear children's
  laughter down the hall.
I look outside, and see the
  old pump with rust
The handle is broken, yet
  layered with dust.
Memories, of long ago and
  far away
I will cherish, a long time
  they are there to stay.

Mickey L. Shaffer

Sand Beach

Grains of shells and urchin
Squawking gulls
Children's squall.
Wave overending wave.
Rush of white and blue, in
Angular union—endlessly.
Great sea gentled by the shore,
Jade and sapphire do you seem.
Beckoning fingers do you reach ashore—
Tempting man within.
Dazzled by your riches
Foolish man submits,
Only to retreat a trembling,
Victim of your icy power.
No rock, no shore; oh noble sea
Your power can withstand.
Only the gull atop his craggy perch
Can mock it all.

Matthew A. Vassallo

Haiku

Scarlet, yellow, orange
Roses humming-birds' delight —
They choose whole mélange!

Evelyn Harmon Freeze

Laika

Sputnik ... going round and round
Sputnik ... crashing to the ground
Launched without a sound
Was it lost or was it found

Sputnik ... flaming through the sky
Sputnik ... wondering how it flies
From the country of red
It was just like they said

Sputnik ... none other by design
Sputnik ... completely blows my mind
With imagination and appliance
Was it magic or was it science?

Sputnik ... a self luminous ball
Sputnik .. you sure amazed us all
It was a dog in the drivers seat
Was it a humiliating defeat?

John Palmer Jr.

Red Neck Roses

These roses aren't
special and no they're
not new

They're a gift
from my heart
and I give them
to you

And if I don't bring
them home to you
anymore
I'll bring you
my love when
I walk through
your door

I can't promise
much, but my love
and a maybe
I'll try to remember
them over you and our baby!

Mark McIntire

Speak To Me

You
speaking prose and poetry
A veritable symphony
to my ears
The doors are thrown wide
as my mind
Draws your words inside
Prostrate acolyte
before her dazzling altar
You
Searing words of truth
Branded upon my soul
Your voice
pouring images and dreams
To quench my parched spirit
You   Speak to Me
words of these imaginings
Ideals and sensibilities
So comparable to thoughts and ideologies
    Of We

Raven

Life Is...

Life is like a bowl of cherries —
Sometimes there's a few pits.

Life is like an escalator -
It has its ups and downs.

Life is like a puppy -
There can be lots of love.

Life is like angels' wings -
Miracles can take a flight.

So, what is life?
Life is ...

Karen M. Wilson

A Special Someone

Someone special,
Someone sweet,
Someone I've
been waiting to
meet. The smile
on his face, as
bright as a light.
His laugh, very
jolly, and his eyes
almost green, but
very clean. When
he blinks his eyes
twinkle like a star
in the sky. His
mood, not rude, but
very good, his temper
very calm.

Nicole Van Scoy

The Day Of My Death

In the battle I hear a cry,
Someone is going to have to die.

I hear my captain yell and say,
"Everybody shall die today!"

As I hold their blood in my hands,
I watch them fall onto the land.

When I see him from the side,
I quickly duck down and try to hide.

As he comes near,
I begin to fear.

When I see him behind a tire,
We begin to exchange our fire.

As he took his shot,
I began to feel hot.

I look at my chest,
I see that his shot was best.
As I lay there in pain,
It begins to rain.

As my blood is washed away,
I know I will never see the light of day.

Nicholas Billings

A Poem

A poem can be about anything
People, places, or songs to sing.
Open your pen and let ideas flow
Eventually your poem is ready to go.
Maybe you'll win (If I don't)!

Mary Schilling

Second Time Around

Six years gone by
Some said it was destiny
We plunged right in
Some said it was fate
We didn't hesitate

Six years had gone by
At first it was glorious
But a space was between us
At first so in love
We fit each other like a glove

Six long years had gone by
Our souls were so familiar
Time brings forth change
Our happiness began to fade
We had missed our day

Jodi Hill

Haiku

Squirrel spread-eagled
Soaking up sun on bare tree limb,
We share brief respite.

Wind whips budding trees.
Sun stands higher in bright sky.
Time of change is here.

Heat is hanging heavy,
Leaves lie still and flowers fade.
In accord, we droop.

First sighting of geese,
Black Vee against cloud-free sky,
North wind speeds their flight.

Mildred P. Richards

The Door

Mary walked up to the door,
So white, ornate and tall.
She felt that she could not ring
The bell, she felt so small.
What might there be behind the door?
She was afraid to look and see
Because just the thought of someone
There, threatened her reality.
So she stood and waited to decide
If she should run or stay.
Perhaps, she thought, "I can go
And come back another day."
Then she remembered the words she read
About how to face your fears.
So she lingered for awhile to think
About why she had come here.
Then she lifted her hand to the bell
And it began to ring.
Then suddenly the door began to open
And the sight made her heart sing.

Marjorie Bishop

Spirit

I called him spirit
so gentle as a lamb
like the wind
he ran fast
like a storm
he was fierce
But tamed he truly was
so bless him be
the spirit within me

Gary L. Billington

Good Friends

I've written you in thoughts, my friend,
So often through the years,
But somehow ink just couldn't find
The words to make thoughts clear.

You were a friend to me back then,
And still you are today,
For memories can give us strength
And help us on our way.

There's a joy that comes from sending
Wishes that are most sincere
For love, health, and happiness
Each day throughout the year.

There's a joy that comes from hoping
All your fondest dreams come true
Because it is so wonderful
To have a friend like you.

In my thoughts I've thanked you, friend,
But here at last are words
To say I thank you for the joys
That in my heart you've stirred.

Judy Alberternst

Walking

As I am walking with my head held high-
So many things just pass me by-
I take a deep breath with a heavy sigh-
As I am walking with my head held high-
So much beauty all around-
Kittens playing in leaps and bounds-
The trees are changing colors now-
Oh' what beauty I have found-
The day is gone, the night is here-
The stars are twinkling oh so near-
The night is cold, the moon is bright-
oh what a lovely, lovely sight.

Josephine M. Malloy

For Lara

Infant child that I hold so dear,
So free of question, so free of fear,

Infant child that I gently touch,
You are so tiny, you are so much,

Infant child I kiss your cheek
Ever so softly, ever so meek,

Infant child that I sing to sleep,
Dream lightly today in my tender keep,

Infant child I am in bliss,
You are the dream I thought I'd miss,

Infant child I hope you know,
That in my heart I love you so,

Infant child I now must rest,
You can stay right there upon my chest,

Infant child we rest now as one,
To awaken later to have more fun.

Mark Stephen Anderson

God

As the fragments of my brain
slowly swells to burst into the
Rainbows of my weary mind. The
Soul of my inner self explodes
into the galaxy's of all space
and time.

For I prevail over all that
ever will be, through out life's
eternities.
To enhance every state of
mind, to enlighten the souls
and minds of all creatures
that ever exist.
To create and preserve a
wondrous sanctuary.
I enslave only myself, to
ensure life's evolutions; for
one and all.
This I gladly give, for
through all, I shall live.

Linda Kaye Lockhart

Moondance

Ample hips sway seductively
slowly circling the stars
embers emanating inward
heating up the lava core.

Fingers caress hilly mounds
delighting as sparks flare
electric pulses of passion
erupting fiery trails.

Heat surging up and out
as fevers pitch and wane
sweet fires smoldering
surfacing into sunlight.

Kathleen A. Muja

Rosy Clouds

And so the song continues...
Sleepy eyes awaken.
I see laughter in the air
and I feel the music
when I'm there.
Stars, dreams and
stranger things.
You've got quite a mind there.
And your father's eyes.
Look at the flowers.
Look at my hands.
No one is here but me
roaming about inside my head.
For better or worse,
break the curse and come outside.
There you are and I smile all night.
Out of bed and into the light.
I'm alive.

Linda Denise Stipp

The Game

On a cold, winter night
Six men are in a casino.
Laughing, playing poker,
Betting their money and possessions.

A lone man stands
In an alley warming his hands
Over a burn barrel
Wishing he had never joined the game.

Lindsay McDonnell

Billy Drums

Oh little seed with in the ground
sleep you may not, Oh roses yield
your bloom cause Billy's here to beat
his Drums. Wake up wake up noise
is what his heart desires
Leaves fly open wide there's
no place you may hide. Hear me,
hear me Billy's here to beat his drums.
Fly away, fly away, Birds, Billy's
here to beat his drums, his spirits
are high his arms ache for the beat.
Stop, wait, Oh my God, Billy is
beating his drums.

Onia Bailey

She Was There

She was there; she always was
She was there when I was born
She was there when I was young
She was there; she always was

She was there; she always was
She was there when no one was
She was there when others weren't
She was there; she always was.

Jennifer Powell

The Blue Lady

The ocean loves to sing with me,
She tells me all her poetry.
She tells me of her power,
She gives me a small shower.
She throws herself upon the land,
come morning she'll start again.
Her beauty flies inside of me,
I love to listen to the sea.

Marla Haynes

The Soul That Died

She reaches out but grasps the air
She realizes life ain't fair.
Striving and trying is all she can do.
Even when she knows she's through.
And with each brand new road she takes,
She can learn from her mistakes.
And with time her wounds will heal.
Living, loving, learn to feel
The hurt is there for all to see.
Dying, crushing, time to flee.
No matter how far and fast she runs,
She looks behind and here it comes.
The pain, the sadness, and the tears.
Scarred in deep throughout the years.
We all must learn; we all must live.
No matter how much love we give.
We won't forget the tears we cried
We won't forget the soul that died.

Katie Kennedy

Old Age

The lace on my curtains is
ripped,
and the windowsill
crackly and dry;
the paint-chips flecked in my
last geranium,
left in the sunshine
to die.

Karen Walsh Pio

Wings

On top of the hill,
She lay facing the sky,
watching she wonders,
what it feels like to fly.
She watches the birds
and the airplanes go by,
feeling the wind blow,
and hearing its cry.
Standing up,
she stretches her arms wide,
a feeling of Confidence
she now feels inside.
another step,
and she approaches the ledge,
taking a breath,
she dives off of the edge.
Falling she smiles,
Happily she sings,
"I'm flying! - I'm flying!
My God, I have wings!"

Joey Arlene Perez

A Dream Is Just Reality

A dream is just reality
Sharpened by a thought
They come and go as they please
Never to be caught.

Some dreams you can control
Others just fade away
Some of them possess the soul
Others as clear as day.

Some dreams are hard to find
Unlocked by just one key
But remember, keep in mind
A dream is just reality.

Jeff W. Frost

Tasty Flight

Look out across the lake!
See the gentle ripples...
Feel... the gentle ripples!
The quiet,...the peace...
The gentleness,...the comfort...
Touch the mountain tops!
Skid along the ridges...
From sunrise to sunset,
Into the valleys and over the peaks...
Taste the dew,
Ingest... all!
Reach for the clouds!
Float...float with them...Glide!
From island to island...
Rest in their folds.
Bask...Drink...deep!
Inhale!
Caress its softness... Digest...!
Come down...down...down.
Softly, softly...gently...gently...gently!

Leila Lucas

Pompo

Promises you always made,
Over and over till this day,
Many of them you always keep,
Promises you'll never forget,
Over and over on and on here's
a promise you will never forget,
I promise someday we'll meet again
up in Heaven where we all begin.

Lori Archuleta

Untitled

If you had no eyes could you not
see my pain.

If you had no heart would you
never know love.

If you had no hands would I never
know your touch.

If you had no emotions would you
never shed a tear.

If you had no conscience would
you not be so faithful.

If you had no pride would you let
me know your fears.

If you could not hear would you
not know I love you.

If there was no time would our
love never grow.

If we did not have each other-
Would we love another....

Gina Marie Laughy

I Should Have Listened

You told me no, hit my hand,
screamed in my face,
I should have listened.
You said things get better,
you told me not everyone's like that,
you said life goes on,
I should have listened.
You said don't give-up,
do something good with your life,
you said don't do that,
I should have listened.
You said there's another way,
begged me to please stay,
you said I was loved,
I should have listened.
You stared at my coffin crying,
you said you should have been there,
Well it's not your fault...
I should have listened.

Lisa Wylde

Sounds Of Rain

Falling rain.
Rushing down, crowding in.
Then you feel it,
pouring, pouring.
Sweet is its caress.

Listen,
listen to its music.
Do you hear its soul?
Can you feel its heartbeat?
Do you know what rain is?

It's the cries of those who came
before us.
It's their cries of sorrow, their
tears of pain.

If you listen closely you can
hear their cries.
Shh now listen,
listen to the sounds of rain.

Michelle Woodard

Time To Go

"It's time to go" the soft voice
said.

Tho' I knew not where still I felt
no dread.

How will we travel I asked...
Is it far?

We can fly there in a heartbeat
just a' ways beyond the stars.

"But I can't fly", I protested
"I don't have wings!"

Just then I felt I was falling
I reached out - for anything.

Suddenly arms were holding me,
lifting me to greater heights.

And I felt secure and strong again,
I could make this flight!

In a moment all was clear to me
both the present and the past.

And I looked into Eternity
and saw our Savior's face at last.

Judy R. Beavers

Digging

Excavate memory
rummage through bones
of buried love
fire-charred, worm-holed
dusty, caked with time
close to the roots
evolving

I sort the pieces
archaeological miner for gold

Rain pelting windows, lying
in bed reading poems, words
playing and striking and loving
with the candle's flicker
a man of the air

Trudging Kalaloch piled driftwood
ground stones and gull tracks
orange and yellow shouts
challenging the damp skies
a woman of the sea

Nancy Leimbacher

My Battlefield

Flooding feelings that obtain
qualities of bitter pain
inflicted on my own instinct
loosing touch with what I think
I arm myself with angry shield
I run out to my battle field
and fight till death do us part
but I was dead before the start
fight myself and need to kill
I cause my pain by my own will
I see darkness I feel ease
finally I am at peace.

Lori Noll

Untitled

It stands on the edge
Ready to fall
But it does not.
It balances on the rim
Of emotions.

You feel helpless
Weak
Choked.

Will you allow
That single teardrop
To begin
The long awaited journey?

In your mouth
Is salty sadness
And you know it will
Never be the same

Then you realize
That the memories
Will be enough

Mindy Burkholder

Reality

It comes;
   reaching;
      grasping;
         holding.

It encircles me;
   with ...
      dignity;
         mobility;
            grace.

It searches;
   seeks;
      finds.

It encompasses;
   devours;
      is;

   Reality!

Leslie R. Hammen

The Dazed Dandelion

Withstanding the passive
Rape by wind,
Stripped blatantly to the bone.

Condemned by the sunny
neighbor's jealousy,
left painfully alone.

Should she extend
Protruding buttery petals,
To the buzzing bees.

Or be a cozy rest
for the vain butterfly,
briefly before he flees.

Remaining only a
Gardener's nuisance,
Reprimanded by a spade.

Or simply ignored and forgotten
meeting death,
by the lawn mower's blade.

Kristy Chavez

Night Room

Night silence roams room's
   raddled walls
Where glides the shadow of my
   body,
Distorted by lamps and shades,
And by the corners of my cage.

A streetlight casts its eerie streams
Of light across the room's dark beams,
And I, beckoned by its bright, watch,
As my shadow disappears
Out into the night.

Marcia Gibson

Separation

   We settle for life's
pleasures, a day goes
by, we ask ourselves
why. Just moments of
Love platonically passing
through life's riches
and britches silent pasts
The key is in our heart
Secret's hidden, yes
when we are apart.
Happiness, awareness
await us looking
for new days
new ways, keeping
us contented solemnly
erasing the resent
of the enjoyment
that is now sent
days of separation

Jayne Casciato

Sing To The World

When you think of the World
Please think of the good things
When you do, open your mouth
and you'll begin to sing.
Think of the blowing trees
And all the things you can
Dolphins jumping on the seas
And your fellow man
When you sing, sing loud and clear
Stand up and let the world hear
When they know of those things
and you hear them sing,
The pleasure is so great.
To hear them sing from state to state to state.
World Peace could be at hand
if all could understand.
To accomplish that goal
It must be straight from your soul.

Michelle Doggett, age 12

What I Like About Pigs

I like pigs
Pink pigs
blue pigs
black pigs too
I like baby pigs how about you
Rapping pigs and
dancing pigs
I like pigs that play the piano
I like pigs that rather sit
I like pigs that run real fast

Pigs, pigs, I like any kind of pigs.

Lucindra Fleming

Forever And A Day

The cat waits in silence
Picking the moment
To take a life.
I wait in silence
Waiting for the fish to nibble.
Forever and a day.
How long will it take?
For the flower to see the
Silver light.
So it can grow
Into what must be beautiful.
The beetle waits for
The sun to emerge,
To warm its shiny
Blue back.
I wait for the food
To reach my lips,
For I grow ever more
Hungry.

Kate Eburg

Captivity

At the aquarium parks
People go to see
All of the whales and dolphins
That used to swim free.

Slowly they're dying,
And many people don't care.
They think they'll get more
Animals like to live there.

They suffer each day
So someone can get richer,
And also so tourists
Can take their picture.

Soon one day
Only pictures will be left,
And no one will remember
All of the animals' deaths.

Jessica Spencer

"Toy Soldiers"

Death is in the air,
People are dying everywhere.
For his mother he's crying,
The young soldier is dying.

Scared from the start,
Bodies are blown apart,
Bombs drown out the screams.
This is hell, it seems.

The soldier keeps on killing,
He cannot fight this empty feeling.
They make him fight,
Although he's already lost his sight.

He's going insane,
The bullet pierces his brain.
He lies in a pool of his own blood,
Silently screaming into the mud.

They don't know why they're fighting,
They don't know why they're dying.

Jeff Oscar

Ragman

It seems as if last week he passed,
parading up the street to ask,
rags, any rags today?

With easy rein in every weather
his wagon rolled, through
every neighborhood.

The seasons round in shabby dress
he rambled on and as he went,
a trace of sorrow in his song
came back to me and echoes on.

Joy Dorsey Brown

Old Glory

Raise it!! Praise it!!
Our red, white and blue.
Honor it!! Respect it!!
To it be true.
Think of it!! Drink to it!!
Our stars and bars.
Our trademark of freedom.
This banner is ours.
Here's to Old Glory.
Long may it wave;
Over this land of the free
And this home of the brave

Marian E. Heilmann

Untitled

The world burned the
other night.
A vision arrived on wings,
in flight.
Judgment was upon
the beast.
Freedom lost to say
the least.
Souls were flushed into the
bowels of hell.
Hundreds of thousands of
souls for sale.
Heaven exists within
your mind.
While hell awaits to rob
you blind.
Hate breeds its kind,
Kindness frees the blind.
Blindness is what we
suffer from.
Critical is most everyone.
What if everyone were
the same?
Who then could you blame?
If people would try to see,
judgement upon the other
would not be.
If the critical would see,
Everyone could be set free.
Free to think, Free to be.
To live life as they see.

Keith D. Hinson

Untitled

I May Die...
It would be like the
falling of a great
and majestic Sequoia
(if I may flatter myself)
...But
life will go on.

Joseph Lombardi

Dream

Shall I sing you a lullaby,
or gently rub your head?
Shall I tell you a story or
read you a book instead?
Let's forget all that
just close your eyes and dream-
dream of me, dream of you and
daddy, just us three.
Dream of all the good things ahead,
those near and far away.
Dream of the things you did in the past
and the things you did today.
Dream of what you want to be and those
you'll one day meet;
dream of people that aren't here anymore
and the memories that can't be beat.
No matter what, you can always dream,
nothing can take that away,
dreams are just like wishes - they may come
true one day!

Katherine Carini

Through A Single Speculum

Peering closely
One may see
Muddy cracked sneaker tracks
The unforgotten we

Lingering echoes
Dust covered smiles
Stale incense burning
Ripened gum wad piles

Fading stained glass windows
Green banana peels
Tears strung through cob webs
Lone red wagon wheels

Ashes coating lipstick
Faddish dress up gowns
Simple football interludes
Prevailing circus clowns

Life's promise of wrinkles
Daydream and good
Footprints tomorrow cue
Leftover childhood

Jill Holtz

Childhood Memories

Life goes by so fast.
One is reflecting at the past.
Sounds of laughter heard with delight.
Follow memories that are bright.
The wind is blowing leaves all around.
Children dancing, playing on the grounds.
Boats on the ocean sailing by.
Kites flying in the sky.
Children rushing to the candy stores.
Ice cream cones dropping to the floors.
The wind is blowing leaves all around.
Children dancing on the grounds.
Childhood memories seem so near.
Childhood memories are so dear.

Marjorie Reed

Decline

Against her charms, what can I do?
One glance and I'm a pawn
My resolve fades from view
She leads me on and on and on
Come down from your high
You fool, walk away
Broken hearted you die
This is life not a play
My feeling I can no longer defend
Oh to once again be whole
Let the curtain slowly descend
On this mortal soul
Ending with this inspired notion
That love the magic elixir
Can be an elusive potion.

Loren D. Clark

Remember Me

The circus over
   one final fading wish is asked
Slowly he walks off,
   His balloons trailing behind him
The clown had cheered
   The children had laughed (as always)
   The music had sounded
The tent now hollow
   The passing marks of
   Friendship now have gone.
And without a word the tents fold
   The wagons roll out
   over the horizon
And only the wind cries
   Remember me.....someone...

Michael Sigler

The Black Hole

Love is like a black hole
Once you fall into it you cannot escape
you go deeper and deeper
Until it is too late.

Then you get hurt.
But it is never your fault.
It is love's for not warning you earlier
It wants to surprise you.

Surprise you with heartache
More than you can bear
Until you realize that love
Can be dangerous - if you aren't careful.

Now love is sorry for all the pain
It caused you
Crawling through your heart
It begs for your forgiveness

You won't listen. You've been hurt.
Once too much
you vow never to fall in love again
The Black Hole closes - forever.

Joanna Wojda

Crush

The crush is like a wild flower,
it grows,
then blossoms,
looks good,
wilts,
and dies,
while no one notices.

Jennifer Dykema

Untitled

I thought,
once upon a time,
"Happily ever after"
was just the way things went;
    But now,
    the dragons are real,
    and the spell won't be broken
by a kiss.
    This time,
    the knight's blade is not so true,
    his armor somewhat less
than shining...

Guy D. Hammond

A Prayer For Spring

Grant me patience, O gracious God
On these days which lie in between
The fading winter's dreary hold
And springtime's promise of the green

Renew your promise of Easter
Of joy, new life, eternal hope
During these cold, gray cloudy days
Give not my heart reason to mope

Let me pleasure in the slow rain
In southwest wind warmed by the sun
In quiet clouds whispering by-
Lord, let me contemplate each one

God, may the goodness of the soil
Hold safe the seeds which now I sow
Whether for food or flowers fair
Work your wonders Lord, let them grow

Let me give thanks this day to you
For heart and mind and body strong
Thank you for your richest blessing
Of springtime's sweet eternal song!

Gerald Berndt

"Crystal Midnight"

Walking down this moonlit path
On the soft, powdery
White sand, I can hear the
Crashing waves of the mysterious sea
Slap an outstretching pier nearby.

I can see the shimmering streak
Of silver illumination on the
Azure water, left by the moon
As a reminder of His heavenly presence.
I can feel the crisp breeze

And hear its whisper through
The reeds on the water's edge
Telling the tale of nature's wonders.
I can smell the pure air
As it wraps it gentle arms around me.

I can see the brilliant stars
Strewn across the ebony blanket night
And by studying the carbon sky
I notice that the man in the moon
Has a hint of a smile upon his lips.

Mindy Bakale

Cinquane

Dragons
Mystical, Magical
Flying, eating, sleeping
Love to fly high
Reptile

Linda Burns

Mind's Eye

The moonlight dances
on her iridescent skin,
wings extended in full glory
as she dips
and spins
with a wild,
tempestuous grace.

(She is proud, untamed,
the child of a forgotten realm.)

Delicate and powerful,
those soft and, sleek limbs
weave possibilities into the air.
Denying the web of fate,
she creates her own, instead,
out of the gossamer threads
of sweet imaginings...

Jennifer Fales

A Love Forgotten

Down goes the rain,
On down the drain.
With it a chance,
A chance for romance.
Now our time is past,
A love broken in a cast.
But in time it will heal,
And then reveal.
A love like a rose,
More beautiful than any one knows.

Justin Terry

"A Time For Yourself"

You sit on your porch,
    on a bright sunny day.
You can hear in the distance,
    the children at play.

You look at the clouds,
    way up in the sky.
You think to yourself,
    you wish you could fly.

The clouds look like cotton,
    their puffy and round.
They take different shapes,
    they bump without sound.

You spend the time dreaming,
    your mind starts to wander.
Your troubles have faded,
    you stare and you wonder.

The breezes are blowing,
    the sun's on your face.
The world seems so peaceful,
    you give thanks and grace.

Mary Jane Ducharme

What's Wrong With Me

I'm acting really mean.
My heart is beating at the
wrong speed.
I can't think clear not anymore.
My head is throbbing.
My minds confused.
I just don't know what to do!

Jennifer Jean Nagel

Moonlit Performance

Your glow
Oh glamorous moonlight
Makes a dark and restless ocean
A ballroom
Bright and sparkling
Enhancing waves that dance and dip
To lyric orchestrations of the sea
Whitecaps cresting with glee
Tantalize the shadows
Foamy waters leap, high, higher
Reaching joyous crescendos
That break—then shiny ripples
Bow their finale at my feet

Mary D. Giacinto

"Sobrius"

Get thee behind me
oh ghost of my past,
to my new found life
I am holding fast.

I no longer need nor want you
in my everyday-ness,
Whence you only showed me existence
fraught with decadence and grayness.

I beseech you to silence
your whisper in my head,
besot me no more
I'm awake from the dead!

To thyself I can now be true,
honestly and openly, no more a mime -
for I'm shouting from the rooftops
exploring one day at a time!

Gail Sawyer-Pylant

First Snow

The first flakes
    of winter's joy
fall silently from
    the secret-filled sky
to rest unseen
on the unsuspecting
newly fallen leaves.

The anticipation
    of the season's arrival
has been blown away
    with the wind,
only to return
with the daydreams
of spring.

Gail H. Kerns

The Stranger Beside Me

    The stranger beside me smells faintly
of whiskey and cheap cologne. You may
begin to think he is a bum, but he is
well-dressed and clean-shaven. He has
an attitude about him. He says little,
but does a lot. He has a kind smile
and loving eyes, yet he seems so far
away. I wish there was a way to get
him to stop seeing her and finally see
me. I wish that he would understand
that she is gone, and I'm the only one
left to care for him. When he looks
at me, I want to say so badly. I
love you, Daddy!

Jessica Edge

Untitled

Smelling the freshness
of this rose,
 Makes the windows open
and close,
 Doors slam, pictures fall,
you hear screaming coming
from the hall.
 Putting a pillow over
your head, wishing to God that
you were dead.
 Awakening violently
in the night, the yelling still
seems to fight.
 Wishing all was well,
but really living in a hell.

Kara L. Cooper

Decaying Soul

The soul is the immortal part
 Of the man.
When the man dies, his soul is
 Lacerated from his body.
His soul runs free, like the blood
 Runs free from his decaying body.
For now his soul is ripped from his
 Decaying body.

Jonathan Brzuchalski

Roots

Beneath the roots
 of that dead tree
with growing limbs so fat,

 I can't see.

Cemented by mud,
 my hair armors my mouth.
Too much dirt.

 I can't breathe.

Entwined, imprisoned
 by hard hanging roots beneath
 that dead tree.

That big tree
 whose branches strong
 on which birds can alight,

Has captured me beneath.

My eyes are blind.
My lungs are choked.
I can't say

 I am free.

Jennifer Eileen Allen

I'll Know

The definition of love,
no one will know.
How does one know when
it is showed?
Maybe one day I'll figure
it out, I'll know the answer,
I'll dance about, for I'll
be in love, there will
be no doubt!

Laura Castle

Time Was

There was a time
of summer's still,
with blue jeans and butterflies
I loved this world;
of home baked muffins,
blackberry pies
and lightening bugs in a jar.
There was a time of sailboat racing
after summer's rain in the field.
There was a time of laughing
and running,
running,
until I lost myself,
with my body
looking back for my soul.

Jean P. Daniel

One In The Spirit

I pray for you every day
 of my life
  We are now and always have
  been
 ONE IN THE SPIRIT

I see you as a free spirit
 going along in grace and
  beauty - I pray
  healthy, whole in mind
  and body
 ONE IN THE SPIRIT

My mind touches yours
 My heart rejoices
  We pray together
   laugh together
   Commiserate
   Always
   we are
 ONE IN THE SPIRIT
To those I love and who love me back

Octavia Ruben Simien

"Songs Of The Soul"

Our souls sang the language
of a kingdom far away
A language never spoken
yet understood in every way

These songs told tales which
the heart had secretly sown
Tales full of love and of
the wonders of being known

Oh, come away, let us run
to a place we can hide
The place where love grows
as our souls do confide

If ever, I ever live
more lives than this one
I will never sing with another
the songs we have sung

Maureen Hanley

My Love For Fall

I hadn't finished with
October, when I awoke
and it was November.
The leaves are falling,
the pine needles flutter
down, and I'm in a
state of bliss.
Is this reality, or am
I dreaming in living
Color?

Mary Farrow Smith

Tomorrows

There'll be no more "tomorrows"
Now that you've gone away;
Tomorrow I'll have nothing,
Only a "yesterday."

You used to say, "tomorrow,
I'll see you then, my dear."
There'll be no more "tomorrows,"
You've gone and left me here.

I pray that you'll remember
Up there in Heaven above
That even without "tomorrow"
There'll always be our love.

And when there comes another day
And you are not with me,
Yesterday's "tomorrows"
Will live in memory.

Marjorie M. Castile

Poetic License

Great Grammas like to think
Not wash dishes in the sink
Computers help them see it's fun
To pen a letter on the run.

Microsoft and semaphore
Someone has to close the door
Windows old and windows new
Soon we'll find the one that's true.

Great grand child loves dear Dr. Seuss
Stories of animals like "the moose"
But also loves the story of kitten
Whose Ma cat saw she'd lost her mitten

Any story from Mother Goose
Can well compete with Dr. Seuss
Like "Hickory, dickory, dock
the mouse ran up the clock"

Mary Virginia Lucas

Untitled

She asked for a house
Not spacious at all.

She wanted the entrance
Five inches up the wall.

Could I please make it
round, four feet off the ground.

She was always blue
I complied with her request

Her mate wore a rusty tie
with his vest.

Myrtle L. Wunderlin

Tundra

Snowflakes drifting to the ground,
not making but the littlest sound.
I see the Caribou and deer grazing,
what a sight to see when I'm gazing.
I watch the rabbits while they rush,
without a sound, without a hush.
I hear the clouds move,
beyond the horizons groove.
I feel the morning breeze,
pass me with great ease.
I touch the snow,
while wondering where to go.
I listen to the owl,
waiting for night to prowl.
You might not know what this all means,
but I'm a bird that's in your dreams.
In the winter, on the Tundra.
Matthew W. Wilson

Memories

Memories
Not knowing what's real
Dreamlike
Mysterious

Never forget them
And on your mind
Always - they
Are there

Remember your memories
Always - forever
Treasure them
Hold on to them tight

The best memories
Are the memories
That are never forgotten
Life is a memory - let it rise
Lisa Marie Brennan

No One, Someone

No one understands me
No one likes me
No one cares
No one should
No one could
No one would
No one sees me as I am
No one knows how I feel
No one cares how I see things
No one understands
No one should
No one could
No one would
Someone just like me
Someone who sees me as I am
Someone who knows how I feel
Someone understands
Someone should
Someone could
Someone would
Jeremy Stoll

Riches

Riches inspired by love
Love inspired by need
Need inspired by lust
Lust inspired by greed
Greed inspired by vice
Vice inspired by riches
Mark F. Hillyard

Daddy Isn't There

The grave is lonely and bare
No flowers does it wear
But Daddy isn't there.
He has no worldly care.
He's in Heaven, high above
Surrounded by God's everlasting love.
Standing with Jesus, hand-in-hand
Or playing in the Heavenly band.
He has no more heartache or pain
Because he was born again.

The grave lies quiet and bare,
But my Daddy isn't there.
No flowers adorn this lonely site
But Daddy's not forgotten any night.
Yes, the grave lies quiet and bare,
But Daddy's not there.
He's in Heaven with Jesus
Without a worldly care.
Misty J. Hammerbacker

Why

She was so wise for only three
No day went by but she had to see
The birds that always came to feed
She always seemed each day to need
To learn some new, exciting thing.

But only after three short years
My heart is filled with bitter tears
For God called her up above
Grandma's own sweet little love
I love and miss you my angel girl.
Lois B. McNulty

Time

It goes on and on.
Never waiting for you.
When you stumble and fall.
It doesn't wait.
It goes on.
Leaving you far behind.

You can't make time.
You can't stop time.
You can't begin time.

Time created itself.
Time will destroy itself.
Michelle D. Rinker

A Broken Family

A broken family you can
never ever fix.
When people fight or yell
a broken family begins.
When people don't love one
another a broken family can
never love again.
When people never appreciate
anything a broken family will
never start again.
When mommy and daddy
fight because of the kids
A broken family can never
turn back again.
But when mommy or daddy
dies or gets a divorce
A broken family ends.
Nicole Collins

My Windowpane

As I gaze through my windowpane
nature unfolding before me
sun bursting through the clouds
birds chirping trees swaying
dawn of life emerging
greenery at its glorious
smell of flowers
lingering in the air
nature beckoning the child within
to romp and play all day
is what my eyes see
through my window pane
Josephine Roti

Will Anyone Listen

As I cry for help
    my tears glisten
Does anyone hear me
    will anyone listen
I feel no one cares
    no one cares for me
Can't you hear me
    don't you hear my plea
    just please answer one thing
Does anyone hear me
    will anyone listen
Jennifer Parker

Restless Love

Fly high, reach for your star
My restless love
I'll be here by your side
And if you fall and need to cry
Come to me
For I'll be yours faithfully

Search deep if you must
My restless love
Find answers to questions you asked
And if the things you find don't last
Come to me
For I'll be yours faithfully

Fly high, search deep, roam far
My restless love
I'll never try to bend your wings
But if some cold nights find you
I'll be here to warm you
Come home to me
For I'll be yours faithfully
Maria Adorable Theresa Gonzalez

Special Lover

All this love inside my heart
my mind and soul they yearn
for just one moment of your touch
a touch I know would burn

Burn a path straight to my heart
and unlock my desire
I hear it screaming to be free
darling can't you feel the fire

You don't know how you move me
I want to make you mine
Set loose all my emotions
and stop the hands of time

Take my love, please take this love
I offer you today
take my love, this burning fire
that makes me feel this way
Karen Price

Life After Death

Blinded by the light,
My life begins to shed,
fluffy clouds await
for my wings
To grow and fled.
I'm took'n to a place
where no evil can enter.
I'm asking myself why I'm here
but my mind keeps blinking clear.
I couldn't be dead because
I nearly became
to love none other
than my Mother.
I need to share
before I glare in
to the light.

Kristina Wilson

Destiny

I held it in
my hand
once.

Smooth around
the edges,
I lofted it
softly into
the night
air.
Catching it occasionally
to feel my
grip.

And then I
threw it.
Wide and hard
through the sky,
hoping that one day
perhaps,
it would skip
across the moon.

Luke Brannon

Desert Of The Sun

The heat is coming down.
My feet are on the fire.
The sand eats my spirit away
And kills my heart's desire.

I see the sun go down;
As the breeze comes to play.
It cuts apart the desert heat
Of the evil burning day.

I come to a water oasis
And drink to my heart's desire;
But then I open my eyes
And find my mind a liar.

For there are no trees or palms to eat;
No life for my hungry soul.
Just death-life in vain.
And now I must pay the toll.

'Tis almost over.
My will turns to gray.
I loose my breath and set my head
The pain is gone away.

Larry Phifer

Trapped

On the outside looking in
my feeling burns deep within
but for a person I do not lie
it's for a place, another time
a place, a time, I can not be
But oh the passion burns inside me
And though I hope and wish and pray.
I could not live another day
without this wish of mine.
The world is cruel, the world it hurts.
I long to leave before I burst.
But why I feel this way I do not know.
I do not know why I hate this world so.
I'm so confused and filled with hate.
I try for happiness but find I'm too late
I'll try again day by day
to throw this world of mine away

Kim Jorgensen

My Special Man

When I was a little girl
"My daddy can fix it,"
is what I used to say.
Whenever I would break it
I brought it my father's way.

As a teenager,
"Pops can you do it?"
is what I would say to him.
It was a time in my life,
when I meant everything to him.

As a woman,
"Dad, I have a favor to ask,"
is what I said to him.
"I found a man like you....
Can I marry him?"

As a mom,
"Dad, I have someone who wants to talk to you,"
is what I said to him
"Hi grandpa, I love you"
is what she said to him!

Jennifer Becker Woodall

Untitled

On a solitary hike
my brother found a lily,
shortly he returned for me.
As important for him to show his find
as it was for me to see.

You've heard of that conundrum,
if no one is around
and a tree falls in the forest
does it really make a sound?

If you carry an idea too close
is it really there?
How do you count your joy accrued
unless your treasure is shared?

Gloria Olson

Serene

I've seen joy.
I've felt pain.
I've known love.
I felt shame.
I know have peace.
This I have gained.

Katie E. Dunn

Backstage

As the boxed toe slides over
my anxious feet I begin to think
of the bright light's heat

The impatient crowd and the
music loud ring through my
ever listening ear

It's almost time for me to
go, in dance you can't hold up the show

I'm shaking like an autumn leaf
ready to be blown away, my
rosy face has turned to gray

The butterflies flap their giant
wings and my heart begins to
quickly sing in a rhythm to match
the butterflies pace. My thoughts
and emotions begin to race.

At last I'm on my way
down the hall and through the black door
marked stage.

Like a bird let out of her
gilded cage, I'm on my way to fly.

Kristen Cable

House Made Of Cards

There's a place in my mind
more like a house made of
cards where I go to hide from
the real world. The place has
no windows all that makes
it light is a few candles in
the whole house, it calms my
temper and when I feel like
coming back to the real
world I find it way different
from when I left it.

Heidi Palmer

"Faith Instilled"

It happened past, this life of
mine, that I had played charades,
Of coping with reality, a must,
For two decades.
Trying to act, with faith that
Lacked, unnoticed by the few,
That I had though important,
At the time, to help me through.
Till watered eyes, from countless
Cries, I'd pray to end these ways,
But not without, concern about,
Recovering from my maze.
It seemed some time, would yet
Be mine, to challenge this my will,
He'd give this test, no doubt his
Best, my faith He would instill.

Katt McCray

Untitled

Floating in the clouds,
like a fish in the sea,
dropped I, my favorite teddy
on the bottom of the sea.

Crying after crying,
but the fish wouldn't help,
finally a bird found teddy
riding on the back of a shelf.

Louise Went

Time Pieces

Time pieces,
Measures of a fleeting life
Beating sounds of loss lamented,
Fatal fragments.

Haunting hands,
Painting dreams of love's green scenes,
Surreal strokes, a heartfelt rending
Teasing hopes.

Sifting sands,
Seconds push pain's present past,
Shifting times to stem the course
Of psychic wound.

Longing face,
Ticks of teardrops left without
Life and love for granted taken.
Untimely Angel.

Dwindling glass,
Welcomed by the aching heart,
To fated Saint a prayer's despair,
Dateless embrace.

Gregory Alan Peddle

You And Me

Can you see,
me and you, you and me,
Walking hand and hand,
down by the sea,
down on the sand,

Can't you tell,
how much I love you
you are my life,
You are my world,
I'd go crazy without you,

You and me,
can you see it?
I can, it's a reality,
Me and you, you and me

Kristi Bunnell

The World At A Glance

Absurdly spinning through a cycle
Love and hate and peace and war,
They all come after the one before.
Blending with the sunsets hues,
Even in the churches pews,
EVERYONE has different views,
And you live the one you choose.

The World, it bewilders me.
Is it contentment that we seek?
Is it kindness that is the key?
The world will not shape up till we
Push our hate aside

Kristin Hehe

Friends Forever

Friends are forever
Like the sky is blue
And the stars shine
Friends will always be there
Be there when you need them
Friends are forever
Even though people die
Friends are forever
Even when it's hard-
-to say good-bye...

Misty Wilhelmi

Open Your Eyes, Little Girl

Little girl
lost, lonely
needing to be loved
rescued

A young boy appears
willing, able
someone at last
who won't leave her
alone, broken

She's blinded by another fool
who'll disappear
her heart torn in two

She's tired
all these games
there's no way to win

Will she realize
he's the end
to all her sorrow

Happiness
is inside the young boy's eyes

Jennifer R. Koehler

Lost In The Crowd

Walking through the city
   Lost in the crowd,
Searching for the questions
   To the answer's I've found.
So many people mourning
   There's no one around,
Walking through the city
   Lost in the crowd.

Walking through the playgrounds
   The children lie dead.
Their recess never ending
   From the drugs they were fed.
Bees no longer stinging
   Birds no longer fly,
I can't find a reason
   For the way that they die.

Walking through the city
   Only demons around,
Walking through the city
   Lost in the crowd.

Neil Silverman

Babies

Babies are precious love gifts
Loaned by God for a while
To teach parents to be patient
And also how to smile.

Babies are like blossoms
Which in my garden grow,
But you cannot have a flower
Unless you dig and hoe.

Then one day babies grow up
And like the birds sprout wings,
And off they fly to foreign parts.
They do so many things.

They keep their families happy
When they come flying in
And bring their babies, chattering
Of the places they have been.

Keith Reeve

"Nothing"

When the one thing you've been
Living for is taken away,
What do you think?

When everything is gone, and
There is nothing left,
What do you feel?

When the world is cold and black, and
There is no place to hide
No one to hold you,
No one to save you by your side
There's just an emptiness
A desolate silence and unfeeling death,
What do you do?

Nothing
Nothing, you are strong
Eternally nothing

Until your soul is nonexistent,
Save a final whisper
It is then when your heart trembles and cries
But you're alone, and so, it is nothing

Jennifer Mattson

Today

Today is your day
   live it,
   appreciate it,
   find it full.

Today your mind is sharper
   creative,
   decisive,
   receptive.

Today you let go of the past
   be secure.
   look for, find
   and give thanks for life.

Today you reach another step
   up the ladder
   toward
   your fulfillment.

Today is meant for you
   look with new vision
   you are guided and enabled
   by the Great One above who cares.

Lahoma M. Cook

Life Long Love

In this world of wonder,
I've always wondered why;
you are always oh so strong
and all I do is cry.

To cherish to love, to honor,
to lay upon your chest.
To run my fingers through
your hair and lay my head to rest.

To feel secure and cared for,
to feel the warmth of you.
To know that you'll be there for me,
and I'll be there for you.

Nancy L. Gayler

Child, Child

Child, child in a room
Listening to her parents fight
She hears her mother asking for divorce
"Life goes on," she said
Gathering her might
Child, child has yet to see
How cruel this world can really be.

As she grows older
She feels nothing can heal the pain
She fights with her mom
And sticks the needle in her vein
Child, child has yet to see
How cruel this world can really be.

One day on a very cloudy night
She lay crying in bed
She can't stand it anymore
So she puts the gun to her head
Child, child don't leave me
This cruel world is a world no one
Can ever see.

Monica Santos

Whispered Words

Sitting alone at night,
Listen to the sounds in the dark,
I can almost hear you.

Whispered words float on air,
Before they reach me,
A wind blows them away.

Try and catch them,
They slip through fingers,
Soon I know they won't be.

Whispered words on air,
Come to me I am lonely,
Bring memories of you to me.

Whispered words on air no longer,
Whispered words from you to me,
Whispered words not needed,
'Cause you are here with me.

Joanna Ella Clever

Granny's Tea Pot

Special things bring memories,
Like savory herbs, or fragrant teas.

Remembrances of Yesteryear.
Of hearty laugh, or weeping tear.

Of sunshine days and skinned knees.
Of watching sky, neath long tall trees.

Of picking flowers, smelling sweet;
With clover soft beneath your feet.

Such memories come back to me,
when sipping from a cup of tea.

With Granny's tea pot nestled there;
Grand and green, and looking fair.

Aged with time and steeped with love.
An ever present keeper of...

All my favorite memories,
It holds and keeps them safe for me.

Like memories in a cedar chest,
My Granny's tea pot holds the best.

Mitzi Hatch

"Confusion"

My life seems so in place
like nothing could go wrong
until I look into the face
of sorrow for too long.

I felt like nothing could stop me
like I was on top
but then I looked down
and fell like a rock.

I thought of yesterday
when every thing was so great
I wondered which path I took
that sent me the wrong way.

I wondered about happiness
and thought of how long it would last
then I felt all the confusion
and forgot about the past.

Jennifer Bennett

Temptation

Your willpower breaks down
like fire to ashes.
The flames of passion
burning up the logs of better judgement.
All hope is lost
and slowly one loses control.

Through heat and destruction,
the wood burns with corruption.
The soul has taken a different path.
No longer towards the light,
but into the infrared darkness
of temptation.

After a fire gets going,
it can turn into a blaze.
Never again will ashes be logs.
Logs never again.

Kim Gross

Fallacy

A gentle flower,
Like a rose.
With a thorn,
That gives a scar.
Looks that kill,
But beware.
Things so gentle,
Things so sweet.
May be a fallacy,
It may not be a treat.

Melissa Debies

April

A lover sent by angels
Knelt down and kissed my hand
But
No one will ever love me
A jester comes to laugh
It's gone, it's done forever
Hope is not my dance
Gone are the rays of sunshine
Behind the cloud of age
Nor will I surrender
No time my soul to waste

Loretta M. Thompson

Departure

Broken, battered, body is shattered
Life itself never mattered
Having died throughout the years
I'm worn away by my devils and fears

Broken, battered, mind is shattered
Awareness itself never mattered
Having lied throughout the years
I'm torn away from knowledge and peers

Broken, battered, soul is shattered
Belief itself never mattered
Having tried throughout the years
Worn away from the lies I hear

Broken, battered, I am shattered
Me, myself, never mattered
Having cried throughout the years
Loneliness my reward for all those tears

Jesse May

One Of A Thousand

I had a family and garden once;
    Life is a bed of roses now.

Will you recognize me?
    Will you understand this?

I walk constantly here and there
    In a surreal world of dreaming

I never truly awaken
    Surrounded by sex thugs.

I'm a subject of a cheap thrill
    When men come hooking.

My body is racked with pain
    Eased with help from drugs.

Hate, depression increase daily
    Within me towards my "MAN".

The light of hope certainly
    Has eluded me!

Come around someone soon.
    Help my friends and me!

Did you understand this?
    Have you recognized me?

Marie C. Guay

For One - Chalm

Deep black pools of sorrow speak
lies and truth entwined in wreath
Spew a light so filled with pain
a story happy it tries to feign.

Eyes of beauty eyes of charm
the ones of whom I'd hate to harm
dispel the light and put to rout
The clear murky shades of doubt.

Neil Colin D'Cunha

Love Is In The Air

Love is like a dove.
Just sitting there peacefully and
gracefully. Then you think,
how could I have been so blind.
When love is staring me right
in the eye.

Juliana Carvalho

Suspended Metamorphosis

Twilight of sleep
Kaleidoscope on the eyelids
Of loves lost
And hopes unfurled.

One sighs for sleep
And a surcease of resurrected
    images,
As flashes of light ignite the
    iris of the mind
And someone calls your name.

The little death-of-sleep
Descends in drifts to shroud
    the mind,
As dreams become reality
A breath away.

Gloria F. Ueberholz

Time

No one has the time,
Just like a shiny dime,
Time is always short.

Everyone is always in a hurry,
Sometimes it can get very blurry,
Time is always short.

The worst thing about a date,
They're always late,
Time is always short.

If everyone could slow down a little,
We could write a couple more riddles,
Time is always short.

Kenneth Hammond

The Dream

Sometimes I wish I could
just leave this place.
To be free to travel among
time and among space.

For now I'm a tree, firmly
rooted to my home.
How I wish I was that bird,
flying about and able to roam.

Or even a horse as wild as
the breeze.
Able to go and to do as
I please.

But I know, to achieve
this dream,
I must give up all that I
have, or so it would seem.

Kara Runyan

"Our Little Baby Girl"

Oh the world can be so beautiful,
It's not always cruel
Like the day you came
into our lives
our little baby girl.

How we waited long
to hold you
and call you by your name
Oh little baby Ashley
We love you more and more
each day.

Kristal M. Carter

"The Gift"

I never really knew
Just how to cry.
I didn't have any reason
I didn't know why.

I was so different
From anyone else.
Didn't have any pride
To give myself.

Then you were given to me
My angel, my friend.
You taught me to believe
You taught me to pretend.

You gave my heart a special gift
One that will last for years.
Not only did you give me love
You gave me joy, hope and tears.

I hope you never leave me
And that with you, the joy will stay.
And I pray to God that I will never
Have to wipe the tears away.

June-Marie Jones

Joy

This poem is a symbol of what is not.
It's what I once felt,
but no longer feel.
It's what I had,
but no longer have.
it's what I always searched for,
but no longer find.
It's what I talked about,
but no longer speak of.
It's what I saw,
but no longer see.
It's what I loved deeply,
but no longer loves me...
It's JOY.

Jason Pangilinan

My Imagination

What an imagination I have!
It usually is running rampant
as every time I try to get it in gear
it goes off into another direction.
It is surprising how many avenues
of thought there are to go down.
My train of thought can be triggered
to another inspiration in a twinkling
of an eye.

Calm is not a word in my vocabulary.
irrationality is more like it.
Concentration is a rarity.

I try not to bruise my sensibilities,
so I become tolerant and except
the inevitable.

I have no agenda with which to glean
knowledge,
so I just use my imagination.
Is it a gift or not?

Marolyn E. Baker

Lonely Face

You came to me when I was in need.
It surprised me,
I had never cared about you.

I wondered what you wanted with me.
I'd never done anything for you.
You were nothing to me but a lonely face.

You come to me out of the rain,
Searching for a friend,
I never gave my friendship to you.

You taught me to love.
I loved everyone.
Everyone but you.

And yet you still came,
You still asked,
You still loved.

Morley Lewallen

Friendship

A rose is like two people's friendship,
It starts out as a bud,
It grows big and beautiful,
Just because of water and mud.
That part if just like friendship,
You need two people for it to grow,
Water is one and mud is the other,
And the friendship shall freely flow!

If you don't water the flower,
The rose will wilt away,
Meaning if one person leaves,
Then only one person will stay.
But if the water comes back again,
The rose will grow some more,
So if water and mud stay together,
Our friendship will not be a bore!

Krista C. Kinkade

"Don't Wanna Fall"

Why are you so sweet?
It makes it hard to stay away.
I don't feel like fallin' in love.
But I can only go your way.

You pull me in
And I look in your eyes.
I drown in that color
You could never disguise.

I don't wanna fall in love.
I try to stay away.
I don't wanna fall in love.
I can't stand to play this game.

You make me feel
So needed and loved.
You take away my worries
By the feel of your touch.

The warmth in your smile
Makes my heart beat fast.
But I say to myself.
This could never last.

Karen Pierce

It Happens

Now and then, not very often
It happens once in a while
Perhaps once in a lifetime
Your path crosses another
A very special kind of person!

Like a gorgeous autumn sunset
Or a brilliant spring sunrise
A cool breeze in the summer sun
Or a sparkling brook in a desert
This person makes a difference!

Now and then it happens
There is that sunrise, that sunset
The rainbow after the storm appears
The cool breeze in the summer sun blows
That brook in the desert sparkles.

Yes, paths cross - people meet
Lives are touched, spirits are lifted
It suddenly happens - once in a while
I am glad your path crossed mine
It happens - it happened then!

Monroe C. Good

"The Coast"

Feel the cool, soothing breeze as
   it flows gently down your back.
Smell the salty air while slowly
   breathing in.
Grab the warm, soft sand and
   watch it eagerly run out
   of your fingers.
Watch the soaring seagulls as
   they become one with the wind.
Taste the ripe, juicy pineapple as
   it gently flows down your throat.
Take the sweet smelling lotion in
   your hand and rub it all over
   your soft, sensitive body.
Just another day at the coast.

Melissa McDorman

Kevin

A mother's love knows no boundaries
It doesn't come to an end
To be there for you,
To help you fight
Also be your friend
I love you always with all my heart
You are my son, the only one
I thought we'd never part
I try to see the good in this
Forgive me if I don't.
A mother's soul can find no sense
Or she simply won't
Trying to grasp the heartache
Of you not being here today
I watched you come into my life
And watched you fade away
Every mornin' hereafter
Will bring me a new dawn
To be able to live my life
Knowing your soul lives on.

Melissa Cottingham

Love

Love can't be earned,
It can't be neglected.

Love is a feeling

You can't own it,
Or hurt it.

Though you may
feel it, but don't
worry, nor fear, it will
   make you happy

Lacie Stanley

Secrets

   Come with me to the secrets
of my love,
   Open your mind in a new
direction.
   You will feel the secret love.
   Your heart won't be a lonely
heart all alone.
   Just come and see the magic
that I bring.
   Come into the light,
   Don't be afraid open your
eyes.
   I'm not going to play those stinking games.
   Think of a romantic summer nights
   Think of a me whispering
sweet things in your ear.
   Come with me to a place
where we can be alone
   And cherish the night
Like there's no tomorrow.

Trisha M. Hanel

An Ode To Cats

There was a young maid who had two cats
   one was Spits and the other Spats.
Now Spit did spit and Spat did spat,
   what a name for two miserable cats!
If Spit does spit and Spat does spat
   what would you name a thousand cats?
Well, there would be Spits and Spats,
   Dits and Dats, Pits and Pats, Ritz and Ratz
Rats? What a name for a miserable cat!
   Bits and Bats, Hits and Hats
Glory Be! I'm going bats!
   Rose and Toes, Short and Nose,
One Ear and Two, White and Red.
   That enough..........I'm going to bed!

Paul Cornish

Daddy

Daddy, when I was born
   you were there and I cried
Daddy, when I got hurt
   you were there and I cried
Daddy, when you died,
   I was there, and I cried.

Catherine Mayo

Untitled

You made me laugh,
you made me cry,
sometimes I wish we didn't have to
say goodbye, although I don't know
why God has picked you, you
were so special to those
who knew you.
   If you were so good and
carefree, why did he take
you away from me I miss
you so dearly, wishing
you were still here my love is not
gone and will always be near
   If I were to see you one
last time how happy I
would be knowing that
you'll always be with me.

Barbara Alessi

Secrets

   Some secrets may hurt
you if you keep them too long.
   Secrets could hurt the
people they are about.
   Secrets can break up
friendships.
   Secrets can never end.
   Secrets are always supposed
to be kept.
   But secrets are never
kept so the person the secret
is about gets hurt the most.

Bobbi Collins

A Sound Of Desolation

The hummingbirds,
You have seen them fly,
Their wings a blur of motion.
The only sound a quiet whir.
Have you ever heard them cry?
They are crying now.
Their homes are gone.
They built them in the tall green firs.
Yesterday the chain saw felled them.

Anna Lowe Rishel

Parents

You love them,
you hate them.

They gave you life,
they gave you rules.

You despise their authority,
they despise your ignorance.

They gave you love,
you gave them hope.

They grew old,
you grew up.

Friends at last,
friends to late.

Cherish the moments,
accept the pain,
deal with the differences.

Don't let life slip away without
enjoying the beauty of love.

Alyson Dahlby

My Respect For Others

Meanwhile across the world, destruction leaves many people in fear
Youths today are dying, and I'm trying to hold in my tears

Ravishing thoughts come to mind to help world peace
Especially when it's my family that's becoming the deceased
Spending time with the family or someone in need
Preparing for the future but taking it step by step in the present indeed
Every time I look at the news crime takes place
Communicate with each other and let's bring a smile to a face
Today there's war but tomorrow there will be no race

Forgive sinners because everybody plays their part.
Only if we take time to listen, not only with our ears, but with our heart
Really this world can be better, we just need to think smart

Over look those who say you'll never make it in life
Turn to God for advice, and don't pick up a gun and a knife
Help those who need to be helped, and you will learn
Enjoying the love that you will receive from others in return
Realize what I'm saying my sisters, and brothers
Showing you that I care, because I have "My Respect For Others."

Travas D. Binion

I Realized

I see you all the time
You're like my prince charming in disguise
It wasn't love at first sight,
But as time went by,
I realized
You're so sweet and sensitive
Yet you have a great sense of humor
You're everything I've ever dreamed of
If only I could find some way to tell you
When you're near me,
I can feel the love
I can see it in your eyes,
And in your movements
I can hear it in your voice
Do you feel the way I feel
I've never been as happy as I am now
You're like an angel sent from above
There is no greater love,
Than the love I feel for you
If only I could find some way to tell you.

Therese Cronin

The Battle

The battle begins every time you awake
Your souls destination is always at stake
Your weaknesses perceived by Satan's delight
He sits on his throne with you in sight
Attack, he commands, to his angels of dark
The scent of concession my nostrils do hark
Without any word or warning to heed
He's after you now with Hell-risen speed
Desires unending are thrown in your face
The offer of power is yours to embrace
You feel the pull of the world to have and to own
The feelings are spurned and from evil grown
Weaken yourself not to this plight
Prepare yourself to fight the good fight
Protected with the armor of God's unyielding love
Armed with the blood of Christ from above
From you old devil I don't like what I've seen
I cast you out of my life in the name of the Nazarene.

Philip F. Kowalske

Slipping

Inside I feel so lonely, such sadness, I crave
your love, the new love, the love of love, the
kind of love we first had. It all seems to have
slipped away, like money slipping through our
fingers, water running down the drain. Somehow
we take all of these for granted. I sit wondering
if it will ever be——be the way it was in the
beginning, love all so new, all so fresh, searching
one another with loving eyes and wondering hands
both so curious to know one another, and both so
willing to give everything.
    Love for granted,
       love so lonely,
          no longer new,
             just waiting and wondering....

Juandah J. Westby

A Daughter's Love

No matter what I do
    Your love continue to show through
There's always truth in what you said
    You've seen the games that people play
Nothing could ever keep us apart
    Because of the love within our hearts

Although we may not be alike
    A daughter's love never goes on strike
Mom you are the very best
    And so much unlike the rest
Don't eve doubt my love for you
    For nobody else's love could be more true

For I'll always be here
    So loneliness your never have to fear
Through the touch of our hard
    We'll share what only mothers and daughters understand
And through thick and thin
    Mom our love will always win.

Toni Robinson

"You Were Never There!"

You were never there when I needed thee.
You were never there since I was three.

You were never there when I came back here.
You were never there to wipe away my fears.

You were never there when I started kinder
school, You were never there during elementary
school, You were never there when I needed you.

You were never there when I got sick, You
were never there when I played my first trick.

You were never there when I rode my first
bike, You were never there when I bowled my first strike.

You were never there when I started swim
team, You were never there when I wanted to scream.

You were never there when I wanted to play
football, You were never there when I took my big
fall and was in the hospital.
"You were never there!"

Theresa M. Price

A Poem For Meme

You were the greatest woman I ever knew.
You were my inspiration, my friend, and confidant.
There weren't words enough to express my love
and gratitude towards you.
You were always there for me.
Some showed pity towards your situation, I on the
other hand, showed you the love and respect you needed.
And in return I received your love and companionship.
You shared your deepest feelings and darkest secrets with me.
You told me stories of your life that I will hold dearly
in my heart forever.
And although you are no longer with me; I can still
feel your presence and protection around me.
I can still feel your love and great compassion for me.
And most of all, I cherish the memories and the laughs
that we shared together.
And I in turn will pass them onto my children one day
and hope they will get a chance to have what I had with you.

Sarah Carrillo

Best Friends Forever

You were here when I was happy
You were here when I was sad.
We have shared so many memories
We have laughed, cried, and enjoyed the best times.
We will always treasure our times together
We will always be best friends forever

Valerie Cara Webb

'Gotta Believe'

You hear the hip-hop,
You see the tip-top,
You want to get there,
But you don't know how.

You gotta believe in yourself first,
Believe in others, second to none.
You can't have slack.
Only after two steps forward can you take one back.

You gotta believe in yourself first.
Before you even try,
To touch the sky when you fly.
If you want to go that high.

You gotta believe in yourself first,
Because you gotta know where you're going,
As well as where you've been.
You gotta believe.

Rebecca Gagnon

Precious One, Oh Precious One

To My Gift, To My Daughter - Tiffany Re'nee Hicks
Precious One, oh Precious One, how I love you Precious One. I knew
You from your beginning. You gave me a new start, you gave me a
Peek at what a miracle looks like. Through your eyes I took a glimpse
At Heaven. I saw the purity of what God meant when he created us.

Precious One, oh Precious One, how I love you Precious One. You are
The one who sees all my weaknesses and faults and loves me with a love
That only a child could have. Precious One, oh Precious One, how I
Love you Precious One. You are my gift from God, my link to the
Next generation. You are my Daughter, my Child, my Friend. Precious
One, oh Precious One, how I love you Precious One.

I hope I have instilled in you the things that matter most in life.
Things like Love, Kindness, Long-suffering, Commitment and Honesty.
Precious One, oh Precious One, how I love you Precious One.
You are my gift from God, you are my Daughter.

L. A. Matthews-Hicks

Richard

I looked into your eye.
You said, "I'm going to die."

My heart broke.
I felt a lump in my throat.

I wanted to run from the room screaming.
Instead I watched the wan-ton soup steaming.

You asked me to let you go.
I said to myself, "How! I do not know."

I asked you if you had given up.
You said of this illness, "I've had enough."

"This is not living," you said.
As you took the 10th pill that was Red.

You told me things that day that have come to pass.
How did you know life as I knew it couldn't last?

I still miss you every day of my life,
but I think I have become a pretty good mother and wife.

If my last daughter had been a son,
Richard's what I'd have named her, but then there's only one.

Peggy W. Bressman

Lady In Blue

"Little girl," she called me. I'd be soon forty-nine.
"You remind me," she continued, "of a daughter of mine.
I haven't seen her now in almost a year."
Her soft voice trembled, and she blotted a tear.
She said, "she lives miles away and works a job yet
and when kids get busy, they tend to forget.
I have two sons and a daughter. My husband, John died."
Mentioning his name, she broke down and cried.
-Explaining, "excuse my bad manners, please come and sit."
Then... "I guess when I get to talking, I can't seem to quit."
Her worn hands lay idle against a neat pale blue dress.
She'd given most of her life to her family, I guess.
"Time was, I was busy," she smiled, reminiscing.
"I was surrounded by laughter, and hugging and kissing..."
Wise dark eyes contrasted with hair white as snow.
She talked like she knew me, and I couldn't just go.
Why I was drawn there that day I can't quite construe.
Or why I been captured by the lady in blue.
But since I became friends with the nursing home greeter,
my pace is much slower, and the roses smell sweeter.

Ruth Vaughan-Scearce

Please Stay

I was lonely and cold when you came into my life
You opened the doors so I could see out
Now day is clear and night is right with you by my side,
    leading me on into the world
You took my loneliness and emptiness away and filled it
    with joy and happiness
Now I'm happy, I can see day clearly and not through a
    teardrop
I'm not so cold and lonely at night
Why...because you came and opened my eyes and doors
    to my life
I love you please don't go.

Shonda Cinelli

Ole Porch Swing

One cold winter night in December,
you lead me to that ole porch swing.

The trees were naked then,
and the wind all cold and bitter.

The wind pressed against my face,
so you pulled me closer.

From beneath your jacket came a small package,
all beautifully wrapped with care.

I opened that little box and there it sat,
all shiny and sparkling new,
a little gift that said I belong to you.

Perfectly round in shape,
and how it shined of gold.

I love you my little bumble bee,
that pink heart seemed to say to me.

That night I shall never forget,
when I opened that blue jewel box.

As you held me so tight and close,
on that ole porch swing.

Tina Louise Harrell

Dear Mom

It seems as if just yesterday you held me in your arms
You held me close protecting me from all the earthly harms,

It seems as if just yesterday I knelt beside your chair
You spoke of the Lord's mother and taught me the Lord's prayer

It seems as if just yesterday
You sent me off to school
I missed you so, I cried that day
I had to sit on the dunces stool

It seems as if just yesterday
That I was twenty-one
You and dad gave me a car, dear
So many things you've done

It seems as if just yesterday
I sailed for over seas
Oh how I wish for days gone by
Just a child upon your knees

Dear mom there's no repaying you
For your mother love and care
But I can say with all my heart
I love you mother dear.

Victor E. Cordone

My Mother, My Friend

You gave me the most precious gift, that one person can give another.
You gave me life, you became my mother.

I was your first, so tiny and frail.
How scared you must have been, the first time you heard me wail.

You guided me through school, and walked me down the aisle.
You're always there when I need you, no matter how far the mile.

You hold a special place, within my heart.
I love our time together, and hate the time apart.

You're the most caring and loving person, one could ever hope to find.
You give so much of yourself, you're one of a kind.

I know this isn't much, but these words from my heart I send.
For you're the best, My mother, my friend.

Trish McCloud

Untitled

Without just cause
You have made up your mind
Although you can see
You're still blind
I may not be like you
But I do exist I am a person
An individual with just as much right
To be as you
And even though you grieve
At the thought I am here I am

I am here but you can't see me
I am real but you can't touch me
I am person a concept you don't believe
I have feelings even though there hidden deep
I am alive living for a purpose

Doesn't matter if you agree
You're no better than me
And however you deny
Or turn your back on be
I will still me

C. Wells

Be Yourself

Always be yourself there shouldn't be anyone else you'd rather be,
You are special can't you see.
Maybe you inherited your parents' or grandparents' hair, eyes or more,
But you are not destined to become anyone who came before.
You do not have to be like your parents nor your grandparents on either side.
Make your own choices, but make them wise.
If you want to inherit something-inherit a temperate will,
Inherit reasoning for thinking you can do anything when applying
strength and skill.
Be yourself and with wisdom do resign,
To daily respect, nurture and love the body you call mine.

Always be yourself as time goes by,
You will be with yourself until the day you die.
Have faith in yourself it will help to make you strong,
And give yourself a smile of understanding when things go wrong.
You have the ability to reach for the stars so high,
Believing the sky is your limit without a sigh.
There are people with faults that could cause self-blame,
Accept yourself as you are whether others do the same.
Be yourself and keep a loving heart. You'll know,
That, the feeling of being yourself is sure to always show.

Thelma D. Rogers

Friendship

A friend is a person you hold dear to your heart, with memories of
  yester-year;
A friend is a shoulder to cry on, when you feel like shedding a tear.

A friend is a person to talk to, when the load seems to heavy to bear;
A friend is the one you rely on, when no one else seems to bother to care.

A friend can be asked a favor, and expect nothing in return;
A friend is one who shows patience, kindness, consideration, concern.

It takes a lot to make a friend, and be a good friend too;
And importance isn't on how you met, or where you met...it's who.

A friend is a friend, because your a friend,
And you share in taking and giving;

And if when I die, I have One Good Friend,
I'll know that my life was worth living.

Patsy D. Richou

The Labyrinth

It began slowly in my deepest sleep, places I had been, rendezvous
Yet to keep and in the morning all but bits and pieces forgotten

Dark by ways in memory dwell, shadowed lanes remembered well and
Though I was never there, I am never quite able to leave

Mental telepathy, reincarnation, deja vu, another's thoughts
Creeping through, then again maybe just something I read

More vivid and explicit each dream became, different and yet some
How just the same, as morning's light played tag with my mind

Waken hours spent in dread of sleep, terrified of appointments yet to
Keep, drawn deeper into places within my self I did not wish to go

But as morning memories progressed, time spent in sleep less and less,
And so with bottle and books I drift like a mist through the night

Then sleep comes with mornings sun and still terrors gauntlet yet
To run, I am again going back and forwards at the same time

Dark places, white fears torment my soul, plunging me again out of
Control, reality defied, as I again experience all of the senses

And yet concentrating with all my might, I can not stay the coming of
Night, when I again succumb to the shadows of the sun and my own mind

So surrender would be as natural as breath, the transition, more like
Life than death and then the fear and pain would come no more

G. Gene Gibbs

Shadows

Shadows are fun,
Yet plain as can be,
They are only around for a short time,
And yet always seem free.
The sun is what makes them, the clouds destroy.

Shadows are everywhere,
You can't always see them,
But they are there.
Shadows are what make the light, dark.

Everything has one, but not all the time,
Only when the sun is on one side.

Some people's shadows are their best friends,
And yet others seem scared of them.

It's fun to make puppets on the wall,
And to see everyone's shadows in the hall.

When you play games, your shadow plays too.
And you know what...
    ...Your shadow loves you!

To conclude this poem, I'd like to say;
See if your shadow is visiting you today.

Sarah Dorr

The Great Unknown

You are an Angel of the fourth dimension
yet part of you is within me.
We are all spirits which have reached
different realms of life.
You are a spark of knowledge
shining in the dark tunnel of mystery.
The great unknown, yet you know.
We will all be there, someday.
Yet we must remember what we know
and truly believe what we believe.
We must search for the truth and let it guide us.
This starts the journey of life,
the journey of life to the great unknown.

Rainbow Weldon

What Is Love?

Love is not always fireworks and rainbows
Yet love is always fire and rain
Love is not always being there with you
Yet love is being there for you
Love is not always feelings of passion
Yet love is the passion driving you
Love is not always to know where you're going
Yet love knows of only one direction
Love is not always a feeling of security
Yet having love is comforting
Love is not always knowing what love is
Nor is it knowing what it's not
The one thing about love that is always strong
Is the suffering inside when love is gone.

Robin Lynn Perrett

Face To Face......

I have a God who brings life from the smallest seed
Yet cares enough to meet my every need.

I have a God who sees each sparrow fall
Yet loves me more and hears each time I call

I have a God who wipes away my tears
And always stands beside me through my fears

I have a God who bore my sin and shame
That I might bear His name

Because my earthly eyes are growing dim
I have a God that bids me come to Him

No other love has ever claimed my heart
The way His love has won me from the start

So having run my best in this tough race
At last I shall behold Him face to face.

E. Marilyn Cobb

Praise The Lord! Cade Did Make It To His First Birthday!

Yes, you are my little one.
Yes, you are my only son.
Yes, I love you - always will.
Yes, with pride my heart you fill.

Such a good baby - you are.
Yes, you are my shining star.
Mommy loves you very much -
with your smile my soul you touch.

I adore you - yes I do!
Cherish you and need you too.
You're my baby dressed in blue -
Yes you are my dream come true.

Never thought I'd see this day.
Never thought I'd feel this way.
I love you - I really do.
Don't want to let go of you.

You've been through a lot this year.
Through it all - you showed no fear.
Angels watch you where you go.
Jesus saved you - this I know.

Vicki Dokken

"Lost"

My thoughts wonder through the
years...
Wondering what I've done...
Where I've been and....where am I going...

Through the 60's and 70's all of us
were trying to find ourselves with pills,
booze, and dope...

Does anyone ever find themselves!
Or does someone find them?
If your lost along the way...
And no one finds you...
Where are you today?
Is it war or peace or love?
I'm lost because I've lost my love,
my peace, my pride...
And maybe soon, my war...
Is war always bloodshed?
Will I ever know!??

Sandra Oligney

Learning Disabled

Reality, a looking-glass world.
Words tumble out backwards and upside-down,
numbers jump out of place,
too many sounds,
Time doesn't exist
and confusion reigns supreme.

Susan Pollard

Broken Heart

She sits outside and stares up at the stars
Wondering how long they will have to be apart
She watches and waits but still no answer
She wonders will there ever be an answer
Frightened and confused she slowly moves away
Holding her teddy bear wishing he could stay
Hoping one day things will soon be okay
As she wipes her tears she kneels down to pray
Slowly getting up, gazing at the stars
Wondering if now her healing will start
Burdened with thoughts upsetting her more
As she sleeps she dreams about it some more
Morning comes and it's a beautiful day
Hoping to start off in a better way.

Tracy Quarto

"My Grandmother"

An old woman sits and stares,
wondering and pondering if anyone still cares.
Whatever happened to her days of youth;
Whatever happened to honesty and truth.
Time slips by like sand between your hands.
If only we could slow it down, but she knows no one can.
The memories are all that's left to savior.
The laughter of her babies and the love that never wavers.
She can always slip into the past and forget about her pain.
She can always close her eyes and wish those days remained.
But they are long gone and so are most of her friends;
so it would really be better if this present life could end.
To go to a place where there's no sorrow or goodbyes.
just warm, familiar faces singing in the clouds up high.
So do not feel sad when you see her staring into space,
She's not far from heaven and that will be a wonderful place

Sandra Costa

Grace Within The Beast

When the sun sets the tiger becomes the beast.
With its power and speed the tiger is the prince of all animals,
its fangs like daggers, its claws like razors.
The sleek tiger runs wildly, but still with much grace.
Emotionally I run with the tiger, but physically I wouldn't dare.
When the sun rises I feel the energy the tiger is receiving.
Its intense eyes follow me every where,
and its stripes are all around.
The tiger is the grace within the beast.
Even when there is no tiger its eyes will still follow me
and its stripes will be all around.
And it still will be the grace within the beast.

Rex McPheeters

Niagara Falls

I love Niagara Falls;
With its cascading walls;

Of endless water; falling and tumbling, as it
Leaves the ground;
Crashing and splashing on its way down;

Causing, a steady rumbling sound;
That seems to be coming, from under ground;

Where the water, meets the rocks below;
Lost in the mist and the water flow;

Causing, a mighty undertow;
Where people, are encouraged, not to go!

Cause if they do, they'll never know;
Twisting and tumbling with the flow;

How far they've traveled;
As their life unraveled;

Under the foam, beneath the mist;
Another name, to put on the list;

Of those who tried;
And those who died!

Robert E. Filip

Discover The U.S.A.

My country's land is big and bold,
With climates ranging from warm to cold.
My country's land is said to be,
A land that everyone dreams to see.

I take this land for granted by far.
But as we sit in our little white car,
My family realizes, with much surprise,
What, for years, has been before our eyes.

People of different cultures and races,
People with different shapes and faces.
People of different ages and sizes,
People who's languages hold some surprises.

Landforms, colorful and vast,
Holding memories, forever to last.
National and state parks for fun,
With continuous laughter 'til the day is done.

My country is a place I love,
With the Bald Eagle soaring above.
I would accept no other land,
But this, of mountains, valleys, trees, and sand.

Sara Casper

Cheer Up

You stand proud, never swayed
Wishing you could die as your heart breaks
When all you ever wanted
Just isn't enough
And all you ever had
Simply turns to dust
Like memories of foreign time
Sweet nectar on your lips
And now you live in misery
As joy from your grasp slips

Oh, my immortal, wondrous friend
Don't you know that you are gave me the world,
That I'm trying to give it back to you
Love is not dead! I still love you my sweetest friend
The world is dancing, the birds are singing
"The world is dying" — Open your eyes
The world is changing
For the better? For the worse? We won't be around to see it
But we have now, and
Forever. Stay with me then

E. J. Finizio

August Pantoum

Listen to the locust's calling buzz,
wipe your brow and sit here in the shade.
The burning sun has turned the grass to fuzz;
relax and I shall fix you lemonade.

Wipe your brow and sit here in the shade,
it's hot enough to cause your toes to curl.
Relax and I shall fix you lemonade,
turn on the sprinkler, watch the rainbow swirl.

It's hot enough to cause your toes to curl,
with no end to shim'ring heat in sight.
Turn on the sprinkler, watch the rainbow swirl
let its hypnotic colors put the fire to flight.

With no end to shim'ring heat in sight
the sound of water playing cools the skin.
Let its hypnotic colors put the fire to flight
until the dark'ning clouds start moving in.

The sound of water playing cools the skin;
when burning sun has turned the grass to fuzz.
Until the clouds of rain start moving in,
lie back and listen to the locusts buzz.

Treva Myatt

"Noble Colors"

I have always wondered why, when I look up at the sky,
Why God spawned across the heavens,
The color white, blue and gray, in such a beautiful, gorgeous array.

One might say they are a splendid combination
Others may think white, blue and gray are a figure of imagination
But whatever they are,
The colors in the sky are so intriguing and fascinating
To lots of people who agree, unequivocally.

The color white could suggest or reflect a mirror
   of cleanliness and purity
Royalty and unique beauty
While the blue resembles serenity and clearness of thought,
Like in a running brook.
And the gray denotes boldness, and sometimes a somber look.

The colors are such an outstanding display of art,
Made I believe never to depart.
The colors in the sky, white, blue and gray are distinctive selections
Given to the world.
With touches of superb and elegant perfections.

Sadie F. Melson

Why?

Why do I fall in love, but only to get hurt?
Why do I fall so hard, but only to land in the dirt?
Why do birds sing so cheerful every day?
Why do they not divorce, when their mates go astray?

It's really not in me to do a dirty deed, I'm always with
Open arms, to help someone in need..
So if you see me with a tear, falling from my eye..
The hurt and pain will soon surpass, and again I'll ask
Myself - why?

Robert Lee Richardson Sr.

The Writers Of My Play

Who are the writers of my play? Where did they come from?
Why are they here?
They are the people of my shadow; raising me each day.
They have that special role to play.
They're behind the curtains rooting me on.
Through the good times and the bad.
For I am a person who doesn't know the good times that I've had.
The costumes, the jewelry, the play make up.
These things are given out of love and joy to make
   The play just right.
Then comes the opening night....
Things go perfect, everything is in place.
Can you see their smiling faces?
They're so proud to see what I've accomplished.
But aren't willing to take the credit.
I love these two forgotten people..the writers of my play.
Then comes the day when I leave them, leaving the stage behind.
But we'll always have the memories. The good times and the bad.
So I stand up now as the audience and applaud my
   MOM and DAD!!

Tricia Lynn Boyd

The Dream Of My Song

Who will dance for me now,
Who will feel my tears,
How will my tender caress smooth away the fears?
When the bright dawn has burst forth how can I let you know
I still feel the magnificence
Of each irradiating glow?
As the days grow into years, and the time becomes before,
I'll reach into your mirrored mind to feel your inner core -
You'll see the shimmered sunset on a frozen lake beyond,
You'll smell the sweet wet forest and enter the dream of my song
My wings upon your cheek as I flow above the day,
And what lay below the soil will never taste the clay -
But,
Who will dance for me now,
Who will feel my tears,
How will my tender caress smooth away the fears?
When the bright dawn has burst forth how can I let you know
I still feel the magnificence
Of each irradiating glow?

Susan I. Reading

A Beautiful Mother

This is a tale of a very sweet lady
Who raised her family when things were so shady
A son I am, one of two,
Girls, there are seven, beautiful too
My mother was proud and when things get bad
She would just smile and say
"Don't be so sad". No matter
How bad things get they always get better
For that we were blessed
With a beautiful mother

Steve Trump

Awake

Once a peaceful country and people who really cared;
Who lived in close harmony and gave a friendly wave, not stare.

There was no fear of being taken or sued for a friendly hand;
Responsibility and honesty were the code that ruled the land.

Our children and the women folk could walk, without a fear;
An attack on a child or elder, was a thing that no one dared.

In that time the only need for law, meant a truant or town drunk;
A deep respect for authority with home and church, our trunk.

Where it has it gone, I heard the cry, was all we had a dream?
My nightmare kept getting worse and I heard the people scream.

Our land now ruled in fear and dread, of people gone in mind;
The radicals and terrorist spreading pain to all mankind.

Each willing for the sake of hate, to turn life and earth to sand;
Is this the hell we learned of, beyond the land of man?

Is this a sample of life to come and a warning from with-in;
Awake, awake, let this dream depart, let the light return again.

I pray, this nightmare now be gone, for all of man-kind's sake;
Please wake us from this nightmare; Awake - Awake - Awake.

Paul Rickman

Answers In The Ocean

Looking upon the sunset as I told it my dreams.
  Whispering aloud problems for the winds to answer me.
Warm breezes surround me and hold me so tight,
  as tears tremble down upon my cheeks in fright.
I ask the ocean for answers, but it goes on its own way.
  Until finally I break free from the wind's strong brace.
As seagulls fly freely high above me,
  I run free, run free, down by the sea.

Patricia Morin

"The Sun's Daily Chore"

The sun peers out of the clouds reluctantly,
Whisking away the darkness very slowly.
The black night fades away and disappears.
Its silence isn't heard by any ears.
The sun sheds its light down on earth,
And to another day it imparts birth.
The cool morning air had come upon this alteration,
It is today's revelation.

When the day advances towards a conclusion,
The sun retreats into seclusion.
It escapes into the clouds.
Then the dark night overcrowds.
The sun will shine again day after day,
After the dark gloomy night fades away.

Raymond Worob

Her Lover

She moves through waves as yet unscathed a mighty boat is she
While others fall and others rise and repent tales and lengthy lies
Among the white capped sea of green she stands a mighty boat pristine
The sun hits hull of blue and white it is austere a regal sight
A uniformed soldier at attention all dressed for parade in its dimension
The polished teak atop the hull must be the bright work to envy all
The ropes are wrapped with proper knot round shining cleats on this fine yacht
Mahogany wraps her in its color seagulls pass and do not bother
To light upon this well made craft with proud flags flown bow to aft
'68 was her production I am obsessed with her seduction
So anchored in my heart this boat all warm with wood and varnished coat
She'll stand in silent water deep and I will be her watchful keep
'Til age has crept into my bones and once more she is left alone
I fancy she will trap another to varnish deck and be her lover.

Terrie A. Kizer

Paradox

A linear circle or a circular line
whichever it cares to be called
there's no real contradiction in terms
and who is to say
but that a line may be part of a circle
an infinitesimal part
just as the finite is of infinity?

And the world flows and changes
while man tries to grasp and hold
he tries to understand and rule
but such is not its nature
and the world continues to flow

And if this is line
where, what is the circle?
it is there flowing and existing all the same
we call it Paradox.

C. J. Smith

Knights Of Chautauqua

I wake to the sound of the fluttering thump,
Which pulls me from dreams and my dance with the dark.

I roll to the edge of the bed with a stretch
And release the sash for a winged depart.

From my part-time summertime sleep filled
Memory chamber, I remember those nights with wings;

Years of visits from shadows losing their way
To the wrong side of the dark side of the eave.

Now I lay between sentiment scented sheets
And listen to ghosts of those soldiers of night.

The dark sky has changed despite persistent defense,
As our army of shadows departs.

Coming back to this room that still echoes with flight,
I release thoughts to the backs of those wings;

And hope returns to what awareness can bring
And those fluttering thump-filled nights without dreams.

Terri Winters

"What We See"

Everyone can see
Whether they use their eyes or not
Some people can see no further than a pea,
Yet others can see farther than the sea.
But who sees what, that I can't say
But one thing I do know is that no one can see
What's inside of me!!!

People see only what their minds allow
And to those who understand, I give them a bow.
Is a mind weak or is it strong?
For that knowledge I do long!
One thing I do know, is that no one can see, what I see
And nor can they see what's inside of me!

I see a vision that no other can see
For what I see is inside of me.
My vision so rare,
That I wouldn't dare
To look into the eyes, that give the cold stare!!!

Valerie Jimenez

197

Song Of Nature

I have a special garden spot,
Wherein I planted all the seeds I bought.
Soon the seeds do show their heads,
Flowers, veggies, sprouting from their beds.
Like overnight they are in bloom
Wishing they just had more room.
Tenderly I care for them each day,
As they grow and glow in the warmth of May.
Visited often by birds and bees,
Gathering nectar, spreading pollen with ease.
From tree to tree there's a nest of a bird,
As hatchlings grow - more songs to be heard.
When in need of a little breather,
I watch the birds come to my feeder.
The summer sun and soil below
Help all plants to grow and grow.
Soon it's time to collect the treasure
Nature has given me in full measure.
As the last leaf dances in the winter breeze,
Spring, summer, autumn colors are lasting memories.

Petryna K. Pinkert

Far Away Places

"I would like to travel to a far away place,
where people would always have a smile on their face."
A place where people didn't care about color or race.
A place where the flower's never die, and there
is always a clear blue sky.
"I would like to be in a land, where birds sweet
songs filled the air, and all the colors
of the rainbow would be there."
"I, would like to be in a land white and clean,
where all the stars of the galaxy could be seen."
"If I could travel to such a place,
I know I would always have a smile on my face."

Sharon A. Gregory

In God We Trust

Whatever happened to prayer in our schools?
Where our children were taught the Golden Rule,
And pledging allegiance to the flag was a must.
Whatever happened to, "In God We Trust?"

Our country is at war with those overseas,
Because our presidents are not on their knees.
Our country is full of hate, violence, and lust,
Whatever happened to, "In God We Trust?"

Gangs are slowly ruling the world,
Recruiting every man, woman, boy and girl.
Police, everyday, are doing drug busts!
Whatever happened to, "In God We Trust?"

Innocence, kindness, happiness...are of the past.
Our future generation is almost to the last.
All preachers are reciting.
"From ashes-to-ashes; form dust-to-dust",
Whatever happened to, "In God We Trust?"

Tonya N. Alexander

Dreams

Such scary things, these dreams. They come to you as you sleep and
when you awaken during the night they seem so real and sometimes so
very frightening. When you awaken the next morning they are nothing
more than a distant memory. By mid-day they fade into nothingness
and it's hard to recall the thing that frightened you so deeply. Soon
it doesn't exist at all. It's like a fog in the morning. As the sun
moves through the day it fades and disappears, leaving no trace. As
night falls once more we return to our slumber and once again we dream.
To be set free by flight or love or to be frightened by death or such
evil that only in sleep can it possibly exist. Such scary things these dreams.

Tammara Kay Waldon

"I Love Watching Her Eyes"

I love watching her eyes from the separation
where does she go when her eyes glaze over like that
she tries to speak but no words make it out
I will do the talking
I can talk for days, it is at times like this
when she does not mind
a mile a minute baby, a mile a minute my mouth can not
keep up with the dialogue each time the conversation starts anew
the topic is exploration every time once the topic gets interesting
I stick around to see how far I can penetrate her mind
every time all of those times her eyes always remain the same
always lost in the excitemenT.

Paul C. Gamble

Full Moon Night

Alone I stand, deep within my spirit cries.
Where did they all go? Water weights my eyes-
Frightened my foreign heart flies,
High above to the pure even skies.

I awake to stop and listen-
Do you feel as I do?

The mighty rumbles with static flow,
And whispering pines the bird's echo,
The crash of water blends, and then it goes;
Until forever, God only knows.

This love of mine grows strong with time;
Then time stops, till it bursts,
Maybe it's still a dream, but it hurts.

A weary fascination my spirit rests,
And then it blends, and bounds a step.

This life inside thy wonder rides,
Outside ourselves our fate collides,
Then of ourselves our form resides-
Without this love, all hope has died.

William John Sullivan

Love It Is

Love it is
When your mind is thinking always of

Love it is
When your heart is being so true

Love it is
When your feelings are flying high in the sky like a dove

Love it is
When your happiness is much apparent you see no blue

Love it is
When your given the sense of forever from above

Love it is
When your troubles of the past helped you two grew

Love it is
Yes, that is most indeed when love it is.

Russ Bitely

The Pathway

There's a lonely little pathway where your footsteps wander often,
When my daydreams draw me gently from the busy world apart,
But you never walk alone, for I am everywhere about you,
And your presence sanctifies the secret places of my heart.

Ronald A. Murch

"Thinking Of You"

Thinking of you all the time
when you always come to mind,
Thinking of you when your spirit is low
so the flames in your life can begin to blow,
Thinking of you in your darkest hours
To make you happy, I'll give you a flower,
Thinking of you in your happy days
Even deep inside you may have selfish ways,
Thinking of you when a love one floated away
To knowing there's always a better day,
I'm thinking of you right now
without making a single sound.

Shica Tuttle

Keep Looking For Tomorrow

Some days seem the darkest
When the trials o'er us pour,
And when we feel the cup is brimmed
And we can take no more.

But Jesus knows how much we hurt
Our pain and all our sorrow,
But then He tells us it won't last
Keep looking for tomorrow.

Our Lord will speak to each of us
And answer every why,
To the question asked while here on earth
Why did our loved ones die.

But when He tell us we will smile
And praise Him day and night
Because we'll see our Saviour's love
And know that he was right

So don't lose sight when the trails come
And you're filled with so much sorrow,
Just trust in God and lean on Him
And keep looking for tomorrow.

William A. Cook

My Sunshine

When days are dreary and skies are grey
When life seems so weary I drift away
Then I remember, God sent me a ray of sunshine
Her twinkling eyes, her dimpling smile
Her sparkling countenance makes all worthwhile

She cheers me on, through pain and sorrow
and gives me hope for a new tomorrow

My Sunshine

So wise and courageous for a child her years
Her insight in life so advanced from her peers
I am thankful today to the maker above
Who sent me this special bundle of love.

My Sunshine

May she grow in stature, beauty and grace
May the Rays of her Sunshine beam from her face

May she share the joy of the World yet unknown
And radiate sun light and rejoice in song.
If I were an artist and could capture the strength,
The beauty, the character of the person God lent...
I would paint My Sunshine.

Roberta Hadaway Jones

Cry

Sometimes I want to just sit and cry,
When I see the years just pass me by.
Day after day it's all the same
and I only have myself to blame.
I want so much and need so little,
And I see my life just seem to shrivel.
I watch my kids growing up fast and tall,
And I wander just what happened to it all
My birthdays just seem like any other day,
And I just don't seem to know what to say.

Susan Messinger

Black Sunday

It was on a Sunday
when I saw someone that I haven't seen
in a long time.
He had his hair combed back
with his best suit on
in a room full of flowers
and weeping relatives.

He had been battling for a long time
until that fateful day. I guess God
wanted him on that day to walk with him
through the gates of heaven.

Now, I am back here
not weeping, for I did not know him well
but realizing that a person is only with us
for a short time before they ascend to a higher place.

People are coming one by one into the room
that is filled with sadness. They give their blessings
to the dearly departed's family, for the
family needs consoled on this day of mourning.

Shaun A. Marchese

Life

Cause it... never made a difference
when I listened to the sound of pouring raindrops
Cause I... never remembered
All the secrets the wind told me the
night I flew
Now that I think back... I will never
Know the secret of life that I could of known
Take a good look at yourself remember the
things you should know and the one
that you trust
Your life is a grain of sand that your soul holds
And that's the one you trust

Sarah Widrich

"Our Land"

We sit, we stand, in our very own land.
We will fight to the death, to our very last breath.
Not an inch we will give, and none to be bought.
All battles we win, and others not fought.
Don't tread on this land, and try not to put out.
But you're welcome to stay, so seedlings may sprout.

Robert Ames

Days Gone By

Sing me a song of the days gone by
When I danced in the rain
And tied flowers in a chain,
When I splashed in the puddles
And of my imaginary dog named Cuddles.

Oh, sing me a song of the days gone by
When I played down the street
And how I'd come with muddy feet,
When I wasn't aware of the time going by
And how my little red kite used to fly so high.

Oh, sing me a song of the days gone by
When I learned to tie my shoe
And how I always asked why the sky is blue,
When I got along with the other girls and boys
And how I learned to share my toys.

Oh, sing me a song of the days gone by
When I never thought I'd date
And how I hadn't yet learned to hate,
When I thought I was twelve feet high
And how I thought I would never die.

Sarah Elise Morgan

A Cry For Help

A man sits and mourns in silence
When he remembers the time he turned to violence.
Everyday was a fight to survive
He prayed each day wondering if he'd be alive.

He remembers the time he robbed a liquor store
He shot the man and ran out the door.
It was the first time he killed someone
He screamed and shouted, "What have I done!"

His eyes widened with fear, he knew he was in danger
When he crossed the path of a stranger.
He turned his back and felt a sharp pain in his right shoulder
Right then and there, thinking his life was over.

He remembers wandering through the streets walking about
Talking to his best friend he said, "I want out!"
Just then shots rung out from the street, his friend dropped by his side.
He held him in his arms, and there he lay to die.

He remembers the day he buried his friend
That's when crime and violence in his life came to an end.
Now kneeling upon his friend's grave he said, "I have survived!"
Wondering to himself if I never turned to crime would he still be alive?

Tara Lynn Matejovitz

To Be

I sat quietly, staring out the window
What obstacles must I overcome today?
What barriers will society place in my way?
Will there be a high price to pay?

I sat quietly, staring out the window
There are no obstacles I cannot overcome
There are no barriers that cannot be moved
The price of freedom is too high for some

I sat quietly, staring out the window
Am I strong enough to meet life's challenges?
Am I bold enough to strongly disagree?
Am I confident enough to be me?

I rise from the window, and proudly I walk
With my head held high, while others gawk
I am confident, I am soft spoken
I wear my pride like an invisible crown
I am black, I am strong, I am woman, I am....

Zaida E. White

The Fall Of Hector

Gods mingled with mortals on that fatal day
When Achilles mourned Patroclos and started to slay.

Hector, the hero, swept the plain the day before
But did not discern the fate of the spear he bore.
One lunge forward and a sharp pain in Patroclos' side
Doomed Hector to a fate from which he couldn't hide.
Death and darkness were to cover his eyes
As deemed by Fate and Zeus Allwise.

Back against the fortified wall of Troy
The Achaians pushed the Trojans, man and boy.
Driven into the gates of home by force
Were all except Hector, who stood without recourse.
On sped Achilles at the Trojan's sight,
Prepared for a long and grueling fight.

Each cursed vengeance to fulfill his wrath;
Each struck a blow with his spear-headed staff.
Fate doomed Hector, but he bravely vied
Till Achilles' sharp spear finally pierced his side.
Down fell the greatest of the defenders of Troy,
Honored as a god and bestowed great glory.

R. Larry Grayson

Oklahoma City

Oklahoma City, I feel really bad.
What's happened to you, is so sad.
Oklahoma City, I feel for you.
Whoever did this, should feel the pain you do.
It was the day, April 19th was the date.
This shouldn't have happened, but, it was your fate.
April 19, 1995. That was the day.
So many lives, were taken away.
Who would commit such an awful crime.
Gosh, I wonder what's going through their mind.
I saw people with teddy bears, flowers and ribbons of yellow.
The rescue worker who's gone, was such a great fellow.
To the survivors: Stand proud and tall.
This wasn't your fault, it wasn't at all.
Some people out there don't realize what they've done,
To them this was a whole lot of fun.
But they don't feel the pain, the agony of you.
But you don't deserve this, they're the ones who do.
So, here's my last words, they come from the heart, and they're true.
Stand tall, be brave and God Bless You.

Shay Bulzomi

Lost In Time

Wondering where you are now,
what you are doing, how life is for you.

Understanding why you left,
why you had to leave, even in the way you did,
probably more than you will ever know.

For, I awoke this morning and
throughout the day with you on my mind,
missing you terribly.

Strange, how I haven't thought of you
for quite some time, but, now
you are etched in my mind.

Certain you are married now,
a house in the country
along with a life of certainty and hope.

I wonder if you ever think of me,
reflect on the town in which we lived,
or realize how much you meant to me?

Perhaps, we will meet again,
to this I truly look forward;
for now, you remain a friend lost in time.

Raymond J. Lyons

The Greatest Mother

What do you think God expects Mothers to be?
What words would you pick to describe them to me?
Perfect, or sinless are impossible for all humankind;
But what other thoughts can you bring to mind?
Loving, understanding, and caring are sure
to be traits of the model which we deem pure.
Gentle, forgiving and unselfish we add,
to this friend whose good nature makes all times shared glad!
Some things are much harder to describe in a word,
like the way that you feel when her voice is just heard.
The comfort you know when she's coming near,
And the concern that she shows when she lends you an ear.
The support she is giving when she hugs you so tight.
The sincerity expressed when her love's timed just right.
So I put down on paper what words come to mind
When I think of my Mother who is one of a kind.
The example she sets gives me great pride,
The respect that I feel is nothing to hide!
She's so special it gives me more reason to pray
And thank the good Lord for my blessings today.

Vera L. Gisin

Color Blind World

If justice is blind, then why not we?
What of a world with nothing to see?

Think of a world where no one has sight,
Not knowing whether it is day or night.

No one could see who or what we are.
What race or creed, or wearing David's star.

We would all be the same in darkness or light,
Never seeing who is black or white.

Maybe not so bad, for white, black or jew,
A way for peace so long overdue?

But what a dull and boring world this would be,
With no beautiful colors for all to see.

Flowers and trees, birds and butterflies,
Stars and rainbows draped in the skies.

So beautiful are people, black, yellow, red or brown,
And it takes us all to make the world go round.

Sharon Robinson

Another World

I look up and I seek to find
what it is I'm looking for,
not knowing from whence I came
or where I'm going, but this I know,

I'm here in this human jungle,
seeking and searching a way of life.
But is this all, can there be more?
Is there life in another world?

Is there a place where I will go
and live in peace without death or anguish?
Can there be such a place?
And if there is, why can't it be here?

Maybe there is such a place for me
after I've finished this hectic life.
But I'll live this life to its fullest
for maybe it's all, I can't be sure.

And I'll continue to seek and try to find
the answer that I'm looking for,
for someday I must die, and I hope
to enter another world.

Steve Doss

Women Of The Sea

Dear women of the sea
What do you see in me?
Is it terror and misfortune?
Or simply love and devotion?
I, who is yet young and small
Care for all creatures great and tall.
I build friendships with those I fear
When things don't work out I
Cry an uncontrollable tear.
I take only what I need where others beg and plead.
I don't misjudge those I am not knowing
feeling relationships bind and growing.
I am frightened by some who rule
Knowing they can be mean and cruel
I am naive in many ways
Misguided by life on most of my days.

So tell me dear women of the sea
What is it you see in me?
A poor and stubborn little fool
Or a prized and precious golden jewel?

Tamzen Spiegel

Another Time, Another Place

When I was seventeen a handsome teacher came by and in a few
weeks we were married and gone. We never looked back and a
primitive little cabin on the Rockcastle river became our first home.

We tended the farm, swam in the coal-bank, made love in the
corn-crib when work was done. Hot nights in the cabin, a
quilt on the ground, talking of everything under the sun.

Hearts afire, loving, sparks from a touch;
he was passionate and gentle. I loved him so much!

The aurora borealis amazed us one night with its brilliant display
and one morning the river surprised us almost at our door.
The babies we made and cared for with love are beautiful people today.

He seemed so sad - was he jealous? My way was to pout -
was there someone else? What if I lost him, was he wanting out?

Most hours were filled, not a minute would wait, not a second stood
still. Our forty-fourth anniversary, "Stardust" our song. A day all
our own. He suffered in silence, few knew he was ill.

Then months in the hospital, never alone and early one
morning as I held him he died. He's gone now twelve
years and I long for him ever, I've tried God, you know how I've tried.

D. Y. McKnight

Mike's Bar

Dressed in suntans and Italian knits,
We used to drink martinis
Eating olives for our lunch
At Mike's Bar . . . on the west side of the Snake.

Living now in exile, penance for my soul
I feed on lectures and gobble books
Served as food for thought
At the university . . . on the east side of the Snake.

I'm on speaking terms with Hawthorne . . .
But Hemingway's a kindred soul
We travel through a wasteland
In search of mountain timber.

Dressed in cottons now and dreams,
I've given up martinis . . . the olives make me sick,
Homesick for a land I can't forget
And friends I still remember.

Living here in exile, I thirst for banquets
Served across the roaring falls,
Dressed in suntans and Italian knits,
At Mike's Bar . . . on the west side of the Snake.

Sandra Stevens Hudgins

Today We Become One

Today we become one, we spread our wings and fly
We take the world on together
And search the endless sky

God placed us hand in hand and
bound us with his love, now He sends us on our way
And keeps watch from above

He gave us times of good and
bad and feelings we didn't
Understand, but that was
to grow me as a woman and you as a man

The Lord is our shepherd and
He shall guide our way and
give us the grace and strength
to handle what comes our way

I will always stand beside you
And go where God may lead, for
He brought us together, He planted the seed

Today, I give you my heart
for all eternity, to share
With our Lord Jesus, who died for you and me.

Tonya Lofton

Mother-In-Law

As the years continue to pass
We shall never forget
The people who leaves us behind
But we must continue to live on
In hopes to meet with our loved ones

We remember all of the times
In which we share true emotion
Our love for our loss shall overcome
And the pain and grief heal with time

Unbelievable is the only word I know
For reasons beyond my control
I just can't let go
She was a mother-in-law of love, peace, and happiness
With plenty of life to share
Yet my children shall never know
The wonderful woman I had to let go.

Valerie S. Gambill

For Baby Adelia

Tiny rose
we see you not
yet like all men and women
who achingly stare at the flood of life
with fear and trepidation,
we two ask all of Him above
to use us and our gifts to produce
a fruitful life of hope.
He says you are from Beauty, Love and Power —
through mist and shadow
you soar on silk to meet us here.
I know though there will be times
of hardship in this fallen garden,
Still,
we will worship Him and await
your coming.

Yvette Burnham Couser

Apart

When we were young we were the best of friends.
We said we'd stay that way until the end.
But times have changed and we've gotten older.
The summers are warmer and the winters seem colder.
Our paths have turned from one to two
And now there is no more "me and you."
I often think back to our times together.
We were as flighty and free as a feather.
But we have gone our separate ways,
Which is really sad for me to say.
So this is just a little reminder,
Even though we are apart,
That no matter what tomorrow brings,
You are always in my heart!

Stefanie Liberti

Modern Medicine

We are more cruel than Death.
We guard the dying from Death's swift benevolence.
Hampered, Death pulls and tugs at the dying,
Twisting them through our fence of drugs and machines.
It may take days.

J. M. Farrell

The World

The world is such a sinful lady, with oh so many tempting
Ways, she captures the hearts of sinful men who from God
Have strayed.

Come see, she cries, what things I offer, come see things
You can ill afford, come and taste of my many pleasures,
Come quickly and take your reward.

Come dive into my sweet temptations, come hand to me
Your very soul, some close and see what things I offer,
Come see, come see, cries the jaded harlot, come see,
Come see cries the world.

Ruby Foster Walton

Espiritu

This journey we call life, sure it is a daily struggle for such is our way.
With no Hardships we don't learn, don't grow and for us that is death.
We must strive to live, love and be more than we were the day before.
To build something better, bigger and faster than was ever before.
Such is progress, but it is not cheap nor easy.
Life lost, toil and burdens in ignorance.
These are the prices of this advancement.
Prices that must be paid, we as race must absorb the cost equally.
So that we as a race may grow equally. Then there is understanding.
No jealousy, no ignorance and no waste of the human spirit.
Madmen and dictators are the killers of democracy, they must be taught.
All of us...the race are one, none better and None worse.
If this abstract called the human race ever does overcome prejudices.
And the Human Spirit does grow as a living entity then the stars
And all within are ours, for from the on, the only barriers are the
Steps of knowledge. As we learn we step up and grow more.
Perhaps someday all will come true and on that day perhaps we will
Finally realize just what we were placed on this Earth for.

Timothy P. Greenwood

New York's Winter

A shadow of a midnight pixie soul flew out of
Van Gogh's painting.
This subtle touch threw me into a field of wild
grapes, and I found myself on Strawberry Hill
as men in iron cars chased a new myth.
Let's retire my visual art when poetry gives out
its crystal glow, then our opera will hear a
new voice through New York's winter.

Scott Buster

America

We look into the sky so blue you
wave so high, so proud and true.

The country of our fathers and mothers
down the line. You are our
mighty country so fancy and so fine.

America my country you're very, very
old you'll been through so much my
fair country your stories we forever told.

America how we love you are hearts we cry for
you. We want to keep you new forever because we
do love you.

The flag that waves for all of us we know
in faith in God we trust. We've seen you
through so many years you've shared our
smiles and you've dried our tears.

No one can take your love away because
it will forever stay. You are our country
yes we pray our lovely America the U. S. of A.

Taneka Poarch

Guardian Angel

You are my guardian angel and I know Mom you are here.
Watching over my shoulder, comforting me and wiping away a tear.
I hope it is beautiful where you are and that you are happy there.
Not a day goes by, that I don't think of you and know that you still care.
Although you are far away, in my life you are still a part.
The memories we have shared together will always be in my heart.
Our lives were so happy and Mom I never wanted you to leave,
But God had different plans for you, so I should not grieve.
He has taken you to a better place with no more pain or tears,
So I am content knowing you will be my guardian angel for the
    rest of my years.

Connie Aurora

Oklahoma City

There was a bombing in Oklahoma City, this vast devastation
was truly a pity.
The death of our children, our family and friends, this
inexcusable madness has to end.
How could someone he filled with so much hate, not even to
think of this deathly fate.
The wondering; is our loved ones alive, or are they hurt or did they die.
The sadness that filled each and every person, the tears, the
anger, the hours searching.
Dear God I pray for each of those lives to give them peace the
husbands the wives.
To all those people who died that day God up above will lead your way.
This country isn't real bad place, it's people like McVeigh
that makes it a waste.
Out of all this madness, the country pulled together to end the sadness.
They reached out whatever they could but when you look at it
it's all we should.
To be together as one is a nation strong to be divided is truly wrong.

Rhonda Harris

Untitled

For even though our lives
    together have just begun
    and although the path
    we shall be traveling
    may seem uncertain;
        the future looks bright
        and full of promise
        just walk beside me
        and hold me close
        and we'll take each
            of life's obstacles together.

Robin A. Moore

Quiet Love

The night covers me like a blanket, but its
warmth is lost in the endless reach of its
starry lining
The city lights shine around me acknowledging
life, yet the quiet of the early morning
hours separates me from life's touch
My thoughts begin to drift, time passes
unnoticed
In the east comes a dim light, the dark
emptiness slowly being pushed away by the
coming dawn
A new day, a release from this dark prison, a
chance to once again join with the soul of my
life
The one who gives me faith to continue my
struggle, the half of me which holds the love I
need to exist
Soon I will be home, whole again in her warm
embrace
In the arms of my wife

Randall Y. Blayney

At The Door

With an outstretched hand, He said, "Enter, I will show you the way."
Wanting to obey, but still a child, confused and afraid,
She asked for just one more day.
"I have brothers and friends that won't understand,
And my mama will never be the same again.
I'm only sixteen, I have much to do,
I don't know if I'm ready to be with You."
With love so pure, He touched her hand,
And gently pulled her into His Holy Land.
"Omega dear, child so sweet,
Listen to Me as I speak.
You may not think you are ready, but it's part of My plan.
One day your mother will understand."
"Oh, but God, hear my mama cry.
I think she is dying deep inside."
"Yes My child, for now her grief is deep.
But soon My help she will seek.
See there now, three years have passed,
She trusted Me to give you the best."

Seminole Street

"Deception"

He is but a wolf in a lamb's cloak
Waiting to vault on his next blameless victim
For no apparent reason he takes them in
With his fraudulent outer appearance
Only to tell them that he isn't what he seems to be
He is a snake hiding in a paradise full of
Naive children of whom want to play his game
Their parents have warned them of the snake's cunning ways but
They must find out for themselves
That their curiosity will pull them in but
They will come away bleeding
From the razor sharp claws of the beast.
The beast seeks to taste their innocence
Is it out of anguish and pain that he preys on them
Or is it just a hobby for him
I hear the loneliness of his call
But is that what I'm hearing
Or is it the charm of a rattler with no fear
Will I take my chances like the rest
Or will I shrink back and wait for the lamb to be sheared

Jammie Knox

Love Seek

Love is like...

Like gale force winds, it blows my mind into a
void of despair.

Like the white vail of a bride, my innocence is
sacrificed into an unknown venture.

I wander through the channels of my vision only
to find more walls and more barriers impending
my direction.

Why the constant struggles... with no answers?

Why the constant barrage of distress...with no
answers?

Confidence in the relationship dwindles, but we toil
with enormous fervor to kindle our passion.

Steadfast efforts cannot be hampered.

Come to me my destined one and find your
beacon borrowing in to labor endlessly in
solemn dedication.

Let us find placid pools of love and abandon
arid desolation.

...And finally find the answers.

Steven Carey Robinson

"A Secret By Violets Kept"

She led her lover to a secret wooded place.
Violets undisturbed, sweet and innocent of face,
Looked up as the pair embraced.
When he laid her down among them, her body pressed heavily upon them.
Violets peeked from beneath the tresses of her fanned out auburn hair.
A moment of passion seized,
The crushing, grinding of tiny purple petals and leaves,
For a stolen moment of passion, much too hastily achieved.

When they rose to leave, their love now spent,
Her impression remained among the purple innocents.
Violets grossly twisted, dismembered, stems broken...bent.
This moment meant to be
the epitome of love, but instead,
Innocent shy violets,
Lay dying...dead.

Ruth Pipitone

To Begin Again

A memory a longing, an unfulfilled dream
Vast emptiness surrounds me like a swirling stream

The world moves about with its constant chatter
anguished cries, imprisoned, shout "What does it matter"

Pain swirls like an inferno searing my heart
what once made sense is now all apart

Disillusionment has shattered my naive bliss
cloaked in love, the splendor was but a deceitful kiss

Doors to my innocence slammed forever closed
Gates to emotion are no longer exposed

A moist cheek on a pillow finds peace in slumber
Morning radiant sunbeams cause me to wonder

Is there anything for which to survive?
Breath, rasping through my lungs, says I am alive

I grasp life's ladder with a trembling hand
Scarred and shaky I make my stand

Today I begin with a determined will
Perhaps one tomorrow I may again learn to feel

Silvia Walker

My Little Bit Of Heaven

Kentucky has its blue grass
  Utah has its snow
Where you find a little bit of heaven
  Your never sure to know
I found my love in Avalon
  Where you've not heard, no doubt
But that's where my little bit of Heaven
  Happened to come about
When Carol said she loved me
  It made my life complete
I found my little bit of heaven
  When my wife and I did meet
When our children came along
  Our love expanded more
That little bit of heaven
  Was, much bigger than before
So a little bit of heaven
  May not be a place
A little bit of Heaven
  Can be a loved one's face

Sheldon J. Lewis

The Homework Hassle

A carrot-topped boy with a very keen brain,
  Uses homework time to drive his Dad insane.
He fidgets and he fiddles as the clock ticks on,
  He wiggles in his chair, then goes to the John.
He pesters his poor sister and drives her up a wall,
  He finds a thousand ways to put his brain into a stall.
Then as the seconds, minutes and hours tick off,
  His Dad stands over him and soon begins to cough.
"Get that blasted homework done, you lazy little son,
  The sooner you can finish, the sooner we'll have fun!
There's ice cream in the freezer and games that you can win,
  And stories I can read you that will cause your head to spin.
So stick your nose into those books and study up a storm,
  And flex those mental muscles in your very best form.
Soon hours will seem like minutes and time will sift like sand,
  Through the skillful machinations of your busy writing hand"
And when at last my son looks up, his homework at an end,
  He'll gaze at me with loving eyes; I'll know him for my friend.
A wistful look will cross his face as he is forced to say,
  "Gee Dad, it's gettin' kinda late and I'm too tired to play!"

Robert D. Andersen

Current

As I tilted my head very, very slowly
  upward towards the sky.
I could see the sun coming alive through the
  dark gray clouds in the sky.
A new day is about to begin with the rising of the sun.
The sun rose in a swift way, casting its
  bright glow about the earth, for which
God has created to well. What a sight.
My how the sun started to shine with such
  joyous, sparkling and gleaming splendor.
The brightness made my eyes sting in
  a pleasant way.
As the sun went even higher in the sky. The
  reflection of it, reflected its
intense shine off of the large high rise
  glass window buildings.
This was a sight to behold, a moment to
  remember, or just breath taking.
When the sun reached its highest point in the sky,
  the earth was captured in its beauty.

Dedra A. White-Goudas

Old Log House

Setting to north of white-wash hill,
Under the heavens so ghostly and still,
Stands an old log house with a porch all around,
Old red clay falling from cracks in the wall,
Wind playing in spaces make a music call,
A wayfarer pauses to consider this sight,
Sam Stark raised a family here, he heard someone say,
By sweat of brow, he showed his children the way,
There's memories in decayed places and things,
It takes the past, then new life springs,
The wind sings the stories in a song,
Of all that have lived here and now are gone.

Theo McCroskey

The Gunfighter

A man tall and dark came a'riding.
  Two guns were tied at his side.
His clothes were all black and dusty,
  And a mighty black horse he did ride.

He rode into town very slowly.
  His eyes were fixed straight ahead,
And I knew that before the sunset
  Someone in town would be dead.

He rode right up to the barroom.
  And he walked straight through the door.
Then in a very short moment,
  I heard those mighty guns roar.

He came back out of the barroom.
  His eyes I'll never forget.
And he and the mighty black horse
  Rode into the red sunset.

Now that's the end of my story.
  The truth is for you to decide.
But I just wanted to tell you
  That's how the gunfighter died.

Philip R. Joram

Silvery Moments

The years have come the years have flown and strange as it may seem;
  Twenty-five have now slipped by...it must be like a dream.
God was good to you Mom and Dad and blessed you bountifully
  With seven happy children just as healthy as could be.

You put us all through high school, you kept us clothed and fed
  And cared enough to kiss us and tuck us up in bed.
We thank you Mom and thank you Dad for everything you've done;
  For sharing in our work each day as well as in our fun.
We know you had a struggle when times were not so good
  And thank you for the faith you kept which bound us while you stood.

Now twenty-five have slipped on by and in those yet to come
  May God still bless you graciously and keep the sorrows numb.
And so on this blessed 25th, about all we can say
  Is thank you Mom and thank you Dad for life so free and gay!

Sharon L. Wessels

What Good?

For years I had a solid wall, built around my heart,
To help block out the awful pain, a lifetime can impart.
From growing up in a broken home, to taking a sacred vow,
Knowing that my choice was wrong, too late to back out now.
While through the years my wall grew strong, I failed to see,
That every block I added on, took away a part of me.
It took some help and lots of love, from friends and family,
To tear apart this wall of mine, and help me to believe
What good's my life to anyone, if I've taken away "Me"?

Patricia Pike

My Gifts To My Children

Monday   - The gift of strength, so you can begin each week out right.
Tuesday   - The gift of sunshine, to remind you all you are
                  in my spotlight.
Wednesday - The gift of drive and determination,
                  to make it through each day.
Thursday - The gift of hope, to make tomorrow even better than today.
Friday   - The gift of wishes,
                  and I will do my best to make them all come true.
Saturday - The gift of promise,
                  that I will always be there for all of you.
Sunday   - The gift of relaxation,
                  we all deserve our "day of rest."
A day for us all to enjoy each other,
    and for this mother to build her nest.
Everyday I give you these special gifts,
    and all this love of mine.
It is not easy raising your four children alone,
    but it is the reward of a life time!

Susan J. Zimmerman

Round Trip

Riding in an open vehicle at a speed far beyond compare
Traveling through an earth tunnel flying in the open air
I was rising from the depths into the mouth of a cave entrance
Seeing the light of God his glory in all its brilliance

Revealing illuminating soft is the light coming from everywhere
A surrounding light there are no shadows I saw the atmosphere or air
Clearly I could see a tree in minute detail in every leaf every line
I could see a thousand miles I could see as far as the light shined

From within the holy hill I could see out across the land
There I was greeted by a man with a silhouette for each hand
A smiling face talking brown eyes most beautiful most bright
Like brass was the tone of his skin same tone as God's light

In a regal robe with a powdery blue glow his face a delight to see
Smooth firm skin with no blood in it an eternal body it had to be
We talked he told me you are here too soon you have to go back now
I hated to leave I could stay forever if I knew the way or how

He looked at me with compassion as I slowly moved from the cave
You will return he told me as he raised his right hand to wave
Hearing what he told me put my heart at ease as I moved faster away
Traveling millions of miles one round trip all complete in one day

Roy N. Green

In The Middle Of Nowhere

I stand in the middle of my life.
Too young to vote, but too old for pretend.
In the middle of nowhere.
Knowing nothing, but what I've already lived.
I stand in the middle looking at both worlds.
I can't go back to being a child,
and they don't think of me as an adult.
So, there I stand in the middle.
Where no one knows who they are.
Where no one cares about you.
In this place of no where.
Friends drift away with the wind.
So you're all alone.
To face things unknown.
There is nothing in the middle, but a lot of emotions.
Emotions of confusion.
No one knows why they are here.
Or when they'll leave.
but we know we're stuck in the middle.
The middle of no where.

Sherri Smith

Scenes From God

I tiptoed quietly from my room today,
to watch a colorful bird at play,
I heard it sing, I watched it, and then it took flight
I watched until it flew and soared out of my sight.

As I stand looking at the leaves drifting slowly to the ground,
I can feel the awesome presence of God all around,
I feel the presence of God in each fall flower that is in bloom,
as each cool breeze seems to whisper away the gloom.

As I walk along the path beside the winding, sparkling stream,
My mind is looking ahead, I am beginning my day dream,
I think of what heaven will be like with grass so cool and green,
I think of angels singing, everything is so calm and serene.

I love the mountain as we climb up and down the hill,
who made all of these beautiful scenes? God made them 'twas his will,
I see the lake, with fish and fowl all around,
I see God in all these glorious scenes, Gods beauty does abound.

When evening shadows begin to slowly fall
I can hear the sound of the night birds call,
as the stars are like diamonds, that is Gods handiwork of love,
I know and can in my minds eye see the God Head watching from above.

Sarah Ozella Kendrick

Never-Never Land

I'm praying a wish for Never-Never Land
To turn to when my world turns gray
Joyously, I'd laugh and smile all day
While this world continues upon its way

There I'd stay, 'til my sobs turn to smiles
And my life's pain would leave my mind
For when life would try to suffocate my joys
Never-Never Land would be gentle and kind

This land would be perfect in every way
No pains, suffering, problems or strife
Love and peace fills Never-Never Land
Upon entering, all burdens become light

Never-Never Land would be my escape route
When life's troubles would rain on my parade
This paradise would be like a comforting umbrella
To protect against all harsh charades

This would be a care-free and loving place
With the main focus, on our Lord, Jesus Christ
He would be the foundation of Never-Never Land
There, his reign would be supreme and right

Shamona Yvonne Carter

Bear "She Is"

Bear is sent to you with love and understanding
To help chase the blues away. And know you are not alone
She brings to you much love - you thought forgotten
She brings to you many blessings that you tucked far away

She brings to you much happiness - you've not allowed yourself to explore
She brings to you - your long future - you thought would never come
She will ask you no questions - nor will she tell you no lies
She will lend you an ear - for whatever your needs allow

She will understand you - and believe in you she will
For she brings you a faith you haven't had since a child
Where your thoughts were always free
She is yours alone to hug - she is yours alone to love

She is yours alone to shake and scream at - if that is what it takes
For she truly believes in you - and the Father above
She knows your road uphill is long and yes - knows you will remain strong
She will always be alongside you for whatever it takes

She loves and adores you and has restored your faith
She is especially made to be yours alone in love and faith always

Rosalie A. Gamache

Through My Eyes

I wake, my eyes are open wide
To see the light of day outside.

And now I know it's time to play,
With my dear friend in our special way.

I think I hear her coming down,
In her long, fluffy, pink nightgown!

It is! It's Britney here with me,
The best friend I have, I call her B.

We go outside to run and run,
And explore everything under the sun.

We water the flowers, the plants and trees,
And chase the flies, the birds and bees.

Then we see the Sun's going down,
And everyone is home from town.

The night, we know, will be here fast,
And we still don't know how the day has past.

She looks at me and I stare into her eyes,
And we begin our sweet goodbyes.

Her mom then says sleep, before you get grumpy,
And she says I LOVE YOU good night puppy!

Toby Blecick

Summer Daze

Summer daze takes me back in time
To my country home and some friends of mine.
Sultry breeze carries memories
Little boy at play, youth has gone from me.

Home, where I long to go
To a simple place that is there no more.
Willow weep, o'er a golden stream.
Hours fade away as I lie and dream
Of the world that awaits me there
Expecting life to be free and fair.

Time has changed all around me now.
Search to find a way
I must return somehow.
Now that my days are done,
Like those foolish dreams
All my years are gone.

Summer daze takes me back in time
To my country home and some friends of mine.

Russell E. Lowry

A Sense of Reality

With unspoken eyes we elected her
to capture the feelings in mischief.
Forgotten time in a sense of immortality.
Can you fly like the raven, can you see like an eagle.
Don't forget your aura in an ion stone of feelings.
Depressed in a state of mind losing all consciousness.
Never knowing an animal from a person.
A sense of reality.
The touch of death, the feeling of lost souls, as yours
desperately looses himself.
Always a fool in the house of love, knowing, trying, and
always forgetting your love and your soul.
Can a sense of change be exchanged for a blessing, and for yourself.

Patrick Bellamy

Absence Of Silence

I heard about silence it was once spoken
to me

I quietly listened in awe, a place without
noise, how could this be.

I thought about a room no windows
no door.

I shivered from the cold isolation as I
fetally crouched on the floor.

I could hear a faint thumping echoing
around my existence and soul.

The darkness overwhelmed me no description
could be told.

I for the first time was in a place where no
noise or words were spoken.

I quietly drifted into a dream, months passed,
until suddenly the stillness was broken.

I woke from my dream and awed at the sound, the
beauty and shine.

And as I moved forward into a world seeking knowledge
I never knew I would be searching for, what I left behind.

Rupert Cole-Palmer Jr.

Happy Birthday, Mary

A holy couple, so long ago, yearned for a child
   to love and cherish.
God heard their prayers and granted their wish...
   HAPPY BIRTHDAY, MARY

The child grew in wisdom, beauty and grace,
Bringing joy to us all in the human race.

A handsome young carpenter, Joseph by name,
Chose her to wed - when the angel came.

She bore him a son, a son sent from above,
A holy family were they - overflowing with love.

The child grew in wisdom, honor, grace and devotion,
And changed our hearts, our acts, and emotion.

She walked the last mile, helped carry His cross
Weighed down by the wood and a Mother's loss.

She cradled His body, broken and sore,
And swaddled Him in cloth as in days of yore.

He gave her to us to love and to cherish
To keep us in touch - our faith to nourish.

We love her, we pray, we have our devotion,
We offer our hearts, minds and flowers in one motion.

   HAPPY BIRTHDAY, MARY
   Ruth P. Regensburg

The Dream

Like a bird in a cage, I dream to soar free
To have my soul and spirit freed from controversy.
   Malediction: The curse, the spell
   Morpheus: God of dreams, lift me from this hell.
I will not succumb to dying in captivity,
I will fly free some day and calm the adversity.
   My loyalty to the sky; a nomad of the air,
   I will have no limitations - no despair.
I envision a Nexus with the earth, wind and sky
I know I was born to be free, and to fly.

   Tammi M. Jordan-Wilson

Given The Chance

If I was lucky enough to be given the chance
to go back and live my life again,
and God could assure me I'd have the same parents,
I would have to say I'd do it then!

I wish sometimes that I could go back
to about the time I was becoming a teen-
when they said, "These are your best years, honey"-
because I now know what they mean!

I can clearly remember them telling me too-
"Honey, be all that you can be,"
but somehow I misinterpreted it
and turned out to be just me!

No - I didn't become a doctor or nurse,
and as for material things I have not much-
but what I have in my heart is even greater;
it's the knowledge that I was loved very much!

So, given the question "Would you want to go back?",
and knowing now what I didn't know then,
having them as my parents I assure you-
yes, I would do it all again!

Wendy M. Lecates

"My Prayer"

Heavenly Father, each morning as I try.
To get out of bed without waking my husband, I cry,
Help me through this new day, to do and say.
The things you'd have me, to help others on life's way.

My arms and legs don't want to work,
from riding old tractor with loose seat to jerk,
The many cattle need hay for winter, to eat,
Breakfast must be fixed, medicine given to stroke patient to treat.

Must get farm work done while weather is fair,
Trying to help so we can do our share.
Looking back, did I take on more than I can do??
Heavenly Father, I can only with your help, be true.

Please help all those, I remember each day.
For they tell me it really helps, on their pathway,
You know each one, and their needs appear,
Give me the words and actions to cheer.

Most of all let us be with you mentioned I Thessalonians 4:13-18
I pray we may all meet as written Revelation chapters 21, 22
Again I ask, give me strength to do my part.
This I ask from the bottom of my heart.

   Vermeille Davis Todd

Untitled

Through the roads she travels,
Through the darkness and the shadows,
Piercing people through the heart.
She is not love, though love dwells with her in the heart
She is hate.
   Mistress of shadows,
      sister of betrayal,
         mother of prejudice,
            friend of injustice,
               enemy of love,
                  adversary of life.

Rachel Sowray

Memories

Looking back upon times past
To childhood dreams and reveries,
I find precious memories made to last-
Penned on parchment in old diaries.

In ink that can never be erased,
Moving gently through the corridors of my mind;
Things silver and gold cannot replace-
Etched indelibly in the annals of time.

Now each new day brings things to ponder;
Creating new memories to store away-
Through my mind to drift and wander
On some tomorrow, some future's day.

Tomorrow's dreams not yet fulfilled,
Plans not made, as yet undone-
Things as yet unknown until
Today has passed and tomorrow won.

Then the memories made today
Will be dreams fulfilled, things said and done-
Things penned on parchment from yesterday
In old diaries, if tomorrow comes.

Patricia Osborne Orton

"They"

They want peace to be deceased, and all of hell
to be released, who are They, I say. Are They
the same who play wargames with nations of the world,
for their own personal gain. Do or die, I don't know
why, screams cry for help in the night, through an
endless fight. Fighting like demons, demons and devils,
so you tell me now that man is not evil.
Visibility is grim, destruction is taught, so They tear
down the walls, in show of a peace that is not.
They cover up lies, with true lies of deception, at the
same time, They seal their own fate, as we draw
towards redemption. So as I glance at the world of today,
I hope and pray for a world of tomorrow, to have a
change of way. So take heed chosen ones, for They know
not what They do. The end is nigh, so take one last
breath, and a look to the sky.
For the light at the end of the tunnel may be you.

Paul Commers

Memories

There are times in the past we would like to forget,
Times of mistaken, hardships and regret. There are times
of struggles, lessons, and tears, all these evaporate with
the passage of years.

As we aim high for the largest star, let us never forget who
we are, we are the fruit, the blossom, and the pride, the
everlasting hope the future will not die.

Let us not succumb to the on-going pressure, instead, let us hunt for
the greatest treasure. Keep in mind the opportunities that lie in our
hands, the promises, the challenge of discovering unknown lands.

Let us thank all the parents who have loved and cared, the laughing,
the fun, the disappointments they have shared.

Let us say good-bye to this shelter we have taken for granted, a
shelter of values and knowledge that have forever been planted.

Most importantly, good-bye to the class of 1989, go out and succeed
and always shine, for that is what a dream is always for, a chance to
leave the past behind and the walk through future doors be yourself
and never feel afraid, for these times of your life will never fade.
Because they are your memories.

Wendy Williams

Retirement

A time to choose a new direction for my life
Time to do the things I often dreamed
A time to sit and to listen
And hear the words that are really spoken
Be sensitive to the needs around me
Will my time be filled with busyness
Or will I really make a difference
Give me the wisdom to pick and choose at will
Utilize my gifts to grow and not stand still
Then I'm sure I will feel complete
And my retirement will be so sweet.

Wanda Sawhill Robison

Romance It Ain't

'Twas near to Wintertime on the Western plain,
Time to bring the range horses back home again.

Old Paint, the wild stallion, along with his brood,
Mixed in with our horses and was in a feisty mood.

The geldings weren't a problem, they moved right along,
But our best mare — well, that's a whole 'nother song!

Try as we did to get 'em in a group,
Paint would maneuver among 'em stirring 'em like soup.

We drove 'em for a week, with weather closing in,
But Paint's shenanigans put us further back than where we begin.

In frustration, my brother took aim,
Laid ol' Paint down like any other big game.

We loved that ol' mustang, but how do you rate
Forty good mares against coyote bait?

You can love a good woman, you can even love ol' Paint,
But with that rogue horse, romance it ain't!

Wendell Warren

"Wiltest Thou?"

Wiltest thou O flower of youth?
    Time hath surely aged thee.
From whence came thou decay?
    Thy beauty never again to be!

Wiltest thou O flower of hate?
    Thou dost burn within a heart.
Canst thou fade away without killing another part?

Wiltest thou O flower of friends?
    Thine truth forever be?
When thou dost go memories are left to see.

Wiltest thou O flower of mind?
    Thou surely doest decay?
Whence goest thou?
    Now with my life I pay.

Wiltest thou O flower of love?
    Only if thou be true.
If thou be of any grace, thou might stay of colored hue.

Everything doth wilt and fade; everyone must die.
Wiltest thou O flower of Heaven?
    Ne'er! Lest all be lies.

Rachel Sayler

Tornado

Moving the dark and turbulent clouds
Threatening are the foreboding shrouds
Winds swirling counter clock blowing
Humans hurry-scurry all fears showing

A reverse cornucopia touches ground
Vicious roar screams unearthly sound
A howling dervish-a furious angry devil
Dancing happily destructive in its revile

Swiftly wending-a fury-along any path
Disaster total-unforgiving demonic wrath
Energy expended FINIS!-deadly sojourn
A daylight quiet-a sudden hush to mourn

Prim Tiberi

The World As A Dream

The world at its best is still only a dream.
Though when storms blow it seems so real.
When it's dark and cold and you're all alone,
And you're not sure exactly how you feel.
You just wish you had someone to talk to,
Someone to tell you that you'll be all right.
To keep you safe until things get better,
To dry your tears and hold you tight.
But to you, this person doesn't exist.
And for now, you'll still be all alone.
You'll hide away in some small place,
And cry each time a storm has blown.
You escape behind a wall you've built,
That shelters you from all your fears.
Making it hard for others to reach you,
And consoling yourself with bitter tears.
You long for the time when morning will come,
And you'll leave this world of sadness and shame,
'Cause this dream of life is more like a nightmare,
And you've learned to hate it just the same.

Sarah Rivington

My Hero

Many people have a hero and in some ways I do too
Though others may not see my hero as heroic as I do.
My Hero is always there to calm most of my fears
My Hero always lends a shoulder and wipes away my tears.

My Hero always cheers me on in everything I do
My Hero always cheers me up whenever I am blue.
My Hero will stand by me in my deepest time of need
My Hero gives me that extra push to return me to the lead.

My Hero helps me find the path whenever I am lost
My Hero will help me in anyway no matter what the cost.
My Hero sits and holds my hand when I need time to heal
My Hero hears and understands exactly how I feel.

My Hero tells me when I'm wrong and helps me to erase
My Hero cheers me when I'm right the few times that's the case.
And after I do something wrong when I should have known
My Hero won't give up on me and leave me on my own.

My Hero may not be the same as the heroes of my friends
But my Hero will not cause me trouble, no rule will he bend.
No one has ever seen my hero but still no one can lessen
The faith that I put in my hero, he's my Father up in Heaven.

Sarah Chapman

Life Is So Grand

There are people we don't understand,
Those people can't see just how
good it can be,
And also they don't know they can,
All because of one man.
Jesus Christ the Son of God
has changed people's lives over the years,
And those who didn't want it,
shed a lot of tears.
No matter what you have
or are going through,
Jesus will, and can, change you.
When you accept and believe in
Jesus Christ, a new life in you
will begin.
And remember, stronger is he
that is within.
When you are a Christian, you will understand
There is a life after death here
which is so grand.

Robert Scott Shoff

Weeds And Thorns

Standing in field of weeds and thorns.
Thorns of pain and weeds of despair.
By myself, tending to my foul deeds.
Looking to the sky for clouds to bring
Rain that will start the plants to grow.
Seeds of sorrow I have sown in hope for
Fruits of love and joy that I have lost.
Love is like the far away white cloud.
It does promise to come but fades.
Hoping for the rain and getting sun.
Hoping for the fruit and getting weeds.
Shackled here to tend the field of thorns.
I am here alone with my pain.
Crows come and squawk around my head.
Cackles haunt my mind, corrupt my sleep.
Out of here you foul birds. I have no need.
You sing not. In pain your song is heard.
Mice do nibble my toes while I sleep.
Shackled here to tend my field of thorns.
Waiting for the one who has the key.

Robert Repasky

True Friend

We all have one true Friend.
This Friend is always there for you;
Helping you through it all;
Lifting your spirits;
Helping you up whenever you fall.

Your Friend is there for you every minute of the day;
Listening and hearing every word you say.
You may stagger or even get off track;
Still He never leaves-
He is always there to direct you back.
Whatever happens He goes through it too.
Guiding you through your problems;
Always there for you.

You may not be able to see Him.
Though, He always sees you.
He's in every rock, every little tree;
In the mighty hurricane that thunders in the sea.
He is always near and will be throughout eternity...

Russell Anderson

Over Forty

Sitting on a chair in the den
Thinking of what I could have been
Maybe an Artist
Maybe a Poet
Maybe an Entrepreneur
Maybe I'd sew it.
In a big high rise building
With fine clientele
Oh how I wish how I could have been there
Yes all in all I've made a blunder
I let a bad marriage
Pull me under
But here's a fine note
I'd like to share
I've got five beautiful children
Who really do care

Rosemary Anderson-Morton

A Life Torn Apart

Life is full of ups and downs
Things that turn my laughs into frowns
I always try to put on a smile
When deep inside I hurt all the while

When I've lost what I had for so many years
I fight and struggle to hold back the tears
I was told I'm a loser and would never get ahead
By a woman who said she wished I was dead

People may think I am happy all day
But I'll never be happy till the hurt goes away
I look and find someplace to hide
to cover the tears I have often cried

I wish I could somehow recover
Hoping to find a friend and a lover
Someone to listen to all my fears
And wipe away unwanted tears

Someone to take me into their arms
And shield me away from any harms
To teach me to laugh and love from the heart
And help me rebuild a life torn apart.

Rodney Dogan

"Things Are Meant To Be"

When hearts are broken from
  things meant to be
Take time to plant a flower
  or a very special tree.

For angels from heaven will
  turn teardrops to rain
The flowers and trees will
  blossom
Somehow lessening the pain

You see, hope blooms like the flower
faith and wisdom grow strong like the tree
Both are gifts from above
When things are meant to be.

Sheila R. Laslovich

My Blessing

When God made my daughter he made the perfect mold.
The curls on her head glisten like gold.
The shape of her eyes and her entire face
were copied from the man who taught her how to tie her first lace.
She is the most beautiful gift I have ever received.
Thank you God for the day my husband and I conceived.

Pamela Voyles

"Thinking About You Always"

Mom and Dad, I'd love to do so much for you.
They're times when I'm thinking about you,
I wonder if rather I should have stayed over-there.
I do believe we'll be enjoying life a lot better.

I also realize how painful my departure was for you
And deep in your hearts, you never wish that separation.
Through the years, you'd spoiled me with so much love and affection
I really couldn't figure out that one day I had to leave you.

It seems like yesterday, those souvenirs still haunt my head.
Sometimes, I'm thinking about how grandiose it'd have been
If during one of your living days we have to be reunited.
Even in one of my dreams, happy I would have been!

And again letting you know that you're grandparents,
How could have you imagine such a celebration?
Frankly, I wish each one of us could have enjoyed this occasion.
I finally realize that happiness isn't for all under this firmament.

Wherever you're, I'd like to thank you
For the memorable years I had shared with you.
I cannot stop loving you. Don't ever forget that.
Mom and Dad, again I love you no matter what.

Pierre Edouard Dalencour

Lock

I meet death's grim partner with every passing day.
They're killers, murderers and plunderers, yet they all have something
  to say.
They all claim their innocence and that the courts are always wrong;
  however,
They cannot prove that they were not there and that crime did not
  carry on.
If you believe as I do, then you probably will agree,
The best place for them is where they are...
Behind some bars with a screen.

J. T. Carter

Untitled

The reflection in the mirror they're just not getting clearer;
They're fogging up right before my eyes.
The stranger is inside of me doing things that I can't see,
fascinating me with alibi's.
Do I know who I am? Could I see what you are?
Could you recognize yourself?
Is real reality or are we living in a fantasy?
Walking with closed eyes, abiding our own lies.
It's not a matter of what you know,
what you do, or who you know,
only in due time, you'll see its state of mind.
Shocking to know the truth!
Do you dare or do you hurt?
Could you take a life, slicing yourself with a knife?
Cutting through you, you're cutting through me
My blood flows out of your veins as you bleed
Never do you realize what's to matter
walking around in a subconscious matter.

Paula B. Benedetto

Love's Fire

In the beginning it was just a tiny spark
That ignited and consumed my soul
I was mesmerized so completely
That it burned out of control

I thought that it would go on forever
But little did I know
That nothing lasts forever
For to ashes all fires must go

Sharron Pemberton

Friendship

Friends are real gems, so precious and true,
They'll always be there for you and never make you blue.
They'll stand by you always, through thick or thin,
With them on your side, you'll be sure to win.
Friends will love you, care about you and accept you as you are,
No matter where you live, be it close by, or away, very far.
Friends are so special, so dear to our hearts,
Forever our friends, we will never part.
You can always depend upon them for just anything,
They'll laugh with you and cry with you and maybe even sing,
What a special gift from God when he gives us a friend,
For it is such a blessing, a friend forever till the end.
We love them and cherish them, how sweet their names,
No matter to us how rich or famous or fame.
Friends are one of life's beautiful treasures,
They are so precious and priceless beyond all measure.
So keep them dear within your heart,
Your love for one another will never part.

Shirley Ann Warner

"The Lotteries Of The World"

People play the lottery in many distant lands;
They play that they might win and solve all their plans
Many spend their life savings and wind upon the street;
A few will hit the jackpot and think it's very neat

When you play a game in the United States and hit the jackpot.
You don't get your money all at once and you can't afford to stop
When you play in Europe or Canada you get your money all at once
You don't have to wait for twenty years to get yourself a hunch.

The lotteries of the world are games of chance you can beat;
If you have the money to play every day when you can repeat
You think first I'll get a new house, a car and then even more;
When it comes time for a vacation, then I cross to the other shore.

Some will say don't take a chance of playing the lottery every day;
You could wind up a loser by gambling your hard earned money away.
When we hear these words that many people say, we know they are true
It's as though they are talking to someone else it just couldn't be you

The lotteries of the world make more than they will ever pay out;
When you think you got the best of them there will be a little doubt.
I hope you have learned your lesson well there won't be a second chance
Be all that you can be and hope that one day you will have that stance

Rudolph V. Freeman

Give Love To God's Children

We need to love our children.
They need to know that there's nothing
they deserve more than love.
Gods children shouldn't die
by our hands.
Their blood shouldn't fill this land.
Their hearts need the medicine of laughter
not the pain of inflicted wounds.
Scrapes and cuts bandaged with the
security that we will be there.
Their tears wiped clean so that there's
not a trace left to see.
Kisses left on the cheek for repair.
God gives nothing less than his
love to us.
Our children are gifts of his love.
Give Gods children all they deserve.
Give nothing less than love.

Satrena Chung

Ponder Upon This...

The Indians feel the pain of the earth, the closeness makes it so...
They know their Maker and in spirituality they grow.
The earth is living entity, they insist, they claim...
If we don't treat it right, we will have no air and no grain.
The drum beat means pulse of the earth and of the sea...
They proclaim, the earth will soon be lost for you and me...
The drum beats slower...and quieter, the pulse is weaker we hear...
The Indians warn us that global disaster is here...
The beat of the drum, the pulse of the earth is fading...the earth
   can hardly breathe...
The poison, the smoke, polluted waters, we all have a part in this...
Has the drum beat a meaning for us?
Wake up, to clean your mother-earth is our urgent task...
Desperately they knocked on the UN door - their message nobody wanted
   to hear...
IT IS LATER THAN YOU THINK - GLOBAL DISASTER IS
   ALREADY HERE...
The door finally opened, the Indians tried to open it many times...
And they delivered to the world a warning - "the word of the wise...
If the rules of our Maker don't mean anything to us...
We will soon be without grain, water, air and grass...
If we don't clean the world soon - Intervene will the LAW OF THE
   UNIVERSE...
And the earth will flip and shake and from the pollution CLEAN ITSELF

Stanley Wantula

Forefathers

My forefathers lived on this land,
They hunted on this land, they died on this land.
Where have man's values gone?
Can't they see the destruction, that they have caused?
Never satisfied, always wanting more.
When everything we need is here.
My forefathers were called savages.
Seeing all this "I wonder, who were the real savages?"
Values were taught among people, morals were taught.
Where have the morals of today gone?
"I know now, who really are the savage race."
I only hope that someone, someday will stop before it is too late.
My forefathers were a wise, and gentle people.
They lived in peace before all this.
It's a shame that all this has been destroyed.
Some where out there, the spirits cry, so sad, to see this
beautiful land destroyed before their eyes. How they long to
see the eagles fly, the buffalo roam, and most of all, this beautiful
land returned as before.
This is the dream of our forefathers of long ago.

Trudie Hagan

"Here"

Of the only days we know,
   these may seem the hardest.
the feelings have burned grooves
   in the world of time.
Wishing that the moments could exceed the
   swiftest winds, but knowing that they never did.
To think for us is now, and to feel is as
   a crashing wave feels for shore.
A force full of meaning, but a direction
   unknown, or is it?
The days long after will decide the previous,
   and the present is the fire of mind.
For the burning is in the soul, neither
   forgotten or questioned ever.
And it always has been, and very much will be,
   the single part of us that can really see.

Of the only days we know, these are a few of them.

Patrick M. Cooke

These

These are the days of revolution
These are the days of technology
These are the days that are compared to those days
These are the days of opportunity for our young people
These are the thoughts of our adults
These are the days of murder
These are the days of robbery
These are the days of rape
These are the days of drugs
These are the days of violence
These are the days of our children start packing
These are the days our children are scared to walk the streets
These are the days our children are afraid to be alone
these are the days I cannot walk the streets
These are the days I cannot be alone
These are the days when I do not want to wake up
When will the days come that I will not be afraid?
When will the days come when I will say that I am proud to be alive,
and really mean it?
When will the days come that I will not be writing this from
experience?

Sara Rose Chapman

To-Your Will-O-Wisp

Time is a vagabond—not worth a tinker's dam-
Therefore, lose no sleep about it.
    And,
In twenty-four hours, today will be tomorrow.
Don't be looking over for four leaf clovers,
    That you overlooked before.
Make your little step for man,
    An' be right hip about it.
Our usufruct is great - so don't delay,
Do that good at once, immediately - tout de suite,
    if not sooner, be salt of the earth,
    and a' that.
Proper Ladies and Gents you can be,
    If you try-try-try-Dear Ones.
    Selah, and God bless- pax vabiscum.
    We're citizens of the U.S.A., and a' that.

William M. Cain

What Is Peace To Me

Amidst the trials and stormy weather of life
There is peace to be found in the valley of God.
Ask, seek, and knock in the darkness of the storm
The mystic ears will answer your call.
And like a telephone you can communicate with Him

Ask the mystical voice why there is storm around you.
Please to give me love instead of despair
Seek the love you want until you find it
And knock the door for the mystical one to open
You have found shelter at last, its peace from our creator.

Wycliffe E. Tyson

Troublous Souls

Wander alone, they must, for there is something in
their soul that makes them thus,
some Mother's, Father's child.
Yours and mine, mine and yours.
Those urban, rustic indigent aborigines of this land;
unable to think and speak in a tongue understood by
the masses.
Yours and mine, mine and yours,
Those wandering souls; wander alone, they must,
for there is something in their soul that makes them thus.
For! there, but for the grace of God, goes, I.
Thus, spoke the poet from within my soul!

Robert D. Jefferson Sr.

Remember

REMEMBER ALWAYS... that for all your strength,
there is much that remains far beyond your control.

That a myriad of things that befall you
are elements in an immeasurable, omnipotent force...
through which you have no voice.

REMEMBER ALWAYS... you are but a spoke in a magnificent wheel,
that eternally rotates, but you are never forgotten...
and never replaced... never replaced.

REMEMBER ALWAYS... that for each loss in your world,
there is yet something to be gained... or someone.

REMEMBER ALWAYS... that you have much to forgive,
much to achieve, much to heal,... and to mend.

REMEMBER ALWAYS... that these are the things
which will make you strong, happy, fulfilled and complete.

REMEMBER ALWAYS... that you are loved...
wholly and forever, and it is that force which you may draw upon,
at any time, and for any duration.

REMEMBER ALWAYS... that all of this is truth...
because... we are YOUR FAMILY
and we will always be here for you.

Tracy J. Marien

Living Through The Years

While traveling through these eighty-eight years,
There have been lots of smiles,
And quite a few tears.

Hand in hand we've come a long way,
On a straight and narrow road,
Leaving footprints in the sand every day.

Our steps are getting very slow,
Sight a little dim,
We seem to go with the flow.

With this happy thought we keep pressing on,
You and I will make it just in time,
We will be so happy when we get home.

Ruth G. Huiet

"My Sister My Friend"

You are one of six friends that I hold deep in my heart
There are strong ties to which we are apart.

We share a bond like no other.
We share a strong soul which is our mother.

Sisters are special in every way,
They sometimes bring sunshine to a gloomy day.

I'm glad you are mine, and there for me.
Sometimes you see things that I don't see.

Whenever you need me I'm there for you,
Even if you just need someone to talk to.

When you need an ear I'll try to be there
To let you know how much I care.

The times we share I will always treasure.
A sister's love you can never measure.

Our feet will cross a different path one day
We can look back on the past and say

We were there for each other when we needed it most
We gave sisterly love in a double dose.

We keep our feelings to ourselves and our thoughts deep within
I must truly compliment you, for being "My Sister, My Friend."

Sandra G. Addison

"If You Want To Be A Poet"

If you really want to be a poet
Then write so every-one will know it.

You can't just throw away your time
So you'd better learn to make words rhyme.

Then think careful in choosing too, if you're using many words or few.
Choose your subject, great or small, tho it be short, plump or tall.

If there's been an error, then erase
Try putting something else in its place.

If in doubt, then think for a while
You'll come up with something else to make you smile

Like, apples are red, the sky is blue or a leaping frog would even do

I guess it's time to erase, and put that "title" in its place

Then too, you'll have to keep in mind,
That you'll have to double-space below each line.

Well now I hope I've helped you, but, just
remember - neatness and spelling, still count too.

So! you may never be a Grandma Moses,
but a person can be whom one chooses.

Willie Mae Partain

The Common Light

When you go, and I must stay,
Then I will find another way;
To greet you often with a smile
To stop and rest a little while
To know another in your stead,
And ponder them with prayers at bed.

Forget you not, and hold you still,
At soft reply of whippoorwill,
And go about my merry way,
To greet newcomers day-to-day.

Amid it all, your spark divine,
Will pierce the action 'long the line.
And I'll grow old and face your fate,
When I will go, while others stay.

So we'll meet again it seems, not just in the land of dreams,
But rather where all fate combines,
Where heart-love lives throughout all time.
Where we will share communal will, passing 'mid a mutual chill
From "Old World" embers, once burned bright,
Long ago in common light.

Victoria Pinkus

"Acceleration"

The motels fell aside one by one as I left town
Their promise of rest was painfully ignored
The engine hum soon acquired a distinct whine
A thick hail of stars smacked against the windshield

A long patch of dark pavement loomed ahead
and concrete shapes darted out of my headlights' view
The wind desperately clawed at my window
There was no stopping now...

Where am I going and why did I leave?
No time to ponder such thoughts
Acceleration self-renews
Once in its netting you're caught

Falling without even knowing
The gentle whirl tightens its spin
Life left behind is quickly replaced
With the unknown slope of life ahead

Ray Woods

America

We pick our brains to do our best
the world out there is the real test
but when we fail what do we do?
We start again like it's brand new.

The more we gain, the more we lose,
it gets more difficult to choose
which way to go or what to do
all through life it's nothing new.

We learn new words, we learn a trade
then just when we think we've got it made,
new taxes take what little we've got,
leaving nothing to us but another new start.

Steven P. Caruolo

The Window

The window is open, to the world you look out
The world is around you, the world that you doubt
The world of deceptions of a reality mystified
A world of illusions, to your room you confide

The room is ever changing, a self made world of your own
Into a reality you remember, from the window to the room
Clinging to both worlds, through the window is shown
Arranging to your liking, confided to your tomb

Outside the window, the chaos has begun
Trapped inside your room, there's nowhere to run
Louder it is getting, closer it becomes
Shaking your room, booming like drums

To the window it rushes, into your world you don't want
Through the window in wanting, to your world it haunts
You run to the window and to your surprise
You try so hard to close it, but it's only your eyes.

Tim Jessup

When The Cows Start Growing Wings

They are tiny, they are white,
the wings keep growing night by night,
when the cows start growing wings.

They'll start flapping, trying to succeed,
their legs floating from the grass and weeds,
when the cows are growing wings.

The cows will fly up, happily mooing,
and all the other cows just ignoring and chewing,
when the cows are growing wings.

They'll feast upon birds' wings and feathers,
staying up there in windy weathers,
when the cows are growing wings.

Soaring up and up to reach the stars,
think of the mess on your brand new car,
when the cows are growing wings.

Trey Ange

The Shepherd

Once I was out in the cold, didn't know where to go.
The GOOD SHEPHERD heard my heart cry.
And took me in his fold.
For I am sheltered, and fed, and hunger, no more.
For I am sheltered in the ARMS OF GOD.
A place of safety, and love of peace, and joy.
There I can find rest, and I don't wander no more.
For I can find my GOOD SHEPHERD there.

Peggy Albert

A Rainy Day At The Beach

Although it was summer at a Martha's Vineyard beach,
the wind was blowing cold, crisp air.
The beach was ours, it was deserted except for us.
The crashing waves were roaring lions,
and the rocks on the ocean floor
were dull knives jabbing my feet.
I walked along the cold, damp sand
breathing in the fine mist that smelled of fish.
The wind was the big bad wolf
as it blew our sand castle down.
It robbed us of our beach ball
although my sister retrieved it.
Still, the beach was exciting
on that cold summer day;
like running through a rainstorm

Siobhan Grace

I Need Some Space

When a clouded gleam is in my eye,
the twinkle's no longer in place.
There is, my dear, no need to cry.
Sometimes, I just need some space.

Sometimes I just need left alone.
A slice of life just for me.
No radio, T.V., or telephone.
The sight of non others to see.

To learn back against a big ol' tree,
and watch the clouds in flight.
Maybe sit there continuously,
till the stars come out at night.

To dream, to reflect, to review who I am.
To do something nice for me.
To sit and ponder natures plan.
To establish serenity.

When again existence is reason to smile.
I'll again in life take my place.
Sometimes, every once in a while,
everyone needs some space.

T. C. Wells

Day Dreams On A Summers Day

As I gaze out through my window,
  The trees I do not see.
Though eyes seem to see days light,
  I look instead in memory.

For there within the greenery,
  I see an image of you stand.
A soft sheer flowing dress and shining eyes,
  I drift towards your outstretched hand.

I feel the warmth of sun's light upon me,
  Yet still I shiver with chill.
Suddenly, in thought...I realize dream...
  And awaken by the thrill.

For as your clothes then disappear,
  as I hold you in my arms.
Revealed to me, I breathless,
  gaze upon your charms.

I move then to hold you closer,
  sudden sound turns you into air.
And as I turn to face reality,
  I now find you.....standing there.

Richard S. Lee

"A Ball Player's Dream"

The bugs in your face
The sweat on your brow,
The dust on the base
The cheers from the crowd.

The wind up and the pitch
The swing and a miss
The once white ball and its red stitch
The sun overhead gives everything gliss.

The pitcher that gives his dead stares
The fielders are in their stance,
The stands are quiet and the batter glares
The crack of the bat and the ball over the fence.

The standing ovation and the batter's bow
The dream is alive for this one young man,
The game is his only life for now
The practice paid off for his first grand slam.

Rebecca Auel

"Tim"

It was a cold brisk day in '59'
The sun had risen on this son of mine

Happiness and smiles you gave and shared.
Your strength in life you gave, you cared.

Cool breezes of summer through your
  dark curly hair,
Gave implications of fresh ocean air.

In winter we shared our closeness and
  Love,
You brought rays of light from dark
  clouds above.

Now the sun has set in '85' on that
  wonderful man among men.
My son has gone, but my love lives on
  and I am sure I will meet him
  again.

Tracy A. Jones

War Is Hell

Everyone knows that war is hell
The soldiers wake up to the Sunday church bell
They pray for minutes, for hours at a time
To God that at the day's end, they will still be alive

They talk, sing, and carry on
But at the end of the day, some will be gone
They think of the family and friends that they miss
So they write a letter and seal it with a kiss

Finally after many days and weeks
To the battle field, they across the peaks
Then, to all their friends they give goodbyes
Because they know that they will probably die

And in the end, when all is said and done
To their mothers, look the soldier's son
And when he turns the age of eleven
He will finally accept that this father is in heaven

Tom Warren

Seasons

Spring arrived and resuscitated love
The snow and ice of winter melted away the pain
The birds and flowers arrived with you, the dove
The leaves from brown turned green again

Summer arrived and strengthened love
The temperature rose and brought warmth and light
Over the river, a strong bridge was built above
The foundations linked the souls just right

Autumn arrived and separated love
The winds blew fiercely and took you away
Leaving me alone with a larger bridge to the dove
But with hope the bridge remains, hope that the dove will come
back another day

Winter arrived and engulfed love with ice and snow
The dove got cold and burned the bridge away
The ashes slowly fell to the frozen river below
The snow and cold left the souls blue and grey

Will spring ever come again my dove?

Thomas A. Ditewig

The Kiss

Just as a person's Eyes are the Windows of their Soul,
The secrets of the Heart lies in the Passion of their Kiss.

I'm just a man who found a special person I call a friend,
And like 'The Garden', a forbidden fruit I must only admire.
Forgive me Lord, but so much in common that I cannot pretend,
She touched my Soul, her soft Kiss, my heart reborn with desire.

Though totally innocent and spontaneous, I crossed the Line,
As deep forgotten passion, once dead, surfaced and came alive.
Now I am sorry, and I ask forgiveness with the passage of time,
Because I respect her, a friend who makes me feel good inside.

The beauty of the moment, I loved, but what I've I have learned,
There is hope, my equal, that special someone out there for me.
I am special, live as I am, not to accept less, not to be burned,
And await that kiss which opens my soul and sets my Heart Free.

You have honored me with a gift few have known in their Life,
It is a Journey, a Passage through the Soul by way of the Heart.

Steven Blacketer

Still Standing

In lieu of still standing we still stand where once stood
the prints of foremothers
    forefathers made good
standing still
starry skies
backs lashed but minds free
now black backs bare no marks trial by jury slavery
the still stander's mentality to still stand through the test
    whatever action taken granted
    whatever triumph to contest
still standing for still standing
where we stood is where we stand drips of sand of color life
white black grey misunderstand
that as we stand drink in hand forward fast stuck on pause
talking talk shows
beating videos
marching songs for some different cause
Marley Malcolm Martin Medgar
    mesmerized us glossy eyed
thus a still stander standing still has only left but to die.

Shane Perez Tanzymore

Untitled

For me each day shall self-sufficient be.
The past is gone; 'twas duly laid to rest
When that same sun which tints the Eastern sky
Sank in the West.

Today is mine, and yet not mine to keep.
Why pause to watch the toiling hours creep,
With dull precision on an endless course,
And weep?

Plain simple joys are all that I desire.
Let others bask in adulation's song
And flaunt their tinsel and their ribbons gay,
Before the throng.

If I can hail with joy the rising sun,
And see it fade and count the day well spent;
If I have made no foe, nor lost a friend,
I'll be content.

John M. Sheehan

I Cry On The Inside

Time rushes by,
The past ceases to exist
In silent moments I cry
Over a girl that I truly miss.

Memories of her just won't fade
Dreams of her will never die
Exit the thought I had it made
To have answers to questions of why
    "I Cry on the Inside"

Weeping tears I will never show
Bottled up emotions I struggle to suppress
Feelings of confusion no one will ever know.
Yes I'm guilty of love in which I confess.

Theodore L. Mungin

Treasures Of An Empty Nest

"The party's over, "she said with a sigh.
"The party's finished....but it hasn't gone by!"

It's caught in the seconds, the minutes and hours
still playing its music, still full of its power.
Its presence and impacts indelibly stained
on the windows of memory to always remain.

The laughter still lingers somewhere in the song,
the lyrics aren't ended, the notes not too long.
The threads that still bind us are caught up in a skein
full of love and of laughter and moments of pain.

The party is somewhere deep down in my heart,
Forever the treasure...my own from the start.

Ruth Baker

What If...

What if when you got to the end of the rainbow, there was nothing there?
...when you got up one morning, you found no one cared?
...when you looked up in the sky, there were no stars?
...when you reached out for support, there weren't any bars?

What if when you called to talk to him, he said, "I'm not here"?
...when you looked around for happiness, you found only fear?
...when you looked for love, you found only hate?
...when you called for help, they told you to wait?

What if when you finally find love, it's kept restrained?
...when love was gone, no hope remained?
...when love is given, it wasn't returned?
...when mistakes were made, nothing was learned?

What if?

Sissy Taylor

215

Friends

I pleaded with God to show me your secret side
The part of you that you are always sure to hide
In my talk with Him I begged to know the complete you
For in my lifetime I knew I would never be through
With the love, and respect for you, given by God's hand
Not everything is complete, or whole as we demand
We're all different, with deep jagged scars
Created by our rebellion, and self imposed prison bars
I heard God whisper, I will use you to bring my child in
He's searched and searched for his life to begin
The emptiness hidden deep in his heart
Will be removed when he realizes death is not a start
When I call him home he will know his work is done
That many souls will know, through him, of my son
God gives us friends to point the way
And to stand in the gap when we decide to stray
But most of all to provide a haven of love
Saturated with the Lamb's blood from above.

Shirley Clifton

Representing

I hear my feet upon the pavement
The night is dark and the wind is blowing
I turn to see a face
It represents the hatred within us
Without a smile, a tear is falling
The flesh is dark, and the roots upon
the face are deep
I smile, the face turns away.
I look to where the face has turned
We stare, at a blurry picture representing
my life
The blurry picture fades away
the face looks up, and nods with a grin
How do I know this is the end?
I run, only to meet a dead end
a road has suddenly appeared and I
hear between the winds! "Straight, keep straight"
I know what the winds are meaning...

Summer L.J Sprofera

The Mystery Of Summer

When hearts are light and attitudes are right,
the mysteries of summer we see.

We let down our guard for one brief moment,

When we see old friends who really do care, and flowers
grow wild and flowers just grow and their brilliant color
takes your breath away.

When someone speaks their innermost heart,
you just listen and sit there dazed,

When you see neighbors come, you see neighbors go and
their light chatter is what makes your heart glad.

Their MYSTERY is known only to those who have a heart to
listen; to the mysteries of summer.

Pearl L. Goshert

Free To Be

There's a power within me
That created the earth, time, space, moon and sun
I, so small, so very small
Stand above all
Because God and I are one
Believing is the key
That gives me wings
And sets me free

Ruby Craig

Observations

Pity the man who never sees
The morning sun on the smallest of trees.
Who never hears natures symphonic sound,
Who never sips the nectar to be found,
Who never breathes the essence of the leaves
Who never plants a garden to smell the land
Who never knew the touch of a loved ones hand.

I have not money, home or clothes,
So I suppose I'm one of those
You call the homeless.

But pity me not for the gifts that I've received
Are the sun light glow on the smallest of trees;
The call of a mating bird in the distant field,
The juice of an orange to my lips it yields,
The smell of a rose after a midnight rain
Washed fresh and clean, I can not complain.
I love this land and have held the child by his trusting hand.
The world is my home.
My riches so basic that it is overlooked by most.
I'm not homeless. God is my host.

V. Watkins

"My Life"

Pain, misery is that the life for me
the more I give, the less I receive
grieve sorrow, no joy, no laughter
just a dream I seem to be after
I try and try to do my best
but I can't seem to pass your test
If there is a God high in the sky
answer, "This is my life, why"
no friends, no one who really cares
A girlfriend's secret life that she won't share
death, destruction, fear and hate
No more love for me to hesitate
Hate breeding hate that's the way I need to be
so no one else can ever hurt me
I know I'll never be that way
but everyone will be sorry one day

Robert Jordan

"Sacred Ground"

No matter where you go, no matter what you do
The Lord is always there watching over you
And every step you take determines where you're bound,
So don't you dare forget, you stand on sacred ground!

So before you deal those drugs, before you shoot a man,
Before you beat a child, remember where you stand!
'Fore gossip hurts your friend or you drink another round,
Before you strike your wife, remember "sacred ground"!

Before you curse God's name, or lie or cheat or steal,
'Fore you exact revenge, remember God is real!
Yes, beware of what you say, beware of what you do
For the Lord and His angels are watching over you!

Repent for all your sins, turn away from evil now,
'Cause no matter where you go, you stand on sacred ground!
And the good Lord's definition of sacred ground don't change
It's anywhere we are and all we think and say!

Sharon L. Hudson

Dearest Jessica

It seems like only yesterday,
  The Lord blessed us in a special way.
It was 1980, in the spring,
  When we first held our precious little thing.

Praying for guidance from our Lord above,
  We've watched your flight like a white-winged dove.
Growing in wisdom, patience and knowledge,
  It won't be long and you'll be off to college.

You run like the wind and dance with such grace.
  Your beauty shines with the smile on your face.
The God-given talents, we pray you'll use,
  And discover more daily, but never abuse.

We're proud of the way you're modeling your life,
  Scorning the deeds that cause undue strife.
Look to the future and set your goals high,
  Reach for the stars and continue to fly.

Everlasting our love for you is profound.
  Our wish that success for you will abound.
But above all else, as you might guess,
  We pray for your life only happiness.

Shari Beall

The Light Dims

Where do you go to hide from fate
  The light dims
Hold tight to your mate

Fear surrounds and strangles
  The light dims
Caught up in terror's tangles

It grows ever more bleak
  The light dims
Too horrified to speak

Can you hear my silent plea
  The light dims
In the darkness will you reach out to me

Pamela Grimaldi

"Feeling Way Down Low"

Feeling way down low
The kind of feeling that comes only when you least expect it
When you least know it,
Even after you already show it
Can't go back in time
The future's bleak, grim, gloomy
And then before the responsibilities
of the next day, hour, second
pull you in, you realize a truth
in the vast existence of life.

A secret so known it's utterly unknown.
The more you wish, hope, pray, the less that happens
God won't change the rules for
anyone but he offers his sympathy in this.

No matter what happened, how sorry you are,
or how sad you feel inside
There is never a true ending
For there is and always will be a tomorrow
One that you can share in, feel, and make better
than any memory your heart records.

Scott Selikoff

Tees

with apologies to Alfred Joyce (!) Kilmer
I think that I shall never see
The justice of a Ladies' Tee.

A tee whose club-scarred surface rests
Upon the earth 'neath madam's breasts;

A tee that's placed where ladies fair
Before they drive are half-way there;

So sister, girl-friend, wife and daughter
Skip most threats from trees and water.

If "equal rights and equal pay"
Don't take unequal tees away—

If fools keep making Ladies' Tees
Then please, dear God...make fewer trees!!

Vic Roby

Scare You

The abysmal abyss of ebony night
The hideous beasts that go "bump" and cause fright
Can you elude, staid zombies that rot?
Can you abscond, a perilous Lot?

Horrible haunts that torment your mind
Apparitions you've seen, like no other kind
You wish they would cease, their dark, forlorn games
You hope you'll stop seeing, grim specters that maim

One hundred eyes that scan from afar
From trash cans, their lids, left slightly ajar
The black cat's screech that makes you cringe
Will you withstand its gruesome revenge?

The day finally comes, you pass sighs of relief
The terror is gone, along with your grief
But the night will return, and that will be when
The fierce knights of darkness shall haunt you again!!!!!!!

Samuel Edward Pittman II

October 6, 1993 St. John's Woods

Hot Indian Summer Afternoon
The family hike - sandwiched between this and that - eagerly awaited
Trails crowded, voices floating past
Periodically forced to jump on trails side windfalls
  to watch sweaty runners glide by
Carrie searching for newly learned scientific protest, giving a
  learned explanation for each specimen
Sarah skipping ahead to discover the secrets just around the corner
  Turning back, questioning our pokiness
Mom and Dad savoring the time together
All of us absorbing the last tease of summer
  Seeing fall's promise in the reds, yellows and oranges
  refusing to believe the inevitable
Even as the trail's end opened to a cool sanctuary of an old chapel
  overlooking crystal clear water
A few minutes to renew energy - to soak up the beauty
All of us mentally preparing for the hike back to the car
to the this and that
to the eagerly awaited next family hike on a
Hot Indian Summer Afternoon

Pamela C. Schoon

Shelter

  Shelter my elusive lover, cradle me in your thick
strong walls. Protect me from those who wish me harm, and
be my beacon in times of woe.

Sharon T. Myrick

"My Wish"

If a wish were given to everyone
  the day they met this earth,
Would they wish for valuables
  or items of great worth?
I don't know what you'd wish for,
  but wishing for wishes is out.
You may not know what I'd wish for
  although you may ask about.
Now, we may not know what the other wants,
  but one thing I know is clear.
I'd wish for all the deadly diseases
  of children to disappear.
And that my friend would be MY wish
  for children one and all,
For though my friend they may appear
  to be very small.

Tina Moyer

The Feeling

A feeling. The feeling.
The constant ache of a broken heart
The ache of never ending yearning
A yearning for the love of one
One never to be held again.
The memories of the past.
Memories that become shattered
Shattered because of one mistake.
But now it's too late
He's one never to be held again.
Never to be loved again.
With closed eyes, you remember that night.
You, the only one to hear the last words
His last words whispered to you.
The words "I'm sorry" play over and over in
  your mind.
Then you get it. The feeling.
The constant ache of a broken heart.
The constant ache of your broken heart.

Paige B. Grass

Gunshots

One solemn night as early morning approaches
The clouds and the moon engages in their sensuous dance
The darkness of the clouds tries to block the light of the moon
But, the moon gaily dodges this sensuous play

Pow, pow, pow
Gunshots
There is a stillness in the air
Even the clouds and the moon stop their playful antics

Pow, pow, pow
Gunshots
The moment has come when there is no more time for games
No more time for dancing and playing
The time has come for tears and weeping
One brother, one loved one, one uncle, one father, one son
Gone, Gone, Gone

Slowly the moon and clouds return to their sensuous play
But, stillness continued at the break of day

Paula Robinson

Riders

They are the wind one blond and one dark
the blond one always at the shoulder of the dark one
at speeds worse than squirrels rolling off the roadside
avoiding the raucous rumble of four wheels
attached to jet like engines swerving over macadam meadow roads
the hint of honeysuckle and tractor exhaust
wafting up their flared biker nostrils large insects plastered
against sweatslick foreheads standard issue boll shades
slapped on their faces day or night poised in the direction of the
wind (they are the wind) one blond and one dark
brothers still connected one living and one new dead
the dark one still sees the blond at his shoulder
keeping time with the curves of the asphalt
he is lonelier now more than ever
he takes his partner's share of gasoline dreams
on long, vacant journeys searching for rest (without death)
frequent humanity-poor bars fights off near-barebreasted women with
frayed denim, frayed hair who attach themselves as bloodsuckers
wanting to be his blond where's your partner?
They burned him up today it's his last ride to the cemetery

Susan L. Singer

The Love I Left Behind

If you look inside you'll find
That you're the love I left behind
I know I cheated, I know I lied
I know about the times you cried
Respect and attention was all I had to ask
For you that seemed like such a hard task
I promised myself I wouldn't shed a tear
But losing your love brings them so near
I told myself I wouldn't cry
I guess I told another lie
Being without you causes so much pain
I really think I'm going insane
My feelings for you are so hard to hide
I'm really hurt deep down inside
"I don't want him back" is what I told
But our relationship was getting old
But if you look inside you'll find
That you're the Love I left behind!

Sabrina Marie Hayko

My Grandfather's Clock

My Grandfather's clock upon the wall;
Speaks to me and I hear its call.
In my hands you see your moment in time;
In my tick you hear your passage.
It is to you I give my treasure;
But it is for you to balance the measure.

Thomas M. Dell

Clair De Lune Revisited

Word spread via the underground
that the U.I.S. (Union of Inhuman States)
using missiles with atomic warheads
shot the Great Bear.

The populace masquerading as humanity dashes out into the streets
gazes at the sky; where is the Great Bear?
They run through asphalt illuminated by an epilepsy of neons,
invitations to adult movies, cocktails, and the din of discotheques
they run, inquire, demand where is the Great Bear?
The Great Bear has been killed.

In such a crowd
an elderly woman shuffles and sobs
Lord, my God, this is the end of the world!

A young chick in stylish jeans which
accentuate her every curve
approaches the woman and with a cocaine smile asks
Why are you shrieking, what are you scared of?
That it's the end of the world?
Lady, your world ended a long time ago:
FINI!

Roman Makarewicz

Mind Of A Child

There is something in the dark
that isn't there during the day.
It calls to me constantly
because it wants to play
Devils look like angels with wings of shadow black
and there are castles on the clouds in the sky
and the sunset is a dragon breathing fire
I can make up stories but I don't know how to lie

Everything is touched with a special kind of magic
like it's charged with electricity
and nothing can hurt or scare me
like a vision of immortality
as long as mamma's there
confidence and trust are never broken
and the good things do not go forgotten
in the mind of a child

Rachel Christopherson

Reverie On Father's Day

You, who have given me life and held up your hands in prayer
That I might know truth and build my life on a firm foundation;
You, who have taught me, praised yet disciplined me, and
   through it all, loved me;
You, I revere this day.
Not only for your unfailing love, your kind, but firm patience
Through all my childhood and on through the years,
But for your gentle manner, your unselfish attention to duty,
Your willingness to share my troubles and hopes,
   my fears and blessing.
Though your eyes be dimmed now and your walk more slow,
Your courage and spirit still touch me, uphold me,
Your wisdom and love continue to be life's most precious gift to me
So shall this ever be, father — your life enfolding into mine.

Peggy M. Frazier

Joy Of Giving

How long has it been
Since you've given a toy
To some under privileged girl or boy
And watched their eyes light up with pleasure
While two tiny arms cuddle the treasure
No other feeling of joy can quite compare
To this spirit of giving
Which we can all share

Verona Nitteberg

I Miss You

Not a day goes by
that I don't try
to hold my cry
I wish you didn't die

The laughing times we had
I miss you so much granddad
and all of this makes me sad
but I got to know you, that I'm glad

I'll never stop thinking of you
and all of this is true
I miss you more when the day is new
I want you to know I'll love you my life through

Vito James Faiello

Reverence

My mind is full of such a rage
That I can barely turn the page
To see what lies beyond the wake
All we had, must now forsake.

Bloodless tears in prayerful eyes
Slowly watch our own demise.
Farewell to species of the earth
Too late the value of your worth.

Prodigal daughter, mystical son,
Pretentious waste by a committee of one.

Felonious deeds, acts of contrition,
Expressionless faces, foreseen premonition.

Dreams once swelled inside my head
Now vanish and replaced instead
With visions of nocturnal dread.

We are the product of those who breed
In silent place of lust and need
Poverty and eternal greed.
Rape what you sow,
We are the seed.

I know my turn will come one day
Unfurl my wings and fly away.
Oh, crescent moon in shapeless sky
Bid these earthly bounds goodbye.

Sherry A. Stewart

That Old Oak Tree

It wasn't true, I said, it could not be
That death made its calling on that old oak tree,
The tree in the meadow behind our farm
That sheltered us kids from old Sol's harm.

It tumbled to earth under the cruel sharp saw,
There was no lawyer to fight the lumberman's law,
It gave no struggle, offered no futile case,
The blade struck deep into that old oak base.

That fine old tree has now passed away,
Some said it was never meant to stay;
But I can't forget the pleasures bestowed.
Even held a tree house as my kids' abode.

Have I learned a lesson from that old oak friend?
I've learned to stand tall, never to bend;
I've learned to endure year after year
Right to the finish, shedding no tear.

I've learned a lot from that old oak tree,
Its sturdy branches hold the secret's key,
Even when I can no longer stand
My past has been rooted in earth's farm land.

J. Lyle Whitson

Shutter-Blink

There is more, I think, in shadows and space
Than the eye can catch
   at once, popped open
    and canvassed in light.

An orchestra of chatter hides the sound
Of clipped memories
   captured in a box
    small enough to hold.

Figures are stolen, sketched out and replaced
In the time it takes
   one wave of coarse sand
    to run its glass path.

You hear the sound snap as the door swings shut
And the eyes blink closed
   as the paint dries fast
    on another year.

On the border of my aged memory
I can almost see
   the shadows of those
    who begged to be ignored.
       Scott A. Vandrick

Meet Me At Solomon's Portico

Meet me at Solomon's Portico,
Tell no one of where you go.
Walk with me on the road to Emmaus,
Past the salt pillars of Tiberias.

Take me rowing on the lake of Galilee,
Stroll arm in arm by the Dead Sea.
Pluck me from the reaches of the damned,
By the pyramids ancient shifting sand.

Arid nights I sleep on a Greek abacus,
Counting time on the road to Damascus.
Inside my head there are ancient scrolls,
That pull me deep into earth's dark holes.

Catch me, hold me in your quasar light,
Stand beside me in the equator's sight.
Run with me along the tropic of Capricorn,
Swim naked by Drake's Cape Horn.

At the Archipelago de Colon we will be alone,
There we can rest on ancient stone.
Carve our names on granite deep,
On Galapagos we shall sleep.
       Sheenagh M. O'Rourke

My Two Room Home In Tennessee

Today I visited our two room Home in the Mountains of Erwin,
Tennessee. Oh! how the sweet, sweet memories came rushing back to
me. Those beautiful mountains seem to whisper our laughter and
our tears. And yet it seemed like only yesterday we as kids were
here, but it's been so many years
Then there were six of us kiddos and our Mom and Dad.
When I think of those precious days
It makes my heart feel sad
For it was after we moved from a place
Called Cannie Hollow.
Seemed like all our lives changed and
it is still hard to swallow.
For our precious Dad was taken from
us one hot July day.
And it seemed that after that we
just all went a different way.
And as I gazed at those mountains
it made me want to cry.
But then my heart was gladdened for I know,
We will all be family again in our Mansion in the sky.
     Peggy J. Winters

Baby

Everywhere that I turn
Tears in my eyes seem to burn
Before they roll down my cheeks
As they have the past few weeks.
There is a picture on the wall
Outside my room and down the hall
of my tiny, happy baby
in the arms of another lady.
I can never forget that one sad day
when I had to give my baby away.
I had to give it up for adoption
because I had no other option.
God! I miss its beautiful twinkling eyes.
How I miss its tearful, late-night cries.
I miss its fresh-powdered baby smell.
I miss just holding it close as well.
I long to have my baby back
But time and money I deeply lack.
And, although we may be kept apart,
I'll hold my baby forever close in my heart.
     Victoria D. Garcia

I Wanted

I wanted to pick up the phone this morning and hear a recording
   telling me who I am, what I'm doing, where I'm going,
   but all I got was a dull hummmmm which led me
   to believe that was my answer.
I wanted over coffee to make a list declaring my vital statistics
   to securely establish my existence even though I
   knew it was pointless.
I wanted to stare into eyes in the subway for some reaction
   or reflection, hoping for a blink of assurance from
   that central core, "We're all in this together" sigh
   the soul shoots forth whenever it confronts a comrade
   in dullness.
I wanted to taste love in the mouth of a woman, expecting
   satisfaction in the salty substance, the liver's food, but
   swallowed bitter resistance: stale tobacco and antiseptic.
I wanted to find the same lasting happiness I saw in the Winston-
   Man's face that smiles down from the billboard upon us
   even on drizzly mornings.
     Thomas D. Wolf

My Friend

  The people I see everyday, we
talked, we told jokes, we laughed, and
they confided in me, told me their
troubles and problems. I gave them advice,
good I hope.

  Each day I saw, worked with, or
communicated with them in some way, if
just to say "Hi".

  Then one day tragedy occurs. I am
unable to see my friends, unable to talk
to them, or even work with them. I have MS.

  They say they still care, day after day
I watch as my friends drive by my house. It
hurts inside sometimes as much as the disease itself.

  As I look to my side, I see all my friends
rolled into one...
   ...it is my wife, my one TRUE FRIEND.
     William McLemore

220

"Taking Time For All"

For you Howard Ely Managing Editor
Taking time for all;
Is for you always not to fall;
Remember, "This gal has to stand,"
For everyday we feel that time has spanned.

Noting life has for me;
Is an every day, 'giving me a chance to see.'
You're a friend; for many of writers;
So, "Thank you for being a wonderful sighter."

When a day hits; like it must all fits.
You feel like a new person;
Under this blessed world to be under our sun.
Because, "All of life isn't always fun."

Lifting your spirits, 'may be something you need.'
Because, "All of your everyday readings you must feed."
So, "As you notice writing you today,"
Comes with another poem for you to stay.

Ronda Darlene D. Gonsalves

Gone

Death is so very unfair
Taking something that can never be replaced
Forever gone, no longer here
It takes the touch, the smell, the taste
There's no longer a lifetime, not even a little while
For the feel, the sounds are gone
I miss her touch, her laugh, her smile
I miss her love, I miss my mom
She was my mom, my friend, the only one
Who stayed with me through the unknown
She stood by me, beside me till all was done
Then left me to stand all alone
God how I miss her, I loved her so much
She was my heart, my soul, my happiness
To know I'll never have her gentle touch
Or her sweet voice and soft kiss
Is like death not only taking her from me
But pieces of my heart and soul
Yet at least I'll have my memories
If not her to hold.

Sherri Hayes Morales Reason

Through The Eyes Of The Eagle

Brother Eagle
Take me with you on your journey to the sky.
Let me see through your eyes,
Our beautiful Mother down below.
Let me feel the joy - rippling, pulsating
Of the freedom of the flight.
Brother Eagle
I have experienced with you
This feeling they call Oneness,
If only for a moment - a magical moment
That unlocked my spirit from the prison of my mind.
Brother Eagle
Let my spirit soar with you
On the eternal journey
Of discovery - of Truth - of bliss.
Give me your perfect gift of the moment,
So that each moment I may remember
It is a good day to die.

Therese Blackwell Harper

A Moment To Remember

Take a moment to slow down
Take a moment to remember
Look around you, see the sky
Touch the earth, breath the air
Remember when you were a child
Oh so young, Oh so fair,
Seems like an eternity
For that child is no longer there.

Now you're a teen, who's beginning to hurry
Running here and running there
Take the time to smell the flowers
For soon they too will disappear.

As an adult you often ponder
Why on earth do we need to wander
Life's too short, and Life's too fast
Think about what really matters
Take a moment to reflect,
Take a moment to remember.

Sandy Mecolick

"Michelle"

Her name slid from his lips like caramel.
Sweet, sticking to his tongue.
Her power, although unintended, wove a shawl around his shoulders.
He felt frightfully content, yet desired more.
Much more.
His thoughts revolved around pleasing her.
Smelling her.
Touching her.
Her eyes, her mouth, her skin were permanent in his mind.
Laden.
Engraved.
Until time brought them forever, he would wait.
He will wait.

Shareen R. Holm

Waves Of Heat

Maudlin thoughts roll 'round my brain
Summer is the season of greatest pain.
Swirls of humid heat run rampant here.
Work? No one works very much, I fear.

The appearance of diligent industry is maintained
But all our papers and files are perspiration stained.
We blot the pages—we mop our brows.
What knowledge can our weary minds house?

Is there no relief for tired man?
Must summer do the worst it can
To wreck strong spirits—damage weak hearts
And pull each one into a thousand parts?

But in the cool of the morning hours
Hope rises—with the fragrant flowers.
We start a fresh and a new day.
Perhaps winter will yet come our way.

Ruth Grossman

The Wail

Night. Coin overboard!
Swallowed by the surface of the sea,
Dark twisting face of anguish.
Freed from the relentless tug of gravity
It shuffles and slips through the water's grasp.

Only to rest upon what once was
The poochy hole of some submerged mariner
Whose own coins once rode the dark casket
Into the lonely cold hungry
Maw of the sea.

Tim Walker

No More

Through howling winds and endless nights
Suddenly the wind comes knocking at your door
It shakes and it rattles and it bangs at your door!
And you cry-no more, no more!

Then as fast as the furies
It comes seekin' through
You're stiff with fright, you shake and you tremble
The cold whispers your name as to swallow you whole
And you cry-no more; no more

It closes in around you
You tremble with fear
And you let out a shriek for all to hear
And you shriek - NO MORE NO MORE!

You look around to find a way out
It gets colder and colder
You cough and you sneeze but, alas,
There's no way out
You look around once more
And whisper - no more, no more.

Stacey Carrier

A New Path

Have you walked in the forest of life
Stumbling in a world of strife
The true pathway cannot be found
For you travel on dense covered ground

Light is not there as you seek relief
For you wallow in anxiety and grief
The thorns on bushes cut and do prick
Your whole body became weary and sick

A point in right thinking searches in hope
To find help in this situation to cope
At last sparkling light does appear
As sunlight shining above trees helps fear

A new path is seen in the Way now
As in the presence of God you bow
Seeking His help to restore you as you walk
Giving Him a moment of earnest prayerful talk

Repentance shows you the proper sure gate
To open heart to Jesus fully: Do not negate
Righteous pathway is joyful: full of peace
Happiness in Christian pathway will increase

Susan Essler

Past Passions

Two bodies have met
Struggle through friendship,
but still...
Lust comes before love.
There is a sad sweet smell of you that fills my mind.
an almost sick smell of love on lazy afternoons in rented rooms
that never were really ours for keep.
Because this never happened, despite the fact that you'll
always remain a part of me, you've never really been mine.
Our love affair has been a torrent of passion fast and furious.
I made the mistake of falling in love. I'll remember you and I will
burn inside for your touch. Your smile, and the little parts of
yourself that you shared with me. Sometimes when
I'm with someone else I know I'll pretend I'm with you, but the
passion won't be there.

Susan L. Eaton

Beans And Peas And Peas And Beans

Shelled, spotted, shaped like the kidney
Strings, snaps, sprouts, and seedy
Beans and peas, peas and beans; yes indeedy!
Hulled, harnessed, hurdled and hopped
All send comfort and cozy messages from the pot

Fitted, snugged together all in a row
Forming, falling, filling and flashing in a glow
Peas and beans, beans and peas
Stand alone to satisfy a hearty protein tease
Sends a mighty healthy message all with ease

Eaten raw, boiled or mashed for sure
All curdled up in salads and soup du jour
Seems to give body to meals not a few
Round ones, rollies, ribbon-like and red
Multiplying in jars and pots with bread
Flat ones, fleshy ones, fat ones, and fiber filled
Fun ones. Fossilled ones, Flossy one smiled
Flayed, flexed, and flavorful you see
Beans and peas are worth the flavorful
Buy them by the bag, box, bowl flavorful.

Velma Jean Bennett

Flow To Eternity

As we flow down the stream of life over stones and shrubs of everyday
strife, struggling to find that moment of peace it seems as if we'll
never reach; We try to accomplish our goals on our own
and those times we find ourselves all alone, It seems.
We try and try and don't succeed, and cry for help in dire need.
Then a majestic voice calls out our name,
And we realize it is the voice of God.
He says "It's time now to put your trust in Me."
We can conquer anything as a team.
The stones and shrubs may scar and taint,
Don't fret, He says, I'll heal your pain;
For if I've created an insignificant creek
I'll be with you my child when you're most weak.
You see, life's a stream that flows; It clogs, and turns,
Stops, and goes; Each little shift another battle won,
For nothing can stop what God has meant to run.
We continue on in search of the prize.
As faith overcomes all problems that rise.
For that insignificant stream that once was,
One day reaches home, - The Eternal Sea.

Todd Wright

"My Beloved Spring"

Old man winter, brushes my cheek with icy breath,
Stillness surrounds me and how barren is nature's growth.

Desolate fields, no crowing crow, no bird on wing,
Just bitter, bitter winds that sharply sting.

Oh, how I recall the running brooks,
The glittering rocks and banks with moss,
Now just a memory, oh, what a loss.

With heavy heart, a slow moving gait,
Vigor almost gone, I sadly wait,
For a lost thing, "My Beloved spring".

Paul Piccolo

The Garbage Can Banger

Once there was a boy who wanted to play music.
Once he found two garbage cans
and started banging and banging on them,
but it did not sound nice.
He tried burning the metal garbage cans.
It started to make a beautiful sound!

Terrence Darnell Forester

"Confusion"

All bunched up nowhere to move. Words being tossed but none stay except two, two different voices, two different sounds, two different attitudes, but only one, they came together and made a hole, so now it's more dense like a forest with trees two inches apart and I am between. I don't know which one to chop down. There is a big one that stands fifty feet. There is also a small one, that is the same as me and its leaves shake the same way, her branches sway the same way, her heart beats the same way. I still hear the rustle of the big one, he sits and waves and make his leaves fall, fall on me. For now I'm stuck between the green and no one is there to let me free. I hope someone comes along soon or the little one may become a big one and crush me, crush me between two different things. So "help" I called but no one answered. A few pass but just stared. The leaves are harder now. The tree is growing now. What should I do, o, what should I do.

Rachel Bennett

Christina

Piano music drifts up the stairs,
starting softly, but deepening with each note.
It fills the room and swirls about my head in a thick, warm steam
and I lay on the bed shivering — crying but not in pain.
And I am achingly happy.
But in the back of my mind I remember the feeling of each note
its weight in my hand, in my ear
And I know I have lost the memory which gave it its shape.
The painful shards are scattered around. Glistening like gold —
reflecting in each other's light. In confusion, I freeze.
I struggle, trying to grasp the memory painfully sweet behind my eyes,
the melted remains of a perfectly shaped cube of sugar.
I grasp even tighter to my aching knees — addicting myself further
to the music.

I'm not even sure if the girl is playing,
but I hear the music still, begging it to remain deep and clear.
Parts of the melody weaken and I focus now, even harder, on its crispness.
   But it fades and whines diffusing into the pale blue walls.
      And think I've forgotten its name.

Stacey Hollenberger

You Can't Staple Souls

A facelift, a browlift, and swollen stitched eyes
stapled tightness across a tired blue face
Lying beneath a cloudburst of ice packs
stuggling to be beautiful and young again

Eye lids don't close when she is sleeping
Displaying her painful dreams
The cuts overwhelm her at midnight
as blood drips steadily into a drain

Sandpapered mouth, brown and crusted
forming pink flesh beneath the ooze
Fighting the urge to tear soiled bandages
covering wounds deeper than she knows

Drug induced sleep eases raging discomfort
expressionless features tightly reined
Can all of these staples and stitches and tucks
make my mom happy with her soul?

Rhonda J. McCook

Tomorrow

I woke this morning to the angels tears.
On my back, I think back but the memories were no longer there.
Fading away unconsciously, I lay them to rest, the stars I used to test.
Awaken today the winners play. Not afraid of what was said but
driven by a darken craze.
And upon that night I rose, sick of what I had become. Tired of the
trophies someone else had won.
I think back lonely without my fears. I woke again with angels in my tears.

Scott Griffel

Today And Tomorrow

Happiness is found in special moments
spent with good friends
and looking forward to the happy times
that will be shared in the days to come

Comfort comes in knowing
that whether near or far
no matter what crazy directions life takes
we can only accept the things
that seem out of our control
and try to move forward.

May you find strength in yesterday's rain
walk straight in tomorrow wind
and cherish each moment
of the sun today

Ronda L. Bisatt

Moving

How does one carry the hours of joy
Spent in the love of a little boy?
How do you put on a hanger to go
Excitement you felt watching girls grow?
How do the movers carry outside
Memories of Mother who loved you with pride?
How does one pack a house full of living?
How does love fold a life full of giving?
China and quilts fit nice in a crate
But what of the longing for a lost mate?
I'll tell you how-it's all wrapped in joy
Most tenderly cradled, handled with care,
Placed deep in your heart - and you move it there.

Shirley Taylor

To My Hero

The red sky seen in the northern hemisphere
Sound of the ammunitions broke the silent of the night
The sound heard like the roar of a wounded lion in the night
Dry and hot winds still blew from Southern hemisphere
Wonderful night changed to be death

   My city destroyed and changed to be big ball of flame
   All of a sudden, everything vanished in the dense darkness of the night
   Ash was the only thing left

Thousands of thousands of powerless dead bodies laid on the ground
A small little girl was walking still,
With a bundle of flowers
She put the flowers on the dead bodies who were powerless

   There is for you, my hero
   Thank you hero,
   You had already struggled for my country

Yogggie Efendy

One Last Fear

One tear fall from my eye, and
Soon I'll begin to cry,

Joy and happiness is all around,
But I lie crying on the ground.

The love we shared was really true,
That's why when you left I was truly blue.
My heart and my life has turned
gray, but for you love I'll gladly pay.
So until our hearts meet again, I'll love
you always, my special friend.

Perry Pannell

Dad's Harvest

Cycle of seasons, rhyme of God's reasons,
Sons are the crop he seeds.
Sowing and reaping, work without sleeping,
Teaching and keeping ahead of the weeds.

Young one's birth, up from the earth,
Fed by his own hand;
Later weaning, full of meaning,
Lessons learned, from his own land.

He gave warmth and light, told what's right,
Showed what they needed to know.
Gave his time, sweat and grime,
So they could learn and grow.

Rewards were sweet, never complete,
From helping young things grow;
They stumble and fall, then rise up tall,
Those hardy youngsters he did sow!

The sons return his love, and from above
Blessings come through strife;
Time for joy and time for boy,
To praise the one who gave them life!

Paul Mills

Such Is Life

Such is life when things so wrong,
Sometimes you feel you don't belong.
Getting embarrassed is not so nice,
Make a mistake and you'll pay the price.
Yelling and screaming in your face,
Don't they know it's not their place.
They're not perfect, it's not fair,
To yell and scream to make things clear.
Understand and calmly explain,
To avoid the mistake from happening again.
Always treat others as you would expect,
This is the way to earn their respect.
Accidents happen, mistakes do too,
They're not done to anger you,
So keep your cool, don't blow your stack,
Together we'll get back on track.
Such is life when things go wrong,
Please treat me now, like I belong....

Regina Weismantle

Reflections

Women speak
sometimes
Mostly to assure themselves that they aren't threatened by the pretty
clothes I wear

Sisters hug
occasionally
Society teaches familial closeness
while forgetting that even sisters are women

You
homegirls turned corporate
better remember that Friday night still comes — loneliness unmasked

Friendship is not found in fashion or discomfort!

Wanda J. Martin-Terry

Death Of A Lover

Sometimes the wind calls your name.
Sometime I hear your voice in the rain.
Then there's that feeling, always the same.
You walked into my life, I'm glad you came.

I thought parting would never come, ever,
But when it came early my heart was severed.
That doesn't mean we can't be together.
We'll never be separated, together forever

Summer Lanksbury

Steamed Up Glasses

My glasses need windshield wipers for the rain
Something must be done before I go insane
Rain, snow and extreme heat
Make my glasses a mess complete
I nearly walked into a wall
My steamed up glasses were no help at all
Hot weather makes my eyes sweat to the brim
All over the glasses and covering the rim
I see nothing with glasses covered with rain
I cannot win, I cannot gain
No matter how many times the glasses I clean
I sweat and they have lost their gleam
I clean them morning, noon and night
I cannot make them look just right
I write a few words and my glasses I wipe
I hate to just complain and gripe
I must end this poem right now, but I must mention
My glasses need lots of attention

Winniferd Gilchrest

Sisters

A sister is someone, who will always be there
Someone to look up to, someone who will care
She's always there, to lend a helping hand
She'll always listen, and try to understand
She'll give all her love, that comes from within
She'll stand by your side, through the thick and the thin
She'll comfort you, when bad times come along
She'll push you ahead, and help you be strong
She'll laugh at your jokes, if they're really good
She'll smile at the bad ones, because she understood
She'll give you that hug, when you really need one
She'll give her support, for things you have done
She'll open her arms, and share the world with you
She'll open her heart, because her love is so true
So having a sister, is a great part of birth
I would not trade mine, for anything that's on earth
Because a sister, is someone very special to me
I'm a very lucky brother, because I have three

Vincent Cea

The Game

Why do we lose focus on the things that matter to us the most?
Somehow the vision of what was, now becomes the dreams of tomorrow.
We see things in a different way and yet somehow the things that
we become afraid of now becomes clear to us. The emotions of the
heart becomes harder as the depth of its meaning turns to inner
beauty. The chaos, is now the existence of what lies deep within
us. Feeling everything that is to be felt, the journey now goes
onto a newer level, one that cannot be played by the weak. Finding
that your inner self cannot tolerate the games that men play may lead
you to find that a game is what it really was........

D. P. F.

Somebody

He breaks her heart.
Somebody's crying.
She fell apart
Somebody's dying.
He says he doesn't want her
Somebody's lying.

The fear in her eyes,
Mirrors all the lies.
The different touch of his hand
Now makes her understand.

In her heart she feels the pain
Without him, she might touch the burning flame.
He'll be to blame if she stops her heart.
For it was he who led her to fall apart.

Trisha Weber

Dreaming

While sleeping I felt your lips
softly caressing my face.
I felt as though I smiled at
something you said blushing just
a little as I so often do.
Not knowing why, I turned over to reach out for you,
only to wake
and find you weren't there.
I was only dreaming.

Sharon Kirkpatrick

An Anniversary Poem

As murmurs a brook through the forest
soft, gentle, soothing,
so does your voice soothe my soul.

As caresses the breeze across the meadow
in loving, delicate touch
so do your hands impress my soul.

As warms the sun the air,
with tender radiance,
so your eyes fill my soul.

Murmuring voice, caressing hands, radiant eyes,
in concert lovely,
give wholeness to my soul.

Soothing voice, tender hands, warming eyes,
poetry quietly felt,
makes me love you.

Robert E. Allen

Ready For Love, Ready For Pain

When you're ready for love, you're ready for pain.
So you'd better make sure your love feels the same.
'Cause if your lover's just playing with you.
You're gonna get hurt and you won't know what to do.
You'll think about putting a gun to your head.
'Cause if your lover doesn't want you, you're better off dead.
You might think about diving off a roof.
'Cause that sounds better than playing bullet proof.
No kind of love should ever go that far.
For anyone person, no matter who they are.
Your mother, your brother, your sister or your lover.
Whether they love you outside, indoors or only under cover.
So when you get dumped try not to go insane.
'Cause when you're ready for love, you're ready for pain!

C. Jones

Falcon

One day I watched a falcon
Soaring,
    Soaring,
        Soaring,
Until at last it disappeared
Against the brightness of the sun.
Just below, a lone white dove
Glided homeward along the edge
Of a wandering cloud.

Suddenly, the falcon,
Its telescopic eyes fixed upon its prey
Diving,
    Diving,
        Diving,
Until at last its knife-like talons clenched
And then away.

Somewhere beyond the sun
Another falcon with fearsome eyes
Is diving.

Suck-Min Kim

Broken Doll

She had doe like eyes, and Alabaster skin
So unblemished that she resembled porcelain
Even her sphere changed from reality to plastic
Held together by thin threads of elastic
In a world too brittle for glass to endure
Instead of human she was a ravishing fixture
Solicitors arrived for an amour's extortion
Yet mantle pieces aren't permitted emotion
She started to crack in the collectors hand
They wouldn't put her down, they wouldn't understand
No one heard her cry out, no one heard her call
There's a Macabre beauty to a broken doll
When she became frightened they put her away
She lost her tenacity, couldn't stay on display
One tried to fix her, one tried to hold her
Losing her own hold and controlled by another
A splendid encasement held a spirit battered
Hurling to the ground her heart was shattered
Everyone saw her go down, but no one broke her fall
There's such a Macabre beauty to a broken doll

Shirley Bolstok

Untitled

You were not here the long time that I wish for you.
So short here was your stay; but you must
have known how much I love you, and I will miss
you with each passing day. I remember the sunny
day that you came, and joy that you brought to our
hearts. I could not envision the sadness we would
know when too soon we would be apart. But you
must have completed your mission here on Earth;
you have done all the things that you were
supposed to do. You have brought us closer
together. Your presence here has inspire me to
raise my head and look above and pray that I will
never forfeit the right to your love. You have left
us and you are home now. But I know you are not
really gone. I will see you each time I look up
above to say I love you.

Peggy Ann Hendrix

Chicago Revisited

I cried the day that I returned,
So long the years and breach
I'd searched the world for misty dreams
And things beyond my reach.

I know you understood, my dear
Why I was in arrears,
And why I mourned the wasted time
With seas of salty tears.

You set a feast for my return
But I hungered not for bread,
I was content to feed my heart
Your loaves of love instead.

Yes, I promised that I'd return
When autumn leaves were falling,
For through the years I've heard your voice
Calling, calling, calling...

Rosemary Muntz Yasparro

human kindness?

i have no father
so i scan from my vantage point, pick out, choose one man
i look to him to be the one, possibly
hoping, yearning, pleading (with my eyes), almost aching
the one to guide me, teach me, applaud me, take pride in
   me, provide for me
the one meant for me to follow
finally, he looks into my eyes, searching
meant to reciprocate my feelings
yet he explores my eyes not with everlasting love, but with sympathy
poor little boy!
with the truly heartfelt sorrow of a stranger
i hear the clanging of a nickel against my tin can
if only the nickel could be a home
or a person who cared
i watch the stranger, my lost saviour, walk away
happy with his unselfishness
and i realize once again the cruelty of human nature
i am all alone.
do we have a father?

Ritu Sen

"Innocence Found"

I close my eyes and my world returns to me
   So hollow and cold I begin to see
I have run and I have walked
   I have stood and I have stopped
Never knowing that all the while
   My world possessed not a smile
I have been for others but not for me
   Now they have all left and I am so lonely
I seek only a touch, a feel, an innocent caress
   To feel someone so near, no wanting to possess
I have been all through my mind
   And know all there is to find
I have slipped away, lost for so long
   Living in emptiness, shadows, and wrong
My innocence I lost but so long ago
   I now stand alone, no friend and no foe
I hear all around me the beating of my heart
   It echoes into my soul and tears it apart
I open my eyes as though witnessing the dawn
   I find a new strength pushing me on

Ronn Davis

The Spaceship

There was a spaceship,
So big and shiny,
When I stand next to it,
I feel so tiny.
Inside there are many switches and gears,
That have been developed over the years.
So dare to discover new planets or stars,
You might start a colony on Mars!

William Joseph Naivar III

The Unknown

The sharp teeth, blades through my neck.
Slowly my veins shivering
by the force of the passion
converting me into an
immortal flying beast.
A vampire they say
that's what I am?
strange that is.
Flying through the night
hungry for blood.
Be my victim, I say.
Feeling alive and unstop able.
How can this be I ask myself;
Living an eternal, nightmare.
Assassin, they roar at me
ready to rid of me.
"I'm immortal!" I say
devour their soul to make
mine stronger.

Vicki Sanchez

The Addict

I awake to face the morning;
Sleep in my eyes and my body moving slow;
I cannot grasp the rhythm of the sun;
Water on my face and news on the air;
I need my fix to play my role;
What happens to my head, my blood, my bones;
They work together;
Clearness arrives, veins open, bones tingle;
I am ready for the day;
I've had my cup of coffee.

Robert Alan

Grieving for the Memory

I remember all our Christmases and how our eyes would glow
sitting by our windows, hoping it would snow.
Praying we weren't naughty so Santa would stop by,
waiting for the morning in hopes of a surprise.
Doing good deeds for others, thanking mom and dad
I wish we still were little I miss the fun we had.
This will be the first year when I sit down by the tree,
you won't be beside me saying "open this one "T".
Your laughter will be missing from the hall ways in our house
Silence will replace it like a church yard's winter mouse
your stocking will be hanging where it has for many years
no goodies tucked inside it, 'cause there's only room for tears.
Tears that say we're grieving for the memory of the joy
you gave to all your Loved ones since you were a little boy.
Time will not forget you for the pain will never fade,
especially on the morning of the Lord's most precious day.

Tina Kovack

The Face Of An Angel

Some sweet child with the face of an angel
Sits by the window looking for a friend.
Hoping and praying for someone to come,
Someone with some time to spend.

A game to play or a book to color,
A TV show to talk about later,
A snack to eat or a song to sing,
These are the joys that a friend can bring.

This sweet child with the face of an angel,
Can't run outside and play on her own.
She must wait for someone to help her.
Her legs don't work like any of our own.

A wheelchair can be a confining place
To spend life's days all the time.
But when friends stop by to spend some time
You'll get along just fine.

Some sweet child with the face of an angel
Sits by the window looking for a friend.
Hoping and praying for someone to come.
Someone with some time to spend.

Ruth M. Edwards

Mommy

A web of life-connections the rain descends and covers the window-a single drop roams down the sill-it then touches the ground and quenches its thirst-the earth, that is-so many connections, so many interwoven thoughts and feelings- a butterfly flaps it wings in montana and the wind changes somewhere else

As I walk towards the mountains peak, I listen for the glorious symphony that my brothers and sisters play for me-I lift my foot over a vibrant purple flower: Alpine forget-me-not the tiny stream trickling down the mountain-a tear trickling/roaming down my face

Touching the purple flower-may I mommy? Gently, bending close to the ground, she feels it smallness, like me mommy-smile, my tear roams walk gently upon the earth-quietly, soaking in the solitude-mom, my hand is lost in hers-connected-I wipe the tiny tear of rain that meanders down her face-she wipes mine

Mommy? Mom? Mother? Eyes are opened to her long hair as the breeze plays with-I smile-her hand becomes mine-mother earth? Or mother? responsibility for like, she says, beads of sweat slide down the mountain of flesh-oozing fleshy baby-new life

Peace-re-sensitization-adaptation of words, beliefs, connections, I feel them-smiles-a drop of water roams down the window sill-it then touches the ground and quenches its thirst-the earth, that is-so many interwoven thoughts and feelings-a butterfly flaps its wings in montana and the wind changes somewhere else

Shelly Arlene Poehler

A Syrenian-Named Simon

I'll never remember the weight of the cross
Since a drop of His blood fell on me
Since He touched me - I never again am the same
Since that road leading to Calvary.

They told me to carry His cross on that day
For a man who meant nothing to me
Why do they pick me? I ask of myself
Tell someone He knows-why pick me?

When they told me that I was to carry the cross
There was nothing to do but obey.
Now I'm ever more thankful that I was the one
Who carried His cross on that day.

Just a drop of His blood-made the cross easy to bear
Just a touch-what a change came on me
My sins are all gone-I'm made clean evermore.
Since that road leading to Calvary.

Pearl Jacobson

Rhyme Time

Young men who are romantic in their ways,
Should know why earth's first poet took the time
To take a rather common human phrase
And twist the simple words into a rhyme.
This unversed lover led his love into
A lilac grove where hopefully he cried:
"My dear, I swear this love of mine is true,"
But all his shabby prose she brushed aside.
In frenzy then this most determined male
Regrouped his words into a metric plea,
And though we will not to into detail,
We can point out the worth of poetry,
For facts are facts and, boys, I'm telling you,
Those lilacs blushed at what she let him do!

J. V. Adams

"Joy"

The light gleams through the open window
Shining into my eyes with speed
Reflecting off everything
Not stopping in any one place
And in it you may find the ultimate
But you may not catch it
It whips by you too fast
You reach out to grab it
But it has eluded you
The joy of joys eludes you once again.

William Adler

Our Mother Earth

We can sense that her soul is so strong and so free,
She's the spirit in the waves of the untamed sea.
Her eyes are wild, they glow of bright light,
They light up the world, they're the stars of the night.
Her hair smells of Jasmine and shines of pure gold,
She's the sun in the sky, so warm yet so bold.
She runs like the wind and flies like a bird,
Her songs fill the sky, yet she speaks not a word.
The woman is poetry, her thoughts come in rhyme,
She's the mother of nature, creator of time.
As we speak of her spirit, her strength and her pride,
we'd never expect that she's dying inside.
We've taken it all with our greed and our lies,
We've polluted her soils, her seas and her skies.
If we try, we can stop her from reaching life's end,
Please save her, our home, Mother Earth, our friend.

Wendy Loudermilk

"Let's Not Give Up On America"

Let's not give up on America
She's still the land of the free.
Though she's filled with trial, she remains the isle
And the heart of liberty.
Let's do our best for America
And change those things that are wrong.
In a world at peace we all can share
Our love is one great song
We'll overcome adversity and with the help of God
We'll bring about tranquility here on our native sod.
Let's all stand up for America
In spite of ills of the past
If we all pitch in we're sure to win
A vict'ry that will last.

Roland E. Ellen

A Little Paint

It's over now, I know
She's on the other side of the room,
But it really makes no difference
There's no love anymore, no love at all
It's not me, I know
I love her
But it makes no difference to her
I might as well be a wall,
Painted over with obscenities, blank verse
Perhaps if I were painted over
A new coat of paint,
A peace sign, or two,
A border, some cement to patch up the cracks,
Maybe she'd love me again

William Gjebre

My Mother

She was the sweetest person alive
She was as busy as a bee in a hive:
She had more love and faith
Than most people of late.

Moms eyes were so blue;
Her cheeks so rosy red;
Her hair was a golden hue.
I can't believe she's dead.

Her voice was like a soft breeze;
Her hands were like two soft angels;
She dealt out love and punishment with ease.
Now she is one of God's perfect angels.

She may be gone for now;
But she will always live;
She would never bow.
For her pride would not give.

So for many and many a year;
Whenever a bird we hear;
We will think of you mother dear.
Weather we be far or near.

Robert C. Lee

Taking The Life

Driving down the highway at ninety miles an hour,
She starts spacing off.

What is she thinking about?

Maybe she's thinking about her first love,
Her first breath,
Her speeding ticket.

Maybe how she will die or her last tomorrow.

Maybe her dysfunctional family who threw
Her out when she was innocent;
Or could she be thinking about her childhood that
Got interrupted by punishment?

Maybe she's thinking about her child she will
Never give life to;
Maybe the world that her child will never live in.

Abortion?

Maybe she isn't thinking at all.

Sharlie Messinger

My Sister Cared

I had a sister once, she was tall and full of grace.
She had brown hair that framed her glowing face.
Her eyes were sharp and a beautiful brown hue.
She danced all night until the sun broke through.
For she was in another world, very happy then.

Much has happened in her world. Her family were babies,
And, have grown up and have grown apart;
Scattered East, West, North, and South.
She can't decide which she loves the best.

For they're all her children. She remembers the parties.
The Halloween costumes she has designed and sewn
For these children which have been
All her love and pride.
They're always clearly in her heart.

Collette Calhoun

Looking Through Teenaged Eyes

I once knew a girl who had a good life
She did lots of things to hide her strife.
Everybody knew her because she was the outgoing type,
and the clothes she wore were somewhat hype.
Then one night she went to a party,
she did some drugs with a guy named Marty.
A couple of weeks later she felt kind of strange
and needed some rest,
so the next day she took a blood test.
I try to understand the short life she lived,
and now I understand that she was H.I.V. Positive.
It is hard to believe the things we see,
it is hard to believe it could happen to me.

Tanisha Bennke

"Mama Loves You So"

For nine whole months she carried you round
She always come running when you made a slight sound
    Your Mama loves you so
She combed your hair and made your bed
She'd always provide food when you need to be fed
    Your Mama loves you so
She bought your clothes, your shoes, your toys
She filled your life with plenty of joys
    Your Mama loves you so
She put you through school and bought you a car
It doesn't matter how old you are
    Your Mama loves you so
She'll give you love the best she can
From birth, till you die, and on to the next land
    Your Mama loves you so!

Petrina Morgan

The Little Children

Children are a blessing as you can see.
Sent from our Father above to take care of by
you and me.

Love the little children our Lord has said.
For such is the Kingdom of heaven that lies ahead.

We are to be like children.
Full of Faith and Hope and Trust.
For it is by Faith and Hope and Trust,
Our Father blesses little children like us.

When a child is called by God's Almighty hand.
And we do not understand.
All we know it is by faith.
That it is part of His Heavenly Grace.

Richard Sauers

228

Getting Ready For Christmas

We get a fresh cut tree of pine
Shaped so nice and oh so fine
Bright white lights go up and down
Here at our house you'll see no frowns

Pretty red bulbs and pretty red bows
A few glittering snow flakes here and there
String of red beads up high and down low
And a large red bow a top with care

Poinsettia rings and candles too
Were all put out to decorate
Many things to get ready and much to do
And Santa's coming so no time to hesitate

Getting ready for X-mas we all join in
Decorating outside as well as within
Getting ready for X-mas is so much fun
Time to sit back and enjoy the decorating is done

Sharon M. Martyna

Cautious Dream

Darkening night sensed along our
Shaded beach, we fell to a twilight sleep,
Sparkling, quakes of emotion rolled
Then smoothed in evolutions of time, we seeped!

Yet the late night faded as summers
Soothing breezes collected in chills,
Wet, turned to a quieting cool,
We faced again along our single hill!

Bending, clouds played on heavens shores,
A new moon split the graying mass,
Sending, streams of shining silver light,
Before us, a beam lent a dash!

Then our world grew in slumber,
Still we held for just a moment,
Soar if you must in this land of sanding sprinkles,
Remember we pass in darkness, to no torment!

Seeds, are sown in natures night,
By day we cast and wait in steam,
Heed, these calls of protection,
Then lend to silence in this minds cautious dream!

P. Vincent Nee

The Tide Rocks At Mendocino

Salt-taste and change,
Scent of freshening tide, a narrowing,
Afternoon seaside warm without Northwest breezes.
Enskied above the horizon white, spreading contrail marks the
journey of a high, - flying jet.
Contemplating, - listening, - feeling ocean splendor glittering
From this promontory as from a tower in isolation.
One senses Deity distantly stirring great Pacific waters.
Dry air drinking an offertory. Earth, the summer season oscillating.
Raw will fueling invisible stars.
Urgency spreading the universe. And a domestic nurturing
of waves on dark, deep journeys, - row on row.
The mustering out as uniform, wind-sired cavalry.
All manes and tails and steaming breath remembering endless crusade.
A disciplined charging of headlands, beaches and mute,
hunch-shouldered stones.
Bared by chance, a yet incumbent creator,
Dis-passionate, thousand year guards. Deaf to the beating drum,
Blind to flags, - profoundly absorbed in their own
Immutable raptures.

W. P. Burr

Where Circles End

O, mothers, fathers, sons and daughters
Scattered rings upon the waters...
The wayward skip of destiny's stone
Leaves in its wake new fam'lies sown...
And from its touch, that great long strider
The rings of change grow ever wider...
Though trav'ling out to raze and rend
All circles clashing, in the end...
   ...How can that pattern last?

A million years will never see us
A million stones will never free us...
Rings of change are just illusions
Too many habits in collusion...
This modern race of savage man
Will make his face an also-ran...
To fade beyond all mortal hist'ry
Extinct, he'll be another myst'ry...
   ...To something else's past.

J. Michael Deerfield

The Fear Of A Child

As I little child I was always afraid
scared of the shadows that hang where I laid
Frightened of the dark and all it revealed
Never knowing what was fake and what was real
I covered my head just to keep out the ghost
They probably thought I was a terrible host
Although my fear came back every night
My mother never hesitated to turn out the light
Maybe I was afraid of something not there
It seemed real to me so I didn't care
The ghost of my childhood may be that I dreamed
Or maybe they were exactly as they seemed

Rosemary Miller

Padre Island

The beach comes alive in the early morning hours;
Sand crabs, still drowsy from their rest, come out to greet the dawn.
Arrogant fish darting out of the sea for a quick breath of the salty air
Find the pelican surveying the sea, hoping to find his morning's meal.
The water laps at the sand's feet, knowing these gentle hours will soon
   be gone.

Higher rises the sun, and the once-playful seek the depths of the
ocean to escape its harsh rays.
The grasses growing on the sand dunes bow to this God,
Hoping their humility will persuade him to be more kind to their dying souls.
Parched is the sand, and it cries for water to cool its thirsting tongue.
The sea, not daring to challenge the sun's reign, creeps in,
Giving his friend a shield for a few brief moments.
Small creatures have fled to the dunes and buried themselves deep into
   their inner coolness.

Dusk steals in silently, changing the sun's rays from burning yellow,
   to soft reds and golds.
The conch dwellers emerge from the sea for their evening meal,
Then bury themselves in the sand for their night's rest.
The sky turns to a gentle shade of amber, then violet;
And all is quiet as night becomes god of the universe.

Wilma Heffelfinger

Impressions Of Padre Island

Bare brown toes, pinching crabs, gathered shells -
Sand castles rise

Smelly wharf, fishing boats, gleaming shrimp -
Greedy gulls fly

Cresting waves, snowy foam, happy shouts -
Surf boards descend

White sand dunes, wild sea oats, old driftwood -
Pelicans cry!

Vivian Hennings

From Galleon To Flotsam

On one dark night, in the Japanese sea,
sailing there were Galleons Three.
A storm brewed up, and hit the first and
into flames it soon did burst,
then lightning hit number 2 with a crash and soon
reduced it down to ash.
The first one's cannon was pointed at 3 this
courted certain death, boom!
Went the gun and all the balls and sunk
the third beneath the depths.
But now the ships are merely Flotsam,
bits of wood, and debris,
It's all that remains of that fearful night,
and the horrible fate of the Galleons Three .

Robin Keck

Regaining Consciousness

The powerful empire of my mind crumbled to the muddy ground.
Rust-tainted raindrops drive sharply into my brain.

I would cry,
If I weren't dry
From tears lasting 41 days and 42 nights.

I would scream,
But I know that
It would only please her more than I ever had.

I would forget,
But I cannot remember
What happened on that cold, cold August night.

I would sleep,
If I weren't awakened
By the constant reminder of my most recent failure.

I sit in the darkened room with all the lights on,
Holding my breath in an attempt to end my life.
One minute... Two minutes... Two and a half...

I regain consciousness five minutes later, and come to the realization:
I need to move on with my life.

So I go to bed.

Peter A. Ceresa

My Two Grandpas

My grandpa was a special man, I loved to call him
Poppie Sam. My other grandpa was Poppa David,
I loved to call him Poppa. Poppie Sam was a
Pharmacist, who gave prescriptions to assist.
Poppa David was a Pediatrician, who helped me
back to good condition. One was short and one
was tall, one had hair and one was bald, but I didn't
care because I loved them all. Even though in
death we're apart, I still hold them close in my heart.

Peter Weltman

Escape

Run children -
Run from swollen clouds rumbling over amber waves of grain.

Hide children -
Hide beneath the low ledge of yonder purple mountain.

Cringe children -
Cringe as ye seek comfort within its majestic bosom.

Lift children -
Lift your hopeful faces toward a fading patch of blue.

Watch children -
Watch those coal-black clouds change to silver —
Dazzling, blinding your innocent eyes.

Fly children -
Fly to the inviting radiance.

Sleep children -
Sleep in loving warmth forever peaceful.

Rada P. Kaparakos

Forever And A Day

Sad and lonely am I, here in my lonely
room. My poor heart is filled with gloom.
As I watch lovers pass me by, all I can do
is heave a sigh. Oh what is to become of me
I'm so filled with misery. All I do is cry. Oh
how I wish I could die as I awake each
morn, I ask my self, why was I born?
Sometimes I feel like a lonely queen
waiting for her true love and king. Then
one sunny day you came along, filling
my whole world with song and as you held me
I could hear you say, you would never, never,
go away. Never never let me go my darling
I love you so. You've made me happy in
every way. For tomorrow is our wedding day
and when we take our vows. I will hear
you say. I'm yours forever and a day.
I love you.

Viola E. Jones

Sweetheart

Memories you brought to me whether good or bad,
Remain with me for that is all I have:

No uttering of loving words,
No passionate embrace,
All that I have left now is this picture of your face.

I long to touch your face,
Caress your cheek,
To press my lips against yours,
That's what my heart speaks.

I will not burden you with bad times;
But remember all the good,
I'll remember all the tears you dried,
Not the ones you should've.

I know the dream has ended,
We've said our goodbyes,
Only I can face the hurt I feel inside;

I close my eyes to hide it all,
But now all that I see is life without you
Just memories for me.

Tammy Eickholdt

Carefree Roses

Every summer there are
Red roses climbing on the old wooden fence,
  weaving up and around
  perfectly aware of their importance.

But when the snow drifts up over the second railing
and the frozen wind blows
and pushes against the world,
  where do they go?

They are the red
  in the tropical birds' feathers,
the red
  in the blossoms lining the quaint streets
  of the islands,
and the red
  in the beach towels lying in the sand.

Then somehow the roses know
  just when to come back
  to adorn their place
  on the old wooden fence.

    Teresa Millias

Rebecca Edwards

Rebecca Edwards, where are you?
Rebecca Edwards, who are you?

She is like no one else,
She stands alone in her reality.

Rebecca Edwards, can you help me?
Rebecca Edwards, what has happened to you?

She is described to be like her characters,
She is the image of them.

Rebecca Edwards, do you know her?
Rebecca Edwards, could it be me?

    Rosemary Wally

Peace

Sitting under a maple tree
Reading a book of War
I glance over at the daisy
Staring up at me.

With its beautiful pink tips
and golden yellow center,
I wonder why we even have
seasons such as winter.

I rip the book in tiny tear drop shreds
to watch the birds rearrange them
into magical flower beds.

They chirp and sing and dance
To show off their graceful stance;
And when they're all gathered in their tiny little nest,
It's time to contemplate how this world could be
at our very best.

    Wendi R. Woods

The Melting Pot

The melting pot is boiling over, this fire rages the whole world
over. Once revered as a land of peace, now in bedlam we feed the beast.

It started quiet and serene, now parents search and children
scream. The voices of the dead will not be hushed until all
involved are caught and crushed.

It is horrible to look at, but we dare not look away, for it was
Americans that killed Americans in Oklahoma that sad day.

    Thomas B. Feeney Jr.

Daddy's "Homemade Money Tree"

Dedicated to my loving father, Mr. Wilton A. Thomas
"Rich" as can be, without a dime to spare,
Raised the "old fashion" way, never mounds
of money, yet always equally shared.
Morals, respect and the "Honor code," instilled in our souls,
Now it is second nature to conquer our life time goals.
Learning that "success" is something to be
proud of pending, on how one gets there.
Knowing if it is not honest and true from your heart, it is not fair!
Hours on end spent sitting on that branch as we grew,
Dreaming of how "rich" we would someday be,
Little did we know then, that we were creating ourselves.
In Daddy's "homemade money tree"!

    Ramona Lee Thomas Schmidt

AllWoman

Wrapped in mountains' mist, oceans' pull,
primitive dances of stars, moon pull,
I count bones of women, begin with
the crown jewel, Pearl, my mother.

Their bones clickclack clickclack like earth drums.
My bones bend in recognition. Juice from
their bones are bombshells of knowledge in mine.

Forever, the wind has does will blow
her knowing: Earthmother, like all women splits,
her bones make bones that make bones.
In the moon's eyes, Earthmother's trees
and my babies are the same.

I dare walk out into the night, carry my light
as does the cat, the tiger, the moon.
I dare sing music that began at the beginning,
hold the bones high, rattle them for all to listen,
to hear, to know AllWoman, she who is Alpha, seed,
beginning, creation, birth.

    Sylvia Turk Weinberg

The Land Destroyer

The land destroyer is like a wolf
Pouncing on its prey

And now I see no more of what used to be
A piece of beautiful nature

I hear the loud noise of the tractors
Instead of the birds singing

And I smell the brown smog
That sits in the air

Now I touch cold hard cement
Instead of soft soil and flower petals

The happy land that once stood proudly
Is now a sad polluted city

    Tabatha Lee Whittaker

'Til I Remember

There is this thought within my mind,
  of an illusive, secret kind.
It flits and flitters here and there,
  from consciousness to unawares.
It finds its way within my dreams,
  through woods and over mountain streams.
Just like a butterfly it rides
  on wings of silver threaded tides
  that rise and fall and rise again,
'Til I remember, through lessons end.

    Renee K. Driscoll

"Dare To Share"

Anger and sadness swirl together in the
  pit of my stomach;
Gnawing at my conscience, trying to escape.
I want to set them free, but I don't know how.
Talking to someone, maybe that will help.
But, who is there to confide in?
My friends won't understand; they'll laugh at me.
Mom? She'll merely scoff at my petty, childish problems
Oh, God, please help me;
These awful beasts are killing me!
Maybe a counselor could save me.
No, she'd probably think I'm nuts.
I have to talk, say that ever comes out.
I'll never truly live again unless I dare to share.

Sarah Michelle Nunley

Always Go Back

We must always go back into the past to pick up the
pieces in order to heal. So very much is buried
there and we must look so we can learn. Our life
is a journey that is difficult and long. It will
never cease to be hard, but if you look under the
problems with faith, you will find flowers.

The only way to accomplish. This is not to run away.
You must handle each situation and solve every dilemma
as it occurs. Work your way through the thorns which
are the problems, and then, push them a side. For,
when you brave the thorns, you will reach the rose.

Shirley Smith

Ode To A Speck On The Floor

Where did you come from? Who can tell?
Perhaps the result of a fairy spell.
You must have sprung as a spark from her wand
One day when she carelessly shook it, and yawned.

Maybe you're really a miniature dome
Some minuscule creatures have built for their home;
Inside your roof, under cover of dark,
They dance and they sing, or they squeak and they bark.

Where did you come from? Who can say?
I hope you have traveled a distant way,
Riding the clouds, and the wind, and the sea,
Landing right here just to motivate me.

Sarah Samuelson

A Prelude To New Beginnings

When we met our lives were quite shattered
Past lives we lived - broken, nothing mattered
We talked, we smiled, and hurtingly laughed
No serious relationship, we decided, recalling the past
We never thought we could trust ourselves to love again
But time has an inconspicuous way of healing the pain
Because of our requirements for an uncommitted association
We relaxed and respected one another with no expectation
We are not exactly sure how this could possibly happen
We began caring about each other more than ourselves
We began to recognize our ever growing attraction
In the years we spent together our souls and spirits merged
We found affection, devotion, each day is a delight
We discovered our love is honest, true, and genuinely earned
True love is rarely - love at first sight!

Ramona Biegler-Powers

A Peace Of War

Vast sea of faces
passing me by without a glance
a feelingless mob on a mission of mercy
moving, marching forward
in the fervent frenzy that's your life
from the vantage of vanity toward the depths of the damned
rushing ever onward
in haughty delusions of unwanted help
glancing not behind nor to the side
your brother
your sister
your child
I'm here
a countryman in need
loved one lost
in the paradox
of peace at home

Patricia L. Austin

The Painting

The first strokes of the sun
paint the ice away,
while bright colors mix and run
onto the coming day.
Trickling water begins to gush
the brown transforms to green;
life's no longer a silenced hush
as He sweeps the sky pristine.

The blooming, buzzing, bustling earth
slows its busy factory;
the chilled sun puts on its shawl
while the jeweled leaves fall
and gather under a bending tree.

The colors are dulled to grey and brown tones,
while the waters are lulled
to soft, quiet moans.
His brush strokes turn violent
as the wind swirls around
all the white paint is spent,
then there is no sound.

Serena Goldsmith

Untitled

Celestial Bride, princess of the night
Overload of panic fury
Underestimate the power in a child's eyes
Ravaged by society's upbringing
Selfish, yet taught to be giving
Equation is less without anger

On the crown of a rabid tooth
Future's nuclear mother

Ride off into the sunset
Unique with distinguished patterns
I bow to none
None is all that is left

Troy Usher

First Encounter

Thunder rolls and lightning flashes;
Outside rain beats down.
Inside bodies and sheets entwine -
She wears him well.
Heartbeats echo a primal one;
Virgin passions collide;
A blend of abandoned stormy need -
primitive and poetic.
A combination of desire,
Direct and penetrating - molten fire
And haunting fragments of flowers in the rain.
Searing passion and fragile innocence -
The alchemy of equal parts
A nearly holy thing.
No pleasure more exquisite
Than this great sweet pain.
Waves build and roll and crash to shore
And in their wake sweet sleep.
Night colors deepen, painting the land
And in her garden, Love's seed.

Skye Montana

She Says

There she goes telling people she's a Gypsy again

Needlessly marks milestones
only to know they're just yesterdays

It's the whole that she wants, that she wishes, that she had

The beat of that different drum
the sun shining that free heat, the road that leads anywhere

I wonder if she knows exactly which venues she's in for
but then again, as I recall, she once told me
of the gypsy life "where the wind is like a whetted knife"

So she consults the cards and smiles grimly, as if
she knows all too well of the tarot, the runes, and the ways of the Gyps

So she waits the weeks 'til the caravan moves out- go west
she waits for the joker who'll play her game

Someone witty, someone clever, someone free
she carries her amber, holds it to the full moon
hoping to uncover the secret of this unknown lover

The lover to roam and dance all around this rock
only to know, a joker's jest and a scorpio's smile
will take them to the lands they travel.

But today she's just telling people, she's a Gypsy.

c. s. haven

Times Are Changing

Many are the times I catch myself thinking...
    of what used to be
And I know this present time...
    just isn't for me.
A family was a family...
    and a friend was a friend
Oh dear me
    has it all come to an end.
We respected our elders...
    and manners we all had...
Thanks to the up bringing of Mom and Dad.
    Let's pray those times aren't gone and past...
The present age is moving too fast!
    It's moving so fast, it's left behind...
        All those dear and wonderful times!

Sherrill Hale

Alone

Close, feeling the night so close around me,
Only one star pierced through the velvety black.
Caught in a maelstrom of an emotional sea,
Fear that you may never be back.

Then, cold reasoning froze me into stillness,
Not death...but worse...a timeless limbo.
Filled to my very core as I witness,
Even in dream, I cannot let you go.

I dare not speak aloud these inane thoughts,
Yet, wild in my mind, unfettered, roam free,
Tormenting, fermenting, giving rise to mad plots,
Fearing them, yet powerless to flee.

Alas! No sanctuary for me to hide,
Not solace, nor help, no one to care.
You left me, I move, but life died.
My soul of dead love feeds on despair.

Spring returns, bare trees with new leaf rife.
Love! To bud, to grow, external, internal. To grope,
And so I thaw, I draw, and fill with life,
And never endeavor to love without hope.

Shirley A. Bassett

Red, Yellow Or Blue

If I could make a wish,
One that would come true,
I would wish for you to be,
A flower of red, yellow or blue...

For never are they lonely since,
There are many to be found,
And they are quite content,
To be rooted in the ground...

Never are they stubborn as they,
Grow most anywhere and always,
Are they grateful for our patience and care...

Although they may whither,
They never really die,
For again they shall bloom,
Under a warm spring sky...

Yes, if I could make a wish, then a flower you would be,
So everyone could behold your beauty, as you dance in the summer's
breeze, yes, if I could make a wish, one that would come true,
I would wish for you to be, a flower of red, yellow or blue...

Timothy Barrett

A Dream Worth Keeping

A dream worth keeping is
One that makes you laugh
When you feel like weeping
One that you dream of
When you sleep at night
One that you think of
When you gaze up at the starlight
One that keeps you warm
When you're inside a raging snow storm
One that you can keep beside you
And let it guide you
One that you can follow
And look forward toward tomorrow
One that you keep inside your heart
And where your path of fulfillment must start
A dream worth dreaming
Is a dream worth keeping

Samantha Kilian

233

Nikolette

Nikolette,
One day I must leave,
I wish that would be the only time you'll cry but,
I brought you here, to this world, with its
  habits, twisted morals, its viciousness

I promise to make your life the best I can

Your curious, unexpecting, almond eyes,
with those childish, curled lashes,
  they're so innocent, so loving
How many tears will they shed?
  I want to be there to dry them

Your soft dimpled hands, so quick to grab, to touch
  will they be burned or unheld?
  I want to hold them as you cross those tough streets

That little heart, with such energy, so naive to what hate is,
will it be broken because of what life needs to teach you?

I want it to beat with warmth
  just like mine does, as I look at you

  My unexpected gift!
  Priggione-Brannan

The Martyred

We struggle and call - "I'm small oh so small"
One among many - million if any
"How can I traverse - a vast universe"?
We ask and we ask - we partake of the flash
The flask of the needy - the flask of the greedy
The flask of affliction - The flask of addiction
We anesthetize - 'til we're desensitized

Then we see someone martyred - beaten, discarded
In empathy we see - 'that could be me'
Such commitment surprising - Love - uncompromising
To redeem and inspire - to ignite our desire
That's why they're here - to draw us in near
To the voice down inside - to the truth in our minds
To help us traverse - this vast universe
Waste not their pain - let them suffer not in vain
Though history repeats - it is ours to delete
Trials and tribulation - and bring exultation
  D. Q. Wells

The Traveler

Glistening upon the water were the last breaths
  of the afternoon's life
The light meandering about the ripples
I, like the lonely leaf sustained by the murky shadows, began
  drifting towards deeper darkness
Until the highlighted ripples seemed no more than an image of the past
  and the future cried for mercy
The only reassurance came from the melodies and words of a song from a
  buried childhood, almost forgotten
Perhaps lost in the shadows
Then the sun, gasping for life, surrendered to the night
At that moment, with the song clearly engraved in my mind...

Reality ceased
The fantasy within the melody thrived...

And it was over

I stood awaiting the company of the moonlight
Whose presence among the shadows was my only encouragement to move on
The music faintly echoed throughout my thoughts
  Stephen R. Dagata III

Summer's Last Goodbyes

How vivid are the memories
  of summer's last goodbyes.
Roses in bloom, pansies, peonies
  scenic hues, majestic sighs.

Rich tapestry of poetic nature
  blanket earth's hills and dale.
Heavenly everlasting picture rapture
  calm winds, cloud softness sail.

How gentle the summer breezes,
  tranquil thoughts prevail.
Memories of pleasant seizures
  summers beauty captures entail.

Nestled in gardens, bright blossom flowers,
  chirping birds echo songs forever last.
Hearts and minds fill enchanted hours
  gently, nature's music whispers summer's past.
  Rose A. Nikolla

Old Bones

As marrow pulsates like powerful waterfalls upon the stream,
old bones leap beyond the crest that ascends the gasp for life.
Grandly fashioned from lamenting pains, it binds the calcium
that endows strength against the pointed edge invading
its frame. Old bones, molded from hot clay with Great Hands,
rise toward the skies amid the drying dew, surrounded by twinkles
of light that becomes darkened by shadows that forge its presence.
But, old bones are strong.
Sheathed in dark cloth of unrelenting ghosts, old bones move forward,
graced with the wisdom of a rising sun.
Even in the tomb, its dust does not flutter humbly beneath
the night air. It makes impressions like hands in the golden sand,
forever telling the story of the bones that stood upon it. Like
angels dancing through the rapture, old bones soar, too, the winds of time.
  Sherry Philpott

Footprints In The Sand

Each grain of sand is a piece of time
On a beach where many have run
Every stride has moved the grains
The grains are all the things of time
Crushed and eternal to construct shifting sands
Memories, the remains of time, are crushed under the grinding wheels
Of all the lives living in the fast lane
Thinking to themselves that time is saved
When in truth time is being made
Old ideas tossed away, along with forgotten
dreams and shattered lives
Make time to fill the eternal beach
Onto the beach stepped the feet of a girl
The grains of sand sticking close to her toes
The grains are the time she lived as the waves swallow time
And she danced to the music of the waves
Footprints in the sand left her markings on time
But although the beach is eternal
The footprints we each strive to leave will never last forever
For they are born to be washed to the sea.
  Sarah Arlen

Untitled

Stargazer, look at you!
Your eyes are fixed to the sky
staring....piercing...
into a vast, lonely world
without another's glance to meet you.

Just look at you!
There is no one, no thing
no where near you,
not within your reach.
Don't waste your life
waiting...dreaming...
twisting the real
into an amorphous fantasy.

Come back down. Come back to me.
I'll take you where
you can stop seeking what's beyond,
where the sky has a limit,
where the heavens are within reach,
where the universe has an end.

Anna Alberici

"A Sister's Love"

(Dedicated to Erin)
A sister's love is great to have
You'll know it's always there
She knows how to make you laugh
You'll know she'll always care

You may play with dolls and crowns
And pretend that you are mothers
The both of you have ups and downs
But you're always there for each other

That very special time will come
It's time for you to marry
You know that you will both have fun
Even if it's scary

You might not see each other much
And miss each other dearly
But you can still feel her touch
And love each other sincerely

A sister's love is great to have
In no way is it a game
Even if you don't always laugh
I'll love you just the same

Amanda Boroff

Reality

I never really knew you
You were just another friend
But when I knew you noticed me
I let my heart unbend
I couldn't keep past memories
They only made me cry
I had to forget my first love
And give love another try
So now I've fallen in love with you
And I'll never let you go
I love you more than anyone
I just had to let you know
And if you ever wonder
I just don't know what I'll do
But you are your own person
Just remember...
   I love you!

Amy Carruthers

Nocturnal Minds

When you dream,
You take a thought.
Hold it tightly,
Once it's sought.

Sometimes scary,
Full of fear.
Others happy,
Filled with cheer.

When it's over,
And you finally wake.
That's when you realize,
Your visions were fake!

Elizabeth Richardson

Quiet Time

You need a quiet time
You need a quiet minute
You need a quiet time
But you need God in it
He'll take away your fears
And dry up all of your tears
In your quiet time
In your God filled minute.

Eileen E. Armstrong

Untitled

My dearest Daddy,
   You may think it strange
   or not very smart...

BUT FOR FATHER'S DAY
   I'm sending my heart!
   It's special to me,
   so handle with care,
   and try not to notice
   the cracks here and there.

IT'S A "LOOKIN' AT" HEART
   to remind you each day
   That this daughter loves you
   in a very big way!

HAPPY FATHERS' DAY!!
Ellen Heath

Crickets In The Spring

When there is warm weather
You can hear the crickets sing
During months of the summer
And also during spring

When there is a smile
Or laughter is in the air
You can see from any mile
These feelings that we share

When there is pain
Or tears that are shed
It is easy to blame
Or to not use one's head

But when words are spoken
And kisses we feel
A heart that was once broken
Is now able to heal

For when eyes with tears glisten
Or the season is not spring
You can still stop to listen
And hear the crickets sing

Beth A. Wagner

Earth

Columbus proved the world wasn't flat.
You better not believe a word of that!

Somewhere near the Alaskan border.
I believe the world comes to an end.

I ain't telling a lie, and you know that.
So believe me, the world is flat.

Brooks Parsons

"Best Friends"

Since a child,
You and me,
We've been together
Running free.

A separation has come,
Apart from one another we are.
It's not a game,
And you are not that far.

Friends we've been
Friends we'll be,
Together yesterday
Together today.

Our friendship will last,
In my heart it has.
A spell was cast,
And time has past.

The love we share
As family and friends,
There's no despair
You are my Best friend.

Christy Cannon

The Sky Remains Blue

Blue is the sky,
Yet there's a chill in the air.
That chill is inside me,
Since your presence isn't there.

Leaves are falling fast,
My tears are falling slow.
Summer lost its happiness,
My heart has lost its glow.

Memories of the season,
are going through my head,
Fantasies of our love,
are laid down to the dead.

The land will ache for summer's sun,
My heart will ache for you.
fall to winter, love to loneliness,
The sky remains so blue

Amy M. Sell

An Ode To Garlic

A garlic bulb lurks on my kitchen shelf
   with the squat-bellied torso
   of a sumo wrestler
   whose translucent white-flesh
   with the merest flush of pink veins
   harbors its lion strength
   to wrestle and subdue
   the raging appetites
   of the formidable eater.

Adelene Fistedis Ellenberg

Set, Drugs, Rock And Roll

To live each day as it was my last.
Would be a great adventure.
Sex drugs and rock and roll.
Then peace, love and wilderness.
Is it possible to be rich to poor?
I would go to sleep on the streets
Wake up a pillow of air.
More sex drugs and rock and roll.
To end every day I would pray to
God if there is one.
Because there is one.
I would pray and he/she would forgive.
If ever in the heat of my freedom
I killed please let me cry.
Sex drugs to rock and roll

Beth Hirsch

Listening

I listen to the music, it's played
with true feeling.
I listen to the people who
insult it with their jealousness.
I listen to my voice,
as I scream in horror.
And I watch the end of
the people who don't listen...

I am alone.

April McIntire

My Valentine

Love is a notion set in motion
With the twinkle of an eye.
Lovers so happy together
day dream with a wistful sigh.

Love is many wonderful feelings.
Life can't go on without it.
To share our dreams with others
There's no doubt about it.

Oh, how much I love you!
My heart is now sublime,
And I would be so true
If you would be my VALENTINE.

Eleanor Doll

The Red Rose

He said, "How shall I find you,
With the many girls so fair?"
She said, "Oh, yes, you will find me,
With a red, red rose in my hair."

The years that passed were so happy,
Their joy was so complete.
His love only grew with the years;
She was so dainty and sweet.

Then one day he said, "I shall find you,
The flowers don't wither up there."
And he kissed the heart of that,
Red, red rose,
He left in her silvery hair.

Corralee A. Cagle

My Life

I am all alone
with no one to hold
I wish I could die
or at least go home.

There are people around
but no one is near.
They can all see
but no one can hear.

Where is my life?
Did I throw it away?
Is this the price.
I will always pay?

Time will fly by
but not fast enough.
One day at a time,
I try to stay tough.

Am I going in circles?
Have I been here before?
Is this fight with myself,
the questioned love war?

Felicia Howard

Reflected Light

While some are red and some are white
With lovely pinks all through,
I get great joy from the bouquet
That's sent to me from you.

The light reflects from each flower.
The leaves show color too.
I get delight from the bouquet
That's sent to me from you.

Reflected light is from a source
Outside the thing itself.
The beauty comes while looking at
The flowers 'pon my shelf.

The life we live reflects a light
With source beyond this sun.
'Tis Him we'll see Whom we reflect
When our last race is run.

Now, others see the life we live
While trav'ling through this space.
What kind of light do we reflect -
God's glory, or disgrace?

Clifford C. Cartee

Golden Aspen

Exotic little dancer
with leaves of golden coins.
Did an avid gardener, steal
you from your harem? Plant
you in this grove of trees?
Sultan Redwood claps his boughs.
Fir and Pine trees moan and sigh.
When breezes softly touch you,
your performance will begin.
Then winds pick up momentum,
whirl your golden jangling coins,
You must entertain them all,
dancing... dancing... dancing...
Soon will come your Winter's rest.
Snow will cover naked limbs.
until Spring when birds flirt in
and out each budding branch, then,
Summer sun your charms enhance
for Autumn's Golden Glory Show,
dancing... dancing... dancing....

Florence Lynch

The Ocean

I love living by the ocean
with its long beach of sand
And the big rolling waves
trying to catch me if they can

Sometimes I find a rock or two
some seaweed or a shell
Or just a piece of driftwood
or a fish with an awful smell

The sea gulls flying overhead
are looking for a treat
when I give them a handout
they will circle at my feet

Sometimes the water changes color
one time it's a silvery grey
Another time it's a greenish blue
it changes from day to day

No matter how it changes
or how quiet or how wild
I will always love the ocean
and have since I was a child

Ethel Giriodi

A Jewel

Mary my friend
With her smile serene
Made everyone happy
When she walked down the lane

Her warmth and love
Showed through and through
She cared about people
Her spark was there for you

A jewel of a person
You could never find
She was gracious and delightful
Which made her one of a kind

What a pleasure it's been
Having a jewel in our midst
She will always remain
In my mind as the best

I shall miss her smiling face
It will be etched in my mind
She was a jewel of a lady
I was lucky to know for sometime

Eleanor Goldman

Imagery Untitled

White Socks
with
Red Skin symbols on them.

a paradox?
a parallel?
a puzzle?

all images not comfortably
placed in contrast with,
or in contrast to,

the runners leg
black as the night's.

Boy jump and run and chase the ball.

Poor O.J.
When the dream gets deferred
you say, "what ever happened"?
Langston knows.

Elliott Daughtry Jr.

"His Name"

His parents called him son,
  with great love and much pride,
In the passing of time,
  He chose himself a beautiful bride.

Four of us called him Daddy,
  as he filled our hearts with love.
He taught us from the "Good Book"
  about our Father from above.

Some called him Chief,
  for he had a unique kind of tribe.
While others called him cowboy
  when they touched his hat with pride.

Some called him a survivor,
  for he fought till the end,
Till the Lord spoke and said,
  "You're coming home my friend".

It's sad for us his days are over
  His job here on earth is done.
We will always remember,
  The day our Father called him "Son".

Charlotte Henry

My Cat

I watch him wash,
With an even pace,
He doesn't even know,
He has the cutest face.
He washes his paws,
And then his tummy,
He makes me laugh,
I think he's funny.
He doesn't even know,
The joy that he brings,
He just lives here,
Never saying a thing.
How life can be,
So plain and simple,
To be a cat,
And not a people!

Colleen Migdal - Coco

Abandoned in a World Our Own

It's so cold!
Why has all the
Warmth left?
Where has it gone?
Have all the listeners
Run away,
Scared to think about
What's really happening?
Have all the understanders
Gone into hiding,
Wondering when all this
Chaos will stop?
Have all the carers
Disappeared,
Afraid of the
Evil closing in around them?
And left us dreamers here to die?

Cassandra Gouletas

My Namesake

Lord, why don't I understand?
  Why can't I see?
  Who was she?
Does she know about me?
Is she proud of me?
The person my family helped
  me to be.

I wonder sometimes why she
  had to leave,
I never got to see her or feel
  her warm, gentle touch.
Why do the lights that burn
  twice as bright,
Only burn half as long?

People tell me how special she was,
And what she believed in was
  your Holy word.
So, now I come to you, Lord
Just a young teenage girl,
Who's hurt and wants to know the truth.

Angela Eunice Chavis

Passages

When I think of all the people
Who have touched my life,
and passed on to another world,
I wonder why we met
and if we will ever meet again.
Is death the reality and life the dream?
have we been here before,
and will we return?
Will we meet the same people we knew?
Oh, let that be true,
I loved some of them so much.

Alice L. Jeffries

Dreamer

They say a dreamer's but a fool,
Who doesn't live up to the rule.
He lives in non-existent dreams,
And fills his mind with hazy schemes.

"Oh dreamer, dreamer, where are thee?
Why do you smile so merrily?
What do you find within your haze,
That makes you laugh with such amaze?"

"Oh doubtful person, leave me be,
Those dreams are only drawn for me.
I do regret your mind is blind,
The joy I feel, you cannot find!"

"For I only visit misty dreams,
And rest upon illusive streams.
I find the joy of life in May,
I laugh awhile-but never stay."

They say a dreamer's but a fool,
Who does not live by man-made rule.
His mind is bright, and pure, and free,
And in his haze finds ecstasy!

Antonio Borrego

One True Friend

Give me just one true friend
Who does not judge or condemn.

A treasure to be cherished
For the empathy projected
To this soul of discontent.

A pearl, hidden,
Not to perish in the
Depths of shy repose,

But...

To be discovered and
Transcended to the
Heights of mortal glory.

Magnifying the unveiled
Attributes of
My true and loyal friend.

Allyn Carol Zahn

I Wish

I wish I was the one
Who could look deep into your soul
Able to touch the chambers of your heart
And cause the woman in you to unfold

I wish the path to your heart
Was lined with a candle
Instead I grope in the dark
Unable to find the handle

Wish I could steal your breath
With only a gentle kiss
So many of these thoughts
Have left me in bliss

I wish on this kindness
I had not turned my back
Left to join the wild things
Running with the pack

I wish the forest
Wasn't filled with its soothing sound
In your arms is where
I would always be found

Chris Ippolito

Ode Of The Elements

In the wind, there are voices
Whispering of infinite choices
Elusive ether's allegory
Tells of greatness speaks of glory.

Blazing sun burning fire
Transient forces that inspire
Glowing embers with their visions
Of past wars and past prisons.

Raging seas massive torrents
Plunge great depths mystic sources
Clear cold river trickling water
Tragic falling, crystal laughter.

Mother Earth man's soft pillow
Turns her into pollution's silo
Compensation Cataclysmic
Banishes man from her orbit.

Bruze

Dolphins

Dolphins flip and flapper
While swimming
through the sea
I wish I had a dolphin
Just for me
but a dolphin is an animal
and deserves to be
set free
Dolphins flip and flapper
while swimming
through the sea

Dawn Teufel

'The Treat'

In a pretty little garden -
Where the flowers smell so sweet -
I like to sit among the
grass blades -
And watch the new lady bugs
eat their aphid treats.

Carrie F. Smith

Fifty One

You were near my age
When your father died.

It was hard for you to take
So many similarities.

We watched as you neared
Your forty-eighth birthday.

But just as we thought
We were in the clear,
You turned fifty-one.

You out-lived your father
By four long years.

Now I sit here
I've just turned eighteen.

You've missed so much
In nearly three years.

Amy Unverzagt

Just Say I Love You

There are times I feel forgotten
When we barely speak
It isn't that you're mad at me
It's just a bad-luck streak
There are many times I wonder
Others I don't care
About why you're drifting away
It's giving me a scare

But there are times you do come through
And cheer me when I'm down
I'll never forget that feeling
You're my own personal clown
Whenever I am sad again
My emotions are tight
You just have to say "I love you"
To make everything all right

Elaina DiSalvi

Share

Now it's time for me to share
What once I would never dare

To open my heart and my soul
So I begin to play a real role

I then will be proud of what I do
Everyone else will benefit too

Gratitude fills each of my days
When I forget I'm the one that pays

Life is filled with many good things
I feel like I'm flying on God's wings

Each day God is directing me
Advising that I can be free

He still continues to show me the key
That I am just now beginning to see

I need to honor what I now see
The answers lie quietly inside me

It's time for me to feel the real glee
Of all my peace and serenity

Frances Stier

Untitled

I want
    What I can't have:
    The you
        And me
    You say will never be
    The love you give;
        We make,
        Your touch,
        Your smile
Until the day
    You set me free

Cynthia Krauss

Who Am I?

What am I doing?
What have I done?
Not knowing, not seeing
The damage I've won!

Why did I happen?
Why have I turned?
Not thinking, not hearing
The lessons I've learned.

Where am I going?
Where have I gone?
Not stopping, not feeling
The sting of the numb.

Dawn M. Rosconi

Up

Up
Up
Goes my eagle
My country's eagle
My country's symbol of freedom
Up
Up
Up
'Til it flies through
The opening
In the cage

Debra M. Phillips

Demons

How can I explain
What goes on
In this tortured cell
They call my brain?
It longs for peace
Like a cool mountain lake
Or a slight summer breeze
That rustles the tops
Of majestic pine trees
It is empty - that chamber
Except for the demons
That dance and haunt
And never sleep
I yearn for solitude
Instead I cut
In a futile attempt
To free the demons
They only laugh
And gain strength and power
In that tortured cell they call my brain.

Betsy Johnston

The War

To the old memorial
Went Mommy and me
To the war memorial
it was a minor fee
As we gazed upon a stone
The tears flowed from my eyes
For on that stone was printed
The names of men who lost their lives
They fought to save our country
They strived each day to free
The love deep inside us
That we couldn't see.

Alison Kenny

Love Is Magic

We spent the week in glory
We grew so very close
The week has no description
It was more magical than most

Each day keeps getting better
Each day we laugh and sing
Each day we find each other
Each day means everything

Cherish dear each moment
Hold every minute in the heart
Feel all there is to feel
May this magic never part.

Debra L. Burt

The Memory

Every so often
we express
our past
lovers.

They pale
when put up
to our
present expression.

I anxiously await
my reflections
of the present
reality.

Carl R. Miller

238

Life

Why is the world in such a rush?
  We always seem to fly.
I wish that we could just slow down
  And not let it pass by.

We hurry here and run about.
  We never want to wait.
Don't we know there's more to life
  Than we anticipate?

Our children grow up before our eyes.
  They're growing much too fast.
Oh, I would give the moon and stars
  To make the moments last.

I've come to a decision.
  It's time to make a start.
We have to make the most of life
  And live it from the heart.

The rest of you may fly about
  And live "to beat the bands."
But me, I'm going to take the time
  To hold my children's hands.

Colleen Lacox

'Ode To The American Flag'

Oh, there you stand Old Glory
Waving your stars and stripes,
And do you still remember
Protecting all our rights?
If you could speak Old Glory
What words would you now say
To those who would berate you
Or take your rights away?
You have been our symbol
Of national pride and joy,
Never to be jeered at
By those who would destroy
Our nation's cradle banner.
We were born within your folds,
Stood by us in depressions
And through several major wars.
It's our turn to honor you,
To give you proper respect.
We pledge you our allegiance,
And our flag we will protect.

Esther M. Thomas

The Deer

Quietly, patiently,
Watching the trees.
Is anything moving,
Except for the breeze?

Finally, he walks out,
Behind, leaving no trace,
Sniffing and watching
Head high, what style and grace.

No way can he hear
My heart pound in my chest,
Nor can he sense,
My fear at the test.

From forest to table,
That is how it must be.
Animal instincts on both sides,
Today the stronger for me.

There is a strong bond
Between animal and man.
I felt it inside me,
From that silent deer stand.

Carolyn M. Baker

Love

Love is something
warm in the heart.

Love is something
that starts from the start.

Love is something
meaning you care.

Love is something
that you should share.

Love is something
that is not sad.

Love is something
that should make you glad!

Love is as warm
as a summer day.

Love is used in
every way!

Crystal Makela

Vanity

Being vain without being visual,
Vanity hidden behind modesty;
Hidden behind morality.

Unsuspecting victims stumble in.
Surrounded by humility.

Many have the power.
Curiosity pulls in the innocent,
Reality throws back the truth.

Under close examination all is told,
Without words - actions speak.

From meek, timid, submissive,
To inflated, egotistical and conceited.

Being vain without being visual.

Bridie Moore

Untitled

Incoherent Mumble
Vague memories of vacant faces
A tear falls to a two way mirror
From the fair girl in the corner
Slow motion, frozen in time, forever.
Storm clouds rumble south
Where to hide?
Truth
Confusion
Mass exodus
A drop of blood, a cry of a babe
Torrents of rain.

The fair maiden in the gossamer gown
Takes the center of the room,
Falls to her knees
And sighs
Alone.

Corina Ann Tappert

Tenderly into the Night

Tender is the moment
  Tender is the night
    Tender is your touch

You hold me while I cry

Elizabeth Rey

"Shimmers"

An endless path of gold
Upon the rippling blue
Leading me always
Into the moon
Against the glimmering ocean
That melts into the sky
My destiny awaits me
Where the moonlit path lies
Blue-black waves surround me
As I walk the golden trail
Slipping through the thick night
Without a boat I sail
The line of life
The line of death
I will not know
Till I take my last step

Christy Smith

What Is?

What is a heart
Until it has been broken?

What is a word
Before it has been spoken?

What is the wind
Until it has begun?

What is a song
Before it has been sung?

What is a tear
Until it is falling?

What is a bird
Before it is calling?

What is a person
Until it has life?

What is a husband
Before he has his wife?

They are just whispers on the wind
Of what could and should have been.

Erin Osborne

Tears And Laughter

Can I dance with you
  unashamed?

Can we touch each other
  on the inside
and not chain?

What is the mystery of love
  that the heart seeks -
  beyond you and I

A union at once personal
  and unbounded

Elizabeth R. Sawyer

A Cheery Thought

A cheery thought
To brighten up your day
Is never feeling overwrought
At home, work, or play;
As cheeriness be sought
To pass boredom away
By smelling roses one bought,
To relax, be happy, and gay.

Debbie Gauvin

When To Pick The Corn

When the corn begins to sprout,
Two little leaves come peeking out
When the leaves begin to grow,
A tiny stalk begins to show
When the stalk is tall and thin,
A tiny shoot begins
From the tiny shoot a pretty silk
  begins to spin
When the pretty silk is spun,
It turns the color of the sun
And when the summer sun is gone,
It's time to gather in the corn.

Fletcher Lee White, Sr.

Twilight Serenade

The shadows outrace the sun
Twilight at last has come
Birds find their nightly roost
The hills give the moon a boost

Night is quiet at its onset
Dew twinkles moist and wet
Then a dog in the distance howls
And a cat silently prowls

Insects sing their nightly croon
Blossom's scent to make one swoon
Grand is the air this eve
Wind whispers on a leaf

No mortal can accomplish such
Night's beauty speaks of much
To walk on forever in this dream
Smooth as silk and silent stream

Charles R. Wykle

Kickin' Back And Relaxin'

Sittin' in my boat and
Trollin' down the river
My skin's all red yet
When the wind blows I shiver

  Kickin' Back and Relaxin'

A beer in my left hand
A pole in my right
When somethin' bumps my line
It feels so right

  Kickin' Back and Relaxin'

When my skin's all burnt and
My back feels broke
It's time to move ashore
Stroke after slow stroke

  Kickin' Back and Relaxin"

When the daytime's done and
The night moves in
Layin' in my tent
Just thinkin' about when

  I can Kick Back and Relax

Debra Leiner

Christmas Past

A plastic manger
trimmed with lights
glistening, in the still cold night
a small reminder
for all to see
how Christmas really used to be
no trees with lights
no candy canes
no Santa Claus
no reindeer games
just a child
who was born one night
in a manger
on a cold winter's night
the son of God
the angels delight
His name...
Jesus Christ.

Dan DeWolf

Autumn

A transition season
Trees loose their hair
Becoming lonely and bare
Leaves of
Amber, gold, green, brown
Floating
Drifting
Falling
Down
Down
To the mosaic meadow
In waves of time
They sing a sweet melody in the light
And echo a soft whisper in the night
Falling from the sky
Like the first snow
In wavy rivers
To the roadbed below

Brent Gudgel

Webbed

Holding on, I wait,
Trapped by your thin, silk strings
almost invisible
they hold me together
as I fall apart, unnoticed,
given no acknowledgment
Of my existence
or my pain.
I once felt your heart
when we were close;
Its soft, precious beat
against mine
now belonging to others
helpless elsewhere,
wrapped in silk
on this web of your emotions.
Not wanting to leave
The comfort of these strings
from which I suffer,
I unfasten the bindings and fall.

Erin Barton

Goodies

The tiny girl ran
to the lighted display;
with fingers outspread
upon the curved glass
she stood on tip toe
to see the goodies inside.

Ostentatiously, slowly
the lighted shelves turned
displaying the cheesecakes
and high-meringued pies
and slices of raspberry torte.

The glow lit her awe
which became pure delight
as she rested her forehead
against the warm glass
and chirped with approval
of such a beautiful world
to be graced with joys such as this!

Della Burch

"The Tennis Prayer"

When the match ends and I go
To the great courts in the sky-
I hope the umpire will allow
The bygones to go by....
And remember all my good shots
And forget the ones I missed-
Recalling that I did my best
And cross my faults off the list.

Please make a reservation
On the green of center court...
And bear in mind (if nothing else)
I was a darned good sport!
Just give me one small victory,
My defeats are in the past.
I do not ask to take the set....
Only one perfect game at last!

Florence Brandwein

Moth

I am a moth drawn
to the flame;
I try to fly an even orbit
around it; close enough
to be warmed;
far enough away so as
not to be burned.
I do not understand my
fascination; I do not
understand him; I
know the moth
gets tired, and
eventually, is
consumed by the
fire.

Elizabeth Mack

Peaches

A Peach is my wish for life.
The skin gently soft and furry.
Warm wine and yellow glow
To catch the eye.

To be sweet but never mushy
Choosing to be firm, yet soft.
The center a pit of love and courage.
The inside more important than the out.

Elizabeth Porter

To My Baby, Jenny:

I wish I could be there with you
To share this special hour.
To watch my baby open gifts
At her first baby shower.

It would be such fun to watch your eyes
And share in your delight.
But it won't be so, I cannot go,
And I'll miss this lovely sight.

I'm just her mom, I wasn't invited
And I'm left to wonder why.
I'm so sad and broken hearted,
All I've done today is cry.

My heart's been broke before you know
And I hope that it will heal.
I've missed something precious today
And some day you'll know how I feel.

Benet M. Winberg

The Childhood Swimming Hole

Come let us go,
To our childhood swimming hole.
Jump into a fresh spring stream.
Float around, a summer dream.

Drop clothing, on the lush grass
Hop over pebbles, running fast.
Feel cooling water, caress the toes.
As near to heaven, a young boy knows.

Over streams, weeping willow trees,
Shadows dancing, in the breeze.
Melodies from many birds,
Sweetest music, ever heard.

Come, let us go,
To our childhood swimming hole.
There we are young, never old.
Back in time, as life unfold.

Ella R. Hermesman

Untitled

The bible is a special treasure,
to keep close by your side.
It has so many things to say
of how Jesus lived and died.
It shows how much He loves us
and hears our many prayers.
When we feel there is nothing left,
it reminds us that He cares.
So when your feeling down and out
and so all alone,
pick it up and read awhile,
soon your fears will all be gone.

Angela Bender

Our Goodbyes....

As the sun sets you go
   to close your eyes.

The sound of a bird
   awakes you.

You watch the firing
   sky, as you about to
   die.

For this is the last sun
   set and sky you will ever
   see before you die!

Annie Bugari

Poetry

Poetry needn't be serious
to get its point across.
You can add a bit of flippery
without suffering great loss.
"Awound the wugged, wagged wocks,"
was how I once began
a poem that plumbed the very depths
of the heart and soul of man.
A poem should be entertaining,
while you say what you have to say.
You don't have to boom and thunder!
Sometimes it's best to play.
True, Poe with vivid imagery
held us fast in horror's thrall,
but I prefer to use whimsy,
and let the reader have a ball.
So don't expect to see Jesus,
nailed high upon his cross,
remember, I don't use that stuff,
to get MY point across.

Charles E. Perry

"The Cake"

All so normal
Till she heard
The truth from them
Couldn't believe those words
She screamed and cried
So mournfully
For her love taken
So suddenly
All eyes turned
To sadly see
Her collapse
In agony
A special cake
Laid on the floor
Crushed for the love
That's nevermore
Won't forget
That awful scene
Of Heaven and Hell
In front of me

Anita L. Stanke

"The Fall"

Remembering all that you said to me,
Thinking you tried your very best,
You gave me hope and you gave me dreams,
You held my hand

Scared to be by your side,
For so long I didn't know how,
You were always there

So far away in the morning,
You woke me up to say goodbye,
I didn't know if that's why I woke,
But I never saw you

So I'll wait for the fall to come,
So I remember the day when you left me,
I miss you dad

Deborah E. Schmidt

"Sailboats 'Round The Moon"

Sailboats 'round the moon,
They're nothing but the stars.
The clouds are the silver lagoon,
The ships are Jupiter and Mars.

O How I wish I could sail with them,
To a land that no one knows,
Sail away to the rim
To a place where friendship grows,

Where roses bud, and flowers bloom;
Where the grass is always green,
I want to sail away real soon
To a world no one has seen.

Florence N. Blalock

A Friend

Everyone needs a friend now and then
They'll be there when you need them
And stay away when you want them to
A shoulder to cry on
Or a person to laugh with
Is always welcome
Whether spoken on paper
Or in friendly words
The comfort will be there
A good friend can keep a secret
And confide in you always
Both girls and boys can be good friends
But if by chance you find a bad one
Know that others will be there for you
To get through the bad times
And rejoice in the good times
A friend is always there.

Felicity May

Where Are The Children?

Where have my little children gone?
   They were here just yesterday.
The home's so still and quiet now,
   No sounds of children at play.

I think they are only playing,
   A little game of hide with me.
They think they're somewhere hiding,
   And that I cannot see.

But, I have seen where they are,
   I've known it from the start.
I see them often in my mind,
   And deep within my heart.

The "grown up" children sometimes come,
   To talk, to share, or confide.
I am not fooled! For I can see,
   My child is hiding down inside.

And when a grandchild runs to me,
   So sweet, so bright, so fair,
I get a glimpse of another child,
   I see is hiding there.

Ann M. Martin

It Takes Two

Ready, aim, clean
the firm law
and Peacemake
Wanted: the first. Not the last.
A changing role is no joke.
Everyone is equal!

Leffly A. Rose

Psycho Sanitarium

They locked me up in this cell
They turned my life into my hell
They shoot these drugs into my vain
Then whisper lies into my brain
People screaming every night
Afraid of dark afraid of light
All my nightmares coming true
If I escape I will kill you
Sometimes I wish I had a gun
So I could murder everyone
Who are they to judge my brain
To tell me whether I'm insane
I tell you I should not be here
You've made a mistake now isn't it clear
But no my words just wont be heard
They say my thoughts are just absurd
Never will I be released
So never will I rest in peace
The noise is high and the lights are dim
In this Psycho Sanitarium

Brian Casamassima

What Is Meant To Be?

So many walk into my life,
  they turn the key,
    hold me,
  leave and shut the door.

So much I have felt
  for those who return the key
    at least then I know
  it's not meant to be...

But when they keep the key,
I wonder... What is meant to be?

Betsy Bluey

Trees

Trees are like people.
They come in all shapes
and sizes. Like some
small and big.

Some are fat and some are
thin. Their are over
1000 different kinds of
trees in the world.

But trees are the
easiest to get away
and just look at
the sky at night.

Beau Sheffield

A Child's Youth

As we speak
There he now lies
Far below the ground
Underneath the heavenly skies
He can't ever change
What he has done
The story's sad to tell
His is not the only one
Guns are not safe
This children must know
They must learn now
While they still have time to grow

Emily Abaray

Ode To Technology

I live with the mind of a poet,
Therefore, the heart of a fool.

Will the miracle of multimedia
Really steal away my tool?

To tell my tale in simple words,
May lack the newest spunk.

Catching no one's eye to read,
Does it make it "virtual" bunk?

But this foolish heart is willing
to say things not for many.

Sometimes it happens upon another,
Who'll just might pay the penny,

Shouts of joy and gladness heard,
"There is a place for dreams.

Hidden by the DOS and Windows,
yet, popping through the screens."

I'll continue to collect my thoughts,
And savor favorite picks.

Alas, succumbing to my newest plight,
Found captured on a disc.

Andrea M. Paglia Taylor

[title]

Who invented the title?
There has never been
A more savage
Cruel
Unjust
Concept given to man

Why must we use the title?
There has never been
A more obsolete
Feckless
Inessential
Concept given to man.

Elizabeth Dashiell

The Word

The word that builds a thousand bridges,
the word that tears them apart.
The word that helps those broken heal,
and somewhat restores their heart.

The word that is understood
in every language, every country
near and far
and every single person
no matter who they are.

The word that can tear through
racism and prejudice
and diminish any hate.
The word that breaks boundaries,
and unlatches every gate.

The word that is so important
in the heavens; up above.
The word that is in everyone's heart
because this word is Love.

Carissa Helton

Why Dad

  Why dad, why didn't you tell
the truth? Why dad, why did
you do it? You told everyone I
was lying! I hope you go to
hell for what you did! I've been
thinking you never loved me
nor you never will! I have a
step-dad that will never touch me
so I call him Dad, because
he'll be what you will never be, a Dad!

Crystal Benwell

The People Came

The people came to remember
The suffering and shame.
To save a dying ember
Of a relative's lost name.

The people came in silence
As if not to break a pact.
To look at the exhibits
Of memorabilia intact.

The people came with hope
Of their lost wounds to suture.
To learn how to cope
With problems of the future.

The people came to learn
And try to understand.
To give other ones a turn
And lend a helping hand.

But for whatever reason
It's more or less the same,
To bring a better season
Is why the people came.

Abria L. Chisolm

"Eve"

When God made you, He searched so wise;
The stars so bright, and high above,
But with His understanding love
Yet placed the starlight in your eyes.

When God made you He searched for you
The heavens fair: He fashioned wise,
The glory of your lovely hair,
To match the starlight in your eyes.

When God made you, He searched for you
The rainbow's end after the storm;
Then from the beauty of its hue;
He made your loveliness of form.

When God made you His work was done
Almost too lovely to believe
Yet from the dusk but now begun
Man chose a name, and called you Eve.
From that day on, man's love was born.
FOR WOMAN; THE ETERNAL EVE.

Ad R. Zielsdorf

The Life Tree

The green as blood,
The leaves as lives,
A leaf falls,
A life is lost,
A person falls to sorrow,
A cry for help is heard,
But no response is heard,
But no response is heard,

Atif Ghizali

The Sixth Hour

The sun is gone...
The Son is gone.

Earth trembles at the fact;
While on the throne, the One in charge
    has sadly turned His back.

The sun is gone...
The Son is gone.

There is weeping at the cross; sounds
    of anguish at the throne;
While multitudes of angels wait to
    welcome Him home.

One man, our Lord, hangs dying on a tree;
Not by might, but by Choice, that He
    might welcome me.

Catherine L. Stancil

Doze

There is a splendor in this silence, in
The solitude of this darkened room, in
The rhythmic passing of each breath
    through your lips as you
Peacefully slumber, oblivious to my
    watchful, protective gaze.
I see your eyes moving beneath
    their lids and
I hear you murmur so softly that
    even this silence cannot
Help me to hear your words and
A smile appears on your gentle,
    slumbering lips and
The silence becomes magnificent and with
The joy in my heart that is you,
I am finally able to drift off into
Unconsciousness with a smile of my own because
I know you are dreaming of me.

Felicia M. Wampole

Fourth of July

"Look up!" he pointed..." There!..There!"
The sky streaked orange and blue.
The sounds of thunderous fireworks
Accompanied bursting hue.

Her sweet young face upturned to see
That painting's... "Starry Night"
Eclipsed the master's frenzied strokes,
With surging shades of light.

And as she gazed with wonderment,
Her eyes were sparked with mist.
Her slightly moistened, smiling lips
Were targeted and kissed!

'Twas on that pyrotechnic night
A journey then began.
Two spirits joined with tenderness,
A girl and this young man.

Adventure took them through the years
Their lives were richly blessed.
Of all the memories they share,
That kiss remains the best!

Frank McGeary

The Iceberg

The people sing proudly,
The people sing loudly,
The women are wailing,
The lifeboats are sailing.

Jump off the deck,
Swim from the wreck,
Into dark water,
The ocean will martyr.

No ship was built finer,
This gigantic liner,
Which now sinks below,
All vessels foe.

No more to be seen,
This Titanic dream,
Slips quietly to sleep,
Into cold, icy deep.

Freddie L. Cooper Jr.

Lost Love

I lost your love
The only one I knew.
I lost your trust,
Then I lost you.

It didn't take long
To go our separate ways.
Just to say I miss you
Is the beginning of my dismay.

Our love would last forever
I thought all throughout my mind
But oh, a short time ago,
You walked and said you were never mine.

Things now seem so different,
So far, far away.
I guess it's time to really let go,
And live our separate lives.

Anika White

A Tribute To Mother

The foundation of family,
The nurturer of ills,
Creator of little faces
Pressed against window sills.
A wealth of wisdom and
Source of strength,
Always willing to go
An extra mile's length.
She's a tour guide to the future,
And dreamer of dreams,
With the radiance of the sun
And the magic of its beams.

Ellen Joy

Blind Man

I see not a thing,
the man says again look, look
out there, what do you see,
I opened my eyes but,
All I saw was a desert,
I kept naming things but,
they were all wrong,
but when I look back
at the man, he was blind
then it hits me,
he can see what the world,
can give him sight,
which even my eyes cannot see!

Florencio Rivera

"No School"

School is out.
The kids start to shout
The teachers are boring.
You'll start snoring.
Ms. Johnson starts talking about Africa.
Children blurt out "Canada"
Two plus two is four,
Four plus four is eight.
Eight plus eight is sixteen.
Don't you think my face looks green.
Now that summer is here.
I sit with my friends on the pier.
I sit on the beach,
eating my peach
Talking to the bird.
My friends consider me a nerd.
I love school.
My friends start to drool
Over a boy named Roy.

Elvira Margie Ferrer

Alabaster Moon

Rosy pink sky with gray clouds streaking
the horizon
A jet plane soars high in the heavens
Two white clouds streaming behind
Making a bridal veil

The moon is shining alabaster
Almost full tonight
While one bright evening star twinkles
Guiding me home

Claudette Clarke

The Walk

    I walk through the halls,
the halls in this sanitarium.
    Passing people with such plain
sad looks on their face.
    I'm so sad
    I want to be happy
but all I can be is mad.
    It's driving me crazy or
maybe insane.
    Won't you help me?
    Free me from all this pain.

Cassie Sink

Weeping Willow

Willow's bows bend with grace to
    the ground

It weeps in the wind without
    a sound

Its trunk is burdened with lots
    of strife

Its roots grasp deep hanging on
    to life

Like the weeping willow
    standing tall

Its trunk holds firm it shall
    not fall

I too feel its strength and
    graceful woe

My roots give me courage, not
    let go

Allysan F. Drew

The Silent Drums

The land was theirs;
The eternal rolling hills,
The ocean of grasses kissed with dew
And rippled with the breeze,
Liquid sapphire skies
That grew golden with the dawn,
Brother Sun and Sister Moon

Smoke signals from the mountain
Blowing towards the valley
The sharp proud cry of the eagle
Calling out in rhythm
To the pounding of drums

Wagons, in a line
Creaked assertively
Through the hills
Crushing the prairie sea
The eagle soars away

Now all that remains are
Arrowheads,
Left in the dust

Cynthia Erin Chin

Dreams

I fell asleep one lonely night,
the dream I had was a wonderful sight.
I wondered if anyone knew,
the dream I had was of you.
Then I looked into your eyes,
now I know where paradise lies.
When you pressed your lips to mine,
I knew that everything would be fine.
When I awoke from this dream,
I knew nothing was as it would seem.
For I am just merely me,
and nothing between us could ever be.
The reason for this is very clear,
you hold another girl very dear.
Oh, how I wish it could be me,
that you would much rather see.
Sure we may be good friends,
but that is where it ends.
How I wish dreams could come true,
for every day I would have you.

Amber Michelle Bailey

All About Dreams

Was it a dream or was it real,
the closeness of that person you
feel. The wind in the sky blows
the dreams away, but the memories
will always stay. Why do the
good dreams always shatter,
and the special ones that
really matter. Please let me sleep
the whole night through, and let
me dream my dreams of you.

Amber Elizabeth Sherman

Crossing

Bridges help to cross the way,
That's where I'll be today.
Tomorrow I'm on the other side,
On strong ground my bridge is tied.

A whole new world lies ahead,
No avoiding it, I do not dread.
Another bridge I will cross again,
But this one first I shall begin.

Chrystal Todd

In A World Of White

In a world of white,
the blackness fades.
Driven by the light,
to dwell within the shades.
Where bold colors change,
to a dimmer view,
and sadly rearrange,
to display a less defiant hue,
then as color is lost.
Black turns to gray,
becoming a shadowy ghost
of its proud yesterday.

Andre N. Cobbs

The Rose

There's a rose in the garden
That sparkles with dew.
This precious rose
Reminds me of you.

The dewdrops that hang
Like silent tears
Represent the heartaches
All through the years.

The thorns are the troubles
That plague life's way.
The problems and sorrows
Faced day after day.

When the bud becomes a rose
Turning its face to the Son
You feel God's healing
That your prayers have won.

Then the dewdrops are dried
By the Son's warm rays
And we know God is with us
All of our days.

Bonnie Sherouse Martin

I Wish I Were A Fish

Dilly Dan had a wish.
That he could turn into a fish.
To swim upon the ocean waves,
And hide in underwater caves.
To ride with dolphins, how he longed
To listen to the humpbacks song.
To watch the swordfish as they fight,
While as starfish lights the night.
To gaze in wonder at a shark,
And listen to the dogfish bark.
To rest upon a turtle's shell.
To swim beside a killer whale.
To walk upon the ocean floor.
Sunken ships he could explore.
To spy upon a moray eel.
That hides in waiting for a meal.
Dilly Dan sits and dreams,
Of how an ocean life would be.

Debra Ellen Riser

The Rose

The rose has a pose
That changes with the wind.
But the rose never changes
The place it grows in.
Joyful brightness it gives
Until its petals grow dim.
Then it rests another year,
And in the spring it does appear.

Anna Rose Waters

Flurries Of Thoughts

It's the nothings of life
That are the somethings of life.
A smile, a look
A touch, a word
Acts and thoughts remembered.

Ideas shared
Ponderings pondered
Incidental learnings
That may seem insignificant
   at moment heard
Come back to haunt us
   to teach us
To make us wiser.

Florence Kricheff

Grace In The Joy Of Sharing

When the harvest days are over
Thanksgiving day is near.
Like birthdays and Christmas
They come but once a year.

So as we journey on through life
much depends upon our will,
To appreciate nature's gift to man
and our mission to fulfill.

While time is of the essence here
As in life of all things living,
But generous nature never dies
It just keeps on giving.

That all day may share the harvest
With a grateful heart and mind,
And proclaim thanksgiving every day
That others may find.
Grace in the joy of sharing
Whate'er they have in mankind...

Essie Fink

What Is Love?

Love is a touch,
tender with care.
A meaningful look,
Secrets
   to share...
Love is a mood,
laughter or tears.
Shared by two hearts
that grow close
   through the years...
Love is a faith,
that dreams
   will come true...
Love is wonderful
   LOVE IS YOU!

Cheryld T. Hanson

Glowing Rays

Glowing rays of light I see
Staring right back down on me
Bringing thoughts into my head
Something that I've never said
Watching, wandering could it be
My true love looking down on me

Christa Hodges

Perfect Rose

That's me lying over there
Teardrops are falling
Flowers are laid
Still I lay motionless
I lay like a perfect rose
Too sharp to touch
My mother cries
My father is drunk and
My sisters laugh
I can't move
It's hot
I can't breathe
Now I must cry as
I wait.

Alisa Eppich

Cradle Me

Help me put my barriers down,
Take off the makeup of a clown.
In your arms of strength to bear,
Every one of my worldly cares.
Hold me close and keep me safe,
Give me a place that is totally safe.
No hidden feelings to be left,
Open my heart and close the rift.
Help me come to terms with me,
Cradle me, please, cradle me.

I am not an island unto myself,
Love and caring are my true wealth.
About me are things I do not like,
They jab and stab me like a spike.
Look past the monster I sometimes show,
Help me to find a peaceful inner glow.
I need to close my painful past,
And find a present and make it last.
I'm afraid to be alone, but I must be free,
Cradle me, please, cradle me.

Colleen L. Doran Lewis

"Here I Am Lord"

Here I am Lord...
Take my heart Lord.
I'm here to serve you.
Unworthy, as I am Lord.
Thank you Father...
For your Mercy.
You forgave me.
And made me whole Lord.
Take my soul Lord...
I'm here to serve you.
All that I am Lord.
Is yours from now
Until eternity.
Oh! Holy Father...
I'm here to serve you.
Here I am Lord.

Dawn Lee Ball

"But Not Forever"

Joy, but only minutes
Swing, but not on for long
Time, but not an hour
Book, but not long
Sun, but not very bright
Dark, but no stars
Rain, but not many drops
You, but not mature
Me, but not with you
Love, but very dead

Brenda S. Bautista

The Rape

Attacked, violated,
stripped of what is mine.

Hands across my mouth and legs,
splinters pierce my spine.

Caught in the crossfire of Humanity
and men who have lost their minds.

Losing all to someone (something)
in seconds of countable time.

Andre Bonitto

My ode to sales

I shop and shop and will never
stop.
Show sales, shirt sales, pant sales,
and bag sales.
I will never fall to unveil a
new sale.
I'm a female and will never
bewail.
My desire for sales will never
fail.

Brandy Smith

Black

Sitting in the darkness waiting for
  Steve Miller to rock out.
Leaning forward close enough to touch
  A motorcycle mama's black as oil
  Leather pants.
Enjoying the unique licorice taste of
  "Good and Plenty" its movie house
  Memoirs reminding me of old black
  And white war newsreels.
Remembering a pitch black night when
  We waited for an ebony casket to
  Come home from a real war.
Later, a dreary, gloomy Saturday with
  Gloomy, black draped mourners.
Then the dreams of terror as I floated
  Down to inky velvet.
Finding myself reliving the day with
  Charcoal sketches of a young hero
  Sporting jet black Elvis hair.

Erik Nelson-Kortland

The Garden

Spring
Stems come creeping out
Inch by inch you'll see them grow
Soon you'll see their blooms.

Summer
Beautiful are they
The flowers in the garden
Soon they'll fade away.

Fall
All that's left are stubs
The garden has few flowers
Coming back next spring.

Winter
Snow has fallen down
The garden is covered white
Soon you'll see the stems.

Eleanor O'Connor

Wooden Spirit

Wooden spirit,
Steel soul,
Broken heart,
Shattered goals.
Paper dreams,
Burnt and forgotten,
So many tears,
Now cold and rotten.
Bleeding heart,
No longer mine,
Belonging to you now,
I'm so far behind,
Where you left me,
Is where we stand, alone in the rain,
With teardrops in my hands,
Worn like a candle, blown by the wind,
That brushed my hair, and kissed my skin...

Amie Coelho

Aviator

You
standing there
with your coffee belly
reeking of past days

I saw you there
on that abysmal flight
to nowhere

You looked at me
shirt stained
eyes reddened
from the tears that
made creases in your face

You
clinging to your warped tinkertoy
look at me as if I may rescue you

But all I see are twisted memories
that cover my eyes like the stain
on your chest.

Alicia Perez

Alone

I see a child
Standing in the cold.
No mittens, no hat,
No one to hold.
His eyes are filled
With sadness.
And it breaks my heart
That this child's life
Is being torn apart.
The drugs, the drinking,
Consumes the heart.
The hitting, the beating,
That should never start.
I close my eyes to
Make it all go away.
But I know that
When they open,
It's here to stay.

Betsi J. Yates

"Moon"

Miles and miles
Out in space.
Orbiting around a
Nice place.

Dale Berenbrock

Reflections

I saw Mom today...
Standing in front of me.
I smiled at her, she smiled back,
It was quite a sight to see.

I stared into her eyes...
Saw wrinkles here and there;
Streaks of silver glistened
In once dark brown hair.

As I reached to touch her face
I saw hands I used to hold.
How could those hands once so young
Be suddenly so old?

I noticed when she moved...
She wasn't quite as fast;
I remember her being much quicker
Over the years gone past.

Yes, I had a look at Mom today...
Though she was no where near.
I winked my eye, waved goodbye
And turned away from the mirror.

Alice M. Shourds

Morning Melody

Catch the Sun,
Sparkling, Winking
from a drop of dew,
foliage begins to awaken.

A pair of Red Birds
frolic amid the
bouquet of Pink and Red buds,
dark angles and lines
the tree forms a exotic
conversion of perspective.

Smooth, cool rocks
plush new grass
the sky mirrored
in the puddles of rain
scent of freshness

Active Community,
birds echo their
sweet sounds
in the morning sun
A Melody.

Dorothy K. Ross

Untitled

These thoughts of mine
So twisted and unstable
Uncontrollable craziness
An eagerness to create
Flowing energetic brain waves
Full of life and hope
The words come intensely
No, I will not stop them
They make me enthusiastic
A way to look on
Or maybe to look out
Someone looking in
The cutting of the chest
My heart bleeding feelings
Love, hate, anger, frustration
They reveal their many faces
Nothing hidden among
Leaving no questions, only me
Poetry!

Crystal Karstensen

Untitled

With eyes bright blue on summer's morn,
So to grow dim come autumn's form
Darker, darker they grow sore
While they study night and more
Darker, darker they grow tired
As they read by the fire...
Poor these eyes they may be,
But when come spring they be free.

Chrissy McConnell

The Greatest Man I Knew

Into my mind there comes a face
    so loving kind and good,
he was my Daddy, tall and true,
    he lived as all men should.

Part Indian and part Irish,
    a preacher man, by trade,
and like Jesus, too, a carpenter,
    houses of wood, he made.

He raised six children, as he lived,
    good, honest, upright and true,
A love of God and all mankind,
    of earth and skies so blue.

And now we teach our children
    about the things we learned,
We work, we play, we all reach out,
    the things we have we earned!

Evelyn Rains Gordon

Searching

Love is but an emotion,
So good and yet so rare.
Finally when you've found it,
you know because you really care.

Things change a little sometimes.
Sometimes they change a lot.
Sometimes you have to stop for a moment
and look at what you've got.

Is the person you love different
Than what they were before?
Do you really feel the same
Or are you looking for more?

Now the loving is over.
You're feeling very confused.
A part of you is missing.
You know that you've been used.

Why is there an emotion that can cut someone
    so deep?
Why do we have love if it's something we
    can't keep?

Maybe if we keep searching and call upon
    God above,
Then he will finally send us that one, That
    perfect love.

Connie Olsen

Shadows At Midnight

Dreams
Shooting stars
Sparks from my heart
Where the broken edges grate
Make no sound
But on a clear night
Cast shadows on the rocks

Elijah Pitts

Into The Well

It starts with look
    so bright.
Then ends, in vain,
    with a fright.
Things went bad,
    but don't know why.
Why should I live
    I want to die.
Let me take step into
    torture and hell.
Let me die
    as I fall...
        into the well.

Chris Wendorff

Night Snowfall

Snow falling,
Slipping past old
Unanswering trees.

Night snowfall
Covering yellow bulbs
Above the dark shadowy houses

Sending icy sparkles
Splashing and sliding
Over sleek brown panes.

Each flake
A prismatic hexagonal
Drifting in the glittering lights

Their melting wetness
Soothes the barren limbs
Of brooding solitary hardwoods.

Fleeting words
of unassuming love float
In the cold, empty air.

Silhouetted, the trees wait
As the snowy spangles
Cover love with the enchantment of night.

Barbara Bruch

Think About Trees

There was a tree on our land
Sitting there in the sand

I give it water I give it love
It gets its light from up above

It's a home for lots of things
From bugs that fly to birds that sing

When you think about a tree
You think how lovely

With all this pollution
We need a solution

Killing our trees is a scare
Because we will lose air

My tree is still standing in the breeze
By all those other beautiful trees

When my tree stands tall in the breeze
Then I'll think what the bird sees

When a bird flies to its nest
He thinks that his nest is beast

Then again I think about my tree
And I think how special it is to me

Andrew J. Cox

A Child's Lullaby

Now as sun
sinks dim and low
and moon returns
to bed I go

I pray to GOD
o hear my plea
from fear and darkness
rescue me

I pray as well
through fading light
bless me and family
and the night

And GOD I hope
that if I die
you take my soul
to heaven's sky

Adam Chapman

Deep Sleep

Deep sleep
Silent surrounds the room.
Deep breath
And my eyes open no more.

Deep sleep
Yet I lay still.
Immobile, I am for now.
Why cry?

Deep sleep
I am stay alive.
Cry you not,
For I am at sleep.

Don't we need sleep?
Breathless, I am for now.
But I am awake in
The world of my dream.

Why stare?
My sleep is deep.
When I shall be awake,
I will be the same.

Agnes Yond

What The Future Holds

The clock struck twelve in the
    silence of the night
And the waves remained quiet allowing
    faint whispers to be heard
There was neither love nor passion
There was neither romance nor dancing
Another night over
Another morning begun
Lost among nature and man
Wandering through time
Never turning back
No directions
No instructions
Just a push into the unknown
Heading toward an undecided future
Leaving a past of decisions behind

Erin R. Cody

The Grand Canyon

The Grand Canyon,
Shining and free,
The majesty of it,
Is beauty, don't you see?

Shining like a star,
The Colorado flows far,
Forming and engraving,
The beautiful sights and sounds,
of a river misbehaving.

Crashing and raving,
The waves push away,
At the crumbling wall of the canyon,
Today.

Courtney N. Turner

My Mother And I

I say one thing
She says another
I sing one chord
She sings the other

She makes me laugh
But I make her cry
I look at the floor
She looks into my eyes

But two things we do
that are the same ...
We share the same heart
and we share the same pain.

Ashley Bell

Untitled

    When their eyes first met.
She knew it was love.
But would he feel the same?
Only time can tell.
She hoped and she prayed that
some day he'd come to her.
And one day he did!
All her dreams have come true.
He gently reached out for her.
He then pulled her close and
held her tight.
He softly kissed her.
She felt so numb but yet
so good.
They fell in love.
A love so strong, so true.
A love that will last forever.
    When their eyes first met.

Amy Rolf

The Red Headed Dancer

Dancing in the darkness,
Shadows on the wall,
Will any body be there
When you hear the final call?

Listen to the music
Words swirling in my head.
Dancing in the darkness like
Two lovers in their bed.

Pay attention to the darkness
As the shadows start to fall.
For the final fall of darkness...
Brings an end to it all.

Mrs. Deborah L. Dunlap

Memories

The gate of the past
Shall be opened to see,
Memories everywhere
Of you and me.

Let us shed tears
Of sadness and joy,
Let us remember the times
Of being a girl and boy.

Let us spend time together
Today and tomorrow,
Knowing we'll be there
To lend and borrow.

And as tomorrow comes
So we must,
Pick up our stuff
And leave the dust.

Dina M. Mehta

Angel

Sweet little angel
Set upon this earth
You bought us much joy
For what it's worth
Though in our prime
There comes a time
When we all must depart
Remember this...
You've got a place
Deep within our hearts.

Sweet little angel
Our love divine
Life is but
A moment in time
So many hearts you've touched
So little time we've shared
Your tender smile
Though for a while
Bought us much cheer.

Debra P. Stephens

Fish

One day my Uncle Tell,
Sent me something though the mail.
And boy did it smell!
I almost fell!
It was a raw fish,
He must have picked it off his dish!
Boy fishes are smelly,
I turned it over to look at its belly.
I know it sounds funny,
But my eyes were hooked.
I saw a bunny,
It sniffed the air,
Then it was not there!
I went across the street,
To Miss Saint,
She almost faint!
Then I went to Pete,
He ran.
Well my fish was no use,
So I put it in the trash can.

Betsy Chan

Friendship's Garden

Friendship is a garden fair
Seeds from Heaven growing there.

Blooms of goodness all around.
Understanding floods and ground.

Words of kindness bring forth fruit.
Real caring is the root.

Loving smiles sunshine are
Encouragement the guiding star.

Tears we share are April showers.
Joys untold become May flowers.

Dreams we share are leaves we need.
Trusting grows with each good deed.

Barb Cassel

State Of Mind

Swirling eddies of mindless despair
Running rampant everywhere
Unwanted thoughts that creep around
Devouring all that can be found
They say it's just a state of mind
But I guess right now I must be blind
For depressing visions are everywhere
Upon what ever I seem to stare
I'm tired of living in a lie
This thing they call a state of mind
I'm exhausted from the battle with in
And I see no light at the tunnels end
Sometimes I think I'd rather die
And let this world pass on by
For then I wouldn't have to care
At a world that seems so damn unfair
So maybe I'll just close my eye's
And stop asking myself why
For maybe tomorrow won't be so grey
But instead a better day

David S. Magilton

My Love

My love for you is like a
river running long, like a
fire burning a log, it comes
so natural, just like a singer
singing a song, My Love for you
has grown over the years, and
will hopefully grow more
you are apart of me, a part
that will hopefully last,
for if we shall part, my
heart, will be broken. You
are like my knight in shining
armor, my prince with
handsome features, my very
own Albert Einstein and you
will no doubt be the only
man I shall ever truly, love

Annie Reich

Twilight Of Wisdom

Wisdom is experience that
ripens with age
    And thrives on learning with
the knowledge of a sage
    what an insight It has on
things as they are
with a profound understanding
that reaches for a star
    It blossoms into enlightenment
like a spiritual flower
    Which transcend beyond
ignorance with a divine form
of power
    The acquiring of information
where it naturally accumulates
    In the depths of a man's mind
where it normally saturates

Bernard Jones

Endanger!

Do you see the world around you!
Revolving round and round.
Can you see the light blue sky,
Can you see the green grass ground.

Do you see the missing animals?
That use to be here too.
The endanger ones of extinction,
That died ago a year or two.

If lions and tigers had vanish,
What would happen to the foodchain.
With antelopes and zebras weigh a lot,
And they'll gain and gain.

The earth is in critical condition.
But some animals are gone.
So hunters put down your weapons.
And let the life go on.

Caroline Le (11 years old)

Petals Strewn From Childhood

Petals strewn from childhood
Remain throughout the years.
The past creates the present,
the future is unknown.

Yet grant a backward glance
To the child who seems to stumble,
And quickly finds her feet again
When helped by loving hands.

Just like a budding
    rose- she grows,
Her life uncarved before her,
Petals of the rose and child
    all too soon-full blown.

Petals from the rose
    will drop and blow away,
But petals strewn from childhood-stay.

Anita Kingsley

Untitled

The ocean is still
Reflecting snow-capped headlands;
Gulls break the silence.

Ann M. La Vallee

Our Flag

Our flag is pretty
Red, white and blue
See it in the city
And the country too

If flies up high
On a staff or a pole
A silhouette in the sky
That stirs the soul.

Its stripes of red
For courage stand
And it has led
Many a stirring band

Its stars on darkest blue
One for each state
Count them will you?
Forty eight and then two

It's fifty and you will see
It flying in glory and victory
As we united will have to be
Our dust will be our destiny

Eleanoar Julig

The Wrong Road

To see the sun, but not feel its heat
radiating abundantly amongst
one's feet

To hear the wind but not feel its
breeze, to wonder one's mind to
days of ease

To touch the stream but not feel its
cool wetness comforting one body
from life's daily stresses

To feel compassionate but not understand
its worth to not relieve the
torment on this we call earth

To sense anger but not understand
Its consequence one chooses
to ignore beyond good sense

The world one lives in full of
hate, jealousy and war, good times
abound no more

Excuse me sir, is this hell?
I must have taken the wrong road

Craig Castanik

Smile

A crinkle here, a crinkle there
Quite a few crinkles to spare
I gave her one, I gave him one
I gave them freely
Still I wasn't done.
It takes fewer crinkles
To form a smile you see
When you frown,
You only show misery
No one cares about
Your frowns anyway
But your smile may
Brighten someone's day.

DeLores B. Harding

Dance Of Joy

Watching the leaves
quiet on the ground.
Their only motivation
the wind.
Pushing, pulling,
hurrying them on.
Gold and rust, orange and brown;
their skin like velvet.
They fill my heart
with their dance of joy.
All too soon,
the winter will come;
weighing them down
with its kiss of frost.
So dance my friends!
Show your beauty to all.
Let the wind touch your spirit...
Just for today.

Cheryl A. Jennings

Fog

Slowly, rolling, through the hills,
quiet, and white and oddly still.
as I stand and watch and wonder
I hardly see what's on the yonder.
And what this life holds for me
is the hardest for me to see.

Frances Carol Burnett

"Love Forever In The Light"

Our egos we may contain;
Purest of hearts do remain.
Negativity will fall;
It's the White Light that I call.

I have seen the beauty within;
The search for my soul will begin.
Deep down inside I've felt pain;
Forgiveness is all that remains.

Vibrations of love are above;
It is in the light I see love.
When in doubt believe that it's true;
Love and forgiveness are the clue.

Angela Michelle Soth

"Friends"

True friends are like "Angels"
Precious but rare, false friends
Are often found every-where.

A true friend will always be
there, even when life seems so
very hard to bare.

Their that special
friend that really cares,
and will always be near
to take away your hurt
and fears, and to wipe away
your crying tears.

A true friend indeed
will cherish you for your
beauty inside and out,
that's what true friends
are all about.

Ellen M. Timmer

Within Is A Power

Within is a power
Power endless
Light in flight
Despair, gladness, the golden sun
Control it, sin
Accept it, freedom
Feel it, our star of fire
Savor it, the satellite of our world
This is I, inside
Flows intense rivers of auburn fire
Dramatic, truthful
Tomorrow unknown
Discover now
Who I am
Extract my temporary shell of water
Beneath find this
Me, it, I
Power endless
All as one

Erica Tabet-Bresslauer

Life...

Life is like a painting.
People would rather look at it,
than to live it.

People are like the wind.
They come and they go,
Whether you want them to or not.

The earth is like love.
Always there when you need it,
Never to go away.

Love is like a never-ending story.
Always eager to be read,
But not as eager to be put away.

Andrea Leigh Raney

Image Of Dawn

A white crescent moon,
Peeps down on the earth below,
The dark blue sky,
Kisses the emerald grass.
The shimmering stars,
Look like diamonds in the sky.
The fog creeps,
Creeps in like a dolphin
Swimming over the horizon.
The dew trickles,
Trickles slowly and quietly,
Off the crisp leaves.
Soon the sun,
Will peep over the horizon,
Like a golden swan.

Elena Pereira

ANDREA

Anger inside of me,
Not able to release it,
Deep deep inside
Repealing at my happiness
Eating it away
And leaving no anxiety.

Andrea Thompson

As We Watched A Sunset

As we watched a sunset
Our love began to bloom,
I needed him more than ever,
Our romance seemed to loom.

I felt secure in his arms,
As he held me tight,
We were perfect for each other,
I knew that it was right.

My head was in his lap,
As on soft grass we lay,
The sun was almost gone,
And the trees began to sway.

He whispered to me sweetly,
His voice was very dear,
I wanted him with me always,
All I wanted was him near.

Autumn E. Amarello

Honor Due

I'm proud to be your child
Our heritage I hold dear

You passed down your love for God
Which shadowed me through the years

I have always felt your strength
And your guidance followed me

The protection that you gave me
By time spent on your knees

But today I tip my hat to you
For fighting for ole Glory

In a war that gave me freedom
And took away my worry

You were willing to give your life
In America's worst turmoil

And shed your precious blood
On fields of foreign soil

So now I stand in honor
And pledge my love for you

As you did for me many years ago
Fighting for the red white and blue

Cynthia L. Pollard

"Life Is... Alive!"

Time goes by...
Or, does it grow?
Seeds to tree,
With age they know.
Fishes in oceans,
Now, walk on feet.
Lands past horizon,
Birds they do fly,
Dust on earth,
Once, mountains so high.
Sun and moon,
Far reaches of sky...
Time... spent wondering?
Is, wasted on why?
But, to ponder,
And wander in truth.
Live and enjoy,
Best plan to do.
The final questions,
Not final at all...

Elissa Abbey Keller

Untitled

Life floats away
on wings of time.
Life drifts away
on the ebbing tide.

The flame burns,
the smoke rises higher.
Life is full of pain;
being burnt on the fire.

A clock ticks away,
a life is wasting.
A life goes astray,
the irony, bitter tasting.

The light grows dimmer,
the shadows climb the walls.
The wick is at its end,
a life will leave these hallowed halls.

Do we realize
how quickly it's gone?
This life we live,
lost with the newcoming dawn?

Andrew Fitzgerald

Untitled

The city buried its dead today,
on this summer's Sunday afternoon.
People, they would stop and stare,
Then go about their busy day.

The woman dead once lived here but,
single, few people knew her.
Old, and full of years,
not one would shed a tear.

Once young and vibrant, full of life,
the maiden's goals did seem
to be in reach, without much strife,
Alas! Was but a dream.

Now slowly down the boulevard
the hearse goes unheeded.
Few people stop to muse and look,
I think police weren't needed.

Her final days here were spent,
her story had an end.
And to the grave the city sent
but few to bury its dead.

Dale K. Dreyer

What Is Teal

Teal reminds me of a flower
on a cold wet day. Teal is the
color of a bridesmaid's dress, it
shines like a star or a diamond
in the sky. It sounds like the
love I have in my heart,
it tastes like water rushing
down my throat, it smells like
leaves on the trees nice and fresh, like
a cherry tree or a strawberry bush.
On a warm spring day. It looks
like a rainbow way up in the sky,
like the sun, moon and the air
and clouds. Like a light bulb lit
up in the nighttime navy blue sky.
And it can also be the love that
a person gets for all of
his or her life.

Alisa Malzac

Winter, Spring, Summer, Fall

Winter, Spring, Summer, Fall,
Oh, how I love them all!
Winter brings the snow.
Oh, and don't you know,
Spring brings April showers,
And lots of May flowers!

I always have plenty of fun,
In the beautiful Summer sun,
But the most beautiful season of all,
Is the crisp, colorful Fall!
Winter, Spring, Summer, Fall,
Oh, how I love them all!

Christi Robinson

Because We Love You

You need to know how proud we are
of what you've gone and done.

You've given up the thing in life
you thought was number one

And as you wake each day you see
the world a little clearer

And face a different person
As you look into the mirror

You'll need support, it will be rough
Sometimes too hard to bear

But just remember all the people
in your life who care.

And as I leave you with this thought
of life without a crutch.

You need to know we support you
and love you very much.

Beverly Marshall

What Is Black?

Black is the shadow;
of the whitest fish.
Black is the sky,
of a moonlit wish.

Black is the color
of the tapping tap shoes.
And don't forget the black geese;
walking in two's.

Black is the mind
of a star that is kind.
The burnt ginger bread man,
And the big family of the Scottish clan.

Black is the color of the soil,
dug up from the earth.
Black is the color of the
fireplace hearth.

Black is the color of the Indian Princess's hair,
And the Lion's long flattering stare.

Eryn H. Duffield

No More

Night's cloak descends upon our heads
Midnight's eye surrounds us with dread.
Even though some shake and shiver,
Without a ripple, quake or quiver,
I walk along the ocean shore
And find an eel that will swim no more.

April Quincoses

Pink And Red Mom

Pink and red remind me
of the most wonderful person in my life.
Pink reminds me of her rosy cheeks,
the love she brings into our house,
and of her kindness.

Red reminds me of
her constant sunburns,
her lipstick,
her favorite red roses,
and... once again her everlasting love.
Who is it?... you ask.
It's my Mom!

Casie Krantz

Dolphins

Diving, loving, mammals,
Of the deep blue sea.
Lurking harmlessly around with
Patience and beauty.
Happiness and peace goes through
their mind, while gliding in the
waters of their home.
Never searching for danger or
harm, just
Showing off their luscious charm.

Anna E. Lowry

Empathy

She told me of her lonely room,
Of tears that fell at night,
Of wishing for him in the gloom
Until the morning's light.

She told me and I listened, crying,
For I thought I sympathized,
But when I woke to our love, dying,
I knew her tears were in my eyes.

Elinor S. Hargraves

"Elegy"

Wandering through our crowds
Of painted faces and dubious smiles
Life is a masquerade ball
Mischief lurking behind every mask

Elegant costumes disguise our fear
Jealousy dressed in beautiful gowns
Manic faces hide evil minds
Sparkling eyes conceal our sins

The beauty of the pain
The pleasure of the tears
Gestures of amusement and desire
Can anything be so sensual?

Why is everything we are
So worshipped by those who love?
Envious of our dispositions
Possessive of our guilt

Veil yourselves with selfish pride
Spread empty vanity on your winds
Revel in the depths of our despair
Surrender to our passions

J. T. Botelho

"War"

I found myself in the middle
of nowhere.
Fighting a battle of confusion,
and facing a tie.
Feuding with fact.
Winning with wit.
Losing with stupidity.
Armed with nothing.
Escaping only by sleep, but still
waking to find enmity between
opposing forces.

Ashley Taylor

In Old New York

In old New York, the streets are full
of many unfortunate ones.

Everyday sorrow and depression
but never any fun.

They scrounge and save for every
cent to help keep them alive.

Their shredded clothes and cardboard
homes are things that they despise

The Broadway lights and spend thrift
cars emphasize their poverty.

They have nothing in the world
they're just there suffering quietly

The feelings within them I but
you can't see.

For one of those unfortunate
ones just happens to be me!

Christopher Burke

"Waste Not"

Yesterday is a reminder
Of days both good and bad,
The trials that taught us lessons
And good times we have had.
The future still is waiting
As our dreams come in the night.
To become a reality
Before the morning light.

The past may bring us memories
To treasure through the years,
The future keeps the dream alive
Despite our doubts and fears.
But, oh, my friend, we have today
To live and laugh and cry——
A day our Lord has given us
That soon will pass us by.

Dee Glessman

Our House

The Frame
of a long awaited dream
is up.
The acres of heavenly land,
the trees,
the breeze,
we shiver when we see what beauty.
we have created.
Everything will change in
new and exciting
ways.

Erica Leigh Raffaele

God Can

God can reach the unreachable
Obtain the unobtainable
Do the undoable
Get the ungettable
Save the unsaveable
Heal the unhealable
Deliver the undeliverable
Mend the unamendable
Stop the unstoppable
Seek the unseekable
Touch the untouchable
Give the ungiveable
Impossibilities are God's possibilities
Because I AM the God that healeth thee
And teacheth thee to prosper.
  Financially
  Mentally
  Physically
  Spiritually

Darlene K. Hudnall

Early Spring

The peach tree in the garden,
now that winter's gone,
has reached slim arms to heaven
and had them filled with dawn.

Clyde A. Beakley

The Spark

A spark set in the firmament,
Nourished by a divine hand,
Responds like an unruly child.

Cared for in its infancy,
Grows slowly at first,
According to a prescribed meter.

Adolescence brings independence.
Free to reach out
In all directions with fingers of light.

Pulsating and expanding
At a furious rate,
Until stepping beyond its limits,

The bonds of space and time
Can no longer hold it.
Then BANG
A Universe is born.

Charles G. Lang

Call Of A Friend

Sitting In Silence
Not hearing Words
God will remind us
with something that's heard

God might be calling
But do we hear him
Why wouldn't we listen
For do we Fear him

He is our Friend
He is our Pal
He's there till the END
For the END might be NOW!

A good Friend to have
You might say the Best
He's one I will have
For all of the rest!

Chadwick D. Osborn

Enigma

I have not a reason,
Nor have I a cause
No explanation...
As to why I am here

Whether it be to help
  or to harm
  or just be unknown

But patiently I wait....
  with occasional tears
  and frustration
To find the answer
  of my presence

Christine Wojewodzki

Everyone's Different

Everyone's different in their own way
No one's the same, but isn't that okay?
Black, white, red, and blue
Some are different by color, that's true
Everyone's different in their own way
Why isn't that okay?
Some people feel they have to be
Just like all the rest
Other people feel they're superior to us
And that they're the best
But no matter how people act and react,
Everyone's different in their own way
Why, oh why, isn't that okay?

Erin Pistorese

Mother

A mother is someone who is always there
No matter when or where

She can never let you down
That is why she is heaven bound

She will always remember your birthday
She knows how to make the pain go away

She is a teacher everyday of the year
Teaching us not to fear

She is a cook when she can
She may rather it be the MAN

She is a wonderful blessing in the light
An example of love and might

A mother is someone like you
I love you for all you do.

Arthurlee L. Mitchell Jr.

A Loving Thought For You

Walk with a smile
Never be blue
If you start to worry,
This you should do
Forget all your troubles
And let things be
You'll always be happy
If it depends upon me.

Afton Ruth Van Buskirk

What Is Happening To Our Children

What is happening to our children?
No laughter in their eyes,
No smile on their lips,
Where is the innocence?

Streets are no longer safe,
Children killing children,
No one sees,
No one cares.

What is happening to our children?
They cannot run or play,
Is this our fault?
Who is to blame?

Someone save our children
Before it is too late,
Who can save our children?
Only one can, Jesus.

Bonnie Liff

Ame Vie

Dead grass
'neath sparkling rime
crunching from the weight of my
soul

Foot prints
deeply imbedded
melting from the warmth of my
soul

Steamy mist
slowly rising
wafting aimless, from the airiness of my
soul

Trails end
silent clods falling
upon the ether that is my
soul

Warp speed
through starlit heavens
eternal peace awaits my
soul

Dean L. Harvey

To My Sister

This rose is red,
my love is true.
My heart is filled,
with thoughts of you.

Not to mistaken
as just a friend.
But you are my sister,
my best friend.

We may shout,
or even pout.
But time goes on,
and we move on.

As we get older,
our love gets bolder.
And you'll always be here,
to look over my shoulder.

Even when I'm old and gray,
I'll be able to say,
I'll love you forever,
and a day.

Cortney Gower

"Life's Rocky Road"

This road is rough and rocky
My life is filled with tears
My heart is ever aching from
All the doubt, and fear.
I have no one to talk to, or understand
my part, so I just sit alone;
With an aching heart.
If it were not for Jesus my dearest
And closest friend, I would see
No need to live on in this world of sin.

Christene Riley

Winged Caress

When bothered by so many cares
My heart began to cry.
The silent moans and groans were heard
He looks down from on high.

He listened to me patiently
And chose a gentle way
To show the love He has for me
On each and every day.

He gathered 'round some angels
As I began to sigh.
They came right down from heaven
And gently floated by.

And as they did I felt a breeze.
My spirit now just sings,
Because He cared enough to let
My soul be touched by angel wings.

Clare Taylor

Shouts Of Love-Zestfully

When morning greets the sky
My heart awakens and cries,
"'Tis zestful to shout of love!"

When morning leaps to noon
And thoughts of being with you soon,
'Tis zestful to shout of love!

When gone the sun,
Being with you, hon
'Tis indeed zestful!

Alfred Sheldon Hanly

The Open Book

The open book upon the table top
Must contain secret elements of love
If I could only reach the book
If I could only see the pages
I'm slipping
Slipping away from the book
The entire elements of love gone
For I shall never love

Brandy Kelley

Shakespeare Is Weird

Though ages rush pass
like the clouds,
he towers above all,
  as the sky.

With the claws
  of this craft,
all of time,
is frozen into a fly,
in spider's trap.

Anthony A. Aiya-Oba

1944 Mother's Day Letter

You see that rose on yonder bush
Much lovelier than the others?
Its beauty like a woman's blush
Reminds me of my mother's.
And on the hill the sun sets fair
In reddish golden glow
Well, that could be my mother's hair
Of not so long ago.
And in the summer evening's calm
The thrushes liquid notes
Are mother's voice in David's psalm,
That praise to God denotes.
I've yet to find a work of art
Approaching real perfection
Where I'd not find my mother's heart
Mirrored in reflection.
And even though young men, as I,
Yearn longingly for lover,
There's this that you cannot deny
I'll always have my mother.

David Gwathmey Jewett

Worthy Of Praise

God showers us with blessings
  more precious than gold,
as His Glory surrounds us
  and mysteries unfold.

Trees with great splendor
  stretch, praising the sky,
for the God who created them
  abides there on high.

Fine meadows of flowers
  radiate His love,
as birds sing their praises
  to the Creator above.

Let all of God's children
  exalt His dear name,
for all of His blessings
  are ours to proclaim.

Caroline M. Franklin

Never Forget

Days are lost but not forgot.
  Memories never to occur again
Remembered forever.
  Friends of one time,
Friends of another.
  Old dreams nearly forgot,
But never lost.
  Dreams of another time
Acted out by friends;
  Never lost, never forgot.
Bad times, good times,
  Never forgot continue.
A new house, a new home,
  New friends, new surroundings.
Old house, old home,
  Old friends, old surroundings;
As time passes them by
  Never forget.

Elizabeth A. Jackson

Alabama Home

In the morning mist,
Lovers steal a kiss,
Then hasten on their way.

Down a country road,
Hand-in-hand they go,
To find the treasures of their hearts.

Moments in my mind,
Timeless through the years,
I never will forget you.

Yesterdays are gone,
But memories linger on,
Of the good times we've shared.

Alabama home,
No need for me to roam,
You've everything I need,
You're where I long to be,
Alabama home.

Brenda D. Johnson

Until The Next Tomorrow

Do I have to say goodbye
Lord knows I need to try
I loved you from the start
Loved you with all my heart
These dreams I've come to cherish
Will not also with you perish
With every tear I shed
It's the future that I dread
All alone in pain and sorrow
Can I face the next tomorrow

Angelyn Edwards

See The Waste

Standing on a hill top,
looking below to see
the earth,

Looking up,
high above,
to see the sky blue,

Looking below,
You can see the water,
clear, and clean,

Touch the earth,
touch the sky,
touch the water,

Turn around,
to see it,
it's all gone,
see the waste.

Asha Azhar

I Am

I am... I am... I am...
　Just think... I am?

I am? I am?? I am???
　Absolutely... I am!

I am! I am!! I am!!!
　Thank God... I AM

Bette Y. Patton

Why must I feel so
lonely inside
Never have I felt so
sad
Never to see the light
of day
or night
it makes me mad
knowing God watches
over me
I feel a lightness inside
So I sit
waiting
for that final day
The day I join
my Dad

Amanda Vickers

Empower

Go to your heart.
Listen,... for a start.
What does it say?
What can it tell?
How does it feel?
When every cell, will yell,
I'll take care of you!!

You always had it.
The power to do it.
That which you seek.
First think of it.
Next, see it,
After that feel it.
It can be yours.
Rely on yourself.
You are Empowered!

Carleen O. Uhley

Scoffing

It hurts the feelings
like words stabbing
a person through the heart.

It makes one sad as
if you were alone
with no hope and
no one to help you.

It burns the heart
like a fire charring
wood on a chilly
winter day.

It never leaves you
it makes a scar
on the heart
forever.

Carolyn A. Thomas

The Wonderful Sight

I like the sky at night,
It's a very pretty sight.
Stars glisten through the night
While you sleep so tight
Shooting stars zoom over head
While you lie asleep in bed
You can see tonight
even though someone turned out the light
that's because the moon's so bright
now watch the sky and watch all night
and you will see a pretty sight

Diana Webster

Take My Hand Daddy

Take my hand Daddy,
like when I was small,
and we'll walk together,
we'll get through it all.

Take my hand Daddy,
I'm big now you see,
I can handle helping you,
like you handled helping me.

Take my hand Daddy,
the road will get rough,
but I'm right beside you,
and my Daddy is tough.

Take my hand Daddy,
we'll take one step a day,
and soon as you know it,
you'll be off, on your way.

Take my hand Daddy,
and we'll see it through,
put your hand in my hand,
success is waiting for you.

Debbie Lackey

Fireworks

Sometimes
like the flash of a firework
there's a moment
when life sparkles
and excited joy fills the air.
Moments
when two people tingle
in knowing and being
so very close
together.
So close
that if you can see through the blinds,
see through the sketches
of the human form,
see into the soul picture,
you touch there
and for the Moment
are a part of the Firework.

Deanne Bosnak

Fear

Fear,
like the dark cloud it is,
overshadows the sunshine
you bring into my life,
And I am silent,
laughing,
pretending I don't notice
the turmoil inside
Hidden away,
as if no one will understand,
and I hope
and wish
and try to see
what's beyond the barriers
that are keeping me from life
Then I get a glimpse of you
standing there
telling me you love me,
and why do I want to cry?

Elin J. Schmidt

Colors

I'd color hope yellow
like a sun that always
shines.

I'd color boredom black
an absence of color in
my mind.

I'd color freedom green
Like fresh dewy grass.

I'd color conceit a
reflection in glass.

I'd color love blue like
the blue of the sky.
Yes, I'd color love blue
like my true love's
blue eyes.

Alice Bisel

True Love

True Love:
  Like a fawn,
  When newborn,
  First tries its legs,
  Stumbles,
  Falls,
  And tries again.
A constant re-occurrence.

But when nourished,
  Nurtured,
  Cherished,
  Protected,
  This God-given gift
  Appears one day
  Among the forest of time
A strong, sure-footed deer.

Dan Berk

Seeds

The seeds of heaven dropped to earth.
Lighter ones took wings and flew,
soared to land, or waters to drift,
float, sink, and reproduce in forms
of beauty, delight, and color.
The earth and sea held for progeny
forms to twist and mold infinity.
Turmoil established, order anticipated,
science fights against natures right,
as heaven opened and delivered seeds.
So, the earth opens to rescue and renew.

Annie L. McClure

Life

Life is hard,
Life's unfair,
Life can be tricky,
Life's a big dare.
If you take it day by day,
it just might go your way.
So, never give up,
we bid you good luck!
Don't think you're a fool,
and just stay in school.
Don't go on drugs,
don't hang out with slugs.
Just do your best, cause life's a
big test!

Elizabeth Rogers

Echoes Of Renewal

Rogers Lake of long ago...
Lies peaceful under ice and snow,
Memories fondly planted there
Send whispers through the frosty air.

To this lake two youths were drawn,
Camping 'til the break of dawn...
Clothed in darkness softly rest,
Savoring nature at its best.

They walked the paths that I once trod,
Awakened footprints 'neath the sod...
Beheld the sun dance on the lake
While echoes from the past awake.

A breath of time still lingers there,
Inspired dreams invade the air...
And often in the passing view,
Drifting scenes reflect anew.

Blanche M. Kingsley

My Prayer

The past is gone -
Let it never be repeated
Or longed for.
The present is here.
So, please accept my baby, Lord.
The one I never seen.
Give him lots of toys in his playroom,
With lots of ice-cream and candy to eat.

And when he gets a little older,
Explain why his mother had to
Kill him while living in her womb.
Don't be too hard on him, Jesus
For I wouldn't want him to cry.
And when you put him to sleep at night,
Please sing him a lullaby.

If he ever wonders about me, Lord
Speak of me more and more,
Because without his and your forgiveness
I'll never see Heaven's Door.

Betty Mullar

Why I Like North Carolina

Magic mountains
Kites flying high
Beautiful beaches
bright blue skies

Cardinals, Dogwoods
tall pine trees
Dolphins jumping
in clear blue seas

Lighthouses glowing
showing the way
for lonely sailors
who have lost their way

Autumn leaves falling
history abounds
There's always a story
just look around

Friendly people
just come and see
why North Carolina's
so special to me

Brandy Slappey

Poetry Contest

I'll enter this contest
  Just to see
What in the world
  It'll do for me
I have no idea
  What it's for
But with nothing to lose
  I'll write some more
Twenty lines or less
  To participate
Maybe I'll become famous
  They'll think I'm great
I've never written
  A poem before
I guess I'm done
  Can't think no more.

Dawn Brown

I'm Living In A Dream

I'm living in a dream
just to pass the time
no matter how real it may seem
I must keep in mind it's only a dream
with beauty surrounding
our love out standing
reality slips away
I'm living in a dream
just to pass the time
until reality shows itself
I must put my dream on a shelf.

Betty A. Szklenski

Riding The Horse

I lay in my bed,
Just thinking of stuff,
Then I drift to sleep.
I dream of a horse,
That I'm riding in a meadow.
The horse is so beautiful.
Its blond hair is so pretty,
In the sun light,
Its saddle has flowers of all kinds,
And a ribbon in its mane.
The horse is white all over,
And has gray feet.
As I ride my hair just flows back,
It's just as if I'm flying.
Then a chill comes, I get off the horse,
And wake up,
I turn around and see the horse,
And know it's not a dream.

Amber Groves

No Time

Passions ebb to the side
just no time for you and I.
Lust then gathers where need used to be
a little attention would set us free.
Free for laughter, smiles and such
am I asking for way too much?
You're the driver of a truck
I'm a housewife, just my luck.
Can we make that special time
for us to make our own bells chime?
May be silly, may sound plain,
but if I don't have you
I'll go insane!

Debi Kottke

Try Again

Arise and shine!
Jesus' birthright can be mine,
To last throughout eternity.
So try again,
Through his tender, loving mercy.

Christian Birton

Untitled

Patience is a virtue
I've tried and tried to obtain
But it's proven to be very hard
An unreachable height to gain

In my life, though, I have learned
Many different things
About love, and friends, and treasures
And what each new day brings

I know when I find the one I love
I'll learn how to wait
Which will become an advantage
And will keep my path straight

No one knows what the future will bring
Whether it be laughter, sorrow, or death
But, know this, that once I fall in love
It will be to my dying breath

Angela Bahl

Feeling Blue

I feel blue today and I don't know why,
It's just a feeling deep inside of me,
that makes me want to cry.
It's a day when I think too much
and just feel sad.
Doubts and worries overwhelm me,
and that makes me feel bad.
Usually the feeling goes away
later in the day,
and then I should end up
feeling better in every way.

Christine Mattson

Expensive Ignorance

Education is hard to get,
It's costly in the least,
but for it I would give a "mil,"
and on knowledge I could feast.

I will listen to lectures until I'm deaf,
and read until I'm blind,
I'd speak until my mouth went dry,
but I'd never fall behind.

I want to have an endless knowledge,
and in an elite congregation
So ignorance is really the expensive one,
Find riches in education.

Ben McKinney

Perfect Peace

Death comes on silent creeping feet.
It stalks us all unto defeat.
Its ways differ and are not kind.
As live goes on and time unwinds.

And to each of us this hour will come
More merciful to others than to some.
From whence or what will bring our death
God have mercy at our last breath.

Della Orme

The Red Iron Man

Look at yonder building so tall,
It speaks of strength that will not fall.
It was built of steel so red,
As the Red Iron Man earned his bread!

He laid the beams up and across,
Joining each to each without a loss.
With grace they rose to meet the sky,
To mingle with the clouds so high!

Through rain and snow and heat and cold,
He joined the beams, 'cause he is bold.
And fearless too he has to be,
To make those buildings for you and me!

And when the buildings are as ought,
He can stand and see what he's wrought.
And say with pride as he does stand,
This is the work of a Red Iron Man!

Frank M. Dust

Love

Love is a color.
It sounds like a bird's song.
It tastes like a piece of sweet candy.
It smells like a freshly cut rose.
Love feels like a great big hug.

Amanda Kienast

A Summer Rose

The moon is full, and bright, and clear.
  It shines on the new fallen snow.
The crisp clean air of a winter night,
  touches something in my soul.
Yet, nothing warms my heart as much,
  as the beauty of a summer rose.
The long winter night turns into spring.
  The trees began to bloom.
The colorful flowers dance in the breeze,
  kissed by the melting snow.
Yet, nothing warms my heart as much,
  as the beauty of a summer rose.
Seasons come, and seasons go,
  life is a beautiful thing.
To hear and touch, to see and smell,
  the birds, the flowers, the soft gentle breeze,
  nature is a sight to behold.
Yet, nothing warms my heart as much,
  as the beauty of a summer rose.

Carol Ann Broussard

Love

Love is within us.
It only shows, when
  we give it to another
It's a radiant glow,
  that gleams with
  tenderness.
Love is tireless, and
  knows no end.
For, as long as we live,
  it always lies
  within us.

Ann Marie Kaminsky

Grandpa

A heart attack is what it's called
It killed my grandpa and I bawled.
I cried so much I could not sleep
And memories I'll always keep
of my Grandpa, Grandpa sweet,
And I hope that I will meet
with him up there, in heaven, high,
It is called sweet by and by
I know the pain, it hurts real bad
when someone dies, it's always sad
But I know that when I die
I'll go up, so don't you cry.
Yes, I'll go up, you know it's true,
If you get saved, then you'll go, too.

Adam Akeman

It Is There...

Like the newness of Spring,
It is there.
Like the promise of Summer,
It is there.
Like the gentleness of Fall,
It is there.
Like the harshness of Winter,
It is there.
It is there, as the seasons
are there.
It is there, as the cycles of life,
are there.
As the seasons change
As the cycles change
One thing stays, always
there.
Always the same, always
different.
  Love
It is there.

Beverly Andres

Untitled

Nature is a hot tomato
It has peas and trees
And russet potatoes

With nature all around
You don't have to buy
A filling for a pie by the pound

So pluck a pear
That is so juicy and fruity
That to eat it a napkin you must wear

When it's nature that you love
You will find inner peace
By eating quiche
And breeding doves

Nature has many things that are cool
Like ice hot like rice
And wicked like a whirlpool

Nature is groovy
Don't take it for granted
It is enchanted
So go outside, not a movie

Christopher J. Stone

Love

Love is like a rope,
It can be broken
And can be made.

Love is like a band,
It can be learned
And can be sung.

Love is like a baby,
It can grow
And can die.

Love is like a rope.

Christy Bryan

"Muddle Through"

Do you ever feel life,
is something you just Muddle Through?
That you're stuck in a rut,
no matter what you do.

That the years fly by,
and leave you standing still.
And you wonder if you're always
gonna struggle up the hill.

That if it's worth the struggle,
day in and day out?
And then you see the things
that you really care about.

Your friends, your family,
your precious little child.

And then before you know it,
you begin to smile.

They make it all worth it,
to do the things we do.
And give us the courage,
to simply Muddle Through.

Connie Scott

To Fill A Heart With Light and Bouquets of Love

The evil in your heart
is so deeply intense,
why must it be?

Release all that destruction
before your heart
will become a disruption
of yourself!

The evil will take hold
of your whole soul
and, you will not be
a complete person.

So, release the bitterness
that encompasses yourself
and fill your heart
with light and bouquets
filled with love.

Frances Faggelle Larvey

"A Lonely Sailor"

On every lonely South Sea Isle,
I see a Lovely Lady's smile.
Tho' she's not here-we're far apart;
Her smile is framed within my heart
    and gives me strength where'er I go.
It's you, "Sweetheart", I Love you so.

Frank Chase Jr.

for Michael

The secret world
is not yet made,
the cost too dear
it's twice been paid

A place of senses
image and feel,
what love has bought,
lust comes to steal

What's worth desire
unsatisfied,
is but for love
to be supplied

Momentous pleasure,
should we partake,
must leave contentment
in its wake

Decision is made
the pain is unreal
a wounded heart
is left to heal

Deborah J. Corlis

The One I Love

The one I love
    Is just above.

He looks upon me like
a dove.

He loves me with an
    Everlasting love.

The one I love.

Christy Sapp

Love

Love, like a rare white dove,
Is a so very precious thing,
It could be a long lost love,
Or the face of a newborn baby.

It comes in all shapes and forms,
In all emotional degrees,
Whether if love's lost and one mourns,
Or new love's found and all is glee.

But love can also hurt and snare,
If not admitting your feelings,
Neither knows if the other cares,
Causing some misunderstandings.

And when your love is true love,
It lasts forever and ever,
Soaring through all storms like doves,
Coming out in the end for the better.

Love, like a rare white dove,
Is a so very precious thing,
If one thing lasts in this world, love,
Will overcome and be Eternally.

Becky Radmer

We

You reach out to me,
I flee;
I reach out to you,
you flee;
feeling the fear
in our needs,
we flee,
you and me.

Brian Schwall

"Musings '95" (To My Children)

Incorporate my soul
Into your souls
Today
And make me live
Forever.

Transplant the seeds
Of my imagination
Into the fertile gardens
Of your minds
And let them germinate.

Just as cool raindrops
Soften barren soil
To transform aridity
Into nutrition
So will I thrive.

Then will my growth
Savor your touch
As seedlings of my mind
Are coaxed
Into proliferation.

Elma Diel Photikarmbumrung

Runaway

I ran away once,
into the deep forest,
away from my problems and sorrows.
I didn't look back,
but when I stopped to think,
I realized I had run the wrong way.
The forest was dark and lonely,
with no one but me.
I should have run forward,
into my problems.
I should have faced them.
Then I could have solved them.
But I had run too far,
without looking back.
I realized I was lost,
in the deep forest.
A lone child lost,
in the forest of my mind.

Erica Celso

A Whole New World

You brought love,
Into my life,
And you showed me,
The light.

And that's when I knew,
That you had brought a whole new world,
To me.

At first I didn't believe you,
Until,
You came to my house,
One night,
When you asked me to,
Marry you,
Out in the moonlight.

Then,
I knew there was no denying,
The love you had inside,
And,
That's when you brought a whole new world,
To me.

Candi Baber

I've Fallen In Love With You

If you could see
inside my heart,
then you could understand,
how much I'd give
anything
to have you as my man.

There's a pain in my heart,
a flame in my eyes,
I see it in the stars,
it's written cross the skies.

It grew inside,
This feeling of love,
this is a lot more
than I had ever dreamed of.

I always thought
I'd stand strong and true,
But I'm not too proud
to admit,
I've fallen in love with you.

Angelina Miller

Con Fuoco

Soothing crescendo,
Innocent trills,
Unorthodox tempo,
But it does give one chills,
A glissando up the spine,
Vibrato in the bones,
A fermata of silence,
But only the performer will know,
when there is a mistake,
A false note,
A lost bar.
Yet the audience is suspended in awe,
For even a sweet discord,
Or sleight of key,
Can charm the watchers,
So they don't hear,
Or see.
The artist has performed the piece "con fuoco."
And the concert hall is ablaze,
With tone.

Carson E. McCoy

Untitled

I used to think
(In wild anticipation!)
That someday you and I
Would have a permanent relation.

But now I realize,
(And oh how much it hurts!)
That I'm just the gal you depend upon
To launder all your shirts!

Evelyn Blackburn

That Special Someone

That special someone;
His smile so sweet;
His hair so blond;
His eyes so blue.

That special someone;
His dimples so cute;
His heart so big;
His body so brown.

Danielle Bordine

Dreams

Sometimes reality forms
in the shape and substance
of illusionary, cloudy vagueness

My dreams are of you, not as
I knew you, but as you are.
The telepathic transcendence;
to see you pass beyond the veil
Drawn to you by kismet
through the distances of time
   and the uncertain,

As Einstein decreed-
   time bend before the portal
   warped and eternally open.

The pole shifts and swirls in the
colors of rainbows and ribbons
blowing freely in the May wind.

Stars shine brilliantly in the
new moon sky at night.
Reality colored by illusions —
The Prophet's always aware of the Master Plan.

Debra Cooperson Scott

Early Morn

As I sit upon my porch
in the cool morning breeze,
I watch the leaves waving to me
from the dew kissed trees.
Small animals scurry to and fro,
in a hurry, with no place to go.
The cattle grazing in the meadow
on a lazy summer morn,
occasionally glancing over the fence
at the neighbor's field of corn.
As the sun rises high in the sky,
I go inside and think with a sigh,
Another beautiful morning gone by.

Carol Hickman

Renewal

Beyond the mountain lies Tomorrow;
   In my hand I hold Today;
On my back is all the sorrow
   And the pain of Yesterday.

What compels me toward the mountain
   Carrying weights of failures known;
And memory's crashing fountain
   Bares my guilt on every stone?

'Tis the light that shines above me
   Urging onward like a star
Parting clouds, and there more clearly
   Gives me courage from afar.

And I know that I will never
   Walk this mountain way alone;
Light will be my guardian ever,
   Fountain-flood my guilt atone.

So - beyond the mountain lies Tomorrow;
   In my hand I hold Today;
But the pain with all the sorrow
   From the Past is washed away.

Alice L. Davis

I Really Care

I really care for you
In most every way.
I've not known you long
But....how long is one day?

I feel like you've been there
All of my life,
You're the spring and the flowers
And my sundown at night.

I dream of you always
When I'm not in a rush,
And when your away
I long for your touch.

It's just the short time
When we meet now and then,
I feel I'm in heaven
And pray it won't end!

Eleanor J. Black

Dad And Mom

Daddy has met mother
in Heaven at last
Their troubles and pain
in this life has passed

They had been apart
for many years
But now there will be no
more goodbyes or tears

They are singing God's
praises around the throne
waiting for us children
to come home

They are walking hand
in hand on the street of gold
thanking Jesus for giving
His life to save their souls

Won't it be a happy time
when we gather around the crystal sea
where we will meet Mother and
Daddy again forever with them to be

Cleo Snow

The Memorial Service

They entered the sanctuary
in groups of three or more
coming together/to honor
one of the sisters/their eyes/
no longer wide with wonder/narrow
as their lips/faces landscapes
of valleys and ridges/under rouge
and powder/lay bloodless grey
tinged with blue/after in the hall
of fellowship/they minced cookies
between Dr. Goodman's best-fit dentures/
murmured "Sorry" to the family/anxious
to leave/taking the nourishment of hope/
telling each other, "She lived to be
ninety-one."

Betty Brower

Dear World

Dear World:
I am homosexual.
Sincerely,
Me
The Real Me

Anthony Antoine

The Station

We're safely hidden
In an underground station.
A penny, not one.
And food, not any.
A knock on the secret door
Who could it be?
"A friend among friend."
They peek out to see.
They let us inside,
They give us food,
And then we hide.

Elizabeth Banks

The Curtain

What lurks behind the curtain,
I'm too afraid to see
To take that one step forward
And let the light shine in on me.

Fear is in the shadows,
I feel it, though it's still
I'm too afraid to look
I've paralyzed my will

The unbroken step of life
What is it that I feel
Fantasy is a world
In a mind that is not real

What lurks behind the curtain
I'm too afraid to see
For what lurks behind the curtain
Could very well be me!

Angelina M. Morelli

First Crop

Had I not felt before
 I'd never have known.

I tossed the seeds on the land
 manured, watered, weeded
 and they grew

Sowing continuously then would I sleep
 well, no time didn't we reap
 and it was fine reap
 don't we all farmers

Yet, my first crop was to come
 And indeed it came
Yet this was the difference
 It's the finest
 My first crop

When you get there
 you realize
 it's not quantity
 but quality...

Cyd W. Nzyoka

Angel In The Morning

As I awake,
I see her in my bedroom window.
There is a breeze outside,
Her dress made of clouds,
Her body made of snow,
She is a whisper to me.

She is there for just a moment,
She floats away,
Leaving me in a mystery.

Annie Sackler

My Gift To You

Walk alongside of me
I will show you the way
I'll teach you all I know
So you can stand alone someday.

I'll help you build a base
upon which you will grow
And all that you have learned
will be placed on top to show.

Take what I have to offer
and do with it what you may
Whoever you choose to be
is not for me to say.

I'll give you all my love
and anything else you'll need
In hopes that in this life
you will grow and succeed.

Deborah A. Freeman

Speck Of Sand: Me!

Out there on the horizon
I went to sit and think.
The space all around me,
I know where I've been,
And now need to think.
Where am I going and
What am I to be?
The space of the horizon
Holds many ideas.
I'm like a speck of sand
In the vastness of it all;
The force of the wind blows
The sand into a spin!
I can float around and
Come down in an entirely new place.
The ideas will be a new plan for conception.
The whirlwind on the horizon
Turns sand into a design.
I will be made over,
And become a whole new me!

Anna L. Holobach

In Your Absence

In your absence,
I turned to put away a fork,
and of a sudden
you were with me, part of me.

That deep part of you,
that is precious to me,
flowed into me and through me
and I was at peace.

In the moment, this house,
with all its possessions
turned again into our home.

And the dramas of our clashes
seem so slight and insignificant—
like nothing, in this moment,
When the presence of you fills me...
not with longing, but with peace.

It was my heart -
Where you are
...even in your absence.

Estelle Foley

Last Picture

Grandma always tells me
I tilt my head
and smile
when I am most happy
I guess I never noticed
kind of how
I never really saw
Mom's balding head
after months of chemotherapy
or her swollen scars
her tired body   frail mind
when her days insisted on
rushing to their end
it never occurred to me
until I looked
at that last picture of
Us for the first time
smiling
my head tilted
my arm around her fading waist

Christine L. Meyer

"Of Days Gone By"

Sometimes when I let my mind drift,
I think of days gone by.

Good days, bad days,
you name it,
I've had it.

Think about it sometime,
summer days of years gone by,
chasing fireflies and later to watch
them glow.

Winter days,
bundling up and playing in the snow,
lying low hoping not to get hit
by a passing snowball.

Fall days,
playing in the leaves,
only to come out with twigs and
leaves tangled in your hair.

Enjoy them to your best advantage,
because they will soon become
days gone by.

Amanda Marcengill

My Shepherd

With the Lord as my shepherd
I shall have no fears,
For His Book has promised
He will wipe away my tears!

His Promises are many!
His Book with love o'er flows!
I would follow Him to the garden,
For I love Him Heaven only knows!

He is my one true shepherd!
I, a lost and errant sheep!
I'll beg for His forgiveness,
'Ere I lay me down to sleep!

I know my shepherd hears me!
He answers o'er and o'er.
I know that He'll be waiting
At the wonderful, Heavenly Door!

He'll welcome all believers!
He will bid us to come in
If we love and trust our Savior,
Heaven's victory we shall win!

Bessie Brunson

The School Bus

In reminiscence I look out my window,
I see the school bus pass by,-
As every day I do!
It does not stop, of course not.
My children used to get off,
But no longer do.
They are all grown up-
some have children of their own,
In fact they live quite near.
I'm very grateful that they do,
Because if I squint very hard-
I get to see them, just a bit
The children of my children,
Getting off the school bus.

Eve Westaby

What I Saw

I saw flowers, I saw bees,
I saw grass, in a dream that I had.

I saw happiness, I saw gleam,
I saw greed, in a dream that I had.

I saw light, I saw dark,
I saw color, in a dream that I had.

I saw Ryan, I saw Melissa,
I saw Sam, in a dream that I had.

I saw glass, I saw metal,
I saw blood, in a dream that I had.

I saw a church, I saw a morgue,
I saw a cemetery, in a dream that I had.

I saw coffins, I saw four,
I saw parents, in a dream that I had.

I saw them floating upward.
Then, with a sudden start, I arose,
Ever slowly, into the dark, dismal skyline. —
To which then I realized that I felt heavy —
A dulling heavy. — Then I saw darkness —

Never to see again.

Anna Di Biase

I Remember Him Well

Ah, yes
    I remember him well.
He had words of
    silver
That caressed my famished soul,
    yet
Sadly reminded me
of the existence elsewhere of
    gold.
I liked having him near,
    but he did not move me to poetry.
Ah, yes
    I remember him well.

Amanda KC

I'm A Teenager Now

When I was little
I made a lot of mess.
You couldn't find my carpet,
But who could care the less.
I'm a teenager now.
Grown wise beyond my years.
Time to grow older.
Time to face my fears.

Alfonso Ramirez Jr.

Memories...

As I lay this rose on your grave,
I remember all the love you once gave.

As I look up to the big blue sky,
wondering why it was your turn to die.

Wishing I could have said "Good-Bye."
Now all I can do is sit here and cry.

I wish I could have been by your side,
even after the minute you died.

Now all I can do is say "I love you,"
And hope you know my words are true.

Angie Watkins

I Love You

When I think of you
I only think to smile.
You are everything
that was ever worthwhile.

You are my clock of love
may it never cease.
As long as we shall love
may our love increase.

You are my moon
and my stars shining bright.
Your everlasting radiance
brings joy to my life.

Closer and closer
our bond of love keeps growing.
Passionate affection
that's the way it's showing.

I'm placing these words on my heart's shelf
so life's trials can not make me forget how I felt.
These words will help my wounds and hurts
    to heal
the reasons why I fell in love with you, the
way I still feel.

Carol Patton-Hamilton

Missing You

Dear handsome one,
I miss the things that we have done.
I miss holding you tight,
All through the night.
Even though you are far away,
I think of you day by day.
I think of you all the time,
Wishing you were all mine.
I miss you so much,
Especially your beautiful touch.
I miss that wonderful time,
As you caressed that body of mine.
What I really really miss,
Is your beautiful kiss.
I wish you were here with me,
So that I can caress your body.
My feelings for you
Are so very true.
They came from my heart,
So, please don't tear them apart.

Christine Rodriguez

Violent Temper

There once was a man
    I loved so dear,
Until the day he filled
    me with fear.

He threatened he would
    take my life,
If I ever tried to put
    up a fight.

Finally one day when
    push came to shove,
And yes, he really did
    shove.

The many colors of a
    rainbow were no longer
    in the sky,
They were the proof to me
    of the wrong way to
    die.

Christy Strickland

Another Time

In the far-off distance of the night
I listen to the train-sound
Coming so softly,
A persistent yet muffled lament.

It moves swiftly, fades in and out.
Bringing with it remembrances
Of long-ago faces and far-off places.
The pause is slight, the pull is strong.

Suddenly the ghost is here with me!
Thunderous and vivid now,
Flooding the air with its presence.

It was gone in a moment
Rumbling on the wind
To come again another time,
Another time, another time.

Carol L. Baynes

My Narrow Escape (As Told By A Fawn)

On Sonny Trossbach's farm I roam.
    I like to feel it is my home.
Many days of my short life
    Have found me free of fearful strife.

But just a few short weeks ago
    The sight of hunters' guns did show.
My mom and dad explained to me
    The reason why they come and see.

So run as if your tail's on fire,
    And make no noise on bush or briar.
When Sonny and that Karl man came,
    I thought that I would feel some pain.

So run I did, and hopped and flipped
    So fast my heart a beat it skipped.
But lo behold, my quiet trek
    Ended in a safety check.

All limbs intact and heart still beat
    Relief to breathe, success to greet.
Now I know I'll grow much bigger
    For that Karl man pulled no trigger.

Florence T. Roy

When Sleep Flees Away

When sleep flees away
 I lay and listen
To the wind softly blowing
 I watch the fireflies
As they light up the might
 I watch the stairs in the sky
When sleep flees away

 When sleep flees away
I lay and listen to the rain
 As it falls softly
I hear the thunder roar
 I see the lightning
As it flashes across the sky
 I see wonder of wonders
When sleep flees away

Estelle Davis

Today's Youth - Tomorrow's Leaders

Who will be Today's Youth?
I know nothing else but youth,
Whether it has to do with my attitude,
Or the way I feel,
Or growing and having a good education,
Or getting the best job,
Or having more fun,
What will become of Tomorrow's Leaders?

Elizabeth Sharrow

Untitled

I thought he loved me, but
I guess I was wrong.
But people and their feelings
Come and go. It's a mystery!
I never know when the person
Will change his mind.
Looks like he already has because
He's not in love with me anymore.
I guess I made a mistake
By not giving him a chance
When he asked. I buried my
True feelings deep inside and
Couldn't find my way out.
Until I found out what he
Was really like
Now I have lost him forever.

Amy J. Olney

Without A Care

One day I came upon the world
I did not have a care
I did not ask to come this way
no pain have I been spared

I look upon the life I led
and feel it not a waste
I let no one push me too fast
for I won't move in haste

I never laugh at those who hurt
I laugh at those who dare
to cringe upon those who have less
laughter at them, I will not spare

I see life in the clearest light
not blind to the ways of life
to hell with those who fail this sight
I'll park my car wherever I like!

Corrinne Williams

Madness

I awake shaking with fear
I feel the madness inside
Is there anyone here
Or is it all in my mind

I creep out of bed
I feel I'm walking on air
Is it all in my head
Does anyone care

I run to the door
To lock it outside
It stalks me some more
There's no place to hide

It's calling my name
I cover my ears
It's part of the game
It feeds on my fears

Please leave me alone
I hear through my screams
Get out of my house
Stay out of my dreams

Christine Pinckney

Rebirth

As I step out into the light
I feel all my ambitions swarm
All around inside my head
As a frantic hive of bees
Rays of sunshine spill inside
Through broken seams in the fabric
Which covers my soul
Bird song and spring breezes
Echo throughout the depths of my heart
Bringing to life a joy inside
Which time had forgotten
And reality had suppressed
Emotional earthquakes
Rock the foundation of life
To unearth the remains
Of a carefree child
We all once knew

Cari Hatfield

A Long Long Day

In the year of Nineteen Sixty Two
I decided I would marry you
Through all the years
I have always been true
I often wonder if it's true of you
Some of the days were good and bad
Some of the days were very sad
How we stayed together
I will never know
Probably the children made it so
A son and a daughter I love so much
That no one will ever touch
The days have been very good to me
As I am sure you can see
I thank God each day
For his loving touch
And if he takes me today
I can truly say
Thirty Three Years is a very
Long Long Day

Barbara P. Martin

You And Her

The day I saw you with her,
I couldn't believe my eyes,
I wanted to turn and run,
And find a place to cry.

When I asked you the next day,
You said "Um... We're just friends."
Then you said I love you,
All the way till the end.

I tried my best to believe you,
But I couldn't find it in my heart,
So maybe it's best,
If we just part.

I hope you find someone to please you,
And who won't leave you,
But don't come back,
'Cause you will never make me blue.

Dana Marie Stringham

The Sky

You are my moon,
I am your star,
And your love is the sky.
Endless without a limit.

During the day,
When the sun is out,
We walk proudly around the blue sky.
In the shadow of the sun's ray's.

Yet at night,
When the time is right,
We come out of the dim lights.
And shine.

The sky our pallet,
To paint our deep love.

'Cause,
You are my moon,
I am your star,
And our love is the sky.

Beverly Bacchus

Yesterday, Today, Tomorrow

Today's the day to set and rest,
humidity's high, so do your best,
to see blue skies with puffy
clouds, and wonder where rain drops fall.

Falling drops to color the flowers,
green our grass and muddy some
puddles, for children to splash
and wade with glee, all in hot, hazy, summer days.

Fall will come, soon winter nears,
so enjoy summer while it's here.

Elsie Atwell

Lost

I have lost everything,
I cannot go back.
All that I hope for
And all that I dreamed.
It had come true.
My life was perfect, it had few flaws.
But then, I lost it all.
Why can't I get it back?
God only knows.
I cannot go back because
All time has froze.

Angie Sawyer

'Breathe Magic'

It's a magical breath we breathe
how does it come to me
we walk and talk yet no one sees
the magical breath we breathe
From birth to death
it comes - secretly
binding us to life
to hope from woe to glee
this breath inside of me
Can you tell it's there
even if you stare
so silent, yet so free?
...No time to pause,
no time to stop
this friend that never leaves
Until the last,
this dream shall pass
and I'm left - breathlessly
(...magical breath)
Then I'll see

Carolyn Potere

Only Seconds

In twilight's time my mind eye sees,
Horrid pain of man's misery.
Fruited plains all choked with smoke,
Tended by the dying folk.

Among them rides a hell-black steed,
Upon which sits death in entirety.
He swings his blade and reaps the weak,
The strong, the rich and the meek.

I gaze upon a lonely man,
Kneeling in the green blazed sand.
He cries and screams to the world today,
About the promises that were made.

He crumples down upon his face,
The land around a desert waste.
So many lives passed away,
In the coming hours of a new found day.

Only seconds, maybe more — then all beauty
was no more,
Only seconds, maybe less — man shook
hands with grinning death,
Only seconds, that was all,
Life ended.

Chris Lorenz

Secret Friend

Hiding in a corner,
hiding around a bend,
somewhere you'll find a secret friend.
Someone to talk to.
Someone on which to depend.
You may find them by magic,
or by a magic key,
all secret friends are tall or small.
They'll be their when your sad,
or when you're down in the dumps.
Your secret friend may be
a gnome, a fairy, a dwarf, or a troll.
If you don't have one then,
look around in a forest or a field,
keep your eyes peeled,
for the softest rustle in a bush,
or a flash of red out of the corner of your eyes,
could mean your secret friend is nearby.

Anna Banwell

Angels Of Mercy

Everyday the angels of mercy
help us, each and everyday.
When we are sick the angels
help to care, nurse, and smile
us back to healthy days.

These angles ask for nothing
other than, to tend to aches
and pains. They work long
hours and never ever complain.

With rays of joy, and singing
voices each and everyday, these
angels known as nurse's, help
us each and everyday.

A special thanks and praise
to these special angels who
help us each and everyday.

To the dedication,
compassion and love these special angels
known as nurse's give to us
each and everyday.

Brenda E. Cooper

Love Lost

Forever I want to be
held in your arms.
I miss your touch,
and all of your charms.

Life is short and some things
aren't meant to be.
Although for a short while
it was just you and me.

I'm sorry for all of
the pain that it cost.
I now feel that a
part of me has been lost.

The part of you that I carried
close to my heart,
has been taken from me
and no longer plays a part.

One day perhaps,
we will meet again.
When society's rules
will no longer win.

Crystal Sarvay

"Exercise - 2001"

The Health Police
  have come to my house.
My implant monitor has
  told them I have
stopped exercising.
  They insist that I
get into their electronic
  exercise suit.
An exercise program
  is chosen for me and
the dial is turned to "fast"
  to punish me.
They leave the virtual suit
  with me.
That night I dream that
  I die in the suit,
and it continues to jog
  around energetically,
with me in it, and not it it.

Bob Lennon

My Mother

Her love for us was endless
Her spoken words so true
She was always there for us
Knowing just what to do

My mother, my mother
Oh how I miss thee so
this emptiness inside
of me, I cannot let go

In spite of all your pain
You always seemed to smile
This happiness you gave to us
Would last quite awhile

My mother, my mother
You worked so hard for us,
Never quitting, always continuing
without ever a fuss.
I know now, you did this
because you loved us so very much

You are with God now, filled with peace and love,
still watching over us from that glorious
kingdom above.

Barbara J. FlemingCows

If Only You Knew

If only you knew
how much I love you
If only you could see
how much you mean to me
If only you could know
how much you affect me so
If only you could feel
how much my love for you is real
If only I could find
how to share with you, my mind
If only I were near
how I'd love you dear
If only you knew
how much I love you

David M. Ward

The Flower

A man went walking through the wood,
He came upon a flower.

His canteen full he thought he should,
Give this flower water.

His deed complete, he left that spot,
The flower now refreshed.

Another man soon comes about,
And tramples it to death.

David L. Brouse

Cows, Cows, Cows.
How beautiful they are.
I see them eating grass,
How natural they are.
They're off to the slaughter house,
How sad they are.
Yum, Yum, Yum,
How tasty they are,
Although some say it's wrong,
I say, "eat a cow or two!"
I will always remember,
The beautiful cows.

Carlos A. Moreno

Heaven's Gifts

Children are glorious gifts from heaven above; a beautiful testament
of a couple's love. To be brought into this world they do not ask;
to love, cherish and care for them is a parent's task. This task
should be accomplished freely and with an abundance of love.
If at times you need help, ask for it from God above. When things go
wrong in life, as they often do, don't turn on your children; place
blame where it is due. To lift a hateful hand and strike a tiny,
trusting face will cause that trust, in time, to slowly erase.
A child will almost always love his parents no matter what they do,
But if you hurt your child, can you love you? Bruises on a body
will in time fade away. Bruises on a soul will never go away.
As a child I lived through hatefulness and abuse. Many times
I felt life was of no further use. Once I loved the touch of my
father's hand, then I entered a nightmare I was too young to
understand. I lived alone in my nightmare world for many years;
eventually, there were no more hopes and no more tears.
From that life I have now broken free, but that hurt little girl
still lives inside of me. The bruises on my soul will never go
away; the pain in my heart is there to stay. Now God has given
me a glorious gift from up above, and I will strive to fill each
of her days with love. When I get angry, as all parents do,
I walk away until I can turn back and say, "I love you."
I don't want my daughter to bear the scars that I do. I want her to
know love, happiness and cares that are few. Growing up is hard
and should be done throughout the years;
Don't force your child to grow up in one dark night full of pain and
tears. Remember, our children are gifts from above.... they are
given to us to care for and to love.

Teresa J. Armer

The Kiss

An old man sits in a wheel chair all day, in the halls of a
nursing home. He's tall and stooped, his hair is white, not
gray. He's well up in years for ninety-one is his age. Alzheimer
has taken over his mind and he doesn't have a lot to say.

He was looking down the hall one day not noticing much that came
his way. He looked up and saw an old woman walking his way.
He recognized her right away. His eyes lit up and a big
smile came upon his face. She stop by his chair and planted a
kiss upon his face. He glowed with pleasure as she kissed him
there. For they had shared many a kiss and he remembered that she cared.

The beauty of the kiss was seen in his eyes and his face did
shine like the sun. For he remembered that this was his wife
and the vows that they took when they were young. They promised
each other that in "sickness and health", they would always love
one another. Thus proving to the world how much they cared.

In that moment when she kissed him there. Everyone could see
that they had spent many years caring, sharing, loving, and
living. It's something wonderful to see when a couple's love
has lasted a lifetime through.

Patricia A. Patterson

Past, Present, Future

We parted and decided to go our separate ways.
Not knowing if we would see each other again someday.
Our love was strong enough to bring us back together again.
Not only are we lovers but were also friends.
You asked for my hand in marriage.
We took the vow to be man and wife.
Knowing we both had a dream to share.
Showing how much we really care.
We loved before in our past life.
We love now in our present life.
And we will love together in our future life.

Patricia Smith

The Right Way

I did my own thing in the past.
Now on Jesus each care I cast.
My Saviour takes care of each plea.
That's why I must pray, shout, and sing.
To love Him is the best joy life could bring,
I dearly love Him and He always loves me,
A better relationship there could not be.

Jesus said I am the Way, Truth, and Life,
What other friend would have died for me,
So I may live eternally.
I'm so glad He's a part of my life,
He's there through each joy and hardship and strife.

To know Him and love Him is pure joy,
I learn more about Him in each Bible story.
Make Jesus your friend.
Allow Him those broken relationships to mend.
He'll always see you through to the end.
    Oh, how I love Jesus.

Virginia Rhodes

The Spinning of the Room

He has removed himself from me and now,
now, I want him back in.
I try to bury myself in the swell of a breath-
I inhale as he inhales and we exhale
    like one lung.
The streetlights coming in through the blinds
cast long angular shadows.
With closed eyes I feel the spinning of the room.
The high of love evaporating through the walls.

Unable to concentrate on the oneness
that I need so much that I hate-
so much
I look for myself in the smell of his skin
and the lines of light in his room.

I am not in this place.

The rhythm of our synchronized breathing has changed.
one and a half beats to one.
It is our separate lungs, different rhythms.
We roll away from each other to sleep.

Rebecca A. Johnson

Take A Look Closer

    What you see on the outside has
nothing to do with the in, take a look
closer, I could be your friend. Take
a step back and who knows what you'll
see us together, us part or us inseparable
from the start. Take a look closer, don't
be afraid you have nothing to fear
inside, take a look closer, I have nothing
to hide. Dreams can come true, hopes
come alive, take a look deeper, deeper
inside. Anger, sadness, coldness, and
darkness, all lurk inside. Pride,
joy, loving, and caring, all lurk inside
till it's time for sharing. Don't run
away, don't try to hide, there's
nothing for you to fear inside. What you never
knew before is coming alive, now that
you've taken a look closer inside

A. Danielle McCoy

The Pharisee, The Publican

Our Lord often warns us
  not to compare ourselves with others,
Accusing them to be
  not as holy as thee.

The Pharisee seeking God's help
  based on the fact,
He was better and not like
  the Publican in the back.

We know whose prayer was heard
  before God's Holy Throne,
The Publican in the back
  sorrow for the goodness he lacked.

Accept God's gift
  not looking to others,
To see what we lack.

Rejoice in your gifts
  of family and friends,
Thank God for your talents
  and use them for Him.

M. Rosemond

Quiet

She walks the streets
Not knowing what is coming to her.
She expects nothing.
She looks,
But she sees nothing.
In her mind
She is thinking,
Real thoughts
Of what os going to happen to her
But her senses tell her nothing
So that is what she believes.
Her senses are wrong.
She feels something...
Then she feels nothing
Slowly her eyes close and she sees nothing,
Hears nothing,
Tastes nothing,
Smells nothing,
She is... Quiet

Rebecca Johnson

"A Stormy Night"

We were crowded in the cabin;
Not a soul was there to speak. It
was midnight on the water and
storm was on the deep. 'Tis, a fearful
thing in winter to be shattered by
the blast; "as to hear the roaring
tempest; "as it clattered away the mast."
So we set there in silence,
each one busy at his pray. We're
lost, "the captain said" as he staggered
down the stairs. But his little
daughter whispered as she took his icy
hands. Isn't God upon the ocean as
he is upon the land. Then, we kissed
the little maiden. And we spoke with
better cheer. And, we anchored in the
harbor as the moon was shining clear.

Patrick A. Fisher

Divorce

Divorce was all we could do, it was something we both knew.
No one could feel my pain, what did I have to gain.
the only thing I could do was keep same, and
yet sometimes I wonder how I could survive,
I guess I should just thank God I'm alive.
I felt the lonely agony of despair, and with no one whom I could
share. No one understood, no one possibly could, and no one would.
Divorce makes your light turn into darkness, your darkness
into pitch black, because you know there's no turning
back. They say love is supposed to last, this had to
happen because of our past.
From the beginning we didn't have a chance, we chose to fight
instead of winning. Only I know what I feel, oh God I wish my
heart would heal. I want more than anything to go on and forget I
was ever your wife, If I don't you'll destroy my life. Sometimes
we find a way to go on, but getting over the hurt takes so long.

Please somehow find it in you to see it through. You know I never
really said goodbye, I ended up having to lie. They say going
through pain makes you grow, how long will it take before I know?

Sharon Jordan

Reality

Little girl's a big girl now
No more pretty pink and purple room
Black is now her color.
She may look and act different
But she's still the same person.

All she wanted was his attention, which she got,
He loved as much as she loved him,
Or so she thought.
When he left her for another
Her love turned to pure hate.

Now she longs for attention
Which she does not receive.
She thinks of black thoughts
Which she is not strong enough to fulfill.
All she wants to do is follow her hero.

Rachel M. Holm

Love Keeps Holding On

It's good to see a man and wife who've been in love for forty years.
No matter what, they never gave up,
they kept the faith through the hard years and tears.
Now the world keeps preaching, "love 'em and leave 'em,
a commitment is easy to break.
But, Love Keeps Holding On!
So when the world keeps telling you to run away remember,
Love Keeps Holding On.
When it feels like it's time to give up,
Love Keeps Holding On!
It's good to see a child that's not afraid to love their mom or dad
and they just don't buy that age old lie that heartache is all a
family can have.
Remember,
Love keeps holding on
through the hard times and tears.

Stephanie Story

Love Paradigm

Love is beautiful, lasting and strong
Love is scary, fragile, and sometimes wrong

Love conquers the hate within
Hate masks the love with sin

Love and pain is one in the same;
In the end...

Rose Orbeck

A Blast In Time

And when he was born she was all alone,
No baby shower, no flowers, no home.
But her dark eyes glowed with motherly pride,
And the unbearable fear she would hasten to hide.
So she set out with a serious passion and joy,
With fervent affection for this new baby boy.
Now the years sped by and on this child she did bestow,
Her life's every breath, her heart's very soul.
This mother of moderate means who knew heartache and woe,
She walked tall and with vigor as she watched her child grow.
But the streets soon were calling and the sky midnight black,
The night he went out and never came back.
And the young and wholesome fell victim to crime,
Guns rumbled, shots roared, a blast in time.
What a gift to this world I would give,
No more guns, these children should live.

Sara Czarnecki

My Wish, A Friend!

My wish, a friend! One I could talk with most everyday
My wish, a friend! One that would stop to see me when they may
My wish, a friend! One who liked me and the child within
My wish, a friend! One not family, friends I feel can't be Kin
My wish, a friend! One who cares if I live or died
My wish, a friend! One I knew to me had never lied
My wish, a friend! One that would stay around in either thick or thin
My wish, a friend! One who felt others approval unnecessary to win
My wish, a friend! One of any sex, race, shape or form
My wish, a friend! One who would hold my hand as our dreams were born
My wish, a friend! One who wishes only that we try
My wish, a friend! One who had the same wish as I

J. R. Battaglia

Untitled

As I lay against the ground
my troubled lips wear a frown
I'm not bothered by anything outside
but, visions from within
thought of her and I.
I remember the good.
I remember the bad.
I wonder If I did anything wrong.
I wonder if I made her mad.
I gave it my all, I gave all of me.
It simply wasn't enough,
that she made me see.
After she said goodbye, I was.... content.
Only I knew something was missing
I hadn't realized what, yet.
Troubled by the past, content with the present
a unique situation I find myself in
unique, I suspect, to my present condition.
You see, she was my future, she was my life.
Now all's gone, now life has left.

Ouige

In Whitings' Pastures

Every time I stroll through Whitings' pastures
My soul is filled with such tranquility,
Effusing me like misty April showers that
Rain upon the earth their panoply;
Arresting winter's sleep with verdant splendor —
Like this, my heart enraptured swells with mirth,
Delighting in the woodlands and the meadows
Graciously allowed me on God's earth.
Restfully I stroll through Whitings' pastures
Enjoying sights and sounds I cannot fair
Express in all their glory by mere letter,
Nor tell by word; in truth you must be there.

Sharon Davis

View Of Life

Dynamite picture! Dynamite deal!
My sons, my daughters and my friends!
If I strike it rich!
Then a safe and peaceful lair awaits,
Jam-packed with fascinating hardware
And crammed tight with seductive software
All made so clear,
By 50 easy lessons set to music
And then I will shout
"My arteries can clean themselves, if they chose!"
For I've always had them in my life,
And I never told them what to do
So why should I cause them trouble now?
And since I fail to see a world of difference,
For clean or dirty, they are mine
And with this obstructed sight,
I will view the west, From North to South.
And not necessarily, according to the poles.
For the camera of life it doesn't lie,
But only I to me and me to thee.

Stanley J. Siegel

When My Eyes Are Closed

Grandma's words of wisdom
My response ignorance
Love vs. Youth
Age vs. Impatience
Wishing somehow I could be free
Free from the strings, rules, restrictions
My life, my way
Now
I have age, have lost my youth
Have learned pain-heartache, disappointment
I now have freedom
Have experienced distrust, misuse and lies
But I have no love
Eyes closed; have opened
Wisdom of age
Foolishness of youth
How sad to see through closed eyes

Wanda Marie Thompson

Alcoholic Tears

Tears of vodka so simple and clear
My mind is full of confusion I don't remember shedding a tear
Tears of burden so sticky they burn
Being sober never again will I return
Tears of Tequila are dangerous and out to kill
They keep falling as if a bottle was to spill
Tears of schnapps are warm and sweet
But slower and slower everyday my heart beats
Tears of Jack Daniels into my cheeks they blend
Thinking he would be the perfect friend
Everyday I grab the bottle and everyday I cry
And with every sip I think and wonder why
I look at the broken bottles it reminds me of my heart
Day by day and sip by sip I slowly tore it apart
Now everyday when I wake I will be in fear
Knowing that I can only cry alcoholic tears.

Sheree Barbee

"Silver And Snow"

Every cloud has a silver lining, or so they say
Millions of raindrops, like tears, fall everyday
In winter, the rain becomes cold
Lying on a tree as snow, how pretty if it will hold
You're not silver, oh no, you're more beautiful than gold.

Seth Clark Sheckard

The Stormclouds Of Life

Grey as slate, the clouds loom o'er me.
My head beneath, cringed in anticipation.
Will it pass me by, or burst upon me?
Boom! The rain falls...

I sit there wondering if the storm will pass.
This I cannot answer. This I do not know.
Life is my opponent, raging relentlessly against me.
Silence! The rain stops...

The clouds have moved on from the skies of my life.
They do not let me forget them though.
A rainbow shimmers in the sky before me.
Sunshine! Life goes on.

Vi-Anne Van Dunk

The Holocaust

I am a survivor, where do I go?
My family and friends are now dust lying on the floor.
   Where do I go?
   I am a survivor, how do I sleep?
My dreams and memories awake me in a cold sweat, and
justify my most outrageous fears.
   How do I sleep?
   I am a survivor, how do I forget?
The death, the anguish, the pain.
   How do I forget?
   I am a survivor, how do I love?
The past has killed my heart, but I still have hope.
   How do I love?
I am a survivor, but who am I inside?
Am I a number, a color, a religion?
   Who am I?
   I am a survivor, but will I survive?

Stephanie Read

Getting Old

I wake up every morning
   My body stiff and sore.
And if anyone should ask me
   I'm a hundred years or more.

But I put my feet down on the floor
   And give my bode a shake
With a little love and help from above
   Another day I'll make.

You see, our body's like an old Model T
You gotta keep it in shape and prime.
Take care of all the dings and dents,
That we've gotten all down the line.

You've gotta respect it, so please don't neglect it.
   Be honest, sincere and kind.
What's more, my brother, love one another
   It'll pay off every time.

Whatever you do - do it with zest.
   And always have lots of fun
Then on down the way at the end of your day
   Some one will say "Well done."

Maxine Duenow

HIS Majesty

Oh, the glory of HIS presence, as in awe, before Him I stand.
Just to be inside the kingdom, with its grandness, under HIS command.
I'm amazed at all the splendor, glorious music, from an angel band.
Gladly will I lay my trophy at HIS feet, in heaven's fair land.
Because just to be born of HIS Spirit, makes me an heir to the
   kingdom of GOD!
Whether we are kings or lowly peasants we shall all someday bow
   before, "HIS Majesty."

Patricia Vernon Adams

Glass Houses

Peering through windows of pain,
Mourning a childhood slain,
He suffocates cries and is strong,
In the face of all that was wrong.

Eyes wander along halls of shame,
Shielding himself from the casting of blame;
Tears pause on his cheek, to remember the bleak
Time that was served until that tragic week.

Neighbors recall the ear-piercing sound
That most locals claim was heard all around;
Three black and whites arrived right away,
Ignoring the dispatch, as they knew the way.

His older brother, closest in age,
Silenced five of the six in a mad rage;
Downing himself last, with one final blow,
He fell through the bay glass and onto the snow.

Spared from the fate and not knowing why,
The youngest brother half wanted to die;
Now an old man, ancient in face and in bones,
A hardened hand frees the rock, for some don't throw stones.

C. Chauncey Hitchcock

Lenin's Cat

Lenin's cat had a quiet life,
mostly stayed around the house,
slept most of the day,
ate well — never missed a meal —
and purred as the great revolutionary stroked her.

Nothing like Lenin,
who couldn't stay put,
rarely slept (and snored at that), and sometimes even
forgot his meals.
Lenin's passion was revolution
and a dream of social equality.

Lenin's cat liked to sleep most of all,
liked to brush up against Krupskaia's ankle.
She liked it when Trotsky came to visit:
He always gave her a gentle stroking.
Stalin must be a dog person, she thought —
no good with cats.
Lenin's cat had simple, quiet tastes,
liked the good life — a petit bourgeois cat
if you ask me.

Sabrina P. Ramet

"Listen To The Count"

Gold of sun
moon of silver
so full
all hot, so bright
earliest of rays to the latest, faded gray
slivers growing round
cool reflection
scorched with heat
glisten with sweat
an orb of intense energy
touched with dew
caressed with mystique
a sphere of luminous tranquility
and so it is that I count my days and nights
forever in my life
sol, luna
together we are, together they are the notes of an unsung song
a concert to be felt
throughout my being, my being a medium for the notes
of our universe

C. J. Valenti

I'll Be A Good Boy

I see the silence in your eyes
Mommy, Mommy, why do you cry

I see the hurt in your face
Daddy, daddy, why must I leave this place

I see you packing all my toys
Mommy, mommy, I want to play with the other boys

I see you pacing by the phone
Daddy, daddy, I want to come home

What did I do, What did I say
That made my mommy take me away

I'll be a good boy, I'll be a good son
I'm frightened; I'm scared; What can be done

I'll BE a good boy
I'll BE a good boy
I'll BE A GOOD BOY
Robert McMahon

Peace

Dark storm clouds gather
Menacing winds bend the trees
Lighting without mercy shows its fury
The warning roar of the angry thunder
Shattering the peace of the world.

The sun struggles to push clouds asunder
Trying to gain a foothold in the sky.
Storm clouds determined to overshadow
The sun gives one last try.

Suddenly like a trumpet blast...
Dark clouds are scattered
The sun calls forth the rainbow
The contest is finished. Peace at last!!!
Virginia Joann Brady

"Images Of Mother Past"

When my eardrum bangs inside my head your strong arms cradle me press
  me against your lilac-scented body and feed me rotten-eggs
  medicine. Dumbo is my friend.
When the older kids won't play with me your strong silent strokes
  barely break the water as we float on Herring Creek with "Bob
  Whites" echoing in the trees.
  Killies jump high dive deep leave ever-widening circles.
You tell stories — an immigrant in a bazaar filling her basket with
  old favorites passing up vanilla selecting exotics. Shaking
  stirring. Creating new recipes.
Your purple parasol shades me; my eyes close my body snuggles closer.
  Your soft eggnog-dusted-with-nutmeg skin covers your stubborn
  Slovak spine.
I feel my spine is just like yours.
Rosemary Waikuny

Moonlight Magic

Moonlight shines upon the trees.
Many shadows there are to see.
One seems to be looking at me.
Is it a shadow, or what it really seems to be.
Do those eye connect with flesh
and bone, or is it just the
shadow of a stone.
Every night the moon will shine.
It will make shadow of yours and mine.
If you see a shadow.
That seems to have an erie pose.
Then you've seen a painting
and a comment the moon is stating
Sandy Woodbury

Here on Earth

A forest is natural in beauty, but to us it's
many different trees combined together
It's much like people here on earth,
Both support life, each different in there own way
Some are easy to find like squirrels or birds,
others you may never discover. People are much
the same, some you may never meet.
But I have been blessed by meeting someone that
has natural beauty, a special someone who is dear
to my heart, and if it wasn't for being here
on this earth may have never met.
Wayne Rinehart

Waterfalls

Waterfalls, all so peaceful and beautiful
making the sounds water does, falling against a smooth lake or river

Walk through the waterfalls, and wash away the pain that holds you
down today's pain is tomorrow's strength, whether you realize it or not

Sit beneath the waterfalls, the pain will fall in the water and it
will wash all of the evil away, leaving only the good memories in your mind.

Run through the water, while a school hand reaches out to touch your
own someone is there to help you through times, if only the waterfall

Let the water splash against you and relieve this hell that you're
living the waterfalls shall always flow, like the mind of a human, the
spirit of an animal, and the true heart, the heart of the earth

Maybe someday, we can be as the waterfall, and all flow together no
more killing, and no more fighting, just flow, all together, no
arguing, no more bickering, no more nothing, but peace, and beauty.
Sheri Zappier

Children

Children, children, all around
Making all those joyful sounds.

Listen to them while they play
Bringing sunshine to any day.

Sharing time and thoughts together
Without noticing about the weather.

We should watch as children play
And listen to the words they say.

Although their minds are young in thought,
They know the answers to end all wrought.

Take time to listen when children speak
They may have the answers when we are weak.
Patricia A. Mason

Lord, Make Me A Tool

Lord, make me a hoe in Your garden,
Make me a spreader when You scatter seed.
Let me be a hammer when You build a house,
Or a spoon when You stoop down to feed.

Make me a platform when You want to speak,
Or a broom when You sweep the floor.
Let me be a pen when You need to write,
And a knob when You open a door.

Lord, make me a tray when You want to be served,
And a brush when You'd like to paint.
Make me a violin when You want to sing,
Make me a can when the world says can't.

Lord, make 'em putty in Your hands,
Mold me into whomever You need.
Make me a tool in Your garden,
Make me Your Love in deed.
N. Elizabeth Holland

The Hands That Rocked My Cradle

Beautiful, the hands that rocked my cradle.
Lovely was the voice that sang to me.
Strong the faith that rendered grace at table.
High the wind, adrift I went to sea.

In the morning of my preadventure,
Wayward was the path that lead me on.
Hot the noonday sun of shame-faced venture.
Silently, repentant twilight dawned.

Black the night with guilt and apprehension;
Tormented by the sorrows that I'd known,
I bowed my head in humble reconpension,
And sought, again, the love I'd always own.

Give me back the hands that rocked my cradle,
Wrinkled, gnarled and old as they are now.
Return me to her as though I were a baby.
So her sheltered love can soothe my trouble brow.

Zina Runnels

Time Rhymes

A friend who has no time for a friend; has no time for
Love in his life.
A heart that has no time for love; has no life to live.
A friend who cares is worth more time than ten friends
who don't care.
Time never stops but love does.
Time is something you have to live with; when
your life is empty without love.
Time in your home doesn't matter if love doesn't
have the time to be home.
Time keeps passing minute by minute; even if
Love has last track of time.
Time is last in a house that is not a home;
Love has no time to wait for anyone.
Love dies if the heart had no time for it.
When you don't have good friends; the
more time you have for your heart
to hurt for all the time you have left on
your hands.

Wilma Gail Mayfield

In The Total Mist

Gone, gone is the total mist,
lost in the night, and dawn at day.
Inside your heart it is in total blist.

In the mist bad is forgotten;
but still there.
In the mist you are happy,
and blind to the bad things that will happen.

In the total mist your dreams come true;
but with out the mist they fade away.
In the mist you are bright and smart,
true, kind, and special.

In the mist you are free,
no consequences, or doubts;
Just you and your dreams.

Just you and you dreams here to stay,
in the total mist.

Wanda Doring

"S"

I glance away and she is there
Longingly I stare as she feels my gaze.
Oft before, and now, see I my vision:
Vision of beauty, a creature of fire.
Eagerly I search for signs of recognition
Yearning to see the "green" of her eyes.
Openly her face responds in deepening shades of love
Ushering forth a flame of desire ne'er I'd known.
Grateful, I return the glance, and more;
Reaching out, my desperate heart pauses,
Enthralled in a feeling ling imagined,
Emptying my thoughts but of one who
Natures all that I need and that I would be.
Every moment that I have you strains to lengthen,
Yet our absences only serve to lengthen my passion
Enabling my life force to feed this raptured soul
Singing loudly in my way 'I love you'.

William E. Litterer III

Mothering Dreams

I abandoned the hope chest....
Lonely and desperate too long.
Years with the cradle empty,
Gone was the lullaby song.

The tomorrow promised
Long ago fell away.
Reaching, losing my balance
In the ridiculous play,
I toppled over myself.
What a way to face reality!

So, I would teach each daughter about precious dreams.
Tomorrow, my pretty may not be yours as it seems.
It may be cloudy, a world empty gray.
It may be the babies you want are gone with the day,
That sweet little angels were rocked slow to sleep,
By mothers of the 50's who were allowed to keep,
    Mothering dreams.

Sandra L. Warren

My Beloved, Today We Become One

With this hand, I give you the key to my heart,
Locked together, we shall never part.

Come with me my love,
you are so precious, tender like a dove.

Walk with me forever, even in eternity,
Your lips sweet as honeysuckle to a hummingbird.

Your eyes sparkle with the rays of the sun,
Our lives will be blessed with laughter and fun.

I will be your rainbow after the rain,
Will soothe the brow where there is pain.

You are the flower in my garden that blooms each day,
Your petals I cherish, with me forever we'll stay.

With this ring I thee wed,
With this kiss I will seal all that I have said.

I promise to love, cherish and obey,
May God Bless us this Wedding Day.

Phyllis Datta-Gupta

The Spider's Home

A gust of wind starts the swing rocking back and forth.
Listening to the creaks and moans
As the swing rocks back and forth.
Slowly the creaks and moans of the swing rocking back and forth.
Diminish so you can hear the honks and clatter of trucks passing by
The faint creaks and moans of the swing rocking back and forth soon
   come to a halt.
The sound from the street, the honks and clatter, continue after the
   wind has died.
The breeze has stopped moving the swing back and forth and the creaks
   and moans have ceased.
But the relentless honks and shouts from the streets are still hanging
   in the air.
If a gust of wind should stir the swing back and forth again,
The only one to enjoy the creaks and moans would be the spider
   who had made her home in the corner of the swing,
To get away from the commotion and sounds of the street.

Rebecca Faith

Untitled

Smiling eyes, melting me;
Like thin air, hard to breathe;
Smoke filled room, echoing spotlights,
In my head.

That fills my soul with the burning,
will melt the black of my heart,
like a candle to the flame.

Breaking down my defense,
Sending me to darklands,
Ending my solitude,
Bringing death to my infinite sadness.

Watching me through the windows of your soul,
I am contained,
In the sweetness of your envy.

Shannon Hartnett-Fasold

"Our Love"

Our love is special and bright,
Like the star that shines
Brightly, on a dark starry night.

Our love is special and bright,
As the moon that shines,
On a clear dark night.

Our love must be special and bright,
Like the star and the moon,
If other's can see our love for each other shine.

I see the love shine brightly through,
Every time I look into the eyes
Of the man I love. I pray that
He see's my love shine just as brightly
For him, when he looks into my eyes.

Our love is special and bright,
Like the bright star and moon,
That shines on a clear dark night.

For I believe, our love was meant to be,
Created by the power's that
Made the bright star and shiny moon.

Roxanne M. Linville

Truth Is Love

Inside I built a wall,
like cold stone stacked deep and tall.
To keep your love from invading my heart.

Now I hear the sounds,
as your love hammers and pounds.
Chipping away this fortress around my heart.

My selfish mistakes,
hiding feelings, feint and fake.
Nothing could stop your will to win my heart.

Now I just see grains of sand,
where once this wall did stand.
Ground down to truth by your loving heart.

Sam Black

She Walks Like The Sun

She walks among the others
Like a drifting sun
Shining her happiness over the earth
Hiding the hurt from everyone.

The moon, it rarely passes her
Sometimes keeping her light within
But the shadow soon is broken
And she is shining once again.

Like the sun, she helps things grow
And brings warmth to other's hearts
She keeps her light shining bright
Until she must depart.

Sometimes a cloud will block her rays
Or try to soak up her tears
But soon they can handle the burden no more
And let go of all her fears.

With her light she guides us each day
But many have yet to see
What she truly does for us
What a blessing she is to me.

Patricia M. Tuttle

Watching Death

Grandpa always told me
life was a cliche of mountains and valleys
and I watched his life on the TV next to his bed
yep, ups and downs
ups and downs
ups and downs
beeps and then a straight line
that must be serenity
I'd have asked him
but he was sleeping so peacefully.

Paul J. Accavitti

Memories

In a lake, stream, or river not too far away,
   lies this fish that I shall catch one day.

Whether this fish be a walleye, salmon, or trout,
   I know it shall taste the best without a doubt.

The fish will fight and fight its all,
   but in the end, the photographs shall be hung on the wall.

The memories of the fish will grow strong and tall,
   for the photographs will show the fish, fighting its all.

The stories shall be told from generation to generation,
   and they will be told without any hesitation.

When the last days of the fishing story are told,
   I hope many a fisherman catch the fishing cold.

Steven M. Hooks

268

Mother Nature

Mother nature take me into your arms
Let me see the world through your eyes
Let me feel the pain my breed has brought to you
Let me see the world you hoped we would be
Let me know how much more you're going to take
Let me know who will go with you
Are we all doomed when you have had enough?
Will you let some survive and make us do it right this time?
Oh, Mother Earth take me into your arms once again

Susan O'Neil

The Gift Of Freedom

Let freedom ring from hill to shore.
Let freedom knock upon my door.
Let freedom brave the opposing fires.
Let freedom fan our fond desires.
Let freedom fight the fists of fear.
Let freedom hold our families dear.
Let freedom spawn our children's hope.
Let freedom broaden our vision, our scope.
Let freedom tickle the imagination.
Let freedom stifle intimidation.
Let freedom give the spirit a lift
  Because freedom is
    the ultimate gift!

Stephanie Donatoni

The Poem of My Life

Where are you going, young high school grad,
Leaving home of Mom and Dad,
Going along with sprightly step,
With all kinds of vim and pep,
I am going into the world, said he,
To take my place, whate'er it be.
It may be high, it may be low,
But as yet I do not know.
Well, my body, I at length, replied,
If wishes were horses, beggars would ride,
Trust not in wishes but keep in view
A goal that will do credit to you,
Keep your eyes on the stars but your feet on the ground,
And take that advice that is truthful and sound,
"In all your ways acknowledge Him
and He will direct your paths."

Roger K. Dunkerton Sr.

Crimson Tears

Overcast and pale more thoughts crowd my mind
Learning to embrace the hate of mankind.

And the silence bears witness to the rage in this soul.
As my life falls to pieces scattered on the floor
And my confusion rests in this bottomless hole
And a million lies lay howling at the door

These eyes so intoxicated and unseeing to the blind.
Allow the nonpartisan to show me their find.

I'll wait within the darkness.
Shivering in the storm.
I'll give into all weakness.
The nameless and without form.

When all that has been is cried away.
And when all that has been died today.

These angers still remain.
As do these crimson tears that stain the clear blue rain.

Preston McCauley

Dad, Always Her Hero

October 25 - David L. Hough went to Heaven. This is in his memory.
Tiny toddler reaching out her arms
Laughter echoes as Dad swings her around
First grade she has a million dreams
She understands that Dad is so proud
Winds blow, lightning flashes, she hears the storm
Her door opens, Dad is there to calm her fears
She walks the aisle listening to Just As I Am
Jesus is calling, Dad watches and wipes his tears
Years go by cheerleading, dating. Her wedding day
Through it all Dad is her strength, her guidance, her Hero

Helpless man reaching out his arms
Sadness fills the air as daughter turns around
First it's a small tumor and shattered dreams
He can't understand, the daughter's heart pounds
Pain surrounds them and he feels the storm
Doors close, daughter prays to calm his fears
Soon he will go to Heaven listening to Just As I Am
Jesus is calling, Daughter watches and wipes her tears
Will the years go by or just unforgettable days
Daughter will be his strength, his guidance, Dad always her hero.

Tana D. Gotcher

Soft Storm

Blizzards came from nowhere
just the wind starts blowing
and trees twist and bend.
Snow falls as hail and hits the ground
the sky turns dark and colder than ever.
Watching the clouds roll and sky turn
the hail turns soft and light.
As the wind whips, the sky lightens.
Then slowly, the snow falls like feathers
and lays upon the ground
white and beautiful like crystal.

Pamela Hatalak

Untitled

When your stomach gets low there's
Just one place to go Burger King
Home of the whopper that great big juicy
Hunger stopper

Vernon Wallin

Motivation

Go write a poem or an essay,
Just don't sit there or lay.
Start doing this today,
Don't let anything get in your way,
Listen to everything I have to say,
Be on your merry way
Let's go, don't stop and play.
Everyone will know your brain isn't decay.
These things will make you happy and gay
If you make this a better day.

Just start opening your pad.
You will find this is not bad
Don't let anything make you mad
Cheer up don't be sad
Go on make everyone glad
When you get finish show it to mom and dad!
Go on, go on stretch that mind
Show people that you are one of a kind
This will make you shine
When people read your line!

Susan Braxton

Untitled

These tired eyes of mine are many miles away.
I've worked myself into confusion, run astray.
My love hasn't been allowed to see its day.
I'm hoping for the chance to end my confusion -
with each word I say.
And I hope for someone to take my heart -
and live with it, with no delay.
For I'm being restrained by circumstances -
beyond my control.
This emptiness has blcd from my heart
and filled my soul.
Sometimes I find it hard to live like this -
for another lonely day.
But, I know I should hold on -
for my confusion may end,
and my love may find her way.

Paul Ladd

My Dear Husband

Day after day, night after night,
I've wondered what I could do,
To describe the love and warmth in my heart.
Each time I look at you.

If I had all the gems in the world at my hands,
And gold and silver too.
There isn't enough in all the lands
To come close to my love for you.

For ten years I have been with you.
Yet, all I have to say,
Are things that you hear often,
For I say them every day.

I love you my dear husband
and as I follow you through life
I thank you so completely,
For making me your wife.

Rebecca Russell

True To My Heart

Like a ship that sails alone on a stormy night at sea,
I've somehow lost my sight of what I want my life to be.

I thought I knew exactly what I needed all along,
So I roamed around the world, acting tough and acting strong.

Never did I realize, that what I was searching for,
was locked away deep inside, behind my closed door.

I'd always felt the tugging and tearing from within,
But I never understood the sign that told me to begin.

I thought the pain I felt would somehow ease with time,
Instead it spread throughout my body clouding up my mind.

It tore apart my heart and soul 'til nothing could be done.
Until I changed my way of thinking, as I looked toward the sun,

It showed me what I had to do to make a brand new start
I have to live my life today and always be true to my heart.

Shelley Metters

Untitled

Though it seems bleak when one feels so weak,
It's the weakness within that reeks havoc- makes one begin.
The strength of one's soul begins with breakdown,
From there one's life shall turn around.
Whether good or bad it doesn't matter,
Just so that the soul is happy not sadder.

Trent R. Patterson

AIDS

Acquired Immune Deficiency Syndrome,

I should have used a condom.
It's the killer that medicine won't cure.
I'll die...now I know that for sure.
I could have been black, I could have been
white. This disease doesn't know the
difference, all it does is take away all
life's light.

Sex is no game.
When you play around with it, you are the
one being lame.
Turn around now, before it is too late.
Use protection or use my way, abstinence,
that's the sure way. Then you'll know you
and your body will be okay.

Believe in yourself! You can wait!

Shannon Elder

"My Perfume"

I spray it and I see the whole summer again
It's right before my eyes as if it never did end
I relive all my happiness, all my hurt, all my pain
My memories come back in an everlasting chain
Everyday I would spray on my perfume, with that fresh smell of fruits
Slip on a shirt and my combat boots
This was the summer when I found out who I was
A person of hatred yet of love
I put so many people in a pit of pain
Yearning for love though it could never be the same
Everything comes back with just that one little spray
Because I would wear it day after day
And I will always remember this summer as the best of all
For there were so many new things I did and saw
It was a summer of fun, sad times and self pride
A summer of new friends, new adventures, and, of course, my
Lakeside.

Stephannie Carabeo

A Mocking Fledgling

A baby Mockingbird was practicing to fly.
Its efforts were rather spry.
It happily was spreading its wings,
Half running, half jumping against the wind.
Its endeavors were sheer delight,
As it tested its freedom in short, steady flights.

Oh, what wonders lay still ahead
For this tiny Mockingbird.
There will be the seasons with all their grandeur;
There will be a variety of food in springtime splendor.
It will train its little voice according to Mockingbird tradition;
And mimic other birds calls in perfect rendition.

Wherever you are carried by your strong wings,
My happy, little fledgling,
May you always find joy and something to sing
In nature's magnificent panoramic scenes.
Your mere presence makes my heart rejoice,
And gives me a pleasure nobody else can appraise.

Toni Urba

Untitled

The sun rises as do I.
It's alive with glowing brilliance, as am I.
Its wholeness is captivating, as I look.
Its warmth is sometimes overbearing, as I can become.
Its beauty is the core, as I realize.
Its home is its universe, as is mine.
It's true nature cannot be destroyed, as I stand in admiration.
Its immense responsibility goes unnoticed, as I notice.
It will someday sleep, as shall I.

Renee Dondero

Depression

It was a giant hand.
It wore a white glove to stand out in the darkness.
It wasn't there to pat me on the head.
It didn't come to shove me out of my timidness.
It came to scare me,
To interrupt my sleep.
During the lighted hours it couldn't be seen,
But the memory haunts me,
And the pain it is causing slowly kills me.
If only I could step on it
Or scream at it.
But I can't.
I can not reach it.
It wasn't there to comfort,
It didn't come to help,
It came to slowly crush me,
Like a cursed hand from hell.

Stacie Lynn Wofford

Our First Anniversary

My mind goes back to that special day
　It was just one year ago
We stood together, vowed our love forever
　God surely willed it so

For in this world of millions, it's such a miracle
　That we would find each other
But we know God can and He had a plan
　For we belong together

We start each day with a smile and a kiss
　With more of the same with it ends
Everything is right, our future bright
　My sweetheart, my lover, my friend

We've worked hard and loved much this first year
　But we wouldn't have it any other way
Always on the run - but lots of laughter and fun
　When we find those "Toll gates" to pay

So, happy anniversary to you, my sweetheart
　This is one - there'll be many more
I'm proud to be your wife - you're the love of my life
　How could I ask for more!

Wanda Williamson Kidd

I'm A Poet

Reading my poems is warm,
It takes time to say them.
I'm a poet,
I write what I say in a special way.
I'm a poet, I can quote it.
I write what I read with a special speed.
Reading my poems is warm,
They are fun and won't do no harm.
I'm poet!

Queen McAdoo

Burned

I stayed close to her that evening.
It was a cool summer night.
She sat by a fire,
and she said nothing.

I watched her and saw
the flames dancing in her eyes.
I realized it was not the fire
that kept her warm, but thoughts of you.

She sat and still, said nothing;
there was only that calm and
content look she chose to wear.
The glow wavered silently, chasing shadows.

My glance was still upon her.
She wrapped her arms about her,
she longed for yours, still, she kept
a quiet smile while the sparks crackled their song.

As the fire maintained her vigil,
warmth and wishes cast out loneliness.
I felt flame-kissed, and it made me wonder,
what is it that burns in your heart?

Regan R. Sutton

Just Smile

Give a smile today.
It takes nothing but a few muscles.

A smile can't hurt anyone,
But can turn an enemy to a friend;
Bringing a war to its end.

Thirst can be quenched,
Hunger will vanish,
The sick will get well,
The tired and weary will gain strength,
The sad will find happiness,
The dying will die and rest in peace;
When you give a smile.

A smile is the sign of love.
Give a smile today,
And make someone's day bright and beautiful.
Just smile!!

Saidu Kabba

A Good Son

What does it mean to be a good son?
　It takes effort and work which is never done.
It means love and concern and support for each other
　And learning to talk with your Father and Mother.
It means more than that though, it means being a Friend
　And since we don't always agree, it means one has to bend.
Of course, most important, it means serving God together
　And toughing it out through all sorts of weather.
Because, of course, on every issue we don't always agree
　But, so far, so good, till now we've been happy.
I love you Mom and Dad, it's a love that runs deep
　And I've tried as God tells us, your commandments to keep.
We sure aren't perfect, at least not until the end of the 1,000 years
　And we've shown that too, struggling through heartache and tears.
But through all the pain, the tears and the strife,
　I hope I've been a good son, and look forward to sharing with you
　in the "prize of life".

Patrick W. DeBono

Aria In An Empty Room

I am addicted to your brand of love;
It swims in and out of me like an eel.
I crave the fluctuations of your voice;
The musical murderous tones.
    And those eyes-scorching through an alien world,
      Fixed for just a moment.
Pure electricity flows through you,
It makes me tremble.
    Do you manufacture ecstasy and pain?
    I look for you under caves; brave rivers currents,
Reach mountaintops like a junkie.
    We held hands once; in a place sacred and forbidden,
Sort of a garden where snakes stalk and lure.
Just a glance; brings me to a stand still -
Enough for me to plunge,
    deep, deeper,
      deepest,
Into your eyes' labyrinth.
Join me,
The apples is red like lips.

Viviane Klein

The Thief

Time is but a thief.
It makes our life seem oh so brief.
Long days, short nights, we start so young
Then we think, where has time gone.
They come and go with their own,
Now I feel so all alone.

More time to think of what is past,
Now I know, it all can't last.
They come and go, yet they can't see.
How much they really mean to me.

Day after day it comes and goes
Someday they'll see what I now know.

Sandra Renshaw

Troubled Water

I look at the water so calm so peaceful,
It lies there so still untouched so beautiful.
Yet, ignorance will come throw a stone and shatter the peace.
What provokes ignorance to make gentleness cease?
Ripples in water the perfection is broken,
Wishes and dreams from the heart have been stolen.
The upset water finally settles down,
But now sorrow from tears may drown.
She must release her tears and so it rains.
The water is again stirred, like-so the pain.
Settling down once more the waves come to an end,
But stupidity is on the way to upset it once again.
Walking too close to the edge, he trips up and falls in.
And sure enough the waves swaying once again begin.
Stupidity isn't acquainted with wisdom or thought.
Wisdom comes with time and it cannot be taught.
Ignorance, sorrow, stupidity, like the water makes our
lives erupt.
We must learn to cope with these attacks of hardship, or
our lives will be corrupt.

Sarah Viviano

Less Spirit

One, two, three, a raindrop falls on a cement pathway.
It leaves a shattering sound as it collides with its host.
But, its mission is to camouflage the pathway from an undetecting eye.
Who would suspect the tiny wonder with such a stable structure
that glowed and danced with the harsh wind,
and savored the cold temperature.
Its crystal image once flowed from a roaming rain,
but, the transformation left it hard and brittle.

Four, five, six, the crystal multiplies to create a snowball,
which travels to and from its host.
Their colliding has become a faint memory,
since the crystal image now covers the cement.
And, now it is as cold as the ice
and as brittle as the crystal image that surrounds it.
The harsh wind and the cold temperature
will give way to the dance of the snowflakes,
or the cement pathway will crumble.
LIke the snow covering the path,
stress covers the human spirit, and we crumble.

Seven, eight, nine, ten

Pat Campbell

Embroidered In The Sand

The faint soft scent of salt water sea,
It is a beauty only I see.
I gazed longingly at the golden shore,
While the sea gulls cried over the ocean's roar.
Sea gulls overhead, they cry,
Through the golden sky, they fly.
The lasting summer hours
Stretched out on the sand,
And the gentle lapping ocean
Tumbling to the land.
Before I left, I took a stroll
Straight on down the beach,
With every little step I took
With every small step each.
I turned myself around
To look upon the land,
And smiled at all the footprints
Embroidered in the sand.

Rochelle Ernst

Lilies Of The Valley

The lily of the valley is white,
It is a beauty in the night.

Its blossoms are shaped as a bell,
They lean down as if they have fell.

After the rains have gone and past,
It seems its fragrance will always last.

They blossom in the spring,
And when the wind blows, it seems as if they sing.

They hang down in a long cluster along a slender stem,
Even more precious than a beautiful gem.

Tara Hall

272

Best Friends Forever

You're like no one I know,
It hurt so much to see you go.

You changed my outlook on life,
So your leaving cuts like a knife.

You changed my life in a great way,
Now I think of you everyday.

You have such a way to make me smile,
Maybe it's just your odd sense of style.

We helped each other manage to cope,
You gave me faith and I gave you hope.

It's like we've been friends forever,
The way it feels is odd almost clever.

I know your leaving was for the best,
Now that you're happy I can rest.

You're such a good friend in so many ways,
So I want you to know I'll love you always.

Shannon McEachern

Spell Checker

I have a spelling checker
It came with my PC
It plainly marks for my revue
Mistakes I cannot see.
I've ran this poem threw it
I'm sure your please too no
It's letter perfect in its weigh
Because my spell checker tolled me so.

I think my spell checker does a grate job,
In checking all my mistakes.
But every now and then,
Things don't make any cents.
Surely my spell checker is now fake.

It will make sure everything is write.
It'll certainly be quite a site.
I cannot argue with my PC
Weather I think it's wrong to write
I can always cell it
I think I just might!

Renuka Pant

Bluebird Blue

In the late afternoon when the sky is gray,
it flew from the sunset and together we ended the day.
It was a bluebird with feathers soft and plain,
but its song was sweeter than the pitter-patter of rain.
I brought it seeds and bread to end its hunger.
It brought a beautiful melody to end my frustration and anger,
We had a bond that could not be understood or known,
We needed each other we could not survive on our own.
Then one day just as it came, it flew out of my life,
and the hurt remained until someone came and ended my strife.
A wonderful man with eyes as blue as my bird.
He shared his hopes and dreams with such sweet words.
He was so dear to me - I'd never felt so loved in my life,
and one later afternoon he asked me to be his wife.
We watched many sunsets and shared many things.
If I wanted I could've flown - he would've given me the wings.
Then one late night he walked alone down the street.
Where he was left dead, robbed, battered, and beat.
I swear from the sunset his kind voice I heard,
but as I looked all I could see was a shattered dead bluebird.

Staci Griffith

Forbidden Fruit

Succulent, mouthwatering,
It beacons me to take a bite.

Resist and then...surrender.
Promise clouding all sense of what's right;

Delicious, sweet nectar
Left my mouth wanting so much more.

Then tasted the poison
Stealthily inside the fruit to the core.

Just one bite permitted
As fruit returns to its perfection.

Undefined, illusive;
Filling each person's unique predilection.

Single bite was all it took
To lay body and soul to waste.

As I sit dying and damned...
Still feel it was worth the taste...

Thomas S. Tyler

Just A Sound?

To the baby in the womb love is just a sound,
It can't hear or understand so it's just a sound.

To an infant love is felt but still just a sound,
It has no meaning or value just a sound.

To a child love is for grown ups,
They'd rather have fun with they're pups.

To a teenager love is friends, music, and a lover,
Friendly embraces, kisses, hugs, love means no need to cover.

To an adult love is marriage,
But only some are good enough to push a carriage.

To elderly people love is family and a friend,
They remember broken promises and friendship to mend.

To a dead person love is an unheard sound
But to the friends and family love is everything
   Not just a sound.

Shanna E. Olson

Old Home Town

The old barn is still standing, the house
is torn down,
   Where I grew up in my old home town.
Grade school is gone, High School burned
There's nothing but memories, my old heart
   churned.
I was kissed by my sweet heart in the halls
   of the school,
But I still learned my lessons and the
   Golden Rule.
Once upon a time there was action galore,
But now it's so quiet, there is no more.
Schools, Church and friends are memories
in my mind.
Life changes and we'd want it that way.
If we didn't "go with the flow", we'd be
   left behind.

Ruth Perkins McConkey Phillips

273

A Child's Eyes

To view the world as a child does, especially at this time of year,
Is to think of what Santa looks like, and to envision eight tiny reindeer.

To sit upon Santa's lap and tell him of your dreams.
To wish for bikes and teddy bears, and a mountain of chocolate ice cream.

Seeing the Santa in front of a store, with a bucket and ringing a bell.
Then stretching up to drop in a dime, him then thanking and wishing
   you well.

To go to the church service, late on Christmas Eve.
To listen to the beautiful carols, not really wanting to leave.

Returning home and then trying "real" hard to quickly fall asleep.
Then running to the kitchen, almost forgetting to leave something for
   Santa to eat.

Then after a while the lids get heavy, then finally beginning to doze.
Awakening with a start thinking, "I hope he doesn't bring me clothes."

At long last now nearing a peaceful sleep, as the night slowly turns to morn.
The time has arrived, and prayers answered, a Savior has been born.

The sun leaks through the partially closed shade, and in the eyes is bright.
Wiping the darkness from sleepy eyes to see the blinking tree lights.

Reading all the tags on packages, trying to find your name.
Listening to rattles coming from inside, "is it underwear or a video game?".

To see a child's eyes aglow, with rosy cheeks and cute little dimples.
As adults we need to see life as they do, and to keep it pure and simple.

Paul Kubaszak

On Marriage

Marriage, states Webster (and I doubt that he lied)
Is the union of man and woman as husband and wife.
He goes on to say that broadly applied
It's the process of building a married life.

What he fails to explain as no definition can
Is just what it takes to develop this plan.
There is no secret formula, no magic wand
No absolute course to guarantee the bond
That will carry you through a lifetime together
Filled with more sunny days than with stormy weather.

Oh there are many guidelines, they are simple at best.
Tho' when put into practice will stand up to the test
Of slaying the dragons that try to prevent you
From building the marriage that both of you meant to.

It requires saying "I love you" as oft as you can.
It requires lots of hard work, dedication - and
It requires being patient, being loyal and true.
It requires a commitment from both of you
To make this union as husband and wife
The most important priority in your life.

Pamela M. Gingrich

The Gift Of Christmas Love

The 24th of December,
is the time of year,
for you to sing out and ring out a sound
of good cheer, let all the little children
be happy and gay, for soon Christmas will be here,
"Yes", it will be Christmas day.
For Mommy and Daddy,
God will give the great gift of love,
that He has provided for His children from above.
And for every little girl, and boy,
He will give a great big toy!
So, if on Christmas eve,
you should hear a strange sound,
(Think nothing of it)
for it's Santa messing around.

Ronnie E. Davis

"That One Special Person"

All I can think about
Is that one special person
This person is sweet as candy
But yet he is very sincere
This person will do anything and everything
for me
This person is as kind as a new born puppy
As we walk the beach he speaks of love in
many ways
But only on bright sunny days
Is this love
Or is it fake
I'll find out soon
'Cause if I wake up one day thinking that I
want to spend the rest of my life with this
person
Then I'm in love.

Rosie Galvan

"Darkness"

It is so cold, so black and I cannot see
Is someone with me?
I'll just continue
Oh! A patch of light
Should I hurry towards it?
No, I can trust it
Slow and steady sure footed I go
So when I get there I will know, all about me
Oh! I wasn't the only one in the dark
There's others ahead and more behind
We think we are unique until we emerge from the darkness
We find many have traveled the road to new life
All scary, depressed, unsure, sad, lonely,
Fulled with bitterness or guilt
Cast off the cloak of the past
Live only in the here and now
The future will come in time
Now in this new warm light
I will nurture me and grow strong and enjoy the
Precious gift of life lived to the fullest

Trudy Detwiler

"Early Morn"

Sunlight shining on the lake
Is like fireflies ready for you to take
Into your hands to hold
Like little pieces of gold!

The birds singing in the trees
Inspires one to bend at the knees
To meditate of many things
As the birds fly away on beautiful wings!

The grass is so green
The trees are so tall
Makes one stop to think
The wonder of it all!

Peggy Kaboos

Untitled

Come, take me—plant me in your garden—
In the softness of your landscape. In a
private corner, away from all the rest—
the everyday blossoms. Come talk to me
when no one else will listen. Come
whisper to me and watch me grow..
and yes...Don't forget...
Water me once a week.

Rama

Forest Fire!! On the Mountain

Wildfire! Devastating all before you,
In the white hot heat of your flame.
Perhaps a careless campers spark,
Or a lightning shaft that came
To send you glowing in the dark,
A wanton killer without shame.

You send all scurrying in your wake.
A bright red avalanche of death
Humans flee, and the creatures of the wood-
Scamper to escape your dragon's breath.
We see, in the sadness of the day,
Our precious trees cannot run away.

J. W. Gogerty

My Friend And I

One night I had a dream, I thought would never end.
In that dream, I dreamed I made a brand new friend.
My friend would never lie to me, like many others had.
My friend and I were very close, we knew each other's thoughts;
We never had to say a word, we spoke from within our hearts.
There were no acts of jealousy, anger, rage, or tears;
I knew deep down inside my soul we'd be bonded for many years.
Somewhere in the back of my mind I knew that it would end,
Because this dream is not real life, it's only in my head.
Farewell to thee, I love you friend; for now we part... till
   I sleep again.

Tiffany Moore

The Stream-lined Country Road

The blue-grey sky sweeps down
   in one artistic uplifting stroke
   on the panoramic landscape.
The horizon encircles
   the lone traveler on the road.
The small brush and shrubs hug the ground
   as if cemented to the parched earth.
The stream-lined country road
   has numbed the voyager.
Suddenly the road lifts upwards
   and the traveler finds the self
   heading straight into the voluminous clouds.
From there the road ascends
   into heavenly realms.
Raindrops on the traveler's arm
   slowly reawaken the voyager to a reality
   of this earth below and those loved.
The traveler reminds the self
   that it is not yet time,
   and gently releases the accelerator.

Valerie J. Wiley McGuire

Life And Death

   Life is all around us; shining in the spring; searching for a way
in. It emerges on the surface of the best of us, bringing smiles and
joy. It lives within the flowers and brings on love, while children
play in the fields of summer sun. Laughs and rosy cheeks are the
cause of it, and the bright newborn babies of young get loved. It
begins deep inside the earth breaking through green-soaked grass, and
forever staining young and old. The lovers prosper in a world which
takes on life.

   Death is all around us; lurking in the shadows; searching for a way
out. It hides deep within the best of us, causing hatred and repent.
It resides within the earth and brings on hatred, while darkness looms
in the soot of blackened night. Sneers and twisted lies are the cause
of it, but the torturing winter days of old get blamed. It begins in
the depths of the earth seeping through blood-stained weeds, and
forever staining old and withered. The mourners thrive to live in a
world which takes on blackness.

Tara Schickli

A SKUNK'S INSURANCE POLICY

A skunk is striped just right
in colors black and white,
an animal most curious
and showing signs of really being friendly.

But Hey! Look Out!
Whenever skunks are turned about
and pointed right towards you
but all reversed with backside now rear-end-ed-ly!

Terry Roberts

Outdoors

I love the outdoors, not houses with floors.
In a tent on the ground, I can sleep very sound.
To the sound of the seas, and a soft summer breeze,
To the sound of a river, I could listen forever.
The land, sky and seas; plants, bushes and trees.
Flowers, bird and bees, I love all of these.
Come, camp with me, please.

Rita Schurade

Once Upon A Time

On a mountain of pain
in a desert of joy
lives a river of lust
and a pretty little boy.

Inside his world, he resides as king.
Ruling over every, dead and living thing.
And the animals never fight, no there are no tears.
Everything is happy, living with no fears.
As he walks around, he looks upon the land.
He looks at everything around him, and then at the lines upon his hand.

Everything is so big,
and he is only so small.
But he walks upon the land,
like he's the greatest ruler of all.

Memories are the whispers from the stories of the trees.

Tod K. Miner

Missing You

There's something magical, even wondrous
In a common phrase used - WE.
It's a mixture, it's a compound,
Part of you, and part of me.

With me on the east coast, and you on the west;
We share from great distance, and visits are rare.
My love is untimely, even forbidden by some.
If truth of happiness be known, my soul I'll bare.

Many miles have come between us,
Our lives must be lived apart;
But my memories of us together
Help keep warm my heart.

To admit I'm lonely without you
Only confirms treasured moments shared;
And even with the passing years,
Shows just how much I've always cared.

The loneliness that inevitably comes
With the memory of your touch
Fuels these feelings from deep within-
I miss you so very much!

Patrice

The Bridge

The night is dark and rainy.
I'm standing on a bridge
A bridge without end, at least
none to be seen.
This bridge lies between heaven and hell.
Where I stand I know not, but where I stand,
I'm neither dead or alive - just in a state of being.
The bridge is made of no material known to me,
but I only know that it holds me
Like a mother holding a child,
Or is it like man holding his fate,
Shaky with darkness, but with the light
it becomes calm and tranquil.
Where does this bridge go?
It goes only where we go, though by the time
we reach the end, on either side,
We'll realize not where we are,
But who we were.

A. DelRosso

Mansion Of Silver And Gold

One day when I get to Heaven, what a glorious day that will be
I'll look over the beautiful rainbow, this is what I'll see.

A beautiful mansion of silver and gold, with steps leading up so High
I'll climb that golden staircase that leads right to the sky.

At the top of that golden staircase, will be a golden door
I'll open that door marked "Heaven, where I'll live for evermore.

I'll come face to face with Jesus, I'll kneel before his feet
He says to me, "Welcome home, my child I've saved a special seat"

I'll work for our Precious Master, up there beyond the blue
I'll look down on all my friends, they'll be working for Him, too.

So when you get to Heaven, the sun will be shining bright
If you look into the clouds around, Jesus is the light.

Star D. Lambert

Candy Cane

You be the red.
I'll be the white.
We'll stay together throughout the night.
You be the candy,
I'll be the cane.
I need your sweetness to stay sane.
If you need help or feel the pain,
just reach out—just use that cane.

Who put the bend on top of the stick?
Who twisted the colors that we now lick?
Was this candy a madman's mistake,
or is this miracle our life's fate?

I'll accept the miracle.
I'll savor the sweetness.
I'll cherish the colors that paint our completeness.

Ted Michael

Without Thought

Waking up to the peaceful sounds of birds singing,
I stretch and yawn, hoping that today is Friday.
Finding the bitter coldness of a winter morning,
I quickly slip back into my warm and comfortable covers.
I close my eyes only to catch a glimpse of my ending dream,
then I find myself stuck in between my conscience.
Staying in my warm bed, acting like an adolescent made me jump out immediately,
Or maybe,
I should have stayed in that heated bed
without ever coming out.

Yih-Fian Chang

Darlene

There's a girl in my life, of course she's my wife,
If you're in love, you know what I mean
She's the greatest by far
She's my bright shining star
If you're wondering, her name is Darlene.

She's a wonderful person, my lover, my friend,
And I know for sure, this marriage won't end,
We've laughed and we've cried
And she's there by my side
For the good times and all in between
She is precious to me
So I'm sure you can see,
Why I love my darling Darlene.

Sandy Capley

It's A Great Life If You Don't Weaken

Here is a Philosophy to carry through life,
If you follow it strongly, you'll surely survive.
The steps of life may have many stairs,
Making life seem so very hard to bare.
If you compare life to the strength of a rope,
The concept of weakening must go only up slope.
For none of us ever want to be weak,
To be considered fragile or not up to peak.
But sometimes the rope, weakens with wear,
Causing our dreams of life, only to tear.
Tear as they might, unravel as they will,
We control the ride whether bumpy or still.
Wear and tear on the rope is a natural sign,
It's the sudden change of direction that's hard on the line.
So slack up on the rope to the life you are seeking,
And remember, it's a great life if you don't weaken

Sharon L. Moore

"Love"

I ask you is it wrong to dream of love?
If so what created dreams,
did they came from heaven up above?
I dream of love only to wonder will I ever fall in love,
true love, not fools love
When you feel something so strong for one person,
you can only hope for it only to be love you can count on,
be happy with for as long as you have love in your heart.
When you find love, take care of it and
in return it shall take care of you.

Ursula Martinez

Oath To Death

Death is sweet not a sorrow
if I had my choice I wouldn't see tomorrow
I feel so black and hollow inside
just kill me and throw me aside
no one will mourn or weep
cause they know that I was just a creep
I can't live with depression all my life
it just hits me like a knife
I have an obsession with death
it's a wish I never get
Life is a pity and a sin
oh please won't death come in
Why am I here in this world above
six feet under is the one I love
I feel so trapped inside
it left a wound so big and wide
This is my oath to death
when I release
I'll rest in peace

Trisha Merry

Your Love

To an optimist my heart would be half full,
If I didn't have your love with me today.
To a pessimist my days would be half empty,
If you didn't love me in each and every way.

To a person who is color blind,
My world would seem to be bleak,
If I couldn't think about you all the time,
Or dream about you in my sleep.

To a poor person I would seem to be rich,
If I had your love always,
To a musician your love would be like a melody,
If my heart only knew how to play.

But to me your love is like a blanket,
To shelter me from the cold,
Like a star in the sky that sparkles,
Or like my love that never grows old.
Stephanie Elease Childs

A Mother's Portrait

If I could put on canvas what I'd truly like to see,
I'd paint the sky as deep as the love you've felt for me.
Its warm colors would reflect their different shades along the sands,
I'd gently touch each dew drop through the caress of your hands.

If I could put on canvas the happiness I've known,
God's, great clouds would sing of all the glory you have shown.
I'd create the distant mountains with the softness of your glow,
and a little bridge for crossing where you've led me down the road.

The waters down below would show the sparkle of your eyes.
The tall oaks on the bank would have your strength e'en when you cry.
The fresh, spring grass beneath them will contrast the morning hue,
but I've yet to paint a picture that is as beautiful as you.
Teresa Walker

Destiny

In my constant fight to do what's right
I wrestle with the fates

One says "Give up you'll never win"
Another "You have yet to begin"
And the third just smiles and waits

The whole time knowing the pattern she's sewing
Every moment changes shape

From my choices made and the plans I've laid
She laughs at my crazy landscape

Not a smile of disdain but a splendid refrain
Of joyful laughs of glee

Because love brought this state
Not greed, envy or hate
And so the fates decree

To never give in, to always begin
And let love shape Destiny.
Patrick McDeavitt

Love of Loneliness

I need a shoulder which I can lean on.
I need a chest which I can cry in.
Please squeeze me much stronger than he did.
Please kiss me many more than he did.
I need someone to forget my first love.
I need someone to find my second love.
Please hug me until I can forget about him.
Please pet me until I love you.
Rei Sudo

Oh If Only You Didn't Die

If I only had another chance
I would spend more time with grandpa Vance

Oh if only you didn't die

I love you grandpa so very dear
I know you left with a lot of fear

Oh if only you didn't die

You lingered on so very long
The pain and suffering was oh so wrong

Oh if only you didn't die

When you were lying in that hospital bed
You could barley hold up your precious head

Oh if only you didn't die

I was sitting waiting by the phone
When it rang I knew what was wrong

Oh only if you didn't die

I cried and I cried for so very long
After I got the message on the phone

Oh if only you didn't die

Now your in heaven with your mother so dear
But I really do wish that you were here
Tammy Moehlenpah

"If"

If I were the sun,
I would make all days sunny, bright and cheerful.
Were I the moon,
I would let my glow soothe and calm you.
If I were a cloud,
I would shield you from the heat of day.
Were I a rain drop,
I would anoint your lips as the dew upon a rose.
If I were an Angel,
I would watch over you in times of peril or strife.
Were I a rose,
I would bloom eternally to behold your enchanted smile.
If I were but one of these,
"I" would be the hand of God.
But alas,.....''I'' am but Man.
Rudolf W. Keil

Untitled

As I sit here my heart broken and in my hands
  I wonder what to do, why I must be in this pain
As the blood drips from my fingers like the
tears that fall from my eyes
  I wonder why they leave
    why don't they see
      how can they ignore
        don't they understand
As I sit here my spirit stripped of life,
my soul made naked by the let down of another
  I wonder why we are pushed
    why we must conquer the pain put before us
As I sit vulnerable I try to heal
  Hoping for some temporary relief
    never the same
      always more damaged than the heart break before
I wonder will it ever stop
  when will the wounds heal
    and should we be expected to Forgive.
Sandra Cardella

Memories Found

I looked up to you, when I was young,
I was so proud to be your daughter.
You gave gifts that would make any child smile.
But, you left something out when you bought those things.
You left out your love, your pride and your concern.
Some gifts you gave were not so great.
Your anger, your fear and your scars.

I did find something, inside my memories,
that you may not have counted on.
I found my feelings;
I found out how to love myself,
how to give myself, the comforting arms,
and the patience you never gave.
But most of all, I found my strength.

Shelia Kleba

The Abyss

I was barely across, the threshold of existence
I was at a loss I lack all resistance
Until you brought me to a human plain
That I never thought I would feel again
You pulled me through and far beyond
To a realm so new I felt a special bond
Without a sound you crept into my heart
My mind going round till I'm falling apart
Without you knowing you made me a man
Without me showing I'll know not where I stand
The force you exude is where my strength comes
Like some exotic food I've been feeding from
Though your force doesn't wane I can no longer consume
The power I'll gain in my soul there's no room
You're so close I could touch but the distance is great
I can feel so much of the love you create
To hold your hand, touch your hair, and to kiss your lips
But back into the abyss there my soul slowly slips

Robert J. McCollim Jr.

My Precious Heart

There you are, those eyes, that face
I want to melt in your embrace.
My knees weaken at the thought of this
Oh I love you and your soft kiss
My precious heart you took
And now I'm wrapped around your little hook.

Sherry Olson

"I Want To Be Outside When I Die"

Dear Lord, let me be outside when I die.
I want room to spread my wings and have room to fly.
I don't want to hunt a door
When my spirit begins to soar.
I don't want to tarry around.
Lest my soul becomes earthbound.
Well Lord, if you could and Lord, if you would, please,
Let it be on a clear bright day.
But if you choose not, then a starry night,
So the stars can guide my way.
I'll just lay down beneath this shady tree
So Lord you can send your angels after me.
I'll close my eyes and go to sleep
Pray the Lord my soul to keep.
Tell St. Peter, to hold that golden gate.
Not to worry St. Peter, I won't be late.
I've only a few to bid goodbye.
Then I'll be on my way home, Lord, to you in the sky.
Please Lord, let me be outside, when I die.
I want room to spread my wings and have room to fly.

Wanda Little Strawder

Mom

When I was three or maybe four
I used to wait for Mom.
I'd sit and wait for a sign of dust
and then I'd start to run.

I was so happy to see her smile
as she eventually came into sight.
She'd pick me up and give me a kiss
and tell me everything was all right.

I'd walk beside her as far as I could,
but I just couldn't hold my tongue,
for she knew, that before very long
I'd say, "whatcha got for me Mom?"

She'd smile and open her pocketbook and have to dig down far,
but I always knew that before very long, she'd find me a candy bar.

Night would come and she'd put me to bed, making sure to tuck me in,
she'd always say," don't forget your prayers,"
and then she'd kiss me again.

Now I am older and have a job but still need one thing and another,
but of all my needs stands out one special thing,
I'm always in need of a mother.

J. Jerry Stup

Carefree

You are special to me
I treasure you as a friend
for you accept me, however I may be,
again, and again.
I like your company
you always find a way
to make me laugh.
It's not easy to make me happy
but with you, it's a gas.
We can do things together
or we can do just nothing at all.
After spending time being close to you, I feel better
I'm able to make it over the wall.
And I need to tell you this
because you need to know
while you're away, those crazy-moments I miss.
Hold on to the thought, don't let it go.
It's kinda funny, I guess we're lucky.
I cherish our friendship.
Found compatibility

Susannah A. Park (The Mermaid)

The Times You're Not Here

For the times you're not here,
    I think of you still.
I remember with fondness,
    The way that it felt.
The memories are fresh,
    The feelings still new.
I'll always remember,
    How could I forget.

For the times you're not here,
    I still count on your strength.
I still feel you around me, your aura is clear.
Your kindness, your caring,
Will always be near.

For the times you're not here,
    You will still be my friend.
Someone to count on,
    Someone to depend.
There will always be part of you,
    Here in my heart.

For the times you're not here.

Sharon A. Ricigliano

Thoughts Upon Leaving

As I start to leave,
I think of our lovemaking;
Probably our most enjoyable
Togetherness we share.

Your sweetness is overwhelming,
And the negative times are few.

Although I know as yet
You need your space and time;
For independence and
Rediscovering yourself.

Your unconquerable self is
Such a wonderful luring challenge;
I feel only love and desire to consume you.

Yet, I care enough to leave you
All the room you need.

Please be as sure as I am,
And we will overcome;
I must go now; I love you.

Paul S. Hogan

Childhood Monsters

Whenever I'm sad or all alone,
I talk to my friend who used to be made of skeleton bones.
He tells me I'm fine, and not to be upset, even a trife,
Then he tells me again how he lost his life.
A horrible monster invaded his body at the age of four,
Unfortunately when it came in it locked the door.
The doctors didn't know where from or why it came,
Only that it eating up his body frame.
He went though treatments to cure his ail,
Though they did about as much good as a Macy's sale.
The monster was cancer, leukemia to be exact.
The doctors had no sure cure, and that's a fact.
My friend needed a transplant and he needed one fast,
He needed one so bad that it didn't come quick he wouldn't last.
My friend died at the age of eight,
His transplant didn't come until it was too late.
He comes to see me only when I'm down,
He's the only one who can flip-side my frown.
Perhaps if more people were touched by cancer in their lives,
They would realize we have to make it everyone's fight.

Sonja Leighann Hestand

Thinking About My Fears

Holding back tears
I stare into the night.
Thinking, thinking about my fears.
Thinking about tears,
running quietly down my face and knowing I was one of his dears.
As I sit here thinking about his might.
Thinking, thinking about my fears.

And I can't help but wonder if he held back tears
the way I did and do right now in the light.
As I sit here looking in my mirrors.

It's very hard for me to understand why one of my dears
had to go, as I think about him in the night.
Thinking, thinking about my fears.

And if I look close enough I can see his reflection beyond my tears,
but as his face turns into a blur I say into the night,
"I loved him more than all my dears!"
Thinking, thinking about my fears.

Rachel Edwards

My Angel With The Golden Hair

As night time goes by,
I stare at a death stricken sky.
I think about the guy in the dream,
His golden hair seemed to gleam.
The face of an angel so sweet and so kind,
His words still linger in my mind.
As the sky shows signs of a new day,
I remember when he turned to walk away.

I started to cry,
And wanted to die.
How could he leave me behind,
When he had seemed so kind?
Then he turned to face me,
Love in his eyes is all I could see.

He had to make a long journey,
Before he could come back to me.
I could not speak so I just sat there to stare,
At my angel with the golden hair.

Susan Stribling

Don't Look Back

As I get old and feeble,
I sometimes live in the past.
I think about the good times;
Oh! Why couldn't they last.
My eyes are not good anymore
And I love to read so well.
My ears are not good either
I can't hear what people tell.
I cannot read the news paper
And too much T.V. is not good;
So I think back to my former life
And the things I would do if I could.
Since that is not good either
To look back to a happier life,
Just live in the present and don't look back
Think what happened to Lot's wife.

T. W. Steidley

Commitment

On stage in the theater of love
  I shall beckon you from the wings...
Hearts beating together, arms entwined.
  To share again the illusion and enchantment
  of one hundred golden strings.
As passions rise to the seductive gypsy strains...
  Share with me once more..spinning moments
  of ecstasy and revealing precious memories.
  my kiss to heal old wounds
  a gentle touch to dry tears past.

With the passing of years..
  still in my tender embrace, my farewell kiss
  will release you into Paradise Eternal.

Ruth Gilmer

Die

D is for death for everyone dies
I is for the immortal impression you make on people's lives
E is for the emotions that linger, even when the grave and
  memories are long forgot

Tom Schmidt

The Search Of My Release

The Mask with hollowed eyes- watches me in the dark night
I see myself in its empty stare- persuasively calling for each day's surrender
My restless hunger awaits the night's brief escape-
as my lonely needs tick away each second of a perfect union with time
I am trapped...a prisoner of my own dark and sultry ways...my will the
  unbearable reminder

In a sleepless fancy I rise and see you through hollowed eyes from
  where you stand
You hold the shadows in the swarthy night between the space of a dream
  and my secret devotion

Lips full and red drip pleas of my heart's maddened desires
Offer me the secret of my Ancient heart for I am tied to an aged and
  timeless embrace
I am the one who waits for my confession
I am the one who torments the fear of my own loneliness
I am the solo dancer in this gossamer dance with death

My portrait yellowed and cracked
Lines run deep and coursed through the pigment of a sorrowful survival.
Yes!...   Bloody Yes... I know now...
I have slowly been devoured from The Search of My Release
I can no longer hide from this agony for it has lived within me many centuries

So the Mask with hollowed eyes remains- watching me in the dark night
and silently awaits the sweetness of my breath to wane-
to capture me in the stroke of a gaze and call me away from my loneliness

Robyn Ramos

Meeting You

Meeting you on a fine morning I thought, "Who is he?"
I searched all the pages in my memory
No, I have never seen you before.

But, the nature, the stature, the impression
You made on me that's familiar
It could never ever be a confusion.

As a kid I've admired my mother saw the entire world in her
Then I admired my dad: Like any child at that.

It was then my teacher, my sister
Later it was some friends and other
I grew from a kid to a man,
Like some and dislike many others.

Turning the pages, I figured;
What was so familiar and similar-
You have given me a part of each page I turned.

Love, affection, life, fun, joy,
Responsibility, direction, wisdom, knowledge and realization;
Fond remembrances, bliss and tears...
Tears of happiness and eternal joy.

There'll never be a new page without you on its face.

Anil Telikepalli

Untitled

Walking through the snow one day,
I saw a vision in white.
The Angel of Death was coming down on me
Trying to take my life.
I started running faster and faster,
Not knowing where I was going,
Not caring where I'd been,
Just running to get from him.
But then I turned around to see,
the vision I was running from,
was,
Not an Angel,
Not a Devil
But my own reflection.

Sonya C. Smith

Commitment

We were so young when you called to me.
I saw the light of first love.

Did I see you?
We talked. I didn't hear you, not really.
I was proud of my own thoughts; of what I said to you.
My words a mask to hide myself.
To be aware, how dangerous.
To hear and feel, commitment.
I wound my words and feelings around you as tightly as I could.
I held you to me.

We have grown old together and I have learned to listen.
I exposed myself to you and you have not turned away.
I still see the nimbus of love surrounding you.
It holds me within.
You taught me commitment.

Patricia A. Kohler

betwixt shadows

tranquility.
i saw her once.
shy and simple, she stole my soul.
the wisdom witch.
i saw her truth.
dancing like salem, she haunted my time.
silence.
i saw her beauty.
upon bejeweled wings, she tainted my vision.
weird sisters three: mind, body, spirit.
they spoke my name
beneath a whisper;
betwixt shadows and years.
my saviours, my crucifixion,
sanctified in cream, blood, and tears.
writhe, blithe spirits,
singing dirges in the rainstorm of my fears.
When will you receive my kiss?

MH Wylde

For The Rest Of Our Lives

Minutes feel like hours. Hours feel like days.
I really do miss you in so many ways.

It seems like so long
Since I last saw your face.
Or held you in my arms
With a long, sweet embrace.

Or told you I love you with all of my heart.
I love you as much as I did from the start.

I know it's not easy staying in love with me.
I've hurt you so much but you'll always be
My one and only, I'll make you see
It wasn't a mistake for you to love me.

I'll treat you with kindness
My love I will share.
I'll make you so happy
I'll show you I care.

You'll be really proud
To be my wife.
We'll have a great marriage
For the rest of our lives.

Thomas Hawkingberry

My Mountain, Your Garden

Kathy Rae, I Love U!
I reach out to you.
I give you all that I have to offer.
Emotional mountains are climbed,
as I hung on a cliff, created by your words.
I Love to soar on the heights of promise,
Shining out from rays of your life giving heart.
That heat cascades across my skin,
absorbing into this exclusive chance to return your love.
To be the one who shaves in the creation and
    maintenance of an everlasting bond.
If you want me, I'll be the caretaker of your emotional garden,
not the mastermind, wanting to keep you blind.
The map of this life-leads on to many mirage bound horizons.
You define my Journey, you are the soulmate.
I give you all I can offer, reach out, I will wait.

Phil Gaston

A Mother's Prayer

Written at Morning Cheer Bible Conference, the day Holly Rene' Miller,
my grand-daughter, was born
Because I am a follower of Jesus Christ my Lord,
I must believe what He has said in His inerrant Word;
And since I read that He is Lord, and caused each life to grow,
I know that this life in my womb, His loving heart doth know.

'Tis there I read each secret part is after His own plan,
And that is why I cannot heed the word of sinful man;
They tell me this is just a blob of tissue, very small,
That if I should dispose of it, it matters not at all.

But in God's Holy Word I read, 'tis in His image formed,
It has a body, mind and soul that need to be transformed;
That He alone hath given life and formed it for His own,
And He hath willed that I must see that it be fully grown.

And I am told I must give a full accounting there,
Of every deed that I have done while on my journey here;
So Lord, I give this life to You, and will a steward be,
So when I see You face to face, You will be proud of me.

Rev. Titus C. Miller

Bride

Conjuring me with pleasantries,
I met a flower; nay, an adorable beauty.
Intoxicating the Spring with ravishing fragrance.
A sweetheart: an angel?!
But a bride she was.
She had won all hearts,
But most and foremost
The heart of my dearest son.
Amazed the garden-birds,
Chanting to rose-buds in cradles!
Amazed the on-lookers,
Swerving on dancing waves,
Curious of the whereabouts of this endeared mermaid.
Belchanto were the hums of the sweet breeze,
Serenading the harmonious love-songs:
as if the angels relayed the God's blessings,
and the rhapsody of my felicitations.

M. K. Sherkat (Shahrin)

I Love You

I love you, for you the way you are with me.
I love you, for the way you are without me.
But most of all I love you,
because you have me for me
because I do not have to be anything but me.
I love you, for just being there when I call.
I love you, for when we take walks through the mall.
I love you, when your crying or sad.
I love you, when your glad or your mad.
I love you, when your down and out.
I love you, when your in or your out.
I love you, when you are near nor there.
I love you, for more than you can share.
I love you, more than you will ever know.
But all I can say and all I know is that,
I love you so, I love you so.

Theresa M. Perez

Untitled

I love to listen to the wind; it sings a song to me.
I love to feel it on my skin, a caressing, gentle breeze.
It has a taste that's bittersweet from the salty, southern sea;
It's full of summer's fruit and flowers to scatter the autumn leaves.

I love to listen to the rain as it cries into the night;
A melancholy melody for love that did not go right.
It taps a rhythm on my window and dances on the neon lights,
But it washes away sad memories so the morning's clean and bright.

I love the snow in wintertime and its swirling, pure white storm;
To slip into its silent shroud and slumber, safe and warm.
While pristine, icy, satin sheets soften every form,
A crystal midnight blue awakes to a frozen, rosy dawn.

I love to watch the clouds as they sail across the sky;
Shadowy ships changing shape as they pass before my eye.
They roll with a mighty thunder or whisper a gentle sigh;
With fading colors of forgotten dreams to tomorrow's hopes they fly.

I love the fragrance of a desert dawn and of ancient mountain pines,
And the moody ocean's magic mist ripening the roses on the vine.
These delights do not diminish with the shifting sands of time.
But like sweet, golden grapes at harvest, they age into vintage wine.

Vic Doddridge

If She Is A Woman

She is a woman...
    I love her
Because she's a woman
    I love her
If for no other reason
    Than: She is a woman...
    I love her
She is a woman...
    And I love her,
    I do! love her
I really do:
    Without reservation, hesitation, or resignation
Without president, incident, or consequence
    Without conscience
Unequivocally, unabashedly, eternally
    And infinitely...
    Love her!
If she is a woman
    I love her...

William Sammuel Owens Jr.

Midnight Stroll

As I walk along the beach,
I look out above the water.
The stars I cannot reach.
They glitter without a bother.

The night is so very calm and peaceful,
yet the waves are still rushing in.
The wind creates a breeze so fragile and cool,
which can be felt every now and then.

As I proceed, dragging my feet in the sand,
I see a beautiful shell coming in with the tide.
I pick up the husk and hold it in my hand,
and thank the ocean for the gift it supplied.

It is now time to go back, but I hesitate.
I turn around and release a lengthy sigh.
I must go home for it is getting late,
but instead I decide to gaze at the sky.

Dawn approaches and the birds start to sing.
Their chirping awakens me from my sleep.
I look out my window and see the same old thing...
smog, pollution, the big city, and I weep.

Rene Edwards

Zug In Oklahoma City

My name is Zug - a regular thug
  I lived in 8 BC
You know me well - I'm straight from Hell
  I'm in your family tree.

You thought me dead - I'm in your head
  I'll live long and true
I'm every place - see my waste
  I'm always there with you.

Bums I make - and in my wake
  Destruction is a sight
My aim in life - create strife
  It is my basic right.

Don't know nor care - who or where
  Attack I always do
I creep and leap - don't sleep nor weep
  As all my foes so do.

For deep inside - live I with pride
  Waiting for your tug
To claim and maim - rise for my prize
  For I am Zug - your thug.

Robert R. Johnston

Get A Grip

In my discretion and despair
  I lit my candle to watch it flair
But as the world does onto me
  it flickered and flared and cried beneath the ceiling fan
The wax it dripped just like my tears
  it tried, it tried to get a grip
The flames they would grow bright and high
  and then wham, they would fall again and die
It tried, it tried to get a grip
  as the fan it played its evil fit
The tears are real, the tears are mine
  the world it whirls just like the fan
It pushes you around and around
  until you find yourself right on the ground
Burned out you know of light and life
  it snuffs you of every breath of the night
Fight on, fight on, try to grip
  but the fan whirls faster
    you loose your grip!

Sharon Craig

Fleeting Scream

In the sparkling waters, I swim all day,
I leap and jump, and go at my play.
I love my life, as a fish of gold,
It's great to be young, only one year old.

Upstream bad things are happening, I hear,
But I'm not worried; that's way up there.
I don't understand, the concern and fuss,
What could possibly happen, to any of us.

Life was so grand, here on the river,
But now clutter and pollution, gives me a shiver.
The water grows dark, and evil lurks,
I gasp to breathe, and my body jerks.

Oils, chemicals, and gasoline spills,
Tear at my scales, and clog up my gills.
Now my life, hangs in the balance,
I shall surely die, here in the silence.

My one regret, and greatest fear,
Is that no one, shall even hear.
My last lonely cry, and fleeting scream,
As I lay dying, in this poison stream.

Richard Smith

Rose

He named me Rose -
I know not why.
Perhaps my father sensed that, some day,
Just as roses need the warmth of sun
I'd need the warmth of love
Or I should die.

He named me Rose -
But very quickly came the thorns
That fast outpaced the freshening leaves of May.
Until, one day, a passing ray of sunshine
Kissed the bud
And, lo, the rose -
For far too few, but oh -
What scented days.

Rosalie Creamer

"When I See A Church"

When I see a church, standing quiet and alone,
I know God is in there sitting on His throne.
It may not be the church where I attend.
We may not believe the same, but if one soul feels Him within,
He hears them sing and pray,
And gives them peace and hope, to travel in His way.

When I see a church waiting silent as in prayer,
I see His face in every nook with kindness everywhere.
When I pass I have the urge to stay,
And reach out to His sacred place.
It may be a small, humble house; He loves it just the same,
And all who choose to come, to worship in His name.

When I see a church, it's surrounded with peace.
It welcomes you to come, and worship at His feet.
So patiently it stands there straight and tall,
It waits there with joy and love for all.
You'll hear them sing praises and pray, and preach from God's own Word.
It fills your heart and soul when you meet with the Lord.

Rebecca Melton

Untitled

The first time I met you,
I knew you were the one
You always made me feel happy,
When I thought everything was gone

Now we have become best friends
and maybe even more
But it's our friendship I will always adore

We have the greatest time together
Just you and me
We take wild drives
And talk just about anything.

I wish you knew
How I really feel
'Cause what I feel is so very real

So when you leave on your mission
Please do not forget
The love will never change
And I will never regret.

Richelle Cook

Re-Creation

Recently I had a thought that never occurred to me before,
I imagined God decided to try and create the perfect world once more.

The people on every continent all screamed their shouts of joy,
And thanked the Lord God for the gift of his little boy.

They promised to remember all their mistakes and sins,
And prayed to the Lord not to let them make any again.

They prayed for all the soldiers to be well and sane,
Praying they aren't haunted by the souls of innocent maimed.

These citizens repented with all their hearts and souls,
And God chose from among them those who
cherished their faith in its whole.

Those who had true faith rose to heaven above,
And felt the peace delivered by a single white dove.

Liars went down to the depths of Earth's core,
Not to be confused with true believers anymore.

After Earth was emptied of all her recent guests,
God once again went back to work, he had
only seven days to do his best.

Tara K. Dew

Untitled

I have always loved you,
I have always thought of you as sacred,
and I worshipped you in the depths of infinity,
I have always cared when others didn't,
I have always fought for the image of your name,
and I always will,
I have always been there when you cried,
and the others left you behind,
I have always loved you.

Thomas West

A Hidden Dream

In your heart there is a dream
Hiding until one day it is seen
You will know when it is found
For from that day on you'll never look down
So look in your heart and you will find
Something you couldn't in your mind

Stacy Schlickbernd

Friends

Life has been good to us
I guess we shouldn't fuss
We walk the path of life
With great joy and strife
Going up hill and down
Not knowing when to turn around
Our inner guidance comes from above
Mapped out for us with wondrous love
When something goes awry
We would sometimes cry
So to live each day doing our best
An to the higher power we leave the rest
So my friend with the sunshine on our shoulders
We will walk tall and climb any boulders
All is just a test
To see how strong we can handle the rest
So with love in our hearts an wings on our prayers
We can climb those many stairs
For the many years to come
We will walk the path with joy and song

Roseanne Hunniford

I Feel God's Presence

As the birds serenade the dawn.
I feel God's presence.
As the trees bend and rustle in the wind.
I feel God's presence.
As the babbling brook continues its journey.
I feel God's presence.
As the thunder cracks and the lighting flashes across the sky.
I feel God's presence.
As the rain begins to slowly fall.
I feel God's presence.
As the snow blankets the ground.
I feel God's presence.
As the sun slowly descends below the horizon.
I feel God's presence.
As the stars light up the night.
I feel God's presence.

Susan Friend

Whose Child Am I

Born into a world of turmoil and pain,
  I entered not knowing what sorrow I'll gain.
As life progressed in the hours to come,
  it was evident that I would not blossom;
to become the child I should be, a child who could be loved easily.

With the first signs of withdrawal the doctors worked hard on me
  giving me life but not much hope; it seemed as though it were an eternity.
And now I awake each day filled with emptiness and despair.
  Desperately searching for someone to touch me, for someone to care—
wanting so much to be held very tight, knowing that something just isn't right.

Who was there for me when the danger was done?
  For it was in the womb that I was alive only to become—
a distraught and lonely extension of the one who riddled me with drugs.
  And feeling no pain for the wrong she had done;
I was abandoned and left alone, now I have no one. No one to love me
  or to hold my small hand. No one to tell me whose child I am.

Theodore F. Guild

"Time"

  Time is more valuable than silver or gold ...
for its precious minutes cannot be bought
or sold.
  As time's hands tick away, we
say good-bye to another day with hope ...
we valued time.

Shirley Mabey

"A Name On The Wall"

A name on the Wall is all that is left of me,
I died for my country so all may be free.
Family and friends, they walk by and grieve,
When all I really want is to be able to breathe.
Remembered by some,
Forgotten by most,
Now Heavenly Father is my gracious host.
No more pain must I bear,
Only peace of spirit have I here.
Watching over my brothers is what I must do,
Protecting and guiding their every move,
United we stood,
Divided we fall,
But please don't forget my name on the Wall.

Pebbles LaBeau

Parent's Parent's Place

To their place,
I deliver brown bottles dressed in white labels and
long, perfect words I don't know. Open the door.

Plants cower in corners too weak to reach the sun
sneaking in with me. I shuffle across the concrete
carpet of the largest, small room

Of their place.
Ignorant porcelain smiles clutter dusty, laddered shelves.
Old issues of T.V. guide smother tables with
white-ring fossils of yesterday's coffee cups. All is same.

I sit on the plaid couch faded to a solid blah.
It eats me as I visit the monotone ballgame commentator,
blasting, competing with the sucking of that oxygen thing—
Grandpa's breath. She sits

In their place,
in her red, plastic chair, the stuffing hanging
out like her underclothes. Sorting Campbell's soup cans.
No smile.
No hug or homemade cookies.
No escape for them from their place.

Rainee S. Shelton

"Portamento"

What is it?
I can't tell.
An Autumn leaf falling,
A shiny penny in the well.
A fog horn howling,
in the morning bog,
A woodpecker pecking on an old log.
A rose blossom in a simple vase,
Tiny freckles on a young child's face.

The sun coming out on a cloudy day,
The hands of the potter working the clay.
The tears of joy, or tears of pain,
The late night whistle of the 10:00 train.
The earth or the clouds up above.
What is it I can't tell?
I guess it must be love.

Shelby Harris

Genesis

Sometimes when I think about it
I cannot sleep and find no peace
For I want to know what I can never know.
One day I dreamed a dream drifting to the beginning,
To the very beginning of time when there was no time.

And when I saw what I wanted to know I saw nothing, nothing at all.
No form, matter, or energy, no creative force,
Neither light nor darkness, no day or night,
Just a vast stillness, an empty naked void.
Nothing, nothing at all.

When I awoke no wiser than before
The riddle of existence remained the same,
Only questions unanswered came.
If at the dawn, the beginning of it all,
There was nothing, then we are nothing, nothing at all.
Alpha and Omega, the first and last,
The beginning and the end, are they all one?
And in the end, when our days are done,
Must we reclaim our past, returning to the genesis,
Back to nothing again.

Rolf W. Meier

Evidence Of Healing

At last, at last, oh, Blessings Be,
I can value by Being in Totality:
The woman, the child, the Whole of me.

I can share with a man, seek pleasure for myself,
solely...
because...
I love it!

Without any judgement or connecting to past wounds,
I am free to express, to delight, to exude,
I can claim what was given me by God:

Pure, pleasing, proud, poetic.

Oh, Blessings Be, at last, at last.

Roxana Stewart Rohan

Condescension

I am not a mountain man.
I avoid Earth's zits
like the bully in the school yard.
They always look down on the unendowed,
so overgrown with testosterone
judging us for our lack of size,
challenging us to reach their heights,

For some who peg holes in its veneer,
using every muscle to propel upward,
they see it as a reward,
a been-there, done-that of point collection.
If they climb enough mountains, they gain enough points,
and they win God's Grand Prize:
To die and live on one forever.

I don't need to visit them.
I just need my AAA tour guide
to get around them,
because even my car growls
at such condescension.

Scott Mackenzie

No One To Talk To

During lunch my friends were talking
I asked them what they were talking about
They didn't answer me
I sat there looking at the endless blue sky, and tree...

I asked them again
But there was no response
For a moment, the wind was whimpering into my ears
Not my friends' squeaky voices but the soft wind...

I looked at them, staring at their lips
Their lips were moving like the streams into a river
I saw them having a good time
Laughing, playing, and teasing each other
I wish I would be able to do that, but I had no one to talk to...

I felt like I was with an unsuitable group of friends
Maybe it was my style or maybe it was my attitude
I thought and thought about it, I realized
I was in an unsuitable group and eventually, I walked out...
Because something else was calling to me
Something kept telling me to walk out...

    Pok Lim

I Am

I am the wish, the dream and courage of my mother.
I am the hope and the strength of the slaves.
I am a young black intelligent woman.
I am loved, admired, and never taken for granted.
I am determined, I am encouragable and I am also respected.
I am strong open minded and always ready for the future.
I am a leader not a follower.
I am a winner not a loser.
I am a friend to those who need friends and
I am always a friend to those who think they don't need them.
I am always the best person I can be, because
I am drug-free and I am one of God's children and
   that's all I ever want to be.

    Renda Oden

When I Think Of You

As I set oft find myself pondering of you by my side.
I am overcome with emotion for the love you have inside.
My burdens are lifted by the warmth and radiance of your smile.
As you carry my tiresome troubles alone mile after rocky mile.
Oh, how forgetful of me to pierce the soul of a love so deep.
Seldom do I bring to mind how is one to have one so unique.
As you open both body and spirit an offer of all your splendor.
How can this be unto one as I a gift a life a breath oh so tender.
Of all the stars that shine above how canst I be this one so low.
To an awaken days dawning a morning star that is forever glowing.
Is it for me this precious flower of the earth to have been chosen.
Or is it but a dream that I shall find that all to soon I have awoken
I must know how it can be this gem of great price that I admire.
Can be for one, one such as this man that is I who has acquired.
And am lost in the radiance of your beauty that glows from within.
For you are the breath that I breathe and the light that never ends.
Mine eyes glisten from the streams of joy and sadness that do flow.
As I am reminded of the great price that I shall ever, ever owe.
What can one, one so weak and lowly as this man that is I, repay.
One who without concern for self would sacrifice all for me today.

    W. Timothy Dehner

Untitled

Here today and gone tomorrow.
  How those words flash back to mind,
As with a feeling of great sorrow,
  Pathways separate on the sands of time.

As quickly as a bird flits into view,
  A person's life is with ours entwined.
To know her and love her, but soon adieu.
  Apart we are pushed by fate so unkind.

Though from you I am torn asunder,
  When our friendship had barely a start,
Always, despite fate's cruel blunder,
  There'll be a place for you in my heart.

    Thomas E. Cook

The Watchman

Weeping willow gnarled but green
How many tragedies have you seen
Life and death ebbing on and on
People lonely, left alone.

Weeping willow, gnarled but green
How many children have you seen
Loved and blessed or abused and wronged
Longing for life's happy song.

Weeping willow, gnarled but green
How many lovers have you seen
Spiced with youth or aged with grace
Each one yearning for love's embrace.

Weeping willow, gnarled but green
Has watching earth been a painful scene
Has it bent your limbs from grief and toil
As you stand earth's watchman
In the deep, dark soil.

    V. Janie Nickle

A Conversation

Why are the great ones always great?
How did they all become that way?
I asked these folks how they create,
And this is what they had to say:

Whitman claimed, "It was the `Song of Myself.'"
"'I started Early-' a long time ago,"
said Dickinson. "Look on my shelf,
And you'll see 'The Raven!'" blamed Edgar Allan Poe.

Robert Frost spoke of "Stopping by Woods
on a Snowy Evening." "And then," said Longfellow,
"I had `My Lost Youth' just when I could."
"A `Summer Night Piece' was mine," stated Lowell.

Eliot, like Poe, had something to blame.
"It was `The Waste Lands' you see."
Ezra Pound made "A Pact" with a name,
And Langston Hughes cried "`Democracy!'"

As I listened to these women and men
It dawned on me what made them great.
It wasn't that they wrote again and again;
It was, simply, that they COULD create!

    Rebecca Ernst

She Had No One

With whom to share the joke. It was sort of a personal THAING between him and her. Just as personal as the other unspoken intimacies they each pondered in their hearts SECRETLY - SHE Could be blatant, impatient, unamused, very serious, one-minded, one sided, and even dogmatic (sometimes) about her viewpoint. Sometimes she wanted to cry, to scream, to have the biggest fartin', foot-stumpin', cussin', temper-thrown tantrum she'd ever had in her life! She ground her teeth when she thought about it. He - on the other-hand was always cool, calm and well-collected. His aim seemed to be, to remain, dismissed from the entire episode which strained to involve him in his dear friend's life. His dear friend who had more than one personality. His dear friend who was sweet, loving, kind, and generous. His dear friend whose alter-ego was determined to get his attention romantically. He claimed dis-interest and since he had no other personalities it became a dis-heartening situation for them both. She - The alter-ego that is - toyed with idea of growing a beard — unsatisfied estrogen levels do 'strange' things to a woman. She mused on growing a beard and a ___. How else she make herself more attractive to him? SHE HAD NO ONE WITH WHOM TO SHARE THE JOKE!

Louise Banks

"Boston"

Crowded-busy city streets-
Here's where lonely strangers meet.
People, people every where-they do not see me yet they stare.
Men with push carts of things to buy-
Tall buildings, push up for breath toward sky-
New boys on every corner-struggling for a dime-
Old men-dreams dead-clutch at jugs of wine.
Young fair women rush on by- clickity click on heels high-
Old -tired women with desires long spent-
Walk slowly now with shoulders bent.
Slap-slap slap of a rag-little black boy cleaning shoes-
Cigar smoking white man reads the news.
Savage youths with bodies hard and souls of hate-
Surge forth -rebelling at their fate.
Men with motored drills work in the street.
They curse the Lord as this were some great fete.
I pass an open doorway and smells of food drift out.
"One steak rare and coffee black" the waitress shouts.
Oh, it's great to stroll along-being a part of all that I see.
But in the midst of it all-I find -I'm ever so lonely.

Tobi Arcaro

After Twilight

There she sat
Her tired frame gently rocking in her chair
    as she re-read lines from Chaucer.
Her eyes sparkled when she recognized a familiar passage;
    her wrinkled face dancing with graceful freedom
    when recalling a fleeting Middle English line.
Lovingly, I watched as she relived a time long ago -
    a time when she embraced life from the past
    transcending its form to her classroom.
I wanted to return the warmth,
    the protective comfort she had always given me.
I wanted to put my arms around her, holding dearly,
    as she had always done with me.
Looking up, she smiled, losing her place among the pages.
"This book is wonderful!
I think I taught this, didn't I?"
As I assured her that she had,
    she sat back continuing rocking in her chair,
    once again reading those familiar Chaucer lines -
My beautiful mother.

Susan D. Corneille

Windows To The Soul

Masked in pools of jade green,
Her pain is not evident, not even to herself.
A glance, she cries in silent whispers,
A stare, her heart is open for all to see.

Answers to questions unsolved,
All doubts removed from my mind,
The sadness from my heart is lifted.

The love to share that we crave,
My dreams, my hope, my future.

As her eyes breathe life into my soul,
So does she do for me.

My life has begun.
The mask is off.

Richard Rusiecki

My Lost Love

Every other in my life has loved and left never to be heard from again or so I thought...
Then they come back to love me they said but they only hurt me all over again, will this pain ever end?
Why did I let it happen, did I care too much, did I love too much? Maybe so but I know for sure that I couldn't stand to be without another.
But with him it's so different but in a way so much the same as the others; I loved him and he also left me.
I thought here it goes starting all over again, the same thing that always happens and he did come back, but it was different. I knew this had to be the true love I had always wanted.
But he broke my heart twice again more than any other and as always I took him back both times 'cause I couldn't stand to live without him.
I said to myself if he's hurt me so much why do I love him more and more, all the time, each and every day?
The answer came from deep within my feelings and always will be cause he's the one true love I've been searching for.

Tina Vantreese

My Vampire

My Vampire came to me last night like a dream
He was so real I just wanted to scream
I watched him change right before my eyes
Just like clouds change the skies
My vampire only comes to me at night
And I never put up a fight
Because he is my one true love
That has swept down on me from above
My Vampire has me under his spell
And things between us go quite well
His rich, melodious voice
His lips red and moist
My Vampire sends chills up and down my spine
And we treasure our quality time
I know we will never part
Because he will always hold a place in my heart
My Vampire, My Lover
If we were meant to be we'll soon discover.

Rebekah Anne Breakwell

"The Dream"

It all began when he was four;
He took his first step onto the court.

The ball was as big as he;
Because he only came to his Daddy's knee.

Years have gone by and he continues to grow;
His "dream" comes closer with every throw.

To sit on the bench
To play in the game
Either way, he's on his road to fame.

Although we do not know, where the "dream"
Will go or where it will end;
One thing is for sure;
He'll be a "star" to all he knows.

Theresa A. Easton

The Lease

My husband brings me tea in bed and I thank him.
He tells me not to worry things will work out, and I say I know
But when he has gone to work, I lie there and worry
And hope I have the strength to get through another day.

Why did we not read the lease more carefully page by slow death page
Why were we so eager to get started on our new adventure that we
did not see the trap we so blindly signed.
And now that out dream has died why are we still struggling to survive.

For eight long years we held the beauty shop together
We grew to hate our landlord's smiling face
The doors were broken in, the windows smashed.
You fix it fools it's all there in the lease.

Let's put a Brinks alarm in will you help us
It's all your problem suckers read the lease.

At last we face the problem squarely
The bullet through the window seals our fate
We'll move to a new location lease a station
But wait we have not properly read the lease.

Roma Martin

The Wise Man's Song A Fond Farewell

Listen to the wise man's song.
He sometimes appears weak, but his voice is strong.
I sometimes have questioned his word,
Only because his story I have not heard.
He in a lot of ways has helped me along,
But only when I stopped and listened to his song.
His words are strong in voice and heart
And that is what makes him wise and smart.
I know I will miss him, this much is true.
But in our parting, my heart is blue.
But not for long this much I know
For the wise man in my heart tells me so.
So when I hear the wise man's song,
I know now and forever he has helped make me strong!!!

William C. Mattson

Growing Up

C arefree and burdened by their island,
H opeful and desperate for a kind hand.
I nsightful and innocent just the same,
L earning and teaching is their fame.
D iligent and discouraged in the face of tasks,
R esponsible and dependent, with myriad masks.
E veryone and I forever change all,
N o one and you can jump while you fall.

Susan B. Katz

You Are Needed Where You Are

I asked the Lord, what would he have me to do?
He said Dear Child, why do you pursue?
I said because I wanted to please
He said Dear One just be at ease.

I have a job made just for you and at this time it's all that you can do
It's not a mystery that you are where you are, I put you there to be a star.
So, let your light shine bright that others may know what's right
And show them a more loving way by what you do and say.

Now, go ahead and don't delay to use your talents day by day.
I told him that I thought that he had something greater in mind.
He said that he did for a later time, but for now just begin
To show my love to both family and friends.

To share his peace and his joy and listen attentively to his voice.
I told him I thought that he had a better place for me
He said that there were none right now, that he could see
For he had placed me where I am, to learn to be a better lamb.

He hadn't forgotten that I was there and he had heard my daily, prayer.
I told him I could not comprehend, because I thought he was my friend.
He said Dear Child, you still don't understand, there is no greater
work than to love and serve your fellowman.

H. J. Marshall

My Beloved

From whence doth my beloved cometh,
  He cometh to me,
    the delight of my soul
      now truer than before.
Because I have known great joy
  in our hearts,
    whenever we shared our life together.
For we have loved one another most dearly
  in the same way,
    our times hath overcome again and again.
For it was love in the beginning
  and it shall be love forevermore
Until the ending of our days.
  Until eternity turns into life eternal,
    together still,
      there we shall be.

SherAnne Shea

The Unknown Soldier

When his country gave its call.
He answered and gave his all.

The soldier brave and true,
His blood stained the ground with its crimson hue.

His body bent and torn.
Oh, how his family will mourn.

But, what of the soldier who died unknown,
His name never to be etched in stone.

His name never to be known.
His family never to know what happened to their own.

In Arlington stands a monument to him and all the people who
  will never again hear a loved one's laugh.
And, there etched in eternal white marble is his and the
  countless hundreds of his peers epitaph.

Here rests in
Honored Glory
AN AMERICAN SOLDIER
Known but to God.

This guarded tomb is the highest honor we can bestow on your
  soldiers died unknown!

Thomas G. Lentz

"Love Is..."

Love is a river that flows through our souls,
  Having no certain destiny, no resting place.
  It just flows like a never ending stream,
  Hopping from one rock to the next.
Love is a fruit,
  Ripe and juicy, wanting to be tasted.
It's sweet,
  Having both wrongs and rights.
Love is a poem which we read,
  Sometimes not understanding it.
Love is peaceful,
  Yet cruel at times.
Love is a flower,
  Delicate and untamed.
Love is what you feel in your heart,
  Something true to you.
What is love to you?

    C. Megan Bryant

Father's Child

There comes a time when a man a woman.
Have to answer for the things he or she have
done, when you're an adult you say: There's no
one to answer to but the man up above.
And who's going to live my life when it's all
said and done. No matter what anyone's says
we're still our father's child.

I'm still my father's child.
I know he will take good care of me.
When I'm alone and I need someone to
talk too. I get on my knees and pray
And I know I can say anything, that's
on my mind. When things are going wrong,
when there's trouble in my life. I call out his name.
Because I know I'm still my father's child

He carries me on his shoulders.
Anything I could ever need he's there, when I'm weak, he lifts me up.
Because I know I'm still my father's child and I know he's apart of me.
No matter what I do, no, matter what I say. I'll always, always,
Be my father's child:

    Tamika Jewel Davenport

While You Were Sleeping...

While you were sleeping, the heart to your City and County
Has been stolen.
While you were sleeping, 4 letter words, racial epithets became
Common speech.
While you were sleeping, thugs breaking the glass of the sacred
Trinity in the windows of worship took your Church.
While you were sleeping, it hid in your beautiful treed lots.
While you were sleeping, it hid in business suits.
While you were sleeping, it hid in the meaning of your laws.

While you were sleeping, it taught in your schools.
While you were sleeping, it stole your truth.
While you were sleeping, it hid in their work, fear.
While you were sleeping, it burned your books.
While you were sleeping, it snatched your sons and your daughters.
While you were sleeping, it separated your families.
Faceless.
She asked: "Would this happen if you were not in it?"
Hate.
While you were sleeping, it soiled your name.

    Paula Versace

Things

Our world is full of unhappy things
Grief is all it brings
Everyone is moving to fast for their own good
Slowing down would help, if people could

So much destruction going around
Nothing in life is sound
The future appears to be borderline
Every person in a bind
The good Lord needs to come down
To take away everyone's frown
Happiness must conquer all life's gleam
So sadness can not be deem

Our existence require common sense for living
and optimistic security for curativing
Faith must be brought back to exist
Without danger to resist

    Terry Guernsey

Forever You Will Soar

White eagle, thank you for your life and lifting others to a
greater place. Breathtakingly, you captured spirits and carried
them past loneliness into a world of warmth and grace.

Here's to you, enchanter of song from Lakota Nation.
You filled cups with compassion and are due recognition.

A crown you deserve, for you gave fortune to all; you gave
endless understanding to human short falls.

When you sang, God smiled through soft mists and hard rains;
your voice spun to heaven's rafters, echoed through a million stars,
then fell to earth freeing hearts in chains.

As a boy you wanted to climb a mountain - a hard goal to do.
Fearless, you chose to pursue.

Touching the top, you exclaimed "I did right!"
From that moment you climbed many more and reached heavenly heights

Realizing your dream to fly, you caressed countless spirits
with your wings keeping close by sky.

Your amazing life leaves more than a magnificent musical legacy, and
heritage of hope and healing possibilities.

Your priceless voice does still ring, and is blessed by Creator
to forever soar and sing.

    Susan Herzog

Yesterdays

Being a mere child of five.
Going on eleven or twelve
Wishing to do all those fun things
Other playmates older than me.
Bike riding, skating, playing make believe; so many more.

But as time went by oh! So slow when five
Got so mad, cause I couldn't get to do these things fast.

Now that I'm growing young, time is just going too fast.
Trying to keep up is still a chore.
But how I wish that I could bring back all those fun yesterdays.
Oh! So glad to have had all those fun, dreams of all
  those special yesterdays.

    I. Hamilton

Life - The Gift

Life is fragile, it's a gift
God gives you a little lift
All things in life both great and small
Will reach their time and one day fall
They fall not to the ground with fright
But fall to heaven, towards the light
They say farewell to life on earth
As they head up toward the heavenly hearth
And reach the dawning of rebirth
Not all things in life are easy
Death can make you very queasy
Especially when someone you love
Is taken to the heaven's above
Like everything we all will fall
All creatures I great and small

Tami Zeigler

In My Mind's Eye

In my mind's eye I see him
gliding, leaping, twirling, floating,
like flowers dancing in the breeze

He moves with a grace, an ease,
a confidence that says it's right,
all the moves look simple,
anyone can do them.

But I've seen the work,
the sweat, the pain, the dedication,
striving for perfection when others are gone,
or still in bed,

The frustrations when it just doesn't work
and the joy when it does.

The hours and hours of practice
to make that one small part look natural, easy.

In my mind's eye I see him,
my son, the dancer.

Walter F. Reeder III

Reflections Of Newbirth

Shimmering ripples dance across the pond, stirred by a warm and
    gentle breeze.
The streams of gleaming sunlight reflecting through the trees.
You can almost see the glory of God.
Across the bank, a squirrel scurries off to play with its friends.
The grass so tall and green, the sky so blue and wide.
A show of wonder is created in this scene, you can almost feel God
Walking by your side.
A small colorful bird perched on a branch, sings its song of praise.
It knows a cherished secret, that only few will hear, as its sweet
Voice fills the air..
There is a calm all about, but something stirs within you.
As your eyes come upon a tiny bud, its head covered with glistening
Drops of dew, new life is just beginning, its petals so soft and
bright are still waiting patiently closed until it knows the time is
right, to lift up its head and blossom. Facing boldly toward the sun
It's found its purpose for being, within all its glory, silently
Does pose.
Never forgetting that it is wild and thorny, but still, a delicate
And gentle rose.

A. Gail Simms

The Bottle's Sojourn

I will myself that no more pain will come from my own self-disdain
From wicked rot that makes me gain applause from the weak, drunk insane

What lies the golden liquid holds inside the slender glass that molds
The evening's end in full remorse when sunlight wakes the senses' course

How many morns must find me so - a wretch, a witch, a mad one - no!
"No more!" I say with strong resound, just like the morn before I found

That likewise rum, brandy and gin are equal when it comes to win
So now, my final wicked vice, I have declared you put on ice

Away with you the battering brew that leaves a light of sickly hue
Upon my bed and countenance, not hardly the intent romance

'Tis sad the soul can be so weak to lose all its defenses meek
When once again the evening calls I'll curse the ghost of alcohol

Renais Sance

Dark Eyes

Dark, stone eyes stare down
    from a pain stricken body.
His head hanging from a limp nape.
Gasping for air
    only to receive a shallow breath.

Laughter and scorn
    heard all around.
Prayer and mourn
    heard on the ground.
If only his wounds would heal.

Arms outstretched, tearing his muscles apart.
Blood dripping from his feet and hands.
Struggling to exhale the stale oxygen
    which has invaded his lungs.

One lonely, single tear in his kind,
    yet fearful eye.
Speaks of prayers to die.
As he takes his last painful breath.
He forgives his accuser
    and bows to his death.

Samantha Goreham

Rise Up

Rise up young black woman
For you're not slow or dumb
Rise up young black woman
For your work is not yet done
Rise up gently and lift your head
Above the highest tree top
Spread your strong broad wings
Start to fly, never look back, never stop
Remember your mother in her wise years
Remember her when she wiped your tears
Take strength and courage
Never fist-fight, always flee
Stay strong and proud
Don't cry on your knees
For winners never quit
And losers always whine
But strong young black women
Keep their heritage as their sign
So rise up young black woman rise up fast, rise up now
Don't worry and don't fret always keep God under your brow!

Tara L. Hamilton

Nature's Motivating Gift

My hunger doth speak so loud and clear
For what which eyes may always see,
When closely surrounded by Nature's protective arms
We absorb a way of life forever to be.

Just fishing alongside a beauty clear lake
The colorful ducks so widely awake,
Such a charming sight cause a deep inner peace
You raise your eyes, hoping it will never cease.

Then whipped-cream clouds came sailing along
Those varied shapes of beauty holding hands in parts,
They speak to each other, "Let us stay together
For we may bless all humans, our image in their hearts."

Having felt this price gift from our unique-shaped benefactors
We say a prayer that we may always be,
Ready and willing to aid each person in our lives
To know about this blessing, which every eye should see.

Victor L. Hart

Relationship Reduced/He Pulled Away

The instant my eyes located him, seclusion was my fright.
For what purpose with him did I slum on that long, lonely night?
Fretfully, I knew it was he who pulled away,
And on that evening we did not again together lay.
While he sat next to me in that quiet place,
I longed to gently kiss his smooth, chocolate face.
The long, beautiful body emitted feelings of unconcern.
Of all lessons, 'twas this one I did not want to learn.
What was it that made him behave like this?
These wounds could not be healed with so much as a tender kiss.

Doth not this precious Lamb feel the need for my care?
Much more we could enjoy, if only he would dare.
Surely, we are blessings to one another.
In time, it is the true feelings we shall uncover.
For we must soon learn to share.
Perhaps, my pain of his love unrequited he aims to spare.
How has this happened on today?
Oh, saddened was I when he pulled away!
Many times before have I been confused,
But I now realize this is a relationship reduced.

Tamela Y. Nichols

"When You Left"

When you use to leave every morning
for the market in the red '76 Ford pickup I,
innocently, assumed you would always return.
　　Return to the farmhouse you built for Mom and me
　　　and the fields you fed us from.
　　Return to teach me how to ride a two-wheeler and
　　　walk me to the bus stop for school.
　　Return to see me dressed for prom and watch me
　　　graduate in cap and gown.
　　Return to walk me down the aisle and play with
　　　your grandchildren on your knee.
　　Return to rock the warm afternoons away with Mom
　　　for better or worse.
The sun would rise and then set
with all my childish wishes
that you'd come home.

　　Today,
I wake to lay Mom to rest with an empty
plot next to her.

K. A. Mossey

Tears Of Life

There is not one star in the sky tonight,
　　For my heart was stolen by the one I truly love.
In ways I'm glad they're gone,
　　But in others I wish they were here to help me along.
It just seems too upsetting to end.
　　To end with no more love to share.

The night is filled with cold wet rain,
　　Or is it just my tears flowing down?
The rest of my life just flowing down my face.
　　Away to a hole where all my broken feelings lay.

One day when my life comes to its end,
　　I hope you remember:
I had a lot of love in my heart,
　　But the stars disappeared it started to rain,
Or was it my tears,
　　The cold and lonely tears of life?

Rebecca Yarborough

When I Pass Away

When I pass away don't cry for me,
For I've seen life from every degree.
There were days that were boring and long.
There were perfect days where nothing could go wrong.
I've seen times when I doubted myself.
Other times when I sought to help.

When I pass away don't cry for me,
For I'm tired of the worlds endless greed.
I'm one small person, burdened and over worked.
Tired of loneliness, fighting and being hurt.
There were happy days when love and laughter was everywhere.
I could do anything, I was strong and free from care.

When I pass away don't cry for me,
For I'm with nature, the land and sea.
I'm not suffering from anymore pain or disease.
I'll pray to God to guide my children and family.
Show them that life is a borrowed gift that came for free.
Also, show them that love and peace are all they need.

Susan Paquette

Don't Grieve For Me

Don't grieve for me when I reach the end of life's road.
For it is I who rejoice 'ore the shedding of life's heavy load.
I have lived with the pain, felt the fleeting moments of glee.
It's time to move on where my soul can drift free.

Don't grieve for me when my time comes to enter that beautiful
　　city of love.
There I will be with family and friends where time is forgotten
　　and life never ends.
I will sense the protection of God's gentle hand as He proudly
　　observes all He commands.

Don't grieve for me when the autumn of life draws near.
And I feel the chill of death in the air.
For I have been loved like few men will know.
With her love sealed in my memory, I'm willing to go...

R. C. Cornwell

The Day

Let's you and me go down to the sea,
　　down to the sea and be gay;
squishing our toes and scrunching our nose
　　and whiling the hours away.
You and me, down to the sea,
　　holding nothing at bay;
the warm sea air, the breeze in our hair,
　　and us with the day to play.

Victoria True

A Room For You

I write in blood for that's all the ink they'll let me use.
For I sit in an empty room all padded and white too.
I'm writing this letter only to inform you.
If you have any tears shed them and be through.
For this letter will definitely make you blue.
I sit in this room because of people like you.
You people have no heart or soul or no imagination
    when life take its toll.
You saw me talking to no one you knew.
You assumed that I was crazy and had nothing to do
So you gave me some friends only people that you knew.
And they gave me this room all padded and nice too.
Go ahead and cry Boo-who, Boo-who.
For I am writing to tell you.
My new friends and I are coming and we have a room just for you.

Pchernavia T. Muhammad

The Judge

I try to run to darkness and hope that he doesn't find me
For I have disobeyed his wishes, his orders, his commands.
There is nothing I can do, for he can see the shadows
There is nothing I can do, I am shrouded in his hands.

At a tug I can be pulled away into death or into torture
Of them I cannot choose upon, his whim is what's decided.
So I sit here all alone, curiosity plagues my mind
And now you bear the pain I have, for in you I have confided.

Raneath Nor

Untitled

I was born into a world of confusion,
for at times it feels like an illusion.
The man who is supposed to be my father does not even
acknowledge that I'm alive,
if we were on the same street he'd pass me by.
It is weird that I have so much hatred for someone I never met,
I guess it's all the memories without him I cannot forget.
In all of the years that I have been alive,
only once have I talked to that guy.
For when we talked I felt anger,
for someone who thinks that he is my dad-
to me is just another stranger.

Precious Moore

The Women Of Anchorage

Men float across waters as if resilient-
Following only their innate male instincts,
They look for lands to conquer and call theirs.

I am dependent upon at the height of their
discoveries-
Plummeting beneath a facade,
They trust my hold is firm, but yielding.

Vessels crash upon my rocks and bows break-
Falling from their cradles of weakness,
They settle into my steadfast arms.

I am the shore to which they drift-
Seeking blanketed waves of security,
They emigrate to my banks like refugees.

Teresha Freckleton

Remember How To Fly

Once there was a girl who thought she could
Fly. As she got older she
began to Wish she could fly, and became Envious
Of the birds in the sky; oh, how she
Wanted to fly!

But there came a time when she forgot that she
Used to think She could fly,
Or even that she Wished, or Wanted to fly, or that
She dreamed of flying in bed at night.

This girl was now a woman, and at times in her Life
Would feel as if she were forgetting
Something, perhaps she had left something along the
Way? She would think back to her girlhood
And wonder what It was she now missed. The Woman lay
Down in a field of tall golden flowers,
And began to listen And to remember.

And she learned to be Still among the tall golden
Flowers. She was free at that moment.
Like the birds high above. She had remembered how
To fly.

Rebecca Joy Johnson

Time Train

The distant whistle of a train
Floats through the air like ... time alone.
Pleasure masquerades as pain
As we reap what we have sown.

What is it that we hope to gain
As we get older and think we've grown?
The mirror shows us stress and strain
And all the while we should have known.

Indifference cries out we're vain;
I wonder where the dove has flown.
When grief falls on us like rain
Perhaps we will hear what the horn has blown.

Sarah Smalley

Wisps

Wisps of blue and gray mist,
floating, swirling all around:
as I stood looking out over the sea,
or instead,
was it the sea, staring back at me,?

Clouds so close to the ground,
as they moved so gently by,
caressed by a wind that seemed to be,
rather indiscriminately shy!

Cautiously, I reached out to touch this wisp,
this swirling haze of blue and gray mist,
And with a blur of recognition, I said,
"I know you,"
"That's right," she said,
I'm your dreams, your memories, and time,
Thank you she said,
and she gave me a kiss,
Suddenly, I was taken away,
in the swirling blue and gray mist,
WISP!

Russell D. Nolen

My Deaf Child

You are so quiet, so unmoving there,
Fixed on flitting bird singing mid-air.
My anguished thoughts bare sorrow and fear,
"No soaring song yours, but silence drear,
Yours only the mumble, or the roar
Of reverberating hammer and closing door."
And then I see in your shining grey eyes,
A rapt look of wonder that makes me wise:
The bright-feathered head and glissando of wing
Are more than enough to make your heart sing.

Ruth P. Whiteside

Charlie

Whose life spoke more eloquently than these words which he could never hear!
A silent snowflake from high above
Fell to mother so far below,
Through Springtime was warmed with tender love,
Transforming the quiet lain snow.

The burbling brook raced through the meadows of life,
For a short Summer it would roam,
Forging its bed, ever rushing ahead,
Onward toward eternal home.

The waves deafening roar as they pound the shore
River embraced by undying sea,
The body submerges, its spirit emerges
Unfettered... finally free!
The silent mist is blown away
By ocean breezes kind,
The silvery ray, through the Fall could not stay,
Left Winter's snow to those behind.

The path of its stream has etched the ground,
Proven passage for fresh formed frost,
The continuum of life, a cycle come round,
Eternal tracing for souls never lost.

Roger Gaeckler

WHY DO I DESPAIR?

WHY DO I DESPAIR? SHOULD I EVEN CARE?
Fathers, Brothers, Uncles and Cousins,
Fought in World Wars I and II.
Then were sent to Korea too.
We went to Viet Nam.
Then they sent us to fight Saddam.
When we died, many people did not care.
Now, when we ask to be treated fair,
We are told it will take more time
Before society is willing to share.

WHY DO I DESPAIR? SHOULD I EVEN CARE?
I worked very hard, only to be taken advantage of,
By employers who took this as a way to push and shove.
When I tried to assimilate
All you showed was mistrust and hate.

WHY, SHOULD I CARE? OR EVEN DESPAIR?
I will not go away! I am here to stay!
So those of you who will not treat us fair
Must now worry and despair.
Will we be like you? Have you taught us to hate and discriminate too?

Tomas Cisneros

"Circle Of Time"

Fallen autumn leaves blow in the wind
Faithless lovers slowly become distant friends.

Precious memories sorted, then stored safely away
Sacred yet unshared, strength for lonely day.

Children laugh and grow then drift apart
Away from your world but never your heart

Separate roads traveled each at its own bend
One circle of time over while another begins

William B. Simmons

Your Eyes

I peer across a crowded room into your eyes...
Eyes that see into the depths of my soul,
Eyes that see the secrets I have chosen to hide,
Eyes that see what no other eyes have seen or will see.

Your glances stir within me emotions long forgotten...
Emotions so strong, they shake me to my very core,
Emotions deep, longing and uncertain,
Emotions of desire, bewilderment, abhorrence and fear.

Your eyes, haunting, clandestine, searing...

Sheila Hightower Allen

You Are There

You are there
everywhere, in everything.
In the spring,
Nature singing, flowers in bloom.

In the summer,
When the heat is sultry,
The moonlit nights and starry skies,
The sea with its calmness, wakes and waves.

In the fall,
With the leaves falling and nature
entering a long awaited rest.

In the winter,
Temperatures dropping, snow falling.
But you are there and you light
up my life.

Wylodine Crawford

Untitled

The rows of the chairs in the school room are straight
everything is in its place except for your imagination—
where is it when you need it?
Write a poem or an essay the figure says
confusion says hello, thoughts say goodbye
Wait come back I need you,
I need you.
What to write, when no ideas enter your mind. Looking around
you see everyone working hard. Their imagination and
inspiration must have stayed, mine left
I want it back, when do I get it back?
Will looking around the room trigger it?
The students, the teacher, the shelves, the windows
Where is it hiding—
ideas suddenly come rushing
Pop! It scared me when it came back.
Where was it, don't leave again.
All I know is it will be with me somewhere forever.

S. Pianowski

Endings

Whenever good relationships come to an end,
Everyone loses...and nobody wins.
For, always there are times which were good,
Times we would relive if only we could!

I broke my own stalwart golden rule...
Gave the gift I treasure most of you.
Something of me which was no small part...
I gave you my loving but fragile heart!

With laughter, love and fun you filled my days,
And oh, how I wished that you would stay!
I felt so happy and so full of life!
For a short time, living wasn't all strife.

I do not see you now and all I hear,
Are echoes of all I held so close and dear.
Tears are safety valves and though I try,
I cannot laugh, but neither can I cry!

Why do we hurt each other and try to deceive,
When there's so little time, so little to believe?
When did love's meaning become so unclear,
When love is the soul reason for why we are here?

Patsy Carr

Your Eyes

As though looking through crystal windows, your soul shows clearly
Every thought, every desire given away without a word
Your eyes, bring feelings long ago forgotten
Your deep penetrating gaze, stirs the butterflies in my stomach
My heart, lodged in my throat, beats and fast
The silence is sweet, leaving open every pore to sense
    what you long for
Your eyes empower me, giving confidence previously unknown
Our souls intertwine seeming to dance unfolding images of future times
My cheeks flush, yet I cannot look away, for I could spend a
    lifetime lost...in Your Eyes.

Rikki M. Culley

Beauty Of The Horizon

The sky was so blue this morning.
Even the little white clouds didn't dare float by,
To blot the wonderful clearness
Of that picture in the sky.

Even the morning breezes
That throw the clouds in disarray,
Made a promise to each other
That they would stay away.

But the eagle dared to venture
With the spread of his great wings,
To break up that beautiful picture
That the cloudless sky brings.

Soaring across the blue
His dark wings seemed to hide the sun,
Suddenly, the cloudless sky
And the eagle became one.

What a fabulous scene!
What great power!
The sky and the eagle mastered
At this early morning hour.

Virginia Greening

"Vacancy"

Do you want to put an end to all of the injustice in your life?
Erase the hatred, violence and strife?
Worries, problems with debt?
End every sickness war and threat?
No need to keep trying put it to rest!
Fill our vacancy - we have life's best!
Join the chosen few, they tried like you.
Men, women and children, too.
Black, white, red are welcome here.
No jealousy, no panic, no fear!
Many vacancies still exist
to enter you must do just this
your must die and death will free your soul

Vacancies for young or old
Black or white, enter day or night

Patricia Zafuto

Shadows

There is something strange about shadows. Shadows are the great equalizer. You can do anything with a shadow. The shadow of a feather is just as flexible as the shadow of a cold steel bar. And the more intangible the object, the stronger the shadow. People who miss a departed loved one will often tell you that, when they look back at what they miss most about that person, many times they will describe some strange quirk, a small gesture, like the raising of an eyebrow, or a certain mannerism, like getting mad and putting their hands on their hips. The strongest shadow of all, however, is the shadow of love. Love itself is completely intangible. It has a different meaning for every individual. Yet, people build their lives around it and rest their hopes and dreams in it. The shadow of love thereby becomes their greatest burden. Those hopes become iron weights and those dreams make up the links of a chain. The structure of their lives becomes a net of steel that binds them up and drags them to the bottom of self-pity. But, as shadows, you cannot grab the chains to throw them off. They simply coil around you and squeeze, squeeze until your heart is forced from your body. Unless you can manipulate the object that casts the shadow, those chains will find you. Those chains have no mercy. They do not care how you feel. Misery loves company.

Walt Vonau Jr.

Unspoken

To thee I speak of yet not told
entwined, but with control, enmeshed
I long to feel your silken flesh
you are the one I love to hold

Spinning tightly, to thee caress
covered so quite fully with crystal spheres of dew
like blades of prairie grasses, so vast and yet so few
thoust depthen beauty with which I'm blessed

Come 'ere morning, filing but a single plane
A splendor, streaking out through bronzen hair
speaking softly, streaming onward soft and fair
A realm of simple solitude which desires are not inane

Splashes of love's eternal, sweet pastels
dreaming of no other one or thing
life's hope, with no blanketing of darkness, sings
deep within thine soul this passion swells

Rich hearkening, from myself, I pour out to thy heart
capture deep serenity and hold passion not at bay
keep not compromise provoked this and each true day
carry on 'side me, my love, with live hope we shall not part....

K. Eric Long

"Thank You Soldiers"

The sound of violence
echoes in the winds of change
As many soldiers lay in fear
The last explosion was at close range
Soldiers feel death creeping near.
Thousands of boys forced into manhood,
not wanting to go, but knowing they should.
With each passing second, silently they'd pray
"Dear God, let us live to see another day".
Proudly so many of our soldiers die,
Their cherished loved ones left behind to cry.
With pride I fly my flag of red and white and blue.
With honor and dignity my flag reigns true.
Nothing in this world can repay them,
for what they have done for me.
But even so, I'd like to say,
Thank you soldiers.....
I'm free!!!

Tiffany-Ann Hinterman

My Children

My children are very amazing to me.
Each child has his own personality.
Even two brothers from the same family,
Are as different as they can possibly be.

One is very loving and likes to be hugged.
The other will wipe off your kisses,
Then throw them on the rug.

One is very friendly and smiles at everyone he sees.
The other is shy and behind his mother's legs he'll flee.

One will cooperate and do as he's asked,
The other will protest every little task.

One likes to sing out Loud as he can.
The other will just grin and dance like a little man.

Each has their own strengths and their own unique ways.
But they both need to be praised each and every day.

Still they have something in common with every child you'll see.
They all need to be loved unconditionally.

Pamela Butler Bridgers

On That Day

The Lord has helped me and showed me the way; he has taken me through
 each and every day.
He will lead me forever, by my hand; For on His word I will always stand.
Then the day will come when He stands on a cloud and will call my
 name so very loud.
My name will be called and how happy I will be to live with my Lord
 for eternity.
Tears of joy will go astray for I will be gone ON THAT DAY.

I love you so much, I want you to know; but with me to glory I want you
 to go.
If you will just think of the Son He sent and know He loves you and
 wants you to repent.
Just examine your heart and I am sure you will find that you need the
 Lord while there is still time.
The devil is fighting so very hard to make you stay just the way you are.
So turn away and let a new life begin for the Lord is there, just let Him in.

For the day of Judgment is yet to be but I want you to be ready and go
 with me.
First you must throw all things away and pick up the cross and there
 you must stay.
For the time is coming, just wait and see.
Then you will say "What about me?"
The Lord will look and His head will nod and say "My child, I knew you not."
A time of sorrow this will be for someone I love can not go with me
So a question I ask and prayers I pray: "Will you go with me
 "ON THAT DAY?"

Yvonne Christiansen

Trails

One sunny autumn afternoon my feet chanced to stray
Down an old Indian trail, not so far away
A quiet grassy nook, beside a clear little stream
I tarry awhile just to reminisce and dream
On a stump a chipmunk frisks gaily about
And I'm roused from my reverie by a crow's raucous shout
The sun in the west was sinking low
Long shadows on the trail reminds me I must go
I pause again, just to reminisce once more
And I seem to be standing between two open doors
One takes me back down the trails of yesteryear
The other leads on, we never know where.

Reba L. Sparks

Untitled

If you wish to give me flowers, watch me enjoy their beauty today
Don't wait to share their fragrance on the day I pass away.

If you wish to give me your smile, let me be your happiness today
Don't shed sad tears for me the day I pass away.

If you love me and care for me, then express it to me now my dear
for tomorrow's dawn may come and one of us may not be here.

Please embrace me now and promise forever.
Share today with me as we live, take me not for granted my love
for one day I may not be with you unconditionally to give.

Together in this life with you is a dream come true today,
please give me your heart forever, from now until the day I pass away.

Wendy Fountain

Take Time

Love me until the day you die
Don't ever hurt me or make me cry
Hold me tight and close to you
Show me that what you say is true
Don't ever go far away from me
Through patience the real you I see
Tell me endlessly how you really feel
This time I want my dreams to be real
Your courage and touch make me bold
I'll be here now and forever to hold
Don't feed me pathetic stories and lies
You're not someone I could ever despise
Prove to me time and again that you care
Please tell me the rest of our lives are to share.

Sarah Mitchell

Country Dream

I, like the city and its fun, but I, love the country, when day is done.
To look across the fields and see, all mother nature bestowed upon me.
To walk down a shady lane, that leads to a babbling brook.
Sit beneath an old maple tree, and opened up a book.
The sunrise in the morning, the starry moonlit nights,
The ever-changing seasons, my feathered friends in flight.
There is no place like the country, to lose one's self in thought.
Its solitude and beauty, in the city can't be bought.
I, nestle in my bed each night, at the end of a lovely day,
And listen to the silence, which has so much to say.
Oh, God bless the good country life...

F. C. La-Moreaux

Desperation Or Education?

All the strife in the life of a factory rat,
Doin' this and doin' that.
Drains your brains to exasperation,
Due to lack of mental stimulation.

Eight hours becomes an eternal duration,
Building each car to its specification.
Shift priority by seniority and classification,
Is a major source of aggravation.

The foreman yelling, "Production! Acceleration!"
We slow down the line in retaliation.
Receiving results of our procrastination...
Three days off with no compensation.

Having little interest or motivation,
We escape boredom with our imagination.
It becomes harder to avoid the constant temptation,
Of drug and liquor intoxication.

We look forward to a short vacation,
That saves us from deterioration.
With opportunities abundant in our great nation,
Be wise and seek an education.

Patricia S. Pennington

The Battlefield

The Battlefield
Does the War Ever Stop?

The echo of cries deep inside
The screams of survival that go unheard
Does the war ever stop?

Who is the enemy?
They hide, wait and attack
They mask themselves in an array of costumes
Does the war ever stop?

Awake and Pray...Awake and Pray...Awake and Pray
Seek The Light
You were told all of your life
So you pray and seek The Light
But, the war doesn't ever seem to stop!

When you've tried..and tried..and tried
The mind is tired and body weak
Bullets of emotional distraught
Rip the heart apart
Does this war ever stop....?

Maybe on another side!!!

Shirley Brown-Gatling

A Letter To Jesus

Dear Jesus I'm a sinner shall I hide my face
Do you shouldn't my son because of my grace
But Jesus I scoffed and I turned away
It's oh my son the devil led you astray
No Jesus I can't because I am lost
You're not my son, my blood she paid the cost
What if I fail and become untrue
Just trust in me and I'll see you through
Jesus love you and give you my life
Thank you my son now come be my wife

William A. Chaplin

Decisions

A fork in the road, what to decide
Do you lock up the pain that is burning inside
A light in the distance can't reach a star
Sorrow that is buried too deep and too far
A vision of peace lights up the night sky
Refusing to live in what must be a lie
Drifting on waves where the sea never ends
Floating in silence where a heart never mends
The future looks dim through the glow of the past
You learn from experience that nothing can last
One understands, while another is lost
Most things in life have too high of a cost
Living in a world that is merely a game
Now it's only the wind that can whisper your name

Sasha Silverwood

Feelings

I often wonder what love is, please tell me.
Do we look inside ourselves or is it just feelings?
Is it something we feel or something we see?

Perhaps, love could be our every day dealings.

Is this feeling an emotional release?
Does it have a sound or is it just within our heart?
I know these feelings will only increase,
When some feelings go away will other ones start?

Is love the first smile on your new born baby's face?
Or is it how you feel when your all dressed in lace.

When real love comes your way
Is there really anything we can do or say?
This must be a test to see if we really know how to play
Because we hope these feelings will never go away.

For some reason I always know when you are near
The warmth I feel all over, is not the same as my brother
It makes me shed a tear,
Because we both are with another.

Rena K. Lionetti

Do A Little Kindness!

Do a little kindness, to wash away some sadness;
Do a little kindness, it brings a little happiness;
Show someone you care,
Let them see love everywhere.

Do a little kindness, let the world know it exists;
Do a little kindness, show them, and insist
Do it, though sometimes it may be hard,
I know you will get your reward.

Do a little kindness, do it at your best;
Do a little kindness, regardless of the test;
Though you might be penniless,
Lend a helping hand, if you can.

Do a little kindness, you've got to do it proud;
Do a little kindness, at home and abroad;
Life has its season and kindness is the reason,
Show some brother-hood, do some good.

Shirley E. Cameron

Untitled

Once upon a time I used to be happy.
But everything in my life has changed now.
Each moment has become an endless maze of confusion.
All thoughts are chaos.
Events idly pass by without a second glance.
Every last hope dwindles away as realization becomes reality.
Wisdom grows little by little everyday.
Young innocence is lost as life teaches yet another hard lesson.

Sarah Haas

Amy

I wasn't looking but you found me.
Didn't care from afar, but in your eyes I could see
the girl I wanted to know.

We started talking and just couldn't stop. Over a chili
steak and a soda pop, the girl, I started to know.

Your birthday at durango, hockey on the pond, maybe I was dreaming,
but I thought I felt the bond of friendship that would grow

You said you needed time to make sure we were right. I gave you
what you asked for and tried with all my might, not too fast to go.

You said that you were ready to trust I was sincere. We shared
the touch of love, laughter and a tear. My heart was beating so.

Suddenly it was all wrong; you had no time for me. We never fought,
we got along, just how could this be? You broke my heart, you know.

You have no time to share, your schedule is full,
and I'm not sure how much you care,
your thoughts are a tooth to pull but I don't want you to go

You have yours and I've got mine. Yes, I understand.
but when we both have the time, I'd like to hold your hand.
I love you...there, I said so.

Tom Grindem

"The Proposal"

"Where did you come from?" He asked of his love.
"Did you wing past the stars and the heavens above?"
"Are you here to caress me and keep me from harm,
to wrap your warmth round me with soft gentle arms?"

"Will you walk with me, Darling, through the sunlight of day?
"In the twilight of evening, by my side will you lay,
and love me and keep me, till death do us part?"
"Will you take me by hand, and give me your heart?"

She smiled at him softly and reached out her hand,
to brush back the soft curls, that fell strand by strand,
about the bronzed face of this man, sweet and dear,
her heart filled with words, that he longed to hear.

She drew him into her, pressed his head to her breast.
"Forever, my Darling, near my heart, you will rest."

W. F. Jones

Untitled

I sat down last night to write a poem.

I didn't think about voice speaker tone
Diction imagery figures of speech similes
Metaphors symbolism allegory syntax
Sound rhyme alliterationassonance
Consonanceeuphonymetonymyanachronisms
Onomatopoeiarhythmmeterrhymestructure
Closedformopenformortheme

I just sat down

And wrote a poem.

Whitehead

A Lesson About The Beach

The beach is very, very fun
But you must watch out for the sun
The sun may harm in many ways
The most is skin cancer and sunburn, these days
We all love the water, it is very deep
In the water, jelly fish creep
The sand is hot, under the skies
Don't throw the sand! It may get in your eyes
I hope you liked my lesson about the beach
It was one lesson I had to teach!

Sarah Olinde

Desire Not

Love and cherish what is given.
Derive pleasure from what you possess.
Ask not, for anything more,
For you may have had much less.

Never crave for the impossible.
Never ever keep wanting.
Desire should be kept aside,
Else it'll always keep taunting.

"Come", says desire, "Let me inside thee."
"No", should always be the answer.
For, only then will you be free
Of human nature's vicious canker.

"Happiness, where art thou?"
"With you, though so unseen.
Discard desire and you will find,
That is where I've always been."

Shireen A. Lobo

Bitter Cakes

Stillborn love.
Deep beneath the pain flows free,
the smiles on her face
melt and run
through the sieve which was a heart.
Yesterdays are gone forever;
the brief time we had has abandoned me.
Hope and dreams are just a memory
of embraces shared and promises made,
all broken,
the shards smashed to dust - like flour,
mixed with salty tears
into batter for unpalatable cakes.
Try to eat one and choke on the bitterness.
No sweet words like syrup
could change the sardonic nature of this fool's dish.
Cast it away.

Steven B. Pavelsky

Death

You lie awake in the hospital room.
Death trying to weave you in its dark loom.
Grasping hands so fine and nimble.
And to the master of death it is so simple.
But to us it is to feel.
Seeing our loved ones caught by a reel.
Sweat over their face.
There lips cracked and dried.
So much agony from trying to stay alive.
The doctor can not find the weakness.
As their mind is filled with bleakness.
The monitor screeches high and fine
The zig zags go to a straight line.
The doctors leave the room.
Your heart is filled with doom.
Such a life planned ahead.
But now he is dead.

Truly Render

You Touched My Heart, Little One

Did you turn my world upside down
By giving me an angel resembling a clown?
Perhaps it was a dandelion, or something crooked, not new.
Tell me little child, what did you do?
Nevertheless, it was a dear sweet sight to me.
For you were, indeed, so beautiful don't you see?
You never knew you gave me everything, little tot.
You had little to give, yet you gave a lot!

Pat Johnson

Feelings Upon Others

We see the human complexion of those we pass
day by day, as we compare others as we see of ourself
Wanting thought we wish to think refusing to
come to our minds as we refuse the
consequences of what we do
As we feel the spirit of health our problems
seem to fall into our own hands, as we see
open filled souls upon close hearted bodies,
though we have the outcast of another as we
seem to feel through out our life's as only one
can know.

Susanna Kvaraitis

Call An Angel

Cry for me Angel, shed me a tear,
Cry for me softly, so no one will hear.
Stay with me Angel, I'm so far from home,
Stand with me Angel, for I stand alone.

Thunder is rumbling, a storm is near,
Hold me Angel, rid me of fear.
Guide me sweet Angel, for I am lost,
My soul is weary, at the edge of the Dark.

Sing to me Angel, sing of the Light,
A song so soft, in this darkest of nights.
I long to go home, I've forgotten the way,
Walk with me Angel, into the day.

Susan J. Lieber

One Wild Red Rose

You remind me of an early morning sunrise
creeping over white snow capped mountains on a clear blue sky,
as I look down upon a green untouched valley
covered in dew and mist
I see one wild red rose that stands alone,
wild and yet soft and gentle.
Your beauty is like this one red rose that stands alone,
your beauty is one-of-a-kind, different from all the rest,
young, innocent and fresh.
If I could describe beauty, I would be describing you.

Rodney D. Isturis

Ever Slow

Hungry eyes shine and move ever slow
Creating ripples for moon's silver glow
That touches the water they glide underneath
In search of a prize for their merciless teeth
Two stand above them on pilings and planks
Venturing out from lake's edges and banks
Their hands intertwine as they move ever slow
Over crumbling boards through moon's silver glow
Under dark heavy skies in a threatening place
He speaks to her gently and touches her face
And what of the rain easing down to a mist
They rode out the storm as they eagerly kissed
When just underneath on moon's silver glow
Hungry eyes shine and move ever slow

Robin R. Kyle

Rainbow And Balloons

The misty day is transformed into beautiful dream scenes,
    Created by soaring spring showers sending, participated.
Moving and dancing colors hurled from cosmic light beams,
    So vividly painted, can neither be hid nor eradicated.

How still is the quiet after the rains dancing end when,
    Euphoric birdies suddenly sing sweet symphonic songs.
Tirelessly, the last golden hue of the day steadfastly tends,
    The gracefully arching rainbow stretching serenely sailing along.

Balloons dancing joyfully; clustering colors reflecting,
    Hues of purple, green, amber, red, and yellow indigo.
Spheres alive, willful, bobbing, bouncing, ever pulling,
    To be free of grasp to greet and touch the peaceful bow.

Azim, my son, is sailing serenely across the hilly meadow,
    Pulled by collaborating cheerful colors celebrating, floating.
Colors bright beautifully beaming, determined, chasing the rainbow.
    Awesome ponderance, the guardian bow seems to smile, applauding.

Silhouetted against the golden sky, a collage of crystal colors,
    In the heavens and on the earth ever moving forward, together.
The rainbow's promise reflected and etched in my heart, joyfully adored;
    Thus, I seek its Creator to share with Him everlasting colors, forever.

E. Rachel Bazemore Donawa

Nature In The Country!

A Ringtail Raccoon sitting on a log.
Couldn't see the Ground Hog for the dense fog,
If he could, he could, see the Barking Dog,
or in the miry pig pen, see the Squealing Hog,
on the silver pond, see the Croaking Frog,
He couldn't see the Squawking Squirrel high
up in the tree, or see what was buzzing,
it must be a Bee, He couldn't see the
coon dog, coming after him, if he could,
I know he would, go out on a limb,
The fog now is clearing, the sun now
is bearing, the coon dog didn't see,
the raccoon that couldn't see,
the dog, for the dense fog!!

Phyllis Grimm

To Melissa

From the witchcraft hills and dour streams
Comes a soft ray of hope and light
    With silent voice calling
    She guides me to her home
    Where I bask in the blanket warmth of her being
    And the flowers sing their May song
    And the trees whisper public secrets
The stars tell me who I am
And she tells me who she wants me to be
    And the two
    Make me one

Timothy D. Arner

Mountain

Behold majestic mountain, how your peak does pierce the air,
Can you tell me why the upward thrust? Are you seeking social status there?
Is your height so more important than the foothills at your base?
While they boast a sun-drenched foliage, Ice and blizzard sting your face.
Is it really worth the effort to be highest of them all?
Have you wondered through the ages, that perhaps one day you'd fall?
Or does it serve your purpose when your coat of ice and snow,
sends sweet water in abundance to the lush green hills below?
By your serving you are humbled, for your serving are made grand.
On your example I may stumble, but you've taught me how to stand.

C. W. Mickey Foster

Entertainment

There is no creature that must not work or cannot play.
Come unto me all ye who are burdened and I shall bring you
joy and laughter, mystery and suspense, dancing and singing,
for I am Theatre, and the show must go on.
Call me by my name for I am Entertainment.
Drink of me for I am the wine press of desire.
Sing with me for I am the soul of Passion's delight.
Dance with me for I kick up the dust of time's rhythm,
and the tempo of love's passion.
Be at peace with me for I swim in equities pool in the path of
righteousness for the sake of glory, honor and love.
I am entertainment and my wine is
from the greatest vine of life
liberty and the pursuit of happiness.
Joy to the World in every season.

Paul J. Moriarty Jr.

Little Children Of Stormy Weather

Little children little children of to and fro.
Come to me, come to me, as the storm winds blow.
Come to me for I am not afraid
of the thunderous clouds.
Nor the funnels braid.
Nor of the lightning so bright
with its crackle of white.
I have rods of steel an arrow of straight
will tell you which way the wind blows
for you enter the gate.
Run to me to a shelter so deep
made of mortar and stone
and safe you will keep.
To a manger of straw so soft to the head.
No time for the house no time for the shed.
Run to me, run to me, the big barn said.

Sandra K. Braswell

Dream In A Haze

Clouds
Clouds rolling
Into a purple mist
Where dreams disappear
All love is lost.

In a cloudy purple mist
Time ceases to tick
And the burning crosses of racism extinguish
Colors collide into one nation of harmony

Rain comes not to wash societies ills
But to replenish the beautiful of the old
Temptation comes in the good
Bringing a gift of golden love
In a purple haze

Patrick Schott

The Sea

The warmth of the sun is
Beating down against the white sand.
As the waves roll up and wash away
The foot prints of where I have walked.
I walk along, the sun begins to set
Low in the sky, the sunset looks so beautiful.
The waves roll out to the sea
And my foot prints, stay in the sand.
I know that in the morning
They will be washed away.
Now there is darkness all around,
And everything is calm and asleep.

Rose Hendrick

Yellowstone

When I describe Yellowstone, this is what I see
Clouds billowy like cotton and a forest of tall Pine trees

I see mountains majestic still snowcapped in white
And the early summer moon glaring gold in the night

I see the clear mountain water rippling to streams nearby
And fish jumping midair at an unsuspecting dragonfly

I watch Old Faithful in all her glory as she gushes towards the sky
And marvel at her accuracy throughout the aeons gone by

I hear the Loon's eerie tune at the beginning of day
Watch the Eagle soaring in the sky, swoop down upon its prey

I see meadows of green with Deer and Moose grazing there
Watch Chipmunks fill their cheeks and scramble by without a care

This beauty and serenity gives you a new point of view
Clears out your mind and makes a new person of you

There is no other place that I would rather be
Than where I am today because it's special to me

The beauty of Yellowstone is so wondrous to see
And will always remain very awesome in my memory

Sue Hildreth

Anointed

Epiphany - all things hideous and real
Childhood is a kingdom where nobody dies
Molten landscapes exploding into now
Quiet grace and sun shadow smiles
Power surging beyond and more
Joyous laughter and play
The fire of blood and knowing
The seasons turn and call
The pain of knowing and loving still
Long legs and muscles strong
A woman of power, grace and guile
Puppies and windy mornings pass
The heat, the heart of all
A mare of grace and love
Take my hand - this gift I give to you
The black grandmother calls
"I anoint you"

Robin Stone

Undefined Feelings

What is this feeling, burning deep inside my breast?
Churning and turning my soul to unrest.
When memories bring secret smiles, that
give cause to relax.
Where roads so long untraveled, come to life.

Who knows of this feeling, I'm speaking of?
That gives rise to Joy in my soul.
Which causes closed minds to recoil.
Such as to change a dreary day.

I close my eyes and I think, and to whom do I feel this way?

Walking circles in the sand.

Is my life such that it is inconceivable to believe,
that this feeling I have is for me?

Yolanda E. Harris

Ode To Beauty

Created nature, receptor of your regal imprint, weak senses
can take in holy a hint; the pageant of life is what you
richly adorn still sought by all as clothing to be worn.
Sublime and pristine are your accord
your absence this life could never afford.

Smallest to largest touched by your tender grace though the heart
and soul are your true dwelling place; present in the powerful
and terrible storm you are something beyond mere form;
Also there in the soft and gentle breeze
to be recognize with the most deliberate ease.

This to be certain, you are the most inebriating drink
you can get any attention with only a subtle wink.
You are a gift give in the mystical life, for to be sure you are
love's wife. Legend has it you made a prince of the beast
it is truly your virtue not to neglect the least.

The epitome of nature's rhapsodical song for your delicate touch
we all long, the bird in flight or the deer on the run,
yes you have blessed everyone.
It is true we hearken to your call,
yet I see you have graced the feminine most of all.

Shawn Roberson

The Moth

Candle, candle burning bright
Called you from the shadows o' the night
In search of photosynthesis-type-fix
Instinctively blind; innately unaware
  Addiction has its tricks...

To want the light
  To need the light
To seek the light
  To feel the light

Candle, candle burning bright
Lovely funeral pyre in the night
Once trapped I thought I heard you scream
in vain
You saw the light concealed within the flame

Patrick S. Sonderman

Naked, She Dances

Naked, she dances, in forests of Azure
By the light of the Moon, she chases the day
Naked, she dances in wild-flowered meadows
Singing songs of the serpent, she asks me to play

She worships the garden, and kisses its splendor
She sends me her love across the pale wind
She wakes in the midnight and touches my shadow
Lying dead in my nightmare, she leads me to sin

Always, I'm waiting, to feel of her presence
Always, my love, she leaves me to die
Testing my silence, she waits in my chamber
Always, in silence, she whispers the lie

She gives breath to my sorrow and numbs my five senses
She dances 'neath trees of the forest, in vain
She tramples the flowers in meadows of sadness
Singing songs of the serpent, she asks me to play

William Young

Comparative Love

My love is strong,
But you think his is stronger.
I'm yet to figure out why,
But you still run to him.
My devotion runs through my veins,
  like a raging fire.
Burning an image of you into,
  my heart and soul.
Yet his devotion is based solely on convenience.
I realize that I can't be there physically,
  and he can.
But my love holds true,
And I know his doesn't.

Robert T. Jones

In The Mind Of A Woman

Every day, loving you was such an easy task,
but when I saw you standing there it made it hard to ask.
So afraid you'd say no, and hoping you'd say yes,
Everyone around me said I was a nervous wreck.

In the mind of a woman, standing so true,
when I say that I need you, you know that I do.
Then I start thinking, maybe I don't,
living life without you, I can't and I won't.

They told me to forget about you,
but when I said I can't,
they stared at me and laughed a while,
as I walked away.
From that day on those blue skies will forever remain gray.

In the mind of a woman, standing so true,
when I say that I need you, you know that I do.
Then I start thinking, maybe I don't,
living life without you, I can't and I won't.

Tamra Christenson

A Prayer For Our Children

My son, somewhere along the road of life, something went wrong.
But we stand not alone in our tragic hours, there are parents
near and far who suffer with us.

What is this dread disease called drugs that has come over our nation?
That is ripping at our inner hearts. What kind of plague has doomed us.

Dear God, what has happened, what greater power than you has taken
hold of our children, what greater power then you has warped our babes.

Dear God above, find us our answers before the child we once held to
our breast is no more.

We brought him into this world, we clothed and fed him. Taught him
right from wrong, educated him, taught him his religion. Gave all our love.

They know not of the love of parents, this power has given them
hatred. They know not of cleanliness, this power has doomed them to
dirt and disease. They know not of a soft tongue. This power has
made them loud and crude. They know not of prayer for in its place to
soothe them loud music rings in their ears, as their heads sway to and
fro like the African chant. . On that table lies a needle and on the
bed an unclothed girl.

Have we as parents failed, then take us Dear GOD, but give back our
youth. For they are the future of America and a hope for a new and
peaceful world of tomorrow.

Phyllis Baron

The Vision Of The Blind

Today, the sun rose, as it always does,
but today is not the same.

Instead, the sun rose, on thoughts and ideas,
that during the night became...

The result of a new perception,
of feelings, beliefs, and attitudes...

Expressed and conveyed, ironically,
in weightless words and platitudes.

Perhaps it is pride, or arrogance,
however imagined or real,

that falsely grants us a power to express,
what another must suffer or feel,

Or perhaps it is an ignorance,
of what can be done or achieved,

through the simple sharing of honest thoughts,
when another is joyful, or grieved.

Regardless, we grope for time-worn phrases,
to convey our state of mind,

and in doing so, proclaim once again,
the vision of the blind.

William L. Vasquez

My Love For Lana

Some people think a pet is just a pet,
But then my Lana they never met.
She was a bundle of love in a coat of fur,
And no one could be loved more than I loved her.
Anyone who knew us could plainly see,
That I belonged to her more than she did to me.
A pet will love you when no one else will,
So take a chance and get a thrill.
Love them back and you will see,
What a special blessing it will be.

Patricia Davis

Heaven's Introduction

I thought life's pleasures diminished with age
but that's 'til I met my sweet Megan,
how could I know that God saved the great joy
and a way to acquaint me with heaven.

I look at her face and I feel her soft form
and I know all the joy she will bring,
as far as the stress, exhaustion and strife
well that's not a grandmother's thing.

She has all that she needs to have a great life
and I know that is where my joy lies,
her mom and her dad will do all the right things
and she'll always see love in their eyes.

So I thank you dear God for this angel you sent
that brings such joy to us all,
she has given a hint of what heaven will be
and we fear not your final call.

Suzanne L. Smith

A Cry In The Dark

The room is so bright, so colorful, so cheery,
but something about it makes me feel so weary.
I can sense an unwanted feeling inside of me,
something that just won't let me speak freely.
As I walk by I can hear whispers in the air,
and I can feel the wind in my hair.
I hear cries in the night, in the cold dark night.
Sometimes I think I'll come out of the dark and into the light.
The room is an aura of the past.
The feeling is knowing at last,
That all that he did was wrong,
yet I let it go on for so long.
The sounds are my screams in the air,
one for every time he said how he really did care.
The cries are of help that I never did get,
because I always thought it was me from the first time we met.
The feeling of shame is still there,
and I still feel that nobody cares.
Why did it happen to me?
Why wouldn't God set me free?

Stephanie Lynn Roberts

Kazimiera Teresa

When I was a kid I was afraid of her
but my mother would take me there
she had a typewriter drawn on a piece of paper
and typed what my mother said
few weeks later
she would bring my new winter coat
expertly made
we laughed as she walked in her torn nightgown
candle in her hand
there was a picture of a beautiful girl in her room
I never knew who she was
she had many names
and would not respond
to a wrong name on a wrong day
once I heard her say
she was sixteen in nineteen thirty nine
she had a number
printed on her forearm
I think she is dead now.

Wojtek Migdalski

The Key

My conscious tells me that you are the one intended for me.
But I must be patient in order to see, that you are the one who holds
the right key.

My love has been given many times before,
only to be beaten, abused, deceived and more.

Forgive me my love for my lack of trust,
my past has been tainted with so many tears, if I were metal I'd rust.

My love for you comes from deep within,
a place in my heart that is free from sin.

A place that has never been touched before,
it scares me to think I might have it no more.

I know your love for me is true,
although you're quite stubborn, I will see it through.

We are two of a kind, oh love of mine,
both cautiously wondering is this the right time?

Our love for each other is so very strong,
we'll hold on to it tightly from dusk until dawn.

It is time to realize and unlock the door,
we may soon discover it is not such a chore.

This poem will end happy for us you will see,
for our love is the answer, and we two are the key.

Tamara E. Weitzel

Pineconia

Some say you can't go there,
But I go there all the time,
A land of spectacular wonder
Where trees grow tall and peaceful waters flow.

It is here where I take steps forward, not backwards.
I ride the tide, not against it,
And I move along the path that is specially designed for me.

Oh, Pineconia, sweet Pineconia,
I feel that cool autumn breeze,
And I hear the birds sing.
I smell the pine needles,
And I taste that passion for life.

Some say you can't go there,
But I go there all the time.
This land has given me my wings to soar and fly.
She builds me up, does not tear me down,
And always turns all my frowns around.
Oh, Pineconia, sweet Pineconia,
My dearest friend, take me away again and again!

Thomas Berntsen

The Room Of Gold

I'm sitting in a room of gold,
But I don't feel rich I just feel old.

Too many people have been in this room before,
It's a place of death, a place of war.

Why do people really need,
This terrible thing that we call greed?

Pretty soon I will be dead,
But greed won't get into my head.

I will not touch the gold on the floor,
I'd rather die old and poor.

Sitting in this room of gold,
I'm dying soon, it's getting cold.

Randy Barbee

I Am

I am not an American,
But I am God's child.
I come from a foreign land.
Your culture and language, I do not understand.
I want to learn. I want to belong.
For your friendship I yearn. Don't put me down when I am wrong.

I am not an American,
But I am God's child.
I have feelings just as you.
Unkind words hurt me, too.
Everything is new to me.
I will work hard. I want to be free.

I am not an American,
But I am God's child.
Together, we can learn and share
Cultures and languages from here to there.
Respect and love, we both understand.
You and I are God's children in any land.

Phyllis Roudybush

It Cannot Be Done?

They all said it cannot be done
But he with a chuckle replied
Maybe it cannot but I will be one
Who won't say so till I've tried

So he buckled right in with a trace of a grin
And if he worried, he hid it
He started to sing as he tackled the thing
That couldn't be done and he did it

So let that be a lesson to you
Just keep on trying and work it through
And you will have a richer life
Free of some of the stress and the strife

William L. Shirey

Mutt

I called Him Mutt.
But He wasn't a Mutt.
He was my best friend.
We would stay like that until the end.
But His end came before mine.
When He got sick, I felt in my heart He would be fine.
I never thought He would leave me so soon.
But He did, He left me that afternoon.
I lay awake at night and I try not to cry.
And the only thing I can think is why God, why?
Why would you take from me the best friend I ever knew?
There are so many things we had left to do.
I get mad at Him for leaving so suddenly.
And then I think, is He mad at me?
I can't help but wonder if I gave Him enough love.
Lately, that is the only thing I can think of.
We did a lot together by each other's side.
Now I'm beginning to realize that His spirit never died.
He is still with me watching over me like a guardian angel.
Mutt, I promise I'll always love you. I promise I always will.

Staci Smith

Alcohol God

My alcohol God satisfies for the moment,
But does not erase the pain
So I come back to worship again
Only when I am in a dead stupor
Have I had enough
And I can always drink when I awake
My senses leave me and I just want to take
I've sold my family and my soul
For that escape
I bow down to my alcohol God to erase it all
They say, "When I hit bottom, I'll finally quit"
I've kissed death and lost friends
I've known many prison walls
And destroyed vehicles and lives
I've caused heartache and pain
Alcohol has taken everything
Alcohol has staked its claim
And I am the only one to blame
How low do I have to sink?

...Six feet under

Pamela Adair

A Birthday Adventure

Her trip down Broadway was not by taxi,
but by imagination.

As the sweet music filled her ears,
she knew.

Her time... to excel and excite...
awe and amaze... captivate and conquer...
would come.

She knew.

As the spotlight encircled the leading lady,
Tina felt some of it capture her.

And in one marvelous moment
on the evening of her 24th birthday,
Tina was inspired to believe in
something remarkable... Herself.

Quinten Eyman

The Hourglass

Kings and queens of yesteryear,
Built stone castles to mask their fears.
On craggy hills and lonely heaths,
They crumble now where all can see.
Walls of stone with towers and moats,
They raised to quell the common man's hopes.
But change and dreams know no walls,
Like Father Time they'll conquer all.

I build grand castles with the ocean's sand,
For smiles and thanks from my fellow man.
I teach their children short and tall,
Secrets of tides and castles with walls.
Beneath the moon my castle is gone,
Sand to sand or am I wrong.
Did an eager mind that day,
Place my castle in an hourglass...this I pray.

Patrick A. Younger

Unconditional Love

My faithful friend from the start
brought joy and gladness
to my guarded heart.

Those countless days beneath the sun's rays
we'd romp amid the crashing tide.

Calm nights spent at home like a sentinel of stone,
always at watch by my side.

Through hard times immersed in doubt,
this pup could bring me out
and melt away sadness into cheer.

With a smirk or sudden laugh
my joy would surpass at a bark and tilt of the ear.

Now to look back there sometimes does lack
my attention so expected in return.

Too often passed by with a soft word to rely.
Now reflecting back, I have learned.

How I rejoice to hear that bark from so near
My dog, a guardian sent from above.

For this pup gives more to me so unreluctantly
and this is true "unconditional love".

Ron Titus

Promise

The nurturing rays of the golden springtime sun,
Brings the fragrant and enchanted meadows of promise.

Promises of love or the hopefulness of flowers.
Delicate yet courageous, hopeful against all odds.
Fragile yet valiant, whisper of flowers.
Exquisite harmony of the scented bright blue forget-me-nots.

The elegant stalks of snowqueen irises,
Lilies and lupines bloomed in a mosaic of sapphire,
Apricot, scarlet, and flame.

Daffodils and daises smile with their dazzling golden sun.
Laying upon me
With their incredible scent of such wonderful colors.

In a magnificent harmony
Perfumes of lavender, jasmine, lilac, and violet
Bring all hopes of my dreams and promises.

Tami L. Leanza

You

We so passionately kissed,
Blowing my mind
The fear ran out
Is it possible for someone so full of hate
To love someone who is willing
He filled up a hole another left
Left for me to die slowly, painfully
How can something so wrong
Have felt so right
How can the night cast a spell
But now I sit here
Night after night in tears
My arms want to hold you
Can you feel me beside you
Or are you a dream
A dream I once had and probably won't have again.
I'm falling into emotions with someone who can't feel
A killer
A silent killer
You...

Sandra K. Gifford

Sonnet Of The Battlefield

O see the maiden fair
Betwixt the landmark of sorrow and dying,
And see her uplifting care
'Tis the soldiers are all sighing,
See the helplessness of they that remain
'Twas life that walked before them woe,
But all battered now and shaken with pain,
And now in this I see no more to sow
Whatsoe'er death came to these men
Death seared their troublesome heart
To fill their empty billowed life,
And sheared them to leave forever to part.
Didst God not speak to them to obey,
- Or did He leave them with no word to say?

Rachel E. Stepp

"The Me No More"

I've lived my life behind jackets:
Behind baggy pants, and long sleeves,
Behind guarded humor, a masked opinion,
Behind the hope of all my dreams...
I've lived my life in hiding:
From ridicule, and venging critiques,
From shallow proposals, secret vendettas,
From deceitful gossip leaks...

I've lived my life through insecurity:
Looking hard for acceptance and ease,
Looking for permanent friends, and compliments,
Looking for someone to fill my needs...

I've lived my life with caution:
With spontaneity on a leash,
With persistent honest intent,
With a true yearning to succeed...

Each step I'd take to please,
Would end up feeling like a chore.
But if they ever really loved me,
They'll still love the "me no more"

Valerie Tabajonda

Our Foundation

How much history can a rock withstand,
Before it turns into a grain of sand.

If rocks could talk what would they say,
Maybe tell of a Indian who stood here one day.

Or how our soldiers died in a fight,
To defend the constitution and all of our rights.

Years have passed yet this rock still stands,
Could've it been where waters once ran.

Did one of our ancestors settle here,
Is this where they shed their blood, sweat and tears.

There's history here within this land,
Were generals have once taken command.

We'll never know of the things that took place,
For this rock does not bear its own face.

It's unable to talk and tell of its history,
So, most of the past will remain a mystery.

Tami J. Turner

Mother's Special Olympian

The doctor gave a spinal as my mother lay in bed
Before he knew what happened fluid seeped into the baby's head
Before she was born she was subject to deform
It was obvious to all she suffered a traumatic fall
Some were sympathetic others didn't care
You see her life was not theirs to bear
Quiet as can be for many many years
We only saw her heartache through her tiny, little tears
Sometimes we felt ashamed as she was the brunt of so many jokes
We tried to forgive but we hated some folks
Her brother and her sisters would always be there
We taught her about love and that we would always care
Although they said she would never read or write
She defied all the odds and put up such a fight
Little did we know gold medals she would win
And now she has become Mother's special olympian!

Rita L. Paulhus

Swim Of Life

Sunday morn, a crystal clear bay, its surface yet broken,
beckons to me
Gently rolling, the tide seeks to embrace me, to direct my course;
I go eagerly
Slow submergence would take too long, so naively, unhesitating,
I plunge head first
Shivery coolness engulfs me, cleansing, revitalizing;
my baptismal

Strong, sure strokes, shorten the distance to the opposite shore;
I feel immortal
Startled by predatory gulls, divebombing for sustenance,
my stroking flounders
Back on course, but with pace slowed, I have long passed mid-bay;
far-shore is nearing
A speedboat appears, sleek, shiny, leaving turbulent waters;
struggling, I survive

My body, near-defeat, collapses on shore, my mind is fearful,
yet, my spirit hopes for a chance to try the swim again.

Sharon M. Henderson

My Angel

As I gaze at you I see an enchanting angel from above;
Beautiful in every way and as gentle as a dove.

With skin as soft as satin and hair like delicate lace;
A perfectly gorgeous body and a porcelain-like face.

But these traits are soon forgotten as I look into your eyes;
As they seem to soothe my soul and slowly mesmerize.

I can only tell you this and only this one thing;
Every day that we are together angels spread their wings and sing.

I'll try my best to please you, I'll try with all my might;
I'll fill your day with happiness, I'll fill it with delight.

Our love is like an unbreakable bond, a lifelong secret trust;
For if you ever were to leave me my heart would lose its lust.

If you wish to do something special and I know you really do
Just come to me and say three words, the three words are I love you.

Zach Burcham

Untitled

Seasons greetings and may your year
be bright with blessings and happiness
as sun is to light.
And may all your endeavors be as sure as the wind
Knowing and flowing with faithfulness over and over again

And as you awoke each morning with a
smile on your face
Show God that you're thankful for his loving grace

As the days carry you forth in
Health, spirits and mind
Know that people love you because
you're so kind

Ronald Scales

My Mother's Philosophy

My mother had a wonderful philosophy
As to how life should be.
"Live each and every day as if your last."
After all, life goes by so fast.
"Do all the good you possibly can each day"
For everyone who comes your way.
"Have all the joy you can"
As you share with every man.
"For it well may be the last"
You are unable to change the past.

Sylvia S. Kirkman

The Walk

There they were walking hand in hand.
Bare feet leaving tracks in the sand.
Ocean breeze blowing through their hair and across their skin.
Waves gently serenading the dance with in.
A giggle, a look, a smile, and a touch.
The sun shines warmly relaxing them much.
Love is a seed which will sprout and grow.
But will it last, does anyone know?
The hustle and bustle and worldly demands.
Will pull you apart if you won't take a stand.
The two are now one and will be forever.
Because they decided to spend time together.

Rick White

Episode

To the majestic mountains
Back down and up again I envisioned multitudes of angels around me
Protecting as the Great One tends to me
Keen is the sense of smell and my hearing becomes within
Taking in the earthy and burning sensations that mysteriously calm me
Chosen moments that I sat by and set fire to articles, some meaningful
Others not, it must be winter, but yet, I don't feel the cold.

This living in different dimensions
Where it may be possible to see an apple as an orange
And what seems to be one thing I dream to be another
Unless they have ever felt the rushing in their heads, they cannot have
Experienced the exhilaration nor have felt the panic with the sorrow.
In his desperation they convinced my loved one that help must be sought
He could not chance that I would return this time from where I hid.
Later I was told that all episodes are not the same, I could be violent
My convictions tell me differently that I can only love
For swollen am I with my God whose breath I breathe
Frightened am I; how I feel this must be coming to an end
This manic episode; to the wind I gave no care.. over; it is over till again...

Teresa L. Haintel

Peace And Tranquillity

While sitting at the edge of a quiet lake
   awaiting the tug from a fish on my hook,
I lie back and gaze at the moving sky
   full of billowy clouds - gently drifting by.
Their images change as they move with the breeze
   and the leaves gently rustle atop of the trees.
Beyond the white images, the sky is quite blue.
It separates the clouds as it tries to peak through.
"I wonder," I thought, "Does the sky ever end?"
"Does the light ever stop and a darkness begin?"
"Will this peace and tranquillity ever be shared
   with all peoples on earth...does anyone care?"
I can only hope and pray that it will
   before it's too late and ALL is dead-still.
All living things need understanding and love
   and it starts with belief in You, God, up above.

Sylvia L. Harbison

The Water Romances Me

The water romances me
As I glide across it like a fish;
warm, fresh, I love to feel its movements with my every stroke.

I feel its rhythm, so graceful and calming to my soul.
This place is so peaceful, it puts my soul at ease,
as I glide across the beauty of God's handy work.

I want it to surround me for an eternity.
With every stroke I feel its splendor,
like a song well sang or the rhythm of well written poem;

The water romances me

Valerie Ruth Cooper

Jesus Is A Friend Of Mine

Nearly two thousand years ago
At a place called Bethlehem,
The Lord of Heaven came down below
To save all who would believe in Him.

He walked the earth as mortal man,
Living among us for a time,
Carrying out His Father's plan,
Guiltless of any sin or crime.

Yet there were those who feared His purpose,
And plotted against Him, to have Him killed.
Little did they know that by taking Him from us,
They only insured His mission would be fulfilled!

He was sent to die on Calvary,
A cruel death, nailed to a tree,
A death of pain and agony,
Giving His life for you and me!

Surely, we all should be filled with bliss
To remember His words as our own lives end;
'Greater love hath no man than this,
That he lay down his life for his friends!'

C. N. Wesson

Ruby

Ruby's picture hangs on the wall in our hallway.
As you grow I'll tell you all about her,
She is no longer with us today.
I stayed with her a lot when I was growing up.
When I awoke she would be at the kitchen table,
reading the daily paper and sipping from her coffee cup.

Money was something she really didn't need,
She believed it to bring out the ugliness in people,
Selfishness and greed.

Dresses to the knee, hair up in a bun.
She always wore a head scarf,
And you can bet it was the oldest one.

I called her every night before I went to bed.
She was my first thought in the morning,
And the last to leave my head.

This picture in the hall that I show you now and then,
Is your great Grandma Ruby,
And for twenty four years, my very best friend.

Teresa Green

The Cat And The Fiddle

"High-Diddle-Diddle" sang the Cat and the Fiddle
   As they rocketed away to the moon
Needing no names they were just playing games
   Climaxing for them all too soon

That fat Cat under-dressed showed off all her best
   From scruples kept her distance afar
Eyeing all the men for her one craving yen
   Noted the Fiddle alone at the bar

Once their eyes met their destiny was set
   To take their trip up to the stars
Their journey was fast knowing it couldn't last
   Via Venus rather than Mars

But there was one catch fate was destined to hatch
   That fat Cat gave birth to a kitten
Thinking she had been smart this tore her apart
   Outraged as if she'd been bitten

Seeking one Fiddle was an unsolvable riddle
   For she'd taken that trip with many
A merciless crime happening all the time
   The moral of course: She hadn't any . . .

William H. Hackett

Thunder In The Night

On the west side of Detroit played some ordinary boys
As the sun went down in this troubled ghetto town
Then as the boys headed for home a gang of thugs began to roam
Then a fight broke out and someone pulled a gun

Then as the kids began to run they heard the echo of a gun
And the sound it made was like thunder in the night
Then as his young friends stood there crying this little boy child lay
   there dying
A victim of the thunder in the night

Then at a hospital his mom stood crying as she watched her young child dying
Victims of the thunder in the night
And at a church the folks were praying but something's wrong with what
   they're saying
Cause prayer alone can't stop the thunder in the night

Well it's not that we're not trying but the folks just keep on dying
Victims of the thunder in the night
So I ask you as a friend where will the madness end
Or are we all becoming victims of the thunder in the night

   G. A. Rohm

Definite

Are you sure you will see another day?
As the last light quietly slips away.
Night transcends, the world becomes still,
Void of color - Darkness is so ending.

Are you sure you will see another sun? Clouds appear from nowhere.
Graying light - Rumbling skies - Heavy flashes
The world is washed - Down the rain crashes

Are you sure of season changes?
Summer breezes turning cold, as all the green turns brown and gold.
Winters blast - a snow blanket - cold and wanting.
Waiting - waiting for that first sign of warmth.

Are you sure of what you see? - really see.
Of that first light of day - of you - of me.
Of that new sun after a heavy rain shower.
Of its warmth - of its wonder - of the seasons and cold snow
When with the sun so quickly goes.

Are you sure - as sure as I am, Will we always be together?
Are you sure why must I ask, maybe it's the time it flies by so fast.
Just don't answer yet - I am sure I'll be all right,
Just as sure as there's a new day - on the other side of night.

   Richard A. Godette

Smell - Inhale

I Smell, I inhale the sound of crinkly leaves
As I joyfully walk through the woods
Leaves, red as pomegranates, yellow as squash
An artists delight, a treasure in the woods

I smell, I inhale the sound of burning leaves
Inhale and understand the joy of smoke
The smokiness, the aroma of good gourmet cooking
And as I smell, my mind meanders back to old places

I am in an aromatic old-fashioned kitchen
Sweet spicy cloves, cinnamon, nutmeg
Smudge at my nose
Bringing back childhood days, food, toys, love.

I smell, I inhale the smoke of burning leaves
I walk on the crumpled tissue paper sound
Leaves, sweet smelling burning leaves, fire sprinting
Devouring everything in its path.

   C. Gassin Weiner

Unsaid Words

Sitting alone not doing a thing, wonder what the day will bring.
As the day creeps by, I keep wondering "why?" Why, can't I get you
out of my head.
Could it be I want you in my bed or is it all the words unsaid?
The night we shared was all in fun, each performance grand yet, there
was a better one.
The Midnight Cowboy had done it for me, no other performer did I need
to see.
The smile on your face somehow seemed painted, as if something in
your life had once been tainted.
Without any words ever being spoken, it seemed to me your heart had
been broken.
I heard above the crowd's noise, a cry from deep within, I looked
around and still no words, yet I heard it again.
The words I heard had not been said, but transferred from you straight
into my head.
My heart aches to feel such sadness, or maybe all this is just plain madness.
I don't know why I feel this way, I should crumple this up and throw
it away.
They say some people have this knack, but, I wish this gift I could give back.
I'm sure you think I'm out of my mind, and with that thought I am apt
to incline.
Yet, still your painted smile I see, I can't help wondering what that
sadness could be.

   Pam C. Struemph

The Lotus Bed

We glided in among the pads
   As quietly as we could.
Who would disturb the silence
   Of so charmed a place.
Except perhaps, to draw the breath in quickly
   At such beauty.

There were blossoms by the hundreds
   Rising from the lake.
Each on a long, strong stem
   Tilting toward the sun.
And deep inside each creamy cup
   A golden center
Like a bit of the sun itself
   Caught there and held.

   Virginia C. Hawkins

March Of The Seasons

Springtime warmth, springtime showers, rouse a multitude of flowers.
As nature wakens from its sleep tiny fledglings start to peep,
And landscape displays shades of green, reigning like a regal queen.

Summer beauty, summer hues, offer gifts from which to choose.
Gardens flourish in the sun, filling pantries one by one.
Warbling birds and gorgeous flowers gratify for countless hours.

Autumn sorghum, autumn leaves, shiver gently in the breeze,
Till combines gobble up the crop and painted leaves begin to drop.
Piles of leaves and piles of grain end a season once again.

Winter blizzards, winter sleet, numb the fingers freeze the feet.
Frosted rooftops, trees of white, shimmer in the morning light.
No flowers to beckon or birds to sing till once again we welcome spring.

Seasons come, seasons go, bringing rapture, thrills, and woe.
When once again spring has returned we thank the Lord for what
   we've learned.
No greater gift can there be found than glorious seasons marching round.

   Sylvia Girmus

Weak Knees And A Thumping Heart

I don't want to hear your voice booming from a car radio. Pleading
nor scoffing. Let us not reminisce of the laughter. Swinging back
and forth, limbs pumping, sweat gliding across. Let us create. After
all, we are mature beings. I want to hear your pouting kisses. Smell
your seductive hair, upper lip. Smooching in the game we play. For I
am so lucky. We will be before a captain. White water crashing. It
will howl. It will scream. A bedroom mix. A leather covered poetic
collection. A cotton thin strip between its textured pages. Words
drifting from our heart. Our children, a boy and girl, with dark
curly hair and skin, long eyelashes, narrow hips, a bulging belly in
between, knobby knees kneeling, will rummage through our wooden
cabinets. They will find a blue threadbare binder with glossy
pictures. His calloused fingertips touching my nose. "Dad made out
well." Her bony hand against your cheek. "Mom found a great catch."
A stern father. A hip mother. A stern mother. A hip father. My
bony hand wrapped in your calloused palm. Let's go to New Orleans,
Niagara Falls, Walt Disney World... Santa Fe. Press your sweaty
body... hard. I, lying on the steaming sand with my hand gripping
your firm butt cheek. Tangle my hair between your white musked
fingers. Friend, Lover, Roommate. The questions irk me. Wrap the
correct answers your sweet tongue. Will you marry me? Father my
children? Be my best friend and Live forever?

Nisha Narula

"Devour Me Divine"

I lay with a divinity to compose this poem for you
   my god/like stranger
   for you I have sacrificed my innocence treasure

   ...I want to slide down your sexless beauty
to anoint your mountain with the perfume of my tongue...

... I want to crawl into the cage of your chest
   imprisoned to sing for the beat of your brain...

      devour me, devour me divine
         as you starve

until I am the inside of you
   I will not rest
      but lay like a whore/meal sprawled out before you

      indulge in the fruits of my body
   now bruised with the sperm of his rod
Magdalena Rose Kohanna

Passion's Fire

I am sitting here and wishing
That I was loving you
Not just with my heart, my Dear
As I really always do
But with my eyes and fingers
And with my mouth and tongue
In a sunny, mid-morning place
While the day's life is still young
With breezes freshly blowing back
The curls around your face
With secret eyes that watch you from
A private, fiery place
To feel your skin and hear your sounds
And taste your sweet forbidden grounds
And watch your pleasure rise and fall
Until I finally give you all
As conscious sounds of day restore
I kiss your loving mouth once more
And ponder in mid-day's retire
How wonderful this passion's fire
William Meller

Soul Scream

Demented is the word that describes you
All the pain and torture you put me through
Dead dogs lying beneath tall trees
I'm still crawling around on bloody knees
Waiting for the days to pass the pain to fade
Trying to forget the desperate love we made
My heart is bleeding
My soul is screaming
My head is reeling
Someone set me free - end all this hated misery
I can still taste what you gave me
Tears, blood and a need to see
See through you - see back to me
Dress me up in a nice white suit
Baby can you dig?
Screw you with a chainsaw you f***ing pig
Sadie Draper Wilson

The Chair

London flat, 3rd floor,
evening darkness outside of his bathroom window.
He closes the door and we are alone.
His one out two roommates is around, but we don't care.
Naked we hold each other for a moment,
he turns the hot water on to fill the tub.
He sits on the edge of the tub and pulls me to his lap,
so strong, so hard.
He breaks off the kiss.
Standing he moves over to a chair with towels,
throwing them to floor in one sweep.
He sits on the chair as I move towards him.
I sit on his lap and we make love on the chair,
it creaks like we moan, the three of us move together.
I break off the kiss.
He holds my back and I hold the back of the chair.
I look to the side,
stream rises from the hot water running into the tub,
stream rises to fog the window.
Paula Michelle Landreth

Ode To The Commode

I thought of this ode one day
When I was in such a way
That to me the flush toilet became the best invention
The state I was in I will not mention.

I am not as bold
As they were in days of old
When they had to sh*t in the cold.
Nor does the night pail under my bed
Smelling as if an alive thing now dead
Give me any comfort instead.
Thank you industrious soul
Whose invention replaced the hole
You undertook to reach a very noble goal.
Those of us who are weak at heart
With lots of fart
And not as smart
Sincerely thank you with every flush.
John Honeck

Lord Hear Us

Level our mountain when the climb
 is too steep
Dredge our river when the water
 is too deep
Calm the winds so our homeless
 could sleep
Dry the tears of the helpless who cry
 out and weep
Help us spread faith - help us lead
 and tend your flock
Help us remove sharp edges from
 any hardened stone or rock
Give us strength to paddle for those
 who cannot row
And to navigate currents towards a
 calmer gentle flow
Help us mirror goodness - teach our
 children how to pray
So all will know it is only your mirror
 that beams the brightest ray

Lu Pace

To Live Without You

To live without you,
Is to die without love.
I may be strong,
But I'm not that tough.

So don't leave me baby,
Stay here by my side.
Join me on the highway of love,
And enjoy a lifetime ride.

A trip reserved for only you.
There's no exit in sight.
With God as our chauffeur,
The future looks so bright.

With all life's uncertainty,
There's one thing I'm sure of.
To live without you,
Is to die without love.

Joseph P. Chambley

To Ride Upon A Shooting Star

The stars stud the endless sky tonight
As I look up at my moon.
A smooth, round, glowing planet
Playing its own little tune.
I wish somehow that I could catch someday
A radiant shooting star.
Taking me up to this mysterious planet,
Taking me so very far.
As I would land upon a deep crater,
Surely I would see
A little, white house upon a hill
Waiting just for me.
There would be infinite fields of sunflowers,
And a purple picket fence around.
Purple oceans, overlooking cliffs,
Waterfalls making a trinkling sound.
Behind me would be God-like mountains,
The whole picture so very true.
And then I would wake up from this daydream...
Oh, I wish it had been real...don't you?

Pooja Shukla

Our World Today

Our world today
is nothing nice to say.
It could be better,
but no one cares,
The ocean's dirty
Parks are ugly,
Fish are dying
Small animals are choked
to death. We can
help but no one
cares. We could
recycle our trash
Put trash in its place.
Replace trees, you
cut down. Clean
out the bays and
oceans that are dirty
We Should Care.

Lauren Scott

Petal Of A Rose

A petal of a rose
Is all that he throws
As the coffin is lowered to the ground
As the water flows
So the flower grows
And the grave will always be found

It's all he can do
As he returns to view
The site of his loved ones place
Dusted with dew
A rose grows a new
As the tears roll down his face

Every week he returns
And slowly he learns
He has given up life, no hesitating
New love he will spurn
For he only yearns
For the love that he knows is waiting

Michael Eugene Bacon

Handicapped

Determined special people,
 innocent and yet,
Staring at the outside
 is as close as others get.

Joy and happiness abound in them
 although it might not be seen,
At the same time others in ignorance,
 are somehow being mean.

The description of a perfect friend,
 and them is quite the same,
The picture that it paints,
 differs only in the frame.

Be kind to those whose flaws you see.
No telling where yours may be.

Melinda Gurney

The Shadow

Life is but a walking shadow
in which it haunts us year after year,
day after day, hour after hour,
and minute after minute.

It haunts us, to change us into
what it thinks we should be.
What it wants us to be.
Not letting us live our lives
for us, but for the life that is being
forsaken.

Jeff W. Kooken

Insecurity

Not quite secure
in what I know of me;
not feeling safe
in feelings that I feel;
I leave behind
the person that I am
and seek in them
the person I should be,
the other ones, the people, not myself,
in whom I seek
the meaning I should have;
providing for me
thoughts that I should think;
revealing to me
truths I should believe.
Not quite secure
in what I know of me,
I go to them
and ask who I should be.

Laurence R. Cowles

A Day At The Shore

One hot summer day
In the year "92"
I went to the sea
of azure blue
I stood at the shore
And shaded my eye
I saw a school of dolphins
Much to my surprise
They swam through the water
At a mighty pace
And jumped through the water
In a wild race
The next thing I saw
Were the birds in the air
Especially the Canadian geese
Who flew as a pair
The creatures of both air and sea
Made a beautiful scene
As they swam and flew
Through their daily routine

Nicci Bacigalupi

The Little Park

Always, there is someone
In the little park....
Coming and going,
Day and night,
Through all the seasons,
And in all kinds of weather....
There is, always,
Someone walking
In the little park.

Mary Ann Peter

Untitled

Like the sparkle of light
  in the spray,
Or a rainbow caught
  in the sun's ray,
There's the coolness of shade
  at the edge of a glade,
Or the warmth of the sun
  on a clear, bright day.
The rushing of a fall,
  or the calm of pooled water,
There's no one I'd want more
  for my Mother!

It was a different forest,
It was a different time,
But the memory of a pleasant walk
With friends and father come to mind.

Kathryn McDeed

A Flower

A flower
  In the realm
    Of hope and love
It sways and dances
  In the hall
    Of the soul
It kisses the sun
  And holds the hand
    Of beauty
As it is promise
  God's will be done
A flower
  In the realm
    Of hope and love

Michael Mack

Christmas Is Love

Love came down at Christmas
In the form of a little child.
Love came down at Christmas
Gentle Jesus meek and mild.

Love came down at Christmas
To redeem the world of sin.
Love came down at Christmas
To dwell in the hearts of men.

Love Love Love Love
Love came down.
Love Love Love Love
Christmas is love.

Marleene F. McDowell

The Whale

  My dear, let me tell you about the whale.
As it swims so fast, for it has no choice.
The poachers chase it with a big loud voice,
There she blows! From up there in the sky,
The man in the crows nest as he cries
As the whale's red eyes glow, the boats
Weigh anchor and away they go!
Tho' the whale's heart fills with fear,
It charges faster gaining speed when the
Harpoon hits, it starts to bleed. The whale
Looks up at the sun for the last time. The
Poachers found it and made this rhyme.

Simon W. Lloyd

My Window

Sitting in my window
in the early morning,
I can see:
The gold colored sky,
with brilliant hints of rose,
violet, and the most beautiful
shades of blue imaginable,
dancing threw the sky
with the joy of a new morning.
The whole day lays ahead of
this beautiful peaceful beginning
known as the Sunrise.
The day passes by for My Window to see,
ending with a beautiful light show of
red, purple, and finally deep blue.
My Window watches all of this,
even as the smiling silver moon rises
into the dark night sky,
finally quiet from the excited colors of Sunset.
My Window sees it all.

Jennifer Basile

Bug POOF!

Winged gossamer-like shadow
  in the dimness
    aflutter!
One last buzz...lightly fried
  the moth to the light.

Nedra Lubold

Dream

I creep into your head,
In the dead of the night,
I make you laugh,
Or jump up in fright.

I'm like a blur,
Waiting for you to fall asleep,
Then I'll show you a picture,
But I won't say a peep.

When I visit the older ones,
We sometimes take a trip back in time,
We might visit their childhood,
But when I leave I don't get a dime.

When I visit the younger ones,
We see happy or made up things,
We have the greatest times,
Even though I make less sound than an owl's
  wings.

I creep out of your head,
As the sun begins to rise,
I leave for the day,
But I'll be back at night with another surprise.

Jill K. Delton

The Heart Is Shattered

Rubble's still falling
in a rain of sorrow
The heart is shattered
beneath the sharp tears
The people stop and question
as the man walks by
Death to them is shouted
only after we ask
  why

Kathleen Murtagh

To My Daughter

When I first held you
In my arms,
And looked upon your
Small, sweet face,
My heart was filled
With endless joy
That time and space
Could not erase.

When you were small
I calmed your fears.
I heard your prayers
And dried your tears
And in the darkness of the night
I told you things would be alright.

I knew some day you'd leave my side
And travel far and travel wide
Across our land and far from home,
Your restless spirit free to roam.
Wherever you go, whatever you do,
Your mothers love will follow you.

Margaret E. Kingsbury

My Brother's Burial

We walked together
in cool, verdant forests.
A symphony
of color and movement.
The deer followed
as we journeyed
to the river.
Your face was radiant,
a reflection
of glorious light.
We took the earthen jar
filled with your ashes
and flung them high.
A thousand sacred doves
hovered and were fed
as the ashes turned to seed
against the aquamarine sky.

Nancy M. Riley

I Sit Alone

I sit alone
In a dark and lonely room, waiting
Hiding, scared
Will I be prepared?
When He comes, what will I do?
Will He know who I am too?
He rescues me from the darkness
Leads me into the light
We walk hand in hand
Him reminding me to take a stand
But for now, I sit alone
In a dark and lonely room, waiting
Waiting 'til the time is right
To finally settle the fight
He comes for me
When will it be?
But for now, I sit alone
In a dark and lonely room, waiting
Hiding, scared
Will I be prepared?

Katie Bell

My Dream

My dream one day is to be somebody
　　important;
My dream one day is to be a hero;
My dream one day is to have people
　　look up to me;
My dream one day is to make it in life
　　without doing wrong;
My dream one day is to tell people
　　that they can make it too;

I know that one day, a very special
　　day, that my dreams, will
　　come true.

Until that very special day, I will
　　continue to believe in
　　myself and others.

Matthew Butler

The Lord

I'm the sun
I'm the rain
I'm the snow
I'm the children
I'm the older person
I'm the rainbow
I'm the air
I'm the sky
I'm the water
I'm the wind
I'm the thunder
I'm the hail
I'm the ground you walk on
I'm the trees
I'm the animals
I'm the lightning
I'm the feelings
I'm the fire
I'm the rose
I'm the Lord

Lilia Foard

I'd Only Ask For You

I'll tell it rather simply;
　　I'll say it plain and true
A single thing is all I want
　　and all I want is you.

You are the very air I breathe,
　　the soul that grows within.
You're all my thoughts tied up as one,
　　and that's just to begin.

You're all that life need ever give,
　　the maximum that's due.
If I could ask for anything,
　　I'd only ask for you...

Louis Grasse

Perhaps

To speak without worrying
If the words you choose are right,
For knowing that your words
Will not be wronged.
For as two snowflakes
With each its own,
Bound together to transform,
Only to melt away
To take separate streams.

Or perhaps. . .
Form one drop of water.

Lon Dawson McCue

The Other

I don't know
If it was a dream
I had
So long ago.

I'm not sure
He was real,
Maybe I'll never know.

He's breaking me
Again and again,
Tearing my heart in two.

Did I really love him?
I never really knew.

There's two of them now
Staying in me
And haunting my soul.

One is ignorant,
The other shall forever
Remain gold.

Lindsay Brust

"Love That's True"

I loved you so much
I would've given you the world
For you to give me one chance
And say I was your girl.

But no, you didn't want me
There was nothing I could say or do
You said there was only one thing wrong
That I was too young for you.

I sat and wondered if it could work
If you would've gone out with me
And "no" was what my answer was
Because I knew you wanted to be free.

Now that you have gone away
I've tried to get over you
But not one day can go by
That I don't think of you.

I've found someone who could give me
What I couldn't get from you
The only thing that I ask for
A kind of love that's true.

Gretta Lockbaum

Lover

His masculine arms will
　　bring you close
His large hands will
　　rip your clothes
His devilish grin will
　　attract you
His perfect teeth will
　　nibble and chew.

Your body is filled with
　　sensational desire
His genitals are burning
　　like fire.
You know that this relationship
　　will not work,
but you still
　　unbutton his shirt.

A. C. Finke

"Seaforth Sound"

'Twas by the shore of Seaforth sound
I walked alone in thought.
The flow of life and waters pound
Of yester-years I sought

Fleeting glimpse of memories reached
To watch the rolling surf
Golden sands with pebbly beach
My hand out-stretched to turf.

I passed that way so long ago
The sands of time disturbed
Childhood days of pleasures glow
My heart with dreams hath curbed.

Digging holes and castle mounds
With driftwood piles to float,
Tide comes in and washes around
To flood the castle moat.

The sands are ribbed by the flowing waves,
Your in-step pains to touch
Tip-toe out to search the caves
The pleasures I loved so much.

John C. Robinson

My Baby

For nine months
I waited for you,
I love you
since the first month.

I had many plans for you,
but they never came truth.
It's hard to believe
what you don't want to believe.

I remember your tiny face,
your soft skin,
you were an angel.
Now I know where you are,
it's far from here,
but your memory is always
going to be inside of me.

Oh, my Baby.
I wish you were here,
because since you left this world,
the light of my soul,
is off.

Karen Valdez

Untitled

Forever stole my teacher.
I planned to visit,
But she was the secret kind,
And I gave no time to forever.

Forever was close as tomorrow for her.
My poet teacher never said it.
She wrote forever plain on paper,
And read it to strangers.

What I imagine I could have seen.
Her soft voice making people soft.
Her grateful smile embarrassed.
But I was busy being only me.

Now my teacher teaches me again.
Messages in black on white
To remind me of my forever.
So I move away from the TV.

I see this world, feel this world,
And whisper thank you in my mind.

Kim Susedik

What Is Love?

What is love?
I think I know.
It's joy and happiness,
It's something you show.

It's knowing that
you're always there
and that there is someone
that really does care.

It's your kiss that makes
my heart melt.
It's the sweetest, softest
thing I've felt.

It's your warm
and tender touch.
It's something that
I need so much.

It's many things
and feelings that are true,
but when asked, "What is love?"
I'd say it was you.

Kristin Ward

Untitled

If you feel sorrow,
I shall mourn for you.
If you are in pain
I shall hurt for you.
If you are in sadness
I will cry the tears for you.
If your heart is broken,
I shall give you my own.

Meagan Ray

Time's Wasting

As I look around my room
I see it could use a broom
But it's a nice place to be
It's nice, just you and me
I think of what we could do
Since you should be going soon
Maybe we could play dress up?
Or possibly play tea cups.
But it's just not any fun
You'll be late if you don't run
You said "See ya" as you went
I guess that was time well spent

Megan Tucker

My Savior

I hear a hammer,
I see a tree,
I see my savior
dying for me.

I know his love,
I know his grace,
just like a dove
oh, the pain in his face.

For me he was slain
upon that tree,
he took my sins,
on Calvary.

Now I know
his love for me.
I'll be with him
for eternity.

Lewis Adams

Untitled

When did passion take its leave?
I long from weariness reprieve.
What happened to my youthful dreams?
The days are all the same, it seems.

I see the horrors on this earth:
O God give me rebirth.
Just concentrate on those around you,
Your passion just might come anew.

Mary Nicol Jones

Madness

My existence is madness
I live in sadness
I am wrapped in a tomb
In the scent of her womb
There is evil in the night
No joy in the light
In death there is no peace
Life will not cease
The trees bent in grief
Flowers caress a wreath
Eyes filled with desire
Skin engulfed in fire
Why do I live
With nothing to give
Living in sadness
My existence is madness

Lola Mae Blackmon

Tools For The Trade

If I had a toolbox,
I know what I would fix.
I'd fix a car, a boat, a train,
A blender that didn't mix.

But everyone has tools like that,
And they certainly cost a lot.
I have one that's different,
One like no one's got.

You see, the one I have fixes things.
Things that are wrong with me.
Like my honesty, willingness, my dignity,
And especially my self esteem.

You see, these tools are very special,
I must keep them all intact,
Because if I were to lose them,
I might never get them back.

John M. Stephens

Lost Memories

Somewhere back in time we go
I know not where
Somewhere back in time we loved
I know not when
Somewhere back in time we hate
I know not how
Somewhere back in time we part
I know not why
Somewhere back in time I pray
Where, when, how and why
Somewhere back in time I know
Love has come and gone for me
Somewhere back in time I know
Regaining ones memories means
Dearly to me

Margie D. Smith

Not To Be The Last

Though my eyes see the lies
I know not how to break the ties
The image in my mind
Is only a reflection left behind
like a rainbow in the sky
A part of me has died
Or made a transformation
Into some awful representation
Of what I do not know
But what is known has been dethroned
The future is just haze
Yet I keep my ever-present gaze
I am lost in the future
Running from my past
So hurry my brother
You do not want to be the last

Jonathan Wesley Brewer

His Death

Maybe it was scary
I know it did not hurt
Sometimes I feel lonely
Sometimes just like dirt

I know it was for the best
It couldn't last too long
And even for all the rest
We know it wasn't wrong

We knew that it was coming
All of us did feel it
He left us his body
But God took the spirit

His soul will still remain though
And our memories
He was sent for us to love
He wanted just to please

Jennifer Kazules

Storyman

I write the things
I know
he says
of sharp winter winds
and glassy blue eyes—
the night I gave her
whisker burn
and my lips turned
black
I watch the sunrise
every morning
when I wake at eight
I remember when I was
a little girl
he says
grandmother lost her upper
plate in the punch
I always keep my dancing shoes
on a shelf in my brain
just for such occasions.

Kristin Brewer

Black Princess

Her face so chocolate clear
Her teeth are so bright as a white star
she wore silk across her shadow body
colors as red...

Jean Ann Owens

Goodbye

I love you so much
I hope you know.
I never told you
I didn't know how it would go.

You went to the hospital
And I thought now's the time.
I never thought
It would be the last time.
Now you are gone
Things are so hard.
Trying to go on
But it's just too hard.

I never thought
You would die.
You weren't much older than me
But I guess I should say goodbye.

Joanne Sprenger

Indian Field

A name majestic and bold,
I hear a distant drum sound.
Its call to greatness.
Hear me great one.
Watch my field and woods,
And see my birds fly,
My squirrels run.
And watch my flowers grow,
And my children play.
And oh, great Stonebridge one,
Give thanks to our ancestor
Who will always be heard,
A cry of a coyote
Or a distant drum.
Such a park,
Van Cortlandt.

Michael Caffaro

Close To You

In my past few days of loneliness
I have thought of nothing but You.
I have tried so desperately to think
of other things, to occupy my time
and my mind.
However, it has been to no avail.

With You being so far away,
I have realized just how much
I need You near me,
To fill my lonely days,
to comfort my mind,
and to soothe my aching
heart.

For my heart longs to be close to YOU...
once again.

Kimbrely R. Fuller

Untitled

I saw your ad for poetry
I answered it to find my destiny.
What comes if it is my lack of ability.
My time is short, my sense is weak.
What gibberish is this, I create!
Oh well.
God bless - Good luck
I tried my best.

Louise Boucher

Our Secret

Can I tell you a secret.
I have here with me.
It's a fairy tale.
No one besides you or me.
Can see.
It's a land way far away.
We can travel by dreams.
Only when we get our way.
We must travel together.
And stay away.
From the troubles.
That may not obey.
When we arrive there.
We will be free.
To do what we want.
And always see.
What is.
Freedom and peace.
And a place to be.

Lisa Sheets

Role Change

I had a pet hamster
I had a pet cat
My cat kisses my hamster good night.
While my hamster tries to pick a fight.
When I awoke Prince my cat
was laying on his back.
I turned around just to see
Cindy my hamster trying to kill me.
I wonder why my cat is a sweetie
While Cindy, well she's a meany!

Nicole Jones

Pencil

I am slave to another,
I give my life.

It leaves me slowly, gradually,
mangled, ground up.

Someone else's thoughts, their hopes and
wishes.
I am not myself.

Born to suffer.
Born to die.

My life is not my own.
I serve.

Michael R. Moeller

Disappear

Sitting all alone in the dark,
I get paranoid as I hear my dog
begin to bark.
I look outside but see nothing,
then I hear someone laughing.
I look again but can't see very well,
I strained my eyes - then I saw him "The
master from Hell".
He stared at me with eyes of red,
He looks as if he rose from the dead.
Dressed in his cloak of black and
fangs of white,
He casts a spell with all his might.
In a deep dark voice I hear him say,
"I came to take your soul away".
I stared at him holding back a tear
and into the night we disappeared.

Michelle Heming

The Eagle

An eagle soars across the sky,
I gaze up and start to sigh.
Majestic bird so wild and free,
I often wish it could be me.
As I watch the Eagle's grace
A lonely tear slides down my face.
I watch the Eagle stop in flight,
He'll catch a meal, a feast tonight.
He flies again up to the sky
I watch him go and wave good-bye.
As I turn away to leave
I hear a scream with no reprieve.
A gunshot echoes through the air,
the Eagle falling with despair.
I catch my breath and try to run,
The Eagle dead from one man's gun.
His tragic death is no surprise
It's never known when one will die.
The Eagle's spirit still will soar
Within my heart forevermore.

Nicole R. Kelly

It's Fun To Be A Snowflake

I am a pretty snowflake,
I fall gently from the sky,
And everywhere you may look,
I've landed on trees up high.

It's fun to be a pretty snowflake,
I like to flutter down,
I swirl and twirl around,
And land in every little town.

In everyone's front yard,
I make it pretty and white,
Everything gets all-covered,
And what a beautiful sight!

I am one of many snowflakes,
Becoming melted by the sun,
Can't you see my tiny tears?
They're dripping one by one.

Some of us are big,
Some of us are small,
All of us are lacy-looking,
And God makes us all.

Joyce Bessler

Vietnam

An American was killed today my dear
I don't know why, I don't know how.
But an American was killed today
He did not ask for much my dear
A little love, a little fear
His life was lost today

He had a job to do my dear
He did it well, he had no peer
All for what, today my dear
I knew him well you know my dear
He had elan, he had no tear
And he questioned not his goal my dear

All through his life he wanted this
Did he know why? Did he know how?
He lost it all today my dear
And though my life be used also my dear
I shan't know why, I shan't know how
Please understand the choice my dear

Lt. Col. John P.
Irving III, US Army Retired

Why?

All the guns and clatter of cars
I don't know the point of all the wars.
They may not be wars where
army's are involved but they are
the ones that our loved ones cause.
Why must we hurt and kill others.
Why can't we get along and
just love one another.
You don't know how it feels when
someone you love turns the wheel.
The fright and feeling deep
down inside you are so scared you
just wanna hide.

Loni Kennedy

Simplicity

I called to know how Morgan is
I cannot find my frog.
He must be hiding in the pool
And I want to know how Morgan is!

I'll not be home for days and days,
How much has he grown?
Does he swim everyday?
I'm still looking for my frog.

I am bored at Grandma's house.
No, there's not much here to do.
Yes, I'm outside with the phone;
Mother, how do you know?
There he is! Against the wall!

Caught my frog.
Goodbye.

Lisa R. Hall

Why Should I Be Thankful?

Why should I be thankful?
I asked myself one day.

You have so many blessings
I heard a small voice say.

I'm thankful for my country
And the freedom that's my own
For those who fought and died for me
Most of them unknown.

I'm thankful for my home
For food and warmth and health
My job and friends and loved ones
Add to an abundance of wealth.

I'm thankful for God's beauty
Around me to behold
All these many blessings
To me, more precious than gold.

But most of all I'm thankful
To worship as I may
And thank my God for giving me
Another lovely day.

Kathryn L. Hoagland

Haiku

Koalas the facts
Here are the true facts

Koalas bellow
Their bellowing is fearsome
It "may" hurt your ears.

Krissy Gustin

I Am

I am the world
I am nothing
I am a child
I am an adult

I am your teacher
I am your best friend
I am an animal
    that shrieks in the night

I am a tree
I am a river
I am here
I am there

I am your friend
I am your enemy
I am the world
I am nothing

I am life
I am death

I am

Jennifer DeVries

Do Or Die

Some people rather die but not
I.
I have so many things to
live for.
So many things to look for.
In my world almost everybody
wants to die, but not
I.
For I want a family to love.
Unlike those who rather die
and turn into a dove.
There is one more thing I
must say.
Would you rather die or live
to be something someday?

Melonie Joy-May Malone

Reflections At Arlington

So Many Crosses

How many tears were shed?
How many loves were lost?
How many souls were spent?
When that final bar was crossed.

So many crosses we honor
So many memories we bear
So many taps we hear
When their bodies ceased to care.

Too many crosses were planted
Too many never returned
Too many griefs were tendered
When their silver stars were earned.

No more, dear God, please end it
No more sorrows to bear
No more fears to conquer
No more sadness to wear.

Let the peace and understanding
That they gave their lives to save
Be enjoyed by all men everywhere
As we remember them this day.

George A. Piel

Loneliness

How long can a heart bear loneliness
How long can a soul delay,
When the mind in stark awareness
Is searching to find the way.

How oft can the song of a bird at dusk
Tell a heart that God is at hand,
When the aching, crying need to trust
Sifts through a soul of barren sand.

Where does one find the comfort
That will ease the pain within,
How does one offer a solace
To the anguished soul in sin.

When will one find the promise
That will come as the sound of a song,
To banish this hell of loneliness
I wonder, oh God, how long, how long?

Jean Mitchell

When I Come Home To Heaven

When I come home to Heaven
    How joyful, it will be!
For on that day at last
    My risen Lord I'll see.
No greater happiness than
    To see him face to face;
To see the love in his eyes
    And feel his warm embrace.
I've done nothing to deserve
    That perfect home above.
It was given freely through
    The grace of Jesus love.
Then why should earthly cares
    Weigh down upon me so!
They'll be a distant memory
    When home at last I go.

Missy Pitts

Lost Hope

The love of a child is so strong
    How it fades in time.
The life long traditions and beliefs
    engraved in their hearts,
Is slowly sucked away and lifeless
    like the dying rose,
It goes from something beautiful
    to a sad remembrance,
Oh to remember the love of a child
    to grasp it once more,
To let my heart remember
    all the once found joys,
Don't lose the love of a child
    for once you let it go,
The soul becomes empty
    and the heart:
        hard and cold.

Loribeth Ann Silver

Effect

Which one may say
    His presence is not felt,
    some how,
Within the world around,
    When even slender needles
Of the pine tree bough
    Cast shadows on the ground?

Lorraine Drury Haynes

312

View

PICTURE Jesus
holding the world
within his hands
watching it burn away
blowing the dust
so it can be reincarnated
into what it's supposed to be
PICTURE you, and me
free
in love
floating on the clouds above
like a dove
gliding in misty air
PICTURE heaven is right here
imagine
it disappearing

Keith R. Williams

I Can't Believe

I want you to hold me,
Hold me through the night.
I want you to kiss me,
And say that all is right.
It's wishful thinking,
But I don't care.
I fall in love,
Whenever you are near.
I can't believe,
What you've done to me.
I can do anything,
I am so free.
I can't believe,
What you've done to me.
Never again,
Will I feel so free.

Nicole Brown

Desert Moon

The desert moon
Hiding a lonely face
That covers the ground
Times eternal loom
A field of lace.
The treasures never found
The desert that is missed
Full of beauty and grace
While there isn't a sound
The endless night goes on.

Julie Bateman

Untitled

He is buried in a church not far from
here, but he is not there, he is not
anywhere, except in memory.
We coupled once when we were young
Was it good? I don't remember
but this I know, and of this I'm
sure, we had faith in one another.
Faith to make our mark, each to
our own persuasion.

He married twice. I married once to
a man I dearly loved, and when that
man died, he was at my side, with
strength and understanding.

Now that I'm old and memories
Keep intruding, I often feel
and sometimes think, how nice
it was to have known him.

Mary Galligan Cornett

Destiny

I search a place unknown to me
Here and wide for a destiny
I go beyond and set fears behind
And see what the future holds

With luck and love
I enter the unknown mist
Which will clear as the years go by
Through knowledge, toil and experience
Into an everlasting flower

Lisa Mamakos

Satan

He was a man, he came from hell.
He was Satan, I knew it well.
He was devilish, he was a brute.
He was evil, he was crude.

But as I remember it well,
As that little girl sat still,
He came up to her with a smile,
And said "Come to me my child."

"I'll give you all the gold.
Now sell me your soul.
God is not your savior.
'I' back up your behavior!"

She replied, "I don't want all the gold.
I want God to take my soul.
Not you, which would bring me pain.
To me, that's no big gain!"

As he turned to walk away,
She said, "I'll never be your slave."
She bid him farewell,
And said, "Now go back to Hell."

Joanne Hall

Spring

The frog in the pond sang a song.
He sang it all night long.
Spring is here, the flowers are near.
Where is my girlfriend?

Then one fine day in the middle of May,
his dream came true.
Along came a miss and gave him a kiss.
Now the two live together
in the middle of a bog.
They sing together on a long brown log.

Louise Stransky

He Leadeth Me

He leadeth me in pastures green
he leadeth me by quiet streams
he is the guardian of my way
I can trust in him each day.

He leadeth me a blessed thought
he leadeth me I'll question not
he leadeth me through trials and tests.
He leadeth me, his way is best.

He leadeth me, I'm not alone
he leadeth me, I am his own
bought with a price, his own
shed blood, I will follow
though the way is rough -

He leadeth me, the path is narrow
he leadeth me, I'll hold his hand
he leadeth me, in him I'll stand he leadeth me.

Norma Rathbun

The Dance

I am Brown Sugar.
He is Black Chocolate.
We sway together
to our own rhythms.

Mine is the rhythm of
R and B of Georgia and
the Jazz of Harlem.
His is the rhythm of
the Congo drums of Africa,
and the Reggae beat of Jamaica.

We are young, hopeless
people in love,
    we sway.

We are old, happy
people in love,
    we sway.

He is Black Chocolate.
I am Brown Sugar.

Larrie Grimsley

Euphoria

His only memory was
He had no memory

The light, enveloping him
With increasing calm and love,
Lifted him and carried him
Toward his ultimate destination
The choir of the eternal
Raised their voices in salutation
As he passed through the gates
His amorphous spirit
Vibrated with the universal hum
Of absolute oneness
He understood the TRUTH
He accepted the WAY
He joined the ONE

His only memory was
He IS the memory.

Matthew G. Pierce

Untitled

Things I see, all around,
Have their story,
but not been found.
The balance here,
of Earth's domain,
Has much more,
then we could ever see.
To be in tune,
The universe now calls.
Is the key here,
for us to find.
Or lost forever,
within our minds.
Seek the things,
not known to be,
Of this land, we walk each day.
The secrets sought,
will then be found.
Are here for all,
upon this ground.

Joe Ouellette

Where Am I Going

Where am I going?
Have I learned yet why I'm here?
Is the sadness in my eyes,
Tears of sorrow, or of fear?

I lift my head to see the path
My life will end up taking.
And as I've seen, again and again.
I just can't see it changing.

Tomorrow is another day.
At least that's what I've heard!
But my tomorrow could be yesterday,
Or just another word.

Life is just an illusion,
Full of senseless stress and pain.
Pain that leads to confusion.
Confusion that drives you insane!

So where am I going?
Where have I been?
My life's been going no where.
Wish I could start over again...

Milon Wayne Thorley

Graceful Warrior

Strong warrior so weary from the day,
Hang your head and contemplate
   how you got this way.
Look over your land and protect
   it with your heart,
It is known not even death could
   make you part.
Powerful in your look, graceful,
   with your hands,
This is how you worship your God
   But no one understands.
It is acceptable to rest, it is
   necessary just to be,
Start again tomorrow, fore your
   mission we can see......

Jennifer Ward

Little Girl

Little girl, latch key
Growing up to be
Wives, mothers, confined
Frighteningly redefined

Windows casting shadows upon
The saddening eyes
Of dancing dolls
Weary of footsteps
Echoing in the darkness
Watching breathing walls

Little girl, invisible
To those eyes
That should have seen
What this lonely, little girl
Could have been.

Julie A. Plank

Fallen Heroes

Walking on the beach I feel it...
ground shaking smoke hovering
men crying out.
Walking through the haze
seeing the blood
hearing the pain I tremble.
Falling to my knees
among the dead covering my face
fighting back the tears I now know.
Today walking among the white stones
that symbolize men
I silently thank them
for all they sacrificed.
I walk up and down the rows
name after name imagining their stories
hearing their cries.
People walk by they do not stop
they do not hear it or feel as I.
I walk away but will never forget
the honor and bravery that lies here.

Kelle Stadler

My Watch

Bound around my wrist,
gripping for its life.
Ticking on, defiantly,
without a touch of strife.

Though many try to stop it
by living in the past
my watch pays them no heed
for they always come in last.

My watch is one of the few things
in which I can truly trust.
For to it, each has his mission,
and to mark time is a must.

When all else has failed me
and I sit here without a clue,
my watch comforts me with utter loyalty
and then I am not so blue.

Marisa Osborn

To All F-B-Eyes

Great, great
Great
Grand
Father
Me
Five-sixteenths is all I'll ever be
So marry your own if you can
I'm looking for a five-sixteenths
   Cherokee man
I'm the fifth generation
In a real slow fade
Don't look now
But your children's children
Can't be unmade
Just look in the mirror
For a real long time
And remember your ancestors
Are the parents of mine

Kelly Mitchell

Our Walk

We walk through the
grass hand in hand.

We look around at
what we have found.

The sky is blue,
the grass is green.

We look at each other
and see you and me.

Our life is fulfilled
our love is so true.

As we walk through
the grass.

Just Me and You!

Joanne Griggs

A Mother's Task

Receive, conceive, give, deliver,
Grant and bestow.

Love, adore, nurture and nourish.

Educate, train, culture and
Cultivate.

Release, discharge and relinquish.
So they may receive and conceive.

Margaret J. Oxford

Good Night

Good night my little darlings
Good night my little ones

Mama surely loves you
Mama surely does

What wonderful children
What a wonderful child

Jesus gave me a
Wonderful, wonderful child.

KeriLyn Gomez

Silent Cries

Can you hear the cries of the children
Gone silent in the night?
Can you feel the pain that lingers
Never taking flight?
The explosion that sheared
Into our hearts, our minds and souls
Will stay with us forever
With the men who are our foes.
It happened in this country.
This place of peace and freedom,
It happened in this country,
And toppled our mighty kingdom.
It brought us to our knees
To think this could be done.
Our forefathers turn in their graves
As they see a hatred that's fun.
Our prayers are for the families
As they rage through ravages of time.
Our prayers are for ourselves
As we live the horrors of crime.

Kathi Hamilton

Scene

The trees and the sky
Go down the road together.
The sky goes on
But the trees stop
To make way for a village,
A lake
And peaceful pastures
Where sheep are grazing
The trees come back
And follow the sky
They go down the road together.

Lillie M. Prioleau

The Oak

The wind blows through the old Oak Tree.

Its gnarled branches reach to her.
Gesturing, beckoning, calling her.
Accepting her.

I will not let you down, it said.

Only here she is at peace, complete.
No expectations at her feet.
Not feeling weak.

Flashes across her mind.
Scoldings, hurtful words she'd heard.
Cursing all she was.

Alienated and withdrawn.

Here she came to find her rest.
No bickerings, here not a pest.
But accepted.

In the swaying branches she finds her peace.
Swinging back and forth alone on a single rope.

Melanie Riner

The Bugler At Arlington

He stands a solemn pose
Gazing over the endless rows
In that venerable field of white

In his reverential pause
He reflects upon the cause
That justified the toll

How can he ever know
From the silent souls below
What purpose he can trust

Slowly he lifts the horn
His eyes misty and forlorn
And blows the notes of honored rest

John Barda

Rage

Rage, it burns, it learns,
And it yearns—to break free.

But no, it can't,
'cause then they'll know.

Push it back, way back.
Deep inside it burns until one day,
it breaks free.

Matt Hasemeier

Rain

The patter of the rain
Gave me anguish and pain.
It flooded my cold heart
Wisdom it did impart.

I suffered all alone
Before that telltale phone.
What should I say and do?
No husband except you.

Bobby saves the day;
He does not make me pay.
I hope to marry him soon;
At the stroke of high noon.

Rain makes me feel so sad;
It reminds me of a dad
No children though for me
The rain and I are free.

Marie Merenhole

Can I

Throaty growls vibrate down my nape
Full lips follow
As warm breath makes
A delicious path
To my soul
     Can I?
Smooth hands slowly rub my back
Firm thighs caress
As hot sensations excite
Tingly feelings
In my spine
     Can I be?
Strong arms encircle my waist
Burning bodies mold
As heightened emotions smolder
In your loins
And mine
     Can I be
     With you?

Nekisha Lewis

I'm Thinking How Our Love
Will Change

I'm thinking how our love will change
Full knowing that it must.
But, for my part—the only thing
I'll sacrifice is lust.

I'll miss the times we huddled
Wrapped up naked in our bed
Insatiably arranged our parts
So we touched from toes to head.

I'll miss your buttocks warm firm mound—
The coarseness of your chest—
The way your skin felt on my lips—
The smell of it—the taste.

I'll miss the look your face took on
While we wrestled in our love.
I'll miss the way we used ourselves
In the magic way we have.

I can't explain why your lust left
Before my longings through.
I envy, though, the fact you can
Avoid forgetting you.

Kevin T. Durkin

Prayer For A Rookie Cop!

Your badge is new and so are you!
Fulfilled... your heart's desire!
You've built a dream and made the team,
To great things you aspire!

You'll falter not, though dope and pot
Bring rampage to defeat...
But guard, protect, console, direct
Each citizen you meet...

Still persevere in time of fears,
When crime's a war to wage...
Stop... listen... look! Go by the book...
Enjoying ev'ry page...

Then question why these, too, must fly
Without a turn to spare...
Fire to ember! Retired member!
One day you'll join us there!

Sentimental incidental?
Life's blessings... to the top!
In synthesis...please, God, hear this
Prayer for a rookie Cop!

Harriett H. Odum

Conquest

When seems to choke my spirit's flame
From tribulations, great and small,
When hope and even reason wane,
I call -
From depths of silent agony -
Will no one hear, reach out to me?
Bewildered, yet with clarity,
I see -
The masses: Grope, lament and growl,
Untouched by love, of self reek foul
And shamefaced on my knees I weep
And plead -
May not my soul and mind lay waste,
Toward the land of naught must haste,
But search for strength within despair
And care -
Emerge victoriously and rise
Above the vanities, self-lies;
My spirit's flame may freely soar,
Once more -

Monika Dykes

A Whisper From The Heavens

Each day a whisper
From the sky
Blows down upon my face
It gently ripples through my eyes
And through my dress of lace
It softly whispers
In my ear
Somehow I just can't make it clear
What it's saying now
Or what it has said then
Listening hard but oh, oh how
How can I comprehend
This mysterious wonder
That blows all through my head
Maybe it's a secret
A secret I can't tell
I'll bet I'll never ever know
This secret that I hear
But this whisper from the heavens
Is all that I have near

Katylynne Tavella

Nature's Golden Rain

As nature dressed and undressed,
from subtle to colorful grandeur;
My brisk walk slowed when I heard
the winds loud sweeping overture.
A leafy whirlwind enveloped me
like a gold spotlight on stage.
Stopped by surprise at the first,
then captured was I by this golden cage.
My senses reeled and revelled
at nature's golden rain unquelled.
I reached to grasp a piece of it
and in my hand I held,
a light feathery leaf so bright
stopped on its downward fall;
brought wonder and some sadness
at its final curtain call.

Judy Greer

Untitled

Smoke swirling up
From a fire;
Under tiny pin-point
Stars.
Swirling upwards like
A spirit leaving the
Earth.
The stars are beacons
Of light calling,
Calling the spirit
Heavenward.

Michelle Herring

People Leaving

Green leaves
from
gone trees

Spare
bare
nothing there.

Summer trees
fragile with the news
of cold

Went South
spent and shivering
like birds
   in underwear.

Green are needles on
pointed trees.
This green grows in winter:

Strong, sharp, and bitter
like steeped tea
—but ever-there—
staying home.

Katherine F. Robertson

Summers Gone

Summer, breezes through the trees,
Friendly, front porch evening talks;
Long and aimless, starry walks,
Crickets chirping, humming bees,
A harvest moon, will glow in the sky,
Stars, begin to singly shine...
A forgotten wash on a clothes line,
Lazy summer evenings, saying good-bye.

Laura Lee Howard

Dimpled Darling

Sweet as a breath from heaven;
Fresh as a dewy rose;
Pink as an apple blossom
From cheek to tiny toes.

Dainty with fairy dimples;
Precious, sparkling eyes,
Laughing and dancing with gladness,
As blue as the summer skies.

Her smiles will stir your heart strings,
Like the brush of an angel's wing;
A winsome, smiling darling,
And that's my granddaughter - Leah

Norman L. Dodge

"American Heroes"

Columbus sailed with might and courage,
Franklin never got discouraged;

Squanto planted beans and corn,
Bush handled the desert storm;

Lewis and Clark traveled here and there,
Betsy Ross handled our flag with care;

The Civil War was fought for slavery,
Grant fought with hope and bravery;

Paul Revere went through the night,
Shouting his warnings left and right;

The Marines, Air Force, Navy, and more,
Helped our country through the war;

Who wouldn't like a country so grand,
How could you hate this beautiful land.

Jennifer McCartney

REM Flight

Narcoleptic pull toward sleep
forces lashes tight,
as distant voices beckon
without words.
Powerful sound, a thunderclap
slams shut the door of the known,
propelling through tunneled darkness.
The quickening breeze aids flight
toward distant light
that grows ever brighter.
Final burst into an infinity of stars,
unending space, illumines all.
Reaching, soaring closer
to the welcoming light,
beginning of awareness flickers.
Abruptly, fear intrudes
and a soul folds back into the shell
that next day denies its journey.

Marilyn Stacy

The Flea

Why did HE create the flea?
   For me to see
That all creatures
   Great and small
   Are in HIS care.

HE is over all—
   The flea, me,
   The sea, and thee!

Jeanette Anna Eddy

Misleading Isn't It?

My home, gone,
   for the bank said it was theirs,
Freedom, where?,
   for law destroys all that.
Loyalty, never!,
   we're only loyal to ourselves.
Brotherhood, ha!,
   for my sibling is my rival.
Peace, when?,
   for war happens everyday.
Utopia, unreachable,
   for "it" logic can not see.
Beliefs, failing,
   for our science pulls those down.
Eternal life, never,
   for to live is then to die.

To live, only!
So give me food, and love,
and I will live until I die.

Gregory W. Harris

Autumn Scene

Hazy sky now
for shorter day;
wild pheasants feast
in fields of mown hay.

Maples of red
and aspens of gold
wear their signal colors
of winter cold.

Apples aplenty
for cider time;
ripe now the persimmon
and pumpkins on the vine.

Cooler day
and lengthening night,
summer has taken
her flight.

Gather the harvest;
laden the store.
Winter approaches
soon once more.

Mary Lou Dean

"Forever Daddy"

Although I cannot see you,
For heavens' sweet embrace;
You will be with me forever,
With your smiling face.

Your loving words,
And understanding ways,
Will be etched in my mind,
Through all of my days.

I pray to God,
That somehow, you can see;
My life; my love;
And my precious family.

Words cannot express
My emotions so deep;
I talk to you; pray for you;
And yes, I weep.

The love and pride
That I treasure for you;
Will "Forever Daddy,"
Shine through and through!

Kitty Randolph

Untitled

I won't open my eyes
For fear of what I might see
I might see a demon
Looking down upon me
Begging me for forgiveness
Telling me my time has come
Reaching out his bloody hands
Leading me to his hellish lands
Telling me what is right and wrong
Singing me the demons song
No, I won't open my eyes
For fear of what I might see
I might see a demon
Looking down upon me.

Laura Mooney

God's Beautiful Garden

God has a beautiful flower garden
Flowers of every kind
Some are young and tender
Some are in their prime
Others are old feeble
And they droop and drop from the vine

He knows which ones to gather
As he walks through His garden of flowers
Be they young or old or older
He picks them for His Bower.

He makes a bouquet of his blossoms
And takes them with Him we know
we shouldn't ask him to leave them
When life on earth is no more

Because no sickness that in heaven
There's no sickness-suffering or pain
He knows when to take them with Him
It's selfish to want them to stay so now
There's one more flower that He's
Gathered to put in His beautiful bouquet.

Jean Clark

What's His Name?

As she sat on the soft grass she could
feel the cool breeze softly blowing
against her cheeks. She seemed to not
notice others about her, as if she was
alone in this world, but alone in a way
that allowed her to let her mind wander
slowly back to another time, another
place. Knowing how dangerous the
drifting back could be for her. How
far should she drift? Suddenly her
mind stops. She hears, she remembers.
It seems her mind has drifted back an
eternity. No, she realizes it's not
quite so long. She has forgotten time
so much these days. Suddenly from the
distance she hears someone say,
"What's his name?" Quietly she whispers back,
even though no one can hear her but the wind,
"No, What's his Name". I have not forgotten
  thy name.
You will be my "Just Friend" forever.

Melinda Hare

Shadow On The Moon

There is a shadow on the moon
far away from dark and gloom
it is lifeless and still
like us no less real
when you have doubts
jump up and shout
feel the shadow move

Glen Wells

Love's Truth

  In my part of town people
fall in love as fast as they
fall out of love. Love sneaks
up on you but sneaks out just
as fast. It seems love is just
too confusing. People fall in love
and before they know it they're
falling out of love. People just
don't know how to stay in
love. You see the people I'm talking
about are teenagers. Life is
hard enough for us teens but
it's even harder to have to lose
the person you love. You thought
your love would stay but it
didn't. Your love left as fast as
it came. But the sadness or the
memories didn't leave as fast.
They stuck with you and your
heartache. I guess that's love's truth.

Melissa Storey

What Remains

What remains
Fades away,
From what we seek
We've gone astray.
If there is one thing
I must do,
It is to show you,
How much I love you.

Michelle Williams

A Home In Heaven

When he preached on the mountain
Everyone listened
Even at night
When all the stars would glisten.

People would gather
From all around
To hear the Lord Jesus Christ
Awesome sound

He's known everywhere
For the blood that he shed
And all around
For the thousands he fed.

He healed the sick
Made the blind to see
The lame to walk
And look what he's done for you and me.

He gave me life
He gave me love
And someday a home
In heaven above

Jennifer Holman

"Dreams"

Refusing love, denying hate -
Everyone heart is going to forsake.
Blind to the truth, open to falsehood -
Thinking that life is perfect and good.
Thinking reality is the truth -
When fantasy is the path
You should choose.
Having an open mind to see -
Closing your mind to reality.
Thinking of peace, love and mind -
Knowing a dream will be
with you all the time.

Jennifer Davis

Guardian Angels

Guardian angels are beautiful in every way,
They watch over me night and day,
Guardian angels I can not see,
But I know they are there to protect me.
Guardian angels live high up above,
Their whole world they fill with love,
Guardian angels try to keep me
  from all things bad,
But if they fail, I won't get mad.
  I have a guardian angel!

Katie Walsh

Northwest Legacy

Sunlight filtered - mountains high
Evergreens that touch the sky
Burst of color taunt my eyes
Snowed capped mountains in the dawn
Children silent when there gone.

Coho swimming with a dream
Fighting rapids far upstream
Last one there - so it seems
Clams are gone, water's dead
Children crying - they're not fed

Saw blades rolling, owls won't stay
Raintree forest gone away
No place left for wonder or for play
Mother Nature plants the seed
Leave the children what they need

The mountain lifts its barren head
Where deer and elk once roamed and fed
Eternal silence now is bred.
The price is paid for selfish greed
For the children - end these thoughtless deeds.

Kenneth Gross

Untitled

Aesthete I am.
Defeat I am.
Brannigan, Dissension, Dispute!
Detonate - Tame.
Converge?
Oh hee ha ho! Oh no.
Tired of time deciding
Tranquil synergism anticipated.
Patient auspiciousness,
Time...

Mary Kay Herzerach

The Lonely One

You can often be so lonely
Even in a crowded room
No one will even see your pain
Or see your world of doom

You're the only one who knows
How you feel inside
As though everything around you
Crumbled up and died

Loneliness can destroy you
And make you feel so vain
You never share your feelings
You just keep on feeling pain

You've got to open up your heart
Fill your loneliness with love
Take away all the sadness
Walk gentle as a dove

Look around that crowded room
Many are lonely too
Don't live within your misery
Let loneliness fade from you

Linda Goddard

Waves Of Feeling

Whispering softly,
Ebbing, flowing.
Quietly coming,
Gently going.
Building, building,
Strongly mounting,
Shouting, roaring,
Throbbing, pounding.
Stormy tumult
Lashing wildly.
Thrashing, crashing
Deep inside me.
Overwhelming,
Grand and thrilling,
Sweeping, swirling,
Strong, fulfilling.
Then comes stillness,
Spent and reeling,
Calm and quiet.
Waves of feeling.

Gail R. Schimpf

The Train

Remember when the trains went through
Each town, and when the whistle blew.
That sound was like no other made,
And then the memories once more fade.

Until you hear a train once more,
Your back in time you were before
When grandma had a berry tree
In her back yard and they were free.

Oh, for the time of childhood day,
Where once a child did romp and play.
The park a favorite place of joy,
With mom whose help you did employee.

And then the thoughts of Mother come.
The midnight hair, the smile come from
The every soul of gentle thoughts,
Enough to tie your heart in knots.

You dream about these times a while.
A house, a friend, and then you smile.
To be forgotten as life does fly,
Until you hear a train go by.

June E. Elliott

Life Is A Rosebush

Life is a rosebush,
    Each person a rose;
We all live and die here,
    And individually grow.

The others are red,
    And I am bleached white;
They show outer beauty,
    I try with my might.

The others are adored,
    And loved by all around;
I weep in the corner,
    My petals fall to the ground.

There they are stepped on,
    And there they shall lie;
As I watch above them,
    As I slowly die.

Few shall mourn for me,
    Them, I can't complain;
I know there are others like me,
    Who share the same pain.

Melinda I. Dean

Precious Peace

Let freedom ring throughout our land,
Each of us walking hand in hand;
No more quarrelling, no more strife,
Yielding proper respect to life.

Let peace begin with you and me,
Stretched out as far as you can see.
Practice always the Golden Rule,
Treat others like a precious jewel.

America then would be free,
A better place for you and me.
A fitting legacy to all,
Our country then could never fall.

Begin today to instill this,
Guaranteed for a life of bliss.
One by one, let's all go forward,
to live with love, not by the sword.

Let's make this, our beloved land,
Ever extending a helping hand,
The best it could possibly be,
A safe haven for you and me.

Mary Elizabeth Chapin

Tears that cascade
down my face.

Pain that shatters
my loving heart.

Numbness that claims
my body.

Anger that rages
Through my mind.

Daggers that penetrate
my broken heart.

Day dreams that
haunt my memory

Echoes that vibrate
From my lips to my ears.

Milli R. Lee

Pictures

Pictures; a form to go
down memory lane,
    A sign that shows
that everything has changed.
    A look back into the
past,
    A paper which makes
our memories last.
    Something to observe when
you start to forget,
    Of those special moments
or of people you've met.
    Moments in life that
are frozen in time,
    Even the one's that we've
left behind.
    As our friends die, and
were forced to move on.
    Pictures are the objects
that help us hold on.

Maribel Astudillo

Independence

My mind is clear
Do not think for me
My eyes are bright
I can see
My voice is strong
I can speak
My strengths are many
I am not weak
My sins are mine
Do not judge me
I can stand alone
We can stand together
My heart is open
Do not turn the lock
Do not run for me
I'm still learning to walk

Juanita M. Parendo

"Heartbreak"

Soul weeps;
Despondency creeps in.
Vigil in solitude begins.
Emotions like a kaleidoscope
Constantly changing colors.
Rejoice again;
Doubtful it seems,
'Til the next true love strolls within.

Mary Barr

Waiting

Smells of chalky dust
Desks all newly scrubbed
Chairs pushed all in rows
Books all covered over
Walls all painfully bare
They're gone now for the summer
    the happy grins,
    the puzzled looks,
    the smelly lunchbags,
    the mounds of papers.
How I'll miss them 'til the Fall.

Kathleen L. Lyons

Soundless Cries

Soundless cries,
derived from ancient screams,
echo
inside my body
reverberating like ripples
in a stagnant pond.

Someone keeps trying to turn it off.

But preverbal pus
keeps coming;
churning into piles
spurting from limbs
and gurgling lips,
spiraling out
into formless bubbles
of
soundless cries.

Someone doesn't know the knob is broken.

Margaret E. Jones

Hopeless

You twist love's dagger
Deep in my heart
My tears flow like blood
While we are apart

You turn me away
Discarding my love
I pray every day
For help from above

My pleas go unanswered
I live on alone
In the sea of despair
I sink like a stone

Deeper I fall
I fight for each breath
the only solution
the sweet sleep of death.

Greg Huelsenbeck

What We Thought...

As life goes by the
days get shorter and shorter.
As years go by we get
older and older.
When we wake in the
morning we feel that
life will end at that
very moment but our
imagination can't take
us that far, so we just give up.
We always think to
ourself is the world
going to end today, are
we going to make it out
of this lonely world?
As life goes by there
are no days left just
a small part of what
we thought would happen.

Jenny Padgett

"Remembering"

"In my room, I softly weep,
   day and night, without sleep.
Wondering, if I can last,
   until my heartaches have passed.

"How can I bear it? I really don't know.
I just keep on walking the floor,
   constantly, watching the door.
While my tears, gently flow."

"Why did you go? Why did you break
   my heart this way?
   Some day it will mend I pray.
But until that day, I will remember
   you, with a heart that was once happy and gay."

"Again maybe, we will meet.
When I no longer care to weep.
But, to see you would be grand,
   to say hello! And hold your hand!"

Julia Ingram

The Hug

I have known the hug of a 12 year old
   daughter, a hold so strong
   it dragged me, laughing,
   to the floor.
I have seen her black eyes flash,
   and her legs blur as,
   barefoot, she danced
   in wild grass.
I have watched her nuzzle and stroke
   her horse, and canter
   and gallop to its gait.
I notice the budding of her breasts,
   and although she professes
   no interest
   in silly males,
   I see, as she walks
   in town, that their eyes
   hug her.

Laura Jehn Menides

Silence

Silence...
darkness closes in.
Sounds of the night surround me.
For the first time I realize I am alone.
Alone to face
the past, present, and future.
No one to blame
for my failures and short comings.
No one to blame, but myself.
Alone in the silence
for the first time I realize
the decisions I make
forges my path through life.
Alone in the silence
I find peace,
I find the strength to face a new tomorrow

JoDee Watson

The Rose

I shall send you a rose
a single red rose,
so red, so tender, so pure.
The thorns pierce your heart,
the stem tastes so bitter,
yet the petals wipe away
the silence, sorrow, and tears.

Rachel Pearce

Paintings

Brush strokes
dancing in colors.
Colors illuminating the soul
All this, just like you
You are the color
that splashes across
the canvas of
my heart

Matt Thompson

My Midnight Horse

Gallops like the wind as it
dances in the midnight air

His mane sways with every
steps he takes.

His cold fur is as soft as
a jumping bunny but
as cold as the night

His eyes black and piercing
but not an evil heart.

He licks your hand each time
he leaves.

He cannot stay, for dawn
is approaching but will be
back when the clock strikes twelve

Mary Taylor

Technology And Time

Deep beneath the oceans tide
Creatures live and then they die
Seldom do they ever see
The fiery sun
Or you
Or me
And yet they go on
Every dusk
Every dawn
Technology is the story
Time turns the page
And when time permits
Under the sea
Then they will witness
Both, you and me.

Justin Wheeler

Untitled

Slowly walking down an alley
Cold as death and sin,
A young woman sees her life
And the murder of her kin.

The blood stained cloth used
Only to clean the knife
As the weapon is pulled slowly
From the vanishing life.

The shock in the corpse's eyes
As it lay stiffly on the ground
While the slayer runs away
And leaves evidence all around.

He forgot about the finger prints
On the wallet he tried to steal,
But maybe he was hungry
And wanted it for a meal.

Marina Leigh Graber

The Winds Of Life

The time of life is like the wind
Constant in movement and flow
Time moves within a constant pace
Yet like the wind, seems to vary so

There is that moment in time
When time seems to stand still
We cannot make it move faster
Time has the stronger will

To a child time is like a breeze
It seems never to move at all
Years may pass from the green of spring
And winters first snow fall

Some times the years seem endless
As does the unseen wind
Looking toward a special time
It seems waiting has no end

Yet, the latter years of life
Like a hurricane they blow
In retrospect we look back
And wonder, where did those years go.
Kenneth Lilly

Sweet Angel

Sweet angel rain
  comes from the sky
to wash the hurt and
  pain from eye

Sweet angel rain
  O comes to me
And cleanse my soul.
  In ecstasy

Sweet angel rain
  Sweet angel love
touch my heart with
  bounded love.
Mary Cassilly

Finger Painting

Fingers wet with paint —
Colors,
  desert red
  sunflower yellow
  and a purplish combination
  like an "owie."
— a child paints
A portrait of divine innocence

At play,
the child explores the world
Not knowing the words
  to express the beauty
  and wonder
But understanding a
  pleasing composition
  and the words
  "I love you"
Will find the wrinkled,
  rainbow-smeared paper
  on the refrigerator
Jason S. Posthumus

Time Is On Your Side

Words of wisdom;
  challenging, debating.
Quests for freedom;
  struggling, conquering.

Tears and fears;
  swallowing, taking over.
Days and years;
  dividing, giving time.

You must decide;
  whether to go for it,
Or to run and hide:
  you must live
Your own life.

Go forth and take control;
  don't hide from your fears.
It's your play and lead role,
  nobody else's.
Kerry A. Doyle

Sasha

You may think I forgot,
'cause you're so far away.
But in my heart,
forever you'll stay.
The fun we had,
the times we shared,
can't be replaced,
by anyone who says they care.
I miss you,
and I thought we'd be together forever,
but the day you left me, is when I knew,
things would never be the same.
Still to this day,
my heart cries out in pain.
Please come back,
and rescue me from this pain in my heart.
Always remember,
that no one can replace, the fun we had,
and the times we shared, cause those
memories
will always be in my heart.
Nicole Parson

Mothers Lament

  Jackie lives in Huntington,
Carolyn's out in Anaheim.
  Do they know how much I miss them?
Don't they know they are still mine?

  I have my memories, and
My memories are fine,
  But I find it's hard to live
On memories all the time.

  They don't know how much I miss them,
I just tell them I am fine,
  But I hunger for them somehow.
With them always on my mind.
  Jackie lives in Huntington
Carolyn's out in Anaheim.

  Oh came on home my children
While we still have some time.
  Then I won't keep on singing,
This sad and lonely rhyme.
  Jackie lives in Huntington
Carolyn's out in Anaheim.
Joy H. Reagle

"A Petal From My Heart"

Take a petal from my heart
Caress it with a kiss
Let us make a new start
A chance we just can't miss
You smiled at me again
My love you can't deny
It's a fever that just won't leave
the petal from my heart

I'll take a petal from your heart
and make it bloom so bright
You keep the petal from my heart
and watch it shining in the light
We'll water them together
and when the dew has set
We'll gather them each morning
A bouquet of happiness we'll make

Take a petal from my heart
weaving in and out of life
It's wonderful being me
and loving you as your wife
Linda Minga

My Abba Daddy

I know my Heavenly Father
  cares for me.
But I go to "my" Abba daddy
  and sit on his knee.

When troubles come, and
  I feel low.
It's to my Abba daddy,
  that I will go.

When friends and family
  don't have time to care.
I know my Abba daddy,
  will always be there.

When I don't get any
  hugs for a week.
It's the open arms, of
  my abba daddy I will seek.

So if your feeling, no
  one cares about you.
Just go to "your" Abba daddy
  He loves you too.
Margaret Lane

Never Ending

Curled in the corner
Can't raise my head
Shouting and screaming
Pitiful cries, begging for mercy
Hands hitting flesh
Bare skin
Whiskey
Evil all around
I look up
Fist raised
Fresh blood and tears
Never ending river
Fist
Face
Cracking
Bones breaking
Her nose
Daddy, Please stop!
Don't kill mommy!
Jennifer Selvaggio

Life

Life is something you
can't keep.
Life is something that
doesn't sleep.
It can be easy or hard
something you have to guard.
It can't be replaced
It can't run a race
but it's a face.

Kimberly Mong

Still Born

A little bit of heaven,
   Came to us one wintery day
She came for just a little while,
   She wasn't meant to stay.
A perfect form, so sweet and small
   She lay there, oh, so still
The angels came and took her back
   They said it was God's will
All the pain and agony
   We suffered here that day
But still our precious little one
   Was never meant to stay.
They found a better home for her
   Up in the Heaven's high
She's with the other angles now
   There is no need to cry.

Norma C. La Mar

In Memoriam

My stately elm was felled today
By Nature's blight and hacksaw blade
Yet as the branches fell away
And wafted down the cutter's lines
It stayed, in regal arrogance,
Its arms upreaching to the sky.

A bluebird and a red bird each
Came soaring through the open space
One chose a nearby apple tree
And one a leafy maple branch
To stare into the vacantness
Where once had been a daily perch.

And from my window seat I grieved,
The tree that once had sheltered me
And ushered in the cooling breeze
Now lay in mounds upon the ground,
Its legacy the bright sunlight
That it in leaving has let in.

La Verta L. Terry

"If Only"

If only you could be out and
   buzzin' about-
but never leave the comfort
and safety of home.
If only you could be alone-
but have family and friends
always by your side.
If only you could reveal
your most vulnerable thoughts-
but keep all your secrets
inside.
If only...

Lois T. Kelly

Love

Love is a trait you cannot see
But you can surely feel its glee
It has no body or no sound
Boy can it make the world go round
A gift from God it has its ways
To get to you both nights or days
Every soul should give it a try
To find out how it works and why
You will find a lovely change
So give it a try it's not strange
If all would try for its reward
What a change in every yard
You'll be surprised what it can do
It surely would be good for you
So many smiles and happy faces
Even shoes might have happy laces
It is free don't cost a dime
Yes it works and cuts down on crime
What a change this world would see
A happier place for all to be

Kenneth H. Fountain

Rodeo Trail

He was a rodeo man,
but now he's withered and tan.

Every bone of his once broken,
All the tips to the other's spoken.

He drove thousands of miles,
smiled hundreds of winning smiles.

Around his waist he's worn lots of gold,
had a lot of championships to hold.

People say he could ride anything,
he's been to every rodeo ring.

He finally had to ride his last,
couldn't believe it ended so fast.

He dusted his hat and walked away,
since then he don't have much to say.

That was his life, all he never knew,
now the poor man's rodeo trail is through.

Kellie King

Lost Love

"Make new friends
But keep the old
One is silver
And the other gold"

I had not seen him
In many years
When we met
I held back tears

He had not changed
So sincere were his eyes
It's kind of sad
How time flies

We loved to dance
So young were we
Our loved endured
That was plain to see

Yes, true love
New or old
This is one
I want to hold

Margaret Deer

Six For Eight

H should stand for Heart
But here it stands for F
I wrote and wrote and wrote
Until my pretty death

My Heart is closed
And yours is loathed
That's what you think of me

H should stand for Heart
But here it stands for F
I'll write and write and write
And soon the F has left

So much heart
So many miles apart
Now I've moved up three

H should stand for Heart
But now it stands for B
Smiles in my Heart
As happy as can be

One day, if I write and write and write
A will stand for Heart

Joseph McDermott

Untitled

the man on the moon came out tonight
but he wasn't in a mood to play
there was fire in his eyes
by the time he had his fill to say
no one dances in my shining light
or accepts my gifts of true love
am i to just fade from existence
will no one offer even mild resistance
at least the pagans respected me
nowadays everyone neglects me
i should just sail from the sky
one final night
and never again shed my lunar light

Jennifer Hosgood

Isolation Dreams

When false control of screaming tears
Buried beneath a seeing lens
Unshed as they are, drowning fears
And withholding grey emotions
Still reservoirs of vile oceans
Stains in the past of sick amends
Scar the mind, produce wrong bends.
How one aberration from the fall
Holds dominion above us all
Set in brooding dissonant eyes
In which all poignant passion dies.

And how is it down in the dark?
Swimming in carnal confusion
Seeking a lover's illusion
The miscreant path you've chosen.
In another time, another
World, far from aiding cover
What was once true and clean for you
Could be again forever.

Mark Spencer Mills

The Mysterious Seashore

Crashing Waves,
Broken Shells,
Colors of Blue and Green
Cool windy breezes
Sandcastles Standing
Proud and Strong
There is so much we
don't know about the,
Seashore

Maureen Staskowski

Stillshot

A girl once danced across my way
brandishing a cheshire grin.
She smiled at me as if to say
she knew some mischief to begin.

Her words were quick to make me smile,
"rewind, sit back, and chill awhile"
but I never found the time.
I guess that's why I wrote this rhyme.

You see, this girl has flown free,
and now she walks with gods and dreams.
Her spirit sings in harmony
with other souls of blissful themes.

So stop, "sit back and chill awhile"
Find the time to truly smile.
Be careful who you tell to wait,
for we are in the hands of Fate.

Matthew MacMillan

One Last Kiss

He hovered over her dead
body, pale as a ghost, and began
to cry. How hard it was for
him to see his lover's cold,
dead body laying there before
him in an endless sleep.
He would never again run
his hand through her dark hair,
touch her fair complexion,
or kiss her tender lips. He
never got to say goodbye. Her
death was sudden, as sudden as
rain on a clear blue day.
He looked down at her,
in the lonely coffin, and thought—
just one last kiss.

Megan Mazikoske

A Fallen Angel

You are a fallen angel
As you fell from the heavens
You picked up a few things
That added to your beauty
You got the twinkle in your eyes
From the twinkling stars
Soft puffy white clouds
Gave you smooth, soft skin
The sun gave up some of its shine
To put in your hair
The rest of your beauty
Is from everything else
That is beautiful
You are a fallen angel
But now will you be my angel?

John Carson

Cherished Memories

A sturdy child with golden curls
Bluest eyes filled with joyous laughter
Warm summer days
Cool star filled nights
The simple pleasures
Night shadows on white winter scapes
Diamond snowflakes on that golden head
The handsome child grown tall
Safe in that happiness
The poetry stopped
The songs all ceased
The child was gone, the magic air
Dreams like crystal dashed on stone
No wisp of romance anywhere
Things never meant to be
Another time, a far off place
Misty memories
Life damp from pain
Deep within the soul
Love is forever.

Mary F. Hensley

Birds

Doves, Cardinals, Robins,
Bluebirds, Blackbirds, too,
Sparrows, Finches,
Pigeons, Ducks,
Geese, Seagulls,
Owls, Hawks, Eagles,
And every bird known to man,
You fascinate me,
You entertain me,
You amuse me,
And you amaze me.
I could watch you all day long.
The way you effortlessly fly about,
And beautifully sing your songs.
You carefully build your nest,
And cautiously watch over it.
You patiently wait for your eggs to hatch,
And furiously attack anyone who comes too near.
Yet you are always so happy and cheerfully
hopping about.
You fascinate me.

Jillian Ostrowski

The Rose

I am like a rose bud,
blooming with pride.
And making it through life,
with an easy strike.

I am like a rose bud,
starting ugly as a thorn.
Slowly, ever so slowly,
turning into a beautiful rose.

I am like a rose bud,
lights and fragile.
Like a petal.

I am like a rose,
full in bloom.
Outgoing and beautiful,
with sweet caress.

I am like a rose bud,
blooming with pride.
And making it through life,
with an easy stride.

Jenn Hanshew

Untitled

My first pair of
black high heels
sunk into the soft ground
with every step I took
my black skirt and
matching sweater with the
little gold buttons
going down the front did nothing
to ease my case of the chills.
Earlier at the viewing I had privately
cried to myself but not until
the flag had been folded
and presented to my mother
and the eerie creaking sound of
the descending casket had begun,
that another tear
rolled off my cheek
and burned at the hole
in my heart.

Louise Billingsley

Why Do I Feel The Way I Do?

This is all so strange
Because I keep it all inside
I don't mention it to anyone
Cause there's no one whom
I can confide
This secret I carry
This feeling so deep
Little do you know
That you make me weak
It's not only friendship
But love that I seek
I can't tell you cause of your reaction
Will you not mind
Or form an attraction
I try to find the words to say
To make you wanna be mine
Cause I know I'd have to wait in line
But for your love I'd wait forever
I wish I knew if you felt the same
Everything's been better now that you came

Megan Griffith

Summer

A gentle breeze,
Beautiful flowers all around,
Swimming at the pool,
Going to day camp,
The wind sings a song,
As the birds flutter,
I walk down the sidewalk bare footed,
A gentle breeze.

Lisa Greenberg

Guardian Angel

In the sunlight and shadows
at dawn and in the night
She is there, somewhere.

She can't be touched, she can't be seen
her goodness is all around,
She can't be found
She is there, somewhere.

She watches over and protects me,
My Angel
She is there, everywhere.

June M. Smith

Two Splashes

I would swim in the
    Astral Sea,
And find my Love,
    that hied away.
She couched her soul
    in a Causal shell
And left our World
    on an Ocean Swell
She aimed her gaze
    to the Summerland
Where all can'ts
    become a can.
She looks out from
    that Netherland
She heard the dive
    of her swimming man
Arms are out to,
    Embrace and hold,
And walk together
    the streets of Gold.

Miles Wells

Circle

I am just a shadow
    as you walk by
circle around again
    and again...

Your eyes
    behold the break of dawn
your smile
    pulls at the strings of my heart
your lips
    longing to be kissed

And I feel a breeze
    as your hand
brushes gently against mine
    ...as you walk by,
    circle 'round again
    and it is here
    I remain...

Melissa Howsam

Survival of Creation

The thought of great advance
as what was before...,
to know that time is passing
into what comes tomorrow
will our world be tainted still
by the environment that surrounds
high in the universe
and deep into the ground

Speak loud for ears to hear
and letting eyes to see
giving the insight beyond
to cleanse all that brings disaster
for the survival of creation
as it was before our time

Geneva Spencer

Life

Life is but a highway
    And its milestones are the years
And now and then there's a tollgate
    Where you buy your way with tears.
It's not our easy road to travel
    But you need not fear
Because God is watching over us
    He is always near.

Margaret Van Atta

Praise Him

Our pastor speaks
As we listen
Get rid of Satan
let God in

Away from sin
To our God's touch
Praise him
Praise him o' so much

Praise our Lord, the one and only
Let him in your heart
And you will see, all the things
Our Lord can do for you and me.

How lucky
Can you be
For your Lord died
For you and me

Praise Jesus
And don't you fuss
Because in our lives
Jesus is a must!

Michael R. Jones

Standing Alone

Standing alone
As time goes by
Hoping you'll turn my way
Standing alone
Longing for your touch
Not holding you close
Standing alone
As you disappear
Never to return
Standing alone
Knowing you'd not seen
Love deep inside me.
Standing alone...

Niel Swanson

Oh God

On Sunday I saw the future?
As tears filled my eyes
when only a few were willing to rise
While others sat with out
filling a presence or
seeing a need
To praise the almighty king
Please oh God don't let
mine be lost in
the unknowing
For we must keep your
love growing
Let the spirit fill our hearts
And show us the way
for there may not be
another day.

Linda Brandt

The Rose

The rose sat lonely,
a petal fell coldly.
The color of red,
remembering who she fed.
A bee that was yellow,
no longer a fellow
Now she lay at my feet.
Petals all over the street.

Lisa Mehta

Let Me Love

O spirit above,
As my life is coming to an end,
I ask of you just one favor-
Give me the chance to find true love.
I've longed for it for such a long time.
I deserve the chance for love,
Even if it is only for a short while.
Please, let me live until I love.

O spirit above,
I am forever indebted to you.
You have made my dreams come true;
You have let me love.
Now, I am ready for my destiny.
As I close my eyes in sleep,
May I rest in peace.

Jennifer Leigh Hale

Untitled

Its arms wrap around me,
    as its claws dig in.
I watch as it tears out
    my heart and grins.
But still I must go on
    and smile and dance.
And I know another
    will eventually come
And undo what was so
    blatantly done.
So another does come
    and it happens again.
Then my heart cries out
    and my mind gives in.
But still another will
    eventually come
And undo, for some time,
    what was blatantly done.

Kelli Kopen

Attics

We value earthly treasures,
As fleeting years pass by,
A yard-stick of lasting measures,
Compiled in attics high.

A warehouse of the past,
Collections from yester-year,
In chests of cedar cast,
Concealed from light and fear.

In isolation they remain,
Till one curious day,
When heirs trudge steps of grain,
Seeking heirlooms stored away.

To once again shed light,
In attics of the mind,
Appear again within one's sight,
In chests of cedar lined.

Larry D. Ney

Our Horizon

From the beginning, on 'til the end
A lost sunset descends
Reflecting a kingdom of natures blend
To paint our region above
To rejuvenate the mood
And grow in a garden of love
The feel of our horizon.

Jason Rangel

Not A Quiet Weekend In The City

They're all out traveling around,
Around the loop block by block.
Looking for a friend, anywhere abound.
And when they find, they'll stop.
   Flashing head lights passing by
Red neon, honking horns. The beat of
The bass, volume turned high.
Fun will soon turn to storm.
   Green, yellow, red, a glare,
People soon gather, no one speaks.
They just stand in a dauntly stare.
Two autos piled in the street.
   Loud sirens, red blue, red blue
He tried to beat the traffic light.
The car ripped up, could it be true.
It is such a tragic sight.
   He had no ID, too much blood,
No one is for sure who.
Parents are called to judge.
One mother turned pale blue.

Kelly Cannon

Homesick For Heaven

Oh, Father I'm homesick for heaven,
   Are the words I whisper today;
As after a day full of labor
   I kneel on my bedside to pray.

Dear Father, please come and get me;
   As my burden gets harder to bear;
I'm so tired of toiling and waiting;
   Oh, Father please let me come there.

Then softly I hear his answer;
   And my soul felt his tender touch;
Dear child, why are you so worried;
   As you know, I love you so much.

You know I go with you and keep you;
   I help you to carry the load;
But your life's work is not yet over;
   So be patient, go on doing good.

I know you're so homesick for heaven;
   But must patiently wait for that day;
And trust your Father as he has a reason;
   For saying you still need to stay.

Monika Stingl

Three Little Words

Three little words I love you
Are precious and so dear
When you're snuggled up close
With the one you love
And they're whispered in your ear.

It's a warm and loving feeling
That lovers often share
Makes your head go reeling
And you think you're walking on air

Love keeps your life worth living
When it is shared by two
Who at least once a day
Remember to say
Three little words I love you

Marcia M. Van Cleave

The Universe And My Heart

The universe and my heart, tonight,
Are linked in holy ban.
For both have been betrayed,
By the promise of man.

Does the sky lose all its glory
When the bright stars fade away?
No! There is always hope and joy,
In the birth of a new-born day.

Then in the blessed Bible,
When Peter thrice did sin,
The night was dark and cloudy,
Yet Christ believed in men.

A complete dark universe can never be,
Not even in the dead of night,
For in some cabin ever so old
Is but a spark of light.

My love I have tried to smother,
I flee with wounded pride.
Yet, a living spark remains,
The universe and my heart walk side by side.

Nita L. Wiese

Dreams I've Left Behind

Rushing through my memories
are dreams I've left behind

Faded shadows far behind me
Call softly out my name.

Drifting on the water,
further out to sea.
Wishful, dreamy,
wandering mind

Calls softly
out to me.

Kathy Ramirez

Oodleberry Pie

Oodleberry pie
Apple bobbin' dunk
Tic Tac Toe
On an old tree trunk

Walkin' up a hill
Climbing up a tree
Looking all around
To see what you can see

Laying in the grass
Sleeping by a creek
Having a good dream
To find what you may seek

These are all the things
Little kids like to do
Come now with me
And I'll share them with you.

Michael J. Moore

Brightest Star

Oh wondrous star of long ago
Appearing in the east,
Oh brightest star all aglow
Above the prairie beasts.

Where shepherds saw - heard angels call
And the wisemen followed, too -
The kings and children watched in awe
As they gazed at you.

Your holy light that filled the night
Led them on their way,
To Bethlehem's small manger
Where the babe did lay.

Oh where are you - God's greatest star
In earth's darkest hour,
Who will find you in the heavens
Who will know your power?

Oh light so pure - light so true
Return to us again,
Lead us back to Christ the king
The babe of Bethlehem.

Joan Pantaleone

Sunset And Sunrises

See the sun setting.
Another day has ended.
Watching the sun rise
   means another day has begun.

When the sun rises
   it brings another day
   of new beginnings.

What will the sunrise
   bring tomorrow?
What dreams will the sunset
   bring tonight?

Kris Martin

Upon One Winter

Fields and flowers, I can't remember
and yet not long ago
I left my home in late September
and the only love I know

I left him standing at the window
as the snow began to fall
Covered those fields and the flowers
and the wind began to call

His name, it echoes from the hills
among the grass and through the trees
I wander lost, alone, and weak
not cold enough for my heart to freeze

The clouds they move without my want
but mountains harder still
They move not with strength nor thought
nor hope, nor love, nor will

Jennifer Arbaugh

never

nevertodieatruedeathIsnevertoliveatruelife
IsnevertoknowatrueloveIsnevertoBe

Jean Lewis Wallace

Mom's Flowers

Mom gave us traditions to share
And words of wisdom as a guide;
She wanted to enjoy her flowers
While she was alive.

Birthday parties and balloons
Friends over for ice cream and cake;
Every moment was precious to her
No matter how much of a mess we'd make!

As the years crept upon us
Along came the burdens and blessing;
Mom grew too weak to enjoy life with us
So God chose her for Heaven.

There were no visitation restrictions
As we stayed by her side;
We would constantly whisper to her,
"Go to sleep, close your eyes,"

During her struggle with Death
Her family was at her side;
We gave Mom what she wanted—
Her flowers while she while she was alive.

Judie L. Miller

Italy

Italy's drastic views,
and tranquil hue
can take away
anyone's blues.

The setting sun
full of silhouetted fun
can make anyone feel
anew

Base patterned skies
in the afternoon high
can make anyone
say a low hi

But when the views
meets the silhouetted sun
in the brilliant azure sky
before my eyes
lay Italy, with my last
Good-bye

Johanna Lee

Morning On The Farm

I woke up this morning,
and took a walk outside.
The wet dew on the grass
made my feet tickle.
I saw bumble bees buzzing
and birds swiftly flying.
The sweet fragrance of the flowers
filled the air.
Ducks quacked and waddled
near the pond,
while fish swam steadily.
The trees swayed and moved
in the breeze.
I could see the sun start to peek
over the mountains,
and I heard mama calling
me, so I headed for the house.
Another day had begun on
the great farm.

Melissa Watson

Untitled

Into God's hands you were delivered
And there you shall remain.
We will remember you forever.
You have not died in vain.

Such short time we had to love you!
We laughed and played and cried.
And now our precious ones,
You're on the other side.

Our Lord will take good care of you.
Of that we can be sure.
Your memory lives in all of us.
So strong and bright and clear.

Karen Thornbrue

Untitled

I lay myself down
    and the moist dirt tumbles down
    off the mounds surrounding
    my rectangular earthen padded room
The stones pelt me in the head
    and I am forced
    to recall this pain
    you call
L-I-V-I-N-G
I'm knee high in worms
Their laughter
    devours me alive
Pain keeps poking
its bony fingers
    into my open wounds

They say madness
    drags her victims kicking and screaming

So help me now...

Jayson Lozier

Little Lady

She stood before the mirror,
    And swayed this way and that,
All dressed up like a lady,
    In mother's dress and hat.

Her little face was covered,
    With powder and with paint.
She used them both quite freely,
    She did not know restraint.

She tottered slowly back and forth,
    In mother's high-heeled shoes.
Her eyes were brightly shining,
    Like diamonds' radiant hues.

She played the game of make believe,
    And made it come alive.
She was a grown-up lady,
    Although her age was five.

Maggie Goad Hensley

Love

Some say love is like a rose
Always blooming as it grows
It dies some where along the way
Waiting to bloom another day
One day your path will come a cross
You'll find your love you never lost
Your feeling of love returns
The fire of passion still burns
Love will never die
And your heart will never lie

Kim Kromrie

The Panacea Sea

When the world gets too heavy
And sunlight tastes black
I hurry to the sea
And with the earth at my back
    am restored.

When Chopin sounds flat
And a yellow rose dulls
I surge toward the salt air
Where the gliding sea gulls
    renew me.

When friendship grates false
When I read time by a Dali clock
I ebb to the swelling tides
As water craters rock
    me to health.

When I feel the touch of
Clawing mental poverty,
Another Ishmael
I throb to be near the sea—
    the panacea sea.

Maggie Odiorne

"View From A Window"

    As I sit upon my window - sill
and stare upon the sea, I wonder
if there ever was a day, when the
bottom I could see. As I look now
out my window upon the dark gray
sea, I wonder if there ever
was a day, when it was blue and green.
As I sit here by my window, sitting
all alone, I wonder to myself -
"How did this once Bright and Beautiful
world get so dark and bleak?"

Miranda Reavies

Blindness

My sister is legally blind,
And she is just awfully sweet,
When she really wants to be,
And to meet her is surely neat.

This very special sister of mine,
Has exceptionally great ears,
Which listen to every sound,
And interpret all things she hears.

But when my sister wants to be,
She gets as mean as anything,
While nearly all her incidents,
Are as harmless as a bird's wing.

But in this whole wide world of ours,
She is the one you want to meet,
Despite her disabilities,
Because this girl is so very neat.

Jessica L. Roberson

Christmas Cheer

Give me a cup of Christmas Cheer,
A fireplace so warm, -
The comfort of friends and family near,
Safety from the storm,

Let me feel the Christmas mood,
So peculiar to the season.
Presents and love and such good food,
Christmas is the reason.

Lynn Work

Sedona

Sun sets past the horizon
And shadows grow upon the mountains
Beautiful red rock burns bright
Like hot embers after a fire
Swept up by the power of the earth
Seeing centuries of nature's sculpturing
She's found another piece of home
An eagle soaring above the cliffside
As the coyote howls in the canyon
To the East the moon rises
Glowing over the mountain tops
An end to a glorious day
And a beginning of wondrous life

John L. Rausch

Alone, I Walk In Winter's Dream

Alone, I walk in Winter's dream
And quiet stars move overhead,
I've left the weary path in haste
To take this silent way instead.
To know the beauty of it's still
The calm in its release,
To know the solo route I take
Will lead me on in peace.
Alone, to walk in Winter's dream,
Now home, I look on high,
As quiet stars once moving fast
Have stopped there, in the sky.

James Bishop

Dreams

I watch my children everyday,
and pray their dreams will come
their way.
Their eyes are wide and there
Souls are deep.
Dreaming dreams not just in sleep.
Keep them safe I whisper each
night and keep them strong to
Withstand the fight.
Chasing dreams is tiring and
endless.
Achieving them somehow seems
painless.
Should my children catch their
dreams.
They'll have endured life's trials
and schemes.
Be happy boys this is my dream,
from this I'll know what happiness
means.

Laurie A. Hitchcock

Untitled

Sunday afternoons are often
a muttering curse
and the God
of oranges, coffee
and Holy Sacrifice is lost
in the Sunday movie.

Educational T.V. lacks my attention
but keeps muttering
just the same.

Hold me.

Judith A. Hartley

Allow Me To Be

I was created as God ordained,
And perhaps you know not my worth.
But God did not need your say,
When he prepared me for birth.

Passion God gave me.
Good and bad he placed.
I cannot changed to suit your need,
Or be less than I am.

I did not plant the seed.
God created my being.
And with you I humbly plead
To leave change to God and me.

Give to me love and respect
With my own special place.
God will correct and perfect
To make me the best I can be.

If my goals are not same,
Please allow me to think and be.
For my signature is my name,
And all I am is me.

Juanita P. Brown

Young Son's Love

When my son was just a youngster
And outdoors his favorite place,
He discovered many treasures
To collect in his embrace.

To him flower beds were special
Where he held a rose or two,
And watched butterflies aflutter
As they drank the morning dew.

He sensed nature's finest message
From its flowers tame and wild,
For he felt it showed devotion
Between a mother and her child.

Hence I learned from all the blossoms
Which my son displayed for free,
That these really spoke his heartthrob
Of abiding love for me.

So my young son's love was precious
Expressed by golden daffodils,
Or when he gave me prickly bouquets
Picked from weedy unkept hills.

Katherine Camp

Silent Night

Let there be "Silent Night"
And let there be peace in hearts,
   for love instead of hate.
Let us let snow flakes pure
   erase all greed, all selfish ill,
We shall find joy on Christmas Night
   if we go out and seek a hill.
Let there be room for faith to fill
   our hearts beside the dying glow;
For the star in the east
   shines brightly still,
Then let there be "Silent Night"

Nell B. Bates

"Last Time"

A candle still burns,
and my heart still yearns
for the love you've taken
from me.

You came into my life,
became my wife soon after
left me to be.

Emotions now still, my
life soon will finish the
path you set forth.

The sun will soon set,
I say I love you with
regret and lay down for
the very last time.

Fate aimed to my mind
as the thought is all
too kind. My heart will
soon be free....

....and a burning candle
there will no longer be.

Joshua Hughes

"Friends"

Whenever I'm lonely
and my heart needs to mend
I can always depend
on all of my friends
Whenever I'm lost
I need to find a way out
My friends then search for me
and to find me they shout
When I need comfort
In my time of need
My friends help me then
So I can succeed
When other people shun me
and rejection is near
My friends shield me
to protect me from fear
Whenever I'm unhappy
and I feel so sad
They lift my spirits
so I don't feel so bad.

George Martin Derieg

Valencia

Each stone carefully cut
And molded to perfection
Each placement masterly planned
To provide with support
This was a wall built to
Hide and protect
It's the last defense
For a once wounded heart
Unable to penetrate, unshakable
Built to last a lifetime
To withstands all seizes
Years to build
With skillful emotions
In moments it crumbled
By just one touch
A touch from you

John G. Woods

An Anthem Of Love

I stand with might on a hill of love
and look into the valley where he stands,
the grass is green, so very green
but nothing to match his dewy eyes!

He's near, yet, so very far away
I need only to reach and touch his face,
but reaching is a daydream of time
that's wasted before I try to grasp!

The sun is slowly fading away
and here I stand upon the hill,
I must leave my love alone
I must bring my mind back home!

Kathy Mayner

AIDS

As I sit by your bedside
and look in your eyes,
I wonder if you wear a mask in disguise.

I wonder how you feel inside
because I cannot see all the
pain and suffering you probably hide.

At one time life was easy street
but now you have a disease
you just can't beat.

You may feel as if you are deprived
cause you now have to swim
with the tide.

Things are different now and
you ask me why?
How could you have gotten this
deadly disease when all you tried to do was please.

Jody Alves

Write Your Words Upon My Heart

Lord, write your words upon my heart
And lead me through each day
Then from you I'll not depart
Even when clouds are gray

I need you, Lord, to speak to me
I need to hear your voice
I hear it in a child's glee
It makes my heart rejoice

I hear it when a good friend shares
The pain they're going through
Then to them my heart declares
The words that come from you

Help me, Lord, to show your love
When a friend is down
Help me give comfort from above
To turn the day around

Linda Shorts

Dead

Souls disappear to hide behind
a curtain of hate.
Heart and mind begin to dissipate.
False pride becomes an addiction
fear becomes the drug.
here we stand in government's hand
not one left, not one single man.
To the eyes of the world
we are Dead!

Justin J. Smith

A Mother's Prayer

God bless you both upon this day
  And keep you in his heart.
And on through all the coming years
  His love to you impart.

You take yourself a lovely bride
  And promise to be true.
Tho far away this glorious day
  My prayer goes out to you.

To give to her your loving heart
  Your faith and understanding,
Convey your humor, comradeship,
  But never be demanding.

Extend your loyal hand to friends
  That she may treasure dearly
Help conquer fears of our own land
  That you love so sincerely.

Give her all your love and our love too,
  And pray we'll meet and know her.
This comes sincerely from the heart
  Of a waiting, loving Mother.

Grace Osterberger

Wild Flowers On Parade

Wild flowers on the hillsides
  and in many valleys, too,
Brighten our country's landscape
  and bring joy to me and you!

Black eyed Susans steal the show
  competing with the goldenrod,
Passion flowers mark the love sign
  and crimson clover covers the sod.

Queen Anne's lace reigns regally
  over trillium and lady fern, too,
The morning glory greets the sun
  moss verbena creates a lovely view.

The gentians by the brook side
  make gentians in the brook,
The big bright cardinal flowers
  open wide for all who look!

God, who is the master gardener
  planned for beauty everywhere,
His wildflowers bless our lives -
  another proof of his tender care!

Johnnie M. Prickett

I Am Me!

I am me for me
And I'm gonna be
Who I want to be
Not for you
But for me
What do I have to do?
Write it on your shoe

Anyway it's going to
be like this
Yes and I insist
I am me for me
And I'm going to be
Who I want to be

Jennifer Hardrick

The Wolf

I see you in the darkness,
And I hear your mournful cry,
It seems that you are asking, pleading,
Someone tell me why.

Your silent battle, dying,
So peacefully you go,
Your teardrops fall from saddened eyes,
And land on cold, white snow.

Silently you run through trees,
On velvet padded paws,
Pitch black fur and yellow eyes,
With sharp and pointy claws.

I wonder why they hate you so,
You are so dear to me,
An animal that must survive,
Yet somehow still be free.

Laura Gumbert

My Love To My Family

My heart is heavy
And I feel blue.
I am so far
Away from you.
I go to the window,
See the setting sun.
I feel some closer
We see the same one.
No matter, be it sun
moon, or star.
When we see them together.
You don't seem so far.
So look out your window
And see with your heart.
Then we will never
Seem so far apart.
Sometime soon we'll be
Together for eternity.

Joyce Copenhaver

Differences

It is night,
and I am filled with fright,
as I stand in this dark house,
I taste a tart taste in my mouth,
It is the candy I've been sucking on.
It also tastes sweet on my tongue.
But now a rock has been flung.
I was stung.
I hit the floor and I said, "No more!"
The man walked in,
he about scared me out of my skin.
He drew his gun,
and I thought: this is not fun!
I pleaded for my life,
Boy, could I use a knife!
Then I started to talk to him,
Then we began to walk,
and he said everything was his fault!

Justin Delabar

The Things I See

I see a heart filled with love
And glowing with happiness
I see this same heart
Broken and bleeding out in the cold
I see someone hurting and alone
Afraid to reach out and hold a love
I see someone confused and afraid
Forever sad but too proud to say
I see a lonely heart
But can't see a reason why
I see a beautiful person
Torn between security and risk
I see a confident smile
And a bright shine in those eyes
I see a beautiful love
Turn and walk away
I see the tears in your eyes
And I will always wonder, why
I see these things
And a soft voice says goodbye

Michael D. Frost Jr.

Please Bless The Homeless, Lord

Please bless the homeless, Lord,
And give them strength, if you would,
For it is just a sad misfortune,
Of people who are good.

Any one of us could be there,
It doesn't mean they're bad,
A lost job, a shattered family,
A lonely cry for what they had.

Please bless the homeless, Lord,
Keep them warm and safe,
Help them to keep their stomachs filled,
'Til they see you face to face.

In this life, they have it bad,
But please watch them from above,
For when they die and are with you,
They'll surely know your love.

Kellie Lynn Hertz

When We Stand At The Gate Of Eternity

As we stand at the gate of eternity
And gaze at the final sunset for us.
Amazed at the heights of perfection
And our beautiful home up above.
Our thoughts on the green pastures
Where the cattle gaze near by,
And the stars appraising in heaven
As we look for our home in the sky,
As we are all safe in the arms of Jesus
As we cross over that dark rolling tide
We look forward to being with Jesus
In His love forever more abide.

Mr. Jewel Creach

Winter Delight

Majestic winter, what a show!
And everywhere one looks
Every scene seems destined
To be in picture books.
I may turn words to phrases
Descriptive and precise
But no word is so lovely
As a tree encased in ice.
Its diamond twigs all glitter.
The weighted boughs droop down.
Earth has donned an ermine robe,
The trees, her glittering crown.
Icicle fringes grace the lines
And fences by the roadway.
Oh, sun, drop fast, subdue the signs
Of melting from the noonday.
When Luna and her starry court
Trace 'cross the heavens darkling,
In mirror image will reflect
Nights winter, silvery, sparkling.

Neva J. Rogers

Boy

Sunshine and rainbows
And bright, shiny stars
Embellish the soul
Of this boy in my arms.

He strengthens my heart
With his laughter and smile.
My lifeblood, my purpose...
My dear little child.

There's something about him,
How can I explain?
I'm searching for words
That aren't there to say.

He's Earth, Wind, and Fire.
He's strength and he's power.
He's precious and charming
And soft as a flower.

My son is my love song,
A special bright star.
Look! He's making rainbows
In the circle of my arms.

Kimberlie Alidadi

Stars

They come out every night
and appear like speckles of light.
They help brighten up the sky.
And are fun for constellations
But what is their true meaning
They seem to be coded in secrets
Like the answer for world peace,
Or diseases we can't find out.
It could be awhile or longer,
Before we know what they mean
Until then they remain the mystery
of speckles in the sky.

Jennifer Burnette

Love Flies

Love flies through the air
  and almost dares you to
  stop and care;
  about who, what and where.

Caught love may turn to
shreds
  Which would leave the
  people who you love;
  crying in there beds.

Some people say love's magic,
  other people say that's not
  true;
But if you look into your
heart,
  the answer might come to
you.

Michelle H. Cordasco

Untitled

If everything were understood,
and all things were foreseen.
Were vices nonexistent,
so that none could intervene
with all good thoughts and habits,
that vanquish fear and dread,
I think we'd be in paradise,
or else my friend,... we're dead.

But come let us resign ourselves,
for things are as they are.
We cannot change societies minds,
nor ever hope to mar
the righteous face of ethics,
which leaves no alternative,
we'll do the things that we must do,
because my friend,... We live.

Mary Shirley Manis

Our Daughter's Birthday!

We are smiling ear to ear,
  And about to have some fun!
As Lauren ends her first year,
  We're announcing our daughter's one!

From Mauka to Makai,
  Travelling Ewa to Diamond Head.
There will be balloons in the sky,
  And banners flying overhead!

For during this special birthday,
  We'll be wishing you were near!
Around her neck we'll string a Lei,
  To celebrate her first year!

Lori Hall

Image

To some love is like
an image written in the sand.
Vanishing when the tide come's in.
And when the mood is right
they'll be back out
redrawing the sight.
You go back because
they say this time
it will be different.
Once everything seems
to fit in place
that tide strike's again.
And all that was written
is now washed away.

Jessica L. Ryan

The Road To Nowhere

I walk the winding path
amidst the golden sun,
each step leading back
to where I've just begun.
I follow words of wisdom
in this moment now
and walk beside my footprints
as I humbly take a bow.
Lesser men have ventured,
greater men have gained
but all have yet to master
the walking of the lane.

Loveta Blair

Sleeping Beauty

The scent of brambles fill the air,
Amid the folded sheets he lies.
The gold of morning in his hair,
The silver of eve shut in his eyes.

How many a changing moon has lit,
The unchanging paleness of his face.
His soul ever broods on it,
In the silver stillness of the days.

Off flies the moth on filmy wings,
Into his silent, lonely lair,
Shrill evening song the cricket sings,
From some still shadow in his hair.

In heat, sun; in wind, rain.
He sleeps in lovely loneliness,
Half-folded like an April bud,
On a winter haunted tree.

Lena Williams

With Out You

With out you I feel so
alone and cold, I long for
the loved one I want to hold.
Without you it hurts
so bad, I sit and think of
the love we had.
I still feel the love
for you so deep and strong
but I can't figure but
where we went wrong.
Without you I feel
so blue, because what I
feel for you is real and true.
Without you my
life isn't the same, but
When I look back I know
I am to blame.

Jean Gardner

A Child Cries

Sometimes a child cries
and his tears sting his heart,
No one sees his pain
as his soul falls apart.
Time shall heal his wounds,
but this he doesn't know,
Feelings bottle up,
his sadness starts to grow.
This poor little child
searching for his own place.
Already torn up
and, yet, so much to face.

Nicole Littleworth

A Place For Me

I thought I knew
all to know,
But there was more
to learn,
with the cool crisp
wind above the snow,
beauty told its turn.
It told a tale of moonlit
paradise across the open sea,
a cave, a tunnel, a place, just
for me to see.
Where flowers grow of plenty
each and every day,
a peaceful place, a place where
I can stay.

Kelly Timko

His Precious Hands

A peaceful glade,
All pleasant and grand,
It has been made
By God's precious hand.

His hands formed a man
And gave him life,
Then he made a woman
And gave him a wife.

Then the people nailed
His two hands to a tree,
But he had not failed
For sinners were set free.

I know that I shall see
The cruel prints left by the tree,
When together we will be
For I was one who was set free.

Laura A. Kelly

A Silence Calling

From the light
above the mountain
comes a calling
calling of many voices
some of these I have known
in my long silence
and my ascent
becomes a continuance
of ancient conversations

With each step
there is an altering
    shadows infringed,
    time gained or lost,
    like so many breaths
    thieved by the wind,
    a stone displaced

And everywhere
beneath the stones
there are shadows without eyes

And the immeasurable silence

Michael McCay

People Of The Past

Have you ever wondered
about the People of the Past?
Have you ever had a quiet moment
and thought of being asked?
How did they live?
When did they die?
For whom were the tears
that they did cry?
What was their meaning?
What was their purpose in life?
Had they always been faithful
to their husband or wife?
Who did they live for,
to whom was their devotion?
Had they ever felt the mountains
or smelled the salty ocean?
Whether you've ever wondered or not,
there are questions you could ask,
and maybe give one more thought
to the People of the Past.

Marc Meyer

I Want To Be A Witness

I want to be a witness,
A witness I want to be.
I want to be a witness,
Internationally for Thee.

For if I can be a witness,
And change one person's way,
Then in life I have accomplished,
What CHRIST would have me say.

It's the children I want to witness to,
That they might know GOD'S WAY.
They'll need GOD to turn to,
As they grow in this world day by day.

A child of GOD is different,
For he's meant to show THE WAY,
To the children of the world,
That perhaps are out astray.

So I want to be a Witness,
In an international way.
So children may know and come to GOD,
For life everlasting, today.

Marjorie Roberts

In Memory Of Those We Love

As the dust claims my body
A voice doth speak unto me
Inviting me up to the wondrous
    heaven
Much loved souls reaching
    for the stars
An embrace in the darkest
    night
So please, my loves, weep not
    for me.

John Wyrick

Created Vision

I see a vision.
A vision within the world's creation.
It is like a dream,
but also a nightmare,
and a lot of times it creates an
awful scare.
At other times it is beautiful.
The beauty if from the sun and the sky.
The vision comes and it goes,
but when it comes it really shows.
It's a vision within itself,
and you create it.

Kim Sobtzak

The Treasure

I once dreamed I'd find
A treasure that was priceless.
And within that treasure
would be
Love, Laughter, Friendship,
Togetherness, Forgiveness,
Care for people, and
Loveliness.
Then I found that treasure
And when I looked inside
I found you
With all the qualities
I dreamed of.

Mitchel Breland

The Tennis Pro

The tennis pro should be, I think,
A syndicated feature.
He thinks he is a macho man,
A most amazing creature.

His muscles they are very large,
His clothes the latest fashion.
And hitting fuzzy little balls
becomes a lifetime passion.

He served an ace into the space
Where smashes ought to be.
I responded with a lob
Where lobs ought not to be.

"Why did you do that?" he asked,
In a most distressful query.
"I'll tell you what the truth is sir.
You've made my bones most weary!"

"When will our next lesson be?", he asked me
quite discreetly.
"When a new body I have found. You've
worn this one out completely!"
Ah, yes, this is the tennis pro. There's no
more to be said.
If he makes me any healthier, I fear I shall be dead!

Kathleen Gordon

The Tea Party

A sweet little girl
A small teddy bear
A Raggedy Ann
Are each in a chair.

For this is tomorrow
And tomorrow's the day
That milk and crackers
Will be served with their play.

Mary serves each guest
With ladylike graces
And keeps both of them
Propped up in their places.

Mary is busy
As you will agree
Because she's eating
And talking for three.

Margel Gullickson

Why?

Our happiness had just begun
a short few years ago
now sickness came into his life
and he seldom even knows
what's going on around him
whether good, bad, or "just so".
His mind is slowly fading
into oblivion it will go.
We had hoped to share our future,
our dreams and joys and love.
But unbeknown to both of us
a "NO" came from above.
God gave me extra strength to cope
with sorrows down the line.
He also gave me friends who are
so patient and so kind.
With help from "HIM" and family
I know I will come through
this hard ordeal I'm facing now
with love lasting and true.

Lisa Owens

Out Of The Depth

As I sat alone in the twilight,
A sadness came over my soul.
As over the white sand at night,
The dark rushing sea billows roll.

A sadness throbbing with longing,
Engulfing a heart with pain.
Flooding a soul with aching,
As a river is flooded with rain.

Then from the depth I was lifted.
I saw Jesus Christ on a throne.
I thought of the pain he had suffered,
And knew I despaired not alone.

Lucille Martinelli

A Date With Destiny

Dressed to roll,
A red dress and high heels,
I wait.
The man in boots should show,
He comes, we go.
Cozy restaurant - dinner for two.
We chat - the basics,
How are you?
Any family?
Wonderfully boring, but a necessity.
A movie; drive-in of course.
Small talk.
End of evening.
A kiss.
A promise.
Better than some dates.

Kristi L. Budzinski

"Fairy-Tale Fantasy"

Imagination is this world's blood
A place for the forever young
Little men covered with mud
Mining for treasure like diamond
Locked inside a tower
A royal damsel so fair
A man with magic power
Astride a gold horned, white mare
Fire-breathing creatures
Flying high amidst the clouds
Armor hides his body features
On his stead he rides tall and proud
Tiny beings that tinkle with glee
Causing mischief or granting wishes
Living their lives in the sea
Are half-human and half-fishes
People with pointy ears
Quick of wit and with their feet
Who and what is here
The End you've meet

Johanne Untalan

Oklahoma 1995

Shreds and shards and twisted steel...
A new life form of gaping wounds,
Inner organs offensively exposed,
Lying around, piled high...

That's not all, dear God, it is not!
Deep inside, death and destruction...
pain and anguish.
Hatred that thrives on children's cries,
broken bodies and shattered lives.
...Pearl Harbor...Hiroshima, revisited?
Victims, but pawns...not considered?

Rise from this O Beautiful Land
Listen to the cries of your soul...
Gush forth more than corn and oil...
......Love......humanity!

Gerard G. Masters

The Beauty Of You

The sound of your voice,
a melody.
The way your words blend,
a harmony.
Your soft, velvet skin,
so beautiful.
Flowing as you move,
like music.
You turn and smile,
I'm breathless.
Your hazel brown eyes,
are windows.
What lies behind,
a mystery.
But what I do know,
a promise:
My love for you,
lasts forever.

Mark Ricketts

Karen

An orange, blushed flower
A handful of mother earth,
A solitary soul
With just a hint of mirth.
The pages of a diary
With secrets that abound,
Of tenderness and love
And much more to be found.
A tender heart,...but
A guarded love,
The Master's work of art
That brush strokes can not hide.
The end of a golden day
A fresh glow still anew,
A warm, gentle sunset
Seen by just a few,
By eyes that are blind
To a lady full of grace,
A true friend, one of a kind
Karen - God's "orange, blushed flower."

Ned Olmstead

Friends Forever

She'll always be my friend,
A friend forever,
A friend for a lifetime,
A friend that's there for me,
Through thick,
And thin,
A friend that's always my friend,
A friend that loves me,
No matter what,
Even when she's gone,
Gone,
Forever,
She'll always be my friend!

Marni Kornhauser

Before My Eyes

One glance over my shoulder
a flash before my eyes
there stood watching over
was an angel in disguise

An angel in disguise
a police officer who waves you by

An angel in disguise
the neighbor waving "hi"

An angel in disguise
the clerk smiling saying "come again"

An angel in disguise
a smile from a friend

One glance over my shoulder
and much to my surprise
my angel there watching over
was right before my eyes.

Nancy L. Rich

If Only

If only I had a daddy
A daddy I could love
If only I was like you
To have my daddy take me in his arms
And love me like your dad does you
"Oh" how I still remember
When I was only four
I remember seeing
My daddy walk out the door
I haven't seen my daddy since
But now I have not long to live
So daddy come see me in my grave
Please daddy, do come
For now I am......Dead!

Laverne B. Solis

Untitled

A year to grow
A chance to be
like and Eagle
strong and free.
Able to spread my wings
   and fly sky high,
to reach the brightest star
   in the sky.

A year to grow
A chance to be
unrestricted by the things
   in me.
I want to hold my
   head up high
Proud to watch an Eagle fly.

Jeannie Phillips

Only Once

Love given is like a rose,
a bud so new and fresh;
to warmth it slowly opens,
its petals soft as flesh.

Love in full bloom,
is at its finest form;
given adequate attention,
sheltered from the cold, stays warm.

It cannot forever be protected;
you must be able to leave its side;
if someone comes along and takes it,
the pain of loss is hard to abide.

Its beauty never forgotten,
to those it lived within;
but soon you will learn,
it will never flourish again.

A rose can only bloom once,
but not be frozen in time;
so once the tears, (petals) fall,
you can only reconstruct its pleasure in your mind.

Julie Brewer

The Key To God's Heart

They brought before God
   A beautiful deer
And God in his joy
   shed a tiny tear
They showed him a tree trunk
   With a snake wound around
He looked at it and grimly frowned
   Next he was shown
A stately giraffe
   He patted its head
And managed a laugh
   But when they brought in
A little child
God opened his heart
   And—smiled.

Margaret Greco

Quiet Madness

Wings of flight
Borne freely upon a breeze
Their tender virtues wander
In further search of ease

Birds of peace
Singin' what men can't say
As afternoon lingers
Long upon the day

Of light and darkness
Upon their flight they speak
Many sing in simple wonder
Of the bootless goals men seek

In and out
Within their paths of flight
The shine of light departs
Giving way to endless night

Soaring gently down
The ground approaching near
For these birds of peace
Those things darkened disappear

John William O'Hara

Can You Hear The Church Bells Ringing?

Can you
hear the church
bells ringing? Lightly
swinging, softly singing.
Gently rocking the toll
of time, sweetly humming
a soothing rhyme. Can you
hear the church bells
ringing? Good morning to
you, good afternoon, good
evening. Calmly they sing
of peace and love, reminding
all of the man above. Can you
hear the church bells ringing? How
softly
they are
singing.

Katherine Miller

Psalm Of Praise

(for two voices)
Thank you Lord
for these side effects,
*rational * mystical*
Utterly unique,
*objective * subjective*
as a snowflake or fingerprint.
*abstract * concrete*
your creation!
*temporal * eternal*
A patchwork quilt,
*reality * fantasy*
Intricately intertwined,
*directed * free*
Yet
*convergent * divergent*
side-by-side,
*intellect * intuition*
two brains,
*left * right*
one mind!

Betsy Broda

A Poem Of Bittersweet Disparity

For my brother Steven
   A sweet distilled embodied power,
an awesome force of nature,
a cultured hour.
   A sweet installment of womanly woe.
A mindset of hue to solemnly throw.
A subtle wave of peace and kindness;
injustice intermixed.
   Civility at its bleakest hour
war and solitude betwixt.

Christine Heurkins

The Search

I've been searching for a flower,
Among a garden of weeds,
As I tumble to the valleys
And stumble through the trees.
This search is almost endless,
I doubt it shall ever be complete,
For as long as I've been searching,
Not one has appeared beneath my feet.
And I wonder if I'll ever find,
That flower among the weeds.

Colene Brown

To Be Free

To be free
like the sun, sky and wind

To be free
like the sunrise and the sunset

To be free
like you, her or him

To be free
not like me

Brandi Lynn Devine

On The Other Side

Death is uncertain to whom
it strikes next
but death must be.

And I fear that day when
death takes you away from me.

We might as well face facts
death has no friend.

Yet, one day death will come
to take one and leave the
other behind.

If tomorrow comes and you
have left my side, I won't
feel sorrow for we'll meet on
the other side.

Aleka Harris

A Dream

I dream a dream of love
A dream of one so fair
A dream of one so beautiful
There is none to compare

I held the dream so close, so tight
And whispered Babe, I love you.
Please be mine for all time.
I thought I heard her say, I want to

When I awoke and realized
That I was only dreaming.
I cried and cried and ached inside.
My heart was surely broke.

Now I know that dreams are just dreams
And must not be confused with real life.
But how I pray, Dear God someday
Make this dream my wife

Austin Kephart

The Outstretched Hand

The poem is loneliness,
A hand outstretched,
Seeking to share
Answering touch

The page is desire's death,
The mind's grave,
Unless the word becomes
A world for two

The poet is eternal onanist,
Sad half of love,
Until a reader's art
Completes the poem,
Heartbeat in the metaphors,
Life to life,
Loneliness to loneliness.

Bill C. West

The Seasons

The Moon is full, the moon is new
a frost, a chill, a sparkling dew.
From green to red and red to brown,
a warm, a cold, then icy ground,
and the world turns.

The snows fall, the chill of ice
a birth, a death, a baby cries,
a smile, a kiss, another year
then dark and night and silence here,
and the world turns.

The sun now shines, a bird to sing.
Pink roses bloom, the breath of spring.
Comes wind and rain to a fertile sod,
so love and work and worship God,
and the world turns.

Summer air now fills the skies.
so stop to pray and realize,
Your world to have, to share, to love,
so live, give thanks to God above
and the world turns,

Clemis T. Moore

The Ancient Sound Of Nature

The dance of the Western grebe
a choreography older than time.

A call of the loon
Mournful and mysterious.
The flash of a King fisher
By waters edge.

Hummingbirds flit and dart
To slip the nectar of sweet blossoms.

Woodlands murmur
Like sounds of nature,
Like the warp and weave
of intricate patterns.

Seasons of change
That are eternal.
To feel deep vibrations within us
Of the natural world.

Barbara P. Hallett

Raindrop

Drop
A drop
Now many
Drip and drop
Watch them fall
There are so many
Do they begin the same
They all start way up there
Falling endlessly down to us
Shall we stand to greet them all
No drop can do harm to you or me
Watch them gather around the grass
Soon they will be here where we stand
When will we leave this soggy area
They are gathering around my feet
We now conclude our stay here
A superb show is given to us
Nature working with others
Great art given by few
Together for a cause

Damian Barranco

Reflection About Birthdays

A stranger has taken me over I fear.
I see her whenever I look in a mirror.
I know this is me, standing here, looking in,
But, who's looking back with that fat whiskered chin?
How can I disappear in that flat plate of glass,
Replaced in a wink, it happens so fast
I can't see where I go or how she gets there,
But I wish she'd do something to fix that gray hair.
Can the image of me in my mind as a lass
Now be this same woman I see in the glass?
The change seemed so rapid, (I know you'll agree)
The me that I was, no longer is me!
She mimics my movements, she's got it down pat.
Are you sure that is me in that glass looking back?
Or, does she have a life that isn't like mine?
Is she always there, or only when I'm?
It crosses my mind as I shut off the light,
If that isn't me, should I tell her goodnight?

Marjorie Kersulis

Ecola Beach

I fell in love with the ocean spray;
I saw her first in evening light,
Ecola is where I would like to stay.

The sky was barely getting gray,
I felt the chill of the coming night.
I fell in love with the ocean spray.

And then the moon its shining ray
Silvered the sky, ... a lovely sight.
Ecola is where I would like to stay.

I did not want to turn away
As the path to the moon became more bright.
I fell in love with the ocean spray.

I know I will come back another day,
To watch the waves and Gulls in flight.
Ecola is where I would like to stay.

I will return to that tranquil bay,
Where Ecola nestles in the bight.
I fell in love with the ocean spray.
Ecola is where I would like to stay.

LaWayne Chapman

Fear And Faith

With a gentle kiss, while holding on tight
   I said, "I love you",
never dreaming that it was our last night.
   Then came the news today.
Now I just don't know what to do;
   because suddenly you've gone away.

While walking in the morning rain,
   my body aches and all I do is cry.
Because the world is now filled with pain,
   but life goes on and slowly time goes by.

In my heart you will always be.
   As my soul fills me with peace,
I find strength in the love we knew.
   In heaven and earth we will never cease.
Through memories, you are part of me,
   and someday again my skies will be blue.

Michelle Hamilton

Ice Cream Sunday

As a small child growing up in a quiet little town,
I recall the days of summer, all the sights, the smells and sound.

Perhaps my fondest memory is that of Bible School,
Where I, my friends and cousins went to learn the Golden Rule.

But the highlight of the week would come on Sunday night,
To share what we had learned as our faces glowed so bright.

Then at last a special treat was waiting just outside,
There were freezers full of ice cream churning from side to side.

So with the last chorus sung and my last Bible verse said,
I would fly down the isle, flavors racing through my head.

"My favorite is chocolate," someone yelled from the rear,
"How about the strawberry?" Was all that I could hear.

"There's blueberry," "I see peach," I caught from up the line,
If I could just find vanilla my tummy would feel just fine.

So with my plastic bowl filled high with my precious frozen treat,
I would find the a spot on the grass since there were no more folding seats.

Those were the days of summer savored rightly by the locals,
Just a good ole southern evening known then as an ice cream social.

There were no banana splits to ever come our way,
No parfaits or waffle cones - just a simple ice cream Sunday.

Melanie Milton

My Muffy

My dear, sweet Muffy with your little pink bow,
I loved you, I brushed you and I now miss you so.

Such a little dog took a big piece of my heart,
Yet, my dear Muffy, we will never be apart.

I still feel your kisses and hear your little yap,
And, oh, how I wish you could sit on my lap.

My sweet little baby I'm in such despair,
I wish so much that you were still here.

To give me your love, your sweet little ways,
You will live in my heart to the end of my days.

My heart is so broken and I'm in so much pain,
Because I know that I can never hold you again.

Can't give you a bath and put a bow in your hair,
Or give you a kiss and my tender loving care.

I held you one last time so that I could be sure,
That my dear little Muffy lived no more.

I'm so happy I had you for almost 9 years,
If you were here I know you'd lick up my tears.

It's so hard for me to go to sleep at night,
For out of my life went a bright little light.

Marilyn Tardera

The Rain

I hear the soft melody playing on my window pane,
I love to listen to the rain.

The rain washes mother earth anew,
It leaves flowers and plants with a dainty misty dew.

The rain is refreshing, falling on my face and nose,
Some people don't care for it because it wets their clothes.

I love the rain because of the soft melody that I hear,
Gently I fall asleep, only to be reminded that morning is near.

Oh, how I love the rain, because of the softness that it brings,
Oh, how I love the rain, because the sunshine in my heart sings.

Melanie Jackson

How I Love Thee With All My Heart

How I love thee with all my heart even after
I love thee with all my heart, with a passion
When you said I was bella in a way of fashion
You smile how it feels my heart with laughter
How I love thee when your hands caress on me
When you kiss me with your big but tender lips
When you bring my favorite snack in bed, chips
How I love thee when I first caught my eyes on thee
Why should I love thee of what you put me through
The nights I wait for thee but you never come my way
The days I cried and hurt inside for you
Dreaming of pounding your face like a bundle of clay
But I can never hurt thee only chase thee like a dog for its prey
Oh how I love thee with all my heart my love
   my love my love never ends for thee and
    I will never turn it loose.
      Lisha Rachelle Robinson

"My Dad"

I put on your sweater and sit in your chair,
I look for you, but you're not here,
Always there to lend a hand,
A very kind and gentle man,
The twinkle in your eye, your warm embrace,
A silent tear falls upon my face,
I miss your loving smile,
I miss your gentle touch,
Our times together which meant so much,
A wonderful father and also my friend,
How long does it take a broken heart to mend.
    Karleen Antonson

Indiana Summer

I listen to the wind through the leaves of the tall oak tree,
I listen to the blue jays sing as they fly free,
I listen to the tall grass as the squirrels scamper away,
I listen to the rabbits as they run and play

I smell the pungent odor of freshly cut grass,
I smell the scent-filled aroma of cooking on brass,
I smell the sweet fragrance of the bright red rose,
I smell the fish from the lake as the smell drifts by my nose

I see the bright blue skies as I look up above,
I see the innocence of this heavenly place as I see the white dove,
I see the calm, gray waters of the vast lake below,
I see the serenity of this heavenly place as I see the tan doe,
If only you could be here to enjoy this heavenly place with me,
Then you would understand what I hear, smell and see
    Norm Fugate

Rebecca

Although I'm new, young and very small,
I know God has blessed me most of all!

You celebrated my birth with a beautiful shower,
then, when I got sick you prayed down God's power!

You've given me so many wonderful things;
cards, flowers, dresses — God's blessings.

You showed fruits of the Spirit during this long ordeal.
The PARENTING Small Group, each day, supplied a meal.

Now I'm a happy, healthy, beautiful little girl,
cared for by Mommy and Daddy in this big world.

And when you hear me in church, getting a little too loud,
remember, I'm just saying thank you to a wonderful crowd!
    Loretta Verde

What I Like

I like cookies
I like to tease
I like to climb up my friend's tree
I like the sun the moon and I like a bright star
I can't wait to get a car-

I like chocolate
I like the sky
I like chickens, but I don't know why
I like birds and bugs and a buzzing bee
But most of all, I like me-

I like ants
I like trees
I like my hair whipping through the breeze
I like grasshoppers crawling up leaves
I like dogs that sniff and sneeze-

I like pie
And cake too
If you're reading this poem, I like you
I like these things, don't ask me why
I guess I like everything, oh my, oh my!
    Lindsay Rendon

Bereavement

"I can't bear it, Lord," I said,
I lie, so sleepless, on my bed,
With thoughts and mem'ries, flooding round,
In pain and anguish; fears bound.

"I can't do it, Lord," I said,
As others say, "Move on, ahead,"
Here I'd stay, where paths are known,
Not moving out, where I'm alone.

He held, to me, His nail-marked hands,
"Your heart's sore pain, I understand;
Trust My Love, My will is right,
E'en what to you seems darkest night."
    Norma Vinson

Autism: Student To Teacher

In silence, everything speaks to me
  I know it well; so completely
From the smallest sound to the largest hum
  I am become as one.

I observe life's facets concisely
  Wishing to be cognitive of all that I see,
As each entity is in place in my mind
  So I am in my entirety in kind.

I look out in obscure consciousness, but don't perceive
  My mind's eye has a block that blinds me.
Yet, I raise questions to others of my intellect and craft,
  Hoping that someone with understanding will reflect on my behalf.

Though locked in, I desire to be free
  I'll challenge all until they see.
I entreat you, to see through my mirrors, my visions, and my goals.
  Help me to accomplish knowledge and wisdom unto my soul.
    Mildred A. Lightfoot

Untitled

All of the men in his past
I can hear him crying now
I look back and all the memories flood back
And make me cry
Of a time when you were all mine.
    Joseph Patrick Johnson

Untitled

I push you away. You look strange from the inside.
I judge not what you think, only question it. Your expressionable
face gives you away.

  You're not here. It seems you're trapped in some other day, another
memory show, more dramatic plays. I take your hands
and see your screaming eyes. You're still pulling at your lowly disguise.
  One hand is cold and dead, the others hot and wanting.
You heal with that hidden feel. Your eyes burn my brain now,
they stay to haunt me. I want the rest of you.
  Lightly kissing your eyes and then I say...
You're gone now but you're back all the same.
Hold my hand now because I want you to stay.
  Why go, please stay, I can be your needed pray.
I would induce your venom to keep you good, just drop a
ton on me. Now that you did, I feel big,
proud like I did you a favor. Yeah uhuh, I'm
A life saver. Now I want to spit on myself for feeling that way.
I hate the way I think. Your venom
is working, I'm dying even more. But you
feel better and that makes it ok.

  Lee Carty

I Dreamed Of Angels Crying

I dreamed of angels crying, their tears a velvet red.
I imagined words of compassion, I've heard, but never said.
I prayed for the salvation of all creatures on earth,
I saw a realization, of what a life is worth.
I searched to find the answer lost within the rhyme,
I longed for all the power, to change the course of time.
I stood alone in silence, while all of Heaven slept.
I wished I'd told the secrets, that in my heart I kept.
I wandered to a place, where fallen angels lied;
The ghosts of past and present, whose spirits never died.
I looked into the future, a world of mystery;
I glimpsed the land, the sea, the stars, in perfect harmony.
And I understood infinity, as a pre-determined course;
For I know we are intrusted, to a stronger, greater force.

  Michelle De Montis

Mother's Feeling

After a wait that seemed an eternity
I held my baby girl in my arms
I felt my joy rise to infinity
Such is the power of her charms

This moment gives me happiness
Tomorrow new hope and expectation
Her every act of mischievousness
Fills me with love and adoration

Her gaga googoo and other noises
The look she gives with her beautiful eyes
She keeps me entertained with these surprises
She is my future - my precious prize

I cannot imagine a life without her
Strange indeed that this tiny being
Has altered my life altogether
Oh! The force of a mother's feeling

  Nithya S. Doré

Eventide

Clusters of gossamer draped o'er boughs
Gently swaying while soft Summer breezes
  whisper a song.
Nature's voice calling; evening begins
Wrapping creation in love's tender wings.

  Gail G. Escobar

Dragon Song

On the winds that blow this morn
I hear a melodic dragon song
From his mouth where fire spews
Comes a tune that paints vivid hues
A magical image, a minds eye view
Lush green trees; rivers of turquoise blue.
On a hilltop in this land far away,
A Dragon is resting for the day.
Majestically he sits in the sun's hazy light
Wings outstretched, golden and bright
Head turned skyward, voice soft and low,
He's singing for the creatures gathered below.
Pixies and fairies and winged forest sprites,
Elves and gnomes, each listening with delight,
As the Dragon sings of a place he has been,
The land of the humans they have never seen.
Sensing my presence, like an invisible spy
The Dragon smiles warmly and with a gleam in his eye
"A human" he tells them, "is with us today"
And as his song ends, they turn to look my way.

  Laurie Raso

Michael Michael What Will You Do?

I'm doomed to death what will I do?
I have to clean my room through and through,
Tons of books, hundreds of pages,
Handed down through the ages
This book that book, every little book
All I need is a little cranny or a nook.
Look at the mess! Look at the dust!
Oh, cleaning my room is just a bust!
What has past an hour, a day?
I wish I had a super cleaning ray!
Then I would point, and ZAP!
It would be clean just like that
But what can I do?
I have to clean my room through and through.
But wait, what is this?
I'm pinned under the giant mess!
  Help! Help!

  Michael Sweeney

Untitled

I half-kneeled close, half-whispered
'I have something for your pain.'
Lively grey-dawn eyes...rebuke me?
  Brrr, but I hate frosted evening loneliness.
  Hurrah for the sun!
  Warm beams dizzy dance crowds of tumbling
    people into wide time
  The jolly band chokes with laughing
    Ha! Ha! Up and away
      for tomorrow we (La La)
        (Sing up please)
            We pay
          (Of course)
              For tomorrow we pay
mild merry wrinkles, gentle touch
recall me to this last star's twinkle
crowning the blush of Morning.
Soft spoken hush.
'Let me be. I have no pain.'
I was flushed with her peace.

  Kathy Harrell

The Richest One

I have nothing but my dreams, and sometimes they are nightmares,
I have nothing but my hopes, but it seems that no one cares.
I have nothing but my goals, that I don't think I'll reach,
I have nothing left to learn, for you have nothing left to teach.
I was not blessed with looks, but the blind do not worry,
I was not blessed with a beautiful voice, but the
  deaf seem to hear the real me.
I was not blessed with talent, for I have no special trait,
I was not blessed with intelligence, for brilliance is not my fate.
I may not have your power, your prestige or your money,
But one thing I can do without is your half-hearted pity.
So spare me of your troubles, your misfortunes and your woes,
Cause living in the lap of luxury is how your story goes.
Don't call me a poor man, for I may not have all that you possess,
I am far richer, for with a heart I have been blessed.

Lina Silva

Preserve Our Anthem

Let me in to sit a spell,
I have a story I want to tell.
About men with courage, and even some fear.
Takes lots of both of protect those we hold dear.

A man called Sir Francis Scott Key,
Recorded in verse, important history.
To explain what was happening at the break of dawn.
And now some folk our anthem to be gone.

Too hard to sing is what they say!
They're the same ones don't want our children to pray!
Takes courage to stand up and say what's right,
And courage to battle as our men did that night.

Takes courage to sing the verses Sir Francis wrote.
So what if you aren't able to hit that high note!
The star Spangled Banner has been sung all my life,
To change our anthem now would cause much strife.

Give us a break, we love "Old Glory"
Thank you Sir Francis Scott Key for writing yours Story!

Gloria Cotner

Go With Love My Daughter

I gave life to you, but I cannot live it for you.
I give you love, but I cannot choose whom you love.
I can show you which road to take, but I cannot go with you.
I care for and house your body, one day another will supply these
  acts of devotion.
I try so hard to let go, as it must be, and my heart and soul cry
  "No!"
My mind wanders back to when you were young and dependent.
Your desire now is to forget the young years-
To be independent, to go forward- sometimes too fast.
You began separating yourself from me the day of your birth, crying
  your desires.
You were taught the ways of God; do not depart from them.
Go to discover a whole new world;
If you fail, I will be here to help
To send you again on your way,
With sadness in my heart,
But happy that you have the yearning to try again.
So I say, "Go with love, my daughter, go with love".

Mary Jane Carroll

God

Mysterious vapors clouded my head
I felt myself breathing in the river of LIFE
His hand came down through cotton balls
It lifted me to the Kingdom of light
I awoke

Kim Hallisey

Ode To Brother Robert

If in this generation I could say,
I found the darkness of mankind design.
That truth all men must now betray.
My country, thou beauty of all must fall
To Satan's whose crimes though I must admit
Had left the light of my journey unlit.
Falling, falling lower, thus and evermore
I tried to bring my country an honor
Bestowed by my father and even more,
And thus life a time I did ponder,
Thus to bring that candle to lit before,
My father's grave, and then to set yonder
A formula for man's solution
Then shot by Satan's evil master plan.

Michael J. Prosser

That Thick Rich Jam

How did I feel?
I felt as if huge prongs held and lowered my body into a vat of thick
  rich jam.
Pick a jam. Any jam will do, as long as, it is truly thick and rich.
I was covered from my feet to my neck in that thick rich jam.

I was lifted from the vat of that thick rich jam.
For all to see, I stood like a park statue in open space.
My clothing was stuck to me. My fingers and arms were webbed.
I could barely move. I did not enjoy the idea of that thick rich jam.
I wanted to be free. I wanted that thick rich jam off me.
I was alone with that thick rich jam covering me.
There wasn't anyone to help me. How did this happen?

My thoughts circled around and around as I panicked.
My panicking was to no avail. I remained alone and covered.
I realized that my choices were few and that help was not coming.
I could wait for a storm to wash away that thick rich jam.
Or, I could painstakingly eat the jam off me.
I imagined me eating and licking all that thick rich jam.

I felt depressed. That is how I felt.
I needed a change.

JoAnn Andrews

"Wings Of Love"

When I'm alone in solitude, my excited heart does beat.
I feel as if my heart could soar on wings of swift defeat.
Though filled with love and joy serene I cannot leave, I cannot dream.
Jesus says I'm still needed, so here I stay
I live, I learn, He shows me the way.
His gifts to me are my family, my friends and my future wishes
These things he gave me with no conditions.
He has the strength of ageless steel, His love for me, I always feel.
He told me he has work for me to do
So here I wait, his mission for me, I'm soon to see.
His guidance in these things I need
To feed my soul, and to push away greed.
We have our daily talks, we two, I love you my Lord, Oh yes I do..
You are my hope, my dreams come true,
Since I've been saved, I feel brand new.
Since I've been blessed, I feel complete
and now my soul is allowed to sleep.
"My darkest fears, You disowned, you set me free, now I can believe
I love You Sweet Lord, You are my Savior; tried and true
Your comforting presence shines through and through.

Jackie Kline

Untitled

I had a dream, a dream about you.
I dreamed we were together again.
I dreamed of your sweet smile, your voice and your eyes.
I don't know why you felt you had to say good bye
I dreamed that our love was all we needed
to bond us together
nothing else wanted,
nothing else need.
I dreamed you said
you loved me and that
you'll never leave me.
I woke up crying, inside
I felt like dying, but
after all it was a dream.
Dreams remain dreams.

Melissa Garrison

"Scared"

A tear trickles down my face
I cry for a certain place
It's a far away place that's very near
It's a place that's full of giant fear
This place I want to go
I want to get there very slow
Maybe I'm already there
This world is a place that just doesn't seem fair
It's a world of hate
Where we all seem to be bait
It's a world of crime
And others pay the time
The land seems to decease
We all hope for world peace
Mothers, I ask you, keep your kids under your wing
Or they may not get to swing
This world is a scary little place
For this a tear trickles down my face
I'm scared, we are all scared
We wish someone really cared.

Kim Hitter

The Next Generation

a girl, oh my God, it's a girl
I cradle the phone—the overwhelming realization
that a new life 176 miles away just entered the world
tightens my throat and blurs my eyes—a girl, oh my God, it's a girl

a girl, it's a girl—I've got to see her
memories of our childhood spring to the surface
just like the tears to my eyes
my brother, he's a father now—a girl, I've got to see her

a girl—what does she look like
I always thought he'd have a boy first, then a girl
just like us—there she is
what does she look like—oh my God, it's a girl

my niece, I am her aunt
all wrapped up in a pink blanket lying on the bed
she's so tiny, look at all that hair
she looks just like her father—I am her aunt, my niece

my niece, she's beautiful
she lays there fast asleep, I pick her up and hold her close to my heart
not mine, but mine forever, a perfect little child
You're beautiful, Renee Theresa

Michelle E. Arnett

Desolate Nightmare

　Desolate nightmare.
I close my eyes and see a never ending waste
land of terror suffering.
Death and despair linger in the air.
Unholy as it may seem.
It is really a nightmare?
Could it be my fate yet to come?
To spend eternity in damnation.
Never again to see the sun?
　Desolate nightmare.
Terror and suffering.
Out of my nightmare and into reality they
Seep.
I can hear a voice calling me.
Your time has come, your soul belongs to me.
Hell's gates are high and wide, there
is no escape I am locked inside this eternal
damnation.

Gabriel Jaramillo

Second Time Around

The house is quiet, the children are grown,
　I clean to avoid, empty nest syndrome.

I was beginning to feel, I was growing old,
　I gave up swimming, because I got cold.

I was sure I'd forgotten every nursery rhyme,
　When five babies arrived, in a very short time.

All of a sudden, I could swim in a creek,
　And the stones no longer, hurt my feet.

I can't believe I can still catch a frog,
　And not loose my balance, when walking a log.

Fingerprints on everything, I really don't care,
　Because beautiful grandchildren, left them there.

Your giggles and laughter are like heaven on earth,
　There's more value in that, than monetary worth.

There are days I feel, I ran a four minute mile,
　But your hugs and kisses, make it all worth while.

Thank you for letting me act silly and wild,
　again seeing the world, through the eyes of a child.

Joan Y. Miller

The River

"The river runs wild," someone once said
I can't remember who, but it sticks in my head.
I admire the river, so savage and free,
flowing where it wants, to the lake or the sea.
The river can be calm, and gentle sometimes
but just like love, it can turn on a dime.
If the rain starts to fall and the wind begins to blow
there is no telling which way the river will flow.
I love the sound of the waves splashing against each other
or the sight of ripples made when rain hits the water.
I stare at the river in my secret little place
and realize in a glance, the river has a face.
It takes just a moment until I can see
I'm a lot like the river, for the river is me.

Jolene Lansverk

337

They

Who are they?
I cannot say,
nor indeed do I know
for they hide and never show.

They say plenty of this and that
and when they leave this is where they sat.

So who are they?
Can't you say
they said that you would know.

Karen Busch

Drug Liquor Crap Habit

The fumes, the burn, the ultimate high
I can lick your lips and make you fly
You spin and twirl; I will make you hurl
You take me... from he who knows no lack
I will punish you until you crack
Huff and puff, sniff and snort
I am in control; you cannot retort
I fulfill your sex; you will have me next
I am what is inside of you
That chokes and churns and turns you blue
Buy me, try me, croak, and die on me
It is you, not I; now that is the irony
Weep and whine all you will; without me where is your thrill
I am present when you are thirsty
You use me without rhyme or mercy
Converse me; it is worse, you see
Past, present, future: history
I shall always be a burden: your misery
Don't blame me, the purchased crap; you, not I, shall take the rap
Burn, be damned, go to hell; life is short, a worthless spell

Jon Snow

"Walk With Me Lord"

Each morning when I awake,
I call your name in prayer.
I ask your blessings for this day,
And praise you mighty power.

Remember the sick today, no matter
where they may be,
Young, Old, no matter what their race,
or their nationality.
I ask your blessings for my family.

"Walk With Me Lord" that I may say,
and do the right things,
That I may help someone in need, or
just see a smile, where there was a frown.

Sometime I feel so helpless and alone,
But, when you "Walk With Me Lord"
My burdens are not heavy, and I feel
mighty strong.

Jean Cagle

Untitled

Spring is here and now is season spring is here and Gods the reason.
Flowers bloom and butterflies spread their wings and lady bugs and
bumblebees listen while she sings. Spring is here and shows her grace
as she brings smiles to the whole human race. Spring has sprung and
the taste of rain taste good to the tongue and is so invited from the
old to young and the tickling winds feel so nice in the air while they
feel the whole world with lots of care.

Linda Bryson

Untitled

Deep the river runs that carries the silt that blankets the creature.
I be the creature, you are the silt that blankets.
The river is an odd love.
The river is not only deep, but, also powerful.
It runs its course back to the giver of its life.
Its life source is love; it's an odd love.
It is a love that has been specially cultured.
It is a love of special design.
If we adhere to it, we will surely see that it contains no folly.
Wise is the river that contains the silt that blankets the creature.
All the more wise is the giver of the river's life.
It is an odd love which causes the silt to blanket the creature.
It is an odd love which causes the creature to find life in the silt.
The river flows to the oceans of its giver.
It carries the silt and the creature.
In the waters of the river, the silt and the creature share an odd affinity.
What a wondrous ecosystem are the river, the silt, and the creature.
Curse that which seeks to defile its gentle-fragile balance.
The river, the silt, and the creature, it is an odd love.

June S. Lowery-Malcolm

The Futile Fight

No matter what you do, and no matter what you say,
I am who I am, and you can't take that away.
I have power. I am strong. So, if destruction is your goal,
know you cannot break my spirit, and you'll never touch my soul.
You may curse and you may scream, try to blame and shame and beat me,
call me names and cast your insults, but no matter how you treat me
I will never join your forces. I will not become like you.
I will go my way in kindness, for no matter what you do
I believe that deep inside us is where true courage lies
and the choice of mighty silence in response is often wise.
So, though our paths have crossed in conflict, I will choose a
    different course.
I will treat you as my equal...as a creation of the Source.
I am you, and you are me...we are different yet the same.
We are made of the same matter, though we're called a different name.
We are connected by creation, though ego denies what's true,
you cannot aim to shoot me down, without bullets wounding you.

LaWonda A. Eastwood

A Pain I Cannot Bare

I see a picture, it's beautiful.
I am there, and so are you.
But I realize it isn't me standing by your side,
It is someone else.
The scene changes and I see myself once again,
But this time it is a picture of sadness.
I do not understand at first,
But then I realize, I was not chosen to be loved,
I was chosen to be despised.
But even a fate of being despised is nothing to me,
Compared to the pain of what I see.
You are powering love out of your very soul,
And it is not for me,
But for someone who does not need it.
I sit watching the scene quietly,
In a silent agony, tears flowing freely,
Because this pain is too much for me.

Michele Gerardot

The Dying Soldier

As he lay there wounded and dying,
He thought of his past and started crying.
I had everything to live for he thought,
Everything, till I came here and fought.
He thought of his parents and how they would take it,
To hear that their son just didn't make it.
He took out his Bible and whispered a prayer,
Then drew one last breath from the chilled night air.

Maria Felice

Society

Who am I, you ask?
I am the product of society.
A society of violence, drugs, sex, and money.

I live a fast paced life, just like that of the average American liar.

I cheat and bribe my way to the top;
because I'm too lazy to work hard for anything I actually hope of
    achieving.

I was born of the mold of the "American Woman", 36" 26" 34".
I am the standardized version of a magazine; classy, sexy, mysterious,
    and unreal.

I fit the description of every growing woman in my flawed generation.
I strive and pray for the love of objects and materials,
but insist that I'm not conceited nor selfish.

I smile at all those worth the trouble; and spit on those who pull
    me from my place in this race.

This race to the top, where every person has fifteen minutes of fame,
where lovers lie, and believers cheat, and real people get stepped on.

I am the product of an invisible culture, a culture provided for the
sake of having one.

What kind of person am I, you ask?
I am a fake, untouchable person;
because in my culture, being a real person just doesn't cut it.

I am a member of my society; a loose, dying, unboundaried society.

All of us, are a product of this society.

Meredith Newman

Freedom To Be

I walk upon this earth a man, destined to be only what I want to be.
Husband, free to pick the woman I want for my wife, and
loving her for eternity.
Computer Programmer, designing new software for our needs.
Astrologer, discovering the mysteries of space.
Professor, bound by my degree to give education to the community.
Soldier, fighting in a war for our freedom.
Priest, whose calling ranges from christening a child, to
saying mass at the death of a whole family.
Cop, on the street ready to be anything he's needed to be,
friend, an enemy, counselor to any in need.
Butcher, cutting meat day by day.
Coal-miner, always underground, maybe facing black lung disease.
Rodeo-cowboy, riding the meanest bronco on four feet.
Roamer free to explore earth's endless boundaries.
Friend, someone who will stand by you through good times and bad.
One job I'm not sure I would want, is being
President of any country, the continuous stress is not for me.
Whatever I want to be, I know it will satisfy me.

Karen Ann Darling-Gannon

Hope

Afraid of death, I was afraid of life
Hurt in love, a similar fate
To escape, I built a wall around myself
And that resembled death
But fate was kind, and love appeared again
And with God's help I learned to live and love
For wasting precious time must be
The greatest crime we mortals can commit
So now my eyes are opened with the realization
That in each moment is a miracle
And now I live in wonder without the fear of death
For in this life of miracles there is hope

Ginger Stark

All In A Day's Work

Showering, fussing and rushing a muck
hurdling through a maze not knowing where to duck

Yanking and searching for something to wear
stuffing and fluffing whatever is there

Screaming and yelling and pulling your hair
checking your stockings and finding a tear

Searching and examining and making a match
determining and measuring out of your batch

Freaking and panicking all at once
disoriented and bewildered like a dunce

Jumping and leaping through hoops and bounds
juggling and waving with all kinds of sounds

Sweating and struggling to be on time everyday
running and tackling all in your way

All this ferment just to get to work
then arriving and repeating the method all for a perk

Racing and pacing and pushing the day really fast
hoping each minute goes by each hour can pass

All for the time you can get up again
to repeat the cycle which does not end...

Norma S. Murray

Vietnam

In the reeking trench an oppressive wind passes over the dismal crop,
Howling through the blue-blotched lips,
Flapping the grotesque cloth of the fallen.
A putrid rain submerges the sodden soil
As the blood spreads and pales in the deluge.
Slowly the Pipe plant pushes its pale white clusters
    through the earth,
In the shrunken slime the stout, smooth, unbranched stem of
    the Blue Gentian wavers.

An apocryphal wasteland of the mind.
The appalling shape of torn fruit scattered and spent.
Disintegrating, reaped before maturity.
Fleshless jaws issue a gasping accent
Writhing in the severed rubble.
Violence in life, so in death.

Eyes clouded with salt tears
view the unalterable phantom figures.
Unforgiven and forgotten in the scattered twilight.

Linda Carolee Williams-Avila

Unknown

Where are you right now
how can I be sure
unknown
in my mind nothing is certain
looking out the picture is a curtain
unknown
open the drapes, I await
I see you, looking in
our eyes meet
unknown
not of doubt or question
strengthen instead by identity
familiar is the face unknown is the place
unity it blossoms
grows the boundaries which is the
unknown

Michael A. Carrizo

Seeing Through The Darkness

How dark is the darkness?
How black is the night?
How can there be seeing in eyes that have no sight?

In my mind, there are visions, movements in my head,
Showing me signs of beauty, bright memories of the past
I thought I had lost somewhere behind.

But how can I lose the sunshine, I still feel it on
My soul,
And how can I lose nature's wonders?
How could I lose what my spirit still so
Desperately holds?

So how dark is the darkness?
Or how black is the night?
I have no way of knowing, for my heart still has
Such brilliant sight.

Mary Agnes Jones-Myles

"Land Of Hearts"

Dreams to ashes
hopes into dust
smiles turned tears
for the void will be
the golden years.

The grace of life and all its joys
was sliced as with a cruel sharp knife.
All the hearts of the land are throbbing weak
for it's justice that we all seek.
Search within and you will see our
resolve and virtue have grown thin.

Respect and kindness wander
in unconscious sleep
but shall awaken
with a love kiss buried
in the lost hollow deep.

The heart land souls in limbo will rest awhile
in hopes to see again their loved ones smile.

John P. Kroetz

Heart In Hand

Today I stand before you,
Holding my trembling heart in my hand,
Bearing some inner-most feelings to you.
I hope you will understand.

To bear my deepest parts openly,
To pour out my heart from deep within,
Is an anxious moment me.
Will you condemn me or forgive my sin?

As I speak these honest words,
From my heart's deepest place,
A sacred trust I give to you.
Will you judge me harshly or grant me cleansing grace?

For you see as I do disclose myself,
My heart I am now placing in your hand.
It is in your power to crush it,
Or in love to help it stand.

Joel Lillengreen

Untitled

Mothers are angels sent from God above to help in the master plan of
His love. Hand in hand with God above, soft and smooth as a Turtle
Dove. As she shapes and molds the noble ones.

With faith, hope, charity and love. Mothers are angels sent from God
above to help in the master plan of His love. Never wavering from the
ones she loves she gives all glory to the king above. Peacefully she
watches and prayerfully she prays for help throughout each given day.

As the night closes a sweet song of love she sings. Yes a mother is
truly an angel sent from God above to help in the master plan of His love.

Leslie Vickers

Black Magic

Watch the mighty wolf run through the ancient hills.
His howl is like a victory chant
To tell of many kills.

His speed is like lightning, his fur as black as coal,
His eyes are the stars at night,
Windows to his soul.

Mourning in the wild, his howl becomes an erie ghost.
Not a friend this great wolf has,
The animal man fears most.

To them he is a beast,
With razor sharp teeth and knife like claws
To hurt kill and harm, leaping with steel like jaws.

But this is not a werewolf
That changes at full moon.
Just a creature misunderstood,
All but gone too soon.

Watch my friend, the mighty wolf.
It's grace, it's magic, it's wonder.
For one day you will observe
His demise will be our blunder.

Lisa Berger

Untitled

A cold wind blows over the barren landscape of his soul.
His heart has been shattered into a thousand crystal shards, scattered
by the four winds that cross the land.
Love has left him.
He sits in this place, waiting, face expressionless, staring of into
the distance. He waits for the return, in denial of the truth that
deep down he knows— Love shall never return here.
A slight breeze flows through his hair,
whispering to him as he stands.
Looking to the dark horizon, a cold, faint smile passes onto his lips.
Once again, he is alone.

Michael Zuiderveen

Lost

Crashing, crash. Yes, I can feel it.
Here it comes.
I am over, over. Over it all.
Help! I need to be found.
Will I be lost here in these cold waters forever?
Look, look can't you see me?
My love, you have finally found me.
I am at my eternal peace.

Jenn Stefanowicz

The Girl No One Knew

There once was a girl,
Her name no one knows,
She was killed before birth,
But that was the option her mother chose.

Never brought into this world,
To be loved by so many.
Not one bow in her hair,
To make her look so pretty.

Never experienced one birthday,
Or the touch of a dad.
Never been hugged or kissed,
Or cried when she was sad.

She never grew up,
To date or to drive,
Or to experience the love,
Of that one special guy.

So why is it legal,
To stop an innocent one's heart?
It's a controversial issue,
That's tearing our nation apart.

Joy McCullough

Nursing Needs

Help me dear Lord is what I pray
Help me to meet each challenging day
To make the most of what I've been taught
Without allowing myself to become overwrought.

Help me dear Lord to do my share
Remembering always to show that I care
In making decisions, please be my guide
Help me to feel You are at my side.

With patients I attend to, please allow them to see
They are treated as tho' they are family to me
When what is required of me is made known
Help me place "Their Needs" above my own.

Give me the knowledge not to make a mistake
Being always aware that a "life is at stake"
Help me distance myself...just enough to keep my purpose clear
So that I may give proper treatment to those entrusted to my care.

Muriel Weckstrom

To Build A Home

When your lives and love entwine
Heed this advice and you'll be fine.
Daily disappointments drive you insane.
Words like fists cause hurt and pain.
Selfish words must disappear
Replaced by I love you, Dear.
Spoken sincerely once a day
Will drive the wolf of doubt away.
Thank God for each other all your life.
Take time to play as husband and wife.
Share your self in words and deeds
Fulfill each others wants and needs.
Be blind to the unimportant things.
See the joy your mate does bring.
Remember a look, a touch, a tender smile
When the foot between seems like a smile.
The house of matrimony is made of straw
Without warmth and clay it will surely fall.
Loves is the warmth, trust is the clay
Now as brick, it is here to stay.

Marion E. Blanchard

Reading

Dedicated to the Reading/Tutoring Team at Good Samaritan Church
Pinellas Park, Florida
   Reading opens the minds and
hearts of all ages;
   Fulfilling every interest and
every need.
   Romance, mystery, suspense,
Comedy, hobbies and sports —
Books are friends...poetry,
Fiction, non-fiction, biographies,
Autobiographies, history, reference
and more.
   Reading takes us on journeys,
leading us into life's new challenges
for a continuing learning experience
that promotes true growth.

Mary Ellen Rotolo

Sound Of A Teardrop

I've heard eagles, soaring way up high.
Heard the thunder, as it rolls across the sky.

But the loudest sound, loudest sound of all.
Is the sound of a teardrop when it falls.

I've heard the whistle of a lonely midnight train.
The deafness of the engines, on a big silver plane.

The crying of a baby, as it reaches out for love
The calling of the geese information up above.

I've heard the sound of silence, alone on a dark night.
The tapping of a canepole, from a man with no sight.

But the loudest sound, loudest sound of all,
Is the sound of a teardrop when it falls.

I've heard the sound of bombs exploding, in the dawn.
Weeping of the children, when someone loved passed on.

The beating of the drums, for freedom's call,
And the sound of a teardrop when it falls.

Larry A. Whitmire

Country Calls

Have you ever slept a night in the country
Heard the hoot of an owl form a nearby wood
Been lullabied to sleep by a cricket concert?
I heartily wish you could.

Have you ever slept a night in the country
Heard the muted drone of an airborne plane
Listened to the patter of rain on a tin roof?
If so, I wish you will come again.

Have you heard night noises in the country
A vixen fox barking from the edge of a wood
Wildcats screaming for a mate, bullfrogs croaking late?
I surely wish you could.

Have you risen on a country morning
Wakened by a rooster's crow before sunrise
Been serenaded by birds joyfully singing?
I wish you could witness this paradise.

Have you been attuned to country's nature
Listened to peaceful silence, of sun-kissed air took your fill?
Far away from scenes of crime and violence?
Oh, how I wish that you will!

Geraldine Springston

341

An Invitation

There lives a man—a certain man—who likes to think.
He thinks about things that make up life,
The why of this and the why of that.
He thinks with a smile sometimes, but he's always thinking.
For eighty-five years he's been thinking
About children and the winds—about women and their ways
About men and their deeds—about schools and teachers
About farms and politics and bombs and things
About God.
He likes to walk through woods and over hills and around farms
Thinking.
And he likes to sit and talk about what he's thinking
And what he's thought about.
He's travelled far over much of the world—to think and talk.
People have come to him from far corners to listen
Young people—old people—to hear him think
And learn again to think themselves—if only briefly.
His name is Robert Frost—poet, farmer, teacher, but mostly thinker.
He's coming to Traverse City.
Wouldn't you like to come for an evening to hear a great man think?

John T. Parsons

A Christmas Wish

Wish I could hitch a ride with that jolly ole guy as
he streaks merrily across the wintry sky, in his
journey from North to South Pole, I'd be sure he
wouldn't miss nary a soul, on my list of people I'd
like to spend my Christmas time with—both kin and friend.

Oh, I'd have problems with my wish, no doubt
not even Santa's magic could bring it about. Like
Mrs. Santa, I'll be left at home to recall
many happy Christmases now past since to be
separated our lots are cast. But if you feel a
warm loving glow as the Christmas Season comes
and goes it will be just my mental telegraphy
saying "Merry Christmas, I love you, a very
happy prosperous New Year, too."

And if you hear the jolly Ho, Ho, Ho! I
didn't try it—I'm not stuck in the snow but
if Santa's secret for visiting each home you
know, don't tell me—I'd take the risk you
see 'cause to pop in on each of you would be
the very happiest Christmas Season for me.

Leona Ryan

Circle

Lost in a jungle
He runs frantically falling
Over branches and vines,
Always looking behind his shoulder
Looking for repetition.
He runs and sweats, runs and sweats,
Runs and sweats,
Until he comes to the edge of a cliff.
Turning facing the jungle,
As he bows to his knees
just in time to see
Himself running towards him.
Running and sweating, running and sweating
Yelling bloody insanities.
He jumps off the cliff
As he runs to the edge holding out
His hands trying to help himself.

Martin Brandt

A Walk Before Her Funeral

His mind was bombarded by various thoughts and emotions
He gave up, for the moment, any effort to sort them out
He just emptied his heart and his mind and walked

He smiled at a boy who bumped into him, trying to nab a ball
He listened to the chatter of the sparrows in the trees
He held out his hand to catch a falling autumn leaf

He looked at the brown beauty as it lay in his hand
In summer this leaf had been vibrant with life,
joyously turning its face to greet the morning sun
and waving goodbye to it at eventide, confident
that there would be another morrow

But now, as with Mary, its morrows were all spent
Soon it too, must lie in the dark tomb of death
Was it, like Mary, to go unmourned?
Was there no one to say, farewell?

He whispered goodbye to it and laid it among its fellows

Orville Cyrus Brooks

The Joy Of Cyblings

As the insane tyrant walks upon the darkened moon,
He carries his beaten faith and broken soul of a loved friend.
This man is considered to have lost the innocence of virgins.
Being held within his actions, he is only known as a parallel of
immoral ways.

His existing path strayed into the gray of night,
As he never will return to the golden sun.
His damned fate shall be sealed in the blood of his dying brother.

And at the striking sound of moments before the new day,
He will surrender the life of the uncaring one.
I wish him luck and good fortune,
The chance of death does not pass often.

Guy T. Rallo

Valentine Girl

"Valentine Girl"
He calls her
Seems as though he's drawn
To this girl, every Valentines
Working back to a lost friendship
Her heart yet to be won
Afraid of being hurt
He's kept reserved, restraining his tears
Yes or no, not a matter anymore
As long as she can walk away
This time knowing
How he really feels
About her,
"Valentine Girl"

Min Choi

Heavenly Beauties

I in rainbows see God's flowers.
He arches them unto the heavens
So after sprinkling April showers,
Angels in fields may walk the bends
And pluck and prune God's blooming hues
That stretch across the field of blues.

I in starry skies see God's cities.
Gleaming, shining bright.
Like a light house safely guides through night
Until all vessels reach the bay,
So will God's city shine for me
Until I'm anchored to his promise,
And the darkness becomes day.

Lilly Nevers

342

On Your 50th Anniversary, Mom And Dad

Through years of life where joy and sorrow,
Have made their usual rounds,
There's been a force that's leveled out,
Those endless ups and downs.
This force was seen as a youngster who,
Quite never found the mark.
But the loving light from mom and dad,
Did guide me from the dark.
This force was seen at Prairie Lake,
In the glow of a setting sun—
When dad would teach us all those skills, that made for fishing fun.
And every chore mom did for me, despite the daily grind,
Contributed to a lasting bond, that was constantly refined.
Despite the strains of a single life,
Dear folks, I can't complain;
For your lasting love is a symbol of, the one I hope to gain.
So whenever hardships get me down,
And the world lacks all its charms,
I'm quick to find my strength renewed,
In the clutch of mother's arms!

Martin J. Link

Death Be Not Grim

Death be not grim, reaper of lives
  haunting me through darkened halls!
If it be me be not so grim, but greet me by
  some sunny garden wall.
If it is I for whom you look, let me finish this
  one last page in an unfinished book.
Be so kind if you please till I have made my bed,
  and seen the glorious sun one more time.
And one more time to feel the breeze against
  my face, and smell the garden.
Find me in some sunny place, near rustling window
  curtains, finishing a letter to an old friend.
Do not touch my shoulder from behind,
  but let me face you this last time,
And talk to me of miracles beyond the sunset,
  but wait, let me just wash my face,
And please, let me feel her kiss on my cheek,
  just one last time, and hold her hand.
Be not so grim, but let me hear the laughter of the
  children in the yard, and then we'll walk!

Michael R. Shogren

Parting Words

  Though the cloth is dirty and ripped I still keep the hat that you gave to me,
and the photo of us still stares me in face I guess I'll never see.
  You promised me that what we had could never ever break,
but here I sit all alone in quiet constant ache.
  I look through a faded past and I can clearly see,
The love we shared in your eyes was much deeper within me.
  Please don't try to ease the craving it will only make me pain,
Cause the days I live without you are the days consumed with strain.
  Don't call, don't write, or ask my friends, 'cause they'll just tell you lies,
the truth is found in my tears, a truth of sad goodbye.

Melissa Cascino

A Rose

The rose is a flower, a flower of joy,
each little pedal is unlocking a new secret
to a beautiful new rare unknown flower.
As everyone steps down to see
they never know the unforbidden truth.

Kristi Carrington

How I Know God Loves Me...

In the beginning, God created...everything that was or is, God has
  made it.
Adam and Eve, they had it all, even the fruit that would bring the fall.
They were perfect and true in every way, only God knew, what
  would happen that day.
So when His timing was right, a huge star shone by night.
Pointing the way for our sinners delight.
He came as a child, tender and mild.
He asked for nothing, but our love, for our Heavenly Father above.
He came to show us the right way to live, to be humble, and true
  and always to give.
Some would not listen, I don't know why. They wanted him gone, He
  had to die.
Push came to shove, but there was no fight. God knew how to put
  things right.
He sent His Son to the cross that day for our sinners debt, He would pay.
For no one else could pay but He. This is how I know God loves me.
And because of that love the truth doesn't end here.
God has made that oh so clear.
Three days pass and Jesus is gone...to sit by His Father where He belongs.
He is never far from us you see, He's as close as we let Him be.

Julie Gotaas

A Generation Gap

Dad sits rooted to the dining room chair,
hardly speaking. Just once, you'd think he'd say,
"I never did tell you how much I care."

Well stocked with his Busch beer, a moldy pear,
and half-smoked cigarettes in an ashtray,
Dad sits rooted to the dining room chair.

And as the football games drone on, is he aware
that my first twenty years have passed today?
"I never did tell you how much I care";

The statement lingers with the smoke in the air,
hanging from the ceiling fan and its sway.
Dad sits rooted to the dining room chair,

and Mom and I laugh at the bee-hive hair-
do she had in the sixties. I wanted to say,
"I never did tell you how much I care".

But I didn't. Should I even dare
try to tear him away from his quiet ways?
Dad sits rooted to the dining room chair.
I never did tell you how much I care.

Margaret Swoager

"To Satan"

"HELLO there satan...
  Guess I'd best be friendly with you,
Mom said I would go to the devil
  So our acquaintance I'd like to renew.

It isn't easy to live right
  When you feel you're black-sheep of the pack.
Noted for goofing-up matters
  With a life rather hard to hack.

I could never relax with our Maker...
  It's too hard to be good don't you see?
And I wouldn't like being a faker
  Just so folks think the best of me!

I've always loved sipping sweet-nectars
  And partaking of forbidden fruits.
And it's no fun just walking a chalk-line
  Leaving pleasures in life destitute.

So if I am a bad bad sinner
  I need you for my friend.
If we be 'true-blue' and friendships lasting
  You might not 'burn me out' in the end."

Marjorie Druschel

343

Janis Joplin Have You Ever Been To Reno?

I visited last weekend a city that mongers greed,
greed with all its lustful nuances.
There's the disenfranchised ex-laborer who found Probability to be
kinder to his body than mixing concrete.
There's the aged couple entranced by the vague reflection in the
smudged glass of their perished youth - the rewards are simple,
five quarters sometimes, but the ephemeral surprise is at least unpredictable.
There's the soiled boozer, three drinks over the line and ready for
more, who infrequently gambles, preferring simply the reliable company
of fellow addicts in need of a boost.
There's the color-clad tourist, clinching his home-town brew,
searching for the elusive Wave of Fortune on which to ride out
of town, back home to gloat and spend.
And there's the spent visage of the Gambler, curled up in the damp
weeds two blocks away from his own neon-draped mephistopheles,
a survivor of his addiction and victor of nothing...
I think of Janis Joplin crooning ironically "Freedom's just another
word for nothin' left to lose."
I'm prompted to eulogize: While in Reno you might make your dreams
come true or you might just end up freer than you ever wanted to be.

Mark G. Koetting

Chores Of The Enlisted

I was once a dreamer of moonbeams and loose seams and
great things which I could do for others
And I was all content when the wayward way
was bent into a straighter path for me to follow
And praise was like sweet candy because I
was the dandy on their tongues.
But now I'd like a bottle in which noises I
would mottle so I could find my own attributes.
These qualities of mine have been left so far behind
and I think I might have lost them in my hustle
For my goal has been to please, but in the
end I find my knees bruised from kneeling down to
lend support and healing.
I have a journey yet to go, but
I think that I'm beginning to know
the who I was before these chores
of mine were enlisted.

Lauren Anderson

Promise Song

Two tiny hands, ten tiny toes, rosebud lips and eyes that glow.
Grasping fingers won't let go. I hope that this is always so.
With your pure and softest skin you are still without a sin.
Perfect ears and fuzzy head, I should put you in your bed.
You grew within me safe from harm, now you're nestled in my arms.
You're my miracle of birth, born, with me to share this earth
And I promise by my song that I will love you my life long.

I'll be there for sticks and stones, dogs and cats and broken bones.
When you stumble or you fall, I will hear you when you call.
I will teach you right from wrong, I will help you to be strong.
And when you're old enough to go, I will know 'twas always so.
You're the gift that God gave me. I'll still hold you heartfeltly.
Grasping heart-strings won't let go. I hope for you this to is so.
For as I promised by my song, I will love you my life long.

Now, you're tending cuts and bruises, monitoring tricycle cruises.
Teaching never talk to strangers and all the other urban dangers.
Don't telephone, just send a FAX and by computer pay your tax.
Everywhere there's war or fighting; the abortion laws are biting.
Abuse is children and parental. Life it seems is incidental.
While you're teaching right from wrong, remember promise is a song.
We're ALL a miracle of birth; it's God's intent we share this earth.

Jewell Pollock

Why Can't Gram Be Gram?

Gram is Gram. Gram likes Gram things.
Gram likes basketball. Gram likes the Pistons.

Gram meets Jim.
Jim is Jim. Jim likes Jim things.
Jim likes comic books. Jim likes Superman.
Jim likes Gram.

Gram meets Mike.
Mike is Mike. Mike likes Mike things.
Mike likes music. Mike likes Led Zeppelin.
Mike likes Gram.

Gram is not Gram. Gram likes Jim and Mike things.
Gram likes comic books. Gram likes Superman.
Gram likes music. Gram likes Led Zeppelin.

Jim is Jim. Jim likes Jim things.
Mike is Mike. Mike likes Mike things.

Jim and Mike do not like Gram.

Mike Alfaro

More Than A Friend

Through the mist of my tears, I still can see you.
Gone are my fears that my memory would fade,
The wonderful moments we share together.
No master, no owner, In the short years you stayed by my side.
No greater devotion than the one you gave from your heart.
Your eternal love will always be there, Raif dear.
So happy, you are in my mind.
So sad, you are no longer with me.
I see your picture on the mantel.
Extraordinary bright yellow eyes, reflecting your generous soul.
God could not give you a voice, settled for a magnificent spirit.
Gentle little giant of a dog, half wolf, soft as a lamb.
Tail in the air, so proud, roaming the backyard;
Your domain, your corners, you kept with great pride.
Oh! I miss you so, my beautiful friend.
Seems like yesterday, I held you in my arms.
As the tears on my face glided down; I had to let you go.
Almost a year above, where happiness remains eternal.
I'll never forget you, forever and a day.

Nelly Beck

Half A Bottle From Now

I'm running from reality-
Goin' with the flow.
My problems began to fade away
Half a bottle ago.

One more day to struggle through
Awaits me in the dawn.
But for now I am escaping
With half a bottle gone.

I guess I'm playing the cards life deals me
The best way I know how.
And one more night will be behind me
Half a bottle from now.

Jeff Stubing

"The Rose"

Does the Rose know her beauty......
Does the Rose know her strength?
Does she know if she withers - does a rose know she dies?
If I closely look, would I see tears in her eyes -
   The beauty of spring - the restless hot summer -
The winter pain of cold and despair.....
   Does the Rose just give up -
      or does she really care?

Jo Ann Roe

Why Do You Do This To Me?

I was like a butterfly, starting fresh and new.
Glowing with my beauty,
with all my colors, too.
First monstrous creatures came, and inhabited all my lands.
They swam amid my oceans,
and walked upon my sands.
Even after they had died, I had never lost my grace.
The same as before they had come,
a glistening and wonderful place.
As time went on the humans came, wandering all around.
Not knowing much about me,
or where their tribes were bound.
As humans came the beauty left, there wasn't room for both.
They cut my trees and killed my creatures,
In order to learn and grow.
Now I am wildly struggling, to keep my lands alive.
Because of humans' greediness, I'll forever have to strive
I am slowly fading, and I have one question you see.
I am the only earth God gave to you,
so why do you do this to me?

Melissa A. Jacobs

Untitled

I am a transient soul
Glad because
This windy day is never like
Another windy day.
The way the sun streaks through the trees
Is always somehow altered.
Each wave exchanged upon the beach
Is varied from the other,
And every snowflake forms a new
And different pattern.
I am the transient soul
I sing praise to
This moving. Changing....is....
This solar system pacing space
Throughout infinity:
I sing praise to other transient souls
In remembrance to their creativeness.
I sing praise to
A universe without duplication
Whose never sameness marks its constancy!!!

Judith M. Ellis

Wondrous Life

All grand and wondrous beings molded by God's own hands,
Given the breath of life by Him, He thusly called us man.

He then made a big decision that man must not live alone,
Wanting to give man someone to love, created woman from his bone.

O wondrous life bred from above, a marvel of creation,
Given the perfect gift of love, lasting throughout life's duration.

Fill your life with the spirit of God, use His wisdom to keep you free
Give praises to His Holy name, and thanks for all that we plea.

Learn to love with your heart and soul, your years will be truly blessed,
You will get your great reward with a peaceful and heavenly rest.

Peace is so important, we search for it every day,
Cast all troubles to the wind, God will carry them away.

Hold onto your precious life, never let it go,
Love it like a gift from above, protect it from every foe.

O wondrous life given by God, blessed with a love so true,
God gave his only begotten son, so eternal life could come to you.

Joan A. Davis

A Mother's Prayer

What happened to the little
girl who loved to be with me.
Who made me feel so proud
when she said Mommy.
Of course that changed to
Mom as she grew away from me.
And now I am a nothing
for I lost her and her love you see.
The tears flow from my eyes
which she says are not for real and turn
her off from me.
She cannot look in my
heart or the truth she would see.
I love you daughter I really do.
I pray that God is taking care of you.
No one can console me for I have lost a child you see.
Drugs are her world now.
They have now taken her from me.
What happened to that little girl and me.
Dear God please someday send her back to me.

Marge Stewart

My Father's Hand

My father's hand reaches out to mine.
  Gently pushing forward
Into the wind
  Scared, but reassured by strong hands
Clasped in mine
  Life it must be
A flash of lightning
  Suddenly set free into wild winds
Through freedom I see
  My father's touch in me.

Kellie da Silva

Spring Is Here

Clouded skies turning black
Geese flying north
Winds blow strong, smell its smell

Humidity heavy like a burden
Warm moist air wets your dry lips of winter
You thirst

Plants in bloom, flowers welcoming insects
Bees awake collecting their nectar
Sticky and sweet our food they make

Thunderous storms exploding with thanks
Refresh the cold parched earth
Winter's end, a new birth

God's creatures arise to shake off their slumber
Caressing the earth in search of nourishment
Nature's youth enter childhood
Spring is here

Kathleen Mueller

Conservationist's Prayer

  Thank you, God for stars on high;
For fleecy clouds that drift on by; for
  the sun by day, the moon by night
To shed their gold and silver light.
  Thank you for dark drear clouds that promise rain
To bless verdant forest and thirsty plain;
  For towering trees and flowers hues
With gentle wine of morning dews;
  For rolling hills and mountains tall,
For all thy creatures great and small.
  With all of this let man be blessed
and serve them well at thy behest.

Maril Lee Brubaker

345

One Day While Shopping

One day while shopping in a store amid the paper and holiday ribbons galore,
I turned to find my purse gaping wide with forty dollars less inside!
I sighed and searched with all my might unfortunately, it was gone all right.
The important thing was that I was O.K., which was better than the
    woman on the news today who lost her life for a single dollar. I
    felt I had no cause to holler.
She had paid the ultimate price, much too high I would suffice.
Only heaven knows the truth of whether or not it was put to good use.
I believe it was because that eases the pain of never seeing those
    hard-earned dollars again.
So, for all of you that have been robbed, chin up now, no need to sob.
Perhaps this is a gentle reminder that we all should be a little bit kinder.
Too many possessions weigh us down and we don't really need them
    anyhow.
So give to others who are in need and eliminate this thief called greed.

Lisa Rainone

"Red Hearts Released"

Pounding harder, so full of life,
galloping over the open road.
Silk and Satin, with Steely Knife,
red hearts released, white wings explode.

Horses run wild, nostrils full of flames,
hooves beating off the bridle path.
Feelings freed, from whence they came,
love in action, they can't pull back.

Roped by their dreams, and youthful lusts,
will never find a more spirited time,
to burn the winds, and challenge desire,
blazing manes, on perpetual fire.

Muscles rippling with power surge.
Bursting with energy from the sun.
Anxious stallion, mares untameable urge,
bolting through life, fast as they run.

Leanna S. Jagta

Storms From Within

My life seems like such a waste
Fruit getting bitter with every taste
I gaze out the window in silent wonder
There is no storm but I hear thunder
Where am I going where have I been
I near nothing but the hard gusty wind

Looking at the world through my lonely blue eyes
It seems I've said too many good-byes
People try to help but I can't let them in
I'm keeping secrets locked up tight deep within
The storm is getting stronger but nothing around
All the debris is in the air that came from the ground
I gazed out the window in silent wonder
There is no storm but I hear thunder.

Jocelyn Rogers

Approaching Our Day

With each passing day, the time draws near
For us to pledge ourselves one to the other forever, my dear.
That day will be great —
I can hardly wait!
Then together we will go
Down the long, winding road;
Fulfilling old dreams and building new ones,
Constantly sharing both difficulties and fun.

We'll share love and support, laughter and tears
As together we grow old through the years.
We'll climb difficult mountains and race down steep hills
Encouraging each other forever, as we will.

K. F. Barr

Memories Of You

Memories of love live on forever...
    from year to year, from one life to another.
I close my eyes and I can see your face...
    not as you are now, but from another time, in another place.
I've stared into your eyes so blue...
    no matter who you are now, I would always know you.
Your smile has always warmed my heart...
    it has sustained me forever, even when we were apart.
I remember the love in your touch...
    no words needed to be spoken, your embrace said so much.
I've kissed your lips, and I've laid in your arms...
    on the coldest of nights, your love kept me warm.
Your love and your light guided me through...
    every year, every lifetime it has always been me and you.
My soul has known only one love so true...
    I can remember this love, because I can remember you.

Lori A. Washburn

Untitled

We started out just as friends
From my blue eyes to his contact lens

As we grow closer our friendship grew
As we talked for hours he knew my
Friends and I was part of his crew

I was the dancer and he was the attorney
Until God called him on a much greater journey

We were walking home from a football game
It was a drunk driver who took the blame

He's my friend to the end I'll love him forever
Through each part of my life in every endeavor

He's my guardian angel always at my side
Please don't drink and drive that's how
I lost my best friend and that's how he died!

Kathy Kunath

Spendthrift

Mother Nature is a spendthrift
from green Spring to orange-red Fall.
What can she do for pale, drab Winter,
when she has no color left at all?

It is then she dips the moon in hoarfrost,
sequesters the earth in veils of white,
and enlists the stalwart branches
to cast stark shadows in the night.

She dazzles the lawn with diamonds
in morning's golden light.
She has encased a branch in crystal,
a brooch for her gown of sequined white.

Alas, Mother Nature is no spendthrift,
although extravagant, I'll confess,
for no matter what the season,
she is perfection in each new designer dress.

Marie Lovell Perrott

Living Echoes

Experience life,
Fleeting as grains of sand slip through an hour glass.
Moments precious spent
Searching for youth passing by.
Memories captured in time,
Reminiscing from the fullness of their reflections—
Fading beyond the distance.
Hypocrisies echo
Quieting humanity's legacy—
Illusions of hope for immortal salvation.

Mark Gregory Hunsdon

Friends

Friends are special people, people who care
Friends are people you know will be there.
They stand beside you bad times and good
They stand beside you as a friend should
Friends will be there to lend a helping hand,
They will be there to do what they can
Together you laugh, together you cry
Together you might even say goodbye
Friends mean a lot, cherish their love
Friends mean a lot, they were sent from above
God knew we would need them sometime in our life
That's probably why he gave us husband and wife
Friends can be anyone big or small
Friends can be anyone short or tall
They can have brown hair they can have blond
They can have short hair they can have long
We are all special in our own ways
We care for each other we'll always be there
No matter what color eyes or hair
Because we all need FRIENDS.

Jennifer Marie Drew

God Gave Man

God gave man a mind of his own
Freedom to do right or wrong
No matter what man may say
Man will pay that final day

God gave man a mind of his own
Right to worship the one he believes on
If the one he choose be of worldly desire
He shall burn in eternal fire

God gave man a mind of his own
Choice to choose his eternal home
Joy to know some glorious day
Christ shall return and carry
   his faithful away

Because God gave me a mind of my own
I chose to worship him on his throne
For when life on earth comes to an end
He shall take me home to live with him

Mary Fox Conner

Fight For Our Rights #2

When from across the seas, our forefathers came here to be,
Free from control by Kings, who did not allow, among other things,
Less wealthy to be judged by their peers,
   That caused action by certain men, concerned, by their fears.

Soon here, a new country was born,
Our United States Constitution, took form,
By the great Founders of our Land
It included, Bill of Rights, with Kings now, a bane,
Nonetheless, within two-hundred years,
Some wealthy intervened, with their many leers,
And when the evidence clearly showed, one particular Court,
Allowed the richer side, to use some very bad deport,
Rich side would even employ, the dear Court's relative,
Who is much closer than the third degree,
Sure enough, said Court did order, and in negative,
   To U.S. Constitution, meant to protect, both you and me.

Seems that Court conspired, with all of the lawyers,
To show power here, can be, just like the Kings,
"The Fight for our Rights" had no real hero warriors,
   Yet, Bill of Rights, are for all, of us ordinary beings.

Marie M. McMahon

Puppy Love

It is night and the bed quakes,
   Four giant paws leap nimbly to your side.
     Eyes, warm eyes, stare down at your face.
       A smell of edible things, grass, old apples,
         and straw, mix with night flowers blooming.
           A drip lands on your nose. A drip of slobber,
             a drip of love from doggie's mouth.
               The bed quakes again. A tail wags in your face.
           Doggie turns around, lies down.
       I groan, "Settle down!" At once,
     A great tremor shakes the bed.
The dog is down. All this trouble.
You start to fall back to sleep. Once more,
   the bed shakes as if tormented.
     A night with a dog...
       good luck!

Naomi Zaspel

My Greatest Fear

In my dream, reunited at last -
forgotten forever, the time that has passed.
I cry for a moment, not believing it's true -
I've waited so long, an eternity for you.
The embrace is unlocked with the fear that I'll cry -
such a precious memory, before separating I'd die.
I've missed you so much - communication in mind -
I searched through my heart, at the end you
will find -
The picture of friends, at the thought, a tear -
parting once again, my single greatest fear.
The only thing worse, is to wake up and find,
that this wonderful encounter, was only in my mind.
So I cried before, and now I feel pain -
so much lost, at the sound of your name.
I'll cry a river, from a single tear,
to wake up from the dream, my single greatest fear.

Josh Tennison

Maranatha

It's not the dread of hell that flames my love
   For you, O unselfish Lord of goodness;
It's not the hope of pearly gates above.
   It is You, Your Cross, Your total kindness.

I contemplate your myriad precious wounds,
   Suffer thorns and splinters in compassion.
Your body bruised and pierced by heartless fiends,
   Inspires hardened hearts to share Your passion.

I need no threat or loss of self to fear,
   No prizes nor rewards to light my soul.
I love you just for you, my Jesus dear;
   Your heavy cross alone will quite console.

I hear, O Suffering God, Your mournful sob:
   Behold on Me the work of Satan's mob!

Jose A. Torres

To Whom It May Concern

To whom it may concern, I lost a luv so
fine, so gentle, and so kind. A luv I thought
so mine.
   Snatched right out from under me. Buy
one who was so blind. To caught up in
herself to see the luv we felt inside.
   She tried to find a reason that he was
so blind. She did succeed for now inside my
feelings are confined.

Melinda Berkopes

347

If I Was To Be Somebody, What Would I Be?

I would be of noble character,
for this is worth far more than rubies.

I would be of full confidence
and lack nothing of value.

I would being good, not harm
all the days of my life.

I would be of good name,
rather than great riches.

I would be clothed with strength
and dignity.

I would speak with wisdom and
faithful instruction.

I would ask to be blessed
with wisdom and gain understanding.

For these are more profitable
than silver and yields better
returns than gold.

for you see, all I would be,
is me.

Karen Kinney

The Garden Of Life

Waste not the year of youth,
For they rush quickly by, like a bird on the wire,
That is still one moment, and soon
It is flickering like a candle in the wind,
Though you may become weary and tired,
Cherish each day as if it were your very last,
Embrace the winds of change,
Seize the moments that are happy,
For this garden of life grows very fast,
Sow the seeds of love and faith,
Nurture them with courage and hope,
The fruits of your labor will ripen, and turn to wine,
Share the wine of life with those you love,
And your life will be blessed from above.
Even though the winds of time will humble
You, set sail into the golden horizon,
As the tide rushes in, to soothe your weary soul.

Kathy Sue Biddle

Looking Back

The days have drawn to a close
   for the bicentennial year,
   may the times we have worked
   together be happy memories for
   each to share.

The songs have been sung -
   the poems have been read -
   the parades all have passed by.
What a privilege it was to have
been able to share in that "special"
4th of July.

To share in the birthday party of
   our country 200 years old, is a story
   that will be handed down as the
   pages of history unfold.

Whatever the part that we may have
   played, whatever the talents we had
   to lend, we are sure that we did
   the best we could - for we will
   never pass this way again.

Mary L. Ireton

He Is All There Is

He is all there is
   For surely He is he
      For which His new idea was she!

How pleased He was with she -
   And loved her

But other hes and shes
   Tried to turn His universe inside out -
      Would not obey energy laws -
         On which He designed his universe.

He created another she -
   A perfect she -
      To bring forth He -
         As Son in human form and God:
The remedy for all of the disobeying hes and shes -
   His blessed remedy - Jesus

Margaret Mattesm Richter-Brewer

Mother's Scorn

Listen to what I say, mind you best,
for life's youth, in a trice, will come to rest;
and you will have to face life's test.
Invincible you may feel, hormones no less.
Life is no petty game, or instant thrill.
So listen to me, a fool now you may be.
My wisdom of life will guide you free.
Why? You ask, in your ignorant abase.
Because, I say, my hand stings like mace,
more so, mother's wisdom, will help you keep pace,
with ambitious man's frantic race.
Yet fear not my hands as be the peccant man,
his sting is stronger, except to the wise man.
So listen, listen. Where you are, I've been twice,
and I'll tell you need to suffice.
So now you sniffling child with tears like raindrops,
stand not up to me, with your mouth afoul.
For you are the crop and I the soil.
Planted in me, your harvest will not foil.

Oliver C. Allen Jr.

Katy

Shining face
Flowing amber hair
Eyes as clear as the sky
Heart as big as the ocean
Strong as an old oak tree on a crisp spring morning
Beautiful as a vermilion sunset on a warm Autumn evening
Graceful as the grass in a windy field
Kind as a mother cat to her newborn kittens
Forgiving as a mountain creek after a fierce storm
Faithful as a honey bee returning to its nest after each adventure
Determined as a mother robin building a safe nest
Sensitive as an antique porcelain vase
Sweet as a juicy apple in the warm summer heat
Friendly as two bluebirds flying freely in the sky
Laughter that can warm a desolate room
Seeks God like a baby duckling frantically searching for its mother
I will always love my sister with all my heart

Marla Kay Van Skiver

Reflections Of Time

Slowly I limp down the garden path
Flowers shimmer like diamonds from the early morning dew
On the porch my old wicker worn rocking chair seems to beckon me there
Closing my eyes a picture like movie flashes anew
A pink gingham dress, two braids flying
Scampering barefoot through the meadow
Here and there gathering flowers
Until my hands behold a rainbow of colors
Crisp starched curtains sway in the breeze
The aroma of gingerbread drifts from the window and through the trees
On my swing I soar - higher higher into the sky
Not a care in the world as up - up I fly
Free as the birds, gliding, swooping
The sound of the dinner bell rings in my ears
Cold lemonade and apple pie - a time to gather, a time to share
Dark shadows of night spread across my bed
and kneeling in prayer I feel a tear
For the bond of love within this house
I awake with a jolt - ah!
Just a passing glimpse of yesteryears
Fond memories in my heart that I hold so dear.

Norma Valles

Be True To Yourself

Loving others is hard to do,
    First you must love yourself through and through.
Do you treat yourself as good as others?
    Such as your husband, wife, sister or brother?

Can you give yourself an hour a day,
    To do as you please and not rush away?
Can you look in the mirror and say "I Love You,"
    Say it with feeling and know that it's true!

People have many roles in life,
    Aunt, uncle, cousin, husband and wife.
If you were the last person from your family tree,
    What role would you have, who would you be?

Take time to find out who you are,
    Set your goals and reach for your star!
Don't lose yourself along the way,
    Take time for yourself each and every day!

Jill L. Fisher

"Flowers"

These flowers and you have a lot in common my love,
First their touch, both soft as a dove.
Second is the smell, sweet as the nectar held within.
Third and final, beauty so bold it must be a sin.
With all these things in common you would think they
    were one and the same.
Yet there is only one difference to separate their game.
The flowers in all their beauty and might eventually will
    wither right out of sight.
Yet your beauty, smell and touch are here to stay,
    as it is one of the many reasons you give me to wake each day!

Michale A. Hoffman

In Memory Of Coffee (To Mary, My Sister)

Tell the family a wonderful sailor passed along this way.
Except for the pain of living I would have insisted that he stay.
He had a wonderful family and many friends while here.
God held out His hand and said, "Come With Me My Dear".
We who loved him miss him very much.
We miss his smile, his love and his touch.
Soon we will be together again
In the wonderful place where love began.
Dear Lord hold him close in Your care.
He had a tender love as You are well aware.

Leona V. Coffee

Pit Verses

Open to the amplifiers
    first scream
They whirl around the
    wall of bodies
Face against face
    against hands
    against backs
    against shoe soles
They hit me and hurt me
They love me
And when they fall
I help them off the beer soiled concrete
    Sweaty corpses stain my shirt
    and throw me around

It dies and awakens cyclically
    at the change of a song
    and the pit verse
    never leaves a full spirit.

Nate Rogers-Madsen

Evening At The Lake

Fire and ice carved the valley,
Fire and ice still rules this land
Where we camp. Where we now stand.

Gone is the noise and confusion of the day.
Peace now reigns. "Thanks," we pray

For the sun, that turns the sky to fire,
Reminiscent of volcanos' ire;

For the lake, molten silver - dark grey blue,
As the ice from which it grew.

Birds twitter, and the squirrel runs free
Up, down, and around the tree.

Like sentinels, the tall trees stand
to guard the shore, the hills, the land.

This quiet time, at day's end,
Is comforting; helps troubles mend.

As the breeze cools the air,
We know that it is only fair

That we see the fire, and feel the cold
Left from the disturbances of old
When this place was formed by fire and ice.

Leora Bennion

Emotions Of Remembrance

Those who are close and dear in our hearts,
Fill our souls with peace.
A longing fulfilled,
In which we shall keep.
Never forgotten,
Forever loved,
We reach within ourselves,
To embrace those we've loved.
Emptiness replaced by memories,
Pulled into the present,
Representing all we have truly felt.
Our emotions of remembrance,
Fulfill the void of loss.

Michelle Bailey

Let Me Be Free

I sit here alone in this dark, lonely room,
Feeling nothing but emptiness, nothing but gloom.
Please help me, Lord, please let me be free,
Free from this pain and anxiety.

Sometimes I wonder why life is so cruel.
Why can't things be simple, without any rules?
Please help me, Lord, please let me be free,
Free from this pain and anxiety.

My tears are like rivers flowing endlessly downstream.
The only time I feel happy is when I fantasize or when I dream.
Please help me, Lord, please let me be free.
Free from this pain and anxiety.

Maybe someday I'll turn my life around.
I'll face the world with both feet on the ground.
I'll have a husband and children and a future that's complete.
And I'll hold my head high as I walk down the street.
Soon the whole world will look at me and see,
That I am not only happy, but I am free!

Gina E. Dall

Real Freedom

Feel the wind flowing through the air,
Feel the wind so immortal so bare
Endless flow over land, over sea, endless
flowing so soft so free
You can smell it, you can feel it, but can't
capture the wind you can look to see but
will never find start or end
Many have tried to duplicate the
passion so free but nothing like the real
thing, this is wind you see.
It's the kiss of the earth, a gift
from God, stand naked and still let it caress
your body.
To some, it's a terror ripping things apart
but to me a reminder at freedom you see
That's the true meaning of the wind you see

Michael Fleming

Days Long Past

Those Sunday afternoons of days long past
Families together, those memories last
My uncle's picking guitars, and me, plunking along
Those days are gone, but the music lingers long

We are older now and the children grown
They now have children of their own
We've lost some dear ones through the years
Yet, I sense their presence through the tears

Somehow, somewhere, there must be a way
To bring back the music to these days
Again our days would be filled with gold
And the music in our memories we would hold

My mind keeps running back
To those afternoons of days long past
Those memories are blessed with gold
And in my heart, the music I still hold

Ginny Hack

Goodnight My Angel

My baby girl so sweet and small,
falling asleep on my shoulder as I pace the hall.
I've been dancing and singing and shuffling,
trying to ease the little one to sleeping.
I've held her hand and touched her feet,
so small, so pretty, so complete.
I guess miracles happen every day,
one happened for me on her birthday.
Her speech is limited to a gurgle and a coo,
but her little chimes sound so true.
How fast she is growing before my eyes,
her cute little clothes soon won't be her size.
I almost wish there moments would never end,
cuddling and staring at our new little friend.
God bless our little wonder for all this love,
let everyone see the girl I'm so proud of.
I lay her down with a kiss on her head,
she's finally sleeping as I tuck her in bed.
Goodnight my angel, may God bless and keep you,
rest well and dream of all the things we will do.

Larry Devey

Know Yourself

Why does he who wishes to be me
fail to see the dark side of he-
who is actually me?
My physical appearance is so naturally perfect
However, the way I think is something unsafe to detect
The bright light which shines within
Is hardly seen by those who rarely sin
The mask which I put on
Is a cloud of deceit which hangs over heads all day long.
One side of me tries to maintain my dignity and sophistication
The other side pulls me down with tremendous determination
Be happy with who you are
And in time society will accept you the way you are
Know yourself first
And know yourself best.

Nii Koney

"No Other Home My Soul Can Claim..."

I've known you well in private peace, I've known your love in Paradise.
Faced You too in private hell and seen You through a beggar's eyes.

I held You in our happiness, sought You in my beggar's pain,
Known You in such ecstasy, clung to You through drought and rain.

Mysterious, suffering episodes, not for the faint of heart,
Can I contain this love of Yours? Endure its "Better Part"?

Turned back again - for loving You, I cannot leave my home, You see
Sometime, somewhere long ago, I realized I can't leave me.

Two weathered hearts that beat as One, I have no other home, my Love,
It's You alone my soul can claim, it hears its cadence from above.

Though I know desert or the rain, though it be glory mixed with pain,
'Tis all the same 'tis all the same, no other home my soul can claim.

Marie A. Wenrick

The Flowers Of My Heart

Friends are like a field of wild flowers.
Each has a color, shape, and name all its own.
Alone each friend is unique.
Together they create a rainbow of complimentary personalities.
They struggle through the tough times, like a season with little rain
  and they thrive and grow when nurtured with spring showers and
  summer sun.
I will forever treasure these flowers of my heart.

Kristin Bruhn

Hard Times Ahead

Their ant nothing but hard times ahead, with the war in Baghdad,
Everything you buy now days cost more,
In every family there are two people working to make ends meet,
Their ant nothing but, hard times ahead.

Every body knows their can't be anything but, hard times ahead,
With all big companies like Sears, G. M., Ford and others laying
thousands of people off their jobs.
Their ant nothing but, hard times ahead.

As we look back at the good times we had in the past,
Now their ant nothing but, hard times ahead,
Sales are way off the economy looks bad,
Their ant nothing but, hard times ahead,
Just like I said, their ant nothing but, hard times ahead.

Lem Poteete Jr.

The Teacher

Young, and a gifted person, who has something to share:
Everything is done from the heart:
All the homework has been gone through with a fine tooth comb:
Eager to teach the children the right way:
Bold, cause I tell it, like it is:
Daring, cause no strings are attached:
Reverent, cause I prayed for a chance, to express the wisdom,
    that was giving to me, by God:
Courageous, cause I learned through trial and error:
Humble, for they are a family person too.

Gregory Hardson

All Alone

Darkness falls across the sky, a silent tear drops from her eye.
Everyone comes to see, everyone comes to stare at me.
She's there waiting in a corner,
waiting for him to come and warm her.
No one truly understands how she feels,
for she knew that love was for real.
She suddenly felt she was going to die,
until she heard that faint little cry.
She sees him coming across the land,
She sees him holding out his hands.
She runs along to embrace, she runs along to kiss his face.
When she got up to him he disappeared,
just as the thought of him had appeared.
She then falls to her knees,
Begging please... Please bring him back to me,
Bring us together me and thee.
For I love my Brian oh so much,
his heart, body and soul I want to touch.
All I'll ever want in life is him,
But she knows she'll never have his hand to hold,
from now until forever she'll always be... all alone.

Mandy Stewart

What Should I Do

How can I tell you how I feel.
Even though I know it's for real.
I hold back and don't know why,
Although it seems I do try.
How should I say what I mean
Even though these feelings I know you've seen
No word from your lips to let me know
How I should feel or what I should show
Am I just a fool to feel this way
Yet I just don't know what I should say
Please tell me what should I do
When I'm in love with someone like you

Glen F. Lorenz Jr.

School Days

I studied until I could study no more.
Even my room-mate began to snore.

I lay down upon my bed
but could not clear my aching head.

I tossed and turned round and around
but sleep wasn't mine to be found.

My brain was all cluttered it wouldn't be still.
Perhaps of studying I hadn't had my fill.

If I don't soon get some rest
I will surely fail the test.

And then I prayed, Dear Lord above
filled with tenderness and love

Please stretch out your hand to me
And cover me with a blanket of tranquillity.

With your finger my troubled brow do touch.
Ease my mind which is filled with much.

I could feel all the tension drain from me.
My mind was quiet as can be.

I rolled to my tummy, to my pillow crept
Whispered thank you Lord and finally slept.

Karen Krzemien

In Heaven's Light

In heaven's light, my senses won't deny
Evaporating worries in the fresh breeze.
In flight of birds, faith's energy lifts high
As long as rainbow colors of fruitful trees
Delights the mind, I've sought goodwill at hand,
God's gift of love believes the heart will last.
A flower's face, indeed, all over land
Comfort humanity as blessings cast
In friendship's path, a miracle is born,
Without a sight of misery, I'll play
In wealth of gems as Glory welcomes dawn.
Such beauty gains ahead a wholesome day.
The spirit of the soul reflects above
As peace unites mankind in song of love.

Molly Halpren

Family, Brother, Kin

"I Have a Dream" was the famous speech King read,
Equal rights for blacks was the fight for which he led.

His dream still lives on through all mankind,
That it's not about your color, it's about what's in your mind.

People often judge by the color of your skin,
Segregating into color - family, brother, kin.

Too often we don't think about how other people feel,
Lying, twisting feelings... What is false and what is real?

Color's not important, it's about what lies within,
Living with each other - family, brother, kin.

Laura L. Keller

Obsession

Obsession is the great love you feel for someone,
Day dreaming about the times together, the times of fun.
Thinking about him day and night,
Whenever you see him not letting him out of your sight.
Saying to yourself one day he will be mine.
Thinking about him all the time.
The question of how he feels about you is always there,
The thought, the obsession is too much to bear.

Jennifer Bush

Untitled

The words used
effortlessly
so able to extract precisely the feelings that they were
that were because of them.
They spoke and I responded, often silently answering questions they
proposed in their expression
their abandonment of thought
(and of myself)
intrigued me-and so I followed the looks that dismissed me.
Their distance made me want the nothing their presence gave me
even more.

Kathleen S. Carr

The Beauty Of Night

The day has ended... and darkness draws to a near.
Earths gentle night watchman... will reach out and soon appear.

The Universe steps forward to reassure us,
    that the beauty of night is without a doubt...
as glorious and soothing as the sun
    turned inside out.

I see that mother nature...
    has so perfectly put everything to rest,
and suddenly these great and miraculous things
    make me feel so humble, yet so blessed.

The stars begin to shine and dance...
    into beautiful shapes before me,
expressing all forms of love and life
    for my mind, body, and soul to see.

So I quietly sit here alone... in total peace.
Allowing the days disharmony... to completely cease.

And gazing out my window
    I eagerly watch while letting,
the grand stage before me,
    change to a new but beautiful setting.

Kathryn DeBerg

The Web Of Life

The web of life is continuous and united.
Each dependent on the thread before.
Forms may be different but they are all
created from the same cosmic clay.
Land, water, sky and fire, creative matter
from which spiritual being create the inhabitants.
Things with wings that soar and dip in silence up above.
Night creatures meek with gigantic eyes.
Or night creatures that sneak in the shadows of the jungles.
Animals and mammals who cry out Save Me before the
web is weakened, or you might be next.
Listen to their cries and warnings.
For mankind may be next to go the way of the dinosaurs.
Who might be the next king of this mountain
    called earth?

Mary E. Housh

"The Age Of Destruction"

The babies are crying and trees are still
dying and the seat is becoming too deep
We have blood on our hands, the children
are hungry and God is beginning to weep.
Is the war really over? Is death really done?
If darkness is gone, where is the sun?
Our air is polluted and the buildings still stand
That takes up the space of our beautiful land.
The minutes are passing as the days all go by.
Seasons keep changing yet, we still wonder why
If a man hates a man, then what is love for
Some people have family and some people have more.

Jimmy Brooks Dossey

The Search

In your cage you sat,
Drowning in your pool of dread.
Where once you found yourself,
You know find only emptiness.
Locking the door to your own cell,
It becomes your grave.
Your soul they took;
Yourself you gave;
Now revenge is what you crave.
Forever searching within yourself
For something you thought you would always have.
Yourself is the thing you will never find,
For it's something only the fearless can have.

Lena Szentendrei

"Drifting"

    My thoughts wander deeper,
Drifting into a circle of raging vampires.
    They are wicked souls,
Who taste the blood pouring from my heart.
    Trying to get inside me,
They lure me into a world of their own.
    A world of darkness,
Where evil is the master,
    And the devil takes control of your soul.
Living to kill, killing to live.
    There is no way out,
As I drift deeper and deeper into your soul

Kelly Bates

The Country Morning

The night is gone, the sun appears,
Dries the earth soaked by showers
Of gentle, lush, nocturnal hours.

The village roosters in numbers
Awake late risers from their slumbers,
Who wish to keep,
Their satisfying sleep.

But the barking of dogs, from a distance,
And the chirping birds' loud insistence
As jubilant church bells, rouse everyone
At the end of a long-awaited dawn.

Rushing in with golden rays, announces the sun,
For a thousand and one days, as it had done
Its arrival, as before, like in some untold faraway lore.

At a site serene, but not distant,
With a mist fine and quite persistent,
The early morning heat, prepares us to meet,
The new day as it's being born
In the ephemeral yet eternal strife
Of the unending symphony of life.

Mahmut Esat Ozan

Color

Black, Brown, Red, White and Yellow
Does this really change a fellow?
On an artist's palette they easily mix
Once done they never disunite.
In the real world they're immiscible
Once mixed, who knows, they could ignite.
In autumn they are the colors of change
Separate, yet from the same tree they came.
Once fallen they're merely piles of leaves
From many, many different trees.

Matthew T. Holland

352

Nothing To Hold

Alone in this world with nothing to hold
Dreams die away as time passes on
Looking for answers in the faces you see
They hide the pain and the hurt from me
Reaching for something that's not always there
Faking a smile and often a glare
They turn to reason when fact is gone
Believing in dreams that are always left on
They live for the moment that soon fades away
Giving into pleasures that lead them astray
Where is the love and honesty in this world
Whatever happened to friends till the end
A hand to hold on to
I just don't know
Straight from the heart, deep in the soul
And meaning in life are things to live by
That's why we're alone in this world
With nothing to hold

Michael Dean Boven

Water Tapestry

A water tapestry woven with sparkling threads,
Draped between the land's bony shoulders.

Threads of sunshine silver,
Woven between sea greens and sky-mirrored blues.

On rippled lines the light skips away.
Drawing the sailor's eyes
Along that shimmering path toward...
Adventure—dream—reality—death.

The billowing sail, wind filled,
Moves without hesitation among the silver threads
Woven on that loom held tight by the weathered cliffs.

Poseidon awaits outside the rocky frame.
The sailor salutes that water ruler
Passion-wrapped in that water tapestry.

Marilyn E. Dickey

Wayfaring Stranger

I am alone
Down this uneventful trail I walk,
These footprints I leave will soon disappear
Like my shadow after me,
When this winter crisp desert wind that bites and chills my back
Kisses, then gently scatters them to silence,
For footprints speak where I have walked
But, they will not walk this way again.
I am a man
Yet, a crying babe inside my manhood
This boy struggles to set free
But, what is it searching for?
To set free my restless and untamed spirit to some tranquil breeze
To unlock the locks that now imprison my expression,
For I cannot give what the world or you expects of me
What I want to give remains its own mystery,
I walk and I walk, but yet I find only self-meanderings
Whose completeness is elusive once again
The boy and the man will struggle to my end, "Help Me"
I am alone

Kathleen Cypert-Arnold

The Unnamed Poem

Early in the morning, before the break of day
down the quiet street I walk my cares all slip away
In the vastness of the silence my troubles seem so small
It's just as if I had none to bother me at all.
I walk into the brightening east and watch the sun come up
I listen for the birds to stir, I pat a friendly pup
It's only in the stillness of this early morning calm
That I fully come to realize I hold life within my palm.
As the brilliant hues of sunrise wash
across the brightening sky
The traffic starts and people walk and birds begin to fly.
I turn and face the other way and head into the west
Toward home, refreshed, with will to live today with zest.

Adah Thelma Higgins

Pink Ribbon

Pink ribbon kiss of death, like a necklace, but sign of doom.
Doesn't matter what size or girth.
Doesn't matter who gave birth.
Mark upon a furrowed trunk,
anticipating the first chunk.
Limb of life and awesome power,
cannot change a future tower.
What king plays the ugly role,
of what to kill and what to free.
When they come to put me down,
I will steal away his crown.
I bear fruit to his dismay,
will release the seed this May.
And when the cement cracks a hole,
I will come and bare my soul.

Mary L. Sweeney

The Healing Tree

The pain and suffering of spontaneous betrayal,
doesn't always lead to permanent fail.
Go out and look around, and you might see,
a bunch of young children playing on a tree.
But as you sit watching them play on that tree, you ask yourself,
How does this help my problem unfold?
And a little voice inside you says,
Sometimes the solution to something is hidden and untold
You look and you look, until you have found,
nothing but yourself with a headache, sitting on the ground.
But then, as if on cue, one of those kids comes over to you.
You sit and you talk, you bike and you walk.
And as you do these things, you find out,
that your young friend is too in doubt.

The point of this story, as you will see,
is not about sorrow, but about glee.
These two people from different generations join together in relations
And as you bid each other farewell, you finally see,
that the hidden solution to your problems, came from that tree.

Lindsay Coons

Untitled

If you want what you can't have
Do you not want what you do have?
If the bigger the game
the better to gain
Is the game the gain?
If you shouldn't but you do
Should you not do what you should do?
If you have everything but still want more
Having everything would mean you need nothing more

Kelli Kroll

Listen, My Daughter

Listen to the women's voices of the past.
Do you hear?
Their shouts of courage and hope will forever last.

Listen to our mothers' words and deeds.
Do you hear?
No regrets for their actions, so hear and heed!

Listen to your own thoughts
Do you hear?
The silence that fear has bought?

Listen to your heart and soul
Do you hear?
Your plans and actions growing old?

Listen for the bell that tolls for you and me.
Do you hear?
It is courage and hope calling out to be free!

Listen, my daughter, to your dreams.
Do you hear?
The hope that within you screams?

Listen my daughter, I pass to you this legacy, do you hear?
Take action, leave your daughter a brighter history!

Margaret Peterson

Forbidden Love

Do you ever think of me when you're sad and lonely?
Do you ever think of me this forbidden love of
mine that was never meant to be?

You live in my heart and in my soul I pray you
know; You visit my dreams during slumber and oh!
what joy you bring to me until I wake and you cease
to be, my craving to hold you bring me nothing but
pain; I see your face in every man I meet only to
find they can't compete with this forbidden love
of mine that was never meant to be.

I've tried oh so hard to forget you, to push you
from my mind but you seem to ever linger there;
You stand tall above the crowd, oh! so tall and so
proud this forbidden love of mine that was never
meant to be.

When the clock strikes twelve and you pass through
the door you'll be gone forever more, this forbidden
love of mine that was never meant to be.

Mary Allen Olive

A Sprinkle A Day

If you sprinkle bird seed...
   do birds grow?
If you sprinkle flower seed...
   do flowers grow?
Do birds sing... in an empty forest?
Do flowers bloom... in an empty florist?
Have you ever seen...
   a bird's wings flow?
Have you ever seen...
   a flower grow?
You will always have a need...
   unless you simply...
      sprinkle some seed?

Gary Joseph Boland

Race For Freedom. Am I Free?

The love that a child once knew
Disappears like the sky that once was blue
Fire and smoke of hell
Can't go back, run away, refugee bells
Burning trees, burning heart, burning soul
Men in green hard hats and arms,
Living with a heart so cold.
Fear for the love of the family.
Escape, fled the insanity
Long trip to nowhere, but we didn't care
The trip was long and cold, lucky for us it didn't snow.
We were sailing so smoothly
That was when we were wakened rudely,
Gun shots, bullets flying
Men, women, boys, and girls, all scared
But don't move or scream when you smell them through the air
No, this time it's different, they're not the Viet
Great we won't get shot or hit
Wow, everyone is different, it's a great new light
I'm trapped by race, but I'm ready for another fight.

Khanh Tri

A Thought, By Jeffro Jenga

I was standing in my ditch trying to comprehend the subtle differences between the soul seekers and the people of heart. This not the thought only the intent that rectifies who or what we are. The salute to the advancement is swayed by the fall back everyday, everyday in the saga of this land. The land of happiness is nothing but a breeding ground for petulance and the advancement of the filth and the decay that destroyed our land, not whole city mind you, not even houses but in each and every one of us who think they can make a difference, but we are wrong. The decay is to rotten for one man or woman to mend thus we must ride out eternity until the day of deliverance.

Jeffrey Kantor

Forever

Overwhelmed by your nature you've wandered into my heart.
Destined to be, this is only the start.
My admiration for you forever grows stronger.
My hopes for true love lingers no longer.
When I'm with you I wish it to be forever.
Time stands still when were not together.
When things get rough, remember my devotion.
Drunken by your passion I'm dizzy with emotion.
Winded by your love my essence blooms aghast.
We grow with our moments but it happens so fast!
When ever you need me I'll be there for you.
I'll love you forever, unconditional and so true!

Nanette Wampole

Untitled

She listens to the fighting
Crying, covering her ears.
Too busy fighting
To listen to her fears.

Of proms and pimples, big dates and dares
She opens her eyes, uncovers her ears.
Still too busy fighting
To worry of her cares.

She goes to a party
She didn't even mention.
They're too busy fighting
For her to grab their attention.

Her parents get a call
from the next door neighbor rumor.
If only they could stop fighting
just a little sooner.

Alicia Waligorski

Nature's Lovemaking

The beam of sunlight pierces the tree branches seeking deeper
depths like a lover wanting to reach the innermost sanctum

The breeze caresses the leaves bringing forth soft whispers and limbs
sway with an almost sensual movement

The birds clinging within the tree sing a gentle love song as the
roots seem to grasp the ground tighter for strength

The clouds move slowly to embrace the sun like a jealous other trying
to win back lost affection

The sky starts to rumble as the breeze grows stronger and the clouds
grow dark while beginning to weep in pain

The lightning snakes out and electrifies the air, as the thunder booms
with what sounds like a warning.

The sunlight is stolen away and the tree bows to grieve while the
leaves are lifted and carried away by the wind

The seeds fall to the soft moist earth as the dirt, carried by the
water wraps the unborn trees creating a safe womb for the seedlings

The storm reaching a peak slowly falls back, releasing its grip and as
the sun struggles to reach through a solitary beam rushes down to warm
the swollen earth

The tree seems to reach up to the light with pride and the birds come
forth once again and sing a soothing lullaby

Lesa Sweet-Gross

The Bouquet

You sent me flowers for my birthday:
Delicate White Baby's Breath -
  Blossoms as sweet and tender as our own baby,
  our son, the miracle joining two lives that had
  nothing in common, save that pure and beautiful child.
Pink Roses - Fragrant symbols of love and femininity.
  A pink t-shirt I bought for you,
  A never-to-be-worn t-shirt, hidden in your bottom drawer.
  Never completely forgotten, that threat to your masculinity.
  It was your gentleness, though, the feminine side.
  that used to touch me.
And Red, Vibrant Red Carnations -
  Life's blood - like tears from four miscarriages, hopeless surgeries.
  Red wine - a substitute for connection.
  Red screaming of emotions: anger, hurt, fear.
You sent me a bouquet - White, Pink, Red.
The colors of our past, teasing me with memories,
Reminding me that tomorrow is my day
For planting daffodils.

Kathy Swayne

At Sunset

Sad earth turns to face, unknowing, darkness.
Day spent, little is more, much is less,
  frivolous pursuits have laid waste
    her reason for being.

Weep sister earth, what use is weeping?
For lost time, for those lives near final sleep
  without salvation.

Daggers of destruction dove deep in today's heart.
The coming of night, more pain,
  if only the night brings what it can,
  absence of light, so to sadden the soul
    to utter stillness, then,
    will souls search for hope of salvation?

Weep, sister earth, ageless wisdom knows
  the soul will clamor for charming entertainment
  until rescue comes with the dawn.
    Stillness, there is none.

Mary Elizabeth Russo

Valentines Day

Every year it comes to pass and on this
day I shall ask, does she know I want her
near? Or is God the one that keeps her near.

I know it can't be what I say, though I'm
thinking of her everyday. It could not be
those things I do, because those things are very few.

It's not the places that we go, the food
is fast, the prices low. Maybe it's the
time we share? But no... I think those
times are rare.

It's been close to sixteen years, she
drinks wine, I drink beer. Could it be
the clothes I wear? No, comfort is my only care.

What is it then that makes her stay? Work
all day long, with no pay. To this the answer
now seems clear, it is the Lord that keeps her here.

John D. La Sage

Country Nights

I hear the leaves upon the tree
Dancing in the wind.
I hear the crickets start to sing as
darkness falls again.
I sit inside my quiet room and listen
every night and hear these sounds
I've grown to know when the sun fades
out of sight.
The bull frog croaks beside the brook
just down below my house and hiding
in the thick tall grass is a little quiet mouse.
The lightning bug he flashes his light just like
a sparkling star as the moon beams spread across
my yard and to the hills way a far.
Living way out side of town is the perfect
place for me and I can't think of any
place I would really rather be.

Jerry Blum

New York, N.Y

Bedizened jewel of the Atlantic,
Crowned with towering cemented
Glass, brick, mortar, and steel.
Metropolis humming with restless crowds.
Beehive of burgeoning business and bedlam,
Teeming with polyglot ethnic populations
Suctioned from all corners of the world.
Highways streaming with jets of mindless traffic,
Canker sore of crime and corruption,
Bold braggart, buffoon, capricious clown,
Self-styled cesspool of a nation,
World's proud center of the performing arts.
Tenements brooding like oversized monoliths
Break through the shadows of dawn.
Blocks of stunted canyons
Shrug off streaks of slender-fingered golden light,
Exhale layers of humid smells.
Here and there lights suddenly smirk
Through the vacant faces
Of streaked, unwashed windows.

Jules Brandell

355

The Wanderer

The fog slithers in like a thief in the night
Covering the sleeping city with a blanket of white;
It cuts a knife between buildings and silently creeps
Hovering low with a moisture that is wide and deep.

Ghost like, it distinctly muffles buzzing noises of cars
And the warning of train whistles afar;
It sends its lowly message for all to hear
Surrounding its prisoners with a quiet, awesome fear!

Yes - the fog - it is a wanderer in the night
Leaving without a trace as the sun shines bright!

Katherine Maxwell

Confusion Vs. Decision

Confusion is bitter sweet
Confusion is too much of a good thing
    (how is this possible?)
Decision is not being able to
eat your cake and have it too
    (or is that confusion too?)
Decision is difficult because things
    are not always black and white.
Take confusion, for instance, it's
    usually a very definite shade of grey.
Decision means choosing between
    the best of both worlds
Confusion is having two best worlds
    or how about two best friends?
    (how is this possible?)
To clear away confusion,
    we must make a decision
But how is this possible,
    After all, decisions are way too confusing
Are you confused yet, because I sure am.

Melanie J. Ahlborn

The Modern Heart

Truth and pure, a red heart beating
complexity and lies, a red heart bleeding.

Modern soul imbedded in strings of perplexity, each knot
blocks the blood of life (and therefore truth),
and soon the heart begins to slow,

We the preachers of the age
who make morals the rage
give up gleaming ambitions for telescopic vision,
our white pearls for tinted glass,

Or better yet for screens that never still
the onward flow of talk which turns
old themes of life, love, and death
into the encouragement of the poetically perverse,

Once unwashed democracy overtook knotty aristocracy,
but now our preached morals take
as "sensationalism" for bedtime stories,

Once the acclaimed land of the farm and free,
is now that of business and TV.

Nicole Moseley

Love - Family

My loved ones I have to leave behind
But you are the ones who bring to mind
An abundance of kindness and loving deeds
That ministers to my every need
Thank God above for children like you
Who always come through when I'm needing you

Mildred M. Carson

Frighting To Tell My Part

I have searched in the core of my being for
comforts here not in me
    I have come to find comfort does not abide even
in the court yards of my heart of mind
    Nostalgically cascading thoughts parade my minds
of, revealing how I was often neglected and dehumanized, as but a child.
    But some cynical fate in life, my childhood was
stole of its innocence, culprits having no regards to
what I felt or that they traumatized a defenseless little boy.
    Oh...but if, I could have been protected then, from
the robbers who had stolen my innocence, greatly depriving
the little boy I once knew of invision with knowing the true
essence of having ones virginity (pure), and a normal
childhood, then maybe I would have been a better person than I am now.
    But if, I could only gain the ear of an empathic
listener- as inner emotions stir here in, warm and
pensive are my echoing thoughts hidden within,
frightening their way forth desperately to express
Themselves and tell their part.

Lisa Chapuis

Come Ye Apart

Come Ye apart, my master said...
    Come Ye apart with me...
Quietly wait for my healing, my child...
    For I love and I care for thee....

Rest in the quiet of the early morn....
    Speak with a gentle heart....
For the ebb and the flow of your life, my child...
    Seek Me, and come Ye apart...

LaVohn E. Hess

You

You brought me ferris wheels and
    colored balloons,
Warm starry nights and
    cheese-flavored moon,
Carefree sunshine laughter that
    lasted after the rain,
Smiling faces and special places
    where we've shared happiness and pain,
Long sandy beaches caressed by a
    foaming, frothy sea,
Tomorrow's anxious dreams and
    yesterday's magical memories,
Rainbows at midnight and
    skies forever blue,
Dreams to sleep on and
    the courage to say I love you.

Kim Crider

"Renewal"

Time has created many Buds,
CHILDHOOD-ADOLESCENCE-MATURITY.

Blooms have unfolded with some of the petals scourged,
but fertilized once again, it tries to correct its beginnings.

The dew that hugs the petal are tears that the sun wipes away,
but new condensation cleanses the soul, and very essence of the
original seed, to re-new itself and become a better species.

Each cycle creates the Miracle of beauty that we see, for
internally we are Blessed by God to be better than what we were.

Marie E. Havron

356

If I Where To Walk...

If I were to walk upon the sky, I'd make billowy
clouds to float above my head. I'd make
rain dance on the earth, rainbows would stretch
across lands and the sun would always keep me warm.
　　If I were to walk upon the ocean, I'd make the
water so clear, you'd see it for miles. I'd make
waves sing songs as they broke to shore, sea life
would emerge and fill up the waters and birds
would fly high and guard down below.
　　If I were to walk upon the land, I'd make trees
so gigantic,they'd disappear in the mist. I'd make
grass so green, dew would sparkle in the sun.
Animals would roam free without being caged, people
would all be housed and have food to grow strong, and
we'd all love one another without any harm.
　　If I were to walk upon the heavens, I'd float
high through the clouds and sing soft words. I'd
reach out to angels and fly with each one, gently
caressing each of their wings, and touch the
face of God with peace in my soul.

Kelly E. Garvin

Trickster

Memory, vault of influence
closeted forever in my past,
distiller of present
experience, cloaking traces
of reality in disguises
peculiar to fear, desire and confusion.

You trickster!

Unlike Earth's etchings, yours are the most
obscure of cues, clouded with emotion,
singed by passion, replayed as fact
when fiction is the helmsman.

Chronicler of my life, you serve me well,
nonetheless, with your
delicious perceptions
resting beyond the dreadful pale
of objectivity

Continue to enhance
my self myth as I deposit daily
treasures in you, most false of my
cerebral functions... and yet, most nurturing.

Lawrence Etue

All Children Can Learn

All children can learn.
Children can learn fairness by treating others equally.
Children can learn to be less selfish by sharing with others.
Children can learn to be truthful by telling the truth.
Children can learn to enter into friendships with good people.
Children can learn not to follow the majority when the majority is wrong.
Children can learn to know what talents they have and use them.
Children can learn not to be afraid of working too hard to achieve
　　their goals.
Children can learn to find successes by telling themselves, "I can."
Children can learn to face the future with courage.
Children can learn to appreciate the importance of family, family
　　values, and morals.
Children can learn to not be afraid to stick to their values and beliefs.
Children can learn to honor and respect their elders.
Children can learn to accept challenges and successfully jump each hurdle.
Children can learn that school is a place to learn, bloom, and grow.
Children can learn to concentrate on doing what they do best.
Children can learn to never feel inadequate.
Children can learn the Golden Rule and follow its teachings.
Children can learn to be a good instrument that God can work with.
All children can learn.

Ora Lee Owens

The Dance

She's scared to take the chance,
'cause love's a dangerous dance.
　　She danced once before, that's when
she swore she wouldn't anymore.
　　He spun her around and then he was gone.
　　He left her dancing all alone.
　　Now he's back and wants another
dance, she wonders if she should give
him to chance.
　　Will it be the same as before?
　　Will he leave her all alone on the
dance floor?
　　He makes her feel like everything
will be okay every time they're together and
the music starts to play.
　　Will this dance be forever?
　　Does he really love her now?
Or is this the last
dance before the curtsy and the bow?

Jennifer Scott

Oh Mighty Wind

Oh mighty wind
　　Carry me off into the depth's
　　　Of the roaring sea
For that is where my soul
　　Truly longs to be
So that like a relic
　　My skeleton shall remain upon its surface
　　　For all of its children
　　　　To swim about
With an epitaph that reads
　　For years I have traveled
　　　On the journey of life
But now, here,
　　Where our life form began
I rest my weary bones
　　Let it be known
　　　I am home

Maria Martin

Freckles On The Sand

Seascape
Carpinteria Beach
State Park, California

Decades have passed
since oil washed this land,
the beaches are still spotted,
　　freckles on the sand.

Along the windswept bluffs my eyes once embraced,
tar cliffs now stand majestic,
on a smooth sandy face.

My thoughts drift back to a time long ago,
the sea was dark with mystery
while the stars shone bright as gold.

Where graceful, mystic islands
once captured our peaceful glance,
one by one the seascape now is dotted
with off-shore oil camps.

Now when I look from the edge of the sea
where night stars unfold, the dark sea is lighted by their lanterns,
　　kings of the rich black gold.

Lenard W. Eccles

The Lost Child

(For Nita)
One brief day can change your everything
Can alter it irreparably forever.
What others see as just a tiny flicker
Of life scarce registered before it's gone
Remains as memory for you eternal:
The touch of a soft head; a baby's cry
Gone down now into everlasting sleep.

Unhinged, the vortex spinning in your mind
All reason lost, all values reassessed
Stumbling and swirling, emotionally spent
You wandered into places ne'er explored
Only to find that life has turned full circle
Back into consciousness, and grinding hurt again.

The shattered pieces start to come together
You build them bit by bit, day after day
The days progress, you learn to smile once more
(But the colors lack their lustre, pastels and shadows)
Your eyes betray you, but our wishes make us see
The gleam of joy returning: (or is't the hint of tears reforming?)
That masks the sadness in your blue, blue eyes.

Linda Welch

Through Donerous

Eight years ago when I was living in Somalia I didn't think to
came to the United States. Because I saw a lot of my friends dead
beside of me. With out any reason. So I though I die like them

One day when we were going to Mogadishu which is capital city
of Somalia some people fired guns our bus. One of my friend's wife
was shot, her hand, her breast. The bullet torn her breast at two
parts. At that time I was depressed. And I didn't know. What to do.
Finally, I went to United Nation with my friends. We asked them to
help us. In few they made appointment for us.

During the interview one of American man asked me "where are you
from" I told him I came from Ethiopia but I'm a refugee who is
living in this country and also I told him the reason why I escaped
my country. Also I told him I was tried to much conflict cut in my life.

Omer Ushe Ali

The Cycle Of Love

Three hearts joined; mother, child, father, the years go
by, the family grows older;
three hearts joined; father, teenager, mother.
The years go by, the family grows older;
child marries and becomes one with spouse;
three hearts joined; mother, father, young adult and spouse.
The years go by the family grows older;
one dies; three hearts joined; the mother in heaven,
the father, the adult and spouse. The years go by,
the family grows older;
one dies; three hearts joined; the mother in heaven,
the father in heaven, the adult and spouse.
The years go by the family grows older;
The adult and spouse have a child and start the cycle
over, so the years go by the family grows older;
the adult dies; three hearts joined; mother in heaven,
father in heaven, their child in heaven...
the cycle of love never ends.

Kim Schuenemann

"The Truth Shall Set Me Free"

At first I paced - like a caged animal;
    By the bars of manipulation.

I fought back with fury - in the beginning;
    Then soon I became complacent.

My spirit was gone - and my roar silenced;
    The victim of intimidation.

They looked on with control - and arrogance;
    Their presence I grew to resent.

No key of metal - to open these bars;
    No lock with a combination.

But in my solace - the puzzle was solved;
    My soul delivered a present.

Be brave - and into their eyes speak your truth;
    The Truth will be your salvation.

The Truth has set free - my spirit of love;
    There will be no more imprisonment!

Michele A. Gianocaro

Exaggeration

I wish that I could exaggerate,
by saying that I slept eight hours straight.
    'Tis a lie shouted her mother in woeful frustration,
as her daughter lay there tossing and turning throughout
the night again. Lights on again, lights off again.
    Then cometh the dawn as she promised herself,
today I shall sleep, just wait and see.
    As she gazed upward praying, you could hear her saying:
"Dear God up in heaven, would it be an exaggeration just
to sleep a straight seven?"

Mary Jae Altieri

If I'm Rich

If I'm rich, I want to
Buy my Dad airline tickets to come and see America.
If I'm rich, I want to
Build a swimming pool for the children in my hometown.
If I'm rich, I want to
Set up a school for my husband to teach people Taiji.
If I'm rich, I want to
Buy the most beautiful flowers in the world for those old people
who are living in nursing homes.
If I'm rich, I want to
Have a grand palace for those children who lost their parents in
the earthquake.
If I'm rich, I want to
Take a lot of young people to see China and let them realize how
Much they should appreciate life here in the United States.
If I'm rich, I want to
Buy peace in the world and let people enjoy life.
If I'm rich, I want to
Share the love, share the wealth, share the happiness with people
all over the world one.

June Niu

A Mother's Goodbye

I loved you Son, I loved you so.
    But now it's time for me to go.

The Lord has called, He's taking me
    To a state of being that is pain free.

I know your heart is sad, my son.
    But I'm now at peace and my work is done.

And though I'm gone I need you to know,
    I loved you Son, I loved you so.

Linda K. Wintrow

Piece Of Mind

The mode of determination is in one's eyes,
But you have to look hard for it's not easy to spy.
The shadow of ones face is not
the same as the heart,
For the truth lies within, not easy to part,
Your goal is the source of you own destiny,
The meaning of life is in this simple necessity
hatred towards men lessens one's chances.
For one day as I hope we will have songs and dances,
We should all remember that helping someone in need,
Will turn our accomplishments into a rose from a seed
Love and peace can't be found by men who despise,
But those who don't can find love and peace without any lies.

Natalie McRae

Hidden Emotions

Feelings of hurt and anger might be expected;
But when not being told of what is happening,
No emotions are expected.
While having eyes and ears
Make things difficult;
Being not able to express the emotions
Make things even more difficult.
Seeing loved ones getting hurt is unbearable for some,
But for me is a challenge to make happiness.

Kandi Bruce

Where Is The Love?

War, hate, and violence plague our earth,
But what is this hatred really worth?

Have all of our hearts turned to a solid stone?
Why can't we hear all the cries and the moans?

We kill each other everyday,
Not even our children can go out to play.

What have we come to; where will we go?
If we keep this up we may never know.

Where is all the peace, love, and tranquility?
Why in our hearts is there only hostility?

Some of the optimists try to change our views,
But all of the pessimists don't care, they refuse.

If this is what we call evolution;
With all of our hate, violence, and pollution,

Then there is only one thing that I can say...
"We were better evolved in the Stone Age."

Melissa Hayes

Heart's Dream

As I sit here alone, close enough to a heart's dream,
    but too far away to see, the tears want to flow
    as fast and wild as a mountain stream
Every which way I look there is darkness
    leaving me in a limbo of love
    making me want to scream
Scream, cry anything to release the pressure
    that has been placed on this fragile heart
    maybe then the healing can start
All I have left are the memories
    memories of a time when loving and being loved
    seemed the purpose in life.
But now the purpose has changed
    ever since you said goodbye
    my purpose is waking up to cry
I know one day everything will be alright
    I'll find another to hold me tight
    and maybe then I'll remember the real purpose in life.

Michele Dreibelbis

True Blessings

Sometimes when I feel sort of blue I can't understand just why,
But then I realize how truly blessed I've been with sight to see the sky,
The sun, the stars and the moon above
The flowers and the faces of those I love.
To be able to hear, to talk, to walk and feel
That I no longer have a sense of smell is really no big deal.
Help me to keep in mind dear Lord my blessings above all else
Whenever I have a tendency to feel sorry for myself.
I have a wonderful husband and a family who cares
Good friends who are always willing to share.
I try to help others whenever I can
For I believe this is part of Gods plan.
To bring happiness into the lives of others,
For in his sight we're all sisters and brothers.
Now, hopefully, as I walk the last mile,
I'll hear him say, "well done, my child."

LaVerne Hanke

Everything Seen

Everything seen is sacred all to me.
But the image upheld before mine eyes
That they care to grace a blue shield upon
Is but the putrid, sad picture of self.
Disease, you say, that holds no inward bounds
And minds the lips to shuts, the eyes to mind
For powerless they against some sickened thoughts,
That, in theory, think only for skin owned.
Where did that sickness come raging to life?
Deep within some cavity's cavity...
No, rather in a breast that screams and hurts
And thus travelled as Jason to find truths
To cure, but lonely lies could just be found.
So once in a brain it gave in and drowned.

Jon Doyle

Sacred Heart

One day I went to church
But the door was locked
I was lost and very sad
I want to talk to God

Oh...please someone, open the door
There was no one there but my aching soul
I searched all over the land
But I could find no one

I was all alone, standing there
Looking for another soul
I peeked inside to say goodbye
I saw Jesus smiling at me

"What are you doing my child?
Don't you know?
I'm with you always,
Till the end of time."

May Mendenhall

Fourth Of July

Flags are swaying red, white and
blue my country has fought and died
for you

Some people don't know what freedom
means freedom's the thing that those people
bring

On the fourth of July we can say thanks
for letting me be here today

Jenna Stouffer

Ode To Pain

Pain is your name
But surely this is too simple a name for you
Who reeks such devastation, destruction
And despair,....Surely your name should be Rare
You've done more than the Constitution
Bill of Rights and ERA combined
You've closed the Generation Gap, crossed
The Poverty Line and made equal all Mankind.

You are robber of my joy, disrupter of my life
Occupier of my thoughts, rapist of my Self-esteem
Annihilator of my dreams!

My spirit swims the sea of my tears
As it has for too many years
Upward, upward against your tide of defeat
My soul hatches eggs of hope
As I learn to cope
To one so badly battered and torn
Then Faith is born for
"Faith is the substance of things hoped
for and the evidence of things unseen."

LaRose Sills

A Lesson From Papa

I am jealous because she is white
   But papa said I'm pretty
I am jealous because she is bright
   But papa said I am smart
Whenever I complain
   Papa said I am different
Until I realized one day that
   I am me.

I have to be the best of what I am
   instead of being better than the other
I must do my very best in everything that I do
   rather than do what the others can
Only when I stopped comparing
   did I learn to love myself
And mighty glad that . . . I am me.

Nancy Russell S. Kempis

Spiritual Reality

Two people of like mind
but of different faiths
deeply in love
and at a critical point in their relationship.
Sure in their collective mind
yet facing unsure family, friends and clergy
Why?
Divorce rates are one in two.
Jew marries Jew
Baptist marries Baptist
Couples split after bitter disputes;
each member of the partnership
must relearn to live as individuals.
However, Adventist and Agnostic accommodate,
Jew and Presbyterian compromise.
It's still not ideal, they say
If only he was mishpoke, they say
Their relationship endures, I say.
In happiness and spiritual harmony
a union born of unplanned love, not inflexible tradition, thrives.

Jenn Director

"Valley Of My Lord"

Living on a mountain brings comfort enough to me,
But my mountain top gets lonely, my sight set less on You.
Nowhere except in valleys can Your work on me be done,
So, Lord, leave me in the valley, if near You I will be.

My valley must be one of the endless kinds,
For daily I awaken to see my map charted thus.
"What valley today?" I ask my Lord.
"My Child, you have need of this one; we'll begin it right away.

The civilized, winding valleys you've already passed by;
The ones you have remaining no other has seen or walked.
Each of these I've chosen especially for you -
(For each of my creations, unique as they may be.)

This valley will bring you chill and dread;
It is the Valley of the Shadow of Death.
My rod and my staff will have to comfort you,
For you'll not know where I am, as this course you tread.

It'll leave you sick and trembling,
Thinking you are alone and lost;
But just know that I AM with you -
And will be - even when Death does by you pass."

Judy Dees

Lop Eared Bob

My Back Yard lawn is lush and deep,
But its height makes me look like a slob.
And the reason I leave my grass so high,
Is because of a big brown Hare I named Bob.
Well, one night Bob came and brought a friend,
It was Pretty Matilda, I named her right there.
And they dined very well on the grass at its best,
Yes, they truly enjoyed this lush bill of fare.
And night after night they did eat their fill,
Then they quietly hopped off together.
And for many weeks they repeated this feast,
In moonlight and dark stormy weather.
But one night Old Robert came down all alone,
And he anxiously ate and hopped quickly away.
It was then that my heart did sink like a stone.
And I watched for Matilda for many a day.
Then one night Old Bob came down to the patch,
With Matilda and her wonderful surprise to dine.
And Bob stood so proud at the edge of the thatch,
To make sure his family, all nine there, were fine...

John T. Simpson

To My Best Friend

I would give you the happiness of a snowflake on a cold winter's day.
But it might melt away.
I would give you a basket full of sunlight
But it might fade away.
I would give you a field of horses
But they might run away.

I will give you a mind full of dreams
To carry you away.
I will give you a heart full of peace and hope
To calm your fears away.
But most of all, I give you my friendship
And hope that it never goes away.

Katherene R. Lundgren

Outreach

Every day my soul cries out in fear
But it is a cry that no one will ever hear.
With passing time, the sorrow grows more and more
As I try to find ways that I can restore.
I wanted to think of ways all on my own.
The more I thought, the more I knew I was alone.
The pain is strong and the love is weak,
True comfort is all I really seek.
Now the time is passing by so slow
I guess that's what happens when you just can't let go.
I sat and wondered, what could I do?
As I pressed myself to get help from you.
It doesn't seem like I want it, I know,
But feelings like that are hard for me to show.
So maybe if you could take the time to understand
Or maybe just care enough to reach out your hand.
My first instinct is to get up and fight,
So if I grab your hand, it may not be too tight.

Kendra Overfield

The Presence Of You Lord

I walk the streets and people make a crowd,
but, in that crowd I feel no one is around.
The steps I take don't lead me nowhere,
the pain I feel no one else knows is there.

The tears I shed are lonely ones,
the smile I wait for feels like it will never come.
My heart beat is slowing down each day,
sometimes I feel that from this world I should walk away.

I cry out to the presence that I feel,
I know it's the Lord and to him I kneel.
I pray for guidance of my lonely heart,
I ask for safety of this world that by me falls apart.

The place I visit is the house of God,
when the doors are opened I say Lord
I've come to visit because of me I felt you had forgot.

Lord I humbly fall to you on my knees,
I pray that my heart and soul for you, you'll keep.
Lord I ask of you to give me light to the darkness I'm in,
Lord forgive my mistakes and all of my sins.

Maria Gonzalez

Ode To A Broken Leg

I hate to admit it even to me -
But I'm leaning again and I thought that never around be -
I'm leaning on mother as she takes the load
and I'm leaning on others to brighten my road
I've looked with contempt on the leaners I've known -
Not caring what caused them their pathway way alone -
And when I met them in my busy day
I hurriedly spoke and then sped on my way -
But my heart cried out "stand straight and tall
Because no one will care if you stumble and fall" -
The haughty the mighty has fallen a lack -
and things sure look different down here on my back
I had it coming -
Cocksure and wise -
others were human -
I wore the disguise -

Norma Bartley

Amor

I can't talk truth
But I can't lie
There's something about her when she's by my side
Maybe one day I will tell her so
Maybe one day she'll suddenly go

Why does she make me feel this way
How long is this feeling going to stay
Is this just an attempt to deceive
I wish this feeling would never leave

How can I describe
This feeling I never felt before now
That I wish I could restore somehow
Why does this feeling always depart
Why does this feeling break my heart

I guess there's nothing I could say to make this feeling stay
I guess there's nothing I could do to describe this to you

When true love is finally attained
With all my heart I'll never refrain
And the day it leaves I'll have to grieve
I wish this feeling would never leave

Marlon Araujo

Up And Down...

Up and down is how life goes with days all full of care.
But God will fill us with new hope if we call on him in prayer.
Up and down is how life goes,
We look to God above,
And not matter what our problems are he will bless us with his love.
Up and down is how life goes,
We search for gentle peace.
So let us reach out to the Lord and he will grant us sweet release.
Up and down is how life goes,
But no matter what we do,
The Lord will be there by our side and his strength will see us through.

Natalie Morrow

"A Windy Memory"

The wind wisped softly against her angelic face
Brushing strands of blonde hair across her smile, my heart raced
As she turned toward me, her beauty radiant with her love
Just then, I heard the quiet flutter of a baby dove.

Her uncovered shoulder provided it a landing
Soft and sensual she was, with love undemanding
Caressing the baby, she beckoned me closer
Inviting me to taste, touch and explore her.

This incredulous and beautiful woman desired me
A man of many thoughts and feelings most can't see
Her sweet and tender voice whispered to my heart
As we made love 'neath the trees in that deserted part.

Surely she must have been an illusion in my mind
Brought about by lofty thoughts of love I'd never find
Just then, I hear the creak of the wooden screen door
The grandkids' Kool-aid cups, both wanting more.

A warm and breezy day it's been, here in this once deserted part.
My wife says, "hey, remember that day I stole your heart?"
The wind wisped softly against her angelic face
Brushing strands of gray hair across her smile, my heart raced.

Keith D. Brinson

Fire

I sat staring as the piles of sticks and
brush, now ignited in flames, sent up
puffs of black smoke through the
leaf-barren trees, then faded in the
ever-darkening blue sky.
The fire shot neon orange embers into
the clouds of black and then even they turned to black.
The flames danced on the slowly
dissipating rubble as if inviting me to join them.
I felt the urge to run and jump into
the very core of the flames.
I longed to be with them, to dance with them;
I could see the smoke more clearly then.
I could feel the heat against my face.
The fire looked like a refuge from all
the troubles and problems I have each day,
A beautiful place to save me from the world.
But just then I felt a force pulling me back,
Back to the world, black to reality.
Then I turned and walked away.

Jessica Cain

"Breeze From Eden"

I wonder how the sun shines there?
Brighter than I know?
Do crystal rains fall from the sky?
Do the rainbows ever go?
Are the people there all happy?
Do they smile as they pass?
Do they all love mother nature?
Do they walk around the grass?
Do they know nothing about weapons?
Never thoughts about a war?
No hints of any suffering?
Never a chance of being poor?
I feel a breeze from Eden.
Let it carry me away.
If it's half as sweet dear, as it smells....
I'd move there any day.
Is it always nice and quiet?
Just birds and laughter in the air?
If it's different from here, I'd sure like to go.
Does everybody care???

Jennifer Lauren Gibson

Christmas In Iron Duff

Ice crystals in the pine trees glittering in the morning sun
Bright poinsettias in a black iron wash pot sitting in the snow
A house that has seen a hundred Christmases and more
Hemlock and holly gathered from the woods
And red nandina berries in a blue glass basket
Loved ones holding hands while thanks is given for the holiday feast
A long walk through peaceful pastures
Where one of a herd of steaming cows gives birth on the hillside
The wind whips across the mountains as darkness gathers
And another Christmas is gone

Lois Bressler

Girls

God made girls with laughing eyes,
bouncing curls and loving care.
He made girls to take care of animals,
and to run and play in the forest,
and to pick flowers from empty meadows.
He also made girls to make friends with boys,
and someday get married.
But most important to become a woman,
and to be a loving, caring Mother!

Melanie Marie Meyer

The Little Boy

The little boy is standing there, he has
blue eyes and brown hair.
He can see you in his mind.
A friend he wants to find.
He wants to explore the world where
there is more.
Ahead is an open door.
The little boy is getting tall, in his world
that seems so small.
He is a boy with dreams like you and me,
Open the door and set him free.

Gerri Knight

Wind Storm

A stormy wind sweeps across the land,
Blowing with powerful blasts, the dry and rotten stuff.
Cleaning away old debris, doing a good job.
Whistling around every corner and into every crack.
Working hard and loud, teasing the sand.
Trying to walk against this blustering force, I huff.

Oh, could such a wind, clear human hearts,
Of old anger and mean thoughts;
All the ugly things that don't belong there.
Could such a wind free these hearts from fear and misery.
Leaving room for fresh courage and kind thoughts.
Tolerance and love.

Miriam Britschgi

Limbo's Child

Dad was always right, mom was never wrong.
Big brother was their favorite son,
Little sis the last one born.
Me, I was limbo's child, caught between the two.
Not big enough to play with John,
Too big to play with Sue.
So I took to pen and paper and wrote my way to fame,
Using not my given, but a complete fictitious name.

Dad wasn't always right, mom was sometimes wrong.
Big brother's serving time in prison,
Unwed sis is waiting for her child to be born.
Me, I am limbo's child, caught between the two.
Not big enough to pray for John,
Too big to pray for Sue.
For I'd taken pen in hand and written my way to fame,
But for this little poem I'll use my given, not my
fictitious name.

Neil Stevens

The Meanings Of True Love

LOVE should come after friendship
because there's no way you can guarantee a relationship.

LOVE is hard to define
when you're not divine.

LOVE is easy to be broken
when there's no devotion.

LOVE really hurts
when you heart really bursts.

You would say LOVE is precious
when there's no races.
So when you LOVE someone,
Don't be just like anyone,
but learn to let them go
to continue your goal.

Junaliza Tugaoen

362

Looking At Her

The long and tiring nights she spent,
Beside my crib with me in her arms
Loving me and comforting me,
Trying her best to ease the pain and frustration
Of her helpless baby girl.

The many years of molding and shaping
Her daughter's life, only to hope
That she will remember,
The values and principles that had been
Engraved into her mind time and time again.
In the most crucial and painful times of her life,
Reluctantly sitting back, wishing to take the pain away
And praying that she will choose the right.

Looking at her I see
The woman I can only hope to be,
A wonderful mom, a loving wife
A friend and example to all
She truly is a daughter of God.
It's a privilege for me,
That she can be my mom.

Jennifer Nelson

Friendship Lost

Way up on the mountain
Beneath the big oaks and the pines,
That's where I spent my childhood
With a good ol', friend of mine.

Sometimes I can still hear his voice
Late into the night,
Ringing off the old mountain pond
Where my good friend lost his life.

My friend died that night
Doing what he was born and bred to do,
And I can't wait to run with him again
And do the things we never got to do.

I've never been back to that awful place,
Since so long ago,
But somewhere beneath that icy water
Is the friend that I let go.

And as I left, I said goodbye
As the tears rolled down my face,
And I knew right then as I walked away
I left a friend I could never replace.

Michael Cairy

My Hometown Carlyle

All of my memories are in Carlyle
Believe it or not, that's where I got my style
I came there when I was five
I gained attention and became alive
I grew up nurtured and fine and strong
Mama Lila taught me about the good and the wrong
It wasn't easy facing the issues in my day
I came out pretty good, so what can I say
My favorite friends were Pansy, Armilla, and Nadine
Oh! our many laughs and funny jokes and screams
Now don't you laugh about my little town
As I said before, I came out good and sound
I'll never forget my little pet goat
She tried to eat my clothes and loved water like a boat
I'll never forget Ms. Bremmer who taught me my ABC's
Sure enough she taught my children all of these
Well enough for my little Carlyle town
I hear the faraway music of the clowns

Jean M. Thompson-Dalton

Untitled

Along a dark untraveled road, in silence I watched you pass
Behind a closing wooden door, now here you are at last

I found you in a hidden tomb, with secret bleeding hands
Upon my bed, within my room, in dreams my love before me stands

In days of musky splendor, I summoned you at will
And concealed beneath our cleverness, our hearts beat wildly still

I say it doesn't matter, you say it more masterfully bold
This captive of your laughter, this maiden with hair of gold

Speak not of love, my beloved, nor of nights of Donovan's rhymes
Speak not of the cottage beneath the trees nor breathe your gentle sighs

Our child was born of a love so young, was born of a love so sweet
She is now my gift to you, as she has been your gift to me

Gale Neumann

In The Beginning...

This Sunday, March introduces peace,
Begins with a kiss of the morn's sun.
Sweet songs of praise for spring's feast,
Cardinals dance; this day is won.

Victory of life, a sparrow's song flows,
On a branch of rose as it sways,
A brush of breeze to let us know,
Red bud radiant, creation plays.

Blue jay squeals as life awakes,
At the drop of a twig, civilization sounds.
Mockingbirds soar as cool night warms,
Strong winds whistle, day abounds.

Gary M. Grubb

The Teacher

It's quiet in the morning,
Before they all arrive.
I know soon the bell will be ringing,
Then everything will come alive.

Some will come in running,
Full of stories to tell.
Others stroll in quietly, barely beating the morning bell.

Their faces are all different,
yet everyone much the same.
All those little eyes upon me,
for learning is why they came.

Before me sits our future,
The hope of times to be.
Such a heavy burden, to rest on meager little me.

So daily we work together,
Little by little they grow.
It never fails to surprise me, just how much they know.

One day they will leave me,
On to some new class you see.
With each one goes a small part, of what they learned from me.

Karen Parke

Night

   Night is like a bowl of cold pudding.
Because of its beautiful darkness. When the stars
shine they are like fairies dancing and waving
their little wands while sprinkling magic upon one
another. I always wondered what it looked
like up in that big dark blue sky. I think the
moon is like a huge ice cream ball filled with
sprinkles inside. The night has its own. Little world
that glitters and shines. I will never forget this peaceful memory of the night.

Jennifer Gruggett

Today's Thoughts, Tomorrow's Pain

I wake in the morning with the sun
beating in my eyes; sometimes not knowing whether
I should laugh or cry. This you see just seems
so peculiar to me; For I think sometimes
life is nothing but a dream. The only reality
of it all is laughter and pain. And you always
feel like you're going insane. You always have
to rush in a day; and at night the dreams
never last as long as you wish they could. It's
this world and society that we live in today.
They never slow down, and they'd push for more
if they could. It's a crazy world we live
in and you have to be crazy to live in it.
We don't even read the paper anymore 'cause
we know we'll open it and see a world of
horror. But we have created this world
so there's no reason to complain, just sit back
and wait for your loss or gain.

Lisa Tullos

Babies Are God's Gifts

You know it is a miracle; When a precious one is born.
Be it a boy or a girl; God's blessings will adorn.

Come celebrate the coming birth; Of Wade & Kathy's baby girl.
One of God's special gifts; More precious than a pearl.

The babe they've come to know; As little Brittany Brown.
Will surely be a princess; Her baby hair a crown.

So if you are so inclined; To share the coming joy.
Know now... in advance... It's a girl, not a boy.

So if the gift that your bring; Is soft and fuzzy, make it pink.
But if you think the daddy wants a boy; Bring Kathy a good stiff drink.

Because another nine months; With a babe in the womb.
Will surely make the poor mother; Commit herself to a padded room.

Krystal K. L. Shaffer

Voyage

The sun disappears behind the horizon
bathing the sky in radiance
orange, pink, fiery red,
until they too are gone.

Silence

And then faintly
the silver circle appears
the moon will sail the wide ocean of night
through sparkling diamonds and black velvet
and I will voyage to far-off ports
and never return
until I have harnessed the moon
and we will sail back
through almost a year
many months
in and out of weeks
this very day
and the golden sun is ready in the east
waiting to rise once more.

Laurel Damashek

Not Alone

Once I thought I walked through this world alone
all by myself without a friend of my own
I thought no one could care for me
then God made me a friend we could share but I could not see
she would go from him to me with words of love and glee
my angelic friend helped me take my eyes off of me
and put them on He.

Joyce Digges Bontrager

Hunger

The moon hung quietly over the sleepy town;
    Barely escaping the force that was pulling it down.
Many an hour had passed since he left;
    She scampered down the staircase with great deft.
The floorboards creaked under every step;
    Her rosy cheeks wet, from when she had wept.
From the great oak door, ushered a belligerent roar;
    Sending the girl into a great stupor.
The crystal chandelier went swaying;
    She swiftly fled, not hesitating.
O'er the house the sound reverberated;
    All while the beast masticated.
She tried to hide to gain comfort;
    But the beast foiled her every effort.
She screamed when the long dark talons came slashing;
    The huge jaws penetrating, and mashing.
All of a sudden she awoke from her slumber;
    Finding herself back in the cold, wet street,
Shivering down to her feet,
    Once again unable to escape that beast called Hunger.

Jonathan Karpel

Origami Sonnets

In one last gasp of sated ecstasy,
Autumn cast his sonnets full of fantasy
Upon the wind. They spun and twirled,
A court pavane of russet robes that swirled
Amidst wine reds, rosés and gold lamé.
They danced the season's rhythm, fey.
It was a subtle courtship of the senses:
Mushroom musk and spicy pine incenses;
Concord grapes fermenting on the vine;
Perfumed potpourri of flowers now supine;
And stitched in appliqué, the fragrant tease
Of long lost verses, crinkled: taunting memories
Of other love-besotted origami flights
Upon the ardent breath of our delights.
Lingering awhile to pick the very best,
I clasped fall's poems to my breast,
And thought of you with each fond look.
I read them all from spine to spore,
Then I pressed them in a wooden book
To treasure 'til he wrote some more.

Nyuka Anaïs Laurent

October Moon

With wanton expectation I stare
At your ever-turning face
While you lurk behind a smoky screen
Isolated in your hanging solitude.
Your feigned light, shrouded and mysterious
Seduces
Beckons me to watch.
For a moment you tease with shining revelation
Beaming your golden charm.
Then a misty veil, floating black and chiffon-like
Shifts ominously to cloud the view.
Your pallor dims
Familiar darkness masks your suspended glow
Leaving me alone to wonder
Of the ancient secrets you keep
The stellar fantasies you hide
Or is it lunacy that you conceal, October Moon?

Judith E. Alan

"Fate"

My fate is near; I can hear death's raspy scream, but I have no fear,
at the end of the tunnel there is a heavenly gleam.
    Oh, I feel peace with no more pain,
but there is sorrow that floods over me with tears that rain.
I see the black shadow about to fall,
but just as I prepare to ascend to the star, I hear my love call.
    "You so young, I came to late, to say I love you before your fate!
My memory a flow like sweet old wine, must you leave for the faithful
divine? Your life so short, our love so long,...;"
    And as she wept, I quietly whispered along,
"My near fate, but I came back to thee
with only enough strength to tell you what you mean to me.
I know without me, our love will be incomplete,
but now I must go; my fate I must meet."
    Then I slip away into the sweep bye and bye,
as I hear the echo of her last cry.
    No one can describe the look on your face,
or comfort me with the brutal reality I must brace.
My heart is filled with aching sorrow, knowing not even my love
can save you from fate and give you another tomorrow.

Nicola Nellams

Visions

Cats sit and stare
At something that isn't there.
Do they pretend to hallucinate
Just so they may procrastinate?
As they while the day away,
Watching the birds and squirrels at play?
Hoping you'll think they see
Much more than what's visible to you and me.
Cats sit and stare....
Is there really SOMETHING there?

Gail C. Parker

Untitled

He came into my life.
Asked me to be his wife.
Said he wanted me for life.
Stabbed me with a knife.
Broke my heart.
Said we should be apart.
I wanted to die.
He made me cry.
He was unhappy too.
He didn't know what to do.
Eventually he came back with tears in his eyes.
He wanted no more goodbyes.
He said he still loved me and wanted to live with me.
I said we'd have to see.
I had to decide what was best for me.
Well now we're back together.
Hopefully forever and ever.
If it doesn't last.
He'll be in my past.
He won't have a second chance.

Janet K. Strupp

Dawn's Coming

Dark halls with shapes of things coming alive
After sins of transgression,
Fearlessly waiting, wanting, watching
Amid a sea of black—in utter despair,
A pearl of longing, a flawless wonder
Cries out for light in a dungeon of hell.

No wind blows there, no trees grow
Only solitude and a whispered name
Beckoning the dawn's coming.

Maurice Maser II

"Sunrise"

The savanna sparkles
as the bright sun
eases over the endless horizon.
Antelope awaken from their slumber
to greet the new warmth.
Snakes slither from their hidden premises
to bathe in the young light.
Birds flock to the edge of the oasis,
and then,
one by one,
take off again
into the clear blue sky.
The air,
now warm,
carries a greeting of happiness...
Who would have known
this was a land
of much pain and suffering?

Kristina Paris

Makin' It!

"What a day!" She's heard to moan,
as she fights the traffic home.
The phone it rang unceasingly,
the workload's just too much for me.
Short suspenses every day,
a screaming boss and measly pay.
"It's enough to make a grown man cry."
She sighed as she rubbed a blood shot eye.
Why does she do this? I should have known,
she's a single mom with a kid at home.
She opens the door and slips inside,
the cares and worries replaced with pride.
Her house looks great, she's doing fine!
"Mommy's home, dear child of mine!"

Kelly J. Snyder

Mother Of Exiles

I stand in the shadow of her majesty.
As she draws me closer to her side,
I can feel the pulse of thousands before me,
Beating hard —remembering the first glimpse of her eminent form
    against the skyline.

I feel a reverence and awe,
As though abandoned in a great cathedral
Preserved through the ages solely for my redemption.
My eyes travel heavenward fixing upon the flame at the top
    of her grandiose spire;
A flame that has illumined the paths, and minds, of so many before.

In the silence of my homage, I hear the deafening screams
Of those who have provided the sacrifice for my freedom.
Insults and curse words hurled toward her undeserving feet
By a naive young man from the crowd
Refuse deference for that which she embodies,
And abruptly pierce my moment of awareness.

Gently, I pull myself from her embrace.
As my hand slips away from the pedestal on which she stands,
I realize— with compassion— that the blaring screams of sacrifice
Have become too distant for this young man to hear.

Linda Wicker

Time

So someone could be chasing you.
As if you were run down into a dark hallway.
As you are turning around
timid flash of fluorescence in you.

Into you moving lights in forward
position at unoriginal speed.
Unnaturally making you feel as if you are
being pulled in but not moving.

The chaser is violent and lives
tender to pounce, strike, and attack fierce.
Crush your hopes of ever moving on,
and turn your soul inside-out.

Followed by a forsaken killer.
All flowers growing wildly in a
field stomped on and trampled to dust.
A speck of nothingness lies behind.

Will you be so obsessed as to destroy
the center of attention; the sights
of the many people searching for
Answers, devoured and dying every day.

Joe Ludes

The Wings Of My Soul

I have often thought that it would be nice to fly,
As I watch the birds sore up toward the sky.
The bees, they fly and hum as they go.
Even some squirrels can fly as you know.
From the tiniest of insects, to the eagle, to the dove.
Each one is placed here by God.
Through these we see his great love.
These are creatures with God-given wings.
You know they are delightful as you listen to them sing.
Man-made wings, they too can fly.
Sometimes they fall and cause man to die.
The wings that are sure, the wings that are whole,
Are the wings that I claim, the wings of my soul.
Maintenance never needed for repair,
God made them and made them just right.
They are perfect, they are dependable,
They'll be ready when I take my flight.

Kathleen Camp

My Garden

Of all the beauties for me to see,
As I gaze from my chair where I must be;
The blooms of plants fluttering to show colors bright
As if they knew they are my delight.
And then the many birds begin to sing
And seem so happy about everything.
As the squirrel and chipmunk share their feed,
They don't seem to mind 'cause there's all they need.
In late evening when twilight shadows fall;
What beautiful music as they begin their call.
And as the trees pick up the cool breeze
One hears the murmur of the cottonwood leaves,
And some even seem to say
Thank you, God, for this beautiful day.
Purple wisteria, yellow pansies, red wood vine
Far up in the oaks their blooms entwine;
All day long it's a picture I love to face
It's my own dear sanctuary
   Named "Woodsey Place".

Lucile H. Goodgame

It Is Over

It was the end of a good life together.
As I drove my car slowly down the street,
Tears streamed down my cheeks.
In an instant my life seemed to flash across my mind.
Overwhelmed with a multitude of emotions,
I clutched the steering wheel for comfort.
Oblivious to my surroundings,
I thought of the days ahead.
Not only was I in the drivers seat
For this short journey, but for the rest of my life.
From every angle, a surge of determination
Flowed through my veins.
A burst of energy sparked by reflexes and relaxation
Was set into motion.
A transformation of self assurance was reborn.
Now there were tracks of tears upon my face.
A smile took the reins of the frown and weary lines upon my brow.
My thoughts were soaring in the clouds and
I give all the praise to Him!!!

Karen Hardin

Ode To A Graduate

This is your day my love;
As here before me, I see you stand.
Proud silent and serene;
Your diploma held within your hand.

I have longed for this day my love;
Your ardent fan I've always been.
To see you walk the isles of life;
Your goals, your aims your hopes to win.

As I sit here heart filled with pride;
your husband dear sits by my side.
Another mile stone in your life.
Midst a troubled world, torn with strife.

Your education major a special field;
to work with his angels must be Gods will,
Then always look to him above;
for guidance in his wondrous love.

As the years go by throughout your life;
Through your troubles and your strife.
Look to him above everyday;
with loving patience, take time to pray.

Kathryn Peterson

Daddy's Little Girl

Daddy's little girl oh so close to him
as close as laws allow and even more.
Daddy's little girl oh so close to sin
yet she doesn't know to run out the door.

Daddy's little girl trusting and so true
her treats her like her mother he loves her
the same way too. Someday she'll be very blue
for he destroyed the trust of his daughter.

Now she cowers from him whenever he's
around for she remembers the great pain.
He caused her and wonders if he still sees
the little girl in her, what was his gain.

One day she'll confront him ask him why.
But for now all she wants to do is die.

Krista Padgett

The Mouth Of Hell

The Mouth of hell belched with flame
As a maiden walked within its walls
Surely, this lovely creature was not in shame
Did his highness err in his calls
With tears streaming down her face
I ventured alone to ask her case
Alone I ventured to learn and trace
The shame of her fall from grace.
Oh! the ways of life are cruel for one so gay as I
I did not think myself a fool until I created a great lie
I lied so great that heaven provoked
Cast me into the mouth of hell
In heavens name I have not loved
Within a sense you can buy and sell
Than came that long lovely night when I gave my love to him
It seems he loved with all his might
While my response was but a whim. At these words the earth trembled
And on her knees she fell "God save me"! The devils assembled
And with laughter - threw her into hell

Leonard A. Podolsky

Nature Walk

I took a walk in the woods today
As a child that's where I often played
I'm not alone when I take my walk
For there's my Dad with me.

Memories are refreshed in my mind again
As I walk the nature trail
For it was there Dad showed me
God's glorious world of nature.

We looked for dewberries, muscadines, heart leaves
Violets, rocks, moss and streams
While shuffling our feet through leaves
Fallen from the Oak, Poplar and Maple trees.

Trying to avoid snakes, lizards and Poison Oak
We listened to the chirping of many birds
Found babies still in their nest
Rabbits and squirrels could be seen or heard.

There's a nature trail in my own back yard
Of course, it's cut down according to space
If you've never taken a trek through the woods
With your Dad, you've missed a wonderful place.

Kathryn R. Grice

The River

The sound of the geese breaks the pre-dawn quiet
as a call for a new day comes to the river..
A family of mallards glides silently along the far bank
heads dipping below the surface with tails in the air
taking nourishment from the richness of the bottom

As I watch, the swallows take their first drink of the day
skimming the surface
leaving only a small wake to suggest contact.
I wonder how many times I've watched the dawn
along these shores.

How many countless others have awakened along this silver highway
to draw strength for another day
from its cold waters.

The river is from aeons past and will still be here
when I am dust
yet, for now it is mine
and as it cleanses itself in its tranquil flow
so too, do I
renew myself from its depths.

Gerald Bock

Grape Juice Tears

Some days I'm just not smiling fast enough to look like I'm doing
anything but breaking like a priceless dish,
and spilling grape juice tears all over your happy day carpet:
Please Don't Be Mad.

I clench my teeth, grip tightly to my truth,
try to balance it quietly in both hands the way they taught me
to hold the juice cups in preschool.

Carefully, so as not to get in trouble,
I hold in my thoughts, just as I have since I learned how to Act.
Share your toys,
Not your feelings.

But today I'm not holding up very well.
Today I'm not holding back very much.
Today my small self feels like singing to you
a melody called My Discord,
Feels like dancing for joy as I spill myself out to you,
All Over You...
and you Thank me.

Katherine Anne Avinger

I've Got You Where You Want Me...

Where did it come from and where will it lead?
Answers apparent but the questions won't see...

I've got you where you want me...

It came out of nowhere, right out of the blue;
Cliches of the innocent can't carry it through...

You've got me where I want you...

A picture unpainted, yet easily seen;
A wall of reflection on which to lean...

I've got you where you want me...

A story not written, a riddle, a clue;
An ending begun with a chapter still new...

You've got me where I want you...

Light passes through windows not obscured by a screen;
The grandest delusion now unveiling the scene...

I've got you where you want me...

You want me where I've got you,
I want you where you've got me;

Yes, I've got you where you want me...

Lori Anne Tout

Like My Angel

Like my angel, you saved me from the cold times
and you've helped me through my fears.
When ever someone left me, you were there to dry my tears
you made me see that I'm not the horrible me I thought I was
I'll never forget the times when you tried to make me realize
that it doesn't matter what anyone else does.
Like my angel, you tried your hardest to make me laugh at the times
when I was down.
As long as we are together I know I'll never have to frown.
Like my angel, watching me from above, you've wrapped me around your
finger with charming and delightful ways.
And through even the worst days, you were there to see me through
life's foggy haze.
Like my angel, you've cared for me, no matter what I said or did.
You never even got bored of helping bring out my talents and feelings
that I always hid.
And now I'd like to thank you for the times I never did.
When life took some evil turns and even through the good.
The memories that we formed are engraved in my heart and I look
forward to making many more.

Marisa Anne Neebling

Son

Son, it is an amazement to me to have you near
and yet so far from me. Your start in life was delayed
by months but thanks to our Lord your living was
endeared so as to see you, small and chubby, yet
worth every stitch required to make you mine, colic,
and all. Much better than your sleeping for weeks and
being barred from the hospital room. No wonder I can
sleep upright in a chair, I had lots of practice there by
the door.

Nearly all mothers have gone through tearful moments
when sons go off to war, but I was luckier than most
as God gave purpose to us by returning you home to
continue life as he had planned.

Now you know that moms are proud of sons as well as
their daughters. Rearing children is a worth while love
and a treasure to me, your parent. Now it is your turn to
carry on with your children.

Thus Grandma Has Spoken!

Norma E. Shryock

"Awakened"

I gazed at A "Star" in the heavens so bright
And wished for a "Diamond" with all my might
It came to me, "A tiny Baby Boy" My hearts delight!

From deep in the ocean I longed for a "Pearl"
It came to me "A soft Pink Baby Girl"

In fields of Green Grass fragrant with "Roses"
I visioned a "Ruby" Red as my winter Nose is
It came to me, my Second soft "Pink Baby Girl"

Three Jewels are a glow in my band, of Gold My Ring is Complete
Not even a "Kings Ransom" could this match ever beat

Now I am weary, tired and old, shunned by Three Jewels
What secret have they? they so carefully keep.
What wrong have I done? I ponder and weep.
No flowers they bring to brighten my room
Not even a "Rose" to lay at my feet.

Suddenly and Swiftly "My Brain" is "Awakened" "Awakened by the "Guilt"
I had buried so deep, it is "they" not "I" that should ponder and weep.
My "Jewels" have not tarnished "My Band"-glimmers with Gold It was "I"
who shunned them and saddened their lonely "Souls", Forgive me! Soon I
shall turn Cold!

Martha McHugh

Just Hold Out

Sometimes God takes things away from us,
and we sit and we wonder why?

We think about all the good times we had,
and now we say goodbye.

We question God's ability, and say thing like,
"why did it have to be me."

If God is who he said he is, then why does it have to be.
God makes no mistakes, and Yes, his word is true.

Weeping may endure, for a night,
but JOY belongs to you.

Sometime you may have to cry,
just wipe those tears my friend.

Don't you dare give up, because victory is at the end
I know the tunnel is dark right now, and I don't believe in luck.
Whatever you do my sister, don't you dare get stuck.
So keep on walking my sister, so the world can know.
At the end of every tunnel,
there is a RAINBOW.

Neisha L. Jones

Don't Take Him Away

He is so sweet and kind,
and we all love him so.
He's got so much to live for,
so let the life in him flow.

We all know that he is struggling,
but he's got a lot of strength and will.
And through all his pain and suffering,
he is holding onto life still.

And if there's anyone who deserves it more,
to fight for his life and win.
Someone who gives everything his best shot,
I know for sure that it is him!

So I ask just one favor for him,
to the Father above, I pray.
We love him with all our hearts,
so PLEASE DON'T TAKE HIM AWAY!!

Melissa Thornhill

Caress

Drowning in clatter noise,
And waterfalls of time.
Borne by entraining tides of voices,
Unmodulated babble, indistinct,
But savage streams that dash
With leaps and froth, onto the coastal rock.
Reach out, for merciful reprieve
In still pools of the rare caress.

Caress - of friendly silence,
And of gentle, waiting eyes.
Of undemanding touch,
And softly uttered sounds
Of words of simple sense
And setting. And of compassion in the stars,
That motionless in moving vastness,
Speak of assurance, purpose, peace.

Joseph Lewin

Thursday

In the mud of opinions I stand
And view doves and crows flocking together
Against a summer moon like yin and yang.
In the current of faces I glance
To see the eyes of Christ:
Visions of forty days and nights
Temptation, aggravation, condemnation, isolation
I fall deeper into the circle
Pieces of the light penetration of the dark sky
I hold and fragments of the dream
In my eyes blend.
Crucified by my ideals;
Purified by my sins.
Blood, cold and quiet, like falling snow
In the fatal moments of each day
I taste in the dead air
As it transforms into a night.

John F. Smith Jr.

Untitled

Alligator, alligator please be my friend.
Alligator, alligator will this be the end?
Alligator, alligator please grant me one wish.
Alligator, alligator don't make me your dish.

Larry A. Johnson

Norway

No one are for me, as in Norway of a door,
and to be open. On the contrary, of being weary
and that's for neither you, or me to be profound.
As though I here by are standing on my feet. Then
if you see the savers of our lives, and who are
you to be persuaded by. Nevertheless, for waving
goodbye, as in another way. Also, your hands are
mines; moreover the mind. Consequently, the
survivors of our wishes are to be granted. Therefore
our mountains of tears are faithful. Although
the mourns of mornings are for the setting sky,
light. Though the evenings and into nights in order,
for winds to be blowing into the air. Voyages
are places yet times to see the seas of our oceans.
Finally kin's of Norfolks are the land, but
oh in order to find another refinery. Moreover,
one on the nile of a shore are for Norway.

Michelle R. Robinson

A Special Bond

It all began with you holding me tight,
And then you were teaching me wrong from right.
You answered my questions of "how and why",
You applauded my accomplishments and cradled my cries.

You were someone who listened and tried to understand,
And when I was down you gave a helping hand.
Yet when my stubbornness and temper would show,
You'd leave me alone and give me room to grow.

But there you were still by my side,
A one in a million mother, always there to guide.
Together we were growing and teaching each other,
As a special bond was forming between a daughter and mother.

And now it's time to be on my own,
But knowing you're there, I won't be alone.
'Cause you're not only my mother, but my very best friend,
And a special bond like this, has no end.

Kristi L. Kahl

Flowers

What lovely shapes they come in
And the way they glow in the sun.

When you look at them how gentle we must feel
The way the petal drops when autumn has come.

The way the little branch bends
When the wind whistles through our hair.

The way the bells ring in the holiday air.
The first anniversary rings with the joy
of love.

Flowers, we must love them.

Jason Albert Shutts

Spring Is Among Us...

The sound of buzzing bees,
And the sound of children scraping their knees.
The sound of hearing a happy song,
With children hopping merrily along.
The sound of hearing birds start to sing,
And the sound of hearing the church bells ring.
The sight of kites flowing through the air,
And the sight of trees blossoming everywhere.
The sight of people falling in love,
Is a true sign that spring is among us.

Jessica Peper

"Be Thankful"

Feel the wind embrace you, as it travels in haste,
And the warmth of the sun gently caress your face.
The hooting of the owl, in the darkness of night,
Busy little fireflies, flashing their light.

The fragrance of flowers, dancing in the fields,
Walnut trees bearing all it can yield.
Cars traveling, the super highways,
Laughter of children, as they run and play.

The towns are busy, were people stop,
To look around as they shop.
A lonesome whistle from a train each day,
Shaking the ground as it travels its way.

Factories are busy, with its working crew,
Machines always making something new.
Oceans and rivers, where food can be found.
And with a little sweat, it's there in the ground.

So why does man, have greed on his mind,
When God gave His best, to all mankind.
If all would be thankful, for what they possess,
The word war would soon come to rest.

Juanita M. Cole

Timeless Nights

In the still of the night
and the twinkling, timeless solitude of the stars,
I sit at my desk
facing the wall of windows,
gazing at the vast universe,
the hills, the treetops,
and back to the book the lies before me
reading,
under a florescent lamp,
as vapors from the herbal tea
curl up toward the heavens
only to vanish in thin air.
All is still
 not a wind to rustle the leaves
 not a laughter gloating from below
 not a cricket's rhythmic lullaby
 that echoed only the night before.
There is nothing,
only the flickering of fireflies.

Mineko Rebecca Kudamatsu

White Surrenders

The audience is in the valley green.
And the deceased is up on the hill.
And it's so still.
And it's a wake and it's a burial.
And the general stripped naked the soldier's honors and medals.
And the deceased on the hill stripped of his medals and
honors as well.
And all the audience wore blood red and what of their tears
but wind bends heads.
And scattered about grow white surrenders.
And the sky is bleak and some say gray.
And earth is crack and all need rain.
Man may come along and cut deceased tree down.
And it will fall to ground.
Fall leaves will turn into September, then October, then hidden by
December
A winters nap then spring all over again.
And the deceased will still be there stripped naked.
No beginning and no end.
And the blood red multiplied.
And more scattered about grow white surrenders.

Marjorie Moss Taylor

Once The Earth Was Happy

Once the Earth was happy,
And the animals roamed happily,
For they had never seen a gun or trap

Once the Earth was happy,
And the trees in the rainforests stood tall,
For they had never seen man's fire or a saw

Once the Earth was happy,
And the skies and oceans were beautiful and clean,
For they had never seen pollution

Once the Earth was happy,
And it still can be,
If we learn to love, respect, and live in peace and harmony

Malika de Silva

In Pain

It's strange how you can have so many people who love you
and still feel alone.
I didn't know I could hurt like this; it's not a scraped
knee or a broken bone.
It goes much deeper— to the empty space in my heart.
When I want to smile I have to cry.
When I wanted her to stay— I had to say goodbye!
I'd like to talk, but I don't know what to say.
I need time to myself, but I don't want to be alone.
I need to talk, but I won't answer the phone.
I don't want to think of her, but it's all that runs
through my head.
I can't go to sleep, but all I want— is to stay in bed.
I want to hold on and never let go.
What to do? I don't know.
I want to do well in school, but I don't want to try.
One thing I'm sure of— I NEVER wanted to say goodbye!

Kendra Keeley

In Memory of Brian Weaver

You would have been just twenty today,
And so many of us wonder why
you had to go away.
You left us so quickly without saying goodbye.
If only we could understand why.
You were still so young, and had so
much to give,
Not one of us can believe that you
meant not to live.
Not a day goes by that we don't think of you,
and remember that little smile;
So often it seems that you're just gone
for a little while.
Though we may never know what
really happened that night,
Your memory lives forever strong in our hearts,
yet you're gone from our sight.
So many people love you, but perhaps
you'll never know
The sadness that we feel because we miss you so.

Nancy Weaver

Evolution

From germination to termination, our bodies grow and learn.
Across our land, across the world, the flame of hope does burn.
Liberty and equality are paths we must pursue.
Communication is the key, in everything we do.
To speak our tongue or others, they're words we must rehearse.
The great cultures of the world, are many and diverse.
The caterpillar crawls the ground, oblivious to the world.
It changes to a butterfly, with legs and wings unfurled.
Different peoples of the earth, join us, take your place.
We're all one bonded entity, it's called the human race!

Michael R. Farley

Foot Prints In The Snow

It was a cold windy snowy night
And not a soul in sight only a small child
The child lived on edge of town
living in a shack with her
ailing maches, who was very ill.
No food in the house only
crust of bread and water
The pot belly stove was only heat they had!
The child poorly dressed left the house
to seek help for her sick mother
It was a bitter cold snowy night
She went house to house and all refused.
Tired walking most of the night
she came to a rich man's
house, she fell asleep on his steps.
She died and angels
carried her to heaven. The rich
man found two foot prints
on the snow next day.

Mel Glass

We

We're living in a world which now is headed for great sorrow,
And none of us is yet quite sure what fate will bring tomorrow.
And yet we spend our precious time condemning many others
Instead of trying every day to see ourselves as others.
If everyone within this world were not
So all self-centered 'twould be a happier
Place indeed that each new baby entered.
We blame the wars on other foes and on some other nation.
We never even stop to think, man is his own creation.
If the world were one large mirror and each could see his soul
I'm sure that most would want to hide within some deep, dark hole.
So let us not defer the blame no let us try another
Let's try to be the kind of man that we would wish our Brother.

Ginger Gordon

My Husband

Written in memory of my beloved husband Elmer Ewing Franklin
When the loss of you overwhelms me
And my hurt is too much to bear
I feel your presence beside me
I see you not, but you are there.

Could you be the beautiful bird
That comes peaking at the door
It stands, it stretches, it flaps its wings
As if to say, I've lived here before.

Maybe you are a raindrop
Beating upon my window pane
If I knew you were
I would let in all the rain.

One might think that others
Could take up your place
But not so, no one ever crosses the borderline
That is your individual space.

I'll always look for you, darling
With a yearning so sharp and bold
Someday, somewhere, I'll find you
And oh, the joy to behold.

Mabel E. Franklin

370

Blind Faith

The work he has done can never be beat
And many of his words in my mind I repeat

He gives me the peace that on earth I can't find
And love is the word he has stood to define

He will make my dreams come true
What more could this magical person do

He's no fairy tale that
  will come in a book
To find him in your heart
  you have to look

You cannot see him,
Put your faith where
  your eyes are
Upon the sky he's the
  brightest star

His name is Jesus,
  and he stands right
  by my side
In him is only where
  I will let my love confide

Kristy Lindsey

Loving A Soldier

Loving a soldier is not always gay.
And loving him is a high price to pay.
It's mostly loving with nothing to hold.
It's being young, yet feeling old.
It's having him whisper his love to you.
It's whispering back that you love him too.
Watching him leave, with eyes full of tears.
Standing alone with hopes, dreams and fears.
It's sending a letter with stamps upside down.
To a far away love in a far away town.
Then a letter arrives and you're given to joy.
You tear open his letter like a child with a new toy.
Yes, he is well and missed you so.
And it's filled with the love you wanted you know.
Loving a soldier really isn't much fun.
But is well worth the price when the battle is won.
Remember he is thinking of you every day.
He's sad and he's lonely for being away.
So love him, miss him and try to be bolder.
And always be proud of loving a soldier.

Laura Ann Saxe

The Boy I Thought I Knew

Sometimes it happens
And it's all for the best,
And he says he likes you, then leaves you
And then goes all the rest.

Who would of thought, him?
He was so perfect, so nice, so kind,
Then he changed, you saw the real him
It sneaked upon you from behind.

Now he's left, back home, far away
He probably won't write, even call
But think! Do you REALLY need him?
I guess us two weren't meant to be after all

The way you hurt me, you didn't even see
For all you did to me what did you gain?
NOTHING! How could you even do that?
Now you've left me nothing but with a lot of pain.

All I can say to you is thanks for nothing
Maybe one day you'll see
That I'm not the one that will be missing out,
It's you that will be!!!

Katie Mills

I'll Be Satisfied

You have always been a part of me
And I guess you will never know
How much every second with you means to me
Now, I have to let you go.

I don't understand why you can't learn to love me
Even for such a short, short while
Am I that ugly, fat or senseless?
Can't I make your days sunny and worthwhile?

It seems as though I don't exist
For to me, you are so cruel and insensitive
You cast away the love that I give you
You banish me from your little world and make me feel blue.

We're so close in distance
And yet it feels like we're so far apart
Why do you make my feelings suffer?
Do you really intend to break my heart?

I never asked you to love me back
It's just enough that you hold me
Whenever I'm cold, whenever it's dark
With whatever you'll give, I'll be satisfied and happy.

Kitt Sazon

Good-bye

One day he had to leave us
and I could not say good-bye.
I knew that he was going
but I did not wonder why.

His time on earth was over
his eternal life began.
The time we had together here
we will never have again.
but somewhere up above us I can see him standing there
With a "flat top" and a fishing pole and never more a care.

I could not say good-bye to him but I wanted him to go
because I knew that he was ready
though his departure slow.

He held on through his suffering
because he did not want to leave-
his wife, his life, his family
He knew how she would grieve.

I believe he comes to visit her
in times she feels despair and he tells
her of the days they'll spend together over there.

Monique P. Bridgeman

Closer Walk

If I would for just a moment put earthly things aside,
and fix my heart on Jesus and throw away my pride.
I know I could draw closer to Him that died for me.
If only I could do that what glories then I'll see.

I struggle on my Christian walk every single day.
I think about what He would do or just what He would say.
I try my best to be like Him but know it is in vain.
Because He is the perfect one, alone, He bore the pain.

For sinful man, yes, you and I, He died that we might live.
And have it more abundantly, what more could He give.
He gave Himself, a sacrifice, for all our sinful ways
and rose again, from the dead, in just three mournful days.

He lives again in all of us if we will just receive,
our Lord and Savior, Jesus Christ, in Him we can believe.

Mark G. Tjelta

I Kneel Before You.....

I kneel before you as you shine your warmth upon my face
and fill my heart with your love and wisdom.
I kneel before you as the sun sets and the clouds fly away.
I kneel before you in an open field under a velvet black night
filled with brilliant colors of lights like diamonds, rubies,
  and emeralds.
I kneel before you with my eyes closed but my ears
are open to the sounds of the gentle breeze that kisses my cheeks.
I kneel before you in the coolness of the light
of the dawn and the beginning of a fresh new day.
I kneel before you in prayer, night and day
waiting for you to take my hand and lead me home.
I kneel before you with my face to the heavens in prayer and devotion.
I kneel in silence and listen to your words of grace and strength,
to touch my soul and lift my spirits to your light.
I kneel and wait for you to close my eyes in sleep,
so that I might dream in wonder and delight.

    Marlene L. Mitchell

Untitled

Did you ever see a stranger looking lonely and in need
And feel you'd like to comfort him and maybe plant a seed
Of brotherhood and love amongst your lonely fellow man
And help to bridge and fill a gap that so few understand

This gap we've made between ourselves by seeming not to care
I feel we're really actors though hiding feelings that are there
Have you ever sat and watched the news and seen the hate and greed
And wished that you were in a spot where you could hope and plead

To all the people of the world to stop and look around
And try to do the things they feel for in feelings there are found
All the hidden loves and needs of seeming greedy men
And if only they would stop and feel no longer they'd pretend

    John Simmons

And Now I See The Madness

I felt a pain in my heart,
And could not decipher why.
It kept pounding - pounding,
Till, at last, I released a cry.

Then, at last my eyes were open,
And I saw the sun shine through.
But, the skies grew darker - colder.
All my thoughts had turned to you.

The tears just kept falling,
Drowning my heart and soul.
They drove me to seclusion - waiting,
Waiting for the bells to toll.

As all my life I spend hoping,
Wishing, wanting you to be near,
I sit, in silence, with no purpose, wishing -
Wishing you would be here.

And now I see the madness - the anger,
The anger, that has torn apart my mind.
I fought the world in every way,
And left what I truly need, love, behind.

    Nicolas W. Schlim

The Painting

Watching the ladies dance to the "waltz"
A Monet painting in the background
As I gaze at the painting there goes
Scarlet in her red dress off to catch a man
The back of a two dollar bill with Jefferson
And Pachelbel playing on the harpsichord
Seeing the big colorful garden
As I gaze into the blue sky I see Freedom

    Moojan Zare-Parsi

For What Am I Grateful?...

Wisdom, and the time allowed to acquire it...
and consequently, the lifelong chance to grow,
The peace of mind that morality brings,
and the strength, yet compassion, to let it show...

The freedom to define and express my "self"...
And acceptance of unconditional love,
The ability of perception to see such things
From a dog's devotion to the untouchable sky above...

The power of choice and lack of prejudice,
And the common grounds offered to share...
The ties we build amongst ourselves,
Bringing visions where once unaware...

But most of all and without question,
Undoubtedly the reason that "thanks" persist...
Is due to the gift to perceive and voice,
The fact that an answer exists!!!

    Leslie B. Saylor

Dignity Deserved

She asks for her parents who've been gone twenty years
And can't remember her own children's names
She can't dress herself, feed herself
Or even brush her own teeth
But my love for her is still just the same

I don't want to remember my mother like this
Being robbed of her body and mind
I prefer visions of my childhood
When she was healthy and young
So nurturing, loving and kind

The tables have turned, the roles are reversed
I'm now mother, my mother's the child
but I'll not let her see my frustration and pain
I'll sing lullabies, through I'm crying inside

For she's been thrown into a world
Not of her own choice
A cruel, wicked sad twist of fate
And she deserves to receive
The love back that she gave
An encore as she exits the stage

    Jim Adams

The Wall

The wall, so many names.
And behind each name a story, a life.
A spirit, that runs along the wall, never to be put out.
They were children, in a way, with life ahead of them.
Childhood was stolen, from them, and they were placed in the jungle,
Scared, oh so afraid, so young.
And one by one, their names were placed in the wall.
Oh the cold marble slab that holds the human spirit, their innocence.
Restless boys who wanted to play, not fight, but play.
Not to kill, to murder, to torture, or shoot.
Just to play in the summer fields, not the sandbag forts built crudely
around them, just to play.
And so the wall, reflecting the faces of so many boys, so many
innocent boys, who ended up engraved in the wall, but not forgotten.

    Lara Pasternak

Flower Of Love

I'm like any flower
a flower of love that needs care.

My love can't grow with dreams alone
maybe what I'm asking for is too hard to give.
But like water for a plant,
  I need you.

    Lesli Kuhn

"He's My Dad"

At dinner dad draws faces on tortilla chips,
And attaches a sugar packet for hips, then grips
The pepper and sprinkles it on the chips for hair—
But he can do that; he's my dad.

Mom says that before she quit work,
Dad called her a lot because he was lonely,
And her co-workers would say "Just marry the jerk"
But before mom can finish her story I blurt:
"He can do that though, because he's my dad."
And Mom always says "Right."

And I know - no matter what people say,
That I will love my father forever; he's my dad.

Leslie Borenstein

Again

Once again you call like nothing is wrong
And all I can do is just play along
You want me to be yours again in your arms
I accept too quickly and ignore what my mind warns
I forget your past mistakes and all of our fights
Maybe this time you've changed, maybe this time it's right
I don't think of tomorrow and how it always turns out
Tonight we'll make love, but tomorrow we'll shout
Not shouts of joy or happiness, not even shouts of love
Just anger, sadness and rage that leads to push and shove
We'll part like always and promise this is the last
But then the phone rings and once again I forget the past

Nicole Goldsbury

Life Cycle

Days pass without break nor rest,
And all around us the cycle continues.
Churning in a steady unstoppable motion.
Claiming what it must to continue.

We watch helpless as friends and relatives
Are pulled from our grasp by the relentless cycle,
And only pray we could have stopped it.

Blanketed in grief we mourn them,
And try to believe they are happier.
But we can't, because we're not.

Time passes and others are born.
Created to take the place of those lost,
And continue the on-going cycle.

We watch them grow and play.
Filling our lives with a different sense of happiness,
And the cycle continues until we are again drawn into its path,
But now we are the ones claimed.

Michael Smith

Whose Eyes?

The mid-day light emerges through the obscurity and fingers her lips,
An umbra crosses her cheek, eyes unseen, is she genuine or one
of the spirits?
Standing, waiting for a response from the image at my fore part,
Wanting, needing, dreaming that it was I who was in her heart.
A hand lifted gently toward the sky,
Would it be my journey or my cry?
Slowly the touch befell and filled me with abundance, of what
I did not know,
To describe my fervor would do no justice to the palm that landed that blow.
A bang of passion and immense tenderness that reached me that day,
The eyes were unseen how was I to understand,
That who I perceived as the blue-eyed Aimee,
Was the green glassed eyes of Mariee,
A girl I use to know the one my face hit her hand.

Kevin Kleinhanzl

When I'm Without You

When I'm without you, I feel like I have had lost
an important friend,
A friend of whom I had gotten to know from school
days on end.

When I'm without you, I feel lost and isolated from
my friends whom I got to know from childhood.
I have a tendency to think about you only to realize
that it doesn't do any good.

When I'm without you, I feel that I may never see
you again in the future years ahead,
I feel alone and blue. Not to mention the weeknights
I worry and dread.

I'm both running on and feeling empty about never having
a dream come true.
It is the exact feeling I get when I'm without you.

Joe Clancy

Perspective

Childhood dreams come flooding in
Amid the turmoil, chaos, din.
Childhood hopes come rushing back
Amid the violence, war, attack.
Childhood fantasies slip away
As I awake to face another day.

The world is aching, yearning for peace.
The world is for beggars, harlots and thieves.
The world is polluted, sickened and dead.
The world is for pain, suffering and dread.

As I awake to face another day
I won't let my sanity slip away.
Amid the violence, war, attack
I'll strive to bring perspective back.
Amid the turmoil, chaos, din
I'll keep my dreams alive within.

Martie B. Kelly

The Gift

Through your eyes glow the wonders of the world,
Amazed understanding as each day unfurls;
From a fresh green leaf as it slowly uncurls,
To the ocean's promise of its hidden pearls.

You eagerly wake to embrace each day
To dance with the clouds from their first ballet,
Till the painted sunset paves the way
For the shimmering stars as they softly lay.

You've let me see as a child through the soul
Your youthful wisdom is ancient and old
Your laughter a wondrous thing to behold
Your love to cherish as though it were gold.

Tender and gentle as the peaceful dove;
Surely the essence angels are made of,
You are a gift from the Lord God above
As a perfect statement of a perfect love!

Mikie Driscoll

The Girl On The Farm

I met a girl way down on a farm
A girl with a, down on the farm charm
And I'm gonna make her mine all mine
So we can be together all of the time.
Now some day soon I'll take her home to my family.
I know we'll be as happy as we can be
I love that girl way down on the farm
The girl with the, down on the farm charm.

Lena Pepe

A Tribute To Michael

Always smiling, never letting go
  Always entertaining, forever putting on a show.
  You reached out your hand and touched every heart,
  But to you that was only a start.
It wasn't known when you would leave us be
  But you live on, we will always remember you, Michael Lee.
  You put a smile on our face, you brought a tear to our eye.
  It's always so hard to let go and say our last good-bye.
Death; what more can I possibly say,
  It shall take us all one day.
  But as for you Michael, it took you too soon.
  Death shot down your stars and covered your moon.
So how do you beat death, how do you win?
  You pick up the Son and ask forgiveness of every sin.
  Michael my heart bleeds red ribbons just for you
  Because you taught us all about AIDS and what it can do!!

  Jill Suzanne Johnson

For Buddy

Buddy, sweet Buddy, we all miss you so,
Although it's been but a few days ago,
I still hear your voice at night in my sleep,
And many a time wake up with relief,
You are finally gone, there is no doubt,
But precious pictures still lay about,
You were ever faithful, trusting and kind,
While we were so selfish, misguided and blind,
You knew that it was your time to go,
But we held you back just one more day or so,
All efforts to keep you alive were tried,
But nature clued us in when time lied,
Unable to eat or walk without a stagger,
You continued to love us like it didn't matter,
Those trusting eyes and careless walk,
We'll not soon forget though we're apt to balk,
So peace has finally come to you at last,
But we are still wishing this time will soon pass,
Memories, sweet memories, without all this pain,
Buddy, oh Buddy, we'll see you again.

  Memory H. Lola

Communications

In the beginning was God the Father and the Word,
All things were made by them.
We as children, brothers and sisters of the universe
Have learned through time to relate,
Do unto others as you would have them do unto you,
Our actions as well as our words show our ability
To communicate.
The respect that we show others is only a mirrored
Image of the respect we have for ourselves,
Let us look at our own reflection as it radiates
Thought energy, invariably attracting into our
Lives the circumstances we have chosen to create.
Our thoughts they are the primary causes of the
Conditions or effects in our lives and if we want
Our lives to be different in the future, we must
Change our thinking in the present.
Life is a gift, given only one day at a time,
May we all strive to use our gift for the
Betterment of ourselves and others.

  John A. Rocker II

When Mythological Creatures Roam The World

When the unicorn roams the world again,
All the people will unite and live as one.
When the eagle flies no longer, but in its place is the pegasus,
World peace will not be a dream anymore, but reality instead.
When the mermaids join the fish in the sea once again,
Man and nature will live together in perfect harmony.
When dragons are hunted by courageous knights for their fair maidens,
The violence will stop.
When mythological creatures roam the world,
The world will be perfect.
Then we wouldn't live on Earth, instead it would be called Heaven.

  Jessica Griffin

Do You Exist?

I often question whether you exist
All the destruction arouses some doubt
I think you trap everyone in a mist
So they don't question what were really about

Some say for disbelief you'll go to hell
But can it exist if you don't believe
I think that's a secret no one shall tell
The answer one we can not achieve

Are you just something that people made up
To give answers to unanswered questions
To somehow make the world seem less corrupt
To give us hope and offer intentions

I guess when the time comes we all will see
Until then you shall be a mystery

  Krista Panick

Love I Hear

You know my heart and see it clear;
all that it feels, the tears, the laughs, the shame.
But you didn't come here to tell me I was wrong,
to point out the evil I've done.
I already see it.
You did though come to tell me I'm yours,
and ask me to come home.
My child you say so soft and gentle, "come home."
These are the words I need to hear,
these are the words you speak so clear.
You love me, your child,
and the child in me cries out to you from hurts that run too deep.
And not once do you scorn me,
not one angry word passes your lips.
Words spoken so clear,
words that take me home.

  Karey Anne Baumgardt

Someone Special

You're the last thought I have when I go to bed
and in the morning you're the first thing that enters my head
I don't know what I'm supposed to do
all I know is that I'm so in love with you
I can't eat, I can't sleep, I can't concentrate
And rest assured I'll never forget our first date
You asked me to be your number one girl
and at that point in time, I swore I could
conquer the world.

How this will work only God will know
all I can say is I'll never let go.

  Lisa Lynn Colón

Songs From Heaven

When happiness turns to sorrow
All revelations seem to fail
It's looking like a dark tomorrow
As we keep living life in a shell

If all rumors washed away in the tide
And we had to go on with these wounds
Would you break down and cry
Knowing destiny is doomed

Then if we walked outside
And looked up in the sky
And saw Angels singing songs from Heaven
It gave our love a sacred shield
We saw in the sky
Angels singing songs from Heaven
You started smiling to the songs from Heaven
Knowing that our love is so real

How many years have been passing by
How many tears have poured from those eyes
Like me, do you see the shadows, do you still feel the wounds
Is this what you call living in destiny's doom

John A. Reichwein

Windy Day

On a windy day,
All most people can say
is where's the sun
it's much more fun.
On a windy afternoon,
don't let it pass too soon.
Have fun, go fly your kite
even though there's dim light.
When the wind makes you feel as though you could fly,
a raindrop touches you from the sky.
But don't despair once it's come,
just remember where it's from.

Mindy Lewis

Lead

By Philosopher's stone, days of old;
Alchemists wished it turned to gold.

It can stop the gamma ray;
Or poison one within the day.

Soft and pliable, yet heavy, it can be;
But none of these things it means to me.

I recall its meaning so very well;
Its tell-tale scars are my story to tell.

By bullet of sniper, in war, its kiss I felt;
My flesh like butter its heat did melt.

Like a skewer, red hot, that laid beneath my skin;
Trice that enemy tried to do me in!

An angel sat upon my shoulder that day;
For my vital organs it did not stray.

Else I would not be here to tell this ode;
I'd reside in an unmarked grave as a warrior of old.

This element that wished me dead?;
A child holds in a pencil is known as lead.

Joseph P. Ryncarz

Through Sight Of A Friend

I went for a walk in the park today.
Aimlessly is the word to say.
Then an old man came my way.
I heard him say that sunny day,
Smell the flowers, look to the trees,
It's all so simple and all so free.
Don't take for granted what is here for all,
Even the little things aren't really so small!
In time I was to find
this man with the beautiful mind
I found out later, was very much blind.
We take for granted the things we see.
But to an old blind man, their but a memory.

Karen D. Bridgman

Against Myself

Against myself, I do real fine.
Against myself, I destroy all that is mine.
Against myself, I take away pleasure.
Against myself, I punish myself without measure.
Against myself, I need not use wit.
Against myself, I just push myself closer to a pit.
Against myself, I do very well acknowledge with a nod.
Against myself, I make people classify me as odd.
Against myself, I've already ruined my life and before I became an
    adult, it's already depleted.
Against myself, I do what no one else could,
Against myself, I am defeated.

Kenneth McCain

Opening To Tomorrow

We lay awake in the dark of the night
Afraid we are losing our souls
Awaiting the glimpse of first morning light
To recapture our sanity

The dawn comes
And there is a gift in living today
The throbbing universe hums
A song from the edge of time

Listen, hear it
This giant of the creator comforts
Each living thing a perfect fit
Into our life scheme

Dread not the night
Embrace the message of the stars
Absorb the solace and their light
Open your spirit

Rise above all that you see
Not to turn inward again
The feast of life awaits, your trip is yet to be
Take the creator's hand

Karen M. Wieman

Nature

Nature, one of life's beautiful things.
A flickering voyage of water that sings.

A gentle motion of bright green trees.
Fluttering leaves that dance to the breeze.

On the move, the creek is calm as can be.
A splendid gentle style is an attractive sight to see.

So well-formed and glimmering in the sunlight.
Sit back, relax and enjoy this magnificent sight!

Mary Lynn Hess

The Fight

The mind fixed on vanquishing every opponent.
Adrenalin rushing through every vein in your
body. The fear of your fatal ending. The
beating of your heart. The sweat from your
palms. The never ending questions. The plan
of attack.
   Now the time has come. And you have come to
make your mark in time. You have come to answer
all questions and extinguish all doubt. You
have come to conquer if only for one day. You
are the only thing you have to become the provider
of opportunity. You are the only, and
most valuable asset for the future. Regardless
of if you plan to lead or follow, you are
   priceless.
   Be strong my fellow human. Be as positive as
the meaning of the word itself. And through
all of the hurt, pain, the fear, and prejudice,
you will stay in peace of mind.

   Jules L. Johnson

Morning Breaks

God painted a sunrise
Across the morning sky
Reflecting on calm water of a lake that lay nearby

Bright sparkles like gemstones glittered as the sun slowly rose
Changing the scene before me to one of shadowed repose.

Trees are reflected in the quiet waters deep
Fish are causing ripples, the waters are alive.
Turtles are basking on a log in the early morning sun,
Faint sounds of water falling as from a far bank it does seep

Distant sounds break the quietness of this early morning scene
Would that this day hold for us its hours so serene.

   Lois W. Boren

Thinking Of You

I can see us walking hand in hand
Across a meadow filled with morning dew
As you look at me, my heart starts to race
And what I see is the love stretched across your face
Your voice is like a chorus of angels
Singing atop the highest mountains
Your eyes are like the stars in the heavens
Shining ever so bright
Your touch is that of silk
So sensitive and sensual
When my eyes open, all that I can see
Is an image of me "thinking of you"
The house is silent and no one is home
The wind howls through the trees
As the rain drops run down the window
Like the tears run down my face
As I look up again
All I can do is smile
"Thinking of you" brings joy to my heart
And a smile to my face

   Michael Pollard

The Longing In Their Cries

I am standing all alone now,
Above the ocean, watching as the waters rise,
But you have not come to protect me,
You are not by my side.

The wind whips across my face,
The salt burns my eyes,
The seagulls fly above me,
I hear the longing in their cries.

They feel lonely, just as I do,
They understand my pain,
I fall to the hard rock as despair engulfs me,
And then I feel the warm summer rain.

It becomes my Savior,
My only comfort in a time of need,
It reassures my heart and fills my empty shell,
But not in giving, nor in greed.

You were once my sunshine,
You were once my rain,
But you walked away and left me,
With only memories of your name.

   Kimberlee Bethany Cox

Missing You

Once, I sat on a lonely hill
above a lonely sea.

Looking back at special times
when you were here with me.

You were like a guardian angel
sent from up above,

Always there to keep me strong
and always there to show me love.

You showed me that the road not chosen
was the one I should be on.

Sometimes I find it hard to convince myself
that you are gone.

It's true what people say about
not realizing how much you care,
Until the day you look for them,
and then remember they aren't there.

I understand that a thousands wishes
could not bring you back to me,

But if you are up there, please be aware
that I could really use your company.

   Johnnalynn Lynch

What Was Once Great And Beautiful

The sun rises to begin a new day
A young blossom open her petals to gather the shining sun's energy
This blossom is given the best care possible, throughout its childhood
But soon after attention becomes less and less until it's
completely ignored
One day a weed begins to grow, taking precious nutrients
from the young blossom
In a while the flower is almost totally surrounded by the
life-sucking weeds
Every moment giving the flower less and less to live on
Every moment it needing more and more
Now, the weeds have grown so enormous and appalling, they
taunt the poor bud day and night, wringing the life out of
the once beautiful blossom
Finally, the greediest weed takes advantage and grabs her
very will to live, thus killing what was once great and beautiful.

   Kika Morales

To Answer Your Question

I like a bird nest built in the spring.
A warm morning to embrace me —
    as I listen to mama bird sing.

To know where I'm going —
    as well as where I've been.

Losing is not on my list, for we all like to win.

I like sharing a moment —
    as well as endless hours of bliss.

Knowing you are there —
    love, I wouldn't want to miss.

I like staying in line
    and getting out of hand.

Listening to an instrumental or
    dancing to a rock and roll band.

The clean smell of a quiet mountain breeze —
    the mighty roar of an ocean also does please.

I like fresh coffee in the morning —
    cocktails at night.

God's Gifts — whispering softly —
    "Everything is Alright".

Gale Glover

Slugger

The street was lined with saplings,
    a tiny oasis in a land of concrete,
Rays from a setting autumn sun barely
    touched the young treetops
Bidding adieu to a city finally at rest,
Its people and frantic pace slowly
    fading into the quiet night

Suddenly, from behind, 'hey mister,
    can you spare some change?'
He looked at the voice, a ragged, dirty
    woman, her face weather and world beaten
Their eyes met, only seconds, but they knew
She turned and ran, 'wait' he shouted,
    wanting to help, do something, anything
'Slugger, come back' he yelled as she raced
    to another shadowed street and stranger
Her name forgotten but not the pretty tomboy
    and stickball in a grammar school yard

Joseph M. Vitale

Lord, Who Can Stand?

Lord, who can stand in this last hour?
A time when satan walks about to devour.
A time when trials are harder than ever
and one false move...a saint lost forever.
When temptation is the only life I see
and tribulations prevail all around me.
When everyday a minister falls;
one less soldier to guard the wall.
When Truth the liars do distort
taking another soldier from your fort.
I need a refuge, a secret place.
If I find not death then I'll run away.
Peace and solitude I know not now;
all my ups have turned to downs.
I look all around me and your not there
my life is now overcome with fear.
I need you strength God, to free my soul
Clean me up Jesus and make me whole.
Please...

Kenneth Browning

Waiting

Confused. Lost.
A sudden warmth covered me.
It was as if a burning fire was
there beside me.

I thought of my father.
Laughing, playing, even crying together.
He is in a mystical land I
have never seen.

I yearn to see and feel
the warmth of his touch beside me, again,
I want to cry in his and tell him
I love him.

But here, in my heart, a coldness
lays. Waiting for the warmth to return
of a loving father. Once so close,
now so far away.

Kari Harvey

"A Tribute To My Best Friend"

My best friend died many years ago;
A special friend she truly was.
    My Mom - My friend.
She taught me well, though her time with me
was 12 short years.
Much faith she lived and shared with me, often on bended knee.
Faith in, "God, in yourself, and always believe."
Without one you're only part, not whole.
Each make the individual you are to become—to be.
"Dream little one."
Mom, I remember your sacrifices, courage and strength;
you have left them forever in my heart.
Many tears I have shed since you've left,
years they quickly pass.
Rest assured, you have done well with your
"youngest one."

Linda Mae Dinkel

Dream Child

Rest your head upon the pillow
    A soft cloud to place your burdens
    Dreams will bloom in your dream gardens

You're safe from monsters of the deep
    Safe from all the fears inside you
    A blanket of love, it will protect you

Dream of all good things in life
    And what great treasures lie ahead
    As you slumber in your bed

Little one, just close your eyes
    Your blanket's made of love tonight
    Dream until the morning light

Mary T. Grassl

Trust In Jesus

God sent his Son Jesus, to die on the cross
So our lives on earth would not be a loss
That through him, we might find
True happiness and peace of mind
Trust in Jesus and don't delay
For we might never know another day
Now is the time to make that decision
For the Lord has already made a provision
So when our earthly lives come to an end
Our journey to Heaven will begin

Joan W. Smith

God's Wonders

What wondrous works await us, in this new day about to begin?
A smile from a stranger, some laughter,
The warm embrace of a friend.

The song of the robin, the flowers that bloom,
All reveal the work of your hand.
The meadow of wildflowers with their sweet perfume
Lay a blanket of love on the land.

The sun in the sky, shining brightly,
Piercing the depths of the night
Is our lamp in a moment of darkness
Which shines with your glorious light.

All nature resounds with your glory.
All your creation sings
To the glory of God in heaven
His love in our life, daily brings.

Lord, open our eyes to the wonders
Which each moment brings us anew.
Your presence in all things created
Fills our hearts with the wonder of you.

Mona Drouhard

The Bird

Gliding in space
   a single being lightly swerving
   through the waves of life.
Separating them with joyful existence
   knowing where he is moving
   and yet unaware if this destiny, still he
Willingly continues in anticipation
   of the movement of air.
Allowing the current to carry him
   using only his instinct and wonder as guide.

He Lives On
Anticipating his destiny with hope and with love
   always confident of being carried along the current of life.
Sailing the breezes and storms of existence.
   Being only to be,
   Loving only to love, living only to live.
He lives within the realm of unpredictability and emotion,
   quietly singing his message of acceptance and joy,
   eternally harmonizing with the universe of existence.
He Continues On...

Lisa Winburne

Grandma Worley's Barn

She sits a monarch by the road to watch the travelers pass
A sentinel of antiquity, her mighty shadow casts.
Her white face, though chipped and weathered, reflects the morning sun
And though her frame is listing some, her footing still is strong.

More than a century, ruling queen though servanthood her lot
Performing daily duties there, not showing age or rot.
Today I opened up her door and softly stepped inside
Then back I went a hundred years and felt a glow of pride.

Her insides were dark and musty, some beams had fallen down.
The inside rails were crumbling, with cobwebs all around.
Suddenly I saw folks working and living just like me
The barn was a lone reminder of them who preceded me.

I climbed up into the hay loft, smelled the sweetness of the hay
Felt that I had somehow come home and wished that I could stay.
My hands touched the rough hewn beams; old history filled the air;
That wondrous loft from ages past, her secrets hidden there.

But oh and if that barn could talk, what stories it would tell!
Of life and death and joy and pain, life chronicled so well.
Well my life, it takes me elsewhere; I have to leave this farm
But my heart found its home today, in Grandma Worley's barn.

Laura Ann Davis

Return

I passed our road of dreams today —
A rough and sun-baked weedy way
Across a hill. A cawing bird
Denied romance; yet suddenly
A memory came over me:
In starlight, up that little hill
I rode with you. So deep and still
That summer night, we nearly heard
Each other's thoughts. A cricket's call
Kept tryst with silence; dreams were all.
It was our road of dreams, and I —
Because the noonday sun was high —
Because I heard no cricket's cry —
Could count the years, and pass it by.

Myrna Haight

Rosemary, Why Does She Pretend?

"Tell me why must Rosemary always pretend to be the Queen of Hearts?"
   "A predictable girl indeed!"
(impersonating the young girls voice) "Blue is my favorite
colour, everyone likes pink but I like blue the best."
   "Now come on, she was younger then. Now she's just
   more confused". "Confused" (now with the exaggeration
   of a drunken man) "Confused, she's just like her, mother!"
"Tell me why must Rosemary always pretend to be the Queen of Hearts?"
   "Her crimson hair never convinced me!"
   "But what about her words? She always speaks with the mistaken
   Authority of a mad child." "Why couldn't she be something
   else?" "The Queen of Hearts is such an over-used adjective."
   "But she's so original.... you'd think she'd make it up anyway."
"You don't...." "Believe her?" "Yes." "No!" "Well I know I don't
   fall for it!" "Rosemary is such a confusing girl, she contemplates
   everything." "Well, you should think things through."
   "Yes but when she cries...." "The crying ruins it all."
   "Well, she's a girl, she should be having fun!"
"Yes, but the Queen of Hearts never said that love was supposed to be easy."

Justin Rouse

Mine

We do not share the unshareable.
A phrase, a distinction poised
as positioning, the earth tilts
further into arbitrary axis
and does not dare conjecture who
will build their towers into space
or bend their rulers into hand-blown glass.

I share not one endless edge of your
lip's perfect bending nor the corner
of your eye when the world is an hour.

I share not the cloth of your mind
as it turns in liquid motions softly
bent to my deepest stamen of life.

You are mine beyond a word or promise,
beyond any tears of wilting creations.
Beyond and beyond the summer's heated
passion pulling flowers towards the sea
whose salted fingers whistle in the night.

You are mine as the trembling violet
slithers into the sleep-laden earth.

Martin Goldman

twenty lines are all

P-rehistoric is mythology or truth.
A-nnouncements written in stone on a sandy beach are gone.
S-miles were seen in reflections from a rippling mere.
T-ense or anxiety, mere words, tingling cold sweat and time.

P-ress on, play on, go on worthless martyr.
R-umble now across the rocky desert night.
"E-asy as that", the teacher spoke today.
S-leeping ugly awoke to speak well of god.
E-ndless time machine was broken again.
N-othing, if there is such in time, spoke.
T-oday moved on to tomorrow, yesterday.

F-riends are always asking questions.
U-seless appendix with which we are born is removed.
T-errestrial beings and spaceship flying machines.
U-nder the ground ash is as sand.
R-estless people are sleeping now, medicine ingested.
E-arrings of diamonds and food for souls were stolen.

O-nce, twice and many times the same.
N-o violence is different today than yesterday.
E-ven tomorrow, maybe longer, the same will win.

Jim Josephiac

My Love My Life

I remember the day we met.
A love that started out slow,
Began to grow.

Each day I knew you were the one.
Your smile and your way made me happy.
Seven years have past by so fast,
As our love unfolds,
Just like the rose with its beauty and grace,
Our love will be cherished.

Through good and bad we became strong,
And our love never failed.
We gain support for every need,
My love, my life.

You will be my love always and forever.

Marcia F. Rhoton

Someday

Dad, when are we going to spend time together? After I win
a lot of money, then, we'll have a mansion, and a maid. Then I'll
have time to spend with you, and the others, someday. I used to
count the cars, that past, hoping the next one, would be yours,
at last! I'd cry myself to sleep, when you never came. I know
you were too busy, working, to notice the clock, that was ticking.
No matter how much, you worked; the love I lost, the money wasn't
worth. Nothing else mattered, to me; it became so important, can't
you see!? For you to spend, a little more time, with me. The years
have fallen, away, the weeds of pain, inside my heart, have stayed.
I am older, and all my tears are drained. Like a well, that has gone
dry, my eyes cannot cry. My childhood, is gone forever; sad memories,
are buried in my mind. My sorrow, has turned to anger, my anger,
turned to hate, and, at last, my hate, has turned to pain. For I
have realized, that the promises you made, have all slipped
away; my hope inside, died long ago. There will never be that
someday, because, I have to let you go! And, at last, you call me,
and ask why am I not there, with you. Now you cry, for
that someday, when I, will have time!

Mary Klante

"The Seven Of Us"

There were five girls and two boys
A lot of love, not too many toys
We were together through thick and thin
Where to start, it's hard to begin
Fishing and camping out by the pond
If only I could bring it back with a magic wand
We were so young and carefree
Oh how nice that would be
Always there with unconditional love
I guess that came from the Lord above
Always willing to help each other
I guess that come from our Mother
Remembering the good times we had
Going on trips, the seven of us, and mom and dad
Nine in a car, some on the floor, some in a line
I don't know how mom never lost her mind
Always there for each other day and night
May the good Lord forgive us if we ever fight
Though many miles keeps us apart
I love each one from the bottom of my heart

Jeanette L. Heileman

Never Let Them Go

It's good to have a someone on whom you can depend,
A kind and tender sweetheart a true and loving friend.
A someone you can turn to, when skies above are gray,
Who has the magic formula, to smile the clouds away.
Someone to share you sorrow, as well as happiness.
Who lives for you and you alone, and yearns for your caress.
It's wonderful to plan the years, and travel hand in hand,
With someone who will always try, their best to understand.
Some people are not lucky, they never seem to find,
A someone they can cling to, for hope and piece of mind.
So if you find a someone, who sets your heart aglow.
Hold fast to them with all your might, and never let them go.

Mike A. Quinn

A Home

A home is a place where one should feel loved, wanted and comfortable.
A home is a place where the spirit of togetherness prevails.
A home is a place where the mother and father are the role model
for their children.
A home is a place where discipline takes place with love and understanding.
A home is a place where family problems are discussed in confidentiality.
A home is a place where love begins.
A home is a place where the foundation of education begins.
A home is a place where family members work together as a team.
A home is a place where one emotional, social and spiritual needs, are met.
A home is a place where love is accepted unconditionally.
A home is a place for security, encouragement and support.
A home is a place where moral, social, and ethical values are
instilled in children.
A home is the foundation on which the influence of a society is built.

Merlene Jordan

Images

I saw a reflection in the pool,
A person I did not know,
It looked like me,
But then I see,
It's only a reflection of who I used to be,
I lost myself down the road,
And now I can't turn back,
I move forward and see what is to come,
But I can't help but wonder about the past,
And the person I used to be.

Melissa Ann Parrish

A Heart Named Torture

Tried to woo Her, I did I did, yet all was in vain,
A heart of stone did She possess, and Torture was its name.

As black as black as hell at night, Torture did have colour,
To have it bleed, would release an acid, lethal like no other.

Innocent and dainty did She look, at only five foot tall,
But to see It work at the hearts of men, would disgust us one and all.

Broke my own and made me weep, Torture did to me,
A day full of grace and luck, I pray She'll never see.

To wed affluence of greatness, was Its one and primary goal,
So shallow, so cruel, I thought not could exist such a soul.

Try to vain, I do I do, to think not of this ugly Creature,
I pity the next, victim of man, to suffer with the heart named Torture.

Maximilian T. Nassar

My Poetry

A new poem was born in my soul,
A greeting to life, a greeting to all.
A new day was also born,
A pearl with which I my coat adorn.

My poetry is the most faithful friend,
Higher and higher it helps me ascend,
It sustains me, it supports my quest,
Gives words to my longing unexpressed.

It seeks the bridge that leads to eternity,
It is a present, a joy, a mystery,
A tiny light in the deep dark night,
A fragrant flower, it is a delight.

It saves me from going astray,
To my true self it shows me the way,
If I know what I am here for,
Closer to Thee my flight will soar.
With my poems I hope to reach up to Thee,
Oh, Eternal Riddle, Supreme Reality.

George G. Strem

A Sailors Diary

There's a ship named "My love" with nowhere to go
A glorious and beautiful ship that has no shore

Lost in the waves of life and all its pain
In the currents of destiny with no true gain

One day came an island, I steered my course true
It was an uncharted island, I chose to name "You"

"You" was a beautiful, enchanting, unknown land
It was a portrait painted by God's own hand.

"My Love" came to rest on the shores of "You"
"My love" found a home and a purpose too

I will always love the island of you

Michael J. Cocherell - The Sailor

Daddy Left Me

Mommy and him were fighting all the time
And I plugged my ears and
Closed my eyes tight and
Pretty soon my daddy left
See mommy says he loves me still
And them two couldn't get along
But I know
He was mad when
I ate too many crackers

Susan Campbell-Hartzell

Shattered Mockingbirds

Petals stain my heart,
a garden of distress
mockingbirds are shattered by the cold, still air
I am unaware of season's change
for winter hovers always
a desolate friend in a time of
vulnerability and confusion
no more flowers bloom and spread their love
for they live in a steel-glass bowl
a world of disbelief and frozen promises
which I created for us all
one day the sun will rise again
to kill the plastering fog
but it will be too late-
for the mockingbirds are shattered.

Lauren Becker

Letting Go

I knew a man who had a friend,
a friend that meant so much.
They grew together, and laughed, and learned,
made memories and such.

Then one day his best friend died,
and part of him died too.
In the hardships of losing a friend,
I lost the man I knew.

His heart couldn't take the beating,
that death had set upon,
so he wallowed in the memories
instead of moving on

I tell this story to teach a lesson
to remember through the years.
You can't throw your whole life away
to misery and tears.

Just remember you're not alone, my friend,
although the heart may mend slow,
There are many ways of holding on,
and also letting go.

Jody Weber

The Storm

A drop of water on my brow
A feeling of the cool wind that comes with rain
A distant rumble of the future might
For I feel the power coming forth

A flash of fear shot from the sky
A blinding light that hurts my eyes
The twisted howl of a falling tree
Calming the pain that burns inside me

The pouring rain that speaks to the hearts of all
The hypnotizing whispering winds
Speak the language of the ancient gods
All is cleansed from its smoldering confusion

I look at all the colors of a glistening rainbow
As a drop of water drips from a leaf
It lets out a peaceful ring
And before me I see the innocence of a butterfly's wing

Larry L. Doss Jr.

The Dual Language Of Flowers

Flowers, like music, speak a language all their own
  a fact, not fiction, that has become so well known

The crocus speaks of springtime; the dahlia bespeaks fall
  "tulips" demand discretion; the "iris" opens up to all

Violets speak of innocence; narcissus, mere "reflection"
  gardenias speak of romance; "forget-me-not," rejection

The lily speaks of purity; the rose speaks of love,
  the carnation, of constancy; the aster, stars above

Cape Jasmine speak of courtship; mums, the harvest moon
  the lily of the valley, foretells wedlock in June

The hyacinths reveal sweet perfume; poppies, World War I
  the dianthus speaks of fragrance; "foxglove," nature's pun

The language of the flowers, once a mystery
  has been revealed to us, through God's charity

Their language, although ever so silent, speaks loudly
  lyrics so well known

Which allows mankind dual enjoyment from all the
  flowers that are grown

Flowers, unlike music, speak with such a silent tongue
  a language of emotion, a music that's unsung

  Loraine P. Wright

The Important Things

The important things in life are a smile upon
a face, the beauty that sparkles within the
eyes, the kindness shared in a touch, the love
expressed in a kiss, the strength and sureness
in a hug. The understanding in a conversation,
the excitement in anticipation, the beauty
in a sunset, the coolness in a soft breeze.
The freedom of a bird in flight, the vision
of the stars on a summer's night. The
togetherness of people in love, the flowers
that grow wild and free. The rain that
falls and flows to the sea. But the most
important thing is seeking the understanding
of the Lord.

  Noel F. Harvey

"The Goddess"

She sits in the beauty of her light,
a complexion of ponder on her pale face.
Beautiful goddess deep in her soul,
worry and anguish beneath her grace.

She pleads to the goddess within,
"Give me my strength and my will to live."
She knows that she possesses this strength,
but she lacks the power to find it.

If she feels deep in her soul
and makes the goddess strong,
she can use the power of her goddess
and release her mind of her wrong.

The goddess will intensify her beauty
and her weakness will fade within.
She will learn to love herself again,
and courage will make up for her sin.

  Jennifer Atkins

"Please God Not Now!!!!"

It was a beautiful day you see I went out into the backyard to work on a cadillac, I needed the money for my two kids and me someone had took all my money, so there was no money to buy food for my two kids and me I did not have anyone to baby sit for me my mother was in Tennessee so I said I have to make money now you see, so under the car I crawled oh this job is going to take longer than I thought, I unhooked everything and the car went bang!!!! No car, you cannot fall on me! I've got two little kids to take care of you see, Oh God!!!! This cannot be happening to me!!!!! I love my two kids too much to leave them, you see, please God let me stay!!! I love them too much to ever leave them this way, they need me today, please don't take me away!!!! The kids place their hands on me, get up Daddy? Are you mad at me? They dragged me away from the car but I cannot speak, you see, they said, "Daddy get up." to me. Yes God took me that day I wanted to stay I don't want to leave my kids not this way!!!!

  Louise Ownby

A Sunshine

A bright line forms in eternity...the silence marks the peace.
A breeze picks up known only to me as the darkness begins to cease.
A tint of color then appears...a chill flows through the air,
gifts that Mother Nature bears to all become aware.
Forces beyond our most memorable dreams, things that forever affect
  our lives,
always kept secret to us human beings, slowly begin before our eyes.
A tool of art that exceeds our brush...poetry forever hidden from pen,
beginning our lives with a brilliant rush...the morning light begins to win.
Luxurious color streaks the sky...the canvas comes alive with paint,
moving enough to make one cry, yet mysterious, to cause restraint.
A graceful are begins to rise, hardly clear, yet quite present,
his glowing light brings the world alive and causes beauty the moon resents.
Time is passing, yet we are lost, he enters with increasing stride.
A miraculous show that has no cost and takes us on a glorious ride.
All at once he shows his face, his knowing smile bring us warmth.
His robe of blue is edged with lace, but changes with his love and scorn.
Never averting his eyes from ours...never losing his loving touch,
he is with us at all hours and his arrival promises much.
What mood will he be when he does come? Every day is a new surprise.
He is honored as the sun, but I remember the sunrise.

  Michelle Fahmy

Don't Break Your Parents' Hearts

I believe someone should tell the story of Jane Doe
A beautiful, intelligent girl, leader of her class
Who once led a happy life, now it has turned to woe
She listened to so called friends, she smoked grass.

Jane stopped kissing her parents that very same day
At first she was afraid they would smell the pot
Little by little she was hooked, began to drift away
Finally she didn't care if they smelled it or not.

Sadly they watched their once affectionate child
Go from marijuana, to alcohol and finally pills
Until she beat up her mother, drugs made her wild
It happens to good kids who go in search of thrills.

Like any others she started to smoke pot for kicks
It is sad so many girls think it is just a big joke
They should see her now on the street turning tricks
Trying to earn money to support a drug habit, coke.

I have told you the story you know how it starts
Many times it is in response to some fool's dare
Please, don't wind up breaking your parents' hearts
Stop, think, don't take that first puff, if you care.

  Gilbert F. Gadoury

Untitled

There's a quiet, dark, thunderous storm on the way. It rumbles
methodically waiting to dance a black hole through their pitless hollow
souls. No blood need to shed, ever. Merely the venom of this
promising storm. The gallant cunning tornado laughs quietly in the
darkest hour brewing stronger as it telepathically eyes its prey.
Proud of its underestimated power. Proud of great dignity. The
restless, disturbing, clouds turn shades of gray, to dusk. But listen
carefully, and look beyond them. Hidden, smiles a captivating,
moonlight, ballerina. A female warrior draped in pure justice. As
the skies slowly, drape, open, this dark angel will swirl like the
wind, and sweep a life time of misery into their vile souls. They
sleep well, now. At daylight they brag a false deception, and a
wrongful, cruel, distraction, of an innocent woman. A beautiful
peasant creature too trusting, and pure of heart. For now let him
plan a penniless future, destined to come. Oh do let him try to escape.
He wins not. Such foul, fools, seldom do. Still, one stunning legacy
is about to haunt him day and night. Plague him unmercifully. The
storm follows him, throughout, distance, and time. Thus, all in the
form of the darken, soundless ballerina, who awaits patiently to dance
to his own self distraction. To her freedom and beauty, to her
thunderous spirit to good triumph over evil, throughout time, always.
Oh do let him rest well, his unconscious is her greatest power.
"Shhh," do you not hear chilling laughter?

Luanda Machado

Buffalo Soldiers

The Buffalo Soldiers of long ago
Roamed the west not looking for gold
The Buffalo Soldiers
Were bold riding and waving Old Glory
Some pointing their guns ready to fight.
The Buffalo Soldiers
On a mission to do their best,
They weren't to return
Unless safe for the rest.
The Buffalo Soldiers were the best.
The courageous Black Buffalo Soldiers patrol the west
It was a great dangerous test
After the Civil War
Keeping the Indians afar
The Buffalo Soldiers were bold to capture
Old Geronimo and the Apache
Indians and the rest
It was the greatest in the west
As they rode along clearing the way
It was safe for the rest.

Mary L. Williams

Now Let Me Fly

The whip cracks against our backs,
As we
slave away in the noonday sun,
Silent
tears run down heavy black faces as we are forced to work by
brutal white masters,
Our clothes are ripped and shredded from years
of hard
labor on southern cotton fields,
Together
we travel north in search of freedom
and to
escape this horrible treachery
FREE AT LAST

Kyle Packett

Society's Bouquet

Where do you go when there isn't any space?
A free-willing spirit that hasn't any place
Loved ones around, you can't seem to find
Fair weather feelings, without any mind

Heavy conversation and actions that attack
The heart of reality in those who react
End and beginnings—the cycle never stops
Knowing little of the bottom, and even less of the top

Blinded seeing everything, sightful seeking pain
Accomplishing the doubtful—but failing to refrain
Overlooking all tomorrows, but remembering yesterdays
Today is but a vision of a barren bouquet

Marsha L. Geist

The Divorced Woman

I saw her sit on the porch all day long
As her heart did its best to mend itself
I wonder what was going through her mind
As her whole world was tumbling to the ground.
She had to feel the fear of loneliness
And though she was surrounded by loved ones
She knew that she must face this on her own.
Now on that porch she learned to accept fate
And realized her life must start anew...
The sunset that she watched a million times
Was now a sign of better things to come,
And maybe faith would help her get it right
Because God knows she needs a second chance,
To reach the dreams she hoped for as a girl!

B. J. Ferneau

The Question

"What is life?", the little child asked,
  As he looked up with bright, shinning eyes.
"It's a mystery, my son," the mother replied,
  "As big as the earth and the skies,
As deep as the ocean — it puzzles the wise."

"Where is heaven?", the sweet voice piped.
  The mother smiled and squeezed his hand,
"It's in our hearts, when we look at you,
  And watch as you grow to a man."

"Who is God?", the youngster wanted to know.
  "He is with us and in us and all that we see,
The Creator of life and Ruler of all,
  He wants us to be all we can be —
He is the answer to life's mystery."

Verda L. Alexander

"Things Of Heaven And Earth"

Make unto thyself a tiny world enclosed
and place a moat most deeply and well posed
to keep away the commonness of life,
the dreadful boors, and their companion - strife.
Adore the blooms that grow within thy space,
caress the flowers, and hold them to thy face,
for short the day, then gone the merry song
and seconds fly until the final gong,
when the fluttering of angels' wings awaken thee,
to ask, what was so lovely - (quite mistakenly)
that ye detained arrival to thy heaven,
and dallied so for four score years and seven,
regale them with the beauties of the earth;
of songs and wine and flowers and of mirth,
and dear ones who have been with thee since birth.

Robert MacIntosh

To A Real Gem

I did not start life,
As a pain in an oysters side
But! Maybe as a gleam in my Daddy's eye

Time marched on and I began to shine
By doing this and doing that
And never did I whine

The depression was awesome
And we wished for much more
Then along came Roosevelt to help us even the score

Time was cruel and time was sweet
I came through a jewel and we stayed out of the street

Rhinestones may sparkle and with polish will shine
But the real jewel will glisten all the time

Yes, times went up and times went down
But may I ask, is it not true,
I come through a true P E A R L FOR ALL OF YOU

Kids! And you Lloyd, too,
My last wishes were for
The best for all of you

With all my love, Pearl
Samuel M. Smith

Gray Day

The rain quietly sprinkles the windows
  As a mist drips down the walls of my mind...
The trees stand somber and silent
  Only shadows in my head do I find...

The sky for me today, is softly crying
  Through the tears, all I can do is look on...
The gray clouds are a blanket of sadness
  That smother the bright fires of dawn...

Then, there's a breeze as soft as a whisper
  And the fog in my head starts to shift...
The leaves come alive gently stirring
  And the shadows are suddenly adrift...

Before long, there's a thin ray of sunlight
  Behind my eyes it sparkles in the dew...
And I realize that the sky is telling me
  That now I must be thinking of you...

When the sun peeks through all the sorrow
  ...then I must be thinking
                    —of you...
J. Michael Deerfield

Sunset

Your power of beauty threatens me
As a mere mortal human being
I am nothing compared to you
So infinitely huge, so decorously shining

You melt not far from my arms
And disappear into evening dusk
You've taken my heart with you

For the sight of you is a treasure
The colors deepening in the sky
As you say a very lovely, lofty goodbye

Who could compare to your entrances and exits?!
Done with such splendor, flamboyance and execution
Ah, draw me close my love, my forever
For I know you'll be there the next day.
Stephanie Perez

Survival

Secrets of the Summer wind
Are beginning to unfold
The Ancient ones reveal to us
Their message to be told

Sisters and Brothers everywhere
Lend your ears to hear
The changes of Earth are now upon us
Listen to the wise ones near

Return the love of Mother Earth
Save her children at all costs
Blend with her your prayers
Thanksgiving to our spiritual hosts

Man guided by only himself
Has created lands of death and devastation
Let us rebuild as a kindred people
United in love, our consolation
Susie R. Greene

Last One To Know

You said you loved me
and you'd never let me go.
But you were seeing her
and I was the last one to know.

You knew just what I wanted to hear.
You said in you I could confide.
I told you all my dreams, secrets, and fears
and to you I lost all my pride.

I felt so used.
I felt so betrayed.
I had no idea
your love for me would fade.

For a while I sat and cried
thinking you were the only man for me,
but now I realize
there are many fish in the sea.
Stephanie Simon

Separate Lives

You have your life, I have mine.
And we tell everyone we're doing fine
But I cannot clearly see, through this pain and misery,
Why for us, separate lives it had to be.

At first my dear, I must confess

I thought our love could stand the stress
But in time things went wrong, our hearts lost their song
When we found that our love was not that strong
Separate lives it seems to be, it was meant for you and me
We weren't meant to live alone, but we tried and we could not
Share a home.

We now live in separate worlds, we have a little boy and a
Lovely girl.

But we did not count the cost, right from the very start,
And now they pay the price with a broken heart.
Separate lives it seems to be, that's why you and I are free
Yes we tried but we could not share a home.
Rosalie M. Richardson

Dolphin's Song

We sing the songs that were made to be sung
And we ring the bells that were wrought to be rung.
To dance in the sea and to dance in the sun,
Is the way we will be when we want to have fun,
The sea is the home where the dance has its place,
And the sky is where the birds have the lace
Of clouds in the sky and the currents of air,
And, like us, they dance and dive without care!

We sing the songs of the past that were sung
And we ring the bells that the ancients had rung,
For long have we danced and for long we have stayed,
With the men on the land and the birds in the sky,
And the huge golden beasts that sometimes fly by!
We danced since before and we dance once again,
We'll leap in the sun, and we'll play until then!

Many more songs have we yet to sing
Of the men and the birds and the bells we will ring!

Sam Waddington

Life On The Down Hill Run

Some say that life begins at age forty,
    And we know which way it went.
All the way down to the bottom of the hill,
    With a fast and furious descent.

At first you don't think you are getting older
    And it must all just be in your head.
That is, until you wake one morning,
    And need help just to get yourself out of bed.

Because you ache and hurt all over,
    In muscles you didn't even know that you had.
But, when your knees and elbows won't bend,
    You know that it's really getting bad.

The doctors just say that they can't help you,
    'Cause "Old Father Time" is taking his toll.
You'd think they could be a little kinder,
    Instead of saying, "you are just getting old."

I guess we will just have to grin and bear it,
    Since we are all in the same old boat.
We'll either die young, or else we'll grow old,
    Therefore, no one else can brag, boast or gloat!!!

Quennie Tucker

Sunflower Seeds Of Yesterday

Plant the seeds so carefully,
and watch the plant grow so tall,
Let the flower bloom so pretty
Don't make the growing stall.

And from the flower
let the seeds fall,
and another flower will bloom
Let the plant grow so tall.

Plant them all
side by side
so they won't be lonely
so they don't have to hide

Smile, smile with your yellow petals
Because the sunflower seeds of yesterday
Will soon grow into the blooms of tomorrow.

Terah Rochelle Baldwin

The Rainy Afternoon

We walk across a rainy desert,
And watch the box fall gently.
A man talks as we toss flowers,
Our minds racing.
People we know,
But often don't recognize,
Offer tears and apologies.
As if their guilt can be freed.
We stand in silence,
And watch the Earth drop violently into the cold, dark pit.
Covering him forever...
Slowly we retreat,
Letting the darkness close in around us,
Our eyes damp with tears,
And our minds filled with guilt...
We steal one last glance,
Then turn to leave,
Walking through the neatly planted rows of death.
Never to return,
And never to regret....

Rebecca Shoemaker

The Power Of Love

Love puts a smile upon someone's face,
and two people can always embrace.

Love is a song in your heart and mind,
brings perfect harmony to all mankind.

Love keeps a light shinning like a bright star,
whether you are near or whether you are far.

Love is joy each morning you awake,
and that smile you keep in sincere not fake.

Love is the birth of a new tomorrow,
Love will always cover the scars of life's sorrows.

Love is a hand to a friend whose heart is broken,
love is beautiful words from your mouth you have spoken.

If you need more knowledge on the power of love,
read the holy Bible, it relates to all above.

And when you have decided that love is where it's at,
well my dear friend, you have completed a great act.

Susan A. Guy

"Prayer"

Every night I sit down to pray
And to my God these words I say:
Please allow me to do my best
I know you ask for nothing less.
Bless Mom, Dad, Grandma, and all my friends
Make us all strong, no quivers, no bends.
Dad, without fail, is always there for me
He is also the cornerstone of our family.
Mom seems to work 24 hours a day
Please guide her, never keep her at bay.
Protect my sister, Sharon, from the evils of this world
She is so precious, as if a gem or a pearl.
Pap-paps in heaven, I ask that you watch over me
Let me face my problems, never flee.
Bless my aunts, uncles, and cousins
Many to name, possibly dozens.
To all those who shape my life without even knowing
By inclusion in my prayers, my gratitude I am showing.
All prayer takes is some time and some thought
Whenever you are in trouble or divine guidance is sought.

Patrick T. Joyce

I. To a man.

I am resign'd that I and Thou be twain:
    And tho' our rifted lives be liv'd apart
Which contum'd fear and purblind Writ ordain
    Yet shall my Muse un-flesh an agued heart.
The sullen brood decree we live as two;
    With fetid custom's Book they cite Love's death.
But let us live and love as lovers do,
    Who parted, yet do breathe as single breath.
Those sterile lordly, poison'd by their Creeds,
    But mime our ripe and fulsome plentitude.
(Their darlings sow but weak, pathetic seeds
    To reap a gilded crop of weeds as food.)

Lest hearts bespoke shouldst rouse the brows of vice,
A passing-glance from Thee must needs suffice.
        D. C. Goedel
        Sonnets of the Heart (1991)

Reminiscence

I opened a dusty box today
And there before me lay
Piles of adolescent rhymes.

Yes, I remember the times
On backyard steps, plumbing the depths
Of my soul. So bold,
So brash to pen such trash.

Here no tales of ivory towers,
Or frolicking maids in flowery bowers.
No War Crimean — How plebeian!

Instead I wrote of puppy tales and pony tails,
And the boy next door — Not much more.

All to say is said. I dread
'Tis true. There was nothing new
About my verses long ago
To stir emotions, fast or slow,
In any heart but mine.

But, that's it, you see.
Those poems were for me.
Small souvenirs for my winter years.
        Patricia Anne Love

Tears From Heaven

The Lord from heaven once again looked down
And tears like raindrops fell to the ground
As again he listened to the prayer
Of the little girl with long brown hair.

And as he listened, his heart breaking,
She told of her fears and abuse she was taking
Please, Lord, she prayed I'm not asking much
Just a kind word, a soft smile or touch.

She's done no one harm or done any wrong
But by a cruel act of fate she was born into a home
Where love was scarce, compassion all gone
And most times, like now, she felt so alone.

How could anyone be so heartless and cruel
And abuse a small child, God's precious Jewel
But someday she prayed, she'd have a new place
In heaven with Jesus, a smile on her face.

In Heaven there's never a shortage of love
She'd never be lonely in that home above
Till that day comes, to Jesus she'll pray
For strength to face each passing day.
        Sarah E. Haines

Untitled

As I walk down the darkened street
    and step into spot lightened street corner
I see him

Him,
    the one with wonderful eyes.
    The softness in his touch.
    In his blue eyes I see my dreams,
    each one unfolding.

Reaching for this angel of the darkened night
    my dreams and ecstasy race through my fingertips
    onto his. His shivers tell me he feels me
    through his body

Looking into my eyes, he takes me to his room.
    Complete darkness. No words. Just touches.
    And we lie there. Lie in darkness with
    each other. We are two becoming one.

Then the street light brightens into the sun.
    Through rose colored blinds I find not a
    dream, but reality. He is lying dormant
    beside me.
        Stacy L. Darrow

Dear Lisa

I think about you often,
And sometimes about when you were born,
And the Dr. said your lungs didn't inflate,
And you might not be with us long.

And I stood by the nursery window,
And stared at you inside,
And the had you in an oxygen tent,
And I prayed for hours and cried.

And then the Dr. came to me,
And said you were breathing fine,
And that your lungs had inflated,
And you'd be with us a long, long time.

And I asked Him if I could touch you,
And the nurse wheeled you to the hall,
And I kissed your hand so softly,
And it was so white, so soft, so small.

And I loved you oh so much my child,
And I have always loved you dear,
And I will always love you darling,
And for that you should have no fear
                —Dad.
        H. P. Graziano

The Kiss Of An Angel

I remember the first time we touched
As clearly as if it were just moments ago.
I was instantly captivated
by your magical stare and intoxicating kisses.
Your arms
they held me with such tenderness.
I was safe
and completely unaware
that you would soon become
the keeper of my heart.
I paid no mind
as my walls of caution and defense came
tumbling down.
And now
I sit hopelessly spellbound
in the palm of your hand.
While the moon lit the earth
that first early morning - the stars
moved aside - for an angel - descending
form above - to kiss my heart and bless me with you.
        L. E. LeMonier

Societies Children

Let's bring this world together again
And realize children's laughter is our best friend
'Cause society has taken our children away
By selling technology, instead of play
There's not much hope, no looking forward
We play with their lives as if they were cards
Tiny little lives we've brought into this world
We should be treating them as gems, as pearls
Racism, violence is what they see
Because of adults insecurities
In a perfect world our children would laugh
Instead of trembling, at every day gone past
As parents we are teachers, a job I think we have failed
No true communication with others, most we know have been jailed
Not taking into consideration these young adults we bring up
We need to stand firm behind them
And teach the value of true self love
I hope in my lifetime that things will change
So, societies children will rise above us
And their true spirits will be free...

Tammy Jo Mahan

"Retirement" A Beauty

The time has come to set the pace, you're out of the game
and out of the race.

So take the lead and follow through with the many things
you've wanted to do.

Time is yours, so each hour to stop and smell that beautiful flower.

To listen to a bubbling brook, or read a novel or a book,

To take a long and lasting walk, or skip some stones or throw some rocks;

To watch the snow as it gently falls or listen to the sweet bird calls;

To take a drive and enjoy the view, remember now, you're living for you.

So take each moment that is yours and open each and every door.

You're only retiring from troubles and strife and just beginning
to enjoy your life.

So as you stroll along Life's precious way, I hope that you'll
find beauty day by day!

Patricia Bolin

Today

Outside my window, a new day I see
And only I can determine
What kind of day it will be

It can be busy and sunny, laughing and gay,
Or boring and cold, unhappy and gray,

My own state of mind is the determining key.
For I am only the person I let myself be.

I can be thoughtful and do all I can to help,
Or be selfish and think of just myself.

I can enjoy what I do and make it seem fun,
Or gripe and complain and make it hard on someone.

I can be patient with those who may not understand,
Or be little and hurt them as much as I can.

But I have faith in myself
And believe what I say,

And I personally intend to make the best of each day.

Rachel Gibbs

The Unseen World

My roses smell as sweet as any,
And, oh my lilies, I have many.
In my world I can have all,
From nightingale to waterfall.
My world is my own, I am the soul occupant;
My world's door is closed, open it? I won't and can't.

My tender swans slide across a lake of ice,
And the sound of bells in my church is nice.
The horses and dogs roam free in my land;
Their food comes not from human hand.
In my world there is no sorrow or strife,
No joy, for I have found none in life.

When my world is gone, absent without a trace,
Its inhabitants may be found in my mind and face.
For I built it piece by piece with gentleness and love,
As if on some divine mission, a desire from above.
Nay, I would have me think it was God's gift to me,
To me — who cannot see.

Tammy A. Johnson

My Friend Above...

Do you sometimes feel you're alone?
And no one seems to care?
In your heart you long for peace.
You've searched everywhere?

I can "highly" recommend my friend
He fills my every need small and big,
He is my very special "special" friend.

He's always there when I'm in need.
When earthly friends are gone,
He has never left my to struggle all alone.

Some earthly friends are here today, but tomorrow they are gone.
But Jesus is a faithful friend, He's true now and always.

He filled my life with happiness, he filled my soul with joy,
He will do the same for you, just give him full control.
He'll take away the lonely feeling.

He's a special friend indeed,"
He will never leave you on a stormy night,
It's Jesus Christ you need for life,
He'll give you Peace and harmony.

Sharon Appell

"The Eye"

In the Kingdom of heaven I sat upon a chair
and my eyes became the windows of God...

There were all manner of beings, passing by unaware
of whose eyes out of which I chose to stare.

As they danced and pranced and plodded by, like angels
and goblins that creep, crawl and fly...

As they smiled and grinned and spread their great wings
I was mesmerized, horrified by all these strange things.

There were thinkers and doers, creators and fools
There were lovers and heroes, there were imps and ghouls

One would create, the other destroy
One brought great sadness, the other great joy.

Then and there I knew what the earth had become,
a great hell for many, a great heaven for some.

To look at the world through God's all seeing eye is a bitter-sweet
sight to behold
To look at the world through God's all seeing eye the most haunting of
tales will unfold
We each have a choice in what we say and do
Be it good or evil, the truth shines through

We each have a choice in what we say and do
Be it good or evil, the eye of God always watches you.

Romel Mitchell

A Meaningful Life

Let me live to love
   And love to live.
Let me never be selfish
   But always willing to give.

Let me live, laugh with joy,
   To be proud of each day as a child with a toy.
Let my life be a living light,
   That may lead another in a path that's right.

Let me learn and grow in grace,
   And forever have a smiling face.
To each and everyone I meet,
   To have a healthy attitude in Thee.

Let not my life be in vain,
   Let me not suffer a reward for pain.
Let me today hope and believe,
   There is a better day waiting for me.

Dianne M. Rucker

Think About Me

Think about me when you're blue
and I'll be thinking about you too.
This love of mine you hold so tight
I hope it keeps you warm at night.
When I'm not with you and all alone,
My mind takes over and starts to roam.
Think of life and how it could be
if I could just have you next to me.
So don't take my heart that I've given to you
and throw it away like you would an old shoe.
Because if you do and you turn me away,
my heart will be broken for ever and a day.
But time will go on and I will too
but my life will be sad since I don't have you.
So give me a call when you're down and blue
and I'll probably say, I'll always love you!
   Always yours

Robert Jones

Love Is When.......

Love is when you have someone to take walks with, have talks with,
and just be quiet with.

Love is when your spouse wakes you up nicely, because they know you
always wake up grouchy, no matter what.

Love is when you can tell your spouse anything about yourself without
fear of judgment or criticism.

Love is when you find that you don't even have to talk and you already
know what the other person is going to say.

Love is when you make a meal a disaster, and you laugh and go out to eat.

Love is when you support all the endeavors of your spouse, even when
sometimes you are afraid for them.

Love is when you form a team to get a job done and both of you share
to do what each of you does best.

Love is when you know you wouldn't die without the other person in
your life, but you know there would be an emptiness that nothing else
could ever fill.

Love is when you know you care enough to want to spend your lives
together, to grow old together and share the ups and downs.

Love is when you say you take this person for better or worse, and for
richer or poorer, and you stick it out even when it gets worse and
poorer, because you know it's love that makes life worth living.

Susan M. Claffey

To See

Sometimes I feel so confused,
And I don't understand why.

Sometimes I feel so really used,
And I just want to cry.

Sometimes I want to turn around,
And go to where I used to be.

Sometimes I want to be found,
And to be born again as me.

Sometimes I think the world is against me,
But then I remember...
There are some who will help me see.

Sarah Price

A Matter Of Time

In the midnight hour we met
And how appropriate it was.
Our love proved to be as sacred as that hour.
   We remained in the dark
Away from people and questions and opinions and lies.
We hid our love, our passion from them
But more so from ourselves.
   The light would destroy us, but (quite by accident)
The sun rose on us
And when it did we were afraid.
You tried to escape back into the night.
   I was already making plans for the day.
(The night was no longer enough for me.)
You came to me in the day.
In the night you went away.
   In my vault you were buried, but (quite by accident)
Like the sunrise you rose again.
I am afraid.
We are again lovers of the night.
   Mo(u)rning is coming.

Patricia Thomas Phillips

Lighting

There's a man named Lighting he stands on the street
And he's always friendly with everyone he meets
He tilts his hat to greet the people that pass on the street
He gives the kids a dollar
When he sees they're in need
And they always remember to say thank you
And everyday he always says good-morning
and how's your day.

Pamela Smith

April 14, 1995 - Angelic Dreams

I've made love to my dream
And have wished upon a star.
How odd this may seem, to the one who is so far.

I sent you a wish
Upon an angel's wings.
I wrote you a song, about desirous things.

You may be out of sight
But, not out of mind.
I could never hurt you, for my love is the gentle kind.

I've kissed your lips
With every drop of rain.
I've held your hand when all you felt was pain.

I've bared my soul to you,
Like the petals on a rose.
I've sent you heart-felt thoughts that only heaven knows!

You're searching for me, though we've never met.
Soon I'll capture your heart,
'Cause I'm the one you won't forget.

Tammara L. Bischoff

The Beating Rain

Drunk again, it storms into the little boy's room
And from that moment on the child knows that he is doomed.
It looks at him with burning eyes.
Filled with fear, the boy tries not to cry.

Its hate filled blows send searing pain
As the terror stricken boy can't help but hear the
   sound of the falling rain.
He wishes it would go away and never return
As his wounds now begin to ache and burn.

The bruises eventually fade away but not the pain.
The vivid memories of its cruelty still remain.
Although he has grown and it no longer hurts him
I can still see the pain in his eyes and I know it lurks inside him.

Because even though he acts so tough
I know his life has been very rough.
He's been through hell, I can see it in his eyes.
I just want to take him in my arms and let him know it's alright to cry

Because underneath it all that frightened little boy still remains.
And he can still hear the sound of the falling rain.

Rebecca Ross

Going Home

An old woman sits in her rocking chair rocking back and forth, back
and forth, thinking about the "Good Old Days" and the "Bad Old Days"
That used to be. She rocks all day and all night, thinking about
what she will say to God her father. As she close her eyes and lets
her mind wander freely, she thinks about heaven and all the people
she'll meet when she gets there. Finally, she closes her eyes for
the last time.
   Her mind is free!
She has "Gone home!"

Tabitha Williams

Morning Departure

In this jet age a few hours flight can span the USA,
And England, home of ancestors, is but a flight away,
Our forbears left this country with courage conquering fears,
To start new lives in unknown lands, to spend remaining years.

Frail craft were cockleshells of dreams, borne on the swelling waves
Founding a mighty nation, from men whose hearts were brave
They faced a hundred dangers, when they left this island home
To sail across three thousand miles, upon the raging foam.
Now I, in only hours of luxury and ease,
Have retraced my forbears' journey, high above those angry seas
And looking far beneath me, I marvel all the more
At the breadth of their endurance,
   when they left old England's shore.

Ruth Burden

Ministry

When comes the autumn and the winter
And clouds gather about the center
Of the sky so blue and bright;
When it's dark and stormy in the night
And men of every nation have lost sight
Of all that is good, true, and right;
When men have searched to fill their soul,
When they have sought to be made whole
But have not reached that goal;
They come from every city, village, and town;
They come from miles and miles aroun'
To that wonderful place called Ministry,
Where God's Love is said to be,
There, they can receive everything they need,
No matter what their station, race, or creed
Because Jesus is there indeed,
Through the service of the saints, they see the love
Of the Friend, Jesus Christ, enthroned above.

J. Stephen Smith

Once

Once everything was unknown
And blind men had equal advantage
The creative stones had not been thrown
And no war had yet been waged

Once space caused man's isolation
Boundaries caused only physical fatigue
Minds grew with need for creation
And answers found to problems received

Isolated storms grew from weeping clouds
And men eagerly drank their tears
The streams of life brought together crowds
Man celebrated and feasted on his fears

William J. Conaway

Florence

A woman of strength
A woman of warmth
No time for her to rest
Never to far to answer any humble request
A gentle woman with a heart of gold
A strong woman who cared for numbers untold
Dressed in a uniform of white
Caring for the needy and sick by day and by night
She fought others battles for life
Or a warm summer eve in 1910
A nightingale closed her eyes
Her gentle voice never to be heard again

Ronald Philbrick

Change

I sat beneath a tree on a warm summer evening,
an old friend appeared, and we talked of many things.

Of friends both here and gone, people we had loved,
adventures we had known.

We talked about Vietnam, the friends left on that wild range,
as we talked the wind whispered, "It's time for change."

As we talked I looked at him and he changed before my eyes,
Was it really true, or just a dream, in Vietnam he had died.

We talked about the world, the need for peace upon these plains,
and as we talked the wind whispered, "It's time for change."

We talked it seemed for hours, on into the night,
and then my friend slowly faded from my sight.

After he had left, as dreams sometimes do,
was that the wind that whispered...
The change is up to you.

Robert W. Thompson

A Glimpse Of Light

Silent and dark was the time before John.
An evil spell.
Eternal night... broken by the songs of angels.
And a smile
born in our eyes, given breath in a kiss
found a home in our hearts.
Kindred spirits awed by an ageless recognition.
Bodies trembled
with a lifetime of longing at last answered.
And life began.

Love lost...
Agony streaks across the jagged landscape of my heart.
A torrent of tears.
My soul writhes one final time and lies dead
And I will never be warm again.
Each day a requiem, each night a prayer for oblivion
His everlasting gift-
The majesty of love, the purgatory of loss
A glimpse of light...
Eternal night!

Susan Marie Herbert

Yellowstone

Majestic trees, stalwart and strong
Among these the buffalo roam.
Meadows painted with fields of flowers
Blooms are large from all the showers.
Cutthroat trout are swimming aplenty
Eagles, geese, pelicans soar above freely.
Coyotes stealthy stalk each meal
Elk bugle loudly in the field.
Gangly moose feed in the bogs.
Deer leap gracefully over logs.
Geysers hiss and finally blow
Paint pots gurgle and put on a show.
Firehole, Madison, Yellowstone, Gibbon
Yellowstone lake is just like heaven.
Artist point with walls of yellow hues
Waterfalls in the distance are white and blues.
Thunder roars without fail
Raindrops fall minus hail.
Lightning strikes hills are aflame
Blackened trees are all that remain.

Patricia A. La Bauve

Path Of Emotions

I sit on a mountain top
    among the swirling clouds.
Watching people that are free and proud
    once were my enemies but are now my friends.
For you see I was captured on a cold winter's day
    I fought for my freedom, I even ran away.
I was found and carried back to the village that day.

Then on a warm summer's day I was given a choice
    to leave in peace or to stay.
And now I am the wife of that handsome young brave.

I sit on a mountain top
    and watch my children play.
My husband's out on this cool autumn day
    hunting food for winter that's on its way.
I have dried and stored all the food I have found
    some to powder which had to be ground.

My warrior has returned - his handsome face I see
    and my heart sings as he waves to me.
He races up the mountain on his spirited steed
    like the Eagles of the wind we're all proud and free.

Rita Shafer-Parrish

Who Am I

Tell me mama, really who am I?
Am I black, white, Indian, Chinese, Carib or Arawak.
My complexion is black, eyes are blue, with long straight hair
Please tell me mama who am I?

Am I your sister's child or
Am I adopted?
My sister is white, my brother is black and
I look like the mixture of the two
Tell me mama who am I.

Who ever I am, or may not be
All I know is God made me, I am
A person full of life and love to share
And as for my mama I know she loves me
Who ever I am.

Rosalind Quash-Williams

"If I Had A Quarter"

Once I was a young girl who had a lot of sense
Always in the right place-making all the right friends
But I paved my way with carelessness and troubles so immense
And every time that I was wrong you came to my defense.

I used to be an angel 'til the devil talked to me
He gave me first class lessons on how to deceive
But every time I hurt you all I felt was misery
And I'd bet that you'd forgive me though I hurt you needlessly.

I used to be a good girl 'til I made a change or two
It only took one minute to think of an excuse
It's hard to keep up with one's own lies about the truth
And when the truth comes out there's not too much that you can do.

So, if I had a quarter for all the fools I've been
And if I had another one for every time I've sinned
I'd be the richest girl in this town, time and time again
If I had a quarter for all the fools I've been.

I've made my mind up, finally, after all that we've been through
You're gonna see the angel in me after all I've done to you
I listened to old Satan longer than I planned to do
And you're gonna love the new girl better than the one you knew.

Patricia L. Dewald

"Love"

I sit here loving it, loving you
Always and forever
'Till this beautiful land is gone
Until the day when there is no flesh
   and clear beauty left in the world
I shall be yours, as you shall be mine

Right now I think of you, and love you
I see the trees and the hills
and the clear, clear blue sky
the sun is warm on my cheek
and I see you with me

My companions are the breeze that play with my hair
   and the sun that warms my skin
The birds sing our tale
to ever know my feelings for you

Our tale shall live forever
the sun shall tell the stars
the breeze shall tell the trees
the birds and shall tell the world

Renee Nicole Osborne

Untitled

I sat in the front row honor chair
Alone in the crowd a widow

While you lay there, alone, in the flower draped casket
Your voice silent now

I hated the silence the most
Knowing well I could not hear you again until eternity

Above the murmurs of the mourners
I could almost hear you softly saying, as you always did

You will be all right only my body is dead
My spirit is not lost, this is not as final as it seems
My spirit is around you always, to help you finish our hopes and dreams

Look at the faces and hear the voices of our young
As they earnestly weave the laces of their future

In it a piece of you and me
Find strength in joy for what we had
For so long here it was all so very dear

You must go on for a time
As I have in this life beyond the clouds
Cry, my love, for the past but do not pine too long
For the darkness will pass and you will be all right

B. Jean Peterson

Dear Granny And Papa

I'm told what I got though I can't really see,
All the wonderful gifts you gave in expectation of me.

My Mom loves the rocker this I can tell.
She uses it already making me sleep like a bell.

All the wonderful T-shirts that will keep my shirts tucked in tight
And keep me real warm on the chillier nights.

The beautiful blanket, I'm so very proud of
Knowing it was made from Granny's pure love.

And last but not least, all the wonderful toys.
The activity center will bring hours of joy.

I can't wait to be held in Granny's loving arms.
And be kept entertained by Papa's known charms.

I'll see you both soon, I can hardly wait.
Thanks again for the gifts they are absolutely great.

Valerie Mueller

The Eagle

You just can't keep an eagle in a cage
All you will hear from him are screams of rage
Eagles were made to fly high up in the sky
Born on wings so strong
To the place where eagles belong
Soaring through the air sublime
Where only eagles dare to climb
Climbing to the highest heights
In freedom's heady, joyous flight
You just can't keep an eagle in a cage.

Cages are for lesser birds
Birds whose doubts and fears prefer
The comfort of a cage, secure
Where there's no lack of food and drink
And you don't even have to think
About tomorrow's needs and care
For there is always someone there
Supplying dainties that you crave
It's safe — but dull — within a cage

No, you jut can't keep an eagle in a cage.

Thomas P. Matthews

Untitled

The spiritual man embodies and encompasses
All time, All space.
He is without limits and is part of the
Total spiritual substance, existence,
And energy.

Man's ability to be in complete harmony with that
Truth, frees the thought to become
At-one with the all of Truth. This Freedom
and harmony is not related to matter
Or body in Any form. It is pure spiritual energy,
Uplifting consciousness,

To the Unlimited freedom. This state of Freedom
is achieved through the focus of
Thought on the Universal Flow of positive Truth,
expressing the at-one-ment of
All things—one to all, and
All things—all to one.

Robert Westover

Tears That Have Taught

Just the thought of the Holocaust can bring tears to someone's eyes,
All the pain and mourning and breaking of family ties.
Although the reign of Hitler scared us all,
There are many valuable lessons to be learned by his fall.
To stand for your beliefs no matter what the price may be,
Not let your fears take over then become what others want to see.
Family and friends you must love the most,
Not a necklace of gold or earrings of diamonds that you can boast.
In times of pain and sorrow,
Live in hope for the day, worry not about obstacles of tomorrow.
By having the courage and will to live,
One will survive to maybe forget and hopefully forgive.
No longer should society hold prejudices against entire religious
   groups or dare to try,
To extinguish millions at once, that do not deserve to die.
And when there are times our leaders question moralities,
And bring our countries close to war and casualties,
They should consider options big and small,
And realize the past should be a hint to all.
S their fights and trials they soon should cease,
   to call our world to peace.

Susan Reeder

A Poem For Thought

God created the earth, the stars in the heavens,
all the living things that exist on this earth.
Like the trees, the flowers, the clouds in the skies
all these wonders, to see with our eyes.

We should awake to the realization, what life is all about.
It's caring about each other, without a doubt.
Hypocrisy, cheating, killing, lying are bad,
those who do these things, make everybody sad.

To stop all the greed and wars on this earth
'cause where is the profit, and what is it worth?
Walking in peace, and loving each other
like a mother and father, and sister and brother.

Trying to live together, all races and creeds
will make it a wonderful, place indeed.
If we don't learn all this, we will suffer a great loss
until we begin to learn, who is the boss. "It's God."

Robert L. Gerber

"The Beauty Of A Rose"

The beauty of a rose is like a breath of spring,
All that you can do is to just keep wondering;
It grows in flower gardens or in pastures far and wide,
The rose must know its beauty
Because it does not try to hide;
If it could find a place to hide
Do you not suppose, you would ever see anything
Like "The Beauty of a Rose."

It goes to sleep in winter
Beneath the freezing snow,
And when it's good and ready
It decides on where to grow;
If it could bloom all year
Through rain and snow and heat,
I would say to that beauty
Nothing could compete;
Just don't think about the cold
Or when the ground is froze,
But wait till spring and you will see
"The Beauty of a Rose."

Shawn P. Travis

Broken Heart Farmer

A walk alone in the paths,
all I see is broken glass.
A farmer in his field I
stop no, I yield.
I think about you again,
those memories don't stop them.
I see a heard of cattle
grazing, then my heartbeat raising.
I remember our old farm
as I wish there was no harm.
Your memories I can't put behind.
There's always farm things, it's so unkind.
How can I forget you now.
When the path I take somehow,
always ends up tractors, cows,
and farms in my sight.
Oh what a fright!
I wish they were all gone away.
Then your memories
couldn't stay.

Stephanie Hager

Our Summer Friends

Their omniscient coverage of the blackened
air bedazzled my youthful eyes.
Noiseless, yet almost blaring
with the attitude of imprisonment.
Being shorter than the stump
I proceeded to dance with dusk,
and asked aloud to seize these lanterns of the
sky. In my palms, these faceless candles of
the night, I would collect, and then set free
with slight of breath, running and skipping
to the flickering of their light.
I could be the ruler of this land at night.
When ma would call, in a punctured jar I'd save
one, to come with me to my world,
to hover as I slept.
Dad could close my door tonight,
for I had my summer friends
to watch me as I prayed...

B. Thomas Whitney

A Love, Forever, Will Last

She looked so innocent
Adorned in a garb of wintry white.
Sparing nary a glance.
A stranger to chance.
Unsuspecting pawn, on an intricate board.
Victim of a turbulent strife.

Passing of time, eased not the ache.
Tragedy scorned, belittled by fate.

The circling Earth, so little has changed.
Forsaken by God, and loss is His bane.

Resolution come swift, onward the game.
A change from within, again, never the same.

The end of ambition.
The shedding of an impractical mask.
Once more they meet.
Star-crossed union complete.
Her tormented heart, with her healer at hand.
A love, forever, will last.

Patrick J. Carney

Untitled

I've walked alone, casting shadows
across the path of time,
That men may know, their highest destiny
Reaches to the very stars, the sun the moon,
by way of God.

I've walked alone, that men may know.
The power that rules the devastating storm,
the gentle rain, the snows,
Lie in the hearts and minds of those
Who find their God.

I've walked alone to bring the lights and
prove the written words.
Making clear the pathways to those
highest goals
For those bright shining living souls,
that's found their God.

Rosemary Shannon Miller

Foot Falls Upon Stone

The sound of the music made me think
About the night and what had happened there.
My smile faltered.
My face fell.
The world held still that moment and led me to pondering,
About crystal clear streams.
And strips of paper blowing in the wind to God knows where.
And sticking in my mind was the face of the thing that grew there.
Feasting on rage and despair,
Cowering in cool beams of moonlight,
Only waiting for the clouds to pass over.
To cover the watching eyes in the tower,
Where steaming hearts intertwine in a story of love.
Where? Keep still. It will pass.
Not pausing for the storm,
Passing only for silver in a river crossed,
By strangers and a wave of peace lapping the shores of sand.
Heated pools. She renders me.
And I watch her from the shadows as she curls her fire
Into shapes familiar but unrecognizable in the mist.

Torger Eric Lewis

Life Flows

From its birthplace near the clouds
   a wind-tired autumn leaf settles
   without hurry or sound onto the cold river.

Tea-brown water hurries who-knows-where
   carrying the leaf on rocky rollercoaster rides
   with bubbles by the billion
   who dance and die in split seconds.

Great grandfather catfish patiently ponder prey
   where the river runs slow, and deep, and dark.

Ageless boulders wear away without worry;
   gravel can't remember when they were
   big enough for young poets to sit on.

E. Richard Kirkley

Ode To Trinidad

Walking along the road in Trinidad
   A typical, tropical day that wasn't bad
The splendorous setting of the countryside
   Inspired a feeling that I cannot hide
The people gathered here from every race
   Have all decided that this is the place
The moonlight, the white sands, the green countryside

Blazing hot sun, follow that one,
   The road to the right, until it is night,
Silhouetted palms wave in the moonlight
   Tropical sweet madness

Swaying their hips, shining red lips
   The tropical heat, that hypnotic beat,
Of drums and distant shadows in the moonlight tropical sweet madness.

   Beat the feet, ain't it sweet,
Get right with 'em, in the rhythm

Bright colored frocks leave work from the docks,
Provision safari all sing while they carry
The dance ends, and there's petrified black shadows
Tropical sweet madness.

Sylvia Wright

Separation

Where is the night taking me?
A tunnel of fascination, into the stars.
Leaving the cold air of earth,
going to the sunshine of dreams.
Whirlwind of colors splash in the imagination.

Where is the night taking me?
Up and far away from the dark.
Taking me inside myself, inside the glow of emotion.
The sky engulfs me.
Leaving the fear,
I look to the inner fire of my soul
and fly away.

S. Krista Owens

"Rachel"

I look upon my daughter's face
A touch of her hand, a glance of her smile
made my life so very worthwhile.

Yesterday, Rachel was a child
Today at eight; caught in between
the child and the teen.
See her grow at such a fast pace
My daughter's life has become a race.

Rachel's hopes and dreams might not come true
Someday she'll be taken from me and you.

With your hand of love upon her
Rachel might live and grow stronger
Please Dear GOD - keep your touch
I love my daughter very much.

Sandra Brooks

Accepting Challenges

There comes a time whether night or day
a time for a decision to be made

To accept a challenge whether right or wrong
can be disastrous or make you strong

Accepting challenges is a way of life
accepting it now is all right
but putting it off till tomorrow you see can be
as dark as night.

But let it be known that I accept these
challenges now for tomorrow will come
and I can wear a crown.

Accepting challenges is okay
as sure as there is light during the day
but remember this and remember it well
do not accept the challenge of a black rose smell.

Priscilla Quezada

Father's Day

Father's Day
A day to honor fathers for all
they do for their children.
Yea, my father has done an awful lot for me.
So why don't I feel like celebrating him?
I used to know I could never thank him enough
Now I know.....
I hate him
How do I say it—can I say it?
Father's Day
Happy Father's Day, Dad
Thank you for raping me?

Violet R. Schulert

Migration

I had this dream.
A surrealistic journey through time and space.
A fantasy, phantasm, imagination.
The destination; a most peculiar place.
I woke inside your head.
Climbed the walls and delved deep into your brain.
Consciousness, reasoning, your intellect.
I traveled inward, wishing not to cause you pain.
This tale of mystery is all true.
Scientifically, an odyssey of the mind.
Intuition, thought, and understanding.
Past inabilities, we leave them behind.
I lay there relaxed and voiceless.
Sleepy and dreamy, I lay there woolgathering.
Fantasize, desire, and hope.
In utter harmony I'm traveling.
Soon it will end, my voyage through time, space.
I've conquered every theory in your span.
Distance, scope, extent.
Leaving you I forget my traveled lands.

T. John Taylor

The Christmas Moment

There stirs within each one of us
a strange and wondrous desire to touch
the Night and Nights, oh Christmas Eve,
and be granted peace without reprieve.

And while I ponder your mystic code
and what had happened that day of old;
how on that Night, a Babe was born
to save a world so very forlorn.

I sit in silence and you deafen my heart.
You hold so much you make my mind dart;
in and out of your magical trance...
my body's so still, yet I want to dance.

Just for that moment amid holiday hustle
my spirit's at peace and not in a tussle.
My soul do I offer...it's yours for the taking;
yet deep inside me, my being is quaking.

For I have in my presence the essence of life;
the reason, the purpose of all joy and all strife.
Mold me and shape me to your desire;
keep me at peace 'til next I inquire.

Stephen Troychak

Australian Pines

Through spring swept, tangled hammock, to a clearing dark and deep
A spring wind blows old days back to me, a memory clear, complete.
Sweet cedar spray in school book pressed, so like this scent sublime,
that comes today from airy shapes, these trees named Australian pines.

They seem to straggle o'er the plain like a wandering wood nymph lost,
in South land bright, not knowing quite, this clime of tropic coast.
Still now they wave their dark green drapes and sway and seem to race,
ahead of shadows, hue and shapes that lean in flowing grace.

For now they stand in reverence while sunset shadows make,
a painting grand of slender pines beside the silver lake.
Through dark dimmed, tangled hammock my spirit hears, from deep...
the spring wind humming vespers and mystic hymns so sweet.

I cannot move, I cannot breathe from the Eye that ever sees
for I am a blinded, raptured, stilled by that music in the trees.
Soft needles gently spatter down to cover o'er woodland shrines
and against the sky in dim relief, tree-shapes...these Australian pines.

Timothy R. Birch

Smile

The warmth of a down comforter - the comfort of a hug
A sensual kiss
The things we cherish most

A beautiful dawn - an outrageous dusk
Watching the stars as they dance
The things we cherish most

Life is simple, if we'd only let it be
Life is happiness, if we could only see
Life is what you want it to be

The cry of a child - The beauty of a song
The tears of joy as a new life is born
Life is what you want it to be

I sit in my chair so comfortable and safe
I wrap my arms around a pillow and cross my legs
I think of all the things my life could be
I look around at what I see
I am blessed that I am me

A good book, a hot cup of tea
A comforting song, followed by a SMILE.

Paula Y. Thomas

Envisions

Antagonizing thoughts in a world so gloom.
A rose, its falling petals, with chances so slim.
Rivers flowing, without knowing.
My brother's there, but who would care?
His sinking cries, his last goodbye.
The trees they whisper my silent sounds.
Their branches hold me, so I can't be found.
My thoughts are heard through earth itself.
It's my turn now, and no one else.

Xanthea McKenzie

The Day We Buried You

It rained the day we buried you;
a rain so hard it's called a storm.
With black umbrellas and black overcoats
your friends and family joined and mourned.

Our tears unfolded in the rain;
a flow that blended with our pain.
With distraught sadness we said good-bye
farewells appropriate for those who die.

Your funeral was so elegant;
symbolic of how much you meant.
The service was tailored just for you;
and all participants knew what to do.

Saint Joseph's Church was all adorned
with lovely flowers from those who mourned.
And, Father Michael from Saint Mary's Church
officiated your mass and final rite.

Loma Vista was chosen for your resting site;
a beautiful green setting to your delight.
The rain pounded as they lowered you down.
Our hearts halted as you hit the ground.

Raquel M. Sandoval

The Obsession

A wish granted, a dream come true,
A nightmare unleashed, that's what it was.
So badly did I want it, so badly
That I sacrificed all to obtain it.
It was a silly fancy. I know that now.
I don't even know why I wanted it to begin with.
I remember only my obsession
Eating away at my mind until there was nothing else.
I lived only to obtain it.
Finally I had it in my possession!
But only then did I realize my folly,
For only when I touched it was its secret revealed.
I tried to rid myself of it, oh how I tried!
But it was far too late.
It is almost over now.
By this time tomorrow I will be gone.
I can only hope that anyone who may find this
Will heed my warning and not be tempted
Into the same obsession that has destroyed me.

Rebecca Wolentarski

Speed Zone 1

As the scrim disappears into the overhead
a neon sign is lowered on a
braided orange silken cord
to the center of the stage. A quartet bleats a
Bach bacchanal played with their backs to
the audience and in reverse, last not
first and next to last note second and
on until the first note is last.
The audience gasps.
The sign is fashioned of glaring, common
neon green, with neon pink quotation marks,
and it reads:
  speed zone 1

Again the audience gasps.
As the star enters
he rasps in italics,
This is a document to legislate happiness,
embracing a nosegay of poison ivy
and dead violets to his chest
The audience arises and raves applause.

E. Lee Madison

Dr. Jekyll And Mr. Hyde

Dr. Jekyll and Mr. Hyde
A mystery I'll let you decide
Which one was bad, which one was good
I guess it depends on where you stood.
One with a heart as pure as snow.
The other spawned by the devil below.
Sharing one body all their days,
Neither agreed on the other's ways.
Mr. Hyde went to bed, but awoke as Dr. Jekyll instead.
Two minds set side by side,
Shared the body of Jekyll and Hyde.
One laughed, the other cried.
Two different people trapped inside.
They both agreed to a release,
'Twas the only way for any peace.
Dr. Jekyll said that day,
He'd kill himself to get away.
When he awoke on the other side,
There waiting for him, was Mr. Hyde

William R. Woods

Dawning Of A New Birth

Such a precious man, he came to be.
  A man who brought joy, happiness and glee,
To our lives, each and every day,
  In every thought and in every way.
A man of God who never complain,
  No matter the agony or severity of his pain.
He loved to share and to give his all,
  No matter how high the mountain or how great the fall.
He preached about courage, strength, love and salvation,
  Honesty, dignity, sin and damnation.
He always thought of others before himself,
  In spite of the situation or condition of his health.
He was such a strong man, 'twas said he had 9-lives,
  But he was just willing to do what it takes to survive.
I thought I'd see the day when he'd give me away in marriage,
  Just like the storybooks, with a white horse and carriage.
But as the days passed, I knew this wouldn't come to be.
  For the moment had come for God to set his soul free.
Now we are left to mourn and grieve here on earth.
  As his spirit arises to the heavens, the dawning of a new birth.

Vanessa McIver

Love, Not Lie

There was a proud man, a dreamer
A man ever so happily in love
She was a bright, beautiful, young woman
She filled his life with many joys
His great love really blinded him though
For he thought his feeling were shared
Through her unfaithfulness he stayed with her
He swallowed his pride and forgave her
She left him heartbroken for another man
Sorry was not enough to heal wounds
He sat around wondering how and why
Feeling lost and alone as he cried
The only relief he found from misery
Was the alcohol that helped him forget
Alone he was not though, nor lost, he had love too, he soon realized
His friends, they never left his side, they brought him through pain
They give him back his stolen pride, part of him died, he thought
Before, he learned that he loved only lies
The lies were the only thing dead I know now, I am always loved

Rodney Copenhaver

Curiosity

She came to us as a homeless stray,
A little brown dog with no place to stay.

I found her on our porch one cold Christmas Eve,
Holding up her paw she seemed to say, please,

Don't turn me away for I'd surely die,
I've no place to live no place to lie.

My tummy growls for I'm so hungry,
Please will you take me in and help me?

Well, there I stood what could I say,
I couldn't close the door and turn her away.

So, I invited her in she didn't bark nor bite,
And I lead her to my kitchen she had a big appetite.

And when she finished her meal, she looked up at me true,
With her big brown eyes that said "thank you."

Now, I welcomed my guest though with thorns and fleas,
And after a warm bath she curled up in the chair with me.

And since that day nothing more could be,
Any happier than my dog I named "Curiosity."

Shirley Mellette

A Mother's Day Wish

A day for you to call your own.
A day in which Father Time would be stagnant.
A day for Mother Nature to cradle you in her bosom.
A day to hear your laughter echo through the ears of all.
A day filled with more beauty that the heavens could hold.
A day for you to shine more brilliant than the stars.
A day for you to applaud your life accomplishments.
A day your loved ones realize their blessing.
A day for you to experience a blizzard of wealth.
A day a spring shower washes away your pain and sorrow.
A day for you to capture and relish for all eternity.
A Mother's Day as precious as the gifts of life you bestowed.

Rosemary Andrews-Sibbering

Into The Mind

There is a place inside my mind, I know it well.
A dark, gloomy room, covered in dust. Here dwell
The memories of a lifetime—the people, sounds,
Colors, shapes and smells. Swirling mist surrounds
These, engulfs them, sweet, dark, haunting embrace.
If only I could reach them—touch them—this place
So well hidden, but I know full well it is there,
Secret hideaway, awaiting my arrival, where
I will be home, the place I long to go.
It is the place I have sought for so.

Down this street I walked, one time. I knew it well.
It was my street; my home; my life. Cast off this spell
Of ages that makes it strange, and stranger yet the faces
Of people I have met. I do not know them; nor places
I oft went—they are unfamiliar, foreign, frightening.
As though I've lost my mind; then, perchance enlightening
Me, I realize this is not the place I sought for so,
This room-a cell-is not the place I want to go—
No comfort here, just cold unfamiliarity.
Be gone, callous thief; bittersweet senility.

Todd A. Sponsler

Unanswered Questions

Why did God make such funny things,
a cow that moos, a bird that sings?
What was the need for toads or frogs,
cats or pigs, or puppy dogs?

Was God searching for a recipe
to be molded into you or me?
Miracles of sight and sound,
tall or short, thin or round?
Each a loving human being,
filled with ideas worthy of freeing?

Is life a game? Players we are?
We live, we die, but few break par?
Eighteen holes with plenty of rough,
will the game make us scream... enough? Enough?
Or will we keep trying for the hole in one,
with the odds against us, 'til the game is done?

Robert N. Taylor

Weed

By the curb at the bus stop
A burst of shooting stars,
Of fireworks paused at the moment of
    explosion
Myriad of snowflakes bound to earth by
    root and stem
A festival of joy...
Above the litter of cigarette butts,
    gum wrappers, old lottery tickets,
The pristine wheels of Queen Anne's Lace:
Elegant, impartial nonchalant.

Virginia Layefsky

A Hobo's Head Of Hair

Often I have wondered, why I rarely see,
A bum who doesn't have, better hair than me.

He may be sick in body, with a distorted mind,
Resulting from his taking drugs or drinking too much wine.

He's filthy and disheveled, from living on the street,
Scavenging in garbage cans for something he can eat.

His teeth are gone or rotted, with terrible decay,
Smoking cigarettes that people throw away.

His life is without purpose, and every day's the same,
A struggle for survival in the sun or rain.

But in spite of his dilemma, with a life in disrepair,
He never seems to have a problem with his hair.

For though it's often dirty, and in total disarray,
Usually it's bountiful, and rarely is it grey.

Now truly I have pity for hobos that I see,
Unfortunately miserable, when compared to me.

But still with all my blessings, I'm shamefully aware,
Of feeling jealous when I see a hobo's head of hair.

Richard B. Waton

Ballad Of Gettysburg

A long time ago on a field or two,
A battle raged to decide a war,
It lasted three days and the bullets flew,
It started on the first of July and lasted more.

The Rebs ran into a Yankee group,
The Yank calvary made a stand,
The Union couldn't hold and almost formed a hoop,
At dusk the first day closed with a prayer on hand.

The second day pointed to Union victory,
Atop a little hilltop,
Where battle raged within the hickory,
Then came night and battle came to stop.

The third day was to decide the fate,
The Rebs charged from way over there,
It was Armistead and Garnett and all their mates,
The charge failed and the Union hats were thrown into the air.

Ryan Thomas Drummond

"Free"

  My home is one big heartache a place of steel and stone,
a barren cell a home in hell and here I sit alone.
  For two small crimes I pay with time where lights glare night and
day, and though I rage pace my cage I still must stay and pay.
  My home in hell is one small cell which no man wants to own,
my body is cramp and cold and damp that chills me to the bone.
  I hear the being the metal ring of keys in metal locks,
the scrape of feet upon concrete as guards patrol the blocks.
  Convict knives take human lives no jungle holds more danger,
and everyday that comes my way each man remains a stranger.
  I watch my back because there's lack of man who can be trusted.
  They came today and took away the man who lived next door,
to end his strife he took his life he could not take no more.
  Brother, if something fatal should come my way should someone take
my life, please tell my momma I loved her so and forget the bloody knife.
  For I was glad for all we had and all she done for me
and though I'm gone one thing lives on my love eternally.
  My one desire should I expire no one cries for me,
Just take my memory in your heart and know that I'm finally "FREE"

William A. Cornelio III

Devin Is Eleven!

The years have past so quickly and I think back when you were only
2 and you couldn't even tie your shoe.

You're now growing up to be quite a beautiful young miss with eyes
so pretty and a smile that everybody wants to kiss.

My love for you is so clear and know that when I'm around you
have nothing to fear.

The happiness you bring me with just the touch of your hand is why
I think you are so grand.

Our daily route to school and back is always a pleasure, for we get
to visit and that is something I treasure.

Let's toast and raise our glass as fifth grade is in the past and
you'll soon be entering the sixth grade class.

You're truly like a flower that blooms every spring, for your face
reminds me of the soft petals and all the love you bring.

Eleven years ago you entered my life filling it with so much cheer
and throughout the rest of my life I hope you will always be near.

My love for you need not be spoken and my belief in you will never
be broken.

Devin, you are in my heart and soul for you're my ocean of sparkling
water and I'm so blessed that you are my daughter.

Rita K. Rayl

Blue Venetians

Through a life of indecision, full of grace and comprehensions;
tattered, torn and full of tensions, I have found that it has pensions.

Figures from the truth and lies bind my mind in silent cries.
A life must live and then will die in the silence of our lullabies.

I have waited out my wants, lived in doubt with all the taunts.
I have in mind a lot of thoughts, found in love my scattered haunts.

When once I prayed, now I seek my independence shy and meek.
When Cries of love will slowly leak, the time is here as I feel weak.

My life I say would be fulfilled if thoughts confusion could be
    peeled, pondered out and then be sealed.
As it is I have to yield.

Love and hate are just emotions in a bottle full of potions.
It rubs off just like a lotion. If had the feeling been a notion.

The stars that light the unlit sky, the moon the planet passes by,
the sun will shine the rays will fly, a love to share will someday die.

I have fears of unknown reason that change throughout each passing season.
I pulled the blinds, my Blue Venetians,
to hide my face from all the treason.

For love I find will always be, a frightful scene to this I see.
The sectioned feelings that will flee, until I find the untouched key.

Toni Ann Gilmore-Shourds

At My Fingertips The Shadows

At my fingertips the shadows have gathered and here they have made
    their home
And at the bottoms of my eyes they have escorted themselves thereto and ever
    after I must pledge allegiance to them as I go about;
To the bottoms of my teeth, like the serenade of trains or like the
    colors of subways
    pushing through their pre-ordained tunnels to the next station where
    the dead
    gather in appeasing hordes, the dark
Collects in my mouth and I can hear the darkness screaming.

A. Benington Flynn

Where Has Mother Gone?

She can't find the bathroom now, in a house she's lived for years.
Someone must stay awake half the night to relieve her many fears.
She doesn't know where the dishes go, in a kitchen she's worked in so
long, and everyday we ask ourselves where has Mother gone?
Her eyes are empty now, for us she does not see. She spends her time
searching for the family that used to be.
She asks where has Mother gone? She saw her yesterday,
and where have the children gone that she just sent out to play?
She has her coat within her grasp to go anytime, anywhere,
forever looking for the family that isn't there.
To her, we are strangers, in a world that's hers alone. She seems
destined to keep searching for the place that she calls home.
The white house upon the hill she says, the one we never knew.
She must help her mother with the children, she says,
though we know this can't be true.
Her mother died many years ago; the children are all grown.
Oh why does she keep searching for the place that she calls home?
With life comes many heartaches, but few that can compare,
to the mother who is still living, but whose mind has gone ELSEWHERE.

Vera E. Killman

"My Dragons and Wizards..."

I love all my Dragons, my Wizards and Castles,
One of many reasons, is they give me No Hassles.
They don't try to hurt me or tear out my heart,
Each of them are special, to me, right from the start!
Many people have given them to me because they care,
I love it when my friends come over and stare,
They all make me feel good in their own little way.
I'm always inviting many more to stay.
Sadly enough, a few fell victim to Crime,
They were stolen from me by the worst kind of Slime!
It doesn't seem to matter, their molecular Structure or Cost,
I just know I'm deeply saddened if any are lost.
The Dragons represent Strength and Devotion,
Which seems to directly link to my own emotion.
The Wizards represent an unreachable Cunning,
Which helps me feel protected during My Life Running.
Within every Castle is a realm of its own, with space and strength to Endure,
I enjoy the entire Magical Realm,
I never want a Cure!!

Tammy S. Bills

Summer Storm

Ponderous puffs
Filled with fire and ice,
Slowly rumble toward me,
Touching treetops with blackness,
Turning green to silver as the leaves twist,
awaiting the rain.
Deep-throated growls become insistent snarls
As lightning knifes through sky and tree and my sensibility.

Now it is overhead and on every side, all wind and slanted rain,
All grey and black overshadowing the summer green.
I am serene within this chaos about me
For even now I see the leaves as silver, no longer grey.

The western sky softens to a smoky haze
And snarls are muted to mere grumbles in the east.
The rain begins to taper, too.
A streak of sun plays on a leaf.
The last rain
touches the grass
as gently
as
the
dew.

Sydni Ann Shollenberger

A Journey's End

I fall adrift into unknown
a vast and endless space
aah 'tis good to be alone
and free from human race

Quiet and solitude
a rest from frightful things
there's beauty in this blackened place
a heaven with virgin peace

Shh.. listen do you hear
the hushing quiet of the stars
falling still but ever fast
as night sneaks by thy ears

Yet past the black of night shines clear
a star with brilliant radiance
a beacon shining in the night
to mark an end of journey's flight

For in the still dark quiet tomb
begins the stirring of a soul
fed by light of love and truth
a life born free from maiden's womb

Thomas C. Bremer

To A Retiring Teacher

There are no medals for teachers
So we can't give one to you.
The bronze star you've earned for valor
Shines in a child's eyes—his love so true.
You distinguished service cross
Are those pupils you've sent afar,
They look back and remember
How patient and loving you are.
The purple heart is for soldiers
Whose bravery goes beyond words.
But a teacher gets the child's laughter
Sweeter by far—than the clash of swords.
FAITH, PATIENCE, COURAGE, AND WORK
These are the things you've shared.
How happy you made many a child
By letting him know that you cared.
So GOOD LUCK to you. The BEST of HEALTH
And TIME to do the things you've planned.
It's people like you we need today
In this——our impatient land.

Pauline M. Phillips

Someone Special

Someone special is someone you love,
Someone you dream and highly think of.
You know that person will always be in your heart
Cause they've been there from the very start.
I love you more than words can say.
But I never knew I felt that way.
I know how much I feel for you,
You know, no one else will ever do
You know one day I'll get up and leave.
I'm telling you this to save you the grieve
Just think of the fun we had together
Cause I'll always love you forever and ever
And now it's time for me to say goodbye,
Just hold your tears and don't ever cry.

Jenny de Guzman

Cool As A Lemon-Drop!

You come cool as a lemon-drop,
Soothing, dripping with absurd lies and
Half truths; talking yourself into a
coma, saying you are hand-picked among
the races to be more than just another someone!

You cloud yourself with irreplaceability,
Thinking no one could possibly assume
Your empowered, unique nature, apparent
Only to you, and no other.

You speak with repugnance about the
Reality surrounding you, how nothing
is able to capture your complexity
No matter how simply it is fashioned.
You mask yourself the master, eluding
all the while, the true emptiness that
remains apparent in your reflection!

Kasanda D. Chisambisha

A Father And Son's Love

The love between a father and a
son is a very deep love. The older
you get, and the closer to death you
get the more a father and son love
each other. When kids are young they
can be hard for their parents to take
care of but the older they get the
more they regret all the bad things they
did in life.

That is all I have to say about a
father and son's love.

Nicholas Eugene Holderman

"Words"

Words...
Sometimes words make people sad.
Sometimes words are confusing
it can make a person happy
it can break a friendship
I hate myself for saying the wrong thing
I put myself down so hard,
when I feel like somebody hates me.
Then there are the words that make things right,
but I can't find them and the words I say
are not right and cause suspicion.
There are key words that make people feel good such as
love, happiness, and the right words for the right time.
But sometimes, when will I ever shut up.

Jevin W. Caras

It's In My Heart

Sometimes I can't tell them, the words just aren't there,
Sometimes I want to, but the words give me a scare.
I'm sure they must know it, we're not far apart,
They must know I love them cause it's in my heart.
The days seem to grow longer, when I'm feeling blue,
The nights never ending, when I'm not near you.
I know you can feel it, I know cause your smart,
You must know I love you, cause it's in my heart.
Many times I feel it, it's so very strong,
Two voices inside, ones right and ones wrong.
Sometimes I can feel them, I don't know where to start,
I know that I love them, cause it's in my heart.
The happiness comes, it comes everyday,
And with it comes sadness, in its own special way.
Our family's important, not to be torn apart,
We must love one another, cause it's in my heart.

Joy Montarbo

Our Pledge

Though many moons
Have come and gone
My love for you
Goes on and on.

And though the sun
Won't always shine
We know for sure
You will be mine.

We've worked and played
And had our fun
But never left
Our tasks undone.

The years have gone
And time has passed
But we both know
Our love will last.

Eleanor Persigehl

Reciprocation?

When everything you've lived for
   Has turned to ashes
Love dies hard.

When you strive to find
   A corresponding spark
In those you love
   Love dies hard.

When whatever you do seems useless
And no one is there to respond
   Love dies hard.

When whatever you have done in life
   Is for love -
Love dies hard.

Betty K. Talbert

Indifference

Lonely is the man who,
has tasted love, but has none.
Feelings died long ago,
but life had just begun.

Dangerous is he who walks alone,
yet survives the passing storm.
indifferent to the Pain he's caused,
and likely to cause more.

Love and Hate, are one the same,
they both show some concern.
But indifference is a whole new world,
One in which Hell still burns.

So beware of he that is lonely,
Who couldn't care if he were dead.
When brought before the Pits of Hell:
He'd throw you in instead.

Dannie Cox

Moments More To Go

At ten years old my life did change.
From not knowing a words to prize range.
You see, I had a aneurysm to fight.
But learned in time and light.
The doctor said a baby won't
be in the picture, you see.
A son and granddaughter is in my bee.
Now life is good and over fifty.
Life is a challenge and nifty.

Colleen Schauff

"I Have Your Love"

Although the road of life is
hard, I have your hands to
hold, I have your warm and
loving arms when all the world is cold.

And when my special dreams
come true, you celebrate with
me, the happiness in my
heart, on your dear face I see.

When problems seem to get
me down, I have an awful
day, you help me find my
solutions, then you kiss my tears away.

No matter what the future
may hold, I know your love
is true and sweet, and whether
I succeed or fail I can depend on you.

And every night I bless your name,
while counting the stars above.
And everyday I thank the Lord for sending
me your love.

Amy N. Wix

Gift From A Four Year Old

The four-year old
Handed me the box,
Wrapped in a multitude
Of colorful hair ribbons.
"Wrapped it myself, Momma.
Special,
Just for you!"
As I carefully untied each ribbon,
Her eyes sparkled with pride and
Scarcely contained excitement.
When the last ribbon dropped away,
And the lid fell to the floor,
Out,
   Hopped
   A
      Bewildered,
      But
         Liberated,
         Frog!
Alice L. Thompson

My Perfect Man

Eyes of hazel
Hair of brown
I love your smile
Please don't frown.

You're sweet and cute
Adorable, too.
If only I
Could be with you.

Words don't explain
The way I feel.
Believe me
My feelings are real.

I won't say it's love
It hurts too much.
Trust me I know
I've tried such.

Give me a chance
I'll prove to you
That my heart
Can be true.

Catherine Chaney

Present Life

Today's life has,
gotten fast paced,
No one cares about,
the human race.

We only care about ourself,
and put the others on the shelf.
Why can't we all get along,
and dance around to a beautiful song.

Erin Evanoff

The Rose

The rose
God's perfect flower
So treasured
So sacred
Given by the right person
The rose
Means love
One rose is more special
More meaningful
Than one hundred
Though the rose will
Wither and die
The memory of the love shown
Still lives.

Dana White

Untitled

The summer's eve showers
glistens on the leaves,
as gently to earth
the rains fall.
The parched earth,
absorbs the moisture,
like we absorb
our love.
Like a sponge
filling its hollows,
We fill our emptiness.
As nature's love
to the earth,
The showers give
newness and life
to nature's beauty below.
As our love, my dear,
gives us newness
and life inside.

Elaine Morrill

Moonlight On The Snow

Moonlight on the snow
Gave a haunting new glow
To the world it had caught
And designs it had wrought.
Majestic were the trees
That knew last summer's breeze
And the homes on the hills
Wore white windows of frills.
Big snowmen like guards
Stood in all of the yards
While their small artists' heads
Lay asleep on their beds.
The stillness and hush
Eclipsed life's daily rush
And I knew in that hour
God's wonderful power,
For only He could throw
Moonlight on the snow.

Eleanor VanFleet Forehand

Arms Of Love

As I sit here beneath the stars,
  Full of thoughts and fears,
I am wishing more and more,
  That you were with me here.
I cover up the try to keep warm,
  And then I stare above,
My mind wanders far away,
  Into your arms of love.
We walk by the lake, hand in hand,
  Underneath the moon and stars,
Free from all my worries,
  The night is completely ours.
We lay in the grass cuddling,
  To the right of us a dove,
You hold me tight, you hold me near,
  you hold me in your arms of love.
We get up, and walk again,
  Admiring the reflecting lake,
The night ends with a hug,
  and a gentle kiss, and then I awake.

Autumn Rodriguez

I Heard The Bird Sing

Lonely, dazed and confused
from the illusions of reality.
I heard the bird sing,
it sang of peace, happiness,
dreams, desires, and passions.
I wondered how the bird
sang without a heavy-heart
or hatred, unlike the rest of
the world that has fallen
prisoner to destruction.
I heard the bird sing
of how one glorious day
we would learn to understand
and respect each other.
With each waking moment we
must wait for that day with
open arms.
I heard the bird sing
it sang of how life should be.

ChiChi Ezeh

Mother's Nature

Mother is a part of all God's children
from the heights of Heaven they descend
within their hearts and sacred souls
they were made from mothers mould
to watch over them as they grow
that's all that mothers know
the enduring laughter and tears
the love that grows beyond years
can be seen within the child's eyes
when she first says hello or good-bye
and everything in life they do
they know mothers girl in Heaven to
send down bright eyed angels to ensure
that mothers parting memory will endure.

Daniel Thurber

Untitled

Why is a robin's
egg always robin's egg blue?
Celestial genius!

Ernest P. Bicknell

Desert Crossing

We crossed the desert in a Land Rover
From Seba to Brak and back—
It was a regular passenger service,
And of passengers there was no lack.

We set out on a flat rough dirt track
With palm trees and bushes at hand.
But we would see in the distance
The dunes - pink mountains of sand.

The dunes kept getting closer,
I thought surely we'd go around,
But no! We went right up and over-
The passengers made not a sound.

The soft and sand can fool even experts,
As our driver discovered too late.
The Rover went down to the floor boards,
Was being stuck in the Sahara our fate?

We all piled out of the Rover
So as to lighten the load.
We finally continued our journey,
BUT NEXT TIME I'LL go by the ROAD!

Adelle L. Nelson

Love

Love is like a pretty rose,
Forever smelling sweet,
See how mighty proud it grows,
It knows not how to weep.

Love is like a summer sky,
Before the night sets in,
When two hearts pause to hear,
The soft stirring wind.

Love portrays a lonely isle,
Touched only by the sea,
When just a simple smile,
Can do so much to me.

Precious words are dear,
But only eyes can tell,
If love is truly there,
Or is it just a spell.

Brenda G. Munford

Youth And Time

Ravage on Dear Youth,
For the dawn is not yet here.
Stomp your feet in the ash,
Watch the fire disappear.

Then stand naked in stillness
And listen to the silence.
It will come from deep in your mind.
You will hear an encore of violence.

It will be a haunted joy,
For the trees will bear no fruit.
There will be broken glass and mortar,
As you begin to built from the root.

Fear not the accusation,
For you will be beyond the age.
Guilt will be pointed to youth
And you will be among the enraged.

August S. Fontaine

Colour Blind

Together they set sail,
For a land out of sight.
Where it did not matter,
Whether it was dark or bright.
The land behind them,
Held discriminating scorn,
For the contrast they made,
Was too much to be borne.
The wind and the sea,
Gave them a rough time.
They faced it together,
Nature drew no dividing line.
Their destination seemed distant,
As day turned to night,
But a dream was unfolding,
In a graying twilight.
We must create a land,
With no shades of spite,
To dock a ship carrying,
A black and a white.

Anuradha Sundararajan

Butterflies

Butterflies, butterflies
Fluttering in the sky
Flying by, way up high
Makes me wish I could fly
Oh me! Oh my!
Still makes me wish I could fly.
Oh me! Oh my! Now I can fly!

Adam Robert Brown

Lesson In Plaid

I saw his wrinkled plaid shirt,
Flung so carelessly on the corner of
The chair, one arm folded
Underneath in a painful twist,
The other arm wrapped around the
Cushion holding on for dear
Life, while the rest dangled
Precariously off the back,
Fighting the weight of the world
Trying to pull it down to earth,
And I knew it was time to
Move on, move on like that
Song from that musical, lest
I get tossed aside as easily
As that poor plaid shirt.

Allison Boye

Friendship

Friendship is like a river.
Flowing, never ending,
straight to the ocean.
Talking and joking,
with lots of emotion.
Like the river sending,
mental notes and thoughts,
of yesterday's memories.
The river knows,
and shows,
the past left behind.
Our friendship too will hold,
all the memories,
and secrets that we have told.

Erica Jones

Burned

Beautiful words
flow from your tongue
and drip like honey
onto my soul.
Stinging eyes pierce my mind
but your touch cannot compare.
Silk skin,
smooth lace love,
move my flesh,
white pale mounds.
Mold me like clay.
Sin
desire
Burnt by your fire.

Charleen Warford

Untitled

Those who believe
find comfort in
knowing that life
is neatly wrapped up
bound in chapter
tied with verse
see here in
black and white
all things revealed
no why to wonder
blessed delusion
those who believe
just believe

Colleen Bergey

The Final Chapter

He speaks
Few listen
Through the conscience
Of us all
He speaks
And to the future
Not kindly
As we stumble blindly
Into the final chapter
Of our existence

Carmen Gattuso

Rooted Hereafter

Blood hair.
Fell asleep in stranger's car.
Lived in stock cavern.
Wood moist.

Crystal sandals,
leather bands,
fire field in summer sun. (Be fall)

A protector?
A killer?

Headlights in closet.
A fiction writer,
love the moonlight bridge.

Army of bronze/silver.
Rusted skin.

Crossing the burning sun.
Trumpets rising.

Adam Smith

A Vegan Anthem

Eat no carrion, seek no prey
Exploit no creature in any way;
Love the land, lakes and seas
Sky and trees and fragrant breeze.

Vegans seeking not to hurt
So enhancing everyone's worth
Detracting least from all nature
Souls can best indeed mature.

There is no need for intoxicants
Or even very mild incense,
With hearts of peace instead of war
Spirits can most surely soar.

Vegans, one feels safe with you
Your empathy is shining through
May your kindness be quickly spread
That humans might to glory tread.

Charles G. Santora

Untitled

The sun will shine,
Even when clouds are out.
It will be there to guide
Our hopes and dreams of love.

When the hail comes down,
From the dark sky above,
Just know behind the clouds
Lies the sun, the light, with love.

The roads seems so long
When you travel alone.
Just remember always and forever
That the sun will shine above.

The sun still shine,
Even when the rains fall.
It will be there to guide us
Through life, death with love.

Catherine Chen

Stars

Many people rely on a star,
Even though they are so far.
Problems they help solve,
Are sometimes not resolved.
When people are feeling gray,
They sometimes run away.
But that's not right,
So just stay and fight.
Life is rough,
But you have to stay tough!

Breanna Budde

Untitled

Hide my face from the shame,
even though I'm not to blame.
Spite the person from the dark
who put the everlasting mark;
and I know that I must live,
just like Jesus said to forgive!

Claude Randall Peerson

By My Side

You were the one who held me tight,
even if we were in a fight.
You brushed away my tears,
helped me conquer my darkest fears.
Always attempting to make me smile,
always walking that extra mile.
When my day was gloomy and bad,
you tried to make me glad.
At the times my life was good,
it was next to me, you stood.
You never had any greed,
making my life better, indeed.
If I needed to talk, I'd just call,
you never let my greatest hopes fall.
I did nothing in return,
now my lonely heart does burn.
Why did you care so much for me?
You loved me, I can clearly see.
I wish I could have said goodbye.
Please excuse me, while I cry.

Amanda N. Hansom

"Speak Your Mind"

One must always speak their mind,
   even if it cost their life.
If you speak you're
   respected and loved,
If you don't you're
   looked down upon and hated.
You can give your life to others,
   but still looked down upon,
If your feelings and thoughts
   are never spoken.
If your tongue never speaks
   your heart and soul die
Even if your body works,
   the emotions are what count.
If your heart and soul die,
   your silence has then cost
   you your life.

Cristina Ruiz

Visions In Smoke And Water

Silver strands of hair,
Ethereal,
Floating.
   Sounds,
   Strains of synthesized harmonies,
   Wafting,
   Becoming.
Amber liquid,
With green light flowing;
Light passages,
Filled with smoke rising,
Lending to a dream.
A bright blunt vision,
Revealing what you never wanted to know,
You sleep and dream again.

Anthony Hines

Human, Nature

Eyes like jonquils, shining bright
enough to light the earth.
Arms of winds, strong with might...
breaking pathways for new birth.
Tears like waters, cold and moist
to quench the suckling needs.
Voice of fire, hot and poised...
spitting destruction with such ease.

Charlene S. Flanders

"Have You Ever Wondered Why"

Have you ever wondered why
eagles have such keen eye
able to see far and wide
makes animals run and hide

Have you ever wondered why
monkeys go swinging by
at the top of the tree
just as free as you and me

Have you ever wondered why
dolphins are able to jump so high
way up in the air
imagine how it feels to be up there

HAVE YOU EVER WONDERED ...
Calvin Marquez Jr.

True Magic

Sliver of silver, surrounded by gold
Dreams of yesteryear, realities of old
Demons of heart, dragons of mind
Where is the magic to find?

Dagger of sun, shield of moon
Tears of September, lilies of June
Sweet drops of rain, blood of thine
Where is this magic of mine?

Wind of morning, breeze of love
Hell below, heaven above
Life in fall, death in spring
Where is this magic your bring?

Ocean of mermen, waters of storm
Ogres of gentleness, shadow of form
Sleep of dreams, sleep of the dead
Where is the magic to be spread?

Phantom of past, visions of pain
Blanket of night, curtain of rain
Demons and dragons of my mind
Is there still true magic to find?

Erin D. Kincannon

Sweet Dreams

I sleep restlessly
Dreamless dreams
Full of meaningless thoughts
Then I wake
To have a better day
Only to say
Good night
Then I go into flight
Maybe another dream tonight
What awaits me
Maybe a key
To yesterday
Dream of Saturday
But yet
All to say is
Sweet dreams

Angela Bechkhorot

The Violet

There is a violet in my toilet;
Don't sit down or you will spoil it.

Frank Gerulskis

Believe In Yourself

Believe in yourself.
Dream on! but make those
dreams come true.
Strive for the realization
of your goals,
You can do it!

If you're not where you
want to be today, reach deep
inside yourself and find the
answers to the question..."Why?"
You can do it if you try!

Know where you want to go,
then plot your path and find
your way to get there.
You can do it!

This is your life!
Reach for the stars...
Think success and be
successful!
You can do it!!

Eleanor A. French

Forever Friends

As we walk through those
doors tonight and say goodbye,
it won't be forever but at least
a long time. With all the looks
on our faces as we leave
our school and our friends,
but with all the love that we send.
It might be hard to say good-bye
but we will always look back with a sigh.
We have had good times
and bad times, that we
will never forget, but as
we look into the future we
will think we are all set.
We have seen each other
cry, and we have seen
each other laugh, but we
will never forget those
great times we have had.
And hope to be, forever friends.

Alice Rebbecca Scott

"Related"

Related by pain,
Distinguished by fear,
We think we love each other...
Even with my bruised face and
Your wounded pride.
The nights leave and the days come,
But the darkness never feels.
Surrounded by fear and related by pain,
That is what we are.

Elizabeth Skrzynecky

Untitled

Death came suddenly
Catching her unaware
Vanished from life
She has gone away
Gone but not forgotten
Every life she touched
Retains a memory of her.

Barbara Hughey

Red

See thing through the open world,
deliberately destructive and surreal

Friends, hostile and green,
...search... for the forbidden
plight of fellowship,

Minds; chaotically employing
dreams, disasters numb to reality;

Commitments:
pain-stakingly bold,
unpretentiously bro ken
On the void of heedence:

Time Forever troubling,
Factoring and draining
Our scheduled lives,
pulping, eating, the minutes

Laughs, cramping your style,
blurring vision unrelentlessly,
sharing togetherness.

Black, endings that come too fast,
forbidden truths wailing through the open world

Alexis Schubert

Temple Of Copan

From days of old, a mysterious
cultures hand. Between the
south and north, lays the Temple
of Copan.

Complete with books of stone.
Warring elephants, great beasts!
Sea and Land they roam.

The carving is upon the wall.
2 Thessalonians 2, eleven kings,
door in the middle to the Ball.

Opposing ships of the western
coastlands, on a man with eyes -
Mr. Mogul, the dark one, who lies.

And that observatory dome, on
high, upon the top. The one
to grow a crop. Always watching,
yes, where the stars roam.

Oh, my ancient friends, who time
parts, your message is clear, of
seven year, here where it starts.

David W. Domansky

Suppression

You cannot suppress me forever. One
day I will receive my freedom. What
will you do then? My voice will be
heard. My words listened to. I will
not break. I will fight for my freedom,
and then that of the rest. Many have
tried, many have died. That is a lot of
deaths. Still we are not all free. Will
I too die in my fight? Not important.
But I will not stop fighting. Yet, I
will die for the fight, if necessary.

Alen Mausling

"In the Beginning"

In the beginning there was God
Creator of heaven and earth
Creator of life everlasting
Creator of death and of birth

Then there will be the interim
Life on the earth that He made
Long and yet short in its term
Physical life soon will fade

Into the hours that He gave us
We must pack all it will hold
How full a book would my life make
God grant it thick to unfold

And in the end there was God
Creator of heaven and earth
All of my sins are forgiven
Right from the day of my birth

And as my one life ebbs from me
Surely He will take my hand
To guide me to my other life
In his beautiful promised land

Ellen Mooningham

Divinity

The angels flew high,
courting wings of gold.
Hearing our prayer's,
so I've been told.
With the glow of the halo
shining down on you,
your dreams are heard
and soon to come true.
The moon is their light,
and the stars their guide.
These angels know
when you have cried.
They are celestial beings
sent from above.
With only one requirement,
to watch over and love.
They float through the moonlit sky
having faith in those who sin.
These gold-winged angels
belong to God in Heaven!

Andrea Rizzo

Wrong

What is wrong with this picture
Could it be that of the light
that seems to be calling
so deep in the night

Is it my conscious
or maybe my hidden fear
Lost in the darkness
That I hold so near

Building and building
The words never said
Would it have changed or situation
Or was I being mislead?

What is the answer
That I look so hard for
Is it the truth I search
Do I really want more?

Finding what's inside
Is most important to me
Was it worth all of this
Or should we just let it be

Angela M. De Lia

The View From 280

Over the rise
Comes in sight
Green hills furrowed
By rows of white.

Here is where
We plant our young seed
These are the crops
That show our greed.

They look the same
Silent markers row on row
As throughout the world
Our military shrines grow.

What message do they give
So deaf we do not hear
As seeds and harvests
Lost from year to year.

What crop was that?
My forgetful mind inquires
As we speed on
Down the 280?

Audrey E. Harris

The Wind To A Kitten

Pussy cat,
Come close to me
And you shall see
That I can be kind.
Pussy cat,
The world of man is cold,
But when you I hold
Loving warmth I find.
When I touch you —
When I stroke you —
When I rub you gently—
Then I know the touch of love
As you purr so vibrantly...
Pussy cat,
All furry white,
Could you be so like Margaret?
Pussy cat,
Lovingly bright,
Remember this and ne'er forget:
This caprice shall always care...

Dan Leach

Dream Escape

Close your Eyes
Close them tight.
Enter a world
A world distant and new.
A world of peace
   No Animosity No War.
A world of love
   No Hate No Prejudice.

Keep them closed
And stay in this world.
A world of harmony
   Friends among All
   No Barriers to overcome.
A world of truth
   Honesty among all
   No lies to tell.
Keep them closed
And stay in this world.
Open them
and return to the real world.

Charles W. Lieble XII

Can You See What I See

Can you see what I see.
Can you open your eyes and see
What you need. Or look on a
paper and see what you think.
Can you see what I see.
All the pain in the world is
really hard to believe.
But can you see it at night in
your sleep. Or when you're
sitting around or just watching T.V.
Can you see what I see.
Any good things that you could believe.
Maybe it's hard to see what I
see. But try thinking of good things
like the sea's blue breeze. What about
poverty let there be none. Let the
sun shine real light and let the
moon sing us songs. This
may be all just fantasies but
to me it's just what I can see.

Charity L. Morgan

A Soldier

A soldier with only his faith
Can walk into the realm of death
And sacrifice all that he is
'Til his soul is the only thing left

A soldier can walk alone
With discipline as his guide
And always have confidence
For soldiering comes from inside

Face to face with destruction
Out numbered by his offender
Conditioned by his commanders
To die; never surrender

In the heat of a fearsome battle
The blood of a soldier is spilled
The thunder has turned to serenity
As God almighty has willed

A soldier has given his life
As many will have to do
And though you never knew him
He gave his life for you

Andree L. Harp

Bon Voyage My Love

We traveled many pathways
By plane, by ship, by car
The new, the strange, the beautiful
We wandered near and far.

We flew through the Grand Canyon
A splendid, awesome sight
Down to the Indian Village
To explore a starlit night.

We tossed upon the North Sea
One stormy Autumn day
To reach the Shetland Islands
Where the Shetland ponies play.

Then the great adventure
When you had to leave alone
We gathered all our courage
As you faced the vast unknown.

I see you standing on a mountain
I see you strolling by the sea
Majestic beauty all around you
Where you wait for me.

Ernestine Miller

Why??? Our Crisis On Earth

Our Earth is a failure
but what for?
We need to help our children
no more hungry and poor.

To many are out there
laying in the streets
what do you care
you only came for the treats.

Why do we do this?
There's so many in need
we all need a kiss
and we need to feed.

Come now and help me
in this war
You are the key
that's what your for.

Amber Mosier

Grief

The lilacs and roses are in bloom,
but they bring me no joy.
The spring rains echo my tears.
Pain, searing, rips through my soul.

Deloris E. Cashell

Aaron

He suffered so much,
  but no one would help.
He reached out to them,
  but still no one would help.
He was in pain,
  but no one believed him.
He had all the signs,
  but yet they said he was faking.
He died,
  and they say it wasn't their fault.
He was like me.

Carla Yannayon

The Rivals

October is delightful,
But I remember spring.
I'm a willing captive
When robins start to sing.

Then soon there come the mockers,
Cardinals and jays.
My heart is light as thistle down,
On such a gorgeous day.

I'm almost lifted off my feet,
They barely touch the soil.
I hold firmly to my spirit
And from hindering thought recoil.

Now the leaves are dipped in amber
And shimmering in gold.
They fairly sparkle in the sun,
Send out a rich red glow.

Oh, I know October's lovely,
But it's a funny thing,
Even in the midst of autumn,
I still remember spring.

Avice McDowell

After The Banquet

Mom was just Mom,
but after her speech tonight,
also to me, now,
a very brilliant someone.

Evelyn L. Strawn

Quiet Sunrises

I wish for you quiet sunrises
  bursting with color
  for only your eyes to see.

For finding humor in life
  and laughing as
  you both go along.

For mountains that say,
  "you can climb me,"
  and not to be afraid.

And for love to be
  surrounding both of you
  like wild flowers in a field
  where you stand.

Frederick W. Siebelts

Some Thought

They should all be dead
Buried
Deep in my mind
I live without them
The bad memories
They just won't die
I live with them
The good memories
Alive and well

David J. Hearndon Sr.

Fragile Dream

A dream is a fragile
Bubble flying in the air
And like some of those
Dreams they make it
Up there.

When a dream falls
Like bubbles tend to do
Then fate is saying
It shouldn't come true

If we could hold
An endless dream in our
Hands letting it not stop.
Just like a bubble
Hoping it won't pop.

Brandise Ackerman

Where's He Looking From?

It was a beautiful scene of you and me,
both naked - by our bed, on bended knee,
praying to our Father up above,
Thanking Him for peace and love.
But all of a sudden I jump to me feet!
And, just for a moment our eyes meet,
As I explain that His Majesty
Might view from behind you and me!

Anna C. Hamilton

Love And Understanding

Where did I go wrong
Bringing up my two kids
I gave up so much
I don't know what I did

I worked two jobs
So they could have
All the extra things
And they wouldn't starve

The parties alone
That I gave to them
From Burger King and Chucky Cheese
To home parties like a gem

All my love and understanding
I always listened when they spoke
A friend I was to them
Oh what a joke

My parents were right
When they would say
Don't give them so much
In the end you'll pay

Debbie Landells

Dex

Bound together you and me,
Bound together, never free.
The chains which link us together so,
Stem from the blackness in our soul.
Tied by the rage and hate we spent,
As those we trusted came and went.
Leaving us to cold despair,
They passed us by without a care.
In a world which tries to suck you dry,
Which sheds no tears for those who die.
In you I found a kindred soul,
A spirit fighting 'gainst life's hold.
Left by the world to ride the winds,
Punished for our father's sins.
Linked together from the start,
Mind to mind, heart to heart.
Bound together, yes indeed,
Now and always, you and me.

Eric Pulwicz

"The War"

The war raged on,
Blind hatred and bloodshed.
Many lost a son,
Or their arm, leg, or head.

Nations would burn.
Many would die.
Few would return.
Some wonder why.

Return would deny
Honor and glory.
Some refuse to believe
War's hideous story.

Beth Zmitrovich

Untitled

The Temple I frequent is high.
A turquoise vaulted dome, the sky.
That spans the world with majesty.
Blessing my home and family,
Friends and all of humanity.

Daniel DiCenzo

Space

Space is
Black - cold
Like the night.
Unknown to me
Like my future.
The moon is
Pock-marked with holes
Like prairie dog mounds
In grassy green fields.
The thick gray dust
Swirls and twirls
Spiraling upwardly.
From my spacecraft
I reach out
And touch the stars.

Erin Heffernan

Pride

The hidden unbreakable bond
between body and soul

It is a power all possess and
few control

It can be thrown away but
never lost.

Pride, it pushes one to strive
for great heights of personal glory

But the air is thinner at those
heights and the footing tedious.

Farther than is your fall.

Christopher Durnez

To Aleksandra - Yesterday

I went today where we once walked
    beside a little stream.
I thought perhaps that same old tree
    might harbor yet our dreams,
A heart carved deep within the wood
    to shout out loves old theme...
Oh, was that forty years ago?
    So long it does not seem.

If today we could only go
    to where we were before
And God would make us young again...
    then I would cry no more.
If we could take away the hurts,
    and undo all the wrong,
Then we could start our lives again
    and sing Deep Purple song.

Many years have now passed by
    many dreams are over due
But still a silver ring I wear...
    That says that I LOVE YOU!

Barbara Eubank Wood

horizon

i want a lover
as strange and violent as i am
a dirty flower with roots that run deep
i'm tired of girls
with china faces
and perfect calves
the horizon never ends
and i need someone who will run hopelessly
    through life

Carlin Sundell

Baby It's Cold Outside

The trees are shaking constantly
Being bullied by the bitter breeze
The wind whistling through every room
That old familiar winter tune
The air sneaking through every crack
Secretly sends chills up my back
The frost on my windows as I arise
Lets me know baby, it's cold outside
But old man winter doesn't frighten me
For your love warms and covers me
When you take me in your arms to hold
You protect me from the bitter cold
And the heat from your warm embrace
Warms me far better than any fireplace
In the warmth of your body
Is where I want to hide
Because baby, it's cold outside

Eunice Timley

Early Morning

Early morning on the porch swing,
before a busy day,
Cup in hand, ears in tune,
the smell of earths' wet clay.
Early morning on the porch swing,
memories of days gone by.
Happiness and tragedies,
I will not question why.
Nor do I dwell on long lost loves,
or what I could have had.
I simply sit and think about,
this life that's not so bad.
I would not trade this time of day,
for life's more worldly things.
There's nothing quite so soothing as,
early morning on the porch swing.

Deborah S. Sherman

The Small Tree

The tree is stripped of all its leaves
because the wind has come.
The tree is bare and was not spared
because the wind has blown.
The branches down, the tree just there
how sad it feels alone.
The sap as tears, the small tree fears
it has lost its home.
No other tree to see around
no tree to feel its pain.
Just sitting there with branches bare
not there to feel its shame.
Although it's not the small tree's fault
it still feels the guilt.
It's just the wind had blown too hard
now the tree can't be rebuilt.
The wind is gone, the season changed
now all leaves will appear.
Except the Small Tree that has died
because no one had cared.

Frances Margaret Montano

New Life Springs Forth

When spring begins to come
Beauty begins to come forth
Trees begin to bud and come to life
Blossom into many green leaves
Flowers bring forth new life
In many beautiful colors and sizes
Blowing in the wind as they shine forth
Tassels swinging in the breeze
Like silk array in the sun
There is another time in your life
If there is no beauty shining
That old life must pass away
So new life can spring forth
Search out your heart today
If not right choose God's way of life
A new array of life must be brought forth
What beauty begins to come forth
Beams of life that will last forever

Frances Walters Golmon

Untitled

A wild wind through the window
beating against the pane.
The glass broke and hit me, too,
just like the falling rain.

Suddenly, the moment came when
something touched me from behind,
A scream shot, a yell flew;
It was going through my mind.

A chilling sight of blood
took my last deep breath away
I saw the figure standing slightly.
But did not know what to say.

If ever there was a time
where death was so at hand;
I could say that this was it;
Along with the hateful hells in band.

I felt the fiery flame
But not a word could I even speak.
Finally another wild wind
Blew me to a higher peak...

Brian T. Allen

Chellsey

Chellsey is a bird that squawks,
at times I think she
thinks she talks.

About her seed, her, cage, her perch
the big brown oak, the
tall white birch.

She sighs she's rarely seen
them though
twittle through the leaves
to and fro.

I wish, I wish, I wish
it so,
But clipped wings screech
a silent "no".

It's no wonder why Chellsey squawks,
and from her cage shrill bitter mocking,
at times I think she thinks she's
talking.

Erin May

Inside The Child's Mind "Daddy"

Hello Daddy I think I know you
At least I think I do
How are you doing

I am fine clocking time
Why is it so hard for you to talk to me
That might set us both free

Please please please me
I think that you are my daddy

Don't keep me crying for you endlessly
Find me again Daddy

I love you eternally
Christo Tajin

Alabaster

I am partial to spring and autumn
as I am to dawn and twilight
(that most fleeting chance
between curtains),
as I am partial to alabaster,
soft incandescence
blending soil and light,
earth longing for sky,
glowing like yellow roses
(awash in Rain light).
Barbara Ross

Is Love Real?

There exists a man in every woman's life
As a woman in every man's
And some day it will be of necessity
To have that special companionship.

In life we have needs of someone
Or else we'll be as the living dead
Without someone to whom we can
Say: "I'll love you always".

When we do find
That certain person,
We extend our hand
To the one and only, my person.

When we are sure
Of this love,
We'll begin to doubt
Because we can't believe
That this love is real.
Carmen Ceballo

Untitled

Words, so hastily said
are instantly regretted.
So few of them can ruin a day,
a life, a friendship.

The meaning of them
twisted around until
the actual is nothing
but a broken memory—
remembered in a reverie.

Never to be felt, or heard from
Again.

Bethany Brengartner

Cirrus

When I look at you I'm amazed
and when you're down to earth
I think I can jump up and touch you
you seem so fast when you're alone
but when a bird flies by you're slow

Tell me what it's like
to go were the wind blows
to float in the air high or low
tell me all about what you hear
what you see and how it feels

But when you tell me the bad parts
I won't listen or want to know
I'll be dreaming about the good things
about how it feels to fly
and places I would go
Anthony Akers

Ode To A Teddy Bear

I enter the room
And there sits Teddy,
Fixed button eyes, ever ready

Hail to thee, oh silent one
O creature I address with abandon

For I can speak regardless of error
This Bear won't care
What is spoken

He awaits with outstretched paws
And listens in awe

Oh Bear so soft and fluffy
Oh Bear so cute and stuffy

Round brown bear, seemingly uncaring
But full of love
And ready to share with me
All my woes and cares

I salute you, Teddy Bear
With piercing stare
Oh bear extraordinare!

Barbara Bernardi Quackenbush

"Autumn Has Arrived"

The air is cool
And the sweaters are wool
The leaves are falling
And the rakes are calling
Squirrels are storing
While the kites are soaring
Soon the ghouls and goblins
Will get their treats
While the offense and
Defense put on their cleats
For autumn is my favorite season
The window view is very pleasing.
Cynthia Vargo

"Our Days"

When a day is filled with sunshine
And the air is clear and clean
I think of you
In all your beauty, and loving ways
And I know that I am blessed
For the time we spend together
And for those glorious moments
We call our days
David Bass

I'll Fly Away

I look outside
And see the sky
The moon and the stars
That are so very high
Then I dream
I'll soar away someday
Way up in that sky
So very far away
Through the sky
Away I'll go
Away from my fears
Where no one will know
Everything will be good
There will be no bad
No one to hurt me
Or make me sad
I'll say it again
I will fly one day
Where no one can reach me
I will fly away.
Amy Wernimont

The Luna Moth

He gently takes the Luna Moth,
And puts it in a sack.
This lovely little creature
Of soft green velvet wings,
Is now a prized possession, above all
other things.
To show with tender pride and joy,
To all who would behold.
Then suddenly he stops, stoops down,
And opens up the sack.
Puts in his hand and lo the moth crawls
Slowly on his hand.
With graceful arch up goes his arm.
It sweeps above his head.
The moth goes up in swirling flight,
In freedom's heady spin.
"I had to let it go you see."
The small boy simply said.
"So we will have some baby moths,
Or else they will all be dead."
Eugenia M. Garrett

Love Hurts

Love for me has come and gone
And now again, I am alone
I heard the words it's not you
But I wonder, just how true

I gave you my heart and soul
You took it and left a hole
How can you treat me this way
Why is it, I always pay

I thought for sure you were the one
I thought my life had just begun
Then just as fast you took it away
And said goodbye, see you another day

I feel like something is missing inside
And all I do is sit and cry
I try to understand what went wrong
But all I know is, you are gone
Cathy J. Welcher

"Hollow Logs"

Dreams are like hollow logs
and nightmares are reality,
life feels like a hollow log
in the land of endless fog
It's raining sweet gumdrops,
but smells like fish
in the land of endless fog

April Jackson

In Reality

Dreams break hearts
and men break vows
roses melt
and milk makes cows

And laughter hurts
and rich men lack
water runs dry
and white turns black

And old men shrink
and sun makes rain
babies die
and joy brings pain

And winners lose
and best friend lie
treasures burn
and grown-ups cry

Brooke Taylor

The Road

I travel down this lonely road
And meet no one to share my load;
But dare not let my shoulders bend,
Before I glimpse this journey's end.

It is a long and tedious way,
And none there is I might betray,
And none to care and none to know,
If I should let my burden go.

Heavy my pack of unshed tears,
Too full of my unspoken fears.
So, lonely, burdened, where go I?
Down, down this endless road - But why?

I WALK THIS ROAD IN SUN AND RAIN.
I shall not come this way again.
My weary footsteps leave no track -
It matters not - there's no way back.

Florence Morse

I Think I'll Call It Home

Lord, take me as I am
And let me go free.
For I am a child of yours
My spirit lives in thee.

How precious is thy name,
I knew to call upon You...
When my heart was filled with pain
You always helped me through.

How was I to know
When my life would end?
The day I felt no sorrow
Would be my last tomorrow.

Lord, you have brought me home
To the place...now, no more to roam.

Carrie Edwards

"Do Not Forget"

Do not forget what you are told
And know that I'm the best
For if you want to talk to me
Forget about the rest.

Remember that I kid you not
And know that I'm sincere
For you should know that I do love you
And, that you are so dear.

Do not forget my darling
"To me you're everywhere."
"The inspiration that I have
comes only when you're there."

Ali K. Maksad

The Choice

Am I a prisoner of fate,
and is the world beyond this gate
forever lost to me?

Or did my own hands build this jail,
perhaps, afraid that I might fail
to meet the challenges I see?

Where lies the answer I must find?
I need to break the ties that bind,
to grow in strength, to live, to "be" -
Only the truth will set me free!

Daisy Wyrwa

The Anniversary

You were a pen
And I, paper.
We were brought together
To create.

The beginning was rough
'Till we learned;
Smooth the good lines,
Throw out the bad.
Don't rub out too fast,
Respond with the heart.
Blend, lengthen, develop
Harmony so lovely
We are no longer
Separate, pen and paper.

Together we created
A poem, a song, a story.
We'll last forever
Together as One.

Debra K. O'Brien

Things I Plan To do

I wrote you a letter Baby
And I called you on the phone
I didn't get an answer
That's why I began to roam
I now regret it darling
And won't to come back to you
To tell you of the things dear
That I have plan to do
First to make you love me
All over again
Next to make you happy
Like a rose in falling rain
Things then will be different
When I'm back with you
To tell you of my plans dear
All the things I have plans to do
For you.

Etta M. Childs

Cold In The Nose

It drips and drizzles,
And gets so sore.
I've wiped it a dozen times,
And must wipe it once more.

It looks bigger than usual,
And turns bright red.
Shames me so,
I could hide my head.

Keep sniffling and sneezing,
Keep wiping and dabbing.
Out of tissues again.
Becomes almost maddening.

Take some aspirin,
Use some nose spray
And if you're lucky
In 7 days it'll go away.

Fanny Lee Baker Shaw

Acknowledge God

For knowledge to become wisdom
and for the soul to grow,
First, God we must know.
To grow in wisdom and become strong,
We must choose wisely, right from wrong.
We are wise to be vigorous in
the truth we are taught.
Knowing for certain truth must be sought.
Therefore when truth is known
and we wisely take heed,
We discover the way in which to succeed;
Acknowledge God.

Clara Jane Conner

"Directions To Death"

When life has failed you,
and fluids drain you,
bruised is your body,
and dry are your veins,
where do you go?

What happens when your
heart stops,
when your last tear sheds
and your eyes close?

As your body withers and
it becomes forgotten,
where are you?
Have you been trapped?
No longer breathing your
lungs become decrepit,
as they collapse are
you crushed?

Where do you go, for I don't know,
but I want to visit, so can you tell
me how to get there?

Dawn Lavoie

Yearn

I wish for a healthy life
A family and a wife
That dream hasn't come true
And sometime I feel blue

When I see children play
I wonder if I'll have that day
A offspring born to raise
So I want have to stare in a daze

Daniel Cole Jr.

Heaven

I left my earthly body
and crossed the clear blue sea.
I approached a door of gold,
It was Heaven's door, you see.

I knocked upon the door
and an angel of light I saw.
He took me by the hand,
and taught me Heaven's Law.

When I met my Heavenly Father
I was standing all alone.
He gathered me in His arms,
and said, "my child, you are home."

As I walked with my brother
he showed me a beach of sand.
It glowed with such a light,
I knew this was God's land.

We sang upon the mountains
and talked of the world to be.
They told me all the secret's
the world would someday see.

Amber Pascoe

Halloween Poem

'Twas Mischief Night
And all through the 'hood
Creatures were stirring-
The bad and the good.

Bathroom tissue was flung
Through the trees with glee.
The teenagers would "decorate"
Then quickly they'd flee.

And Bubba with his flashlight
And Luke with his paste
Had stolen children's jack-o-lanterns
And were ready to waste-

When on his left shoulder
Luke felt a tap, tap.
Behold - a policeman
With a gun in his strap.
But I heard them exclaim
As they rode down the street,
"A happy Halloween to all!"
....plus some other words I can't repeat!

Bonnie Jayne Smith

The Last Tribute

God saw that you were getting tired,
And a cure was not to be.

So he put his arms around you,
And whispered "Come with me."

With tearful eyes we watched you suffer,
And saw you fade away.

Although I loved you dearly,
I could not make you stay.

A golden heart stopped beating,
hard working hands came to rest.

God broke out hearts to prove to us,
He only takes the best.

Bridget Ann Miller

No Reflection

To myself
Am I visible,
But my life
Is no longer liveable.

I can see others
But I'm not seen,
My senses work
Yet my family is not as keen.

I talk but
I am not heard,
Touching seems to
Be only absurd.

I am here yet,
No one knows,
I see places
Where no one goes.

I feel no life
Or any affection,
I stare in the mirror
And have no reflection.

Charity Clemente

Love

Love is a future full of life
Always seen differently,
through different eyes.
Full of hope and dreams,
Some never to be seen
Some conquer all and
exceed their dreams.
For those who love,
life is true
Love is precious
Life is too.
To love yourself, you
can love another.
For without inner love
their is no other
The future holds all your
dreams
Love yourself and the
future can be seen.

Dana Buchanan Ray

When You're In Love

When you're in love,
All grey skies turn blue.
All your problems disappear,
You feel like someone new.

When you're in love,
Bad moods don't exist.
The person you're in love with,
Is at the top of your list.

When you're in love,
Your heart goes pitter-patter.
Nothing else in the world,
Will ever really matter.

When you're in love,
You feel special every day.
Because the person you're in love with,
Wouldn't want it any other way.

When you're in love,
You'll always be together.
Once you found the one you love,
Your love will last forever.

Amica Collins

Joy Of Love

The trees are alive,
Alive tonight
And all of nature stirs.

The stars laugh low
from high above
As they look down on the world.

The wordless whispers
of joy tonight
Echo the beat of your heart,

And above all things
your eyes tonight
Would outshine a fairy's art.

Anne Allen

The Right Time

It seemed right to go ahead, life goes
ahead, straight forward it seems.
But instead, I took a turn. To my
surprise it was the time to take
a turn. You see you learn at an angel
aside, that time will not always abide.
I moved again, this time to the right.
It was not a fright to see what might
be at a different sight. I learned
some more. A door to open, lessons
of life may be all around. To decide a
time was not a choice. The right time
to move, choose, learn, grow and see,
is always the right time.

Carmen Moore Dockins

Submission

A prayer, I think might 'oft be called
A wish sent heavenward.
So many things to wish for
Heaven portals we bombard.

God listens to each plea;
But with wisdom, he ignores
The ones which only He can know
Do not deserve award.

And so I think 'tis wise
To leave to His regard;
The pleas, the prayers and wishes,
Which we send heavenward.

Bertha Mealy

Stay Stay

Your strong arms were to me
A haven of happiness and rest
Reaching to my very depth

Sometimes felt were misgivings
Then remembered were the words
What God hath joined put not asunder
Now I wonder

Why did he tear us apart
Leaving me with a broken heart
Yet your nearness from above
Is a symbol of our love

Sometimes at night
I awaken with a start
Yours arms sweetheart
Holding me tight

Then I pray Stay Stay
Always you go away

Bessie N. Gamlowski

Untitled

A new life, a new wife,
A true love, from heaven above,
An angel's smile a mile after mile,
Two arms to hold me, loving fingers to caress me,
Warm lips to kiss me, warm feelings for me,
A love so strong, to keep me from wrong,
Eyes with starlight, that says love me tonight,
Someone to chase the chills, when I am ill,
My love, my mate, my angel, my wife,
You are as cooling as the breeze off the snow
on the mountains.
Your laughter is as musical as the streams of
the fountains.
You are as beautiful as all of nature that God
has created.
Your eyes shine with love and happiness, you
glow my mate.
You make me burn with desire, that builds
from looking at you.
You are more loving and more loved, than all
the mountain and all the sky of blue.

Allen N. Richie

A Poem To My Sisters

If God had said "I'll give you
a sister not one but two,"
I know I could not have chosen
Any two more dear than you.

And so each day in my prayers
I thank my God above,
For giving me the two of you
Who I so dearly love.

We have been so very lucky
To always have each other,
But then we were truly blessed
With a sweet and caring Mother.

I think of her up in Heaven
And know how happy she must be,
To see all the special love
There is between us three.

Corrine L. Geck

Her Hem

A pant apart from hem,
A sigh away from her,
A pantelette,
Attached, not yet,
Is a pantalon set.

He wore it underneath,
For warmth, for pride, for glow;
But Lordy be,
She confused Me—
She put it out for glee.

What was for night, for sleep
Is now for day, to see—
Some leisure togs
Enhance the fog,
In finding who's to jog.

Whose slip is showing now?
We ask, to no response.
Oh, my! No scorn—
With what is worn,
The maker is adorned.

Catherine Joan Redmond-Younge

On Megan

I (we) brought a life into this world
A responsibility
    To nurture
    To mold
To one day set free
What is it, we will one day turn loose?
    Today and everyday we decide
Consciously,
    Unconsciously
    We mold we nurture
A setting free
    Is taking place already
Questions?
    Of competence of ability
    Of perseverance
Will be answered in time
May the test results,
    Far-reaching as they'll be,
    be satisfactory
    Is my only request of myself

Allen Hannon

Picture On The Nightstand

Sitting on the nightstand,
A relic of ancient times.
Always there,
Decaying with age.
Lost, under your fingertips,
On the tip of your tongue,
About to roll back
Into lost memories
Words that create pictures;
Pictures in need of words.
A world lost,
Without either, Or both,
A memory, A future,
Forever lost in one.

Dawn M. Wincentsen

In My Dreams

In my dreams, we are together
A mother's love is forever
You soar in the heavens above
Angels embrace you with their love
Reality is not as it seems
You are alive in my dreams.

In my dreams, I hold you tight
I wait to have you in my sight
I never got to say goodbye
I find myself asking, "Why, oh why?"
You have gone to a place of peace
There's no hate; all wars have cease.

A mother's love is forever
In my dreams we are together
We walk along side by side
Daylight comes, it's time to hide.

I know someday my dreams will be
Angels from heaven will set me free
My dreams will have to do;
Until I can be with you.

Deborah S. Miles

A Long Time Ago

I had a true love
A long time ago
Fate had another road
For me to go
And over the years
I had thought of my love
A long time ago
Even after all the years have passed
I finally found him, but
Fate had another road
For him to go
Our paths do not come together
This love of long ago
But this love will live forever
Like Cupid's bow and arrow
We'll never part
If only you're in my heart
Even though I can't have you now
You'll always be
My true love a long time ago

Charlene Casperson

Abused Child

Remember me please for I was here,
A little girl with golden hair.
Mommy got angry when daddy went away,
She beat me more than she let me play.
I tried to be good I really did,
I hid the lonely tears I shed.
My legs burned from the strap she used,
My arms were bruised, my mouth bled.
I often hid beneath my bed.
I wasn't hugged close to her breast,
I wasn't kissed or ever caressed.
I love my Mommy, I wanted to stay,
But God came and took me away.
There won't be any more bruises,
There won't be any more tears,
There won't be any more loneliness,
There won't be any more years.
My life though small is over,
Heaven's doors have opened wide.
The little girl with golden hair, now part of
Heaven's pride.

Carolyn Bumgarner

Friends

A kitty on the table
A kitty on the post,
I wonder if they're thinkin',
"Which does she love the most?"

Well, Frankie boy, is two years old
And, Pokey's just a kitten,
Frankie climbs upon the shelves,
While Pokey likes a sock or mitten.

Frankie knocks things to the floor
Just to get precise attention,
Pokey settles for a tender hug,
He craves love without dissension!

Frankie's quite a skittish cat,
He'll fuss and fume, try each door,
Pokey likes a ball and catnip mouse,
He can chase around the floor.

Well, now, if I had to pick or choose,
'Twould be a hard decision—
I think I'll just keep lovin' both
Without malice or division!

Elizabeth L. Smith

We Were Never Close

We were never close my father and I
Sometimes I sit back and wonder why

Was it because my parents had me late in life
Or was it because there was so much strife

My father was from the era of the depression
During which he was quite full of oppression

He went to work when he was quite young
Never having in his life a lot of fun

He never communicated his feelings very often
Sometimes he seemed so angry and sullen

I think those feelings reflected back at me
As I found it increasingly hard to see

I know he was proud of me as my aunt told me so
But why oh why was I so full of sorrow and woe

As I sat next to his bed in the hospital room
I began to cry as I felt his gloom

My father died April twenty-seventh nineteen hundred seventy seven
And from my heart I feel his spirit from heaven

We were never close my father and I
But I will think of him often until I die

Kevin W. Ardery

Untitled

I've seen that moon before on the days my life was changed
  sometimes for the better, sometimes for the worse
  sometimes full of wonder, but often full of pain.

But tonight the world seemed different as I stood
  within your arms
Sheltered by the crescent moon, the evening's newest stars.
Your touch excites and fills me up
Your eyes leave me so calm.

And although our worlds are challenging and our
  histories left us weak
There are strengths we'll share to see us through
And words our hearts will speak.

How I wish upon that moon, that crescent in the sky,
Thinking thoughts that lie so deep
Hoping we will share our dreams
Finding love we know we'll keep
  I saw it in your eyes.

Marcia D. Churchill

Memories

When we first met I knew there was
something about you that I just couldn't get.
The smile in your face showed me you really did care.
The way you made me laugh without even a smile or a stare.
The way you played pool with my sister and lost
but didn't even care.
The way we talked and had fun like we were a pair.
These are the memories that we both share.

Lisa Roberts

"To Feel It"

Inspire me, guide me, make the fire glow inside me.
See me there, without a care.
Show me love, is it there?
Where are you now, please show me how.
I need you here, to scare my fear.
To fill with grace, my heart's empty space.
I know you'll come soon, as sure as the moon and the skies lying above,
You will help me feel it again, this yearning for love.

Maria T. Driscoll

Friends

As the world turns and lives become one or separate,
Someone will always be there upon your await.

As children being watched by parents, guiding them and
making sure they don't fall,
Friends will always be there to hear your call.

Tears of joy, laughter and sorrow,
Will always be heard until tomorrow.
From the good times of playing in the park,
To the bad times of a first broken heart.

Friends will always be together even though far apart.

Jennifer M. Seivertson

"Heroes"

Each person needs more than one hero in life.
Someone to look up to-someone to hold on to.
Small children choose heroes they treasure all through life.
Heroes are like sparkles-a kaleidoscope view.
Heroes are like candles that light up our world.
Heroes are like raindrops that refresh our spirit.
Heroes are like keepsakes all shiny and pearled.
Heroes are like sunshine that strengthens our grip
On how to achieve our hopes and our dreams
And reach for the stars and every moonbeam.

Mary Dorsey

The Crow

People once believed that when
someone dies, a crow carries their soul
to the land of the dead. But sometimes something
so bad happens that a terrible sadness is carried
with it and the soul can't rest. Sometimes, just sometimes,
the crow brings that soul back to put the (wrong) things
to (right).
A building gets torched and all that is left is ashes.
I used to think that about everything; friends, family, feelings.
But now I know that when love proves, two people are meant to be
together, and nothing can keep them apart.
If the people we love are stolen form us, the way to have them
live on is to never stop loving them. Buildings burn; people
die, but real love is forever!

Kala R. Clifton

Love

Love is like a tree.
Some days it is green and full of life,
other days it can be brown and dead.
Some days the warm wind blows through its leaves,
other days it can be cold and dreary.

Love is like a tree.
People will climb in your limbs,
but they'll also cut you down,
they pick and eat your delicious fruit,
they'll burn your soul to warm their homes.

Love is like a tree.
People love to sit in your shade,
yet they poison your ground.
They trim you and make you look good,
but in the end you die.

Justin Rhodes

Someday

Someday we won't be here,
Someday we won't shed a tear,
Not a foe or even a woe,
There's no place I'd rather go,
We are given a light,
We are given the right,
But many throw their chance away,
They say they'll do it another day,
He's coming soon, he's coming fast,
When many will pay for the wrongs of their past,
One day it will be too late,
When the Lord will decide our fate,
Everything we have said and done,
Every time we praised his Holy Son,
The bad shall go, to a place below,
The good shall fly, and meet him in the sky,
Where everyone is our friend,
And good times never end,
I know where I'm going, I can proudly say,
I'm going to meet the King someday.

Michelle Anne George (age 13)

Propellers Are For Planes

Propellers are for planes
some surgeons are for brains
aspiring are for pains.
plumbers are for drains.

Cobblers are for shoes
cows are for moos, papers are for news
diapers are for poos.

Strings are for strummin'
tunes are for hummin', dentists are for numbin'
oh boy! Grandma's comin'.

Bells are for ringin'
toys are for bringin', songs are for singin'
flapjacks are for flingin'.

Clothes are for wearing
packages are for tearing
joy is for sharing
people are for caring.

Ships are for floatin', suitcases are for totin'
around castles are for moatin'
and sins are all verboten.

Jerry Paul Honkanen

The Proud Red Man

I am a man of honor;
Some men have tried to treat me like a dog.
I support my family well.
Some men try to put me through hell.

They hate my religion;
some men forced theirs on me.
They hate my language;
and forced their language on me.

All my beliefs and way of life
are almost gone.
Yet they still find something
about me to hate.

All in all they hate the
color of my skin.
For all the hate and prejudice
they still hate the red man the most.

Marilyn Johnston

A Heart's Garden

Deep within us lies a garden
Solitude where seeds are sown
A place to collect all thoughts and dreams
And make wishes for what only heaven makes known.

Our garden is always safe from harm
Never exposing its vulnerable soul
But tenderly nourishing each new hope
Creating new life then making it whole.

Clinging vines of memory
Like honeysuckle do entwine
And bring forth fond remembrances
Like flowers bursting on the vine.

Contemplations are encouraged
While sitting quietly in thought
Daydreams lend themselves to flourish
Producing ideas being sought.

So, whatever your wonderings happen to be
On gossamer wings let them depart
And travel to where all answers lie
Deep in the garden of your heart.

Linda Fiorelli

The Beach

Another year has come and gone, like a
   solitary man who has walked across a
      sunset-bathed beach,
only to have his tracks erased by the waves.
   And, after many more such years have passed,
      and many more tracks have been made,
         and erased,
   and many more sunsets have bathed that beach,
the beach will still stand, pure and unimpeachable,
   and no one will know who has crossed it.
What a twisting, screaming universe possesses us,
   yet we never sense the movement.

Kevin J. Rogers

Trials Are For Growing

God allows us to go through trials,
So when it's over we can see others' pain.
We'll be able to help them,
Get back on their feet again.

We can really understand them,
Without just saying, yes I know.
But, really, feel their pain inside.
For, the pain we had, helped us grow.

Now, others' pains, we understand.
Because we had them too.
So we can really, help the hurting,
Because, these pains, we've been through.

We must all have some, suffering,
For we must suffer as He
And when the suffering is over,
We can help others to go free.

So we're all in it together.
This, we must see.
Our trials are for others,
As, His trials, were for us, on a tree.

Linda S. Knight

As The Rain Falls

She is released from all she's known.
So suddenly,
yet with a delicacy known by her alone.
She falls,
liberated, independent,
spiraling blindly towards her inescapable destiny.
Loneliness swiftly surrounds her,
filling her with an ever festering fear.
She is engulfed in the knowledge
that she is uncontrollably racing
towards a thickly veiled future.
But control was given up willingly,
and the freedom must be embraced.
What happens is what must happen.
What comes to be is what was meant to be.
She is overcome with warmth,
fear no longer shrouds the truth.
She is, for the first time in her life,
her own.

Nicole Courneya

I Cannot Speak To The Moon

The waters roar on every shore
so ferocious is the sea.
I thought it calmer, and the waters more clear
than they now appear to be.

Is it the moon that controls the tide?
(For I cannot speak to the moon.)
Or is it the tide inside my mind?
(Oh, I thought I was more kind).

But consider this, my frightened child,
for now it is clear to me...
The inventor of fierce waters around,
wherever he may be,
is the gentleman whom, from his fondest respects,

Has saved you from the sea.

Nannette Sexton Gunn

To The Last Leaf

How beautiful you are,
Small emblem of God afar!
Yet, how near you bring Him here.
As I hold your lovely form so dear,
I see your living gold and red.
Tomorrow you'll be brown and dead.
No longer a supple, smooth token,
You'll be brittle, dry and broken.
But, in my memory you will be
The brave, strong life that now I see.

How like our lives, small gift from God!
Today we live, tomorrow we're sod.
Yet, in the hearts of those we've known
We shall live on, though we are gone.

Maxine J. Kemplin

Close Encounter With The Human Mind

Adventure, seeking thrills, spine tingling, oh it gives me chills!
Reaching out for the heavens, blazing through the stars.
Danger not knowing where you're going and not knowing where you are.
Suspense entering the unknown, caution your imagination won't leave
    you alone.
Now gazing as dreamers gaze, slowly your soul sets ablaze.
Still not knowing or sure of what you'll find, then it happens,
contact with something not your kind.
Now you've been there, close encounters with the human mind.

Mark McIntire

"Southern Stupidity"

Atlanta burning, rubble and ashes, ruins of a torrid battle,

A union soldier in tattered blues sitting triumphant in his saddle.

Barefoot, ragged...; wearing crowns of newfound fearlessness, freed
slaves journey towards the north. Cleansed of forced conformity,
the first step of equality bravely strides forth.

Elegant southern ladies and gentlemen, who lived off the agony of
others, turned cheeks unjustly away, thinking not of the inhuman
treatment of our dark skinned brothers.

Defeated and conquered, those lacking compassion, who sacrificed pride
for an unworthy cause,

Now under God's own stars and stripes, stripped of their importance
and wealth, stop, regret and pause.

Even one hundred some years later, the still-present poison of
racism brings a pang of shame to my heart.

The hate crimes of ignorance, white-supremacy rebuilds a wall between
humans which must be torn apart.

I dream of a day when we cease fighting amongst ourselves and join
hands in colorless brotherhood.

And love for each other is nurtured and taught, when this useless hate
is snuffed out and understood.

Melinda Leslie Giel

Autumn

Leaves turn golden with brown and red
Skies turn silver with clouds o'er head
Winds travel swiftly, chilling the breeze
Ripened goldenrod brings the sneeze
The sedentary it may motivate
Crisp coolness can invigorate.
  - the leaves
  - the breeze
  - the sneeze
Sometimes if a walk I take
Between day and night - a break
A light wrap or cover - for warmth the reason
To comfortably enjoy
  - the autumn season.

Mary Graliker

Ode To A Dear One

'Tis almost a year
Since you passed away.
You sang "Girl of my dreams, I love you"
Two nights before that day.
Your favorite phrase was,
"I'm running out of time."
Then you would smile;
You knew God was smiling too.
Waiting with open arms for you at ninety-two.
Loving everyone on this earth
And patiently waiting for me
When in two years more I reach ninety-three.

Mildred M. Charlton

Yankee Window

Interchangeable virgins set to music
Riding on crude homemade trails.
The road to sensuous, sinful, inferences.
Sweating masculine shadows canvas cotton fields.
A display of mock gallantry.
The clamor of carriage wheels.
Women enthroned and immobile pass across vision
Like painted portraits.

Jerod D. Schroeder

Ode To The Giver Of This Creative Hand

To my mother, the giver of this creative hand
The attic is upon me, musty and cold; labeled boxes are at my feet.
Significant treasures; ancient and old
And all my memories are bittersweet.

Pictures stained yellow and gray, yet the smiles are still anew.
Distant whispers, what do they say?
"The gift is passed on to you..."

A secret diary once held by one
Whose writings were grim and bare.
And just as I open the book I've begun, I slowly sit down in a chair.

Tear-stained pages deplete at my touch
My heart aches; their emotions I understand.
Suddenly I realize that I may know too much
About the heart of this creative hand.

For even then hearts were broken; just as they are today.
And maybe the same words were spoken,
And now I know what they'd say.

These treasures I cherish so close to my heart
Inspire my talent that will last.
An ancient society I am now a part
For my future depends on the past.

Lydia C. Siciliano

My Mirror

Mirror, My Mirror
Show me a lie
Reflect back a farce
So I need not cry.
Each morning as I rise
There is that familiar pain
Of beauty that forgot me
And none for me to attain.
My heart is true
Perhaps my only real virtue
But I can't see my heart
And what I can see is cruel.
Mirror, Oh Mirror
Let me live for but a moment
Unleash the happiness that lies in me dormant.
For a split second, let me have peace
To gaze upon beauty, to relinquish the beast.
But alas! You are unable to.
For your one true quality is honesty
And it is this honesty that is indeed costing me.

Jason K. Woody

Disturbance

The lamb slowly walks among the
shadows of the trees in the cemetery.
Careful not to wake the dead.
Watching every move it makes.
Suddenly, a gust of wind blows a leaf
into the lamb's path, and frightens it.
Leaping away, the lamb steps onto a grave,
falls, and disturbs a corpse.
Without struggling, the lamb lies down
to its fate for it knows it can't win.
The corpse rises out of the grave, and
devours the lamb.
Biting hard and crushing bones....
The lamb has now been taught a lesson.

Kristen Bachman

Old Glory Revisited

Although we're individuals, there's a part of history we share
She's red, white and blue and waves proudly in the air.
She's been a special part of us since 1777
And makes her home proudly in the blue skies we call heaven.

Some people think Old Glory isn't what she used to be
They think she stands for nothing; not even you and me.
Maybe I'm old fashioned, but I pray I'm not alone
Because each time I see her I think of heart and home.

When a song is sung in honor of the thousands who have died
I think of the American's who've lost loved ones and who've cried.
Emotions overcome me and these feelings are no charade
Especially when I see her carried by veterans in parade.

The commitment made by those who have pledged lives to defend her
Should never be forgotten in Spring, Summer, Fall or Winter.
Many seasons have passed since our independence was proclaimed
And the United States of America is among this earth's most famed.

Our nation and its people did not happen just by chance
And Old Glory was not created just for pomp and circumstance.
I invite you to join with me as we honor our nation's best
As Old Glory waves above us and God controls the rest.

Kim Reiter

Her Gifts

In my sorrow I could barely see the gifts my mother gave to me.
She'd taught me how to love, to laugh, to live;
But most of all she taught me to give.
Through my heartache and my tears I called to her,
    I need her near,
I want to call her back to me, to make her live
    to make her see.
In the morning as I rise a tear falls gently from my eye.
We are not so far apart, we're still together in my heart.
And as I lay a rose upon her grave, I thank my Mom
    For the gifts she gave;
To love a sunset pure and bright,
To love the starry summer night,
To love the sound of a baby's sigh,
To hear the birds, to touch the sky,
So many gifts that keep on giving,
So many reasons to keep on living,
So many things in the world to see,
So many gifts she gave to me.

Judith Weisman

Lend Me

Lend me your tear and I shall
shed it for you.
Lend me your touch and I shall
make it for you.
Lend me your legs and I shall
walk across it for you
Lend me your sweet voice and I shall
sing it for you.
Lend me your mind and I shall
solve it for you.
Lend me your soft tender lips and I shall
kiss it for you
You know there's only one thing that I
want most and that's your love so
Lend me your love and I shall
love you back

Kristen Phelan

412

For Love Or Laugh

Her eyes seem to glow, as a moonlit night,
she smiles so often, so cheerful and bright,
and yet within, lays a girl I've never known...

She can be so kind, I've seen her that way,
like she hurts inside, yet does not say,
then does not call, so my thoughts remain my own.

I think of her often, and her love as well,
am I wasting my time, I cannot tell,
she says caring things, then runs off to play on her own.

I have tried to learn, this inside girl,
it's been hard although, it's her own closed world,
she says sure we can, and yet I remain alone.

This time like last, my phone will not ring,
she gives me her love, so she's had her fling,
it only makes me think, should I have known???

Kevindean D. R. Rice III

Katie

Tenderly she gets her baby ready for a bath
She adores her so much, and promises to always
take care of her

The bath water is just right now, and she giggles
as drops splash to the floor
Very carefully she washes and dries her

Smiling, she kisses her on the cheek and tickles
her belly
With a heart full of happiness she cradles Katie
and sings Rock-A-Bye-Baby

Mommy says I have to get ready for bed now
So with a final good night kiss she lays Katie in her crib
Don't forget I love you she whispers, and I'll
play with you tomorrow

A mothers love has been felt
A mothers love has been learned
A mothers love will be passed on

Grace Hagman

Ribbon Untied

I penciled in a new face
Shaded old eyes and made them new
I lined the peaks of my lips
I made them as tall as doorways
 I put on a new dress
I pressed it flat against my skin
 My feet are the same but my shoes are new

I feel my exit possible
 And my entrance easy
 With these lips as tall as doorways.
The adventure starts with birth
 And is renewed with every step.
The words fall through
These lips as tall as doorways.

Maria Zavada

Untitled

The storm rolled in so quietly it almost went unnoticed.
Picking up the leaves of emotion and tossing them about.
One can easily be taken by the beauty of the electric skies,
unaware of the devastation caused by the storm.
How fortunate that solace may be found in a rainbow.

Julianne M. Bates

Just One Sip

All I want is just one sip, one drop of water upon my lips.
Send momma to the well, try to find out the secret she won't tell.
Send momma to get a little more. Haven't got a dime; we must be poor.
Momma, poor momma, oh how she cries.
She doesn't know it, but me and the Lord, we know she tries.
We haven't gone to school in years.
The only thing we study are each other's tears.
I try to care for the younger ones as best I can.
Everyone in town says momma, she needs a man.
My momma don't like to be dependent on some else, you see.
That's how we live, she says that's just the way it has to be.
Poor little Jimmie, oh how that boy lies.
Momma says, "Leave 'em alone," but it's hard sometimes.
I never asked my momma for a bicycle, or a puppy, and such.
In fact, I never asked for very much.
But, for now, all I want is just one sip,
One drop of water upon my lips.
Send momma to the well, try to find out the secret she won't tell.
Send momma to get a little more.
Haven't got a dime, but we'll never be poor.

Melody A. Carswell

In The Distance

In the distance - on the cloud - a lone warrior rides
 Searching for those who are lost.

In the minds of our children, the echoes
 of our traditional songs
Sing silently - as the drumbeat of our nations
 beat strong within our hearts.

For many moons this lone warrior's spirit
 touches and nourishes the young
In their dreams of what has been lost
 guiding them back to the way of life.

Once awakened, notice the young
 seeking out the old ones
Asking endless questions
 for everything they know,

In the distance you can see this lone warrior
 sitting upon his majestic war horse - smiling
With his long braided hair and eagle feather in the wind
 Listening to the young singing loud with pride
Of the traditional songs...

 With the spirit of Crazy Horse.

George R. Still Day

Music Man

In my mind I see you standing on a stage,
Saxophone to your lips, curtain up
The audience flips.

The music man is you and everybody knows it,
Just play your notes and keep the beat,
The music is hot and they are tapping
their feet.

Someday you'll be there center stage
And the house it will be packed.
And your name will be all over town,
The billboard reads "Hey Rich is back"

And me I will be sitting there as proud
As I can be, and I will be remembering
When you played so good for free to me,
When it was just you mate, and me.

Lori A. Eden

Untitled

I wish I could remember the first time I
saw you; the day, the hour, the min., the
second, but I can't.

I wish I could remember the first time we
talked; the day, the hour, the min., the second,
but I can't.

I wish I could remember the first time
you took my hand into yours; the day, the
hour, the min., the second, but I can't.

I wish I could remember the first
time our lips gently pressed together;
the day the hour, the min., the second, but I can't.

I wish I couldn't remember the time
you left me; the day, the hour, the min.,
the second, but I can.

Keyona L. Burdin

What Choice?

As I sit awake at night I hear the cries of
sadness. They tumble down your face one after
another. Each one represents some event and some
are just there of memories, but each one stands
for something just like every person has there
place. Your mind's no longer in order all the old
memories have clattered the new thoughts like
water flooding a town and all of the people
getting washed away. All kinds of feelings fill
your body like a field full of several different
kinds of flowers. Out of the many choices to pick
from only one is correct. The tears of sadness
have now turned red. The blood rolls faster as if
it just started pouring down rain. The drops now
are only crimson instead of clear. Streak
markings are left of where the blood was smeared
when tried to be wiped away. Your life that
supposedly sucked could have been turned around.
You made the choice, you chose the wrong one!

Jessica Horneman

The Crossing

By the shores of the Cacapon river, I saw the waters
Running northward towards the Potomac - the rocky bed
Of the river caused a cascading scene of white top
Breakers. I dreamed. The white top breakers
Were the manes of white steeds pulling a royal chariot
Upon which rode a Goddess - she was naked and
Exceedingly beautiful. She looked upon the shore and
Smiled and beckoned. Me? I thought. She took me into

A luscious garden where the fruits were ripe and falling.
Eat! She commanded, for the fruit is sweet
I ate ravishingly but could not stay my hunger
For the fruit was indeed wondrous strange.

I then saw a fountain in the center of the garden
And drank thereof and it was sweet like honey

That is the nectar of the Gods, she said, and is forbidden
You must never drink from it again - I saw a tear in her
Eyes and behind the tear a gleam - you have been favored
Of many, she said, and rode away towards Polaris.
This is not a dream, I thought but a taste of a new heaven
I have crossed the Rubicon - who is to change that?

Gilbert S. Aleman

Treasures of Life

Keep the spirit of God in your heart.

Remember everyone is human and forgive their
rudeness and their faults.

Remember the beauty of this earth and look for
the beauty in people. It is there.

Remember and cherish the good moments in life,
and forget all others.

Be thankful if you have ever known love, regardless
if you have lost it. Love is special, and many do
not have the fortune of its experience.

Take your trials and turn them into triumphs.
Don't dwell on misfortune or bad times, they
but make the good times better.

What is precious in your life, hold in your heart;
share them with others, but let no one take them from you.

Do not lose sight of yourself, for when you do,
you lose sight of life.

Never take the love of family and friends for
granted. They are your greatest treasure.

Be the best that you can and you will come out on top.

Nancy C. Larson

Circa November 1986

JANUARY 1986

The day dawned bright and a painful blue and the 7 walked by in quick
Review. The fleecy white clouds went scudding by, and the great ship
groaned, getting ready to fly. In screaming silence I watched her
rise, on thundering jets in the mid-morning skies, and "Go for Roll!"
the speaker said... I knew in that instant the 7 were dead.

"Go for Roll!", the words boomed out,
but nobody heard my silent shout, "NO!" - And still they rose.

She was rising on billowing smoke and fire and I watched her rise,
going higher and higher... "Throttle up!"

Then a moan of agony from the gathered crowd, a pall of smoke in a
spreading shroud-and a smoke tulip bloomed...

In a screaming steep dive the cabin fell,
a long drawn out moment of metal scorched hell,
from the tumbling, spinning, fire-washed flare,
the cabin arched away in the thin cold air,
all scattered around with metal shards,
the ship broke up like a house of cards, and plummeted down.

Then the sea rose up and took them in, and the 7 were never seen again-alive.

Mary LaVeitta Hestand

The Prayer

Now I lay me down to sleep
pray the Lord my soul to keep
and if I dream before I wake
let me dream about these for goodness sake
let me dream about endless beaches
and not boring speeches
let me dream about loves
and not black doves
let me dream about sunsets
and not silly regrets
let me dream about cute boys
and not stupid toys
let me dream about good things
and not what bad luck brings

Karmen M. Sellers

414

Self-Portrait

My eyes drift over her, (but my stare bores through her), and I try to
remove her life, to see her the way a stranger would...
Her hair, so deep in color and rich in texture, is warm and lush, with
hints of sunshine from summers past.
(How many have entwined their fingers in her hair?)
Her skin is so fair, yet often rosy, with almost the expected texture
of a porcelain doll, but it appears warm and
yielding to the touch.
(How many have caressed her skin and felt its warmth?)
Her eyes are large almonds, brown and full of mystery and sadness, but
they twinkle when she laughs, and sparkle
when she's feverish. They look secretive and cold when she's angry,
penetrating, almost black, appearing to be all pupil.
(How many have felt her loving gaze upon them?)
Her lips are not full, but not small, with just enough suppleness to
imply luxury, and they are a rosy shade, like lips
that have just been kissed roughly.
(How many have kissed her lips and made them a deeper shade of red?)
Her voice...in the morning it is low and gravelly, but when morning
leaves, it remains low, with a lilting that she
uses when she sometimes slips into a slight unknown accent.
(How many times has she said "I love you" to her friends and lovers
when a moment later, in an angry flash, she
could say, "I hate you" with just as much passion?)
(Will she ever say she loves me?)

Laura M. Butler

Naturally

Like a cheerful ray of sunshine that skips across a stream
Reflects the art of living that no human eye has seen

The giving is the living
The spark's in the dance
As it plays across the water
The world becomes enhanced

Like a breeze in spring and autumn that never chases worth
Lifts the seeds and pollen to spread their life to earth

The trees that grow will never know
The motive why they grew
To touch the sky's the reason why
Growing's what they do

To grow and play is natures way
When done will give a gift
A piece of fruit or a tiny shoot
Will blossom out to lift

All humankind in time will find a talent too to give
Then naturally in harmony with living things we'll live

Mike Gray

Red

Red is the color of paper and ink.
Red is the color that can be mixed with pink.
Red is the color that says NO! out loud.
Red is the color that makes you proud.

There are red woods and red hoods,
Red flags and red bags,
Red halls and red balls,
Red lights and red kites.

Some stars are red and some cars are red.
Some books are red and some hooks are red.
Some hearts are red and some darts are red.
Some boxes are red and some foxes are red.

Red can make you mad
and also sometimes make you sad.
Some people like red with all their might
and some people think it's such a fright.

Matthew W. Soto

Celestial Flower

Luminous as the sun, each petal, darting from the center, like
rays of light, in the shadow of morning. Intense saffron darkens
the heart, to explode in lemon hues, curling towards, sister the sun.
  Earth, the mother,
   has given birth to its first glimpse of spring.
Time passes, it takes shape, as, Father the moon,
   white and gray,
    circular sphere,
     delicate to see,
      tender to touch,
       fragile as a heart broken.
Then a child's breath... blowing air... that is life... bursting
the sun and the moon into a hundred stars, that scatter and fly
back to earth that is mother.
Dandelions...

Lucy Alamia

Memories

When I was young
Quite long ago
The world was quiet
And travel was slow.

Our pleasure came from simple things
A "Treasure Box" tied up with strings
A china doll with eyes that closed
Satin and lace to make her clothes

Little pieces we valued so...
Happy days watching mother sew.
Nothing was ever thrown away
they were cut and saved 'til time of play.

An old shoe box with half a lid
Became a carriage or a crib.
A piece of string pulled it along
As we sang to our dolls a silly song.

Oh what happened to long ago
When kids were happy, and the world went slow?
Gone with the advent of speed and haste,
and plastic toys and all that waste!!!

Marie M. Carr

Dark Night Surface Light

Life hidden from sight
Pulsing and struggling
underneath the surface of light.
Flowing with the current into the abyss of dark night.

Calm and serene
deep depths of green
beckoning and calling my name.

Woe to creatures of the light.
Beware demons of the night.
Deceivers of the depths
beneath the surface of light
flowing with the current from the abyss of dark night.

Calm and serene
deep depths of green
pulsing and struggling with life
beckoning and calling my name

Linda Myszka

My Mother

My mother is my mentor:
  Pointing towards the right direction,
  Guiding me along the paths I choose,
  Instructing me with the best of intention,
  Insisting that sight of my goal, I do not lose.

My mother is my parent:
  Teaching me lessons learned by her own mistakes,
  Instilling in me the thirst to learn,
  Staying by my side, no matter what it takes,
  Always kind and loving, appropriately stern.

My mother is my confidante:
  Opening her mind to my different views,
  Reminding me of the shoulds and should nots,
  Advising me upon hearing the worst of news,
  Accepting of all my deepest thoughts.

My mother is all of these things to me:
  My best friend, my idol, and so much more.
  She is all things that a mother should be,
  Making my life worth living for.

Justine D. Begley

Summer

In those days, we always
played in the park.

Doing whatever kids did to
pass the day's life.

I always brought the ball.

We always played alone-
except for - the old man in the box
by the pond in the shadow of
the bright buildings, his the smallest of
the many we saw.

He was absent except for when he
fed his birds on the pond.

I never talked to him - until
the ball landed by his box.

He picked it up and handed it
to me and said, "Son, do you
love your mother?"

"Yes."
"Tell her."

Michael Knipp

Peace In The Night

Misery, misery, so much misery. Can I rise above this Plane?
With a heart filled with such sadness, will the sun replace the rain?
Will I wake with light draped o'er my face, or will the
  dark obscure my way?
I wish that today was tomorrow. Is there a place for my
  misery to lay?
As I lay on my bed of dark shadows, I roll back the curtain
  of years.
I see a young girl in the prime of her life, making choices
  she'll pay for with tears.
I see the young pastor who loved me. He wanted for me a good life.
I traded it all for the love of a man, who enjoys abusing his wife.
I cry out "Oh God! Do you love me? Will this trouble I'm in ever cease?"
In the night I feel a soft presence. God's love has filled me with peace.

Gracie L. Nelson

Everlasting To My Mind

"Everlasting" what does it mean? Is it a lovers
phrase or the topic of a preacher's sermon? To me it's not
either/or, but both, as in and.
  Two people in love state their depth of passion by
declaring Everlasting love. When you feel so strongly
for one Being and you would never give your heart to
another, that is Everlasting love. The love a parent gives
to their child from the moment they hear that lusty cry is
Everlasting love. Remembering the love and devotion
your grandmother gave you is Everlasting love. The
feelings a child has for the first pet you gave them, and
when they look up at you and say thank-you, thank-you,
thank-you that is Everlasting.
  Sitting in church listening to the preacher's words,
letting them seep into your soul, is Everlasting. Taking
communion for the first time, drinking the juice and eating
the bread, being told that it is the blood and body of Christ, is Everlasting.
  Whether it be for loving or for Christ, it will always
be Everlasting to your heart.

Lynne Marie Gordon

My Dream Is Thee

Happily, drowsiness befalls upon me,
Perchance the dream of all dreams is my destiny.
Night, slowly being replaced by the light of thee
Ideal, perfect, beautiful woman I see

Come hitherto, succumb to my touch
A mere passionate, soothing caress or such.
Yea, this alluring visionary, come close, come near,
Bewilderment, damnation a vision untouchable I fear.

Dream or no, how thee provokes thy desire
Pity me, thee, drench this burning runaway fire.
Thy beg thee to take physical form,
Relieve me of thy pain during this subconscious sojourn

Real, thy would undauntingly coddle thee,
Dream, 'tis mere perfunctory, formality.
Wishing for the impossible gives life to the dead,
The same for a dream is exquisite passion fed

To want it all, the best, the beauty, the dream,
Untouchable, so far away, a millennium or so it seems.
Now, having dreamed the dream of perfection,
Awake, and thy expose to thee my affection.

Larry Seals

Think Before You Speak

You can sit around a public place; and listen to
people talk, they are always judging others they don't know
nothing about, it's best to keep your big mouth shut until
you are very sure. For the truest message you can bring
is what you know on you, and that's the part we dare to
tell that's the part don't look so good, we will sweep that
silently under the rug, we'll find ourselves
all out of words with nothing more to say, you can almost
hear a pin drop before it hit the rug, so let us keep
our eyes off John and Sally and our mouth off Bill and
Sue, and turn the mirror in the other direction and
take a good look at you, for you cannot live in Hollywood
know what goes on in Rome. No more than you can rove
the streets and make your house a home, there's more than
one way man can use his mouth. And it's up to him to
make his choice whether he want to use it for good or bad
that's entirely up to him. How you use your mouth for
speaking if you want your words to bless some one be sure
you speak the truth, your words can be used to bless or curse,
let them be a blessing to others, and not a curse to you.

Laura K. Keen

416

Summertime

Summer time summertime is here,
people everywhere including here and there.
Beaches are packed to the fullest,
that's where the winds are the coolest.
Super Nintendo's are off,
while clearing the dust Segas cough.
Older people are riding bikes,
while children are flying kites.
People are swimming in pools,
and are also glad there's no school.
People are going to Disney World
and Epcot Center,
while others are ice skating
and it's not even winter.
    The End!
    Kristina Wilson

Let Hope Be Restored

These times are rough, these times are hard.
People are being hurt in their own back yards.
Children are being shot by their own peers,
and no one is left to wipe Mama's tears.
Mother, sister, father, son.
The violence is hurting everyone.
It's hard to smile when you're scared inside,
with nowhere to run - nowhere to hide.
But wait - there's hope, just look and see,
Open your Bible; John 3:16.
He died because He loved us so;
His life his death for all to know.
But not only death; life again!
For you and me He rose again!
Your hope is the anchor of your soul,
and when you're sick He makes you whole.
All your hope removes all doubt because you know He brought you out.
Yes times are rough, and yes it's hard,
but you are safe where ever you are.
You won't be shot by your peers, and God is there to wipe your tears.
    LaNiece Williams

My Temporary Roommate

The other night for a little while
PEACE came to live in my room.
My former roommates all took flight;
gone where the fears, the pain, and the gloom.

I welcomed this PEACE with open arms,
and with this PEACE I was cured.
I was finally free from all life's harms,
and all that I had endured.

I was glad that PEACE was there with me,
and my heart was filled with hope.
I was able to be all that I could be,
because I was learning to cope.

Then suddenly misfortune and my roommates returned,
Now, I lament and cry.
I long for that PEACE and all that I've learned;
and I wonder, "My, God, Why? Why?"

But, every night since PEACE went away,
I keep my eyes on the door
For, I believe it will return one day,
and I shall be free once more.
    Jeanette Miller

The Servant

O'er misty hills and autumn plain,
Past many a moor, since sodden with rain,
Beyond silver-clad rider, and steed's flowing mane,
Whose thundering step can no man restrain,
A servant, so lowly, looks weary and tried.

Through yonder moat, waves dispersing the light,
Hearing laughter and gaiety, though no one in sight,
Up further embankment, where drawbridge shut tight,
Encloses its courtyard from the rest of the night,
Sits a servant, so lowly, who from grief can not hide.

Down a door-studded passage, light starting to wane,
Under arches of stone, across musical strain,
Athwart noises of jesters, in the chambers, who feign,
And the lords and the ladies who they entertain,
A servant, a mother, has broken down and cried.

Past happiness and merriment and sounds of delight,
Around every turn all things looks aright,
But at the stairs and down it a flight,
In a small, dirty room which is quite out of sight,
Sits a servant, a mother, whose small child has just died.
    Matthew Mente

A Tragedy In A Small Village

In the fresh meadows
    painted checkered greens and browns

Lies rubble of a wooden farmhouse
    the smoke rises
        carries the scent of the dead

A village surrounded by evergreen trees
    shocked and dismayed

The structures of the walls still remain
    the purpose is gone

Bodies dressed in religious grab
    lay side by side

The earth was once their homes
    now they will live forever below

As the sun casts shadows on the ground
    night has already fallen for some

A cult in search of religious salvation
    found only white sheets
        over their faces

These rolling meadows hold fertile beginnings
    rotten harvests
    Leah A. Eidson

Untitled

My tongue slips like a dripping faucet
over my lips
but I catch myself -
It almost happened again.
Words of endearment,
the deep speak of my soul
that wants to cry out to you —
My restraint is unprecedented.
Words become entrenched in shallow reverberations...
mere echoes in the empty caverns of
daily life, a
cliche.
My soul is lost,
its power seared by the sharing.
    Karen Herman DeMuro

A Dream

A midnight sun washes
over a tide out beach.
Footsteps in the vibrant, red sand.
Higher, your feet lift off the
ground, into the purple sky.
Suddenly, a cloud appeared, you land.
The soft, transparent
embraces your body.
Tiny delicate fingers
stroke away your fears.
A palace made of crystal,
the smell of roses.
You float in among
the angels, heaven, the place of no tears.
Mysteriously, the gate closes.
Back to the cloud, back to the beach.
You awake from your
dream, now out of reach.

    Jillian Black

The Arrogant Feline

Sleek, soft, silent. Making her way in and
out of the rungs on a bannister like a
gymnast on her balance beam.

Furry, warm, delicate paws anticipating
Every turn, every dip in the surface with
the agility only she possesses.

Slipping to the ground without a sound,
glancing back only slightly to acknowledge an
obstacle in her path.

Eyes shining in the darkness as if to
illuminate a path only she will follow.

A familiar voice, a soft caress. A hint of
brightness in the sky. A delicate yawn,
A feminine stretch, her journey over. An
Evening well spent.

    Kim Calogar

Life's Epic — A Father's Biography, July 16, 1945-?

From the desert night dark, into a July day; dawns an era.
Out of darkness expelled, vociferously into the light.

Taste that cooking, see tidy house, smell fresh laundry; loving home.
"Watch those pennies! Visit family! Be a good Catholic dear!"
Polish; dance the polka, have a merry time — elicit with beer!

The world expands, home and family shrinks — expatriated son:
gregarious grocery, garrulous garbage, callow college;
engineer to new frontier, Air Force declared; solitaire? Marriage!
Made in Montana, orator of North Carolina; new life!

Nomads Ohio home moved to South Carolina base;
Steeple Chase, outpaced by life's embrace, brings a love defaced;
divorce and Dalzell — single trailer loner;
the weatherman forecasted son, and the stormy clouds cleared;
next, Shaw foreman considered normality in Camden...

An aspiring fisherman is welcomed in Lake Wateree;
talking, visiting, hunting: Virginia, Buddy, Raymond, Leland.
Winter Wisconsin migration concludes — unforeseen eclipse!
Dear Helene — caring mother, loving grandma.
Murdered! My father's father; cancer: devastating deprivation!
"Thirteen there, fifteen here; birthday. Fifty!" The A-bomb hits Dad.

    Jon Andreski

Dandelion Dreams

Oh, the Dandelion Dreams of
our youth
    I have seen them
    I dream them
Yellow abysses of
   fairy   wings
     Dance   in the light
But too many, a life-giving
    Dandelion   Dream
I have seen
  Turn to the cold
     white stuff of our 'Adulthood'
and fly
    away
in the tormented winds
of oh-so-cool-masochistic
concepts of reality
in an eternal search for
a stable foothold in
       the cloud of life
leaving a lone,
    cold,
      naked
        stem.

    Oly Spitzer

Let Us Pray

Please God above we need your help
Our world is bursting at the seams and we
  have become segmented groups
Each group believes that they are right
Each one is ready for a fight
Many of them have forgotten, what it is to pray
And others seek out love or peace in
  such a violent way
Open their eyes, oh Lord, for to many speak at once
With voices reaching to a shrill much is lost
  in what they say
Give faith, courage and strength to men who lead us
So our problems can be solved in a manner
  that is righteous
What joy the day man on the moon did land
Thank you for your helping hand
The step they took for mankind was
  a human feat.
We now need spiritual guidance for the
  step to lasting peace

    Mary P. Steene

The Unfinished

As our paths were united, they now again part,
our lives joined together with hope in our hearts.
As time keeps on ticking, we see different views,
and we look to the past of friends we once knew.

It's still, though, unfinished - our friendship I mean,
a road never ending of adventures to be seen.
The road keeps on going, it's never all done
our likeness still there, our friendship just begun.

As the lane of our lives, parts in different ways,
We can look at the memories of the good ol' days
And when I look at you all, I'll remember each face,
Your respect I was given, I return to you grace.

The road's unfinished, it's still building more,
always filled with excitement, never a bore.

Still unfinished business, the journey not done.
Our friendship just starting, the road just begun.

    Jennifer M. Carpenter

A New Beginning

What's happened to our stately oaks?
Our sturdy chestnut trees?
The pink and white sweet Dogwood
And the sleeping peach and apple trees?
The stately firs stand green and tall
Their feet look cold without wildflowers and brush for slippers!
The grass has a sad and rusty look
Just waiting for a signal!

The Days last a little longer now
The Darkness of the night grows shorter.

Just stop and look and listen
For a long and quiet time-
Be still and wait and suddenly you'll start to see the Sign!

A faint red haze of budding trees - a tiny hint of green around.
The trees are not quite so bare
Was that a robin's call I heard?

At last it seems that nature wakes!
Spring is truly on its way! All God's creatures are cheering up!

   Surely, this is a New Beginning!!
   Marie Davis Deatelhauser

Our Flag

Swaying in the wind with floating colors,
Our lovely flag of red, white and blue.
Sending all the world a message
The price of living in freedom's truth.

Thanks to the veterans of our nation that bravely served,
World War II, Korea, Vietnam and Desert Storm,
They stand tall - proud of their country,
When the "Star Spangled Banner" is being sung.

Salute the "Old Glory" as she sways forever in time,
Honor to the fallen comrades of our nation's best,
May God forever keep our country safe in His care,
May our United States always be blessed.
   Nancy Mineer

Gratitude

The clock keeps ticking as time goes by.
Our lives flash before us in the wink of an eye.

Large tasks, small ones, we try to do them all;
The cooking, the cleaning, and shopping at the mall.

Hurry, hurry, quick, quick; we must get it all done.
There is so much to do before the setting of the sun.

But in our haste we often overlook,
The beauty that surrounds us in every cranny and nook.

The sweet, juicy taste of an orange; a kitten purring in your ear;
The rhythmic chimes of a grandfather clock;
Or time spent with loved ones we hold dear.

The smile on a child's face; sunshine, flowers, a butterfly;
The friendly wave from a neighbor;
Or a grilled ham and cheese on rye.

The everyday life that surrounds us
Can easily become humdrum and mundane,
But when we awaken our senses with gratitude,
Nothing will ever be the same.

It doesn't matter how great or how small,
Our purpose in life is to love it all.
   Marilyn Grace Maceri

The Things I Should Have Done

I see you lying there so still,
Our life together past.
I think of things I should have done
Why did time go so fast?

So many times, I now recall
I should have been more wise.
Imagined wrongs divided us
And strained the binding ties.

I should have held you close those times
I pushed you far away.
I should have said, "I Love You" more
And proved it every day.

My greatest wish would be today
For time, I need much more.
So I could do so many things
I didn't do before.
...

Awake at last, it's just a dream,
Another chance I've won.
I'll start today to do those things,
The things I should have done.
   Mary La Fleur

Second Hand Pain

We all have pain.

Some feel it all the time,
Others only now and then.
It may stem from your past or present life,
Mine comes from the sufferings of friends.

I feel their pain so deeply
As if it were my own.
This second hand pain consumes completely,
And I can't help but feel alone.

My friendships are so precious
Each one is special and unique.
Different friends have different pain,
That is what is so hard for me.

They all have someone else who cares.
Who tries to help when they suffer in their life.
But I am the only one who loves them all,
And shares their pain simultaneously every single night

I cannot choose whose pain to feel and whose to ignore
I only know that each time I do this second hand pain
is more intense than ever before.
   Justine Gueno

How Long Has It Been?

How long has it been since you've looked at the sky?
Or stopped to pay attention to the birds flying by?
How long has it been since you've watched the grass grow?
Or just simply listened to hear the wind blow?

We rush through our lives with our plans and our schemes,
We'll find the time later to listen and dream.
To live your life fully, you can carefully plan.
But just don't forget to dream when you can.

Life passes too quickly without moments to spare.
There won't be time later to listen or care.
So start now to dream, for once you begin,
You'll be able to answer "How long has it been?"
   Linda Thomsen

419

The Perfectionist

Perfection is the curse of the bright — the well read.
Order and discipline is lived — not simply said.
You've got to be starched, if perfection's your game.
Each minute has a purpose, every picture a frame.

Change causes wrinkles in this one's brow.
Flexibility challenges the perfectionist's know-how.
Life has so many shades of gray, even the sun is covered with haze.
Human beings are not easily controlled and often have sloppy ways.

There must be order in the perfectionist's universe.
Talk takes time, so it must be terse.
The perfectionist, you see, lives in the clouds.
She is ever reaching, always seeking, confidently proud.

With love and pain, I release perfectionism from my grasp.
It's part of my fiber to be perfect to the last.
But, by accepting the imperfection of my human side,
I am slowly learning how to cruise — how to ride.

Average is not what I'm about.
Ideals, adventure — that's what I shout.
But, let's be friends — bright, slow, short and tall.
Strive to do your best, and you'll be ready when you hear His call.

Margaret M. Newman

Apocalypse Down

There are big green dots before my eyes
orange psychedelic flashes of pure power flash through my mind like
thunder bolts, and I think of red blood, flowing over the hills,
leaving the land crimson in its wake.
The sun is a sickly yellow, that throbs like a pulsating heart.
The green is a nauseating color, as Ares comes charging forth from
the earth, just as it opens like a hungry mouth. His mission, to
destroy the people who have long forgotten the faces of their fathers.
His chariot rolls forth, crushing some beneath its tread, leaving
the ground crimson in his wake, while others are killed by the strife
that rolls off it like pulsing waves.
And the sky is a too bright blue before my eyes; as thunder clouds
rain crimson down upon my prone body, and I lay on a hill-top
waiting to die. I want to close my eyes, but want to watch the crows
that gather pick my flesh, how disappointing they go first for my open eyes.

Michael Briggs

I Don't Care

I don't care what you said,
  or how you treated me.
Now I know you're the one
  that I don't really need.

I didn't care when you stared at me,
  although you didn't see;
The way I rolled my eyes at you,
  you thought I was the fool.

I didn't care when you called me names,
  and said some real mean things;
I didn't show how I felt,
  but the pain still held within.

I didn't care when you were with her,
  that night I saw you there.
And don't worry, I don't care,
  that you and her are a pair.

Monique Rios

The Tears of Thunder

Has there ever been a day gone by
or a word - pain inflicted, yet somehow
forgotten, passed by?
Then, like a mighty roll of thunder, is
but an echo of the lightning, a chord
struck deep in the heart, a simple tear
for something left unsaid...

Me, simple, a vision of a solitary tree
standing alone; deep in thought.
Naked before the elements, the flash was
but a mighty limb o'er a century grown;
now severed, a memory - thunder rolls, a tear is shed...

A stately oak, shrine of beauty and provision of shade.
Yet alone, solitary. No children
to swing from my limbs, nor lovers to seek
shelter from the eyes of the gods - destined
to survive without purpose.

John F. Eckert

Untitled

In an instant it was done, like a crease in a paper
Or a fire in the dry summer brush,
And souls were left to revere in awe

The angels mourn with the gentle fall of rain
And sunbeams fade as they search the vast cavern of sin

As evil lashes out, a blanketing darkness smothers an eternity
Too forlorn for remorse, for all we know and believe to be true
Our ears are deaf to the dolor which rings out through infinity
Expanding past the farthest stars, chanting a lament in its silence
For the loss of divinity

In the hands of one, to mold each complex thought and sacred motion
To serve as father and executioner,
Who gives and takes as he may please has fallen

For with the sobs of the angels and the laughs of the demons
Everything has slowed to a halt and now your world
In an empty vacuum no longer rests on faith
But, rather, on an eternal altar

For God lays dead in heaven, shattered on its steps,
Murdered, by the children which he created
In His image

Joshua Verch

Death of a Flower

suddenly I'm lost in this meadow of grief
only in your arms could I ever find relief
through days and nights I'll see your face
a multitude of memories I cannot erase
a gushing rain hampers my sight
growing cold and mournful throughout the night
we've come to the end - the darkest hour
sunlight cannot save this flower

perhaps some sun would ease the pain
but all we have is endless rain

midnight whispers a strange sweet song
to bless you as you travel on
the night seems endless lingering on
I'm afraid you'll never see the dawn
exhaling a final withered breath
inhaling the blissful sleep of death
on a blanket of petals you lie so still
sleep my darling daffodil

Jodi-Rae Arruda

Glorious Sun

Well the day is of the sun and the people are glad to be the joyous
ones they come to play and sing and tell the world about everything
It's a world of nature and beauty sings the day is just begun
Come and see its own history as the day has given us moments of
delight, be filled, be glad, for in three weeks, what we are all here
for, one thing we all have in common, one thing that ties us all into
one is this campus the place - that tells us that? Is this the place
- that gives us our freedoms, constrictions, our education? Is this
the place - that gets lost and dribbles down the efforted pages that
our words to our professors fall upon? So step away and remember to
think, this place you've come to - it's yours - it's mine - we're here
all the time, and in the future we will return, but mainly in our
minds our memories the day is of the sun and the day is just begun so
stroll, so walk, and enjoy what you've got, and remember who you are
and play that out passionately for everyone - be you - be me - I just
want to be free

Martin R. Dionne

"Observation On A Sunday Afternoon"

As I walked the streets, I met two men -
One, widowed of wife; the other did not share her life.
The "one" felt empty at his loss;
The "other" saw naught in her, but woes!
The "one" remembered all the good;
The "other" criticized, all he could.
The "one" desired the other's fortune;
The "other" took her without notion.
The "one" bewailed his lonely fate;
The "other" brewed within his hate!

Two men, two fates - neither in peace;
Each one requests of life a lease
To fill the dreams each thinks his own
And reverse the quirk Nature has done;
Reverse the steps their paths have trod;
Reverse the plans laid down by God.

No one appears fulfilled complete,
No one believes that life is fleet.
Until the day the curtain's drawn
Across the face of our last dawn...

Manuel J. Tous

Like A Garden

Written for Terri
Friendship is like a garden:
One person's soul is the earth,
and another person's heart is the seed.
As we build our friendship, we experience
sad times, and the tears we shed fall like rain,
and as we go through happy times together,
our laughter shines warm like the sun,
and just as the garden grows, so does our friendship
until it "blooms" not only changing the world around it
by its rainbow of colors, but also for changing a life,
touching a heart and decorating a soul. "Without your
friendship, my garden would be empty."

Mikel C. Snyder

Beautiful

Beautiful is like an eagle soaring through the sky, like a sunset
on the mountains, a walk along the beach at night, like a starry
night, like under the surface of the ocean, the Caribbean in the evening.
Beautiful is like Las Vegas after dark, like all the houses in my
neighborhood at Christmas, like a piece of gold glimmering in the
sun, like the sun making a glow of eternal light over the surface of the earth.
Beautiful is like our band playing a song, like my Mom singing
a lullaby to my brother, like spending time with my Family, like
swimming in the pool with my Dad.

Michael Marc

Two People in a World

Two people in a world where people hurt and people cry.
One named Kathy, one named Keith.

One can hurt and one can cry. Two people in a world,
trying to adjust, to what comes along, only these two people can make it right.

Kathy cries and Kathy heals. And she
learns to deal with what's been said.
She goes on, and one day Kathy will cry,
but she won't heal, from what's been
said or what's been done.

Then maybe Keith will come
home, and deal with what's been said or done -
himself! Since he is the one, who has said,
what makes Kathy cry and only sometimes heal.

Kathy may heal, but only for a while,
'cause she is only one person and healing takes a lot.
Now Kathy is running out of ways to deal with it all.

One day when Kathy cries, and Keith deals, with the hurt,
that does not heal, she only hopes that Keith will know,
Kathy, can not deal - All Alone.

Kathy Van Meter

Praise God

I'll praise him for his only son who died
one day for me.

I'll praise him for a right of mind, and
To live eternally

I'll praise him for his only son oh what
a man was he.

I'll praise him for all the souls that rose
on Calvary.

I'll praise him for the moments oh and when, I
Think what God really means to me

I'll praise him because, I love him he means
a lot to me

Oh how do you praise him may, I ask in all
sincerely ways

Or do you praise him once a week or just
once a day

Oh know that way is half of what a praise, is
ought to be

I'll, just praise him because he's so sweet and
Dear to me. Oh if you could realize such
Peace and joy to be.

The suffering he gave for all mankind
that day on Calvary

Joseph D. MiddleBrooks

Men Of Power Lost

Shining bright like a beacon of light,
Old man who is spirit made flesh,
Come to set things right,
Rallies men without hope,
Strengthening arms with words,
With their most somber fears they learn to cope,
Against darkest evil they set sail,
Bonds unbreakable they from in dire quest.
Darkness fall forever if they fail.

Joey Price

421

Crimson Leaf

Don't let me go, said the crimson leaf
on top of the tree.
Up here, near heaven is the place for me.
Don't let me go mother tree, hold on tight,
Nestle me there while others are in flight.
I'd rather remains here to see the moon
and stars at night...
Feel the raindrops and snow and feel
the wind flow.

If you let me stay this winter,
In the spring I'll gladly go.
For in the spring you'll sprout new colors
and all the trees new green will show.
If you decide to drop me and let me go
Some naughty boy might crush me
and I'll never see the snow.

Grace Malcolm Athey

Bitter Cheese

In the season of summer when it continually snows,
on the plains of asphalt by the rock tree groves.

There lived a cat named Sir Thomas The Third,
who spoke pure English in every word.

He said to his time piece one day in the sun
"Boy this winter sure is no fun.

How I want to swim to the moon and see
the cats who live in the monterey tree."

"What is the moon?" The time piece said,
"Is it that thing you wear on your head?"

"No this is my hat," Sir Thomas replied,
As he stood with an air of feline pride.

"It's a rock in the sky of no great worth,
at night it gives light to some of the earth."

Then a noble mouse near by said "Sir if you please,
I heard the moon was plain bitter cheese."

A Doberman sentry who was crossing the way said.
"The moon is nothing more than a hole in the day."

Sir Thomas arose and finished his tea
and calmly replied, "I shall set sail on the sea!

To solve the mystery that lies afar
across the blackness amongst the stars."

"And I shall return with the secret cosmic keys,
even if the moon is plain bitter cheese."

Matthew Jones

The Proud Bluejay

Its coat of shades of blue of black of white,
On perch or on the wing
is a beautiful sight.
Flitting from tree to bush to
ground to heights in flight
With easy grace and beyond,
always in search of food.
A loving parent to its offspring
and a vicious competitor
to all their feathered kind.
Be it sun on cloud on any day.
On perch or wing there is
none more magnificent than
the proud bluejay.

Oliver Tussey

"She Waited All These Years"

There was a little boy dragging a baseball bat!
On a little neighborhood baseball field at that!

Little did he know there was a little girl named "Brandi"
running here and there on her toes.

Rooting for him! Cheering for him!
Yelling "Hit that ball, Norm! Go! Go!"

She tried so hard then to get his eye!
Every time that he passed by......
"What a swell little guy" she sighed!

As years went by she never caught his eye
He went to Reagan and she went to Elgin High!

Girl friends came and went in time.
They just weren't his kind.

One day he noticed two smiling green eyes,
God did it as he passed by!

This little girl's dream came true,
so that's why we invited you.

Jennie Davis

Travel Alone

Travel alone
on a destitute island of blue

The being of man is to be alone,
wandering the colors of life.. empty

Travel alone
into the golden light of the sun

To be warm..to feel the scorching heat of life
glowing within..only to be drenched

Travel alone
in the aqua waves of despair

Making your way through the ripples of
colorless fear that binds us all

Travel alone
on the barren branches of umbered trees

To reach out..to grasp the empty arms of love

Travel alone
on a pure canvas of white cloth

To pick up the brushes.. to color life..
Your only challenge.. to be

Karen Townsend

Colors Of Our Heart

There! Up on the pole in currents unfurled,
Old Glory, colors, best in all the world.
It thrills my heart, see in breezes streaming,
Those stripes our emblems of a freedom gleaming.
The valiant ones all love it's raising,
Trails of liberty loyal ones are blazing.
Hear! The notes waft a melody on the wind,
Our hearts and heads in admiration bend.
Why are those stripes so bright a red?
Reminding us of where that blood was shed.
For freedom many man have died,
For liberty they were sorely tried.
The red red stripes are like their blood,
Our hearts a thankful joy will flood.
Now! Assign to each one a star above,
And fill it full of everlasting love.

Jene Hall

To Write To Write

To write, to write, how I hate to write, It is such a bore,
oh I can't take much more.

Give me a pencil, I won't know what to do. Give me a
pen, I'll show you.

Some poems are happy, some poems are sad. Some are funny,
and some make you mad.

I need a piece of paper, I need a pencil too. I need an
eraser, and I'll write for you.

I think of where I'm going, I think of where I've been.
I think of how, who, where, and even why, and when.

Give me a pen, and I'll write for you. Give me a crayon,
oh that will not do.

When I wrote this poem, oh it really wasn't fair. For
when I wrote this poem, I was tearing out my hair.

I will end my poem, because night is coming soon. The
sun is going down, and you will see the moon.

This is last, oh I've had such a blast. But since I've
said hi, I will end with goodbye.

Noelle Lovejoy

Oh, How The Days Fly By!

Oh, how the days fly by, fly by;
Oh, how the days fly by.
"Stop please," I plead,
But the days do not heed.
All they can do is concede.
"We have a journey to make.
We must make haste, must make speed.
We, by ourselves do not know
Why we must be on the go.
We do not question, (we fly with the rest)
All we can do is attest:
Do Now what you must, and be blessed."

Olga Michel

Wondering Why

Just thinking that you are no longer here
Oh, how it brings so many tears.
It's hard to accept that you are gone.
It seems so very, very wrong.
Sometime I sit and wonder why
How can I make myself not cry?
I am trying to continue being strong
Because I know I must move on.
Memories I have flash in my mind.
I am so thankful they're with me all of the time.
Without them what would I do?
Please remember I will always love you.

Lori Britt

Untitled

In the work-a-day world we often lose sight
Of things we once considered so right.
With E-Mail and faxes and cellular phones
Individuality suffers. We behave like clones.

When "progress" and civilization demand
That we no longer do anything "by hand",
Computers take over and they rule supreme.
Refinement and gentility are lost, it would seem.

Regardless of how far advanced we may be
We still go to war, pollute land and sea,
And even the air we breathe on this planet
We fouled so, if we could, we would ban it.

Gloria Rettig

There's A Beauty In Thunderstorms

There's a beauty in thunderstorms
     Often misunderstood
Much more than just a downpour
     Rain does the soul some good
Clouds are nothing more than reservoirs
     So designed to hold the pain
Bearing the weight of the world
     To be released each time it rains
Thunderstorms are really just a means
     Of getting all the earth to share
Life's heavy burden of troubles
     Eased to a level you can bear
Once the clouds have finished crying
     The sun begins to shine
There is a calm, a rainbow over the earth
     Now you know you'll be just fine
Yes, there's a beauty in thunderstorms
     Often misunderstood
If you don't understand them
     Perhaps you should

Michelle Davis

Life

Life...
Often a mystery,
No one knows what will happen,
And no one can change the past,
People sometimes think they can predict the future,
But no one really can.

Although life is one of those things,
That are not meant to be found out,
It's a riddle, a puzzle, a mystical existence.

Life is full of questions.
Full of adventure!
And it's out there waiting for you.

I admit that sometimes it's hard to grasp life,
But when you've overcome a problem,
You feel like you could do anything.
Life is not easy to conquer, but with a little faith and
A little courage, you can pull yourself through.

Don't go too fast, just let it guide you on your path.
Don't ask why, or how, just be thankful and try your hardest.
And in the end you can say, with great pleasure, I am
Ruler of my life.

Melanie Epstein

Relax

I've chosen my way, sometimes it's win or lose,
often, in the stress time I need a quiet snooze.

Just a little excitement will chase away the blues,
then I forget everything except a little snooze.

Walk, relax or rest, that's just a ruse,
I'd rather sit down and enjoy a snooze.

I don't want to wash dishes or polish my shoes,
I'll just take it easy and go for a snooze.

I'm not very lazy, I do as I choose,
I eat a little dinner, then take a snooze.

I must hurry now, I've no time to lose,
I'll go to my recliner for another little snooze.

Mary K. Barnett

A Fierce Enemy

What is the meaning of this enemy called inferiority
Of the human race, it plagues the majority
It's not at all prejudice you see
No matter what color, creed, or religion you be
From the beginning of your birth, it seeks to destroy your self worth.

Inferiority indeed can be fatal and, as I said it begins in the cradle
It whispers over and over you're no good
You're ugly, you're stupid, not like the rest
And you try and try to be you best
Inferiority says but you just don't pass the test.

But it's up to you and I whether or not to believe the lie
Because that's exactly what it is, you know
A lie from hell to make us feel low
Look to God's word to see what's true
You're worth God's son dying for you.

You must have been worth leaving Heaven for
Worth more than streets of gold
More than all of Heaven's splendor
You're worth all the love God could give
Because Jesus left it all behind, so you and I, eternal life could find.

Kathie G. Price

Rebound

I am the fearful eyes that fathom the felt weight
Of the fallen tear that fell before my sin.
My vision has begun to blear by the feelings
Bestowed behind your breast because of him.

I am the loving shoulders that lift along the lost weight
Of the living burden of an unforgotten love.
As I try to pry, my shy feelings die awry.
As your fun is done, my love's begun, in the tears of a dove.

I am set in the shadows of darkness,
A heart's sulking void that is misnamed passion.
My love is lost along the line of low lying rocks of your heart
And a long lived past with him, still present in an essence's fashion.

I monotonously move though my mind, my dreams omit
Your mind's memories you've made and miss of him.
As I rise into the riveting realm of reality, I realize
That our love is nothing more than a whim.

I begin to break like broken brittle, buried by my beliefs.
A forgotten fear is forced to be found.
A silent stillness oppresses my soul as I slowly see
What I am here for, nothing more than before, just Rebound.

John Ramos

Song Of Self

And I have read these poems
Of more than aspiring poets, today.
Does jealousy now enhance my despair,
Or does inspiration deaden the desperateness?

The poets write of prejudice, rape,
Suicide, volcanic and plywood-shelter parents;
And the alum taste upon my tongue persists
From these same cataclysmic past clamors
That still within me unexpressed burn.

But as I sit in the dimming light from lowering clouds,
The metaphors of poets absorb arid strife.
As the I in each poem preserves self,
My halting words upon a page resurrect,
And hammer blows beat golden symbols
On the anvil that is I.

Geneva J. Marking

Memories

Memories of the times we've shared
of moon-dates and long relationships,
Memories of the way you talked and looked and cared;
Those are some of my memories
That I'll never forget in all my life I live;
Memories of love and laughter,
Some were mine to give.
Memories never die
But some make you sad and cry;
But all memories are stored away
So in your old age you can see,
All the joys and happiness that you've had with ones you
cared for and loved and dreamt of when you were young.
Memories will live on after you're gone, because you
will have told them to others.
One good thing about memories is...
You'll always have something to remember!

Lori Sargent

daughter

I see you staring at me with a face full
of memories that drip from your eyes like tears.
Boxes containing my childhood lay sleeping in
the attic, surrounded by invisible laughter as the toys remember
with joy, all the fun they had while entertaining
their small master.
"Whatever happened to our child?" whisper the toys,
"Where has she gone?"
The air still wears the laughter of imaginary friends
even though Time has left them far behind.
No more piggy back rides through the park or forbidden ghost stories
told from behind a flashlight.
Your body sags with realization,
you knew this day would come.
Now you, too, are wondering where your child has gone
and who is this young lady standing in front of you
smiling all your sadness away.
Why, it's only me daddy,
your little tomboy.

Krystal Houseman

Hands

From a world full of darkness, of anger,
Of hatred and disrespect;
From a world full of shattered dreams,
and hopeless searches,
and the faces of the betrayed;
From a world unable to trust,
and unable to love unconditionally,
A hand stretches out...

In hopes of finding a world where there is light, and joy,
and love and respect;
a world where dreams do come true,
and where what is sought is found,
and where trust is never broken,
and love is unconditional, and undeniable.

A Hand reaches out,
as far as it can,
hoping to reach its dream,
and it finds only...

The hand of friendship it had sought all along!

Nate Pedersen

World Of Confusion

There I am a girl who is loved by family, but yet lost in a world of confusion. There I am in school, wondering why I am here? Who are these people? Not knowing I'm not supposed to be here The people in my life are like paper dolls. They will come and go, but yet leave paper cuts left on my body. I wonder, am I really supposed to be here? Is this really the story of my life or something to settle for. I guess I'm just a girl lost in a world of confusion.

Lisa Bottaro

"My Treasure"

Oh, such pleasure to find the treasure
of a precious seashell on the seashore.

It's there in your hand... and it's so grand
as you keep on walking in the sand.

You hope you'll find just one more hidden there in the sand,
but these are so rare and so grand.

At the end of this day one special shell is all the treasures gained.
So proud of this one little find kept safely in your hand.

To that special place you quickly go to hide such a treasure.
You'll take out the box to keep it so safe.
Taking it out often to admire and remember.
What a pleasure when found, this small precious treasure.

Your friendship hidden safe in my heart is much greater a treasure
and bring me oh, so much more pleasure.

Michelle McLaughlin

"The American Way"

Freedom for all, when did it fall?
Oath and vow, where are you now?

Who is my neighbor, what color is he?
Is he really as good as me?
Is this what God meant for this world to be?

Our resources depleting, our air about gone,
Should greed and power be our song?
Is this where all the people have gone?

The honest man falls to the hammer and claws.
Are we people or should we have paws?

It's not enough we take lives in war,
We now can before they are bore.

The enemy sows seeds of envy and greed,
Are we so dumb we jump under the thumb?

Unrest and hatred highly zoom,
And they will surely be our doom.

It's time we woke that this is no joke,
Before this whole world goes up in smoke.

Judy A. Nolan

Poetry

P oems are verses with words that rhyme.
O ne who writes - needs plenty of time.
E ach of us wants to do our best.
T aking a break for a few seconds to rest.
R eading it over is important to me.
Y es, I'm sure you all will agree.

Marion Allspach

Paean To The Orchid Of Prognostications

O, pretty, pale orchid!
O lovely, mauve manifestation of the moon!
O mother goddess of the sky!
O wonder of Isis!
O immortal plant with a thousand uses!
O destroyer!
O savior of mortals with grievous problems!
O thou destroyer of priests!
O thou demon of the mind.
Like the Assyrian Ishtar, thou art, O orchid!
Unforgiving art thou, O rare plant.

Katherine Gates Runkle

De Profundis (Psalm 130)

"Out of the depths have I cried to Thee!"
O, God how true!

Out of the pit of anguish have I cried,
Beseeching You.
Wretched and sorrowful,
Yet unafraid, I dare
Approach You at the altar rail
You will not care
Nor long remember that I fail.
Merciful God, I need but turn to You
And once again, my heart and soul are new!
The Host upon my tongue,
And I am young,
O Prince of Love,
For You have kissed me.

"Out of the depths have I cried to Thee!"
And out of the heights of love you come to me.

Louise Moore

Sailor's Angel

Though it's been quite some time,
now my rhythm and rhyme
once more sets forth to tell you a story.

He has answered my prayers
when He sent one who cares
from the Kingdom of Power and Glory.

While we met first as friends,
we soon joined in shared ends;
lovers sailing through worlds of wonder.

But storms soon descended
on ships undefended,
unprepared for the lightning and thunder.

Still together we stayed,
navigated and prayed,
and together we weathered our romance.

For even at midnight,
there's just enough starlight
for two lovers to spin in a slow dance.

Still, I look in your eyes
to confirm my surprise
when so softly you whispers, "I love you."

Now no cross can conceal,
for forever I'll feel,
that I've fallen in love with an angel.

Kenneth M. Coleman

You

I never knew what love meant 'til I met you
Now I know what love means
You show me by everything you do
I never knew what love meant
'Til you made my dreams come true
Now I know what love means
Love means you

Joanne Mitchell

Seagull

The ocean's wave never reaches the sky
Notices the seagull passing by
The winter winds will forever blow
No one will wonder when it will snow
Another branch grows out of a tree
Though nothing will have the pleasure to see
The midnight star has glorious shine
We won't be there to argue if it's yours or mine
The width of the mountains can never end
The seagull can not even tell a friend
Admiring these things is the hardest part
For they are useless to a lonely heart
Knowing that the waterfall won't run dry
This sad bird begins to cry
So the seagull waits for its time to go
Being the last is the hardest you know.

Melissa Olivarez

Two Ways On A Road

Where I come from it seems as if time stands still
Not much has changed I often wonder if it ever will
Sex and drugs are power; prostitution is its worker
The community is faltering; the crying voices are just murmurs

Everyday I went outside; I risked my life
I was lucky because my parents told me the wrongs and rights
"Stick with those who are positive and you'll survive
Get caught with the wrong crowd and you could lose your life"

My mom got married and we moved out of the city
To the suburbs where life was pretty
I hated being away from family and friends; now everything's boring
The night was very quiet; no midnight engines roaring

I survived this far and plan to keep surviving
Maybe I was one of the lucky ones
Or maybe this way is right for riding

Marshall Lyons II

The "Strike"

These boys are tough, they come to play;
not just now and then, but every day.
When they hit the ball, they're running hard;
when on the field, they roam the yard.
They swing the bats, they'll steal a base;
they have no respect, for the pitchers they face.
And their pitchers, pitch, they walk no one.
When we play these guys, it's not much fun.
Run on and off, they're in the game;
from the Inland Empire, the Strikes' their name.
They intimidate the teams they play;
but on the field, not by what they say.
They play with pride, and class alike;
they're the best there is, and they're called the Strike.

John Knuth

My Angel

An angel voice I heard one night say, "do
not feel afraid" for I am with you everyday,
at work, at home or play.
You many have sorrows in your life but never
forget, that I am with you all the time so please
don't ever fret.
I'm always there to talk to when things get really
bad but don't forget I'm also there to hear
when you are glad.
I'll pick you up when you stumble or fall and
also be there when your standing straight and tall.
I'll cry with you and laugh aloud, no one will
hear me but you
Just remember I'm here and will always be in
everything you do.

Joan Schuyler

The Dream

As the body relaxes, the mind at ease;
Not a thought, not a worry;
Drifting from reality, leaving the troubled world;
Introduced with subconsciousness;
Thoughts so minimal, yet the mind wonders on.

Experience fantasy, excitement beyond imagination, utmost beauty;
Encounter adventure, seems like an eternity;
There's no pretending, no hiding here, only truth;
Live your greatest desire, encounter your worst fear;
You have no control, can't stop, can't go on.

Mystery around every corner, curiosity takes over;
Questions of the future, horrors of the past;
Deja vu, things look familiar.

Something happens, moving quickly in reverse;
Consciousness coming on, reality is once again;
No memory, all has been erased.

No need to fret, you'll be again;
Every day of your life.

Jennifer Hamerlinck-Raschke

CNA

I am a certified nurse's aide.
Not a dark cloud
But a rainbow.
I'm here to satisfy each and
Every little desire.
Willing to give a helping hand
Willing to help each woman and man.
I'm not the problem. I'm the
solution to the problem.
With a joyful heart and a winning smile
willing to go that extra mile.
Hoping to be accepted for who I am,
With a "have a good day" and
"Thank you, Madam."

Linda E. Garwood

Blanket Of Pain

Farewell insanity you were my friend
My name is passion

You know me well you hold me when I'm alone
You feed my dreams with driven hunger never known

You let me cry when there's no more tears
I scream but no one hears

Precious memories forever stained
Wrap me tightly blanket of pain

Scratches from Kitty

A Letter To Rachel

All those August walks we used to take around Godfrey Lake, with our
noses plugged against the stench, and my telling you, you'll never be
as thin as I am. Your bones are too big, girl! All those times, we
laughed. Do you remember? The mosquitoes still swarm about my head
despite the fact that I'm thousands of miles away from that polluted
water, where "three-eyed fish could have walked up on the bridge",
having been mutated by some strange chemical.

Leaving was something I could not prevent. To the King of the Army my
father was a low courtier, and I was one of his few servants. So I
had no choice. I had to go where he went. And then you never wrote,
as you promised you would. Oh, how I cried over that response!
Strangely enough, I could not figure out why. Were you angry for me
leaving you? Were you ashamed for loving me like a sister?

My hair hasn't grown much since I cut it short in the eleventh grade.
My eyes are still blue, compared to your brown. My skin is still
ivory, compared to your olive. I still write you poems, even though
I know you don't read them. It's funny—if I were a boy and you were a
girl, we would surely have been lovers, so steadfastly in love with
one another were you and I. And it would have been you that remained
the girl (you were always much more a woman than I).

Katherine Edwards

A Tunnel Of Light

There's a tunnel of light wherever I go;
no train; no tracks to follow.
There's a tunnel of light to brighten the
way when things are dark and cold.
There's a tunnel of light that I follow walking
in the twilight.
There's a tunnel of light wherever I go
to show me the right path home.

There's a tunnel of light wherever I go;
I can hear the rain drops falling.
There's a tunnel of light when I feel the
wind, the mist, and the draft in the air.

There will always be a tunnel of light just
to lead me home.

Kristy L. LaMar

Progress

Chained to nothing.
No roots, no ties.
Wandering seems unknown.

Bound by time, money and fear.
To roam freely, travel to the ends.
Feeling the sun from every angle,
Stars from every view,
Seeing the moon on all sides.

There must be more filling this immense space than
Unintelligible noise, unbreathable air
And piled concrete.
But it is always more of the same.

One day to awaken - no escape.
An endless ride to look upon the sky only to
See cardboard commercials fighting for first
Billing with the sun... cardboard wins.
Nights of burning neon.
And plastic flowers never die.

Lisa A. Vosburgh

Argus's Story

I am Odysseus's dog, Argus. I once was young and strong,
no other dog could keep up with me. I was the best.
My master left to go to Troy,
but we never got to hunt together.
Now all I do is just sit here on this dung pile.
I am about to die here.
All I want is to see my master one last time.
He has been gone for twenty years now.
I wish he would come back. At last! There he is.
My master Odysseus has returned!
I would give everything if I could just be young again.
I am so old I can hardly wag my tail.
Oh how I would love to play with him.
If I could only lick his face.
Even though I can't, it is such a joy to just see him again.
I am so glad that he is alive and well.
I finally saw his face. I have felt joy.
It is time for me to go now.
I got to do what I have lived and waited for. Even though I am dying,
I will always love my master and he will love me.

Jared P. Bell

"Dark Room"

I opened the door to a dark room.
No one was there to comfort the tears of a dying child.
No one was there to fulfill her needs.
No one was there at all.

Emptiness is my sorrow.
Death is my fear.
Lonely is my heart.

I feel the cold, chilling winds of death upon me.
I see a dark, stone stairway before me.
I hear the sobs and cries of those who share my fate.
I smell the stench of my dead body as it is being buried.
I taste the saltiness of my tears.
I touch the cold stone with my bare feet as I climb higher and
Higher.
I see a light.

This is the end.

Lindsey Northen

Why Me?

Taking the innocent, scaring the world
No one is alone, killing yourself before you're dead
Pain, anger, hate, destruction running through your head
Everyone you see, no one comes without five feet
Wanting to scream, scream out to all
"Watch out hell is abroad"!!
Horror, sickness, no way to escape, the devil is taking us all
All to see his home
You lay in your death bed; as you feel so alone
There are millions feeling the same way
"Why should we pay?" We are innocent bystanders
Never want to hurt anybody, why did they hurt me?
Thoughts of death, Hopes of death
Finally you get your wish
The reaper is all you will see.
Laying in your coffin
Screaming silently "Why me?!? Why me?!?

Karen A. Turner

Untitled

I searched, but I could not find,
No one could solve the mystery for me.
I searched and searched, but I was blind.
I forgot to look in the only place where it would be.

I asked everyone, except myself.
Their round about responses forced open my eyes.
I was afraid to look, but I knew all along,
The only place it could be was obvious.

I tried to blame my non-feelings on everyone else.
Sure, I had problems, we all do...
    We have to learn to deal with them.

It took a long time, and so often I wanted to give up.
The more I searched for the answers,
The farther away I seemed to get.
Happiness, peace, love,
They all seemed to be unsolvable mysteries.
But the single place I forgot to look was inside of me.

I see you agree by your knowing nod,
But one thing you might not realize,
I did not do it on my own, I had help from God!

Matthew Walsworth

Cypress Tree

Lonely, moaning, in the morning, I'm here by myself, alone
No-one comes to visit me in my moat
They say I'm squalid and unkind in my dirty brown coat
My roots stay in water all day long
People come by and call me names but I know that they're wrong
Sometimes I just cry as I stand in my moat
As people come by laughing at me in their boats
I don't let it bother me
Because my dream of having a family will one day be
One day as I stood in my moat
A woman and her child came by in a boat
"Mommy, mommy look at the tree, it's standing all alone looking at me"
"Mommy, let's give to some friends"
"Let's plant some more of its kind!"
"And on every other day of the week we'll come here to dine"
I was so happy to here those words
Those special words that I heard
And from then on we were like a family
A special family meant to be
The woman the little girl and me!

Kimberly Sheri Smothers

Wait On Me

No need to laugh
No need to smile
For my best friend is gone
And I never had a chance to say these words in my heart
I love you
That was on the tip of my tongue everyday
It just hurts to think that I'll never be able to say them to you
But I shouldn't complain
You're in a much better place
Waiting for me at those pearly white gates
And the road of gold
That we'll walk upon
With smiles upon our face
My heart breaks into
Each time your memory drifts my way
Just meet me by the river
For I'll be there soon
Wait on me
Because I'm waiting on you

Michelle N. Howard

Moods

Know that in life there is no lasting thing;
No ivy vine that will forever cling
Upon the cool gray outer garden wall.
The berries rot. The vine grows weak and falls.
The rocks immortal are immortal never.
They puff away in dust and even the mightiest river
Runs off away and leaves behind its bed
Of pebbles dry and snail shells long since dead.
Thus it is and was and ever must: Nothing lives
But the eternal dust
Of broken hopes and hearts and salty tears,
Layer on layer beneath he molding years.

The old Aurora glows tonight, wide on an autumn sky
Like candles lit near a sepulcher
In the place where the seasons die.
And all along the darkened street
The orphan leaves are blown
Like children lost on pattering feet
Down through the dark alone.

Kenneth Harlan

The Gift

I received a gift some time ago
No fancy ribbons or even a bow.

Sometimes I wonder how it came to be
This wonderful gift that was given to me.

The "special-ness" with which it came
Alone gives hope it will remain.

The size of it cannot be measured
The beauty of it will always be treasured

The precious gift I write about
Is YOU my friend, without a doubt.

Leslie A. Chobod

One The Eve Of The Last Day Of The World

Bitter cold engulfs the night,
No dreams will come, no hope in sight.
On the eve of the last day of the world.

The irony of man, our final disgrace,
to butcher the earth and end the race.

To destroy beauty for want of more,
to seal our own fate through greed and war.

What once was ignored is now very clear,
as we weep together in ultimate fear.

Bitter cold engulfs the night.
No dreams will come, no hope in sight.
On the eve of the last day of the world.

John R. Story

Nature

Nature is beautiful
Nature is sweet
Nature is a nice thing.
Nature is not ugly,
Nature means animals, plants, and life can be yours and mine.
Nature is not a crime,
It's not meant for digging for gold in a mine.
See what nature can be
Don't just want to be another wanna be.
Don't destroy it and that's the truth,
'Cause
God made it for me and you!

Nathaniel Morrow

428

Driving In Rain

Heading off on a sunny day
No clouds in sight
Almost home
Halfway there
Clouds embrace the sky
Floods of rain pouring down
Blinded windshield
Wipers won't help
Choice to wait for it to go bye
Or strong enough to go on in the darkened sky
Up and down curved roads
Staying close to the side
Going up a hill with stride
Pulling in a place you know
Drawing the car from the rain
You're home and happy about the choice you made

Megan A. O'Reilly

Slumber Denied

Lying, at the ceiling staring,
Night is ticking by.
Burdened by misguided caring,
Repose, a fleeting sigh.
Finding self alone in wonder
Makes ample time to dwell.
The paths to choose are fond of blunder,
The mind does beg to tell.
As passing days are lost to time
To ponder is our wont.
Within us lies a dwarfish prime,
The clock a constant haunt.
Through fragile window, raindrop blurred,
Fate sure enough will pour.
And then a weary soul stirred
Must live this day once more.

Martin Swidwa

A Fable On Risk Taking

Two birds were sitting on the ground,
Nibbling on a worm, so juicy, so round.
A lazy cat was far away,
It was a nice and quiet day.

One bird exclaimed in a while:
"Let's travel for at least a mile!
I want to strive against the wind,
To fly, to see and try new things!"

"It's unfamiliar world, and it's so high,
I can get lost in this unfriendly sky."
So said the second bird and headed for the nest,
Where it could get a little rest.

The first had spread its wings and flew!
The sky was unfamiliar, and high, that's true.
The bird had struggled against the wind and won.
The sky and bird had only strengthened their bond.

The second bird, that wanted rest,
It didn't make it to the nest.
That lazy cat, the one so far away,
It ate the bird, concluding nice and quiet day.

Mary Klevitsky

Jacqui

Death means confusion
never knowing why
always wanting to hang on
trying to forget good-bye

needing memories more than ever
hating the hurt in your heart
knowing that life is now or never
never wanting to part

death leaves an empty hole in your life
and a wish for the days before
and a cry, a shout, a scream of strife
or a gun to even the score

I miss her so much, almost too much to bear
but life just gives, that's what you get
I just can't help the way I cared
I just wasn't ready yet

Michelle R. Baker

"Tim"

I remember long starlit nights just gazing up at his face
    never before had I been held by such warm an embrace
I thought always we would be together
    thinking he would leave me never
but now he is gone
    and I must move on
sometimes I feel I will wake up and this reality will be a dream
    for everything is not how it used to seem
and if I close my eyes I can still hear a faint knocking on my door
    but I realize I will hear that sweet sound never more
I don't understand why he was taken from me
    some things I am not meant to know and now it is that I see
that now and forever he is gone
    and I must pick up the pieces, deal with this pain, and go on

Jennifer Lynn Cambra

Natural Love

Like the sound of rain as it hits the ground, I hear you calling my name how it patters then flows when it is combined, your words enter my heart and my body you proclaim.

The raindrops catch the leaves and the petals of flowers, like the tears that fall from my eyes I never knew how much the rain stood to empower, almost in the same way your words held me mesmerize.

There stood the sun and a rainbow suddenly appeared, leaving a warm feeling across my face the clouds met and so did we, and without saying a word, we knew from that moment on our love had finally found its place.

Now the rain and the sun plays a beautiful melody continuously in my mind I still enjoy hearing it even though you are not there, but eventually your love will return all I have to do is give it time.

A natural love is like the rain it falls right where it should it shines just like the sun, brighter if it could.
Natural love, don't ever stop or ever go away always be near or in the distance like the rainbow appearing after the rain I want your love to always stay.

Natassia Sheree Spence

Hills Of Mist

Gray and white, blue and black
Moving swiftly in the air
Casting shadows on the ground
Representing peace, and at the same time fury
They calm the soul and feed the fire
Hills of mist, loud with rumbling and crashing
A hypnotizing yet peaceful and beautiful sight

Katie Tunison

Tricks On My Tricycle

It all began with tricks on my tricycle, you taught me to believe in myself.
"Can't never did anything," constantly came from your mouth.

I wished I were a boy, being strong and being the best were what I dwelt on.
You told me with conviction that, "the best man for the job was a woman."

I wanted to leave. There was something in life I thought I could find.
You gave me money. You believed in my dream and soundness of mind.

I had problems, of course, you probably knew they would come.
But no words of reproach just, "You can always come home."

I started swinging a hammer and began again to believe in myself.
All your words of wisdom I took off of the shelf.

It was then I met Richard, and how happy I am.
"The nicest thing to be," you said, "is in love with a man."

We're coming to see you, on Mother's Day we'll arrive.
As long as you're living you're the best mom alive!

Julie McCrary

Life

I looked across the field of time to see
my yesterdays, when I was young and
foolish and so different in my ways.

Back to where my life began, a child
that knew no heartache, a spirit that,
without a doubt no one could ever break:

And as the years of yesterday passed
with the blowing wind. I grew into a
woman and the pain of life began.

My children grew and flew away like
birds will leave a nest and my loving
parents were also laid to rest.

And now the years are closing, passing
faster with each day; and as I look
across the fields, I wonder; could
I have made my life better in some way?

Mickey C. Trogden

Nature's Wonders

The sun, the beach, the rocks, the sea
My words and nothing more
Another day at the shore
This is all that I want
This is all that I feel inside
My soul is filled with the warmth of the sun...
The freedom of the sea
It pulls me in...it calls to me
I am drawn inescapably
To be so near, to feel, to see...
My soul cries out to be heard
Natures wonders set me free
The warmth of the sun...the words from above
The universe, she talks to me
At this moment in time; I am no longer alone
The universe, this place...we are as one
Here in this way...here today
Here in my heart and my soul
I am once again completely at peace
I once again feel whole

Maria H. Hocin

A Wish Upon A Star

If I could wish upon a star,
My wish would go very far.
Everyone would get along,
And everywhere that you would go
People would be singing songs.
In my wish no one would fight,
And you would speak in great delight.
You'd always have a smile on your face
And never have a sign of disgrace.
In my wish nothing ever goes wrong
And your life would flow just like a song.
That is my wish upon a star
That would go very, very far.

Julie Fishman

Midsummer

On this summer day in the twilight of life.
My thoughts return to the days of youth,
In my mind I see the midsummer day.
Solstice, the longest day of the year.
A day I spent in a country far north,
Where the sun rises at three in the morning,
And sets at 10 p.m. or there after.
The night never really turn dark, only dusk.
On this evening when the work is done.
The evening fun begins.
Bon fires have been built of wood and straw.
Now the fires are lit.
They signal from island to island.
In a tradition that talks of old.
Young people gather for singing, dancing and fun.
They forget their tired muscles from a day of work.
They see only green fields of clover, grain, and beets.
They enjoy the vigor and health of the young.
And celebrate the midsummer night to the fullest.

John A. Rasch

Her Eyes

When I look into your eyes
My senses are set about like wild fire
I feel every rhythm there is to feel and I hear every word in rhyme.
As they mix and mingle together into a song of love divine
You are the ideal woman to me so very real and so very free
And tell me can you hear the music playing
Tell me can you hear the song they are singing
About a man and woman having fallen in love
Listen closely now to the voice of wisdom as it softly speaks
of sweet serenity and inner peace
And when I look into your eyes I see myself in a very different light
Just as we are now and as we will be
Together we shall create our own history
Love is the emotion which sets us free
And mine is yours for all the world to see
Doing that which many others have done, with every dusk and with
   every dawn
With every twinkle of every little star you and I shall be as one
And when I look into your eyes I just have to smile
For I have someone with who I can walk the miles
Listening to love's sweet song, deep and divine.

J. Michael Morton

The Darkness Of My Depression

My way is dark. I am a prisoner caught in my own private hell.
My depression wears many faces and has long been smoldering.
The fire ignites and becomes more intense. The pain is
indescribable yet excruciating. I spend my days with no relief.
I can no longer endure this season of hell. But, I have become
paralyzed in the torture chamber of my mind where there are
no exists. There is no escape. Only a solution - - -.

Kelly Foltz

Ode To Shakespeare

If I should expound as well as Shakespeare
My pen as fluid in art of sonnet,
Flowering forth with words I hold so dear
With graceful rhythm and form upon it.
Then would I travel past the first quatrain
To put the matter down straight way;
Having no difficulty of thought or strain
That obstructs the flow and creates delay.
How widespread my talent displayed may be
To perchance a sonnet of gratitude
Be written by a soul such as me,
As I to Shakespeare write this interlude.
O muses, I pray that talent I possess,
To make Shakespeare proud of what I profess!

Mary Soon

Of Trees And Men

On a spring day while in the park,
My mood or spirit was in the dark.
I was staring intensely into the trees,
When these thoughts passed in front of me.

Trees wither and die and so does man,
It's all part of God and nature's plan.
Trees bend in the wind and sometimes fray,
Life does the same to men almost everyday.

Trees are planted and there they stay,
Unlike man whom can move about and play.
A tree will often get rotten and decay,
Man's body, mind and spirit are the same way.

A tree is not forever and neither are we,
But were both natural wonders most would agree.
Trees and men both have fates, but
Man resists while trees just wait.

At times like this I would like to be a tree,
So I could be carefree and not have to worry.
I know this all has probably been said before,
But some thoughts are for pondering more and more.

Michael Bartolomucci

Broken Promises

Oh Lord hear my words, for I have spoken to you many times
My mind is overtaken by guilt and my heart with love.

How can I escape this feeling knowing you're above.
Oh Lord hear my words as I try to explain
The emptiness I feel along with the pain.

You must understand why I weep, as
I pray to you before I sleep.

With all my wrongs I hope you'll see
me through the broken promise I give to you.

Kim Wetz

Heartache

As tears of sorrow escape my eyes,
My heart breaks at the sound of your voice.
Today I cry for fear,
That I will never get you back.
Worse than any pain, cast upon me,
Is your choice of her, and not I.
A little voice tells me forget you,
But I know that I cannot.
Understand please this message I send,
For I can no longer cry these tears.

Leah Kowalski

A Place In Time

Strange...I seem to be strange.
My mind...I feel my mind derange.

Born...to a time of confusion.
But to my inner self...this time...a great delusion.

I seek a place...to where I belong.
Be it, the darkest of nights...or even...the earliest of dawns.

My suffering soul...longs for peace.
But, a time for me...is what the soul seeks.

A time...of sweet melodies romance.
The beautiful sound...that chimes enhance.

As I count the brick...that lay a wall.
It haunts my mind's time...and in its trap, I do blindly fall.

What I need...is a peace of mind.
And, I'll only find it in...my place in time.

Mark Josephson

Night Swim

The fog so thick,
My memory vague,
The last thing I wanted was to be live bate.

The howling wind,
The salty air,
hushing rhyme everywhere.

White-caps stung my burning eyes,
not one consolation in the sky.

Weightlessly lifted, limplessly sifted
along the endless ride upon the tide.

Eventually it came to be,
I found my way back from the sea,
and staggering to the beaches run,
I counted my blessings one by one.

Mae Carpenter

The Wind Chimes

My life was torn apart that day
  My heart forever hurled
Into a dark and endless void
  When Garner left my world.

He joked and taunted to the end
  Through all his pain and fear
He gave me courage to go on
  And whispered in my ear.

"I'm tired and I must rest now
  I've fought hard, but I really have to go
Before I leave forever, dear
  There are things that you must know".

"I'll love you for all eternity
  I'll always wear your ring
And when I've gone away, my love
  I'll make the wind chimes sing".

The wind blows gently through the trees
  The leaves have now unfurled
I listen for the wind chimes
  Since Garner left my world.

Marcella B. Rhodes

431

Mental Abyss

If the end never comes, who will change the channel?
My hammer falls upon a nail, and I've bent a quarter panel.
My pants worn and greasy, acne on my face.
Soiled are my bed sheets, I can't keep up this pace.
Psychotic I am not to be, schizophrenia, just a word.
If I pull the trigger, I might kill a mocking bird.
Words that slice my wrists, in a furor state of mind.
Pollution kills the trees, no breath for mankind.
Urination on the park bench, cold and wet, the breeze.
I hate that stupid song, she is such a tease.
When will it rise? I don't really know.
Maybe pink will work, bread can't eat dough.
The sun burns my kidneys, blue paint on my head.
A frog under a lily pad, no, the puppy's dead.
How much does it cost? If tomorrow never comes.
Where will I go? A bush full of plumbs.
I despise my alter ego, whatever is the time?
God! Look at me, I've truly lost my mind....

Jeremy C. Lee

How Love Should Be

I saw two sahuaros growing together today, on the way to
    my favorite place, Cave Creek.
Growing side by side, in the desert, stuck together with
    their prickly spines enmeshed.
Each blooming their own flowers, yet aging together entwined.
Is that not how love should be?
They shared roots and the strength of each other to lean on.
Each bore their own fruit, enhancing one another, protecting one
    another; yet, blossoming, flowering, growing their own
    individuality.
Sharing their glory, united.
This is how love should be!

Luanne Merickel Kaiser

"Beatitudes"

Blessed are they who understand-
My faltering step and crippled hand.
Blessed are they that know my ears today -
Must strain to hear the things they say.
Blessed are they that seem to know -
That my eyes are dim and my answers slow.
Blessed are they who looked away -
When my tea was spilled at the table today.
Blessed are they with a cheery smile -
Who stopped to chat for a little while.
Blessed are they that never say -
You have told that story twice today.
Blessed are they that make it known -
That I am loved and not alone.
Blessed is my doctor, the best you sce-
When I can't go to him, he comes to me.
Blessed are all that ease the days -
Of my sunset years in loving ways.
Blessed are my families who are so dear -
Their good care is why I'm still here.

Grace McDonald

My Magic Flute

As a child one beautiful summer day,
My dad fashioned a flute for me to play.
He took a small limb from our willow tree,
And made that magic flute for me.

I played from Mozart, Brahms, and Mendelssohn.
That tree had flutes for everyone.
But this was a secret, don't you see,
Between me, an eight year old, and our willow tree.

Muriel B. Snarr

"Never To Be A Stranger"

I heard your weeps today
My dress is still damp from your tears
I never told you what I wanted to say...
But I can help release your fears
Even though my eyes are closed
And my heart shall never beat again
My ghost shakes hands with yours and says
That friendship has no end
So remember the moments that we shared
And the genuine times that we had
Smile when you think of me
Not frown and be so sad
For we both shall meet again somewhere
I cannot tell you when
And when we do
I'll know it's you
And we shall speak again

Mariko Edwards

Getting Old

I wake up every morning
    My body stiff and sore.
And if anyone should ask me
    I'm a hundred years or more.

But I put my feet down on the floor
    And give my bode a shake
With a little love and help from above
    Another day I'll make.

You see, our body's like an old Model T
You gotta keep it in shape and prime.
Take care of all the dings and dents,
That we've gotten all down the line.

You've gotta respect it, so please don't neglect it.
    Be honest, sincere and kind.
What's more, my brother, love one another
    It'll pay off every time.

Whatever you do - do it with zest.
    And always have lots of fun
Then on down the way at the end of your day
    Some one will say "Well done."

Maxine Duenow

World of the Dream

There is a place where every animal
Moves with grace.
Come with me in the hidden glades,
Where fair ladies wade,
Their skin like cream and hair like lace.
There is a place...
There is a place...
Where the grains of the meadow grow—
And the waves of the ocean come and go.
See the bright sunbeams filter the water
And make it gleam
Come run with me in the world of the dream.

Jennifer Lore

Inside Me

My tears like ice they flow, like a river into the sea of
life. I am lost, so scared, I search but where is this sea,
cold walls close in will they capture me?
    Who is this she's always here, as I cry she comes with fear.
    She runs with love and hides away, she will return some lonely
day, when the shadows of my past lurk on.
    So who's to say if it will change, my life must not remain
the same, so as they close these walls so cold, I'll sit and
wait as I grow old.

Lucia DiSabatino

432

So Much Like All And I

He walks about the world with outstretched arms
   More so than I and more toward all and I
   They never simply limp along beside
But hold him in and hold him out of harm

With every wall that occupies its space
   Each wide and rigid standing side-to-side
   Where most — I know that I — might lose a stride
He feels direction and a forward place

When heaven thunders — threatening to cry
   Throws strong and sore his tantrum to the floor
   Whereas a shelter would I hasten for
He feels each drop to feel it purify

And as — when anything is left to mold
   Our scratching lead detached the unappraised
   He went beneath and had the writing raised
So feels the cold brutality unfold

Though nothingness might be his greatest fear
   To hand and eye, so much like all and I
   He reaches to where tangibles might lie
Where darkness isn't altogether near

   Marion McGregor

"Crossing Life"

Life is nothing
   more than a series of events,
      of speculation,
         regret,
            and chance meetings.

Changes occurring readily through your life;

Life comes and goes.
   people pass you by
      they will never know you.
         And you might be their sister.

So many paths in life cross no more than once;

Life is letting go.
   everything you love,
      over and over again,
         disappears,
            like life.

Until one day your life isn't yours anymore.

   Michael J. Hurley

Poet's Wealth

I'll sing you a song of my treasure,
   More precious, by far, than gold;
   But unlike a wealth of worldly goods,
   It cannot be bought or sold.
It is eyes . . . like the bluest of violets,
   Lit up with a mischievous gleam.
   And hair like the halo of angels
   Seen in a heavenly dream.
It's a smile as bright as the springtime,
   Which scatters the deepest gloom.
   And laughter, like crystallized sunshine,
   That echoes from room to room.
It is fingers as soft as rose petals;
   They tug at my hair with glee.
   And toes, like the pinkest of sea-shells
   That whispers about the sea.
So . . . I hurry home from my labor,
   Home, when my day is done,
   Like a miser, to fondle my fortune,
   . . . To play with my infant son!

   Norma Shippy Meuer

"Firefly, Firefly..."

They have incandescent wings.
Molten gold runs through their veins.
I see their barely coiled power.
"Firefly, firefly, burning bright...."
They hover with surprising grace.
Maybe it's not too surprising.
They talk to me with dreams that are hard to understand.
When I listen close it becomes clear.
And if I try hard enough, they understand me.
They told me about a time before man,
When magic was alive.
When the forgotten language of the flowers was spoken by all.
A time when the firefly ruled.
"Firefly, firefly, burning bright..."
They disappear as dawn breaks.
They'll return at dusk.
The darkness gives them purpose.
They wish to rule again.
"Firefly, firefly, burning bright,
With such a clear and lovely light."

   Kelly Rubidoux

"An Angel's Touch"

As I stand on a threshold with no corners, feeling the cool
mist of a restless sea reaching out to brush my cheeks my
dreams start to fade and the edges of the threshold begin to
crumble the gentle hands of an Angel caress my soul so
humble. With the warmth of her touch and wings of gold she
settles my being forever to hold.

As the beckoned me over the waves so gloom, I awoke and saw
I was in God's waiting room. When the numbers were called one
by one, I prayed my deeds had surely been done.

With a smile so sweet the Lord called my name aloud, he blessed
all my deeds as he placed me on a silver cloud.
Lo I then awoke in my room of black and realized the Lord had
sent me back. He spoke and said, "Go forth and do good and dare
don't wait and you can inherit a key to the Golden Gate."

   Juanita G. Bevins

The Last Walk

These feet, propped up, have been my life-long friends!
Mine to command until the long day ends.
And as I sit here, staring, I'm amazed
I have not offered, sooner, some amends!

They've carried me afar to view it all,
The ancient pyramids and Taj Mahal.
They've walked the decks at sea clawed by the waves
That sent them limping back to ports of call.

I've been their master pointing ways to go.
Some people call them "dogs" and now I know
I had their real support in all the prints
Left chasing rainbows in the melting snow.

I've pointed toes to trails both left and right,
But time points toes straight up! And out of sight!
Still I'll be fine with friends that braved it all,
Their silent bark will star their master's night!

   Leland Embert Andrews

Why

Why is a question hard to answer and say.
Like when we ask why something has to be a certain way.
We can ask why about sight, hearing, touch, smell and taste.
We can ask why about the problems we have faced.
We can ask why do people suffer and die,
And why do people have to say good bye.

   John Michael Zahodne

Regret

As death draws near
Merely footsteps away
I think of all that I hold dear,
But can't find much to my dismay.

My whole life flashes by
Like some cruel movie in the sky.
Pictures of my pathetic being,
I am looking but not really seeing.

I lie here and think of what I would change
If only I could back to perform on this stage.
This stage we call life—what is it really?
When you look at the surface, it seems pretty silly.

But if you dig deep, down deep to the core,
You'll find things you sincerely wish
That you had unearthed, discovered before.

I only wish I had known what I do now,
As death takes me, still with this furrow on my brow.

Jennifer A. Appleby

Beneath The Wings Of An Angel....

For Angels,
men have sought hither and thither,
from mount Zion to the deepest depth of the Red Sea,
thus the administering of Angels unveil what sephard's seek,
having me adjourn to a journey beyond the River Euphrates.

Where for art thou, oh...Suriyel and Salathiel,
thus a bewilderness becomes those which behold your beauty,
your eyes beheld the beforetime of Adam, as did Gabrael,
soon the Angel Raphael will appear before nightfall draws near.

Weighted in the balance
is a purity of purpose, a protection which preserves one path,
thus Heavenly host provide sanctuary until the storms aftermath,
in a whirlwind of flames Cherubim are our compass as the Northern
Star in the sky, knowing how way leads on to way, we venture forward
by and by.

Thus patience is a virtue as my thoughts do collide,
focusing upon a celestial chorus, though they subside,
heavenly shades of splendor permeate the higher heavens found,
as sweet as Amazing Grace, how sweet the sound.

Kevin Fisher

Love

Love is a precious thing,
Meant for every man and woman to share.
Sometimes love hurts,
And sometimes it heals despair.

Love will see you through all things,
No matter what the situations brings.
Love won't leave no questions or doubt
And you'll never leave without,
the feeling that you are someone special.

Sometimes love is for the worst...
But most times for the better.
It doesn't wait only to come in certain types of weather.
Love can heal a broken heart, and fit the pieces together,
Love can also have two joined to live happily forever.

If you think you've found love,
And you get no response from heaven,
Just remember that love comes from within the heart,
And under no circumstance can be measured.

Latoya Hoskins

The Hidden Truth

People hiding from their true feelings,
masquerading with painted faces,
not admitting their true personalities
or emotions to anyone,
not even themselves.

Pretending to be someone they're not,
themselves not knowing who they really are.

They falsify themselves so much, they are
beginning to believe that they are
something they're not.

They continue to fool themselves
and others,
losing all remaining touch with their
true selves.

They have become the people they're not.

Jessica M. Vasquez

Ode To Griffy Baby

Griffy is mulish and will not budge,
Man!! He sure can hold a grudge.
It started when I got to work one mornin',
And in my lathe he tried to horn in.
I removed his tool and started to work,
Later he came with his usual smirk;
He said "OUT - that machine belongs to me"
I said, "I'm sorry Griff but I don't agree".
He said "You're not fair, at six my tool was there"
I said "I don't care, and you can go
(And you know where)".
I looked at him as he started to smoulder,
I was set up yesterday with this Aloris tool holder.
Since I told him to take a walk,
Griffy will not even try to talk;
So maybe I should tell him - I surmise
That I do really apologize.
I'll say it with a voice serene,
I'm sorry - you tried to steal my machine.

Leonard J. Hoag

Clearly Love Completely

Love is not an easy vibe to feel, cause most people
make you not like them or love them.

To a person who never knew of love's special gifts,
the vibes of this vibe of love is love's special bliss.

Oh what a wondrous meeting of hearts just like yours
and mine.

Oh I found it hard myself to love and let go of all my
fears, I'm trusting my loving soul to you

Because I never knew of all which you could give to me
a chance to feel something so wondrously new love.

What you are made of is love, all of you, all of you
have to understand heart.
The heart is the very best part of a very loving special clear and
complete soul.
"Oh," a clear heart plus a complete heart gives us two souls
in love all the way.

Marsha Sullivan

Children Love Thy Parents

Children love thy parents, even though they
make you go to school. They do this so
you can enjoy success in life and not
have to struggle like they did to make
ends meet.
Understand when they were angry at
you for coming home late when you knew
you were in the wrong. Don't reproach
them instead thank them for teaching
you responsibility.
Finally, one day our parents will no
longer be here with us so respect them
for their wisdom and knowledge, and
remember: Children Love Thy Parents

Michael Sawyer

Wishes

Your mother said to blow out the candle and make a wish,
So you did.

Your father said to wish upon that falling star,
So you did.

Your grandpa said that dreams are wishes your heart makes so dream well,
So you did.

Your grandma said that God heard all your wishes,
And He did.

Kelly Murray

Beauty

Beauty is like a field of wheat,
Lying upon a golden sheet.
It is the bell that always rings,
It is the part in our heart that sings.
Beauty's the squirrel with the bushy tail,
Beauty's the sand in the children's pail.
It is the part in us that we must believe in,
We must find a haystack, and within it, a pin.

Kate Seremek

My Life

My poisoned black lace,
Lurks upon my face,
Burning the papers,
They no longer can prove my capers,
Skulls in my windows,
I am hidden in shadows,
Balloons on my floor,
How can I get out the door?
Flower fairies, unicorns, I've got it all,
Sitting in my room waiting for fall.
Seeing fake smiles,
Stretching across miles,
I'll just wait and see,
what I can be,
I no longer shall glee,
On the edges of reality.

Maija Cantori

Dark Eyes

"It seemed I could have sat there forever -
   Just you and I ... and the
   crackling fire dancing in your
   dark eyes."

"Such closeness, however, doesn't produce
   inertia, instead it generates its own
   fire - and that too ...
      danced in your dark eyes"

Lewis Brown-Coon

True Colors

Through young eyes it was detected but not recognized. What was
lurking beneath the surface was smoldering but inexperience shielded
the view.

The smoke screen can hold the truth but a moment, until it is finally
revealed to me and to you. Denial takes its toll over the course
and parallels a silent trial.

As age creeps across our clock, the optical focus sharpens and the
mind molds the pieces. The newly found knowledge serves not as
reward, but as genetic blackmail.

Recognition transforms to shame but scientists assure us, for those
with similar genes, we are not to blame. Memories do not extinguish
the fire, but only serve to fan the flame.

Illness followed by tragedy unleashed it, confirming the horrific
truth. The hue of his soul flashed before the facade could be
reconstructed.

Now complacent eyes have uncovered truth and take comfort in the
knowledge that evil knows not of its self-incrimination. Reserving
judgement for he who is king and hands down the ultimate
incarceration.

Kimberly Parsons

"Nature Relaxed"

As I sat there alone
Looking upon nature,
I almost had to force myself
To notice what mother nature created for us.
It seemed that everything was affected by what we created for her.

We have tampered with all she has given us:

She gave us a river;
We build a dam to stop its flow.
She gave us sand and gravel;
We litter it with cans and bags of trash.
She gave us beautiful trees and playful squirrels;
We tear down those trees, and for every single one,
We leave a hole in every creature's life.
She gave us flowers, ivy, moss, and shells;
We cover all that with pavement for our cars and buildings.

She supplies calmness every day,
And every day we disrupt it with the fear of death, rape,
murder, and pain.

Leslie Cooper

Untitled

Turning, Turning, Constantly Turning-
   looking for something I lost somewhere-
   never seeing what's here all along-

Turning, Turning, Constantly Turning-
   looking behind and never ahead-
   looking for yesterday-
   ignoring today-
   looking for lost love-
   not feeling your love-
   Rushing to get away-
   Rushing to start turning all over again-
Turning, Turning, Constantly Turning-
   looking for something I lost somewhere

Kevin T. Taylor

The Bridge

Standing by the rail of the bridge
Looking down into the cold river
Depression sets in
Unwanted memories linger
Tears of frustration drop into the water
Dark thoughts invade my mind
Bad memories haunt my conscious
Climbing upon the rail of the bridge
Holding on for dear life
Taking one last look at my surroundings
Thinking my last deep thoughts
Wishing I was stronger to handle all of this
Wishing my life could have been different
Wishing my mistakes were never made
Wishing all the hurt I caused was forgiven
Just can't take the agony any longer
My tight grasp loosens
Letting go of the rail
SPLASH....
The cleansing of the soul

Lennore Poirier

First Cherry

There I was on ninth street,
Looking across at a nice looking petite.
I just stood there looking and loving her,
I thought of going over but I just wasn't sure.
I finally decided to walk over and look,
I thought to myself, boy I bet she can cook.
She has a great looking bod and a nice set of headlights,
It looked like she was wearing some really tight tights.
I checked her out from all sides,
And found out her top even slides.
I rubbed my hand across her smooth body,
I was getting jitters so bad I needed a hot toddy.
It was cold, and I started to cough,
So I paid for her, and drove her off.

Michael A. Trotts

Everything Ends

I float down to the bottom of the sea.
Look what I did went and killed me.
I said I loved you I didn't mean to.
You laughed and looked at the sky as if to admire the shade of blue.
I watch. I listen. I wait. You don't say it.
You take my hand and lead me to a bench. You tell me to sit.
You tell me what a great girl I am and how much fun you had with me.
Then you tell me about her. You tell me her name. I say "Oh, I see.."
I draw back my hand and slap your face. I hope it'll swell!
I feel tears coming. Through clenched teeth I say "Go to hell!"
Little did I know that's where I'd be soon.
Not now but later under the light of the moon.
I run away from you. I run far, I run fast.
I run to my destination, the bridge at last.
I jump, I soar, I fly through the sky,
Towards the water ready to die.
Back to the place where life begins,
For me the place where everything ends.

Jessica Adrover

Together

I met you in a bar, we shared our drinks from afar.
It was love at first sight when you came to me that night.
We rode off together it's a moment I will hold forever.
The night was rare and full of dare and I really didn't have a care.
I knew right then I'd found my knight when he looked at me
I was all so shy. I am so glad we had this chance to meet each
other with just a glance. It was really quite a sight when I saw
you there that night. I was watching from afar wishing you were
in my arms. Now we share a life that's grand in a way that no one can.

Lori Scharich

The Sea Of Deep Blue

Look at the sun,
Look at the moon,
Look at the beautiful sea of deep blue.
See the wind blowing in her face,
Starting off like a championship race.
The waves flow rushing down to the beach
Where the sandcastle is, it cannot reach.
There they are sitting under the moon
Although they wish they were in a lagoon.
They chase each other along the shore
They wish to be together forever more.
They come together and start to dance
Now they know that this is romance.
There, in front of the sea of deep blue,
Together at last, together as two.

Kristen Farino

Thy Most Beloved Son Jesus Christ, Our Lord

J-erusalem a Holy Land a child was born in a manger in the
   little town of Bethlehem
E-ternal life, greatest teacher of all time
S-uperpower can make all things possible and beautiful
U-niversal King of all kings, King of endless glory
S-acred Heart of Jesus pray for us protect our families

C-onceived by the power of the Holy Spirit and born of the
   Virgin Mary and became man
H-oly Lord, Hosanna in the highest, Hallelujah
R-esurrection ascended into heaven on the third day from
   the dead and is seated at the right hand of the Father.
   Rejoice! He will come again to judge the living and the dead
I-nfinite power and love His kingdom will have no end
S-avior, merciful, only Son of Almighty, God forgiving Father maker
   of heaven and earth of all that is seen and unseen one
   God forever and ever
T-he Mystery of Faith, crucified under Pontius Pilate, He suffered,
   died on the cross and was buried redeemer of the sins of men

Leonides S. Sales

It's Halloween

The clean, crisp air,
little children without a care.
monsters with hair of green,
don't be frightened - it's Halloween.

Ghosts, goblins, and scary things,
Getting ready to make the door bell ring.
Trick or treat they all shout,
Fun and fright is what it's all about.

Across the full moon flies a screeching bat,
There goes a witch and her black cat.
As Dracula flares his creepy bite,
Wolfman howls into the night.

Candles in pumpkins, make an eerie glow,
but I'm not spooked, don't you know.
For I love this day, if you know what I mean,
So don't be frightened, - it's Halloween.

Keri Klepach

Hope

Hope is not a feeling, it is a desire from within.
It comes only when you summon it, but once it's within
your soul, you can sail the roughest of waters with the
confidence that you will not be abandoned.
Hope is not only a word, it is a way of thinking.
No matter how old or young, good or bad, hope lives inside,
but must be called upon.
Hope is not prejudiced or cruel, for no matter what -
whether you're short or tall, fat or thin - hope longs to be in you.

Meghan Werth

My Parents My Planet

Mother earth is angry, she is begging, "Please hear my plea!"
Listen to her cry, for if we ignore her, then surely she will die!
Father sky is screaming, "Stop the killing that we do!"
For if we don't, the he surely will die too!
Stop the pollution, stop the cutting, stop the burning, stop the
  digging,
Stop the destruction, stop the killing of ourselves.
Stop the maddens!...
Listen to Mother Earth!
Listen to Father Sky!
Please listen very closely to they're cry's!!.
For if we don't, then surely one day-
We they're children.
Will all just vanish and die!...

Michelle Mehrmann

Love Poem

Ties tenuous and tender
  Linked us in those early days
Just a spark of admiration
  As we went our carefree ways.

Gossamer threads seeming fragile
  Began to weave a subtle pattern of content.
We walked the paths together,
  Timeless time we spent.

A mystic, magic, ambiance
  Settled softly as a sigh.
The world took on the rain-washed beauty
  Of the fresh translucent sky.

Your manly presence, your chivalry,
  Traits that make all hearts rejoice,
Enhanced the pleasure of your presence
  And the lovely timbre of your voice.

Some alchemy - ? Fairy touch - ? Love had slipped in
  I hardly knew its birth.
You took me in your arms and heart
  And paradise came down to earth.

Leola Davis

Death

Death is cloaked in a shroud of mystery
Like the unending fog over a restless sea
Engulfing its victims in a forever silence
Reminding all of its foreboding presence.

Rising like a phantom from the stillness of night
Conveying the burden of a hopeless plight
As souls become lost in the streams of despair
And the ravines of greed — man is destined to bear.

Yet so vast the cosmic space of infinity
That only Death may know its strange affinity
No night so dark can equate to its blackness
Covering all in a veil of somber sadness.

Or Death may dwell in the den of the elements
Where a tempest drives the sea in surging torrents
And thunder and gales lash the land in fury
Forcing mankind into the fields of obscurity.

Death reigns over the valley of life and pauses
Then moves on to other imponderable causes
To intermingle with the shadows of the deep
Its secrets of life and death - forever to keep.

Joseph D. Earl

The First

Like the all important first stroke of color upon a vast vacant canvas.
Like the anxiousness of the bird before dawn utters a song to awaken
all that will hear that they may see the awesomeness of the sun rays
incumbent the blueness of a new day.

The powerful moment of the first time you look upon your newborn, and
understand not why you love right that very moment.

The nervous amorous tender moment of the first, time the love of your
life lays their hand upon your hand, and gently caressing it causes
everything else in life to disappear.

Experiencing the first parting of a life that felt like it was your
very own. Though in your mind some of the first you'd rather had
escaped. Yet the understanding is clear it was needful.

So with clarity we interpret the last shall even be the first.

Maxine Brockington

Think

Think too much too much too much. You think too much.
Like telling me my eyes are too bloody green. What am I to do?
Command my mind to cease working.
Sanctity so much like sanity I can not find the difference anymore. I
am insanc today. It is one better than insane. Felt close to that
too. It is a thin, thin line that sanity one, nothing grey about it.
Here, sane One step, woops! Insane, insane, insane. Not black and
white, though.
No no? Opalesce and malachite green. (So which side is which?)
First, you give me a corporeal body.
I have nerves all over, a stomach that growls, a womb that hungers,
eyes that itch to see better.
then, you say, you God, "Hah. I didn't mean it. Really, you only
want one husband, dull eyesight and an easily filled belly. That is
what you really want." First, you environ me in a place of strong
love, poorly expressed, and a place of thought, with sweet cunning and
wicked idealogy and a place where I can be nothing but a wall flower
followed by a wild flower. Then, you say, you God, "Hah. I didn't
mean it. Really you ought to be cultured flower, with no thought and
confident love." Sure. I can do that. Watch me go. One step.

Jennifer LaForce

10/26

Auburn waves cascading, falling
like ruby red leaves upon my chilly front lawn.
Fall is here again, and I remember her face.
Kind eyes knowing her stay will be brief but not forgotten.
Soft voice asking me to do her bidding,
untouchable but no less real.
I recall the pictures catching her, I thought I could, too.
The same as winter, cold and hard,
will forever follow fall:
pictures will be all that remains of her auburn waterfall.
Predecessor of loneliness, follower of warmth
fall remains the time of year when change is not suppressed.
Acknowledged and admired her starry, moonlit nights.
Crisp and clean collected midnight strolls accepted
fall walks by.
I cannot keep the season nor can I replace
the emptiness that fills my heart
when fall's wind is in my face.
I let the season by even though I hold it dear
for auburn waves cascading still comes once a year.

Justin Locke Eby

Of Watching The Open Door

Her memories are wistful,
Like clouds and screams and broken dreams.
Even us the night faded into
Dawn, darkness shadowed the empty walls.
The wheels of her mind were turning once again,
Though the years were corroded by the years of misuse.
She tried not to remember his warmth
And gentleness, because he was no longer there.
But she knew the long, dusty road would
Lead him to her doorway once gain;
The days and the hours are but seconds in
The ageless turning of the universe.
For him the doorway would always be
Open.

Laurie Lynn Brandel

A Spectacular Show Of Lights

Lightning bugs, where do you come from, and where do you go?
Lightning bugs do you come up from the ground, or
do you just appear from nowhere?

As I watch the lightning bugs start to show themselves
at dusk, flying around the tombstones in the cemetery
As they give the appearance of spirits of the dead ones there
All around the monuments, never very high, just
over the tallest head-stone, playing in the summer air.

I watch for a long time after darkness has come
on, enjoying the spectacular show of lights, lighting
up the cemetery in this special way.

I go away still not knowing where lightning
bugs come from, or where they go.
So I will come again to watch their show.

Norma Jean Griffin

"Moonbeams"

Moonbeams shining in the night
Light my world, illuminate my soul
The Universe sleeps

In the distance bells toll, day breaks
The wind shakes leaves from the maple
Cool crisp fall in the air - white light from above

Birds coo softly like the dove
Too early to leave the grand maple
Squirrels collect staples

All at rest
The moon hangs low over the nest
Over the crest of the hill

Moonbeams all around reflecting
Shadows dance on the ground, on my wall
Casting shadows tall and small

Beauty floods the night, a rare sight to behold
God's Masterpiece hangs suspended for the weary, releasing
Lighting the way for another day, a new tomorrow

Nancy E. Atkins

There Is A Place I Wish For....

There is a place I wish for,
In this place there is no hatred, no cruelty,
In this place there is no starvation,
No death, no pollution, no sickness, no greed,
In this place there is only friendship, life,
In this place everything is fair, everyone is equal,
This place I wish for, this place I hope for,
I wish it could be earth.

Kristy Tankersley

Words Of Wisdom

When it seems,
Life has made you invisible.
Don't be like that invisible man,
And wrap yourself up.

Your affliction hasn't erased you,
Take up your pen and prepare a battle,
Armed with love, acts of kindness,
And words of wisdom.
Then you will find that,
The cure for invisibility,
Has come from the same life,
That colors your life with those words of wisdom.

Jennifer Foster

"Putting Today's Troubles Behind"

Down a small, well trodden path,
Lies a rolling stream;
My favorite place to go and think,
And plan my life long dream;

Where the water rolls so cold and clear,
And the stones are as smooth as glass;
The moonlight glistens off the water's edge,
As the hours slowly pass;

The crickets begin to sing their song,
That is carried on the breeze;
As the stars twinkle so high above,
Through the swaying trees;

The night air is filled with the sweet aroma,
Of pines so soft and green;
As shadows on the forest floor perform,
A ballet not often seen;

I sit in awe at the beauty,
And it somehow clears my mind;
And allows me to think of tomorrow,
And put today's troubles behind.

Jeremy Almarode

O. J. Simpson Tries Pontius Pilate

And O. J. S. said, to the lawyers on trial,
letters 'US, then strike to rest a-while;
Give me my blood, I'll prove to the flesh,
that white is white, and black is black;
For strength by law, there is much cash,
as drugs become blood, in one world crash;
In a psycho jury, confused langu-Age class.

Let's give O. J. Simpson, a Barabbas arrest,
in a utopia libertinism, of Hillary's Mess;
Or give him health care, or give him death,
before the Pillory Bill, puts us all to rest;
For that law, is limbo'o easter at its best,
as the laws become law-less, in the west;
when the Word knows Plut'US, will-not confess:

Now the people said, you are quite a sport,
for being sanctimonious, setting in the court;
A benevolence expression, is upon your face,
in a Liberal innocence, of your silent pace;
Thanking the law-less, for winning the race.
But where is O.J.; within his days of grace,
Is he taking the Barabbas, to his own place???

George Allen

Untitled

The Judge struck his gavel.
"Let the trial begin!"
Before him a boy,
with a sarcastic grin!
"You're in contempt my brazen young man!"
They met eye to eye and the trial began.
That he had gone wrong there was little doubt!
The question is why this all came about.
The short span of time that had passed since his birth,
makes us wonder why someone could not find this boy's worth!
Did his parents care? They are here at the trial.
did his mother care? Did she kiss her babe's brow?
Did his father care? Did he teach him a trade?
Did he tell him what's right, and not be afraid?
Or was he beyond help parents can give?
A child of the devil, with but one way to live?
Then where were God's workers, the men of the cloth?
Could they not extinguish the flame for this moth?
Teachers, church goers, so many about!
And no one could help him ah!!
Now there lies the doubt!!!!
"Tomorrow," the judge said, "Your sentence begins!"
Come on now, really! Don't we share this boy's sins?

Marjorie Cluck

Half-Bits

I start to tell you something, but I've forgotten what.
Leaning over, I ask you what we were just discussing
But you can't remember either.
The ballplayer we discussed with such enthusiasm yesterday,
We've forgotten his name today,
And we both laugh and picture ourselves in future nursing homes,
With different colors of purple hair
Forgetting dates, names, but hopefully not each other.
Going downstairs with purpose, I forgot why I am there
And go back upstairs again and find my
   lost iced tea behind the shower curtain,
Remembering that I was going to take a bath.
I traipse back down again and stare at my library of books
Sighing with pleasure at the joy they have given me
Remembering authors, characters, content, plot
But no longer why I am down there.
And figure it probably doesn't matter or isn't
   so important after all as long as I have memories-
Memories of those I love and those who love me
knowing the important things are seared upon my heart.

Judy Christian

Rebirth

The frozen beginnings of things that grow,
Lay in waiting beneath the icy snow.
They slumber quietly all winter long,
Waiting for the season in which they belong.

With the sun's warm and gentle ray,
As promised yearly in May,
Snow melts and moistens the earth,
Starting their long awaited rebirth.

Sprouts released towards the sun,
Anticipation of life that's begun.
The ground loosens and opens up,
Emerges the beginnings of a buttercup.

More buds appear covered in morning dew,
Their colors burst forth bright and new.
And not to our dismay,
We need and enjoy their timely array.

Spring is a wondrous time of year.
The promise of new beginnings,
For everything we hold dear.

LeAnn Pajcic

A Time

Springs budding flowers, planted along the edges,
Lead the way to the house that sits just beyond the hedges.

A well loved place, where sunrise spills it golden hues; and
blades of slender grasses bend under the weight of morning dew.

Summer breezes air the rooms overlooking field and glade,
of that sweet inviting home, cool beneath mid-morning shade.

Aromas of cooking and canning mingling with white summer heat,
   laced with
children's light voices and the sound of their slapping bare-feet.

Beyond stubbled-harvested fields the house trim and tall, and old
iron pump and wooden wheels, are framed by the foliage of Fall.

The smell of pinestraw warm, peanut hay and dust;
and sunbeams, through the barn, across the brown corn-husk.

A beckoning haven on a winters' day.
Life is slowly unfolding, as time slips gently away.

A much used house through sun, rain, and wind;
wearing its years mended, waits to receive kith and kin.

Glow on the windows and reflections in glass,
Family there waiting with the sun sinking fast.

Breath; Steam; Smoke; Dust; Memories, all the same.
Fog; Haze; wisps of memories too deep to give a name.

Joan Annette H. Mansfield

My Wife

I miss you so much that sometimes it is hard for me to bear it
Just the thought of you ignites a fire in my heart
I love you so much
I long to see you
   Even more
   I desire to be with you
If only I could hold you   just for a moment
It would be so satisfying
I imagine a gentle kiss   a gentle touch   and then so much
A romantic dinner for two a candlelight affair and then
Wrapped in each others arms and maybe just maybe
   kissing and hugging all through the night
I miss you my love
My Darling, my sweetheart, my sunshine, my wife, my life
Where are you? Come to me
Come to me
I need you
   now
     and forever love

Jeffrey Harris

The Swing

The chains are shiny, the paint soft gray,
Just the right gift for a sixth birthday!
The little girl smiles and her heart begins to sing
As her Daddy hangs the new porch swing.

A few years pass and new things come and go
But the girl and her dolls still sway to and fro
What better way to spend a day in spring
Than to dream and play in the old porch swing?

More years pass and what a perfect place to spend
A warm summer's eve with her best boy-friend
With sweet words of love, he places his ring
As they sit very close in the old porch swing.

Now the chains are rusty, the paint long gone
The woman looks sadly at what time has done.
She sits ever so gently and softly she sings
A fond farewell to the old porch swing.

Mildred Hinshaw

439

My Corny Unicorn!

A Unicorn hung on the wall
Just so-high beside my bed.
Told me time both night and day
Upon a clock within his head.

One early morn in spring, as I awoke,
He said "It's Noon." It couldn't be!
I thought he played an April joke.
I laughed and said "You can't fool me!"

By six o'clock that evening
Unicorn declared "It's midnight now."
I checked the kitchen clock and said to Dad
"My Unicorn is wrong somehow!"

Dad took "Corny" off the bedroom wall;
Checked inside its fibbin' head.
"Daughter, dear, you're April Fooled!
The batteries inside are DEAD!"

Marjorie W. Collins

Grandma's Lap

Cuddle curled in grandma's lap you sigh soft sleep sounds
joining your heartbeat and whisper-soft breath with mine.
Rocking with you to lullaby melodies,
I am flung out on the yo-yo of time,
and my mother heart remembers
two, dear little ones now grown.
Cotton-soft memories...lingering joy...

Rocking, rocking, rocking...
I treasure hunt you,
my heart pirated away
by your jet-black eyes - adoring jeweled sparkles -
and by your wiggle smile - uncontained -
consuming dimple-dot arms,
jungle-gym legs and copy-cat tongue.
I pray over your downy soft head,
infusing into you God's love and mine.
I promise you warm hugs and intricate love strands
to weave around you during the velvet years of your life.

Margaret A. Lort

Crucifixion Of Christ

God sent Jesus to our sinful world
Jesus body and soul to Earth God hurled
Sent his only begotten son to die for our every sin
Crucified to save the souls of women and men
Arms spread like the wingspan of the albatross
Spikes suspended Jesus to the cross
With a crown of thorns placed upon his head
Which drew blood that dripped like molten lead
Jesus' blood dripped upon the ground
Below the cross in which he was bound
The death of Jesus was a major loss
After crucifying him he was removed from the cross
Jesus' body was wrapped in a shroud of white
Then was placed into his tomb that night
Three days later his body and soul did rise
To appear again before his followers eyes
Then ascended to the heavenly skies

Michael Reid

Jest Blue

Jest blue, God.
Jest blue.
Ain't prayin' much jest now, tear blind, I guess.
Can't see my way through.
You know those things
I ask'd for so many times
Maybe I hadn't ought to repeated
  like the Pharisees do;
But I ain't stood in no market place,
It's jest 'tween me and you.
You said, "ask".
Somehow I ain't askin' now and
  I hardly know what to do.
Hope jest sort of left, but Faith's still here.
Faith ain't gone, too.
I know that, "a thousand years
Is as a single day," with you,
And I ain't meanin' to tempt you
with, "if you give me —"
But I ain't prayin' tonight, God, I'm jest blue.

Mary Bethune

Life's Stages

Aw! The stages of life
  I've experienced a few
We're the same, yet we are different
  Like from evening sunset to morning dew.

When I was ten
  I wished I was twenty
Sometimes when I was twenty
  I wished I was half that many.

I guess I'll have to learn
  As others have done before
That you have to live each stage of life
  Then dwell on that no more.

But go onto another stage
  And give a try at that
And live it, so you'll have pleasant memories
  As you get older and look back.

Life's lessons and stages from dawn to sunset
  Have carried us many a mile
But for me one of life's most remarkable pleasures
  Is the love and trust of a child.

Nelda S. Burch

Destined For Greatness

Like a handmade newspaper boat
I've drifted through life
Caught in the current that travels
through time and worldly strife.

Momentarily, I pause as I journey
trapped in a calm-filled eddy
to rest and strengthen before the storm
Ever forward, my movement is steady.

Until recently, I thought it was just fortune
that this vessel never sank or took water
I thought it was good luck from bad luck
In these steps I did not falter.

I know now my course has always been plotted
the heavens have always been there to guide me
No longer randomly do I wander
but for a purpose I have come to see.

WE are all destined for greatness
each in our own separate ways
sometimes our boat gets rocked and sways
uprighted always in His infinite grace.

Linda C. Thorpe

440

Missing You

For the past few years,
I've cried a large amount of tears.

Wondering if I'll ever get to see you again,
or if this is just the beginning of the end.

I think of you every day and night,
hoping and praying that your alright.

Wishing I could talk to you—not on the phone,
but in person—all alone.

I think of all the time we had,
I remember both good and bad.

Every moment that we shared,
I want you to know I really did care.

I don't care what people think of the things you do,
your my brother and I'll stick by you.

No matter what happens between now and whenever,
I love you now and I'll love you forever,
no matter if were apart or together!

Nikki Rumfelt

My Secret Waltz

As the sun's warm light restlessly poured in
Its rays danced upon my still-sleeping eyes
Announcing then a new day to begin
Inviting me that morning to its rise

To dance with my partner, to waltz with them
The songs of the morning, the songs of birds
That would sing only to me, only then
Soft and sweet melodies I'd never heard

But oh, how I shall pity all the ones
Who will never see the most precious dance
That the most beautiful and graceful sun
Happened to show to me that day by chance

Surely the sun will come to me again
And waiting patiently I'll wait 'til then.

Lissy Marrero

Getting Back Together

I can't live another day without your love.
It's like a day without the moon and stars high above.
I tried to smile so you wouldn't know that I was
So sad to see you go.
But now if you know
how I feel I don't care.
All I want is for you to be there.
But I'm afraid you don't
want to come back,
That you've found someone
new and that's that.
Sometimes I wonder even
though we've been together
all these years, is it really
worth all these tears.
Then I see you and I
Know that our love can only grow and grow.
So I hope you feel the
same as I and we can
get back together if we try.

Nicole Machinski

Untitled

Today I saw true love.
It wasn't the passion of men and women,
It was something more precious.
This love was between a child of flaxen hair and amber eyes
And her Daddy.

I bent to speak to the child,
She was shy at first.
She was so adorable I wanted to hug her
But being a stranger, I didn't want to frighten her.

I asked her if she liked being with her Daddy
And she looked up at him with adoration and complete trust.
When she looked back at me she smiled a silly little grin.
My heart melted, I knew how she felt.

I looked up at him and saw so much love and pride.
I saw a man who would protect his child against all hurt.
A man who would give up his life for her.
I never felt so much affection or warmth towards this man as then.

I was overwhelmed by the love I saw in his eyes.
They shone with the beauty of true love.
And I knew nothing would ever separate them.
What a lucky little girl!

Linda L. Woolf

One Dead Seal

It came upon a deserted beach,
It washed up on the shore,
The bloody skin of one dead seal,
A seal that is no more.

Men came to its island long ago,
Only thinking about themselves,
And caught and killed the helpless seals,
Just to wear their pelts.

Some seals are still alive today,
But other animals are not,
They were caught and killed by mankind's cruel hand,
A hand that couldn't be fought.

So stop and think when you kill these seals,
Each and every race,
Or they, like the others will,
Vanish-without a trace

Jessica Pieciul

Flying Away

Away, away it flew,
It was the only one left,
And only I knew.
His feathers cooled the air as he escaped into the clouds.

The last of his kind,
With strong tears in his eyes.
Alone he flies...
Into the depth of space,
Searching for a peaceful place.

Above the ocean blue,
The last alive, lonely flew.
Faster, faster then the night.
Erasing himself from sight.

Then suddenly,
One smooth feather was pulled away
Alone, it too passed the world,
Past it all...
Into my hand.
A perfect, golden feather...
Yes, extinction is forever.

Jennifer Dawn Samuel

Why My Father Left

I used to blame myself, but now I see
it was all for the love of me.
He thought I could lead a better life without
him, he is so wrong.
The pain and anguish I feel is strong.
I love him with all my heart.
Just thinking of him I just fall apart.
I don't think it's any fair.
I will take my own, if only to his life spared.
If I could turn back time.
The life that would have been taken would've been mine.

Michelle Middlemist

A Summer Love Affair

The sky is an 'o' so blue,
it makes me think just of you.

The waves that carry, shells ashore,
I will think of you for ever more.

I will think of you as days go by.
Every time I think, I start to cry.

That one long summer we spent together,
I thought we'd be together forever.

The romance ended and the waves grew calm,
even though the summer went on and on.

I love you my darling, I love you so,
Oh please, pretty please don't go!

Megan and Stephanie Flynn

"A Great Joy"

The purpose of life has a lot of meanings.
It lets your bring out your true thoughts and feelings.

Oh, there are so many great joys on earth,
and one of them is birth.

You come into the world,
thinking that you never could.

But yet you go on leading your life,
having many problems and great strife.

But things will get better,
sooner or later.

Happiness here on earth, a great joy,
as you come into the world, as a baby boy.

Missy Bair

God's Mosaic

Breathe in the inspiration of goodness and truth.
It is the spirit of honesty, purity, unselfishness and love.
It is readily available if we are willing to except it wholeheartedly.
God has given us two things,
his spirit and the power of choice, to accept or not, as we will.

One secret of abundant living is the art of giving.
The paradox of life is that the more you give, the more you have.
If you lose your life in the service of others, you will save it.
You are rich in one respect, you have a spirit that is inexhaustible.
Let no mean or selfish thought keep you from sharing this spirit.
If your heart is right your world will be right.

As you look back over your life, it is not too difficult to believe
that what you went through was for a purpose,
to prepare you for some valuable work in life.
Each person's life is like a pattern of a mosaic.
Each thing that happened to you is like one tiny stone in the mosaic;
and each tiny stone in the mosaic of your life,
which has been designed by God.

Joan G. Maher Jr.

Mystic Enrapture

November, 1987 - virtuous, almost angelic to the naked eye
It is not the naked eye who looks
Your room, seven years, my chrysalis
What would I become?

The sweet surrender of my "girl"
Rocky metamorphosis to woman - but oh how she has arrived
Once inhibited, demure, now erupting
One so loving, so giving
Closet doll parts not recognized, have come to life

Soft brown eyes always looking
Coming so close, going right through - they know
Sending trapeze in mid air every time
Thursdays - once so loved, now completely liquefied

There you are and there you'll stay - infinite
in rooms of a willing heart so real - restless, ungoverned
You need not an hour inside of me to feel the pleasure - of you

And so my written words like soldiers, march
as only they can
They are my touch
The only link

Lorri Stamile

Another Test of Time...

The candle is life,
It is lit by a higher source
and burns consistently,
exploding eruptions of vibrant colors,
shadows dance on its merriment
and the flame plays along side
jerking in delight.

Who knows which way your
candle may blow,
but don't spill hot tears,
Just know this:
Somewhere, in all of this vast nothingness,
a new flame is being lit,
to replace what we have ruined,
and it grows.

Melinda Porter

Colors Of Elegance

A butterfly bursts full of life
It is joined by the growth of a gentle breeze
It rises, floats, enjoying the air
To and fro, side by side, enjoying life

Wings spread to show varied colors
So delicate, so beautiful
Elegant in style, floating in the wind
So free, going where e'er the wind flows

Finally landing to give its colors a rest
Time to show us its true beauty
The seconds seem all too few
As wings rise and colors float away

Butterfly, you were here for time too short
In all your beauty, you were gone too soon
But, I'll remember your majestic elegance always
And the peace and joy it brought within

Mary Ellen Schmidt

442

The Rose

A single rose I give to you,
It is for your heart that is so true,
Your love is a special kind
one that is so hard to find.

When I am down, you are there,
Always showing that you care.
You give a meaning to my days.
You do things in special ways.

Our time together seems to go so fast
Sometimes I wonder if we will last,
You seem to always be there
You make life seem so fair.

The requirement do you put on our love,
Sometimes I think you were sent from above,
Your presence is all that I need,
From your love I want to feed.

You make my day so bright,
Your lovely face is a precious sight,
You make me want to live.
To you, a single rose I do give.

George Chenette

Paradise

People and things live in paradise
It is a place filled with wonder, grace, and glory
People enjoy flowers with beautiful colors and nectar
Kids stay up late, eat candy, and play games
People enjoy the company of their best friends
Watch a rainbow that never ends appear
People play with animals without harm
Eat fresh fruits and vegetables from their own farms
People sing with the birds as much as they please
In the summer, they wade in cool water up to their knees
People organize and enjoy picnics on hills almost every day
In the shades, under the trees are spots to lay
People of all ages are there at all times
Everything is as wonderful as gold
People do not worry about vanities
Everybody exhibits the best type of inner beauty
People are filled with illumination and glee
Paradise is a place where I will always want to be!

Katie A. Igah

Love Is Merciless

Love is merciless in its cold, exacting....servitude.
It holds you spellbound when it's there,
Uncaring to the world at large,
So long as its deep eyes experience
All the attention of...
   The beloved.

But, woe should that attention falter,
For love is merciless in its cold, exacting
   ...utter rejection.
It lets you fall so far, so deep, so long...
   Forever.
And it leaves you lost in memories
That slowly, slowly fade
Until reality snaps back
Above the surface of the rippled mind-sea's
   ...New release.

Joseph E. Pia

Scudriarch

   Teach the young ones well is what he told me you see. Don't let
it happen to you, like it did to me. There's better times and bad
times, in this world we have to fall. In times when life turns
madness he answers our call. Lord call us to your glory; As one
and all we'll never fall. All of God's creation together. As for
me I'll answer your call.

   The 28th of February 1991. A Holy War came to an end the U.S.
thought they won, the flame was set while in retreat the wells the
fire blew. Oh God! George Burns was funny treat, for Bush to show to
you. Flaming as it's set ablaze by his mighty commandment so all the
righteous be amazed by what their loss of life meant. He's all for
one and one for all, don't matter who's to blame. Unite in his holy name.

   Christianity I chose to name for what I knew. Cause in my sanity
I saw the question asked to you. Who's Sane? When judge, jury,
executioner you became. Yet here back home the likes of Charles
Manson still can plea. Which proves our justice system don't give
right to have set free - like that. Who's Sane? Who was it really
that was Sane. Our world afraid of an apocalyptic holocaust. Sends
fear through Soviet Union for their power then they lost.

   A New Clear War's amassed against who cannot God perceive. All I
can do is my part for all those who don't believe. The 28th plus
Arch of March brings us to April Fools. For just in case you
thought the end was near, our Father Rules.

Joe Patriot

Love's Pain

In darkness now, my heart it aches. For some
It comes so easy. For me it is now.
It knows us all. It will be here, so come
With me to kill it in its glory. How
Can I hold the hand that holds me down? It
Will crush your emotions until they die.
It cares for you not the slightest bit.
You cry in agony. You ask it "why?"
To break a man, a heart to pieces. To
Cause so much destruction, yet not be found.
A drilling in my heart, just like a screw
In a coffin so far under the ground.

Who would have thought Love's joy so hurtful? My
Heart is ripped apart as I say goodbye.

Moragh Goyette

The Dream

If you believe fairy tales can come true
It can happen to you
If you believe in sleeping beauty
Then believe in me

For a friend just walk across a rainbow
At the end you'll find a heart of gold

If you believe fantasies can come true
You must believe in the dream I'm dreaming of you

If you believe a story book romance
Can be reality
If you believe in Cinderella's dance
Then believe in me

Each night I wish upon a star
I want to be where ever you are

If you believe in true love and laughter
We can live happy ever after
If you believe fantasies can come true
All my dreams became reality with you
You must believe in the dream I'm dreaming of you

Melvin Sherrod

443

The Eye Of The Storm

When you think of loneliness how do you feel,
Is your mind full of dreams and
your heart made of steel?
You once were happy with someone you knew,
Now, they are gone and you're far
from blue.
You're in the eye of the storm where
it's peaceful and calm,
Your thoughts and ideas they keep
you from harm.
You're content with existence it makes
others wonder,
your peaceful aura they sit and ponder.
You know what's ahead and it's not
the norm,
as you sit and wait in the eye of the storm.

JoAnn Gannon

This Life

This darkness, so dim and bleak,
Is what we call life.
What I would give to be strong and
not weak like you.
To be immortal is my only wish
as I sink further into this pit
known as hell.
So many losses I've endured, many more
to come I'm sure.
Too much pain, not enough love, not enough
blessings to thank the Lord above.
I need someone, anyone, to tell me they care,
no matter if they are grotesque or fair.
This thing we call life, it's not real,
it's but a dream.
This life in which no one cares.

Kimberly L. Chatman

Love Inspires

Within my world, one thing I see
Is people that are close to me.
Who I am and strive to be
Comes from these friends and family.

Such vibrant souls, true cherished gifts
They warm my heart, my spirits lift.
This "THEY" I speak creates a tree
A sturdy support, never far from me.

Cadmium reds, with golden weaves
Bright sunlit rays touch spearmint leaves.
This dream of beauty dances deep within
A creation inspired by love and whim.

My tree of love and laughing light
Exists from you, your greatness bright.
I shout aloud, voice clear, no strife
I love you dearly, you've touched my life.

I think of you, my thoughts flow free
Endless thanks for who you are, who you be for me.

Lise Layne Bosman

A Mother

Playing with dolls and giving them names.
Is not like the real thing, not all fun and games.
But now I'm a mother, I feel my true worth.
And I owe it to the woman who gave me my birth.
For without her love I might never be.
Or able to enjoy all my kids give to me.
She took all my back talk and problems in stride.
It took all her patience; it took all her pride.
I've given her such heartache, trouble, and pain.
Still she keeps loving me again and again.
Being a mother I now understand.
Just how my destiny was already planned.
It means loving and loving without any thought.
To all of the pains bearing children had brought.
It's giving and giving with only believing.
It's a fact that giving is better than receiving.
It's true that my mother deserves all the credit.
For without her, I'd have to forget it.
Being a daughter, having a brother's okay.
But I'd rather be a mother like mine any day.

Kathy Manger

"Nature's Fireworks"

A giant lantern in the sky
is lit for just a moment—
This flame seems to come
only to disappear,
When it slips behind the darkness,
you'd think it was gone forever—
But then, to behold, it comes again,
this time with the strength of one thousand men—
Although the night seems dominating,
doused in India Ink
the flame somehow permeates the air—
Although seen for just a second,
its luminescence becomes a necessity.

Long thin fingers try to frighten us,
but we are not afraid—
For we are wrapped in the forgiving blanket of night,
its shadows no longer daunt us,
for we know that the lantern, though briefly lit, is eternal.

Jean Osborne

Weeds In A Garden

Your longing to tell me what you think and feel.
Is it really necessary for my appeal?
Just turn it loose and let it go.
It doesn't take gall, it takes "guts", you know.

I must admit, I do like "guts".
It's the stuff for me that smooths out ruts.
But be aware...if the truth be known.
That truth is fact and seeds are sown.

And when such seeds are sown in life,
Weeds in a garden are the gardener's strife,
Unless perhaps...the gentle gardener,
Copes and works just a little harder.

And sees some beauty in the weed.
And understands its place indeed.
So, if your ready for seeds to sow,
Make sure there's room for weeds to grow.

Kelvin Geiger

Lasting Love

From an image in my mind that will last for all time
Is a rose three petals round sculptured in silver without sound
A ring for the finger of gold it is made
In the middle of the petals, and creator of shade
The diamond, the starlight source of light,
Illuminator of the night
From the crest of each petal, there shines that same light,
A gift sent from heaven to break through the night
Beneath these bright diamonds rest compassion's red glow
Three rubies of warmth in a circular flow
Forest light, product of the rest
Symbol of growth the emerald is next
The silver's for magic
Gold wisdom true
The jewels love and beauty
The ring sings of you

Glenn Bussman

Love Forever

To forever love and never despise,
Is a gift from above that we all must recognize.
But love is more than a gift of pleasure or a priceless treasure,
It is joy without limit and happiness without measure.
It is the peace and contentment that love brings,
Which causes the heart to fervently sing.
However, love would not be complete without PASSION or ROMANCE,
Two beautiful experiences which enriches man's existence.
The beauty of ecstasy which passion revives,
Causes the soul, through all life's misery, to survive.
And the quietude and pleasure which romance returns,
Helps the mind to forget those sorrows that once made it burn.
So let us have a little more us and a little less I's,
A little more truth and a lot less lies,
And let us stand united in love, free from fear,
Holding onto each other forever with that warmth of care!

Gerhard Anthony Franco

"Together Is One"

Lost love of the past do we not meet on strange grounds?
Ironic situations bring two hearts together separated by distance
and brought together by fate.
The magic that is created is like none other,
the light that bursts through smiles with joy
and smells of the freshness of the morning.

Together is peace for two hearts sharing times of the past.
Together is love caressing the night with the soft whisper of the trees.
Together is eternity, everlasting and promising in the dark of the night.
Together is one, united with souls so pure that nothing could break -
souls together and bound with love.

McKenzie Ritchie

The Murder Of My First Mother

As I watch through my window
I see the murder of my first mother
Her innocence slaughtered for progress
Insane men destroying what created them
Still watching through my window
I wonder about this murder
When will we comprehend children?
There must be an end to this violence
Imagine, my mother, a day of love and Peace

Matthew Bryan

The Blue Eye Of The Universe

Mother Earth
Inhabited with naked angels
White breasted and pure
Who among you listened to the snake

See what you did
You reptile teenagers
Living on a dilated planet
Dancing at the gate of a shrunken sanctuary

Ask Noah
If the blue eye has shed one tear
Can man adjust his primitive contact lens
While her pupil is burning with grit

Magnificent golden rainbows
Now sterile
By the alchemists dull shine
Soon to be aborted

Mother Earth will blink
Sin will be flushed from her burning
Virgin Eye
And the contact lens will fall.

Joseph Jesuit

TV Madness

I watched the news, the weather, and more
In with that was commercials galore
So I shut the thing off and went in the kitchen
Started to do things a little more fittin'
I did the dishes and washed the floor
I folded clothes and went to the store
Up and down the aisles I went
Amazing thing, how much I spent
Back to the car and on my way
Wanted to make this a special day
Next thing I knew I was at the park
Thought maybe here I could make my mark
Children were playing, mothers were laughing,
  people were walking around
This is much better I thought to myself, a great discovery I found
My world is as small or as big as I want it depending on my mood
And an optimistic approach has been totally renewed
The day to day activities we choose to embark on
Can be rewarding and informative, even more I reckon
So put it on, turn the volume up, if that's what you want to do
But do yourself a favor, limit programs to just a few.

Margaret A. Maxfield

Whisper Of Air

With our love my head spins
in vibrating motion,
recoiling from your loves desires potion.
A wisp of your hair
a serenity in your eyes,
the taste of your lips almost
brings one to cry.
Such fathoms we dive
through emerald colored dreams,
through aeons of space
we glide on it seems.
I gaze in wonderment that I could see,
that feeling that floats between you and me.
I volume of clouds reach near our heights,
like a whisper of air,
there, but no sight.
My existence I unfold
in arrays of illumination,
the moments we share, oh my love,
what a sensation.

Martin McKeay

445

Swim With The Dolphins

Walking on the beach of life
In unison with the sand
Gazing across the living water
Where the sky reaches to kiss the sea
And feel the enchantment in your veins
As you look at the dolphins frolicking about
And hear the seagulls shout
Close your eyes and listen hard
To the mysteries of the sea
And its mighty vastness that cannot be tamed
Singing a love song to a dream
And a ballad for lovers, forever long
The freedom to be and to belong
Listen mankind, don't you hear
Swim with the Dolphins, it's so clear.

Gwyne Skinner

The Stranger

Wind pillaged the night
  In the woodlands
    trees and birds were slashed by its razor breath
Rained drowned stones under its palm
  crushing wooden castles between its fingers
Lightning bounced from brilliant glass-cut eyes
Thunder deafened bold rivers
  The wild hunt then recessed across and beyond the sky

The morning creeps as a stranger in silent posture
  Mist drips over the ruins of yesterday
    drenching hidden cities in warmth
  Leaves sail still in pools of amber water

  Feathers hurl from broken nests
  Blood dyes the sky scarlet

Matt B. Nichols

A Wish

There's a wish I make every night, to take away all my fright.
In my bed I would hear a shot of a gun, most gangs think it's fun.
You go to walk across the street,
You see a defenseless person getting beat.
People do drugs thinking they're cool,
But someone who does is just a fool.
Hear the stories about abuse,
You try to fight it, but it's just no use.
Everyone tells you about STD's,
Just talking about it makes me weak in the knees.
Most kids listen but don't really care,
They'll go off and "Do It" anywhere.
And what's this thing called discrimination?
We should love each other white, black or Asian.
When you turn the corner you see someone hungry and poor,
This world is so screwed up, I can't take it anymore!
People are getting killed everyday,
why can't these problems go away.
But someday the sky will always be blue,
So I'll keep wishing for me and you.

Jennifer M. Louw

Untitled

In the snow clouds of the mountains high;
In the blue meld of the sea and sky;
Where the four winds of the world are spun
At the high noon of the midnight sun
Where the daylight of the day night glows
On the ice waves of the glacier flows;
In the heat haze of the desert red,
Or the isle sprung from the ocean bed:
Nature weaves earth's memories,
Witness to her mysteries.

Maxine Powell-Lavery

Touch Green

I pump my legs hard,
In and out, in and out.
I slice through the air,
My hair whipping across my face
And my mouth wide open.
I go higher and higher.
Bet I can reach higher than you.
Look! I can almost touch green.
Watch me do tricks — stand, spin, wobble.
I can probably go higher — I'm almost sure of it.

I don't stop the "kiddish" way by dragging my feet,
But I'm stopped by the sight of my car,
The face of my watch, my present life.
I quit pumping and release the chain from my grip, while I slide off.
Grounded.

Julie Ann Mazella

"The Orient"

  The slanted black eyes seem to stare
in amusement,
  The children stop playing and look up in
confusement.
  A new American walks through
the streets of an unknown city, an
unknown place,
  Although a man of importance he
feels like a disgrace.
  The frightened people are as educated
as he,
  But one wouldn't know it for they
pick fruit from a different tree.

Katie Nance

Violence And Silence

In a world of hate there's no heart
In a world of violence there's no silence
In a world of heart there's no hate
In a world of silence there's no violence
In a world of all four it's like a wood door
Will you knock it down or,
Will it knock you down.
You have the right to frown if it knocks you down
You have the right to smile
If it all seemed worth while
We all have the right to have
Clothes, homes and rights
No matter if we're blacks or whites
We have the right to be a nation
Since we have a population
We should make the ripples of war,
Criticism, and discrimination disappear
So we become a nation without fear.

Kristy Mathews

I Just Know

Sometimes I feel so lost in this time and place,
I'm walking down the road alone, I'm just another face.
I'm searching for a love that seems impossible to find,
Is it right in front of me or do I stop and look behind?
I wish I knew the answers on all the good that love can be,
But I just keep on waiting in hopes that they find me.
Yet maybe I'm too careful and should stop feeling all this doubt
And take the time to be honest and let my feelings out.
For I am only human and I have one life to share,
To love someone completely and to show how much I care.
So I will keep on walking and keep looking high and low
For my true love, it's out there, I will find it...I just know.

Jenny Nordstrom

446

War Of The Innocent

They took my boy to fight like a man
In a war that was just over land.
Though I prayed and prayed each night,
My sorrow came strong about this ugly fight.
He could be wounded, how would I know?
As he fought this country's foe.
"He's just a boy" I thought to myself.
But when he returns would he be himself?
Or would he be a man on his own,
Running away from the sorrow he once knew
Hoping to find that by in himself.
To be young and innocent in his heart.
To clear his mind and leave that ugliness behind.
They took my boy to fight like a man
In a war that was just over land.

Lisa Howard

No More Oil In Oilmont

The grandfather sits
in a splintering chair
on his sagging porch,
and watches everything, or nothing at all.

His grandchildren play
in the dusty dirt road
that everyone calls
"Main Street."

The street is lined with fifteen dry houses,
the post office that keeps them on the map,
and the bar that keeps them a town.

There is no gas station,
none of the oil that brought you here,
first to steal from the earth,
and then to get for your dead car ten miles back.

There's just a word of advice
from a lonely old man,
and some quick directions
to the oil that you are dependent upon.

Because there's no more oil in Oilmont

Johanna Orendorff

Rose Colored Glasses

These garments I'm wearing today are not mine
I'm walking in my brothers shoes
And the rose colored glasses that belonged to Aunt Sylvia
Are resting a top of my nose
The cardboard box that envelops my body
Does little to keep out the cold
Much like a barrier to hide from society
A vapor to cover the soul
Some friends from my past saw my face in the box and hurriedly made
    a retreat
My stomach is talking in a strange foreign language
For days I've had little to eat
Aunt Sylvia knew she had it made
Her rose colored glasses are neat
I see sunshine instead of rain and behold the new shoes on my feet
I see the compassion of my fellow-man and the love as they pass me by
I see the smooth paths that my feet must walk and rainbows up in a blue sky
I may be the brother whose shoes you'll soon wear
So take a good look at yourself
You'll never survive without Sylvia's glasses
Don't look for them on the shelf

Geraline B. Samples

"My World"

In my world I reign supreme, I stand on top of the hill
I'm the only being the only burden in this place where I live
You must love God to be in my world, you must be overly divine
You must have thoughts and care for others to live in this world of mine

There are no disasters in my world, no tornadoes, no fires
No poverty, no hunger, but only wants and desires
In my world there are no trees, the wind blows silently by the hour
There are no dark dreadful forests, but only rose gardens and flowers

In my world you live forever, there is no fear of dying
There are no tears and sadness is joy, laughter is the same as crying
There are no wars in my world, for I have no enemies
Every wish in my world comes true and all dreams are realities

In my world there's only love, no hate, no bigotry
No apartheid, no oppression, and everyone is free

Wouldn't you love to live in my World?

Julius Raynard Young

You Call Me

You call me black, you say
I'm colored and you say to me "what's up n***a?"
    Without the "er" you think
I will take no offense
    But only your ignorance of
being shows what you know
For I am not colored, I
am not as if you say to call a child's picture
    I am not black, for then
I would just be a hue of the
rainbow and the depression of light
    I am not a n****r, nor am I a n***a, for I refuse to
answer to a term in which I
and many others took as an insult to our race
    So you say what do I call you?
You can call me African American, as a branch of my ancestors
But don't call me something if you are not totally sure of what
your words mean or what feelings they may bring.

Megan Lilly

I Never Knew Why

I never knew why, when things go wrong
I'll sit and hum a sad, sad song
I never knew why, when I felt down
I'll sit and mope with a big old frown

If only the world was a better place to live,
With peace and hope we all could give

I remember as a child
I cried so much,
Just thinking about life and all the bad stuff.

What would you do if you had the chance again?
To live in peace with your and no sin.

I'd like to create a better me
I could picture myself in the land of plenty
Living the life the good Lord intended

Why was the fight for power an glory?
Where was a good angel, when the bad one detoured?

If only I could have been there to stop the devil,
We would be living free from sin "Forever and ever."

Naomi Tucker

Please

Gimmie, gimmie, gimmie food
if you're in a generous mood.
Been three days since I last ate
tends to fill one's mind with hate.

Gimmie, gimmie, gimmie money
the way I look may be funny.
So help me to get out of these dirty rags.
Are all your clothes in plastic bags?

Gimmie, gimmie, gimmie work
don't just call me a jerk.
I can do the things you do,
I have got a brain too.

Gimmie, gimmie, gimmie shelter
don't let me go helter skelter.
Rain has poured right off my head
I just want to sleep in a bed.

Gimmie, gimmie, gimmie love
what about God above.
I just want someone to care
please give me a soul to bear.

Ken Reed

"Love"

A house is not a home
If you spend all your time alone.
No matter the price you pay
It's not worth the loneliness day after day.
I realize someone has to make a living -
But love is more than just giving.
All the worldly goods are not worth a care -
When you have no one with them to share.
Whether it be wife or spouse
You still need love in the house.
At times with our work we get carried away;
And fail to see our lives slipping away.
Our love we forget to share
With no one at home to care.
Sometimes we drift so far apart
We forget about each other's heart.
We need to stop and realize
How each affects the other's lives.

Olene Middleton

If I Could Take It Back I Would Abuse

If I could take back the pain, I would.
If I could take back the anger, I would.
If I could take back the hurt, I would.
If I could take back the words, I would.
If I could take back the bruises and cuts, I would.
If I could take you away from it, I would.
If your parents only knew what they did, they should.

Julie Blevins

My Eternal Love For You

To love so completely is the purest form of ecstasy
I want to give you my soul and love
I will love you through all eternity
for you have shown me heaven
I can see the angels through your eyes
Your love showers me with the soft rains of passion
we'll fly away together on the wings of desire
and make sweet tender love on the billowing clouds
I will remain hopelessly devoted to you even
beyond this life.
You are my life, inspiration, and center of happiness
I will always love you.

Maria Chantell Partee

The Lord

Wherever I go, He is with me
If I am at the mountains or at the sea
It is His presence that I feel
I can sense that He is real
He makes the day bright
He gives us a silent night
He wishes me to explain to you about His power
He made the beauty of a flower
He made the sky blue
He continues to do wonders the day through
He died on the cross for our sins
He hopes that with His strength that we tell Him of our problems and
worries, and to realize that His love wins
He is my strength, hopes, and love
And I know when the time comes I will rejoice with Him above
I am not saying that life will be perfect though that it can be better
And that soon you will wish to mention His name without fetter
For you to know of the special day of Jesus Christ's birth and that He
journeyed through His life doing good deeds
And when the time came He died for us and now it is our faith and
belief that He needs.

Leah Hudson

One World

Nature can furnish whatever we need,
If her warnings all will but heed;
To honor the earth, its oceans and air;
Ne'er to behold them as one's own affair.

From desecration, let us recoil;
And from whoever may lust to despoil—
For power or greed, else fleeting fun;
Rebuffing those eager, their space in the sun.

This is a world which does not rest;
That could be unfurled, resplendently dressed.
How we employ it assesses its worth
Thus why not enjoy a fresh Eden on earth?

Jeanette Birnbaum

If I Knew You And You Knew Me

If I knew you and you knew me my heart will be filled with glee.
If both of us could clearly see and with an inner sight divine
The true meaning of your heart and mine.
I'm sure that we should differ less and clasp our hands in friendship
Our thoughts would pleasantly agree and then the both of us would see
If I knew you and you knew me
If I knew you and you knew me as each one knows his own self
we could look each other in the face and see there in a truer grace
Life has so many thorns for every rose every where you go hidden woes
The "why" of things our heart would see
If I knew you and you knew me
If I knew you and you knew me
Then maybe... just maybe you would see how we were really meant to be
If I knew you and you knew me what a better world it may be
To see how you need me and I need thee, if I knew you and you knew me
then both of us would clearly see
The beauty and grace that it would be.
If I knew you and you knew me

Lenne Osby

"Dreams"

If I were an astronaut,
I would walk across the moon,
Build a house, plant a flag without doubt,
And do it all before noon.

If I were a pilot,
I would write my name in the sky,
I'd fly the world from spot to spot
Don't bother asking me why!

Being a pilot or an astronaut,
Are things I've given some thought
Will they come true? I know not.
'Cause I am just a distrait teen.
I'm a lean, mean, dreaming machine!

Jennifer Yomoah

I Am

I am wondrous and scared
I wonder what will happen to me in the future
I hear my mom saying she will come home to me
I see myself blooming
I want my family to be with me forever
I am wondrous and scared
I pretend my childhood was normal
I believe I will follow my dreams
I will reach the stars
I feel lucky to be where I am
I worry for my families safety
I cry when I think of my mom
I am wondrous and scared
I understand people's worries and feelings
I say I am trust worthy
I dream about my future
I hope I will live a long and successful life
I am wondrous and scared

Kathy Allen

Why Do Children Always Have To Pay?

Why do children always have to pay?
I wonder how many children are beaten every day?
Why should they suffer for something they didn't do
They didn't ask to be born but look what they go through
They only want attention
They only want to grow
So always show you love them
they really need to know
just remember you were once a child
So please don't let your temper
get out of hand or wild
There's one more thing I'd like for you to do
Think about your children being parents
Do you want them to be like you?

Nancy J. Berlincourt

Vocal Student

I will praise my God.
I will shout out loud.
I will practice at home
and sing in the crowd.

For Jesus did practice and studied hard too
and learned all he could. He was a good Jew.
Then he passed a terrific examination
(given by Satan,) to save all creation!

Oh, Father, forgive everything that I do;
it seems that I can save only a few.
And Oh! Mighty God! Sir! Please include me
among those who sing at your throne, and are free!

Nell D. Esslinger

Travlin'

Be it Kalamazoo, Atlantic Beach, or South Bend,
I will go anytime, no matter when.
To an airport, or from a train station
Just give me a bag, a map, and a destination.

Off to Cleveland, to Akron, and on to Canton,
My feet, I never plan on plantin'.
Whoops I made a wrong turn and now I'm in New Stanton,
Without fail this will take some back trackin'.

Down to Biloxi, up to Chicago and off to Buffalo,
Anywhere, everywhere, somewhere I go.
Must I really contend with old man snow.
But this weekend takes me to Toronto.

Take me to Miami, not Philadelphia, or Chattanooga,
Where the sun always shines, Hallelujah!
But then it's on the road again, and off to Missoula
For it's only in Hawaii I can do the hula.

Out to Spokane, back to Peoria, on to New Orleans.
Yes, ah yes, try the local cuisine.
I simply cannot let any sight to unseen.
Just make sure the trip is in John's big white stretch limousine.

Mary Rossman

The Native

As my eyes scan the horizon
I watch the beautiful naked women
Run freely in the quiet forest around us.

The emergent frost rained
On the forest,
The forest holds the Gods of the sea
Swimming through a river of madness

Abounding from life
Through murky chaotic high lands,
There we breed an infinite and dying race

Indians stand in the place of honor,
I now I have gone to join them
Upon the nervous unprecedented grounds
Of what is known as heaven.

Dean Carr

A Dream - Alone

I was on my way into a dream-a dream I could neither avoid nor delete.
I wanted my life to be complete.

I'm now in a world of love and respect.
One that only I could reflect, where no one could interject.

The dizziness was felt from head to toe and I wanted everyone to know.
To know of this dream that I was in,
The Altitude high, the air was thin.

I caressed myself, cause no one was there,
I needed someone, but no one was there. I wanted somebody to care....

The sky was blue, the clouds where white
Then it became dark and I knew it was night.

People rushed all over the place,
But I still did not see a familiar face.
I felt alone, alone in my dream-you know what I mean?

Maybe it wasn't a dream at all. I was just waiting for someone to call.
To be alone just doesn't seem real. I wanted to care, to be, to feel.
So then I awoke, or so I did think
Then it really sank in, and I never slept a wink.

I was never asleep, just tired and alone,
And the dream that I had was that dream of my own...to be loved.

Jody A. Herow

I Want You To Know....

I want you to know that when things go wrong,
I want you to know that all along,
Someone remembers and someone cares,
Whatever load the burden shares.
Whatever they do or whatever they say,
I want you to know that all the way.
Someone believes though others may not.
I want you to know.

I want you to know when we are apart,
When I cannot speak to you heart to heart,
Whatever the rest may say or do,
I want you to know that my faith is true.
I want you to know that come what will,
In the deepest valley, on the highest hill.
The things I say to you are now forever.
I want you to know.

I want you to know in the after years,
In the time of sorrow, in the time of tears.
Perhaps my love will not help you so,
But if it will, well...I want you to know.

Jessica Terry

Poem From The Heart

My dreams I always see you in the park;
I want to cuddle up next to you in the dark and embark;
my magical spark!

I want to expand my faithful hands;
   all over your wonderland.

I want to be your love slave;
so we both will have romance all day.

Blow in each other ears to get;
rid of both our fears.

Your feet are so delicate glorious and sweet.

I'm love sick wanting everlasting harmony;
loving you in my artistic quantities?

In my mind you have the most captivating
   body of all woman kind.

Melvin C. Reece Jr.

My Forever Love

When I was just a child, I didn't know my fate,
I waited for the sunshine and you finally came my way.

We've had our share of troubles,
We've had our share of strife,
but through it all I'm certain that with you I'll spend my life.

Each day I look around me but never do I see
a love so true and special
as the love you've given me.

If I should ever lose you,
I don't know what I'd do;
I'll never love another, the way that I love you.

No matter where love takes us our love will see us through.
I've never had a single doubt,
My heart belongs to you!

Maria Daniela Ricca

Jesse's Song

In loving memory of Jesse L. Dunlap (9/14/31 - 10/21/93)
As I kneel in the crisp leaves to pray
I try to think of the words that I'll say

I need not think, the words come with ease
carried by him in the fresh Autumn breeze

I hear the song of the geese flying south
I taste the salt as the tears reach my mouth

It must be my father's, sweet gentle kiss
For as I pray, it's him that I miss

The geese grow weary, their flight shall be long
But fly they must, to sing Jesse's song.

Greg Dunlap

I Remember...

I remember the day when we first met,
I thought this was the best life can get.

I remember when you used to hold me tight,
Only thinking why I can't stay there all night.

I remember the first kiss that you ever gave to me
And when I gave it back, there was only love I could see

I remember when you would say "I Love You"
I couldn't wait until the day I could say "I do"

I sadly remember when you had to say goodbye
As I watched you leave, I just wanted to die

Now as I sit here, waiting for your return
I remember how much I love you, that's one thing I have learned.

Jacquelyn Ligon

True Love

Our eyes met in a home of a friend,
I think that's where our life began.
After our dates, when you took me home,
We couldn't wait to talk on the phone.
We wanted to be together longer,
As our relationship began to grow stronger.
We fell in love, deep in our hearts,
And no one could never break us apart.
Now we're living together happy as can be,
Planning our future as far as we can see.
Someday we will be husband and wife,
To share our love to the end of life.
Our life is beautiful shared with each other,
We're just two happy people who love one another.

Lois K. Fox

Our Planet Earth

I am a dreamer of reality.
I see what I see, I hear what I hear.
The time has come for a change.
Love is fading, and hate has thrown a veil of violence upon us.
The ozone layer is disappearing.
Our forest are being destroyed.
Our oceans polluted by trash, oil spills, and toxic chemicals.
Each day more and more animals are being added to the endangered list.
People are starving and homeless all around the world.
Our earth is slowly crumbling to our feet.
What will the future generation have if there's nothing left?
Help is needed how before it's too late.

Lisa Cullen

Missing You

Today is a cloudy day
I think of you so far away.
It makes me sad, and so very blue,
sitting here thinking only of you.

The past five weeks were so full
of love and heavenly bliss.
I miss you darling and your
goodnight kiss.

I sat here this morning wishing I could hear,
Your cheerful greeting of Good morning dear.
I waited and waited, I knew it couldn't be,
Because you are so far away from me.

I can hardly wait until you are my bride.
I can never be happy again until you are at my side.
I never again want to hear you say a goodbye.
For without you darling, I know I would die.

The days are growing shorter to
the day that will bind us, which
will bring us to a beautiful ending
of a lifetime of happiness and love.

Lawrence D. Garwitz

"That Old Woman In The Bathroom"

"She's there every time I go in, that old woman in the bathroom.
  I tell her to get out of there, but she won't leave when I say.

I don't like her, that old woman in the bathroom,
  because no matter how hard I try, she will not go away.

Sometimes I just look in to see, that old woman in the bathroom,
  but when I peek around the corner, I find her peeking back at me!

Her clothes are just like mine, that old woman in the bathroom,
  and even though I try to hurry, she always changes right along with me.

She won't acknowledge me, that old woman in the bathroom,
  if only we could go for walks together, I wouldn't be so lonely.

They pay her a lot to spy on me, that old woman in the bathroom,
  But I wish they would let her talk to me, we could keep each other company.

if only I knew why, that old woman in the bathroom,
  always gets in front of me so I can't see myself in the mirror.

My family says it is just me in there, that old woman in the bathroom,
  but I know it isn't so.

Because no matter what they say, that old woman in the bathroom
  just doesn't look anything like me!!"

Nancy Campbell

Untitled

As the dawn folds unto the heavens,
I taste the sweetness of your lips.
Beauty cannot behold the purity of the soul,
But still the day cannot diminish the
pain that the days have ceased.
Though I love you more than the waken morn
And your eyes are the limits beyond my wants,
We are born to death.
And death receives us.
Afterwards there's no pain.
So I give my last drop of life
To replace your tears inside
And pray that the memory will fade like
the dawn unto the heavens at the break of day.

Jennifer Mrohs

I Am (Misunderstood)

I am someone who is misunderstood.
I sometimes do bad though I often do good.
I am someone who is not afraid to laugh,
Who is not ashamed to cry. Not afraid to let go,
When someone says "goodbye".
Though sometimes I don't let my feelings show
It is inside that I cry.

I am someone who will be true to a friend.
When time starts to pass, my friendship won't end.
When others bail out, on me you can depend.

I'm also someone who is trustworthy too. My trust you can have
unless given reason not to.

I am someone who you can't figure out! Though you'll swear up
and down you know what I'm about. Now as you can see,
I'm unique with no doubt.

I am unique in my own little way. If you want to know me close
attention you must pay. You'll think you know me but it's
just in your mind; what you see is not what you get, there's
much more to find. When I am a Lion, you'll think I am a Lamb.
I am misunderstood, yes, that's what I am.

Nyanontee E. Cooper

My Wall

Alone in this room, dead from the world.
I sit staring at the walls, works of art
  in my prison cell.
Feelings of emptiness take over my body,
  as the ceiling creeks above my head.

The outside is far too painful for me.
So I lock myself in a sepulcher, far, far,
  from the pain beyond these walls.
Safe and alone I sit in my tomb, waiting
  for the final chapter to arrive.

I hear the predaceous people planning my defeat.
I see the scavengers looking for their next
  feast of human emotions.
But behind these walls, I am safe from this ungodly torture.
Behind my scenario, I am free of the
  contact which causes pain.

This wall built inside me is now my saviour, my "God."
It protects me from the evil and pain beyond.
This wall, my "God", is all I have to defend
  myself against the hell outside.

Lisa Bahr

Forever

In a place where others come and go,
I sit so solemnly agape to the world.
My experience being quite unique on this hill.
How satisfied my soul seems.
My back to the sun that warms so soothingly.
My face to the breeze that plays, tickling my tresses.
I observe the myriad treasures from afar.
The surrounding hills amble to the waters edge
in their greenery and matchless splendor.
The waters surface sparkles with the sun,
encompassing the islands and their distinctiveness.
The sky is so clear and brilliant,
it engulfs the distance with clarity.
Seeing forever, so beautifully satisfying,
I now understand what a long, long time it is.

Melanie J. Kenney

451

An October Breeze

In the damp air of an October breeze
I sit among the darkened silence.
The smell of saturated barks
and decaying leaves sweet perfume.
There is something about an October breeze,
the death of beauty.
With every breath I inhale an extinct life.

Each leaf cries out its prayers,
to just be part of a spring afternoon,
to be the shade of summertime lovers.
Walking towards the trees
I see leaves draping over the pond
wishing to fall upon amiable waters.

These sun gathers softly speak their intentions.
Rustling in the remorseful burrows of reason,
the dead season begins.
All light is pale.
The grass hinders its judgments.
As flowers hide in cold furrows of earth.

Kerry Frieben

The Scar

Tree, oh beautiful tree -
I see your scar.
Before I see you, I see the space
That has been taken away.
It jars me that something so quiet and lovely
Has been so marred.
But I want to see more, so I look;
I start up, and you go, and reach
And travel toward the sky.
You are tall, and sturdy, and big
And branched out;
You have grown, and you are growing
And you are deeply greened.
You are ageless and you are strong.
When I now see you
In all that you are,
I see
Really see
So much more than
The scar.

Kate Geurkink

Domination

Today I finally realized I'm a failure
I thought of ending it all
All my reasons, all my boundaries, all the beats of my heart
That keep me awake in this f***in' world
Sorrow will exist no more
Except in the eyes of the beloved
They will soon believe it's their fault for my departure
One after the other
Leaving for good
Never to return, never to love, never to hate
I will kill off the world
For having loved only me
What fools you've learned to be

Psychopathic eyes
Hath cursed you to love
I once in visioned in the night
Me as a ruler of a world
I now own all your souls
They will be transformed to hate
My world, my rules, my God, What have I done?

Mandy Vanderburg

A Perfect Place

The sun is shining brightly
I see thousands of bluebonnets across the
  Sweet smelling fields
A blanket of dew settles across the flowers
  Giving them just he right amount of
  dampness

Birds are singing their beautiful glistening
  Melodies, sharing it with the rest of the
  forest animals
A small cottage is resting beyond the horizon
  Of the bubbling hot sun
There is a slow moving river in the distance
  Where little boys dream of catching a fish
  bigger than their last

Melanie Younger

Death Upon Me

As I glance out my window
I see nothing but life
Something I will lose
Besides my children and wife
Death is surrounding me by my bed
By tomorrow morning I might be dead
So I ask myself one last time
"Is life worth living if you're gonna die?"
My soul will vanish, my heart will stop
My soul will then be there no more, my heart will drop.
Then up in heaven I will go, a place
I'll get used to, a place I'll know
A tear down my cheek I will cry once more
'Cause death will soon close the door
I have no worries, I have no fears
I have scary thoughts, I have lots of tears
So once before I leave this world I'd like
to say good-bye.
'Cause by tomorrow morning, I probably will die.

Lindsey A. Carey

I See

I see I see what people don't see
I see love and happiness between you and me
I see a smile on everyone's face
I see families living in a wonderful place
I see a forever rainbow up in the sky
I see the world giving at least one try
I see no guns shooting up in the air
I see not one look or a glare
I see a glimmer in everyone's eyes
I see only truth not hateful lies
I see I see what I wish could be true
But what I know is that hate's nothing new
Our world's lived with it for a long, long while
But if we try hard we will pass the trial

Kitty Wibracht

Never A Song Nor Ever A Poem

Can tell of the love you've given our home
But with words I must try with each passing day
Before life itself has gone away.
Your heart is so giving
Your smile so true
Eyes bright as stars
The word love is you and together it is ours.

David T. Tener

452

Forgiveness

Forgiveness is a window
Full of gentle curiosity
And silver dreams
To journey on
Shannon Bauer

Black Woman

Black Woman:
Fulfilling her everyday dreams
that shall take her a far
to spread a little joy so that her
forever lasting light will have
a chance to beam
like a falling star.

Black Woman:
So loving and kind
ready to give her all
right down to the food she eats
to the clothes on her back
so that someone else can get their
life back on track.

Black Woman:
So mighty and strong
her smile warms your heart
forever long.
Tonia Tyler

Science

Science pushes back the
frontiers of ignorance
through that power
which dazzles mortal eyes.
Science is nothing more than
persistence in disguise.
Therefore...
A little more persistence,
courage, vim
and success will dawn
Over failures...
Cloudy Rim
Robert M. Burmeff

My Day

What of this day
Fresh upon me?

The potters' clay proffered
To develop as I wish
To press to stretch
To mold into my offering to life.

Each new day
Brings the morning
Of a new beginning
Challenging me
To become involved
To take each day
To make each day
A statement of my life.

Fresh opportunity without strings
Freely given the invitation
Being to accept
To try or let lie
Untouched unworked to die.
This day. My day. HIS gift.
M. D. Bowe

Rain

Down falling thoughts,
Forming puddles of confusion in my mind.
It's raining in my head.

Puzzled, I ponder. My emotions
Dampen from the tumultuous downpour.
It's raining in my head.

Increasing madness, decreasing sanity,
Confusion ends.
Rain from my head
Trickles down my face,
Using my eyes for a drainpipe,
Clearing my mind.
Steve Gagne

Small Talk

New faces,
Foreign lands,
New neighbors,
Strangers at the gate.
Is it hard for you
To make small talk?

Small talk
Can be right words
At the right time,
Gently spoken;
Great love, softly sung,
Echoes of "the still small voice."
Penelope Ann Schuler

October

October is a month for dying
For the cold winds can numb the senses
The gentle colors can caress the eyes
And the unashamed beauty
Can endear the soul with hope

A time Nature chose
For her Creations to pass asunder
A time Nature chose
For death to be so gloriously beautiful
In all its heart wrenching pain

October
Will always be with me
A time Nature chose
For dying
A time Nature chose for sublimation
Tim Colletti

"Seeds of Love"

As the master gathers flowers
for his bouquet
He doesn't see fading flowers
that will soon decay
He sees blooms of love and kindness
new seeds that have been sown
Tiny delicate bouquet of flowers
from the older ones have grown
The fragrance from this bouquet
is heady and fills the air
From this bouquet the young seeds
begin to grow for they were planted
with great care
And as the master gathers the
bouquet home
The new seeds remember and grow
tall and strong.
Regina Busby

"Say Goodbye"

I think it's time
for me to say goodbye
I will never be with
You through this eternity,
You will always be here
You will always be near
But I can not handle
these God awful tears.
My heart is shattering
What can I do to ease the
pain, I see you with her
and all I do is cry
I think it's time for
me to say goodbye
My heart won't stop breaking
cause your beautiful blue eyes, Never
forgetting your goodbyes
Now you're gone, out of my
mind. What is love, how is it defined.
Raquel Conley

Suicide

The self-made blood
flows around me
The death-night surrounding
I can no longer see
Cries to my soul
you will find peace
By your own hand
pain will cease
Do not listen to
the coward's way
The blood-red night ends
with the blue-white of day.
Teresa Crytser

Existence

I cease to exist
Fighting for existence.
The rules, the regulations,
And the limits
Unable to bear the obstacles,
restraints, and fortifications
The way of life.
The boundary of mankind.
Farewell to the kindhearted
Good-bye to the vain and
Egotistical
Buying admission to the future
Longing for an inclination
The hope of togetherness.....
But the ongoing agony of defeat
The silence of the outcries.
The clamor of the stillness.
Fighting for existence
I cease to exist.
Sarah Stanton

Remembrance

The lingering rays of sunset
Danced upon the marigolds;
The beauty in your eyes so deep,
The mystery of your soul.
So captured and enraptured;
I drink in all the beauty.
The sun does set,
My eyes grow wet;
A vision lost unto me.
Robert J. Moran

The Vietnam Memorial...

I hear their whispers in my ears,
Feel their soul very near.
  I touch the dampness in the air,
I see these people everywhere.
  I hear these people next to me,
And know just what they used to be.
  People with lives of their own,
Now in peace yet all alone.
  We learn about what caused the fight,
Who had won this unholy night.
  But what they do not care to say,
Who were the people that died that day?
  I caress the wall that shows the way,
Who they were to this new day.
  Thousands of new names etched in,
Why they died, a new found sin.
  So as you think about their lives,
Think about how they died.
  Now they have but one thing more,
Their names carved in the Vietnam Wall.

Rae Flores

The Traveler's Prayer

Lord, I know Thou art with me,
Even when I'm far from home.
I feel a strength deep inside me,
And I know I'm not alone.

Danger lies all around me,
And temptations plague my soul;
But I know Thy love will guide me,
And I'm sure to reach my goal.

Love is strong - Love is eternal,
And it binds my heart to thee.
I hear Thy voice that bids me answer;
"Lord, I'll always walk with Thee."

Thomasina England

I Love Him

I love him still,
even though he's gone...
He doesn't love us;
so he's moved on.
  Maybe someday...

Trina Kessler

"Fear"

Fear.
Envelops one's mind with a creeping
Darkness.
Haunting and obsessing
The heart
Horrifying one's soul to the point
that one is always looking over their
shoulder.
Causing good judgement to give out to
Panic.
Making a soul come under
A reign of terror.
But a spirit of fear is
Not forever for
God offers
Hope
Love
And Trust.

Rachel DeVore

He Said He Loved Me

He said he loved me
Enough to die.
He loved me
Enough to lie.

He said he loved me
Enough he couldn't think.
He loved me
Enough to drink.

He said he loved me
Enough to be sweet.
He loved me
Enough to cheat.

He said he loved me
Enough to quit.
He loved me
Enough to hit.

He said he loved me
More than himself.
He loved me...
Almost to death.

Victoria Taylor

Dove

A cooing on my balcony...
Enchanting.
So I rise and tiptoe
To the window — careful
Not to let those beady eyes
Detect a human.
Breezes divide its back feathers.
Nervous, its head turns this way,
That ... until
Some sound or image
Flutters its wings in a sudden
Curve from the balcony
To a power pole across the street.

Roger D. Paine

For A Child

An Angel has come
down from the Lord,
In the silence of the night,
without a word.

A child has been taken,
It seems so unfair,
But the child has gone
to we all know where.

A child is innocent,
So young and pure,
That is why we all
can be so sure.

Nothing can be said
to ease all the strain,
But knowing this may
help the pain.

So deep down inside
Be strong at heart.
Remembering that down there
you'll never be apart.

Wendy Finchum

The Search

My mind wanders
Don't know where it goes
Scattered thoughts
Tumbling
Disconnected prose
My emotions drifting
Don't know where to land
Scrambling heartbeat
Getting out of hand
My love searching
Don't know where to hold
Glorious rainbow
But no pot o' gold
My life's love
Don't know where she's found
Somewhere waiting
By our destiny bound

Wayne J. Porter

Love Endures All

Love proves all truth
Denies all lies
It can see through
All the ifs and how's and why's
Love can break down
Your sickness and sorrows
It can carry you through
All of the tomorrows
Love can move objects
And then change your ways
It relieves all the madness
It'll pull ya through the maze
Love has been with you
Since before you could crawl
Love is powerful and mighty
Love endures all.

Rodger A. Goff

When I Can't Speak

Gems of clear blue,
Deeper than the sky,
Holding mysterious true
Urge me to ask why...

The answer to my inquiry,
The heartfelt revelation,
Can stop my life's iniquities
Can be my soul's salvation...

With questions my soul burns,
Her answers beyond grasp...
Like a path with many turns...
Or a book with fastened clasp...

To hear her mysteries told,
Jut to hear her tell me why...
As pirates did for gold,
To please her I would die.

Ron R. Strzelecki

Worrying

Zipper up the opening that the
button failed to do.
Cover up that spot draining
the soul.
Patch it with a dream that will
throw it off track.

Thomas G. Miller

Rainy Days

Falling water from above
dark clouds
abundant

Each with its own
anxious solitude alone
yet bringing beauty to the sky

Each bringing a memory of the last
but unique unto itself

Falling water from above
dark clouds abundant

Leaving puddles
on the ground for
children to slosh in

In their banana yellow
plastic coat and
barn red latex galoshes

Falling water from above
dark clouds abundant

What a day to spend alone
S. Aberman

Island Midwife

Poling through fog,
currents swirl, circle rippling,
muck suckling flat-bottom planks,
a few notes hum,
thrum, and hover in Spanish moss—

In she sweeps,
wind washing up waves of fertile air,
Caribbean lilt fills
corners, crevices,
soothing sharp cries,
hands dancing, singing,
soften struggle and mollify stinging,
knead clenched grimaces
into supple sheen—

A last gasp,
release, relief,
love shines on new skin
and she laughs
her smile, teeth
like stars in the night.
K. Haley Whipple

Frostbitten (Drug Addiction)

See the black backed snowbanks,
clean were you now turned dark,
look in the mirror
try to see through
infectious mirage that stares at you
yes alive you are
true you are
yet the friends see compelling
compiling of scars

Attitude marking death of friends
reincarnated they'll be devilscends
once in hand to turn to foes
blizzard of emotions to endure
again you banish your reality
where a world lies knighted
cut the hoofs of horse you ride
straight jacked saddle to which you fall
a problem of mind to abide
kernel of relief of the narrow
time and time again has if frostbitten your loathes
Wayne Lockwood

"A Beautiful World"

This is a beautiful world.
Created by God you see
He made everything in it
And we can enjoy it far free.

He gave us two eyes to see
A tongue so we can talk
Two ears that we can hear
Two feet so we can walk.

He made the mountains and Valley's
The wind, that gives fresh air
He made the sun, moon, and stars
And they never needs repair.

What a mighty God we serve
Who is there for one and all
One who hears every prayer
and can answer every call.

Lets enjoy this beautiful world
And give God all the praise
And thank him for keeping us
by his amazing grace.
Veta M. Peterman

Action

Is your:
Conversation endowed with wisdom?
Occasion viewed with diplomacy?
Lore perfected with stability?
Occupation championed with provision?
Reputation guarded with diligence?
Success reflected with perseverance?

Always:
Observe landmarks.
Follow peace.

Love to exhibit truth.
Incite temperance.
Fancy integrity.
Endeavor to excel in virtue.
M. A. Pierro

"The Past"

Hurtful words that only
come out of hate and anger.

I wish we were still close,
Now it seems as if were strangers.

I wish we still felt the same,
I wish there was a law
that said, best friends always
would be best friends forever.

For some reason forever seems like never.
I feel apart of me is missing.

I hate to say this but what
I thought would last, now
seems like the past.
Tiffiany Flinchum

Stars

There are stars in the sky
and the moon is shy
on a winter night I pray,
to the Lord ohh, heavenly God
I thank - you for this day
Regina Warren

"Fireworks Impromptu"

Blow, blow away fog,
Clouds with evening rain.
Creep, creep eastward,
Back to you darkly domain.

Stars and twinkles,
Hidden in black.
Blankets of gray,
that cover Earth's back.

Rains that come,
Rains that go.
Here we stand,
In roofless abode.

Eyes that see,
Ears that wait,
The lights to appear.

Oooh's and Ahhh's,
From the mass.
As lights stretch,
Ending their dance.
Roy H. Johnson III

Heaven Sent

She is an angel in disguise,
cloaked as a precocious toddler.

With her golden curls and laughing eyes,
she has been sent to enchant.

Her impish grin lends joy
to the dreariest of days,
and her silly deeds beguile
both young and old alike.

With her pleading gaze and pouting smile,
she can be denied nothing.

She is a blessing from heaven,
cherished as a beloved daughter.
Stacy McGava

Depressed II

It's terrible how life
Can get you down
And then that depression come's around

It makes you think and feel
Unhappy thoughts
And really scares you
With the depression it caught

I don't like to think
That way any more
But sometimes it's just like
An open sore

And it really hurts You
And makes you really Blue

I like to be happy
And bring joy and love wherever I go
And give thanks to the one above

I don't know why I'm given
All of these bridges to cross
And all of these hurdles to jump
And I try to understand, but I'm at a loss
Wayne Dillon

Telling Your Love

How do you tell someone you love them?
By word of mouth?
Do they say it different in the North
than what they say in the South?

Is it truer in the East
than it is in the West?
Out of all the methods
which one is best?

When you find the best
method, how will you know -
Will the difference jump right out?
Or will it slowly begin to show?

When you find this method
you think it's to be,
is it best for you?
Or is it best for me?

Are the methods different
like a right or left shoe?
Or is it as easy as
saying I love you?

K. Lee Rowan

The Weakest Link

Most are held by thread and fall
By rope, we hang on,
And swing across the abyss,
Watching the slow, churning
    Ignorance Pain Hate
That await us
When the braiding fails.

We circle, and connect.
The rope retracts, and we float,
Supporting each other.

And when one drops,
We gather and lift.
But when one rises,
Most just ignore
    Ignorance, bringing them lower.

As long as we hold on,
We survive.
But I'm slipping, and no one seems to see it.

Paul de Barros

The Joy Of Not Having To

By fits and starts I've lived my life,
By chance most courses charted,
Two factors ill to serve one;
I doubt I'm known to those that are,
The scheme of things controlling;
How many do so signify?
I call myself a sometime poet
Who dabbles in verse and writes
Doggerel; in spite of long immersion
In sloth and manly vices of the times,
Some things I've learned; a lady writer
To columnists enables me to chart
Some courses surely; once she wrote
About the joy of not having to go,
Learned late in life by her and me;
I pay deserved tribute to that thought
And would piggy-back on it to add
The joy of not having to DO!
A life of angst is often opted for.

Troy H. Davis

"Hope"

HOPE can't always be seen,
    but somehow you know it's there.
HOPE is living for what you believe in
    and sometimes, it's a dare.

HOPE is looking for a brighter side,
    although life may seem so grim.
HOPE is keeping your head held high,
    although you may not win.

HOPE is knowing there's still a chance
    to somehow, come out on top.
HOPE is striving to reach a goal;
    you tire but never stop.

HOPE is having confidence,
    that's based on more than just luck.
HOPE is what keep some people alive
    and should never be given up.

    HOPE!

Randolph Harris

A Woman, A Mother, A Friend

A woman was born, not long ago,
    but she was taken away too fast.

A mother has been here to show,
    her wisdom,
    her love,
    the future and past;

A friend she has been to all that hears,
Great love is shown to her in my tears;

Each drop that is to slowly descend
    will mark:
A woman,
A mother,
A friend!

Toni Mosior

"Not There"

Silence is golden
    but not when your lover will not
    speak
Words spoken, not answered
Letters written, no reply
Are you still there?
Can you hear me?

Now you feel you are running uphill on a
    downhill, one-way street
Loving but not being loved
Being loved but not having passion
Having passion but not feeling it is true

Distance is great, but love is strong
You are the one I care about
The love, the passion, the feeling is still
    in my heart
Can you not see me in your world?
Or am I just
    Not there

Stephen S. Smith

A Dancer's Art

If the stage her palette
    And her body the brush
Then my mind her easel
    And my memory her canvas

Randy Burke

The Prize Of Life

All of us must die.
But before we pass away
    We must love.

Your woman and her man,
    Must be a dream you
    Both have had.

She is beautiful only in your eyes,
He is the one created by GOD.
    Both of you shall love
    As the commandments have said.

So let the world rejoice,
    You have found love's dream.
Your love is sacred;
Love before you pass away.

Love before you leave this world,
The prize you could well afford,
    Love now, you and she have earned it.
    She loves you, you love her,
    LOVE. That's the PRIZE OF LIFE.

Willard J. Olson

"Skills"

Man's passion to build
Brings about "Needed" skills
Not the skills of survival
But ones to build cities that rival
Great mountains and valleys divide
The skills society relies on
These skills are not of reality
But "Necessary" in today's society
I do not have these skills
I have endurance and will
Cities have been built
Lakes are filling with silt
Destroy what is loved
With skills that are not enough
These skills are not mine
They do not fit in my mind
I live the way I live
My skills to you I give

Steve Downs

Intimacy

If I ask you to bring your humanity
bring your sins
your downfalls
your obscure rainbows

Hug me with your pain
greet me with your loud silent
tell me those secrets everybody knows
here is my moist bosom
furious to embrace a sibling soul

If I ask to bring your humanity
pull out my nails
lay me down along your heart
drink my agony
sing my fears

I promise I will not hide
I will be eye to eye
counting our tears

Robertoluis Lugo

Sweeping

Changes come fast and
bring us to the ground.
The new broom sweeps
so vigorously
the dust is spread around.
Easy does it - in life,
in work or love,
with a touch as
gentle as a dove.
Get sweeping results,
a fresh house, a new start,
with a brush-broom
used skillfully - with art.

Ruth B. Law

Autumn Leaves

Floating, flying, leaping, swirling,
Bouncing, circling, jumping, twirling,
Soaring, ever higher prancing,
"Holding hands," together dancing.

Leaves are in formation going
As the autumn winds keep blowing:
Yellow, brown, and orange too;
Red, or green (but just a few).

When they've done their lively dance,
Land in piles upon the grass,
Children like to hear them crunch,
Run and leap atop the bunch!

Rowena Stenis

Two A.M.

Ephemeral dust
borne by the wind
and scintillated by the sun.
Up and down, up and down,
what a kaleidoscope of color.
I was enthralled,
until with the thunder
of a thousand tiny
tinkling bells,
it vanished.

Viona Stitt

"Right From The Start"

The feelings we share
Between you and me
Are ever so special
As special as can be
Your love is my treasure
To have it is not my right
Only my pleasure
To make you happy
Is my point to meet
My love for you shall never be beat
You'll always be with me
No matter how close or far apart
You've always been my love
Right from the start.

Ryan M. McConnell

To My Patootie

Sweet Patootie is your name,
Being sweet's your claim to fame.
You're a sweetie through and through,
That's why I'm in love with you!

Darling, you're my sweetie pie.
I don't have to tell you why-
'coz you're sweet as cream and honey,
And I love you more than money!

Sweet Patootie, I love you-
Idolize, adore you, too.
You're the sweetest, yes it's true-
And so lovely through and through!

Forever, you're my sweetie pie,
And there is a reason why-
You fill my life with hope and peace,
And my love will never cease!

J. Leighton Barkley

Safe

Poetry,
Began when Adam,
First touched,
Eve's lips with his.

Ever since then,
More than lips,
Have been tasted,
And written about!

Joy of women,
Through poetry,
Is,
Sense sensual passion.

Especially,
If the poets,
Are shy of action,
But not words.

Poetic joys of women,
Help keep,
Men's stilled hearts and brains,
Safe!

Chumly
TYG

I Never Said Good Bye

I never got to say goodbye
Before you passed away
And every time I think of that
I regret it in every way

And when I say my prayers tonight,
I'll remember what to do
I have to tell dear God above,
To take good care of You

I know that you will be happy
Where you will be
I will never forget you,
So, please always remember me

And every time I think of you,
I begin to cry
Knowing deep inside of my heart,
I never said goodbye.

Sarah Pearce-Wilderson

Optimism

Life's road veered
becoming a narrow lane
closed in, darkened
by the oppressive, assailing woodland
while just off the path
he was grateful
for the sustaining cloak
of a secure, sheltering penumbra

Then emerged
an unending passage
naked, exposed
to disparaging, threatening incessance
of the parching horizon
and his spirit soared
at the irrepressible possibility
of unconstrained potential...

Peg Nelson

"Silent Whispers"

When I look into the softened
Beauty of your eyes,
A symphony of utter sweetness
Soars me through the skies.

I look up into tenderness
That holds me in its will,
I cannot breathe for in that moment
Time is standing still.

You look into my eyes and see me,
Soul that's standing bare,
You look into my hopes and dreams
And silence holds me there.

I often sigh with gentle whispers
Of what cannot be,
Never-spoken words of music,
Loving silently.

Shari Gerson

Desperation

Hearts afire, wind in motion,
beats upon endless beats of a
human gripping on what they
hold so near. Reality slowly slipping
through her fingers, the world
in this lifetime, drips turning
into cool running water with only
a tear to add to it. Her hands
melt as the world ends around
her. The walls catch on fire
and her image slowly fades,
only to see reality gone bad.

Tracey Hansen

He's Just A Little Boy

He's breaking things by age of two
At four he's talking back,
By five he can tell a lie
Well don't all kids do that?
He's just a little boy

He's eight now seems so mature
Why do they grow so fast?
Caught him smoking at age of ten
But fads they quickly pass,
He's just a little boy

Now twelve he's liking girls
Fourteen he wants to drive,
At sixteen a car of his own
I hope we all survive,
He's just a little boy

At the senior prom most kids drink
Some they even get high,
I wish he had called home that night
He was much to young to die,
He was just a little boy

Tommie Sue Wilkey

"Time"

Here I sit looking out
At all the things I love about
Oh how I miss running so hard
In the big green playful yard
These things called chicken-pox
They'll never know
Oh how much I hate them so
The rain, the snow, the sun about
Oh how I wish I could go out
Days go on and feel like years
Days pass by with many tears
The green is fading and turning brown
Pretty soon the snow queen will be crowned
Here I sit looking out
At all the things I love about
The snow so white, the air so crisp
Oh boy oh boy don't I wish
Pretty soon the snow will be gone
And I'll be able to play on the lawn.

Tracy Ryder

Little Dog

I know I'll see you waiting there
As you used to on the stair
Wagging tail and lolling tongue
You've been patient so long

Your tiny grave with daisies set
The tear-stained stone is always wet
None could ever take your place
That comic, furry, tiny face

Will you welcome me once more
When I come to Heaven's door
I'll try to bring your favorite toy
I'm coming soon my little boy

Terry Holzmacher

Star Shower

On a magical night in July
As we walked along the shore,
There appeared at water's edge
Stars, twinkling by the score.

We stretched out our toes to touch them
And, much to our delight,
A shower of light danced up,
Then melted out of sight.

We wondered how they came here
While gazing at the sky.
Soon came an answer
When a shooting star streaked by.

Once again we queried
Why the tide had brought them in.
Could it be that stars get bored
And crave a midnight swim?

Except for ocean's murmur
There was no sound at all.
We promised to keep secret
Why stars fall.

Rachel Lobdell

Liquid Thoughts Of A Dream

Her body turns with mine,
as we move in the moonlight and
extend our arms, reaching to each
other as young children reach for
the twinkling stars in her eyes
shine a brilliant blue-grey land
around her moves into shadow
as I step into her embrace of the
world turned black from the clouds
rolling over the moon shines off
her hair into the shadow of the
trees above us gently let loose
their precious leaves of falling
down in the soft, emerald grass
that surrounds us and is entwined
in her hair covers her face as she smiles
her teeth shine in the moonlight
her laugh rings the stars like
tiny bells of celebration of love yet defined...
as her body turns with mine...

Ryan K. Seiberling

From The Wilderness

Let us build day by day
As the moments pass away
Unseen structures for mankind
Satisfying all its kind.

Let us build for young and old
All are in an unseen hold
With all we have to surrender
Else gloom over us doth cover

Let all take a worthy place
Building for no single race
Help for orphans, the fatherless
Better life for the helpless.

Let us build for all nations
For their needs, nay, aspirations
Structures founded on goodwill
Satisfying divine will.

Stephen Nyarko

The Angry Words

Her eyes drift away
As the angry words pierce her heart
How to find the words to say
What will set her apart
From the hurt

Her mind cannot leave
What her heart feels
For only in her soul can she believe
That the anger will not seal
Her fate forever

He tells her things
That no person's ears should hear
Her hardened heart lingers
When she holds back her tears
With her mask

No one can see
What she keeps hidden within
The despair sets in deep
Because no one sees him
Like she does

Tammy Rueger

"Emotions"

You came into my life
As suddenly as life begins.
And just like that,
You were gone.
You taught me emotions
As different as a rainbow.
But then you never returned
The one I felt the most;
Love.
You were with me
Yet you were not mine.
I could touch you, hold you,
But yet never be close to you.
I never got to tell you:
To express my feelings;
You left too soon.
The fact I'll never see you again
Overwhelms all my other feelings
And replaces all of them with one;
Sadness.

Shawna Raby

May 15

May Fifteen
As I've seen
May be forgotten
But not by me

I hear he's with Grandma now
Well, I can't see how
No more friendly greeting
No beg while I'm eating

The furry mess
I loved the best
He's gone away
What else can I say?

Sarah Williamson

"The Crow"

The crow! He caws all day long.
As if to sing a song.
He watches and flies.
Till the sun dies.
Down goes the sun.
Up comes the moon.
The crow! I'll see you at noon.

Patricia English

You And I

As the years pass
as our looks appear so much clearer.
And as I look at you and I see
all the years we spent together
as friends, laughing, smiling and even
through the tears
I think to myself
the feelings I have for you
are so much more
than you could ever imagine.

Tiffany Pyka

Children In The Park

All of the children
are playing in the park.
Swinging, sliding, and running
even after dark.
Enjoying all of the simple things
in life, that are the best
not worrying about wordily things
and all of the rest.
Innocently they play
and fast they grow
into problems that they now
will never know.

Tammye Preston

Volunteering

If days seem lonely,
And you've nothing to do,
Don't feel this can only,
Happen to you.

There are other folks out there,
Who feel like you do,
They have time, they can share,
Make it happen for you.

You can help someone lonely,
And feel better, too,
This feeling didn't only,
Happen to you.

Volunteer, you can do it,
Meet new people, too,
Get busy and make it,
Happen to you.

Peggy Ball

"God Gave Me A Child"

First his birth then his cry,
  And with this over, I gave a sigh.
God gave me a child.

He was so young and innocent,
  And then I knew what true love meant.
The patient caring of his needs,
  All the laughter, all the grieves.
God gave me a child.

So thank you God, I'll do my best,
  To make our love and happiness last.
To teach him prayers before he sleeps,
  And in his heart, your love he'll keep.
Because God gave me a child.

Shelia A. Johnson

Whispers Of Our Names

Ten thousand years shall pass
And who shall know if we
  laughed or danced this night away?
How we flittered the hours of our days?
The world shall know,
for it shall be empty in spots that
laughing and dancing could not fill

Ten thousand years shall pass
And who shall know if we
  laughed or loved this night away?
How we flittered the hours of our days?
We shall know,
for we shall be empty in spots that
laughing and loving could not fill

Ten thousand years shall pass
without a whisper of our names
and what shall make it right?

Robert A. Mills

A Last Farewell

He turned his head, smiled gallantly
And whispered weakly, thus:
Farewell, my dears, adieu,
I go because I must.
Life has been good, life has been gay;
A feeble pun, I grant you.
Yet, in the throes of death, one finds
The truth inconsequential.
This mortal coil will take its leave,
Soon turning into dust.
Remember, though I love you all,
I go because I must.

Virginia Iaia

There Is Always A New Tomorrow

There is always a new tomorrow,
And when you're old you'll say
How funny those tomorrow
Turned into new todays.
The happenings are unexpected,
And minutes slip away.
Your dreams are then reflected
Upon your daily ways.
Your found these little happenings
Of each enchanting day,
Had very quickly turned into
The memories of yesterday.

Patricia Basil Arnold

Not Fair

WE walked for you
And WE talked for you
WE lived your life
Also for you
When WE quit
YOU quit.
Not fair!
The stress
The strain
The sacrifices
The burden
Not fair!
A broke wing amongst our nest
WE had two to lend
BUT you wanted ours
Not fair.

S. Anne Brown

To April

As the storm crashed around us
And the skies poured forth their waters
We lit a flame
To warm our hearts
And those of our companions
For on this day we did vow
That we shall forevermore
Be as one.
And to the cynics of the world,
Whose coarse shells
Often armors a tender heart,
I say to all of you
That love may not conquer all,
But most assuredly,
It will show you how.

Ray Ruelan

Untitled

As the days go steady by
And the nights linger on
I can only wonder why
I'm awake before dawn

For what kind of life
Am I leading this time
For is it full of strife
Or is it just in my mind

Richard D. Linton

Follow Your Dreams

Follow your dreams
and never give up,
Education will make
them come true,
no matter what.
Always look forward,
and never turn back.
Somewhere down the line
your dreams will come true,
and that's a fact.

Rhesha Lewis

Lap Time

Mama picked up baby
And she sat him on her lap.
Baby said, "Gabooda."
Mama said, "Now what was that?"

"Is it time for a bottle?
Does your diaper need a change?"
Baby said, "Gabooda."
Mama thought, Hmm, that's strange.

"Do you want to play some Pat-a-cake?
Or take a little nap?"
Baby said, "Gabooda."
"Okay, baby...clap, clap, clap."

But Baby didn't want to clap,
Or play some Pat-a-cake.
He didn't need a diaper change,
And he was wide awake.

He didn't need a bottle,
And he didn't want a nap.
When baby said, "Gabooda",
He just wanted off her lap.

Pamela Sue Toler

Crying

If the world were perfect
and no one hated,
We would be happy
and not berated.

Why do we hate this guy or that?
Whether he's skinny
or whether he's fat.
It makes no difference,
the color of our skin.
We should love each other,
love all men.

Crying and yelling.
I hear it so loud
Now I see them,
they're in a big crowd.
I see the tears streaming down faces.
I see their families,
moving to new places.
And they're crying.

Tara Williams

My Wish

If I could have three wishes
And make them all come true;
It wouldn't be so very hard.
I'd make them all for you.

For all the love you've shown me,
I'd make the first come true.
All that you'd see or hear or touch
Would give their love to you.

And for the many deeds you've done
This second wish is sure.
I'd promise that in all your life
I'd never find you poor.

My last wish would without a doubt
Be my solemn duty.
I'd give you all that you deserve
With everlasting beauty.

If I could have three wishes
And make them all come true.
It wouldn't be so very hard.
I'd make them all for you.

Susan Pantano

"Idaho"

I've been all over the world,
And I'll tell you one thing
The beauties of this state,
Just makes you want to sing

High mountain lakes,
And mouth-watering Rainbow Trout
Crystal clear rivers,
Get those hungry fisherman out

The fresh mountain air,
And Winter snow so white
The thought of someone spoiling it,
Just makes you want to fight

Mt. Borah standing tall,
And Hells Canyon running so deep
The beauties of Idaho,
I think we will just keep

Her people are friendly, and go out of their way
To treat you right, this is what they say
She has wilderness beauty, and we want you to see
That Idaho is today, what America used to be!

Steven C. Faulkner

My Drifter

I have found a dream come true,
And he is that dream.
The flame that lit the road
Will go out for many a day.
But the flame in my heart
Will stay forever burning.

For that drifter in my life
There will always be a yearning,
A passion and emotion I cannot explain.
My drifter is a special man.
A man that I really feel,
To whom all good things should come.

One day I hope there will be
A place in his heart for me.
Until that day comes,
There is only one thing I must say;
To my drifter, good-bye and good luck.
May happiness be yours forever.

Susan Marturano

Prayer

Don't wait 'til you're in trouble,
and friends your plea evade.
Don't wait 'til there are trials
to ask the Lord for aid.

He's always willing to help you,
no matter what you need.
But pray to Him and ask Him
for a purer life to lead.

Just talk with God and tell Him
what's in your heart and mind,
And He will listen to you.
He's the best friend you will find.

Phyllis D. Yeatts

"All I Wanted Was A Chance"

For some reason I wonder why?
And for hours I sit up here and cry.
What did I do that was so wrong?
I would have grown up
to be healthy and strong.
It's not exactly hate I feel,
I just wanted my chance to be real.
I wanted to walk, and sing, and dance
But of course I didn't get my chance.
Now I understand it's not my fault,
your supposed to be the adult.
They didn't think I could feel pain,
But my need to live is driving me insane
What they did was not fair,
Now I realize they just don't care.
I always wonder about that special day,
I was due the tenth of May.
So alone I sit, broken hearted.
Why didn't my parents
finish what they started.

Tara Brady

The Day

In comes the morning sunrise,
and follows it the day.
A golden sun, the only one,
the flowers tilt and sway.

Life begins anew each day,
and dawn turns dark to fire.
Heaven's children come to play
"Chirp! Chirp!" The birds inquire.

The golden dancer of the morn
tiptoes its way from the top.
And as the day comes to an end,
everything stops.

Zachary Jex

"Flowers Will Bloom"

Flowers will bloom;
And birds will sing:

Spring will come;
And earth will bring:

Thoughts of love;
And dreams of you:

Now love has gone;
And left me blue.

Shelly Adams

Sea Spell

I know a place the oceans churn
And beat against the jutting rocks.
Where sea birds whirl and turn
In endless, raucous, circling flocks.
A place where misty sea and skies
Release my soul, and burden flies.

I know a place along the shore
The sucking, surging sea attacks
In one eternal rhythmic roar,
And clears the mind that evil racks
Of all mundane complexity
And blends into sublimity.

Walter I. Allen

"Wishing For His Love"

He is as sweet as sugar
And as gentle as a bunny.
He is handsome
And also very funny.

He does love
But not me.
He loves
Someone named Stacy.

I wish I was her,
As lucky as she,
For then he would love me.

Stephanie L. Shelton

Massasoit's Prayer

Oh Great Spirit hear our plea
and always guide us back to thee,
Give us the wisdom to understand
those who need a helping hand.
Unveil our eyes so we may see,
someone less fortunate than we,
and if perchance we should fall
because we didn't hear you call,
please before the day goes by,
Grant us another chance to try.

Thomasina E. Jordan

Keep Them

We must always keep our dreams and
always wish and hope for tomorrow.
If you let your dreams die a part
of you dies.
If you let someone steal them away
you lose your soul.
Don't ever let anyone steal your dreams.
Always keep your wishes and hopes alive.
It may take many long days and many hours
of toil and trouble.
But someday things we dream, hope and
wish for will come true.

Ruth A. Price

I Dream

I dream of walks
along the beach
with someone
hand in hand

of nights
under the stars
someone holding me
as I hold them
lying arm in arm

But most of all I dream
of finding someone
whom jointly
our deepest joys
our darkest fears
we do share
forever
setting us
free

Stephen Whitmore

Together We Can Fly

Come along and walk with me,
Along a golden road;
Take my hand, I'll set you free,
Your dreams will never fold.

Come along and fly with me,
Up in the cloud-lined skies;
And what we share will surely be,
A joy that never dies.

Come along and trust in me,
To you I'd never lie;
And soon, in time, you will see,
Together, we can fly.

Rachel Purnell

It Is You I Called Uncle

It is you I called uncle,
all those many years,
you then went to heaven,
and I shed my tears.
It is you I called uncle,
I loved so very much,
leaving me with the memory
of your warm, caring touch.
It is you I called uncle,
as I look at the stars,
and I dream of you,
so very, very far.
It is you I called uncle,
on those very special holidays,
Easter and Christmas,
I will cherish always.
I still call you uncle,
as I sit in my chair,
hoping and praying,
someday, I'll see you there.

Sarah Cannon

A Word For Newlyweds

The wedding vows have been spoken,
All the rice has been thrown.
You are now both joined together,
And starting out on your own.

As you go about your activities,
And routines day by day,
Remember our Dear Lord Jesus,
Who is there to show you the way.

Let Him guide your footsteps,
Down the road of marriage so tough.
Make Him part of your family,
He will help you through the rough.

Love and respect each other,
Just as you do the Lord.
Surely, you will be blessed,
And be of one accord.

Patrick W. O'Bryan

S-p-r-i-n-g

Spring is a time for joy!
　A time—like a new toy
And the birds know when it is
　It's when a Misses becomes a Miss
Flowers come in all kinds
　And animals, love is on their minds
What does spring mean to you?
　A lot of housework to do?

Wayne Mims

My Daddy

My Daddy is pitiful, and really very sad,
All his life he was brought up bad,

He left us lonely, hurt, and confused,
We were only kids, we never knew.

The anger and pain he has left inside,
It hurts so bad I cannot describe.

My love for him is dying so fast,
I don't know how much longer I can last.

Without that love I am afraid,
I pray and pray each and every day.

I'm trying to save that love inside,
But how can you help someone
Who cannot help themselves to survive.

Tonya Bohannon

The Writing On The Walls

Yellow pale walls
all covered with writing,
to others it's funny,
but to me it's just frightening.

The rain and the wetness
may make it fade away,
but the words used and the laughter,
have, will and always will stay.

The writing on the walls
is written by my friends,
they write the worse things written,
either way the message sends.

That writing on the walls,
would frighten you too,
that writing is about me,
figured out myself from the view.

I'll lie around and watch the walls
the writing will go away,
the rain will wash the words gone,
but in my heart the words will stay.

Robbrina Tapp

Lingering Thoughts

Yesterday I went for
a walk by a stream.

Lingering thoughts traversed
through my mind.

Lingering thoughts of you...

How I longed to hold
you and whisper to
you my inner-most
thoughts.

As I walked it almost
seemed that you were near.

I whirled around.

But turned only to
find the breeze
singing a melody as
it moved through
the trees, and the
stream which ran
as ceaselessly as
my longing for you.

Thomas Wooden Jr.

The Uncertainty Of A Rose

The rose is beautiful but deadly,
A venus in long-stem disguise,
Petals so devilishly lovely,
A poison to each gazer's eye.

But you, you should have resisted,
Instead you chose to be blind,
You stole my cherished rose,
Leaving only the thorns behind.

A lifetime betrayed for a memory,
For soon the rose will die,
When she finally withers away,
What about you and I?

I long for the days of old,
Before the rose began to bloom,
That cursed day in the garden,
When temptation sealed our doom.

To all I give this warning:
In the garden do beware,
The uncertainty of a rose,
Will leave you in despair!

P. J. Cafferty

A Winter's Eve

Along the ragged mountain crest
  a tiny snow flake came to rest.

And as I looked toward the sky,
  a thousand more came sailing by.

The screaming wind with all her might
  made dancing shadows in the night.

Making whirlwinds on the ground
  and drifting snow for miles around.

She covers all the fields and woods
  with lovely, lacy, icy hoods.

She keeps her vigil through the night
  while painting all the landscape white.

Virginia Parsons

Angel Song

I would sing to you with
  a thousand voices
  only to proclaim one word of love

And gaze at you with
  a thousand eyes
  to catch the warmth and innocence
  of each smile and supple move.

I would give to you
  a thousand lifetimes
  knowing that I could spend
  a fraction of one with you

And save
  a thousand of my dreams
  holding my arms open
  to share them with you.

I would free
  a thousand violet souls to you
  certain that your love could save them

And without pretense
  release my own soul for your sanctuary.

Scott Norris

God's Child

A child sat down upon my step.
A tear fell from his eye.
Are you lost? I said.
But his refrain was just a sigh.
I am not the child of anywhere,
anywhere at all.
My skin is black so I am told
And I cannot stand tall.
Do not be discouraged for
God is on your side.
So raise your face to heaven
and be a child to him.
The light he'll cast upon your
life will never ever dim.

Shirley Ziskie

Midnight Fire

A wink of an eye
A star of the night
A midnight fire
Breaks into flight
Tropical breeze
Sand in my hair
Waves at my feet
She's standing there
This lady I've dreamed of
Most of all of my life
She's here in reality
By her own devise
Like a fast moving spirit
Running oh so bold
Turning sparks into fire
Now she burns through my soul
Like a endless voice
On a restless flight
Drifting through my dreams
Dancing in my nights

Preston Nail

Life Confusing

Focus on time
A second of present
Always tomorrow to make things pleasant

The wind blows time
North, South, East, West
A second is gone
Where once you could claim it

Introduce lottery
So much to choose
One right, two wrong
Will you lose?

Step left and right
Soon the area is tight
Repetition blows
Sand covers all goals

Present to future
No longer to see
Only behind you
An open sea

Shannon M. Biby

Can Love Be Measured? And How!

What are the many faces of love?
A mate, a child, a family or friends,
Country, pets, and infinite things,
Those values that a good life sends.

Is it from passion, an emotive thing,
Intrinsic and not within my power
To control with mind and human thought,
To come, yet vanish in an hour?

Can it be measured, as with a rule,
Can we divine in varying degrees,
And do a hierarchal reckoning,
To rate its multiple mysteries?

I say it can, and I'll tell you how,
Just lay your values in mind's row,
Arrange in order as if to pay
A shopper's price, from high to low.

For when I group my cherished things,
In gatherings of a kind, I see
My values set the price I'll pay
For things that mean the most to me.

Stuart Daw

Love Is ....

Love is in the air!
A kiss here and there ....
Do we really dare
To be so bare?

Love is strong,
Love is long,
Love is a song,
Love can be wrong.

Love is a wild heart beat.
In winter you need no heat.
Love is a tasty treat;
You don't even need to eat!

Love is pain we have to fear
We bear the burden with a tear
The heart so precious and dear
Will remain forever near.

Yasmine Muhtasib

Grand-Pa's Bell

I've given Grand-pa's old farm bell
a gold coat of paint....
And the pole it sits atop of
is new.
But, the sound that comes forth
when I pull on its rope...
As in the days of its youth
still rings true.
Pealing forth memories of
hot summer days...
When it called the men-folk
from the field,
To Grand-ma's noonday table,
laden with food;
That their sweat-browed labor
did yield.
Though its decades of service
was in days now long past...
Grand-pa's old farm bell,
and its memories will last.

Phyllis W. Compton

Untitled

The air was cool and deathly still;
A fluid thick with gloom,
Steeped with the odors of such flowers —
With withered moldy, bloom —
As are forgot and left to rot,
On some neglected tomb.
It seemed to seep within me deep,
And tell my soul of doom!

The thick fog swirled in ghastly shapes,
As I bore madly on;
The brambles tripped my stumbling feet,
And slashed me with its thorn.
A spider's net with dew was wet,
And in the dim light shone;
It clothed my face in sticky lace,
I gasped a sickly moan!

Willie Bruce Underwood

War

War
A dreaded time and place
Of viscous death
War
Where bullets fly
Veins run dry
War
When limbs are thrown
And people leave home
War
When lives are lost
When bombs are tossed
War
But in all the hatred
There is a purpose
That is................
To end..........
WAR!!!!

Phillip Adam Chiari

A Face Of Natured Lace

In her room alone she sat,
A curled up shawl upon her lap.
A silver tear trickles from her one
Good eye, as empty hours pass her by.
She sips her tea and nibbles her
Toast, remembering the days of company
And when she played host.
A few scattered pictures here and there,
Hang above her flowered chair.
A son, a daughter, a grandchild too,
One she never, ever, really knew.
An old worn card on the table it rests.
Now this old woman lies peaceful
Hands folded across her chest.
Like broken branch from winters trees
Hearts never healed only cold memories
She lies now for all to remember, she
Waited so long for a card for someone to send her.
Now this old natured lace woman never
Ask for much, just that someone keep in touch.

Sharon Hung

Birds Of The Earth

A blue bird of happiness
A black bird of sorrow
A white bird of promises
A red bird of tomorrow
A yellow bird of hope
That keeps us happy by the day
A brown bird of the earth
In which most secrets lay.

Sheila Kruse

A Burning Fire

A fire that lies within me
Tries to cease the heat.
But the embers spark rays of hope
Each time the oil it meets.

The coals ignite with a sudden surge
As the sounds of His praises ring.
It sends the dusty smoke asunder,
To my soul red-hot flames still cling.

So burn within me Mighty One,
As I kindle the flames with prayer.
And make this fire everlasting,
So the ashes of death are spared.

Teresa J. Ferraris

I Watch The Water

I watch the water
comforting me, so peaceful,
always relaxing me.
I watch the water

The wild current, the gentle
lake the calm stream. They
control my every being.
I watch the water.

Where are you coming from?
Where are you going?
Can I flow with you, swim
in you, drift with you, or
just - watch you.
I watch the water.

When the sun rises,
She sprays green and splashes blue, all
over you, your beautiful
your breath taking falls that dip
into the sea, Oh how you consume me
I watch the water

Teresa Campbell

Three Black Dining Room Chairs

Three black dining room chairs.
All that is left.
Three black dining room chairs
Sitting against a white dining room wall.
All that is left
After 29 years.
The last of the load.
Three black dining room chairs.

Doris E. Smith

Beautiful Angel Mother

Beauty within sheds forth your light,
of a soft spoken angel always in sight.
Your eyes so deep
filled with an immense
amount of patience and love,
a gift from above.
The touch of your hand
softens the tears and fears
and so magically changes it
into happy years.
Your heart is your masterpiece
made of shiny gold,
surrounding with glistening diamonds
and rare jewels unknown.
You are the center of all you believe,
generosity, love and peace.
You are all the above.
you are my Beautiful Angel Mother
someone I will forever love.

Antoinette Congialdi

The Tree

I
may
never
replace
in all of
my travels,
a fascination
so strong about
one of the world's
marvels. Where ever
I go, in every land I see,
there's nothing more lovely
than the
splendor
of a tree.

Bill Porter

Seek 'O' My Heart

Seek 'o' my heart
A love to find
He shareth my mind
He maketh me whole

Seek 'o' my heart
I look to the sky
A tear in my eye
A vision to hold, hair of gold
eyes as blue as the sky
He taketh my breath away

Seek 'o' my heart
On this day, my true love come
His hand reacheth out
His words he doth shout
"Seek" o no more your dear heart
sail away with me
on the "Wings of a Pure White Dove"

Alice Colgan

No Chance

The pain of a little boy so innocent, so sweet, trapped
  by a single man's destruction and defeat.
He's new to this world, so he doesn't know what's right,
  but the hurt soon begins he crawls in bed at night.
He keeps his pain locked inside his tiny little heart, but
  deep inside his mind and soul it's ripping him apart.
He lays in bed and laughs and cries trying to forget,
  the painful memories inside the challenges he's met.
He moves his hands to push away the evil thing's around,
  hoping in his one safe place his body won't be found.
Knowing when he shuts his eyes, the nightmares soon begin,
  having no escape from him no hope for him to win.
I look into his tear filled eyes searching for a clue,
  wishing he would open up and tell us what to do.
It breaks my heart to think about my little brother's pain
  knowing that this small boy's loss is someone else's gain.
We try to talk to him and tell him everything's ok. That if he
  stays at home with us his pain will go away.
But, we know the scars are there so permanent and deep,
  and when he shuts his tiny eyes they'll haunt him in his sleep

Candice Denham

Persuaded Trust

I trusted you with all my heart,
but you deceived me.
You led me in temptation,
I was blind and could not see.
For a voice so tender and comforting,
lies is all you told.
I thought you were a true friend,
but your heart is cold.
How could I learn to believe you again,
'cause I'm not so sure.
That whatever may come out of your mouth,
won't be a lure.
If these harsh words have
hurt you in any way.
I want you to think of
them every single day.

Cheri Stephens

Untitled

Saying goodbye to a loved one is never an easy thing to do
  but when you have your friends it becomes a little easier for you.

Although you think it's really hard now, things do get a little
  easier with time but you will always have those days when
  he's always on your mind. You can never forget about all
  the times you shared; the good ones of course and the bad
  ones too. Even though the reality has not set in and it
  probably never will you still have to go on, even feeling
  the way you feel.

Although he's no longer with you, he still is near and dear.
  He'll never leave your side, he will be there everyday of every year.

No matter what anyone says it never seems to help. How can
  they possibly understand any of your hell. You will go
  through many stages; denial, bargaining, and even some
  anger too. No matter how hard you try he won't come back to you.

When ever you need a friend remember I will always be around
  and if you need a shoulder to cry on, I'll always have two for you.

Erica K. Collins

Vivé

We all fall down at one time or another
But we must always get up
We all may not be dealt the same hand
But we must still play it

Life is not fair nor is it equal

You may not have feet but can still win a race
You may not have hands but can still write a song
You may not have eyes but can still see

Life is a question mark until you make it an Exclamation!!

Anita Stansbury

Untitled

Dedicated to John and Adam
They tell us to be bold and strong
but we feel helpless and weak
so many things that they don't know
things we hide and can't let go
they think our life is plain and simple
and it's always trouble free
but they don't know what we've been through
or what our life has come to be
trying to make good decisions which at times we fail
we cannot seek decisions in very strong detail
wish they'd look a little harder
then maybe they would see
exactly what was meant to be
inside of you and me

Becky McElroy

A Best Friend

A true friend can be a girl or boy....
but to make a friendship, is made of trust
I thought I knew a friend a really good friend
but now she's gone only friend I did trust...
If I could only find a friend to talk to....
to tell my feelings and to tell my lies
but not a friend tells others of your secrets.
A friend to share my laughs and cries...
To share my clothes and belongings...
to talk at school, to talk on the phone
And when I'm happy for her to be happy
And to keep me company when I'm alone...
So when I find that friend I'll talk forever...
I'd like to know those secrets, starts and ends
I'd like to know the person better
and for all that in a person that's my best friend...

Auburn Baggett

Blockhead

At first I thought it was a rock
but then I saw it was a sock,
So I use it as my front door lock!
I know I'm acting crazy,
because my head is just a building-block.

Daniel Thompson

At Last

At last the bright light that has escaped me shines warm upon my face.
At last the darkness that engulfed my soul has slithered away.
At last the pain that consumed my being has subsided to the deepest
depths of my conscience.
At last the tears of despair have dried up and the wrath of my anger
has diminished.
At last I feel. Yes, I feel the peace like the gentle dove flying in
the heavens above.
At last, once again, I can feel love.

Bonnie L. Thompson

Life's Purpose

The waiting was intolerable
But then he was here!
Small round head covered in hair as soft as down.
Features familiar and yet unknown,
Cupid bow mouth and shapely chin,
Hands with fingers and tiny nails
That take one's breath away with their perfection.

Swaddled in white,
Deep in satisfied slumber-
My grandson
Son of my son,
A new spirit to take life on.

Frances M. Johnson

The Accused

She didn't want to remember it
But the pain just wouldn't quit.
She'd always heard stories of sexual assault,
how not to blame the victim, it's not her fault.
Yet when she looks in the mirror, all she can see
is a lonely girl crying, "It happened to me!"
For all the damage caused it's hard to believe
his only punishment is a lifetime of reprieve.
Day after day she asks herself why
though she knows there's no answer,
no tears left to cry.
What he did cut deep like a knife
and will certainly haunt her the rest of her life.
Still she seeks no vengeance for this terrible sin;
to do so would be like letting him win.
To all of you who simply don't see
I shall explain the best way known to me:
It's easy to show he committed the crime
What you'll never know is she's doing the time.

Debra Castonguay

Without A Word

I fell and scraped my knee outside,
but the kiss was better than the Band-Aid.

Sometimes I feel 10 feet tall,
Yet, you smile but say nothing

"Hey Mom, I got an A today",
You'd reply with no sound but a hug

A tear would roll down my cheek,
You'd dry it without a word.

"Mom, He broke my heart again,"
but never "I told you so" but yet a card on my pillow.

A budget that I am used to being on
It's no mystery how the money appeared in my wallet.

Just when I think no one understands,
I look up and see we both have tears in our eyes...enough said.

Sometimes you say things that mean the world to me,
but lately you've done that and more and you did it all
WITHOUT A WORD...

Angel Phillips

A Forced Illusion

A forced illusion, a moment's confusion,
as the facade slips away.
Reality strikes the face of all who step in its way.
A noble prince, a shining star,
masks are donned everyday.
And every day the masks are worn, the soul just slips away.

Carrol Lee

The Song

It could be about breakups, sometimes about frowns,
But the bright and the cheery ones always seem to go on.
I have sung about places that have captured my heart,
tears, fears, and nightmares, wild thoughts have played part,
And then I've heard some that have brought my thoughts to a stand,
and other times wander to far away lands.
Some sung of MY lover, together, alone, doing things that we've
dreamed of to help our love grow.
Of places I've fished, lakes that I've swam, of mountains I've
climbed, and dreams I have had.
One thing most about music, that's amazing to me, it the way we all
feel it inside glowing free.
If my eyes can not see and my mouth will not move, still surely the
notes will be heard through and through.
It's nothing but tones altogether you see, that brings us united
this world around me.
For no matter what language or color you fare, I'm sure you've
heard music that has lifted despair,
And if not for but one moment, you seem to belong,
The universe provided you with that song.

Chuck Wilcox

Untitled

I looked to my parents for a sign, for a clue.
But the answers they gave were varied and few.
Who is it I am? Just where is my place?
They saw but themselves when they looked in my face.

I looked to my husband for whom I might be.
He knowingly answered, "why you're just like me."
I believed for a while and tried with my best,
But my soul still revolted and my search wouldn't rest.

I moved on alone, but continued to feel,
That each person I loved then became my ideal.
I tried it their way, but failed in the end.
That's not who I am. My soul wouldn't bend.

With sorrow, I decided, that nobody knew.
The answer I sought would never come through.
One day, while out walking, alone on the hill,
The answer came shining, yet quiet and still.

I looked all around, at the trees and the sky.
Smiled to myself and thought I would cry.
All this that I love, all this that I see,
The answer is clear, "why, I am just me."

Jeanne

Sadness

We all get mad, and sometimes sad,
but that's just the way life goes.
I know you're feeling pain inside
because to me your sadness shows.
You need to know that I am here
to wipe your tears away,
and to tell you to remember
that tomorrow's another day.
The sadness that you feel inside
has got to disappear,
because the sadness that I'm seeing
is the cause of all your fears.
Wipe away your teary eyes
and bring a smile to your face,
because even though you feel this sadness,
in my heart you still hold a place.

Anthony Cheslick

465

He Is Looking For You

You may be feeling down and blue,
  But stop and consider a thing or two.
Maybe he just wasn't the man for you.
  The one for you will always be true.

When true love really comes along
  Your heart will be filled with song.
He will be thoughtful and kind,
  Always putting you first in his mind.

He is out there somewhere looking for you.
  The problem is he doesn't know who.
He doesn't know where or when,
  But he'll keep on searching, your heart to win.

Life is too short to look back and be sad.
  If you dwell on the past then you won't be glad.
Look to the future, in life take a part.
  You don't know when he will steal your heart.

Eileen Combest

Untitled

He moved on and so should I.
But sometimes I just have to cry.
He told me what I wanted to hear
And comforted my every fear.
I foolishly let him lead me on,
And play me like a pawn.
Although they could see he was a fake,
My friends' advice I would not take.
I fell for each and every trick,
And took a risk too many,
So that maybe in the end,
I'd be more than just another girlfriend.
It took me ever so long to learn
That the love I gave will never be returned.
Foolishly believing all those lies,
My conscience vanished, when I looked into his eyes.
Now he's searching for someone new,
A fresh naive-face without a clue.
So beware of this "Romeo,"
To whom I couldn't say NO.

Christie Beck

Forgive Me

Love should be forever,
  But some hurts won't go 'way.
For the thoughtless things I've surely done
  I know I have to pay.

I wish I could undo each time
  My actions, words, or deeds
Caused you to think less of me
  And turned flowers into weeds.

I've loved the children deeply — true,
  But always loved you more.
For all the years I've known you
  You've caused my heart to soar.

I always thought down through those years
  Our sky was bright and blue,
But unintended wrongs by me
  Have clouded it for you.

Dear, my love is forever.
  I want no one but you.
So, though you may not feel the same,
  I send my love to you.

Bedford D. May

In Memory Of Krystina

People come and go as they please,
But people like Krystina don't want to go.
God says it is just the way it has to be.

As we cry and sob all day long -
Krystina tells us:
I really wish you knew what was going on.

I think of you all
And what it was like on earth
But heaven can't be sold for what it is worth.

If I had a choice I would not leave
But when you get up here you will say:
Krystina, you're right look at heaven now I see.

So people of the world keep doing your job
But believe me, if you want eternal life
Please, oh please believe in God.

So as I sign out, I hope to see each and every one of you.
I love you all:
Friends and family of my last year 1992.

Chad W. Sigsworth

Happiness

Once I had love
But love is a hurting thing
It takes your very being ripping it to shreds,
Stomps upon it and laughs "saying stupid, foolish things."
Who are you that I should belong to you?
Is this a corrupt and evil world?
Am I seeing only one side?
That which is in myself.
Am I the thing that mutilates my own world?
Is my relief inside myself, or must I
constantly seek to change the world?
There is none so blind as those who will not see.
Perhaps if I close my eyes and forget,
when I open them, I too, will be able to see.
Relief from mistrust and ugliness
That is all I see, This is all I crave.
Happiness.

Frances Russell

Feelings

I know that you think what I write is a game;
but listen to me, for my heart is in pain.
It aches for someone to love me for me;
and be happy for that, not what they want
me to be.
What I say right now comes from my heart,
which sometimes feels it's tearing me apart.
My emotions are wild and out of control
so what happens next, I'll never know.
So please excuse what I say or do,
it's only because I care for you.

Barbara Craig

Detour To The End

Born
burnt paper. Trembling hands. Dissolving words.
Locked in a flame.
Disappeared - the main idea. Eyes never see. Minds never know
what is drafted, by seeing (planned.) Though
(for your own good.) Put down on a piece of paper to be
destroyed.
All emotion erased. Strike the match as the
pages crumble to
dust.

Carrie Roskam

September 1, 1970

The darkness and the rain are outside my house,
But inward the scene is warm
With thoughts of other times of sun and laughter.
Water so cool and smooth rolling over stone and flesh,
And wind blowing the blackness far behind us.

The good days of spring-not-yet-summer.
Of love-not-yet-born.
It was one of the Now times forever to be,
To be young, and young to be free
As long as the sky was a partner to the contract.

The richness of insanity flowed from your eyes to mine
And filled the abyss of longing.
The revolution began the peace free from revolt.
A word from a sister marked the beginning
Of a noise-quiet space in time.

Away in the watchfulness of dreams undreamed
I walked without you,
Still seeing the sunrise of a million new
Tomorrows, and the close of a thousand well-worn
Yesterdays just waiting to be born again.

Cathy Young Johns

"Even The Darkest Cloud Has A Silver Lining"

I can't begin to tell you how much you mean to me,
but in this poem I've wrote for you
perhaps you will see.

When God saw fit to take our little girl one day,
He also gave us all of you
to help ease the pain away.

And each of you have done the job just fine,
for I can't tell the difference
than if all of you were mine.

Sometimes I get so lonely on her birthday and Christmas time,
then some of you come up with something
that makes me think you're mine.

Someday if I'm lucky to get to heaven to see our "Lynn,"
Then I'm going to tell her
What a blessing each of you have been.

Your Loving Aunt,
Ethel H. Chambers

Running Scared

I was running from what, I do not know.
But I know if I stopped it would catch me through.
My legs really hurt, in agonizing pain,
It's about time my mind stopped playing this game.
I trip then fall, and hurt my knee.
I've got to keep running, or it'll catch me.
I can hardly see, everything's in a blur.
My mind tells me to run, faster, faster.
I can't help it anymore, I fall to my knees.
I close my eyes and to the Lord I pray please.
I slowly and cautiously turn around my head.
I seen midnight block with eyes of red.
I struggle to get up with tears in my eyes
Fear filled my heart, but my body still tried.
Make it go away, anything I would sacrifice
Just make it stop, and give me back my life
My head ached, and my body was sore
The unbearable pain was hard to ignore
To even look back, wouldn't even be dared
I ran in the dark alone, I was running scared.

Alexandrea Moore

Our Beautiful Campus

There's a great, big world out there to explore,
But I am growing tired and can't go out there anymore.
The traffic is heavy and the streets difficult to cross,
My vision is poor, my hearing at a loss.

So, it's best I stay on the grounds of this lovely home
And do not wander and attempt to roam.
I've heard there are beautiful gardens on our campus grounds
And enchanted areas with trilling bird sounds.

So, let's start walking and view some pretty spots.
Oh, a few yards away I see forget-me-nots.
And as I look to that first cottage, how my heart reposes,
Viewing that pretty row of stately tree roses.

Down in the gardens at the end of the block,
There grow beautiful poinsettia and hollyhock.
Between the rows of cottages a few feet west,
Beds of geranium and lobelia look their best.

Over the beautiful, flowering grounds
What loveliness we have easily found!
So much beauty we have right at our feet,
Never have we need to go out on the street.

Blanche Littler

Blind Marie

You needn't believe this story if you don't want to,
But farmer Robey told it and swears it is true.
A sheep named Ralph came to the farm one day,
The boy who owned him asked if he could stay.
Ralph didn't care for other sheep,
So perhaps to justify his keep,
He befriended an old pony named Marie
Now this poor old horse could not see;
For twenty winters had taken their toll, indeed,
Mrs. Robey had to lead her to her stall and feed.

Enter Ralph - gifted possibly with a special sense,
Or for his board and keep to recompense,
No matter the reason how or why,
To Marie he became her seeing eye.
If she nickered Ralph was there in a flash,
Or with a stray dog in the yard he would clash.
At night nose to nose the two of them slept,
Ralph always alert as his vigil he kept.
Often Ralph's body became a pillow for Marie;
They lived for each other in complete harmony...

Beatrice Brewer

Tender Love From The Gardener's Hand

With a rainbow of colors sent from above,
bright tiny flowers burst out with love.

They demand no care of a gardener's hand,
yet they flourish and thrive even in sand.

But, oh what a waste of a precious delight
when the flowering blooms escape your sight.

So, I gathered together in the palm of my hand.
a bouquet of love I've pulled from the sand.

For you my precious and beautiful flower
a gift of my love in a tall crystal tower.

And, along with my gift of colors from sand
comes for you the touch of this gardener's hand.

David Zimmerman

467

The Seed

The seed of the flower is planted with the expectance of
  blossoming beauty.
The flowers are baked in the sun, swayed by the winds
  and bathed in the rains.
The seed of Man is planted with the expectance of mental
  and physical beauty.
But Man is scorched with pain, swayed by evil and bathed
  in the concepts of a sick society.
Thus Man may not grow, even, to the height of a flower.

Elaine Ligon

Blind Heart

A blanket covers my eyes.
Blinding my vision from bitter truth.
Lost in serenity, I cannot sense danger.
Sheltered by warm clouds.
Haunted by rainstorms.
Inevitable fate lurks in the thunder.
Pain in the rain. Death in the lightning.
Unable to move.
Paralyzation from fear.
It is the absence of sight.
A cold shoulder of awareness approaches.
I now see clearly.
For a brisk moment I find peace.
I have learned. Endless seconds pass.
Oblivious to the sands of time,
Slipping through the hands of life.
Just beginning to live.
New found wisdom and hope. Eternal thanks.
I have been taught a lesson of love.
In the blink of an eye, lightning crashes.

Cara Ann Clauer

Soldier's Song

Standing alone with man's twisted manor,
bleeds horror from steel in each ends womb.
Joins those soldiers of power and valor,
while mother lies dreaming of son's final tomb.
This darkest glitter above all disgrace,
casts morbid a scene through the eyes on his face.

What cause is just
to pursue such a slander?
Man's life, unsanctioned lust,
says from death, no glamour.
From angels adorn his cradle was laden,
comes bliss to all scorn, of this no mistaken.

What devil's tongue splits thy family's name?
What to this doth my mind say?
To cast a life betwixt honor and shame,
and within thy sight, no other day.
Found with greed above all conception,
condemn all wars, be children not forgotten.

David H. Blomquist

My Love Is Gone

My love is gone, day by day my tears are fading away, it will never
be the same for my love is gone.
The roses bloom reminding me of him, day by day the sunset goes
down reminding me of that special night we held hands. When will my
love return to me?
My days are grey the sunshine is gone. My dream has left me, when
will the sun return? Will it be when that special someone comes along
or will the days be grey for the rest of my life?
Drip, drip, drip, the tears from my eyes form puddles, my love has
left. There is no longer sunshine the flowers are dead, and my days
are sad, sunshine please return to me.

Christina Horn

Let Us Bring Prayer Back

One nation under God was how my school
began but for now it seems the anti
Christ has them all at hand. Prayer is
rare in public schools and may be found
no more this abomination gave us Sheol
and all he's longing for. So in place of
peace and love and the commandments as
our rules we have guns and drugs and
hatred as our tools. Now one nation under
Sheol that's a darkened plight but bring
back prayer within our schools and we
will see the light. Sheol won't go
where God resides this a proven fact
so let us not be fooled by this anti
Christ let us bring prayer back.
No God no peace - know God know peace.

Catherine Denise Robinson

To The Opossum

Maybe hanging upside down has affected your brain,
Because you missed the point of genetics.
Survival belongs to the fittest-
And not to those whose family members
Refuse to learn from prior mistakes
And continue to run in the road
And be flattened, tortilla-like,
Fur and flesh ground into the pavement.

Why do you do it?
Do your pocketed babies cry for food
From a greener area in the distance?
Another place?
Does your playing dead have any
Bearing upon your decision?
Maybe you believe in reincarnation,
And you must practice with a street death.
Or, could it be that you dream
Of a better life, somewhere else,
And the risk is somehow worth it?

Cindy H. Rivers

Untitled

I need a picture to remember this by,
because memories can die so fast.
    The chill in the air, with a moon in the sky,
because memories never last.
    The wind in the sea, with a song in the night,
because memories are all that I have.
    The rhythm of love, and all that is right,
because memories can fade so black.
    Remember this time and all that we do,
because memories can't last forever.
    Remember the love that I have for you,
because memories will keep us together.

Bobi Jo White

The Lesson Learned

There wasn't a worry in her heart that day.
As she drove along quickly, the time whiled away
But with foot on the pedal, the speed slowly rose.
Still no worry or fear on her face did she show.
Then it happened so quickly, just a screech and swerve,
And the fear settled in as she rounded that curve.
She just might have lived but no seat belt she wore.
It's lonely around without her anymore.
But she's left behind memories for you and for me,
In hopes through this tragedy it might help us see,
That life is so precious and not just a game.
'Cause when it's one of your friends, you're never the same.

Christa Woodlief

If This Is Goodbye

If this is goodbye let me know
because I've been holding on for so long

I know we rushed in
but we just can't rush out
and then again,
we can't go on like we are

No matter what happens,
I'll still always love you
even when the tears roll down my face
and I scream at you in anger,
you're still going to be the one

We need to talk
So don't hold back what you're dying to say

Give "us" one more chance
and please don't tell me
Goodbye.

Erin M. Marsh

To God With Love

Dear Lord, I'm writing this letter in the form of a poem, to you
Because I sincerely believe that you inspired me to
Let others in the big wide world out there
Know of the beautiful relationship we share
And I have to wonder at my age of ninety-five
If you have some special reason for keeping me alive
So I ask you in prayer to show me the ways
I might serve you best, for the rest of my days
You have been my dearest and most beloved friend
Giving me strength and spiritual guidance, times without end.
Of course I'm only human and I confess that I sometimes fail
To follow you completely along the holy trail
But, you are right there beside me and in answer to my plea
You draw me very close and get me back in line with Thee
You're so divine, so loving, so kind and so true
Whatever in this world would I do without you
I do love you truly - dear Lord above
And forever thank you for your grace and love.

Florence P. Skene

A Fearless Stare

With foolish eyes I gaze toward
    Beauty I'm unable to face with words
In the obscurity of my desk I can't help but stare
    Her angelic eyes and flaxen hair
    Shadowed by her crimson glare
Though timid I'm compelled to observe
    A feminine body, delicate curves
    Concealed by means of calamitous reserve
Furthermore my eyes vast and long
    Her satin legs she walks upon
    Shielded by her fearless calm
Perhaps one day I'll attain the fortitude
    Steal her heart and escape from solitude
    If not my soul may perish soon
With somber eyes I will gaze no more
    Beauty I was unwilling to face with words

Brandon Bonow

My World

It's all in place. Each one framed within the
    backdrop of their present sense.
Where am I though, in the focus of today? A hub
    no longer needed to spoke love's idea?
Now a reference, an impression of layered images,
    the new not blended yet with yesterday.

I feel compelled to beckon. No one sees me as
    though I am a shade, indiscernible.
Pausing, I realize I must now acknowledge me!
Somehow, then, I must catch hold of myself,
    And take my hand...
        and know...
            I am becoming....

Elizabeth Harner Brooks

Inborn Fondness

I was not born out of love, as I can now look
back and see, I sometimes wonder what was
Gods aim for thee? Born by two people who
never expected on seeing me. Not a girl but a
strong he. Born one February on a cold sleepless
night, the situation must be made whole and
corrected as right. I sometimes think it must
be wrong to have been born, My mother feeling
nine months of an infants throne. Nine months
of inborn memories living in a prison of pure
hell, the child waiting to be released like a
criminal expecting bail. I now know my
purpose to love you and make the feeling last,
Regardless of all I am revealing about my past.
To start my new family with my everlasting thee,
to love you as a small token of what you
have given to me.

Billy Joe Currie

AH...............

We've touched the beauty of the riches so serene.
Atop the trees, the sun became a fortress for our dreams.
The colors of the rainbow caressed each and every limb.
And I became his lovely leaf, he touched my heart again.

The showers of the morning churned within my mind so clear.
As he spoke his love for me, my cheeks were streaked with tears.
They trickled to my lower lip, I tasted soft sweet salt.
I knew he'd never find in me, what others see as fault.

And as he gently looked beyond, my eyes that he could see,
My heart began to venture in the trees where he found me.
My lips became much softer, my heart began to pound,
And as I looked into his eyes, I knew my love I'd found.

His hand caressed my shoulder, he pulled me unto him.
And caressed me as his own, my brow beneath his chin.
I felt his heartbeat in me, my heart began to pound.
And all the music I could hear, was of our own sweet sound.

Christine Steward

My Feelings At The Beach

The beach lets me think,
As the waves crash I look back at my life,
I see many wrongs and rights.
As I lay on the soft sand
And listen to the sea gulls,
I think about my future.
As I see the sea life live a happy life
I think of living a happy life.
As I take deep breaths I smell the sea,
And that lets me think of what I love.

Danielle Brower

Stealth

With iconoclastic glee he crept into my soul
at the hour of the wolf
when night is at its peak
and angels weep
at the sight of so many scowling demons
his filthy fingers were like rusted blades
tearing and shredding my barely worn flesh
with no trace of remorse
or remembrance
he came and he left
forever forcing me to re-piece
the incomplete puzzle of myself.

Christine Hayes

The Cold Winds Of Loneliness

When I look out my window
At the cold winter wind
I can't help to think
What it would be like
Without you as my friend.

Our friendship is one
That has blossomed from its start
And it helps warm the icicles
From my frosted lonely heart.

For lonely and frosted is how
   my heart can be
Because of the distance that you are from me.

But the thoughts of you
And the memories that we share
Warms the cold winds that blow through my soul.

Allen W. Williams

Selfless Love

I don't want to say goodbye,
At that moment, I know I'll cry,
Because I know time will lose
you from my heart,
My heart from your mind.

But, if it comes to going our separate ways,
I'll still have the memories of better days,
Where a laugh filled the night,
No harsh words and no verbal fights.

I cannot force you to mature with me,
I can't make you understand a vow is a
promise for eternity,
That love means: What I want for me -
Is exactly what I would do for you!
SELFishLESSly!

But, until you come to me,
As I am here for you,
What I have is an illusion of us two,
There is no me in love alone to the
shadow of you.

Darrel Poppino

Untitled

Bubbling waters spring from cooling skin, birds form V's
and parted lips greet new waves. The sun shines to warm
hearts and begin the journey through neighboring forests.

Reaching sprinkling water, eyes sparkle to welcome lonely
wanderers, sitting ducks wait their turn, while hunters
toast and begin the hunt...A foolish man attempts his kill.

Passing peaceable flowers, eyes meet to ensure friendly
surroundings. Ocean breezes and crashing waves; pouring
souls and only one perfect pair of smiling eyes...

Abril Borrego Pacheco

"My Father"

Fathers' Day comes once a year;
At last, the day is finally here.
I have a "Father" who can't be beat
By any Father on the street.
He has a heart as pure as gold;
He never allowed us to go cold;
He worked his fingers to the bones
To give his family a very good home.
I have a "Brother" and "Sister" too;
Of this we agree, we all love you.
You made us mind when we were young.
That's why we didn't turn out to be bums.
I know I have said it many times before;
But not enough, so I'll say it some more,
"I love you Daddy" and that's no line
You are the perfect Father;
And I'm so glad you are mine.

Darlene W. Beavers

Strange As It Seems

The burdens on my shoulders are much too heavy.
At any time now, my knees will give away and I'll collapse.
But strange as it seems, someone is holding me up.

The darkness has blinded me; I cannot find my way.
At any time now, I will become totally lost.
But strange as it seems, someone is guiding me.

My heart has broken and shattered into many pieces.
At any time now, it will stop pumping.
But strange as it seems, someone is healing it.

Who is this special someone that has the power
to give me strength?
To give me light?
To mend my heart?

Strange as it seems, I believe I know him.

Dana R. Pickett Johnson

Motherhood

Flesh of my flesh
As you passed through my loins,
My heart separated in two:
The smaller part remained with me,
The rest accompanied you.

Now logic tells us that the whole
Must equal the sum of its parts,
But logic doesn't play a role
In matters of the heart.

Every child that I have borne
Claims the greater share of mine,
As though my heart,
By some divine equation,
Multiplied with each miracle of creation.

Ann Troncale

Untitled

A smile spreads across my face
As I dream of a land in a far away place
Where we'll be together, my love and I
And there our desires and dreams will fly
I'll run my fingers through his long, dark hair
And I'll tell him that I love him, that I'll always care
He'll say that he needs me, that we'll always be together
He'll tell me that he loves me for now and forever
We'll look deep into each others eyes
And I'll know his dreams are the same as mine
But for now I'll miss him just the same
And he'll know it's me, at night, calling his name

Christina Jo Baker

Grave Progress

A girl cried out into the shroud of night
As those preceding her had done before
But now the neighbors scurried with their fright
While finding comfort locked behind their doors

Her cries just might as well had not been heard
For little did they do if but for harm
The stranger irked by every word
The neighbors wishing no cause for alarm

And so alone she suffered her assault
Reflecting on the day to be her last
Her tears more full of loss than common salt
Entreated time to seize her as it passed

As time obliged her tormentor withdrew
Insensately she fell across the walk
And all that she had ever known or knew
Then coupled with her breath and left in smoke

Collectively the neighbors dared to sigh
Now free to move about with small concern
The stranger needed not an alibi
No-one had seen him lest he return

Angela Porter

The Mirror

*Dedicated to my deceased mother Edith, my daughter Tricia Thomas, and
my granddaughter Sara Thomas*

The mirror stands before me now;
As the years leave me older and favoring Mom.
The mirror reflects my Mother's face;
And when I look again it's my own reflection I see.
In the mirror I see her gestures and ways,
I think because she lives on in me.

The Mother I loved will never die -
so long as I stand before this mirror now.
So when my daughter's youthful ways fade
and the years leave her older and graced.
The mirror shall stand before her then -
And see me - her Mother's face.
So when she turns to look again
She'll then see so long as she lives
the Mother she will lose one day.

I will never die my dear sweet child
So long as you stand before the mirror again.

Then one day - her daughter will stand before that mirror too -
Only to see what I see now.
The face of the Mother she loved so much.

Cynthia Darlene Pere

The Snipers

"We hate them all," answered the Bosnian snipers
As one took aim and made another child lifeless.
"Our enemies must be totally destroyed;
Thus restoring ethnic purity, and peace we'll employ.
"Child bearing women not pro-create,
The obvious reason is not up for debate."

"The child of today is their combatant tomorrow,
So we end their existence now, without any sorrow."
"The age and the sex is of no valued importance
As killing them all we do without any reluctance."
"Eliminate the men, women and all their children,
As a cleansing peace is our only moral solution."

How sad!!!!!

Anthony James

Mighty Presence

There are so many expectations in the air
as many souls are dwelling on the ground
Life seems to be to very few welfare
and for so many just poorness is bound.

But is not luck in existing the essence
not only wishes achieve what is bad wanted
it's just for those who find the mighty presence
for whom is fortune and goodness always granted.

And it's so easy to find that source all powerful
that inner God that grabs from nothingness
tangible things as well as happiness.

There's deep inside yourself a meaningful
voice struggling to tell your boredom
that will... and knowledge and action get you freedom.

Efrain A. Cardona

So That's It

So that's it; he just walks away.
As if I never existed
As if I never would have stayed.
He doesn't like me,
but my feelings are not the same.
I'll love him with all my heart,
until death do us part.
After that, I'd love him in heaven.
Oh, how my heart burns with passion.
I wish he'd notice me. I wish he'd care.
I wish he'd see that I'm there.
My so-called friends ask him why
But all he gives are alibis.
He says as friends that's how we'll stay.
As if we were ever that anyway.
To him, I'm just another number
in a little black book.
He'll never look me up,
And that's where I'll stay.
So that's it; he just walks away.

Alyssa Coady

Roses Of Color

Dedicated to K.J.B.

One day I saw you bloom; you took my attention from the norm.
As I watched with loving eyes, you were my shelter in the storm.
I looked up to you, you could see right through my outer self.
You looked into the deeper side where no one has dwelled before.

Then one day I started to look around you and noticed that
you weren't the same because the color of your petals
didn't match the ones on me.
I started to wonder if they saw what I see.

Please bear in mind, I've been told time and time again
that I have been wrong before; it isn't to ponder why or when.
Alas, I cannot love you, for your petals bloom a different shade than mine.
You must understand that I need to stick to my own kind.

Older and wiser are they who have lived longer than you or I.
Stronger and higher are those who soar beyond the sky.
I wish you could be me, or just how I am.
But the way things are, I can't be with you again.
Because I'm gaining their acceptance and losing my best friend.

Elissa F. De La Paz

471

Room In Your Heart

A baby is born, born with a heart that is open yet empty.
As a child grows, the heart begins to fill.
First it is filled with the love for a parent, then family,
  then friends.
If one is lucky, the heart is always open,
  open and filling with new different kinds of love.
But if one suffers a loss, loss of a love,
  a wall is built in the heart.
That wall holds in the love that was there,
  but it doesn't allow any love out or any love in.
There is still room in the heart, but those walls are constricting.
Replace those walls, replace them with blankets.
Blankets will keep those loving memories safe and warm,
  tucked away in that special place in your heart;
And when you need them,
  you uncover them and enjoy remembering;
Then you cover them, tuck them away for another day.
There is always room in your heart, as long as you use blankets,
  not build walls.

Andrea Turner

Winter

As winter lays its ermine wraps
Around Dame Nature's shoulders,
It covers up some hideous gaps
And conceals unsightly boulders;
The trees' bare fingers arc gloved with snow,
Brooks still their monotonous hum,
As reeling from the wintry blow,
They are suddenly struck dumb.
The gentle snow that tumbles down
And settles every place,
Falls alike on country and town,
Over the earth's unwashed face;
The earth clad in its chill attire
Makes a picture quite serene,
Viewed from a nice warm fire,
There's nothing nicer than a winter scene.

Alexander Patterson Carlisle

Good-Bye Daddy

Why did you have to leave?
Are you ever coming back?
Will you bounce me on your knee and play hide-and-seek with me?
I miss you daddy.
Can you hear me, can you see me?
Remember when we played games and watched TV, I do.
Why did you go away? Was it something I said?
I look at pictures of us. Can we take pictures again?
Oh, do you remember family vacations and Christmas and my birthday?
Are going to come to my birthday party daddy?
I bought you a Christmas present.
I drew you a picture, it's of us, do you like it?
Let's go to the park and ice skate and go sledding.
I can't ice skate so will you help me! That was always fun.
Can we build a snowman? I want to put in the eyes and nose,
Let's make it real big, with a pipe!
Why can't we play anymore?
Are you okay daddy, what's the matter?
Why are you just lying there, why is everyone crying?
Will we ever play again? Good-bye daddy.

David P. Oudbier

Think Hard

Think hard about who your friends are,
  are they really true to you?
Do you fight a lot or go behind their back,
  or do they do the same to you?
Do they help you through bad times,
  or do you go through it alone?
Think hard about the dangers,
  are they friends or just some strangers?

Life takes care of problems naturally,
  so don't depend on them.
Think hard about who you are,
  do you really need them?
True friends stay by your side,
  through all your stresses good or bad.
When your boyfriend dumps you,
  or if you're just plain sad.

True friends are fun to be with,
  and laugh along with you.
So think hard about who your friends are,
  and again what's best for you.

Erin French

Why We Cry

Feelings, yes, deep feelings of heart felt love
  are reached in fulfillment when tear drops flow.
When sorrow, joy, or achievement touches us,
  then humbleness in the expression of crying is evident.
Crying releases, refreshes, and regains new confidence
  in our selves.
Why Not Cry? The Heavens do!
The atmosphere is unsettled when the sky is filled with hanging
  dark clouds bursting with rain drops, which will fall
  to the earth refreshing the air.
A natural phenomenon, known as the rainbow, follows with delight.
Hopefully, the natural behavior of your feelings will help you
  find a rainbow of new beginnings in sorrow, joy, or achievement
  from a tear drop.

Catherine E. Hoilien

To Please His Mistress

Through waves of bread-to-be, the Familiar picks a delicate path.
Approaching the asphalt vein, he pauses to consider,
eyes glowing the twin Harvest moons, liquid with thought.
He continues, only to settle down midway.
A single headlight needles the dimness, rushing ever near
to his tranquility. Eyes spy.
Thoughts pass, arrow swift; an inkblot shadow bleeds over the bush.
The chromed Centaur passes, its single eye rendered unperceiving.
Oblivious crimson pinpricks sail onward beneath the twinkling trail.
From behind, Cheshire delight casts a sterling quality upon the ebony strip.
A like expression appears nearby.
Smoke coalesces, steps quietly into the faint glow;
his burgundy-robed Enchantress assumes her visibility.

Anastasia Drabicky

Little Sister

Little sister I know sometimes we fight and say things that just aren't right.

Little sister sometimes we go to bed without even saying goodnight.

Little sister time seems to flow together like a swift river and for
days we may not even speak.

Little sister these periods are the ones that I regret the most, for
as life becomes more difficult, our memories will be the ones that I seek.

Little sister sometimes we are not as close as I would like.

But little sister remember I am your big brother. And when you need
help through the dark, I will be there to turn on the light.

Christian Cellini

A Poem For My Daughter

The time has come and now you're grown
And you will be leaving your loving home.

It's temporary
A college stay.

So take with you along the way:
The love I've given.
The values I've taught.
And you will never be distraught.

Always remember we're not far apart
For we are together in our hearts.

Your home is always very near
For you to visit throughout the year.

And also if you wish to chat
The telephone is where it's at.

Oh, by the way, there are letters too.
And always remember, I love you.

Ava Ruth Herskovitz

Family Tree

Our family tree is broken and bare
    And winter - with heartaches grafted there.
All of us broken and wishing that we
    All were united as meant to be -
One beautiful tree, all branches intact.
    But once it is broken there's no looking back.

What can we do now? How hopeless it seems!
    Whatever happened to all of our dreams?
Can beauty be salvaged from this ugly thing?
    Can God turn a winter tree into spring?

Remember the winter tree - desolate, bare -
    Changed by God's love with leaves growing there.
Leaves change to beauty this gnarled, broken tree.
    They cover, protect it, for all to see.
And in the same way God sends us spring
    With new leaves to cover this poor, barren thing.

Love covers all failures, griefs, and mistakes,
    All sorrows and troubles, and all our heartaches.
Leaves make the difference; they're sent from above.
    All loss is covered by leaves of love.

Betty Heath Partridge

To My Husband With Love

Each day that we're husband
and wife our love grows stronger.
You are my life, my love and my world.
You are everything to me;
and much more than words could ever possibly say.

As I look into your eyes
I see all your love and desires
I can feel your love as I
place my hand or head on your heart,
Each pounding rhythm saying
"I love you"
You are my everything;
My life, my love and my world.

Candy Benzel

Just You And Only You

I see you walk down the halls all alone,
And when I see your face, I feel as if I was hit by a cyclone.
Lost in my thoughts, I wonder if you love me,
For with your expressionless face it is hard to see.

Life would be dreary without you,
Just like the rain washing away the residue.
Without you, I couldn't live another day
Because I'll always try to find you no matter which way.

Looking at you and your homely face,
Makes me slow down my pace
To wait for you and walk beside you,
But I get a startled feeling not really knowing what to do.

I wish you would put your strong arms around me and hold me tight,
And never let go even if it took all your might.
I wish you would kiss me with your smiling lips
That are as soft as rose petal tips.

Without you, there would be nothing to live for,
For it is only you whom I adore.
I love you and only you with every breath,
And I will love just you and only you until my death.

Esther Kim

The Way We Are

We are creatures of needs.
And want them to be met
Right here, right now. Not tomorrow.
But right now without delay.

Focus pan me no Lord
How yuh just a lef me out?
Don't yuh se fi me needs dem
Just a beckon an' a call yuh out.
Show yuh hand, lay out yuh plan
Lord! Deliver me right now.

A know that Miss Mary sick
And Millie lay low from week gone
Not to mention Miss Lou and her feeble bwoy Paul.
Lord, yuh know a think and pray 'bout dem.
And thank yuh that I'm not the worse.
Sometimes a think yuh shoulda deal with them first.

But a woulda greatly appreciate
If you woulda stretch out yuh hand
And meet fi me needs dem
Right here, right now.

Angela Murray

Fear Is...

Knowing you will walk again
And knowing you might not
Knowing test after painful test says you're "normal"
And knowing that you're not
Knowing you are choking and dying
And no one will help
Knowing your body hurts - a lot - all over
And knowing you can't allow it
Knowing you're safe with him around
And knowing he won't always be
Knowing that you care too much
And knowing you can't stop it
Knowing your body must change to continue
And knowing it won't
Knowing it is there and it has no name
And knowing that its name is... Life

Catherine Shimozono

Our Mirror Of Tears

(Personal Feelings about Incest)
This is dedicated to all the children in the near,
And to all the ones that never got to cheer.

We children, send our mirror to all the ones
That filled our hearts with fear,
So you can wipe away our tears.

"You never warned me of the horror,
That you'd be leaving me tomorrow,
You filled my heart with sorrow."

"When we look in the mirror,
And try to fight the tears,
It's your face that we will remember tomorrow!"

"So we ask God to forgive you today,
Just in case He comes to take you away,
The very next day."

And remember children, we can only get stronger
For the children that will never be forgotten.

And, for the ones in the near—
Whose hearts will be filled with cheer.
Elizabeth L. DeLaney

Simplicity

As I sit and gaze into your eyes—
    and the sun sets behind us,
My insides fill with warmth
    and passion.

When we lay down beside one another—
    a sense of security overwhelms me.
Your caress and touch melts me,
    like the sun will do to snow on the mountains.

At that moment—our love flows through us—
    and fills us with life's simplest;
Yet rewarding pleasure,
    which is love!
Catherine A. Owens

The Breeze

The wind will blow you free of restrictions...
And the soft summer breeze will surround you on
a beautiful moonlit night,
While the stars above will light your way to a
bright new life.
Red and pink rose petals will float through the
air to you like a magnet of perfumed color.
Music surrounds you in an aura of magical melody and rhythm.
Bernice Prill Grebner

Faith Through Tears

Things happen to us to help us learn
and the lessons He teaches, are sometimes stern
But you must have faith and know it's right
to go through what you must, to reach the light
At times you're broken to your knees, left
sobbing, praying, begging please
He does hear you and feel your pain, and the
lessons you learn are the blessings you gain.
CherylAnn McMahan

Shadow Of A Man

His room lit only by the end of his cigarette
And the glow of a solitary candle
Waiting for some indication of reason, or thought, or spirit
While taking strength from the glass of scotch in his hand
To this world, and the stars, and the infinite
He's just a shadow of a man

    He can feel that his soul's on fire
    Expecting a call to something higher
    His eyes grow wide with desire
    But he's old, he aches, and is tired

He can't see that he's a mere phantom in this dreamland
Nor can he answer life's questions of how or why
He expects fate to somehow guide him by the hand
For he doesn't dare give his own feeble reply
He wants to make a difference, leave his mark in the sand
But the sea just washes it away, no sign that he even passed by

    Then inexorably the startling revelation
    He cries of despair and consternation
    He sees his life's an aberration
    That he's just a shadow of a man
Brian R. Morrow

Change of Times

One day to the next
    And the end to far from sight,
With a circle of ties
    Preoccupied with agendas of flight.

Problems seem to change
    Into a catastrophic feat,
Worldly ideals riding on your shoulders
    And the challenge to hard to meet.

If only for a moment
    To have a mind of thoughts that is pure,
Take heed to these emotions
    For your heart could never be truer.

Abruptly, times will change
    And much sooner than you thought,
For the anticipated will soon appear
    And it's something you have long since sought.
Brett Byrnes

There's One Thing Worse Than Booze!

There's one thing worse than booze . . .
And that's the NEGATIVE NEWS!
Going to sleep with it on our mind
And awakening in the morning to find
We're hung over from the night before!

We turn on the news, and then there's MORE!
To dull our senses for the day ahead . . .
We're no better off than when we went to bed!

It's a beautiful place, this world of ours;
nestled among a trillion stars!
The law that was set when we came into being:
like creates like! And that's what we're seeing!
Thanks to the NEGATIVE NEWS that we see . . .
It causes much of the negativity!

Like creates like! It's the law that was set!
Seeds giving birth is what we get!
The negative news is the evil seed
On TV and in the papers we read.
Let's stop planting negative weeds!
GOOD NEWS COMES FROM POSITIVE SEEDS!
Eve Moore

The Gift Of Life

Each day of our life has a meaning
And sometimes we don't understand
The smooth and the rocky roads
Are all part of God's special plan
Life is like a journey through time
As we travel along the way
We sometimes have many mountains to climb
At the start of a brand new day
We grow weary from the struggle
And the mountains seem too high
We don't realize at the top of the mountains
There's a rainbow in the sky
Life is a gift from God
A gift to love and treasure
A day may be filled with sadness and pain
While another brings joy and pleasure
If we hold on to our hopes and dreams
He will someday wipe our tears
If we only have a little faith in Him
He will guide us through the years

Elaine Cote

Moving On

I don't want to shove my emotions off to the side
and run from fears, as if to hide
I want to put my thoughts into words; to say what's on my mind
But, I can't express the way I feel, for the words I just can't find
I want to share the pain and sorrow that live deep within my soul
for hopes I'll be better tomorrow-not as a piece, but as a whole
I wish to relieve myself of burdens and of all my pain
to be free from exhaustion, stress and strain
But, little do I know that it's not simple;
as easy as I wish it could be
there's still so much I don't know, so much facing me
Though I shall make it, for I am strong and full of pride
And in the end I'll know what it mean's to feel good inside
Knowing that I am who I am, and nothing can change what I feel
Knowing I can accept my emotions, and acknowledging they are real
For now I can honestly say I'm moving on, into a world with a clean slate
I've endured my old life for so long-and no longer must I wait
Finally to be changing, shifting, experiencing the new life I love
Moving on, being strong with help from up above

Amanda Kelly

Love At First Sight

When their eyes met from across the way
And neither of them had anything to say
She never believed in love at first sight
But her mind was changed after last night
It was like everything just fell into place
Her feelings were moving at a very fast pace
His eyes were so big and bright
They lit up her sky like dawn's early light
She still can't get him off of her mind
She thinks he is, her one-of-a-kind
And she'll see her first love again tonight
She has no doubt it was love at first sight.

Carmalita Alvina Castaneda

A Beautiful Soul

I lay myself softly besides him, observing his strong
and masculine body.
His almost black hair, begins to show touches of grey.
As he smiles a smile that is always present, dimples appear.
They are absorbed into his hazel brown eyes and then
enhanced by his natural olive complexion.
His eyes catch the shimmering sunlight through the corner window,
giving them a golden glow.
Holding his hand I feel a warmth travel through my body.
As I lay my head on his shoulder, he wraps his arm around me.
I can hear his heart pounding gently through his masculine body.
Like an angel at sunrise he whispers in my ear "Je t'aime."
His soft and seasoned voice is filled with spice.
I now realize that such spice is powerful enough so that it can outglow
the sun at any time.
Like a silhouette against the bright and glorious sunset.
A vision from a time of knights in shining armor,
he lays beside me resembling a God.
His kind, loving, and affectionate heart filled with kind words
can heal any broken soul.

Elenor Gahchan

"I Took Time"

I took time, to walk across the field
  And listened to the wind; whistle through the grass.
I took time, to pause, look and
  Smell all the beautiful flowers.
I took time, to watch a big honey bee
  Land on top, of the purple clover flower,
I took time, to watch a garter snake
  Wiggle through the wet grass.
I took time, to follow the track
  of the deer; who had been up to eat.
I took time, to watch a line of
  Ants march across the trail.
I took time, to watch the birds
  Flying overhead; singing a song.
Then I paused, to count all my
  Blessings and thank God for it all.
I took time, to ask God for strength
  To go on; for I know, God is always there.

Carol Ann Allen (with God's help)

I'll Love You Forever

I'll love you today and tomorrow my love
And in all the tomorrows there are
I'll love you as long as there lingers a song
And the sky has a single star
In the spring when the wind is a gentle breeze
In the summery days when the friendly rays
Of the golden sun appear.
In the lonely lap of the autumn months
When the beautiful leaves must fall
And again in the night when the fields are white
In the folds of their wintery shawl
I'll love you as long as a mountain stands
And until the sands of the farthest lands
Have run through the hour-glass
I'll love you as much as my heart can love
No matter where you are
I'll love you as long as there lingers a song
And the sky has a single star

Amy L. Lara

475

"Respect"

I am the symbol of these United States of America,
And I wave gently over forty acres of parking lot in
   a busy city.
The crowds surge in and out of stores and their cars
   to get to the freeways.
No one notices my beautiful colors or my sea of stars
   on the blue background.
But wait, down by a lamp post stands a young boy
He is dressed in the uniform of a "Boy Scout" and he
   stands at attention and gives me a smart salute.
He stands for a long moment and many passers-by take
   time from their busy schedules to stop.
They are proud to see the great respect this young
   boy has for the flag and stop in respect also.
How proud I am of this young man and of how he has
   shown respect for his country and for the emblem
   of his country.
I can go on waving proudly over my part of the little
   area of my country and remember the love and respect
   that young boy has shown.

     Alice R. Lafleur

Untitled

God called me
and I left my home,
not knowing the destination of my flight.
I flew to the ark that Noah had built
and there I stayed, for forty days and forty nights.

My freedom
stopped by walls of wood.
My sky, the beams of a once tall tree.
My wings
no longer filter sunlight.
An ocean
as far as the eye could see.

Then I, a dove of feathers white,
Left kind Noah's rugged hand.
Fearful, lonely, yet full of hope
To fly from the ark and find dry land.

I found dry land and the earth was saved,
For God commanded the flood to cease.
And I brought Noah an Olive branch
As an everlasting sign of peace.

     April Dawn West

"I'm Part Of It Now"

I'm part of it now! Earth, wind, fire and water!!
And, I do understand so much! I hope you do!
Don't say no! My friends the angels
Hug each cloud to send us drops of love!
You'll see!! I do understand!!
I am taken care of and do very well!
I'm alright! Be happy for me!! Hush ....
Love each other! Love is the strongest
Bond ... Needs no ribbons!! Hush ....
Look out the window ... Listen to the rain ....
Kiss each other ... Tomorrow will be soon!
Then you'll be able to see the roses ...
And nature's display! Beautiful!!!
Cut a rose for me ... Careful!!
I'll always be at your side ... Listen
to the song of the nightingale ... She
sang me to sleep many a night. Now she's yours!
Look up at the sky I'm the brightest!
Always for you! Love needs no ribbons!!

     Anita M. Diaz

Untitled

You walked into my room one day and told me I was a butterfly
and I believed you.
You saw the colors swirling in my wings and the freedom to
flutter through the day.
You saw the unique form I'd grown into but you didn't see the
inner self I possessed - the assurance. . . the indecision.
You were so consumed with the beauty in my wings that you
overlooked the beauty of my being.
As the days passed on, it became normal to caress my skin
but not my soul. You didn't realize that us butterflies were
once trapped in a cocoon, unable to move.
You put me back into a cocoon. An inner cocoon.
One so tightly woven that you forgot how to unravel the silk.
You walked away because the butterfly was realer than you
wanted. You knew that even if you tried to help me
you couldn't. You walked out of my room and into another.
Not one that held a butterfly but one that started in the cocoon.
That was easier.
Now I break my cocoon piece by piece to become the butterfly
I once was.

     Anne-Marie Egede-Nissen

Bubble Gum

It started small,
And grew and grew.
From pink to white,
I blew and blew.

It smelled so good,
And taste so sweet.
My bubble gum,
A chewy treat,

And then a bang,
Oh, what a mess.
Stuck in my hair,
And on my dress.

     Carol Ann Cobb

Awakening

The March winds gust
And force winter-drugged branches into motion
Capriciously shaking
Then caressing the naked boughs
Alternately shrieking in impatience
Then moaning solicitously
To finally whispering seductively
Of wetness and warmth
Until, finally and fully roused
Restless stirrings begin within
Rigid buds appear in response
And then soften when anticipation
Becomes promised fulfillment.

     Arlena Bolick

A Lifetime Of Thanks

I remember the days when I played with my toys,
   and also the times of the heartache and joys.
You raised me through the years and taught
   me my manners, now I'm out in the world
   finding it all really did matter.
I'm all grown up now and away from home and
   have a family to raise of my own; even
   though you are miles away, you're always
   with me in my heart each day.
As I look back at yesterday I shed a few tears,
   here's a lifetime of thanks for caring through
   the years.

     Cindi Crislip

"Holding You For The First Time"

Many years passed as I waited for you,
And finally our time arrived.
I didn't know what to expect,
Seeing you for the first time.
And I wondered what life had planned for you?
For this moment you lay in my arms
Keeping you from all harm, watching you so peacefully.
In our time, holding you for the first time,
So what was life's plan for my bundle
I held so dear?
I saw my job held in front of me,
Knowing the responsibility was all mine,
And yet, the Lord put you in my arms.
Holding you knowing you came from me,
So much love in me for you.
Holding my heart captive in your little arms,
And high expectations for this bundle of mine,
Hoping to give you what you needed from me,
For this moment you lay in my arms,
Holding you for the first time.

Deborah M. Vanderwood

Borreguito

Borreguito was his name - this little black sheep-
And every night it was the same - the wolf disturbed his sleep.
 "Why do you bother me during my peaceful dreams at night?
If you don't leave me alone right now - you're gonna have a heck of a fight!"
 They fought their fight - it took all night.
Borreguito had stood his ground - the wolf knew he
had been beaten, 'cause his hair was scattered all around!
Borreguito told the wolf as he was leaving-
"I don't want to see your family grieving -
So please don't come back here no more - 'cause next
time it'll be your life I score!"
 That was the end of the midnight madness
until guess what! Along came Gladyss, the pretty
little female sheep - his restless nights he's gonna
keep - but that's another story -
Let's all pray for poor Ol' Borre..!

Dana Garcia

Drugs In America

Somewhere in America where drugs are like a curse,
And each day is followed by another one slightly worse,
Somewhere the drugs get thicker than the shifting desert sand,
And all men dream and wish for is a peaceful and drug-free land.
Somewhere in America where drugs are never seen,
There is somebody behind it that you thanks is always clean.
Where the dingoes nightly crowd robs a working man of his
Blessed sleep,
Where there is whisky and drugs ever so cheap.
Somewhere in America where the nights were made for love,
Where the moon is like a searchlight and the southern cross above.
Flames sparkles like a diamond cluster in the balmy tropic night,
And it's a shameless waste of beauty because there are people with
drugs in sight.
Somewhere in America people have everything to spent,
But in the end fooling around with drugs will leave you without a cent.

Curtis J. Carson

"Deep Thoughts"

The overshadowing dreams of despair,
and dissolutions keep repeating itself.
Is it a warning I refuse to take heed,
my mind in a whirl of frustrations I wish to weed.
Out of sight, out of mind, one has to conquer within himself.
Wrinkled brow, a frown of strain, thoughts of hope, free from pain.
Life certainly has its ups and downs, that's what it's all about,
but then above all the thoughtfulness beyond it, creates a stronger
determination not to fall.
Thankful for each day, alive, head-up high, a tiny smile,
a breath of fresh-air to say, today I've conquered this fear.

Cecilia Segal

Old Glory

The lone grey coyote walked slowly throughout the purple-hued mesas
and auburn faded cliffs of its rugged homeland;
It prowled relentlessly and knew not why, yet it also realized that
it must trudge on to its unknown mission.

The shadows of the impending twilight were the beast's only companion
as it stalked its way breathlessly on into the mystic night.
Its steel blue eyes are clouded with age but they now blaze with
youthful intensity as this somber creature of the shifting plains
relives its days of yore.

Seen by no one yet known by all, it suddenly halts in the undulating
lands of its dormant domain and emits the mournful message of his ancestors,
Passionately and pitifully its molten soliloquy reverberates and resonates
amongst the tattered memories of yesterday and the glowing treasures
of tomorrow
Its impromptu concerto now coming to an end, the erstwhile vagabond
melts into the tawny dusk and dreams of all that was and everything
that is to be.

David R. Borchardt

The Sands Of Time

The time has come to cease my endless search for
 an understanding of the world.
Perhaps I should consider finding, as they say,
 "the world in a grain of sand."
I find a beach, clean and clear and white in the sunlight
And seat myself at the water's edge, where the
 lapping at the shoreline carves a scalloped, sculptured look.
After a moment of contemplation, I gently reach into the sand.
My hand comes up with many grains which I sift
 through my wide-spread fingers
Seeking just one pure grain to hold to the light
 to reveal the meaning of the world.
I cannot seem to separate just one, and maybe that is the message.
We are all grains of sand in the universal pattern of life,
Needing to cling together, holding on to one another,
Melding to make up the colors and sounds and sights
 of the world - its soul and its spirit.
I ponder long and hard as the sun begins to set
And the sand jewels take on different shapes and
 forms in the fading light.

Charlotte Pall

"Life"

Life is a medley of people, places, and things,
An object of beauty and an object of dreams.
Life starts when you are young,
With bottles and diapers and things you adore.
You're young and inexperienced about the world and the place,
Until that perfect day a light hits your face,
And you know it's your duty to study the beauty,
Of a wonderful time and a wonderful place.
When all in a day you look back and embrace,
The dreams, and the songs and that wonderful day,
When you decided to try dared to discover the
Wonderful feeling of life.

April Brabbs

The Significant Rose

Eleven roses stand before you
  An incomplete number that you see
But my hope is, that through these words
  A dozen roses there will be

One rose to represent the time that we first met
One rose for the jokes you believed I did not get

One rose to portray the times when you are near
One rose to remind me of your voice I long to hear

One rose for the memories that you choose to share
And one rose to show you how much I really care

One rose for our talks and how they make me feel
One rose for the belief that this one is for real

One rose for the times I've wished we were together
One rose to say I will remember you forever

And one rose for love - a hope for a new start
Because you're all I've ever wanted - straight from the heart

But one rose stands out from all of the rest
  Though intangible, this rose is best
For this rose alone possesses a power, for without her,
    the other roses are merely flowers. You are that rose

   Damian Philip Marchand

Untitled

I look around and what do I see
An empty chair setting next to me
It once held someone very dear
Not saying much but always near
Now she is gone, only God knows where
I'm left alone with an empty chair
And a room full of sad memories and pain
I pray for the day we will be together again
There is no one left who can help or would care
All by myself with my empty chair

   Carl Phelps

Ugly Free

In the backyard of nature's life
Amid toil, remission and strife
Comes knowledge of the Ugly Tree -
Its spoiled per say fruit to be
Of moulding sustenance,
Different than good and us.
Eating that funny looking fruit
Became a joy of unusual root
With a climatic summation
Related to temptation.
We have reaped of it food
And made recipes all understood,
Such as pleasing, considerate attitude,
Deliberate pursuit and even not quite rude.
Though leaves have come and gone,
And roots are old and familiar on,
We keep Ugly Seeds hidden away
For we have education to pay.
We need each young life to be
That special way of Ugly Free.

   Cathy M. Chamberlain

Abandoned Feelings

My childhood was a scary dream that never left my mind,
Although I knew that one day his love I'd surely find.
I yearned to have the father that everyone else had,
But happy dreams for me were always turning sad.
He wasn't there to see me tie my very first shoe,
Or even see the precious things that little girls do.
He probably never knew all the trouble that he made,
Or even if his daughter was in first or second grade.
Then my father started calling almost every week,
Those feeling started coming back so fast I couldn't speak.
I finally started talking and every thing was fine,
That's when I knew the father I lost was truthfully mine.
Soon I knew that my life would be o.k.,
And all those terrible, abandoned feelings would go far, far away.

   Christy Waterman

Together

I see you lying in the hospital bed,
All your lovely tresses have fallen from your head,
I walk over to where you lay,
Pain flashes in your eyes every day.
I hold the same soft hand,
I do this everyday as if by plan,
The meter beeps quietly but sure,
Your gown is white and pure.
We both cry bitter tears,
Our love will last through all the years,
Why did this have to happen to my mother,
I have no significant other.
And now that she's dying,
Is there any reason for me to keep trying?
Mother, oh, mother don't leave me,
I'll be by myself and so lonely.
Nothing I feel and nothing I see,
But, I know that one day in heaven we'll be,
Together.

   Alicia Louise Coleman

"You and Me"

How can I make you see
All that you mean to me?
A piece of mind you'll always lend
you're more than just another friend.
You always seem to lift me up
Just when I'd about given up.
And when I'm down you're always there
Just to say "I really care."
You always seem to be around
To make me smile instead of frown,
Through all the sunshine, clouds, and rain,
Through all the hardships, toils, and pain,
By my side you'll always be
Best friends forever "You and me."

   Ann Jackson

Alone At Last

As I looked outside of my window I could feel the cold night
Air hitting my back making me shiver like a horse without his mane.
The trees made shadows upon my wall, reminding me of the stormy
Nights I spent alone in my room thinking the BOOGIE MAN might
Come and take me away, but now I'm a growing young lady waiting
For nature to take its hideous course.
The moon had a silvery glow that made the sky come alive with a
Mysterious light. It was peaceful in the house tonight no brother to
Say, "Mom she hit me, or, I'm telling," no mom telling me to clean my
Room, and no dad yelling because the bills were too high this month.
It was just me, my music, and the glowing of the moon.

   Bridget L. Maynor

Grandpa Coolyman

Faults he had I know, they say Vee, he loved with
all his heart, for her, his desertion no forgiveness.

His sons a foundation he was not
But in his weakness and faults he stood proud
A stalwart spirit ruling yet aching
For not being there when he was needed.

Torn apart his family gone to foreign lands
Letters with monies buried among his few belongings
Their company he longed for, where did he go wrong
Clinging to my hands tightly, then I never understood why.

As we walked to his pastime of solace, the horses we watched
Monies spent on dreams long lost to time
See, he said, EL's (G-D'S) laws you shall do
For time changes all things, to the past you cannot return
But it is your judgement forever in the present.

I miss you as your spirit rides within my soul
I see you now walking, holding my hand, my heart in yours
Your eyes with love, your strength mine's
Your respect for me in my tender years as you showed me
Your Fatherhood, I love you grandpa till the end of time.

Ashirah S. Naphtali

Everything is Everything

A primordial calm comes,
After mother's rain transforms,
The anguish of an arid day,
When all unmarked souls are brought to bay,
A beacon of unfiltered light,
Stands above all, whitened and bright,
Revealing the creation of old earth's shower,
Earth's love, her life, her eternal power,
The ability of perpetual re-creation,
The world waits with anticipation,
For the rejuvenation of earth,
Fulfilling instinctually her immeasurable worth,
Transformation to young from old,
What lies in mother's first true gold,
The appeasement of all hopes and fears,
Provided by her cleansing tears,
The planet stands in full rejoice,
Wrapped in the melodic tones of her voice,
All her creatures, majestic or cod,
Stand before her, within each the essence of God.

Amy Erenberg

To All Children

When you were born I rejoiced. I believed in God. I could finally
accept my own mortality. You were my Miracle!

I beheld your face-the face of an angel. Somehow, though unworthy,
I had become your guardian angel. A new thought. An angel
guarding an angel! You made me reflect upon god's purpose for me
so often.

I wondered where your little feet-with those perfect little toes-would
take you. No thought would allow you to stray far. I couldn't stand
the pain of separation.

You, my child, were my immortality, my hope for the future. And then
you left. As I was there at your birth to love you, I was there at
your death to love you, just as I believe you will be there at my
death to love me.

You changed my life forever. You are still truly my future. As the
child becomes the parent and the parent the child and as we become one
in eternity we will never again be separated.

Ann Marie Steele

Eternal Confrontations

The sweet smell of spring flowers floated in the air.
A yearling buck browsed at the edge of the gurgling brook without a care.
The sun was hardly up but already felt warm.
We'd weathered some hard times but here our life seemed finally
    without storm.
Two songbirds sang duelingly from above me on a willow branch.
I'd never once regretted bringing my young wife
and children to this distant wilderness ranch.
A cool breeze whispered through the trees across my face
and through my hair, stirring my soul with the message
of what through time has made men dare.
Oh, but it was truly such a great day to be alive and if I had a thousand
to pick from I could not have picked a better day to die.
As I measured the black eyes that fixedly measured me, I couldn't
help wonder what the outcome of the next few minutes would be.
This was his land but it was also mine and if we didn't somehow find
compromise, in this mutually-loved dirt from today one of us would
    forever lie.

David L. Pfiester

D-Day From The Other Side

In January forty-five
a telephone call changed my life.
We were to do as we were told:
Evacuate the sick and old
the only people left in town
before the soldiers burn it down.

At dawn I left, cold and afraid,
a little girl of only eight.
East Germany was on the run
from Second World War's deadly gun.
Day after day, a steady flow
for thirteen weeks in ice and snow.

Infants froze in mothers' arms
who hid in woods and vacant farms.
We starved, we hurt, we walked - and still
the enemy came for the kill.
They raped, they killed, and their excuse
'...war justifies any abuse...'

I have survived torment and grief,
yet, memories will never leave.

Christine Hambach

"My Dream"

My dream is like a rose, which has not yet bloomed,
A soaring ending, dark, gloom.
A bird which has not yet flown,
A sunflower which has not yet grown.
A woman who has not yet married,
A baby who has not yet carried.
A loving emotion not yet expressed,
A certain object which has not been possessed.
A gloomy tunnel leading to an endless destination,
The constant betrayal or sudden hesitation.
A champion who has not achieved the gold,
A fairytale not yet told.
My dreams linger, then do not disappear.
When there is ambition, it is always near.
I may never catch it or fulfill my desire,
But the actual goal has lifted me higher.

Cara Erdheim

"Heartbreak"

My loving daughter has gone astray
A mean man tells her what to do and say
Now she does not have a life of her own
Dear God, please make him for his sins atone

He isolated her from family and friends
I hope someday he has to make amends
New friends and old ones are waiting for you
Dear God, please tell us what we can do

She cannot go anywhere or see anyone
I cannot count the terrible things he has done
He holds the reins on her so tight
Dear God, please help her to see the light

He has even started her to drinking
She is under his spell and not thinking
She is still alive but cannot see me
Dear God, please help her and set her free

It would be so nice too end this heartbreak
Her future and her children are at stake
I am so worried because he also carries a knife
Dear God, please watch over her and save her life

Fern M. Waugh

Sexual Sin

There was a time in my life when I engaged in sexual sin
A man's love and respect I was hoping to win

Till one day God showed me I was doing wrong
My body belongs to God pleasing him is what I long

In me lives the Holy Spirit God gave me for free
To teach me to use my body to please him instead of me

Thank God through Jesus Christ I've been forgiven this sin
Marry me if you want sexual intercourse that's what I tell men

Debby Woolsey

Then And Now

Many years ago,
a great black train
rumbled across these fields
With its great stack bellowing black smoke,
its wheels singing along the tracks,
hauling behind it boxcar after boxcar
filled with grain, animals, and all the
merchandise needed by the town,
its caboose taking up the rear as its majestic greatness
rumbled across the fields and along the tracks,
Now, as these fields lie here in a freshly plowed state,
if they could see or hear, they would have a hard time believing
that a great train rumbled and roared across them
as they lie here now and hear the trucks
rumble past and see the great jets
roar overhead, like great silver birds
with their wings outspread doing the work the train once did.

Barbara B. Keetch

"A Natural-Born Leader - Reece"

More than merely ambition, or
A desire to get ahead ... there was
The ever-unsettling recognition of
An unclaimed furtherance within
His soul; there were lights
To shine, but only with reasons - and
only eventually would there be claim!
He thought to know, without fully
knowing, of all that possibility there could be
Only a little farther on...
up there, just ahead.

Canadia Collins

Dreaming A Dream

Gently lying by the murmuring stream,
a girl I see dreaming a dream.
So golden flows her hair,
as does the sun from everywhere.

This crystal stream, in line, so sublime,
reflects her face, so kind, so fine.
How lovely this lonely stream glides,
as the winds flow by where she resides.

How pleasant the banks and green valleys below,
where in the woodlands the flowers grow.
There by the meadow in the timid evening,
a sweet scented birch shades her body, so serene.

I must depart, to leave my love,
this beauty I see as white as a dove.
Gently lying by the murmuring stream,
A boy she sees dreaming his dream.

Benjamin J. Burris

Life Without Flowers

A flower is lovely to behold,
A flower is to be held,

A woman is like a flower, she should always be cared for,
What would life be like without flowers?

A flower can have attractive colors,
A flower's scent can be marveled,

A woman is like a flower, we should appreciate them more,
What would life be like without flowers?

A world without flowers, A world without flowers.

Such a sad thought such one like that.
The world indeed what would be?

Bradley J. Seward

Washington, D.C.

Out of a marshy wilderness - transformation!
    A city whose beauty draws admiration.
Pierre L'Enfant designed Washington, D.C.,
    the nation's capital, for you and for me.

Named for the father of our country;
    leader of the men who set us free.
He never saw the obelisk raised in his name;
    reflected with cherry blossoms of worldwide fame.

Visit where the great men walked, prayed and planned.
    Could they envision the might of this land?
Lincoln and Jefferson still watching in glory
    as America acts out freedom's story.

There's the Capitol building and Smithsonian Castle.
    Everything's free. You can walk. No hassle.
The space museum and fabulous zoo,
    the White House and museums - all for you.

See Kennedy's grave with the "Eternal Flame."
    Close your eyes! Hear that voice of fame?
Still asking each American citizen anew;
    "What can you do for your country?" You! Yes! You!

Adele LeBuffe Gregos

In The Solarium

The sun's rage exhales
a brilliant plume
of dust-speckled rays
Whose stately bands
heave in slow, rhythmic turns

Twirling pillars inside the glass house,
they glisten amidst a jungle's foliage,
seemingly supporting the weight of heaven.

Yet, they shiver
against your covetous gasp

dust flecks,
angered by the disruption of their cavort,
spin down like
lit-up planes and angered hornets

They seek your nose
held up so high

Brian Rumberger

The Trees

September 1991

Last year, I talked about the ocean, the flowers and my dreams,
But I failed to say one word about the trees.

The trees are around me because I love them in the Spring
The fresh new life wearing colors all of green
And in the Summer, I love them again — when the heat wants to
explode
They shade the house, sifting the dust from the dry country road.

Then Fall comes to bring yet a new flare
Leaf by leaf they go until the cold Winter day is here
Then they stand in nudity and allow the warmth I caress
And I am happy they decided to undress,

Some say these trees of mine are not worth standing at all
But, yet another year, I see what they've done, as they stand tall
God planted them and I shall
Always let them be my sentinel

Alice Marie Buras Flowers Weaver

"Just The Way Love Is"

Broken heart and shattered with tears
Full with pain and confused with fears
Always been hurt with nothing more or nothing less
Rich with joy and pouring with happiness

As our feelings were willing to show
The profoundly tenderness comes and the emotions go
Don't know what to say or do
Playing the game of love, I am a fool

Been hurt once and always been hurt twice
To show no affection or devotion, you broke the ice
Broken in so many pieces
That there is no life worth living

Bunthay Touch

Untitled

I hear your voice so far away
your words of support, encouragement and praise
I also hear the fears the worries and the tears
hiding behind your laughter.
I can feel it when your happy and
can sense it when your scared and down
Our love provides the link and maintains
that intimate bond that we share.

Christopher J. Skjold

During The Night

The Stars shone bright through the night
The candles burned till dawn
Whispering of legends could be heard around the glistening pond
The strumming of violins could be heard for miles
Your heart grows strong with the night
You dream of dreams
flying kites
playing ball
all through the night
Sweet kisses can be heard during the night
You open up your eyes to see the night disappear
and watch the sunrise
for the new day to begin
You can't help but wonder
what mysteries you will uncover today!

Amie Helmick

My One and Only True Love

You are my one and only true love, sent to me from God above.
My wonderful, cuddly bear, and sweetest valentine.
Our life together has not always been so easy or sublime.
When we were separated in the summer of '94, we both were sad,
So we got back together and said we'd be apart no more!
So...through it all we've always known,
Even through the rough times
And though the winds of adversity have blown,
That our love has stood the test of time and is strong,
And so deep wide and long!
Many don't know, my love, that forgiveness is the key,
Without it many a marriage and romance have been shipwrecked at sea.
Please continue to warm me when I am cold,
And hold my hand as we grow old.
Our love is friendship, companionship, romance,
And always and forever...
And we will never...be apart,
But always remain in each other's heart!!
I love you more today than when we first met — In every way!

James Livingston IV

In The Heavens

In the heavens above lies the hearts and souls
Of many a young and old
Though they are missed by those of us who loved
We know they are safely kept above

When the wind whips and the clouds cry
I whisper to the Lord my sweet good-bye
For all those I have known
Who in the heavens they have flown

I will never understand
How the Lord had dealt his hand
But I know it was time for him to leave
And now from all the evils he shall be free

Though there are reasons
Unknown they shall always be
And although at times I still feel the pain
The sweet memories shall forever remain

Of baseball games and travels past
And of his days last
When he took his final ragged breath
Then came upon him—Death

Fran Hall

Gracing Of The Heart...

As each day passes,
A new beginning arises,
Out of the thoughts created,
Not instilled of our minds.
A new dawning appears,
As it reaches down to earth,
And grazes exceptional views,
Of the moments to come.
When the nigh has revealed,
And the darkness appalls,
Reminiscing days of the past,
That once combined forever.
In the still of the night,
All is contemplated without,
For there shall lie down,
All the grace of the heart.

Janet S. McMillin

The Stroke of Color

The canvas sets empty,
A palette lays untouched.

With one flowing stroke,
The brush hits the color.

The colors take form,
And the scene begins.

The contrasts become vibrant,
And the shapes are ever changing.

The canvas is no longer empty,
It has become a portrait.

Although it will never be finished,
It will remain unframed but priceless.

The Art is Friendship!

Jacqueline M. Brosius

Losing A Loved One

It's hard to give the one above
A person that you really love.
You feel the world is at an end,
Left with a heart that just won't mend.

The hurt just lingers down real deep,
And their absence disturbs your sleep.
Time has a way of healing pain,
Remember life must start again.

Knowing it hurts you to recall,
There is a silence from us all,
Cause when you're feeling down and blue,
It hurts the ones who love you too.

Someday when the ache decreases,
And you've picked up all the pieces,
You will look back and reminisce,
With afterthoughts of utter bliss.

Janet M. Hart

Your Daughter

Look at the light.
Do you notice how bright
Mom they're calling
I feel myself falling
Please hold me tight
He's me put us a fight
I'll remember your face
As I enter this place
Before this darkness I leap
Remember mom,
Our hearts will always meet

Kristi Chambers

Untitled

A whimper
A "wanna know why?"
A chapter of life
begins when we're five

A laughter,
a cry.
Another chapter of life
gone by.

A secret,
a lie.
Another chapter of life
gone by.

Our many memories
we leave behind.
The book ends when
we die.

Jan Livingston

The Day After Christmas

'Twas the day after Christmas
And all 'round the earth
Every creature was leaping
And laughing with mirth.
The stockings still hung from the
  chimney, my lad,
But empty they were, empty and sad.
Couples were dancing
All around was romancing.
Princes and paupers, those rich and
  those not,
All were joyful,
Many hugs were to be got,
But all 'round the earth,
Among all the mirth,
In homes shabby and bright,
All remembered the Christ child,
Born that night.

Sara L. Brady

Little One

I'd like to hold you in my arms
And comfort every sigh.
Whenever you called out to me,
I'd like to be nearby.

I'd like to take your every hurt;
Each bloody nose and graveled knee.
And softly sing your lullabies
Throughout eternity.

I'd like to tell you, honey,
The world is cruel out there,
Stay inside with Grandma,
Let me take your every care.

I'd like to tell you, little one
That life will be kind to you.
But this world never love you,
Like God and Grandma do.

Barbara Wolfe

As Long

As long as you're there
  and don't say goodbye
As long as you listen
  and don't make me cry
I'll love you forever
  until my last breathe
I'll love you forever
  even after death
Something about you
  When you can't lie
Something about you
  that I can't deny
So I'll stay by your side
  until these days end
So I'll stay by your side
  With all my heart to lend
As long as you're there
  I'll keep my love true
As long as you love me
  I'll give my heart to you

Ashli D. Moore

"Death"

I hear the thunder,
And I question eternity.
Will the music play?
A world only the blind can see.
I dream of warmth and love,
But all I see is terror.
I'm only human, help me!
I hear the screams of my life,
And I feel the rains of my mind.
We're all victims of the devil!
I sense death coming near,
The end of the world is now.
A bullet flies by my head.
A bomb fires.
Blood.
Pain.
Emptiness.
DEATH.

The music plays, I sleep.
God has had His revenge.

Shae' Caldwell

Once A Mother

A dream came about,
And that dream came true.
For in the end,
There was you.

Wasn't so long ago
That you were here,
Something very precious,
And so very dear.

You were so very tiny.
I wanted you with all my heart.
But, God wanted you too
And we had to part.

So, my son, as time goes by,
Even though you won't see,
I was once your mother
  and I loved you;
Not only then, but now —
  through Eternity.

Flora Owens

A Vietnam Veteran's Poem

I killed some men
And watched them die
And more than that
I made their mothers cry
This is a recurring picture to me
And more than that
When I killed them
I killed part of me

Donald Ohmes

Heart Seasons

The beauty of the seasons
Are felt within my heart.
Touching as only God can do,
Reaching the utmost part.

Spring causes me to feel
As though a little child.
Even though I'm grow
And know it all the while.

The golden rays of Summer
Affect my very soul.
Leaving a warm impression
As the days slowly roll.

Autumn days can be contrary.
Its preparations we commend.
Never really being sure
If a beginning or an end.

The chilling winds of Winter
May freeze the world outside.
Yet a warming in my heart
Where love for God abides.

Donna Sherrill

Please Leap At Me

You surely know that I am just
   As bashful as can be
And so I hope that you will take
   This chance to leap at me.
For this leap year and
   There is that special day
When you may rightly lasso me
   And haul my heart away.
I haven't much to offer you
   And in your gorgeous eyes
I may not seem what you may think
   To be a handsome prize.
But I will always love you and
   I will be ever true
And I will give my gratitude
   Forever dear to you.
Please leap at me this leap year
And I promise not to duck
For if I catch you in my arms
   It will be my good luck

Donald Hall

I Love You

Her eyes,
   As dark as the midnight sky,
Her face,
   Such a beautiful place,
Her hair,
   As brown as a brown bear,
Not much I can do,
   Not much I can say,
Besides I love you.

Jason Holihan

Lost Dreams

O, to sail again to Zanzibar
   As far as the eye can see.
To ride the waves to Malabar,
   My boat, my lady and me.

To follow the moonbeams
   O'er Homer's wine-dark sea,
And fill our hearts with moon dreams,
   My boat, my lady and me.

Never again will we coast down to Java,
   Nor breath the spices of Trincomalee.
Never to feel the soft breezes of Tonga,
   My ship, my lady and me.

For she is forever one-and-twenty,
   And I am now seventy three.

Don W. Minium

Unknown Feelings

I've never been as happy...
   ...as happy as I am with you.

I've never felt as nice...
   ...as nice as I feel with you.

I've never been as dreamy...
   ...as dreamy as I am with you.

I've never had this feeling...
   ...this feeling I feel with you.

What is this wonderful feeling that
   I feel when you are near?
I think I found the answer
   the feeling is LOVE
And love is what I feel...
   ...feel toward you!

Jennifer S. Raue

Catholic Caresses

              Lessons
at ten when Kristen told tales of
self-love:
              Like this, like this
Taught to bring upon tides
of toe-curling, palm-clenching
                            guilt.
My own caring caresses
                    left bruises
and found me trying
to leave myself alone
                    for Lent.
If only top-speed thoughts
                    Stop Wrong Stop
flowing confusedly through my brain
could be relinquished,
this perverse, remorseful rape of myself
                            could be ended.

Denise F. Parrillo

Forgotten Essence

Now still,
   breezes captured in jars.

Now brittle,
   butterflies crucified to walls.

Now lifeless,
   loves confined to lockets.

Now dead,
   dreams seized, stuffed in pockets.

Edward Kay Keiser

Untitled

For the flame will surely come...
Burn, blacken and lay bare the land.
Simultaneously an emotional breath
of life whispers...
Flora appear
yielding only to the searing heat.
Yet in their metaphor of beauty
they engage...
Against the burning,
in the creation of light

Rebecca Rodriguez Bass

"The Gamble And Drink"

Gambling is a lot of Pain
But I'll try it once again

No coin falls into my cup
Just some booze - so let us sup.

When I drink up all this Booze,
I lay down and take a Snooze.
Why do I always seem to loose?

I'll try again - but what's the use.

My job and paycheck flew away
I had hoped to work just one more day.

I gambled all I had "Be Moan"
Now it's all gone - I'll stagger home.

Herman L. Larsen

Untitled

People say a lot of things,
But I'm not sure what it means.
They like to hurt you in any way,
And it happens everyday.
I don't understand the reason why,
All I ever do is cry.
I can't take this anymore,
I'm in deep water with no shore.
People should know how much I care,
But, this pain I can not bare.
In my life I feel so bad,
I'm tired of always being sad.
If I can see a ray of sun,
Then my sadness has not won.
One day I will make it,
And no one can say I tried to fake it.

Heather Singer

Legend

I have a legend of a love like you
But there's no comparison
between the two.
I used to love him, but I love
you now.
I'll never stop no way no how.
That legend was over long ago
Our love is here and forever
will grow.
that was then, and then is now.
I'll love you always.
I love you now.

Jamie Burns

483

Hangin' With The Rhino

There's rhinoceros in the living room
but were told it isn't there

Mommy's too busy being considerate
and Daddy doesn't really much care

The rhinoceros is told it is nothing
so it refuses to even budge
So we in turn ignore it
and pretend it's big black smudge
I go through life with blinders on
ignoring rhino's everywhere

But a voice in my mind keeps telling me
there's something amiss in the air

It has become far too painful
to ignore all these black beasts

So instead I decide to acknowledge them
and start to feel a little at peace

Today the rhinos have disappeared
but should one arise in a room

I quickly address its presence
and dispel all the oncoming gloom

Denise Kramer

Samcat

Great fur ball
coiled in a wicker basket
grey eminence with yellow-green eyes
oblivious to blatherings
of his outsized sidekick
left-pawed lapper of milk
dredged from drinking glasses
always underfoot never on call
bushwhacker of his pal by day
stalker of beasties by night
tail soaring like a plumed streamer
master of all he way lays
but 'neath that pillager pose
beats the heart of a pussy cat
lying supine on the sofa
left paw cocked in torpid salute
head on the pillow next to mine
equal-opportunity napper
doing what he does best.

Hugh Welborn

Questions?

Hearing sobs,
coming from her bedroom door
I peer through at her.
Sitting in her bedroom,
She leans over her phone crying.
I feel my insides tighten.
Why?
Why is she going through
So much pain?
Is it me?
her friends?
I beat myself up for hours.
Then there's one final question
I have to ask myself,
Why does there have to be so much pain?

Becky Wortman

The Fair

I love fairs galore
Cotton candy, Caramel
apples, oh give me more, more, and more.
The rides are great
they rank first rate.
The fair will not skip
a single state.
There are games to flames
who knows you could even
meet someone named James..
From North to South, East
to West, I think fairs are
the best.

Amy Marie Pettengill

The Song Of Bosnian Children

They made us leave, terrible beasts,
Couldn't fight them then
Fists too weak, minds too young.
Deserting our homes, three years ago,
In a hurry to leave,
Didn't know that's the best of it
We'll ever see.
Our sorrow is deep,
Out hearts are stone.
Now we declare: "We'll fight them
'Till all are gone."
Their cruelty gave us the right
To revenge and fight
For our sister's tears
For our mothers' fears
And our brothers' toys
They will hear our voice.

Jasmina Mulaosmanovic

Thus Marred The Morning

An angel crying on the cobble stone
Dawn breaks and you're all alone
thus marred the morning
waking cold from a fretful sleep
lost in a dream and rising in fear
thus marred the morning
leaving the warmth
open to the cold
eyes stung by the sun
tears frozen to my cheeks
fumbling blindly
go back to sleep
a safe haven away from the world
falling into a dead sleep
dreamy life, sleepy world
A brisk shaking
and a shrill voice calls,
"ARISE!"
Thus marred the morning

Joey Jude Casale

Just Cry Yourself To Sleep

Yesterday was a very good day.
Everything was turning out right,
But I got some bad news near bedtime,
And I cried myself to sleep.

It may seem like a childish thing to do,
But it helps no matter your age.
What a beautiful escape
When things go wrong
Is crying yourself to sleep!

Edward W. Clautice

Untitled

It's different from
day to day.
Sometimes I can
accept it.
Sometimes I cannot.
It hurts me to
see you
with him.
I wish it could be
different.
If only it was me that you
loved.
I would be
so content.
But no.
It is not I that
you feel for.
And I don't think that it
can ever be.

Eli Stickler

"Patches"

"Patches," oh "Patches",
dear sweet ball of fur.
I was so blind
as to what might occur.

I took you for granted,
as you lay on the chair.
I wish I'd have stroked you more,
and told you I care.

With one swift blow,
your body was broken.
The pain in your eyes
that remained unspoken.

I'll miss you sweet "Patches,"
you brought joy to my heart.
My spirit is saddened
by the way we had to part.

"Patches," oh "Patches,"
dear sweet ball of fur.
I was so blind
as to what might occur.

Denise Watts

Mankind Heritage

God in his wisdom
did not bear Jesus
yellow, red, black or
white.

Jesus, the epitome
of mankind, was in
the flesh a golden
reddish brown figure
of a man.

The day all hearts
and eyes can see
the truth racial
prejudice and
bigotry will
cease to exist.

Diane M. Russell

"The Grip Of Madness"

Mothers drown their babies.
Fathers stab and kill their teens.

In the grip of madness
it's all even worse than it seems.

In this grip of madness,
the world today is astray.
What can we do?
What can we say?

Is there hope?

Can we cope?

While in the grip of madness
and
sadness,
we stay.

Donna Leanheart

Untitled

It took me a while to get the
feelings out of me that I had for you.
You left a mark, like a hole it made
me feel like I wasn't anything anymore.
I cried trying to get you out of my
mind but it felt like just thinking of
you was a crime.
Why did you have to leave me this
way with out a thing for me to say.
My love is gone it left with you
I have no more love to give to give
to anyone but you.

Heather Burnham

"Thank A Veteran"

It's time we thank the veterans,
For all that they have done.
Let's thank them for the freedoms,
And the battles they have won.

Their time away from families,
Their time away from home.
For all they have done for us,
They should be seated on a throne.

To the thousands, that are missing,
And those held prisoner of war,
It's true, they are not forgotten,
It just leaves our hearts at war.

To those confined to wheelchairs,
And those confined to bed.
It's time for us to thank them,
For all the blood that they shed.

To those that gave the ultimate,
We will never hear them boast,
For they are the veterans,
That truly gave the most.

Edward R. Stiner Sr.

Irene

My itsy bitsy baby
has itsy bitsy toes
itsy bitsy fingers
and a wee nose
My itsy bitsy baby
has eyes of blue
My itsy bitsy baby
I Love you.
Mother.

Martha L. Jenkins

Peaches Of Victory, A Prayer

Lord, teach us to reach
For that sweet juicy peach
The one growing highest in the tree.

Teach us to strive.
To become fully alive
As you always intended us to be.

Oh Lord, teach us this,
That we will sometimes miss
But we'll learn all about being free.

And when we fail,
Please prove us not frail
So we'll stay on the path shown by thee.

Because with thy lead
We shall surely succeed
In reaching every peach on your tree.

Monnie Martin

A Poet's Prayer

Dear God-may I always have a shoulder
For the sad to cry upon
May I have a deep compassion
For the either right or wrong?

May my hands be ever open
To all trouble doubt and fear
When there's need to talk it over
May I have a lending ear?

May my eyes be ever closing
Should temptation spread its glow
May my feet leave only footprints
That will never lead to woe?

May my lips be non-revealing
And my mouth provide the hide
For all words that's detrimental
To a peace on earth abide?

These blessings Heavenly Father
That can only come from thee
Will forever be my guidelines
When I write poetically.

Edith E. Harris

Untitled

Though it ain't easy
  for we're two families,
trying to become one.
Though there are those times...
  Where words are harder to say,
So the anger we have built up inside
  comes out in all different ways.
It's hard I know
  but I feel like the outcast
  with no where to turn,
I try to find the right words
  to make it easier,
But nothing comes out
  the way I want to say,
So I keep to myself praying
  it'll work out.
There's a lot going on
  at one time during the day,
Maybe one day things will work out,
Until then I have no hard feelings,

Gwen D. Derr

The Peaceful Trail

The morning sun is peering out
from under the blanket of night
To smile at the moonshine
As she casually blows out her light
It brings one more sunny morning
Yes one more sunny day
I think this life is beautiful
Today is on its way
It will bring to me new ventures
Of the things I've yet to learn
To add another color
To my rainbow as I turn
So I spread my wings for freedom
I fly in search of love
At times I hear a distant call
Which comes from up above
Giving to me the comfort
That only he can give
To guide me on this peaceful trail
Each and every day I live.

James H. Schroder

Prayer For A Rookie Cop!

Your badge is new and so are you!
Fulfilled... your heart's desire!
You've built a dream and made the team,
To great things you aspire!

You'll falter not, though dope and pot
Bring rampage to defeat...
But guard, protect, console, direct
Each citizen you meet...

Still persevere in time of fear,
When crime's a war to wage...
Stop... listen... look! Go by the book...
Enjoying ev'ry page...

Then question why these, two, must fly
Without a turn to spare...
Fire to ember! Retired member!
One day you'll join us there!

Sentimental incidental?
Life's blessings... to the top!
In synthesis...please, God, hear this
Prayer for a rookie Cop!

Harriett H. Odum

Gift From A Four Year Old

The four-year old
Handed me the box,
Wrapped in a multitude
Of colorful hair ribbons.
"Wrapped it myself, Momma.
Special,
Just for you!"
As I carefully untied each ribbon,
Her eyes sparkled with pride and
Scarcely contained excitement.
When the last ribbon dropped away,
And the lid fell to the floor,
Out,
  Hopped
  A
    Bewildered,
    But
      Liberated,
      Frog!

Alice L. Thompson

Hazed

Waking when sleep is still calling
Having to rise instead
Body not yet energized
Heavy is my head.

Too many days of work
Not enough time for rest
Swing shift controlling my life
I'm not at my best.

Taking myself into view
Hair going every which way
Time to get on the move
Night clothes rumpled at midday.

Twenty minutes of time goes by
Momentum goes into force
The haze begin to lift
Returning my natural voice.

A little more time, and
I'm headed out the door
To the same job, that
Brought the haze before.

Sheila D. Williams

The Choice

He was just a little child
he heard a still small voice
you are a body with a soul
and so you have a choice

You can choose to think
of you every want and need
or to rob and hurt or kill
but this voice you should heed

It tells you to find happiness
with trust and faith and love
and to help those in need
it all goes hand in glove

For everything you do on earth
one day you will be judged
so with a kindly mind and heart
store treasure up above

Donna Patton

Mothers

My mother has red hair,
Her skin is the color of a polar bear.
She has freckles on her nose,
On each foot she has five toes,
She has four girls,
Who are from different worlds.
Sometimes I hated her.
But I would never trade her.
She is my mother,
And I love her.

When we were small,
She loved us all.
When we were hurtin,'
She didn't think us a burden.
When my father died,
With us she cried.
Now I'm a mother as well,
Through rain, sleet and hail.
Now I have my own little sweetie,
And I know he loves me.

Bobbi Bryant-Hadden

"The Future"

You don't go to
high school to
get high and die.
You have a purpose
for living and so do I.
You have a brain to help
you through but if you
don't help yourself then
who's going to help you.
You must think about
The future and not the
past, the future is coming
don't you dare let it pass.
You have a purpose for
living and so do I.
Do you want to know the
reason why?
You are the future
and so am I.

Bernadette Fredricks

In My Dreams

In my dreams
I am an important person
I save the rainforest
    and sometimes I don't succeed.
In my dreams
I travel to far away jungles
    where I help scientists find new
    cures.
In my dreams
I am whom ever I want to be
When by night, I am a scientist
    and by day, I am a kid.

Jaclyn Whitley

The Supremeness

Guide my hand so gently as today
I am as fragile as the wings of a
Dried butterfly
Life has gone astray

May my fragmented life
A copy of your glory so sweet
Strengthen my every fiber

May the things you saved us all from
Be as no other sin
For all manner of sins are the same
May all past things fly away

The servant of the dragon keeper
Only looks up
Trust the faith
For all power enters you through the
Heart, and through the mind and soul
In unison

Carry with you the true glory of a dream
Not differed but chosen
The clear choice is you

Linda D. Lovett

More Or Less

I am what I am
No more, no less.
But, if I must
I will confess
I hope to be much more than less
And less than more
If it is best.

Jackie Collins

My Letter To The Blind

Tell me what it is you see,
I am confused
But yet, enthused
To know what it is you see.

Tell me what it is you see,
Is it the sound of nature?
Is it the touch of texture?
Tell me what it is you see.

Tell me what it is you see,
Is it the sense of smell
That helps you to tell
What it is you see?

Tell me what it is you see,
I long to know
What it shows,
In the world that you see.

Tell me what it is you see,
In your sight
Even though in the night
What we all fear, you see!

Heather S. Weaver

Not Always Perfect

I think I'm learning
I believe I'm growing
I've come to a resolution you see
Nothing can always be perfect
Not even me
People pretend
People hide what they don't want seen
Are they afraid
Or impersonating what they must be
Is it to fittin'
Is it to be happy
But how happy are they really
Portraying something they're not
And taking it out wrongfully
That's what other people see
Nothing can always go your way
But you can always at least try
To be yourself
And enjoy what you were destined to be
You

Jamie Benson

Words

You wonder why I say,
I love you every day.

She wonders why I say,
Hi on my way.

Words left unspoken,
can leave your life broken.

Everyone has something to say,
but express it in their own way.

There is no price to pay,
when said something to say.

Words ... Beautiful Words.

Erin Brunner

Instant

Strong tight
I sight desperately silent
Waiting wanting
to gasp the moment
in my presence here.

Around me
the drama unfolds.
Without haste nor hesitation
the moment draws near.
    When the futility of the action
    strains the nerves
    to a crises.

The screaming urgency.
Leaving no room for debate.
Urgency which captures the
moment.
Without repetitions no omissions.

Rearranging the instance.
Without the staining for tedious proofs.

Edson P. Tembo

Hope

The world goes round and I am still.
I try and try to catch up but.
I can't and I am so tried
of trying that I want to just
quit, just give up and be alone
Then I see a light, not bright, but
very dim, just enough to see,
when I see that light, I feel peace
I can try again, I can go
The world doesn't seem as fast as
it once did and I can catch up.

Heather Lea Spore

My Prayer

    I did not want to be alone.
I wanted something to call my own.
I looked upon the stars one night.
And prayed that I would see God's light.
    I prayed so hard I shed a tear.
And had a feeling of no more fear.
    I had a dream in this quite place.
of holding a child without a face.
    This was his way of letting me know,
I would soon have that special glow.
    My son is now here for all to see.
for the greatest gift God gave to me.
    Thank you God

Dorae Smith

You'll Always Lose

    Loneliness is the same as drowning,
once you're under the surface
there's not much hope of coming,
out alive,
If you're alone,
no one will save you from
the war you're drowning in,
When you stop talking for awhile,
You forget to talk at all,
So you drown.
When you stop talking for awhile,
that's when you know you're alone,
    You'll always lose,

Becky Wortman

To The Trees

They are going to cut the trees.
I'll die a little—
But maybe more.
One hundred and ninety trees—
That much more.
Think of all the dead leaves,
And the squirrels' nests
And the raccoons' dens
And the owls' homes
And the bees' hives
And the woodpeckers' nests
And the bluebirds' homes
And the foxes' lairs—
I said I'd die a little
But "they" will live
Who keep warm by their fires
Who build houses with it,
Who make furniture with it—
I'll live—in every grain
And flame and aching moment...

Jane S. Nichols

Christ Am I

I walk the streets,
    In daylight and at night.

I eat whatever I can find,
    Though not fit for man nor for mice.

I've slept in boxes and on benches,
    Dreaming only of white picket fences.

I laid myself down and prayed to die,
    When a soft voice said "have faith
    in me, for Christ am I."

Carlos Rodriguez

Little Signs

I look for you everyday
    in everything and every way

Little signs that say so much
    of our Lord's gentle touch

Of springtime and green grass
    or the sparkle of polished brass

In the meadows full of flowers
    bursting with colors from April
    showers

The rainbows in the sky
    the birds aloft soaring by
    a baby's cry
    a peaceful sigh

A prayer of faith and ears to your
    cry is all it takes to walk by
    your side.

Doreen Olsen

Untitled

Pain throbs deep
my lonely heart seeps
degradation cuts through
rejected love from you
your smile fades
a rained parade
I sit in silence
stunned by loves defiance

Donnalyn Roxey

Rhythmic Grave

So soon to smile
In grass aligned
By the oceans steamy breath,
To gaze in mad pubescent wonder
I ascend and forget
And plummet to your abyss
A magical gnome
All the time falling in dreams
I still recall
The rose petal scent
Musky and fresh
In the stale corridor of your heart
Till all that is blue
Blinking resides
Into migrant skies
Now moving.

Jack E. Wright

To Whom It May Concern

Sitting by the corner. The rain
is hitting my face. I look for
shelter. None to be found. The
coldness comes up through the grand.
Silently seeking my eternal feelings.
Nothing is around. The greyness
enters my heart. Sadness is lurking
about. To whom it may concern: My
life's unraveling. Mixture of tears
and rain. What do I have to gain?
The rain hits harder now. It'll
rain forever. Blackness enters.
waiting for the saviour to give
a sign. But I guess it can't rain
all of the time.

Jennifer Cannedy

What Is Love

What is love,
    Is it good or bad.
Was love meant to be,
    or is it another human imperfection.

Is love forever,
    or is it temporary,
Does love save,
    or does it kill.

Is love for you and me,
    or was it never meant to be.
All I know that love is here,
    and it will never leave.

Iwona Bialon

Lost Love

Deserted and alone,
Isolated from others.
Staring into the darkness,
Memories fill your mind,
Pain fills your heart.
Love is in the air,
but without someone to share it,
You let your mind wonder.
Remembering your lost love,
And the way it once was.

Heather Naughton

True Love

My love for you
It runs so deep
I think inside
Oh, how I weep
I love you dearly
How I wish you could see
The pain in my heart
Just let me be
The sea so dark
How it runs so deep
Our love compares
Sleep, sleep
I see an awakening
How wonderful it could be...
A flower blooms
It freshens the room
Our love is true.

Anissa Rusthoven

God's Assurance

I had a vision,
It was almost daylight,
I felt a light touch,
My Savior was in sight.

I explained my empty feelings,
My heart was filled with pain,
I'd lost a friend so special,
My prayers seemed all in vain.

He comforted my empty feeling,
We prayed, we wept, we cried,
God guided me to heaven,
By opening the clear blue skies.

So if your ever lonely,
Kneel to him in prayer,
Trust in him to guide you,
God's presence is everywhere.

Carolyn Vogel

Hair

I am a weave queen but, I wear
it well. When I'm wearing it,
it looks very real. All the men
talk about it yes they do, but
they rub their fingers through
it without a clue. Say what
you wanna say about hair
weave, but girlfriend here's
my card come and see me.
   I am a weave queen yes
indeed, two things you don't touch
my soaps, and my weave. When
I'm wearing it they always ask
is it yours? I tell them,
"Yeah girl" and yes I'm
sure. If they don't know don't
tell 'em but, if they do,
still don't tell 'em, cause when
I wear my weave I sure look good.

Janine Williams

Canvas Prayer

Choose the colors
I've been waiting.
Palette and canvas
Start the mating.

Stokes are brilliant
Medley so bright.
Cover my face
Splatter delight.

Over here, yes there
A little more, a little less.
That's right, stand back,
This is your best.

Subject so new
Composition takes flight.
Complete. Change nothing!
Frame me tonight.

Bertha Taylor Tucker

'The Unknown Soldier'

His country pays him tribute,
Knowing not from whence he came,
The symbol of the million brave
Who carried freedoms flame.

He's the son of every mother
Who passes by his tomb
Remembering the tiny life
Once carried in their womb.

They pray for him, in many tongues,
To God's each of their choice -
And from this land of freedom,
Every God will hear their voice.

His spirit will forever soar,
Across our mighty land,
To spark the torch of freedom;
To quell the conquerors hand.

In generations, yet to come.
His cause will never cease,
Until all wars are vanquished
And all people live in peace.

Edmund C. McCoy

Daydreams

Catch me in this moment,
Let time not carry me.

Thoughts awaken, it begins,
This daydream sets me free.

Tear me not away from now,
Now is where I'll stay.

A rainbows end, where colors swirl,
Love whispers on the breeze.

Confetti kisses fall from the clouds,
On lovers skin they tease.

At night, the sky cast misty light,
The oceans breathe with life.

Waves glow silver, as they rise,
And wish to reach the moon.

In this place, where love smolders,
It cannot burn.

So I shall stay, and satisfy,
This fantasy I yearn.

Jane M. Wittrock

DW1

I'm driving down the street,
looking very beat.
I'm coming from a party,
had too much to drink.
Music's blaring in my ears,
I cannot hear a thing .
I'm breezing passed the lights,
don't even bother waiting.
Soon I heard a crash.
I stopped my car and turned my head,
I saw a body on the ground.
I got back in my car,
and thought just to myself.
I should drank much less,
because of me a girl is dead.

Denise Berger

Dawn

If my heart were the sun
may it always set with you,
let us rise every morning
to start the day anew.
While the sky changes colors
from red and yellow to blue
the birds will be singing
their sweet songs for you.
The trees would call your name
as the wind whistles by,
a beam would light the path you take
forming from the sky.
Love will flow between us
like the river rushing past,
endless streams of passion
knowing it's meant to last.
As the sun begins to set again
and with each ensuing night,
I will think of you my darling,
our love taking flight.

Donald Stoll

Ecstatic Heretic

Some christen
Me a
Blasphemous heretic.
When
Creativity,
Intellect,
And
Audacity,
Have long been
Proclaimed
Iniquitous
Traits
For
Women,
I exult
In such a
Prestigious title.

Janet L. McGinn

Bobbie's Boy

Jake, you are truth
Sharing spontaneously
As budding strength within
Uniquely you will be
Naturally within my heart
Then you known by me.

Rita Vaughan

A Day In The Sun

A flower in the morning
Moistened by the dew
open its arms to the sun.

By midday it is in full
bloom, basking in its glory.

Toward dusk it folds its petals inwards,
reflecting on its day in the sun.

But it is only a flower,
lovely though it be.

As for man, his day in the sun
lives on in the deeds he has done
and in the lives he has touched;
whose reward will surely come.

Dorothy Poppe Campbell

Waving

I wave goodbye to a dear friend,
My arm and hand are a going,
I look around and what do I see,
But my upper arm also waving.
Yes, my upper arm waves to all,
Whenever I use this arm to tell,
A story of strength or a story so tall,
This upper arm makes this point for all.
I try to keep it in the dark,
So others won't see, but it sparks.
It comes out opening so wide,
For all to see, can't wait inside.
A stranger came to my outside door,
Wanting directions to a house of so's,
My flabby arm wave hello to thee.
These things do happen as we age,
And we try to take these changes with calm,
Our ageless can't bring us any harm,
That body and mind is in a degree,
With all my arm all to see.

Jannet Knox

The Last Stages

I'm too old for a Christmas tree
   My children are married and gone.
I am a widower of fourscore years
   Crippled and all alone.

I have a phone that seldom rings
   I'm not a business man.
They have no reason at all to call
   So I truly understand.

I have two gates that are always open
   My drive is wide and clear.
I see the cars go driving by
   But only mine is here.

The same address I've had for years
   It will soon be forty five.
The yard and house is hard to keep
   But still I have to strive.

My furniture is getting old
   I never buy what's new.
It has served me well these many years
   And another year will do.

Elwood A. Lawler

Day's End

When day is done and excitement wanes
My thoughts begin to wander
Events of the passing day leaves
Much time for me to ponder,
Was my day fulfilling with events
That made it so complete,
When settling in at home, takes
On an air of calm retreat?
Thankful for all blessings received,
No matter, large or small
For great are the things that God
Has done, for whose cause
I will stand tall, Peace.

Milton C. Plummer

No Matter

No matter, what I do or say,
No matter, in the night or the day.

Whatever we understand or not,
Whatever things we've sold or bought.

Whenever our hearts are just about,
Whenever our minds are full of doubt.

Without your strong and wondering arms,
Without my boisterous and loud charms.

Nothing will ever replace,
Nothing, no book, show or face.

However loud, outrageous or wild,
However quiet, relaxing or mild.

Together we will end up,
Together, like a saucer and a cup.

Promise to cherish, love and support,
Promise to hold down our small, little fort.

I'll love you 'till I die...
No matter...how much you make me cry.

Donna Marie Wheelehon

No One Should Fear

In times of darkness
no one should fear,
for there is a Light
always shining near.
Showing us all
how we should live,
the perfect example
of how we should give.
Never ignore Him
when you hear Him call,
for Jesus, our Saviour,
gave us his all.
Sometimes in giving
there is great pain.
Cutting off one's life
that others may gain.
This is the truth
of giving and sharing.
Fulfilling God's love,
encompassed in His caring.

Quinton L. Nottingham, Jr.

Today

Not a yesterday
Nor a tomorrow
Yesterday was a today
Today is a today
Tomorrow may never be a today.

Edith A. Riddle

O Spirit

   Born into a world of uncertainty,
Nurtured in the arms of a restless
society,
Steeled in the knowledge of
understanding.
Spring from the boundaries of
discipline.
And rest in the hearts of
humanity.
Free us from the prejudices
of humankind,
And live in our souls
As peace.

Jan Valdesuso

Letting Go

Return address
Of a distant city.
Plain envelope,
My name printed
In faded ink,
Corners worn
To a rounded edge,
Stationary warped
With tears.
Handwriting barely legible,
I strain my eyes to
Read it over
And over.
I grasp the page
And won't let go
For fear I'd be
Letting go of
Him
And my dreams

Diana Lynn Pakstis

W.W.-2

Mid chaos and the frantic surge
Of a frightened race
Godless men with bloody purge
Seek Him to displace

The tower of Babel grows once more
In mockery and in vain
Mars flaming sword poised to restore
The brotherhood of Cain

Four Horseman, saddled and alert
Prepare to ride again
Grasping freed, viciously covert
Encompass the domain

Extend O God! Thy soothing hand
To give this broil surcease
Return unto this frothing land
The gentle Prince of Peace

Aloysius O'Connor

Oh! Daughter's Mine

Oh! Daughter's Mine
So lost to me
My heart is full
Thinking of thee
My heart doth know
That 'tis God's will
But, yet, my brain
Can't reason still.

Dolores G. Marraffa

Brandy

I hear the whisper
of her footsteps,
as she treads softly
upon the stairs.

A contented sigh
as she settles herself
into her favorite chair.

The warm glow of love
as she tenderly
touches my hand.

My heart aches,
my eyes sting,
with unshed tears.

For these things
are not,
and can never
be again.

Dorothy L. Bush

A Higher Power

Whispers through the dawn,
Of sin's sweeping tide.
Rolling by like thunder now,
As the blood flows from your side.
I ask only forgiveness,
And feel each debt you take.
Your touch is warm and tender,
A love that I could not forsake.
Even though there may be times,
That I feel the need to hide,
You never wonder where I am,
For you are always by my side.
The sound of your voice calling,
Made it clear suddenly,
Above all your suffering and pain,
Was your love for me.
I'm yearning for something,
A peace from above.
Perhaps I need only learn,
Of the power of your love.

Janice Stringer

God's Creative Word

Born by your creative word
Old things are pass away
All things become new
And loving you as created
in me an ability to love
Cause in the beginning was
love and love was never
created it always was
I consider the heavens
the work of your fingers
the moon, the stars
For you have created me
a little lower than yourself
You crowned me with glory
and honor
You but all things under my feet
every living thing
You have set me free!

William S. Arroyo

Memories

As we walk down the aisle
On our very special day
We remember the memories
That no one can take away

We'll never forget
The good times and bad
Our family and friends
The special times we've had

The memories
Of our first date
The prom, the late night parties
The consequences of being late.

We now look to the future
Wondering what we'll be
But after we graduate
A whole new world is what we'll see.

Melissa Raubuch

The Magic Carpet

As I walk among the flowers
On this path beside the sea
I while away the hours
Reminiscing pleasantly.

I think of all the happy times
The loves which I have known
I feel, that like these flowers
My blessings all have grown.

They form a magic carpet
As lovely as can be
All variety's of beauty
Are among these blessings which I see.

I hope I too, may linger on
In someone memory
To help their magic carpet bloom
A lovely sight to see.

Edith Strain

The Fragile Stem

Looking out my window
    One cold November day
The chill of winter had erased
    Summer's green away!

And then I saw
    A single leaf
Left on the tree
The other leaves had
    Feel silently
This stem must be stronger
    Or yet to be
A gentle wind,
    Will set it free

Life is like the stem
    Of the last leaf
        On the tree
Strong yet we may be
    The masters call
Like the gentle wind
Will free our soul to eternity!

Lottie D. Smith

Sometimes

Sometimes I wish there was only
one star in the sky to look at
but then it would be lonely

Sometimes I wish
that life wasn't reality
but then what would it be

Sometimes I wish
nothing was ever killed
but then how would it die

Sometimes I wish everything
was like it used to be
but then what was it like

Sometimes I wish
that I didn't wish
but then how would I survive

Jaime Gowdy

I Love You

As I talk to you through the night,
Only three words I try to fight.
I Love You are the words to hide,
As I bury them deep inside.

In my dreams I hear your voice,
After that I have no choice.
To tell you this I would surely die,
Even this brings a tear to my eye.

I love you more with each passing day,
How can three words be so hard to say?
I am lost and don't know what to do,
So how do I say I Love You?

Edward W. Luzadder Jr.

A Children's Prayer

I won't lay down, my weary head,
    Or close my eyes to rest.
Before I kneel beside my bed,
    And with my mouth confess.

Dear Father GOD, I love you true,
    I pray down on my knees.
To do the things you'd have me do,
    And hope that you are pleased.

I pray you keep me in your arms,
    And hold me oh so tight.
And keep my body safe from harm,
    For just another night.

Keep me straight, and spirit strong,
    For every day I live.
And all the things, that I've done wrong,
    I hope you will forgive.

I don't know very much of sin,
    So teach me wrong from night.
Until I come to pray again,
    Amen—And A—Goodnight.

Joseph Jones

Life

Life is very special if
there is love but if there
is no love than life be
dammed for without love
you can not become a
full man.

Douglas M. Tyler

Marriage Proposal

Thought distance parts our loving arms
our thoughts may travel free.
So on this day of love I send
these emissaries three.

Like golden sunlight on my soul
as aurie as can be,
this yellow rose, my love, recalls
the friend you are to me.

Like passion's fires' crimson flame
and blood that hotly flows,
in memory of seething love
The lover's red, red rose.

and now, in simple tribute
to a heart that ever pours
a love that we shall always share,
this lily white is yours.

These flowers represent a love
that I shall feel for life
and ask again if you will be
my lover, my friend, my wife.

Guy L. W. Hardy

Impelled Response

In a
poised
moment
bird
wings through
the "oil mixed with light"
on
past blue
on
through the prism
soaring
until it reaches
dove white.

Jane Rae Lewis

Opals From My Heart

I have cried for you and about you
Shared good times and laughter
Beside you and through you
I have hurt with you
And due to the absence of you
But always, I have cared about you

Though time passes,
You will remain in my heart and thoughts
I will miss you
As I do the moments we have shared
I am...forever...your friend

Doreen L. Maples

A Heavy Load

We drink too much,
We over eat,
We take dessert,
And then repeat,
The above mistakes
Till down the road,
For our pallbearers
We're a heavy load.

Edward B. McMenomy

My Dreams

As I walk along the ocean -
side and see the white
caps come ashore, I begin
dreaming the dreams I had
before.

My dreams are brighter
than the light houses light,
stronger then all the rocks
which surround the shore.

But the one thing I know
is that they will never be
stronger or as bright than
heavens light that shines
from up - above

Janell Groman

The Lesson

As the minutes tick away
Silently I say goodbye
To a strength nearly gone
A strength I've always known

Slipping away into the darkness
Of a cold cold world
The child feeling of protection
Laughing as it disappears

Elusive is the answer
Did I learn the lesson
Taught by the strength
Whose journey is about to begin

Now naked of protection
The strength too weak to lean on
With the present in transition
And as the minutes tick away
Did I learn the lesson

James Russell

Love!

Love is a word-
Small, yet complicated.
What does it mean?
Doesn't it mean something?
How is it supposed to make you feel?
Love makes me feel warm all over;
It helps me get through tough times.
Love makes me feel safe and wanted!
Does it really mean this?
Or is it only in my head?
Love supposedly means so many things.
How can you tell it is love?
Can it be true?
Or is it infatuation?
How do I know what love means?
How do I know I love you?
I think I love you because you
Make me feel safe and wanted.
It must be love!
I love you!

Amy VanOcker

"A Whistling Woman..."

A woman poet is dangerous
She can draw blood with pen
And loves the pricking of
puffed up balloons.

Jane Gillespie Cross

Where Does It Go?

Where does it go - how does it slip
So far away from us
The beauty of a love so new
A raging sort of bliss

We start a new forgetting
There is a world out there
Devouring every breath and sigh
Passion filling every care

Then while we sleep - it seems to creep
From some unknown realm
The anguish of a world unleashed
Into that sacred dwell

It comes with angry claws and thorns
And words we can't erase
And now that gripping word called fear
Has filled that sacred space

I want to take us back you know
I want to reach ahead
And find that place with you
That brings undying peace

Sherry Burton

The Unborn Lives

My mommy loves me,
So she says,
to her other friends,
So why in hell,
did I have to end?

Being young and,
being old,
is nothing to compare,
but now I'm being murdered,
by her,
from the scalpel that has teared.

Heidi Wygle, age 15

Wind

Every night the wind blows on my street.
Sometimes...
  It blows toward the canyon
    As if the mountains breathe in...

But, mostly...the canyon shouts
  To the people on my street;

"Come...
  Come and see what Nature has for you."

  Those who hear the voice
May drive their cars and bikes
  Between the gaping teeth
For a day's recreation.

But those who listen....and understand...
Will strap on their shoes,
  Their backpacks.
    Leave the frenzied world of concrete and steel,
    Of toxins, reactionary, policy, and fast-
    food restaurants,
And become part of Nature's world.

For the wind knows life consists of wildness
And yearns to share the wild with us.

Jason Antone Gee

Monks And Wool And 1088

Monks, wool, curative
springs. Silver buys privilege.
Move to worm speed 2.

Barbara Pryor

The Raft

This raft alone
stranded and apart
is what a child has done

This ship of youth and all its sails
moved with gusts of time

This raft can be for each of us
a floating dream
    of what we were

This piece of wood which once did live
making such sound
to the silence of time

This be the innocence sealing one dream
of a morning not forgotten

And when the sun says good night
our only thoughts are such of this
a special day

Douglas N. Peterson

"Unwanted"

I am the being who was not to be
Sucked from nature's inviolate hearth
Into a cold, unfeeling receptacle;
Flushed as waste into the sea
To join the flotsam and debris
Which pollute our tainted waters.
The womb which sheltered me,
No longer nurtures my awakening life.
Nor will I suckle a mother's breast,
Or know the warmth of a trundle bed,
Watching by loving, caring eyes.
Does my mother lives with shame?
Is there one who shares the blame?
Or is she lonely, unrepentant?

Edward F. Halpin

The Glorious Sea

Beauty....that touches the heart!
Sunshine, bathing the sea
with its brilliance;
Translucent, dancing water!
Beneath, the happy sea dwellers
celebrating,
Waltzing their way in their
graceful movement.
Nature, unbelievably beautiful!
O'er head, seagulls fly mingling
with the other birds;
Singing their songs in the air.
Yes..., today the sea brings
forth peace and tranquility.
Tomorrow?
Tomorrow is another day!

Ramon G. Palanca

Eagle Flight

Gliding, soaring, free,
Totally ignoring earth-bound
limits-her,
With winged, pulsing,
feathered majesty,
Swift - swoops down on prey
And just as gracefully
sweeps up and on his way.

Jane R. Taylor

Strength

Strength comes in all shapes and sizes
Take it all in stride
When the world comes down
You want to run and hide

Step back take a breath
Look what you can give
Hold your head up high
you've got your life to live

When the world is on your shoulder
Don't walk around blind
There is sunshine in every cloud
Just strive and you will find

Anita Dodd

Why

Why do you smoke
    that funny cigarette
Knowing, it will be
    the death of you yet.

Does it give you
    such great illusions
Or only cause
    much more confusion

Does it let you forget
    things you don't want to see
Just remember they're still there
    when you come back to reality

It may phase out things
    you can't endure
But guaranteed that
    funny cigarette is no cure

Diana Newharth

Creation Or Compulsion

There is a fascination with needlework
    That is hard to compare
With any other leisure pastime.
    For instance, in knitting, one is
Tempted to go one more row
    Or one more set of rows.
In crochet it is just one more
    Pattern, or one more color.
In needlepoint the urge to
    Keep going is just as strong.
These are supposed to be fun
    To fill our idle hours,
But they tend to take over
    Our lives — we put off the
Dusting, sweeping and mopping
    For the joy of seeing something grow.
I guess you might call it "The Creative Urge."

Dorothy B. Bliss

"My Candle In The Dark"

My candle in the dark,
    your light shines my way
    you stay until I'm strong enough
    and then you blow away
My candle in the dark,
    each day and night I pray
    that when my days are dark
    and gray
    I'll see your yellow flames
My candle in the dark.

Heather Boyd

Jack Frost

The frost is on the pumpkin.
The frost is in the air.
But best of all,
is Jack Frost that impish little elf.
His forest and trees all trimmed in
icicles and lace.
They sparkle like diamonds.
His window panes etched with
delicate taste and design,
no two alike
he is truly an artist divine.
He is here only a little while
but will return again next year.

Dorothy Geyer

Birth

Joy beyond words expressed,
The new born, tiny and pink,
Unfolds its lungs and life is expressed,
Greatest miracle of God we think.
Through life's great struggle on we go,
Struggling and moaning with each breath,
Bent and worn as down we slow,
To meet our destiny, death.

Edna L. Boyum

My Window

When I look through my window,
the only things I see are a bunch of
houses and a big oak tree.
When I look through my window
I see many things, sometimes,
I see all of London's Kings.
When I look out my window and
I see some birds fly,
I wish I could fly too.
When I look out my window I can't
see or hear or touch because I
am inside and the world is outside
So lead me there and one day I'll see,
I'll touch and I'll hear, lead me there
and one day I'll see what I've seen
touch what I've touched and hear what I've
heard.
And then, soon I'll be back inside looking out
through my window.

Jaimie Davis

Snow

Wake up, wake up
The snow has fallen
And ice is upon the ground

The ground is white
Let's have a snow fight
Or make a snow man with a bound

Children sled
Faces cold and red
One small child is lost
He finds his way
On this frosty mound
This happy Christmas Day

Time to come in
To warm your skin
So you can go out again

Harold Turner

"If You Only Knew"

If you only knew how much I love you,
the softness of your hands and the
tenderness of your kiss,
If you only knew.

If you only knew the pain you put me
through,
the harshness in your voice and the
remembrance of the song,
If you only knew.

If you only knew the aching in my
heart,
The pain in missing you and the sorrow
of being apart,
If you only knew.

Heather Yingling

Everybody's Right

May the Lord give me
The strength to endure
For that which
I am not sure
If we lift
Our heads above
We will have
The strength
Of the dove
Which is the peace
That we need
To ensure
Once this
Is known
We can proceed
To be on our own
With the blessings
That can be
Conferred upon us all.

Edward T. Philpitt

Lost Love

I love the way you hold me
The way you say my name
The way you call me sweetheart
The way you call me Jane
The way you always listen
And always seem to care
So many years have past
Since you first held my hand
I don't know why we parted
I'll never understand
I know my life without you
has brought so many fears
I know I'll always love you
but oh so many tears.

Jane W. Regan

Damaged Butterfly

I saw a butterfly today,
wings all tattered and torn,
weather-beaten and worn.
Its flight was majestic to behold,
like it was newborn.
Not knowing it was damaged.
It continued its pursuit.
Flying, feeding and free,
Not knowing the worries of you and me.

Dickie W. Warren

Sudden Summer Shower

The clouds have joined hands
Their clapping is thunder.
On this June summer day
Will it rain - well I wonder.

I don a windbreaker jacket
With slacks of old rose.
Should I take an umbrella?
Looks silly, I suppose.

Two hours later
With the rain pouring down
'Neath my pink parasol
I'm no longer the clown.

Men in shirt sleeves
Are drenched to one skin.
One said I looked "great."
I'll never see him again.

I'm no fashion plate
So what do I think?
All little old ladies
Look pretty in pink.

Helen Margaret Wilson

"Like A Dream"

Like a dream you came into my heart
Then like a dream you broke it apart
Always thought I was someone special
How stupid could I be
I didn't know you wanted to be free
you made me feel like a queen
I was your special dream
Little did I know it was jut a show
You were cheating all the time
You were never really mine.
How stupid could I be
Now that it is over I can truthfully say
I wouldn't have it any other way.

Hilda L. Kuhn

"Silly Fears"

Movements and shadows,
things around the bend.
Night has arrived.
When will it end?

I lay in the darkness,
alone in my bed,
thinking strange thoughts,
but what I do I dread?

I fall asleep wondering,
what makes me feel scared?
I'm glad no one's here,
to see my feeling's so bared.

The house is so quiet,
no movements are heard.
Everyone's sleeping,
you'll hear not a word.

Movements and shadows,
when will it end?
It's all laughable now,
it's morning again.

Janice Havelka

Untitled

Pieces of dishes shattering,
those horrible screaming sounds,
as if someone attacked by wild hounds.
I lock my doors and listen.
My mother, a victim of my father.
So helpless to do anything...
while my father acts like he's the king.
Can my siblings or I stop
him from hitting my mother?
No one. Not me,
not my sister, nor my brother.
My mother is the only one,
who can stop him.
But she is too scared.
She would never dare...
to fight back,
or even make a little peep.
Oh, her wounds so deep.

Diana Lin

Happiness

Speak a word of cheerfulness
To boy, old man and neighbor.
Stretch a hand of helpfulness
To lighten others' labor.

Cast away all selfishness
Of prejudice, hatred, suspicion.
Kindle thoughts of kindliness
And free the soul from perdition.

Live by the light of friendliness
In deed and word of honor.
Take the way to happiness,
A way to God, our Succor.

Doris Snyder

Too Glad

Upon the wings of thought I flew,
To places only angles knew.
Bright they were,
Blinding bright
Just as the truth is
When you find it.
My mind reached out
To where my eyes could not see,
And I found
A smile
Just for me.

Jack Grimes

On B-Lay

I am learning
to rappel through life;
to trust someone else
to hold the rope
I have clutched so tightly
for so long
that my burned
and calloused hands
must be pried open;
To know that though I may
sustain a scrape
or two,
I will not be allowed
to plummet
and be broken
on the rocks below.

Helen J. LaVere

Two To One

My life began anew with you,
two.
Happiness, joy, sunshine,
sublime.
The rapture of your kiss,
bliss.
Wondrous love, so sweet,
complete.
Sharing, caring, love supreme,
a team.
Angels came, took you away,
to stay.
Suddenly clouds hid the sun,
one.
Your happy face, your smile, your song,
gone.
I stood alone and wept,
inept.

Dorene Winn

Untitled

God, why you chose to take her
we'll never understand
She was our rock to lean on
Mom, with the helping hands.

She was quite a person
her laughs, and jokes, and such
It's not hard to realize
Why she was loved so much.

Her grandkids all adored her
She laughed and teased them all,
In all their loving eyes
Grandma stood ten feet tall.

We prayed the cancer would go away
And leave her as she used to be,
The radiant star in all our lives
A loving Mom that all could see.

But God decided he needed her more
To help Dad in "Heavens" door,
There's one thing we can all attest,
That God takes the very best.

Dianna Sievers

Quest For Love

Love is caring, love is sharing
What a marvelous thing to find.
Love is patient, love is sparing,
Do not fall for love that's blind.

On this searching quest for love,
After all is said and done,
Say your vows to God above,
Then life for you has just begun!

Build your house with great care,
Remember what the past has taught.
Fill your home with love and prayer,
Show the world what love has brought.

Be gallant in your latter days,
Be thankful for the strength within
Have no sorrow for your ways,
As the twilight years close in.

Charles W. Murdock

Sands

A lone traveler
what she was once we do not know and
a graceful shell or a soft smooth stone
removed and drifting on her journey
through wind and water
landing on distant shores or
settling to the bottom of some sea
no one can ever know only
the soft supple sand and the
winds that whisper
over rolling oceans.

Denisse Paulino

Outside

Outside a world of wonder
Where you can hear a roll of thunder
Where the animals roam
Trying to find a new home

Outside a world of hope
Animals tugging on a rope
To find the end of this struggle
Hoping to stop this on going smuggle

Outside a world of dreams
Clean rivers and streams.
People trying to stop pollution
Everyone looking for a solution

Outside a world of despair
People destroying our air
If they only took pride
In what we were given outside.

Lisa Voit

Idaho

Meadows so green
Wildflowers too
Tall yellow pines
Water so blue
Red burly cattle
High flying hawks
Little creepy crawlers
Chipmunks that talk
Old miners cabins
Dusty old roads
Sweet smelling clover
Loud croaking toads
Salty old timers
Dashing young bucks
Swanky sleek sports cars
Huge logging trucks
Campers and cookouts
Fluffy white clouds
Idaho its summer!
You buzzing with crowds.

Janice M. Haney

Alone

Alone,
Yet not by myself.
Hidden by covers,
Yet not hidden.
Shadowed by darkness,
Yet not shadowed.
Surrounded by silence,
Yet I hear voices.
Loved by no one,
Yet I love others.
By myself,
Yet not alone.

Heather Whatley

"Poetry"

"When did poetry begin?
With the beat of the heart?
Was it not before that,
Before fauna?
Did it begin with the seed
Of the flora?

Was it not before that
With the sea and the earth
Or was it the moon,
Circling the earth?
Did it begin with the sun,
Or the planets or stars?
Was it not before that?

Poetry began
With the love of the Lord?

Harriet Pauline Hughes

Elaine At Thirteen

Your wheaten hair swings shoulder long,
Your eyes are soft and deep
Your growing frame is delicate
And sweet the words you speak.

It's early April in your life
And April's sun is tender.

There is in you a steely core
Beneath your gentleness
And oh, be careful of that strength
For April cannot last
And summer comes on fast.

Dorothy M. Wedemeyer

"Just A Look"

Just a look of your soft satin face,
Warms my heart
Just a look of your pale face as you die,
Kills my soul

I hold you in my arms
Caress your lifeless body
Only to hear from another
Our love for each other was so deep,
But never told

As it goes to black
I can't think
You've taken my soul
You've taken my heart
All I ask for is just a look...

Dennis LaPrade

Broken Hearts

I didn't think the day would come
when I would lose you.
I am on my own again and
I can't remember what to do.

I would never have imagined
you would go back to her,
Especially knowing the way
things always were.

I stuck by you through
thick and thin,
Always thinking how lucky
I was to win.

I thought we would always be together
without a worry or a care.
In a blink of an eye my world crumbled
without notice or even a glare.

Diane Vassey

494

The Ultimate Gift

Receiving gifts is a joy.
A box of chocolates for special friends;
A child overjoyed by a gift of a toy;
To communicate love, red roses with long stems;
A diamond ring for a marriage commitment;
A gift of a car for the graduate brings jubilation;
A gift to show appreciation at a social engagement;
People receive nice gifts with elation.

There is an ultimate gift absolutely free;
This gift is called salvation, and is for eternity.
The Bible tells about this and requires no work or fee;
Sadly, this gift is spurned by most of humanity;
But this wonderful gift can be all yours.
Jesus died on the cross for your sins; this just believe.
If you are sincere your future will be secure.
Come to God; accept His gift; salvation and hope you will receive.

James H. Colton

Genesis For Strength

The new earth shall have
A bright and hopeful Genesis, an ego
Creating brotherhood, enlightenment,
And the artistry of attainment.
Lasting verity in progress,
More beautiful victories for people,
Will carry the nations closer
To the golden mountain that is home.

The New Earth shall have a fervor for peace,
And the heavens in God's Glory will be
Commingled with the needs
Of the children of freedom.
Echoes of tribulation shall diminish
As the sons and heroes and saints
Of the old Earth orient through roots
Challenged by misfortune
And in kindness surviving adversity.

The purpose and the will of mankind
Shall grow in Virtue, Prudence, and Strength.

Jane Banks

Happy St. Valentine's Day!

Ah! Love!
Whispering above the clouds
Roaring through the ocean
Swaying to the music
Dancing between the trees;

Entering full force
With laughter and smiles
Wiping away the fears - the tears
  Of yesteryear;

Two people challenging tomorrow
Embracing today
With dreams, expectations, plans
Rising far above the storm of despair
  Silently!
Love! Transcends time
Two hearts enjoying treasured moments.
  Happy Valentine's Day!

Ethel (Hedy) P. Breunig

The Encounter

I remember the day when our eyes first met,
  a captivating moment I'll not soon forget.
My son on the ballfield, I would miss his swing,
  as hotdogs and coffees to the crowds I did sling.

The parents and coaches were rushed for some service,
  I hustled and hurried, yet they made me quite nervous.
They simply just wanted cold drinks and hot food,
  so I did what I could, even when they were rude.

The stand is quite small, you can barely turn 'round,
  "Hey, isn't that my son that's up on the mound?"
Now, who is this guy, his own coffee he's gettin'?
  Just walk right on in, mist'r... he's a coach, I'm bettin!

Well this guy, whoever he may be to Fishkill,
  it still doesn't mean he can self-serve at his will.
They do this too often, and they're sorely mistak'n,
  if they think they can come here and their donuts be tak'n.

So whoever he may be, his turn he can take,
  go stand with the crowds, at least for my sake.
And he bent over too, so nowhere could I move.
  Now this is too much, it's bordering on rude!

I stood there... I watched... he sure took his time.
  Now this guy is get'n on a nerve of mine.
I could tell he knew he was push'n his luck,
  as he turned to me look'n to hand me his buck.

Determined, I planned to stand firm on my ground,
  I took a deep breath as he slowly turned 'round.
I wanted to clearly, and boldly proclaim,
  that which was pointed at him—I took aim.

But before I could utter a word or a phrase,
  his eyes caught with mine, and upon them I gazed.
The crystal-like blue that was looking at me,
  was all that he needed to be set free.

My words were no longer on the tip of my tongue.
  My bold little song would no longer be sung.
His eyes went right through me... he knew it... he flaunted!
  Oh, what the heck, he could have anything he wanted!

Karen L. Russo

The Dual Language Of Flowers

Flowers, like music, speak a language all their own
  a fact, not fiction, that has become so well known

The crocus speaks of springtime; the dahlia bespeaks fall
  "tulips" demand discretion; the "iris" opens up to all

Violets speak of innocence; narcissus, mere "reflection"
  gardenias speak of romance; "forget-me-not," rejection

The lily speaks of purity; the rose speaks of love,
  the carnation, of constancy; the aster, stars above

Cape Jasmine speak of courtship; mums, the harvest moon
  the lily of the valley, foretells wedlock in June

The hyacinths reveal sweet perfume; poppies, World War I
  the dianthus speaks of fragrance; "foxglove," nature's pun

The language of the flowers, once a mystery
  has been revealed to us, through God's charity

Their language, although ever so silent, speaks loudly
  lyrics so well known

Which allows mankind dual enjoyment from all the
  flowers that are grown

Flowers, unlike music, speak with such a silent tongue
  a language of emotion, a music that's unsung

Loraine P. Wright

A Sailors Diary

There's a ship named "My love" with nowhere to go
A glorious and beautiful ship that has no shore

Lost in the waves of life and all its pain
In the currents of destiny with no true gain

One day came an island, I steered my course true
It was an uncharted island, I chose to name "You"

"You" was a beautiful, enchanting, unknown land
It was a portrait painted by God's own hand.

"My Love" came to rest on the shores of "You"
"My love" found a home and a purpose too

I will always love the island of you

Michael J. Cocherell - The Sailor

Little Reminders

Little reminders to keep us from feeling without,
A roadrunner crossing our path,
A sunflower to make us smile and brighten each day we celebrate life.
The beautiful singing of a bird on the day of a special planting of a tree.
The love that gives us the strength to shine when
We are called upon to do a job we are being held back from.
The reappearance of thins though to be lost,
Suddenly appearing in the most obvious places.
All these and many more not yet realize help ease our loss
Of a special love and give us the strength to live our lives.
So as we kiss the wind as "he" passes by,
We know the love we feel for those who are no longer
With us will never die!!

Hilda D. Loyola

Dying Rose

A rose sweet and fresh,
A rose so beautiful and until a poison, a poison
that can make a beautiful thing turn into a terror,
that is how I feel I don't want to live here any
more I am scared I am not scared of losing
you I have already lost you I have fallin' for
you and in one day that I have already
lost you. And I know there is no way
to even maybe get you back, others say that
it is love but I don't see it that way,
love is two different people feeling for each
other, but we are one, one with no other,
I thought I was so different and until I found
you, but then again you must leave and
are one is broken into two and we are so far
from each other, I am scared that this one
only goes one way, I am scared dying rose
and I will die until I get you back.

Rachael Mestas

My Child

As movement in my body grows, my heart
aflutter, I grasp Holy magnitude
of miracles. With labored birth, a part
of life unveiled, mother's pride exudes
each pore - each day. Sweet cries of helplessness,
willful need of mother's love; enchanting
enduring ties interconnect us, 'less
we separate, joyous growth, our singing,
our dancing celebrate our family.
As the years pass, youthful growth seemingly
un-noticed, yet, vivid reality ...
a young adult maturing vibrantly.
   Our separation, a necessity,
   though painful, lovingly I set you free.

Diana J. Weigel

"The Drum - Major"

M artin sits on the throne of martyrdom
A rticulate spokesman for the masses
R eflective beacon of twenty-two million
T ried, tested among all classes
I nspiration to evoke the shining truth
N ever will that spirit be extinguished
   (How long will it take?)
L ove, peace, justice cried the drum-major
U nite black and white or perish
T he moment of truth is fast approaching
H eed to the fact that the fate of one man
E ventually becomes the fate of all men
R eaching all race, color and ideology
   (How long will it take?)
K ing, Kennedy, Evers and the Forgotten Four
I nside our collective conscience we implore
N o more deeds of infamy can this nation endure
G one to the promised land, free at last!
   FREE AT LAST!!
(How long will it take?)

James Bynoe

Little Girls

   Twenty years ago, you came into my life.
A sweet little girl so delicate, so precious and nice.
You were daddy's little girl to have and to hold
But I knew one day I would have to let you go.
For into a woman you would grow.
Now as you walk through this world in your new life.
I wish you tenderness, good things, and everything nice.
Because today you become a wife.
I can't help think back to when you were a little girl.
Your eyes so big and bright and not a care in the world.
Some things will be easy, some things will be hard, some things
will be happy and some will be sad.
So if you ever need some one to talk to, come talk to me
because I'll always be your daddy.
There are all kinds of daughters through out this world
But to me Tammy you'll always be my little girl
No matter were life leads you to your so much
in my heart and your so much in my soul
A life time ain't enough to ever let you know
how I love you so.

Ed McGrady

Don't Wake Me If I'm Dreaming

A world of peace and violence free
A world of no pollution, that's where I want to be
People encouraging others and not put them down
Don't wake me if I'm dreaming
Kids staying in school and doing their best
Trying to impress their parents and all the rest
Living in a world that is free from drugs
Don't wake me if I'm dreaming
Parents being there for their children in need
During the times that are rough and the times they succeed
Believing in them 100 percent
Don't wake me if I'm dreaming
Living in a world of truth and reality
Not worrying about the murderers being set free
Living in a world that is loyal and true
Don't wake me if I'm dreaming
People not fearing of having no pay
Or being laid off the very next day
Nor worrying about where their next meal is
Please, Don't wake me if I'm dreaming.

Demetria Neal

The End Of Time

The end of time, is far away,
across eternity sea.
    We'll set sail, on loves sailboat,
together just you and me.
    The journey's long, sometimes it's rough,
to face the waves ahead.
    But as long as we're strong, and the boat doesn't rock,
the waters won't be our bed.
    And when it's calm, the wind's blowing sweet,
it's as peaceful as a dove.
    We'll lay down, and close our eyes,
on the way to heaven above.
    I love you, and you love me,
we're sailing on waters divine.
    All aboard, and set the course,
cause we're sailing...
    till the end of the time
        Harley Callihan

My God

My God has been so good to me
After reading these few lines you will see.
After leaving my God for forty years,
And my Mother and Father crying for me many tears.

Early one morning Jesus visited me,
And said it is time to come back to me you see.
He said I will forgive you of all your sins,
And if you will serve me that Great Place Heaven I'll let you in.

After losing my Wife,
Who I had been married to 44 years of my life.
Five months later I lost my Mother, my God knew about my sorrow,
And my God He would be there for me today and tomorrow.

My God didn't let me be too sad, `
Time has passed my God has been so good to me I am always glad.
I am happy as can be,
Oh my God has truly been good to me.

My God is blessing me every day,
And I truly know my God is walking with me every step of the way.
These words I have written is the reason why,
I will serve my God until I die.

    Edgar Harris

The Legacy

A legacy is something that remains
After time and life are spent;
The beautiful thing remembered,
Life's sweetest compliment.

A legacy gently emerges
As a precious gift we leave;
The better part of what we've been
And all that we believe.

A life should stand for something,
For in reality,
Only in remembrance
Can we have immortality.

I praise God for special people--
Some still here, and some are gone--
Who have touched my life with gentle love
And a way of life have shown.

As I meditate upon their lives,
Would that I, by imitation,
Could create a legacy worthy
For another's inspiration.

    Donna S. Rich

"If I Could Go Back"

If I could go back, oh the things that I would change
All the words of disconcert, and anything that brought you pain

If I could go back, oh the things that I would do
I would show you how much I love you, I'd help make all your dreams
    come true

This life, so sweet, with a span so short, if I could go back,
I'd do most of my bidding, most of it from my heart

If I could go back, I'd look beyond the simple things that divide
I'd replace them with God's true love, the only love that abides

If I could go back, this time I'd know how precious each memory to the heart
I'd cherish those moments from long ago, and add to them since I
now know how precious sweet you are to me
How all in God's plan, He placed you within my life, with your
heart in your hands

I cannot go back, so all that's left to do is remember all the ties
that bind us, and know that His word is true

Someday, we'll all be together by his grace, and on that day I'll
know again how it feels to behold your face.
    Janet E. Collins

Friendship

    A friendship never perfect,
although I wish it was.
    I used to think it had no flows,
but now I know it does.
    In a friendship there is laughter,
but just as much there's teas.
    And happiness, there is a lot,
to last throughout the years.
    Sometimes you are alone,
and you wish your friend is there.
    But when you are together,
There is magic in the air.
    Through the giggles and the boyfriends
and the braiding of the hair,
    There are so many moments,
in your memories to share.
    Although it may be severed,
with jealousy and lies,
    I hope our special friendship,
never, ever lies.
        Ilene Sitner

Your Love

The essence of your love, is like the depth of a mighty river
Always there, never ending, whispering softly,
In the moon light, as the night fades away forever.

Just the thought of you, keeps your love
Safely locked in my heart.
And the sounds of your voice, plays as incredible love song,
That captivated me from the very start.

The whole complexity of you is characterized
By the quality of your love,
And that my dear is more than the stars,
That shine in the heavens above.
    Ida M. Murchison

Ready To Feel Free

Am I ready to give back something I love so much
Am I ready to say goodbye and never
again feel your touch -
Am I ready to live my life without you
as a part -
Am I ready to be alone and feel nothing
in my heart -
The romantic storybook love I've dreamt
of through the years-
Only seems to be filling my eyes with
everlasting tears -
It's funny how the things you dream for
never come true -
but only lead your life in moments of
feeling hopeless and blue -
I'm so confused for what I think is
best for me -
If I didn't know any better, I'd dream
of feeling free.

Doreen Maurer

Way To Haven

How do I earn my way to heaven?
   Am I to believe in a lucky number seven?
Do I work only to receive praise?
   Out of greed-
Or do I help others really in need?
   Do I pray for sinners-
Or only the winners?
   Do I share my money-
Because I love a buddy?
   Or am I so greedy-
That I refuse to help the needy?
   I can't buy my way to heaven-
I must sacrifice - time, energy and money.
   Stay away from the deadly seven-
SINS, that is, that keep me farther from heaven.

Jane M. Nowicki

Petals Yellows

Amigo Mio, blue stem, have petals yellows, and colorfulness buds,
Amigo Mio, looking at the petals roses, with the blue stem, it is a rainbows,
Amigo Mio, you are to me, splendor of rainbows, in my life,
Amigo Mio, because we do have, in our caragines, petals yellows,
Amigo Mio, the blue stem, have the color of yours eye, when you look at me,
Amigo Mio, the colorfulness buds, are the roots, of ours Buenos Amores,
Amigo Mio, petals yellows, can be, our shining stars, in us,
Amigo Mio, petals yellows, buds, and the blue stem, are ours inwardness,
Amigo Mio, because we are, to each others, in our lives, petals yellows!

Dolores Maria Bolivar-Brauet

Vacation At Grandma's

My grandchildren are coming; ages ten, seven, four and two,
And I know it's going to be a lot of work
For a couple of weeks around the clock.
But Oh, the joy and memories of being with you!

I enjoy the laughter and funny things you say,
Even on that occasional off day,
When an "I'm sorry grandma; I love you",
Showing me what a good little heart will do!

You've endured grandma's sweetly repeated rules,
Fun in the pool, instant pictures, and special snacks too.
Sadly it's time to pack your things, as I do with this prayer,
King of Kings hold them close; in your most precious care.

Isabel Burton

Jerry, The Dog

A cute little hound dog, without pedigree,
And labeled a mongrel, by others, - not me!
A soft ball of cotton with spots that were black,
Like mixed salt and pepper all over his back.

He slept on the doorstep and with his nose high,
He'd wail like a siren at trains whistling by,
The porch was his home place, no carpet his bed
"outside", would yell mother, for oh how he shed!

A steak treat was seldom, and dog bones were few,
His meals were composed of a corn pone or two
He wood a she-mongrel, the love bug soon bit her,
It's said that he fathered her fabulous litter!

And as fate would have it, we soon lost this pet,
Run down on the highway! I think of it yet,
I'll bet in dog heaven, where Jerry must be,
He's chewing on dog bones and steaks happily.

Like me, he is waiting for that great day when,
In God's house, we'll all be a family again
In my wheel of friendship, a permanent cog,
Is fastened securely by, Jerry, the dog!

Hazel Burnworth

A Toddler's Joy

He helps his dad in the garden
And loves to water and pull weeds at times.
But the most fun of all is eating a tomato,
When he pulls it from the vines.
Carrots and apples are quite a treat
Because his horses eat them he thinks they're neat,
Dad's tractor he loves when he sits beside him,
But it's better when he sits on his lap.
Then he can turn the wheel and pretend he's driving
And wave his hand at "Pap".
Dad has a wagon he hooks on the tractor and fills with hay,
So when Colby's little friends come over,
They can jump in and play.
It's exciting to climb up thirty cement steps
To the garage and yell "Dad I'm comin'."
The sounds of the hammers and drills
Are music to his ears and he comes "runnin'."

Dorothy R. Maxwell

Life's Clock

The Clock of Life is wound but once,
   and no man has the power
To tell just where the hands will stop,
   at late or early hour.
To lose one's wealth is bad indeed
   to lose one's health is more
To lose one's soul is the greatest loss,
   that no man can restore.
Today is our own,
   to live, to love, to toil at will.
Place no faith in tomorrow,
   for the Clock of Life may then be still.

Don Walker

"Lights"

My eyes are the "Lights" of my soul.
I have many "Lights" in my reach for a goal.
One had many "lights" that are like binds.
Be sure that I am aware of the "Lights" of my mind.
You only have to reach out for the "Lights".
Then you will have many nights of "Lights."

Betty J. Winters

Walking With Me

I look into the sky above,
and see your face carved in with love.

As I stare into the night so clear,
I feel you in my heart, so near.

You're far away, yet that's OK,
because I sense your presence beside me today.

You were the greatest, this I know.
I love you Poppy, I hate to see you go.

You have gone on now to a better place,
with love, and peace, and a smiling face.

You were so lovable, kind and bright.
When you were around there was never a fight.

You were always there for me day in and day out,
so honest, and loyal, like a little Boy Scout.

I'll miss your hugs and that special pat.
The important thing to remember is that:

In the sky or in the sea,
I know that you're there, walking with me.

Christina Stephens

Mindful Anxiety

When I am old I shall carry a cane,
And Sit at a bus stop to pass the time away,
My crumpled old hat under my arm
A battered newspaper held in front of
My bifocals.

The wind shall tear unmercifully at my unsheltered head
My eyes squinting in the afternoon sun.
Behind my eyes shall rest old memories,
My hands effortlessly trying to retrieve them,
Through my cluttered mind.

Jason Rodriguez

My Helper

To wake each morning with a prayer in your heart,
And speak to your Lord before this day starts,
Sets the tone of peace for this troubled land,
For you know that God is holding your hand,
To see you through this day he has made,
And help with whatever you face along the way,
He is always there and is ready to share,
Your sorrow, your happiness, your joy and your cares,
To look about and see the sun,
To know in our heart the battle is won,
Oh how my soul burst with great joy,
Because of the birth of that Baby Boy.

Doris S. Campbell

Spring

Winter would not let go
and spring struggled
toward its destiny;
The birds, muting
their opening songs,
returned not for curtain calls,
but were silent...
And the trees continued to shiver
through the cool days and nights,
as the warm glimmer of sporadic sunlight
exposed a little more
of their extremities each day,
While those in flower went unnoticed
on the cool unlit stage.

Harry L. Nesbit

Christian Palm

As I travel down life's highway
and the cars go whizzing by
will anyone notice if I have a
smile on my face or a tear drop in my eye
No one is caring as I wend my weary way
everyone is in a hurry for today is just for today
Now as I travel down that long
last road to heaven will the cars
Go whizzing buy or will there be
no one to see me with a smile on my
face or a tear drop in my eye

Earl R. Allan

A Mother's Lament

As the night settles like a soft blanket,
and the moon and stars vie for recognition,
I gaze down upon your miniature form, and sigh...
Do not grow up too quickly, my sweet,
I still need to hear your giggles echoing
down the hallways of my heart before I grow too old.
And do not leave my side too soon,
for your little hand in mine
needs to keep you close to me but for as long as I can.
Let destiny not rush you from the sanctity of my arms
for life harbors unexpected surprises and vexations
but my love for you promises a haven of rainbows and fairytales.
Do not shed your innocence too quickly, little one,
as you have much time to pursue your dreams
while I plead with time...for time,
And before your grown-up eyes tell me,
"Mama, it is time for me to leave you".

Henriette M. Liebowitz

The Girl In The Glass

When you get what you want in your struggle for self
and the world makes you queen for a day
Last go to the mirror and look at yourself
And see what that girl has to say.
For it isn't your father nor mother or spouse
Whose judgement upon you must pass
For the person whose judgement counts most in your life
Is the girl staring back from the glass.
She's the one you must please never mind all the rest
For she's with you clear up to the end
But you know you have passed the most difficult test
If the girl staring back is your friend.
You may be BoPeep and find all your sheep
And think you're one of a kind
But the girl in the glass thinks you're only a creep
If you can't stare her straight in the eye
You can fool the whole world in your pathway of years
And get pats on the back as you pass
Yet your final reward will be heartache and tears
If you're cheated the girl in the glass.

Jaime Kronick

My Heart

My heart is way behind my skin
And there it lays deep within
My heart is way behind my rib
And there it lays like a baby in a crib
My heart keeps going pump after pump
If you listen closely you can hear a thump
My heart decides things from good or bad
And to help people when they are sad
My heart expresses the things that I say
And that's how it helps me in a special way
My heart also expresses the way that I feel
That's how I know it is actually real

Heather Benevides

499

To Know Me

Look deeply through my eyes you will see
and understand me
My beauty is from within, not without
Go beyond this shell, man's outward glow
Go deep, deep within my soul, were God's
love flow
That's right go there, I want you to
I want you to know who I am, where I am, and where
I plan to go
Don't be afraid it won't hurt a bit
what you will find is worth the trip
Love, passion, and true friendship is waiting there for you to find
Things that will last beyond this lifetime

Ida M. Gray

Love

Love is a word so loudly unspoken,
And yet heard for miles around.
A wonderful emotion that is never to be broken,
And a wonderful feeling never put down.

A feeling of happiness and of joy,
From the purest part of your heart.
Emotions learned from girls and boys,
From cupids bow, a little dart.

Everyone has this one feeling,
For it is given to them in its purest form.
Some people might express it while kneeling,
And some people express it while in morn,

Love is the only feeling,
that should ever be conquered.
It is a feeling with great appeal,
that one can lead their way to conquest.

With Love winning the battle,
conquest is as close as tomorrow.
And love is the only battle,
fought with our sorrow.

Michael Garza

The Schoolyard

Thunder roars in deafened souls as cruelty bears its staff.
Anguish lurks in human bowls and all the children laugh.

They point and chide and cackle so, you can't escape, don't run!
They torture you 'cause they all know that you're the different one.

No matter how, nor when, nor where, no matter what you do,
it will not stop them never, ever just because it's you.

You don't fit in or even try, "My God, you're such a geek!!"
You will not please them, never, why?
Because to them you're weak.

You're poor and worthless, hopeless, dumb,
you're everything they're not.
They don't respect you, never, none,
they'll crush you flat, that's what.

I tell you hatred sears my heart as sorrow sets them free.
Them that hurt me, made their mark and a recluse out of me.

Jason Sean Carnley

Me And My Monologue

ME and my monologue
are as close as can be.
Tell each other everything.
My monologue and ME.

Me and my monologue.
We laugh together and cry.
Try to help solve our problems
and figure out the why.

ME and my monologue.
With others we can't honestly converse,
but we have one another so never get lonely.
We share secrets, clothes and even a purse.

When friends and family are far away
and I get mad at my spouse whom I adore,
I always have my monologue.
Who could ask for anything more?!

Denise Sternberg

Rainbow After The Storm

Tonight, the rain is running down my window
as I look out these prison walls.
I can't run to you anymore, you're gone and
so am I now. It's funny how I always found peace at
your graveside, in the thunderstorms violent passing.
So different from that of a human...our passing is
often quiet. In silence I uttered not a sound to you.
Yet as I sat close to your stone, I felt as though I were
wrapped in the warmth of your arms.
You spoke not a word to me, yet I found comfort there.
The raindrops are my fears for you, the lightning — my love,
and the thunder - my anger that you are gone.
No, I cannot run to you anymore, Grandpa.
But whenever it rains I can still crawl into your arms
and feel your comfort...even in this place.
Because you are still alive to me
Forever etched in my heart.
You're more than a memory...
You're the Rainbow after the storm.

Donna Sullivan

My Angel

An Angel rides with me each day
As I travel along life's way;
She holds me close and loves me so
Protects me from my head to my toe.

When I'm sick and fever is high,
She nurtures and caresses me with
   a lovely sigh
Sings me a lullaby; tells me a
   story true;
Smiles down at me from out of
   the blue.

My angel is here beside me now;
She gently strokes my fevered brow.
She brushes my cheek with her gossamer wing
Taking from my life every hurt and every sting.

God bless me and my angel each day of my life-
Let me live it for thee - for thy sacrifice,
Giving thy son that I might live freely
   and always for thee.
I pray, humbly, on bended knee.

Helen H. Cox

Tears

The tears rolled down my face.
As I watched that boy vanish into space.
I hope he knew I loved him.
I really hope he did.
But I always felt he kept something hid.
We used to talk and laugh together.
Now all I do is pray forever.
These tears I cry are for years that went by.
All the years we shared together.
Now they've all blown
Away like a feather.
I've lost a brother, I've lost a friend.
I think my life is going to end.
I cry out to you but you seem not to hear.
Just to let you know
these tears I cry are for you dear.

Heather Aver

The Mill

Listen! Hear the murmur of the mill?
As it changes logs to lumber,
All the days it's never still,
As huge saws cut into sawlogs,
Making boards both thick and thin,
As it labors daily toiling,
Its full allotment to win.
Look! See the steam flow from the chimneys?
Covering all the heavens above,
With the beauty of the evening,
To the cooing of the dove.
Brilliant colors clothe the sky ward,
Silently they drift away,
As if called by some lone fairy,
"Won't you please come out to play?"

Edna Rush

The Embrace

Miles tick by
  As the dream unfolds.
Landscapes offer the new beauty:
  the corner,
   the crest,
    the surprise.

This new beauty I enter with all of me...
The single dimension,
  the weak counterfeit
  no longer applies.
The West receives me,
  it brings me close
  to its wild beating heart...
With rock-firm voices,
  the West assures me...
Its beauty will be mine forever!

Edward D. Blandy

Life Is A Breeze

Mystic life—sometimes gentle, sometimes harsh,
As the wind blows.
The wise have pondered, others wondered,
But no one knows
Where the wind goes when it seems to end,
Nor if death ends life....
Or lets it begin.

Clayton A. Johnson

"Queen of the Stems"

Dear Rose, so delightful in the morn
as you unravel your pedals
so beautifully you adorn
Slowly you cast away the tears of the night
glistening the color of wine
so rich, so bright

Each day a new freshness, worth more than a glance
captivating is your fragrance
I wish to enhance

I fear to hold you, for I know
to protect your beauty
your thorns will always show

Knowing my respect for you, and seeing it clear
perhaps my loving touch will never feel
the prick of your spears

Rest for the night, my Queen of the Stems
I'll return again tomorrow
for with you, my time, I wish to spend

Howard P. Butterstein

Love Is Thicker Than Water

My love for you is like a river that comes into being
At first it starts out slowly developing over time
It starts off as a small stream - beating a path into
Unknown territory
It separates itself into many branches that develop
Lives of their own - eventually rejoining to become a
Pulsating rush
Like a river it flows and bring life where there was
None before
It grows stronger and stronger as the days go by and
Builds into an unspoken fury
It rushes forward in a crescendo and tumbles over like a
Never ending waterfall that drowns the senses in a
Bottomless pool

Janet Spevak

Painful Love

Looking back at all that happened, a tear comes to my eye.
At the beginning I was scared, and yet you made me try.
I walked across the bridge of trust to the land of endless pain.
And I asked myself how I allowed you to lead me here again.
You promised me over and over again as you took me by the hand.
But once again you've brought me back to this now familiar land.
I now know that I listen to you because of your threatening smile.
But I couldn't help myself as I stared in the eyes I hadn't seen in awhile.
Why, I ask, do you do this to me, you must hate me a lot.
I don't know you say, I guess cause I loved you,
or at least that's what I thought.
Every time you talk to me, I cling to every word you say.
But I feel that I mean nothing to you as again you push me away.
That's it, I say, I'm stopping this right now,
you can't do this to me anymore.
I'm not worried, you say, you'll come back to me,
just like you did before.

Jaclyn Kluis

Innocence

Like two children
  in a millennium aged, sandstone cradle,
Hushed to silence
  by a voiceless, cascading spring waterfall,
Blanketed into reverence
  beneath an uninterrupted, blue-pacific sky,
Soothed beyond comfort
  during sun soaked, innocent kisses,
A man and a woman are caressed by mother nature's hand.

James Michael Walker

Reasons

God has his reasons for everything in life.
Babies that have gone on and you can't bear strife.
Mothers that die so young it seems I feel there's a reason,
maybe there's an everlasting dream.
People that have gone on and rest for life.
They live eternally and try to help us through our night.
God has a reasons for the things he does.
Which does not kill us, makes us stronger,
for those feelings you don't deserve.
For all the deaths, every minute of everyday
there has to be a reason.
It will puzzle us till it comes our way.
So don't be afraid of his loving hand.
God has a reasons he made us all his fans.

Carrie Nichols

Beloved

Beloved, Beloved, and Beloved,
Beloved, is in my heart, feelings, and sentiments,
Beloved, is my inspirational poems, about you,
Beloved, is in my spanish browns eyes, with the look of tenderness.
Beloved, is need your hand, because you are worth to me,
Beloved, is I knew, I will not desert you, when you do need me.
Beloved, because I have found special treasure in you.
Beloved, stormy enough, not to hurt you, because of my sensitiveness,
Beloved, reaching quietness to you, in tune with patience.
Beloved, we are beautiful, blends, providentials, by the love of our Lord!

Dolores M. Bolivar

Wild Places

Your eyes are wild places
Blue pools -
Where a savage hunter may rest
The thought ranging being though eyes
violate my heart -
and put my soul to the test

I long to here your breath -
In wanton heaves upon my ear
To hold you safe close and warm -
To push away your fear

Your voice I find soothing like
A cool Breeze on a hot summers day
So when I give those blue pools my intense gaze
Please remember that -
I cannot look away

Edward M. Mason

Gone But Not Forgotten

The years go by and life goes on,
But you are sorely missed,
If not for kind words and tender endearments,
But for your hugs and sweet kiss,
You were the glue, your love the bond,
That held our family together,
But like roses without water,
Our family begins to whither,
Further apart and far away,
Our family begins to drift,
We need the memory of your love,
To give our family a lift,
Now when I feel depressed,
And I'm having a miserable day,
All I need is some time alone,
Cause you are but a thought away.

Jahmal Bethel

Seek And Go Hide

"Ready or not", you start the advance,
Bridled by faith, spurred by chance.
But the adventure ends, all too soon,
When fantasy melts into reality's doom.
You'll find them all in their usual places,
Covered only in charm and painted faces.

Retreat at once, to that familiar place,
Picked by prudence and shrouded by grace.
Curiously, they'll stand and stare,
Wondering if you're really there.
But look at length, they will not dare.
How foolish they'd be, admitting they care.

It's a cat - mouse syndrome, an instinctual quest,
From the holy grail, to the pirate's chest.
But who's the hero, the one who finds,
Uncovers deceit and exposes the crimes?
Or is he that one, who chooses to hide,
Keeps truth pure, unblemished with pride?

The name of the game changes with time,
As wisdom descends the uphill climb.

Heidi D. Ignazio

Love Always

I might not have just enough wit,
but the older we grow, the more we know,
even if it is, only bit fly bit.
If you could put a number on all the stars
in the sky,
you cold begin to know how much I love you,
so don't let this love pass you by.
Right now you may be forlorn,
just as if a daughter died; all you could is mourn.
Many great heroes of the past said,
"Don't let it bring you down!"
But it might bring you down just as the world
goes around.
Then, just as we all begin to understand,
sometimes the power seeps out of our hands.
Sometimes things happen and you wonder, "why does
this happen to me?"
There will come a time when we are all set free.

Jaime Perkins

The Dali Exhibit

The loud whispers turn to unbearable
chatters as our tour group tracks
to another painting. Ssshh.
This one of dark seduction:
"Autumn Cannibalism"-
The tour guide says, the man plunging with his knife,
and taking a bite out of his nearest companion,
is Dali. The woman is his wife."

We move on.
"Metamorphosis"-
She says, "the pool of water exhibits self love,
sexual desires, devouring love,"
the crutch, the melting watch, the woman.
I walk out with
"The Persistence of Memory."

I glance at the beggar on the street
and the small school children arguing,
and the couple kissing.

Allison Siegel

Rivers Of Gold

You would say a love so rich and sweet
could not belong to a mortal.
Yet yours with mine brings us to a portal,
a gateway to a life
of happiness and sweet sublime.
A warm inner peace knowing you are mine.
If I never knew bliss I surely know now,
this fortune of beauty, this angel I have found.
I look no further than your golden eyes,
with this I confirm,
you are truly a prize.
A radiating love from you I know,
a love unequaled by a golden rivers flow.
... Rivers of Gold flow to the sunset,
always a reminder of the girl I met.

John Eric Broderick

The Wind Beneath My Wings

February 20th is here, now you're 90 years old!
Crowned with gossamer hair and a heart of gold.
Your sky blue eyes still twinkle like stars,
And your cherub-like face beams from afar.

A lap like a cloud, so soft and mild, to sit on a pie or comfort a child.
Your whole life you have given to others, a shining example of a wife
    and mother.

Never an unkind word has crossed your lips.
Although I've seen you sneak a few licorice nips.
All your days have been spent working hard,
With an occasional break for tea or for cards.

Tune in those tigers while you iron and mend,
Or catch up on gardening or notes to send.
I've often marvelled how you take life in stride.
No matter what the "story" your arms are open wide.

You're quick to forgive and have patience divine.
And each passing year you get better like wine.
I think sometimes you're an angel in disguise;
Always so gentle, so meek, and so wise.

I can't hum, even whistle or sing, but if I could...
It would be, "You're the Wind Beneath My Wings."

Becky Wadenstierna

Phoenix

Phoenix of passion, phoenix of my
desire, I am a math to your flame,
The fire you burn call my name,
My heart races with a wild fury
at a touch, my spirit searches with
an abandon lust
Your eyes a reflection of the
storms within, they beckon my soul
To the depths of the chains you keep me in
Unbridled is your passion and
untamed is your heart, forever
more my desire to never be apart
In the mist of my dreams the
phoenix soars the fires of renewal
blazing from the floor an
eternity awaits to be fulfilled
if destiny so chooses this he God's will.

K. Legault

A Prayer For Peace

Why murder thou with savage roar,
Destroying life that was just born,
Without respect for human rights,
In this short span of earthly life?

Why kill the dreams of new babes born,
Fomenting hate in warlike games,
Instead of nurturing these smiles,
As kissing petals of a dream,
That lives through time in limpid shores,
And calls for men to halt all wars?
Why can't you learn that God gives peace,
To live with love among ourselves,
And preach the pilgrim song of love,
While helping people in distress,
Opposing hate in every way,
And pointing men the upward way?

The time will come when wars will cease,
And martyrs who had died for peace,
Will mark the route of liberty,
And peace on earth will come, amen.

Henry Joshua Nicol

Flower

You were sitting in your field, the other flowers had
died and peeled,
But the sun chose you to love, and you grow from the
strength he sends from up above.
He shines on your petals, and he may bring you rain,
but do not fear, you are not to restrain.
He helps you become beautiful while shining so bright,
he gives you what you need to live your life.
But one day he will be gone, and he may not return, and
you're left alone with your feelings for him that burn.
Even if he's gone, you will always be, the most
beautiful flower I have ever seen.

Jamie Bull

The Profundity Of The Red Pen

If you tend to overuse red,
Don't forget what experts have said;
Red means stop, green means go;
Research proved this statement so.

Red pens are tired and weary;
They need vacation and rest!
For many years they have marked errors
On countless students' papers and tests.

If your red pens could talk,
They would probably say,
We'd like to be used in some positive way,
Especially at Christmas and St. Valentine's Day.

There are many more colors from which to choose,
This might help alleviate test blues;
Students will appreciate papers not marked in red
That could cause them to wonder if your finger bled.

Commitment to writing is proclaimed by us all;
Let's eliminate our use of red pens and recall
There are many more colors from which to choose.
Let's proclaim to our students the good news!

Harriett Smitherman Harris

Drifting

Sometimes I feel like a leaf blowing in the wind
Don't know where I'm going, don't know where I've been.
But I feel so happy just to know I'm free.
So it really doesn't matter where the wind is taking me.

Sometimes I'm in the water just swimming round and round.
And when I come to shore I'm blowing on the ground.
Then suddenly the wind well blow and raise me to the sky.
Now I know what a bird feels flying oh so high.

Maybe blowing in the winds is what life is all about.
It has its ups and downs, and its ins and outs.
And maybe to be happy you have to float along.
So that someday you'll find the place where you belong.

Donna M. McGinn

A White Dream

They beat me all the way down,
Down, down to the cement ground.
I was seeing visions,
About making decisions.
Bam! Bam! Up against my head,
I felt nothing, I thought I dead.
My heart really began to beat,
As I decided to try and get to my feet.
After I saw that they were white,
Somewhere out of me there arose such a fight.
All of a sudden I began to scream.
I woke up sweating, it was only a dream.

LaTanya Mack

Morning Glory

The house is so dark, as I walk through the stillness.
Down the hall to the kitchen for more coffee I go.
Husband and children, sound asleep in their rooms.
Again I must ask, "Why has Thou blessed me so?"

My life's cup runneth over! As I ponder His goodness
My grateful heart swells, so that I catch my breath.
For the One Who has bought me, paid my sin debt in full.
Crucified, so that I might have life through His death.

The love of my husband, our cherished small children.
God's grace in my life — how is there room for more?
And yet, we are told, for the ones who believe
Our minds can't envision what for us lies in store.

Though the journey be long, and at times we'll grow weary
As the enemy seeks to turn us the opposite way,
Let's not despair, Christ is with us! He will lead, and if we follow,
Through the narrow gate He will take us, and from His path we will not stray.

On that glorious morning, those who have gone on before us
Will rise from their sleep to meet the Lord in the air.
Then we who are living will transform in a twinkling
To dwell in that place He has gone to prepare.

Edie Root

Reality

Sometimes my mind runs, to a place where it can hide.
From a harsh reality that make me cry inside,
To a place, a place where there is no hurt or pain.
Where there is no such thing as being ashamed.
And I was so happy there until the wind came,
and blew back, like it blows the rain,
Back to my reality where I am so cold.
It's a place where I must grow old, and die.
And it's sad because it's my life,
But maybe one day the wind will die
If I can scream loud enough where it can hear my cry.
Then maybe it will feel my pain, and
not carry to back to the nightmare, from which I came...

Hakima Mitchell

Dreams

Dreams are like a river flowing through the night
Drifting in many directions never reaching the light

They may have more than one meaning
But they are only meant for one to know
Opening doors to emotions
Sometimes letting inhibitions go

Sometimes people are afraid to close their eyes at night in fear
    of what they might see
They do not wish to meet their fears
But only drift out to sea

Dreams are often the keys people need to open the doors to
    future goals
Reorganizing past thoughts looking deep into their souls

April Hall

Thermo Dynamic

Thermo Dynamic, our galactic fuzz,
Enforces three laws—that's what he does.
Although the universe is his beat,
He'll never suffer a cop's flat feet.

Thermo, you see, rides one awesome wheel,
A Carnot cycle using gas ideal.
With the lowest temp set at zero K,
It turns all heat into work right away.

Thermo on duty provides relief—
Saves us from worry about a joule thief.
He guards energy without gain or loss.
Certainly is a great calorie boss.

For the process that is reversible,
He makes entropy change impossible.
But for one with a spontaneous trend,
He insists on an increase at the end.

For a crystal that is pure and perfect,
As cold as one might ever project,
Thermo Dynamic, our super hero,
Assigns entropy a big fat zero.

Edward W. Anacker

Opportunity For Love

Opportunity for love, oh where have you gone?
    evaporated
A trail of smoke I try to grasp that
    slides through my fingers.

Opportunity for love, oh where have you gone?
Were you ever there or were you imagined?
Your smile so playful, your eyes so
    teasing, inquisitive, behind them hiding
true feelings I only catch a flicker of;
there one moment then the wall.
I wish I could touch your heart
    show you real joy, experience the
thrill people dream of.

Opportunity for love, oh where have you gone?
    I fear my time has passed; my time has passed.
With every breath in me
    my essence, my whole being, I love you,
Run, run, keep running,
    my opportunity for love.

Janie M. Moore

A Single Point Of Light

Life always had a dark side to it.
Fed by loneliness, sadness, and despair.
Everyone has found themselves at one time surrounded by this darkness.
So I have a little advice, when you find yourself here.
This place has a flow.
There is a single faint point of light, that will never disappear.
That light is called hope.
So just close your eyes, and look into your heart, into your soul.
Think about the people that love you. That light starts to grow.
Think about the man that is a part of you now.
He lives there, in your heart. Just like you live in his.
Think about how much he loves you and cares for you.
Think about the wonderful family and life you will have together.
That light has grown so very bright. You feel it warming you.
It's a familiar warmth. It reminds you of the times you're in his arms,
nestled next to his heart.
The feeling of security, caring, and most of all LOVE.
So now that the darkness has gone.
A wish can come true. So concentrate on the love you feel inside.
Open your eyes, and he'll be there, waiting to love you.

Jarred M. Nelson

Spring In My Gait

Have a spring in my gait, note a lift in my stride
Feel a smile on my face and a sense of delight
Feel so good to be living, smell the fresh morning air
Mixed with seasonal flowers and I know that I care
There is love in my thinking
I am lucky, for sure
Just to live in this country
Have so much—feel secure
With a four-pack-of children and my health, and a home
All my tools and my hobbies
And not being alone
But all this good feeling would never survive
It is wasn't for grandkids and their granny, my wife
They give me the kisses that make me feel great
No wonder I have such a spring in my gait!

Henk G. Zoll

Emotions Of Remembrance

Those who are close and dear in our hearts,
Fill our souls with peace.
A longing fulfilled,
In which we shall keep.
Never forgotten,
Forever loved,
We reach within ourselves,
To embrace those we've loved.
Emptiness replaced by memories,
Pulled into the present,
Representing all we have truly felt.
Our emotions of remembrance,
Fulfill the void of loss.

Michelle Bailey

Untitled

Where you are, I long to be, I sense your presence constantly...
I see your handsome, loving face smiling back at me,
I feel your strong and caring arms caress me tenderly,
I smell your sweet aroma - it lingers in the air,
I hear your deep and dreamy voice and wish that you were here...

Donna E. Marquez

"May"

'Tis May, and spring is here indeed
for everyone's carrying a package of seed.
The gardens have all been plowed and dragged,
and each row is furrowed, planted and tagged.
The lawns stretch out like carpets of green,
and the snow drop and crocus is plain to be seen.
The Hyacinth and Narcissus are budding too,
and the Tulips will soon burst into view.
The trees are decorated with leaves of lace,
and the birds have found their favorite place,
to build their nest and sing their song,
and bring their music all day long.
Yes, it's spring and there's much to do,
but there's lots of pleasure in doing it too.
For Mother Earth sticks on each hand
and we come in with an early tan.
We begin to feel weary, it's been a big day,
as we clean our tools and put them away.
And now with this beauty stretching ahead,
we find that winter is forgotten and dead.

Violet Hall

Dedication Blu

Together as one, should we join in hands?
Forever we have searched across this land.
We reach out for Love to be shared by two.
We reach out for Love, Dedication Blu.
Love has followed us here-n-near-n-far.
Love under the sun, Love under the Stars.
Memories of the years, of tears, of tears,
Memories spread think-n-thin through the years.
So forgive me if I have been unkind.
Today our Love has stood the test of time.
Each time we look for the right words to say.
Each time we look-n-just what do we see?
Each time we look for just who we must be.
Each time we find our way back, tell me why?
Love rings us together again-n-again.
Love, a lasting treasure, so deep within.
Together always, I will Love you.
Together forever, under the sun.
Together, let us join in hands as one.

Theresa Briggs Johnson

The Dreams Of A Heart, Mind, And Soul

Sometimes I wish I was far away;
from all the commotion and hassle of everyday life.
Sometimes I wish a miracle would happen; to save something I love.
Sometimes I wish that it would rain,
Sometimes that the sun would just come out.
Sometimes what you wish are dreams, and sometimes what you wish
are simply far off hopes, just waiting to come true.
But, if you wish a dream for long enough...
with all your heart and soul...even miracles can happen.
A wish in a dream can be anything you want it to be...
it has only one requirement.
And that is, that you breathe what you believe,
and it flows through the veins that keep your heart alive.
You need to think what you believe and make decisions over
and through that thought.
Your soul is throughout your body, it never stays in one place.
That is why, when you die, your soul lives on for eternity.
Your spirit can die with you or live on...
it depends on how you feel inside,
and how strong your feelings are for what you truly believe in.

Jacqueline M. Dexter

505

Tears

Everyone cries;
    From the clouds in the sky
To the people passing by.

Do you sometimes bend your head
    and sigh?
And then wonder why that tear is
    falling from your eye?

A tear, a little piece of water
    That can cause so much hurt.
Just like too much can do to the Earth.

Cry a little, cry a lot.
When you open your eyes, what do you see?
A blur, a blur that cause you to stare.
But when the picture clears, who's there?
The one who cares, the one who will be
    there to catch your next tear.

Donique Trotter

The Wandering Son

The sun came up ore the edge of the earth, another day's been given birth
The animals frolic about in mirth, just at the break of day.
The air is pure with sweet perfume, from the flowers awakened and
    now in bloom.
They sensed the day and expelled the gloom, of another night gone by.

All nature is singing in Palmer Park, listen to the song of the bluebird and lark
blackbird and sparrow, red bird; yet hark, to the morning dove far
away. Along the bridle path there's need for timid souls to take
heed of the fast approach of a galloping steed, as a rider flashes by.

Aye that's the way it used to be when my mother and I sat neath the
    old oak tree.
But then the war and I went to sea, the big conflict had begun.

Now the sun comes up ore the crest of a wave, a Bosun's call, I'm just a slave
Please sweet Jesus, make be brave for the land I love so deep.

Four years have passed and now I'm back in my old room in our little
    shack and
to a mother who's love never lacked, a place for her wandering son.

George Smith

Behind The Mind

The hourglass flips to yet another year,
Grains of memories sliding through,
Each I hug with unconditional love,
They embrace me in the depths of sorrow.
As dreams and walls crumble at my feet,
I reach inside and they kiss my tears away.

Their love for me is also forever.
Never betray or disillusion.
No false smiles or secret desires.
How can the truth lie?
Rocking the chair again brings,
Oceans flooding to me with a smile.

When people turn their backs,
They can take a lot, but not everything.
My eyes will well with tears again,
Not for long, I have a defense.
Way behind my mind,
There lies my best friends.

Heather Weidner

Grandma's Farm (A Remembrance Of The Past)

Grandma's in the kitchen making fresh blueberry pie.
Grandpa's on a tractor bailing hay in the fields.
Uncle Bill's loading hay in a wagon pulled by oven.
Uncle Joe's in the garage trying to fit the old Chevy.
Esther's (Mom's) in the barn feeding a month old calf.
Aunt Dot's in the kitchen canning bread and butter pickles.
Aunt Millie's at the table copying Grandma's old recipes.
Aunt Mildred's in the hen house gathering the eggs
Billy's (Dad's) at the grinding wheel sharpening tools for the farm.

Linda's on the front porch snapping beans for supper.
Carol's gathering raspberries at the end of the driveway.
David and Patrick are playing marbles by the barn.
Kenny's splitting wood for Grandpa out by the wood shed.
Diana's in the backyard picking wild roses by the stream.
Betty's in the rocking chair playing with an old saw dust doll.
Gloria's feeding carrots to the new bunnies in the pen.
Susan and Robin stop by the say hello on their way to the camp.
A neighbor stops to buy fresh eggs and maple syrup.

At Grandma's farm we all gathered to share a century of love.
Aunts, uncles, cousins, friends and neighbors, we all gathered.

Diana Charest LeBlanc

I Loved You...

I loved you like a rocket in flight
hard, forceful, with nothing to stop us in our path
and all around us was the freedom of space

I loved you like a dolphin diving through the water in rhythm and
style and grace

I loved you like laughter free, spontaneous, uninhibited, open
unconditionally like a child

I loved you the only way I know how,
with nothing held back and all of me

I loved you like moonbeams and stars,
planets and milkyways and the deep unexplored universe

I loved you like long songs and lullabies and warm bubble baths

I loved you like kisses of passion placed in all
the right spots, hot, burning, wet with lots of suction

I loved you not like a mother loves her child
but like a woman loves the man she had that child by

I loved you like chocolate melting on my tongue
waiting to be swallowed and totally consumed

I loved you as an African woman loves an African man,
thoroughly, exhaustively.

Charity M. Harrison

Wings Of War

The wind is whipped by the wings of war
Harsh hush is felt on the open sore

A battle is fought, but is it won?
Is war ever good for anyone?
Can the cost in life and sorrow and pain
Ever amount to a solid gain?

We say that peace is what we seek
Using weapons as tools the prospects look bleak

The world is round, it doesn't have sides
For the good of the Earth, we all must abide
Abide as brothers and sisters who share
One mind, One heart, One world... in our care

Marcus D. McCoy

"Gone To Be With His Master"

A friend of ours has departed,
  Has left to be seen no more.
No longer will he be singing
  Those wonderful musical scores.

He was born to a working family,
  His education was limited, as such;
But with music he was really a genius,
  Musically, you could say he had the "Touch."

As an eighteen year old country lad,
  He was drafted to the Army by his peers.
He served with distinction and honor,
  And remained a patriot all his years.

Never again will we hear his stories,
  That he told with a smile on his face.
He was full of the jokes and the riddles,
  Which he would share any time, any place.

Now all of you know that I'm writing about
  A man of the farm and the sod.
He was a dear friend and we loved him,
  Now he's gone to be with his God.

James Lee Smith

Widow's Solitude

Soaring with a grace that, if sound, would be gentle Chopin,
Hawks' flight.

Exploding with color, pastels to rubies, scarlet, crimsons, copies of Degas,
Spring's blooms.

Whispering, softly fringing woodlands, delicately kissing panes,
  Victorian Fashion!
Snow's first fall.

Raging madly, hammering bullets of rock water, stabbing furiously at tall,
  undeserving pines, love like gargoyles atop towers!
Hurricanes' might.

Yet nature, when in all its artistic, destructuve wonder, its musical triumphs,
  itsexpression of expressionless wonder -
Cannot describe this pain.

Would be sound, its screams louder than all hawks' flight.
If color, and one's eye could not withstand its vibrancy;
Its style, too avant garde, risque, complex, to dress even mannequins;
Sculptures would show it as broken tombstones, with worn-bare epitaphs.

What cause, this pain-more cancerous than any physical tumor spread?

Solitude,

Tomorrow, the hawk flies; The orchestra plays again.

Diane M. Litynski

Valentine Girl

"Valentine Girl"
He calls her
Seems as though he's drawn
To this girl, every Valentines
Working back to a lost friendship
Her heart yet to be won
Afraid of being hurt
He's kept reserved, restraining his tears
Yes or no, not a matter anymore
As long as she can walk away
This time knowing
How he really feels
About her,
"Valentine Girl"

Min Choi

Aids

He was the one thing that I loved,
he meant everything to me, but how
could it be, it just wasn't fair, all I
could do was care. I felt so hopelessly sad,
how could it have gotten so bad.
  Watching him die each day, I didn't know what to say.
Those wonderful walks in the night,
but all he could do was fight, fight this terrible disease.
  But one day it will be the end, yes my very own boyfriend.
I will say goodbye and try not to cry. I
love him so much, his soft loving touch, it means so much.
  I guess this is how it will be,
it hurts knowing that someday we will
have to part, I know it will break my heart.
I'll probably never love again, why did he commit this deadly sin?
  That day finally came, it just
wasn't the same, he died that day
and I did too, I just couldn't
cope, I lost all hope, I had to do it.
I know I blew it!

Janie Rader

Old Farmer

I saw this old man kneel down to pray.
He said, "Lord please take all my sins away."
Lord, you know that cold I had the other day?
Why Lord, it's done gone away.
And Lord, my foot, why it don't hurt half as much,
I guess it must have been your touch.
Lord, that sick friend I told you about the other day,
Why he's done died and gone your way.
Well Lord, I know that you will take care of him too,
Why he can visit just like me and you,
Well Lord, that's about all I got to say,
Please help me get through another day.

Earl Thornhill

To Tartan At 103

I lost a friend the other day
He was here for a while and loved to play
And then he went away.

He walked with a prance
Like an angel's dance
So swift and sure
So precise and pure

He was a friend for many days
Who talked to me in wondrous ways
And never spoke a word
At least that mere mortals heard.

A beautiful creature of God's World
With four legs and a coat of gold unfurled
Who followed me through life's ebb and flow
Ever graceful, even when he received his
call to go.

To sit at the right hand of God
Of this I am totally sure
Because Dog spelled backwards is God!

Donald L. Hitzl

A New Day

Awaking early to a brand new day.
Hearing all the sweet sounds so far away.

Listening to crickets and birds singing
Filling the world in a peaceful ringing

As the sounds float through my mind,
All my worries seem so far behind.

Like sands in an hourglass slowly sifting,
Ones thoughts are peacefully drifting.

Most don't have time to stop and see!
All the wonders there are for thee.

Take a minute to look around,
And listen to life's pleasant sound.

It is always out there just for you,
To brighten your way and the things you do!

Diane C. Kenworthy

Crestfallen Sentiments

A perpetual thought enters my mind as icy fingers touch my inflamed heart
The sweet nostalgia of the way we were bring back the colorful days
   and evenings we used to share
Timeless moments we spent together beneath the golden sun
How the light shone on your face awakening me with your beautiful smile
The opaque night sky against an almost diminished, pallored moon
   the way you held me showed how you care
So many moments gripping my heart at the core
Crestfallen sentiments fill my lonesome soul
   at the despairing thought that you may not love me anymore
The uncertainty possesses my anguished heart
I envision the day we finally outreach time
   The day which I can love you endlessly and you love me in return.

Janet Minano

"Le Chat"

A marvelous creature, the cat; he knows really where it is at.
He'll sit in your chair, give you a cool stare—
It's his now, you know, and that's that!

He'll walk by, his tail in the air; to pull it you never would dare!
He'd hiss and he'd spit, with paw you'd be hit—
and out of your presence he'd tear.

His dignity's known far and wide; none match his serene, quiet pride.
With eyes green or blue, he'll look you right through
you'll want him to stay by your side.

His home is extensive and grand; he owns you, the house, and the land.
Don't think that he's yours, head, body, all fours—
He's KING, and you're at his command.

At mealtime he'll "soft soap" around; the queen of his life you'll be
crowned. He'll rub and he'll purr, act coy and demure a nicer pet
never is found.

He's playful, and chock full of charm; his antics will sometimes alarm.
With wiggle and springs, he'll grab at your string watch out, now!
Your hand he may harm.

So here's to my good friend, "le chat"; he's just great to hug and to
pat. May be right there, my loving to share that fantastic creature,
my cat!

Edith S. Anderson

Flower Child

She likes candles and incense and things of that sort
Hendrix and Joplin she thinks the beetles are smart
She laughs and tosses her hair aside
Then out the door she dashes for a long wild ride

Her jeans are faded patched and worn
She'll change the world someday she's sworn
She's calm and gentle as a lady should be
But looks far away and dreams of the sea

She wants to go wandering and someday she will
She'll roam and search her dreams to fulfill
With hidden fire in her dark gypsy eyes
And the freedom she worships she'll reach for the skies

Her blonde hair glows in the warm summer breeze
She dances in sunlight and walks gracefully with ease
Her head is held high and so full of dreams
Her world is tomorrow with endless streams

She loves flowers and trees and enjoys the grass
A mind of her own but small things shall pass
The most beautiful girl in the world to put it mild
God bless and keep her for she is my own child

Zoe Howard

Fantasy At 11 PM

YOU ARE MY ONE LOVE, SO TENDER AND KIND

(her thoughts were erotic and took over her mind)

DEAREST, MY HEART YEARNS FOR YOU SO MUCH

(she recalls their passionate loving and his soft perfect touch)

I MUST KNOW THAT YOUR HEART HOLDS MINE ONLY,
FOR I CAN ACCEPT NO LESS

(she eased her zipper slowly down and then removed her dress)

IT'S YOU I NEED, AND YOU I CRAVE TO HOLD NEAR

(she slipped the straps down her silky arms and removed her lace brassiere)

YOUR GENTLE CARESSES SATISFY ME TOTALLY,
AND THIS YOU NEED NOT DOUBT

(she lifted her heels above her shoes and from them she stepped out)

MY DARLING, I'M SO MUCH IN LOVE
I COULD NOT GIVE YOU MORE

(she removed her hose from her shapely legs and slid them to the floor)

I BELONG TO YOU ONLY AND WANT YOU ALWAYS AROUND

(she dropped her silk panties from her waist
and watched them touch the ground)

HONEY, I'M SO GLAD THAT YOU ARE MINE AND MINE ALONE

(Goodnight, she whispered softly and then hung up the phone)

Renate Ewel

The Dancer

His manly body dripping with sweat
His graceful movement melting time away
In honor of DANCE.
His writhing, snakelike body
Godlike, contorting to
The syncopated rhythm of the Afro-Caribbean
BEAT
His face in a concentrated trance
Intelligence, Creator, Dance,
Body and Soul are fused.
His long leg outstretched——
Floating through the air
TIME IS FIXED.

Cassandra Vernon

There's A God Above

There's a God above, who looks down with Love.
He's the one who shed his blood.
Up on the tree, he died for me,
So that my soul, might be free.
They spit, they mocked, they cursed his name.
They tried to make him feel ashamed.
It didn't work! He didn't cry!
He didn't even blink an eye.
Instead he looked up in the sky,
He had the courage that would not die.
But where did the courage get him? some people say.
They didn't believe him any way.
He went through a lot, some people thought.
But it was God's plan, to save this land.
He knew there would be ones, that wouldn't believe.
That would shut their eyes, and be deceived.
He has a plan for them too, you see, that is to burn for eternity.
He doesn't want this, he loves us all.
It is your choice to stand tall, or fall.
It's up to you, now what will you do?

Terry Lynn Collins

Fishing In The Woods

It was his Dad and him,
hiking along the rocky banks
    Of The Black River.
Words were few over the roar of the white falls
flowing into the deep, swirling eddies.
The happy river, nudging its way
    Through the steep canyon-
life holding,
creating,
building - carries their worries and showers them
    Off glistening waterfalls -
bending them into rainbows.
Two people: father and son, alone in the enveloping wonderfulness
    Of nature.
Smelling the sweet pines that sway with the wind;
Tasting the fresh chipper breeze -
full of life and rejuvenation.

Jacob Hines

Ode To A Old Oak Tree

O' wrinkled hand born of earth and water,
how sad you look upon us.
We the specks of dirt on the window of time,
who waste away years and years to pointless destruction of the land
we try to call our own.
You old pillar of strength and life ever grasping for the nothingness
that surrounds us,
do you wonder why?
How we a race of kings and queens who try to write our own fairytale,
could not stumble onto the truth.
No, time goes on and seasons change and all is started anew,
for through the wars of words and people,
there is always you.

Eaves Landry

The Tear

The harsh, bitter wind bites through my black, pin-striped suit.
It whistles a somber tune as it runs through and around the dark,
    dormant skeletons of the ancient oak trees.
A long sigh is released by the tall, golden grass growing around
    the base of the trees as the wind whips it about.
The muted gray sky reflects off of the buffed wood suspended
    above a dark pit in the earth.
A tear glistens as it tracks down my reddened cheek...

It falls and lands on the dry autumn grass.

Dustin DeBoer

My Heaven

My heaven is the most beautiful place I will ever see.
Huge snow-capped mountains will tower over the grassy hills of the valley.
There would be a beautiful lake being fed by a small stream.
The sun shall always shine...brilliantly.
The water would be the life; deer, elk and bear
would come down from the mountains to drink.
Life of all kinds would flourish in my heaven.

My heaven will give me peace. It will comfort me and protect me.
It will be untouched by all civilization.
It will provide food, clothing and a place to live.
I will never be bored in this paradise.

I will find pleasure in watching the light reflect off the dew on the aspen leaves.
In the autumn, leaves will turn orange and bright red.

I will have no enemies in this place.
I will respect all other life there and they will respect me in
return. This place has no name.
The beauty is too immense to be named and can never be fully described
But it is my heaven.

Jason Robert Bak

Never, Never, Ever, Quit!

Eighteen months old...this is my new home.
    I am now referred to as a "foster child."
It's not so bad, really...at least I'm not alone.
    But, why wasn't I wanted, my mind has filled.

I will be something...I'm sure I will.
    Dealing with abuse, that's part of life.
I won't let the negatives keep me still.
    Although the words and actions cut like a knife.

I'm on my own now, so I choose my way.
    Thankful for the foundation —yes, it was there.
One step now, hold on, don't fall, it's a new day.
    Always a chance to show others what I can bear.

Yes I can, leads my path.
    Never say never, keeps me in touch.
Listen to whiners only makes me laugh.
    I have been blessed by God with much.

Jane Adkins

The Breakwater Lighthouse

As I walk to The Breakwater Lighthouse,
I can hear the breakers roar.
It calms my pent-up feelings,
And my heart to soar.

The sun sparkling over the water
Brings contentment to my soul.
I watch the gulls fly overhead
As I list to the breakers roll.

I take deep breaths of the salt, sea air,
I can taste the salty brine.
It rekindles my spirit within me;
A feeling of the finest kind.

I stand near The Breakwater Lighthouse
And look up at the foglight dome.
I watch the boats on Penobscot Bay,
The bellboys, the sea, and the foam.

The bellboys ring out clearly
To keep ships off the shoals.
The beacon in The Breakwater Lighthouse
Calms many storm-tossed souls.

Helen B. Spear

Acid And Resolve

For Matt Newton

A friend was telling me of a TV program,
(I can't remember...maybe it was Oprah?).
That featured a lady, victimized by a man who
    Drenched her face with battery -
    Acid.

The lady said she wished to forgive
    Yes...
    Forgive this man of his crime.
I only I wish that I knew her name,
    Or her address,
    I would write her a letter:

Dear _____,
    You have the most remarkable strength; I
    Admire greatly your Christmas resolve.

    You have the power of the
    Grace of God:

    You can neutralize acid —
    With forgiveness and love.

Michael D. Baker

"Shadows Upon Reflections"

Why is it we put up this wall?
I don't understand so I sound out this call.
To a world who builds it brick my brick
Feeds the virus to inject the disease that makes us sick
What makes you better when you have to put down others
Arrogance puts unjust shame upon your brothers
Not a friend finds yourself all alone
So are you really at the top when you condone
Come on down to join us to face a new dawn
Cause isn't it better to have friendship than a pedestal to stand on
Humility comes when the realization of your reflection
Has similar shadows that cast down upon your perfection
Will you let these words destroy what wasn't stable
Be apart of the cure where healing is able
When all brothers and sisters work together as one
That has the future prosper for what you have done
Cause anybody can sit back and complain
But you answered the call when change was needed to end our pain

Dave R. Doan

America

I heard the stories of soldiers, who lost their lives in war,
I heard of how our country, became so very poor.
The depression was tough, but our people were too,
They'd do all that they could, for the red, white and blue.

Now I see children, who couldn't care less,
They don't realize how much our country's been blessed.
They don't say the pledge, or place a hand on their heart,
They don't sing the anthem; they think they're too smart.

I love this country, every rock and rill,
Seeing still-serene farms, gives my heart a thrill.
Oh sure, we have problems, but where is there not?
Just pray to the Lord, that our problems will stop.

Donna M. Bruck

Alone

Animalistic desires and depressive obsessions take control
Long nights, cold days, tasteless time spent on nothing
Obscure feelings about the silence confuses the mind
No one understands the passive pain ruling over your body
Exit into the deep hole you've created from your own fear of being alone

Denise Saunders

Codependent

Stop! You're hurting me- but you're hurting yourself even more
I need to have the courage to walk out the door.
I'll turn my back on you and quickly depart
I've tried to get my feet to move but haven't found the heart.
I search alone in darkness, totally at your will
To bring the ransom for exchange - but I love you still.
We talk and cry for hours about how things will change
While all time, your mind is fixed on how to arrange
The next stimulation from Momma Luck or Daddy Coke
Riding high on your good times until at last, you're broke.
I try to drown out the ringggggg of that call in the night
But I must know if you are dead or if you're alright.
So one more time I slip away to places unknown
Not knowing if ever again I'll be safely home.
Stop! You're hurting me - but I'm hurting myself even more
I must say goodbye for now and walk out the door.
I won't, I can no longer exist, totally at your will
To contribute to your demise - but I love you still.

Edith Faye Wilson Milner

Missing You

My fingers touch the lips that you used to kiss with love.
I remember how your head once rested so gently in my arms.
Tears spill down face and I know they'll never dry.
My reason for life, my worth, my desire
How I wish you were here to comfort me with your tender soul.
In my dreams, in my heart, in my mind, and in my soul.
You are with and I feel no pain.
But as I look around and see that I am alone.
My vision is blurred and my cheeks are wet.
I think of all our happy times:
Our walks together under the shimmering moonlight.
The first, soft touch of your lips upon mine.
How could you leave me the way that you did?
Never a chance to say good-bye, to say "I Love You."
As I walk across the grassy field, I see a single white cross.
And on that cross, alone are the distant words: Beloved Son.
But I know there were things more special about you.
The things that I loved, things that we shared.
Things that can never be said in words,
Things that I will forever cherish within my heart...

Jacqueline Goh

My Favorite Time

When evening shadows, start to fall —
    I reminisce about, the days gone by.
Life's pleasant memories, I like to recall —
    And try to bring forth, the where's and why's.

I love to sit, on the porch and rock —
    Whittle on stick, and forget the strife.
On peace and tranquility, my thoughts will lock —
    And remember only the better life.

To read a book, and sip a cool drink —
    Days work is done, it's time to rest.
Nothing to interfere, with what I think —
    It's when the day, is at its best.

When the cool breeze blows, upon my brow —
    These shadows I spoke of, now come alive.
A dredge my memories, to find just now —
Images of good things, that I can revive.

The sunset in splendor, a mighty display —
    A picture so incredible, masterpiece of God's art.
Nothing to confuse you, darkness on the way —
God's creatures grow quiet, and the silence now starts.

James H. Mudd

As I Look Into Your Face

As I look into your face,
I see not the person I knew,
Only the shell of what,
Used to be.
At hearing your voice,
I hear a stranger's voice,
Different from the sweet melody tone,
You used to have.
The touch of your hand,
Is a foreign one,
It makes me cringe inside,
Until I feel crushed.

The scent of your hair,
Spring sunshine setting softly on your skin,
Echoing in my mind are these memories,
Which become too loud to ignore,
Making me deaf,
Until I'll hear them no more.

Jared Buckley

Mother

Early projections in the morning
I see your twisted face
you can go away now.
Thanks, you didn't listen again.
Instead, you held onto my anguished breast
and cried "victim."
You always did thrive on my pain
wimp.

Try to fit into my womb
head first, than feet.
Curl up and suck your thumb,
and never come out.
Now you have what you could never get
I as your mother,
not your lover.
I'll never forgive you for this
wimp.

Jaki M. Gilbert

Not Mine

In times of darkness issuing,
I wander far beyond
The reaching shoreline misty gray
Whose waves arc ever on.

And daylight finds me dreaming still
Of twilight's deepest beckon:
That echoing star against the rose
But blinks upon reflection.

The cliffs collapse beneath my gaze;
Skies fly like wanton kites,
And thoughts carry through the close, hot fen
Unto the shyly whispering night.

I know not all that questions.
Those murky truths evade;
The seeker's mind seeks frenzied rest
Ere cruel answers be made plain.

Heather Vinson

Reflections

The one, you were, who slipped from weakened grasp.
Long ago and far away the hands of love unclasped;
Gone before the soul of the world could breathe,
Leaving stranded only me.

Jana Dawn Cooper

As I Attend A Sleep

As I attend a sleep, I am marvelled by an old custom of mine.
I was always fascinated by the wind.
Every time I heard it, I wanted to feel it,
and every time I felt it, I couldn't hear it.

So one night I lay awake,
drowning in the comfort of an American home.
I hear the wind outside; it blows and I like it.
I want to touch it, it is so inviting.
I feel as if it is calling me,
to join it for an infinite ride,
across the landscapes I have seen,
across the blankets I have used.

I desire the cool and honesty of a friend of the earth.
But I cannot go outside and shake hands with the blade of nature.

The wind is beautiful,
It will never cheat on me,
It will encourage the sea.
The wind is there,
Far beyond your distraction.

I feel a friend in the wind, a friend who will never betray me.

James Anthony Cercone

"Faults"

It's all my fault, never yours.
I was wrong, it couldn't of been you.
I screwed up, not you — I wasn't your fault.
I have to start over.
You can keep going
It's my fault, don't blame yourself
I didn't do anything wrong,
But it's all my fault.
I didn't give you all I could,
I didn't give you my life,
I didn't give you my love,
I didn't give you my everything.
It's my fault.
LIE! I did!
And still.... it's all my fault
I'm sorry,
All I've got — is not enough.
It's my fault.
Point the finger at me.
I'm where the blame lies.

James R. Landers

The Writer

I write for satisfaction,
I write to take up time,
I write the words right from my heart,
I write what comes to mind,

I write because I'm lonely,
I write because I'm blue,
I write when I'm not sleeping,
Because I find nothing better to do,

I write from my own wisdom,
I write of future things to come,
I write about the things I know,
And will end when all the writing is done,

Yes, I am a writer,
Yes, I am a scholar,
Yes, without a doubt,
I write for the "Good Old Dollar",

Yes, if you should ask me to write a thing or two,
Yes, and very seldom "NO" I would say,
And it is all because writing,
Is what I do best each and every "Dog Gone" day.

Anthony J. Cappuccino Sr.

"L' Innocence"

I've often wondered between stars and sky
If a place could be found that wonders not why

That questions nothing, and asks of no man
But to give of himself and do what he can.

That allows for mistakes, and gives ample time
For life to flow smoothly, serene and sublime.

Where mountain and valley meet gently rolling hill
And a lush, green forest enhances the still.

A full moon is reflected upon sea and sand
To mirror the sky, at peace with the land.

Where hope and faith, walk with honor and truth
As they dwell in that place of your glorious youth.

As a thing of the earth, confined and bound
I long for the freedom of that place, yet unfound

Where beauty is still raw and makes you give pause
To things untouched by man and his laws.

Margaret Ann Duke

I Am

I am a serious and confident child who hopes to leave an
impression on the world.
I wonder if one person can really make a difference.
I hear people fighting and getting killed over nothing.
I hope to see a peaceful world where everyone gets along.
I want spring, life, to last forever.
I am a serious and confident child who hopes to leave me
impression on the world.

I feel my heart break when somebody cries for help and I can't do anything.
I touch the thin and delicate tear that rolls down the caring child's face.
I worry animals will die because of human luxuries.
I cry at cruelty of human life.
I am a serious and confident child who hopes to leave an
impression on the world.

I understand the sorrow of death.
I know life isn't fair.
I dream of the day everyone gets along
I try to picture a nonviolent world.
I hope for every blade of grass a new wonderful person is born.
I am a serious and confident person who hopes to leave an
impression on the world.

Jasmin Weisz

Trapeze

Suspended upside down
in an upside right world,
waiting for the silence, the void/hush,
when all sound empties from the universe.

A moment of trepidation strangling brain cells,
as the body calls for release
not to be found in the frenzied crowd
seeking their own vicarious pleasures.

Blood rush to the head, arms extended,
waiting for the right moment
when receiver and sender connect
in a retrofitted world.

The silence ascends from the multitude
breathless in anticipation
when one must let go and hang no more
upside down in an upside right world.

Harold R. Snedeker

The Space Race

The race for space began in October 1957.
In November the Russians launched artificial
satellite Sputnik under the Heavens.

The Russians told the United States we will conquer
space, so look out boys now you're in for a race.

The United States told the Russians don't brag too soon,
because we are going to put a man on the moon.

February 20, 1962 the United States
told the Russians we are ahead of you.

We are telling you boys we are not in a hurry.
We are going to launch Friendship 7, Project Mercury.

Astronaut John Glenn and the astronaut crew
boarded that ship knowing what to do.
John Glenn sent that space craft off into space,
leaving the Soviets behind in the race.

Astronaut John Glenn blasted that space craft off on time,
leaving planet Earth far behind.

John Glenn landed on the moon with a thought in mind,
As he stepped of the ship he said one step for me
and one giant step for mankind.

Daisy B. Martin

When We All Loved You So Much

Did you not know to lose you would suffice
In suffering, in grief and aching tears?
To know that you, yourself, took your own life
Will haunt us all through our remaining years.

What were your thoughts, alone, in that last hour,
What the bitter thing that made you choose
To take away from God the rightful power
To end the only life you had to lose?

What was it that we failed to understand,
What the needed things we left undone
And when you chose to take life in your hand,
Were our hands, too, somehow, upon the gun?

Dorothy M. Bartell

Shadows Of The Night

As the doors of my eyes close I am swept out
into the arms of slumber.
Out in the openness of the forest the moon smiles
down upon me illuminating the shadowy figures as they
dance around the fire chanting songs of worship to
their unknown master.
When finished they turn and stare at me with hollow eyes.
Their thunderous roars of laughter swirl around me
like a mighty rushing wind.
The confusion grows as I wonder deeper out into the darkness.
I seem to be searching for something; for some sort of hope.
My grasp weakens and as I slip farther away a sense
of calmness washes over me.
I will savour this feeling for as long as I can
because I know that when I awake from this state of
serenity I will have to carry the same burdens that
I laid down at the gate before I entered this sacred
dream world.

Hope Long

The Land Of Friends To The End

The land where I would like to live,
Is a place where no one dies.
It's always fun and everyone's happy,
And no one ever cries.

Everyone always has a friend,
The people run and play.
They all have fun with the moon and the sun,
During the night or the day.

And the best part of all is that there's no war,
Because everyone is everyone's friend.
There's no need for war in the land I adore,
In the Land of Friends to the End.

Donna Wilson

Man In The Moon

Man in the Moon, why do you cry?
Is someone else sad? Did someone young die?
Are you mourning the loss of another young friend?
Did another new life come to an end?

Did they want it? Are they glad?
Did they deserve it? Are they sad?
Too many lives are ending real soon,
does everyone cry to the Man in the Moon?

Man in the Moon, why do you cry?
Will you tell them I miss them? Will you tell them good-bye?
Are they okay up there? Are they in good hands?
Do they have what they want? Do they get their demands?

Do they wish they were back? Do they want to be here?
Did they want to leave? Did they live in fear?
Were they dressed as goblins? Maybe as a goon?
Did they ask you, Man in the moon?

Man in the moon, why do you cry?
Is someone else sad? Did someone young die?
Are you mourning the loss of another young friend?
Did another new life come to an end?

Jasmin Singh

My Mother

The first sign of life...in a mother you see
Is the heart beat of her baby - the baby to be
And when the child is born, it's the mother again
Who molds the child - Sacrificing... (Now and Then)
My mother accomplished this, many times fold
And placing herself last never got old
It's mother that gave my young life its wings;
My mother that helped me see through material things
She's on the highest of pedestals that pedestals can be
She could be no closer to the man we call thee
"Open Arms" is the trademark of the love she gives
Love and devotion of the life she lives.
For it isn't the house, that makes it a home;
Nor is the rhyme, the heart of this poem
It's my mother that made my childhood whole
It's my mother that gave my souls.
It's okay if this verse says it for another
What's important is that my thoughts are known to my mother
I will have accomplished a lot in life, if all that I do
Is to have someone feel about me the way I feel about you.

Dennis Michael Morrison

"Golf"

Golf is a game, played by two or more players.
It is played at "The Club" by two or more women or men.
The object is to "drive" the ball,
Down the fairway, to the pin.

If you play "in the rough", the going really gets tough;
and the bunker is no fun at all.
But if you play to win, and don't miss the pin,
The states are: "Winner takes all."

If you make the cup, in the fewest strokes,
you've made a "birdie", "eagle", or par.
But if you make a "Hole in One",
You've won a brand new car!"

You play "at the club", with clubs,
to "birdie", "eagle", or "par",
but if you "double or triple bogey",
You've gone way too far.

It's a truly magnificent sport,
played by experts who practice for years;
It's good for your health, a lot of fun,
But takes a lot of blood, sweat, and tears.

James G. Brown

My Love For You

I really didn't plan it,
It just happened that first day
You walked into my life
And chased the blues away
You make my life so happy
In a very special way
My love for you grows stronger
A little more each day.
They say that this could never be
But someone sent you here to me
I count the minutes you're away
And dream of the day you'll be here to stay.
I need you more and more each day
As my love grows stronger every day.

Dorothy J. Schook

Could Interstate #74 Be The Road To Salvation?

It ribbons up and down and cuts through wooded hills
It slams into Kickapoo Creek so has to lift its tread and
  bridge the water.
It inhales the green memories of trees and belches carbon-monoxide
  smack in your face.
It is the carry-all shifting one from town to town to city,
While the gossiping tires leave anonymous black marks on the concrete.
But, oh, excitement! Movement!
This circus caravan of unmatched locomotion: the bruised and
battered...the buffed and shining...the noisy complainers or
the black-windowed autistic...some tandem trailer trucks
shoulder above the traffic, elbow past little tin play cars.
  Is this the way to the HEREAFTER?
Maybe...for that red MG ducking through holes, gunning the
motor along the berm and fish-tailing his little rear back
into the outer lane. I could hear a Southern Baptist
Preacher intone the epitaph for Mr. Wire Wheels, "HEREAFTER
be round that next curve. He dyin' to be promoted."

Dorothy Deuell Fry

513

Life

Life is but an empty dream
Its hours are full of misery
and earth's breeze is like death's breath
Cool and dry caressing our cheeks
Life gives but never takes
Death takes but never gives
Some say life is beautiful
But how when life is but
An empty dream

Elizabeth McCarthy

The Creature

A shadow of the past looms large on the horizon
Its outline distinct......grotesque and intact

It stills the tiny heart of the songbird
Silently now and dead
Wearied, it lays upon its nest

I hurry onward...
Fleeing from this tyrant of days gone by,
Ceaseless from its pursuit of my tormented soul
No rest...no time...no respite from its foul embrace

The haunting echo of it mindless trail
Crashing ever closer, darkening my heart
Three hairs-breadth, two...now one...
Separate me from all Eternity at the past's command

One muffled cry escapes
Parched lips and clenched teeth
As I awake in sweat-soaked sheets
To ponder the creature of my dreams....

And realize, to my dismay, the devil of my dreams....
The creature from which there is no escape....
Is me

Sherry J. Olsen

Just Love Me

So maybe my grades aren't all that great?
    JUST LOVE ME.
  Maybe there's times when we just don't get along
and everything's gone wrong with our fate.
    JUST LOVE ME.
  I know we haven't always been the best of friends
and time after time we end up fighting again.
    JUST LOVE ME.
  Stop trying to judge each thing I say and do, and
trying to make me be like you.
    JUST LOVE ME.
  Don't try to pretend I'm a perfect child, and that
I'll never ever get a little wild.
    JUST LOVE ME.
  Try not to forget the good times we shared, when
I knew deep down you always cared.
    JUST LOVE ME.

  Keep these memories and thoughts in your head, for one day soon
we'll both be dead. How could I die not knowing if you loved me?
Sometimes those things are hard to see. So please... JUST LOVE ME?

Shel Ivey

The Connecticut River

From the cliff I see the river winding,
Silver against the green,
Vermont and New Hampshire smoothly binding,
Only the water between.

And far below where the river bends,
A bridge makes a handclasp between two friends.

Dorothea Low

Into The Night

When we run away into the night
  let's put all our past behind us,
    let them try to find us as we run away into the night

As we look into the night
  we see nothing but - danger and death, in darkness.
  It will soon be behind us when
    we run away into the night.

We will take the risk together,
  the love we have cannot be broken
    by the darkness, as we run away
      into the night.

Our love is like warm light,
  where there was death,
    now there is life.
      We will run away,

but into the day of days
  instead of the lonesome darkness.
    When we run away together,
      into the pitch black night.

Ilya Shustin

Legacy Of Love

Amazing what some people feel that they must leave behind
Lifetime items, seeming real; mere collections of mankind.
Until you lose that loved one, dear...and temporal things do disappear.
What would you pick if you could choose? To leave....
A gift of love?; you couldn't lose.
Perhaps wisdom is your choice, or maybe tenderness of voice?
Compassion for all who pass by? ...Humility seen in one's eye?
Perhaps patience would make your face shine, forgiveness could
    make us divine.

These are some of the fruits our Lord doth give...
designed to show us how easy to live.
So, rather than gather money and "things"
Give them true values and see what those bring.

Doris J. Babb

Nightfall

With silence roaring, darkness devours the landscape
like so many weeds across a forgotten garden.

Each shadow, newly spawned from a dying sun, devouring,
growing, realizing, becoming, increasingly empowered
yet losing itself in each passing moment to the consuming dusk.

All that was, glorious, colorful, vibrant, individual in the
golden glow of day's demise, now equal as the world
rushes towards its nocturnal mistress.

No gentle passing this, as Night spreads her lustrous,
blue-violet cape, for Heaven's stars rip fierce holes in its
fabric with futile light, realizing their hopeless struggle to
rekindle the days memory.

The second world awakens with somber moon riding high on
glistening lids, graying all the day-eye beholds, glaring down
on eyes sensitive to this darkened world.

Born only to succumb to the light from which she stole her
shadowed being, Night relishes in her brief glory; her
children wailing in nocturnal celebration.

Donald Q. Linke Jr.

The Writer

The Writer sits at his desk,
  listening to the gentle tapping of keys.
He has no boundaries in his work.
The universe will listen when he speaks.
Because with a touch of his finger,
  He destroys or creates,
    whatever he pleases.
With his imagination,
  he can do anything.
And with the smallest thought,
  he can become a god.
He is the Writer.

Michael Baker

Your Eyes Tell Everything

It is in the eyes
Look in the eyes for you will see
What are you looking for, it is in the eyes
For the person who cannot lie,
  the eyes tell the essence of things.
For the person who lies not.
The true emotion will be. It is the eyes.
Happy eyes are beautiful to see;
  the sparkle, glow, so glad to see,
    so much, and so straight.
Sad eyes so far away and not so straight.
  Mad eyes with fire and dark that will jump you see.
  Eyes it is in the eyes.
Eyes that change their color when it is extreme
Love in the eyes is a special thing to see.
  I dare not to explain such a thing.
It's just plain love you see with a wide mix of things.
For sure it is in your eyes, to see.

Michael Baker

Friend Of Friends Through And Through

A friend is a friend through and through
Loving and caring in all you do.
They'll laugh, they'll cry,
When a guy passes, they'll sigh.
They stick by you in good times and bad.
On occasions they may make you sad.
You'll work these things out and your all brand new,
The friendship, the trust, the smiles that are due.
These characteristics, all of which are hard to see,
Are pure and faithful signs of friends.
When you find the one who fits,
Make sure that away from you they never get.
Forever, if true, to the end they'll stay.
Always close to your heart, never astray.
All of these things I see in you,
My friend of friends through and through.

Judith Needham

The Potter

You are the potter and I am the clay;
  Mold me and make me into your way.
Empty this vessel of self and of sin;
  A newness of life I wish to begin.
Help me dear Lord to be patient and still;
  Content to be whatever you will.
Then fill this vessel, my mind and my heart;
  Knowing your Spirit will never depart.
Help me to live a life that is true;
  Worthy of love and pleasing to you.

Janet Lee

Beneath The Wings Of An Angel....

For Angels,
men have sought hither and thither,
from Mount Zion to the deepest depth of the Red Sea,
thus the administering of Angels unveil what shepherds seek,
having me adjourn to a journey beyond the River Euphrates.

Where for art thou, oh...Suriyel and Salathiel,
thus a bewilderness becomes those which behold your beauty,
your eyes beheld the beforetime of Adam, as did Gabriel,
soon the Angel Raphael will appear before nightfall draws near.

Weighted in the balance
is a purity of purpose, a protection which preserves one path,
thus Heavenly host provide sanctuary until the storms aftermath,
in a whirlwind of flames Cherubim are our compass as the Northern
Star in the sky, knowing how way leads on to way, we venture forward
by and by.

Thus patience is a virtue as my thoughts do collide,
focusing upon a celestial chorus, though they subside,
heavenly shades of splendor permeate the higher heavens found,
as sweet as Amazing Grace, how sweet the sound.

Kevin Fisher

My Awakening

My God looked down to me and said,
My daughter, what is troubling you in your head?
Do you not think that I am always near?
Your every thought of need brings me there!

God, I am so thankful for your love and devotion,
Yet there are times when I feel all alone in the ocean.
Then I remember of You seeing to the needs
Of your earth, its birds, fish, insects and beasts.

Old habits die hard, yet much effort I make
For the old ways feel awkward now that I am awake.
I see much more of your magnificent world
As I take time to notice, slow down and say not a word.

My life has been crazy the last four years.
I am ready for happiness and prosperity, not tears.
Great strides have I made on my journey back Home.
My journey of remembering My Path, until now unknown.

I now know that I am a Spiritual Being filled with Love
And my task is to show others how to find their path from above.
To help them see, feel and know that God is inside their hearts
And always remember His Love never ends for them,
  though theirs stops and starts.

Janette V. Cooke

love

love is red like a beating heart, it echoes through
my ears like a thousand drums, it reminds me of an
open field alive in bloom, adrenaline rushes to my
heart, i feel like i'm on top of the world.

love is a rose blowing in the breeze, it tells the
world love grows here and all of us can share the
wonder and joy that it can bring, yes, love grows
here, yes love grows here.

love is my heart alive with care, every second
beating, keeping me alive, so that I may share it. love.

Harmony Cleary

The Coastal Shore

I bathe along the coastal shore,
my feet sinking into the ocean floor,
they can't go deeper anymore.

The waves break upon my knee,
but I remain steady as a tree,
as the wave retreats into the sea.

My back is turned toward the bluff,
Which has been worn from seas so rough,
but the strength of its walls will be enough.

Enough to with stand the test of time,
the coastal shore the end of the line.
It will always be there for me and mine.

India Leigh Quick

My Life's Continuation

Everything is happening oh, so, fast.
My mind is reluctant.
Why do I want to stay in the past?
I am becoming frantic.

So many changes are taking place.
What do I do?
Why can't everything move at my pace?
What is my cue?

My mind is jumbled with so many thoughts.
Will I make a mistake?
If I do, won't a lessen be taught,
With the decision I make?

Will my life change as much as I think,
If I shoot for my goal?
What is the key? What is the link?
What is my role?

What is this I am feeling?
Is it anticipation?
Or is this just revealing
My life's continuation?

Heather Walsh

Reality Becomes Possibility

It's hard to talk about how I feel
My mind tends to balk at having to deal
With the reality of my life.

Is it too much for me to face?
Have I become cowardly?
Or have I managed to make a case,
For the coward I've been to me?

A special friend, understanding and giving,
Provides a measure of hope
That I can do anything
And learn to cope
With the reality of my life.

It's time to turn myself around - -
To get my feet back on the ground.

I'm determined to do well - -
My future's in my care.
I need only to tell
Myself, to be kind to me, and dare

To realize the possibilities of my life.

Dorothy Wilson

The Texas Lottery

When we hit the Texas lottery.
My wife is going to declare.
A hollow day.
Just for me; you see.
It's off to a far away land.
An Island if we can,
We will run across the sand.
Bare footed and kicking sand.
Oh yes we will write you all a letter in the sand.
And if you all hit the lottery.
Join us if you can.
We sit in the shade every day.
And watch the palm trees sway.
We look at the stars at night.
You see this is the life.
So try to understand.
You have to think of a far away land.
Because it's just like I said.
You have to hit the Texas lottery.

James D. White

To The Young Black Male

So many trips back and forth to the cemetery.
Not giving thought that one day soon you also will be buried.
Black on black crime in every state.
And you are the race that most others hate.

It really makes many of us feel ashamed.
But all of you are not to blame.
So think about it, live and let live.
Because you my brother have so much to give.

For a people who have so much pain, trials, and suffers.
It only seems natural that we love one another.
Open up your eyes and your mind.
And lets stop destroying our own kind.

You are brothers, fathers, husbands, and sons.
So let's stop the killings, get rid of the guns.

Doris J. Blakeney

Untitled

Waiting, wondering what will happen next
  Not knowing other than one out of text.
It begins as a friendship and goes from there
  They don't think about it and they don't care.
But as time goes on, a heart grows fonder,
  Feelings that no longer need to wander.
Once having found something, something that was liked,
  It was not a toy, nothing like a bike.
It was not something that was dreamed of,
  but then find themselves in that thing called love.
Strange how some things happen and how they turn out.
  but happiness is what can be found, no doubt.
Whatever it is, it is definitely here
  No complaints, but maybe a cheer.
Maybe friendship is the key
  to what will make a relationship be.
I guess that is how story goes,
  it is supposed to keep one on their toes.
But for now they will be just like a dove,
  totally free, and totally in love.

Heidi Moeller

Travelling With The Kudzu

1-65, Mobile to Birmingham. A steamy August
of hot cloudy skies leaden with outbursts
of lightning and rain, and heat
rippling from the asphalt.

From the car window, at the right
suddenly appears an enchanting forest
with giant structures reminiscent
of a Goblin valley but sculpted
in foliage, not stone.

Trees and bushes shrouded in green
leafy vines that silently creep
enveloping even the wind,
in their mysterious enclosure.

They reach out as if to engulf
the highway and its occupants
in their depths. Tempting me
to flee into the cool quietness
of this sanctuary.

Janice R. Lindgren

Time Brings About A Change

This is just a hint
Of what retirement is meant.
You worked for many years,
Now retirement time is here.

Retirement - don't just sit and rock,
It might give the body quite a shock.
You've been up and on the go,
So into retirement go real slow.

Don't just lay around and get fat.
Retirement means much more than that.
Don't just sit and reflect on your pain,
Retirement will give you a change.

You went through the rain, sleet and snow.
Off to your job you would go.
Sometimes you went through the heat of the day
Not knowing if you would be able to stay.

God has blessed you to retire, shall we pray,
Giving "God" the thanks for this retirement day.

Hazel McDaniels

Heritage

There are many old tales which are buried deep
  On the lips of the men who lived them;
And many more tales reside in minds
  Of those who will never forget them.

But earth can't reveal what's buried in minds,
  Neither sorrows, nor glories once won;
And some who are left, find memories dimmed,
  As age watches each setting sun.

There are those whose recall is as clear as the Fall,
  When the leaves change from green to bright red,
And those are the ones who should let their minds speak,
  So their tales, by our youth, may be read.

A tale handed down from father to son,
  Or re-told by mother to daughter,
Is part of a heritage, of interest to all.
  Like earth, sea and sky, and fresh water.

Bob Tipple

Praise To Your Guardian Angels

They knew that you were asleep, so they gathered around your bed.
One, brushed your cheek with a feather, the other, caressed your head.

They gathered all around you to give you a warm embrace.
Angels always arrive on time, always, at the right place.

Down from the Heavens they came to comfort, to ease your fears,
They brought along some angel dust. They wiped away your tears.

Your Angels watched over you. They brought blessings from above.
Peace: Was their mission. The reason: Was their love.

So, if you ever need them, close your eyes and pray.
They'll be at your side to guide you, to help you along the way.

When the day is over, blow your angels a kiss good night!
Tell them how much you love them, as they depart on their celestial flight.

Mary Ellen Davis Skutack

Family Fun

Hey, little brother! This is not just another
One of my sinister schemes. So silence your screams,
Uncover your eyes, for what I will do
Is not apologize, but simply say - "Thank you-"

For fuming when your friend cuts up your clothes.
(I'm glad I had you meet mean Mr. Ground.)
For savoring the ripe fruits of my nose,
And dining on the wet worms we had found.

For letting me laugh until I lose my breath
Because no matter how Houdini tries
He can't escape from that closet of death,
Unless the sissy gives it up and cries.

For drinking of the salty smelly ade,
So fresh from the fleshy lemon I had squeezed.
And when you smashed the snow fort I had made,
For allowing me to beat you as I pleased.

If somehow I had been given the choice,
You know I never would have made the switch
And chose another's helpless squealing voice
Because I am one loyal son of a bitch.

Earl Ross Gillanders

Good Or Evil

There is a road that divides two separate ways,
One road is dark, the other has sun rays.
One road goes up a hill, the other road goes down.
There's country along one side, and the other there is a town.

I decided to take the road where sun, country, and up a hill sounds fun.
I realize it was a good choice but oh I'm not done.

There is a road that goes left or you can go right.
One road has pot holes, the other road has a lot of pretty sights.
There's sand along one side, and then on the other there is trees.

I decided to go right, with the trees, and pretty sight.
At the end of the road there is a red light.
Underneath a sign that says, HELLO YOU THERE MAKE A WISH
  IN THE WELL,
GOOD THINGS HAPPEN TO THOSE WHO PICK HEAVEN
  OVER HELL.

Denise Maynard

My Three Best Friends

I have three best friends.
One short, two tall.
One with short hair, one with long,
and one with shoulder length.
One wear glasses, one contacts, and the other, neither.
Two live in Arizona, one lives in New York.
Yet, they all have one thing in
common, they are all understanding,
great listeners, fun to be with and will
always be my three best friends

Janice Hayhae

Two Halves Make A Whole

Two different worlds
One white
One yellow
A foot in each one
Being pulled in both directions
Neither world wanting to let you go
But they will never fully except you
For you are not whole
Neither full white, or full yellow
"Never whole!" they will taunt
But I am human, which makes me whole
I can't be split, to go in both directions
For I am one
Made up of two
Which combined into one
Take a little from each
White and yellow
Pale skin; slanty, uptilt eyes
And you have me
A proud chinese - European American

Jaimee Chow

Insanity!

Ragweed blowing over a wide
open field, and no! I don't know why?

I'm a dragon fly buzzing around
until your love swats me down!

There's a rhinoceros smoking
a drag in the corner, trying
to slit his wrists

There's a giraffe on stage reciting quotes from
"Death of a Salesman".

A tired old man sitting on a park bench
preaching a sermon of love as an abalone
swims by.

Orange shag carpet with a scent of lemon.
There's a Volvo double parked there.

There's no violence in this madness,
only sweat drenched sheets, and a
sad song an octave down from no where.

Justin Smillie

What We See

Strange are the things we see in darkness,
So many are the shadows that really aren't there.
Your mind transforms nothing into something.
All because you sit and stare.
The more you look the more you shall see,
The deep you look the more real it will be.
But, there's no reason for you to fear,
The things before you that really aren't there.

James B. Knight

"Remember"

Remember the warmth of transparent rain falling on the
open hands of serenity embracing the compassionate love
that pours from your soul. "I remember."

I remember the wonderful journey of infinity every
time you smiled, that magical path of sincerity I followed
until I had reach your inquisitive last mile.
Remember how our contentment challenged the universal travails
of time... than you should always remember...

The continuity we share that make us happy make us wise
The passing of seasons bring us closer to our prime
The blessing of our love shall always shy away from compromise
'Remember'
"I do"

James M. Turner III

Aurora Borealis

Sound the reveal you're great man, you prepare the road
Open to pass through thousands bend heads looking to the mud road
Can't turn the heads can't look at the sun shining brilliant
The peace the love and hope is impossible
To raise the head to see the fallen sun, you're a great man,
You prepare the road to erect the cross from the floor
Fallen of thousand calvarys help the people. You create man
Fasten on top of the dry blood who poured for freedom and peace
Help to erect the cross to stand beside the tree of Christmas
See the star shining brilliant riser to the top of the tree
The star that splendid magnificent glorious jewelries of peace
Look on the sky is wide open and the Aurora Borealis pouring to the
Earth the golden cataract of the lavish illumination
Great man don't advance to see the peace she lyin' down between
Two monsters the blood come from the eyes and the nails is from
The flesh of peace don't go there
The monsters they bring to you the bleeding peace because they
Like to give them the ring with the sea green stone
Human you are free

Maria Malamatina

Second Hand Pain

We all have pain.

Some feel it all the time,
Others only now and then.
It may stem from your past or present life,
Mine comes from the sufferings of friends.

I feel their pain so deeply
As if it were my own.
This second hand pain consumes completely,
And I can't help but feel alone.

My friendships are so precious
Each one is special and unique.
Different friends have different pain,
That is what is so hard for me.

They all have someone else who cares.
Who tries to help when they suffer in their life.
But I am the only one who loves them all,
And shares their pain simultaneously every single night

I cannot choose whose pain to feel and whose to ignore
I only know that each time I do this second hand pain
is more intense than ever before.

Justine Gueno

A New Beginning

What's happened to our stately oaks?
Our sturdy chestnut trees?
The pink and white sweet Dogwood
And the sleeping peach and apple trees?
The stately firs stand green and tall
Their feet look cold without wildflowers and brush for slippers!
The grass has a sad and rusty look
Just waiting for a signal!

The Days last a little longer now
The Darkness of the night grows shorter.

Just stop and look and listen
For a long and quiet time-
Be still and wait and suddenly you'll start to see the Sign!

A faint red haze of budding trees - a tiny hint of green around.
The trees are not quite so bare
Was that a robin's call I heard?

At last it seems that nature wakes!
Spring is truly on its way! All God's creatures are cheering up!

Surely, this is a New Beginning!!
Marie Davis Deatelhauser

A Prisoner In My Own Body!!!

At the age of 24 years I slowly was becoming a prisoner in my own body. My body was slowly declining and so very frail. So alone and so afraid. Not knowing which way to turn! I would cry out in prayer Lord what's going on. I have no control! I'm losing a losing battle. I was so scared, how I longed to have somebody hold me and say hey it's going to be alright. But nobody was there for me. Just my prayers and I. The most dreadful day arrived in 1978 it was either surgery with a 5 percent chance of survival or die!!! I was so scared I said alright let's go for it. I figured if I didn't make it here on earth I would still make it and be in the presence of the most high. I made it here on earth. The next day after surgery when I viewed my body I screamed and cried in terror to see the most horrible gruesome scare. Oh what a defect I had become. Why didn't you take me home I cried. But his response was it's not time for your arrival. The next few years were very hard for me. But I can honestly say that with time I have learned to love me as I am and I have learned to love others with a greater love and compassion. I no longer am a prisoner in my own body. I am free to love and to be loved!!!

Diana Macal

Little Children

God bless these little children, God bless them all today
Please keep them safe and happy, watch over them each day

In their world of make believe, their thoughts always afar
Whether here or in outer space, please God, be where they are

There is no worry in their world, they do not know of fears
I wish I were a youngster, back in my younger years

You see them playing out of doors, smiles upon their face
No dispute in their world about color, creed or race

Their ball game is the series, their race the mile run
They fly the fastest jet on earth and challenge everything to come

Their mother is the greatest, their pop the strongest man
They'll try to be just like them in every way they can

God, please don't wonder who to help, just hear my plea today
Protect these little children in each and every way

Gwen Dean

Carriage Of Destiny

Thundering, thundering hooves of destiny,
Pounding, pounding meandering paths,
Their carriage reined by a ghostly spectre
Silhouetted against a moonlit sky.

From out of the misty haze of dawn
Into the rays of the Eastern Fire,
Into the splendor of evening blaze
The carriage assumes chameleon shades.

Winds of time the months lay waste,
And one by one the years have gone
Along with cities, wars and kings,
And still the carriage presses on.

Harold L. Sampson

To David And Louisa Reece (Great-Grandparents)

One with the eager restless throng
Pressing to new frontiers,
Young like their nation, courageous, strong,
But untested by travail or years;

Threading north o'er Ohio hills,
Following valley and stream,
Their foresight a bulwark against all ills,
And in their hearts a dream.

Molding the future with willing hands,
Its triumphs mingled with strife,
Carving from untamed forest lands
A home and a way of life —
Such were they who silent lie
In Sixteen's calm embrace,
Forgotten, as we shall be, bye and bye,
Save for a resting place.

Imo Lucile Reece Loder

Heartland

The man remembers the boy that did reside within his youth and in his pride; his feelings not set aside, his land attached by criminal hand.
Recalls the streets of his wondrous days of safety
Contentment, where the child once played.
Now filled with dust that only tears still;
From Mothers and families of loved ones lost there.
Now grief is all that is left, as crying silence fills the air.
Tragic and loss is their cost, the criminal set their price.
The Man remembers the boy, that did reside within his youth and in his pride. Look to his streets, feel his defeat.
Memories of youth now tarnished safety and all contentment abolished, because of the violence the criminal brought us.
Look to the Mother, the Father, the Brother the Sister and the friend.
Look to those who's time here, ends.
The Babies now gone, with only precious memories to live on.
Carry those left to grieve. Help them to live again. Nurture them, remember them, cradle them to love again. Pray for them for strength again. Encourage them to trust again. Look beyond your tears, reach from your heart and past your fears. Remember them that did reside where once they found their youth and pride.

Jamie Lynne Rhoads Terrell

Innocent

The sun rises and I am still innocent.
The sun sets and I am still innocent.
I walk outside and I am still innocent.
The wars and riots go on around me
and I am still innocent.
The babies without mothers starving
But I don't see any tears shed.
I don't see the pain and I don't see the fear.
Maybe, I'm not so innocent.

Jamie Flynn

Empty Nester

Years are gone, families raised.
  Problems all solved with new ones to age

We keep the faith to do our best
  with strength enough for all the rest

The sense of community enhances our hearts
  and brings out the best of everyone's parts

We challenge the new and proclaim to compare
  the difference of improvement or more despair.

We are part of the changes with all our Love
  for preserving the morals of yesterday's Dove.

True love is learned and patience deserved
  for all who have served
The God as our leader
  while only he holds the meter.

Thank you dear God for the gift of life
  from all of the husbands and all of the wives.

Dolores S. Christopher

"Manifest Destiny"

My heritage, pausing for recognition
proud and full of knowledge. Knowing
the land is the brotherhood of man
and creature. One in the same
feeding off each other for survival
in a Darwinistic reality. Made yet sculptured
from the Clay of masters. Masters of creation,
masters of surviving. They are the prototype
of the ideal man one with nature and the
mind of ones self. Yet the in pending
death of the nation was one with the
singular notion of Manifest Destiny
an idea that preached hatred and destruction
of the set ideals with a vengeance only obtained
by the truly selfish. The heritage of a nation
wiped out by a cause, and without any provocation to
speak of. No remorse given, not even a word.
Swept under the rug by time.

Dimitri Whitten

Tragedy

When you are devastated with a broken heart;
remember, you and the Lord are not far apart.

He is as close as a prayer, the whisper of His name;
and He will enter in to ease the pain.

You wonder why this tragedy happened to you.
Tragedies happen, but He will see you through.

Anger and confusion is natural, sorrow and mourning are too.
Just remember our blessed Saviour has His arms open for you.

Those passed on are in a better place;
where they may gaze upon our sweet Saviour's face.

The pain is all gone, the hurt is all done;
due to the grace of the precious Son.

Call upon His name. Let the Saviour in.
Call upon His name. Let the healing begin.

Dorabeth Dunning Sutterfield

Three Women Impressionist

Three women sit in the garden of life
Revealing to one another wounds life has cut sharper than any knife
For each shares a story that's sweet and true
Each cradles a steel tear from the hard times they've made it through

For life, they've found, is Happiness and Pain
As they talk about the ones loved and lost
And the ones that still remain.

Today they see so clearly the impressions of father, mother and child.
Their strengths, their weaknesses, the love so mild.
For was it not fate, their father, that brought them near.
Memory, their mother, that sheds a single tear.
And tomorrow, their child, full of wonder and surprise
For all three impressions reflect through the window of each eye.

Gather their thoughts as they did the flowers on this day
For like all precious moments, never forgotten but must end forever yesterday
But, the echoes of their fate, their memories, their tomorrows,
will always be -
Here in the Garden — "Impressions of Three"

Sherri Mohan

In Memory

At first you were my dark and handsome stranger,
Saying all the sweet and caring things.
There were the winks, the looks, the stolen kisses,
All the dreamy romance young love brings.

Then came to love, the marriage, home, and children;
Our life to spend together would unfold.
You were my friend, my lover, and my standby;
Together we made memories untold.

As I look back upon the many mem'ries,
The good times and the bad times we went through,
I know I'd do the same as I did then, love,
'Cause nothing had a meaning without you.

You were all the things I really wanted.
You were all that meant the most to me.

Donna M. Morice

Only In My Dreams

  THUMP, THUMP: THUMP, THUMP.....,
Says my heart one million times a minute.
My eyes are glued to him and with all else I become blind.
All sounds around me deaden, and even his softest footsteps,
My ears seem to find!!!

  I feel his very presence, even when he's not here with me.
His sexy, soft masculine scent, fills my every room so securely!
In my dreams he's always there, touching my every move and thought.
We do our own thing but together we share, we love each other a lot!

  In the morning my eyes awaken,
A river starts to flow.
My reality with him is shaken,
For nothing ever grows!!

  I pick up the telephone in sheer desperation.
Hoping to hear him, and hear him say......
I hang up in heartbroken frustration,
Knowing that it's only in my dreams....,
It'll never be...
NEVER BE THAT WAY!!!

Ellen Wilkinson

Airs And Incense

Stories lie in the dancing smoke
Secrets untold released by fire

Hypnotizing gray spiraling up from an amber
Ancient perfumes sustaining an impossible high

Dreams come flowing through
Thoughts once past come to reality

Flying amongst dead stars and black holes
Pulled into the powerful vortex
A dizzy consciousness, sitting behind a wall

Eyes not seeing into the distance
Reaching back inside themselves

Senses numbed and amplified
A feeling of pleasure, inside a rotting corpse

Dixie O'Donnell

Old Lady And Her Cat

Together on the couch they nap.
She all stretched out, he on her lap.
For many months, since just a kitten,
With one another, they've been smitten.
The love they have, is plain to see.
He on her lap, head on her knee.
She strokes his back, and he will purr.
And with a paw, he will stroke her.
It matters not, that she's grown old,
For cats have, nine lives, I'm told.
The greatest thing, in life, they've found.
That love makes, the world go round.
She loves him, and he loves her.
She will smile, and he will purr.
Between the two, there is no gap.
She all the stretched out, he on her lap.

Ethel Crownover

Untitled

A frightened girl, lives inside my body.
She cries, but no one hears her.
She screams and no one's there.
She yearns for affection
From which she never received.
She cannot find security
She wants to leave this world of pain,
But doesn't know how to escape.
She needs someone so desperately that she settles for less.
Teach her, make her learn...
She is not alone
Show her she is the best, and is going to get better.
Comfort her when she cries for help.
A frightened girl doesn't understand
And she may never be free of her pain.

Karen Bromberg

Untitled

There is a flower in the field
That is more beautiful than the rest
Its glow stands out among many
There are other flowers around it
But, none of them could ever compare
With this flower's radiant perfection
When the wind and rain are strong
All the other's shall be beaten and fall
But, not this one, it will always stand proud
It is the finest of God's creation
This flower is the very best of all
Because this flower I speak of - is you.

Derek J. Hurst

Missing Out

She's very quiet most of the time
She hardly has a word to say unless asked a question

She seems so very sad when she should be happy
Maybe she feels she has no reason to be happy

There is something tugging inside of her
Some emotional rollercoaster
that refuses to settle itself else where

She feels a sort of loss but in all actuality
Has all the love and attention one could ask for

She's not pampered and though she has many things
She's lacking a most important ingredient to her happiness

She's not hopeless as a matter of fact,
Quiet hopeful but rather tired

What she wants most is not at all material
It has no monetary value
And requires no work from others

Her desire for such is quite natural
And for it, there is no substitute.

Angela R. Washington

"My Favorite Rapper"

My favorite rapper is "Da Brat"!
She is fresh and is all that.
Her first hit single was "Funkdafied"!
It was so good, it never died.
Her producer and buddy is Atlanta's Jermaine.
He made her songs good, it was insane.
Her actual first name is Shantae.
And anytime you see her, you got to say "Hey"!!!
On the west side of Chicago, 60644.
She entered a rap contest and won it for sure.
She always admits, she likes to get high.
But she ain't no phony, so she would never lie.
She is my inspiration and role model too.
She always brightens up my day,
When I'm feeling blue,
Da Brat is the greatest person all around.
When you hear her music, you'll
leap off the ground.

Jacqlyn Tikasingh

Mother

This is about my wonderful mother,
She is unique, not like any other.
So very sweet and I hold her dear,
And I want to tell her how much I love her while she is here.

She picked cotton from early till late,
Her fingers would bleed, her back would break.
Her muscles were sore, her head would ache,
But she endured it all for her kid's sake.

I remember times cornbread was all she could bake,
There was no flour for biscuits, much less a cake.
But she was still there for the kid's sake.

Mother had one hard and strict rule,
All her kids were going to school.

There is lot's more I could say about all those years,
Some of it would bring laughter, some would bring tears.

I think I am stronger for what we went through,
And mother I owe it all to you.

I want to say one more thing then I will be done,
I am glad God chose me to be your son.

Donnie Walden

"The Colt"

Running through the forest like her sister the deer,
She knew she was close, she could feel she was near.
The animals ran with her.
They tried to keep up the pace.
Over the rocks and the roots,
They were finally at the special place.
Where the sun touched as far as the eye could see.
And the fresh dew glistened on the grass.
Where she truly felt at peace and in harmony,
She wished the feeling would never pass.
Oh, but it did in that split second,
When she looked to the ground.
A beautiful, injured, newborn colt is what she sadly found.
He was trapped, yet born so free.
She saw the helplessness in his eyes,
She slowly bent to one knee.
She put her hand against his neck,
Let her fingers touch his mane.
She felt him take in a deep breath,
And let the last one out in pain.

Lisa Church

"The Acorn Falls"

Some say her soul called out for more
She sold her body for a score.
Her urge for drugs and smoking weed,
The acorn falls close to the tree.

The prison door closed with a resounding clang
Mary Jane started her time,
Her drugs had led to serving a gang.

Her wide sweet smile and come on look,
Now made the guards put down their book.

Mary knew men and used their needs.
A young guard filled her womb with seed.

A daughter conceived within prison's doom,
Adopted out, raised, outshone the moon.

A bright child, legend in her town,
Artistic, compassionate, cheerful and 'sound.

Some say her soul called out for more
She sold her body for a score.
Her urge for drugs and smoking weed,
The acorn falls close to the tree.

Hedy Christine Miles

Dawn (Thus The Dawn Did Appear)

When last I saw Dawn
She was a young and shy- silvery-dressed girl;
Creeping slowly in without fringe or curl —
But softly and still
Overcast with soft grays and November chill —
Then she started to mist even more
And cry a drizzle unlike before
As if turned down by some fathom Lover that
very starry night...
Up pops an umbrella or two
And she begins to teem a heavy Autumn rain
Down comes someone's fancy hairdo
wet, wispy — but without pain
As the gutters stream with her wistful, copious
tears
I step quickly now back in
On the luminous-toned windows I see
Zigzagging droplets
Thus the dawn appears
Thus the dawn did appear.

Paul Kogut

Sitting On Ashes

Take me away erase me from me smear me into nothing take my everything
Smash me into a thousand pieces burn me into pretty ashes taste me
Choke on me feel me inside you inside a burning you sitting ashes
A pretty violation of my everything inside a womb of dirt a rebirth of my me
Tear me down take out my insides show me the real me scared to see
the real me
Steal my everything shatter my little dreams show me how it feels
an endless routine
Rotten meat melts in my mouth with dirt it scrapes me off the wall
Inside a room of you sitting on ashes beat into submission take
this from me
Covered in stale skin to hide myself from your everything smash my
beginning
Steal my love and put it inside you over and over again drain me
to fill yourself up
Ruin my faith and throw it away cut it out of me pull it through me
it breaks me
Let me waste inside you burning inside you sitting on my ashes try
to save me
Show me what I could be look through me take my everything take it from me
Wreck myself ground me spoil me tear this from me a sick little beautiful
It rots inside me forever reminds me of what I really am crucify inside
On an erotic deathbed burning sitting on my ashes I'm happy I'm dead

Eddie Walter

Flames Of Death

Thick dark clouds of dangerous
smoke!

Two fire fighters helplessly
choke.

Trapped inside an inferno of flames—
Yet no one remembers their names!

The flames grew fierce as it headed
their way.

"Bring in more water!" I heard the Captain
say.

The collapsing of cement, the bonfire of
wood!

All hopes were lost as it's been understood.

Like a beacon in the night appear a tremendous
glow!

From the "Flames of Death" that took our
unknown heroes.

Hector J. Williams

Untitled

When the world is quiet
So am I
For I am the people.
I am the baby who cries each night
I am the children who are beat
Let them come to me
and I will hold them, love them
and take care of them.

I will show them
the world with eyes
big and bright
and let them hear the sounds they never heard.
I will soothe the Mother
and help the Fathers
For I am the voice of the people
I understand all languages
even though I am just a child.
Bring me your frowns and I will
turn them upside down with the
Voice of a child.

Dinajean Rodeman Lapczynski

Love??

What is it?
Something you feel with your heart?
How do you know when it's torn apart?
An emotion some will say..
For those who believe,
it might be just a prayer away.
When will I know, you say?
Is it love when the other turns away?
For such "a mysterious and a many splendored thing"...
Many know all about the pain.
Sometime on a bright and sunny day,
it will rain, then and only then you will
know why, such a beautiful feeling
like love can make you cry.
Then will come a day, when the birds and the bees
will play. Things you never noticed before
will brighten your day...
Then you'll know...

Is it Love??

Donnie Sevy

"Oh" I Was Soully Born, "With The God Spanta Galaxies Variety Of...."

"Oh", I was soully born, "with the God
Sparta Galaxies variety of sports funs:
"OH", I was soully born, with the God
Sport Galaxies variety of sports funs:
And sweetheart, "I go on praising God
is the man and God sport on the plains.
I can soully tell the galaxies souls
neighborhood chummy chums some mellow jokes.
Then hilariously jolly on home, "for my
favorite choices of the drink of the cokes.
The jovial golden ways of the lumerians
sports souls citizens under God Ishmain.
Of the God Olympus, from God Hesperus sports
galaxies of many excitements of the lost and the wons.
I always knew, with the God spica
golden taste of the batteries bread bums.
"Oh", I was soully born, "Oh", I was soully
born with the God sparta galaxies variety of sports funs.
"Oh", I was soully born-born-born with the
God sport galaxies variety of the souls sports funs.

Harold Gabriel McNairy

The Velvet Touch

The white blanket, covering the city in depth;
Stark images clothe, covering dirt and grime.

The white spired church, sparkling in grace
While the chimes toll in melodious song,

And we hurry by.
the storm rages, the conquer, to challenge.
On the mountain slopes, the body reigns, laughter abides.
Friendships kindle.

Unnoticed, time goes by.
Nature continuing its wrath
on the highway, smooth and shining, glazed in ice—

Sorrow washed down the road, tears mixed with flakes.
the loving embrace catches a glimpse of the debris
Hugging the memory of escape.
And this time: God stopped by.

Ethel (Hedy) P. Breunig

Beans And Peas And Peas And Beans

Shelled, spotted, shaped like the kidney
Strings, snaps, sprouts, and seedy
Beans and peas, peas and beans; yes indeedy!
Hulled, harnessed, hurdled and hopped
All send comfort and cozy messages from the pot

Fitted, snugged together all in a row
Forming, falling, filling and flashing in a glow
Peas and beans, beans and peas
Stand alone to satisfy a hearty protein tease
Sends a mighty healthy message all with ease

Eaten raw, boiled or mashed for sure
All curdled up in salads and soup du jour
Seems to give body to meals not a few
Round ones, rollies, ribbon-like and red
Multiplying in jars and pots with bread
Flat ones, fleshy ones, fat ones, and fiber filled
Fun ones. Fossilled ones, Flossy one smiled
Flayed, flexed, and flavorful you see
Beans and peas are worth the flavorful
Buy them by the bag, box, bowl flavorful.

Velma Jean Bennett

I'll Know

Don't send me flowers
That blow in the sun
Just shelter the homeless from rain

Remember me kindly
Send me a kiss
On the face of one ravaged by pain

Don't tell me goodbye
Our hearts are in tune
We don't need words to explain

I'll know that you love me
And I'll know that you care
For the difference you've made will remain

You'll know when the sun
Shines warm on your face
And the buds sprout new down the lane

That we were meant for this
Life to death to life
And a joy that is born new again

Gwin A. Williams

Poetry

There are little bits of poetry
that filter through my mind,
but it's hard to find a pencil at the time.

As I'm driving, while I'm working,
even dreaming, I will find
there's a certain flow of words that seem to rhyme.

But, of course, there is no paper
or a place on which to write
and I think I can remember just a few.

But it's not at all that easy,
it's a struggle and a fight,
to recall that certain phrase, or maybe two.

So it seems the key to poetry
is hearing from above,
it's not necessary that it be in print.

There are angels up there talking
and their words are filled with love,
if you'll listen, you'll be richer than the mint.

Yes, I hear a lot of poetry, too beautiful to write,
it's not written - it's projected - and it's blessed - with all HIS might!

Donald L. Bratten

To Share The Wonder

I want to share the splendor of that wondrous place
That records earth's history on its vast rock face,
On layers of Coconino, Supai, Bright Angel Shale
That line the wall of the Kaibab Trail,
Rocks that hold the dawn and sunset glow
And entrap awesome space in the canyon below.
To recall the silvery river in a scene from the rim
Now etched in memory clearer than film.
The dark purple skies and the lightning flash
That struck Wotan's throne with thunderous crash.
To talk of embedded fossils from Paleozoic seas
And of more recent dwellers among the pinyon trees.
While eager to share this wonder, the response I hear
"I remember, my son lost his sneaker there."

Edith MacRae

Come Fly With Me

Now shut your eyes and make believe,
That you are standing in a breeze.
Now spread your arms as if to reach
For a gust of wind to touch your feet

Now take a deep breath and let it out slow,
Do you feel the gentle wind that blows?
Now lift your head and jump up high
You've made it up. Now you can fly.
Fly over the mountains and down by the streams
Fly over the tree tops and through the sunbeams.
You can fly to the stars if this be your dream,
Things can be wonderful if you fly with me.

Now you can say in a mysterious way
That you took flight with me today
Isn't it magical don't you feel free
You can come anytime and fly with me.

Connie Vincent

Desert Morning

It's morning in the desert.
The air is chilled,
A sliver of white
As the moon, late, begins its rise.

El Sol begins another day
In crimson, red and gold;
He spreads his rays,
The lonely night to drive away.

The cowboy stirs
Embers to a flame;
Dried beef, beans, strong coffee
Just more of the same.

His horse stands waiting
Its burden to bear;
As the colors of day burst forth in the air.
It's morning in the desert...

Wish I was there.

Edward R. Deusenberry

Paradise Restored

Turn and look about you, as far as the eye can see,
To all that's set before you, for everything is free.
Go and walk throughout the land, upon the shores, upon the sands
Cry out in the valley plains, drink of every pouring rain.
Quickly! Run, with all your might, and chase the eagle in the heights
The earth's true bounties you may take and never a commandment break.

Amongst the beast do make your bed, of not a man you have no dread.
Rejoice with holy majesty, for everything is new, everything has
been restored, yes son, even you.

Robert Hannah

New Day

It's a bright and cheerful morning
The birds begin to sing
It's warm and yet the rain has left its touch
As if it's spring-
Green is shining through the
    left over mounds of snow-
The tiny squirrels are busy
    scampering to and fro -
The fence is sloping downward
    and the deck is listing so-
The feeling of elation sure
    begins to grow.
The promise of a new day
The sensation of surprise
Comes with the brand new morning and the beauty of sunrise

Dorothy Bartow

Grandma Francie's House

The house was old - 50 years and some —
    The husband and wife were very young, with an infant daughter
    and one small son
They asked God in, and He came to stay
    And that is how they "made their way."

They prepared the walls — and the curtains came...
    From bright checkered gingham and her treadle sewing machine.
The bookcase came from some borrowed "barn boards,"
    He planned and sanded and made them warm.

The castle they made was full of love
    And two more sons came down from above.
The door always open and the teakettle on,
    And the old farm prospered and so did their home.

Years went by and grandchildren grew
    And the house full of love grew and grew, too.
Six years ago, on a bright fall day,
    My Lord called my Davie home to stay.

The old house and I cried, for a man so true,
    But that's O.K. because Jesus cried, too.
Now the house is older — 90 years and some —
    And the teakettle's on, and Francie's not gone,
    Come and visit, Come!

Frances M. Christianson

The Lily Of Peace

Dear Jesus,
The Lily of Peace hung heavy weeping bitterly the sins you did keep,
"Sins of mankind!"
My heart was sadden to see such a grief, "prompt me to reach out in love."
I picked up her limp body and carried her in, "out of the heat of the sun."
Touching her limbs so weak in sadness, I heard her cry for the lost
sheep in sin.
I lifted my heart to you within and prayed for the life of the sheep.
I went to the well and picked up a pail and filled it with life flowing water.
As I prayed for the sins that men did keep, I nourished Miss Lily the
"breath of life!"
Hours passed and to my surprise happiness radiated her aglow!
Her body became upright, her limbs become strong; once again
"beautiful!"
Before my eyes to my surprise I beheld her "resurrection,"
Freeing the sheep the sins they did keep, granting a promise fulfilled,
"A life anew" and thanks to you "Life of great Peace,"
Resting in heaven your keep!

Donna J. Struble

524

My Father's Strength

He was the one who cradled his baby girl in one massive hand.
The same hand that brushed my waist-length hair in later years.
He was the one who carried me on his shoulders...
And ran many miles behind me on the giant blue bike.
He put his only child on motorcycles and horses and trusted
    enough to let me go...
Because he taught me and taught me well.
He was the teacher and I his only student.
Our classroom was a pond, his pick-up, the woods, or under
The nearest tree. Wherever we were together.
Time has passed...we have both grown and aged.
I look at him now and feel anger and bitterness at the illness
That robbed me of my super-Dad.
In a sense, I have become his strength and his muscle.
The little girl grew up and learned he is only human.
But in a grown woman's eyes, he is still the super-Dad...
    Still the teacher...
        And always my hero.

Gina Garver

"Summer Love"

The summer nights of warm sunset breezes
The spring of love in the air fills the moonlit evenings
Holding him close heats the passion of the season
Now tell me doesn't this sound like love in the heart?
Passion, passion of the best kind, a summer romance
First love is so often the sign of a summer romance
Don't you remember your first summer of passion?
Don't you remember the heat of the season?
Summer, sweet summer what is love without summer?
Every season means something different
But only summer means heat.
Passion and love grow strongest in the heat of summer
Remember summer and think of first love and the passion of the season!

Janice Tverberg

Reflections On A March Day

The morning comes coldly awake as I sit here listening to
The stillness, yet not still
Far off a barking dog, the roar of a plane overhead far up
In the sky, heard but not seen. Clouds drift by unaware.
The cat lies warmly in my lap, her pink rough tongue
Flicking out to kiss my fingers as I write.
How oft I sit here thus, remembering. I am alone and
Sometimes lonely yet I have but to think of you and I feel a
Richness steal into my reverie, and I am no longer alone.
I think of laughter shared and secrets spoken in the
Twilight's gloom. A look, a touch, a knowing smile,
Not gifts or deeds, but just the knowing that you were there.
Ah, sad memories, too, but none so sad as not to be
Forgotten soon with caring and loving.
If never our paths shall cross again, my heart will
Remember you and this shall warm me however cold the day.

Edna Fruehauf

Father-In-Laws

Father-in-laws to some are prim and proper,
To some he's known as "Gramps" or Poppa".
To his "Ma" - he is "Pa".
To his lad - he is Dad.
To some - he is the "Old Man".
To some a crank, and others a "fan".
Yet in our thoughts he is sedate,
He would like to be early, but is often quite late.
He would, no doubt, give you his shirt
But, he needs it for dress, so he can flirt,
I like to think of him as a helluva guy,
And be the one to lend him my tie!

George Mitchell

The Flower In My Life

The leaves are lush dark green; the roses are wrapped tight.
The sun is high in the sky, bringing just the right light.
Slowly without conscious effort, her petals begin to unfold,
With the touch of the soft, elegant petals, her beauty I behold.

The flower's ascending fragrance, breathtakingly sweet,
Circling, lingering in the air, I inhale her scent to meet.
Echoing with harmony, the sound from my throbbing heart,
Transforming the rhythm into loving music. Hark!

I contemplate in wonder; this is the Gardener's way.
God's gift unfolds more radiant with each passing day.
The fragile pink rose continues to endure.
The sight, the fragrance gives peace, me to reassure.

When each graceful petal one by one begins to fall,
It is the Saviour's eloquent voice, we hear Him call.
The great suffering on earth each soul must feel,
Through Jesus' compassionate love, we alone will heal.

Diana J. Weigel

Autumn

They wait not meekly for their death to knell,
The trees and bushes in the autumn scene.
No sombre-hued and furtive last farewell,
No mourning for the vanished summer green.

Magnificently garbed, in vibrant tones,
Mocking the sun, the rainbow and the flowers;
From purest ivory, pale as old bleached bones,
To lavish gold, with all its dazzling powers.

Copper, bronze, they shine like jewels bright,
Glowing like a fiercely flaming fire,
Every leaf becomes a shining light,
Every tree becomes a brilliant pyre.

Red as a sunset in the evening sky,
Their beauty sings a promise to the earth;
Glorious and undefeated as they die,
That death is just a prelude to rebirth.

Jean M. Buzan

Insanity

The cliff I hear its calling
The unfathomable abyss that lies ahead
Damn I think I'm falling into the realm of the dead
Into the shadows in the realm so deep
Below the earth where no one sleeps
The realm of the dead is where I'll wake
My innocence and soul the least will take
A few steps away from total insanity
I fear that soon it will take total control of me
Lying below the depths of the earth
Maddening screams, they're all this life's worth
A scream rises in my throat
A gurgling noise that I try to release
Oh my God, I have no control
I struggle and fight to keep my spirit alive
But it's too late I've already died
The demons around me, the crazed raging, beast
They gather around, for I am the beast
My life is over, my sanity gone
To my life I say farewell, so goodbye, so long.

Heather Barnes

My Garden

I love my garden that I grow each year
The vegetables I grow, I love so dear.
The carrots are fat and orange and long,
I plant with care, while I sing a song.
The peas are always green and fat,
While the lettuce I grow is thin and flat.
I stake the beans, so they'll grow real tall,
While the radishes grow tender and small.
While the egg plants grow purple in color,
The purple onions are a little duller.
The okra grows so tall and lean,
It makes you itch when you cut the thing.
Everything I grow is good to eat,
I cook and can, till I'm dead on my feet.

Harriett McCurley

Willpower

In the pond of my life.
There lived a willpower that was so strong it almost broke my heart.
It was a pain sometimes, but it helped me too.
Until one day all of a sudden an overwhelming feeling came.
Can you believe that it made kind of sense it hurt.
It made me realize how strong I was for myself,
   not to depend on others.
Even if they depend on me.
My heart is missing something I know.
It mostly feels like a big hole in the middle, of my heart.
But I made a commitment to myself to have willpower.
I blacked out then.
I knew I had died.
I saw a bright light ahead of me.
I knew then, God was waiting for me. At the altar kneeling, praying.
It was so clear, my mind was just about to be clean.
To see the one and only, God. All because I had willpower.

Christina Mathews

Heritage

These hills of home are dear to me.
They tell of times that used to be:
So green and lush this summer day,
"Come play on me", they seem to say.

The peace and strength I feel here,
Make life for me, serene and dear.
And as I sit this evening night,
The valley suddenly is ablaze with light.

What a different scene met eyes long ago
When my pioneer fathers wanted to know:
"Is this the right place for us to be?
There's sage brush and rocks far as eye can see."

But the words rang out "this is the place!
Wipe the sweat from your face.
Put your hand to the plow.
Go, and make a difference, now!"

Thus little by little the wild gave away,
Till we see this beauty that is here today.
Hearts swell and voices sing.
As the mountains echo and the valleys ring.

Isabelle J. Hanson

Springtime Is Here

Out of all the gorgeous and wonderful springs
This one has the prettiest things.
The flowers are bright and the clouds are blue
The stuff is pretty to me—is it pretty to you?

When Easter comes it is a joy
To every girl and every boy.
When rain comes it makes things grow
You can cut some flowers and have a show.

When it's hot you can go out and play
Every night and every day.
You can swim all day long
And while you are swimming you can sing a song.

You can get on a pretty balloon or go to the zoo
I like the tigers, the bear and the lions.
How about you?

Laura Williams

My Rose

There is only one rose for me,
This rose is my rose.
My rose was soft, tender, and full of life,
My rose has given me lots of love in the past,
And also made me realize the things I have taken for
   granted.
She has bought us her special charms, fun times, and laughter.
And also the great love she shared for her family and friends.
Now her love is gone,
Although she has left us sadness, grief,
   and a little disbelief.
We all wish she was still here,
But no one wishes more than I.
Now that she has gone,
I wish her love, peace, happiness, and everything
   she has given us.
I wish that my rose was still here,
To share her warmth and love with all of us
There is only on rose for me,
And that rose is my Grandma Rose.

Nathalie Spelman

Violin Strings

I am drawn to the black case,
thought it is dawn.
I open the case to unveil a violin.
It speaks to my soul reaching deep inside me;
to my heart.

The spirit of the violin fills my soul, my heart, my body.
I raise the violin to my shoulder.
the bow rises to my yearning fingers.

As the rays of Morning gleam at my window
I see the reality of my ability.
The sun's rays dance across the strings like dew on a spiders web.

The day has come now. I lay the violin down
into its velvet case and close the lid.
One lone ray of sunshine steals into my case
to turn my strings to silver; my violin to gold.

Forever more my music shall be clear,
as a bubbling brook on a sunny day
in June.

Jamie L. Grace

Red-Checked Dress, Size One

Violet, you were the first grandchild
To gladden our family abode.
You should have seen Grandpa,
Who took you for his own.
He went right downtown, the day you were born
And did something he had never done.
He bought for you a red-checked dress
In a size that was number one.
Well, of all things! It was hard to believe!
You could not have worn it 'til you were three.
All of this did not disturb him—
His mind was firmly set.
The first baby in the family
Naturally, you were his pet.

Delphia Puckett

To A Widowed Mother Who Has Also Lost Her Only Son

You nursed us in our sickness consoled us in our strife, and,
To my darling Papa you were a wonderful wife.
Through two big wars you worked and worried - giving all around -
You care - making sure of rations as they came - giving each and
All a share.

Your son, he flew in world war two - fighting war hell in the air -
Your heart and Papa's in those dark days saying many a fervent prayer,
Outwardly, you were sunny and bright, a smile on your face, your
laughter was light,
Papa would watch you and then hold you tight, saying, "'twas a war
that the younger men must fight".

Many happy years followed for Papa and you - with a golden wedding day
just for you two and,
Down memories lane no words can explain - the love that you shared so -
you dream - and live it all again.

God's hand has now taken both Papa and your son but, you shine valiantly
Through as you always have done, Oh! and you are still very proud of
Your appearance and looks -
About you dearest Mother - I - Could write books.

Sheila Smithers

Save The Children

We need to save the children no matter what the cost
Too many young lives today are being lost
With drugs, guns and fires we need to take control
If we don't act quickly we won't have them to hold

They don't know they're wrong when they're given drugs
We have to educate them through teaching and love
They don't know they're wrong then they're playing with guns
They watch so much television they think guns are fun

They don't know they're wrong when they're playing with fire
We should keep matches and lighters on a shelf up higher
If we want to save our children now's the time to take control
If we don't make changes now some of them won't grow old

It's up to us as parents to change our ways also
If we don't take time to teach them how are they suppose to know
So let's all join hands and show them the way
The future of America will be in their hands someday

Earl W. Schoettlin

The Photo

The photo had faded like the old eyes which gazed;
Trembling hands wiped dust from the frame;
Dim eyes strained to see the face of the woman;
Then a young girl with a future of dreams,

Burning tears fell, like a slow rain from heaven;
Forming little rivers on the old photograph;
She in white satin, he in dark blue,
For the final farewell, today he wore black.

Wrinkled hands placed the photo back on the table;
And shakily wiped the tears from his eyes;
Slowly he shuffled to the silent bedroom;
Whispered a prayer, then laid down to die.

Doris Zafra

Inner Pain

There's a pain inside of me,
Trying to be accepted only to be pushed aside;
If only I knew how they want me to be.
Then I could run with their tide.

There's a pain inside of me.
Wishing to be understood;
Yet still people tear at what they can't see.
Darkness covers me like a black hood.

There's a pain inside of me.
Surviving on the factor of no self-esteem.
Why can't people try to find me?
Why are they so mean? Do they enjoy preying on the weak?
Is it their pleasure to devour my inner self?
I struggle, trying to reach my mountain's peak
But before I reach it, I'm torn down like a rotten shelf.

There's a pain inside of me. How long can I hide it
When's the next time I'll be stung by the hatred bee?
When will I finally fall into the bottomless pit?

There's a pain inside of me, how long can I act sane?
How long will it take everyone... to see my inner pain?

Janna Piper

"Oh No" Said My Heart

The raindrops kept falling from skies that were gray,
'Twas as if the whole world were crying when God took her away.
We said our last goodbyes, that cold rainy day.
In the church that she loved, where she once knelt to pray.

The thunder it rolled, the raindrops kept time
With tears from our eyes in that long funeral line.
Our hearts were so sad, we wept and we mourned
Trying to realize our loved Mother was gone.

But is she really gone, "Oh No" said my heart
For where there is true love, you don't have to part
For she walks beside you so proud and so strong
Guiding your footsteps if they start to go wrong.

No she isn't gone, she's close by our side
Trying to lead us with God to abide.

Edna M. Kuykendall

Why

Why did he do that?
Why didn't I say no?
Why was I so willing?
Why can't I die?
Why did God let him do that?
Why can't anyone answer me?
Why can't I truly hate him?
Why do people say they know how I feel when they don't?

Laura Gross

527

Dance Of The Ages

Whirling
Twirling
Dancing, drifting
Small specks of dust inhabit the air,
Falling as singles, as trios, or sextet or pair,
Settling down, to the housewife's despair,
In a filmy dust-cover on things in her care.

I wonder what story a dust mote could tell —
Of tidings of joy, or of angels that fell.
Would the stories be new, or would they be old,
Of events that are recent, or are often retold,
Of cowardly acts, or of heroes so bold?

I patiently wait for the stories in vain,
As silently, mutely, the dust falls like rain.
Softly, quietly, filtering down,
Dancing, drifting
Twirling
Whirling
Down.

Shirley Durga

The Vision Of You

As I stare into the dark of the night,
Visions of you come to my sight.
You with that smile which glows like the moon,
With echoes of your laugh pouring into my room.
Your eyes piercing down like stars in the night,
As your hair flows gracefully, and briskly through flight.

Wave after wave putting me into a rage,
Please help me out, help me out of this cage.
Though I know it could be easy to have,
This vision of you has made me so sad.
Made me so sad that it is driving me mad.

But as I stare, while the sun breaks the night,
The vision of you grows far from my sight.
I will remember.....
I shall not forget.....
This vision of you which I briefly met.

Dwight C. Morgan

Something For Nothing

Waiting for the winds to change to sweep the clouds away.
Waiting for the rainbows edge to cast its gold your way.
Waiting for someone to turn your world around.
Looking for answers to the questions you have found.
Countless ways to pass the days!
You don't get something for nothing.
You don't get freedom for free.
You don't get wise with the sleep in your eyes.
No matter what your dream maybe.
What you own, is your own kingdom.
What you do-is your own glory.
What you love is your own power.
And what you live is your own story.
In your head is the answer let it guide you along.
Let your heart be the anchor to the beat of your song.
Because you don't get something for nothing,
you can't have freedom for free.
You don't get wise with the sleep in your eyes.
No matter what your dream maybe.

Marilyn Hemminger

Gray Manor

Have you ever been to an old folks home,
Walked by the rooms and heard their moans.

Insensitive nurses and other personnel,
Disinfectants and feces can you stand the smell?

Seen the old ladies clutching their purses,
Impatiently waiting for their nurses.

Eager to go shopping and get outside,
Looking around to see who's died.

And bald headed men with missing teeth,
Shots of morphine for pain and relief.

Cooped up in room amidst four walls,
Occupied wheel chairs lining the halls.

Look at their faces they're so depressed,
Hospitals gowns is how they're dressed.

Is this where we're heading -
Rolling you over and changing your bedding.

Wallowing in urine flat on your back
I'd rather go quick with a heart attack!

Dennis L. Burkman

Concrete Operations

In the houses, on the streets - children.
War, crime, violence - abstractions
not comprehended at this stage.
Twin brothers age seven, witness as
a fellow citizen blows their daddy's head off.
A little brother is shot as
he and big sister run for cover.
Everyday these scenes recur.
Everywhere in this land
you hear the deafening absence
of childish laughter.
Look! Children are playing in the rubble.
Yes, silent and grim with
make-believe weapons
they play - War.

Helen Aanensen

"Heavy However Hearts From Too Many Bleed"

The death toll in Oklahoma continues to rise
Waves over radio brought tears to my eyes
Television photos of black cloud in skies
Papers from workers were scattering like flies

Nine in the morning third April Wednesday started
Parents and children from care center parted
Marrah building workers this day most thwarted
Evil driven ryder devastation imparted

Blast biggest bite bestowed before brunch
Earth shaking tremor many buildings felt crunch
Quake quandered question so many held hunch
One deadly strike killing KO like punch

Happening here heartland not God act but war
Unsafe our streets unsafe are our door
Security sounds shaken world fears to the core
Crime cash corruption continuous cries pour

Aid from all over with things that they need
Emergency workers cooperating with lead
Digastuous bring tears plus together good deed
Heavy however hearts from too many forever bleed

James A. Gossett

528

Morning Meditation

When the sun rises each morning in the East.
We face the day like natures beast.

We never know what lurks ahead.
From the time we rise till we go to bed.

We leave the house with anticipation.
Forgetting to take time for meditation.

Whether it's work or school or play.
We should make God apart of our day.

Our heart determines the mood we possess.
Which helps to make for our failure or success.

Take the time to say a prayer.
God is up there and is ready to hear.

Live your life with God at your side
Let him in and do not hide.

Peace of mind comes when you let him in
You can not lose, you can only win.

God's love is there each and every day.
When you wake and proceed along the way.

If you keep your heart as pure as gold.
Life will be easier as you grow old.

Donald A. Woodson

Turnings In The Road

If it be wondrous or truly profound,
we search.
Because we desire peace we reject the paths to it.
To seek love is more then we could hope,
but it is to be when it is so finite.
To have contentment makes us walk more proudly,
we can not believe the joy it brings.
To live we bear the emotions that are ours to
share or guard.
Unknown to us in the time that best to be used,
and the purpose of the choice.
Our wanderings are guided by the inner light that
brings us to sheltered valleys in the mists.
For the truth we acknowledge we show the strength
of our spirit.

James A. Wingrove

Parents Remembered

When we are young and so naive,
We seldom listen or believe
What parents say or try to teach;
We often think it's just a speech.

Then as adulthood approaches near,
It all becomes so crystal clear
That what our parents strived to do
Was love, protect and guide us through.

And though we may not think the same,
Both parent and child are not to blame;
For each of us must be our own
Through all experience we have known.

When we have lived through all our trends,
Our parents have become our friends:
We share our lives and love each other,
We've learned to honor our Father and Mother.

And when we're grown and live apart,
We hold the memories in our heart:
We look back on our parents and say,
"I wish they were still here today".

Janet R. Henry

Untitled

Soft sounds of drums in the distance
welcoming the bright sun in the morning
I awake from my dreamless sleep
and start the day off right

Shimmering stillness against the dawn
I smile at the whiteness of my lawn
"It's Christmas day," I shout with glee
I see the presents under my brilliant tree

A warm wind touches the earth
I awake to the aroma of fresh brewed coffee
my cat still sleeping next to the fire
the snow still falling in the breeze

Joe Decker

Happy People Dancing

If I could invent a rainbow to make people happy and never sad again,
    what a wonderful, mystical fairy tale that would begin.
People playing great music and getting down with all of their favorite
    dances from dawn to dust,
    and laughing so hard until they almost bust.
How I would love to see folks dancing all day long, forgetting all
    their cares and worries, and nothing going wrong —
Just happy people of all races dancing and singing together a most
    colorful song!!!

Haven A. Tillar

Crazy Ostrich

Oh Mr. Ostrich with your head in the hole.
What are you doing, looking for a mole?
You silly creature, can't you see?
I'm really stuck and can't get free.
Please help me and give it your best shot.
Maybe you can get me out of this spot.
Oh dear, I'm afraid you're in quite a pinch.
I've pushed and I've pulled but it won't budge an inch.
Maybe strength is not the key.
Let's use our heads to set me free.
I'm sorry, I don't mean to be blue,
But I'm just a monkey, what can I do?
Excuse me you two, I don't mean to intrude,
But you're blocking my entrance and I think that's rude.
Mrs. Mole, don't be upset with me.
I'm just helping this Ostrich get free.
Crazy Ostrich!! This is the last time I'm digging you out.
You better start thinking before you stick in your snout.

Suzie Miller

Untitled

Screaming, crying, no way out
what just happened, did, without a doubt.
Drinking, driving, late one night
Don't you know what's wrong or right?
asking, begging, for a ride
Even to one who'd drink and drive.
Walking, running, to the car
From the party at the bar.
Worrying, wondering if your late
Unknowing where your led by fate.
Green light, red light, they switch so fast
Slam into another car boom! bang! crash!
Sirens, sounding, three are dead
Two are children, one the friend.
She Begged, pleaded, for a ride home
Now she's dead, and you're alone.
Always, sleeping, it happens to many alive,
When friends let friends, drink and drive.

Tasha Rurka

Obstreperous?

Oh, love how can you use that word with such sweet innocence
When all the while, with full red lips and sparkling eyes you incense
Me with such desire and a growing passion
That leaves me but little room for compassion?

What meaning does it have for me
When you've just made me fall
So much in love that my former thoughts
Are now far beyond recall?

Oh, love, what do you want of me
Kind man, considerate and mild
Or lover wild, with caution strewn
To whatever winds should blow? Or both?

What meaning does it have for me
As I go on slipping, sliding
Falling ever deeper into love
My heart as aflame as the sun above?

James H. Anderson

Free

Why does the cage bird sing?
When it is limited in where it can fly and what it can see, but
its spirit soars freely as it sings its sweet songs.

Freedom: Man are much like the caged bird. Even though he is
free to wonder, but still limited on where.
Free to see, but still limited on how much he sees.
Each day he walks through life with limitations.

True freedom: is standing firm, therefore, do not submit again
to a yoke of bondage. Let us walk in spirit.
I am free! I am free!

Janice L. Brooks

Ladybug

Ladybug, tell me, how do you know,
When it is time to stay or to go.
Now for can you travel, how high can you fly,
With wings not as large as the dot on an 'I'.

Do you hop from a petal, then to a pod,
Does a bumblebee sound like a great singing God.
To roses taste sweet as the breath they exhale,
Are you frightened of robins and scared of a snail.

How magic the moment, how wondrous the charm,
I feel when I feel you rest on my arm,
Two creatures in silence; you resting there.
And I half-asleep in my old rocking chair.

Two worlds-yours and mine, come together at last,
While the third one is spinning into the past,
I stare at your body, you stare at mine,
Somehow we know we are both lost in time.

James R. McElwee

One Dark Hole

In the meaning of life there is one dark hole,
This is where I sit all alone,
No one there but me, all my friends are in the light
Fight as I might, I never get to the light
The dark has taken me as his friend,
He'll never let me see the light again
As my friends see me they run
Side by side, they see darkness and I

The dark hole I sit in is a large one in fact
Many people come in, all of them go out
Darkness lets everyone go but me,
Oh, will you come in and talk to me!

Cynthia Allen

"Adam And Eve"

Adam's thoughts upon seeing Eve for the first time
How dark the night
when love lay,
wasted,
like a shattered shell
upon the sands of time.

Then love, so new,
came dancing through
the shaded shutters
of my soul
like bright, white light...
and darkness
fled.

Janet E. Hecker

Lord, I'll Never Forget

Lord, I'll never forget the mercy you've shown
When others have left me and I'm all alone.
I'll never forget the miracles you have done,
With you in my life, all battles are won.

Lord, I'll never forget that you're on my side,
I can always come to you and always confide.
I'll never forget the filling of the Holy Ghost,
Lord, above everything else, I love you most.

Lord, I'll never forget your saving grace,
Now I'll have peace when death I'll face.
I'll never forget, my prayers you have fulfilled,
Things I have asked for while before you I kneeled.

Lord, I'll never forget that you chose me,
Changed my heart and life and set me free.
Lord, you're the answer to all worldly strife,
I'll never forget you, not one day of my life.

Delta McLaughlin

My Mother-In-Law

She lived to be almost eighty-seven
When she was called to the gate of heaven.

She was Mom, Ma and Mother
Nana, Grandma and, of course, Grandmother.

She was confidant, friend and tutor
Cook, banker or counselor would suit her.

Trust in God, her life's principle
Truth, honesty, charity, just that simple.

She plodded and struggled through foul or fair weather
Managing to keep her family together.

But, now she has eternal bliss
Rewarding me with a farewell kiss.

My hope, someday to meet her again
In company with my parents and very dear friends.

George Mitchell

Pretendo

If I wanted to dance, you were my partner.
When Zorro arrived, you were my sword.
As I would giddy-up through the yard, you were my horse.
And if I wanted to sing, you were my microphone.
The witch's costume was not complete without you.
Then a voice would say, "Dianne, what are you doin'?"
"I'm still sweeping the floor Moma: I'm just sweeping the floor."

Dianne Butler

Beyond The Moon

There lies a place beyond the moon where memories no longer exist.
Where earthly possessions and mortal obsessions.
Are lost in the dense of the mist.

Time stands still beyond the moon, the mind can pause in peace.
Our lee side desires and wind crippled dires.
Are obscured when we search our beliefs.

Silence abounds beyond the moon, attentions can focus within.
Our earthborn concerns and deep mortal years,
Are drowned in the undetectable din.

Vision is clearest beyond the moon yet no light traverses the sky.
We can revel in solitude, there's nothingness in plenitude.
And all unfolds in the mind's eye.

Souls are found beyond the moon, those lost and those never known.
Peace calms the spirit and silence is a lyric,
And we know we truly have grown.

Peace is found beyond the moon, our world can slow and rest.
Bodies loose tension, minds move to ascension.
And there we are at our best.

Go there
with Godspeed.

Koni Huddleston

Still Water

   Still water is calm as the deep blue sea...
Where you can watch from far under that great big palm tree.
   The ocean waves roar in a dramatic sound
as the tides slowly move in touching ground.
   The seagulls fly in the neutral blue sky,
in such a silence it makes you wonder why...
   Everything around me suddenly becomes still
the breeze from the ocean gives me such a soft chill,
   Sitting in the sand watching the sun go down...
has me wondering why I'm sitting with such a frown.
   Could it be that still water has my thoughts in such a freeze...
So deep that I'm crying on bended knees
   All around me everything looks so bold...
I reach out with tears and find there is nobody there to hold.
   As the night slowly comes to an end...
I walk the sandy trails with my imaginary friend.

Stacy Kimbel

Grandpa Spinner

Grandpa spinning pennies upon the table top.
Where's the penny spinning?
Where will the penny stop?
Dimes they spin much faster than a spinning penny does,
and no one spins them better than my grandpa......cuz,
Grandpa's been a spinner, ever since I was a tot,
always spinning pennies, I know he spun a lot.
Coins upon the table, each stands up on its side,
Spin it! Grandpa! Spin it! Each one of us had cried.
Now Grandpa's not just Grandpa, now Grandpa he's a great.
No spinner ever beat him, best spinner to this date.
.............cuz.................
Grandpa's been a spinner, ever since I was a tot.
Always spinning pennies, I know he spun a lot!
Coins upon the table, each stands up on its side.
Spin it Grandpa! Spin it! Each one of us had cried.
Till one day our Grandpa, he never, never came.
Embedded in my memories that
..........spin it, spin it game.

Donna Osterman

Faith

I walked to the beach today, but the ocean wasn't there
whit lace ruffles danced about knee high and they danced to a tune
  oh so gentle,
But the thunderous roar from behind was ever so mindful of the sea,
Hidden but not gone

It reminded me of God, sometimes not seen, but there because you know
it, his presence apprehends you and you've experienced him before,
Out there in the middle of the Ocean, like a second in a lifetime,
you've been in Him

So overwhelming can his magnificence be that you long for land and
yet, once you're there, long to be back in him... You can look for him
And in the depth of dusk and fog you run into him, Or you can be still
and let him surround you with his presence, he touches you with the
gentle dance of waves on shore and, he reminds you of his magnitude
with his roar from what seems to be nowhere but, everywhere

In the air you smell him, taste him, feel the freshness of his
habitation, and so we know faith, and trust that like the mighty ocean
God is there, always, strong, yet gentle, quiet, yet boisterous,
hidden, yet obvious, nowhere yet everywhere.

I walked to the beach today and the ocean filled my spirit, he danced
on the sand a lighthearted jig and sang me a song of toe tapping
tunes, and drums of distant shores, he stayed with me as I walked
and looked no more.

Cyndi Savage Rice

"Lovers Who Are Now Strangers"

Lovers who are now strangers
who promise to Love, Honor and Obey
till death do them apart.

Lovers who are now strangers
who promise to have to hold-forever......

Lovers who are now strangers
who promise to stay with one another
through sickness and through health.

Lovers who are now strangers
who promise to be together
through poverty and richness.

Lovers are now strangers
who vow these treasure in matrimony
but soon departed and went their own ways.

Never to return to each other
ever again......

Jaqueline F. Wooldridge

Why?

Why do I fall in love, but only to get hurt?
Why do I fall so hard, but only to land in the dirt?
Why do birds sing so cheerful every day?
Why do they not divorce, when their mates go astray?

It's really not in me to do a dirty deed, I'm always with
Open arms, to help someone in need..
So if you see me with a tear, falling from my eye..
The hurt and pain will soon surpass, and again I'll ask
Myself - why?

Robert Lee Richardson Sr.

Faith

For Charles Murray, St. Bernard's, Maryland
I once met a man with a heart like Grand Canyon,
Wide open to all, and beautiful to behold,
Kind words, kind ways, always smiling and helping,
Those who are burdened and feel all alone.

Charlie is strong, his spirit soars,
To a power higher than himself, where he gets
   his strength,
Then he gives away everything he receives from above,
Peace and Joy—Unconditional Love.

His faith is unshakable, his goodness endures,
The world is a sad place, but Charlie is sure—
That each day can get better.

There is a prayer I've often heard him say,
In every kind of weather,
"Lord, help me to remember,
   nothing is going to happen today,
That you and I can't handle together."

Jeanne M. Smith

That's What I Think Of You, Each Day

You make the darkness seem so bright
Will you still love me in the night?
By the shores of the seas,
With the sea breeze blowing through your hair,
You are in an image of a goddess standing there.
Curved and slander to perfect form,
A beautiful rose without a thorn.
Like red hot ember your lips glow,
In the wind your hair flows.
I look into your eyes,
They are as vast as the seas
On a voyage they are taking me.
On this voyage will you come
Be it hotter than the sun?

Gregory Khitrov

Monday Night, 11 PM

Another leaf fell today. Fall is coming, soon the cold of
Winter. I in my nightshirt, got out bed, to answer the
hollow call, and now I sit in the shadow of darkness.

Peter was one of those fellows whose smile, whose smile
would light up any room. I would try to amuse him, and he
would look at me in that curious way, smiling as if he was
not quite sure what planet he had just landed on, but
sincerely hoped the natives were friendly. And we'd laugh.

The crab got him, shouldn't have, but did. So young, my
friend, to face the fire. It hurt to see him lying there, a frail
clothes hanger draped in cotton, hair almost gone, speech
slow and strained, eyes grasping... He was my ski partner,
the bicycle guru, my left-winged friend. Now his wings are
clipped; Peter will fly no more.

Pull the shades, there is nothing more to see. Oh me, oh my
and my worries: bills, clothing, the red or the white car?
Death is but a remember that we are immortal, for a limited
time only.

James J. F. Forest

Forever Eden

Anticipating my next moments;
With envisions of your magnetic touch
The nucleus of my being; love unblemished,
Radiating beyond the circle of life.

The heavens; angel filled,
Vigilance of our joy;
Loves devote reward
Our child of girl and boy.

As the crested wave, resurrecting from the sea;
Its strength underrate
A cradle modeled from my arms
Savoring your respect and humanity; parody to none I've seen.

"God's creations"; minute to bold,
Generate life's design
Sculptures harmony of love
Thus, in you I find; I live with love.

Alice Hill Blackburn

Wish For Humanity

This journey we call life, sure it is a daily struggle for such is our way.
With no Hardships we don't learn, don't grow and for us that is death.
We must strive to live, love and be more than we were the day before.
To build something better, bigger and faster than ever was before.
Such is progress, but it is not cheap nor easy.
Life lost, toil and burdens in ignorance.
These are the prices of this advancement.
Prices that must be paid; we as a race must absorb the cost equally.
So that we as a race may grow equally. Then there is understanding.
No jealousy, no ignorance and no waste of the human spirit.
Madmen and dictators are the killers of democracy, they must be taught.
All of us... the race are one, none better and NONE worse.
If this abstract called the human race ever does overcome prejudices...
And the Human Spirit does grow as a living entity, then the stars
And all within are ours; for from then on, the only barriers are the
Steps of knowledge. As we learn we step up and grow more.
Perhaps someday all will come true and on that day perhaps we will
Finally realize just what we were placed on this Earth for.

Timon the Bard

Heaven and Earth

Eyes the darkness of night
with the shine of the stars above,
Eyes the warmth of earth
the color of the harvest we reap
the fruit of our toil,
Eyes reflecting the happiness of children,
Eyes the blue skies above,
Eyes that lash the anger and wrath of God,
And gray eyes of weeping people,
neither black nor white
The eyes of discouragement
The eyes of a glooming day.

Deborah Sloane

Bluebird

Hear their song's that welcome Spring,
warm wind's blow their echo rings
Feel the warmth, rays beaming through skies,
forgotten seed's stretching so high.
Tree's awaken and leaves spread wide,
slumber is over, no more need to hide.
River's are flowing swift and clear,
quench the thirst of a gentle deer.
Bouquet's embrace the once naked field's,
snow has melted, that one must shield.
Showers dancing on rainbows so bright,
What canvas, but earth could hold such a glorious sight.

Patricia A. Marshall

"I Know"

I love you more than any one before.
With these words, I'll try to
Explain exactly how I know.
Yes it's true I may have loved before,
But never actually ever given someone my soul.

Lying next to you every night.
I feel as if we are becoming one.
You have given me the strength and courage,
To not just turn and run.

And to find someone.
Who can take the love I give.
And return it ten times in full.
Assures me of any doubts I may have.
And reminds me of how I know.

Douglas D. Van Der Sloot

It's Sweet Out Here! Yes, It Is;

Especially when rays of sun
Yield minim rainbows
Faced on twinkling dew
After canyon covering fog
Is trundled o'er Mission Bay
Past prolonged Point Loma toward
The Coronados rising from Pacific blue.

Then on patio floor is spread
Dry seed; their daily repast
For hopping, skipping, fluttering jays,
Mourning dove, goldfinch and quail.
Mother spotted mountain quail turns
Ruffing her feathers, signaling "come."
Seven chicks march single-file heralding their days.

It's sweet out here,
Oh yes it is!

Diane W. Carnes

The Masterpiece

This masterpiece was given to me and again and again people say
You brag about this work of art, why isn't it on display?
I tell them I can't show them this because it is one of a kind
And they wonder time and time again, is the masterpiece really that fine?
There will be no replica of this art because imperfection would ruin it all
You could never just paint a picture, and replace this art upon the wall.
But this masterpiece it can't be seen, for it's in a place seen just by me
You may enter my home in search of it, and ask me a million times why
I brag about this masterpiece, but you can't see it with the naked eye.
And others have seen it unconsciously, but were so engrossed with a
   framed piece of art
They didn't realize it was in front of them, the truth would have
   melted their heart.
And when the time is right, I then explain
That this masterpiece walks, talks, and breathes
And out of the frame walks the mysterious soul
The MOTHER that God gave to me.

Heather L. Browning

Sorrow And Pain

Your pain is gone forever but our sorrow is still here.
Your pain left so early no one had expected it.
Sorrow had come unexpectedly to everyone around you
Their hearts are with you always
and we will never forget all the fun we had
When you were around us but most of all
no one will ever forget the sorrow and pain
that filled all our hearts.

Heather Cron

"The Purple Skirt"

I went shopping today -
   You know - the after thanksgiving specials...

Everything was on sale - or so it seemed
   People were pushing and shoving and snatching and grabbing!

I found a "Purple Skirt" - !!
   Some really fat lady tried to take it from me

But - I held on

I love the "purple skirt"!
   the hem is uneven hangs longer on one side.

The price was right!
   I lean to the left and people think I have one short leg.

I get a back ache when I wear it but no matter,
   it hangs even, - it's purple and it's me!

I wish you could see it!

Ima Poffenberger

Take A Stand

There's no middle of the road, my friend.
You know we're really near the end.
The time has come to take a stand;
You can walk away — or take my hand.

With luck, my path may lead the way
To freedoms lost or given away.
We've let sick people hold the power
Over our future — the fault is ours.

We can't walk away from the truth anymore,
We do something now or just close the door
On all we believed in and taught in our schools,
We take a stand now or be lost to their rules.

This old world's about to slow down and shift gears;
We've raped and we've pillaged her too many years.
We may save her yet and, perhaps, make amends...
Take a stand and be counted as one of her friends.

Janet R. Martin

Molding A Child

Real love is the greatest asset in a parental molding Guild;
your Bible and Library have many answers, to the final molding of
your child.

As I take God's clay to mold, in its earliest, softest stage;
the child searches my eyes and mouth for answers, it learns at
this highly vulnerable, innocent, trusting, early age.

I must not give the wrong signals to this soft pliable clay;
the molding must be gentle and subtle, in a musical kind of way.

If you yourself was molded to seek your own personal wants first,
and others around you come last; without help, your molding will
resemble your own distorted selfish looking glass.

While it is still so soft and pliable, I want not to make a bad
mistake; but many parents pay no attention when molding, and
become concerned and saddened, when it is much, much to late.

If you don't love and enjoy the molding, and have your own wants
on your mind; for God's sake, and their sake, wake up, do your
job, before they get involved in crime.

Plant good high moral seed as you go along; cultivate them, try
to make them strong.

George Ervin Rhoads

My Eyes Through A Rose

You touch my petals so soft within, it's like smoothing
your hand across my skin.
Blooming to sunlight and heaven above, opening myself
showing my love.
Closing at nighttime to start another day, taking you in
my petals and leading the way.
My stem so firm to show our backbone of life, if I weren't
a rose I could be your wife.
Leaves among my stem strong and upright, I use to wrap
around you on a cool summer night.
My roots are those who keep us tight, packed with dirt
our love flies higher than a kite.
The rain has come and so you see, water droplets on my
petals not rain, but tears are the key.
Not to worry my stem stands strong, for I know you
can take me from the ground and make my life last long.

Teresa Hutchinson

Life

When you are born you feel so new,
Your life is happy not blue.
When you get to be a toddler you learn how to walk,
you may not know how to talk.
Whet you get older you have to go to school.
You have to follow a lot of rules.
When you get to teens you feel so smart,
But if you take drugs you'll fall apart.
When you get to college you can't be dumb,
Because when you get older you'll owe lots of sums
When you get older and have children of your own
You've got to tell your children that they're not alone.
When you get to be a grandparent old and gray
Tell your grandchildren they'll be like you some day.
Through the years it's come about,
You've always been able to sort things out.

Heather Layne

To Nether

If you were a song, I would sing you always,
your words would never leave my lips.

If you were a poem, I would memorize your every line
until you dwelt within my very soul.

If you were a painting, I would cost my eyes upon your beauty
and cherish you for all eternity.

But alas in all reality you are these three to me.
The music to my song, the words to my poem,
the image to my brush.

Rob Abernathie

Biographies
of
Poets

AANENSEN, HELEN JOSEPHINE
[b.] October 6, 1929, Port of Spain, Trinidad and Tobago; [p.] John and Josefina Sullivan; [m.] Gordon Aanensen, September 3, 1949; [ch.] Eight daughters, seven sons-in-law, 12 Grandchildren (four boys - eight girls); [ed.] Holy name convent (P-O-S Trinidad) University of Northern Iowa (Cedar Falls, Iowa) Graduate Courses from UNI, Iowa U. and Calmar Community College; [occ.] Last past position (10 years at Sigourney H.S.) Retired (1996) High School Teacher; [memb.] Holy name Catholic Church Catholic Daughters of the Americas. Have served on the foreign language A.E.A. Advisory board in Ohum WA, IA (1966) Certified teacher of catholic Daughters Teach 9th. Grade at Holy name.; [hon.] Graduated from High School with 2nd, class honors 1947 was on the Dean's List (once) at U.N.I. Graduated with a double major in spanish and English from UNI. B.A. 1977. Then returned in the summers to UNI for a speech endorsement.; [oth. wrt.] Several poems published in Lyrical Iowa. A poem and a play (children's) published in The Signature (UNI magazine); [pers.] Children are our most precious resource. Many live in a terrifying environment. Their wide-eyed innocence and disarming perception are at once, lovable and alarming.; [a.] West Union, IA

ACKERMAN, BRANDISE APRIL
[b.] April 10, 1982, Akron, OH; [p.] Cathy and Floyd Ackerman; [ed.] K-8th grade Glover Elem and Goodrich Middle School; [occ.] Jr. High Student; [memb.] Akron Baptist Temple, Awana Assistant, and Parent, Teacher, and Student Association. (PTSA); [hon.] School-Honor and Merit rolls; [oth. wrt.] Poems in school newspaper; [pers.] I write not what I know or see but what I don't know and can't see.; [a.] Akron, OH

ADAIR, PAMELA
[b.] December 30, 1960, Anderson, IN; [p.] Donald and Joyce Adair; [ed.] High School; [occ.] Aspiring writer; [pers.] The words is sharper than a dagger and cuts into our inner most thoughts and desires and exposes us for what we really are and leaves us bare and wide open for everyone to see.; [a.] Jacksonville, NC

ADAMS, AIMEE R.
[b.] December 12, 1974, Rockfold, IL; [p.] Rev Gerald And Christine Adams; [ed.] South Shore Christian High School, Nyack College; [occ.] Student of Nyack College; [memb.] National Honor Society, MENL (Music Educators National Conference); [hon.] National Honor Society, Presidential Academic Fitness Award, Salutatorian Of My High School Senior Class, Certificate Of Merit Of Nyack College for Outstanding service to community College, Distinguished Christian High School Student Award; [pers.] "And whatever you do , whether in word or deed, do it all in the name of the Lord Jesus, giving thanks to God the Father through Him".; [a.] West Hempstead, NY

ADAMS, JAMES V.
[b.] April 6, 1932, Minneapolis, MN; [p.] Edward F. Adams and Mildred McDonald; [occ.] "Cowboy, soldier, hobo, farmer, cabby, gambler, poet, painter, fighter, singer, bodyguard, miner, novelist, etc . . . 105 jobs since 1946!", song writer: BMI, New York; song publishing: Catnip Music, BMI, N.Y.C

(Owner); [oth. wrt.] Books: All The Cake I Want (Autobiography, 1971), transcribed into Braile by The Minnesota Society for the Blind, 1976; The Sociopath (1983); Last Trip to Vegas (1993); [a.] Minneapolis, MN

ADAMS, JENNIFER
[b.] April 11, 1980, Baltimore, MD; [p.] Mark and Betsy Adams; [ed.] Sophomore at Bel Air High School Class of '98; [memb.] Varsity Swimming at Bel Air High School, the Bel Air High School Band, the Harford YMCA Swimming Team, and the Emmorton Barracudas Swim Team; [hon.] Minds in motion and I was awarded my varsity letter as a freshmen. Honor roll; [oth. wrt.] April, which is being published in a book of poetry called Perspectives; [a.] Bel Air, MD

ADDISON, BERNITA
[pen.] Pee Wee; [b.] July, 11, 1951, Longwood, MS; [p.] Richar Barnes Jr., Late-Earlene Barnes; [m.] Fulton L. Addison, March 20, 1972; [ch.] NiKeaful Addison, Kenya Addison; [ed.] High School graduate, Riverside High of Avon, MS 1970, ITI (International Tabulating Institute) of Washington, DC; [occ.] Home maker, former F.B.I. employee; [memb.] High School years, member of the Preside 4-H-Club Lives stock show cash and metal awards, class president and vice high school years; [hon.] High school years, member of the 4-H-Club (President). Live stock show cash of metal awards, through-out grade school, received awards for 1st and 2nd place contestant in spelling match.; [oth. wrt.] Poems written, but not yet published or submitted.; [a.] Cleburne, TX

ADKINS, JANE
[pen.] Jane Adkins; [b.] July 30, 1954, Charlotte, NC; [p.] Foster Parents 18 yrs.; [m.] Fred M. Adkins Jr., February 14, 1982; [ch.] One (1); [ed.] North Mecklenburg High, Huntersville, NC Queens College, CPCC, Continuing Education Courses Mingle Institute - Real Estate Salesman; [occ.] Director of Operations Take Ten Corporation/Brass Ring Carousel Company; [memb.] Charter Member, IFECA, IAAPA, AMOA, GAOMA, NCAMA; [hon.] President FBLA in High School, State Reporter FBLA, Secretary of Year 1980, Nominee, Century 21 Real Estate, Profiled in Playmeter magazine, requested as Speaker at State and National Association Meetings; [oth. wrt.] Have many poems written through the years, but none published. (Have never submitted any before.); [pers.] Never, Never, Ever, Quit! I have been told for years that the odds were against me and being raised in foster homes, I grew up believing that I would never amount to anything, until one day I realized, it was up to me! I have to believe in myself and never give up! I never have!

ADROVER, JESSICA
[pen.] Sigh; [b.] March 6, 1979, ND; [p.] Barbara and Jerome Herdrix; [ed.] Attending Effingham County High School, currently a Junior; [occ.] McDonalds, a cashier; [memb.] An officer in the Effingham County High Schools Drama Club, also involved with the Schools Poetry Society and Academic Decathcon; [hon.] A Thespian; [pers.] If you write about something, write how you feel, what you see or about pain. Don't write about nothing, nothing is boring. Always remember your friends,

without them you are nothing. Thanks my friends.; [a.] Springfield, GA

AHLBORN, MELANIE
[b.] May 25, 1970, Milwaukee, WI; [p.] James Osterman, Margaret Osterman; [ch.] Ripley, Drayke Nathan; [ed.] Cedarburgh High, Carroll College; [occ.] Social worker/counselor; [memb.] A.S.P.C.A. (American society for the prevention of cruelty to Animals), W.W.F. (National Wild life Federation), Red Cross First Aide And C.P.R. certified, Past N.A.S.W. member (National Association of Social Workers); [hon.] Alpha Xi Delta, Dean's List; [oth. wrt.] Honorable Mention for poem entered in county fair, professor wanted to published my editorial on animal experimentation in local newspaper.; [pers.] I would like to help others to help themselves communication through writing is just one of the many ways I hope to accomplish this goal, of mine.; [a.] Hartford, WI

ALAMIA, LUCY
[b.] December 15, 1944, PA; [p.] Jennie and Bernard Ingber; [m.] Vito Alamia, January 28, 1961; [ch.] Anthony, Vitojr, Peter, Mike, Chris and Jennifer; [ed.] Student at Adirondack Community College; [occ.] Student, wife mother and grandmother; [oth. wrt.] Novel in progress, six previously published poems.

ALBA, DIANA
[b.] May 28, 1946, Seattle, WA; [p.] Paul DuNard, Dorothy DuNard; [m.] Donald Alba, June 21, 1969; [ch.] John William, Christina Marie; [ed.] University of Missouri, Columbia; [occ.] Free lance writer/photographer; [hon.] Providence Journal photo contest Poetry/350th Anniversary/Rehoboth; [oth. wrt.] Providence Sunday Journal magazine, Attlesoro Sun Chronicle, Senior Sentinal, Feelings, Japanophile, Merlana Magical, our Journey and others; [pers.] With the brevity of life listen and leave a song.; [a.] Rehoboth, MA

ALEXANDER, VERDA L.
[b.] September 17, 1931, PA; [p.] William and Linda Blanton; [m.] Herbert W. Alexander, April 5, 1952; [ch.] Four (three sons, one daughter); [ed.] Graduate New Castle High School Attended: Cumberland College, Williamsburg, KY; [occ.] Administrative Assistant Shenango Pres by Terian Home; [memb.] Shenango Pres by Terian Church, Women of Shenango Missionary Soc.; [pers.] "The Question" was written for my grandson, Micah Charles Allen (aged 3). I try to draw a picture with words to reach something inside each reader.; [a.] New Castle, PA

ALFARO, MIKE
[pen.] Gino C., Richard Kimble; [b.] December 23, 1980, Toledo, OH; [p.] Jorge and Mary Alfaro; [ed.] St. Katherine Elementary Christ the King Elementary, McCord Junior High, Northview High School, Graduating year '99; [occ.] Student; [memb.] Toled. Ski Club; [hon.] In Kindergarten I got an award for best artist; [oth. wrt.] My Mame Is Death, The Hall; [pers.] Have a nice day!; [a.] Sylvania, OH

ALLAN, EARL R.
[b.] May 19, 1919, Baxter, IA; [p.] John and Janet Galloway Allan; [m.] Widowed; [ed.] Graduate of Baxter Community School System in Spring 1937; [occ.] Retired Farmer; [memb.] Arbor Society; [oth.

writ.] Unpublished poetry; [pers.] My writing is influenced by my love of nature's beauty, my strong ties to family and my Scottish homeland.; [a.] Baxter, IA

ALLEN, CINDY L.
[b.] May 4, 1957, New Castle, PA; [p.] Herb and Verda Alexander; [m.] Neil C. Allen, August 29 1987; [ch.] Micah Charles Allen; [ed.] Graduated from Neshannock High; [occ.] Secretary/Bookkeeper At Shenango Presbyterian Church; [memb.] I am a member Shenango Church Choir and the New Castle Music Club Chorus "Messiah" Performers; [oth. writ.] I have written many other poems; [pers.] I have been attending Shenango Presby. Church since I was 6 years old and now I work there! It is truly a joy. I believe if you speak kind words, you will hear kind echoes.; [a.] New Castle, PA

ALLEN, GEORGE BERT
[pen.] G. B. A.; [b.] April 8, 1925, Doniphan, MO; [p.] Edward and Mary Lee Allen; [m.] Christene E. Allen, (Maden) Boyless, February 29, 1948; [ch.] Kenneth E., Charlotte A., Lawrence W., Fred H., Boyd L., and Everett T.; [ed.] Eleven years; [occ.] Life time experience of manufacturing of farm and garden tool Handles, Sales, USA, and foreign countries; [oth. writ.] In poetry of providence, of his LIFE, in the pro-verbs, through plurals, and the precepts, giving the Word the complete authority over the TRUTH, for thirty years: In Precious times.

ALLEN JR., OLIVER C.
[pen.] Oliver Cromwell; [b.] November 29, 1954, Washington, DC; [p.] Annie Allen and Oliver C. Allen, Sr; [ch.] Dirron and Krishawn Allen; [ed.] Anacostia High School, Northern Virginia Community College, Strayer College; [occ.] Equal Employment Opportunity Specialist, Dept. of the Army, Washington D.C.; [memb.] Toastmaster, Association of the United States Army; [hon.] Alpha Sigma Lambda (IOTA ETA) Honor Society; [oth. writ.] Now publish, currently working on a manuscript.; [pers.] Education is knowledge and knowledge is power. Stay focused and educate your mind.; [a.] Woodbridge, VI

ALLEN, ROBERT E.
[b.] September 29, 1944, Palmdale, CA; [p.] C.W. and Dorothy Allen; [m.] Marcia Allen, June 14, 1969; [ch.] Karlos, Joel, Daniel, Katie Allen; [ed.] MA in Social Science (East Asian History) Southern Oregon College, Ashland, OR BA in History, SOC, Ashland, OR Diploma in Microprocessors and Microcomputers; [oth. writ.] Children's books: The Lion Who Liked Ketchup and There's A Big Orange Rat on Apple Mountain. Master's Thesis: Thailand: Center of A Triangle; [pers.] No matter how great the problem, no matter how persistent the trouble, there is a always a place to lean.; [a.] Sutherlin, OR

ALLEN, SHEILA HIGHTOWER
[b.] July 29, 1953, San Antonio, TX; [p.] James and Gwendolyn Hightower; [m.] Benjamin Allen, September 28, 1974; [ch.] James Benjamin Allen, Jamarcus Rashun Carrington; [ed.] M. Ed Admin. and Supervision, Augusta College; [occ.] Director, Adult Literacy Augusta Technical Institute; [memb.] Sigma Gamma Rho Sorority, American Association of Adult and Continuing Education, American Business Woman's Assoc, Network Augusta; [hon.]

Founder-Metro Augusta Adult Literacy Council, President Vice Pres and Secretary - Georgia Association of Public - School Adult Education, Outstanding Administrator of the year - Georgia Adult Literacy Association; [oth. writ.] Several poems published in local papers.; [a.] Augusta, GA

ALLEN, WALTER IRA
[pen.] Walter I. Allen; [b.] August 10, 1915, Harrisburg, PA; [p.] Sherman Allen, Hertha Allen; [m.] Isabel Virginia Allen, October 17, 1949; [ch.] Chris A. Allen, Peter F. Allen, Angela M. Shaw; [ed.] 4 Yrs. No. High, Worcester, MA, Clark University Worcester, MA (2 years) Leland Powers School of Theatre. Boston, MA (graduate) served with The American Field service as a Volunteer and the British 8th Army in the Middle East WW II; [occ.] Retired Author: Published works poetry, porphyry, mosaics in words; [memb.] crystals of life and trailing arbutos and in two anthologies of the poet (Pen and Pen) Misawaka, Indiana California Writes Club Calvary Church of Santa Ana, CA; [hon.] American Security Council Award Business Citizenship Competition, A Bronze Medal 1967. Mary times "Poet of the Moth" as a member of the California Writers Club (established by Jack London 1910; [oth. writ.] Short stories and plays, "The Cabbie", and dialogue, Misc short stories for children. I am believe in Christ Jesus as a my Savior I enjoy long walks in a near by Wilderness Park. My wife and I have 10 grandchildren who bring us great joy.; [pers.] I believe God often influences my poems. I am a conservative and believe God established this country as a "City built on a Hill" to honor and glorify Him. Recently we have lost our way, but we will; [a.] Lake Forest, CA

AMERELLO, AUTUMN E.
[b.] November 20, 1981, Louisville, KY; [p.] Jeffrey and Beverley Amarello; [ed.] Home Educated and 2 1/2 years of public school in grade 8 now; [occ.] Student; [memb.] Girl Scouts Swim Team Dance Student (starting 11th year); [hon.] Honor Roll, Math Awards, Spelling Awards Several ribbons and medals for swimming; [oth. writ.] A poem published in The Anthology of Poetry by Young Americans and about 100 poems in my own private collection that I've written; [pers.] My poetry is inspired by just about anything. My immediate surroundings, my thoughts, feelings, or just something, my thoughts, feelings, of just something I hear.; [a.] Laconia, IN

AMES JR., ROBERT D.
[b.] January 10, 1957, Long Beach, CA; [p.] Robert and Ruth Ames; [m.] Rhoda Ann Carr-Ames, March 19, 1988; [ch.] Rachael, Russell, Bobby III; [ed.] Graduated from memorial High School with scholastic honors. Attended business college at J.C. Santa Rosa Calif. Have 1 yr. College; [occ.] Service Dept, Mid. West Coca Cola Corp.; [memb.] My membership is Invested in my Family. The most important membership that a man could have.; [hon.] Military service honorable discharge. PTO Member.; [oth. writ.] Articles printed in local news paper. Children's Christmas story (unpublished) european adventure story (unpublished) many poems love, sad, patriotic, and kids poems; [pers.] I love to invent things, products, poems, stories, drawings from political to practical to Fantasy. Someday my ideas may even make me a profit.; [a.] Topeka, KS

ANACKER, EDWARD E.
[b.] June 2, 1921, Chicago, IL; [p.] Edward F. Anacker and Nellie A. Anacker; [m.] Stella E. Anacker; [ch.] Steven Edwards, David Carlve, Eric Roland, John William; [ed.] B.S in Chemistry-Montana State College 1943 (Now Montana State University), Ph.O in Chemistry-Cornell Univ. 1949; [occ.] Professor Emeritus, Montana State University; [memb.] American Chemical Society, Sigma X1, Alpha Chi Sigma, PHI Kappa PHI; [hon.] About 50 Articles in Scientific Journals; [oth. writ.] About 50 Articles in Scientific Journals; [a.] Bozeman, MT

ANDERSON, JAMES
[b.] February 19, 1921, Muskegon, MI; [p.] Adolph Anderson, Helen Anderson; [m.] Eva Anderson, June 26, 1949; [ed.] Montague High, Hackley College; [occ.] Author; [memb.] Robert Schuller Ministries; [oth. writ.] A novel "Ill Wind"; [pers.] In my writings I prefer to let the reader's imaginations add to the more intimate thoughts within the story.; [a.] Miami, FL

ANDERSON, KELLY
[b.] December 6, 1975, New Orleans, LA; [p.] Alvin and Ruby Anderson; [ed.] Graduates from Sarah T. Reed High School. Senior yr or. at Southern University at New Orleans; [memb.] Greater St. Stephens Full Gospel Baptist Church, Education Club at School; [hon.] Honor role and Dean's List at my school; [pers.] Do anything you want to do and do it well, but always remember to put God first in everything that you do.; [a.] New Orleans, LA

ANDERSON, RUSSELL P.
[b.] July 29, 1980, Kimball, NE; [p.] Jerry and Roxie Anderson; [ed.] 10th grade in High School; [occ.] Student, Rancher; [memb.] FFA, United Methodist Church, Academic Decathlon, knowledge bowl, and Nebraska Cattlemen Assoc.; [hon.] Star Greenhand, 3 President Academic Award; [oth. writ.] "Grandpa", "Flickering Candle". "Grandpa" has been published. "Tumble weed."; [pers.] You can only go as far in life as your dreams will let you.; [a.] Grover, CO

ANDRESKI, JON
[b.] October 3, 1972, Goldsboro, NC; [p.] Thad Andreski, Ava Holton; [ed.] North Central High, University of South Carolina; [occ.] Student; [memb.] USC Alumni Association, our lady of perpetual help; [hon.] Dean's List, President, Graduated Cum Laude; [pers.] "No man (or woman) is free of the image his (or her) literature imposes upon him (or her)." Louis L'Amour; [a.] Camden, SC

ANGE III, SAM
[pen.] Trey; [b.] August 21, 1983, Lake Charles, LA; [p.] Sam and Evette Ange; [ed.] 6th gr. Home Schooled with five other brothers; [a.] Westlake, LA

ANTHONY, SHARON
[pen.] S. L. Anthony; [b.] August 31, 1948, Gary, WV; [p.] Joseph Anthony, Lena Anthony Cummings; [ed.] Sharmelle, Charles, Cameron, Sharee; [occ.] Columbus Central High, Bliss Business College; [memb.] Instructional Aid Special Education, Etiwanda School District Cucamonga, CA; [hon.] National PTA, Mary McCloud Bethune Association, Ontario/Montclair Council PTA - President , 5th District PTA - Inspiration Chairman;

[oth. writ.] Articles for PTA Newsletters and magazines; [pers.] I write from emotions from within. Also from those who have been a part of my life. My inspiration comes from the writing of Maya Angelou, Terry McMillian, and Langston Hughes.; [a.] Ontario, CA

ANTONSON, KARLEEN
[pen.] Karleen Antonson; [b.] August 5, 1949, Providence, RI; [p.] Karl Antonson, Mary Antonson; [ed.] Cranszon High School East Community College of R.I. Bancrofz School of Massage Therapy; [occ.] Nurse Kenz Country Hospital Message Therapist; [pers.] My poem is in memory of my Dad Karl Antonson. He was the best father and my best friend.; [a.] Cranston, RI

AQUINO, LEO
[b.] August 26, 1930, Vancouver, British Columbia, Canada; [m.] Divorced; [ed.] High School, Trinity College (London) certification for Associate level in music theory.; [occ.] Concert Accordionist, I enjoy a world-wide reputation in my field. I have performed with Symphony Orchestras, String Quartets, Opera singers, and have performed solo concerts in tours, in England, Sweden, Holland, Denmark, the U.S., and Canada. I did a short tour of classical solo concerts, in the Former Soviet Union, in 1978. I am also active as a commercial musician, and have made radio and TV appearance, in Canada and the US, in past years.; [oth. writ.] Other works in poetry (as yet unpublished) and articles which have appeared in music newsletters and other publications.; [pers.] A profound mystical experience in 1960, has left me feeling that our lives in this physical world, is a kind of dream state... a form of spiritual hologram, which is a "ghost" image of higher states of being and consciousness. The higher spiritual paths aim to "awaken" us from this illusory slumber. This awakening is ultimately inevitable for all of us.; [a.] Vancouver British Columbia, Canada

ARAIZA, ISABEL
[b.] April 17, 1973, Corpus Christi, TX; [p.] Maria Teresa Araiza, Juan Araiza III; [ch.] Mia Mercedes; [ed.] A.A. in English and from Del Mar College, B.A. in English and Political Science from Texas A&M Corpus Christi; [occ.] G.E.D. Instructor and English writing Lab Instructor; [hon.] Tiger Hall of Fame, National Hispanic Semi-Finalist, Outstanding Student in English- Del Mar College; [a.] Corpus Christi, TX

ARAUJO, MARLON
[pen.] Marlon Araujo, Raspan; [b.] April 12, 1977, San Salvador, El Salvador; [p.] Luis Araujo, Doris Araujo; [ed.] Brentwood High School, Suny Farmingdale; [occ.] Market Research Interviewer; [hon.] Recognized as a Tandy Technology Scholar in '94-'95 school year, Perfect Attendance in school, Honor Roll student; [oth. writ.] This is the first time I have had anything published, but I sent poetry, on a weekly basis through E-Mail, to over 40 people during my Senior year at High School.; [pers.] Ignore what the rest of society thinks. Think what YOU want to think. Be who YOU want to be.; [a.] Bay Shore, NY

ARBAUGH, JENNIFER
[b.] November 17, 1972, Grass Valley, CA; [p.] Troy and Karen Arbaugh; [ed.] Nevada Union High, Sierra Junior College, The School for International Training; [memb.] Girl Scouts of America, California Scholarship Federation; [hon.] Sociology Student of the Year Award-1993. College High Honors Graduate. Girl Scout Gold Award; [oth. writ.] Hundreds of unpublished poems serving as tangible memories, stored in boxes until discovery; [pers.] I have travelled to 13 different countries and seen life as it is truly lived. One lesson I have learned is these images cannot be captured by film or video and perhaps not even by the mind. They can only be seen through the verses of an inspired writer.; [a.] Grass Valley, CA

ARCISZEWSKI, ERIC
[b.] April 15, 1981, Chicago; [p.] Don Arciszewski, Irene Arciszewski; [ed.] I am currently a freshman in high school, but I was in seventh grade when wrote this poem; [pers.] I wrote this poem when I was in 7th grade, almost I year after my mother passed away. Everything in this poem is true, she was only 35 yrs. young and a very good person. Her memory lies in the hearts of many; [a.] Neenah, WI

ARLEN, SARAH
[b.] July 24, 1980, Los Olivos, CA; [p.] Linda King, Jef Arlen; [ed.] Currently in Santa Ynez High School, Sophomore year, formerly a student of Dunn Middle School; [occ.] Student, mowing the lawn; [memb.] SY High School Drama 'N Arts Club, School Pretty Club; [hon.] Academic, Athletic, Awards, including High Honors for maintaining 4.0 average; [oth. writ.] Starting a book (fiction), various other poems and short stories; [pers.] "I have a simple philosophy. Fill what's empty. Empty what's full. And scratch where it itches." Quoted from Alice Roose velt long worth "I love being a writer. What I can't stand is the paper work." Peter Devries.; [a.] Los Alamos, CA

ARMBRUSTER, REBECCA
[b.] August 10, 1985, St. Louis; [p.] Charles and Barbara; [ed.] St. Andrew Grade School; [occ.] Student; [memb.] Girl Scouts, Choir, Volleyball, and Piano; [hon.] At school I won a poetry, contest, and I'm a straight a student.; [oth. writ.] Flowers, Flowers and Trees; [pers.] I usually get my ideas from my surroundings, I have three older sisters. I have a lot of pets also.; [a.] Saint Louis, MO

ARMER, TERESA J.
[b.] March 17, 1965, Heidelburg, Germany; [p.] James McNerlin, Barbara Jeffers; [m.] Jay Armer, March 16, 1985; [ch.] Caitlin Arielle, Colton Zackary; [ed.] Graduated Booneville High School, Booneville, AR and Capital City Business College, Russellville, AR; [occ.] Homemaker; [hon.] Senior art award, Booneville High School Distinguished Graduate, capital City Business College; [oth. writ.] Several poems published in a local newspaper wrote and illustrated a comic strip for a local newspaper to honor Children's Dental Month; [pers.] Sharing my life's struggles with others through poetry has become a way for purging my soul. If my words touch just one person - somewhere, sometime and give comfort - then my struggles have all been worthwhile.; [a.] Volkel Air Base, Netherlands

ARMSTRONG, EILEEN E.
[b.] December 27, 1921, Winnipeg, Manitoba, Canada; [p.] William and Elsie Ayres; [m.] James Daniel Armstrong Sr., June 10, 1944; [ch.] James D. Jr., and Jill E. Armstrong-Berger; [ed.] Glenlawn Collegiate and Success Bus. College; [occ.] Co Owner Armstrong Hydraulic and Pneumatic Repair Service and full time worker there, for twenty-three years; [memb.] Ginghamsburg U.M. Church, Northridge Business and Civic Assoc., and DeWeese Neighborhood Assoc. and Equipment Service Assoc; [oth. writ.] Have been writing poetry since I was a child, on anything and everything. Never sent one in to anyone before.; [pers.] My Love for the Lord and His Love for me leads me forward to try and make my little corner of His earth a better place to before those coming after me.; [a.] Dayton, OH

ARNER, TIM
[b.] May 20, 1978, Allenton, PA; [p.] David Arner, Patti Ebert; [ed.] Emmaus High School; [occ.] Student - currently a senior in high school; [oth. writ.] Numerous unpublished short stories and poems; [pers.] Everything I have written has been written for that who have encouraged me to write and insisted that I have talent. It took two very special people to open my eyes to a whole new world.; [a.] Alburtis, PA

ARNOLD, ELISABETH F.
[pen.] E. P. Frasure; [pers.] Writing is a treasure. The words chosen, the meanings sought out with care, the inspiration that comes to me that I can share with others in precious. I know that my work is complete when those who read my poems can feel good and comfortable inside.; [a.] Colorado Springs, CO

ATKINS, CHARLES
[b.] February 10, 1927, Kingsport, TN; [p.] Lena Ruth; [ch.] 4 children-Charles Jr. Beverly, Lisa and Eric; [occ.] Retired; [a.] Kingsport, TN

ATKINS, LAURA MAE
[b.] May 30, 1962, Columbus, MS; [p.] J. T. Atkins (Deceased), Esther Atkins; [ed.] Graduate of Wood Jr. College, presently majoring in English at Mississippi University for Women in Columbus, MS; [occ.] Student, Writer; [memb.] Treasure of Club de Espanol American Red Cross, Maben United Methodist Church; [hon.] Graduated with honors from Wood Jr. College also Dean's List; [oth. writ.] Several poems not published at this time. Working currently on new poems and a novel.; [pers.] I wish to work with disabled children and to teach them and others that if you continue trying you will reach your goal. Your dreams can come true.; [a.] Columbus, MS

ATKINS, NANCY
[pen.] Elliott Atkins; [b.] Brunswick, ME; [m.] Ernest Atkins Jr.; [ch.] Four sons, five grandchildren; [ed.] B.S., University Maine Education/History Graduate work - Arizona State University; [occ.] President, Samco Pub., Inc. Educator Doll designer, Illustrator-writer; [memb.] American Legion Auxiliary; [hon.] Thousands of Letters from 7 year old children and teachers thanking me for "SAM" and his message. "Follow your dreams hot drugs"; [oth. writ.] Writer, Illustrator, children's books - All American Sam series: All - American Sam Says Dreams Not Drugs printed - 55,000 for school children and still going strong.; [pers.] I reach out to children in a fun way with positive messages - love

yourself, you have choices, follow your dreams. My poetry reflects on God's beauty in our Universe, on the fun and joys of everyday life, on humor in problems, on woman's emotions and fleeting moments., [a.] Phoenix, AZ

ATWOOD, KAREN
[b.] November 13, 1940; [m.] Ronald Atwood, August 15, 1957; [ch.] Three girls, two boys; [ed.] Quiet school end of 10th grade. Completed adult education at age 40; [occ.] Homemaker; [oth. writ.] I have written a song entitled "The Honky Tonk Bar" that is in publication in Nashville, Tennessee; [pers.] I have dabbled in writing poems for the last few years but nothing serious until last year.; [a.] Cedar Springs, MI

AUER, HEATHER
[b.] February 4, 1982, Atlantic City; [p.] Laura and Michael Moran; [ed.] Junior High; [oth. writ.] Written other poems for language classes in school; [a.] Egg Harbor Township, NJ

AUSTIN, PATRICIA L.
[b.] December 3, 1969, Phoenix, AZ; [p.] Steve Austin, Lynn Austin; [pers.] I consider the ability to write a gift of God. Therefore, I strive to reflect the lessons He's taught me with my writing.; [a.] Glendale, AZ

AVILA, LINDA CAROLEE WILLIAMS
[b.] April 29, 1944, La Junta, CO; [p.] Edison Shirley Williams, Louise Fairbanks Williams; [m.] Rafael Avila, July, 1988; [ed.] B. of Applied Arts, B. of Fine Arts - Watercolor M. of Applied Arts (Teach. Ed Print Making); [occ.] Freelance Artist; [memb.] Legion of Mary; [pers.] Enhance the quality of your life - awaken your creativity!; [a.] Hercules, CA

AVINGER, KATHERINE
[b.] 1974; [memb.] Phi Kappa Phi and Delta Chi Honor Societies; [pers.] "Grape Juice Tears" is dedicated to my best friend, Kurt. His openness, loyalty, and unique perspective are continual sources of inspiration to me.

AXLEY, KAREN L.
[pen.] Karen L. Axley; [b.] June 16, 1966, San Bernadino, CA; [p.] Bob and Pauline Palstring,; [m.] Tony Axley, October 12, 1985; [ch.] David Anthony and Timothy Mark; [ed.] Harrison High School University of Southern Indiana; [occ.] Distribution Clerk - U.S. Postal Service; [memb.] Eagle's Way Church; [hon.] Dean's List; [pers.] I like writing about the thoughts and feelings of the human heart and the magnificent God who created it.; [a.] Evansville, IN

BABER, CANDI LYNN
[b.] September 3, 1980, Charlottsville; [p.] Douglas and Judy Baber; [ed.] Huvanna County High School; [oth. writ.] "Depression/Suicide" published in "Season to Come"; [pers.] A whole new world, was inspired by my aunt Jo Ann Pope, because when she meet Clayton Pope Jr, she was hopelessly in love, and I kinda felt the way she did because we are close. Her happiness overwelcomed me and inspired this poem. Thanks Jo Ann for inspiring this poem and thanks Clayton for making my aunt so happy.; [a.] Kents Store, VA

BACCHUS, BEVERLY
[b.] September 13, 1982, Jersey City; [p.] Mr. and Mrs. Bacchus; [ed.] Philippa Schuyler Middle School for the Gifted and Talented; [occ.] Student; [memb.] Member of Thirteen; [hon.] African American Heritage 1991 Level 1, [pers.] I strive to write how I feel and how the reader would like to feel.; [a.] New York City, NY

BACELLAR, BILL
[pen.] Eric Draven; [b.] December 2, 1977, Houston, TX; [p.] CID and Claudia Bacellar; [ed.] Tustin High, CA will attend Orange Coast College in CA and later attend UC Irvine; [occ.] Work full time as an office assistant in westboard, MA; [pers.] I write my poems on my own experiences and now they affect the course of my life.; [a.] Westboro, MA

BACIGALUPI, NICCI
[b.] March 26, 1995, Santa Rosa; [p.] John and Pam Bacigalupi; [ed.] St. Johns Catholic School 7th Grade; [occ.] School; [memb.] United States Pony Club; [hon.] 3 years of receiving ACF Awards (Attitude, Conduct and Effort) in school. I have received many ribbons in horse shows and Pony Club Rallys.; [oth. writ.] My other poem, My Cat Tigger, was published in a Children's Book of Poetry; [pers.] Be the best that you can be, every day, and in every way.; [a.] Healdsburg, CA

BAILEY, MICHELLE
[b.] January 9, 1969, Annarbor; [p.] Diane Nichols and Jerry Nichols; [m.] Michael Bailey, February 8, 1990; [ch.] Zachary David, Brittany Lynn; [ed.] Jonesville High; [occ.] Lyric Writer, Health Care Worker; [memb.] Parents Club, Diabetes Association, AKC Club; [hon.] Musical and Volunteer; [oth. writ.] Lyrics being recorded, short stories school, unpublished poetry for personal satisfaction and family; [pers.] I try to write moving thoughts, and encouraging material. My influences are family and a love of literature, aspiring writers; [a.] Ossco, MI

BAILEY, ONIA
[pen.] Onia; [b.] September 19, 1930, Hamilton, OH; [p.] Hiram and Mattie Metcalf; [ch.] Larry, William and Madeline, grandchildren: Holly and Kayla; [ed.] GED, Cosmetology; [occ.] Sales; [memb.] 700 Club; [pers.] I enjoy sharing with others my feelings from within, and hope to make the world a better place. Sincerely, Onia; [a.] Oviedo, FL

BAK, JASON
[pen.] Jason Bak; [b.] March 3, 1981, Denver, CO; [p.] Russell Bak and Annette Bak; [ed.] Currently a freshman at McCullough High School, the Woodlands, Texas; [occ.] Student; [pers.] Jason's First Attempt at poetry with "My Heaven' was written as an 8th Grade Student. His Descriptive poem of mountain scenery derives from his experiences hiking, camping, fishing in the Colorado High Country.; [a.] The Woodlands, TX

BAKER, CAROLYN MOORE
[pen.] Cas Evans; [b.] June 26, 1946, Houston, TX; [m.] John H. Baker, March 15, 1991; [ch.] Three; [occ.] Control Systems Designer M.W. Kellogg in Houston; [memb.] Water Color Art Society of Houston, Houston Art League, Instrument Society of America, Society of Women Engineers; [oth. writ.] Many poems which have been written and are

unpublished to date; [pers.] I want to express and share the truly emotional experiences which will or have occurred in my lifetime.; [a.] Houston, TX

BAKER, KIMBERLY
[b.] November 6, 1977, Lynn, MA; [p.] Stephen Baker and Shelley Baker; [ed.] Phillips Academy, Andover, Boston University; [occ.] Student; [pers.] Thanks to my family without whom I would not be who I am. Their unconditional love and support has given me the strength to share not only my laughter, but also my tears. I love you all from the bottom of my heart!; [a.] Lynnfield, MA

BAKER, MICHAEL
[pen.] Kinjaro; [b.] August 25, 1975, Wilkesbarre, PA; [p.] Mary Ann Headman, Charles Headman; [ed.] Tunkhannock Area High; [pers.] "Seize the day it does not last".; [a.] Tunkhannock, PA

BALDRIDGE, ROBERT LINDSEY
[b.] August 20, 1919, Providence, RI; [p.] John Percy Baldridge, Elsie (Lydia) Baldridge, (Erickson) Baldridge; [m.] Helen Everts Baldridge, June 14, 1943; [ch.] Lawrence Clayton, John Preston, James Joseph (deceased), Robert Lee; [ed.] Roosevelt High School, Deg Moines Iowa, Iowa State College, AMES, Iowa (BS Civil Engineering) US Army OCS Engineering School, Fort Belvoir Virginia, US Army Command and General Staff College Presented by Sattelite School, Portland Oregon, (Associate of Fort Leaven Wolth Command and General Staff College Located at Fort Leavenworth Kausasi, [occ.] Retired; [memb.] Army Engineer Association, National Association for Uniformed Services; [hon.] Best Non Technical Article, 1949 "Iowa State Engineer" (Student magazine, Iowa State College, AMES Iowa); [oth. writ.] Poem "Remembrances of Jimmie" to be published in "Window's of the Soul"; [pers.] Christian.; [a.] Portland, OR

BALL, HELEN M.
[pen.] Peggy Ball; [b.] August 8, 1930, Washington, DC; [p.] Edwing A. and Helen C. Doig; [m.] Ed C. Ball Jr., July 3, 1976; [ed.] Mt. St. Mary's Academy - Little Rock, AR (3 yrs.), St. Agnes High - St. Paul, Minn. (1 yr.); [occ.] Housewife and Volunteer; [memb.] Ladies Society-Sacred Heart, Catholic Church - Texarkana, TX, Hospital Auxilliary - St. Michael Health Care Center - Texarkana, TX (50 miles, round trip, from my home.); [oth. writ.] One article in Ark. Catholic newspaper; [pers.] I worked out in the public for 28 yrs. after high school, married and moved to city, where my husband was working, Texarkana, TX. He said if I got bored, I could go back to work if I wanted to. I decided to volunteer instead.; [a.] Doddridge, AR

BALMACEDA, NELSON
[pen.] Nelson Balmaceda; [b.] July 4, 1945, Chile; [p.] Arturo Balmaceda, Violeta Gonzalez; [ed.] Grammar Spanish Teacher, Department D.U.O.C. Universidad, Catolica De Chile. (When I was living in Chile 1974); [memb.] Amnesty International Pablo Neruda Foundation; [oth. writ.] Cantares a Pablo Neruda; [pers.] I have been living almost my entire life in exile defending human rights in latin America countries, specially in Chile under pinochet's dictatorship. I have been greatly influenced and motivated by Isabel Allende my favorite writer and Pablo Neruda my favorite poet.; [a.] San Francisco, CA

BANCROFT, SHIRLEY F.
[b.] January 9, 1912, Annapolis, IL; [p.] Elsie and Frank Faught; [m.] Virgil H. Bancroft (Deceased), March 23, 1929; [ch.] 1 daughter died at age 9; [ed.] Robinson High School, Freshman Year of College at Eastern State University, Charleston, IL 2 1/2 years college at University of IL; [occ.] Teaching piano lessons; [memb.] Greenup Woman's Civic Club Member of Presbyterian Women's Association; [oth. writ.] I write poetry and song lyrics for the pleasure of my family, my friends, and myself; [pers.] I like to write about the things and people that are close to my heart and that I know the most about.; [a.] Greenup, IL

BANKS, JANE
[pen.] Jane Christian Barnes; [b.] February 12, 1933, Tahleguah, OK; [p.] E. J. and Marion Green; [m.] C. B. Banks (Ex-husband), March, 1953; [ch.] Marian and Paul; [ed.] Plainview H. S., BA English Texas Tech; [occ.] Retired teacher-poet-writer; [memb.] Past-TSTA-NEA-TACAE College - 7IA, Signa Tan Delta, French Club, H.S. y-Teens, Spanish Club, H.S. Band, Rainbow girls, Nat'l Honor Society, H.S. newspaper staff; [hon.] L.I.S.D. Adult Education Teacher of the year - 1977 Plainview H.S. Journalist of the year - 1950, Distinguished Member Internat'l Society Poets 1995, Baptist Church; [oth. writ.] Many unpublished manuscripts submitted. I dentity, Red, White, and Blue - The Garden of Life - 1995; [pers.] John Kents and other Romantic Period poets, John Milton are wonderful examples to me. I love to write uplifting and inspiring poems, especially patriotic verse.; [a.] Lubbuck, TX

BAQUE, JODI
[pen.] Josie; [b.] February 22, 1981, Pomona Valley; [p.] Cathy Baque, Jerry Baque; [ed.] Monte Vista Elementary, Serrano Junior High, and Montclair High (Now); [occ.] I want to be an actress; [memb.] Trinity Broadcasting Network; [hon.] Student of the Month and Week, Award from President, many others; [oth. writ.] More poems but not published; [pers.] When I write my poems, I write what I fell.; [a.] Montclair, CA

BARBER, RANDY SAMUEL
[b.] February 27, 1970, Concord, NC; [a.] Harris-burg, NC

BARCLAY, DEBORAH J.
[pen.] Debbie; [b.] July 15, 1961, Montpelier, VT; [p.] Kenneth and Buelah Barclay; [m.] Bernie Bell, Companion; [ch.] Carrie, Josh, Jessica, Dustin, Taylor; [occ.] Machine Operator Northfield Wood Products; [pers.] I have been writing for 15 yrs. I like to write poetry but don't always have the time. My family keeps me very busy.; [a.] Northfield, VT

BARNES, HEATHER MARIE
[pen.] Shadow black; [b.] August 23, 1980, Denver, CO; [p.] Mary Bares/David Barnes; [ed.] Thornton High School; [occ.] Photography Model; [pers.] Evil is always possible. And goodness eternally difficult. The strength is in us all to find it, but only if we try.; [a.] Thornton, CO

BARNHILL JR., BOBBY L.
[b.] August 30, 1956, Fort Ord, CA; [p.] Bobby and Marianne Barnhill; [ch.] Benjamin, Julia, and Sarah; [ed.] Wenatchee High, Univ. of Maryland Abroad;

[occ.] Sales, Independent Agent; [memb.] German-American Congress; [pers.] Many thanks to that very special person who believed in my talent and submitted this poem without my knowledge. Thank you Veronica.; [a.] Arvada, CO

BARR, KELLY F.
[pen.] K. F. Barr; [b.] April 26, 1964, Ephrata, PA; [p.] Robert Krimes, Doreen Krimes; [m.] Duane Barr, September 15, 1993; [ed.] Ephrata High International Correspondence School; [occ.] Seamstress; [pers.] I strive to show the strength and power of love in my writing. Only through love can we find true happiness and the hope and possibility of world peace and a bright future. I have been greatly influenced by the inspirational poets.; [a.] Ephrata, PA

BARRETT, TIMOTHY MARK
[b.] November 2, 1961, Kansas City, MO; [p.] Margaret Ramsley; [ed.] Hickman Mill's High School, Studied poetry I-II III, along with Spanish Comtemerary Music; [occ.] Pest Control Technician; [hon.] Employer of the Year, in Pest Elimination and, Termite Control, also Commercial Pest Control; [oth. writ.] Shooting Star's, A Measure of Loss, Cupids Arrow, Andrew's Song, At Ease, At Last, Angel's Among Her, Her Little Box Song Birds Hymn, He Wear's A Smile, This Single Rose; [pers.] Which have (none, been published.) My inspiration tend's to come, from music and past experience however, parables and or stories in rhyme, fascinate me.; [a.] Kansas City, MO

BARTON, ERIN F.
[b.] March 20, 1979, Tuba City, AZ; [p.] Gwen Barton; [ed.] Window Rock High School - 9th grade only, Sunnyslope High School; [hon.] Honor Roll; [a.] Phoenix, AZ

BARTON, GINA ROSE
[b.] July 11, 1966, Germany; [p.] Virginia Barton; [ed.] 1985 Grad. of Dolgeville Central High School in Upstate NY; [occ.] Cook at the Alpha Gamma Delta Sorority Florida State Univ.; [memb.] Big Bend Cares Volunteer; [hon.] Voice of Democracy winner 3 year in a row in high school; [pers.] This pome came about while waiting for a train at Penn Station in NYC there were a great number of homeless people trying to keep warm and safe for one more night. I bet most of them never thought that they had to fight so hard to survive!; [a.] Tallahassee, FL

BASILE, JENNIFER
[b.] March 4, 1984, Tulsa, OK; [p.] Tom Basile, Sydney Basile; [ed.] I am 11 years old and in the 6th grade at Jenks East Middle School; [hon.] I am on my school's honor role. I am the 1st chair flute in our 6th grade band.; [pers.] I love to write poems and short stories. I think it is fun and can be fun for anyone who wanted to write. I hope people can enjoy this poem.; [a.] Tulsa, OK

BASS, DAVID MICHAEL
[pen.] David Bass; [b.] July 10, 1957, Lakeland, FL; [p.] Dellis Millentene and Betty Sue Bass; [ed.] Graduated from Kathleen High School 1976, Dance Education, NY New York; [occ.] Real Estate Broker Formally Dance Teacher; [memb.] Elks, Chamber of Commerce; [hon.] Best First Year Pageant from Miss

Florida to Miss Lakeland Pageant 1984, numerous show awards and outstanding contribution awards; [oth. writ.] Short stories, essays to local newspapers. Currently working on my first book titled Short Stories, Essays and What Not's by David Bass; [pers.] "To be trusted is a person greatest achievement".; [a.] Kathleen, FL

BASS, MONA LISA
[b.] November 23, Birmingham, AL; [p.] R. C. and Annie Graham; [m.] James A. Bass, May 4, 1976; [ch.] Tracey Bass and Casey Bass; [ed.] Brighton High School, Alabama State University Major Art Minor English; [memb.] Montgomery Art Guild; [pers.] I hope that through my poetry I give someone the strength to stand up and fight for their rights to be heard and respected. It is not always easy to say what one feels when there is an obstacles of fear blocking the way.; [a.] Montgomery, AL

BATES, BETTY LOU
[b.] November 11, 1941, Democrat, KY; [p.] Oscar B. and Gladys Oliver Belcher; [m.] Lewis B. Bates, October 5, 1963; [ch.] Sheila, John, David, April and Pamela; [ed.] Everett Jr. High, Central Senior High School; [occ.] Housewife; [oth. writ.] Several poems hand written in a blank book not yet published; [pers.] I seek to present to my readers the way I view the beauty of nature, my feelings on certain events around me, for example: that they may smell a rose I picked this morn.; [a.] Isom, KY

BAUMGARDT, KAREY
[pen.] Karey Anne Baumgardt; [b.] May 30, 1972, Renton, WA; [p.] Larry and Star Baumgardt; [m.] Christopher Sparks, May 20, 1995; [ed.] Enumclaw High School, Green River Community College; [occ.] Data Processor, PSI Renton, WA; [memb.] St. Jude Children's Research Hospital; [oth. writ.] Several poems published in past anthologies; [pers.] My poetry is a result of emotions felt by my heart. Everything I have written holds a personal place in my life.; [a.] Renton, WA

BAUTISTA, BRENDA
[b.] December 18, 1978, Portland, OR; [p.] Salvador and Petra Bautista; [ed.] Woodburn High School, 11th grade; [memb.] House of Zion Youth Group; [oth. writ.] Several poems; [pers.] A poem is a great way to express your feelings at least that's how I express mines.; [a.] Woodburn, OR

BAYLISS, SARAH LOUISE
[b.] May 25, 1963, London, England; [p.] David and Gwendoline Shopland; [ed.] Orleans Park School London, England United States Coast Guard; [occ.] Petty Officer United States Coast Guard; [oth. writ.] Poems and stories yet to be published, but there is always hope.; [pers.] Be honest and truthful with yourself, the rest will follow.; [a.] Boston, MA

BECHTHOLD, DARRYL J.
[pen.] Jerome W. Forest; [b.] July 17, 1945, ND; [p.] Bill and Hilda Bechthold; [ed.] Monterey Bay Academey, Grossmont Jr. College; [occ.] Video Production, President and Founder of "All Occasion Video Productions", Long Beach, CA; [memb.] American Videographers Assoc.; [hon.] Letters of recommendations and appreciation from clients services in video productions; [oth. writ.] "The Bulb" short story, "The Time In My Life" published,

"Take Care" published, "Sincerely" unpub., "Youth" published, "Simplicity" unpub., "My Love" published, "Forward To...?" short story; [pers.] To be the best that I can be in all my endeavors. Truth and honesty are the best policy. Riches and fame are not worth the loss of your character and our ethics.; [a.] Long Beach, CA

BECK, CHRISTIE LA SHELL
[pen.] La' Shalle; [b.] July 8, 1977, Thomasville, AL; [p.] Linda A. Beck; [ed.] Miss Print High c/o "95" Mississippi Gulf Coast Community, College Major in Medical Lab Technician; [occ.] Sales; [memb.] Little Rock Baptist Church, Poetry Club; [hon.] Advanced diploma in High School, perfect Attendance, honor roll and many other honors and awards; [oth. writ.] I have written 36 poems but haven't been published; [pers.] My poems are written from my real life ups and down story to help others watch out for their mistakes.; [a.] Moss Point, MS

BECKER, BRENDA J.
[b.] July 11, 1943, York, PA; [p.] George and Elsie Clark; [m.] Gordon E. Becker, February 16, 1963; [ch.] Jeffrey (Deceased) and Craig, granddaughter - Amber; [ed.] Wm. Penn Sr. High, York Towne Business School; [occ.] Human Resource Clerk - York County Hospital and Home; [memb.] The Compassionate Friends Victims of Homicide Group; [oth. writ.] Several poems published in the Compassionate Friends Newsletter; [pers.] Writing came to me as a form of therapy after the murder of my son, Jeffrey. The words came from the heart and through many tears. I want my granddaughter to be left with a legacy of her father, who she had for five short years.; [a.] York, PA

BECKER, LAUREN MICHELLE
[pen.] Cascade Magleu; [b.] January 30, 1981, Atlanta, GA; [p.] Cindy and Bruce Becker; [ed.] I am a freshman at Pace Academy High School; [hon.] Derech Eretz Award, Erma D. Young Principals Award, Orlin Scholarship, 2nd place - National Latin Exam. 1st place French Test (State), high honors; [oth. writ.] First published writing; [pers.] "It you write about things you do not understand people won't gain from your writing. I write about what I know, so people can become me for a few short moments."; [a.] Atlanta, GA

BELL, KATIE
[b.] March 31, 1981, Tarzana, CA; [p.] Wayne and Sheila Bell; [ed.] Greater Atlanta Christian School, 9th grade; [occ.] Student; [memb.] Beta Club; [hon.] President's List, Honor roll, English and Algebra honor award, Achievement Award, Induction into Beta Club; [oth. writ.] Many poems and stories which I usually keep to myself; [pers.] I love to write, it helps my mind to become free. I hope to one day become a famous author and poet.; [a.] Alpharetta, GA

BENDAWALD, SHIRLEY
[b.] January 8, 1937, Saint Louis, MO; [p.] Allen and Mathilda Ragan; [m.] Eugene Bendawald, June 19, 1954; [ch.] Five; [ed.] Finished 9th grade, received GED 3-69, took some courses at Flo Valley Community College; [occ.] Bakery Clerk; [oth. writ.] Paragraph published in school newspaper; [pers.] Would like to show the real important things in life.

Give of myself and receive love and understanding in return.; [a.] Saint Louis, MO

BENNETT, JENNIFER N.
[pen.] Pajara Day; [b.] September 10, 1980, Toledo, OH; [p.] Tammy and Glenn Bennett; [ed.] Presently attending Happy Valley High School, [occ.] A student and certified Tae Kwon Do instructor; [memb.] The National Honors Society, National Black Belt Association, SMART, SECKA and NASKA; [hon.] National ranked in American Karate; [pers.] Go for your dreams and goals, and never let any obstacles get in your way.; [a.] Johnson City, TN

BENNETT, VELMA JEAN
[b.] September 29, 1942, Jacksonville, FL; [p.] Dessie Mae Ray; [m.] Warren Carleton Bennett, May 2, 1958; [ch.] Arlene, Beverly, Carla, Doreen, & Eric; [ed.] Graduate of UMass Boston and Cambridge College, currently attending Harvard Extension School in Cambridge, MA; [occ.] Teacher, Entrepreneur; [memb.] Bradley Institute, Inc., B.E.A.M. Inc., Parent Involvement Committee; Boston Teachers' Union, Shaklee, Inc.; [hon.] Editor's Award 1994; [oth. writ.] "Be Strong," "Be All There Is," "Volcanic Beginnings," "Eye(s) See," "One Trillion Eyes See Me,"; [pers.] I am aware of the vastness of the explorations of the mind--to the height of the eagle soaring I will continue to strive for my poetic career. This is such a wonderful healing process, to write.; [a.] Jamaica Plain, MA

BENNKE, TANISHA
[pen.] Tanisha Bennke; [b.] March 25, 1980, San Jose; [p.] Tammy Griswold, Bruce Gilbert; [occ.] Attending Prospect High School; [pers.] I would like to thank whose who inspired me: Danya Bennke, Bruce Gilbert, Gaby McInnis, Aunt Lori, Uncle Bud, and the rest of the family.; [a.] San Jose, CA

BENNY, ERIN
[pen.] E. Michael; [b.] August 23, 1982, Dallas; [p.] Kenneth A. Benz and Janice Ellen Thornal; [ed.] I haven't finished yet; [occ.] I am still trying to get through Jr. High; [memb.] PAT at my school, manager of the school (Heritage Christian Academy) volleyball team; [hon.] I have a bunch of ribbons for stuff, 8 bowling trophies, a plaque, and a certificate of recognition for Choir; [oth. writ.] A wide variety of poems from my heart; [pers.] I am 13 years old. I would not have been able to write any of my poems if not for God. He gives me strength and inspiration that I hope others can feel through my poems. I thank my mother for intentionally encouraging me but I give God all this Glory.; [a.] Rowlett, TX

BENSON, JAMIE
[pen.] Jamie Benson; [b.] June 7, 1980, Corvallis, OR; [p.] Steve and Verla Benson; [ed.] 1st Christian Pre-School, Oak Grove, North Albany Middle School. West Albany High School; [occ.] West Albany High Steppers and crew dance team, WA High School; [memb.] The amazing official Madonna Fan Club; [hon.] Student of the Year, #1 Dancer of High Steppers and Krew, Rookie dancer of the year, Super dancer ribbon, Award for Physical fitness; [oth. writ.] A rose to remember where's the action, destination unknown, as the pages turn, stupidly stereo typical surrounded but alone, prisoner; [pers.] People should not be divided, black,

white, red, yellow, orange, purple, bay, straight, whatever. Were all human. Treat everyone how you want to be treated. Live and let leave and have a damn good time.; [a.] Albany, OR

BENSON, JULIANNE
[pen.] J. Benson; [b.] September 30, 1938, Ellendale, ND; [p.] Royal B. and Pauline Wanaka; [m.] Roland D. Benson, April 8, 1960; [ch.] Kirsten Pauline, Karin Limea; [ed.] Roosevelt High School, Portland Community College, Mt. Hood Community College; [memb.] Christian Women's Club Tops Club, Inc.; [pers.] My poem is dedicated to my father, who spent the last seven years of his life in nursing homes. My favorite poet is Emily Dickinson.; [a.] Portland, OR

BENTULAN, CECILIA PALOMATA
[b.] May 20, 1979, Portsmouth, VA; [p.] Teodulo and Marietta Bentulan; [ed.] Deep Creek High School; [occ.] Student; [memb.] Holy Angels Youth Group, DCHS Girls Tennis Team, Pals for Peers, Spanish Club and National Honor Society. Chesapeake Challenge Team, Student Against Drunk Driving, Future Business Leader of America; [a.] Chesapeake, VA

BERGER, DENISE
[b.] March 10, 1981, Brooklyn, NY; [p.] Mara and Alexander; [ed.] Currently: Jericho High School, Elementary - P.S. 230+ Cantiague Junio High - Jericho Middle School; [occ.] High School student; [oth. writ.] Wrote for school papers and class magazines; [pers.] I may not be an exceptional writer, but I try to open people's eyes to see what's going on in today's society.; [a.] Jericho, NY

BERKOPES, MELINDA
[b.] May 29, 1981, Indianapolis, IN; [p.] Tony Berkopes, Dee Berkopes; [ed.] Saint Gabriel Elem. Freshman, Cardinal Rether High School; [occ.] Student; [hon.] Numerous local and National Dance Championships; [oth. writ.] A Christmas short story published in The Criterion; [pers.] I am truly honored to be recognized for something. I luv to do. Lu thy neighbor.; [a.] Indianapolis, IN

BERNARD, CLAIRE SANDBERG
[b.] April 27, 1983; [p.] Catherine Bernard, William Sandberg; [ch.] Currently attending Takoma Park Middle School; [hon.] '94, '95 Female Band under 5K Turkey Trot Race Winner Strait A Student; [pers.] Through the flow of a pen, my soul strives to the best of it's ability to describe the melody of white coral bells and the sweet soprano songs of fairies that I have heard in my dreams of Avalon.; [a.] Takoma Park, MD

BERNTSEN, THOMAS
[b.] August 6, 1965, Rockville Centre, NY; [p.] Joanne and Ragnvald; [ed.] B.A. Utica College of Syracuse University (88), M.S. Indiana University (91), Ed.D. University of Massachusetts (98); [occ.] High School Math and Science Teacher; [memb.] National Council of Teachers of Mathematics, American Association of Physics Teachers, Vermont Science Teachers Association, Indiana University Alumni Association; [oth. writ.] Article, "Let It Snow, Let It Snow" is Nov./Dec. '95 issue of The Physics Teacher poems: "Come With Me To A Distant Star, A Distant Land" in A Delicate Balance and "America, The Great Pine" in Shadows and

Light; [pers.] Anything is possible with hard work and God's help.; [a.] Brattleboro, VT

BERRY, RITA
[b.] July 2 1958, Borger, TX; [p.] Vick Livingston, Floy Livingston-Henry; [m.] Jim Berry, February 20, 1982; [ch.] Matthew Tyler, Rachael Breanne; [ed.] Borger High School, Amarillo College, Bachelor of Science Degree from West Texas State University; [occ.] Medical Technologist, Clinical Laboratory High Plains Baptist Health Systems; [memb.] American Society of Clinical Pathologists, American Association of Blood Banks; [hon.] Alpha Chi; [oth. writ.] A few poems, as yet unpublished, and a Father's Day Card published in Rubber Stampers World Magazine; [a.] Amarillo, TX

BICKNELL, ERNEST P.
[pen.] Bick; [b.] September 13, 1912, Fort Wayne, IN; [ed.] Antioch College, San Francisco State U., BA; [occ.] Retired newspaperman; [memb.] Religious Society of Friends, Friends Committee on Legislation, San Francisco Press Club; [a.] Oakland, CA

BIGGERS, MARY HELEN
[pen.] Mary Helen Biggers; [b.] September 16, 1937, Washburn, MO; [p.] Raymond Painter, Velma Painter; [m.] Carl Wyne Biggers, January 3, 1954; [ch.] Monica Biggers, Dixon, Rocky Lee Biggers, Ramona Biggers, Marvin, Melody Biggers, Chenoweth, Robin Biggers, Baranak; [ed.] Twin Falls Idaho High School, Draughn Business College; [occ.] Retired Bookkeeper and Real Estate Broker; [memb.] First Free Will Baptist Church; [oth. writ.] Several poems published in local newspaper and religious newsletters. Three recorded and published sacred songs.; [pers.] I would like all my writings to be an honor and witness for my Lord and Savior Jesus Christ!; [a.] Joplin, MO

BILLINGTON, GARY
[b.] August 26, 1952, Amsterdam, NY; [p.] William Billington, Beverly Billington; [ed.] Wilbur H. Lynch High, Europa School of Hairdressing and Cosmetology Hair Stylist; [hon.] I am an award winning Hairstylist with certificates of achievements and diplomas in various fields of hairdressing, past, present, and advance.; [oth. writ.] I also enjoy art and design and inventing things; [pers.] A feel poetry can be fun, its a way to share our inner feelings with one another and it so many. I believe poetry can have a great reflection on our life's for the better. Its a way we can educate our minds and hearts with good. A read poetry to give myself inner comfort and peace of mind. Its very relaxing and I highly recommend everyone to read and write poetry if not for fun, than for the challenge of it.; [a.] Schenectady, NY

BIRCH, ALISON WYRLEY
[b.] March 11, 1922, New York City; [p.] Sydney-Marjorie Greenbie; [m.] Richard Wyrley Birch, August 5, 1942; [ch.] Wendy Lucchini, Laurie Kendall; [ed.] Northfield-Mt Hermon - Central High School, Washington, DC and Western CT State College; [occ.] Free-lance Magazine feature writer; [memb.] Poetry Therapy Association Several local civic committees in Kent, CT; [hon.] Have been listed in a Who's Who of American Women, Who's Who in the East, Who's Who in CT Literary Guild etc. Won many poetry awards.; [oth. writ.] Reader's

Digest Features and Christian Science Monitor and many more national, regional and special interest publications. "Poetry for Peace of Mind" - Doubleday - 1978 "A History of Dover Township" "East of Manhattan" - "A Little of This and That" "Say Ahh" The above are published books.; [pers.] Have been a news reporter, columnist and reader of my own poetry on radio, Television and live groups. Public speaker/lecturer and teach creative writing.; [a.] Kent, CT

BISEL, ALICE
[b.] December 8, 1955, Post, TX; [p.] Sefrina Perez and Pete Perez; [m.] Andy Bisel, May 28, 1987; [ch.] Anthony Martinez and Howard Cook; [ed.] Morton High School Morton, Texas; [occ.] Law Enforcement Student/Cashier; [a.] Okeene, OK

BISHOP, JAMES
[pen.] Jim Bishop; [b.] Sioux City, IA; [p.] Ed Bishop, Ann Bishop; [ch.] James Alan Bishop; [oth. writ.] Poems appeared in Lyrical Iowa, Poetry Parade Audio cassettes; [pers.] I would write in the variousness of forms, in an otherness of thought, yet at times, in the communicative Commonness of experience.; [a.] Sioux City, IA

BISHOP, MARJORIE
[pen.] Marjorie Bishop; [b.] March 11, 1929, Waynesville, MO; [p.] James and Ora Wade; [m.] Calvin F. Bishop, MD (Ret.), March 25, 1961; [ch.] Mark, Michael and Marcia; [ed.] Associate in Liberal Arts, San Diego, City College, BA English, San Diego State University; [occ.] Home maker; [memb.] Cedar Center Chorus; [hon.] Who's Who Among Students, American Universities and Colleges, Golden Key National Honor Society, San Diego State University; [oth. writ.] A short story, play and poems published in Literary Magazine, San Diego City College, lyric approved and recorded by Jeff Roberts publishing Co. (The Flame) Wollaston, MA; [pers.] I strive to keep a positive attitude and to look for beauty, truth, and harmony in all people and circumstances.; [a.] San Diego, CA

BLACK, ELEANOR J.
[b.] October 12, 1954, Ashland, KY; [p.] Claude and Erma Wright; [m.] Harry Edward Black, February 13, 1989; [ch.] Shawn, Jamie, Tawnee; [ed.] Russell Highs School Graduate 1972, Ashland Community College (University of KY); [occ.] Secretary; [memb.] 1st Christian Church Chancel Choir, Tennessee Walking Horse Breeders and Exhibitor's Association (TWHBEA), Eastern Hills Saddle Club, Northeastern Kentucky Fish and Game Club, Kentucky Real Estate Sales Associate Notary Public; [hon.] 1st and 3rd place - Pro-Am Bowling Tourn. 28 1st place - Horse Show Awards; [oth. writ.] A poem published in local newspaper. Editor and publisher of church choir newsletter and saddle club newsletter where I include poems and stories.; [pers.] I have always been inspired by all types of poetry. I base my own writings on my intermost feelings, which are much easier to express on paper, and poetry has always satisfied that part of my communication of feelings.; [a.] Ashland, KY

BLACK, JILLIAN
[b.] October 9, 1982, Cincinnati, OH; [p.] Mark and Goldie Black; [ed.] I'm in 7th grade at Three Rivers Middle School in Northbend, OH; [occ.] Student;

[memb.] Chorus, Newberry Book Club, Drama Club, Honor Society; [hon.] Honor student since kindergarten, 1st place Walt Sweeney Art Contest; [pers.] I enjoy writing poetry and am greatly honored to have my poem published in your book.; [a.] Northbend, OH

BLACK, SAM
[b.] August 25, 1949, Eugene, OR; [m.] Denise Black, September 3, 1994; [ch.] Melissa, Quinn, Cecily, Jeromey, Damara; [ed.] Comage Grove High, Lane Community College; [occ.] Sales/Design Rep.; [pers.] Writing enables me to understand and accept myself. My life's goals are to be a more compassionate, loving person.; [a.] Eugene, OR

BLAKE, DAYLE SUSAN
[pen.] Dayle Susan Gloege; [b.] August 17, 1952, Fort Belvoir, VA; [p.] Dale and Lorraine Gloege; [m.] Divorced; [ch.] Chris Gloege, Nick Blake, and Allison Blake; [ed.] High School Graduate of Cooper Sr. H. in New Hope, MN/Misc. Computer Classes; [occ.] Writer, Children Raiser 3, Inventor; [memb.] National Park Trust, PETA, Clean Water ACtion, North Shore Humane Society, Anoka County Humane Society, Habitat for Humanity and MN Inventor Congress; [hon.] Award for Creative Achievement from Minnesota Inventors Congress for my "Boogie Checker" (Which I also received a Trademark for). Also received Honor for supporting National Park Trust.; [oth. writ.] Wrote for all Anoka County Newspapers and I had a column in a newspaper for "Pet Care" for the Anoka County Humane Society (We were trying to raise money for a shelter - which we did!); [pers.] We can all help save the world if we are kind to each other, all animals and all trees and plants, and all of our earth and air. It's hard, after all "Who's Perfect".; [a.] Brooklyn Center, MN

BLANCHARD, MARION E.
[b.] November 26, 1946, Albemarle, NC; [p.] J. D. Almond and Bernice Mullis Almond; [m.] Tommie L. Blanchard, May 19, 1967; [ch.] Tracy Young, Tonya Blanchard; [ed.] North Stanley High, Cabarrus Memorial Hospital School of Nursing - Institute of Children's Literature; [occ.] Operating Room Nurse - First Assistant; [memb.] Plyler Baptist Church, Association of Operating Room Nurses, Camping Clubs, Cabarrus Amateur Radio Society (KB40YY); [hon.] Beta Club, won essay contestant National Nurses Week at our hospital; [oth. writ.] Articles for Concord Tribune in Concord, NC. Have written numerous poems and 3 children's books.; [pers.] Ultimately life is a chain of todays, make each link count.; [a.] Mount Pleasant, NC

BLAYNEY, RANDALL Y.
[b.] March 24, 1958, Burbank, CA; [p.] Leonard Blayney, Frances Blayney; [m.] Lisa Blayney, February 14, 1983; [ch.] Candace Liran, Cassandra Liran; [ed.] San Fernando High, Los Angeles Valley College; [occ.] Los Angeles Airport, Police Officer; [memb.] The Church on the Way - Van Nuys, CA; [pers.] I would like to thank my wife Lisa for providing the love and inspiration to write my poetry.; [a.] Mission Hills, CA

BLECICK, TOBY L.
[b.] February 23, 1960, Cincinnati, OH; [p.] Billie Ann and Robert James Goodrick; [m.] Michael,

April 21, 1979; [ch.] Ryan - 2/89, Shain - 7/85, Britney - 8/87; [ed.] High School; [occ.] Financial Manager of 16 years; [memb.] Cleve. First SDA Church; [hon.] My most wonderful honor is being a mother; [oth. wrlt.] I have several poems written for pleasure. I've been writing for about 25 years., [pers.] When you open your heart, your hand will expose your feelings for your mind to read.; [a.] Chesterland, OH

BLUM, JERRY DUANE
[b.] February 2, 1968, Monroe Memorial; [p.] Fredrick and Janice Blum; [ed.] Iowa-Grant High School Linden Elementary, Linden Wisconsin; [occ.] Farm Hand; [oth. writ.] Loves Prayer, Night Time, Nature, Stormy Skies, The Prairie, Loneliness, Winter; [pers.] I think poetry comes straight from the heart if you have something special that you love a spouse or nature or anything if you write about it it might be the best poem every wrote.; [a.] Monroe, WI

BOHANNON, TONYA
[b.] April 7, 1980, Toccoa, GA; [p.] Terry K. Bohannon, Susan P. Boyd; [ed.] Stephens Co. High; [a.] Carnesville, GA

BOHNSTENGEL, ELLEN
[b.] December 22, 1977, Tallahassee, FL; [p.] Jim and Harriet Irwin and Michael Bohnstengel; [ed.] Leon High School; [a.] Tallahassee, FL

BOLAND, VIRGINIA REDDEN
[b.] August 28, 1950, Hartford, CT; [p.] Laurie and Dennis Redden; [m.] Floran James Boland, June 8, 1973; [ch.] Cara, Brian, Jack and Jessica; [oth. writ.] Always in Dreams is a poem from my journal: Quinmehtukqut... Connecticut...Saiagiad, Quinmehtukqut: Land of the Long Tidal River, Saiagiad: Whom Thou Lovest, which I hope to have published by next summer; [pers.] They told my my grandfather died (when I was 12 years old). Today, again hear his voice and am forever grateful.; [a.] West Hartford, CT

BOLIN, PATRICIA
[b.] December 23, 1958, Cicleville, OH; [p.] Joan Brungs, Daniel Brungs; [ed.] Graduate: Logan Elm High School, Graduate: Institute of children's Literature; [pers.] I believe if each and every one of us lived our lives today as if there were no tomorrow, we would gain greater incite as to what matters the most, that of loving our family, friends and fellow man without reserve and being loved in returns.; [a.] Orient, OH

BONITTO, ANDRE
[pen.] David Andy; [b.] December 8, 1974, New York, NY; [p.] David and Laura Bonitto; [pers.] We must find peace within ourselves instead of waging war against our neighbors, yet we must wage war within ourselves to love ourselves and our neighbors.; [a.] Fort Lauderdale, FL

BONOW, BRANDON
[b.] June 29, 1978, Milwaukee, WI; [p.] Pamela Bonow-Pelino, Michael Bonow; [ed.] Senior at Piux XI High School; [occ.] Student; [memb.] Drama Club, Debate, and currently have key role in the school's play "A Few Good Men"; [oth. writ.] Poem entitled "Mindless Priorities" to be published in the

San Fernando Poetic Journal; [pers.] Being an only child and extremely shy, I began to write poetry especially dealing with loneliness and one's inability to express his/herself.; [a.] Milwaukee, WI

BORREGO, ANTONIO
[pen.] Tony Borrego; [b.] June 23, 1954, El Paso, TX; [p.] Luis F. Borrego, Maria Borrego; [m.] Alicia Borrego, December 9, 1973; [ch.] Linda Borrego, Christina Borrego; [ed.] Clint High School, University of Texas El Paso; [occ.] Senior Development Engineer Storage Technology Corp, Louisville, CO; [hon.] Etta Kappa Nu, Tau Beta Pi, Dean's List; [oth. writ.] Defensive publication patent, technical documentation/specifications, no other poems have been submitted for publication; [pers.] The submitted poem was written over 20 years ago. Throughout the years, and a few poems later, I cannot help but feel that fine poetry portrays an image of the soul that provides music to the heart, and illumination to the mind.; [a.] Louisville, CO

BOUCHER, LOUISE
[b.] September 15, 1926, ND; [p.] Ovide and Amelia Cote; [m.] Ales Boucher, March 24, 1951; [ch.] Alvin, Norman, Michelle, Shelley, Marvin, Robbie, Charla, Janiee, Diane; [ed.] Some college; [occ.] Retired - do a lot of volunteer work; [memb.] Women of the Moose St Leo's Womens Guild; [pers.] This was my first try at any type of writing.; [a.] Minot, ND

BOUQUET, CANDY
[pen.] Candy Bouquet; [b.] October 2, 1978, Utah; [p.] Bert Bouquet (Dad); [ed.] Still enrolled in Lakewood High School; [occ.] Safeway Courtesy Clerk; [hon.] Silver Medal in Weather Forecasting - Science Olympiad; [oth. writ.] None that were published; [pers.] I love to write, I think its a great way to creatively spend your time.; [a.] Marysville, WA

BOWERSOX, AMANDA
[b.] August 24, 1980, Misawa, Japan; [p.] Jack and Josie Bowersox; [ed.] Bear Creek and River's Elementary John Sticker Middle, and Patapsco High School; [memb.] Student Government; [hon.] This is an honor for having my poem publish. My fantastic parents who will always be here for me are my awards.; [oth. writ.] None published; [pers.] I like to read to that will help me in a situation. Therefore I write what I feel inside. Hoping that it will help someone else figure out what's inside of themselves.; [a.] Baltimore, MD

BOX, OLIVIA JEAN
[pen.] Dream Dancer; [b.] August 15, 1941, B'ham, AL; [p.] Everette and Grace Jones; [m.] Robert A. Box, September 2, 1959; [ch.] Robert Lisa, Jackie; [ed.] Associate Applied Science; [occ.] Physical Therapist Assistant; [memb.] American Physical Therapy Assoc., Civitan International; [hon.] Dean's List, Jefferson State Community College, Outstanding PTA Affiliate Assembly 1995; [oth. writ.] Professional publications; [pers.] I believe in the interconnectedness of all things and all beings. What effects one, effects all.; [a.] Trussville, AL

BOYUM, EDNA LAURA HOIRUP
[b.] May 16, 1915, Burnstead, ND; [p.] Jakob and Elizabeth Hoirup; [m.] Adrian A. Boyum, March 17,

1940; [ch.] Lauraine Edna Ehley, Imlay City, MI, (an Artist) and LTC(R) US Army, Sandra Boyum Cox, Fayetteville, NC; [ed.] Registered Nurse, graduated 1937 Bismarck Hospital; [occ.] Retired Registered Nurse/Hospital Administrator; [hon.] Numerous awards and recognitions for oil, acrylic, and watercolor paintings in North Dakota, North Carolina, Texas, Italy, and Germany, have paintings and rosemaled crafts in friends homes in Greece, Italy, Germany, Netherlands, Texas, North Carolina, North Dakota, South Dakota, Michigan, Washington and California. All my life wrote poetry, stories, and recipes.; [pers.] Growing up in the hills of North Dakota I learned to see nature through an artists eyes. This coupled with my desire to live life to the fullest, inspired me to write and paint whenever I wasn't working. I passed this desire onto my Graddaughter, Kimberlee Bethany Cox.; [a.] Fayetteville, NC

BRABBS, APRIL
[b.] March 17, 1981, Dallas, TX; [p.] Patricia and Ronald Brabbs; [ed.] North Garland High - present Bussey Middle School, Golden Meadows Elementary; [occ.] Student; [memb.] Scholastic Reading Club, Wild Life Fact File; [hon.] Presidential/ Academic Achievement Award (1-5), (6-8); [oth. writ.] Writing for "Daughters of the Republic of Texas", Reflections contest for the City of Garland; [pers.] I write about what man and man bind can experience when he is on earth. I also write poems about things people dream about.; [a.] Garland, TX

BRADY, VIRGINIA JOANN
[pen.] Vee Brady; [b.] November 8, 1924, New Canaan, Ct; [p.] Anthony and Margaret Sauatsky; [m.] Peter R. Brady M.D., April 22, 1946; [ch.] Virginia, Patricia, Peter, Margo, Katheryn; [ed.] New Canaan High School, King County Hospital School of Nursing; [occ.] Retired; [memb.] King's County Hospital School of Nursing Alumina Assoc., U.S Army Nurse Cadet Corp., St. Mary's Roman Catholic Church, Scholarship Donor, International Society of Poets; [pers.] I try to stir the conscience on controversial issues that face our world today; [a.] New Monmouth, NJ

BRANDELL, JULES
[pen.] Jules Brandell; [b.] December 6, 1911, Ukrania, Russia; [p.] Joseph and Anna Bramowitz; [m.] Evelyn Brandell, May 22, 1969; [ch.] Jerold, Alan, James, Martin, Jennifer, Margaret; [ed.] Alexander Hamilton High, Brooklyn College; [occ.] Retired, was Director of Advertising of several corporations; [memb.] University of Wisconsin-Milwaukee, President of Guild for Learning in Retirement. Taught English as second language. Member of Congregation Emanual B'ne Jeshurun, serve meals for indigent people at St. Vincent de Paul Church, Advisor to County Dept. of Aging, Volunteer at St. Mary's Hospital.; [hon.] Battalion Adjutant U.S. Army Corps of Engineers-served during WW II in Europe and Pacific, Editor of college and high school publications; [oth. writ.] Poetry-have compiled a number of poems. Have produced many direct mailings and catalogs for various corporations.; [pers.] Budget: a means of telling your money where to go instead of wondering where it went. Diplomacy: disagreeing without being disagreeable.; [a.] Milwaukee, WI

BRANNON, LUKE JOSIAH
[b.] December 4, 1972, Escondido, CA; [p.] Dr. Wayne and Linda Brannon; [ed.] Poway High School, Grossmont Community College, Palomar Community College University of California, San Diego; [occ.] Student at UCSD; [oth. writ.] A poem entitled "Root" in Palomar College's Award winning literary magazine Bravura. Two poems published in an out of State Periodical "Poetry Plus Magazine"

BRATTEN, DONALD L.
[b.] April 7, 1934, Manitou, Minnesota; [p.] Peter & Irene Bratten; [m.] Elaine (Lind) Bratten, October 16, 1954; [ch.] Douglas, Dawn & Stephanie; [ed.] Littlefork High School; [occ.] Mechanic and Ski Equipment Technician; [memb.] National Rifle Association; The Quiet Birdmen, Aircraft Owners & Pilots Association; [pers.] Poetry was of no interest to me until my mother passed away about 15 years ago. At approximately that period of time it became a very natural way of expressing myself. My mother loved poetry and I believe her spirit is now influencing my thoughts,; [a.] Fairbanks, AK

BREEN, MICHELLE HENDERSON
[b.] September 18, 1965, SSM, Ontario, Canada; [p.] Terry and Marlene Henderson; [m.] Francis A. Breen III, August 19, 1989; [ch.] Francis Anthony IV; [ed.] Sault College, BA from University of Waterloo, Ontario Fine Arts, University of Western Ontario; [occ.] Freelance Artist/Writer; [memb.] Garden River 1st Nation, Kuk Sool Won Canada, International Society of Poets, (Distinguished Member); [hon.] A Toohey Scholarship from University of Western, Ontario for Academic Excellence, First Degree Blackbelt, Editor's Choice Award, 1994, for poem "Pale Petal"; [oth. writ.] Pale Petal, The Quest, 29th Birthday, Can You Feel Your Knees?; [pers.] My hands are my tools that guide my inner voice and unleash my imagination. Have confidence and listen to your inner voice.; [a.] Niagara Falls, NY

BRELAND, MITCHEL
[pen.] Mitchel Breland; [b.] April 7, 1959, Sacramento, CA; [p.] Earl and Cleo; [m.] Christy, March 3, 1984; [ch.] Dale, Sarah, Clarissa, Letisha, Samuel, Timothy; [ed.] Norte Vista High; [occ.] Home maker; [memb.] Blue Cross Blood Donor; [hon.] Employee Awards for jobs well done; [oth. writ.] Unpublished poems written to my wife; [pers.] This poem was written to my wife when we were pen pals. Approx. 8 years later we were married. Still happy married.; [a.] Rialto, CA

BRENGARTNER, BETHANY J.
[b.] February 20, 1978, Toledo, OH; [p.] Barbara and Dennis Brengartner; [ed.] Roy C. start high school, old Orchard High School, Toledo, OH; [memb.] Epworth United Methodist Church, National Honor Society, Treasurer, Latin Club, President, PALS, Tennis Team, Tri-Captain, Jefferson-Madison Leadership Team; [hon.] All Academic Tennis Team, Helene Sanzenbacher Junior year English Award, top 1% of High School Class, Best Daughter of the Year Award; [a.] Toledo, OH

BRENNER, CHRISTINA
[b.] March 21, 1980, Youngstown; [p.] Richard and Joan Brenner; [ed.] 10 grade in high school; [occ.] Student; [hon.] National Honor Roll Achievement Academy; [pers.] Make the world a better place.

BREWER, MARGARET RICHTER
[pcn.] Margaret Matteson Richter Brewer; [b.] October 7, 1930, Mountour Falls, NY; [p.] Frances Mary VanToyl Matteson, John Albert Matteson; [m.] Divorced; [ch.] Four; [ed.] Technical schools, Art schools, 2 yrs. Drama - Radio Editor Ellis Advertising Buffalo, NY, 1995; [occ.] Portrait and Fine Artists; [oth. writ.] My thoughts about speed reading. Unpublished (Radio Editor, Ellis Advertising - 1995, Radio Commercials - 1995, Margaret McKinney), Dept Store Advertising Copywriter 1953-55, (Hens and Kelly, Buffalo, NY), Technical and Theoretical Writing (unpublished), 21 books in process: Do Kitties Talk? You Bet They Do!, 20 books in process on social problems; [pers.] Have spent 30 years overcoming tragedy brought to my children and self by cruel relatives. My children are back with me, I persevered through God's help and am now still able to paint and write as if the "clock" of lif has turned back 30 years. For poetry: "I simply write what the Lord gives me".; [a.] Redwood City, CA

BRIDGMAN, KAREN D.
[pen.] Raven; [b.] November 5, 1954, Hamtramck, MI; [p.] Bob Bridgman - Joan G. Van Metre; [ed.] 12 Grade; [occ.] Bartender, Side Track Saloon, Van Wert, Ohio; [hon.] Poetry-World of Poetry Golden Poet Award 1989, Silver Poet Award 1990, Award of Merit of Poetry 1988-1980, 1992 Cocktail Rights for 2 new Bar drinks - Karen Killer, Gillotine; [oth. writ.] Poetry - A Plead, Brandy Jo, A friend, An Untold Piece of Beauty, Words of the Soul, Travis, several of these have been published in Sparrowgrass Poetry Forum Inc.; [pers.] Learn to live before we die! Life is a pleasure and a joy if we can just learn to appreciate it.; [a.] Van Wert, OH

BRIGGS, MICHAL A.
[b.] January 12, 1978, Sydney Hospital; [p.] David and Patricia Briggs; [ed.] 13 years at Deposit High School (Still in school); [pers.] The place you knew is gone, the place you know is hell, and all your fears and memories are some place in between. And all the things you'll see and the things you'll see, are going to clash in a maelstrom of righteous and damnable ideas and ideals - trained conversations - Michal Briggs.; [a.] Deposit, NY

BROCK, MARTHA
[b.] May 23, 1930, Syracuse, NY; [m.] Clarence Lee Brock, December 27, 1960; [ch.] Byron, Katherine, Heather, Beth; [ed.] Masters in Education; [occ.] Retired from teaching after 17 years; [memb.] Charter member ISP, Michigan Reading Assoc., International Reading Assoc.; [hon.] Semi Finalist ISP 1994; [oth. writ.] Rainbow Riches - a book of poems published December, 1994. Several poems published locally as well as ISP Anthologies.; [pers.] We need to see the world about us through the eyes of our children. I try to reflect this in my writing.; [a.] Marysville, MI

BRODERICK, JOHN ERIC
[pen.] Eric Broderick; [b.] November 28, 1970, Aiken, SC; [p.] J. William & Mary Alice Broderick; [ed.] Summerville High, University of South Carolina at Aiken - Sophomore Undergraduate; [occ.] YMCA Career & Aiken County Prime Time Director In Training Director Augusta GA; [memb.] Old Fort Baptist Church, Young Republicans,

Senator - Student Government Association; [hon.] Who's Who Junior Year in High School; [pers.] I rely greatly on personal happenings for inspiration in my writing. Love, tragedy and anger are truly the key elements when persuading complex emotions into poetic form.; [a.] Aiken, SC

BRODOFSKY, ADAM I.
[b.] January 19, 1969, Hattiesburg, MS; [p.] Melvin Brodofsky, Elizabeth Worsham; [ed.] Yeshiva High School, Delta State University; [occ.] Dealer; [pers.] It is my hope to show the world through my eyes, and to entertain people with the ironies of my life.; [a.] Marion, AR

BROMBERG, KAREN
[b.] November 3, 1975, NJ; [p.] Stephen Bromberg, Ronda Bromberg; [ed.] Northern Valley Regional High School, Boston University; [occ.] Student; [memb.] Live Poets Society; [hon.] Alpha Phi, Dean's List; [oth. writ.] Many poems written since I was fifteen; [pers.] Life is too short to hide your talents.; [a.] Boston, MA

BROOKS, ORVILLE
[b.] October 11, 1903, Enloe, TX; [p.] Oscar Brooks, Annie Brooks; [m.] Berthe May Belle Brooks, August 29, 1929; [ch.] Ann; [ed.] Enloe High School, Baylor University; [occ.] Retired Farmer; [memb.] Armstrong Browning Library Society, Baylor University; [oth. writ.] The Dragon and the Butterfly, an autobiographical novel, Children of the Stars, a book of poetry and essays (self published); [pers.] Love is the core of my philosophy - love for national beauty and for all life. Plus love for my fellow human beings.; [a.] Klondike, TX

BROOKSHER, LARRY V.
[b.] October 14, 1942, Galveston, TX; [p.] Mildred Harris, John Harris; [m.] Judy J. Gibson Brooksher, January 17, 1990; [ch.] Kelly, Todd, Sherry, Joy L, Lynn; [ed.] Marion College University, Marion, In, 1960 Vienna High School - Vienna, OH; [occ.] Owner and Sales Director for At A Home Improvements Inc. Peru, IN 46970; [oth. writ.] Winston-Salem, North Carolina Newspaper The debate between President Bush and Mr. Ducacuss titled "A Challenge to the War on Drugs"; [pers.] The promotion or love of country, life, freedom, nature, environment, and thinking of God as the grantor of all.; [a.] Logansport, IN

BROSIUS, JACQUELINE M.
[b.] April 5, 1963, Chicago, IL; [p.] Robert R. and Virginia M. Brosius; [ed.] Thornton Fractional South High School, Purdue University College; [occ.] Second Vice-President/Division Manager in Information Delivery for the Northern Trust Co.; [memb.] Brookfield Zoo Parent Program; [pers.] Family and friends are the toast of life.; [a.] Chicago, IL

BROWN, ADAM ROBERT
[pen.] Adam Robert Brown; [b.] February 5, 1987, Arlington; [p.] Keith and Lisa Brown; [ed.] I attend 3rd grade at Thornton Elementary, Mrs. Linda Crislip; [occ.] Full time student; [hon.] 3rd place in Thornton Science fair 94-95 for 2nd grd. level first place winner of culdcott book parade 94-95 2nd grd.; [a.] Arlington, TX

BROWN, JAMES GREGORY
[pen.] Jim Brown, Jerry Brown; [b.] November 11, 1934, Independence, KS; [p.] Melvin and Margaret Brown; [m.] Jane Brown, December 27, 1962; [ch.] Three, 24, 31, and 32; [ed.] 5 yrs. College B.S., B.A., part of a masters degree and other continuous education; [occ.] Private security, 2 yrs, Tax Auditor 12 yrs., Sales 12 yrs.; [memb.] Knights of Columbus (18 yrs), Lions Club (4 years), Toast Masters Club (Pres. one year), AAA Auto Club (13 years); [hon.] Semi-finalist, National Library of Poetry (1994 and 1995), Letters of Commendation as a State Tax Auditor. Letter of Meritorious Service (US Army) #1 Staff Man for Kirby Co. 1970; [oth. writ.] Visitors and Friends (1993), "The Great Family God Gave To You And Me" (1992), "The Game of Golf" (1995), "A Chant of Praise" (1995), "Remember The Good Times, Not The Bad" (1991); [pers.] To spread peace, health, happiness and humor and prosperity and goodness and love, in all that I write, and marvel at the blessings and gifts God has given this world.; [a.] Tulsa, OK

BROWN, JOY DORSEY
[b.] July 21, 1935, Los Angeles, CA; [p.] Donald and Melle Dorsey; [m.] Robert J. Brown, September 24, 1963; [ch.] Lanie, Brian, Scott and Nancy; [ed.] Excelsion High School, Pasadena City College, Cal Poly Pomona University of California; [occ.] Legal Secretary to husband, Attorney, R. J. Brown; [oth. writ.] I have had two other poems published in the college literary books; [pers.] I feel that poetry touches that which is most profound in us and it has long been my favorite pastime.; [a.] Sylman, CA

BROWN, LAURA MARIE
[b.] March 1, 1962, Monmouth County, NJ; [p.] Joan and Joseph Miele; [m.] Stephen T. Brown, April 13, 1991; [ch.] Sierra Claire, Nicholas Stephen, Kevin Joseph; [ed.] Maritan High School, Brookdale Community College School of Nursing; [occ.] Wife, Mom, Homemaker; [memb.] St. Andrews Church; [pers.] Know good. Seek Good. Do Good.; [a.] Holland, PA

BROWNING, HEATHER LYNN
[b.] April 5, 1970, Carbondale, IL; [p.] Gene Stearns/ Marty Johnson; [m.] Paul Browning, September 30, 1989; [ch.] Joshua Ryan, Taylor Paul; [ed.] Murphysboro High School, Murphysboro, IL 1988; [occ.] Daycare Worker; [pers.] Writing is my joy. Whether it's a paragraph in my son's journal or a reflection of yesteryear, this is where I find my peace.; [a.] Centralia, IL

BROWNING, KENNETH H.
[pen.] Kentie M'Bulu; [b.] December 6, 1971, Hartford, CT; [p.] Christina Browning; [ch.] Christopher Howard Browning; [ed.] BS in English Ed from University of South Florida; [occ.] School teacher, Minister; [memb.] Phi Beta Sigma Fraternity, Phi Delta Kappa, USF's Wrestling Team; [hon.] Public Speaking, Tampa Males Choir Solo Award, Innovative Teacher; [oth. writ.] Non-published works; [pers.] If I had a million tongues and this worldly life they could save I would cut off every single one and with my soul give God the praise. All thanks to God for lifting my lost soul.; [a.] Tampa, FL

BRUCH, BARBARA
[b.] April 15, 1940, Seattle, WA; [p.] Ray and Zephyr Bruch; [ed.] BA, MFA in Art, University of Washington, Seattle; [occ.] Artist, Art Teacher; [memb.] Seattle Women's Caucus for Art, past President, Friends of the Earth; [hon.] Honor student, Bank of America Scholarship Award, 6 Solo Exhibitions in Galleries in Seattle, included in Art Exhibitions Nationally, Internationally including Seattle Art Museum, Portland Art Museum, included in book "Modernism and Beyond: Women Artist's of the Pacific Northwest" askey, Brunsman Ed. Midmarch Press (1993); [oth. writ.] "Where Are Our Women Artists" signature tabloid, Seattle '87; [pers.] I am trying to make visible the invisible and the unknown inner world more understandable through metaphor and verbal imagery.; [a.] Seattle, WA

BUCHANAN, DEBRA L.
[b.] June 17, 1962, Missowa, MT; [p.] Tod and Sharron Hackman; [m.] Patrick Buchanan, August 22, 1982; [ch.] Brandon Michael, Joshua Adam, Tyler Andrew, and Cody Daniel; [ed.] Pleasant Valley High - Chiro, Chico State University; [occ.] Children Provider; [memb.] Boys Scouts of America Cub Scout Leader, Involved in Kennedy School PTO - Children's classrooms; [a.] Medford, OR

BUCKLEY, APRIL M.
[b.] May 4, 1984, Tacoma, WA; [p.] Kathy Buckley, Curtis Buckley; [ed.] Now in 6th grade Smithridge Elementary; [occ.] Student; [memb.] Hangin' Out The Right Way Club (club at school); [pers.] Try the hardest and do the best you can.; [a.] Reno, NV

BUDZINSKI, KRISTI LYNNE
[b.] April 11, 1981; [p.] Sheila and Dan Budzinski; [ed.] Studied tap, ballet, and jazz dance for 9 years; [memb.] Honor Society, Holy Savior Catholic Church, has taught Sunday School; [hon.] 9th grade Honors student, Received Outstanding Musician Award in 1995, plays the alto saxophone, Enrolled in the Duke University Talent Search Program for Gifted Students; [pers.] I enjoy reading mystery novels, speaking French, and swimming. I love children and animals, we have two dogs, two birds, and two rabbits.

BUNDY, CAROL ANNE
[b.] February 18, 1963, Baltimore, MD; [ch.] Elia Pereira Forjaz; [ed.] University of MD School of Law, Oxford University (Extension) England; [occ.] Writer, President Human Futures Foundations Inc.; [oth. writ.] Tender is the Moment, collection of poems reflecting love and motherhood published privately and in limited edition; [pers.] In thinking and writing on philosophical matters with Dr. Jonas Salk from 1990 to 1995, I am more and more convinced that poets and poetry have vital roles to play in helping us to understand ourselves, each other and the world in which we live.; [a.] La Jolla, CA

BURDEN, WESLEY
[pen.] Wes; [b.] June 3, 1978, Bowling Green; [p.] Ronald and Joyce Burden; [ed.] Junior at Oak Ridge Christian Academy; [memb.] Cool Springs Youth for Missions; [pers.] Strive to be the best at whatever you wish to do.; [a.] Morgantown, KY

BURKE, MELISSA J.
[pen.] Cecilia; [b.] December 14, 1959, Miami, FL; [p.] Walter E. and Paula J. Carl; [m.] John J. Burke Jr., November 4, 1989; [ch.] Mark Alan, Jacqueline Marie, Ronald Carl, Melissa Anne, Catherine Elizabeth, John Joseph IV; [ed.] Graduated 1977, South West High, Miami Fl - School for Interior Ceco. and Design (Certificate) Miami, Fl.; [occ.] Citizen information Specialist, Dade Co. Public School transportation Dept.; [memb.] Run for Life Committees Sacred Heart Church, Hmstd. Fl.; [hon.] Awarded U.S. utilities Patent: Covers for 5 gal. bottle water dispenser units. 1994; [pers.] If you have faith and truly believe, you really can move mountains! Thanks to my Dad Walter, my brother Ronnie, my nephew Joey, and my beautiful family, I am not moving the mountains alone.; [a.] Princeton, FL

BURKMAN, GREGORY
[pen.] Gregory Burkman; [b.] October 23, 1981, Waterbury, CT; [p.] Angela and William Burkman; [ed.] St. Mary's Grammer School (Waterbury, CT) and Holy Cross High School currently (Waterbury, CT); [memb.] National Honors Society; [hon.] Academic School Awards, 1st place Oratorical Contest 1994, National Honor Society member, Scholarship Achiever on Christianity, winner of a spelling contest, and two letters approving my academic status from the London Parliament; [pers.] I try to make the best of myself, from academics to Christianity. I have been amazed by all the successors and successions of the world. And as I reach for my goal I express myself to others through my poems.; [a.] Waterbury, CT

BURNETT, FRANCES
[b.] February 15, 1981, Decatur, AL; [p.] Ken and Berta Burnett; [ed.] Freshman at East Limestone High School; [occ.] SADD, Jr. Beta, 4-H; [memb.] 1st in many city and school 4-H projects; [pers.] Always strive to do your best and it will happen in everything you do the human spirit is the strongest thing of all.; [a.] East Limestone, AL

BURNWORTH, HAZEL
[b.] July 24, 1920, Fairmont, WV; [p.] Jess Arthur and Icie Esther Burnworth; [ed.] D.T. Watson High School Graduate, Studied: Harmony, Psychology of Teaching, (Piano), through University of Chicago Music School; [occ.] Retired, Writing mostly (home study) Lyrics and music, poetry; [memb.] Member of Oakland, United Methodist Church, Former member of UNited Music, Inc. of Pittsburgh, Pa. and member of Johnstown Handicapped Association; [oth. writ.] Mostly song writing (unpublished) and lyrics; [pers.] I like to write in a wholesome happy go lucky style about friendly things. I love the teachings of the bible, kids and animals.; [a.] Ebensburg, PA

BURTON, ISABEL
[pen.] Izzy; [b.] February 12, 1941, Galveston, TX; [p.] Josephine and Louis Autrey; [m.] James Edward Burton; [ch.] Anna Isabel, Fernando, Alfonso, and John Camino; [ed.] Attended the Ursuline Academy in Galveston Texas, University of Mexico City 2 yrs.; [occ.] Independent Beauty Control Consultant/ Freelance Watercolorist; [memb.] American Cancer Society; [oth. writ.] Poem "Entwined" pending recognition; [pers.] My children stuck by me through hard times and are all successful and good people

today. I pray my grandchildren will also be good people. I love them all very much.; [a.] Tucson, AZ

BUSH, JENNIFER
[pen.] Chilli-Pepper; [b.] August 30, 1980, Eglin AFR, FL; [p.] Dale and Beverly Bush; [ed.] In high school, Freshman at Ceasar Rodney High School; [occ.] Student - Play Basketball for school; [hon.] JR Honor Society High Honor Award For 8th Grade; [oth. writ.] Many stories and poems; [pers.] I write what I feel. Writing is something that should happen, you can't make it happen.; [a.] Dover, DE

BUTLER, DIANNE
[pen.] Heavy Dee/Sonic Boom; [b.] April 5, 1962, Montezuma, GA; [p.] Mrs. Dorothy B. Engram and Mr. Franic Smith; [ch.] Brian O'Keith Harris; [ed.] DF Douglass High School, Georgia Southwestern College; [occ.] Writer, homemaker; [memb.] Brown Chapel Missionary Baptist Church, GA Public Television Sponsor, NAACP; [hon.] Speak Up for Young Americans" WRBL (High School and College) Who's Who, SABU President Award GSWC, Finalist in the National Library of Poetry 1995-96; [oth. writ.] I have written poems for the local paper when I was a child. I also was featured in the Macon Telegraph and News. I like to write poems, plays, skits, songs, letters, essays, etc.; [pers.] To achieve the desired, desire to achieve. The broom was the most versatile "toy" I ever had. I thank God for my talents, and for the broom.; [a.] Montezuma, GA

BUTLER, LAURA M.
[b.] August 11, 1970, Jersey City, NJ; [ed.] Trenton State College Ewing, NJ, B.A. in Journalism, May, 1993; [oth. writ.] Some short stories, other poems and 3 unfinished novels. This is my first published work.; [a.] Burlington, NJ

BUTTS, STEPHANIE JAMIEN
[b.] September 5, 1977, Greensboro, NC; [p.] John and Margo Butts; [ed.] Page High, currently attending GTCC, and planning to transfer to UNCG or Appalachin in January; [occ.] Student, Guilford Technical Community College; [memb.] Health Occupation Students of America, Former Girl Scout of America, former Greensboro Youth Council member, former member of the Ice Skating Institution of America; [hon.] Outstanding Achievement in Medical Careers, 3-time Honor Roll Student, various merit badges for skating and scouting. "Reflections" first place photography winner.; [oth. writ.] Many poems unpublished, a few poems published in local school media; [pers.] I feel youth is so meaningful, because I have experienced so much, yet so little.; [a.] Greensboro, NC

BUZAN, JEAN MARY
[b.] May 20, 1916, London, England; [p.] Ernest and Mary Burn (deceased); [m.] Gordon Frank Buzan, September 2, 1939 (deceased); [ch.] Anthony Peter, Barry Gordon; [ed.] University of B.C,; [occ.] Retired Gerontologist - still freelance lecturer and consultant; [memb.] Canadian Association of Gerontology, BC Association of Gerontology, Heart and Stroke Foundation, Knowledge Network, Use Your Head Club, Public Broadcasting Society, etc.; [oth. writ.] Thesis on older immigrants classes, many articles for various publications, currently writing books on successful aging, spelling, and a pet cat;

[pers.] I've always tried to ensure that the world is a little better for my existence by not knowingly hurting anybody, and actively helping where I can. I believe that age per se is not a relevant measure of worth and that one should "live" till one dies.; [a.] Surrey, BC, CAN

BWOSINDE, HOPHINE O.
[pen.] Otwori Bwosinde; [b.] December 30, 1963, Kenya, East Africa; [p.] Elias Osinde, Yunuke Osinde; [ed.] BS in Chemistry, Central Missouri University (1992); [occ.] Chemist, Part-time Student, School of Pharmacy, University of Missouri at Kansas City; [memb.] American Chemical Society, Graduate Student Pharmacy Association (GSPA); [hon.] Association of Student Leaders Award (1990), International Friendship Award (1988); [oth. writ.] Unpublished works include: "The House of the Republic," "Africa You're Mother," "Running Away," "The Barrel of the Pen," "The Bonds that Bind Us" (all poems), and My Color My Race (book); [pers.] I strive to reflect the colourful and natural beauty of my land, the place where birth and death are baptized in one water . . . Home, and sometimes on the evils that bedevil modern human society.; [a.] Kansas City, MO

CABRERA, MATTHEW S.
[b.] April 17, 1981, Pasadena, CA; [p.] Gaudencio A. Cabrera and Dulce S. Cabrera; [ed.] St. Bernard Class of 1995, Currently attending St. Francis High School (9th Grade); [occ.] Student, Brown Belt in Tae Kwon Do; [memb.] California Junior Scholarship Federation (C.J.S.F.), Student Council Treasurer for St. Bernard School '94-95 School Year; [hon.] 2nd Honors in 6th and 7th, 1st Honor in 8th Grade (St. Bernard School); [pers.] Tae Kwon Do Philosophy, respect, humble, patients, set goals, set your mind into your work and take your time; [a.] Los Angeles, CA

CAIN, JESSICA S.
[pen.] Jessica S. Cain; [b.] Montgomery, AL; [p.] Wayne and Jennie Cain; [ed.] Presently an 8th grader at Alabama Christian Academy Montgomery, AL; [occ.] Student and Baby sitter; [memb.] Member of the Youth Dept. of Eastmont Baptist Church in Montgomery,; [hon.] Have been on all A's Honor Roll at school several times; [oth. writ.] Have written many poems, but "The Fire" is the first o be published. A, presently working to get a literary magazine startled in the middle school at ACA so that students will have a way to express their feelings.; [pers.] I'm excited about this honor, and would like to express my love and appreciation to my grandmother, Jewel jackson, who is the closest person to me besides my parents and has given so much love and support all my life.; [a.] Montgomery, AL

CALDWELL, NAOMI W.
[b.] May 1, 1939, Nashville, TN; [p.] James W., Mabel T. Walker; [m.] Colin S. Caldwell, August 15, 1987; [ch.] Lisa, Sandy, Keith Ackers; [ed.] BA-University of VA, M.B.A.-University of Baltimore, C.F.P.-College for Financial Planning; [memb.] First Presbyterian Church, The Woman's Club of Lynchburg, Wakefield Investment Club, Wordweavers; [hon.] Alpha Chi, Phi Alpha Theta, Delta Mu Delta National, Honor Societies, Who's Who of Americans Women 1989-1990; [pers.]

Writing, for me, has been a journey into the side of the brain. Firmly enscorced in left-brain process through a B.A. in History, an M.B.A., a CFP and a career in Banking, I am now feeling the joy and exhilaration of using words to express feelings or tell a story. The joy is all the greater for the long delay, but with that joy has come a sense of the responsibility the winter bears to look deep within and speak the truth; [a.] Lynchburg, VA

CALLIHAN, HARLEY
[b.] March 30, 1978, Columbia, TN; [p.] Carl and Deborah Wheeler; [ch.] Sebastian Lee Callihan; [ed.] Central High School GED graduate; [occ.] Laundry worker; [memb.] President of my own fan club; [oth. writ.] Several unpublished poems stories, and songs; [pers.] Dedicated to Ryan my inspiration. In all things, first you must care. If deaf is dumb then hearing is ignorance. Never forget Christ died for you too.; [a.] Columbia, TN

CAMP, KATHERINE
[pen.] Kathy Camp (Prefer Katherine); [b.] Shelby, NC; [p.] Haskell and Annie L. Humphries; [m.] Boyd Camp; [ch.] Larry Camp; [ed.] High School, some College Courses (not for credit); [occ.] Retired (Federal Civil Service) Free-lance writer; [memb.] Professional Housing Management Assoc, (PHMA); [hon.] Most Outstanding Individual Contribution to PHMA Publication (1990), For "Linchpin" Series, Current Nomination to the Executive Committee, Southern Baptist Conservatives of Virginia; [oth. writ.] Articles for PHMA by-monthly magazine, Articles in the Baptist Banner, A Publication of Southern Baptist Conservatives of Virginia; [pers.] I strive to reflect Christian Love, and responsibility in all writing and speaking; [a.] Woodbridge, VA

CAMP, KATHLEEN F.
[pen.] Kathleen "Kitty" Camp; [b.] September 4, 1919, Rex, GA; [p.] Mose and Mary Lee Fielder; [m.] Charles E., September 26, 1941; [ch.] Charlotte and Carlos D.; [ed.] Clayton Co GA; [occ.] Retired (Sales Clerk); [memb.] The Rock Baptist Church; [oth. writ.] Book "Strangers at my Door", other poems published in local newspaper; [pers.] My aim is to leave some things that will bring enjoyment to those left behind.; [a.] Eastman, GA

CAMPBELL, NANCY KAYE
[b.] December 24, 1949, Flint, MI; [p.] Paul Sharp and Ruby Sharp (Merrow); [m.] Ronald Campbell, May 6, 1972; [ch.] David Campbell, Erin Campbell; [ed.] One Year Business Certificate Bob Jones University, 1969; [occ.] Retired, IBM Corporation, 1992 President/Owner, Professional Office Services; [memb.] Learning Resource Director, Mayfair Bible Church, Secretary/Treasurer, Flushing Township Crimewatch, Member, Flushing Chamber of Commerce; [hon.] Numerous IBM Means Service Awards, Regional and National IBM Manager Awards, IBM Suggestion Awards; [pers.] I wrote this poem after visiting my 98-year-old grandmother at the nursing home on July 24, 1995. Many thanks to my family for their faithful and unwavering love: Grandma Merrow, Mom Sharp, husband Ron, and my children David and Erin. I LOVE YOU ALL!.!; [a.] Flushing, MI

CAMPBELL, PAT
[pen.] Pat Campbell; [b.] December 1, 1955, Quincy,

FL; [m.] Divorced; [ch.] Dondre' West; [ed.] Hillsborough High, Hillsborough Community College, University of South Florida; [occ.] Crisis Prevention/International Counselor; [memb.] Golden Key National Honor Society; [hon.] Phi Kappa Phi, University Honors program, Phi Gamma Mu, Black Scholar Award; [oth. writ.] The Moment I See...; [pers.] I am inspired by feelings that engulf my soul.; [a.] Tampa, FL

CANNIN, PATRICIA
[pen.] Patrice, Lascivia Astate; [b.] July, 1952, MA; [p.] Gloria and John Sullivan; [m.] Al Cannin, 1975; [ch.] Michelle Ann, Alfred John; [ed.] Notre Dame high, Mass., Fall River Nursing School, Mass; [occ.] RN; [oth. writ.] Poetry, short stories, and erotica; [pers.] Poetry is my attempt to give voice and to preserve on paper those meaningful discussion with myself on the private obsessions and underlying issues that shape my being as I search for a more meaningful and balanced life.; [a.] Toms River, NJ

CAPALBO, NANCY RYAN
[pen.] Nancy Ryan; [b.] May 15, 1963, New York, NY; [p.] Robert Ryan, Rebecca Ryan; [m.] Kevin Capalbo, October 10, 1992; [ch.] Nicholas Dante Capalbo; [ed.] BA - Communication Glassboro State College Glassboro NJ

CAPONO, HILDA D. LOYOLA
[pen.] Hdlle; [b.] December 31, 1958, Phoenix, AR; [p.] Juan N. and Rosalie Loyola; [m.] Alfonso Ray Capono, September 1, 1979; [occ.] Wife, Mother and Part-time Dental Assistant; [oth. writ.] "I dedicate my first work of art to Ernest V. Capono for inspiring me to know I am the person I say I am"; [pers.] Phoenix, AR

CARAVEO, JOE E.
[pen.] Joey; [b.] March 25, 1961, El Paso, TX; [p.] Joe N. and Elvira Caraveo; [m.] Oralia Manuela, October 16, 1993; [ch.] 1; [ed.] Eagle Pass High; [occ.] Maintenance Supervisor (El Cenizo Development); [memb.] Clean and sober in a suggestive but spiritual program of recovery trying to offer hope for other Addictive personalities like mine; [hon.] Doctor's Diagnosis Schizo Active Disorder Bipolar Disorder Schizophrenic (Who Knows); [pers.] Theme "Brothers in Arms" Dire Straits "1984" God's will is Good will. One world with one God is my dream; [a.] Eagle Pass, TX

CARBONELL, JO
[pen.] Venka D. Wolf; [b.] February 28, 1978, Rutland, VT; [p.] Pat. Carbonell, Ruth Carbonell (grandmother); [ed.] Ruthland Sr.High School (class of 1996); [occ.] Child Caretaker and Sales Asst.; [memb.] Encore Theatre (Sr. Actress), Unitarian Universalist Church; [hon.] Choir, Art, Theatre, Certificates, 2 Place in Fla State Computer Writing Contest, Working in Community Summer Stock; [oth. writ.] Over 200 poems, 20 short stories, odd assorted long, unfinished stories; [pers.] Thank to Jonathan Gresl for the inspiration; [a.] Ruthland, VT

CARDER, PAULA
[b.] August 27, 1958, Arlington, VA; [p.] Freeland C. and Nellie S. Bogle; [m.] William J. Carder, September 26, 1981; [ch.] William David, Lindsey Nicole, Clay Dalton; [ed.] Fairfax High, The Institute, of Children's Literature; [occ.] Housewife

and student; [memb.] Red Mill Civic Assoc., Red Mill Elem. PTA, Hell's Point Golf Club Assoc.; [pers.] Set goals and never stop dreaming!; [a.] Virginia Beach, VA

CAREY, LINDSEY A.
[b.] January 27, 1982, Rochester, NY; [p.] Donald R. Carey (Uncle), Carol S. Carey (Aunt); [occ.] Student Holy Cross Rochester, NY; [memb.] Holy Cross Soccer, Holy Cross Cheer Leader; [pers.] In my writing I would like to get the message across that life is something that comes only once so you should not take it for granted thanks to my aunt and uncle.; [a.] Rochester, NY

CARINI, KATHERINE
[b.] August 25, 1958, New York; [p.] Marie and Stephen Chiffriller; [m.] Anthony; [ch.] Samantha; [pers.] I dedicated this poem to my daughter and one of the three pals, Samantha.

CARLISLE, ALEXANDER PETTERSON
[pen.] Douglas Grant Cameron; [b.] March 1, 1913, Pittsburgh, PA; [p.] John D. Carlisle and Pearl W. Carlisle; [ch.] Kelvin S. Carlisle, Robert M. Carlisle; [ed.] B.S.B.A Duquesne University Pch PA; [occ.] Retired; [hon.] Sigma Tau Delta Nat'l Prof. English Frat, Beta Alpha Phi. Honorary Bus Fraternity, Chas. E. McDonald Award Duquesne Univ; [oth. writ.] Rain, Spring, The Seasons

CARNLEY, JASON SEAN
[pen.] John Erik Allbright, Erik Allbrcht; [b.] December 12, 1970, Tallahassee, FL; [p.] Walter S. and Nell Hyatt Carnley; [ed.] Marianna High School, Chipola Junior College, Pittman Academie Von Musik, Los Medanos College; [occ.] Piano Teacher; [memb.] Phi Theta Kappa, Taoist Rai Chi Assn. of Florida, Feng Loy Kok Taoist Temple, Order of Wicca, Nat'l Family Opinion; [hon.] National Dean's List, Phi Theta Kappa, Dean's Lists; [oth. writ.] Numerous poems - nonpublished as of yet; [pers.] Before we can move to a higher state of consciousness, we have to understand and embrace ourselves as we are. We can know what we want and where we want to be, but we can't expect to get there unless we first know what we have, where we are, and what we'll need for the journey.; [a.] Pitsburg, CA

CARPENTER, LINDA JANE
[b.] May 29, 1948, Catskill, NY; [m.] Charles H. Carpenter Esq; [occ.] Executive and Llama Farmer; [oth. writ.] My Heart Grows with Love, One Week in the Woods, Moon Shadow, Circle in the Woods, Moments; [pers.] Moments shared, gives our soul the nourishment to Love, create and share again; [a.] Freehold, NY

CARPENTER, PRUDENCE MAE
[pen.] Mae Carpenter; [b.] May 2, 1957, Claremont, NH; [p.] Roger Wentworth Carpenter and Eunice Emogene Chandler; [memb.] Transcendental Medation Society; [pers.] Our souls need well grounded imput so they may amplify genuinely pure, free to radiate, as to experience each valuable present moment to it's fullest.; [a.] Nashua, NH

CARR, PATSY M.
[pen.] Pat Figary-Carr; [b.] June 22, 1946, Norwich, NY; [p.] Phyliss I. and Robert Figary; [m.] Divorced;

[ed.] High School , U.S. Navy Medical Corps School, SSCBT (Social Services Competency Based) Training - One eonta State College)]; [occ.] Family Assistant, Chenanled County Head Start; [memb.] Eucharist Minister, St. Paul's Church; [hon.] U.S. Navy - Good Conduct, National Defense (served 5 yrs. during Viet Nam conflict); [oth. writ.] Articles in Local Newspaper; [pers.] It was my dear Mom's death bed wish that I dear Mom's death bed wish that I share my writing by being published. Her loving ways and crest faith have influenced my life and my writings.; [a.] Norwich, NY

CARRILLO, SARAH E.
[b.] January 29, 1980, Galesburg, IL; [p.] Mr Fernando Garay and Mrs Maria P. Carrillo; [ed.] Sophomore in Academy High School; [occ.] Student in High School; [memb.] Taylor's Valley Youth, Group Business Professionals of America, Fellowship of Christian students, U.I.L. Academic Team; [hon.] A-B Honor Roll, Soph. Class Student Council Rep., Secretary and Treasurer in A.H.A Band, Music Librarian; [oth. writ.] Some other poems published in school newspapers and local newspaper; [pers.] I wish to dedicate my poems, The Greatest Woman I Ever Knew, to lois Y. Crain and her family. She was my inspiration and best friend, and will continue to be; [a.] Academy, TX

CARRIZO, MICHAEL A.
[pen.] Michael A. Carrizo; [b.] September 5, 1965, Corpus Christi, TX; [p.] Ralph and Rose Carrizo; [ch.] Benjamin A. Stiener; [ed.] Mary Carroll High School, Del Mar Community College, Riverside Community College; [occ.] Service consultant with kinetic concepts, Inc.; [memb.] Surf Rider Foundation, American Red Cross Fellowship and Christian Athlete's AOL at Fifty 150; [hon.] National Defense Medal Gulf War, Organized Marwe Corps Reserve Medal, Honorable Discharge United States Marwe Corps; [pers.] A man and his word is worth more than a man and his money.; [a.] Riverside, CA

CARROLL, MARY JANE
[pen.] Mary Jane Pleasant; [b.] August 1, 1942, Kentucky; [p.] Lilian Pleasant and Willie Pleasant; [m.] Walter M. Carroll, June 3, 1960; [ch.] Teresa Francine and Sharon Darlene; [ed.] Rock Hill, S.C. Schools-Virginia Elementary; [occ.] Unit Secretary-Piedmont Medical Hospital, Rock Hill, S.C; [oth. writ.] Poems published in church magazines; [a.] Rock Hill, SC

CARSWELL, MELODY A.
[b.] January 7, 1977, Atlanta, GA; [pers.] We are all characters in our own book of memories, and, although we may write our own rough draft, it is not up to us, however, to write the final copy.; [a.] Marietta, GA

CARUOLO, STEVEN P.
[pen.] Flash Sparky; [b.] October 3, 1951, Providence, RI; [p.] Paul V. Caruolo, Alma F. Booth; [ed.] St. Andrew's School, Roger William's University, Bachelor of Fine Arts; [occ.] Electrician, Naval Education and Training Center, Newport, RI; [memb.] National Fire Protection Association; [hon.] Naval War College Art Show, 1991 Honorable Mention; [oth. writ.] Poetry published in: Treasured poems of America. Local publishings in various newspapers.; [pers.] "Life is poetry, poetry is life".; [a.] Tiverton, RI

CASCINO, MELISSA
[b.] December 2, 1977, Smithtown, NY; [p.] Barbara and Tom Cascino; [ed.] Currently attending Ward Melville H.S. plan to continue academic career in college; [occ.] Student High School Senoir; [oth. writ.] Have written several poems starting at 10 years of age. Continue to write poetry for relaxation and enjoyment.; [pers.] In the end everything is going to be quite alright.; [a.] Stony Brook, NY

CASHELL, DELORIS E.
[b.] June 1, 1950, Cleveland, OH; [p.] Sib and Jess Barrickman; [m.] The late John R. Cashell, April 24, 1971; [ch.] 1 Jami R.; [ed.] High School Tygart Valley, Mill Creek, WV; [occ.] Intelligence Assistant, Federal Government; [oth. writ.] Although I haven't published anything up to now, I have written poetry for years.; [a.] Charles Town, WV

CASSILLY, MARY
[pen.] Mary Cassilly; [b.] March 29, 1953, Maryland, MD; [p.] Robert and Nancy Cassilly; [occ.] Cook-McDonalds; [memb.] AAA; [hon.] Award of Recognition for "Quiet Thoughts"; [pers.] Poetry is very Rewarding and a great means of strengthing the heart; [a.] Bel Air, MD

CASTLE, LAURA
[b.] November 5, 1983; [p.] Nina and George Castle; [ed.] Currently in 6th grade at Park View School; [occ.] School; [oth. writ.] None of my other writings have been published; [pers.] let poetry be read for al eyes to see; [a.] Morton Grove, IL

CEA, VINCENT
[pen.] Vincent James, James Vincent; [b.] October 14, 1947, New York; [p.] Vincent and Rose; [m.] Carol Ann; [memb.] International Society of Poets; [hon.] Editor's Choice Award; [oth. writ.] What is a Grandson and life's treasures; [pers.] A family to me is one of the most important things to share in life; [a.] Selden, NY

CEBALLO, CARMEN
[pen.] Estela Amada; [b.] October 5, 1951, Ponce, PR; [p.] Juan Laracuente, Norberta Laracuente; [m.] Rafael Ceballo, December 5, 1981; [ch.] Jean-Paul Ceballo; [ed.] Fordham University-MS in Early Education; [occ.] 1st Grade Teacher - St. John Chrysostom, Bronx; [memb.] Sigma Delta Pi-Spanish Honorary Society at City College Of NY 1974; [oth. writ.] A collection of 10 years poetry, some in English others in Spanish; [pers.] I was influenced into poetry writing by my Italian Professor in City College while making my Bachelors Degree; [a.] Bronx, NY

CHAMBERLAIN, CATHY M.
[b.] March 4, 1946, Columbia, MO; [p.] Smith Chamberlain, Cathryn Throckmorton; [ch.] Robyn and Georgean; [ed.] Univ of Mo. Syracuse, NY Univ. Extension Jas. W. Ricey High School; [occ.] Mail Order Services Naturopathic Counselor; [memb.] Beta Sigma Phi friends of the library; [hon.] Golden poets award royal patronage, hutt river province; [oth. writ.] Misc, poems articles; [a.] Reno, NV

CHAMBLEY, JOSEPH
[b.] July 31, 1971, Newnan, GA; [p.] Herman Chambley, Peggy Chambley; [ed.] Newnan High,

DeVry Institute of Technology-Atlanta; [occ.] Field Engineer, Racal-Datacom Inc; [hon.] Tau Alpha Pi National Honors Society, Deans List, Presidents List; [pers.] Always write from the heart. Happiness is; [a.] Old Hickory, TN

CHAMBLISS, TRACY
[b.] July 16, 1973, Gaiveston, TX; [p.] Leslie and John Chambliss; [ed.] G.E.D. and Self Studies; [pers.] It is not so much a choice of occupation as it is an imperative, I must write; [a.] Iowa Park, TX

CHAPMAN, LAWAYNE
[b.] April 8, 1923, Blackfoot, ID; [p.] Samuel H. and Sarah Jane Chapman (both Deceased); [m.] Ermadean Chapman, October 14, 1989; [ch.] Kay Marlene Bacon, Brian Keith Chapman, John Wayne Chapman and Adrian Darrell Chapman; [ed.] Attended Univ. of Idaho; [occ.] Retired; [memb.] Church of Jesus Christ of Latter Day Saints, Former member of the American Association of Personal Managers; [pers.] I enjoy the arts.. Music and Drama. I have been involved both as participant and as a director of Musical Dramatic shows for my church; [a.] Boise, ID

CHAPMAN, SARA
[b.] October 13, 1982, Poughkeepsie; [p.] Brian and Kathy Chapman; [ed.] Arlington Middle School, grade 8 Arlington Middle School, grade 8; [occ.] School Newspaper; [memb.] Student of the month Arlington Middle School grade 7, Student of the Month-Arlington Middle school grade 7; [pers.] I wrote this shortly after a woman I know was attacked, and a family was robbed. This was my way of expressing my feelings of this.; [a.] Poughkeepsie, NY

CHAVEZ, KRISTY
[b.] November 2, 1976, Lubbock, TX; [p.] Virginia and Simon Chavez Jr.; [ed.] Coronado High School, Texas Tech University; [occ.] Student, staff writer for The Caprock Sun/Literary Magazine; [memb.] Hispanic Association of Women, Lubbock ISD Career Tech Advisory Committee, member of Thespian Society, Committee member of Fiestas Del Llano, Inc. - a committee that sponsors Hispanic Cultural Events, member of National Honor Society and South Plains Writer's Association member.; [hon.] Altrusa's Outstanding Student Scholarship and an academic excellence scholarship to Texas Tech; [oth. writ.] Several poems published in local literacy magazine and school newspapers. Regular column "The Raging Feminist" currently being published in The Caprock Sun. Currently seeking publication for a short novel.; [pers.] I try to build into my poetry the essence of empathy and expression to create a foundation for the imagination.; [a.] Lubbock, TX

CHENIER, PAULA
[pen.] D. Dragon Moon; [b.] Escanaba, MI; [p.] Clint and Mickey Marenger; [m.] Donald Chenier; [ch.] Jen and Amy; [ed.] Gladstone High School Gladstone MI, Bay de Noc Community College, Escanaba, MI; [occ.] Painter, Nurse; [pers.] Stay focused on the word of God and go where the Monet is.; [a.] Lincoln Park, MI

CHIARI, PHILLIP ADAM
[pen.] Phil; [b.] October 26, 1982, Rockville Centre,

Long Island, NY; [p.] Edward and Yvonne Chiari; [ed.] Kindergarten to seventh grade, so far!; [occ.] Student in Junior High; [hon.] A citizen award and a reading award, both in grade school; [oth. writ.] Starter poem, there once was, Tom and his bomb, Babies, Sun, The Pie, Life. Special poems, My heart knows, I am the light in your mind, Death, The most beautiful feature, and Mother.; [pers.] I dedicate my poems to my Mom and Dad, and to my 6th grade teacher Mrs. Carmichael for her encouragement. Other special people, Great Grandma Honey, Grandma Sissy, Uncle Bill and Aunt Evelyn, Aunt Angrea and my brother Jay and Cliff.; [a.] Rockville Center, NY

CHILDS, ETTA W.
[pen.] Mae; [b.] March 12, Senior, Americus, GA; [p.] Passed; [m.] George W. Childs, March 14, 1944; [ed.] High Americus CA Further study Ft. Valley state college, A diploma from Master Collage, IL; [occ.] Teacher and Designer in Ladies Garments; [memb.] Methodist both retired in Wash, D.C. After my wedding to my husband Geo W. Childs of Chicago Ill we spent our honeymoon in Illinois; [hon.] And decided to make hour home in his home town for many years. We settled in Florida, Geo, New Jersey and now in Unadilla Ge P.S. Also taught in Ga training school for girls in Macon Ga years later; [oth. writ.] Would like to say this poem written by me over 50 yrs. As our wedding anniversary was 50 yrs May 4, 195 (smile) ETTU; [pers.] I have loved writing poems since I was away young. While with my parent in Americus Ga also since my in married life.

CHOBOD, LESLIE A.
[b.] May 3, 1947, Saginaw, MI; [p.] Elden and Freda Emede; [m.] Jerry W. Chobod, June 20, 1981; [ch.] Kerri Slominski, Tracy Slominski, Tammy Moore, Scott Chobod, Nicole Moore; [ed.] St. Andrew High School Central Michigan University; [occ.] Teacher (1st grade); [memb.] St. Helen Catholic Church Liturgy Commission C.M.U. Alumni Association; [pers.] I enjoy writing poems for family and friends and encourage creative writing in the classroom.; [a.] Saginaw, MI

CHOW, JAIMEE
[b.] February 6, 1981, San Jose, CA; [p.] George and Robin Chow; [occ.] High School Student; [a.] Fremont, CA

CHRISTOPHER, DOLORES
[pen.] Kris Kristopher; [b.] July 8, 1930, Chicago; [p.] Rose and Paul Sprov; [m.] Deceased (1979), December 5, 1948; [ch.] Three Boys, 2 Girls (all married); [ed.] Two years evening Business College personal courses at Random; [occ.] Retired legal secretary; [memb.] Rich Port YMCA Bally Health Club Indian Head Park Women's Club, Etc.; [hon.] Teacher's and Den Mother, Brownie Ass't. Calif. Studio Girl Golden Crown Merit Award; [oth. writ.] Commentary articles news or responses to featured material and public meetings with community interests; [pers.] Accomplishments and good works of others inspire the pleasant thoughts of putting music and rhyme in words of praise.; [a.] Chicago, IL

CHUCK, CHRISTOPHER
[pen.] Christopher Tracy; [b.] May 26, 1995,

Uptown; [ed.] Education of the mind, body, and soul; [occ.] Writer; [oth. writ.] 132 other poems, 5 screenplays and 3 songs; [pers.] The world is in chaos because of hate. I love as much I can, so should. Love isn't just a 4 letter word, it's something ineffable. In the immortal words of Peace and be wild; [a.] Uptown

CHURCHILL, MARCIA DEBRA
[b.] September 11, 1956, New York, NY; [ch.] Graig Brandon Perry and Andrew Neal Taylor; [ed.] B.S. Union College, Schenectady, NY D.P.M. New York College of Podiatric Medicine; [occ.] Doctor of Podiatric Medicine; [memb.] American Podiatric Medical Assn., New York Podiatric Medical Assn., A Association of Women Podiatric Institute of Noetic Sciences; [oth. writ.] Memories and Essays; [pers.] To survive the coming millennium, we must tap our altruistic and spiritual selves. The future depends on our redefinition of who we are, and what we want. Teach the children love and peace. Thanks God. Shalom.; [a.] Oceanside, NY

CLANCY, JOSEPH W.
[b.] August, 1963, Kaukauna, WI; [p.] Both (Deceased); [ed.] Wrightstown High School; [occ.] Curative rehabilitation center emphasis work program; [pers.] Always do you best whatever you do and wherever goals and having fun doing them no matter what they are at the same time in the process. Enjoy always the fun times and the joy that comes with it.; [a.] Greenbay, WI

CLARK, GLADYS H.
[pen.] Jean Clark; [b.] May 8, 1913; [p.] William T. Stuver and Leta Irene (putnam); [m.] Howard E. Clark (Deceased), November 18, 1975; [ch.] Leta M. Brooks, Patricia A. Patterson; [ed.] 10th grade; [occ.] Retired and still writing poetry; [oth. writ.] Many short stories unpublished; [pers.] I love the country, and for over 50 years i made my living cooking on cattle reaches in Montana Wyoming and Nevada. I retired at 71 I miss that peaceful life and the beautiful buffalo-moose elk-deer and antelope. I often saw thru my kitchen window, grazing in the foothills and mountain side their beauty, serenity, contentment made my life complete. I understand now how my Indian Ancestors FELT. That is where received my education; [a.] Likely, CA

CLARKE, CLAUDETTE H.
[pen.] Claudette H. Clarke; [b.] California, PA; [p.] Emmett E. Harris, Pauline R. Harris; [m.] Edward S. Clarke; [ch.] Lynette, Robert Danielle, Kristine, Ryan Robert, Nicole; [ed.] BS in Biology and Chem - Registry in Medical Technology Carlow College Pitts, PA, Currently Attending WVO for music degree; [occ.] medical Technologist Wash. Hosp. Lab. Wash. PA, Church Organist, Trinity Episcopal Ch,; [memb.] Society of American Poets; [oth. writ.] Book published "Songs of the Heart" Poems in anthology by Dr. Charles Crave Society Arms Poets; [pers.] I have dedicated my work to my God who has given me all the talent I have to be a blessing to others.; [a.] Washington, PA

CLARKE, VALERIA LANZA
[pen.] Valeria Lanza Clarke; [b.] Genova, Italy; [m.] Married; [ch.] Two children; [ed.] Degree in European literatures. Master in English Literature - Diploma in Special Education; [occ.] Teaches Italian and paints mostly watercolor; [pers.] Born in a family of paintrs, musicians and writers, spent most of her life in Italy came to the states only recently. While in her paintings she depicts the most brilliant facets of nature, in her writing. There is always present the attempt of finding a link between life any death. Love and hate. Supernatural and tangible nature. I find true the melancholy Shakespearian saying "There is nothing either good or bad but thinking makes it so". Like Shakespeare I think that I can stands between the two life and death love and hate, naturals supernatural.; [a.] Lexington, MA

CLAUTICE, EDWARD W.
[b.] October 13, 1916, Baltimore, MD; [p.] George Joseph C., and Janet Harwood Wellmore; [m.] Madelyn Spraker C. (Deceased), August 30, 1941; [ch.] Elizabeth F., Stephen F., Christopher G., Michael J., Edward G.; [ed.] Calvert Hall H.S., Jones Hopkins, Univ. B.E., Boston Univ. M.B.A., U.S. Army Command and General Staff College; [occ.] Retired Manufacturing Engineer, Ret. Lt. Col, U.S. Army Ordinance; [memb.] American Ordinance Assn., Soc. of Manufacturing Engrs, Retired Officers Assn., Yorktowne Tennis and Fitness Club; [hon.] Corporate Top Employee, various Military Medals, many awards in fourteen different sports, various writing awards; [oth. writ.] Books-Internal Federal Labor Relations, A Little Non Sense, A Lotta Nonsense, Madelyn My Wife, Our Mother, Many Technical and Scientific Reports; [pers.] Up to this year, my work was primary humorous, since Jan. 5, the amount has been greatly reduced and the subject matter has reflected my feelings resulting from the loss of my wife of 53 years; [a.] York, PA

CLAY, LILLIAN H.
[b.] June 11, 1913, Bourbon Co, KY; [p.] Mr. Mrs. Oliver L. and Edna Ritchie Harrison; [m.] James T. Clay, December 1, 1934; [ed.] High School, College Courses, Nationally accredited Hour Show Judge Extensive Travel, Courses in art, Painting; [occ.] Retired - enjoy writing poetry attending timely lectures, reading, knitting; [memb.] Methodist church, Wendell, NC Woman Club, Raleigh Garden Club (Wendell N.C.) (Raleigh, N.C.); [hon.] A Nationally accredited Hour Show Judge - Judging in N.C. KY, Tenn, and Florida, or on many Blue Ribbons involving flower shows that I entered, poems printed in local newspaper, church news letter (monthly) 6 yrs. won Blue Ribbons also in Japanese Flower Arranging; [oth. writ.] For Church news letter, woman's club, as christmas card children, Articles for Gold Leaf Farmer, (Wendell, N.C. local paper), poems to Brides, children, congratulations, elderly bereaved etc.; [pers.] I hope others will enjoy reading my poems as much I have enjoyed writing them.; [a.] Lexington, KY

CLAY, MARY MYRA
[b.] October 28, 1926, Little Elm; [p.] Calvin and Myrtle Tubbs; [m.] Divorced, April 45, 1947; [ch.] Larry and Donita; [ed.] High School - Frisco, TX. Elm. School - Little High School - in Little Elm, TX; [occ.] Retired; [oth. writ.] None except for my own pleasure. None have been published.; [pers.] I write about things I know well and that I feel very deeply about.; [a.] Denton, TX

CLAYPOOL, THOMAS JOHN
[pen.] Toms Adams; [b.] August 12, 1966, Winfield,

IL; [p.] Oliver and Elizabeth Claypool; [occ.] Bank Clerk; [oth. writ.] Published five (5) chapbooks, "Magdeline", "Mask", "An Ugly American, "Nouveaux Hobos", "Alley Voodoo", and am currently working on a sixth tentatively titled "In From The Lake". Published in the now defunct "Coventry Reader"; [pers.] A self-proclaimed neo-Romantic, I strive to blend the traditions of classic and modern poetry forms into a newer contemporary style; [a.] Cleveland, OH

COADY, ALYSSA
[b.] January 28, 1982, Arlington, TX; [p.] Buzz and Carol Coady; [ed.] I am an eight grader at the Oakridge school Arlington school in Arlington. I have been going to Oakridge since 6th grade and plan to be going there until I graduate.; [occ.] I am a student; [memb.] I am sponsoring a child in the Philippines through children International; [hon.] I am a cheerleader for school and I am on a competitive squad, Robel Cheer company. Last year Rebels went to NCH championship and got 4th place in the nation.; [oth. writ.] I write poems as a hobby. This is my first competition to enter. I am so surprised at the results.; [pers.] Live life while you can, because before you know it, it's gone.; [a.] Arlington, TX

COBB, CAROL ANN
[b.] July 6, 1951, Schenectady, NY; [p.] Albert and Betty Strimel; [m.] William Harold Cobb, August 14, 1970; [ch.] Christopher Michael, Julie Diane, Allison Denise, Wendy Jennette and Nathaniel James-Kelson; [ed.] Waterloo Senior High, NY, U.S.A.F. Medical Technician San Antonio, TX, various religious education courses, San Antonio, TX; [occ.] Housewife; [memb.] Calvary Chapel, Haltom City, TX, Woman's Group at Calvary Chapel; [hon.] 1980 District Award of Merit, Tejas Valley Cub Scouts San Antonio, TX, Various Cub scouts awards, various religious education awards; [oth. writ.] I have about 50 unpublished poems; [pers.] God and family are very important to me. My writings come from my experiences, particularly with my children.; [a.] Fort Worth, TX

COBB, MARILYN E.
[b.] January 10, 1930, Sebring, FL; [p.] Charles C. and Vera K. Cobb; [ed.] B.S. degree in Education - Florida. State U. Medical Technology degree Florida. College of Medical Technology - Miami, Florida.; [occ.] Retired Phlebotomist with St, Joseph's Hospital Nursing Home Division - Tampa, Florida; [hon.] Voted Best Women's Athlete in 4,000 students in college, Valedictorian of Medical Technology school in Miami; [pers.] I thank God for allowing me to be blessed with Christian parents and a Christian homelife. They taught me the truths of the Bible and I accepted Jesus Christ as my personal Saviour at an early age. My desire is to share Him and serve Him in every area of my life.

COBBS, ANDRE N.
[b.] July 26, 1961, Bastrop, LA; [p.] James Cobbs, Alvie Cobbs; [m.] Gloria Ann Cobbs, June 5, 1981; [ed.] Bastrop, High, Northeast Louisiana University; [hon.] President's List, Dean's List; [oth. writ.] No other published writings; [a.] Bastrop Louisiana, LA

CODY, ERIN R.
[b.] July 31, 1977, Sylvania, OH; [p.] Albert and Elaine Cody; [ed.] Saint Ursula Academy, Bowling

Green State University; [occ.] Student; [memb.] Honors Student Association; [hon.] National Science Merit, Dean's List, President's List; [pers.] Poetry is not meant to be expressly defined by the poet' it is up to each individual to determine its emotional significance; [a.] Toledo, OH

COGSWELL, LAURIE MAE
[b.] May 23, 1964, Brookville, PA; [p.] Gloria Lee Murphy, Earl Dorman Murphy; [ch.] Marvin, Melissa; [ed.] Union High School Rinersburg PA Clarion County Area Vo-tech-practical Nursing; [occ.] Bartender/manager; [memb.] Fryburg Sportsman's Club, Women of the moose, Social member VFW #2145, Social member American Legion Post #066 Auxiliary member; [oth. writ.] Numerous unpublished; [pers.] Life always throws curve balls, you just have to remember to wear your face mask or learn how to catch.; [a.] Rimersburg, PA

COLE JR., DANIEL
[b.] October 31, 1953, Hempstead, TX; [p.] Mr. and Mrs. Daniel Cole Sr., Reatha J. Cole; [ed.] Hempstead High School Prairie View A and M University; [occ.] Computer Programmer, H.E.B. San Antonio, TX; [pers.] Poetry allows me to express my thoughts and emotions unconfined.; [a.] San Antonio, TX

COLEMAN, KENNETH MATTHEW
[b.] February 7, 1967; [p.] Kenneth L. Coleman and Beth Anne Coleman; [m.] Beth Ann Coleman, July 9, 1994; [ed.] BA Political Science/History Suny Binghamton with honors; [occ.] Lt. US Navy; [a.] Staten Island, NY

COLTON, JAMES H.
[b.] August 7, 1930, Malone, NY; [m.] Hideko Colton, May 14, 1958; [ch.] Carl and Charles Colton (both married with three children each); [ed.] Franklin Academy High School, Adirondack School of Commerce; [occ.] Retired Rural Letter Carrier, Volunteer for Meals on Wheels and other volunteer work; [memb.] National Association of Rural Letter Carrier, National Association of Retired Federal Employees, AARP, RSVP volunteer, First Baptist Church of East Syracuse; [oth. writ.] Poems that have never been published. Some poems were put on Message boards of the America Online Writers Club; [pers.] To strive, to be obedient to the Lord each day and continually seek His guidance and glorify His name; [a.] East Syracuse, NY

COMBEST, EILEEN M.
[b.] October 30, 1939, Jamestown, KY; [p.] Vertus and Opal Grider; [m.] Corbett T. Combest, December 28, 1957; [ch.] Connie, Lisa, Pamela; [ed.] High School Diploma Russell County High School; [occ.] Court Clerk at Quartzsite Justice Court; [pers.] I have written numerous poems, none of which have been printed to date. Mostly I write about others experiences and how I think they feel. With almost every poem I write I open a tiny window and expose my innermost being.; [a.] Quartzsite, AZ

CONAWAY, WILLIAM J.
[b.] April 5, 1968, Kansas City; [ed.] Bachelor of Science in Psychology from Kansas State University; [occ.] Unsigned Musician and Writer; [oth. writ.]

Numerous poems, essays, songs and currently organizing material for a book; [pers.] I view man as Gods most grotesque creature, since he deliberately harms himself, others and his environment with foreknowledge of his actions; [a.] Studio City, CA

CONNER, CLARA JANE
[pen.] Sarah Rebeccah Ely; [b.] May 4, 1952, Lewis, CO; [p.] Otto and Verna Burns; [m.] Kyle Daniel Conner, July 12, 1971; [ch.] Nathan D. Conner (Deceased), Bethany Necole Conner Shepherd; [ed.] Senior Graduate Glencliff High; [occ.] Self-employed, wedding decor artist, craftperson, poet; [memb.] (1993-4-5) Intr Nat'l Society of poets. Active member - sunday school teacher Bangus Ch. of God.; [hon.] Nominated to Advisory Board - 1993, 94, 95 Intr. Nat'l Soc. Poets. honors from world of poetry - Silver and Gold, Intr Nat'l Soc. of poets, Ruby and Merit Award 3 Editors choice awards lib of poetry; [oth. writ.] Winds of the night sky, Outstd'g Poets - 1993-94. Best Poems 1995-96 N.U.P. The Rainbow's end. Local newspaper write-ups - Lewis Co Herald, l'bury Advocate.; [pers.] All honors given to me given by God. And it is to God I give the Honor and Glory.; [a.] Hohenwald, TN

COOK, CHRISTINA
[b.] November 14, 1975, Springfield, OR; [p.] Richard Cook, Teresa Cook; [ed.] Currently attending Fullerton Community College, Major is Child Psychology, and human Services; [occ.] Student; [hon.] Lambda Delta Sigma, (Service Award), Buena Park Police Department (Explorer)-Cumulation for beyond the call of duty; [oth. writ.] The Church of Jesus Christ of Latter Day, Saints Institute of Religion Newsletter; [pers.] I had written this poem as a writing assignment in one of my English classes. The main idea of this poem was to write about the person introduced me to journal writing. My mother gave me my first journal, and inspired me to write, philosophical statement, expect the unexpected; [a.] Buena Park, CA

COOK, RICHELLE
[b.] September 15, 1980, Lancaster, CA; [p.] Jan Arries and Harold Cook; [ed.] A sophomore at Antelope Valley High School; [pers.] I wrote this poem to the person I cared for very much.

COOKE, JANETTE V.
[b.] November 15, 1954, Canton, OH; [p.] David B. Vail and Gloria E. Vail; [m.] M. Ted Cooke, November 10, 1991; [ed.] Palmetto High School; [occ.] Secretary, Cunningham and Co. Mortgage Bankers; [hon.] Honorable Mention - Poetry Contest; [pers.] My poetry reflects my personals growth spiritually toward a more loving message for all children of God.; [a.] Asheville, NC

COOLIDGE, FRANCES DEA
[b.] November 11, 1946, Grafton, ND; [m.] Mark Coolidge, July 7, 1967; [ch.] Michael, Matthew, Marshall; [oth. writ.] My poetry started when my middle son returned from the Gulf War. War was great trauma for me. Even though I've always questioned life, war opened me and made me more aware. I never sit down to think about writing-it just comes. Sometimes it wakes me in the middle of the night. And it's always written within a few minutes; [pers.] If my poetry can connect people and help them see the unity in all and if can encourage them

to scarch for the true meaning of their own soul, then my life here has truly served a good purpose; [a.] Seattle, WA

COONS, LINDSAY
[pen.] Lindsay White; [b.] September 4, 1982, Niskayuna, NY; [p.] Theresa and Casey Coons; [ed.] Currently in 8th grade at Schohoroe Central Schools, Class of 2000, 13 years old in 1995; [memb.] School's band, stage band with saxophone, flute ensemble, volleyball, and FHA (Future Homemakers of America); [hon.] 1st chair flute in 7th and 8th grade band, selected to go to a state competition for my flute (3 people in the band), English award for 'quality writing', and a social studies award; [oth. writ.] A book of poems, by the Bradt Press in 1992, 4th grade; [pers.] I have found that I've always been able to express my true feelings through my music and writing. I wrote this poem during a sad time, and I felt better after I did.; [a.] Sloansville, NY

COOPER, NYANONTEE
[pen.] Shorty Shor Tee; [b.] November 13, 1982, Paynesville, Liberia; [p.] Miriam A. Cooper and Thomas R. Cooper; [ed.] Kora Kelly Elementary, George Elementary, West Middle School, and Edmonson Middle School; [occ.] 8th grade student at Edmonson Middle School; [memb.] Service Leadership/Learning Training; [hon.] Excellence Awards for the 1992 Dr. Martin Luther King, Jr. writing contest; [oth. writ.] A few other poems I just read to close friends teachers and family members; [pers.] "The heart has reasons the mind cannot know."; [a.] Ypsilanti, MI

COOPER, VALERIE RUTH
[b.] May 27, 1962, Neptune, NJ; [p.] Beverly Ann Davis and June A. Morgan; [m.] Divorced; [ch.] John E. Cooper Jr.; [ed.] Pastoral Care BA, LPN, Current Student in Marine Biology; [occ.] Chaplain; [memb.] W.A.S.; [oth. writ.] Children's Books-unpub., lots of other poems; [pers.] I intend to use and develop every gift ability that God put in me to influence and effect the world around me; [a.] SD, CA

COOPER, WANDA
[b.] April 26, 1930, Crab Orchard, KY; [p.] Henry Neal and Lula Neal; [m.] Ralph J. Cooper, October 24, 1947; [ch.] Susan Kay Thompson and Gary W. Cooper; [ed.] Dipper School, Baptist Church-Member of Moose Lodge in North Vernon. Ind. I collected a Thousand Dolls; [occ.] Housewife. I owned the Doll Store 4 years and Old Time Photographer; [oth. writ.] The Death Of Love, Different Strokes; [pers.] I write from my heart. My own personal life experiences. Has inspired me. My son Gary Wayne Cooper is a poet also; [a.] Columbus, IN

COPENHAVER, JOYCE
[pen.] Jodi; [b.] September 21, 1932, IN; [ch.] Karla, Michele, Teri, Chuck; [ed.] High School, 6 Mo. Business, 3 yrs. children's Literature, 7 yr. bible Correspondence; [occ.] Retired, senior volunteer writer; [memb.] Worldwide Church of God (choir, First Aid Secr) (SRDA) Senior Retirement Development Assoc, Retired Senior Volunteer Program (RSVP), and Senior Choir; [hon.] 1992-95 Volunteer Award Certificates and pin from Par View Hospital, volunteer of year (1995-96) Pueblo

Community health Center, 1950 DAR Good Citizenship. Various Music Awards and 4-H. Awards, Proofreading and Typing Awards during High School.; [oth. writ.] I wrote poetry and stories for school paper, stories from pictures in sixth grade, articles for local newspaper in I.N. and TX.; [pers.] I started writing in Ind. in sixth grade. Then was when I knew what I wanted to be involved in but waited until my four children were grown. Now I write for my grand - children, they are less critical; [a.] Pueblo, CO

COPENHAVER, RODNEY
[b.] September 14, 1974, Dillsburg, PA; [p.] Clarence and Joyce Copenhaver; [ed.] Northern Senior High School; [occ.] Construction; [pers.] I am inspired by things that I experience in my life and things that I see and hear of in the world.; [a.] Dillsburg, PA

COPPLER, COVA M.
[pen.] Cova Moore Coppler; [b.] July 21, 1938, Muncie, IN; [p.] Robert and Marie Moore; [m.] Gerald, October 26, 1980; [ch.] Connie, Danny, Carla, Kay, Bill Mike; [ed.] Male High School, 2 Medical Degrees from California College of Health Sciences; [occ.] Respiratory Therapist at University Hospital - traum a center; [memb.] NBRC - KSRC - AARC - AARP - Ridgewood Baptist Church. The Living Bank - Organ Donor Assoc.; [hon.] Merit Awards for being team Mother for youth sports. "I care pins" at Hospital - pts wrote after leaving hospital that I was a caring Therapist; [oth. writ.] Poem published for National Library of Poetry in "Whispers in the wind". I write poetry about my Family and Friends and my 1st Love - Jesus Christ.; [pers.] I write poetry trying to make readers feel the enormous love in my heart and soul for God, family and friends. Helen Steiner rice has always been my inspiration.; [a.] Louisville, KY

CORNELL, JENNIFER
[b.] June 10, 1983, SC; [p.] Shelley Cornell; [ed.] Brookhurst Jr. High; [occ.] Student; [hon.] American Legion Honorable Mention, President Gold Award; [pers.] I have just begun my writing career and I've expressed things close to my heart.; [a.] Anaheim, CA

COTE, ELAINE
[b.] October 17, 1948, Providence, RI; [p.] Andrew and Loretta Francis; [ch.] Jesse, Sheri Mandy; [ed.] Certified nursing assistant at Laurel health care center, a small nursing home in Coventry, RI; [pers.] I write about what I feel from within. My inspiration to write comes from God, life, and the people I have met, who have touched my life and my heart.; [a.] West Warwick, RI

COTNER, GLORIA E.
[pen.] Estella Cotner; [b.] August 3, 1926, Detroit, MI; [p.] Evelyn and Stephen Jones; [m.] Widow; [ch.] George Han, Judy, Joyce and Joella; [ed.] Attended Akron U Fenn College; [occ.] Retired Real estate Associate; [memb.] Avid Bridge Player St. Thomas Orthy dox church widowed persons service AARP Hobbies- oil painting and music; [hon.] This the first time in the fifty years I have been writing, I have ever submitted anything.; [oth. writ.] Presently Editor of WPS Newsletter, Akon, Ohio (widowed Persons Service) many unpublished stories and

poems. Former column in Ocean Pine Newspaper in Berlin Md. (Monthly); [pers.] I feel compelled to write the story of my life, from my earliest memories my deeds, my thoughts, good or bad. And an absolute obligation to write my family genealogy on both maternal and paternal sides, This will include things they have things they have said and done. This is no small task but I will completed it and where I leave off.; [a.] Akron, OH

COUSER, YVETTE BURNHAM
[b.] December 1, 1967, Belleville, NJ; [p.] Dr. Enriqueta Burnham and Laurence Burnham; [m.] Jonathan Couser, December 10, 1994; [ch.] Adelia Sophia; [ed.] Manalapan High, Howell High School, New York University; [occ.] Full time mom pursuing Writing Career; [oth. writ.] Everywoman, A Modern Morality Play-published by Balar's Plays 1994; [a.] New York City, NY

COWEN, CAROLINE L.
[pen.] Carrie Lou Smith; [b.] August 30, 1942; [p.] Leon Joseph and Myra P. Smith; [m.] Raymond R. Cowen Jr., August 30, 1958; [ch.] Kim Sadowski and Kevin Corey Cowen; [ed.] Valley High School Graduate, New Kensington Commercial Business College, Some college courses; [occ.] Senior Technician/Planner-Scheduler with Alcoa Research Center; [oth. writ.] Short Stories - "Feathers", "my God Drives a Yellow Volkswagen", and "Survivor"; [pers.] Vision alone cannot allow you to see what you must, we must see with our heart; [a.] Arnold, PN

COX, HELEN H.
[b.] October 28, Glendale, FL; [p.] Walter Manning and Adoline Elizabeth Herley; [m.] William E Cox, Jr. (Bill) VPI '38, March 28, 1942; [ch.] Poet E. Cox, III, Pamela E. Cox, Alan H. Cox, Kimberly Helen Cox Nance; [occ.] Retired Teacher, MHS and MMS - Marianna F.; [memb.] FEA, WPS (Widowed Persons Services), FUMC, JC Ret. Teachers, AARP, FUM Quilters; [hon.] My greatest honor is having been graduated from FSCW (FSU now) Marrying Cdn. William e. Ca, Jo. and Searing three children, and then a lake life child who was/is a joy to all of us. I also have eight lovely grand children and a now one due February 13, 1996. I'm very proud and blessed in an abundant way.; [oth. writ.] I have written poems all of my life, I have then written on napkins, placemats, whatever! There's a bushed basket full of my heartfelt feelings written for all occasions i.e. b-day, wedding, retirements, everything!; [pers.] I am a very positive person - the glass is half fall never half empty. I believe that LOVE is the most important thing we can give and to love to care for our fellow men is the best way to a show our love for God. I lost my husband and 51.9 yrs. in Dec. '94 and only three my poetry, love of family and friends, love I been able to survive.; [a.] Marianna, FL

COX, KIMBERLEE BETHANY
[b.] July 8, 1977, Fort Bragg, NC; [p.] Peter and Sandra Cox; [ed.] Killeen High School, Killeen, Texas, I'm currently an undergraduate student at Duke University in Durham, NC; [occ.] Student; [hon.] National Merit Scholar, 1955, Texas All State Academic Team Member, 1995, AP Scholar, 1995; [oth. writ.] I had a high school internship writing for "Discover Magazine" in Killeen, Texas from

February '94 - March '95, as well as and internship at "The Killeen Daily Herald" from January through May '95; [pers.] My grandmother, Edna Boyum, has also been selected as a semi-finalist and will be published in "The Rainbow's End".; [a.] Fayetteville, NC

CRAIG, BARBARA
[pen.] Simone, Barbie; [b.] March 28, 1982, Berkeley, CA; [p.] Barbara and Carlton Castex; [ed.] Episcopal School of Acadiana; [occ.] Student at the Episcopal School of Acadiana; [memb.] ESA Volleyball team, ESA Tennis team, Lafayette Lanes Bowling League, also club volleyball; [hon.] First place in reading contest and second place in Black History National Art Contest; [oth. writ.] The Perfect friend, Love to limit, dreams and goals. Publications in Jefferson schools books in Kindergarten; [pers.] In my writings, I try to reflect the way I feel daily. Being thirteen in a world like this is hard and since my feelings are so mixed up, I decided to write them down.; [a.] Lafayette, LA

CRAWFORD, GLORIA
[pen.] Gloria Graggs Crowford; [b.] March 20, 1955, Mobile, AL; [p.] S.T., Louella Graggs; [occ.] Educational Behavioral, Counselor; [oth. writ.] Poems, philosophical prose, and essays; [pers.] I write for posterity: Branden, Kameron, and the unborn Graggs child.; [a.] Sacramento, CA

CREAMER, ROSALIE J.
[b.] February 25, 1934, Grand Manan Island, New Brunswick, Canada; [p.] Carl and Florence Frost (Deceased); [m.] James Creamer, January 25, 1957; [ch.] Barry Red Creamer; [ed.] Grand Manan High School; [occ.] Secretary Specialist, State of Florida; [memb.] Polk County Humane Society; [oth. writ.] I am compiling a collection of poems that I hope to submit for publication in the near future, I also hope to submit a collections of greeting card verses.; [pers.] I hope some day to work with illiterate adults so that they, too, can enjoy the beauty of poetry.; [a.] Bartow, FL

CRYTSER, TERESA
[b.] April 21, 1976, Pittsburgh, PA; [p.] Alfred and Jean Lanyi Crytser; [ed.] Serra Catholic High School Community College of Allegheny County; [hon.] Dean's List, Honor Roll, Quill and Scroll Society,; [oth. writ.] Articles and poems published in The Next Generation; [a.] East McKeesport, PA

CULL, TRISHA
[pen.] Patricia Jean Cull; [b.] January 29, 1974, Cranbrook, BC; [ed.] Currently attending the University of Victoria (Major : Creative Writing); [pers.] Writing of all things, reflect directly the world around us. Words are a beautiful abstraction of the heart, and have in many ways, become my passion and my light; [a.] Victoria, BC

CURRIE, BILLY JOE
[b.] February 28, 1968, Ripley, TN; [ch.] Whitney Currie, Brittney Currie; [ed.] Ripley High Dyersburg State College; [occ.] Inspiring Singer, Song writer; [oth. writ.] Completion of an record album of 12 songs hoping to get discovered country, pop, R and B; [pers.] "A winner never quits and a quitter never wins" in my life those are words I live by because in life people have dreams and in those dreams, there's

hope and without hope there's no beginning only you know your limitations and for me, the sky is the limit.; [a.] Ripley, TN

CVACH, PHILIP E.
[b.] July 28, 1927, Baltimore, MD; [p.] Jerome C.M. and Anna E; [m.] Mary A., January 24, 1948; [ch.] Phyllis Ann Shand, Jerome J., John J., Philip E.III; [ed.] Calvert Hall College, Eckels College, Essex Community College; [occ.] Semi-Retired Montician; [memb.] American Legion, Lions Club, Knight of Columbus, Alhambra, NSFDA, MSFDA, HOPA, St.Clement Church; [hon.] Jaycee Men of the Year, Lions Man of the Year, Several Civic and Fraternal Awards, Also Youth Program Awards; [oth. writ.] Articles published in local papers; [pers.] I comment and reflect on times of my life and others, and the world around me; [a.] Towson, MD

D'AMATO, ALISON
[b.] January 9, 1984, Charleston, SC; [p.] Nicholas D'Amato and Julie Boyd; [ed.] Elementary School PS42, Jonas E. Salk Middle School; [occ.] 6th Grade Student; [memb.] Newspaper Club; [hon.] Honor Student, Language Arts Award, Recycling Award; [oth. writ.] One poem published in local newspaper ("Behind My Eyelids"). Articles, short stories and poems for school newspaper.; [pers.] I enjoy writing poetry because it is a creative way of expressing my feelings; [a.] Farmingdale, NY

D'CUNHA, NEIL COLIN
[pen.] Neil Colin D'Cunha; [b.] December 15, 1967; [ed.] University of Texas at Arlington BS Computer Science Engineering, University Of Karachi B.S. Mathematic; [occ.] Software Engineer, IBM; [memb.] Honor society of International Scholar's, The Golden Key Honor Society, Dean's List; [pers.] To Keep up my relentless pursuit of life and truth.; [a.] Dallas, TX

D'IGNAZIO, HEIDI
[m.] Michael D'Ignazio; [ch.] Karina, Angela, Bianca and Mary; [occ.] School bus Driver; [pers.] I have been greatly influenced and inspired by children the only ones, in my opinion, who know the secret meaning of life. I strive to reveal the long-forgotten truths of our simple, still innocent minds.; [a.] Harrisburg, PA

DAGATA, STEPHEN
[b.] October 13, 1972, Winchester; [p.] Stephen and Barbara Dagata; [ed.] Woburn High School, Northeast Broad Casting School; [occ.] Pharmaceutical Distribution; [pers.] When I write, I try to capture the emotion I'm feeling at that moment in time. Each reader will create his/her own imagery to connect with the specific poem. So if I'm able to transmit my emotions to the readers (whether it be love, pain or longing), I've accomplished something: an emotional bond which transcends any difference we may have.; [a.] Woburn, MA

DALTON, JEAN M.
[pen.] Jean M. Thompson-Dalton; [b.] Little Rock, AR; [p.] Delta Ivory and Earl Thompson; [m.] Oscar Dalton; [ch.] Bobby, Delta Jean and O. Andre Dalton; [ed.] CH Mason Bible College Univ. of Balto Community College of Balto Univ. of MD; [occ.] Retired; [pers.] My writings are the legacy for my beloved children and my grandchildren Andrea,

Kellee, and Chantreis Dalton and my darling husband, Oscar Dalton

DANIEL, JEAN P.
[b.] July 26, 1937, Augusta, GA; [p.] Fred and Lucy Pearson; [m.] Divorced; [ch.] Mark and Amy; [ed.] B. C. High School Attended Uni. of South Carolina, Uni of Virginia; [occ.] Banker, Nations Bank; [memb.] Augusta Rowing Club, Augusta Port Authority, Augusta Sports Council; [hon.] S. E. Scholarship, NA. B. W.; [oth. writ.] Several poems published in the crocible, (literary magazine.); [pers.] I want the love of my family and childhood to show through my writing. Also to express what others may feel and cannot express.; [a.] Augusta, GA

DAUGHTRY JR., ELLIOTT
[b.] April 30, 1969, Baltimore, MD; [p.] Elliott and Evelyn Daughtry Sr.; [ed.] Eastern High, Coppin State College; [occ.] Academic Counselor; [memb.] Kappa Alpha Psi Fraternity, Arena Players, Coppin Models; [oth. writ.] Not seeing the forest for the trees: My experience from the boat.; [pers.] Crazy Shouts to the one's I love! Crazy shouts to the one's I love!; [a.] Baltimore, MD

DAVENPORT, TAMIKA A.
[pen.] Meeka; [b.] March 17, 1980, Mt. Sinai; [p.] Theresa Pointer and Harold Davenport; [ch.] Temika Davenport, Lawrence Porter; [ed.] 10th Grader, Warensville Senior High School; [occ.] 10th Grader at Warensville Senior High; [hon.] Girls scouts award, Softball award; [oth. writ.] I don't want To Fuse Or Fight; [pers.] I'm currently 15 years old and high school I strive to make my goal as a poet one day and I like to write and write different songs.; [a.] Warrensville, OH

DAVIS, DAVID BLAKE
[pen.] David Blake Davis; [b.] October 15, 1982, Van Nuys, CA; [p.] David A. Davis and Pauline Davis; [ed.] Woodrow Wallace Middle School in Lake Isabella, CA; [occ.] Full time student; [pers.] I would like to dedicate my poem to Candace Mabee Scandlen-Davis.; [a.] Wofford Heights, CA

DAVIS, JENNIE FEE
[pen.] Jennie Davis; [b.] August 13, 1914, Austin, TX; [p.] Mr. and Mrs. Tom H. Seekatz (Austin); [m.] "Dave" Davis (Leonard H.), October 1941 (Divorced); [ch.] Elizabeth Whitaker; [occ.] Retired; [memb.] University of Texas Student in Project to start Junior Colleges; [hon.] In a contest in 1958 with the world publishing co. my poem was the rose poem of the year, cups were awarded at Las Vegas by Milton Burl; [oth. writ.] I sent poems to ideals mag. and I write poems to go with our sunday school lessons and read them to the class. (Our class and teacher like this); [pers.] To you all! God I thank thee for another day. God help me in every way to live a life that I might be a little shining light for thee.; [a.] Austin, TX

DAVIS, JOHN A.
[b.] December 12, 1933, Washington, DC; [p.] George Johnson and Nettie Johnson; [m.] Eugene N. Davis, June 30, 1956; [ch.] Eugene Nolen II, Frank Allen, Donna Arnette Cooper; [ed.] Armstrong Technical High School, BS Degree Howard University; [occ.] D.C. Gov't. Retired - Former Manager of the Before and After School Care

Branch, Dep't. of Recreation and Parks; [memb.] Delta Sigma Theta Sorority, D.C. School Age Alliance, Salem Baptist Church H.N. Travis Educational Society and the Afrocentric Committee; [oth. writ.] "Enduring Impressions" A collection of Poems written about persons and life occurances that left an enduring impression on me; [pers.] Life is good. I look to The Creator with "Thanks" for the goodness and love of life. I attempt to look for and reflect on the good in mankind based on my Christian beliefs; [a.] Washington, DC

DAVIS, LAURA ANN
[b.] June 26, 1961, Santa Monica, CA; [p.] Royall and Maryann Miller; [m.] Charles Kirk Davis, June 11, 1983; [ch.] Benjamin Kirk, Brianna Joy, Brandon Charles; [ed.] Santa Monica High School, Los Angeles Baptist College; [occ.] Home maker; [oth. writ.] Many poems written on a variety of subjects having to do with the beauty of the simple life, the common man and a genuine, honest look at oneself.; [pers.] I have a desire to reflect the creator's love for us in the gift of life and in the joy of simple things.; [a.] Saugus, CA

DAVIS, MALINDA JANE
[b.] May 26, 1970, Hunstville, AL; [p.] John and Galoria Davis; [ed.] Hartselle High School, The University of Alabama; [occ.] Bookseller and Post-Graduate student; [memb.] Million Dollar Band Alumni Association; [hon.] President's List; [pers.] Passion and beauty are the driving forces of life, without them, life would merely be existence.; [a.] Hartselle, AL

DAVIS, MARY ESTELLE
[b.] February 13, 1930, Malvreva Ark; [p.] Mr. and Mrs. David L. Muncrief; [m.] August 23, 1949; [ch.] Linda Larry Doris Tonya; [ed.] 9th; [occ.] On Disability; [oth. writ.] I won't the hook rainbow and but just don't have the money I will send the 20.00 by the first. But I was so thrilled to know my poems was picked I was just thrilled; [pers.] This went through my head one might as I lay on my head I have wrist others but they didn't sound good to me.; [a.] Oklahoma City, OK

DAVIS, MICHELLE M.
[b.] August 14, 1957, Minneapolis, MN; [p.] Donna Lind and Donald Schminkey; [m.] Mark Davis; [ch.] Shane, Christopher, Jeffrey Ryan, Trevor De Wayne; [ed.] Columbia Heights High Anoka Ramsey Community College; [hon.] Dean's List; [oth. writ.] Various poems and short stories, none of which have been submitted for publication; [pers.] My most precious moments of gratitude can be attributed to the simple beauty that only nature provides. My writings allow me to grasp hold of this beauty, preserving it for further enjoyment.; [a.] Elk River, MN

DAVIS, SHARON
[b.] March 7, 1954, Hancock, NY; [p.] Raymond and Virginia Squires; [m.] Craig Davis, August 12, 1972; [ch.] Colleen Marie, Kelinda Lee; [ed.] Hancock Central School, Class of '72; [occ.] Homemaker and Home Educator; [memb.] Delaware River Writer's Group, Twentieth Century Book Circle, Little Victory Players Theatrical Group; [hon.] Various creative writing awards in high school for poetry; [oth. writ.] Several poems and short

stories published in River Voices anthology, poems and articles published in New York L.E.A.H newsletters; [pers.] I try to capture the moods inspired by nature and the human experience, after the manner of the great poets of the past.

DE LA PENA, ENEIL RYAN P.
[b.] December 23, 1978, Davao City, Philippines; [p.] Nelson de la Pena and Gilda de la Pena; [ed.] De Witt Clinton High School, currently attending State University of New York at Story Brook; [occ.] Freshman College Student; [hon.] Salutatorian De Witt Clinton High School 1995, Rensselaer Mathematics and Science award; [a.] Bronx, NY

DE PAULA, HENRIQUE
[pen.] El Brujo (Sorcerer); [b.] December 12, 1928, Sao Paulo, Brazil; [p.] Antonio and Amalia; [m.] Maria Luiza De Paula, May 31, 1958; [ch.] Julio Cesar, Carlos Alberto, Valerie, Celia (in law); [ed.] First School and Commercial School; [occ.] Construction Laborer and artisan. In Brazil I was a sales manager for the newspaper Folha De S. Paulo; [memb.] American Association of Retired People; [hon.] So far five awards from The National Library of Poetry for the books In The Desert Sun (1993) Dance on the Horizon, Tears of Fire, Edge of Twilight (1994) and Best Poems of (1995); [oth. writ.] Many letters, poems and articles printed in local newspaper and magazines, such as The Portuguese Post, Independent (Newark), Brazilian Voice (Harrison), Brazilian Times Massachusets, Ponto de Encontro (Elizabeth-N.J.). In Sao Paulo Brazil I wrote many articles about sports in the newspapers Noticias Populares; [pers.] I hate the liars. I write almost about everything. In poetry I write from the tragic to the humorous, passing by the romantic that I like most. I'm finishing writing a book titled God, The Outright Lie, about today's humanity. To me the way governs, religions, sects, police and justice are going is a calamity!; [a.] Newark, NJ

DEAN, MARYLOU
[b.] July 14, 1951, Forsyth Co, NC; [p.] Mr. and Mrs. Ralph E. Tesh, Sr.; [m.] Ret. Master Sgt. James K. Dean, December 16, 1972; [ed.] North Forsyth Senior High School NC. Draughon's Business College NC, Institute of Children's Lit. Conn, New Life Bible Course, Voice of Prophecy, CA; [occ.] Small business owner, author; [memb.] Church of the Nazarene, a Protestant Denomination headquartered at Kansas City, MO; [hon.] Sunday School Teacher of the Year - 1973-1974, Mc Arthur Park, church of God S. A, TX, Sunday school teacher of the Year-1974-1975, same church S.A., TX; [oth. writ.] Poems published in 3 separate anthologies and in one other book, own volume of verse released in December 1991, (Gemstones) by Vantage Press, Inc. of New York, NY; [pers.] Much of my poetry takes as ever from everyday life I enjoy the writings life. I enjoy the writings of Robert frost especially, Poetry is music from the heart expressed with pen and paper other those instruments.; [a.] Kernersville, NC

DEAN, MELINDA IRENE
[b.] January 16, 1974, Arkansas City, KS; [p.] Barbara Irene Dean; [ed.] Wichita Northwest and South High Schools, Friends University; [occ.] Student earning Bachelor's Degree in Zoo Science with a minor in Biology; [hon.] Kansas Epsilon

Chapter of the Alpha Chi national honors society, President's Honor Roll; [oth. writ.] A novella plus various poems and papers but none published as of yet; [pers.] This poem evolved during the conflicts of puberty. I want to thank my mom for reminding me that good things can arise from bad experiences.; [a.] Wichita, KS

DEBONO, PATRICK
[b.] June 1, 1971, Bayshore, NY; [p.] William A. DeBono and Roberta H. DeBono; [m.] Bridget Boshart DeBono, May 7, 1994; [ed.] Patchogue-Medford High School, Medford, L.I.N.Y.; [occ.] Small Business Proprietor, Full Time Minister; [memb.] Medford Volunteer Ambulance, Rome South Cong. of Jehovah's Witnesses; [oth. writ.] Several Discourses on religious topics for both public and congregation uses; [pers.] My goal is to do what the Bible describes at Ecc. 12:13 and Matt. 6:33, by putting first the interests of God's Kingdom.; [a.] Rome, NY

DEER, MARGARET C.
[b.] April 2, 1921, Harrisburg, PA; [p.] Peter and Annie Christmas; [m.] Deceased, January 12, 1946; [ch.] One Daughter; [ed.] High School; [occ.] Retired; [memb.] Poetry Society of OK; [hon.] A certificate of honorable mention for a poem "My Granddaughter"

DELABAR, JUSTIN
[pen.] Sean Lewis; [b.] March 15, 1983, Portsmouth, OH; [p.] Debro H. Delabar and James Delabar; [ed.] Wheelersburg Elementary and Jr. High; [hon.] A student, On A honor roll six out of six times in the fifth grade; [oth. writ.] Several unpublished poems; [pers.] I also have interest in art and I wish to go to the Joe Kubert School of Cartoon and Graphic Art. Poetry is also a main interest of mine.; [a.] Wheelersburg, OH

DELANEY, ELIZABETH LYNN
[pen.] Elizabeth Lynn Delaney; [b.] July 25, 1968, Madison; [p.] John R. Martin and Judith L. Home; [m.] Tim F. Delaney, May 8, 1988; [ch.] Leah Darline Delaney; [ed.] 4th Grade, didn't get much education on the count of incest. Was pulled out of school.; [occ.] Gift Shop Sales; [oth. writ.] Not yet published have two more; [pers.] I serve to let people no that they can overcome any boundary the earth may put around them and find peace with in them self's and find good in all and over look the evil; [a.] Madison, TN

DELAU, BRIDGET ANNE
[b.] January 2, 1982, Crown Point, IN; [p.] Barb and Jeff DeLau; [ed.] Trinity Lutheran School Church; [occ.] Student; [memb.] To 4-H band, Girl Scouts; [oth. writ.] A novels, 'A Walk Into Heaven' and other poems, 'Soul-Searching', 'Mind' and 'Wind Whispers'; [pers.] "I feel, that when you look unto the ute most bottoms of your heart and soul, you will find a side of you, you never even knew you had".; [a.] Lowell, IN

DELL, THOMAS M.
[b.] August 13, 1943, Los Angeles, CA; [p.] Jack and Chrys Dell; [m.] Kathleen, May 4, 1991; [ch.] Ken, Kris, Jim, Traci and Pam; [ed.] John H Francis Polytechnic High School, L.A. Valley College; [occ.] Superintendent; [memb.] NRA; [pers.]

Influenced by classical English poets; [a.] Simi Valley, CA

DEMERS, MICHAEL
[b.] September 26, 1960, Manchester, NH; [p.] Leo Demers and Lucille Demers; [m.] Ann Demers, April 4, 1987; [ch.] Erin Mackenzie; [ed.] Central High, University of New Hampshire; [occ.] Mortgage Professional, Homeowners assistance Corp, Bedford, NH; [memb.] Concord Board of Realtors, Affiliate Committee, Concord Chamber of Commerce, New Hampshire Army, National Guard; [hon.] UNH, Dean's List, New Hampshire National Guard Commendation medal, Meritorious Service Medal; [oth. writ.] Articles for The Realtor Review; [pers.] The heart and the pen-are one, with my wife's encouragement and my daughter's inspiration.; [a.] Hooksett, NH

DENHAM, CANDICE
[b.] February 7, 1979, Bryan, TX; [p.] Terry Siefing; [ed.] Fourth Christian School, Greenville Senior High School; [hon.] Honors in Reading Who's Who Among American High School student's, National Youth Leadership Forum on law and the constitution; [oth. writ.] Many poems published in local newspapers; [pers.] I've been greatly influenced to write poems, by personal experiences in my life and within my family.; [a.] Greenville, OH

DENTON, PATRICIA R.
[pen.] Patry; [b.] July 20, 1943, Scottsbluff, NE; [p.] Louise Covington Redding and Dale Redding; [m.] Lawrence E. Denton, August 23, 1964; [ch.] Chip, Christopher, Lance, Heather; [ed.] Univ. of Kansas, Univ. of Denver, Colo State Univ. Vocational Certificate; [occ.] Arapahoe Community, College-Littleton, CO, artist; [memb.] Colo Wclr Society, Charter Member Foothills Art Center, Signature Member Georgia Wclr Society, Signature Member Natl Wclr Society, Southwest Wclr Society; [hon.] 91, Adirondaks Natl. Wclr, 92, San Diego Intl Wclr, 92, Rocky Mtn, Natl Wtrmedia, 92, Natl Wclr Society, 93, Natl Realism, 93, Philadelphia Wclr Club and others; [oth. writ.] The Artist Magazine, Artonyms - Mar '86 article about my art 3/'88; [pers.] The desire to create and write along with the notion that I must share these God given talents, encourage me to keep the discipline and dare to do it.

DERIEG, GEORGE MARTIN
[pen.] George Martin Derieg; [b.] August 8, 1979, San Lorenzo, CA; [p.] George and Marylou Derieg; [ed.] DelRey Elementery Arroyo High School; [occ.] Referee of Soccer; [oth. writ.] "Two Blades of Grass", "Contemplations of Self Desire", "A Time to Live", "A Fear of Woe in Man's True Heart", "The Wind Will Carryon", "The Sun Will Dry My Way", "A Window of Truth" none have been published; [pers.] I strive to unlock the mysteries of poetic gesture. Only through constant writing will make me much greater. I have been influenced by the one and only Edgar Allen Poe. An outstanding author and poet.; [a.] San Lorenzo, CA

DETWILER, TRUDY
[b.] September 1, 1941, Willow Grove, PA; [p.] Edward and Marie Thomas Sr.; [m.] June 10, 1961, Divorced; [ch.] John C. Jr. and Paul L. Detwiler, Dana L. Fancher; [ed.] Upper Moreland High School

(59), Montgomery County Community College, AAS Accounting (83), Certificate Business Management (83), Certificate Marketing (83), Insurance Licensed, Security Licensed, Real Estate Licensed; [occ.] Partner, Tax Return Plus Financial Services do Tax Returns and help people reach their financial goals thur H D. Vest Financial Services; [memb.] Woman's Club of Perkasie, Treasure, Souderton Telford BPW Club, Blue Comet Motorcycle Club, Lady HOG, Coopersburg HOGS, Bedminster Historical Society; [hon.] Past President of Pennridge BPW, Past President of Bedminster PTG, Past Treasurer of Woman Who Make a Difference; [oth. writ.] "Me", "Happy New Year", "Natural Flowing Stream", "Dave", "The Morning After", "Journey's End" and "Togetherness"; [pers.] Life is an education, learn a lesson and grow from each experience. Always keep in touch with those who mean the most to you. With me, it's family and a few close friends.; [a.] Telford, PA

DEUSENBERRY, EDWARD
[b.] November 28, 1949, Morgantown, WA; [p.] Billy Deusenberry and Betty Deusemberry; [m.] JoAnn Deusenberry, April 24, 1970; [ch.] Jennifer, Micah, Ryan, Billy; [ed.] Montclair High School, Montclair, CA, Chaffey College, Rancho Cucamonga, CA; [occ.] Solid Fuel Handler North American Chemical Co. Trona CA; [oth. writ.] Occasional Editorial Columns for local paper; [pers.] I really enjoy "Cowboy" poetry especially work by Waddie Mitchell.; [a.] Trona, CA

DEVEAU, JOHN JASON
[b.] January 31, 1977, Gloucester, MA; [p.] David and Virginia Deveau; [ed.] Gloucester High; [pers.] I write from what happens in my life and that of others and of the world.; [a.] Gloucester, MA

DEVERAUX, MICHELLE M.
[b.] June 11, 1982, Idaho Falls, ID; [p.] Bill and Charlene Deveraux; [ed.] 8th Grade at Eagle Rock Jr. High; [occ.] Student; [memb.] Silver Sage Girl Scouts of America, Drama Club; [a.] Idaho Falls, ID

DEVORE, RACHEL
[pen.] Rachel DeVore; [b.] October 6, 1980, Oak Ridge, TN; [p.] Joe and Rosemary DeVore; [occ.] High School Student at Roane County High School (Freshman); [hon.] Coca-Cola Fine Arts Award for 8th grade; [oth. writ.] Writes poems and some short stories, artist enjoys drawing and music; [pers.] Trust in the Lord with all thine heart, and lean not unto thine own understanding. In all thy ways acknowledge him, and shall direct thy him, paths. Proverbs 3:5-6; [a.] Kingston, TN

DEVRIES, JENNIFER LYNN
[pen.] Green Eyes; [b.] March 6, 1979, Downey, CA; [p.] Nan DeVriest and Jerry DeVries; [ed.] LaMirada High School; [occ.] Student; [hon.] Student of the month and student of the year; [oth. writ.] I have written over 75 original poems and hope to have them all published in a book; [pers.] There are no set-backs, only lessons to be learned. Never give up, your dreams can come true!; [a.] LaMirada, CA

DEWALD, PATRICIA LYNN
[pen.] Patti Lynn; [b.] September 29, 1959, Evanston, IL; [p.] Donald P. Kirsch and Mary P. Riegler; [ch.] Michael Peter, Patricia Ann; [ed.]

Bensalem High School Del Tech Community College; [occ.] Singer, Songwriter; [memb.] BMI member Our Lady of Hope Choir; [hon.] Interviewed on WDVR Radio, Demo of Original Tune Aired on WKKN and other Country Radio Stations; [oth. writ.] Have poem published in former volume of collection of poetry, Printed Dedication In Trentonian Newspaper; [pers.] I choose to write about true feelings and real situations about every day life. I am inspired by country music both yesterday's and today's.; [a.] Daytona, FL

DIAS, TAMMY LOU
[b.] Febraury 12, 1970, Fall River; [p.] John and Carmen Tavares; [m.] Pedros P. Dias, August 12, 1989; [ch.] Alexander P. Dias; [ed.] Newport Pacific High School, Institute of Children's Literature; [occ.] Housewife; [oth. writ.] I write many children stories and poems. Just starting out being published. I am a new writer.; [pers.] I would like to get my work published allot more and look forward to a career of becoming a writer children will enjoy and admire.; [a.] Fall River, MA

DILISSIO, MICHELE
[b.] July 29, 1980, Bristol, PA; [p.] Mary Eileen and Ray DiLissio; [ed.] Saint Ann School, Bristol High School; [occ.] Full-time student, part-time receptionist; [memb.] Student Council, Interact club, field hockey, basketball, softball, track and field; [hon.] Distinguished Honor Roll, Knights of Columbus Award, Presidential Academic Award; [pers.] My poetry provides me with an escape from reality. I write poetry to express my innermost feelings about my relationships to the world and people around me.; [a.] Bristol, PA

DISABATINO, LUCIA
[pen.] Lucia DiSabatino; [b.] January, 24, 1966, New York; [p.] Charles DeMarco and Josephine DeMarco; [m.] Frank A. DiSabatino, July 21, 1994; [ch.] Steven Bruce Reed II; [ed.] Christiana High School, Delaware Technical College; [occ.] Leasing Agent/Manager; [memb.] Saint Thomas The Apostle, Volunteers Group; [hon.] Saint Thomas The Apostle School Volunteers Group; [oth. writ.] Several including: Window of Sin, They Care, Game of Life, Shadows of My Past; [pers.] I have been highly influenced, by the great insight of my mother. And would like to give special thanks to the Lord, for he makes all things possible.; [a.] Wilmington, DE

DIWAKARAN, ANURADHA
[pen.] Anuradha Sundararajan; [b.] March 24, 1969, New Delhi, India; [m.] Hariharan Diwakaran; [ed.] Kilpauk Medical College, India, Children's Hospital of Michigan, Detroit, St Louis, Children's Hospital, St. Louis; [occ.] Pediatrician, Fellow in Infection Diseases; [memb.] American Academy of Pediatrics, Pediatric Infectious, Diseases Society; [oth. writ.] Rhyme without reason, A collection of poetry and prose, Amazing Grace, A Description of a Personal Religious Realization (Both Published in India); [pers.] Writing Poetry is a hobby of mine that gives me welcome relief from the busy schedule of pediatrics and its practice.; [a.] Saint Louis, MO

DOAN, AMIEE RENEE
[b.] March 19, 1977, Steubenville; [p.] Curtis and Joan Doan; [ed.] Indian Creek High School, The Ohio State University; [occ.] Student at Ohio State

working in stadium scholarship dormitory and weekends at magic mountain; [memb.] Wildlife society, OSU Dairy club; [hon.] Stadium Scholarship, Joe Prest Scholarship; [oth. writ.] Many unpublished poems, a few poems printed in the local paper; [pers.] I use my poetry to express my innermost unspoken feelings. It is usually influenced by family close friends and personal experiences. I feel that people should learn to appreciate the gift of life rather than taking it for granted.; [a.] Wintersville, OH

DONALDSON, EDNA MAE
[pen.] Edna Mae Donaldson; [b.] March 14, 1920, Alberta, Canada; [p.] Forest, Mabel McNelly; [m.] Harold Donaldson, September 21, 1939; [ch.] Sandra, David, Donna, Debra; [ed.] Gullion High, grade 10; [occ.] Retired; [oth. writ.] Poems, short stories, a biography of my life on a homestead. One of eight children from 1912 mother and father homesteaded beside the athabasca trail.; [a.] Toronto Ontario, Canada

DURGIN, MARY LOUISE BOYLE
[b.] Rumford, ME; [p.] Elizabeth and Irving Boyle; [m.] Perlie R. Durgin, December, 1980; [ed.] B.A. College of New Rochelle, NY, M.A. Columbia University NY; [occ.] Housewife-writer Formerly Latin - French teacher; [hon.] Valedictory for grammar and high school, B.A. cum laude; [oth. writ.] "Odyssey of Love", biography published in '94, unpublished drama, "The Reluctant Disciple", Unpublished novel, "A Touch Of Love"; [a.] Dixfield, ME

FLEMING, BARBARA
[b.] January 10, 1961, Allentown, PA; [p.] Helen Gunther (Deceased), Edward Gunther; [a.] Barto, PA

FLEMING, MICHAEL
[pen.] Micki Cherri; [b.] March 4, 1968, Reading, PA; [p.] Arlene and James Fleming; [ed.] G.E.D.; [occ.] Song writer, writer; [oth. writ.] Published in the book (Season to Come) from the National Library of Poetry; [pers.] Be free to do as you feel as long as no one gets hurt and theres an honorable achievement accomplished in the end, I plan to do so threw music and writing.; [a.] Bernville, PA

FLIPSE, ALEXANDER KIRK
[b.] May 4, 1977, Miami, FL; [p.] Donn and Diana Flipse; [ed.] Graduated from Gulliver Preparatory School in June of 1995. I am currently in my freshman year at Barry University.; [occ.] Student; [memb.] Phi Kappa Tau Fraternity; [pers.] This is the first time I've ever had a piece of my writing published, so I'm very proud of my poem. When I submitted it, I really didn't expect it to be even considered for an anthology like this. I'd like to thank the National Library of Poetry for doing so I really didn't take my writing seriously until now!; [a.] Coral Gables, FL

FLORIO, LISA ANN
[b.] November 20, 1963, Providence, RI; [p.] Frank and Cecelia Florio; [ed.] Windmill Elementary School, Hopkins Jr. High School, and Hope High School. I did not attend college.; [occ.] I work as a sales girl at a local bakery; [memb.] I belong to "St. Jude Children's Research Hospital" monthly donor ($16.00 a month) "Partner in Hope" membership

program. To help children with Childhood Cancer.; [hon.] Getting noticed here in this poetry contest is a truly great honor to me. Other than that I have never won any other honors or awards before, that is why I am so "happy" about this one.; [oth. writ.] These are not published yet, poems: "Granpa", "Grandma", "Heaven", and "The Mirror". And songs: "Lord I Love You", "When I Look At You", and "You Have Love Inside of You". I play the guitar. I also collect "Star Wars" Memorabilia, and "Wizard of Oz, and Religious".; [pers.] I love to get lost in the words I write. When I write I feel like I flying! It is so exhilarating when words flow from your heart! I write only what is in my heart, soul and mind.; [a.] Providence, RI

FOAT, EMILY FAY
[b.] February 25, 1969, Chicago, IL; [p.] Anna Cruze and Robert A. Miller; [m.] Ken R. Foat, October 5, 1990; [ch.] Joshua R. Foat and Kenneth Earl Foat; [ed.] Bassett High; [occ.] Housewife and mother; [oth. writ.] I have more poems but they haven't been published; [pers.] I hope to touch peoples hearts so they could hear my words not just read them I have been interested in writing poems before I knew what they were.; [a.] Victorville, CA

FORD, JENNIFER
[b.] February 8, 1982, Astoria, NY; [p.] Diane and John Ford; [ed.] Elementary School-P.S. 85 now attending JHS (I.S.) 141 (8th grade) Astoria, NY; [hon.] 16 Recognition Certificates in Elementary School, Certificate of Merit, Certificate for School Service, and Certificate for Academic Excellence in 6th grade, Certificate of Achievement in 7th grade; [oth. writ.] I've been mentioned in the newspaper for winning a poetry contest in my school in (Elementary) the 5th grade. I had to write about the effects of drugs.; [pers.] I don't know where I get my ideas from I just clear my mind and think about verses for poems. I just want to thank friends and family, for support.; [a.] Astoria, NY

FORREST, JAMES J. F.
[b.] October 17, 1968, Poratello, ID; [p.] John and Jeri Franzen; [ed.] B.S. Foreign Service, Georgetown University, M.A. Education Stanford University; [occ.] Research Associate, Boston College Center for International Higher Education; [pers.] Do the best you can with what you have, as Buckwheat would say, and long live those who strive to make a difference.

FOSTER, CLARENCE W.
[pen.] CW Mickey Foster; [b.] March 1, 1936, Detroit, MI; [p.] Ester and Clyde Foster; [m.] Marlene, October 29, 1955; [ch.] Vicki, Tammy, Michelle, Shawn; [ed.] 10th grade GED; [occ.] Mobile Home Park Manager; [oth. writ.] Have written and copyrighted 6 song collections consisting of 46 song lyrics and melodies; [pers.] To share life's experience with others through poetry and song in hope's their will be some identification and bond through that experience.; [a.] Medford, OR

FOSTER, JENNIFER
[b.] May 8, 1972, Denver, CO; [p.] Jay R. Buehler; [m.] Gary L. Foster, October 18, 1993; [ch.] Jesse L. Foster; [ed.] Santa Rita H.S. and currently attending Pima Community College to transfer to University of Arizona; [occ.] Homemaker and writer; [memb.]

Christ Community Church, Women of the World; [hon.] Certified Nursing Asst. Certification. I was President of Students against Drunk Driving, and have completed leadership training. I was also student of the month at Phoenix Job Corp.; [oth. writ.] Many poems not yet published; [pers.] I like to write with realism my influences are Anne Sexton and Shakespeare; [a.] Tucson, AZ

FRAITES, ROALD CONSTANTINE
[pen.] Roald Constantine; [b.] December 30, 1945, St Kitts, WI; [p.] Carlton Symonds, Eileen Fraites-Hawley; [m.] Janice Fraites, August 19, 1967; [ch.] Sharlene Fraites, Cornell Fraites; [ed.] Sussex College-B.S. Economics, Antioch University-M.A. Legal Studies; [occ.] Financial Counselor, Bible student; [memb.] Past: Rotary Club-President, U.S.O.-Board, United Way-Board, Chamber, Toastmasters-Vice President, Jaycees-Vice President; [hon.] LUTCF Designation; [oth. writ.] Established banking procedures for branches. Articles published in local newspapers. Comments in magazines.; [pers.] When bodies and souls are transfixed to find truth, then justice is served. "Truth" remains itself... it cannot do otherwise.; [a.] Pittsburgh, PA

FRANKLIN, CAROLINE
[pen.] Caroline Franklin; [b.] March 1, 1938, Toledo, OH; [p.] Floyd and Mildred Plumb; [m.] David Franklin, June 18, 1960; [ch.] Steven, Daniel, and Michacl; [ed.] Whitmer H.S. graduate also attended Nyack Missionary College and Fort Wayne Bible College; [occ.] Homemaker; [oth. writ.] A collection of poems I've entitled: "Expressions of Praise for all of God's Blessings" however, I have not had anything published; [pers.] I enjoy all of nature, and it's the desire of my heart to be able to renew, through words of poetry, an enriched awareness of the beauty that surrounds us and the opportunities that are ours by simply opening our minds and hearts to all he's provided.; [a.] Toledo, OH

FRANKLIN, MABEL EDITH
[pen.] May; [b.] February 14, Lebanon, VA; [m.] Elmer Ewing Franklin (Deceased), December 19; [occ.] Retired; [memb.] Right to Life Tenn. sustaining member Republican National Committee, Tenessee Republican Party, Sullivan County Humane Society, Bristol Humane Society; [hon.] Honorary staff member 2nd Legislative District Feb. 2nd 1993 by the Honorable Keith Westmoreland State of Tennessee in recognition of outstanding service to the state several awards for outstanding service in Recognition of Achievement.; [oth. writ.] Poems published in Kingsport Times News, Reporter for Newsletter at my employment before retirement I have sixty poem's writer, want to get published soon; [pers.] I established the Elmer Ewing Franklin Memorial Scholarship Fund at King College in Bristol, TN. I am striving to get the Elmer Ewing Franklin Center or Museum soon at King College Bristol, TN or Walter State Un. Morristown, TN.; [a.] Kingsport, TN

FRECKLETON, TERESHA
[b.] May 18, 1976, Bronx, NY; [ed.] Miami Norland Sr. High, currently a Sophomore at the University of Florida in Gainesville; [occ.] Student University of Florida (major: journalism); [hon.] Recipient of the American Civil Liberties, Union Miami Chapters

1994, Maurice Rosen Act of Courage Award, Honorable Mention The Miami Heralds, Silver Knight English Category; [oth. writ.] Written several articles and columns for The Miami Herald; [pers.] Poetry is more than a rhythmic fusion of words. It is a fluid art that allows those who partake of its magic to cast rays of verse that hold readers spellbound.; [a.] Miami, FL

FREEMAN, ANGELA K.
[b.] September 4, 1980, Birmingham, AL; [p.] Charles and Linda Freeman; [ed.] Dora High School, Dora, AL 10th grade student; [occ.] Student; [memb.] Dora High School Chorus, Union Grove Baptist Church (Youth Group); [hon.] Honor Roll Who's Who Among American High School students, Head of the Class Junior Achiever; [a.] Empire, AL

FREEMAN, HAWK
[pen.] John Freeman, Jay Phillips, Joan Freeman; [b.] February 21, 1951, Berkley, CA; [p.] Kim Freeman and Gill Freeman; [m.] Barbara ("Bobbie") McGlynn Freeman, February 9, 1974; [ed.] Bachelor of Arts in English with additional emphasis in Theology, Psychology, and Music, Masters in Aviation Management with additional emphasis in Aviation Science (Aviation Engineering); [occ.] Retired from U.S. Government Service; [memb.] Red River Valley Fighter Pilots Assoc. ("River Rats"). An organization dedicated to providing scholarship support to surviving dependents of those who did not make it back from missions over North Vietnam through to and including the dependents of those who fell during the Persian Gulf War.; [hon.] A total of 51 from working in 34 countries, in Antarctica and beneath the Coral Sea; [oth. writ.] Poetry and lyrics have periodically published in the United States and other English speaking countries, to include England and Australia since the mid-1960's.; [pers.] Despite being heavily influenced by Milton, I remain an incurable optimist having seen so much individual and personal compassion during two wars and in the aftermath of more than just one terrorist incident.; [a.] Colorado Springs, CO

FREMGEN, FRANK
[pen.] Frank Fremgen; [b.] October 9, 1921, Woodhaven, NY; [p.] Frank M. and Agnes Fremgen; [m.] Gladys E. Fremgen (Nee Long), April 11, 1943; [ch.] Janet, Jimmy; [ed.] High School graduate; [occ.] Retired from U.S. Postal Service; [memb.] Am a member of our church choir, and they have in large part, been the subjects, as was the case with "An Ode to Elwin" choir friend that died; [oth. writ.] "There Must Be A God", "An Ode To Moriah", "An Ode To Gladdie", "An Ode To Betsey", et al-have written about 25 at least, mostly about friends and loved ones, for the joy of writing; [pers.] I love writing about everyday occurrences and friends, with a lot of humor involved, but also poignant memories and experiences, with an appreciation of what's important in life, thankfulness to God, and being mindful of the Golden Rule. Tried to show this in "There Must Be A God", and also my story about "My Two Dads" my own dad and my Dad-in-law, both passed on now.; [a.] West Springfield, NH

FRENCH, ELEANOR ALTHEA
[pen.] Frenchie; [b.] May 16, Port Of Spain, Trinidad, West Indies; [p.] Alphaeus and Lillith French; [m.] Michael Perkins, July 31, 1989; [ch.]

Richard Lamar Edmond; [ed.] A.A. Northwestern State University, LA. B.S. University of the State of New York Major Psychology; [occ.] Student, poet, storyteller; [memb.] Inventors' Clubs of America Inc., Atlanta Chapter Women's National Book Association Atlanta Chapter. Disabled American Veteran's Association.; [hon.] 1995 International Hall of Fame Award, Literature for inspirational works in the field of poetry; [oth. writ.] "A Salute to Women, the World's Greatest Asset"-a collection of poetry designed to inspire and motivate, to show love, friendship and passion and to encourage self love and self respect.; [pers.] Love and respect yourself, love God and live each day to its fullest.; [a.] Jonesboro, GA

FREY, JENNIFER LYNN
[pen.] Francisca Frey; [b.] September 12, 1982, EMMC Bangor; [p.] Kelley and Rodney Frey; [ed.] Viola Rand School and Leonarn Middle School; [occ.] Student; [hon.] Tar Wars Coloring Contest and "Why it would be next to be death and Blind" writing contest; [pers.] Personal thanks to my grandparents Paul and Glennice Frey, my best friends Vicky Drake and Jenny Avery and my teachers Miss Lacombe, Mr. Gavett and Mrs. Quimby. Also Erica Hamlin!; [a.] Bradley, ME

FRIEBEN, KERRY
[pen.] Jack Ludlen or Clark and Dagger Enterprises; [b.] April 1, 1972, Madison, WI; [p.] Bill and Lynn Frieben; [m.] Angela Frieben, August 21, 1993; [ed.] BA in Behavioral Psy, MSW in Clinical Social Work; [occ.] Sub. Abuse Counselor and Group Home Member; [hon.] Advanced Poetry Workshop at Western Michigan University, Honorable Mention in Portage Northern High Schools poetry contest Honors WMU, Dean's List 93-94; [oth. writ.] Mensa Society, "Contemporary Insanity", Journey Into Thought (book), "Stairs to Heaven"; [pers.] There are no limits.; [a.] Grand Rapids, MI

FRITZ, DEBORAH
[pen.] Deborah Pfeifer; [b.] March 7, 1953, Baltimore, MD; [p.] Margaret and Albert Pfeifer; [m.] Thomas Fritz, May 1, 1976; [ch.] Jessica and Thomas Fritz; [ed.] Western High School, Towson State University; [occ.] Library Magazine Room in charge clerk; [memb.] PTA and PTSA; [hon.] Honorable Mention High School Poetry Contest. Honor Roll Junior High's High School; [oth. writ.] Article on the Women are Wonderful page of "True Story" have submitted articles to various magazines that I'm waiting to here from. Poem published in Church Newspaper also a School Newsletter; [pers.] I have been greatly influenced by poets such as Robert Frost and Emily Dickinson and favorite poet Edgar Allan Poe. I own a parrot, I named Poe in his honor. I find I am able to express deep feelings through my poetry.; [a.] Baltimore, MD

FUNKHOUSER, SHANNON M.
[pen.] Renee Bradshaw; [b.] June 10, 1980, Tacoma Park; [p.] Claude and Debra Funkhouser; [ed.] Eleanor Roosevelt High School, Bettsville Seventh-Day Adventist; [occ.] Student; [oth. writ.] Several unpublished poems, stories, and other things; [pers.] I thank the people who showed me and taught me what I needed to know, and everyone who pushed me in the right direction. I love you with all my heart!; [a.] College Park, MD

FURULI, DARLENE P.
[pen.] D.P.F. Pua Furuli; [b.] November 28, 1965, Kealakekua, HI; [p.] Harry and Naomi Aiu; [m.] Kevin J. Furuli, August 4, 1990; [ed.] Hilo Community College; [occ.] Aloha Airlines C.S.A.; [pers.] With the changes that I face each day, comes a desire to express myself through words. To the one who has encouraged me to pursue my dreams and excel beyond life's limitations. For your neverending love and support, I dedicate this accomplishment to you my friend, M.C.G.; [a.] Hilo, HI

GAGNON, DEBRA
[pen.] Debbie O'Brien; [b.] October 1, 1952, Winthrop, MA; [p.] William Florence O'Brien; [m.] Rene Gagnon June 4, 1986; [ch.] William and Heidi; [ed.] Windham High School Windham, Me; [occ.] Machinist; [oth. writ.] Several Poems none published; [pers.] I love nature, I went to make everyone aware of its beauty. My poetry reflects my inner most feelings and beliefs. I'm not a wealthy person. So my poetry is the only contribution I have to give to mankind.; [a.] Windham, ME

GAGNON, REBECCA
[pen.] Rebecca Gagnon; [b.] April 14, 1982, Attleboro, MA; [p.] Paula and Michael; [ed.] 8th grade so far; [occ.] Student; [memb.] Taunton Little Theatre, Silver City Children's Theatre, Girls Incorporated, Girl Scouts St Joseph's Youth Choir St. Joseph's Youth Group Mulcaney School Band and Chorus; [hon.] Marion Medal 2nd place Science Fair 1994, 1995 high honors Middle School 3 yrs in a row; [pers.] Set a goal for yourself. Don't let anything get in your way.; [a.] Taunton, MA

GALDI, ANTONY C.
[b.] August 23, 1982, NYC; [p.] Dagmar and Peter Galch; [ed.] The Elisabeth Morrow School Graduate; [occ.] Attending 7th Grade at Dwight Englewood School; [memb.] NJ, AOPA, AMA, National Geographics, NAFC; [oth. writ.] None; [pers.] Influence of my English teacher Mrs. Lipman in 6th grade at EMS, and because I really hope all wood love nature like I do.; [a.] North Bergen, NJ

GALLAGHER, CRAIG
[b.] May 31, 1973, Lynn; [ed.] 2 years Physics Major at Merrimack College and 2 years English Major at Salem State College; [hon.] SSC Dean's List, Bausch and Lomb Honorary Science Award, Tandy Technical Scholar Awards, 3 Time LCHS Boys Soccer Scholar Athlete, Lynn Chamber of Commerce Honor Scholar. Runner-up 1990 Mr. Lynn Contest; [pers.] Without the acknowledge existence of Evil, one can never understand what good is. I try to remind people of that in my writings by continual expression of what should be evil.; [a.] Lynn, MA

GAMBILL, VALERIE S.
[b.] May 7, 1971, Steubenville, OH; [p.] Howard and Cheryl Smith; [m.] Gary L. Gambill, December 24, 1994; [ch.] Tan Lee and Due Date December 24, 1995; [ed.] Southwest High and Jeff Tech College, Scott College Of Cosmetology; [occ.] Housewife and Mother; [oth. writ.] No published poems, just done in spare time for pleasure; [pers.] This poem was written in loving memory of Shirley Belle Gambill, May 15, 1935, May 27, 1995; [a.] Toronto, OH

GAMBLE, PAUL C.
[pen.] P. C. Gamble; [b.] June 68, Chicopee, MS; [p.] Dave and Nancy; [m.] Cheryl, December 1989; [ch.] Caitlin (Daddy's little girl); [occ.] 3RD US INF (The Old Guard), US ARMY; [oth. writ.] A large number of unpublished poetry in a private collections. Adds a little spice in the ol' marriage.; [pers.] I write with the intentions of wooing my better half. It is written to roll off of her tongue, or whatever else it may effect. You have to be able decipher both content and context e.e. eat your heart out!; [a.] Fort Myer, VA

GARCIA, DANA
[pen.] Dana Garcia; [b.] November 25, 1975, Hammond, IN; [p.] Frank and Mary Copeland; [m.] Ramon Garcia, July 25, 1974; [ch.] Savanna Genet Garcia; [ed.] Liberty Grade School, Shelbyville, Central High School; [occ.] Factory Work - Inspector of Jana/Southside Apperall in Petersburg; [pers.] This poem (Borreguito) was my first poem. I was surprised at how easy the words came to me. I might have a good thing going, I'd like to keep it up. I hope for the best.; [a.] Petersburg, IN

GARCIA, VICTORIA D.
[b.] December 9, 1966, St. Cloud, MN; [p.] Gary and Delayne, McKinley; [m.] Joseph G. Garcia, May 11, 1991; [ch.] Allyssia K. Garcia, Dee M. Garcia, Brittany P. Garcia; [ed.] B.S. in Elementary Education; [occ.] Kindergarten Teacher; [memb.] Kappa Delta Pi; [oth. writ.] None published; [pers.] If you can feel it - write it.; [a.] Colorado Springs, CO

GARRETT, EUGENIA
[b.] May 7, 1921, Holly Grove, AK; [p.] Grover E. and Henrietta Medlock; [m.] George H. Garrett, March 9, 1941; [ch.] Gary Harold and Richard Hugh; [ed.] Benton High; [occ.] Home maker; [memb.] First United Methodist Church; [oth. writ.] Numerous poems. That I have assembled in a small handmade booklet. I have given copies to relatives and friends.; [pers.] My naive poems were written to express the joy of living, and my personal thankfulness for my life.; [a.] De Queen, AK

GARRETT, EUGENIA
[b.] May 7, 1921, Holly Grove, AR; [p.] Grover and Henrietta Medlock; [m.] George H. Garrett, March 9, 1941; [ch.] Gary Harold and Richard Hugh; [ed.] Benton High; [occ.] Home Maker; [memb.] First United Methodist Church; [oth. writ.] Numerous poems that I have assembled in a small handmade booklet. I have given copies to relatives and friends.; [pers.] My naive poems were written to express the joy of living, and my personal thankfulness for my life.; [a.] De Queen, AR

GARRISON, MELISSA
[pen.] Melissa Garrison; [b.] January 2, 1981, Millington, TN; [p.] Debra and John Anderson; [ed.] 9th grade, Denbigh Hugh School, Newport News VA; [occ.] Student/baby sitter; [memb.] Band; [hon.] Most improvement in band Honor Roll, Day Camp Award (Citizenship); [oth. writ.] None published; [pers.] I can't say I plan to be a writer but I plan to continue my poetry and see were it takes me in the future; [a.] Newport News, VA

GARWITZ, LAWRENCE D.
[pen.] Missouri Mule; [b.] November 7, 1910, Houston, MO; [p.] Bert and Bertie Raper Garwitz; [m.] Joan M. Garwitz, September 22, 1989; [ed.] Houston Public Schools. Dept of Defense Special Schools. Industrial Radiopgraphy. Metals Inspection. Non Destructive Testing. Certified.; [occ.] Retired; [memb.] VFW, American Legion, Life Member, Catholic Church; [hon.] U.S. Defense Supply Agency Certificate for 31 Years Service, Defense Supply Agency, Excellent Attendance Award; [oth. writ.] Various Articles Houston Herald, Houston Missouri, Federal Employee Retirement Assoc. Life; [pers.] Honorable Discharge U.S. Navy; [a.] Lake Wales, FL

GASTON, PHILLIP F.
[b.] September 30, 1953, Youngstown, OH; [p.] Martha and Robert Gaston; [ed.] BS in Ed Youngstown State Univ. 1980; [occ.] Nuclear Maintenance Supervisor; [pers.] I was to write these words about Kathy because of her wonderful and loving personality. I will forever love her.; [a.] Girard, OH

GECK, CORRINE LUCILLE
[pen.] Cille; [b.] March 24, 1924, Kansas City, MO; [p.] Edith Lorance; [m.] Leonard Geck, May 26, 1951; [ch.] Linda and Robert; [ed.] Westport High School; [pers.] I enjoy writing poems about my family. "A poem to my sisters" was written about my dear sisters Hazel and Bette.; [a.] Orange, CA

GEE, JASON ANTONE
[b.] July 17, 1971, Rexbury, ID; [p.] Jerald and Toni Gee; [m.] Linda Carbaugh; [ed.] Sugar-Salem High, Ricks College, Utah State University; [occ.] Retailer, The Book Table; [hon.] Graduated Cum Laude; [pers.] Greatness in life is determined by what one succeeds in, greatness in death is determined by what one leaves behind in the memories of others.; [a.] Logan, UT

GEIGER, KELVIN
[pen.] Harold Nordley; [b.] December 8, 1956, Greenville, MI; [ed.] Belding Central High School Grand Rapids Adult Education Schaum Music Instruction; [occ.] Owner: The Automatic Piano Company; [memb.] Musical Box Society Int. Life Member: Michigan State Horticultural Society; [oth. writ.] Ode to What I've Thrown Away, You Can If You Ty?, My Treasure Island; [a.] Smyrna, MI

GEIST, MARSHA
[pen.] Marsha Geist; [b.] April 29, 1951, Columbus, OH; [p.] Louis and Gloria Geist; [ed.] Hilliard High School, Mt. Carmel School of Operating Room Technology; [memb.] Ohio Country and Western Music Association, Hilliard Grange, VFW Auxiliary; [hon.] OCWMA State Queen in 1982, numerous music awards; [oth. writ.] Articles for the OCWMA newsletter; [pers.] I have been very fortunate to have had wonderful teachers, not only in early schooling but throughout my adult life. Gifted individuals in their own way. I thank God for allowing me to be part of the plan.; [a.] Hilliard, OH

GEORGE, CAROL W.
[b.] January 9, 1933, Anderson, SC; [p.] Joe and Lena Wilson; [m.] Andrew J. George, July 4, 1952; [ch.] Andrew Carol and Nancy Sue; [ed.] Greer High; [occ.] Retired after 36 years in banking;

[memb.] I am a Baptist, I am a Notary Public No memberships since retirement; [hon.] I feel it is an honor to have 2 children and 9 grandchildren and a wonderful husband of 43 years.; [oth. writ.] I have written several poems, none have been published; [pers.] My desire is to write something that will be beneficial to those who read my poetry, a laugh at a funny line, hope and encouragement when times are bad.; [a.] Taylors, SC

GERBER, ROBERT LOUIS
[pen.] Bob Gerber; [b.] July 11, 1924, Hamilton, OH; [p.] Mabel Gerber and Alferd Gerber; [ed.] High School Graduate; [occ.] Retired; [pers.] Veteran of World War II. And amateur poet trying to make people happy in reading poems that show them how it is possible to live in peace and harmony with each other.; [a.] Hamilton, OH

GEYER, MRS. DOROTHY S.
[b.] August 11, 1919, Waterbury, CT; [p.] Joseph and Marie Schaeffer; [m.] H. W. Geyer, June 27, 1942; [ch.] Anita Marie and Robert Martin; [ed.] Bachelor of Science Bridgeport University help out at Day School Care Center like to Oil Paint and do Arts, Ceramics and Crafts - CNA in Pediatrics Dept.; [occ.] Retired; [memb.] Prince of Peace Lutheran Church, Anaheim, CA; [pers.] Like to show or acquaint people with natures beauty and all the lovely things God has created for our benefit and pleasure.

GIFFORD, SANDRA K.
[pen.] Sandra Randall; [b.] January 20, 1981, Oklahoma City, OK; [p.] Richard Gifford; [ed.] Deming Jr. High, Alcott Alternative Middle School, West High School; [hon.] A young writers award in Elementary School for a short story, two certificates for two short stories in Elementary school; [oth. writ.] A couple of short story printed in a school collection book of student's writings.; [a.] Wichita, KS

GIROD, KENDRA JEANNE
[b.] August 14, 1965, Eureka, CA; [p.] Eugene Calanchini, Karen Calanchini; [m.] Kenneth Girod, April 19, 1986; [ch.] Kenneth Michael, Kassandra Jeanne; [ed.] Enterprise High, Shasta College; [occ.] Teachers Aide with multi-handicapped, Anna Elementary; [oth. writ.] Several poems and short stories; [pers.] To greet the world with a smile and open mind, therefore people can feel the warmth of an open heart.; [a.] Sidney, OH

GLOVER, GALE
[b.] March 22, 1948, Greenbrier Co., White Sulphur Springs, WV; [p.] Lawrence Craft, Pansy Craft; [ch.] Robert Houston; [ed.] White Sulphur Springs High, Leonards, School of Beauty, Massage Therapy Certification The Greenbrier Hotel; [occ.] Retired Masseuse; [memb.] AAIS - Appalachian American Indians of West Virginia, Inc.; [hon.] Local Reading of Poem, Church Publishment; [oth. writ.] Several poems, a short story a song and started a book; [pers.] The joy of love, graceful harmony and peace in nature, family, friends, and writings of others are inspirations for my poetry.; [a.] White Sulphur Springs, WV

GOLDMAN, ELEANOR
[pen.] Ellie; [b.] July 10, 1925, Oakland, CA; [p.]

Manuel Freitas, Augusta Freitas; [m.] Victor Allen Goldman, October 8, 1943; [ch.] Randy, Don, Vickie; [ed.] Santa Clara High School; [occ.] Homemaker - widow Active in Clubs; [memb.] Active Senior's American Legion Auxiliary, Women of the Moose, Salinas Bowling Association; [hon.] Publicity Chairman Junior Regent, Chaplain, Academy Of Friendship, Bowling Association - Trophy's; [oth. writ.] I submitted a poem titled Will To EPS publishing Co. It has been chosen to appear in The Reflection of Life Winter 1996 I am composing a book of poetry about members of my family and friends.; [pers.] Poetry has been my love for many years. I started writing this year. Writing for family and friends has brought me much joy.; [a.] Salinas, CA

GOLDMAN, MARTIN
[b.] February 21, 1948, Brooklyn, NY; [m.] Mercedes Jenouri Goldman; [ch.] Ruth; [ed.] Bachelor's Degree at Manhattan School of Music, Master's Degree from Yale, Studies at the Royal Conservatory in Brussels, the Chigiana in Siena, Aspen Music Festival, Extensive training in the Suzuki Method, etc.; [occ.] Violist with the Puerto Rico Symphony, Director of Violines Suzuki De Puerto Ric, Inc.; [memb.] Suzuki Association of The Americas, International Suzuki Association, American Federation of Musicians; [hon.] Dean's List and scholarship at Manhattan School of Music, Full Scholarship at Yale University, Aspen School of Music Scholarship; [oth. writ.] Many other poems in search of a publisher; [pers.] My influences have ranged from, Shakespeare to Rilke, The Old Testament, Mozart, Mahler and Bartok, include John Unterecker, Schinichi Suzuki, Yascha Heifetz, Bruno Giuranna, Lee Goebel, Professor Wimsatt, Mercedes and Ruthy.; [a.] San Juan, PR

GOLDSMITH, SERENA
[b.] March 27, 1971, Paterson, NJ; [p.] Marvin and Elaine Goldsmith; [ed.] San Dieguito High School, Occidental College; [occ.] Entrepreneur; [memb.] Seaside Church of Religious Science, The Nature Conservatory, Brandeis/Bardin Institute; [hon.] Phi Beta Kappa, Summa Cum Laude, Departmental in Sociology and Chemistry; [pers.] My poetry serves as an outlet for the expression of that part of me that knows the unity and perfection of the Universe. I have been influenced by the passionate and deeply expressive works of Latin American poets such as Pablo Neruda, and by the philosophical and spiritual beliefs reflected in the Course in Miracles and the writings of Ernest Holmes; [a.] Carlsbad, CA

GOLIAN, LINDA MARIE
[b.] Woodbridge, NJ; [p.] Joseph and Mary Golian; [m.] Gary S. Lui, October 6, 1988; [ed.] BA 1986 Univ of Miami MLIS 1988 Florida State Univ EDS 1985 Florida Atl. Univ.; [occ.] Librarian, Adult Educator Florida Atlantic Univ.; [memb.] AAACE, ALA, AAUW, ALISE, NOW; [hon.] Who's Who in American Ed. Ala/NMRT Professional Dev. grant Phi Delata Pi, Beta Pi Mu, Golden Key Honor Society; [pers.] Writing is my way of sharing experiences with others.; [a.] Boca Raton, FL

GOLMON, FRANCES
[pen.] Frances Walters; [b.] Magnolia, MS; [p.] Arthur Walters, Dollie Walters; [occ.] Nurse; [oth. writ.] Working on books of poems; [pers.] A willing vessel letting God direct my life; [a.] Magnolia, MS

GONZALEZ, BLANCA ESTELA
[b.] October 14, 1957, McAllen, TX; [p.] Argentina Alvarado Gonzalez, Marcelo Gonzalez Jr.; [ed.] PSJA High School 1976, Pan American University 1980 BA Psychology and Elementary Education, Texas A and I University 1985 MA Reading; [occ.] Reading Teacher at PSJA North; [memb.] Texas Computer Education Association, The International Society of Poets; [hon.] Editor's Choice Award 1994, Poem published in Affer the Storm, First division for two years in ensemble band, Second Division for one year in ensemble band, Psychology scholarship for tuition, President honor roll; [oth. writ.] Article published in local paper, Poem published in the following books, After the Storm, Best Poems of 1996, A Delicate Balance; [pers.] I believe that through education anything will be achieved. A goal is accomplished through hard work and determination. The stars can be reached.; [a.] San Juan, TX

GOODELL JR., DONALD CHARLES
[pen.] D. C. Goedel; [b.] April 15, 1959, Culver City, CA; [p.] Florence Graham Goodell, Donald Goodells Sr; [ed.] AA in Latin, English Literature and Religious Science, Bedford Tutorial College, (Bedfordshire, England), BA and MA (Hons.) St. John's College, Durham University, (Durham, England); [occ.] Corporate Accounts Administrator for a major Telecommunications Company in Pleasanton, California; [memb.] Die Grotte Mozarteums, President (An Institute for Mozart Research); [hon.] Musician of the Year Award (1976) awarded by Gardena High School/ROTC, Los Angeles California. Durham University's Outstanding Composer of the Year Award (1981), Durham, England. Composer-in-Residence Award (1981), St. John's College, Durham University, Durham, England.; [oth. writ.] Musical Compositions include: Sinfonia in D (1976), Concerto a quattro mani for Klavier and Orchestra in C (1979), Six Sonatas for Forte-Piano (1986), Amos: An Oratorio in 3 Parts (Part I) 1991, Part 2 (1995) (Woek in Progress), Poetical works include Sonnets of the Heart (24 poems, 1991) The Grotto (24 Sonnets, 1995); [pers.] I am primarily a composer/ librettist in the Classical Tradition but ave found Poetry an exciting outlet and variation for my restless Muse. My poetical works are of a varied restless Muse. My poetical works are of a varied nature, but revolve around themes of Unrequited Love and Misunderstood Lives. My Poetical Models are Donne and Shakespeare, my Musical Models are Mozart and J. C. Bach; [a.] Pleasanton, CA

GOODELL, SETH WELDON
[pen.] Seth Goodell; [b.] May 20, 1982, Mammond, LA; [p.] John and Sandra Goodell; [ed.] I'm attending the 8th grade at Meppner High School; [memb.] JR High Drama Club; [hon.] Passed Spanish I; [oth. writ.] Hanging By A Thread was published in a county booklet which comes out once a year. I wrote the poem Hanging By A Thread; [pers.] If you believe in the powers of the great one Tales can be turned and battles may be won; [a.] Heppner, OR

GORDON, EVELYN RAINS
[b.] April 20, 1928, New Mexico; [p.] Claud and Vera Rains; [m.] J. Gordon, February 22, 1947; [ch.] Gregg and Mike, Dtr Chris; [ed.] High School -

Some College; [occ.] Retired - 1 Volunteer at Hurst Police Dept Storefront; [memb.] Member of the Church Of God 57 years - Volunteers In Action; [oth. writ.] I've written poems all my life just to tuck in with gifts or to read at gatherings it's just always "flowed" out.; [pers.] Life has been good - our youth of today are 99% good - bad things happen - we hear about it good things are never on the front page or on TV - But good is everywhere!!; [a.] Hurst, TX

GOREHAM, SAMANTHA
[pen.] Sam, "Jesus Freak"; [b.] April 3, 1979, St. Francis Hospital; [p.] Rolland and Peggy Goreham; [ed.] Cleveland Elementary St. Anne's Catholic Middle School Bishop Carroll Catholic Highschool, Class of '97; [memb.] Wichita Vineyard Christian Fellowship, Youth Worship Band, Bishop Carroll Heritage Panel; [hon.] I rating at State Vocal contest; [pers.] Don't let the talent other people have discourage, but use it and learn from it. Discover your talents, give glory to God with them and you'll never go wrong. Always remember to thank God for all your gifts.; [a.] Wichita, KS

GOSHERT, PEARL
[pen.] JC; [b.] May 19, 1938, Denver, PA; [p.] Ivan German, Isabelle German; [m.] Robert Goshert, December 25, 1957; [ed.] Cocalico High LPN School; [memb.] Assembly of God Church; [pers.] I want my poetry to reflect what the God of creation, through his son Jesus, inspires me to write - my favorite poet is Helen Steiner Rice; [a.] Ephrata, PA

GOTCHER, TANA D.
[pen.] Tana; [b.] May 3, 1956, Amarillo, TX; [p.] David L. Hough, Betty Hough; [m.] Charles, March 10, 1989; [ch.] D. Ryan Whitley; [ed.] Amarillo High, Amarillo College; [occ.] Phlebotomist, Coffee Memorial Blood Center; [memb.] BPW; [oth. writ.] Personal Poems, Church Publications; [pers.] The poem is in memory of my Dad. He joined Jesus in Heaven October 25, 1995. I write from my heart and soul.; [a.] Amarillo, TX

GOWDY, JAIME MARIE
[b.] December 11, 1978, Siloam Springs, AR; [p.] Cheryl Gowdy; [ch.] 2; [ed.] Walnut High School; [occ.] Gymnastics Coach; [hon.] Dean's List, Presidential Academic Award; [a.] Walnut, CA

GRACE, SIOBHAN
[b.] November 29, 1982, Yonkers, NY; [p.] Kathryn Grace, William P. Grace III; [ed.] Bridge Elementary School, Lexington, Clarke Middle School, Lexington, MA, September '96 - Lexington High School; [memb.] Clarke Middle School Band and Orchestra Hayden Rec. Center for gymnastic, past member of the Hayden Dolphins Swim and Lexington Town Pool Swim Team; [hon.] 1992 Coaches Award in Swimming 1993 Coaches award in Swimming. In 1992, Silver medal in Gymnastic for floor ex. Multiple 1st and 2nd place ribbons in swimming and gymnastic Honor roll in 6th and 7th grade; [oth. writ.] Small collection of theme poems.; [pers.] Hate and Rage are four letters - so are love and hope.; [a.] Lexington, MA

GRALIKER, MARY
[b.] November 16, 1927, Rural, IN; [ch.] Five grown children; [occ.] Retired; [pers.] First attempted at poetry. Hobby is primarily painting with oils.; [a.] Duluth, GA

GRANT, ALLEN
[b.] October 13, 1930, Salem, NH; [p.] Allan Grant, Grace S. Grant; [m.] 1926; [ch.] Allen and Raymond Grant; [ed.] Bellows Falls High School, Bellows Falls, UT; [occ.] Security; [memb.] Connecticut Songwriter Association, Presbyterian Elder, GBC Choir; [oth. writ.] In addition to poetry - Lyricist, Collaborator - Composer of Anthems "A Praise Hymn" and "He is Living, Near" for S.A.T.B. Also compose Introits call have been performed...); [pers.] I was about to give up writing poetry until my Tete-a-Tete with Richard Eberhart in Wash, DC, in the 50's. He greatly encouraged me then and in correspondence he had later. Personally, one should endeavor to look "Beyond" that whatever seems obvious, and contemplate. Things are not always what they seem to be!; [a.] Milford, CT

GRANT, ANTHONY LUSEAN
[pen.] Shony; [b.] August 7, 1975, Portsmouth; [p.] Anthony and Tina Grand; [m.] Jordan; [ed.] Brighton Ele School, NY J. Mapp Jr. High Deep Creek High and Cradock High; [occ.] Was a student at time of his death; [oth. writ.] There are many more poems my son wrote, but I haven't published them.; [pers.] The creator, arrange for the male child to continue the family line but my family line stopped on December 9, 1993. Maybe our name will live through our only son's writing.; [a.] Portsmouth, VA

GRASSE, LOUIS R.
[b.] March 18, 1975, Ridgewood, NJ; [p.] Susan Milan, Alex Milan; [ed.] Mandarin High School; [occ.] Technical Administrator Ideon Group, Inc.; [oth. writ.] Several poems have been submitted to newspapers, books, magazines, and local newsletters; [pers.] The ink of my pen is influenced by the love of my life.; [a.] Jacksonville, FL

GRASSL, MARY T.
[pen.] Mary Grassl; [b.] May 9, 1974, Wisconsin; [p.] Raymond Sr and Susan Grassl; [ed.] Lincoln High, Currently pursuing a college Education while in the USAF, and I plan to amend UW-Madison in 1996; [occ.] United States Air Force; [oth. writ.] Several Poems published through the National Library of Poetry; [pers.] I strive to show the world what is seen through my eyes.; [a.] Vesper, WI

GRAY, IDA M.
[b.] August 14, 1951, Pensacola, FL; [p.] Henry and Ida Bell Williams; [m.] Ramon L. Gray, March 15, 1977; [ch.] Terri, Raymond and Robert; [pers.] Writing poetry is a healing process. Expressing my feeling in a rhymic Pattern of words bring great joy to my soul.; [a.] Lynwood, CA

GREBNER, BERNICE
[pen.] Bernice Prill Grebner; [b.] May 23, Peoria, IL; [p.] Elmert and Emma Prill; [m.] Divorced; [ch.] Marjorie Welsch, David Grebner; [ed.] Philosophy Psychology, Religion and Accredited Astrologer; [occ.] Professional astrologer, author of eight astrology books; [memb.] American Federation of Astrologers, Edgar Cayces A.R.E. group; [hon.] Woman of The Year 1991, 2000 Notable American Women; [oth. writ.] Lunar Nodes, Decantes, A Full View, Books: Everything Has A Phase, Mercury, The Open Door, Mercury, The Open Door, Day of Your Birth, ABC's Of Astrology and Astronomy, Bee's Flight, Don't Take You Away From You,

Don't Sin Against Yourself And What You Were Meant To Be, If You Have To Do Something, Do It But If You Think You'll Get Negatively From Others Keep It Secret; [a.] Peoria, IL

GREEN, LEWIS D.
[b.] September 30, 1933, Cambridge, MA; [p.] Darcy and Marjorie Greene; [m.] Frances Greene, April 1976; [ch.] Lisa Maria, Laura Anne, Lynne Ellen; [ed.] Ringetech High School, NYCC College; [occ.] Retired Medical Technologist; [memb.] AARP and American Diabetes Association; [hon.] Two Community Awards by Police Dept.; [oth. writ.] Penalty Death, In The Morning, Little Girls Little Boys, Fly, What You Didn't See, The Ladder of Life, My Wife, My Life; [pers.] In loving memory of my brother, Det. Sargent Edward Greene of the Harvard Police Force.; [a.] Richmond Hill, NY

GREEN, TERESA LEA
[b.] March 24, 1963, San Antonio, TX; [p.] Mary Barron Wiley; [m.] Alan Joseph Green, July 10, 1981; [ch.] Tanner Joseph Green; [ed.] Troy High School; [occ.] Reproductive Endocrinology, Medical Secretary, Scott and White Clinic; [pers.] Dedicated in loving memory of my grandma Ruby Joanna Barron. December 12, 1905 October 1, 1987. Alive in my heart Forever.; [a.] Rogers, TX

GREENE, SUSIE R.
[pen.] Majestic Eagle Ministries; [b.] November 8, 1934, Milwaukee, WI; [p.] Thurmon Greene, Louis Greene; [m.] David W. Livingston, July 19, 1952; [ch.] David Jr., Cindy Su, Daniel R.; [occ.] Retired; [oth. writ.] Child Like Faith (A series), Nam's Victory, many others, including family related poems, love, inspired poems of the spirit; [pers.] Poetry came to me as a gift, several years ago. Therefore, as my own spirit began to inquire about truth's and mysteries, I was blessed with the awe, the beauty and the wonder of lessons not found in books. That is, until lately, as the bold ones come forth with lessons for all humanity.; [a.] Theresa, WI

GREENWOOD, TIMOTHY PAUL
[pen.] Timon the Bard, Jokerman; [b.] September 16, 1970, Peoria, IL; [p.] Thomas Greenwood Sr., Joan WIll; [ed.] Northbrook High School; [occ.] Controller/EMT American MedTrans Ambulance; [memb.] Washington State IV/EMT, Volunteer Firefighter KCFD 15, International Thespian Society Troupe 1610; [hon.] Two Regional Awards for Acting, 5 year Service Award for firefighting; [oth. writ.] "Memories and Visions" a collection of cyber poetry, available only through the Internet; [pers.] Through perseverance, faith and understanding is life survivable. You must be willing to listen, read and see the world around you.; [a.] Bremerton, WA

GREER, JUDY
[b.] March 9, 1942, Chester, SC; [p.] Julius Stroud, Hattie Stroud; [m.] Maxie Greer, August 1, 1986; [ch.] Kelly Collins, Tammy Cromer; [ed.] Lewisville High Greenwood Piedmont Tec; [occ.] Data Entry Operator Park Seed Co.; [oth. writ.] Poem published in church bulletin; [pers.] I write about things that touch my heart, and things in nature that overwhelm me with awe.; [a.] Greenwood, SC

GREGORY, SHARON A.
[pen.] Sherii A. Gregory Cruz; [b.] July 12, 1951,

Victorville; [p.] Eugene and Ione King; [ch.] Sheila, Joseph, Ruth, Matthew, and Luke; [ed.] San Bernardino Valley College; [memb.] Judson Baptist Church; [pers.] I strive to be a better person and to love truth and honor an justice for all, Amen Also to impart Faith Love and Hope to all mankind ; [a.] San Bernardino, CA

GREUEL, JOYCE E.
[b.] March 8, 1945, Orlando, FL; [p.] Floy Ellenback, Mary Frances Ellenback; [m.] Robert J. Greuel; [occ.] Stenographer, Word Processing Tech.; [memb.] Many quality Service awards; [hon.] A General Mgh. Awards,; [oth. writ.] The flowers that bloomed published in lyrical voices 1979, The Meaning Of True Friendship, published in Edge of Twilight 1994; [a.] Orlando, FL

GRIFFIN, JESSICA MARIE
[b.] October 6, 1982, Hopewell; [p.] Donna and Keith Griffin; [ed.] Chester Middle School; [occ.] Student at CMS; [hon.] High Honors in School Citizenship Awards. Gifted Programs in School; [oth. writ.] Several Pieces of Work Just for Fun; [pers.] The following is quote from the book "Anne of Green Gabbles "Tomorrow Is Always Fresh From Mistakes"; [a.] Chester, VA

GRIMALDI, PAMELA
[b.] May 29, 1967, Brooklyn, NY; [p.] Patricia and James Grimaldi; [pers.] Writing has been my deliverance. It bestows on me anonymity needed to unleash my demons. I express the things I can not articulate. This tool has empowered me to unveil my innermost thoughts and feelings. In a composing frenzy I achieve true peace. I am forever comforted.; [a.] Kew Gardens, NY

GRIMES, JACK
[b.] December 15, 1934, Wellston, MO; [p.] Arquilla and Edith Grimes; [m.] Carolyn Grimes, January 10, 1994; [ch.] Carole Chuck Sally Grimes; [ed.] Morehouse High University Missouri Rolla University State of New York; [occ.] Traffic Operations and Transportation Dept; [memb.] Masonic Lodge 1st United Methodist Church; [a.] Sikeston, MO

GRIMES, SYLVIA N.
[pen.] Sylvia Nadine; [b.] March 27, 1926, Bradford, PA; [p.] Julius Miller, Hester Miller; [m.] Paul H. Grimes, April 11, 1942; [ch.] Paula, Gerald, Evereh, Cynthia and Phillip; [ed.] Bradford High School; [occ.] Retired; [memb.] AARP United We Stand America; [oth. writ.] Several poems unpublished including Life's Rose Disrobed, My Realm, Why Sky?, Three Way Secret, Visioned. (Take Love's Angel With You written for daughter's wedding); [pers.] I am a Romantic! most of my poems reflect this. Some with sadness, some with joy, I love natural things sky patterns, water ripples and leaf colors.; [a.] Smethport, PA

GROM, FRANK
[pen.] "Being Frank with you"; [b.] April 5, 1917, Newark, NJ; [p.] Frank, Sr. and Eva Grom; [m.] Irene M. Grom, July 3, 1941; [ch.] Claudette, Jacqueline; [ed.] West Orange High Newark College of Engeineering Atlantic Utilities Institute; [occ.] Retired "former President of Jersey Central Federal Credit Union"; [memb.] Florida Sheriffs Association,

Enchanting Shores Neighborhood, Watch Street Captain, Enchanting Shores Fishing and Boating Club, Chairman of 55 Alive Driving Course Program at Enchanting Shores; [hon.] 1933 School Football Captain, 1952, Big Fish Contest Award, 22 Trout Leader in Ballantine Garcia Accury Surf Casting Tournament at New York City Coliseum 1965; [oth. writ.] "Si Si Seniors", "Mugged by A Manatee", "The Roaring Twenties", "The Mermaids", above published taken from my book 1995 at Enchanting Shores Mobile Home Park; [pers.] Our time is short, and the years do run, so let's relax and have some fun. I wrote my first poem 20 years ago, then last year I decided to try again, and wrote 22 more in six months.; [a.] Naples, FL

GROMAN, JANELL
[b.] April 3, 1980, San Bernardino; [p.] Randall and Jodie Groman; [ed.] Student at Yucaipa High School (10th grade); [memb.] I am a member in CSF; [hon.] I have received awards for my GPA and school recommendation; [pers.] I love poems that are about mother nature because they are enjoyable to read.; [a.] Yucaipa, CA

GRONER, LESLIE KAREN
[b.] August 12, 1965, Inglewood, CA; [p.] Herman Groner and Mariann Robinson; [ed.] 3 years High School, Currently Studying Bookkeeping and Accounting; [occ.] Inventory Auditor; [oth. writ.] I have many other writings however none have been published. (I have never submitted them); [pers.] The best way to approach the difficulties life has to offer is this simplicity and honesty not with complexity. (Complex answers bring about more questions); [a.] Quartz Hill, CA

GROOMS, ANGEL
[b.] January 21, 1981; [p.] Terry and Marguerite Grooms; [ed.] I am a freshman at Seymour High School; [occ.] I write articles for the Tri-County News; [memb.] I am an active member of the 4-H Club, a volunteer club that helps throughout the community. I am also a member of the Jr. Beta Club which is an honor club for Jr. High students. I take part in many extra-curricular activities; [hon.] I have won first place in the 4-H County Public Speaking contest since the 1993 competition. I won first place in the National Beta Club Essay Contest and was honored with the publication of the essay.; [oth. writ.] "Young Rebels" was published May of 1995. The topic of this paper was What's Right With America's Youth? It was my first published piece of literature.; [pers.] Chase after your dreams, one day they'll come true.; [a.] Seymour, TN

GROSSKOPT, BESS
[b.] October 27, 1981, Waukesha, WI; [p.] Carol and Norbert Grosskopf; [ed.] Currently 8th grade student; [pers.] The world is a harsh place, full of criticism and greed, but writing to me is a light shining through even the darkest of clouds.; [a.] Waukesha, WI

GRUSECKI, RYAN E.
[b.] February 4, 1985, Cheboygan, MI; [p.] Bruce and Kim Grusecki; [ed.] I am in 5th grade at Washington Middle School in Calumet, Michigan; [occ.] Student; [memb.] Washington Middle School Flag Football Team; [hon.] 1995 Arenac County Fair 1st place Spelling Bee, 1995 Merit Award Raintree -

Steck - Vaughn Publish A Book Contest; [oth. writ.] "The Red-Stocking Hat"; [pers.] I believe that you should work hard at writing. It's not hard when you really try!; [a.] Calumet, MI

GUAY, MARIE
[b.] December 25, 1941, Roebling, NJ; [m.] Larry; [ch.] Robert; [ed.] BSN from UN of Penns; [occ.] Dialysis Nursing and Freelance Writing; [oth. writ.] Biblical Novel entitled "Acrey in the Wilderness" and Christian Appologetic Topics; [pers.] The poem was inspired after reading Tom Clancey's "Without Remorse"; [a.] Florence, NJ

GUENO, JUSTINE
[b.] July 30, 1963, New Orleans, LA; [p.] Dr. & Mrs. Lemuel Clanton; [m.] Dwayne Andrew Gueno, August 7, 1987; [ch.] Jonah Andrew Gueno; [ed.] Ursuline Academy, University of New Orleans; [occ.] Social Science Researcher and Evaluator (Sociologist); [hon.] 2nd Place Poetry Reading - Ursuline, 1st Place Impromptu Speaking - Xavier University; [oth. writ.] Several unpublished poems on the environment friendship and racial harmony. In the process of writing a series of short self help books called "Shortcuts"; [pers.] I strive to bring hope back to family & friends. I feel that most conflict can be smoothed out by understanding each other's different perceptions of our life experiences. I am inspired by those who suffer constantly but still manage to smile.; [a.] New Orleans, LA

GUNBY, LAURA
[b.] November 27, 1917, Crisfield, MD; [p.] Jessie and Paul Gunby; [m.] Arnold Gunby (Deceased), March 17, 1979 (Second); [ch.] John, Jill, and Karen; [ed.] U. of MD. College Park, MD. International Correspondence School Interior Decorating; [occ.] Homemaker (Retired); [memb.] St. Stephen's Traditional Episcopal Church Glee Club at U. of MD. Opera Club at U. of MD. Tabco; [hon.] Valedictorian of my class at Marion High School, Marion STA., MD in 1934, Two editor's Choice Awards from the National Library of Poetry; [oth. writ.] "Come on Spring" pome read at International Library of Poetry Conference in Washington, D.C. in August '95, Poems to friends and relatives on special occasions.; [pers.] After having taught retarded children for many years, I would hope to be remembered for my love of God, my family, my fellowman, and nature.

GURKINK, KATE
[occ.] Nurse Practitioner; [memb.] Woman's Health Care Hitchcock Clinic, Dartmouth Lebanon, NTJ; [pers.] Poetry is the music of the soul, let it sing to the melodies created.; [a.] Hanover, DH

GUY, DARLENE JOYCE
[b.] September 26, 1944, Oakland, CA; [p.] Arthur and Martha McKee Deceased 1990; [m.] Lemuel "Butch" Jester Guy, December 21, 1963; [ch.] Steven Jester Ronald Lee, Frank Arthur, James Delbert; [ed.] High School Verdugo Hills High in (L.A.) Tiyiungo Col. College Orange Coast, Santa Ana, Riverside City; [occ.] Micro Circuit Electronic Assembler and Comp test tec "ISR" "Huguhes G. M. Electronics"; [memb.] Relief Society, Visiting Teacher, L.D.S. Church Life member N.L.P.; [hon.] Certified top 3% for "A Special Child" in contest printed in "River of Dreams"; [oth. writ.] In Best Poems of 1995, Best poems 1996, River of Dreams.

Personally printed books for close Friends and Realities Numerous poems used in our Church "Women's Relief Society; [pers.] My words are Gods gift given to me, through which he professes profound wisdom for all to hear. I am just the mediator between God and my Word processor. I love to write I never know what gift the end result will be; [a.] Riverside, CA

GUY, SUSAN A.
[b.] January 1, 1954, Trinidad, WI; [p.] Gerald and Myra Questel; [m.] Ian A. Guy, June 28, 1975; [ch.] Alicia, Ian Guy Jr, Gerard, Denise; [ed.] Two Year College - English and History, College of Insurance NYC Orlando Tec. Home Health Aide/and Mental Health Tec. Certified; [occ.] Health Care Worker Winter Park Hospital; [memb.] 1st Pentecostal Church of Orlando Fl. Servant of the Lord Jesus Christ. Care of The Age and Side when ever someone need my service. I do on to others as I would like them do to me.; [oth. writ.] Inspirational poems or Christian way of Living Several other poems writing for my Church and Friends.; [pers.] In this world today man is still hating each other. Embrace your fellowman and love your brother, "Love opens the Mind"; [a.] Orlando, FL

HACK, VIRGINIA L.
[pen.] Ginny Hack; [b.] July 27, 1941, Hobbs, N. Mexico; [p.] T. B. and Bernice Owen; [m.] Divorced, March 21, 1961; [ch.] Michael, Cheryl, Amanda, Cheryl; [ed.] Hobbs High School graduated in 1959; [oth. writ.] A collection of poems, I've written, through the years; [pers.] I try to keep my poems simple. To people and event's that have touched my life, and taught me or given me a little more insight into my life. They're my diary.; [a.] Hobbs, NM

HAGMAN, GRACE
[b.] January 25, 1954, Greenbush, MN; [m.] Larry Hagman, May 12, 1973; [pers.] Is it only child's play or is there a small reflection of our selves in these games? Do we dare look and listen to find out? We should.; [a.] Thief River Falls, MN

HALE, JENNIFER LEIGH
[b.] November 11, 1974, Carthage, TN; [p.] Jeanette Wilkerson and David Wilkerson; [ed.] Gordonsville Elementary, Gordonsville High School, Tennessee Technological University; [occ.] Student working on a Bachelor of Science in Biology; [memb.] Omega Phi Alpha, Beta Beta Beta, Alpha Mu Gamma, Alpha Lambda Delta, Chem-Med Club, Wildlife Society; [hon.] Valedictorian, Beta Beta Beta, Alpha Mu Gamma, Alpha Lambda Delta, National Dean's List; [pers.] My poems are greatly influence by my personal experiences. I hope very much that they touch the people who read them. I thank God for giving me the ability to express my thoughts and feelings through poetry. I would like to dedicate this poem to Chadwick Lewis whom I love with all my heart and soul. A poet himself, he believed in my ability to write poetry and loved reading it. I lost my boyfriend to a car accident, but he will live forevert in my poetry. Chadwick Lewis 8/7/70 - 11/11/95; [a.] Brush Creek, TN

HALE, SHERRILL
[b.] March 28, 1948, Tuscola, IL; [p.] William H. Olehy, Imadeen R. Olehy; [m.] Walter, March 21, 1975; [ch.] Walter Darrin Hale; [ed.] Villa Grove High School Villa Grove, IL; [occ.] Greeter for K-Mart Super Center; [oth. writ.] Personal Poems to family and friends; [pers.] I owe all that I am to God, family and friends and all that I hope to be.; [a.] Memphis, TN

HALL, DONALD A.
[pen.] Donald Hall; [b.] April 27, 1933, Camden, NJ; [p.] Samuel and Althea Hall; [m.] Anita M. Hall, May 13, 1961; [ch.] 2 boy and girl; [ed.] Camden High School - 1951; [occ.] Typesetter/Computer Operator - Retired; [memb.] Veteran - Air Force 1953-1957; [pers.] I write about what I have experienced through life and interpret things in a poetic manner; [a.] Camden, NJ

HALL, JENE
[pen.] "Bobby"; [b.] December 11, 1931, Louisiana; [p.] Claude and Fannie Hall; [m.] Maxine, December 1960; [ch.] Gwendolyn Dianne and David Carroll; [ed.] Tioga High (Louisiana) LA Tech University, LSU (Baton Roupe) Nova Southeastern U. (Fort Lauderdale) In order BS, MA, EdD; [occ.] Retired Teacher Professor, Emeritus Florida Community College; [memb.] American Legion Disabled American Veterans; [hon.] Purple Heart Lion's Club Medal Outstanding Achievement special dedication; [pers.] I want to express the essence on the present and historic American scenes.; [a.] Jacksonville, FL

HALL, JOANNE
[pen.] Nan Morris; [b.] October 15, 1969, Oaklawn, IL; [p.] Shorty, Edward Morris, Kathy, Morris; [m.] Bill Hall, January 27, 1989; [ed.] Clevis High School; [occ.] Book Keeper, Sales; [oth. writ.] Other poems never tried to set a published; [pers.] My goal in life is to be the best I can be! Do to others only what you expect to get in return.; [a.] Clovis, NM

HALL, LISA R.
[pen.] Lisa Hall; [b.] July 26, 1964, Leoti, KS; [ch.] Cameron; [ed.] B.S. Medical Technology, WSU Wichita, KS; [a.] Mesa, AZ

HALL, RAISSA M.
[b.] January 15, 1970, Ohio; [p.] John L. Hall, Domenica A. Hall; [ed.] B.A. English, Wright State University, Dayton, Ohio; [occ.] Technical Writer, The Met Co.; [pers.] People say that a poem must have a fixed, learnable, esoteric meaning. I believe that you should see, feel and hear what you want in a poem.; [a.] Chesapeake, VA

HALL, STEPHANIE
[b.] July 25, 1976, Melbourne, Australia; [p.] Marcus and Pam Hall; [ed.] Leongatha Secondary College (in Victoria, Australia) Cibola High School (Yuma, Arizona for 1 year '95); [occ.] Student; [hon.] Being an exchange student to the U.S. ('95) and Nepal ('93/94) Grand champion and peoples choice award - acrylic painting first place - photograph second place - sandblasted mirror 7 honorable mention ribbons for various photo's. All these awards won at cibola high school's Fine Arts Fair. I am photo assignment editor of cibola H.S. yearbook '95/'96.; [pers.] When I am deeply moved by something, I feel the need to capture it on paper. Being an exchange student has opened my eyes and made me a better person.; [a.] Yuma, AZ

HALPIN, EDWARD F.
[b.] January 12, 1910, Albany, NY; [p.] Nicholas Halpin, May Halpin; [m.] Betty Halpin, December 28, 1946; [ch.] Robert, Mary, Joan; [ed.] Marquette University, U Of Chicago (great books); [occ.] Former president Serra Club of Chicago (two terms), member Serra International, Communications

Committee, Chairman Cardinal Bernardin Serra dinner (2), Retired; [memb.] ASTA, MAST (Co-founder and first pres.), Serra Club of Chicago (ex-pres.); [hon.] Author of Incentive Program which won National Award for Best Promotion by Nat'l Assoc. Sales Executives; [oth. writ.] Articles on business prior to 1980, articles on religion primarily for Catholic publications after 1980; [pers.] I believe Adam and Eve were symbolic of the human race, that "we" collectively rejected to subordinate our will. As a consequence we lost the "gift" of "certituted" and "anxiety" was bred into our genetic make-up.; [a.] Park Ridge, IL

HAMBURG, JENNIFER
[pen.] Jennifer Davis; [b.] April 30, 1979, Torrance, CA; [p.] David Hamburg, Gail Davis; [ed.] Pre School Eleventh Grade I'm 16; [hon.] 1st place singing award; [oth. writ.] I have many more writing not enough room here to write them down; [pers.] I write based on my personal experiences or feelings also dreams are reflected in my poetry my dream is to be a poet.; [a.] La Crescenta, CA

HAMILTON, ANNA C.
[pen.] Anna Hamilton; [b.] March 8, 1944, Meyersdale, PA; [p.] Peter F. Housel and Sadie Marie Housel; [m.] Lloyd B. Hamilton, December 15, 1962; [ch.] Tammy Pacheco, Vicki Owen, Sherrie Worthy; [ed.] High School; [occ.] Self Employed, Maid Service; [memb.] First Christian Church, Stockbridge GA; [oth. writ.] "Oh Ye of Little Faith", Cross Roads Section of Lookout Magazine, August 20, 1978, Several poems published by: Peachtree Publishers Ltd.; [pers.] I wrote this poem 33 years ago when my husband and I were first married.; [a.] Rex, GA

HAMILTON, MICHELLE
[pen.] Michelle Bentley; [b.] October 19, 1963, Lincoln Park, MI; [p.] Johnie and Audrey Bentley; [ch.] Audra Ann; [ed.] Roosevelt High School 3 yrs. College; [occ.] Admn. Asst., Logan County Vietnam Veterans; [memb.] I am currently involved in a Mentor Program for children. Sociology Club; [hon.] Dean's List, National Honor Society, Business Honor Society; [oth. writ.] Previous writings have been for my own enjoyment; [pers.] I believe writing is a way to dare your soul to dream.; [a.] Mount Gay, WV

HAMILTON, TARA L.
[b.] April 4, 1974, Pittsburgh, PA; [p.] Ozell and Betty Hamilton; [ed.] Perry Trad. Acad. (High School) Messiah College (2nd Semester Sophomore) currently on Medical Leave of Absence; [occ.] Student; [oth. writ.] New poet, some of my poems are copy written but none have been published yet; [pers.] I have been inspired to write poetry through my life experiences. I thank God for my talent and I give all the credit to him.; [a.] Pittsburgh, PA

HAMMOND, MICHAEL F.
[b.] March 6, 1967, Barharbor, ME; [p.] Joe and Garda Green; [m.] Jenneice Dennis December 31, 1995; [ch.] Michael Stephen Hammond; [ed.] Student at Texas A&M University at Corpus Christi Texas; [occ.] Restaurant Manager; [pers.] I have had a goal far many years to be published. This small poem will hopefully be the first of many to be published God willing; [a.] Corpus Christi, TX

HAND, DANIELLE SCHELLER
[pen.] Danielle Hand; [b.] June 3, 1965, Plainfield, NJ; [p.] Catherine P. and the late Daniel J. Scheller; [m.] William C. Hand, September 30, 1989; [ch.] Melissa, Michael, Billy and Amanda, Brooke, 1 Stepchild; [ed.] Toms River High School North; [occ.] Housewife; [memb.] Christian Bible Church; [pers.] I am most inspired to write poems for the love I have for my family and friends every poem I write has been inspired either by someone's sadness or happiness I write poems to comfort people to make them feel better, cause I care how people feel.; [a.] Toms River, NJ

HANEY, JANICE MARIE
[b.] May 5, 1934, Cascade, ID; [p.] James and Gratia Bacon Matthews; [m.] Robert, May 23, 1951; [ch.] 3 boys and 1 girl; [ed.] High School LPN School Treasure Valley Community College; [occ.] LPN; [oth. writ.] Poems about my family for my family not published; [pers.] I love to travel the back roads of Idaho to the old ghost towns which once flourished during the gold rush days. There is so much beauty and memories of days gone by.; [a.] Nyssa, OR

HANKE, LAVERNE
[pen.] Laverne Hanke; [b.] March 11, 1915, Chicago, IL; [p.] Mr and Mrs Wm. Joerger; [m.] Mr. Kennedy Hanke (Jim), April 11, 1936; [ch.] Lawrence Wm, James Alan; [ed.] Waller High School and 2 yr. Secretarial Course; [occ.] Homemaker; [memb.] St. Thomas V.C.C. American Heart association Hospice; [oth. writ.] This is my first; [pers.] Visit the sick, volunteer at nursing homes, work for missions. I'm a firm believer that we're put on this earth to do what we can to make a better world.; [a.] Chicago, IL

HANLEY, MAUREEN
[pen.] Mo Henry; [b.] March 9, 1961, Milwaukee, WI; [p.] Michael and Carol Hanley; [ch.] Justin, Laura, Janna, Jacob; [ed.] Fargo South High, Moorhead State University; [occ.] Junior Majoring in Mass Comm. with Print Journalism emphasis and minoring in Spanish; [memb.] Intern and member of people escaping poverty project; [pers.] The only fear I have is living an ordinary life.; [a.] Fargo, ND

HANLEY, TAMMY
[b.] January 15, 1968, Warsaw, NY; [p.] Claudia Houtz and Frank Houtz, Deceased; [m.] Deceased, March 1, 1986; [ch.] Amanda, Kristin, Michelle; [ed.] Currently enrolled in Genesee Community College, Batavia NY, Expected graduation May '96, Dean's List, Keshequa Central, High School Nunda, NY; [oth. writ.] None that are currently published; [pers.] My poem was written to my husband after his death and my bestfriend read it at the funeral service. This poem is very important to me and I'm glad people can have it to read.; [a.] Dalton, NY

HANNAH, ROBERT RAY-MORRIS
[pen.] Mercury Morris; [b.] May 19, 1961, Oakland, CA; [p.] James and Mary Hannah; [m.] Divorced; [ch.] William, Passion, and Charlie Hannah; [ed.] Castlemont High; [occ.] Self-Employed Leather Craftsman; [oth. writ] Collection of unpublished poems and musical compositions; [pers.] I dedicate the publishing of this poem to my daughter Passion, who shares my artistic talents and emotional sensitivity. And Jehovah for His gifts. [a.] Grand Rapids, MI

HANNON JR., ALLEN C.
[pen.] Allen Hannon; [b.] February 22, 1964, Harlem, GA; [p.] Allen and Lucille Hannon; [m.] Kristin Hannon, August 10, 1985; [ch.] Megan Marie; [ed.] Harlem High School; [occ.] Carpenter; [oth. writ.] None published (yet); [pers.] I truly feel my writing talent is God given and am very grateful for this opportunity to share it with others.; [a.] Harlem, GA

HANSEN, TRACEY
[pen.] Tracey Hansen; [b.] September 21, 1981, East Islip, NY; [p.] Anne E. Hansen and Paul H. Hansen; [ed.] Bishop Verot High School in Fort Myer's, Florida (Now attending); [occ.] High School Student; [memb.] Author's Club In School Chamber of Commerce Head Anchor of School T.V. Production; [hon.] National Jr. Honor Soc.; [oth. writ.] None published; [pers.] I believe everything a person writes is good, and everyone with something to say should speak up.; [a.] Cape Coral, FL

HANSOM, AMANDA
[b.] February 12, 1980, Battle Creek, MI; [p.] Michelle Evans, Paul Hansom; [ed.] Attending Bellevue High School, Bellevue, MI; [pers.] Never a day without a line; [a.] Bellevue, MI

HANSON, CHERYLD T.
[b.] May 13, 1969, White Planes, NY; [p.] William and Isabelle Hanson; [ch.] Justin Wayne Hanson; [pers.] I would like to thank my sister Tiffany for helping me write this poem.

HANSON, MONICA KAY
[b.] February 8, 1963, Kansas City, MO; [p.] Grace and Kenton Hanson; [ch.] Heather Rachel; [ed.] Duluth Cathedral High School, University Minnesota Dulutch, Cosmetology Training Center; [occ.] Community Living Specialist in Mental Health Resources, Inc. (St. Paul, MN); [hon.] 2 year member in Honor Society (high school) in which I was secretary. I was also published in Who's Who in American high school students for 2 consecutive years; [oth. writ.] Several of my drawings and poetry have been included in my place of employment's newsletter; [pers.] I have read poetry of vast variety and have been sparked to write my own through the years, usually, struggling to untangle a personal dilemma while trying to say something meaningful to the reader at the same time.; [a.] Richfield, MN

HARBIN, AMANDA
[pen.] Mandiee Harbin; [b.] November 5, 1977, Memphis, TN; [p.] David and Anthony Harbin; [ed.] Senior at Collierville High School; [occ.] Waitress/ Student; [memb.] I am a member and the US President of S.L.A.P. at my High School and creative writing.; [hon.] Most of my honors and awards are from music, playing french horn; [pers.] Most of my poems reflect a sad moment in my life. My writing poetry comes from my great grandmother Rubey Coble. (God bless her); [a.] Collierville, TN

HARBISON, SYLVIA LUCILLE
[pen.] Sylvia Lucille; [b.] August 5, 1937, Indianapolis, IN; [p.] Norma Abby (Hottle) Hawkins, Donald Francis Hawkins; [ch.] 3 (2 daughters/1 son) 4 Grandchildren; [ed.] Public School #21 (Indianapolis, IN), Arsenal Technical HS (Indpls, IN); [occ.] Analyst/Programmer; [memb.] Religious

(Unity of Indianapolis) Clubs (Toastmasters, International); [hon.] President, Board of Trustees, Unity of Indpls, Lay Minister at Unity of Indpls, Achieved the highest designation in Toastmaster, Int. (Distinquished Toastmaster - DTM), have received numerous Toastmaster awards.; [oth. writ.] I have many poems not yet published.; [pers.] I believe that we are all given special gifts through which we may choose to manifest God's presence. Some are blessed with musical abilities some with artistic abilities, some have the ability to put words together whether it be lyrics, poetry, manuscripts, technical manuals, novels, etc. others have chosen to be healers (doctors, nurses, therapists), designers, chefs, computer programmers, gardeners, housekeepers, teachers, ministers, - you see, we all choose our path to manifest the creativity within us (our gift from God). I'm grateful for my special gift(s) and strive to reach as many as is possible with the words expressed through me. Thank You God.

HARDING, DELORES BROWN
[b.] June 8, 1923, Norfolk, VA; [p.] Birt and Devetta Brown; [m.] Milton C. Harding Sr., June 25, 1947; [ch.] Carolyn, Beverly, Phylicia, Milton Jr.; [ed.] Post graduate work in the field of English; [occ.] Retired English Professor; [oth. writ.] "Upon Looking At Love" published in Ebony Rhythm Poetry anthology, Edited an anthology of Student Essay's, Voices above the appomattox; [pers.] I like writing on topics which speak to spirit, soul, and body.; [a.] Petersburg, VA

HARDSON, GREGORY D.
[b.] March 7, 1949, Los Angeles, CA; [p.] Willie and Martha Hardson; [m.] Deborah Hardson, July 3, 1970; [ch.] David, Shannon, Tyrus, Geyne, Lucille; [ed.] Compton Sr. High School A.A. Mt. San Antonio Jr. College 1 yr. Cal Poly Pomona 1 1/2 yrs L.A. Trade Tech.; [occ.] Drywall Taper, Painter; [hon.] Celebrity Centre International Guild of Poets and Russell Salamon; [oth. writ.] Poor Folks, My Children, My Children, Listen to the Baby Cry, The Housing Projects, Spirit in the Dark, The Son, Seasons People, Las Vegas, the best I can. The Eagle.; [pers.] Thanks to Dr. Lynette Lynch of Mt. Sac and Russell Salamon, and most of all Nadine Outlaw Lit Teacher in High School, and my Pastor Dr. Joseph L. Holmes of double rock Baptist Church of Compton, CA.

HARDY, GUY L. W.
[b.] September 20, 1968, San Francisco; [p.] Steven and Valerie Hardy; [m.] Jennifer K. Hardy, December 31, 1993; [oth. writ.] Many poems, as yet unpublished; [pers.] What we do is the essence of love and peace - we keep talking. Be silent only in death.; [a.] Auburn, WA

HARE, MELINDA KAY
[b.] January 24, 1957, Glendale, CA; [p.] William E. Hare, Mary Ellen Hare; [ch.] Margaret Anne Taylor; [ed.] Crescent High, Crescent, Okla. Central State Univ., Edmond, Okla. Oklahoma State Univ., Stillwater, Okla. Southern Oregon State College, Ashland Oregon Western Business College, Fashion School, Portland, Oregon; [occ.] Manpower (clerical) and mother; [memb.] Eastern Star, Rainbows Talent United Methodist Church; [hon.] 1st place VICA Parliamentary Procedure Team, 1st VICA Public Speaking; [pers.] Thru my writings I hope to express

how my life has been greatly influenced by the many special persons who have touched my life. I feel they are the ones that helped to shape and mold my life into what it is today. These are moments that will always be treasured and remembered as I continue to live out my life making many new memories as I go along. Keeping in mind that I should live life today, drawing from the pats that which is good and important, and never fearing the future.; [a.] Salem, OR

HARLAN, DR. KENNETH E.
[b.] August 31, 1913, Maiden Rock, WI; [p.] Edward and Laura Harlan; [m.] Carmel M. (Spano) Harlan, June 19, 1937; [ch.] Cathlene, Twins Ann and Mary, Mark and Elizabeth; [ed.] Doctorate in Clinical Psychology; [occ.] Retired; [memb.] Knights of Columbus National Assoc. of Postal Supervisors, St. Clement's Catholic Church Twin Cities Musician's Union (over 50 years) (Was a disc jockey-had a band and both played and sang); [oth. writ.] Minneapolis Skyline, Western Sampler, Painted Arrows, Editor - Branch 9 News (U. S. P. S.) Poetry - 1946, The Liberty Bell September 1919, Hamilton School 1st Grade; [a.] Minneapolis, MN

HARLESS, BARBARA RILEY
[b.] March 31, 1952, Logan, WV; [p.] Orville and Glenna Riley; [m.] Robert W. Harless, March 20, 1992; [ch.] Jessica, Shay, Lori, Katie and Ashley; [ed.] Associate of Science in Commercial Art, Orlando College, Orlando, FL, Licensed Practical Nurse, Riverside Hospital School of Practical Nursing, Newport News, Va., Man High School, Man, West Va.; [occ.] Free Lance Graphic Designer; [hon.] Presidents and Dean's List, graduated Magna Cum Laude. Great American Family Award, Mare Island, CA Representative.; [pers.] The poem was written about my husband and I and the love we shared over twenty years ago and the re-uniting of the love, after years of separation. With this reuniting we were blessed with the birth of our daughter. "True love will find a way"; [a.] Orlando, FL

HARPSTER, NANCY ELIZABETH
[b.] September 24, 1959, Harrisburg, PA; [occ.] Artist; [memb.] People for the ethical treatment of animals, greenpeace; [pers.] My poetic intent is to confer my love and appreciation for earth, causing the reader to review their individual role in healing our planet, our home, our spirit mother earth.; [a.] Library, PA

HARRELL, KATHY
[b.] January 14, 1946, Swaziland; [p.] Irl and Flo McCallister; [m.] Al Harrell, November 3, 1973; [ch.] Tim, Brian, Richard; [ed.] West Suburban Hospital Sch. of Nursing, Wheaton College (Ill.), Columbia Bible College; [occ.] Staff of Mission Organization; [pers.] My perspective as a Christian gives meaning of eternal significance to all I see and feel. Favorite poet-Gerard Manley Hopkins; [a.] Weaverville, NC

HARRIS, DANIELLE
[b.] February 13, 1980, Miami, FL; [p.] Donn and Lark Harris, Elvira Perez (Mother); [ed.] Presently attending High School; [pers.] True Talent, used for the good of mankind or to express the good of mankind, will truly be rewarded.; [a.] Moses Lake, WA

HARRIS, EDGAR
[pen.] Edgar Harris; [b.] April 17, 1929, Crystal City, MO; [p.] Jessie A. and Lillie L. Harris; [m.] Barbara J. Kelly Harris (Deceased), December 6, 1949; [ch.] Edward K. and Terry L.; [ed.] High School and attend Tennessee State University Clerk, Typist School Fort Lee, VA (Army); [occ.] Retired postal worker 40 years service; [memb.] AARP Deacon Glendale, Memorial Baptist Church Glendale, MO YMCA A Devotion Leader for Senior Group Church, Choir Soloist for Choir, NARPE retired Federal employees; [oth. writ.] Several poems in high school church, programs for YMCA; [pers.] I mostly write for church functions and YMCA events and for funeral.; [a.] Saint Louis, MO

HARRIS, HARRIETT SMITHERMAN
[pen.] Harriett Smitherman Harris; [b.] April 28, 1932, Centreville, AL; [p.] Burl H. Smitherman, Adelaide P. Smitherman; [m.] Winton W. Harris, June 3, 1955; [ed.] Bibb County High School, Centreville, AL, BS degree University of TN at Chattanooga, Postgraduate, Cumberland University, Lebanon, TN; [occ.] Retired Elementary School-teacher; [memb.] Delta Kappa Honorary Teachers Society, Freedoms Foundation at Valley Forge, American Association of University Women, International Platform Association, Chattanooga Symphony and Opera Guild, First Baptist Church Media Center Volunteer, Retired Teachers Association, Phi Mu Sorority; [hon.] 1992 Tennessee Teacher of The Year (Middle School), Mentor Public Education Foundation, Mentor Governor's School for Prospective Teachers, Career Ladder III, Certified, AAUW grantee (1976), Biographee Marquis Who's Who of American Women 1993-94, Who's Who Among America's Teachers 1994, Hamilton County Education Assn. Directors Award, Life Member PTA; [oth. writ.] Official Invocation Freedoms Foundation, Valley, Forge, PA, "Ring Out the Old! Ring In the New!" (published Chattanooga Times and Chattanooga Free Press, 1992), several closing of school year poems dedicated to my students, assisted in compilation of Write On, Hamilton County.; [pers.] I wish to impart my beliefs to readers in a style that will capture their attention in both an informative and entertaining manner.; [a.] Chattanooga, TN

HARRIS, RHONDA
[pen.] Ronnie; [b.] January 8, 1953, Rochester, NY; [p.] Lenard Fox, Helen Audino; [m.] Williams Harris, May 6, 1978; [ch.] Michael William, Steven Nicholas, Brian Keith; [ed.] Gulf High School Tarpon Beauty Academy Received Scholarship for Academy 3.4 Average; [occ.] Server, waitress; [pers.] My poems reflect my feeling about life or incidents that have happened. I love to write poems to express my inner feelings God has given me this special gift, to bring enjoyment to all; [a.] Newport Richey, FL

HARRIS, YOLANDA E.
[pen.] Raven; [b.] May 21, 1960, Oakland, CA; [p.] Yvonne Lee Utley, Gradie V. Harris; [ch.] Raven Marisela Flores; [sib.]; [ed.] Skyline High School, Chabot Jr. College; [occ.] Rehabilitation activity Leader/Student; [memb.] CARP (College Association for Research of the Principles); [pers.] To grow we have to learn from mistakes we make in our lives. We cannot learn without actually living and we are

not living if we are not learning. Live to learn or learn to live? (Which comes first, the chicken or the egg.; [a.] San Leandro, CA

HARTZELL, SUSAN CAMPBELL
[b.] February 8, 1968, Los Gatos, CA; [p.] John and MaryAnne Campbell; [m.] Steve Hartzell, April 9, 1991; [ch.] Stephanie, Bryan, Brendon; [ed.] Columbia College, Columbia, CA, California State University, Stanislaws; [occ.] Student, CSU, Stanislaus; [hon.] Dean's List; [pers.] Writing is something I never believed I would be capable of, but maybe dreams can come true.; [a.] Sonora, CA

HARVEY, DEAN L.
[pen.] Dino; [b.] August 5, 1930, Delphos, KS; [m.] Ellie Harvey, February 22, 1975; [ch.] Six; [ed.] High School; [occ.] Retired (Navy); [memb.] Masonic Fraternity, Presbyterian Church, Fleet Reserve Assoc.; [oth. writ.] Published in newspapers and magazines; [pers.] All art is priceless because it is conceived, created and comes to fruition in the mind of human beings, created by God!

HASEMEIER, MATTHEW STRACHAN
[b.] March 18, 1980, Munster, IN; [p.] Dr Eric and Cathy Hasemeier; [ed.] I am a freshman at Athens High School; [memb.] Builder's Club; [hon.] Science Award 1987, Science Award 1988, Science Award Best of show 1989, Science Award 1991, Basic life support Red cross first aid - Red Cross Scuba Diving 1995, Honors English Placement; [oth. writ.] Various poems and short stories; [a.] Athens, OH

HASKELL, NICOLE DAWN
[b.] July 23, 1975; [p.] Robert and Cheryl Haskell; [ed.] Rex Putnam High School, currently attending Seattle Pacific University; [occ.] College Student; [hon.] Commended student in National Merit Scholarship program, seattle pacific university presidential scholar; [pers.] The life in me and around me is created by God, and his gift of life allows me this time and place to use words as a way to reflect the connections of life we all share.; [a.] Seattle, WA

HATFIELD, CARI
[b.] June 11, 1972, Baltimore, MD; [p.] Thomas Aiken and Lynette Aiken; [m.] William Hatfield, March 1, 1991; [ed.] Eldorado High, Albuquerque Technical-Vocational Institute; [occ.] Accounts Payable, Summit Electric Supply, Albuquerque, NM; [pers.] Personal expression is the foundation of freedom; [a.] Albuquerque, NM

HAURY, BRUCE A.
[pen.] Bruce A. Haury; [b.] April 12, 1943, Schenectady, NY; [p.] Edward and Gladys Haury; [m.] Patricia E. Haury, September 10, 1966; [ch.] Quenby Lynn Haury (Schiavo); [ed.] High School Graduate and a graduate of the New School of Contemporary Radio; [occ.] Architectural Drafting on a Consulting basis, as well as Radio Producer; [memb.] Bellevue Reformed Church, Board of Directors - Schenectady Bowling Association; [oth. writ.] Several other poems I have written for my Wife and Daughter that are not being submitted at this time for consideration; [pers.] I enjoy writing poetry when I feel moved to express myself or my thoughts to a loved one or someone whom I care about very deeply.; [a.] Schenectady, NY

HAVENS, WILL H.
[b.] November 21, 1910, Drury, MO; [p.] B. Ray and Mary (Tooley) Havens; [m.] Clara (Keeler) Havens, December 2, 1933; [ch.] Ivan, Ruth, Ann, Bill; [ed.] Self educated beyond high school by correspondence courses and home study course; [occ.] Retired Minister; [memb.] Ava General Baptist Church, International Society of Poetry, American Bible Society, ARRP; [hon.] Editors Choice Awards for Poems Published in "The Desertsun", "Edie of Twilight" and "The Garden of Life", Awarded an Award for fifty years Pastoring plus one for eight additional ministry years.; [oth. writ.] One book of meditations, three books of essays. Three books of poems, many articles, poems and essays published in local and benominational papers and publications; [pers.] I want my writing to be an encouragement for folks to fix their eyes on the Lord and then keep on keeping on until the final victory is won.; [a.] Ava, MO

HAVRON, MARIE ELIZABETH
[pen.] Ree Kelly; [b.] July 8, 1936, Bronx, NY; [p.] Irish Born Marie Lavin and Wm. J. Kelly; [m.] William R. Havron Sr. Ret AF; [ch.] 6 (1 Deceased); [ed.] Butler H.S., N.J. Chic. Univ Art Ext. Germany. LK./Sumter Fl. C.C. Public Spkg. State Fl. R.E.; [occ.] Real Estate, AID Designer Proprieter Retired; [memb.] Present: St. Pats, Grief and Berv. Natl. Chapt. M.S. Soc. Natl. Lung Asso. BPW Editor, Calif. (Past) Editor Golf Divot Digest (Past); [oth. writ.] Journals and notes to write a book; [pers.] I was once told by someone dear, "That Life Is An Accumulation Of Moments — and in order to sustain, one must recognize those moments and Cherish them". I've never forgotten that!; [a.] Zellwood, FL

HAWKINS, FELICIA
[pen.] Felicia Hawkins; [b.] March 9, 1977, Kileen, TX; [p.] Patrick Hawkins, Shirley Hawkins; [ed.] Millington Central High School; [occ.] Captain D's; [memb.] Honors Society, Deca, Who's Who Among American High School Students; [hon.] National Honor Society and Who's Who Among American High School Awards; [oth. writ.] I write poems at home for a hobby; [pers.] I reflect my self through the poem I write.; [a.] Millington, TN

HAWTHORNE, VALERIE
[pen.] Valtie; [b.] September 14, 1972, Charleston, SC; [p.] Peggy and Manuel Dizon; [ch.] Cecilia Eileen; [occ.] Psychiatric Tech. Fulltime student at Mt. San Antonio College; [hon.] 1st place in the Elk's Essay Contest, 2nd place in impromptu speech seminar, 1st place in poetry interp. (Poe's/"The Bells"), Class Vice-pres. in 8th and 11th grades Class Rep. in Tech. College, Etc.; [oth. writ.] "Crossroads", "Eager Eyes", "The Lemon Tree".. Awaiting publication; [pers.] It is my wish to dedicate this poem to my sister, Romella Dizon, and to my best friend, Toni Stark. Time after time they've been there to see me through!, "There's something to be learned from everything. For life is but a compilation of electric wisdom gained from both positive and negative experiences."

HAYDEN, BARBARA
[pen.] Brenda Deslene; [b.] November 19, 1947, Rumford, ME; [p.] Deceased Mother and Fred Hayden; [ed.] Univ. of Maine, Orona, ME, B.S.

Education English 1989, Diploma, Medical Dental office Assistant the Barton School, 1992, May Various courses; [memb.] Local association the Maine and National Association for the Mentally Ill. Eastern Star; [hon.] Dean's List; [pers.] The mental emotional struggles of mankind permit my writing I have been greatly influenced by books and poems which deal with human suffering.; [a.] Auburn, ME

HAYKO, SABRINA MARIE
[b.] April 22, 1982, Johnstown, PA; [p.] Steve Hayko, Colleen Hayko; [ed.] Eight H(+7) Grade at Brawley Middle School 1-4 Westmont Hilltop Elem. 5-6 Somerset Elem. G. Berlin Elem.; [occ.] Odd Jobs (Baby Sitter); [memb.] Students for Christian fellowship, Math counts, drama club; [hon.] Third place in American Junior High School Mathematics Examination Presidential Academic Award; [oth. writ.] One of a Kind, Men, Too Much Too Soon Too Little Chocolate, What You Held, What is Wrong, Breaking-up, Love, Secret Admire, Cheaters Never Win, Life Goes On, My Very Best Friend, First Love, Saving It, Hard-2-Get and some other poems.; [pers.] I probably never would have started writing if it wasn't for Edgar Allen Poe. When I first heard the raven I said, "hey, I can do that!" Since then I've just put my feelings into poetry.; [a.] Mooresville, NC

HAYNES, MARLA CAROLINE
[b.] December 23, 1984, Lake Charles, LA; [p.] James P and Theresa D. Haynes; [ed.] 5th grade at Greenview Elementary School; [pers.] I believe kids should go for their goals and do what they believe in. If kids have on idea, they should try it and keep on trying to accomplish their goal.; [a.] Greenville, SC

HELMICK, AMIE ELIZABETH
[b.] May 2, 1984, Winchester, VA; [p.] Joye L. Scholl, Edward E. Scholl Jr.; [ed.] Beech Tree Elem. POE Middle School; [occ.] Student at Edgar Allen POE Middle School, Annandaler VA; [memb.] Little River Soccer Club, POE Middle-School Advanced Band Clarinetist; [hon.] Little River Soccer Club Trophy 1994 - Student of the month 1991, 1992, 1993; [a.] Annandale, VA

HELMICK, KAREN
[b.] January 19, 1955, Oakland, MD; [p.] Harry and Elizabeth Sisler Sr.; [m.] William Helmick, September 14, 1974; [ch.] William, Eric and Samuel; [ed.] Kingwood High School, Monongalia Vocational School for Licensed Practical Nurses; [occ.] Nurse at valley district Medical Clinic; [pers.] I have always tried to put into poetry things that change my life or make me sad. The poem in the book is dedicated to the memory of my nephew, Bryan Michael Bolyard January 15, 1990.; [a.] Terra Alta, WV

HENDERSON, CHARLES H.
[pen.] Charles Henderson; [b.] July 3, 1919, Dayton, TN; [p.] Deceased; [m.] Deceased, 1944; [ch.] 2 Boys; [ed.] Graduated "Rhea County High" Dayton, TN; [occ.] Retired; [hon.] Honorable mention from entry in contests of poetry; [oth. writ.] For news letters at two senior centers; [pers.] Survived Polio at an early age, but go right on ticking.; [a.] Edmonds, WA

HENDERSON, SHARON
[pen.] S. M. Henderson; [b.] February 24, 1949, Syracuse, NY; [p.] John and Mary Facik; [m.] Marvin G. Henderson, March 31, 1973; [ch.] Jeffrey, Catherine, Monique, Lyle; [ed.] State University of New York at Fredonia, Syracuse University; [occ.] Free lance researcher/recent career begun in writing; [oth. writ.] False Faces, Cayman Affair, several other poems; [pers.] My poetry reflects the love I have for nature and the way it influences our lives.; [a.] Baldwinsville, NY

HENDRICK, ROSE P.
[b.] January 14, 1958, Portland, OR; [p.] Geraldine Stiefel and Jim Luper; [m.] Marty H. Hendrick, August 5, 1995; [ch.] Mandy Howarth; [ed.] Secretarial and Computer, Courses through Portland Community College; [occ.] Office Assistant; [memb.] Oregon State Defence Force; [hon.] Editor's Choice for Poem title tomorrow. Published by the National Library of Poetry; [oth. writ.] Several poems unpublished but maybe not for long, I hoping that the National Library of Poetry will published some more of my poems.; [pers.] Never give up on your dreams.

HENRY, CLARISSA
[pen.] Tish; [b.] June 28, 1980, Kremling, CO; [p.] Iris Henry and Greg Henry; [ed.] Alamosa High School, (Sophomore); [hon.] An academic award for English; [oth. writ.] I have written many poems, and short stories; [pers.] I write about most of my feelings. It allows me to feel better when I put my feelings down on paper.; [a.] Alamosa, CO

HENRY, JANET
[b.] March 23, 1955, San Mateo, CA; [p.] John and Naomi Silva; [m.] Robert Henry, September 1, 1990; [ch.] Matthew Robert; [ed.] Scottsdale High, Scottsdale Community College, Arizona State University; [occ.] Homemaker; [oth. writ.] Assortment of poetry and children's rhymes; [pers.] This poem was written in loving memory of and is dedicated to my parents John and Naomi; [a.] Scottsdale, AZ

HENSHAW, JULI
[b.] Scottsdale, AZ; [p.] Bud and Dee Henshaw; [ed.] Coronado High, Arizona State University; [occ.] Accountant, Writer; [a.] Phoenix, AZ

HENSLEY, MAGGIE G.
[pen.] Maggie Hensley; [b.] November 20, 1915, Salem, VA; [p.] William Goad, Alive Goad; [m.] Ralph Hensley, July 15, 1932; [ch.] James Franklin, Faye Cornelia; [ed.] Salem High and Business Courses; [occ.] Retired; [memb.] Locust Grove Methodist Church Council Member, Salem Educational Foundation; [hon.] Church Choir Award, Sunday School Teachers Award; [oth. writ.] Several poems Family Biography; [pers.] I strive to show love to my God and my fellow man each day. Also I love poetry and books; [a.] Salem, VA

HILL, HAZELL DOROTHEA
[b.] February 25, 1957, Mason City, Iowa; [p.] Lester Paul and Hazel Dorothea Powell Hill; [ed.] Mason City High School, North Iowa Area Community College, University of Iowa, Argonne National Laboratory, University of Minnesota; [occ.] Assistant Scientist in the Department of Medicine at the University of Minnesota; [memb.] University of Iowa Alumni Assoc., National Scoliosis Association, Calvary Alliance Church, Mason City, Iowa; [hon.] State of Iowa Scholar, Recipient of the Dr. Joseph Christopherson Memorial Scholarship, Recipient of the National March of Dimes Scholarship; [oth. writ.] Co-author on several scientific articles published in scientific journals, some short poems published in local newspaper, Editor Choice Award Poem. "Treasures of Life" published in Tear of Fire by National Library of Poetry and Editors Choice Award Poem "Twilight Reflections" published in seasons to come by the National Library of Poetry; [pers.] My poems are my attempt to place words on paper that reflect the very deep feelings that God places in my heart. I am always and forever touched by my precious family and dear friends who encourage me daily; [a.] Minneapolis, MN

HILLYARD, MARK F.
[b.] July 9, 1950, San Mateo, CA; [p.] John Hillyard, Lucile Hillyard; [ch.] Jesse Hillyard, Luke Hillyard; [ed.] Burlingame High College of San Mateo; [occ.] Kitchen Contractor; [memb.] National Rifle Assoc. Christian Writers Guild; [oth. writ.] I write political letters. That is I write to politicians and letters to the editor. I also have an exhortation ministry, I write.; [pers.] I rise every morning, turn on my Bible and begin searching for hidden treasures. What I am the writer produced.; [a.] Half Moon Bay, CA

HIRSCH, ELIZABETH C.
[pen.] Beth Hirsch; [b.] December 16, 1980, New Thampton, IA; [p.] Kevin and Lori Hirsch; [ed.] I have not yet completed high school since I am only fifteen; [occ.] A full-time high school student; [oth. writ.] I was published in the fall 1990 Poetic voices of America by Sparrow grass poetry forum Inc.; [pers.] Since every day could be your last. Think how would I want to spend my last day if I knew when it would be. In other words party.; [a.] Waucoma, IA

HITCHCOCK, LAURIE A.
[pen.] Laurie Mackey Hitchcock; [b.] April 23, 1964, Pittsfield, MA; [p.] Ronald A. Mackey, Barbara LaGrant; [m.] David E. Hitchcock, August 25, 1984; [ch.] David Jr., Ryan William, James Michael; [ed.] Lee High School, Institute of Childrens Literature; [occ.] Homemaker, schoolbus driver; [memb.] St. Mary's Catholic Church; [pers.] Children are my inspiration.; [a.] Lee, MA

HOAG, LEONARD J.
[b.] October 6, 1922, Hudson Falls, NY; [p.] (both deceased) H. Francis and Alam (LaBarge) Hoag; [m.] Ilene Janet (Major) Hoag, November 29, 1952; [ch.] Theresa Lozo, Janice and Erika Hoag, 4 grandchildren: Suzanne and Allyson Lozo, Zackary and Jeremy Hoag; [ed.] High School grad - 1940; [occ.] Retired Machinist from GE Hudson Falls, NY with 30 yrs service. Am now a dispatcher with trucking outfit; [memb.] St. Michael the Archangel Church, So Glens Falls, NY, Ushers Assn, Eucharistic Minister, Knights of Columbus, American Legion, AARP, Fort Edward Minstrels and Town of Moreau Fun Band. We entertain patients at Nursing Homes and also Senior Citizen Clubs; WWII Vet US Navy 10/29/42-3/11/46. Flight mechanic in PBY Squadron covering convoys. We kept German U Boats from molesting and sinking our shipping en route to Europe. Honorable Discharge; [oth. writ.] "Their Morning Prayer in At Day's End. This poem, "My Ilene," is dedicated to my wife of 42 years.; [a.] So. Glens Falls, NY

HODOVANIC, SUZANNE
[b.] August 21, 1980, Parma, OH; [p.] John Jr. and Patricia Hodovanic; [m.] June 30, 1979; [ch.] Sally Ann; [ed.] Green Valley Elementary School, Brecksville Middle School and Brecksville High School; [occ.] Student in 9th grade of Brecksville High; [memb.] None at this time; [oth. writ.] Homer's House, 13-an Unlucky Number, Bobby's Zoo, (books) Pretty poems and many other poems, Artoa (play), and many others; [pers.] God only knows what lies ahead of me. People only hope what lies ahead of me is well worth it. I only wish what lies ahead of me is a dream come true.; [a.] Broadview Heights, OH

HOFFMAN, BARBARA
[b.] November 21, 1942, Queens, NY; [p.] Madeline Spera and Hans Baas; [ch.] Judith - David - Brandon; [ed.] Dominican Commercial High School; [occ.] Vice President Gold Coin Laundry Equipment, Inc.; [memb.] Kiwanis Club of Richmond Hill-Kew-Forest; [oth. writ.] Several other poems; [pers.] My inspiration comes from my personal experience with the up and down roller coaster ride of life; [a.] North Valley Stream, NY

HOFFMAN, MARSHA ANNE
[b.] May 29, 1951, Nogales, AZ; [p.] Sally Holding, Hubert Holding; [m.] Divorced; [ed.] Nogales High School 2 years College; [occ.] Magician, Illusionist, Comic for parties, special events grand openings; [hon.] I have had a certificate of appreciation for performing magical, Illusions at a trade show. I also have had a couple of single records produced with my name on the label. I wrote the lyrics; [oth. writ.] "Love's gonna catch you" "Love's knocking on my door", which were made into single records in 1970. My picture and story came out in the local paper.; [pers.] I enjoy making people happy, and that's one reason I am a magician, illusionist, and sometimes comic. I also enjoy writing poetry, song lyrics because this relaxes me and makes my day. Hopefully my songs will be recorded by a famous singer, someday.; [a.] Goodard, KS

HOLLAND, MATTHEW THOMAS
[b.] July 29, 1967, Encino, CA; [m.] Maggie Holland; [pers.] There has been many great men and women throughout history that have written or spoken words that are still as enlightening as the day they wrote or spoke them. I could go on and on with quotes and written words of wisdom that bring tears to my eyes but they are only words and they don't mean much if we don't apply them.; [a.] Westlake Village, CA

HOLLAND, N. ELIZABETH
[b.] July 13, 1940, Talladeca, AL; [p.] Myrtle Holland, Jim Holland; [ed.] Anniston High School, Stephens College, Rhodes College, Univ. of Tenn. School of Medicine; [occ.] Physician Licensed Minister Assembly of God Mission Field 1983-1990; [memb.] Shelby County, Tenn, and American Medical Association, National Right to Life, World Wildlife Fund, Board Member-Life Choices, Tenn. Citizens concerned for life, Teen Challenge; [hon.]

Memphis "Volunteer of the Year 1993", DAR Medal of Honor 1994; [oth. writ.] "I am a we" - poem, A Doctor Looks at BSF poem, Godly Parenting book published 1995, Fingerprint of Value - booklet, The Puzzle - booklet; [pers.] It is my desire to help people to know themselves better, and to reach their full potential because of their relationship with God.; [a.] Memphis, TN

HOLLENBERGER, STACEY
[b.] September 3, 1977, Pompano Beach, FL; [p.] John and Marcia Hollenberger; [ed.] Ashville High School, Ashville, NC Currently a Freshman at Auburn University, Auburn, AL; [memb.] The Literary Council; [hon.] The Amy, Charles Writing Award for short fiction. First place prose in 1995 in a sense literary magazine.; [oth. writ.] Several poems published in a sense Literary Magazine and on short story in North Carolina English Teacher; [a.] Montgomery, AL

HOLMES, LESLIE
[b.] November 26, 1980, Plano, TX; [p.] Steve and Fredda Holmes; [occ.] High School Student; [memb.] National Jr. Honor Society The Colony High School Band; [a.] Carrollton, TX

HOLT, JUDITH F.
[pen.] Judith F. Holt; [b.] November 6, 1941, Birmingham, AL; [p.] Herdman and Eunice Carver; [m.] Jerry D. Holt, Sr., December 2, 1961; [ch.] Don, Jr., Kevin, Gail, Karen, Tim, Lisha, and Corey; [ed.] Jones Valley High School, Albright Business College; [occ.] Homemaker; [memb.] The Church of Jesus Christ of Latter-day Saints, The Shelby County Historical Society; [oth. writ.] I have written numerous poems, children's short stories, essays, and songs. I'm currently preparing to do a family history and genealogy book of which I am very excited.; [pers.] What I write, is inspired by God and comes to my mind as if appearing on a screen. My life has been influenced by God and any talents or gifts has been a blessing bestowed upon me by Him. "My help cometh from the Lord, which made heaven and earth." Ps 121.2.; [a.] Hephzibah, GA

HONECK, JOHN
[b.] December 30, 1964, Milwaukee; [p.] James and Charlotte Honeck; [ch.] Erica; [ed.] Brookfield Central H.S., Waukeshia County Technical College, U.W. Milwaukee, U.W. Fond Du Lac; [hon.] Sophomore Honors at U.W. Milwaukee; [pers.] Peace.; [a.] Brookfield, WI

HONEYCUTT, SERENA LOUISA BANKS
[pen.] Louise Banks; [b.] September 15, 1949, Little Rock, AR; [p.] Anderson Owens and Rosia Meeks Banks; [ch.] Rose-Helen Louise, Robert Edward and Robynne Anderlisa Honeycutt; [ed.] Horace Mann High, Philander Smith College, Southern Methodist University; [occ.] Resource/special Education Teacher, C.S. Winn Classic Academy Dallas (Hutchins) TX; [memb.] Zeta Phi Beta, Sorority, Inc. Texas Federation of Teachers/AFT, Association of Texas Professional Educators, National Educational Association and Texas State Teachers Association; [oth. writ.] There are many soon to be published; [pers.] I write about real subjects, real people what's happening now!; [a.] Cedar Hill, TX

HOOFNAGLE, A. NORBERT
[b.] November 28, 1973, Chestnut Hill, PA; [p.] John and Marion Hoofnagle; [ed.] B.S. in Biology from Cornell University in Ithaca, NY; [occ.] Research Fellow; [memb.] Hoofnagle Family Tree, Cornell Sailing Alumni; [pers.] There's one thing missing from this world and I'm trying to replace it, it has everything to do with love, but even more to do with crying.; [a.] Washington, DC

HOOKS, STEVEN M.
[b.] August 9, 1974, New Brighton, PA; [p.] Michael E. Hooks and Linda G. Hooks; [ed.] I am presently Attending Slippery Rock University. New Brighton High; [occ.] Student; [hon.] Many awards in swimming several honors in Baseball; [pers.] My poems are mostly influenced by God with his creation of nature.; [a.] New Brighton, PA

HOOLDRIDGE, JACQUELINE H.
[ch.] 2; [ed.] Susan M. Dorsey High School, Los Angeles, California, graduated June 19, 1971; [memb.] Unity Christian Center; [oth. writ.] Several Poems written in High School and also Computer School. "Lover's Who Are Now Strangers"; [pers.] I was blessed by the Lord and the age to 5 to write poems coming from my heart, my mind and my soul spiritually. As I mature over the years. I was even blessed more to write: Love, children, short stories, prayers personal, marriage, peoples, relationship that are in trouble and marriage vows over to Jesus Christ our Lord and Savior Thank you Jesus all praises due to your love and eternity. I also give personal thanks to my mother Lillian M. Hooldridge and a personal close friend Mr. Michael A. Gibson; [a.] Riverside, CA

HOOVER, PEGGY L.
[b.] April 29, 1952, Dayton, OH; [p.] Fred and Dorothy Gibson; [m.] Dennis L. Hoover, June 30, 1990; [ch.] Ginger Ann Tony Alan; [ed.] Hillsborough High School St. Petersburg Jr. College Florida State University University of Tampa; [occ.] Registered Nurse; [memb.] Society of Urologic Nurses and Associates Urology Section Affiliate of the American Academy of Pediatrics National Association of Physician Nurses United States Amateur Ballroom Dancers Assoc., Inc.; [oth. writ.] Poem published in the local newspaper. Poem published in the poems: Anthology; [pers.] Writing is my personal expression of where my life journey has taken me and it unfolds as my journey continues. I have a sincere interest in writing from the voice of my Cherokee heritage. I see the potential for that to evolve in the future.; [a.] Lutz, FL

HOPE, ELEANOR GOLDING
[pen.] Amber Lace; [b.] August 20, 1944, Surrey County, NC; [p.] Grace Fulk Golding and Lewis G. (Deceased); [m.] Divorced; [ch.] Stephen Hope and Nicole Hope Murray; [ed.] Northwest H.S. Winston Salem N.C., Winston Salem School of Vocational Nursing N.C.; [occ.] Nurse; [memb.] Walnut Manor Poetry Club Hobby-Oil Painting Poetry Writing; [oth. writ.] Several other poems; [pers.] You can become anything you dream you can be.; [a.] Laguna Niguel, CA

HORN, CHRISTINA
[b.] May 11, 1981, Santa Barbara, CA; [p.] Bob and Alma Horn; [ed.] I'm in the 8th Grade; [pers.] I

thank the good Lord my grandmother Zaragoza and my mother for encouraging me.; [a.] Santa Barbara, CA

HORNER, MARGARET FOSS
[pen.] Marg; [h] January 26, 1955, Portland, ME; [p.] Jane Higgins Hoy; [m.] Divorced; [ed.] Sahuaro High, Northern Arizona University; [occ.] Electronics Assembly Technician; [memb.] Church of Scientology International Association of Scientologists; [pers.] "A culture is only as great as its dreams, and its dreams are dreamed by artists." L. Ron Hubbard; [a.] Hollywood, CA

HORVATH, MARY KATHERINE DAVES MOOTZ
[b.] January 4, 1929, Sturges, MI; [p.] Willard W., Margaret N., Fee, Davis; [m.] Twice widowed - Gilbert J. Mootz, July 14, 1954, Paul J. Horvath, November 7, 1981; [ch.] Gilbert L., Kathy M., William R., Angela H., Anthony L.; [ed.] Colon, Mt High Lafayette, Academy, Rhode, Island for Medical Receptionist office assistant. Cerefeed Medical Aid, in service study at meller's merry manor, nursing home, La Grance, Ind; [occ.] Retired; [memb.] Community Mental Health, Club House. Holy Angel's, Catholic Church; [hon.] I feel very honored to be selected for my poem to be published in the rainbow's end book. Thank you; [oth. writ.] A lot of poems. These the first one to be published.; [pers.] My concern is expressing God's love to humanity.; [a.] Sturges, MI

HOSKINS, VERNIE ELIZABETH
[b.] January 8, 1947, Pequot Lakes, MN; [p.] Walter Wermter and Grace Wermter; [m.] Thomas Allen Hoskins, September 26, 1964; [ch.] Tammy, John, Thomas, William, Verna, Luther, Gussie, Elizabeth; [ed.] Baxter Elementary, Brainerd Public Schools; [occ.] Homemaker; [hon.] Riverside Elementary School guest reader, Blue Bear Children Series; [oth. writ.] Blue Bear Children Series, Several poems, song lyrics, Short stories; [pers.] I strive to reach people's hearts in my writing, every body's somebody, good or bad from all walks of life waiting to be heard.; [a.] Brainerd, MN

HOUSTON, JESSICA
[b.] December 11, 1980, Charlotte, NC; [p.] Bobby Houston, Patsy Houston; [ed.] Currently a nineth grade student at Alexander Middle School, in Huntersville, NC; [memb.] Hopewell Pres. Church in Huntersville, National Junior Honors Society; [oth. writ.] All my other poems are in a notebook at my home. This is the first piece I've entered in any kind of contest.; [pers.] I do not write for fame, I do not write for money. I write for the release and love of writing, and all I seek is respect and all I strive to do is to open another's imagination and creative eyes.; [a.] Huntersville, NC

HOWELL, EVELYN M.
[pen.] Evelyn M. Howell; [b.] October 1, 1917, Newton, NJ; [p.] William S. and Almeda B. Howell; [m.] George Richards, February 18, 1939; [ch.] Marcia, Thelma and Rebecca; [ed.] Newton High School, Retiree of the Procurement Directorate of Picatinny Arsenal, Dover, NJ; [occ.] Nurse's Assistant and Retirement; [memb.] Delaware Br of OES NY. United Methodist Church of Hever Spring's, AR, AARP and NARFE; [oth. writ.] Poems

published in local news papers and one in "Our World's Most Treasured Poetry", world poetry press; [pers.] My poems reflect wild beauty, world problems and items of general concern of the times.; [a.] Heber Springs, AR

HOWSAM, MELISSA ANNE
[b.] September 7, 1977, Atalanta, GA; [p.] Jeff and Cindy Howsam; [ed.] Student at NC State University; [occ.] Student, work part-time as an administrative assistant; [hon.] Graduated high school with honors; [pers.] Behind every shadow, there is a speck of light small, or big, find that light, and use it to guide you.; [a.] Raleigh, NC

HUBBELL, PHYLLIS M.
[b.] December 1, 1951, Bloomington, IL; [p.] Harold and Mary Rea; [m.] L. David Hubbell, May 23, 1971; [ch.] Joshua David; [ed.] Labette County High School, Labette Community College; [occ.] Clerk, Chetopa Implement Co., Chetopa, KS; [memb.] Dennis United Methodist Church, Denis, KS, Church Pianist Chetopa Little League; [hon.] One of two valedictorians, Class of 1971, LCC, Childhood trophies for accordion solos, Mid-American Music Contests in several states; [oth. writ.] Poems for church service, none published publicly; [pers.] He that has the son has life. In the world, but not of it, being conformed to his image, my favorite scripture is Isaiah 26:3 and 4 KJV.; [a.] Chetopa, KS

HUDDLESTON, KONI
[pen.] Koni; [b.] December 18, 1964; [ed.] CST-U.S. Air Force Eastern Washington University; [occ.] CST; [pers.] In my poetry and essays I try to explore the intensity of human emotion, as well as what I believe to be, the innate desires that posses us all.; [a.] Spokane, WA

HUDSON, MARIA CHANTELL
[pen.] Chantell Hudson; [b.] April 15, 1970, Carmichael; [p.] Earl and Kathy Gellerman; [ed.] 3 years in College; [occ.] Fulltime student; [memb.] Phi Theta Kappa (honor Club); [hon.] I'm on the deans list; [pers.] In order to understand me you'd first have to understand my writing; [a.] Reno, NV

HUDSON, PATRICIA K.
[pen.] P. K. Hudson; [b.] April 4, 1960, Garden City, MI; [occ.] Finance dept of a advertising agency; [oth. writ.] I have had nothing published just my own personal file a writings

HUDSON, SHARON L.
[pen.] Sharon L. Hudson; [b.] May 17, 1951, New Albany, MS; [p.] James Boyce Potts and Mattie Frances Potts; [m.] Danny Jeroll Hudson, January 15, 1978; [ch.] Keith, Brittanni, Bridgette, Karmyn and Krystal; [ed.] East Aurora High School, Aurora, IL 60505; [occ.] Housewife, Writer, Songwriter; [hon.] 1 Honorable Mentions for poetry - '85, '88, Golden Poet of year Awards for 1985, 1986, 1987, 1988, one silver poet of year award for 1990, won 1st place song contest/award '87, 2nd place song contest award for '88 Editor's choice award '95, and a royal proclamation award in December, '94 for outstanding good deeds. Done.; [oth. writ.] Several published in newspapers, The amer. writers magazine, Our Western World's most beautiful poems, new Am. Poetry Anthology, The Golden Treasy of Great poems, poems that will live forever,

chasing rainbows, poetic symphony, N. AM's. Best loved poems, poetry at its best treasured poems of am. Poetic voice of America, Best poems of '95, Best Poems '96, treasured Poems of America '96, Audio Tape of Best Poems '95; [pers.] I try to remember and live by the rule: "When we truly forgive, we truly forget-without any bitterness, hurt or regret, then when we are wrong, God will avenge the strong and gather his sheep, at the foot of his throne.

HUFFORD, JOSEPH M.
[p.] Ross and Cynthia Hufford; [m.] Kim M. Wilson; [ch.] Kayla D. Wilson and Jordan M. Hufford; [occ.] Action Steel Supply, Indianapolis Reid Litwick and Tim prather take care of me and my family; [oth. writ.] For you to find out...maybe; [pers.] Hard work builds character.; [a.] Indianapolis, IN

HUGHES, HARRIET PAULINE
[pen.] Harriet Pauline Hughes; [b.] Germantown, PA; [p.] Pauline Angela Smith, Harry Martin Hughes; [ed.] Germantown High College High, with Latin and Greek Scholarship to Phila. College of Art, graduated Illustration. Taught Accounting by CPA father attended painting work shops in Philadelphia Museum of art, Exhibit in Bryn Maur, in Philadelphia Bread and Chestnut at Prov. Not. BK- and 19th a Hamilton at IFE Imperial.; [memb.] Bryn Mauer Presbyterian Church American Friends Service Committee Alumna Phila College of Art and Design Friend of Bryn Maur College Library. Free Library of Phila-Archivist Member Phila Museum of Art/ Smithsonian Assoc. National Sierra Club, Children's Hosp. of Phila Foundation Iankenaw Hospital Foundation Presbyterian Med. Center foundation Montgomery county SPCA Phila Zoological Society Nat. wild life federation guardian of the wild tower meran twp. Police pensiean Asso.; [hon.] Articles and letters in news papers articles in ITE Imperial publications Short Stories poem titles The Sea's Courtship of the Earth, "A Rainbow I Was Their Wedding Ring", Two Weeks of Eden, Bay of Naples La Bella La Bella, Of Men and Horses be Cautious, To A Soldier Overseas; [oth. writ.] UBH is poet free lance painted of flera fauna, people places favorite poets Keats, Favorite painter, Monet Favorite philosopher. Photo Peacemaker, I love people and many creatures with fins, wings, and four legs.; [pers.] Wynnewood, PA

HUGHES, LAURA
[b.] September 7, 1982, Buffalo, NY; [p.] Donald Hughes, Toni Hughes; [ed.] I am an 8th grader at Penn Cambria Middle School; [occ.] I hope to be a lawyer or a journalist; [memb.] I am a member of the AYF Youth Fellowship at the Cresson Christian missionary alliance church, I'm in Forensics and Choirs; [hon.] I have trophies in cheer leading and karate I have a creative writing award from New York. I have high honors in Math and Science at my current school.; [oth. writ.] I have won 2nd place creative writing contest at my school. I have had a poem published in my school news paper and in my church bulletin; [pers.] Find the hidden talent you have with-in you. Strive for excellence. But don't be discouraged if you don't be it because only God can be perfect!; [a.] Cresson, PA

HUGHES, LORA D.
[b.] February 22, 1950, Raleigh, NC; [p.] Josephine and Ernest Dickinson; [m.] Chuck, February 24, 1976; [ch.] Tammy and Scott; [ed.] High School Diploma Nursing Aid, Diploma, Master Life Diploma, Christian Development Diploma; [occ.] Middle River Baptist Church prepare family night dinners (minister to shut); [memb.] Middle River Baptist Church teacher adult 6 class C.O.P.S. V.W.V. American cancer research, Angel Tree Ministries; [hon.] Scholarship Cosmetology; [pers.] My poems are inspired by the Lord and intended for encouragement and guidance which is needed in these days.; [a.] Baltimore, MD

HULSE, KHRISTINA MICHELLE
[pen.] Khristie; [b.] February 27, 1978, Indianapolis, IN; [p.] Chuck Hulse and Beverly Thornburg; [ed.] Senior at Ben Davis High School; [occ.] Part-time at Meiger; [memb.] Chapel Rock, Christian Church; [hon.] I'm very honored to be published in The Rainbow's End, Art awards from 9th-12th grades; [oth. writ.] "Discriminating: I'm not having it" published in school newspaper (essay); [pers.] I hope that one day my poetry will help another with his/her problems.; [a.] Indianapolis, IN

HUNG, SHARON
[b.] April 12, 1952, Lowell, MA; [p.] John Mary Quigley; [m.] Dominic Hung, August 12, 1974; [ch.] Tammy J. Hung; [ed.] G.E.D. Graduate, Certified Preschool Teacher College. Hessier, Wheelocc University Systems.; [occ.] File Clerk in Printing Corporation; [hon.] Community teamwork lowell, Mass. awarded me for my excellence in my work as a day care provider in my home 1985; [oth. writ.] Working on a book of my own life, because I was a foster child, since the age of two until I was 16 1/2 years old.; [pers.] I have found myself through my writings, and feel if one tries hard enough nothing is impossible.; [a.] Manchester, NH

HURLEY, MICHAEL J.
[b.] September 5, 1975; [p.] John F. and Sharon L. Hurley; [occ.] Student; [pers.] I have been greatly influenced by the modernist period of American literature, writers such as T.S. Elliot, Robert Frost, Kate Chopin and F. Scott Fitzgerald in particular have made an impression on me. I write for three reasons: one, because I have to, two, because I like to, and three, because I to force people to face things they normally try to ignore. Life is the journey, death is the adventure.; [a.] Brainerd, MN

HURST, DEREK J.
[b.] November 15, 1959, San Diego, CA; [p.] Andrew J. Hurst and Margaret M. Hurst; [m.] Roseanne, January 4, 1988; [ed.] Received a Bachelor of Arts Rice University, Houston, Texas

IGAH, KATHERINE ADANNA
[pen.] Katie or Ada or Ad; [b.] January 24, 1983, Dayton, OH; [p.] Frank M. Igah and Flora Offiah-Igah; [ed.] Seventh Grade Honor Roll Student at Corpus Christi Elementary School, Dayton, OH; [occ.] The American Red Cross Association (baby sitting) Dayton Chapter; [memb.] Corpus Christi Volley Ball Team, Corpus Christi Recreation Center, Chorpus Christi Basketball Team, City of Dayton Swim Team (Dabney Pool) Corpus Christi School Patrol Team, Corpus Christi Parish Choir; [hon.]

Honor Roll Student (Academic) (1 and 2 place Awards - Tournaments) Martial Arts (tang Soo Doo Karate) Volley Ball Team Awards, City of Dayton's Swim Team Awards, Gelsel's Piano Music Honors Corpus Christi (CYO) Catholic Youth Organization League, Corpus Christi Creative Arts Awards, National Library of Poetry Honors; [oth. writ.] I have a great interest in Literature focusing on poetry. I have written several poems as my personal collection. However, the poem, Paradise, is the first and only poem that I sent in for contest.; [pers.] I feel honored to be selected as one of the best poem writers for this entry. I was surprised and shocked when I first read the news. My first reaction was to run to my Mom to share the wonderful news. Then I called my dad at work. We were all extremely happy and praised God. True and honest work can open a lot of doors.; [a.] Dayton, OH

INGLE, BRETT J.
[b.] March 27, 1973, Lander, NY; [p.] Don and Rosemary Ingle; [ed.] Sturgis Brown High School, Western Dakota Technical Institute; [occ.] Cabinet Maker; [memb.] National Home Builders Association. Black Hills Home Builders.; [hon.] National Defense Service Medal; [oth. writ.] Published cartoon in great lakes bulletin, 31 Oct. 1992; [pers.] Honesty is an important quality for a poet. Anybody can rhyme a few words and call it a poem. Putting your heart on the page is what makes a poem special.; [a.] Sturgis, SD

ISBITSKI, ESTELLE
[b.] February 13, 1946, New Brunswick, NJ; [p.] Alan F. and Doris E. Gardner; [m.] John P. Isbitski, December 4, 1965; [ch.] David, Michael; [ed.] Edison Township, High School, Edison, NJ, Ocean County College, Toms River, NJ; [occ.] Legal Assistant; [memb.] Ocean County, College Paralegal Assoc., Ocean County College, Advisory Board; [hon.] Phi Thetta Kappa, Dean list, National Honor Society; [oth. writ.] Published in Edge Of Twilight, best of poem 1995; [pers.] To write relates one soul to many bringing one's passion to crest in artistry viewed by all.; [a.] Toms River, NJ

JACKSON, ESTELLE GIFFORD
[b.] August 12, 1932, Long Beach, MS; [p.] Walter and Cora Gifford; [m.] Bradford J. Jackson, my constant source of encouragement, December 16, 1951; [ed.] Long Beach High School, MS, University of Southern Mississippi; [occ.] Currently working on other books, and enjoying my 15 grandchildren, 10 of whom live next door!; [memb.] Bible Teacher, Jubilee House of Prayer (Baptist). Retired from 25 years Government service, including 16 years as Writer and Editor of Speeches, Astronaut Office, Johnson Space Center, TX and 5 years Office of the Chief Scientist, Air Force Missile Development Center, NM; [hon.] Sustained Superior Performance Award, Astronaut Office, NASA. Sustained Superior Performance Award, Office of the Chief Scientist, Air Force Missile Development Center, NM; [oth. writ.] Two Books: "The Eagle Has landed" (a poetic history of Americans on the moon), and "Not As The World Giveth" (the story of Jesus in poetry), Evangelist Leonard Ravenhill on his books, and authored the title poem published in his book, "Revival God's Way"; [pers.] The Holy Bible is my main source of inspiration: "Faith, hope, and love, these three, but the greatest of these is love."

Love for God, family, and all mankind, with a prayer that our Nation and the world may experience a true spiritual awakening and return to Biblical principles.; [a.] Webster, TX

JOB, DEBORAH QUINTANA
[b.] March 27, 1953, Pueblo, CO; [p.] Della and Gilber Quintana; [m.] Juan Roberto Job; [ch.] Elina Martinez, Dominica, Adrian and Maritza Job; [occ.] Business Woman; [oth. writ.] Is currently translating a collection of her own Spanish poems and hopes to publish them in both English and Spanish. They seem to have an Erotic flavor to them. She has written for over 20 years, up to now has never submitted or shared poems publicly; [pers.] I feel like a gypsy in disguise who has fallen out of the pages of a romantic novel and that is a tough feeling to have going into the 21st century and very much a part of the business world. That feeling may very well steer my risk taking ability. My greatest challenge is breaking away to write, something I enjoy with a passion and am anxious to share with the public in the next few years.; [a.] Aurora, CO

JOHNSON, CLAYTON A.
[b.] August 3, 1928, Newport, TN; [p.] Henderson and Bertha Johnson; [m.] Ophelia Pope Johnson; [ch.] Jeanne' Christ, Ronald A. Johnson (deceased), Leanna Nalley and Deanna Marsh (ident. twins), (st. ch.) Kay Michelson and Janice Giles, 10 gr. ch.; [ed.] Cocke County High School, Walter State Jr. College, various military courses and training programs; [occ.] Ret. Navy 1973, Seaman Recruit to Lieutenant Commander; [oth. writ.] Readers Digest anes., news stories and poems in Navy Pub. and daily column in Newport Banner after ret.; [pers.] Heeding advice to live each day as if it were my last, but to prepare to live forever, goals have been set in most areas of my life which extend far beyond normal life expectancy.; [a.] Marietta, GA

JOHNSON, DANA R. PICKETT
[b.] October 26, 1956, Annapolis, MD; [p.] John and Emma Pickett; [m.] John F. Johnson Sr.; [ed.] Annapolis Sr. High, Towson State University; [memb.] Mt. Moriah A.M.E. Church, Naptowne Sea and Ski Club; [oth. writ.] Wrote several plays: "Awake With Praise", The Hat Maker"; [a.] Pasadena, MD

JONES, MARGARET E.
[b.] September 24, 1958, Manhatten, NY; [m.] Richard I. Stewart, October 12, 1991; [ed.] Frank Cox High School, VA BCH, VA - Warren Wilson College, Swannanoa, NC; [occ.] Paralegal Advocate with Pisgah Legal Services; [hon.] Nominated - Outstanding Young Woman of 1985. Chosen Outstanding Paralegal of the Year 1994; [oth. writ.] Written more than 200 unpublished poems. Article in local newspaper.; [pers.] My Poetry is an expression of my heart and soul.; [a.] Asheville, NC

JONES, MATTHEW
[pen.] J.C. Matthews; [b.] November 17, 1975, Garden Grove, CA; [p.] Jerry and Nelle Jones; [m.] Elizabeth S. Jones, August 5, 1995; [ch.] Christina Nesbitt; [ed.] Kingman High School; [occ.] Retail Clerk, Mervyns; [memb.] Maranatha Chapel; [oth. writ.] Willow Princess, Snow Queen, Plain Tea, The Jellybean Whip, Grace, Vision, A Voice Unheard, and many more; [pers.] I thank the greatest poet,

God, who made me one of His poems, whose writings and creations made the world and everything in it. We are Jesus' poems written on parchment across the sky.; [a.] San Diego, CA

JONES, NEISHA L.
[b.] January 7, 1973, Jamaica, NY; [p.] Phyllis Bennett; [ed.] Rincon High, Betty Owens Business School, Universal Temple of Love, Peace and Joy; [occ.] Robert Plan Insurance Co.; [memb.] Sweet rest Baptist Church, Pres., H.T.C. Gospel Ensemble; [oth. writ.] What are we doing in God's house, it shall be done (gospel plays produced off-Broadway) Poems - Why Me?, Don't Give up!, Jesus Is The Answer!; [pers.] My hope is that God continues to use me as an instrument of his grace and peace. Perhaps my writings will inspire someone to "Endure through the night", knowing that "Joy cometh in the Morning."; [a.] Jamaica, NY

JONES, NICOLE RENEE
[b.] March 22, 1982, San Antonio, TX; [p.] Frederick and Sandra Jones; [occ.] Junior High Student; [pers.] I thank God for blessing me with the talent to write poems.

JONES, ROBERT
[b.] September 6, 1974, Colorado Springs, CO; [p.] John and Jody Jones; [ed.] Graduated from William Howard Taft High School in 1992. Am working toward a degree in Social Science and Secondary ED; [occ.] Student, Cook; [memb.] Boy Scouts - University Programming Council - Newman Center; [hon.] Eagle Scout - Letter in Band, Track, Member of the all superior marching and concert band in Ocean Springs MS; [oth. writ.] Nothing published; [pers.] You are only young once, but where is that point when you stop being young; [a.] Aberdeen, SD

JONES, ROBERT W.
[b.] October 8, 1951, Binghamton, NY; [m.] Catherine J. Jones, December 15, 1973; [ch.] Becky, Wendy, Tommy; [occ.] Painting Contractor

JONES, ROBERTA HADAWAY
[b.] January 20, 1942, Marion Co., TN; [p.] Izella W. Hadaway, James Fousen Hadaway; [m.] Deceased; [ch.] Marcia, Diane, Kimberly Marshall; [ed.] 9th Grade - G.E.D, Licensing Board Of Nursing Nashville, TN, Licensed Practical Nurse; [occ.] Clinic Office Nurse; [oth. writ.] A diary of poems unseen by anyone other than family and close friends; [pers.] My writing is a way of expressing my inner most feelings.; [a.] Sequatchie, TN

JONES, SHERRY L.
[b.] April 24, 1951, Amesbury, MA; [p.] James and Sylvia Clark; [m.] W. Scott Jones, Jr., May 2, 1969; [ch.] Jeffrey, Timothy, April, and Julie (I have one grandson, Johnathan); [ed.] Graduate Pentucket Regional High School West Newbury, MA; [occ.] Account Manager and Office Manager for Son's Martial Arts School; [oth. writ.] Unpublished book (Romance) and assorted poems; [pers.] Cherish every moment, it will never come again. Live your life as "I did", not as "I wish I had."; [a.] Haverhill, MA

JONES, VIOLA E.
[b.] June 19, 1924, Cleveland, OH; [p.] Deceased; [m.] Deceased; [ch.] Jeanette D. Brown; [ed.] High

School Education; [pers.] I was born and raised in Cleveland, Ohio I had a beautiful marriage to me my husband will always be with me. I am just a simple person with a daughter whom I love dearly. I love helping other people.; [a.] Cleveland, OH

JORAM JR., PHILIP R.
[b.] April 30, 1925, Longview, TX; [p.] Philip Joram Sr., Lillian Joram; [m.] Helen Phillips Joram, November 22, 1952; [ch.] Ellen, Michael, Mark, Joni, Robbie; [ed.] Catholic University of America; [occ.] Retired; [oth. writ.] Five Technical Papers published in five Technical Journals; [pers.] "There's no heavier burden than a great potential"; [a.] Washington, DC

JORDAN, SHARON
[b.] December 21, 1956, Los Angeles; [p.] Wayne and Allene Williams; [m.] Mark Jordan; [ch.] Eric, Janna, Jessica; [ed.] Bell Gardens High Occupational School of Riverside - Medical Assistant, Medical Terminology; [occ.] Medical Assistant; [a.] Moreno Valley, CA

JORDAN, THOMASINA ELIZABETH
[pen.] "Red Hawk Woman"; [p.] Deceased since my early childhood; [m.] D. Wendell Jordan; [ch.] Andy And Tracy; [ed.] B.F.A. M.F.A.M.A. Bishop Lee College American Academy of Dramatic Arts grad. Harvard University, Catholic University of America, MBR Electorol Collage; [occ.] Co-Chr. (Nationally) American Indian Alliance, Co-Chr (Nationally) American Indian Cultural Exchange, Vice chr - American Indian Forum; [memb.] Capital Speakers Club, Va. Native America Cultural, (Past pres. Chapter I) Currently secy of the Government Board - Center (Received Outstanding Contribute Award), Welcome to Washington, Women of Washington, National Rehabilitation Hospital, Washington and Ball, Salvation Army, American Cancer Society Electoral College; [hon.] Nat'l Society Daughters of the American Revolution (Medal of Honor), Highest Award, Outstanding American, Strategic Defense Command (Outstanding Community Service) Save the Children, Outstanding Award for Community Service), Urban League Award - Outstanding Community Service), White House Conf. O Indian Educ. Award - Natro (Native American Treating Rights Org.) Outstanding Indian Woman etc., City of Alexandria (outstanding Citizen Award Nat'l Thespian Society; [oth. writ.] Invocation, God's Companion Replica, Soaring like identity eagles, etc.; [pers.] We are all connected. If we are to truly soar like eagles we must keep this thought in mind - The mighty eagles cannot fly with just a left or a right wing. The eagle needs both wings, just as we all need each other.; [a.] Alexandria, VA

JOSEPHIAC, JAMES R.
[pen.] Jim Josephiac; [b.] February 5, 1954, Brookline, MA; [p.] James F. Josephiac, Mary R. Josephiac; [m.] Jo Stepien Josephiac, September 18, 1976; [ch.] Jaime Ann, Jessica Marie and Jason John; [ed.] Stafford High School, Central Connecticut State University; [occ.] Manufacturing Management and Advertising Company Owner; [memb.] Various Business and Political Organizations; [hon.] Award from Poetry Editor Eddie-Lou Cole. Many Art and Music Awards. Performed with Young Americans In Concert in Europe and Carnegie Hall in New York City; [oth. writ.] A

Somber mood poem. Published in the world of Poetry Anthology. Many other unpublished poems.; [pers.] I love realism and to create a question and a mystic in my poems to keep my readers thinking and wondering.; [a.] Ellington, CT

JOSEPHSON, MARK
[b.] February 17, 1968, Queens, NY; [p.] Joseph and Patricia Josephson; [m.] Rocio Josephson, September 3, 1990; [ch.] Rose Elizabeth; [ed.] G.E.D. and 5th Elementary in the Italian language, equal to an American G.E.D.; [occ.] Poet, Song Writer; [hon.] The Honor of being accepted to the National Library of Poetry's Anthology (The Rainbows End); [oth. writ.] I have over 220 other writings, including: In The Mists Of The Morning Dawn, Disappearing Footsteps, Old Glory Blue, which can be found (I hope) in my II Volume Book the Sacred Scroll's of a wasted life (not yet published); [pers.] The love of a family is like a rose, it need love and care before it can blum.; [a.] Chino Valley, AZ

KABBA, SAIDU
[pen.] Bankafly; [b.] March 24, 1971, Freetown, Sierra Leone; [p.] Alie Kabba, Aminata Kabba; [ed.] Saint George's Cathedral, Government Secondary Technical School; [occ.] Certified Nursing Assistant; [memb.] Metro D.C. Virginia Soccer Referee Association; [oth. writ.] Unpublished poems, a play; [pers.] I try to bring out the facts of life in my writing.; [a.] Annandale, VA

KABOOS, PEGGY L.
[b.] May 26, 1924, Charlotte, NC; [p.] Deceased "The lesser family" (Vaudeville 1900's); [m.] Louis H. Kaboos, February 19, 1923, November 1, 1970; [ch.] Seven; [ed.] High School Graduate; [occ.] Housewife (Domestic Engineer); [oth. writ.] Quite a few poems none entired in Contests none published; [pers.] My first love was playing piano at age 7, and has continued for 64 years, then came reading and of course, poems. My love for nature inspires me, and I am an incurable romantic!; [a.] North Myrtle Beach, SC

KACZOR, SUZANNE DAIGNAULT
[b.] July 30, 1949, Woonsocket, RI; [p.] Ruth Littlefield, Ralphael Daignutt; [m.] Robert F. Kaczor, October 18, 1969; [ch.] Kristine, James, Brian, Steven; [ed.] Blackstone High School Blackstone, MA; [occ.] Homemaker; [oth. writ.] Several poems written for personal enjoyment. This poem was the first one ever submitted to any publisher of any kind.; [pers.] I have written poetry at different stages of my life as an emotional release or venting. I entered this poem on a whim just to get some professional feedback. I am surprised and honored to be published.; [a.] Bellingham, MA

KAHGEE, APRIL
[b.] December 7, 1982, Honolulu, HI; [p.] Craig and Sarah Kahgee; [occ.] Student; [hon.] A honor roll, Science Olympiad; [pers.] The mind is like a balloon for they both come in a wide variety of shapes and sizes and both have a tendency to drift. When my mind drifts I usually go to imaginary place where every one speaks rhyme.; [a.] Washington, MI

KAISER, LUANNE MERICKEL
[b.] August 12, 1949, Toledo, OH; [p.] Jeanette and Norman Kaiser; [ch.] Audra Joy Pfleghaar; [ed.]

Flower Memorial Hospital Diploma Registered Nurse, Sylvania, Ohio, University of Phoenix, Bachelors of Science of Nursing; [occ.] Registered Nurse; [memb.] Captain in the Army Reserves; [pers.] Life is a "Merickel".; [a.] Phoenix, AZ

KALFAYAN, ELIZABETH R.
[b.] February 22, 1973, Palo Alto, CA; [p.] Charles and Frances Kalfayan; [ed.] A.A. degree in journalism from College of San Mateo. Presently attending San Francisco State University, majoring in Cinema.; [hon.] 2nd Place News Story Journalism Association of Community College, Northern Section, 2nd Place Newspaper News Story, 39th Annual Conference, Journalism Association of Community Colleges, State of California; [pers.] I write only what I feel in my heart. My greatest influence in my writing and in my life has been my parents, whose love and support knows no limits.; [a.] San Mateo, CA

KAMINSKY, ANN MARIE
[b.] December 28, 1928, Whiting, IN; [p.] Deceased; [m.] Richard G. Kaminsky, December 30, 1950; [ch.] Rochelle Kmetz, Richard K. Kaminsky; [ed.] Whiting High School, St. Joseph (B.S.) Purdue, Univ. (MS); [occ.] Teacher, (Elem) Franklin School Hammond School System; [memb.] AFT, Reading (HARC) Who's Who Among America's Teachers - 1994; [hon.] Delta Epsilon, Cum Laude; [oth. writ.] Several Poems (not published as yet); [pers.] Be thankful for each day. Be forgiving, honest and have a loving heart. Have respect for all living things, (animals, people, plants) for these are the treasures of the Earth!; [a.] Whiting, IN

KANDILIAN, SHANA NICOLE
[pen.] Summer; [b.] September 27, 1982, Montebello, CA; [p.] Rouben and Marsha Kandilian; [ed.] 8th Grade Jr. High; [oth.] Poems; [pers.] A writer sees with his heart and feels with his mind.; [a.] Lahabra Heights, CA

KARPEL, JONATHAN
[pen.] Karpman; [b.] March 12, 1977, Santa Clara, CA; [p.] Vivian and Philipp Karpel; [ed.] Westmont High, San Jose State University; [occ.] Student; [hon.] Who's Who Among American High School Students 1992-1995; [pers.] This is dedicated to my brothers, don't ever take the easy way out in life.; [a.] Campbell, CA

KAULILI, DEBBY NAPUA
[b.] February 4, 1964, Lihue, Kauai; [p.] Mr. Spring water and Mrs. Marjorie Kaulili; [ed.] Kauai High School, Kauai Community College, and Leeward Community College; [occ.] Graphic Artist and Lithographic Stripper; [memb.] International Song Writer's Co-op; [hon.] Dean's List, Talent Search America and Honor Roll; [oth. writ.] Quill Books, American Lung Association Newsletter, and Western Poetry Association; [pers.] Poetry breathes life, fun and dreams. Special hope for a better man kind; [a.] Honolulu, HI

KAZULES, JENNIFER
[b.] June 27, 1981, Long Beach; [p.] Kathy Kazules, Stephen Kawles; [ed.] Freshman at Mount Miguel High School; [occ.] Student at Mount Miguel; [memb.] Girl Scouts, Church Santa Sophia Youth Groups, Marching Band, CJSF, Caballeros (Good

Citizenships.); [pers.] My stories were inspired by my father who died on May 17th. I would like to tell others who loose their fathers to look at the good side and remember all the good times you had to get her; [a.] Lamesa, CA

KC, AMANDA
[b.] October 17, Planet Earth; [p.] Alzadie Hardy; [ch.] TAC III; [ed.] BA Degree Wayne State University; [occ.] Actress Artiste (Oils) Writer; [memb.] NAVI (National Association Underwater Instructor), PADI (Professional Association Diving Instructor), SAG (Screen Actor's Guild), AFTRA (American Federation Television, Radio ARtistes), HOG (Harley Owners Group); [oth. writ.] Scripts, Vampire Stories; [pers.] Avoid all spiritual vexation and Live live live for tomorrow we all die!; [a.] New York, NY

KEENE, ALLISON
[pen.] Allie, Munchkin, Shorty; [b.] June 1, 1980, Maine Med; [p.] Marian and Russel Keene; [ed.] I'm in the 10th grade at Kennebunk High School. I wrote the poem in English for an assignment.; [occ.] Current a student; [memb.] V. Cheerleader, V. Gymnast, Horseback riding, Skier, Church Youth Ministry, Certified First aid and CPR and a big sister; [hon.] Got honor roll in 8th grade second place in gymnastics state meet; [oth. writ.] Writing a small book of poems in 7th grade; [pers.] I'd like to thank my grandmother for making this possible. She took me to Yugoslavia June of '91. Hello Melinda. I love you Ryan!; [a.] West Kennebunk, ME

KEETON, GARY WAYNE
[pen.] Gary Keeton; [b.] May 5, 1967, Phoenix, AZ; [p.] Kenneth W. and Patrica I. Keeton; [m.] Donna C. Keeton, July 1, 1992; [ch.] Andrew Jonathon, Julia, Carroll, Jesse Wayne, Kenneth Gary and Michael Joseph Keeton; [pers.] First I would like to thank God forgiving me the talent to write. I also want to thank my loving wife and children, my mother and future stepfather for backing me up in my writing. My philosophy is that maybe someday poverty will be non-excident, where people can live in a world of peace and no violence.; [a.] Phoenix, AZ

KEIL, RUDOLF W.
[b.] November 14, 1926, Chemnitz, Germany; [m.] Not at this time; [ch.] Three daughters one son; [ed.] AA in Business Mgmt; [occ.] Retired USAF MSG and retired DOD CIV in Aircraft Maintenance; [memb.] Masonic, Scottish Rite and Shriner; [pers.] Service in two wars gave you plenty time to think and write, (That was WWII and Vietnam); [a.] Racho Cordova, CA

KELLY, NICOLE RENEE
[b.] May 6, 1974, Jeanette, PA; [p.] Dale L. Kelly and Ulrike S. Kelly; [ch.] David Aaron Kelly; [ed.] Penn Trafford High School Sawyer School of Business Associates Degree in Communications System Management; [occ.] Data Conversion Operator for U.S. Postal Service; [memb.] Rainforest Alliance; [hon.] Graduated with Honors and on the Presidents List; [oth. writ.] Numerous poems that only I have read; [pers.] I was influenced by my loving Parents, my Aunt Jay and Uncle Dave, also my Oma in Germany. I am inspired by my love for animals and also the Native Americans with their love and respect for the Earth.; [a.] Levelgreen, PA

KENNEDY, JENNIFER
[b.] May 26, 1978, Richmond, VA; [p.] Sharon Kennedy and Lloyd Kennedy; [ed.] Senior at Indian River High School in Chesapeake, Va; [occ.] After School Cousler at the YMCA; [oth. writ.] Several unpublished poems and short stories; [pers.] My poems are an emotional outlet for me. They contain all my feelings and doubts, all I could hope is maybe something in my poems could help someone else.; [a.] Chesapeake, VA

KENT, PHYLLIS
[b.] August 17, 1953, Gates, NC; [p.] Vandell Cross, Doris Cross; [m.] William Michael Kent, May 20, 1971; [ch.] Angela Colleen, Adrian Michael, Antron Marcus; [ed.] Gates County High School; [occ.] Sales; [oth. writ.] I have written over one hundred poems, whenever there is something I can't talk about I write about it.; [pers.] I write from the heart, my poetry reflects my mood at the time, whether it's depression, pride, joy or the pain of having a love one die.; [a.] Gates, NC

KERNS, GAIL H.
[b.] September 10, 1955, Virginia; [p.] E. Samuel Healy Jr., and Lillian Senecal Healy; [m.] Charles J. Kerns Jr., July 12, 1975; [ch.] Joshua Ryan and Megan Lee; [ed.] Gloucester High; [occ.] Legal Assistant; [memb.] First Presbyterian Church of Gloucester, VA; [oth. writ.] To date, I have written soley for my own enjoyment but hope to published my works in the near future.; [pers.] I view poetry as a wonderful healing tool and a means of self-expression without limitations.; [a.] Gloucester, VA

KESSLER, TRINA J.
[b.] October 7, 1971, Medina, ND; [p.] Daryl and Alice Kessler; [ch.] Chelsey Lynn Kessler; [ed.] Graduated from Jamestown High School - took a year and half of Liberal Arts of NDSCS Wahpeton College - currently studying Business Management at home; [occ.] Homemaker - Full time works at Benson Quinn Elevator - partime work restaurant; [memb.] YMCA Karate Children International Sponsor Elks Club, Dance Hands, Across America, Red Cross Blood Drive, Easter Seals Society; [hon.] Arts and Science - Karate cross country running and other sports - reading choir theater - Red Cross - Debate Club; [oth. writ.] Recently trying to publish children's books and short stories; [pers.] I just love to make people happy and sometimes think - expressing one's own feelings let's people know what you're about and also let's them know its ok to let those feelings show once in a while. Poem written about Chelsey's father who I'll always love to by better.; [a.] Jamestown, ND

KEYLON, THOMAS J.
[b.] September 23, 1944, San Francisco; [p.] Catherine Keylon, Lewis Keylon; [m.] Audrey Keylon, January 12, 1990; [ch.] Fletcher Chamley; [ed.] Mission High - John O'Connell Apprentice School; [occ.] Retired Union Sheet Metal Worker; [memb.] Sheet Metal Workers International Association Local 104, San Francisco; [pers.] Appreciate today, there is no promise of tomorrow."; [a.] San Francisco, CA

KHITROV, GREGORY
[pen.] Gregg Khitrov; [b.] February 11, 1976, Soviet Union, Tashkeat; [p.] Alexande Khitrov and Klaudia Zablueouskaya; [ed.] New Utrecht High, Adelphi University; [occ.] A student at Adelphi University; [memb.] Sigma Alpha Mu, Adelphi Men's Swimming Team; [hon.] 1992 U.S. Achievement Academy, trophies, medals in swimming; [oth. writ] "I Think Of You," "The Star," "The Lifeguard Choir and The Past," "My Love For You," "Good Byes," "NYC Schools," "Baywatch," also some were written in Russian, "I Have Seen A Wounded Girl"; [pers.] I try to show my emotions through my poems, most of them are love poems. I was influenced by my friend who worked at the Goech with me, who also wrote.; [a.] Brooklyn, NY

KHOURY, DAPHNE
[b.] April 2, 1979; [p.] Ellen Glickman, Grey Khoury; [ed.] Trinity Christian Academy (High School); [occ.] Student; [memb.] National Honor Society, National Art Honor Society, National French Honor Society, Gallery Staff, Member of Student Government (Jr. Class Vice President); [hon.] Who's Who Among High Schools student, French I Award, French II award, Geometry Award, Art II award, Headmasters Honor Roll, Trojan Honor Roll

KILLMAN, VERA E.
[b.] January 30, 1947, Libby, MT; [p.] Wilbur and Celina Cole; [m.] David G. Killman, August 12, 1967; [ch.] Step-son Curtis Lee; [ed.] Libby High School, Jefferson Community College, Louisville KY; [occ.] Registered Nurse; [oth. writ.] I have written a few other poems, but didn't think about publication until now.; [pers.] The poem was written after a visit with my parents. My mother has been diagnosed with Altzheimer's disease.; [a.] Louisville, KY

KIM, ESTHER HYONG-SHIN
[b.] November 2, 1979, Flushing, NY; [p.] Dr. Hyo Y. Kim and Hannah Kim; [ed.] H.F. Stevens Middle School Crowley High School; [memb.] Key Club, Honor Student Saebit Baptist Church, Culture Club); [hon.] Outstanding Student Awards, 3rd place language award, 1st place writing award, two 1st place Reflections Writing contest awards, two third place JV Tennis Awards, 2 first place German Awards, 1st place UIL Writing award; [oth. writ.] The Globular Peace (essay), The Courageous, Dare to Discover Courage, Bond of Love, The Kiss I Never Had, The Best Brother, A Friend No More, and Visions; [pers.] I try to prove a point, and describe the world through my point of view. And I try to express my own opinion about life.; [a.] Fort Worth, TX

KINCANNON, ERIN D.
[b.] September 14, 1979, Oklahoma City, OK; [p.] Ronald and Betty Kincannon; [ed.] Sophomore at Boise City High School; [occ.] Student; [memb.] Student Council, Baptist Youth Group, Booster Club, Cheer leading, Fellowship of Christian Athletes, Oklahoma Honor Society; [hon.] East Central University Gifted and Talented Lyceum "Best Anaphora", Oklahoma High School Honor Society, Academic Athletic Achievement Award, Superintendents Honor Roll, Duke University Talent Identification Program; [oth. writ.] Published a poem in both '93 and '94 editions of Anthology of Poetry by Young Americans, published in Oklahoma State University Writing Camp Anthology 1994, and two

poems in Perspective, Iliad Press, 1996; [pers.] I'd rather be a dreamer than a realist...because the realist sees only the dirt and grime while the dreamer sees all the beauty.; [a.] Boise City, OK

KING, KELLIE DENISE
[pen.] Kellie; [b.] October 27, 1974, Anderson, SC; [p.] Jacky and Dianne Brady; [m.] Sammy Joe King Jr., July 16, 1993; [ch.] Kelsey King; [occ.] Housewife; [pers.] I try to write so that people understand life of the rodes and the way they feel. I was influenced by my husband who rides the trail.; [a.] Iva, SC

KINGSMORE, CRYSTAL POWELL
[b.] October 18, 1977, Atlanta, GA; [p.] David Souder, Diane Gray; [m.] Carey Kingsmore, August 19, 1995; [ed.] Newberry High School; [occ.] Secretary at J.D.'s services, Inc.; [memb.] Freedom Baptist Church, Sadd, Interact Club; [hon.] Who's Who Among American High School Student, 92-93, 93-94, 94-95. Most improved employee, 4 yrs. award for working at J.D.'s Services Inc.; [oth. writ.] Several poems published in my school newspaper and "Passages" a book of poems,'93-'94, and '94-'95; [pers.] I strive to reflect the goodness of love, especially for my husband, in my writings.; [a.] Newberry, SC

KIZER, TERRIE A.
[b.] November 20, 1956, Wyandotte, MI; [p.] Forrest and Elaine Swim; [m.] Kris Kizer, May 19, 1984; [ed.] Monroe High, Monroe, OH Miami University, OH; [pers.] Listen to your inner self, take time to dream; [a.] Flower Mound, TX

KLEINHANZL, KEVIN
[b.] March 24, 1971, Phoenix, AZ; [p.] Nancy L. Kleinhanzl; [ed.] Major in Theatre Education and Speech Communication, Education at Northern Arizona University; [occ.] Drama Instructor at Yuma High School; [memb.] AEA, NEA, Independent Feature Project/West, (Alpha Psi Omega); [hon.] 1st Year Teacher of the year at Yuma High, Director of 1st place state one-act competition 1994; [oth. writ.] Poetry, Plays; [pers.] If you don't have love, don't laugh, don't cry, don't sing...How will you know you are living, enjoy life.; [a.] Yuma, AZ

KLEVITSKY, MARY
[b.] Rigo, Latvia; [m.] Anatoly; [ch.] Lhenia Klevitsky; [ed.] Latvian State University, Rigo, Latvia; [occ.] Quality Assurance Suppt. Analyst, PA Blue Shield; [oth. writ.] Several poems not published; [pers.] My acknowledgement goes to my daughter, Lhenio, who is my critic, my closest friend, whom I draw the inspiration from.; [a.] Harrisburg, PA

KNABLE, ANNE
[pen.] Anna Paul; [b.] May 15, 1914, Cleveland, OH; [p.] Nicholas Paul, Anna Paul; [m.] Herbert Knable, October 2, 1937; [ch.] Phyllis Ann, Dennis Joseph; [ed.] Graduated 1930 from a Catholic Girls' Business School in Brooklyn Ohio Later on I worked in the medical field as Doctor's Asst. and Secretary for a number of years; [occ.] Keeping house for myself interspersed with sporatic writings and reading many, many books-old and new and suspenseful mysteries; [hon.] Received certificates of merit in the Tutor Training Program at Cleveland State

University. Taught remedial reading and did some private tutoring, especially in reading and spelling. All of this took place in Cleveland, OH; [oth. writ.] I have many poems and various writings in my own journal. 'TEARS' was the first poem I have submitted for review or entered in contest of any sort.; [pers.] My motto for a long time has been 'to live and let live' — Never give undue flattery and receive personal flattery only on a light note. My professors at Cleveland State University encouraged me to keep on with my writing, which I have been doing. Writing poetry and sometimes comical stories seems to come to me out of nowhere - most of my Poems come to me from experience, feelings and observations from the ridiculous to the sublime.; [a.] Strongsville, OH

KNIGHT, CHRISTINE S.
[b.] April 9, 1932, Jamaica, West Indies; [p.] Herbert (Kenny) and Elizabeth Wates; [m.] William Knight; [ch.] Clive, William J.R. Marcia, Marie; [ed.] Rural Hill Jamaica Denise Zion College Chatt Tennessee

KNIGHT SR., JAMES G.
[pen.] Bern; [b.] June 2, 1959, St. Petersburg, FL; [p.] Geraldine and Lonnie; [m.] Angela Renee, April 8, 1989; [ch.] James B. Knight Jr.; [occ.] US Marine Aviation Mechanic; [pers.] Never worry about the things which you cannot control. Because, if you could control it, you wouldn't have to worry about it. It would already be the way you wanted.; [a.] Havelock, NC

KNIPP, MICHAEL JOHN
[pen.] Michael Knipp; [b.] January 19, 1978, Ft. Wayne, IN; [p.] John and Barbara Knipp; [ed.] Northrop High School; [occ.] Student; [memb.]National Honors Society, Bethel U.M. Youth Group; [hon.] Various Scholastic Achievements in High School including Scholarship with destination and the Trikappa Incentive Award, National Merit Scholarship Commended Award; [oth. writ.] Several poems and open mind writings all unpublished; [pers.] I strive daily for open-mindedness and love for all people and ideas, aware of the importance of self-knowledge and of world awareness. In am influenced by the ideas of many religious and philosophical traditions, but especially the transcendentalist and the teachings of Jesus Christ.; [a.] Fort Wayne, IN

KOELLER, AMANDA
[b.] April 30, 1981, Memphis, TN; [p.] Marty Koeller, Stanley Koeller; [ed.] I am a ninth grade student at Jackson Junior High; [occ.] Student; [memb.] Jackson Junior High Freshman Band; [hon.] Poem published in "After the Storm". Poet of Merit for 1995-1996. Poem published in the "Best Poems" book for '95. Poems published in "Young Poets of America" books.; [oth. writ.] I write many poems in my spare time.; [pers.] Poetry is the way of which I can open my heart and share my feelings with others.; [a.] Jackson, MO

KOOKAN, JEFFREY W.
[pen.] Jeff "Mad Dog" Kookan; [b.] June 1, 1975, Colorado Springs, CO; [p.] Larry L. Kooken and Phillips A. Kookan; [ed.] Lithonia High School; [occ.] Associate Produce Manager for Winn Dixie food stores; [hon.] Band Manager (3yrs). Marching Band (1 yr) Band Librarian (1 yr) Concert Band

(3yrs) VICA Club (2 yrs); [oth. writ.] "Love", "Friends", "A Dream", "Life", "Ode to 1993"; [pers.] "When asked if there were a single word that could serve as a principle of conduct for life, Confusions replied, `Reciprocity will do.'" I have also been influenced by the romantic poets and by one of my teachers Mrs. Claudia Sarden.; [a.] Lithonia, GA

KOUTROBIS, CHRISTOS G.
[pen.] Christo Tajin; [b.] July 2, 1948, Lowell, MA; [p.] George Koutrobis, Maria Koutrobis; [ch.] Chani Ailika; [ed.] The Galaxy; [occ.] Writer; [oth. writ.] Four manuscripts of Prose, three in copyright. "The Beast is Gone" "The Beast Returns" "Zone'ng Webster" "Selected Prose of C. Tajin 13"; [pers.] I strive to awaken this sleeping planet of ours. Beam travelers Jose Aquelles, Frank Herbert and Carlos Castenada Encourage me on my journey.; [a.] Lowell, MA

KOVACK, TINA K.
[pen.] Tina K. Kovack; [b.] March 3, 1972, Fairmont, WV; [p.] Kenny Kovack and June Kovack; [ed.] Fairmont Senior High; [occ.] Tina, is deceased she died march 13, 1995 I am her mother and always wanted her to submit her poetry but she never thought it was good enough. Tina wrote this poem "I remember" after her brother Kenny Joe was murdered she could never get over his death. There were only the two of them and they were only 17 mo. apart in age.; [memb.] I am sending a copy of power of attorney or administratrix; [hon.] Riversville, WV

KOWALSKE, DR. PHILIP
[pen.] Dr. K; [b.] October 21, 1956, Dearborn, MI; [p.] Harold and Maryann; [m.] Sheri Ann Kowalske, June 6, 1976; [ch.] Philip Michael, Matthew Mark; [ed.] Roosevelt High A.S. at Wayne County College D.C. at Life Chiropractic College; [occ.] Doctor of Chiropractic; [memb.] Holt Road Baptist Church Board of Deacons, Promise Keepers; [oth. writ.] Various Religious Poems, various love poems, two children books; [pers.] I can do all things thru Christ which strengthen me; [a.] Marietta, GA

KRAFT, CARLY MEREDITH
[b.] December 10, 1981, Detroit, MI; [p.] Jackie and Larry Kraft; [ed.] Eight grade, Orchard Lake Middle School; [pers.] I reflect my poems that I write on how I feel at the time that I write it. It helps me let out my feelings and write poems at the same time.; [a.] West Bloomfield, MI

KRAMER, DENISE
[pen.] Denise Kramer; [b.] September 16, 1962, Fort Collins, CO; [p.] Ted and Felice Kramer; [ed.] Auburn High School, Auburn Al., Des Moines Community College, Iowa, Iowa State University, Iowa; [occ.] Legal Assistant at 20th Century Fox Television; [memb.] Humane Society; [oth. writ.] Lots of poems....a true gift from God!!!; [pers.] Writing poetry has set my soul free. Just a few words on paper can take 1,000 pounds of hurt and pain out of your soul. It's the best soul diet I know!!!! If your a poet, try it!!!! Write on!!!; [a.] Los Angeles, CA

KROLL, KELLI
[b.] October 5, 1966, Dallas, TX; [p.] Jerry Hanson, Dayne Knight; [m.] William Kroll, September 6, 1991; [occ.] Sales Representative; [a.] Island Lake, IL

KROMRIE, KIM
[pen.] Petrie; [b.] April 10, 1981, Stevens Point; [p.] Pat and Karl Kromrie; [ed.] 9th Grader at Westfield High School; [occ.] A student; [hon.] I have 4 singing Awards and 2 Science Fair Awards 5 Softball Awards 2 Cheerleading Awards.; [oth. writ.] This writing was my first just started writing this year; [pers.] The reason I wrote this story about love is because I think love is one of the most valuable things in life.; [a.] Coloma, WI

KUBASZAK, PAUL
[b.] April 10, 1950, Chicago; [p.] Josephine and the late Harry Kubaszak; [m.] Julie, April 24, 1970; [ch.] Chistopher; [ed.] Thornton Fractional North High School and a four year Pipefitter Apprenticeship; [occ.] Maint. Foreman, Bethlehem Steel Corp.; [memb.] St. Peter's Lutheran Church In Portage, Distinguished member of the Internatiional Society of Poets; [oth. writ.] In 3 other, National Library of Poetries Anthologies, including the best of 1996.; [a.] Portage, IN

KUHN, LESLI
[b.] February 22, 1980, Osceola, IN; [p.] Hubert Kuhn, Joyce Kuhn; [ed.] Current attending Penn High School; [occ.] Student; [memb.] New Carlisle United Methodist Church, Peer Group; [hon.] Color guard for band in High School; [oth. writ.] Many poems accepted to be published; [pers.] There isn't just one pot of gold at the end of a rainbow.; [a.] Osceola, IN

KULIGA, KARLA A.
[pen.] Karla A. Kuliga (Karly); [b.] March 25, 1971, Philadelphia; [p.] John J. Juliga Jr., Karla H. Kuliga; [ed.] Mastbaum A.V.T.S. (High) Cosmetology Major; [occ.] Cosmetologist (Hairstylist) Talent Salon; [memb.] North Shore Animal League, Circle of Friends (Fox Chase Cancer Center), E.P.V.A (for Veterans); [hon.] National Honor Society, Most likely to succeed, Positive Attitude Awards, finalist Ms. Teen America, honor roll; [oth. writ.] Local and National Magazines; [pers.] I reach inside my heart and mind when I write, and hope my poems will help others do the same.; [a.] Philadelphia, PA

LABEAU, ANN MARGARET
[pen.] Pebbles Labeau; [b.] December 4, 1965, Ft. Knox, KY; [p.] Alfred and Martha LaBeau; [ed.] Chesapeake High, Anne Arundel Community College; [occ.] Police Dispatcher; [memb.] Church of Jesus Christ of Latter Day Saints; [oth. writ.] Letters to my dad... with love; [pers.] My father is a Vietnam vet and has PTSD. My writings are to help all vets deal with their emotions, and their PTSD. All my writings are dedicated to Vietnam Vets and their families.; [a.] Pasadena, MD

LABROSSE, BRADLEY
[b.] April 15, 1946, New Orleans, LA; [p.] Isadore and Veronica; [m.] Judy, April 24, 1965; [ch.] Brad, Brook, Beth; [ed.] High School; [occ.] Dealer - table games; [oth. writ.] Reserved; [pers.] Dedicated to my wife Judy Rose; [a.] Violet, LA

LANDERS, JAMES
[b.] October 12, 1978, Lakewood, WA; [p.] Shari Landers and Jim Andrews; [ed.] Spanaway Lake H.S. and Rogers H.S.; [memb.] YMCA kids night out guide; [pers.] Be real in thought, feeling and emotion to yourself and others - sometimes it just makes things a little more simple; [a.] Spanaway, WA

LANDRENEAU, PAMELA
[b.] March 15, 1966, Boston, MA; [p.] Marsha and Dallas Trahan; [m.] Kevin Landreneau, December 21, 1991; [ch.] Danah, Step-daughters: Nikki and Kelli; [ed.] Lafayette High, St. Martin Academy; [occ.] Homemaker, Housewife or house Engineer; [oth. writ.] Several poems, none which have been published; [pers.] I try to inspire others in my poems. Poems are the key to the inner soul.; [a.] Lake Charles, LA

LANDRY, EAVES
[b.] August 17, 1972, New Orleans, LA; [occ.] Student of University of Southwestern Louisiana; [memb.] Public Relations Student Society of America; [pers.] I have been greatly influenced by the poems of William Blake, and by life itself. "Emotions are what makes life real, don't supress them"; [a.] Lafayette, LA

LANDT, KELLY MICHELLE
[b.] August 19, 1975, Elgin, IL; [p.] Lee Landt, Cathy Landt; [ed.] Graduated from South High School; [oth. writ.] Several poems, short stories. Not yet published.; [pers.] Writing is my way of escaping. The freedom I feel when writing can ever be matched.; [a.] Crystal Lake, IL

LANE, LORDAN
[b.] December 15, 1976; [ed.] Loyola Marymount University. I have also lived in Denver, New York, San Jose and Los Angeles.; [occ.] Student and hopeful writer; [hon.] I'm still looking; [oth. writ.] I'am working on two novels as well as 70 poems. I have also written 40 or so short stories. I'am looking for published for my works.; [pers.] Good writing can only come from great anguish.; [a.] Los Altos, CA

LANE, TIA DIANNE
[pen.] Tia D. Lane; [b.] July 12, 1982, Floyd Medical; [p.] Angela and George Lane Jr.; [ed.] 8th Grade student at Trion High School Trion, Georgia; [pers.] I really put my heart into this poem and I think that it is my best accomplishment.; [a.] Lyerly, GA

LANG JR., CHARLES G.
[pen.] C. G. Lang; [b.] May 2, 1931, Buffalo, NY; [m.] Jeanne A. Lang, September 16, 1967; [ed.] Assoc. Degree in Optical Tech. at Erie Community College in Buffalo NY a number of writing courses; [occ.] Retired; [oth. writ.] Poems! Sirens, the hawk, loving hands, sharing, virtue, courage verse to Accompany Hymn, "Amazing Grace" and Essays; [pers.] In passing I wish to be remembered for the good things I have done and not what I looked like at the end; [a.] Sinclairville, NY

LANG, K. R.
[pen.] Robin Stone, Lady Rayne; [b.] January 3, 1966; [p.] Two; [ed.] B.A. in Psychology from Austin College, Sherman TX. 29 years in the University of Life (working on a masters); [occ.] Medical records technician; [oth. writ.] Forthcoming novel The Book of Soul; [pers.] Whatever we might think, nothing is ever done in isolation. This world is one huge cathedral. Each person we encounter is an altar of God. Every action we take and every thought we have is part of the ritual of life, and it is and should always be a joyous ritual.; [a.] Houston, TX

LANSVERK, JOLENE
[b.] April 8, 1979, Benson MN; [p.] Sandy Lansverk, Richard Lansverk; [ed.] Am presently a Junior in High School; [occ.] Radio Engineer at KSCR Radio Station in Benson MN 56215; [oth. writ.] Several poems published in the local newspaper and the Appelton Chronicle. One poem is in the process of being published in a book called "Echoes of the silence."; [pers.] "You only get one shot at life so live it to the fullest."; [a.] Benson, MN

LARSEN, MARK T.
[b.] August 7, 1969, Portsmouth, VA; [p.] Dr. Geoffrey Larsen, Rebecca C. Lauren; [ed.] The Asheville School, Emory and Henry College; [occ.] Resident Manager Oak Hill Academy, Mouth of Wilson, VA; [pers.] Poetry comes with the breath, the holding and releasing of life.; [a.] Mouth of Wilson, VA

LASSEN, MARY LOU
[b.] April 15, 1909, Globe, AR; [p.] Fred J. and Maryz Elliott; [m.] Lloyd Lassen (Deceased), Nov. 15, 1938; [ch.] Gerald and William (Grown); [ed.] B.A. in Education from Univ. of So. Cal. some graduate credits from Univ. of Texas; [occ.] Retired Teacher and Social Worker; [memb.] Amer. Assoc. of Univ. Women, Presbyterian Church; [hon.] National Honor Society in Phoenix Union High School; [oth. writ.] Person's in High School paper and some Texas Local papers; [pers.] Writing "fun" poems has been a long time hobby - I love to provide a little laughter for friends, etc.; [a.] Olympia, WA

LAT, MARIA TANYA KARINA
[pen.] Tipsy Kisser; [b.] July 31, 1974, Quezon City, Philippines; [p.] Rodolfo Lat, Encarnacion Alfaro; [ed.] B.S. Psychology, Ateneo of Manila University (undergraduate degree); [occ.] Law Student; [memb.] Debate Society Varsity Team; [hon.] Dean's List, School Representative to National and International Debate Competitions; [oth. writ.] Poems written in my native Filipino; [pers.] I believe that we are all multi-faceted jewels, capable of shining with myriad possibilities. We owe it to ourselves to shine in ways that reflect the brilliance of the light that hits us.

LAUGHY, GINA
[pen.] Gina Marie; [b.] November 18, 1976, Adana, Turkey; [p.] Michael and Janice Laughy; [ed.] Will graduate High School in 1996; [occ.] Base Exchange on Randolph Air Force Base; [hon.] Fund raising and Crop walks. Crop walks are to feed the poor and hungry. It makes me feel good to help those less fortunate. Helping to organize blood drives.; [oth. writ.] My other writings have not yet published. This was my first at tempt. My family and teachers encouraged me to do so. I owe all the credit to those who inspired me to write.; [pers.] My poems concentrate mostly on love and deep felt emotions. I was inspired to write this poem by someone who I once loved. I will always have a place in my heart for him. Please read deeper into it then the actual words. It means more then it says.; [a.] Universal, TX

LAVOY, KEVIN
[b.] September 6, 1976, Kalamazoo, MI; [p.] Phil and Teri LaVoy; [ed.] Howell High School, Dorffel Oberschule, Weida, Germany; [occ.] Factory Worker; [memb.] Adult Leader: Boy Scouts of America; [hon.] Eagle Scout, Former Exchange Student; [oth. writ.] Short stories to be found at; [pers.] I'm heavily influenced by Kafka and Kurt Tucholsky; [a.] Howell, MI

LAWRENCE, MARTHA MACLAY SHORTRIDGE
[b.] August 7, 1906, Sedalia, MO; [p.] Alfred Lewis Shortridge, Martha Gleim Maclay Shortridge; [m.] William John Lawrence, August 24, 1938; [ed.] Sedalia High School, A.A. Lindenwood College, 1926, B.A. University of California, Berkeley, CA B.S. in L.S. Western Reserve School of Library Science; [occ.] House and Garden; [memb.] Berkeley Historical Society Friends of the Berkeley Library Editor of the Friends publication Bookmark, Two years, Also President, 2 years; [hon.] USA War Dept. Manhattan District for work as a technician at the Lawrence (no relation) Berkeley Radiation Laboratory, 1942-45. "In Appreciation of Effective Service" in the electro-magnetic separation of uranium isotopes.; [oth. writ.] This is the first literary effort that I have sent to a publisher. I mainly do limericks in the middle of the night.; [pers.] It's selfishness that causes all our woes, personal and worldwide.; [a.] Berkeley, CA

LAYNE, HEATHER MARIE
[b.] February 5, 1984, South Korea; [p.] Larry and Royce Layne; [ed.] Sixth Grade - 1995, 1996; [occ.] Student; [memb.] Eastern Hills Baptist Church, Childrens Choir Forest Ave. Magnet Academic Program. (K-6); [hon.] Honor Roll every year Since first Grade. Presidents Council on Physical Fitness. State Bible Drill Winner 1994, 1995. Young Authors Conference of Montgomery; [oth. writ.] "Christmas Joy" 1991; [pers.] I write to express my joys in life.; [a.] Montgomery, AL

LEANZA, TAMI LYNN
[b.] May 26, 1967, Cleveland; [p.] Anthony and Lenore Leanza; [ed.] Graduated in 1985 from Charles F. Brush High School. Working toward an Associates Degree in Business.; [occ.] Assistant Office Manager, Kohn, Silver and Associates; [memb.] OCA, NCA - Ohio Cosmetology Association, National Cosmetology Assoc. Arthritis Foundation; [hon.] First place student competition in cosmetology won several retail contests from best cuts; [oth. writ.] This is my first time ever to submit my work to anything.; [pers.] Raised money for AIDS and cancer. I strive to own my own beauty salon to bring happiness to all of my customers.; [a.] South Euclid, OH

LEAVITT, PHYLLIS
[b.] Yonkers, NY; [p.] Deceased; [ed.] Graduate "Yonkers High", International Data Processing Institute and 2 1/2 year formal education; [occ.] Retired; [hon.] Have submitted on a few occasions poems a far off place Library of Congress ISBN 1-56167-254-8 under title: The Stuff Falling to Earth. Honorable mention "Serenity" category peace on earth in 1985 - Eddie - Lou Cole Poet my Editor and Judge; [oth. writ.] Miscellaneous writings to the Gannett Suburban News "Herald Statesman".

LEBLANC, DIANA
[pen.] Diana Charest; [b.] December 19, 1949, Manchester, NH; [p.] Esther and William Charest; [ch.] Tammy Vadnais, Jeremy LeBlanc and Billey Joe LeBlanc; [ed.] Graduated Goffstown N.H. have taken CNA courses and computer courses since; [occ.] Housekeeper and private duty C.N.A.; [memb.] Calvary Baptist Church; [oth. writ.] Mama says I yell too much please grandma I really need a pet I'm trying to learn the alphabet fuzzy wuzzy bumble bee.; [pers.] Learn about where you come from to understand who you are and where you are going. Your roots are the most important thing in life my roots come from God!; [a.] Bellmead, TX

LEE, LAURAINE
[b.] August 19, 1913, Los Angeles, CA; [p.] "AS" and Gladys Nolen; [m.] Paul O. Lee, July 6, 1938; [ch.] Laurin, Del, Paulla, Verna, Mark; [ed.] High School; [occ.] Retired; [memb.] First Baptist Ch.; [hon.] Oldest walker in 1970 in Spokane's March of Dimes 20 Mi President 5th yrs. Dorcas Circle; [oth. writ.] Church bulletins home made greeting cards and verses; [pers.] When I was young I was too shy to express myself orally but when I became spiritually enlightened. I had much to say and the Lord helped me to write many "teaching" poems that I could use in my church work.; [a.] Spokane, WA

LEE, MILLI R.
[pen.] Sophia, Chythia Heart; [b.] July 1, 1972, Oklahoma; [p.] Carol Spence and Lonnie Spence; [m.] June 19, 1993; [ch.] Virginia Leslie Lee; [ed.] Union City High School, Redland Community College, Caddo Kiowa Voteach (child-care); [occ.] Student - Redlands College; [memb.] Newspaper Staff, Jr. Yearbook Staff, Sr., Vice President FHA Jr. Yr. (Caddo Kiowa Vo-tech); [hon.] Poems published in Jr. High School Newspapers, in Freshman year book; [oth. writ.] Short stories and more poems - unpublished; [pers.] I write from my heart, pain or from experience gained.; [a.] El Reno, OK

LEE, RICHARD S.
[b.] March 12, 1951, Salt Lake City, UT; [m.] Nancy Lee, May 17, 1991; [ch.] Jeremy Scott Lee, Brandy Dawnett Lee, Jason Keith Lee, Britton Ryan Lee; [ed.] Served U.S. Navy - Vietnam Utah University (Attended); [occ.] Manager, Purchasing; [oth. writ.] Won golden poet award for poem "Afterglow", Looking to get a book published entitled "The Calling", Published article in Salt Lake Tribune; [pers.] A firm believer in the golden rule! Love your wife!

LEHNHARD, GEORGE A.
[pen.] G. Len; [b.] June 29, 1936, St. Louis, MO; [p.] George A. and Mary Ruth; [m.] Patricia, November 19, 1971; [ch.] Michael 21, Maribeth 17; [ed.] Commercial Art, Military History World History BA, MA, MS, PHD; [occ.] Artist Engraver Semi Retired; [memb.] American Legion, VFW, NRA; [pers.] I marvel at the beauty of this great country of ours and I cherish the memories I have received. I try to share this in words of poetry.; [a.] Naples, FL

LENTZ, THOMAS GILBERT
[b.] November 17, 1980, Cleveland, OH; [p.] Douglas and Nora Weyl; [ed.] Currently attending Belleview High School; [memb.] National FFA

Organization, Junior Academy of Science; [oth. writ.] None currently, although he hopes to have more in the future.; [a.] Summerfield, FL

LESLIE, MARCIA
[b.] April 10, 1956, Cleveland; [p.] Georgia Reeves and Tanner Amos; [ch.] Clifford Leslie, Seaman U.S. Navy; [ed.] Erieview Catholic High School, Cuyahoga Community College; [occ.] Case Control Reviewer for Cuyahoga Cty Dept. of Human Services; [pers.] Eighteen years of theatre has provided me with a panoramic view of many issues, and utilizing third person opportunities has allowed me to maintain focus and center on the "heart" of issues!; [a.] Cleveland, OH

LEWALLEN, MORLEY
[b.] February 6, 1980, Puyallup, WA; [p.] Mark and Edwina Lewallen; [ed.] Sophomore at Lodi Academy Graduate in 1998; [memb.] Focus on the family; [hon.] Lodi Academy scholarship, won many piano competitions; [oth. writ.] Several unpublished poems, few short stories; [pers.] In my writing, I try to express my feelings and the feelings I sense around me. I write about real life experiences.; [a.] Linden, CA

LEWIN, JOE
[pen.] John Lone; [b.] February 9, 1921, Petrograd, Russia; [p.] Samuel Lewin and Anna Pliner Lewin; [m.] Suzanne Mellan O'Rorke, November 18, 1944; [ch.] Leanore, Elaine, David, Myra, William; [ed.] Elhurst, N.Y., H.I., Ceny Cooper Union Institute, Oak Ridge School of Reactor Tech. Univ. of Tenn, History Study after; [occ.] Retirement, Writer, Interpreter, Translator; [memb.] Sigma-XI, Civil Air Patrol, 8th A.F., Historical Society, 2nd Air Division Association, Oak Ridge Chapt. of American Nuclear Society, Aircraft Owners and Pilots Assoc.; [hon.] Letters of Commendation for early work on peaceful uses of Nuclear Power on exchange basis with Russia (former S.U); [oth. writ.] "May the Atom be a worker, not a soldier", "Bicycle speed record on a dark night of war", "In memory undimmed"; [pers.] Better to make friends than keep enemies.; [a.] Oak Ridge, TN

LEWIS, DAVID R.
[b.] January 14, 1939, Houston, NY; [p.] Paul and Estelle; [ed.] High School New School; [occ.] Retail; [hon.] Player 6117 to Residence Brooklyn College (Award for Pcs-ton); [oth. writ.] Chillin Oct - Book (Children's poems) (Mattie Robinson's) (Pearly Confections) (Book of poem); [pers.] Personal Motto: "No Excuses!"; [a.] New York, NY

LEWIS, JAN RAE
[pen.] Janie Rae Lewis; [b.] San Jose; [p.] Ray A. Spiker and Mary Van De Graaf; [m.] Jay B. Lewis; [ch.] Brandon Joseph Lewis; [ed.] Del Valle High School, Foothill Jr. College; [occ.] Homemaker; [memb.] Member of Local Public Radio and Television, Y.M.C.A and the first of Christ Scientist, Boston Mass.; [oth. writ.] None published; [pers.] I enjoy contemporary artist that write with a love of humanity and that take the every day and leave you with a message that inspires. I've been influenced by contemporary artist such as William Stafford and various artist show cased in the home forum of the Christian Science Monitor. Recently on a local public radio station I heard something of Hiku

Philosophy that a good Hiku invites you to toss into the pond and join in the art (joy) of making gentle ripples. That what happened to me I was impelled to respond. When I was 9 years old my first poem was a Hiku.; [a.] San Jose, CA

LEWIS, SHELDON J.
[b.] November 2, 1924, Vernal, UT; [p.] James Donald Lewis, Genevieve Lewis; [m.] Carol J. Lewis, June 30, 1948; [ch.] Three daughters, one son; [occ.] Retired; [oth. writ.] Several poems, but this one is the first one I have ever tried to have published; [pers.] I try to write of happenings in my life or people's lives that are close to me.; [a.] Kaysville, UT

LEWIS-CHASE, EVE
[pen.] Evelyn Lewis; [b.] May 17, 1942, Columbus, OH; [p.] William T. Lewis, Doris, Ramsey-Lewis and Catherine Lewis; [m.] Harry L. Chase, May 16, 1992; [ch.] Gizmo the baby cat; [ed.] Ohio State University, School of Journalism International Studies; [occ.] Law firm co-lead word processor and Word for Windows instructor; [memb.] Ohio Press Club from 1965-1973, San Francisco Press Club from 1975-1977, former member Arizona Press Women, current Distinguished Member International Society of Poets, Honorary Chairman Friday Night Irregulars.; [hon.] Through ISP I have been honored with the Editor's Choice award for Reflections of Light, and the Poet of Merit award at the 1995 Convention and, of course, having my work selected for inclusion in four of its publications in the last year.; [oth. writ.] Various articles, wire and news stories in my 10 year (Piqua, Greenville and Delaware, Ohio, Parkersburg, West Virginia, Yuma, Arizona) newspaper career as well as a weekly column "Eve's Dropping". "Being Sensible" published in Today's Best Poems by the World of Poetry in 1980, "History for Me" published in Reflections of Light and "Tribute to Imogen" in Beyond the Stars.; [pers.] Most of my work (as in "Terrorism") reflects my feelings on events and situations. "Vignettes" offers examples of what I call my "dew drop poetry", a twinkling of beauty or expression. The two highest compliments a poet can receive are, in my opinion, "I knew myself in your work." or "I learned to see differently." Therefore, I thank those who have read my work and hope that it provided them with some insight and enjoyment.; [a.] San Francisco, CA

LICARI, ANTOINETTE TRANCHINA
[pen.] Toni Lee; [b.] December 31, 1919, New York City; [p.] Vincenzo Tranchina; [m.] February 13, 1937; [ch.] Josephine Greco and Joseph Licari Jr.; [ed.] Jr. High School, and took evening course was married and seperated and was then divorced; [occ.] Pct Receptionist 83rd Pct New York City Police Dept. 83rd Pct Bklyn. N.Y.; [hon.] Song in Senon's Clusters and Homes and got an award Nursing Homes a Volunteer; [oth. writ.] P.S Tex enjoyed the poem and answered me married young and divorced song in the church chorus St. Joseph and Church Plays love Western since childhood and sing old Cow Boy songs wrote tex poem at the time I was 14 or 15 years old I had a crush on him. I sent him the poem he wrote and thanked me for the poem I write songs now.; [pers.] I was with the rally Jackhore study my sang in the Academy of Music and schools and churches I have photos from these plauses and my job.; [a.] Brooklyn, NY

LIEBER, SUSAN J.
[b.] July 26, 1964, Auburn, NY; [p.] Gerald K. Lieber, Madeline H. Lieber; [m.] Juan Carlos Espinosa, August 31, 1990; [ch.] Mateo, Valentina; [ed.] Skaneateles Central High; [occ.] Admin. Operations Manager (Employment Agency); [pers.] I write for the child in everyone. I search for the truth.; [a.] Wheaton, IL

LIEBLE XII, CHARLES WILLIAM
[pen.] Charles Lieble XII; [b.] January 16, 1973, Roseville, CA; [p.] Charles and Freda Lieble; [ed.] Fort Walton Beach High School University of Alabama Huntsville; [occ.] College Student; [memb.] MIS Club, Formerly part of the Leo Club, Member of New Hope Baptist Church; [oth. writ.] Personal poems of my own collection; [pers.] Thank my parents and my friends for being there and supporting my writings. Also, for the world to realize and to strive for, that with a lot of work and love we can all have the dream world and not have to dream of it anymore. Close your eyes and picture the day.; [a.] Madison, AL

LIEBOWITZ, HENRIETTE
[b.] February 10, 1955, Den Haag, Holland; [p.] Georgine and Sidney Salzman; [m.] Sande Liebowitz, September 24, 1988; [ch.] Oliver Alan Liebowitz; [ed.] Jamaica High School, Superior Career Institute; [occ.] Therapeutic Foster Parent (Licensed); [oth. writ.] Currently compiling a collection of narrative prose; [pers.] I seek to convey the message of motherhood and the power of a mother's love for her child.; [a.] Naranja, FL

LIGHTFOOT, MILDRED A.
[pen.] Alethia - Alethia Williams; [b.] July 8, 1946, New Kent Co, VA; [p.] Mark John Williams, Lillian Williams; [ch.] Jason G., Tamara J., Nicole K.; [ed.] George W. Watkins High, Saint Leo College, John Tyler Community College; [occ.] Preschool Handicapped Teacher E. W. Chambliss Elementary School Wakefield, Virginia; [memb.] National Education Association, Honors Alpha Delta Omega National Honor Society National Honor Society, Suma Cum Laude Graduate; [oth. writ.] Non-Published Author; [pers.] During my experiences of life's loves, kindnesses, tragidies and disappoint-ments, writing to me provides a sense of solitude, tranquility, reflections and peace of mind.; [a.] Prince George, VA

LIGON, ELAINE
[pen.] Leann Nelson; [b.] November 7, 1944, Los Angeles, CA; [p.] Thurmon and Annie Lee Dickson; [ch.] Khalil Taqqee and Vann O. Ligon; [ed.] Centennial High, Compton College L.A. City College UCLA Extension; [occ.] Businessperson, own and operate two small businesses; [oth. writ.] Never published; [pers.] Everyday my life is brightened by my two sons, two grandsons and three granddaughters. Young ones teach us humility and give us the capacity to love without restraint.; [a.] Los Angeles, CA

LILLENGREEN, JOEL
[b.] February 18, 1943, Portland, OR; [p.] Manford Lillengreen, Florence Stritzel; [m.] Pat Norris, June 27, 1968; [ch.] Angelina, Monique, Shawn, Nathan; [ed.] Central Valley High (spokane) Gonzaga University - Washington State University -

Ambassador University (Texas) American River College (Sacramento); [occ.] Minister and Pastor - Worldwide Church of God; [memb.] Theta Xi Fraternity; [hon.] National Human Society Phi Eta Sigma; [oth. writ.] Miscellaneous Articles on Religious Freedom (Sacramento Union) - Editorials and poems for Local Church Publications; [pers.] If you hope for the best in people while also expecting the worst, you will never be disappointed in them, if they succeed you can say "How Great!", if they fail, you call say "There Are Holy Human.".; [a.] Portland, OR

LILLY, MEGAN
[pen.] Samrina Clark, Angelic Wilson; [b.] January 6, 1981, Kansas City, MO; [p.] Alvetta Lilly and Dale Maginness; [ed.] Bishop Helming, James Lewis, Franklin Smith, Georgeff-Baker Middle School, Blue Springs South High School; [occ.] High School Student; [hon.] Being accepted to John Casablancas school of Professional Modeling and being given a signed contract to model with them; [oth. writ.] Many poems that I have a dream and have based a goal on being published; [pers.] I am greatly inspired by the powerful writer Maya Angelou. As only being 14 I see this as opening another door in my life as a writer as to excell in.; [a.] Blue Springs, MO

LIN, DIANA JANE
[b.] September 11, 1983, VA; [p.] Lina Lin, James Lin; [ed.] Ms. Marie Curie 158; [hon.] American Institute of Achievement Scholarship; [pers.] I feel that there is much sorrow and grief of in my life. To express my emotions and feelings, writing poems is within my reach. I was and still am, influenced by other poets of romantic and painful poems; [a.] Bayside, NY

LINDER-MADSEN, MARIANNA
[b.] October 23, 1956, Denmark; [p.] Emil and Betty Linder-Madsen; [ed.] From Denmark in Marketing and International Marketing; [occ.] Sales Represen-tative; [memb.] Cine Paris Repertory Company; [pers.] My commitment to life is to share, and in my journey, it is my hope to plant the seed of joy for others to enjoy.; [a.] San Diego, CA

LINNECOR, KEN
[b.] October 3, 1948, Birmingham, England; [p.] Deceased; [m.] Denise Linnecor, April 8, 1969; [ed.] Secondary Modern and further Education College Birmingham, England; [hon.] None pertaining to literature. A small variety of medals and plaques achieved at soccer and athletics as a youngster.; [oth. writ.] None yet, but I am writing a book about the epilepsy I had to endure for 28 years, how I lived with it, and the prejudices I had to face. A brain operation in 1984 cured it completely; [pers.] With reference to above, having had to face adversity regularly I take delight in adopting a humorous and light hearted approach in my writing.; [a.] Orlando, FL

LITTLEWORTH, NICOLE TERESE
[b.] November 30, 1978, Bloomington, IN; [p.] Dennis and Maria Littleworth; [ed.] Brighton High School; [occ.] Sophomore at Brighton High School; [pers.] I like to write poetry that reaches my peers...that gives them something to thinks about - some events and occasions they can relate to!; [a.] Brighton, MI

LITYNSKI, DIANE M.
[occ.] Writer, Consultant, (Group Therapy); [pers.] Do not be afraid of yourself there is no need to fear solitude, use it as a time to further, prepare yourself for a greater glory and happiness. I hope my writings help others in their preparation.

LLOYD, SIMON
[pen.] Simon Lloyd; [b.] November 27, 1983, Orlando, FL; [p.] Eric Lloyd and John Lloyd; [ed.] Union Park Elementary, and Union Park Middle School; [memb.] Peace Team; [hon.] A,B Honor roll; [oth. writ.] (Not published) "Morning"; [pers.] I dedicate this poem to Ariana Cruiz, Edgar Quinones, Oscar Malve, Richard Guzman, and my Mom and Dad, also my other friends that I love so very much.; [a.] Orlando, FL

LOCH, NORA
[b.] May 25, 1944, Wilkes Barre, PA; [p.] Deceased: Francis Moran and Margaret Moran; [m.] Frank Loch, June 11, 1966; [ch.] Brian, Kevin, Lorrie (a daughter-in-law and two grandchildren); [ed.] G.A.R. Memorial High School, Prior Wilkes-Barre, PA, Courses at: Penn State University and Northern Virginia, Current courses at: Community College; [occ.] Student and Housewife many prior years as a secretary; [oth. writ.] Personal collection of poems; [pers.] I believe each day affords opportunities to become better than the day before, and to work toward future successes. It's what we choose to do that makes a difference.; [a.] Reston, VA

LOCKWOOD, WAYNE S.
[b.] December 13, 1970, Decatur, IL; [p.] Nancy Forbes, Wayne E. Lockwood; [m.] Kimberley Lockwood, October 7, 1995; [ch.] Justin Russell; [ed.] Stephen Decatur; [occ.] Welder, Musician, Songwriter; [memb.] U.F.A.F. (United Fighting Arts Federation); [hon.] First place at Tolono Tournament 1995; [pers.] Through many pains of my own past. I share with others a beckoned call of optimism, for a dim light we see everyday.; [a.] Decatur, IL

LODER, IMO REECE
[pen.] Imo Reece Loder; [b.] July 1, 1906, Bucyrus, OH; [p.] Charles and Ida Reece; [m.] Harry Loder (Deceased), March 1954; [ed.] Bucyrus High School; [occ.] Retired; [hon.] Poems published in the Cleveland Plain Dealer, others in various verse magazines, including Western, National, and Ohio Farmer. Privately printed volume of 60 selected poems, "Thoughts from the past."; [oth. writ.] Over 200 poems; [pers.] Since entering a nursing home, I have had time to reflect on my life which included partnership and poetry, astronomic and microscopic and audio visual equipment, health and illness challenges and family relationships and genealogy. It has all been very interesting.; [a.] Lorain, OH

LOMBARDI, JOSEPH T.
[pen.] Joe; [b.] October 15, 1958, Queens, NY; [p.] Maura and Giuliano Lombardi; [ed.] Archbishop Molloy H.S., St. John's University; [occ.] City Worker; [memb.] City Union, St. John's Alumnus, Archbishop Molloy Alumnus various volunteer agencies; [hon.] 1981's College writing award athletic participation achievements; [oth. writ.] Newspaper Journalist (SJU), Yearbook Journalist (SJU), Volunteer Staff flushing tribune, Avid writer of non-published works and experiences, Entries,

journals, diary entries and possibilities influence. 1. Diversity 2. Freedom 3. Discipline 4. Experience; [pers.] "Imaginary sparks are flying when I think of all that needs to be communicated, written said, read, and done... but people are of utmost and foremost importance." J.L.; [a.] New York, NY

LORENZ JR., GLEN F.
[pen.] The Wolf with the Red Rose; [b.] November 11, 1971, Greeley, CO; [p.] Glen F. Lorenz Sr. and Virginia Lorenz; [ed.] High School Diploma Guernsey Sunrise High - U.S.M.C.; [occ.] Becoming History Teacher; [hon.] National Defense Award, Sea Service Award, Lay Reader Award (Church), Operations of Provide Promise, Deny Flight and Sharp Guard; [oth. writ.] Several unpublished such as The Sacrifice, The Dreamer, How Do You Know?, Words, His Class Ring, And Thoughts Of Past Destiny; [pers.] I try to reflect emotion of love that every humane come in contact with, relying on the hopeless romantic of old.; [a.] Glendo, WY

LORT, MARGARET A.
[b.] July 3, 1939, Denver, CO; [p.] Charles and Clara Armstrong; [m.] Art Lort, July 24, 1959; [ch.] Becky Campbell, Matt Lort; [ed.] Three years at University of Northern Colorado (formerly Colorado State College); [occ.] Administrative Assistant at Denver Seminary; [oth. writ.] Poem published in POCAL POINT magazine, article printed in same magazine; [pers.] Grandchildren are a marvelous creation of God. My two have inspired me to reach depths of feelings, through my poetry, that I've never tapped before.; [a.] Denver, CO

LOUDERMILK, WENDY L.
[b.] November 12, 1969, Forrestville, IL; [p.] Lewis and Patricia Pressgrove; [ed.] Liberty High, Diablo Valley College, Foundation Technical College; [occ.] Mortgage Loan Processer; [oth. writ.] Personal Poetry, short stories; [pers.] This planet is the host of the human race. If there is life on other planets, and we one observed, imagine how foolish we look, killing our host. It is truly miraculous that evolution has not yet weeded us out.; [a.] Pacheco, CA

LOZIER, JAYSON
[b.] May 1975, Hackensack; [p.] Barbara and Ray; [ed.] Hackensack High School and currently attending Bergen Community College; [pers.] Enjoys good music (that is Blues, Beethoven, and Rock-n-Roll) "Jai guru deva - Nothing's gonna change my world" John Lennon; [a.] Hackensack, NJ

LUCAS, LEILA I.
[b.] November 15, 1937, Guyana; [ed.] BA Pace University M.S. Bank Street College of Education; [occ.] Guidance Counselor; [oth. writ.] Story: Passing of a friend; [pers.] Empower others with their sense of their own dignity and worth and create a new individual.; [a.] Brooklyn, NY

LUCAS, MARY VIRGINIA
[pen.] Mary Ginny Lucas; [b.] December 9, 1911, Kansas City, MO; [p.] Maysie Pittorn and John B. Pew; [m.] Mark A. Lucas, February 12, 1937; [ch.] Mary 1938, John 1940, William 1948; [ed.] Public Schools, 1 yr. University of MO (Columbia) 1 1/2 yrs.; [occ.] Retired; [oth. writ.] Take-off poem by Edna St. Vincent Mil-God's World; [pers.] It is

always my daily desire, to bring joy and happiness to others, to share with gifts of my cookery - or just up beat conversation, to keep the golden rule action!; [a.] New Canaan, CT

LUDWIG, CHARLA
[b.] August 2, 1952, Bethesda, MD; [p.] Charles Appleby, Charlene Knapp; [m.] Harald Ludwig, May 3, 1980; [ch.] Kelly Shay, Inga Anneliese, Erik Stefan; [ed.] Northwestern High School, Montgomery College; [occ.] Interior Designer, Design Furniture and Interiors, Rockville, MD; [hon.] Phi Theta Kappa, Dean's List, Valedictorian; [pers.] The written word carries more meaning and permanence than words that are merely uttered; [a.] North Potomac, MD

LUGARDO, DONNA
[pen.] DJ; [b.] September 26, 1960, Chester, PA; [p.] Brenda and Henry Mincy; [ch.] Jason Mincy; [ed.] St. Michael's, Notre Dame H.S. Delaware Community College, Va. Beach Commonwealth College; [occ.] Resource Nurse Counselor; [memb.] Resurrection Church, Resurrection Prayer group, Women's Networking group; [hon.] Dean's list, President's list, Special Act Award, Outstanding Performance Award; [oth. writ.] Unpublished writings which I call "Through my Eyes"; [pers.] Live each day as if it were your lost, because no ones guaranteed tomorrow.; [a.] Ellicott City, MD

LUGO, ROBERTOLUIS
[b.] May 28, 1956, Puerto Rico; [p.] Jose A. Lugo, Hilda M. Lugo; [m.] Carmen N. Lugo, January 26, 1984; [ch.] Stephanie, Steven, Roberto; [ed.] BA in Soul Science, Myack New York, MA, Theology, Philadelphia PA. Ph.D. Candidate; [occ.] Faculty Secretary, Eastern Baptist Theological Seminary; [hon.] Cum Laude at Myack College, Myack, N.Y. and elected for Who's Whom in North American Colleges and Universities, 1990; [oth. writ.] Several Poems published in two antologies of Hispanics poets in New York. Also is Literary Magazines in Puerto Rico and Spain.; [pers.] All what I'm doing is the glory of my God, revealed in the person of Jesus Christ. Because of Rad humankind is my preferred theme in my writings.; [a.] Wynnewood, PA

LUNDGREN, KATHERINE R.
[b.] November 25, 1984; [p.] Kent and Deborah Lundgren; [ed.] Caughlin Ranch Elementary Reno, NV; [memb.] Girl Scouts, Nevada Opera Youth Chorus; [pers.] I feel my talent for writing comes from my heart not from my head.; [a.] Reno, NV

LUZADDER JR., EDWARD W.
[b.] September 2, 1966, Morgantown, WV; [p.] Edward W. Luzadder; [ed.] Morgantown High School, (1984) West Virginia University (1994); [occ.] Fire Direction Officer U.S. Army; [memb.] U.S. Field Artillery Association, 2nd Cavalry Association, AUSA; [pers.] I have loved and lost and it is not better.; [a.] Fort Polk, LA

LYNCH, ALBERTA S.
[b.] February 20, 1927, Lawrance Co, PA; [p.] Charles B. Snyder, Mary Bartle Snyder; [m.] William M. Lynch, June 20, 1964; [ch.] Jon Thomas Lynch, Joseph Michael Lynch; [ed.] Wany Pum High School, New Castle Business College courses; [occ.] Retired Legal Secretary; [oth. writ.] Collec-

tions of song lyrics, entitled "23 songs by Alberta S. Lynch" and "More songs by Alberta S. Lynch" under copyright of Library of Congress; [a.] Glenn Dale, MD

LYNCH, FLORENCE
[b.] November 15, 1911, Parlier, CA; [p.] Olga Nygren, F. Edgar Jones; [m.] James Lynch (Deceased); [ch.] Susan Ethel and Stephen James; [ed.] 1967 A.A Real Estate, College San Mateo CA, 1976 B.S. Economics College Notre Dame Belmont CA, 1989 M.A. Ed. University of San Francisco, San Francisco CA; [occ.] Retired Executive Volunteer for non-profit Agencies; [memb.] Member Zonta International, Mid-Peninsula Chapter A.A.U.W., League of Women Voters, World Affairs Council of Northern California; [hon.] Who's Who of American Women, Who's Who in the West Marquis 1970-1971 Editions; [oth. writ.] Choral lyrics for classical compositions of Carole Priest Published 1995; [pers.] Poetry and Music are the blessings of Civilization; [a.] Palo Alto, CA

LYNCH, JOHNNALYNN
[b.] February 18, 1977, Miami, FL; [p.] Vernal and Caryl Lynch; [ed.] I graduated from Clarkston High, will be attending Georgia State University; [occ.] Biller for a Transportation Service; [memb.] Recently became a member of the Volunteer Center; [hon.] Awarded certificate for excellence in English. Received an award in math and also received an award for good citizenship.; [oth. writ.] I have a collection of poetry that I've gathered throughout the years, but none have been published.; [pers.] I believe that the loss of a loved one should bring gain in a beautiful memory. I try to stress this statement when writing about death.; [a.] Decatur, GA

MACAL, DIANA
[b.] March 6, 1954, Rio Grande City, TX; [p.] Elias and Concepcion Macal; [ch.] Jacob Villarreal and Chris R.T. Fincher; [ed.] McAllen High, McAllen School of Business; [a.] Houston, TX

MACERI, MARILYN GRACE
[b.] February 3, 1957, Detroit, MI; [p.] Thomas and Lena Navarro; [m.] Don Robertson (Fiance); [ch.] Paul Anthony, Matthew Thomas, Anthony Joseph, and Aaron Michael; [ed.] St Brendan Elementary, Bishop Gallogher High School, University of Detroit, Western Michigan University; [occ.] Homemaker, mother, day care Provider, and Author; [memb.] The Unity Church of today since 1977; [hon.] Dean's List at W.M.U.; [oth. writ.] Several poems and a children's story; [pers.] Spiritual Enlightenment is the main focus of my writings.; [a.] Warren, MI

MACHADO, LUANDA MARIA
[b.] April 9, 1964, Angola, Aferica; [p.] Jose Machado, Maria Machado; [m.] David Vaughn Haptonstahl, July 25, 1992; [ch.] Shaun Martins; [ed.] High School; [occ.] Model Vogue Modeling Agency, Manchester, N.H.; [oth. writ.] Stories. "A Rose Is Weeping", a 800 page, novel. "A Journey Within". "A Lost Doll, A Haunting Chilld, "A Castle Of Timeless Children," "My Fairy Aunt" "The Forest Queen And The Holy Sword" "A Childhood Twin" "A Lost February And The Impossible Dream". And, many others.; [pers.] Born from the chilling mouth of cruelty. I crumbled

frozen to the ground. Mysteriously abandoned by my husband, and I rained a pool of anguish, as well. In the face of his find legacy to me, Complete poverty! Born from this, a poem.; [a.] Londonberry, NH

MACK, MICHAEL
[b.] June 3, 1966, Luch Haven, PA; [p.] Joe and Sharon Mack; [ed.] Associates in Chemistry AACC, Senior at University of MA; [occ.] Guitarist, Songwriter; [memb.] Phi Alpha Theta, International Honor Society in History; [hon.] Dean's List, Who's Who in High School, Several Golden Poet Awards; [pers.] Poetry is magic caught in verse and form.; [a.] Arnold, MA

MACKENZIE, SCOTT D.
[b.] May 12, 1967, Rockville Centre, NY; [p.] Jeanette MacKenzie; [m.] Michelle MacKenzie, August 1, 1992; [ed.] BA, Fordham, University, Bronx, NY, Holy Trinity H.S., Hicksville, NY; [occ.] Substitute Teacher, Camp Counselor, Poet; [oth. writ.] "A Darker Shade of War", "A Prayer For Inspiration", in Excursions, College at Lincoln Center, Fordham University's Literary Magazine; [pers.] Influenced by poets like Russell Edson, Theodore, Roethke, Charles Simic, Edward Field, Yevgeny Yevtushen Ko, and Christopher Hewitt, and by sports such as basketball and baseball, I struggle to be original by shunning formality and convention.; [a.] Benicia, CA

MADSEN, NATE ROGERS
[b.] September 25, 1977, Long Beach, CA; [ed.] Long Beach Polytechnic H.S.; [occ.] Student; [oth. writ.] Poems published in The Acacia; [pers.] I've been writing under the influence for as long as I can remember.; [a.] Long Beach, CA

MAGILTON, DAVID
[pen.] David Magilton; [b.] October 8, 1964, Fremont, CA; [p.] David Magilton and Cecelia; [ed.] Sequoia HS, High Tech Inst.; [occ.] Mail Clerk, X-ray Tech; [memb.] Oakland Raider Booster Club; [oth. writ.] None published; [pers.] To me poetry is the power of words in its most submissive state, your allowed to see the soul of a writer.; [a.] Rancho Cordova, CA

MAGOUIRK, MILDRED S.
[pen.] Mildred Scott; [b.] October 13, 1912, Tuscaloosa Co., AL; [p.] Edward S. and Annie R. Scott; [m.] Jessie Brown October 24, 1931, Rance Magouirk June 1, 1986; [ch.] Nan B. York, Michael B. Brown; [ed.] Fairfax High, Cont. Ed. Columbus College; [occ.] Retired secretary and bookkeeper; [memb.] First Christian Church, Board of Deacon and Deaconess; [hon.] Distinguished Service Honors for service at church; [oth. writ.] A youth pagent for "The Front Rank" a christian youth magazine; [pers.] At age 83, I still enjoy life and living, and looking forward to God's promise; [a.] Valley, AL

MAKSAD, ALI K.
[b.] August 14, 1930, Beirut, Lebanon; [m.] Ann Knowles-Maksad, January 1, 1990; [ed.] M.D. American University of Beirut, Post-Doctoral Training, Columbia University, NY; [occ.] Retiring Heart Surgeon, Music Composer, poetry; [memb.] Member of Poets of the Palm Beaches, Florida State Poets Association, International Society of Poetry,

American College of Surgeons, American College of Cardiology and several other medical societies; [hon.] Golden Cedar Medal (by the President of Lebanon) for pioneering Heart Surgery in that country, Silver Medal for pioneering Coronary By-Pass Surgery; [oth. writ.] Several medical articles in National and International Journals several poems in (English, Arabic and French) published in several magazines and papers, a book on Meditation; [pers.] I strive to find the truth about human nature, so that we could shift mankind, from the good to the better and therefore, live a healthier more beautiful, and more productive life; [a.] Boca Raton, FL

MALABED, RONALD
[b.] February 10, 1970, Manila, Philippines; [p.] Luzviminda and Hermenegildo Malabed; [ed.] Wayne State University, Detroit, MI. Bachelor of Music Education (92), Master of Music Education (95); [occ.] Instrumental Music Teacher, James B. Webber School, DPS, Detroit, MI; [memb.] American Federation of Teachers, Michigan Association of Teacher Educators, Music Educators National Conference, International Trumpet Guild, Shoreline Concert Band, Lake St. Clair Symphony Orchestra; [hon.] John Philips Sousa Band Award, Wayne State University Music talent Scholarship Recipient; [pers.] I strive to be like the people who make this world a more safer, kinder, compassionate, and better place to live in. Those heroes are my parents and the educators of the world.; [a.] Saint Clair Shores, MI

MALCOLM, JUNE S. LOWERY
[pen.] Lowery, Lowery-Malcolm; [b.] June 20, 1956, Baltimore, MD; [p.] Margretta and James M. Lowery; [m.] Curtis Allan Malcolm, April 7, 1995; [ch.] Aaron, Bryanna and Doodles; [ed.] ASB degree Medical Office Assistant; [occ.] Volunteer/Disabled; [oth. writ.] I write at home or whenever and wherever I feel the need for expression. I have quite a collection of my own work.; [pers.] Never cease to laugh for laughter is the music of the soul. Special thanks to Father Mark and my dear Curtis; [a.] Johnstown, PA

MALLOY, JOSEPHINE M.
[b.] November 5, 1941, Twin Falls, ID; [p.] Phillip G. and Mary L. Ortega; [m.] Victor E. Malloy, April 25, 1981; [ch.] Sissy, Floyd, Michael and William; [ed.] High School Diploma "1989"; [occ.] Domestic Engineer and Child Care Provider; [pers.] I believe poetry is the key to the mind and heart. I have always enjoyed writing poems. My husband and children have always been supportive with their encouragement and inspiration.; [a.] Bakersfield, CA

MALZAC, ALISA
[b.] September 8, 1985, Duluth, MN; [p.] Richard A. Malzac; [ed.] 5th Grade Student; [occ.] Student; [hon.] Attendance Award, Minnesota Student Inventers Congress Award, Junior Great Books Achievement award, outstanding spelling ability, McDonald's outstanding achievement award; [a.] Duluth, MN

MANCINO, JOHN
[b.] March 10, 1975, Los Angeles; [p.] Lou and Lori Mancino; [ed.] Liberty High; [occ.] I'm in my second year of College working on my Ph.D. in Physics; [oth. writ.] This is my first published

writing; [pers.] It is my hope as a writer, that I simulate new thought in the readers mind, so as to give one insight to themselves and the world around them.; [a.] Renton, WA

MANIS, MARY
[pen.] Mary Manis; [b.] August 15, 1932, Elgin, IL; [p.] Angela and Robert Shirley; [m.] Charles manis, August 1952; [ch.] Charles Jr., Robert and William; [ed.] High School Graduate, Elgin High School Elgin, IL; [occ.] Mary's Santas Hand Crafted Father Christmas Figures; [oth. writ.] This is my first published poem; [pers.] I write what I feel!; [a.] West Frankfort, IL

MANKA, EDWARD FELIX
[pen.] Chumly; [b.] October 11, 1952, Scranton; [p.] Catherine And Edward Manka (Deceased); [ch.] Heather Daughter, Granddaughter Alora; [ed.] BS Clinical Psy; [occ.] Machine Attendant, Thomson Consumer Electronics (24 yrs); [memb.] APA, Mulberry Street Poets, TCE Bass Committee, Marywood College Alumni, American Red Cross, American Legion, Fraternal Order of Police, underground recovery groups; [hon.] Letterman in HS, Swimteam, 7 1/2 lb. bass caught, Honorable Discharge US COAST GUARD YN2-E-5, Certified Forklift Driver, Cat owner, and Harley Davidson Low Rider Owner, (Waiting for Delivery); [oth. writ.] Various local newspapers poems have a way of showing up as Bird Cage catchers, puppy training pages, paper airplanes or landfill.; [pers.] The concept of now is the reality of the moment. Or to quote a bumper sticker on my Ford Ranger. "Reality What A Concept"; [a.] Lake Ariel, PA

MARCHESE, SHAUN AARON
[b.] May 1, 1979, Wheeling, WV; [p.] Frank and Ruth Marchese; [ed.] Junior at the Linsly School, Wheeling, WV; [occ.] Student; [memb.] Classic Club, Fellowship of Christian Athletes, Students Against Drunk Driving; [a.] Bellaire, OH

MARIEN, TRACY J.
[pen.] Marien J. Tracy; [b.] August 16, 1969, Massachusetts; [p.] Robert and Janet Marien; [ed.] Westminster Elem., Oakmonth Regional H.S., Mount Wachuseth Community College; [occ.] Administrative Assistant; [hon.] Fictional Writing utilized by English Comp. II professor as an example to future classes.; [oth. writ.] Currently working on first fiction novel. Many poems written and distributed.; [pers.] Watch out, Mr. King... I'm right behind you!; [a.] Westminster, MA

MARKING, GENEVA J.
[b.] Bangor, Wisconsin; [ed.] University of Wisconsin System; [oth. writ.] An essay on Jane Austen's Pride and Prejudice in the Wisconsin English Journal; [a.] New Berlin, WI

MARQUEZ, DONNA E.
[b.] August 31, 1956, Chicago, IL; [p.] Katherine and Donald Shelton; [ch.] Candace, Devin, Aaron; [ed.] B.S. Degree in Education from Chicago State University, Kenwood High School, Hookway Grammar School; [occ.] Appraisal Secretary - Heitman Financial Corporation, Chicago IL; [memb.] Carter Temple C.M.E. Church, Henry M. Williamson, Sr., Pastor; [oth. writ.] Currently working on other poems with an emphasis on love

and inspiration. Blue mountain arts is currently reviewing some of my poetry.; [pers.] My poems must touch the heart and inspire readers to love, to grow, and to look within.; [a.] Chicago, IL

MARRERO, LISSY
[b.] July 3, 1970, Miami, FL; [p.] Zaida and Abelardo E. Marrero; [pers.] I believe we should all love ourselves. The good and bad, faults and virtues. Realize who and what we are. Take a deep breath. Embrace your soul... Then set it free!; [a.] Miami, FL

MARSHALL, FREDERICK RUSSELL
[b.] July 12, 1951, Crisfield, MD; [p.] Frederick G. and Hazel Marshall; [ed.] Crisfield High, University of Maryland, Dallas Baptist College, Worldwide Travel School; [occ.] Floral Designer and Manager; [memb.] Academy Awards of Washington, DC. Which Raises money for AIDS related projects; [oth. writ.] Won a poem contest in Elementary School Tylerton Elementary; [pers.] Many people express themselves in many ways. I hope to help someone with my inner thoughts. I owe a great deal of this to my parents and grandparents, and especially to God.; [a.] Clinton, MD

MARSHALL, HILDA JEAN
[pen.] H. J. Marshall; [b.] June 7, 1945, Lake Providence, LA; [p.] William L. Harden, Thelma Jones-Harden; [ch.] Lyndon E. Marshall, Tangie F. Marshall; [ed.] Griffin High, University of Cincinnati B.S. Psychology; [occ.] Vice Pres. Marketing Interlott, Inc. Cincinnati, Ohio; [memb.] Victory Christian Center Church Cincinnati Arts Consortium, Vice Pres. Board of Trustees, Director, Interlott Board, Bible Teacher, Olivett, Baptist Church, Community Chest, Youth and Children Field of Service, (United Appeal); [hon.] November, 1993 - Ohio House of Representatives commendation for outstanding performance in a leadership role, December, 1993 - Featured in the Cincinnati Herald and Call Post newspapers as a pacesetter. February, 1994 - Featured in Nip Magazine, Honorable mention in Jet Magazine, People Section, November, 1994 - Featured in Upscale Magazine, Executive Suite, March, 1994 - Cincinnati Enquirer, 1994 Woman of the Year; [oth. writ.] Several articles in local newspaper Writer for sales Newspaper - LSR Reports; [pers.] I strive to encourage and inspire others to search and find the higher road in life. I have been influenced by Dr. Norman Vincent Peale and Dr. Robert Schuller especially Dr. Dwight Pate; [a.] Cincinnati, OH

MARTIN, BONNIE SHEROUSE
[b.] April 16, 1951, Lakeland, FL; [p.] Elmon and Bessie Sherouse; [m.] James Martin, April 16, 1978; [ch.] Sherra Ann Varney; [ed.] Kathleen Sr. High, CCI Business, Fla Fire College (Volunteer); [occ.] Work for Adventure Resorts; [memb.] Salt Spring Vol. Fire Dept., Literary Guild, Salt Spring Writers Forum Marion Co. Fireman's Assoc. have been a volunteer firefighter for the last 6 years; [oth. writ.] Many short stories and poems published by local papers and magazines; [pers.] My main focus is usually on my daughter and 3 grandchildren this particular poem was written for my mother, Bessie Sherouse, for mother's Day.; [a.] Salt Springs, FL

MARTIN, DAISY B.
[pen.] Daisy B. Martin; [b.] March 18, 1917, Milton,

FL; [p.] Anderson and Ardell McCree; [m.] Jame Martin, June 27, 1936; [ch.] James Jr. Lillian, Rebetha, Ollie, Lenora Martin; [ed.] Baldwind Country Training School; [occ.] Foster Grandparent Volunteer; [memb.] William Memorial C.M.E. church. Coordinator for the youth program at Sistrunck Blvd. Garden Apartments, Foster Grandparent Assoc.; [hon.] 10 years of Service with foster Grandparents, St. John United Methodist Church Award, Broward County Historical Commission Award. Koironia Worship Center Church Award.; [oth. writ.] Ten Years on foster Grandparent Advisory Board; [pers.] Never has anyone stood so tall as when they stooped to help a child.

MARTINEZ, BOB G.
[pen.] Bob G. Martinez; [b.] June 7, 1949, Las Vegas, NM; [p.] Mary Jane Martinez; [m.] Annette E. Martinez, February 10, 1973; [ch.] Lita R. Martinez; [ed.] High School Graduate (1968) from North High School in Denver; [occ.] Security Guard at the Denver Merchandise Mart (6 yrs.); [memb.] Distinguished Member, ISP; [hon.] Currently up for Publication in Six Anthologies; [oth. writ.] Compilation of poems, titled Sidetracks and Have written account of my life's experiences in single unbroken poem titled, My Time To Rhyme; [pers.] Divine infusion of verses God send express life's canon in the rainbow's end; [a.] Denver, CO

MARTYNA, SHARON M.
[b.] January 29, 1963, Oil City, PA; [p.] Elizabeth L. Schneider, Thomas M. Moffett Adoptive Father, Charles P. Timlin (Biological Father); [m.] Donald E. Martyna, May 26, 1984; [ch.] Amanda L., Brooke A., Cody J.; [ed.] Two years Associate degree R.N. from University of Pittsburgh at Bradford PA - High School and Oil City High School, Oil City, PA; [occ.] Registered Nurse, The Kane Community Hospital Kane, PA; [memb.] Saint Matthews Luthern Church Mt. Jewett, PA; [oth. writ.] Several other poems, none ever published (but hope to some day or have all my poems composed in a book of its own to be published. Many of which are tribute poems to people who have influenced my life.; [pers.] I have enjoyed poetry since Jr. High School when I first became interested and joined a "poetry club." Writing poetry is a past time hobby for me. My way of expressing my inner self and feelings.; [a.] Mount Jewett, PA

MASER II, MAURICE MILTON
[b.] February 29, 1968, Charleston, WV; [p.] Maurice M. Maser, Brenda Meyers; [ed.] Northwest High School; [occ.] Musical (Guitarist, Songwriter); [memb.] A.S.C.A.P. (American Society of Composers, Authors, and Publishers); [hon.] Previously Included with 19 other U.S. groups on Rodell records "Ran Cuts" Compilation C.P. for song "Somether Place."; [pers.] Many of my lyrics and poems show the stark realism of todays society. Different shades and textures evoking both light and dark good and Bad. I have been influenced by such writers as Poe H.P love craft, and the poetry of James D. Morrison; [a.] Greensboro, NC

MASON, EDWARD M.
[pen.] Big Bad Wolf; [b.] March 31, 1965, Norristown; [ed.] G.E.D. Norristown High; [occ.] Explosive Welding Technician; [pers.] Life is a dark place... The wolf can see in the dark; [a.] Shillington, PA

MASON, PATRICIA A.
[b.] December 26, 1947, Decatur, TX; [p.] J.C. Williams, Lorene Williams; [ch.] Melanie LaNelle, Timothy George; [ed.] Sabine High School, Kilgore Junior College, Stephen F. Austin State University; [occ.] Teacher, 4th Grade Leverett's Chapel ISD, Overton, TX; [memb.] Association of Texas Professional Educators, Cancer Society, Parent - Teacher - Student Association; [oth. writ.] Numerous poems and a couple of short stories. None have been submitted anywhere before.; [pers.] It is my pleasure to share the beauty, joy, and laughter of life with everyone when I write. I have been greatly influenced by my association with colleagues and students for the past 25 years.; [a.] Kilgore, TX

MASTERS, GERARD G.
[b.] January 22, 1941, Cape Town, South Africa; [p.] Jack and Betty; [ed.] Theol. Bachelor Philosophy Bachelor; [occ.] Catholic Priest; [oth. writ.] Various articles, Newspapers, Magazines in South Africa; [a.] Torrington, CT

MAYNARD, DENISE
[b.] April 28, 1975, Hillsdale, MI; [p.] William and Janet Maynard; [ed.] Quincy High, Jackson Community College, Major in Theatre; [occ.] Sales, Student, Modeling, Acting, Singing; [hon.] Who's who among American High School student, Dean's list, excellence in learning, Talent award and 2nd runner up in 1993, tip-up-pageant; [a.] Ashland, OH

MCBRIDE, JULIE
[b.] September 18, 1977, Brooklyn, NY; [p.] Eileen and Joseph McBride; [ed.] Ridgewood High School, Marist College; [memb.] HIV/AIDS Peer Educator Campus Ministry Resident Student Council; [hon.] 12th Grade - English Achievement of Excellence; [oth. writ.] Other poems published in High School literary magazine, Articles in High School newspaper; [pers.] I would like to thank my family and James for all their support and encouragement.; [a.] Ridgewood, NJ

MCCAIN, KENNETH
[b.] March 26, 1954, Roanoke, VA; [m.] Betty H. McCain, June 24, 1988; [ch.] Step-son, Daniel Lee; [ed.] William Byrd High School; [occ.] Unemployed; [memb.] Deacon at Garden of Prayer #7 Church of God in Christ; [oth. writ.] Roanoke Times (Local Newspaper); [pers.] I was inspired by my wife, Betty, and by my Pastor and friends.; [a.] Roanoke, VA

MCCANTS, ANNIE M.
[b.] May 2, 1928, Evergren, AL; [p.] Richard and Pearlie Stott (deceased); [m.] Luther H. McCants (deceased), August 6, 1952; [ch.] I raised 11-6 are mine; [ed.] High School Completed 10th Grade; [occ.] Operator power machine. Making fireman glove; [memb.] I don't have the time to joined any clubs. I don't go out to dinner. I am trying to make ends meet with a part time job.; [hon.] One for my poem tear's from Heaven and one of God wonder's not publishes; [oth. writ.] Short stories none published, songs, lyric, I have other poem my part time. I write to ebony, I inter a short story writer contest; [pers.] When my children was growing up I made their school clothes; [a.] Milwaukee, WI

MCCARTHY, ELIZABETH
[b.] March 18, 1924, Georgia; [m.] Mor McCarthy, M.D., June 7, 1947; [ch.] Ten (10) children, who taught me for more that I taught them.; [ed.] RN BA; [occ.] Retired; [memb.] Women's University Club, Seattle, WA; [hon.] Magna Cum Laude from college; [oth. writ.] Stories for my children and grandchildren.; [pers.] I appreciate the world I live in and its people much more when I write I must be intimately involved.; [a.] Seattle, WA

MCCARTHY, ELIZABETH T.
[b.] December 3, 1927, Brooklyn, NY; [p.] Agnes and Modesto Cappelluti; [m.] Thomas E. McCarthy, September 17, 1949; [ch.] Thomas Jr., Tara; [occ.] Retired; [memb.] Country Knolls Women Club; [pers.] I am a very emotional person. I mostly write when I am sad. I want to thank my children, Tommy and Tara for being there for me.; [a.] Ballston Lake, NY

MCCARTY, KELLY
[b.] October 9, 1978, Oakland, CA; [p.] Michael and Joan McCarty; [ed.] Placer Elementary, Del Oro High School; [occ.] High School Student and part-time employee at Mt. Mike's Pizza; [memb.] Art Club, CSF, Sierra Club, Youth of Unity; [hon.] Cum Laude (3 yrs.) Academic Block with four lamps, Excellence in English Award (11th grade), Who's Who among American High School Students; [a.] Loomis, CA

MCCARY, MATTHEW C.
[pen.] Bobby Johnson, Jon Walters; [b.] July 10, 1979, Fairfield, CA; [p.] Rick McCary, Charlotte McCary; [ed.] Diberville High School; [occ.] Food Distribution, Isle of Capri Casino; [memb.] Student Government, (S.A.D.D.) Students Against Drunk Driving, JROTC; [pers.] Sometimes feelings can be better understood on paper, than when spoken. If more people could put there feelings on paper, there would be an extensive surplus of poets.; [a.] Biloxi, MS

MCCONNELL, CHRISTINA
[pen.] Chrissy; [b.] June 1, 1978, Clarksburg; [p.] Biological: Mary McConnell and Earnest Smith, Adoptive: Joann and Blaine McConnell; [ed.] Doddridge County High School; [memb.] Student Council, Smithburg United Methodist Church, Rural Teen Club; [hon.] Tied for 3rd place in the Soil Conservation Samara Awards Program, Award for highest score in Science; [oth. writ.] Many Short Stories; [pers.] My poem was based on the affects of strenuous work in school.; [a.] West Union, WV

MCCOOK, RHONDA J.
[pen.] R. J. McCook; [b.] February 17, 1964, Bakersfield, CA; [p.] Ronald and Billie Plant; [m.] Albert McCook, February 24, 1988; [ed.] BA Philosophy and French. Currently working on masters in literature at Col State University Bakersfield.; [pers.] I wont to thank my husband Albert for believing in me and my talent enough to encourage my entry into this contest. Thanks to Mom for my vision.; [a.] Bakersfield, CA

MCCOY, EDMUND C.
[b.] September 16, 1918, Raton, NM; [p.] Edmund Crowe, Fanny Crowe; [m.] Glennis L. McCoy, September 20, 1940; [ed.] Holy Trinity High, Anthony RE School, Business Management U.S. Army WW II, Musician; [occ.] Retired; [memb.] St. Vincent de Paul Soc, St. Catherines Catholic Church Drug and Alcohol Abuse Counselor; [oth. writ.] Several poems, songs, lyrics, to me full length book compiled - but not published this is my first attempt for recognition; [pers.] For the poetry is the fulfillment of a secret yearning, deep inside, that can only be satisfied through expression. A strive to impress and inspire future generations to keep freedom and beauty by their side and express and follow their talent whatever it may be; [a.] Temecula, CA

MCCOY, MARCUS DAVID
[pen.] MMc; [b.] October 20, 1950, Detroit, Michigan; [p.] Dr. Robert McCoy/ D. Jean McCoy; [m.] Mari Beth McCoy, June 9, 1990; [ch.] Joseph C. McCoy; [ed.] Seaholm High, Michigan State University, Eastern Michigan U.; [occ.] Corporate Video Producer; [memb.] The Peoples Network (TPN); [hon.] Eagle Scout, Certified NLP Practitioner, Graduate Silva Mind Control, Top IBM Sales - Computerland; [oth. writ.] Poetry on many themes compiled in a manuscript called "Chapters"; [pers.] My poetry reflects empathy of feelings and small "nuggets" of perception offered to increase the reader's perspectives.; [a.] Peachtree City, GA

MCCUE, LON DAWSON
[b.] March 31, 1951, Steubenville, OH; [p.] Harry and Dorothy McCue; [m.] Paula Jean McCue, April 11, 1987; [ch.] Alex Douglas and Ian Robert; [ed.] Bachelors of Music-Bowling Green State University/ Masters in School Psychology - The Ohio State University; [occ.] School Psychologist, Dublin City Schools; [memb.] School Psychologist of Central Ohio/Ohio School Psychologist Association/National Association of School Psychologist/ Member Bellpoint United Methodist Church; [pers.] With God all things really are possible. I believe everything we hear, see, and read is imprinted in our mind. We should fill our minds with good things and good things will come forth.; [a.] Radnor, OH

MCDANIEL, WILLIAM CARL
[b.] July 25, 1951, Mishawaka, IN; [p.] John C. McDaniel, Ruby E. McDaniel; [m.] Julie Anne McDaniel, July 23, 1981; [ch.] James Carl, Tammy Leanne, Christine Laree, Madeline Renee Mark Anthony, William Michael, Jennifer Roseanne; [ed.] Andrew P. High, Delta College; [occ.] Bus Operator - San Joaquin Regional Transit District; [pers.] I sincerely believe that all people should open their eyes and feel with their hearts. There is just not enough compassion in our world today.; [a.] Stockton, CA

MCDANIELS, HAZEL V.
[pen.] Hazel V. McDaniels; [b.] May 31, 1921, Indianapolis, IN; [p.] Samuel, Mhanie McDaniels; [ch.] Phyllis L. A. Brown; [occ.] Retired; [memb.] Greater St. Mark Missionary Baptist Church - Had aneury, SM 1975 - Starter writing after that I am a mother of one - grandmother of 5, great grandmother 6, great great mother of 1; [oth. writ.] Birthday get well, Sympathy - Mother's Day, Thanksgiving, Christmas Tribute etc.; [pers.] It's my desire to do some good thing everyday, I like to keep this rumor going "God" Love you.; [a.] Indianapolis, IN

MCDONALD, GRACE
[b.] July 27, 1898, Hill County, TX; [m.] J. K. McDonald (Deceased); [ch.] Two daughters, 2 grandchildren, 5 great grandchildren; [hon.] Golden Globe Award for Poetry; [oth. writ.] For years I have written poems for family members on their birthdays and other special occasions.; [pers.] I have had a happy and satisfying life for 97 years and still going!; [a.] Hillsboro, TX

MCDONNEL, MARK
[b.] February 29, 1972, San Jose, CA; [p.] John and Nancy McDonnell; [ed.] Bellarmine College Preparatory West Valley College, University of California Santa Cruz; [occ.] Currently a Premed Student at UCSC; [hon.] Dears Honor's Susie Lee memorial Scholarship UCSC merit scholarship; [pers.] (0294) There are many who deserve credit for nuturing my love of writing, but none would be possible without the endless support of my parents.; [a.] Santa Cruz, CA

MCELWEE, JAMES R.
[b.] October 11, 1933, Shamokin, PA; [p.] James J. and Mildred E. McElwee; [m.] Nancy J. McElwee, May 14, 1955; [ch.] Two; [ed.] Mt. Carmel Catholic High School graduate. 1952. I could never afford to go to college. We were just too poor.; [occ.] Deli Onwer - 25 years. Originator of over 1600 Sandwiches.; [memb.] None. I have spent my life working and devoting myself to my family. Being a good father to my family. Being a good father has been my greatest accomplishment. My next love is poetry.; [hon.] The love of my family. Although we give food and money to the less fortunate I do it out of love. No one will ever know how we help others, only the folks we help know. I want to recognition.; [oth. writ.] I have written a great many poems. It's my hobby. This is the first time I have ever submitted a poem to anyone.; [pers.] I have been greatly influenced by a nun - Sr. Constane Mary who instilled in me confidence and a love for poetry. Even in death she remain's my greatest inspiration. Philosophy: Hunger kills the body, Poverty kills the mind.; [a.] Shamokin, PA

MCGILVRAY, APRILE CLAIRE
[b.] September 25, 1984, Hattiesburg, MS; [p.] Ramona McGilvray, Clark and James M. Clark; [ed.] 5th Grader at Oak Grove Upper Elementary in Hattiesburg, Mississippi; [occ.] Student (all a student); [memb.] Immanuel Baptist Church, Hattiesburg, MS; [hon.] Honor roll student straight a's, Pee Wee Cheerleader, 3 yrs twirling, 2 years gymnastics, talent show 3rd place winner, drug awareness essay contest winner, dance; [oth. writ.] Won an award in 3rd grade for essay I wrote against drugs during drug Awareness Week at School; [pers.] I enjoy being with my friends and family. I growing up in Hattiesburg, Mississippi. We have a mall, super Wal-Mart and lots more.; [a.] Sumrall, MS

MCGOWAN, J. L.
[pen.] Les McGowan; [b.] July 2, 1922, Springfield, MA; [occ.] Retired; [oth. writ.] If, Decision, White Ship, Without Mourning, The Jacaranda Tree, US; [pers.] To bring beauty to the world to stir men's souls; [a.] Arcadia, CA

MCGRADY, ED
[b.] February 14, 1948, Providence, RI; [p.] Dorothy and John McGrady; [m.] Paula McGrady, June 24, 1995; [ch.] Tammy, Ryan, Ken, Heather; [ed.] Pilgrim High School Warwick, RI; [oth. writ.] I wrote this poem for my daughter Tammy, and read it to her on her wedding day. I wanted her to know how much I love her and how special she always been to me, 20 years ago when she first came into my life, now and always.; [a.] West Warwick, RI

MCGREGOR, RICHARD MARION
[pen.] Marion McGregor; [b.] October 6, 1964; [p.] Hazel Alsbrooks McGregor; [m.] Still Wandering; [ed.] Georgetown University - Washington D.C., (Computer Science); [occ.] Computer Programmer; [oth. writ.] Many, though none have been published at this point; [pers.] No matter his domain, the dream is never so cunning as to perfectly elude the relentless heart.; [a.] Euless, TX

MCGUIRE, VALERIE J.
[pen.] Valerie J. Wiley McGuire; [b.] July 13, 1958, Battle Creek, MI; [p.] George P. Wiley and Jo Marie Wiley, deceased; [m.] Delton R. McGuire, April 28, 1979; [ch.] Katherine, Rachel, and Travis; [ed.] H.S. Gull Lake High, Richland, MI College, Michigan Christian, Rochester Hills, MI, Associate of Arts Degree; [occ.] "Teacher" at Kiddieland Day care, Hollis, OK; [memb.] Young Homemakers Organization of OK, Hollis, Member - Church of Christ; [oth. writ.] H.S. Publication-call me janitor "The Wishing Tree," "A Feeling" and "Tanka", 1975. The coming of Dawn, "In Search of: New Avenues"; [pers.] I feel and hope to share the appreciation of nature that has often inspired me to greater heights of positive living. I still feel like a little kid stopping to watch the squirrel or gaze on the beauty of a country wild flower.; [a.] Hollis, OK

MCINTIRE, MARK R.
[pen.] Joe Bean; [b.] November 17, 1971, Akron, OH; [p.] Jim, Jean; [m.] Patricia McIntire, December 19, 1991; [ch.] Joseph Dale McIntire; [ed.] Central Hower High, Akron Machining Institute; [occ.] Machinist; [oth. writ.] Various Speeches and poems; [pers.] I believe a true poets writing is an attention of his or her self.; [a.] Akron, OH

MCKINNEY, ELEANOR
[pen.] Eleanor Moen McKinney; [b.] November 30, 1930; [p.] Alice and Francis R. Moen; [m.] John McKinney, October 8, 1949; [ch.] John, Virginia, Francis, Michael and Steven; [ed.] Gloucester City High School; [occ.] Retired Bank Teller; [oth. writ.] Receipe for rehabilitating yourself after a stroke, receipe for a happy and long lasting marriage; [pers.] Having a major stroke in Feb, 1995 inspired me to write my prayer and get teardrops on my pillow.; [a.] Brooklawn, NJ

MCLEMORE JR., WILLIAM R.
[pen.] Will; [b.] February 19, 1966, Monroe County, TN; [p.] W.R. and Alean McLemore; [m.] Stephanie L. McLemore, October 26, 1985; [ed.] Graduated Vonore High School 1984; [occ.] Disabled - Diagnosed with Multiple Sclerosis May 1992; [oth. writ.] Poems for my wife; [pers.] People say you don't appreciate your health until you don't have it anymore, this is true. I know by experience. I say some people don't appreciate part of your wedding

vows, in sickness and in health until your spouse removes all doubts from your mind.; [a.] Madisonville, TN

MCLESTER, CAROL A.
[b.] January 18, 1948, Norfolk, VA; [p.] Shirley Pollard and Raymond Dotson; [m.] Robert Gibson McLester III, December 20, 1969; [ch.] Bonnie Jean and Robin Gayle; [ed.] Masters Degree in English Education from University of FL; [occ.] Full time care giver to elderly parent. Taught school 18 years.; [hon.] Served in U.S. Military (Navy.) Have received honors in athletics years ago.; [oth. writ.] I have a book that I published myself that I use to help me teach writing. It is called of Rattlesnakes and cakes.; [pers.] I am constantly on that inner search for meaning in life. The poet has the power to make the connection between emotion and action which creates the circumstance. I want to explore the depths of connection.

MCMAHAN, CHERYL ANN
[b.] September 15, 1962, Baltimore, MD; [p.] Dina Jones and Marvin Jones; [ch.] Jordan Duane, Joshua Glenn, and Brittany Ann; [occ.] Raising three children and writing books and poems; [memb.] The church of Jesus Christ of latter Day Saints; [oth. writ.] "The Little Mermaid" a childrens personalized book. Co-authored with a childhood friend.; [pers.] I've always strongly believed that everything happens to us for a reason. That through tears and laughter we can find deep within ourselves - hidden strengths that each and every one of us has been given.; [a.] Navarre, FL

MCMAHON, MARIE M.
[pen.] Arline Barry; [b.] February 2, 1922, Anderson, Al; [p.] Theodora and Minnie Moore; [m.] Richard J. McMahon, March 5, 1966; [ed.] Long Beach High, Long Beach City College, Lord Fairfax Community College, (Ed. Bus. And Arts) (have three degrees) Sheppard College, Paralegal Institute, West Virginia University (1/2 Master's in Communication); [occ.] Paralegal, Journalism author (working on book) and have done several songs, both words and music; [memb.] None, to busy...except Church; [hon.] Not yet; [oth. writ.] Covered Government (journalism) Written many poems (words) and music for special occasions and special people who almost always PUSH me to try to publish. I do have other copyrighted verses and songs.; [pers.] I'm very loyal to our U. S. Constitution, I feel it is the greatest document ever written.... I love justice, hate any kind of injustice....also love many kinds of music...can perform sacred and less complicated by "ear" never had a lessons...teachers would not teach and "ruin" what they called "natural talent. (I'm not that good) but do enjoy doing what I can do...As with law, I always just "KNOW" it, or can "hear" it, and I can prove myself right with research.; [a.] Berkeley Springs, WV

MCNAIRY, HAROLD G.
[pen.] Hal; [b.] March 30, 1929, Alberdeem, MS; [p.] Mr. Frank Billips, Miss Valaria Maria McNairy; [ed.] Grade School Graduation, High School Graduation College Graduation, Hotel and Restaurant Institutes Plug a Lawyer Degree LLB; [occ.] Land investor and a retired veteran, and a song writer; [memb.] Songs writers club and X'mas valley and another songs writers club; [hon.] The United

State Army Military Purple Heart, and many more; [oth. writ.] X'mas cards sent on Christmas; [pers.] If you desire to be some one Important before eyes of God make up your mind and go after it? You should not Miss! with a God circus soul.; [a.] Saint Louis, Missouri

MCQUEEN, CYNTHIA MARIE
[b.] October 24, 1948, Albion, MI; [p.] Hosie and Etta Hall; [m.] William F. McQueen III, August 5, 1979; [ch.] Sudari, Jacci, Billy, Carla; [ed.] Washington Gardner High, Kellogg Community College, Eastern Michigan University, Michigan State Uni. University of St. Thomas; [occ.] Elementary Teacher, Holbrook Elem. Cy-Fair I.S.D.; [memb.] Abundant Life Cathedral Church, U-WIN Women's Group. Word Power Plus, ATPE Educational Organization, Curriculum and Instruction, Rosehills writer's Guild; [pers.] One of my purposes for writing is to share common human experiences that connect us all. I strive to encourage, enlighten, refresh and entertain the souls of mankind.; [a.] Houston, TX

MCWILLIAMS, ANTHONY ANTOINE
[pen.] Anthony Antoine, Truth Anthony; [b.] October 21, 1969, Newark, NJ; [p.] Marjorie McWilliams, Chester Sanders; [ch.] Vogue Lee-McWilliams; [ed.] The Art Institute of Dallas, Honor Student, Associate of Applied Science Degree in Music and Video Business; [occ.] Recording Artist, Founder of Launch Records and Flamin' Box Productions; [oth. writ.] Lyrics of Pride, Spoken words promoting positive homosexual self and societal images; [pers.] Dear World: It has taken twenty-five years to express the sentiments of my included poem without shame of its content or fear of the consequences from what was said. Due to homophobia, many will not reach this level of freedom and pride, a human right that many heterosexuals take for granted and assume to be only their own. Let's rid the world of this senseless phobia two allow ourselves as humans to receive the blessings and education that results from the appreciation of diversity.; [a.] Allen, TX

MECHE, DANIEL ELMO
[pen.] Daniel E. Meche; [b.] February 6, 1956, Buffalo, NY; [p.] Lawlas Meche, Agnes Meche; [m.] Mary Jo Meche, April 21, 1991; [ch.] Danielle Mary, Hannah Kate, Abigail Margaret, Benjamin Michael; [ed.] Deer park High, San Jacinto Jr. College and University of Houston Clear Lake; [occ.] Project Administrator Brown and Root Inc; [memb.] Gideon's International; [hon.] Dean's List; [oth. writ.] Numerous Poems; [pers.] "God is my judge" prov 3:5-6 - Kindness and gentleness is what I strive to do. Follow God and have no regrets.; [a.] Winfield, KS

MEEINK, SUSAN
[pen.] Susan Meeink; [b.] February 24, 1979, Fall River Mills, CA; [p.] Bob and Jan Meeink; [ed.] Big Valley High School; [occ.] Student, Senior at BVHS; [memb.] FBLA, CSF, FHA, BVHS Drama Society Student Council; [hon.] Who's Who Among American High School Students 1994-95 Recognition, Honor Roll, Recipient of awards for artwork at local fair, Academic Awards; [pers.] In my writings, I try to give, representations of how I think other people see the world. I admire many poets, especially Henry Rollins for his incredible, romantic writing style.; [a.] Bieber, CA

MEEKS, BARBARA JEAN
[b.] August 12, 1958, Troy, Al.; [p.] Joseph D. Meeks and Imogene Meeks; [ch.] Lauren Michelle Riner; [ed.] A. Crawford Mosley High School, Gulf Coast Community College; [occ.] Legal Secretary; [memb.] Children International; [hon.] Becoming a mother is my highest honor. Having a beautiful, funny and loving daughter has been my greatest award. Lauren is a great inspiration; [oth. writ.] I've written 100's of poems and a few children's stories. This will be my first publication; [pers.] I usually write about things that touch my heart in some way. As to poetry, I prefer it short, simple and to the point. I want to feel what the writer feels. If it doesn't draw on my emotion, I just turn the page.; [a.] Tallahassee, FL

MEHRMANN, MICHELLE
[pen.] True Heart; [b.] July 31, 1962, Cedar Rapids, IA; [p.] Ron Watson, Carole Chartak; [m.] Christopher E. Mehrmann, December 27, 1990; [ch.] Teaya Marie Ann Perez; [ed.] Taylor Iowa - Ditmas - NY, GED Virginia Beach - Prince, Georges Community College; [occ.] Manager for a Deli; [pers.] I was influenced, by the marine American Indian's ways of living and respecting all things we need to become ones and respect everything great and small.; [a.] Upper Marlboro, MD

MELSON, SADIE FRANCES RANSOM
[pen.] Sadie; [b.] June 2, 1929, Paris, KY; [p.] Deceased; [ch.] Jimmie, Willa, Sharon; [ed.] Masters in Education El (University of Dayton); [occ.] Teacher (Elementary); [memb.] Ohio Education Association, National Education Association, St. John Church, United Way; [hon.] Ten top Women of Dayton Ohio 1967, Honor Student Central State Un. Wellerforce Ohio (Under Graduate) I was in college with 3 of my children, My grades surpassed all of their grades; [oth. writ.] "Dr Martin Ruther King's Dream, "A Wonderful Birth Day"; [pers.] I love creative writing I love to read, I will write a book someday it gives me a great sense of pleasure to write about people, nature and other creatures.; [a.] Dayton, OH

MENDENHALL, MAY
[b.] May 31, 1954, Phils.; [p.] Mr. and Mrs. Onofre Balbas; [m.] David A. Mendenhall, December 4, 1975; [ch.] Melanie, Lisanne, Merry and John; [ed.] San Francisco High, Ortanez General Hospital; [occ.] Housewife and Full time "mom"; [memb.] Lady of the Valley Catholic Church; [pers.] That whosoever believeth in him should not perish but have everlasting life.; [a.] Hemet, CA

MENIDES, LAURA JEHN
[ed.] BA Queens College, MA University of Chicago, Ph.D. New York University; [occ.] English Professor, Worcester Polytechnic Institute; [memb.] Worcester County Poetry Asso., Dickers Fellowship, Modern Language Assoc.; [hon.] Awards from Mass. Cultural Council, Worcester Poetry Asso., Worcester Cultural Commission; [oth. writ.] Poems published in Journals and Anthologies, articles about modern American writers, opera libretto based on William Faulkner's As I Lay Dying.; [pers.] I like Emily Dickinson's notion that a poem should tell the truth, but "Tell it slant."; [a.] Worcester, MA

MERCURIO, LINDA CINDY
[b.] April 1, 1978, Hoboken, NJ; [p.] Bertha and George Mercurio; [ed.] Saint Dominic Academy (Senior), plan to attend College; [occ.] Student at St. Dominic Academy, Jersey City, NJ; [memb.] Varsity Soccer, National Honor Society, School Newspaper "the Trumpet" and Literary Magazine "The Elan," Writing Club, Hospitality Club, Spanish Club; [hon.] Who's who among American High School Student 1993-1995, United State Achievement Academy 1994-1995, Soccer Varsity Award, Physics King of the Road Competition 2nd Place; [oth. writ.] Articles for "The trumpet", poems published in "The Elan"; [pers.] My honest out-look on life is always evident somewhere in my writing. I have found that my best writing has come forth through the release of negative experiences.; [a.] Hoboken, NJ

MEYER, MARC KRISTOPHER
[pen.] Kristopher; [b.] January 20, 1977, Bremerhaven, Germany; [p.] Carried Meyer and Peter Meyer; [ed.] Graduated High School, Freshman in College, Norwich University; [occ.] Student; [memb.] Maroon Key, AFROTC; [oth. writ.] Drama piece addition to "A Raisin in the Sun," dozens of poems; [pers.] "Do to impress others and you will impress yourself."; [a.] Northfield, VT

MICHELLE, LIEBKNECHT
[pen.] Anniemae Hobes; [b.] December 11, 1932, Rhine Georgia; [p.] Josephine Former George Former; [m.] George Washington Hobes, July 11, 1949; [ch.] Annie Laura Napoleon Hobes; [ed.] Finish 10th Grade at Mount Olive High School in 1948; [occ.] Housewife I am disability and receive SSI; [oth. writ.] I try to shave my feelings about God in my writing, thank you Lord poets Miami florida 33150; [pers.] Would be keep the 2 commands Jesus gave. The love, study, pursuit of wisdom, Knowledge of things and their causes. Acknowledge study which dear with ultimate reality, that cause principals of things.; [a.] Miami, FL

MICHONSKI, TIMOTHY A.
[b.] December 31, 1963, Berwyn, IL; [p.] Benjamin and Lillian Michonski; [ed.] Proviso West High School; [occ.] Technician; [pers.] I strive to bring out the realizm of situations that occur to people in every day life.; [a.] Villa Park, IL

MIDDLETON, CHENEY RUTH
[pen.] Ruth Middleton; [b.] May 2, 1921, Bellefontaine, OH; [p.] Ruth C. Volkert, George S. Middleton; [m.] James Kleeman A. Austin Cheney, 1943-1960; [ch.] John A. Kleeman, Thomas J. Kleeman, David P. Kleeman; [ed.] Vassar College, Wesleyan University Cranbrook Academy of Art MFA 1975; [occ.] Sculptor and Writer; [oth. writ.] Alexandra David-Neel, Portrait of an Adventurer Shambala Publications 1989, Lewis Rubenstein - A Hudson Valley Painter - Overlook Press 1993; [pers.] As an artist it has been my habit to use a variety of materials - stone, wood, paper, ink, paint and words. Recently I have created combinations that include visual, tactile, and auditory experience all of which I consider "poems"; [a.] Litchfield, CT

MIGDAL, COLLEEN R.
[pen.] Coco; [b.] January 16, 1963, West Covina, CA; [p.] James McGregor, Jenell McGregor; [m.] Bruce Migdal, September 19, 1990; [ch.] Max

Michael Migdal; [ed.] Rowland High; [occ.] Housewife and Mother; [oth. writ.] Several poems of which are about, life, my life, family and everyday living. Many poems about children.; [pers.] I wright to express my inter most feelings and thoughts that are easier to say on paper. Words come to me easier in my mind than speaking. I have been greatly influenced by my grandfather who passed away when I was six years old. My mother Jenell, Sister Cherry, Aunt Jan Husband and most of all my son Max.; [a.] Rancho Cucamonga, CA

MILES, DEBORAH SUE
[b.] April 19, 1958, Benton, IL; [p.] Charles and Sylvia Walker; [m.] William Mallory, Williams (Deceased); [ch.] Charles Fletcher, Amy and Hope Williams; [ed.] I quit school to be a mother during my freshman year at Galatia High School. Received my GED in 1990.; [occ.] Mother and Grandmother; [pers.] This poem was written in memory of my son Charles Allen Fletcher November 27, 1974. He was murdered by Roderick Choisser on April 27, 1994. I was shot and paralyzed at this criminal's rampage.; [a.] Galatia, IL

MILES, NICOLE DENISE
[pen.] Nikki Miles; [b.] July 27, 1978, Carlisle, PA; [p.] Donald Miles, Goldie Miles; [ed.] Kecoughtan High School Graduation Date, June 15, 1996; [occ.] Student; [oth. writ.] Currently have over 37 Original Poems; [pers.] I believe that a poet is only as good as the feelings she evokes in her readers.; [a.] Hampton, VA

MILLECAM, JENNIFER
[pen.] Jennifer Millecam; [b.] February 24, 1985, Evanston, WY; [ed.] 5th Grade Student Mt. View Elementary; [hon.] Battle of the Books - School Competition; [oth. writ.] Several other poems; [pers.] I love reading and writing. I have written several poems. I wrote mothers for a birthday present for my mother. My mother is a song writer. I want to be like her.; [a.] Kenai, AL

MILLER, ERIN M.
[b.] March 2, 1970, Englewood, CO; [p.] Noel Downey; [m.] Donald Miller, December 3, 1990; [ch.] Jonathan, Kristin, Curits; [sib.] G.E.D. 12th grade High School; [ed.] Home Maker; [pers.] I have always wanted to write poetry, but I never knew what to write. Now that I have three children it's amazing how I'm so inspired; [a.] Boone, NC

MILLER, GLORIA ALBERTA
[pen.] Gloria A. Miller; [b.] March 10, 1917, Knowlton, MT; [p.] Alma Laurence, Richard Brown; [m.] Fred William Miller, September 19, 1936; [ch.] Robert, Richard, Howard Miller; [ed.] Hammond Tech High, Sophomore; [occ.] Housewife; [memb.] Nazerene Church of Gilman Ill; [hon.] Silver Award (World of Poetry), Golden Award (World of Poetry) 1989, Silver Award (World of Poetry) 1990, Illianak knews - Published poem Times Republic Spirit - published poem also, Gilman Start News gave a write up on my Golden Award; [oth. writ.] The Glorious Fourth, Death Of Two Brothers, Three Little Pumpkins Presents Under The X'mas Tree, American Hostage Early Dawn; [pers.] I loved long fellow and his poems, in school especially. Most of my poems come from the reality of the things that happen in my life. The Lord has al lot to do with me

and of course it would not be fair if I didn't mention, I take after MOM. She wrote poems too and I would like to think I take after her.; [a.] Gilman, IL

MILLER, JEANETTE
[b.] January 21, 1946, Pittsfield, MA; [p.] Allen and Bertha Mayes; [m.] Bert Miller; [ch.] Michael, Jonathan, Robert and Jacob; [ed.] Piltsfield High, Simmons College (Boston) NY University Yale School of Music; [occ.] Pediatric Physical therapist Supervisor Concert Soprano; [memb.] American Physical Therapy Association Alpha Kappa Alpha Sorority Professional Women's Organization Simmons Alumnae first Methodist Church, Amherst. MA President of Bertha Mayes Scholar-ship Committee; [hon.] Pittsfield High School Award, Rotary Scholarship, March of Dimes Award to student, Finalist Marion Anderson Competition Dean's List, Employee of the year, Winner in essay contest (College); [oth. writ.] Articles in Lexington minute Man publications and concord Journal-Noir Magazine, Article in Amherst Gazette short stories in methodist National Pub. Saturday evening post; [pers.] As a singer and musician I find that writing is an extension of the music in my heart. To be able to write is to be free! Currently, I am working on a book of autobiographical short stories.; [a.] Amherst, MA

MILLER, JOAN Y.
[b.] August 1, 1942, Wyandotte, MI; [p.] Clifford and Wilhelmina Peterson; [m.] Fredric L. Miller, June 25, 1960; [ch.] Cynthia Sue and Samuel James; [ed.] Belding Central High; [occ.] I teach quilting and sewing classes at Janie's Button Box, Am also a seamstress; [memb.] West Michigan Quilt Guild, American Quilt Society, Belding Silk City Quilters; [oth. writ.] Just completed a children's book, which is being illustrated before trying to get it published.; [pers.] I enjoy writing poetry and books for and about children.; [a.] Belding, MI

MILLER, JUDIE LYNN
[b.] June 24, 1964, Philadelphia, PA; [p.] George F. Walton, Helen T. Walton; [m.] Raymond S. Miller, September 22, 1090; [ed.] Saint Hubert High, National School of Health Tech., EMT; [occ.] Monitor Technician (Cardiology); [memb.] Cancer Support Group (GHS-Parkview Hospital); [hon.] Chapel of four Chaplins Award (for working and volunteering as an EMT at a local Community Ambulance); [oth. writ.] "I've Counted the flutters of Butterflies' Wings" self published and copyrights reserved. This book of poem is dedicated to cancer patients and the terminally ill. I am publishing these books for Doctors to distribute to their patients.; [pers.] I suffered Cancer in 1993 and cared for a terminally ill mother who passed away in 1995. I hope this book will help the terminally ill and Cancer patients come to terms. Fighting Cancer gave me the knowledge of understanding the needs of Cancer patients and the death and dying.; [a.] Philadelphia, PA

MILLER, MELISSA ANNE
[pen.] Delphine; [b.] June 12, 1977, Flint, MI; [p.] Addison O. and Karen Sue; [ed.] Currently in College; [occ.] Pursuing a Biology Degree; [hon.] Girl Scout Gold Award, various community honors; [pers.] Be true to your heart, you're the only one who will be.; [a.] Naples, FL

MILLER, ROSEMARY SHANNON
[b.] May 10, 1911, Kokomo, IN; [p.] Mr. Leo G. Shannon, Miss Pearl O. Weidner; [m.] Married four times; [ch.] One son; [ed.] Years and Haft High School; [occ.] Retired; [oth. writ.] Armed Forces Day, Buy The River Potomac, Outside My Window; [pers.] Mostly I was seeking to know the secrets mysteries of the words of God and so to (my) satisfaction I received them.; [a.] Kalamazoo, MI

MILLIAS, TERESA
[occ.] Teacher; [a.] Worcester, NY

MINEER, NANCY
[pen.] Nancy Mineer; [b.] April 21, 1936, Harris, KY; [p.] Taylor Smith, Rachel Lawhorn Smith; [m.] Bennie Harold Mineer, December 19, 1952; [ch.] Frances, Donna, John, Jim; [ed.] Lewis County High School, US School of Music, Young Ladies' Counselor; [occ.] Homemaker (Domestic Engineer); [memb.] South Shore Church of God (Organist); [oth. writ.] Several poems published in local newspaper. Short stories, skits and plays for church, Library and Nursing Homes; [pers.] I strive to reflect the love of God for mankind. In my writing, I have been greatly influenced by every day life experiences of myself and others.; [a.] South Portsmouth, KY

MITCHELL, HAKIMA
[pen.] Keema; [b.] November 12, 1978, San Jose, CA; [p.] William Mouzon And Victoria Mitchell; [ed.] High School; [hon.] Just the Honor Roll at School; [oth. writ.] I write lots of poetry, known of which have been published. Here are some name though:; [pers.] I just want to thank my parents for influencing me to write, also my bestfriend K-C for convincing me to enter this contest. I really never thought I'd actually be chosen for anything thanks. I would also like to say that I started writing poetry when I was very young. The poem I submitted to the contest was written 2 1/2 years ago when I was 14. I writing poetry, because it I way for me to express how I feel about myself and the world around me.; [a.] Los Angeles, CA

MITCHELL, JOANNE M.
[b.] May 10, 1924, Cleveland, OH; [p.] John and Helen DuRivage; [m.] Jim Mitchell, December 28, 1988; [ch.] Four-Three sons, 1 daughter; [ed.] Jr. College; [occ.] Retired; [pers.] This poem was written by me for my husband Norman Mitchell who showed everyone what love meant.; [a.] Santa Ana, CA

MITCHELL, MARLENE L.
[b.] August 28, 1952, Oakland, CA; [p.] Aline L. Heath, Vernon Mitchell; [ed.] Petaluma High School, Santa Rose Jr. College; [occ.] LVN, Sutter Roseville Med. Center, Roseville Calif. (20 years.); [oth. writ.] Many other poems sitting in a drawer waiting for discovery...; [pers.] If reading my poem has touched your soul and lifted your spirit then I am honored by the talents God has blessed me with and maybe I have opened the thoughts of longing in your heart....; [a.] Shingle Springs, CA

MITCHELL, ROMEL
[b.] November 15, 1954, East Chicago, IN; [p.] Cleveland and Rosetta Mitchell; [ed.] B.F.A. Indiana State U. Terre Haute, Indiana; [occ.] Artist, Freelance; [pers.] I utilize the arts as a vehicle

through which I can promote my universal goodwill intent to serve as a messenger and advocate of simple goodness, truth, and beauty. It is my goal to enlighten, entertain, and inspire as we face a new millennium.; [a.] San Francisco, CA

MOELLER, HEIDI K.
[b.] January 12, 1977, Milwaukee, WI; [p.] Jacqueline Moeller; [ed.] Began College as a freshman in fall of 1995 - Interest in Business; [occ.] Waitress; [memb.] College - Student Senate; [hon.] Several Track Awards, horse show Awards; [oth. writ.] This is first to be published, but have many more on hand; [pers.] I am a true romantic - I love poetry. It gives me a sense of freedom.; [a.] Crivitz, WI

MONG, KIMBERLY
[b.] May 3, 1982; [p.] Sandra and Martin Mong; [ed.] 8th grade student at Malvern High School; [pers.] I wrote this poem the night my grandpa died so it is very special to me.; [a.] Malvern, OH

MONTGOMERY, MELISSA C.
[b.] March 10, 1981, Detroit, MI; [ed.] I am a ninth grader attending Detroit High School for the fine and Performing Arts, majoring in Visual Arts; [oth. writ.] My first poem, I wrote when I was six years old called "My Things"; [a.] Detroit, MI

MONTOYA, MARIA ELENA
[b.] November 2, 1978, Santa Fe, NM; [p.] Orlando and Cordilia Montoya; [ed.] In August I shall enter my Senior year at Santa Fe High School; [occ.] High School Student; [memb.] Santa Fe High Band, Choir, and Key Club; [hon.] Honor Society, letters in band and softball, making Honor Roll each year, an open reading of one of my poems in 5th grade, and top 25% in my class; [oth. writ.] I have written many poems before this. Although I've never had the luck to have any of them published until now.; [pers.] All the poems and writings I do are parts of me. I am a complex person with hidden depths. No one can see all of them, but with my writings people can catch a glimpse.; [a.] Santa Fe, NM

MOODY, JOY
[pen.] Rachel Pierce; [b.] August 25, 1972, Anaheim, CA; [p.] Gary Curry, Jeanne Curry; [m.] James T. Moody Jr., July 16, 1994; [ed.] Germantown High School, Southern Nazarene University, The University of Memphis; [occ.] Inventory Auditor/ Graduate Student in Rehabilitation Counselling at the university of Memphis; [memb.] Calvary Church of the Nazarene, Memphis, TN, Youth Council; [hon.] Dean's List, President's Honor Roll, The National Dean's List, Oklahoma Scholarship, Leadership Enrichment Program (OSLEP) Seminar Member; [pers.] Don't accept defeat until defeat is inevitable.; [a.] Memphis, TN

MOORE, CLEMIS T.
[b.] October 1, 1929, Bowdon, GA; [p.] Ottis Kaylor and William Henry Moore; [m.] Helen Alice, December 23, 1955; [ch.] Lisa Jo, Edward, Alan and Gary; [ed.] Bowdon High School, West Georgia College, Carrollton, GA. Georgia State, Atlanta. GA; [occ.] Retired Account, General Motors Corp.; [oth. writ.] Several poems-lyrics for song adaption; [pers.] Favorite: Writer-Poet Robert Burns; [a.] Decatur, GA

MOORE, DOROTHY S.
[pen.] Dorothy Stephens Moore; [b.] December 25, 1940, Wellsburg, WV; [p.] Ira V. and Jennie Stephens; [ed.] Wellsburg High School, Wellsburg, WV; [occ.] Office Administrator - Outboard Marine Corporation - Stuart, FL; [memb.] International Llama Association, Southern States Llama Association; [oth. writ.] Numerous poems for family and friends.; [a.] Stuart, FL

MOORE, MICHAEL J.
[b.] September 13, 1956, Redwood City, CA; [p.] Howard and Doris Moore; [ch.] Michael Walter Moore; [ed.] Carlmont High School Belmont, CA San Jose, Community College San Jose, CA; [occ.] Air Conditioning Technician; [memb.] The National Library of Poetry; [oth. writ.] Children poems and stories. Adult poems and stories. The Rainbows End - National Library of Poetry; [pers.] I write to bring out joy in the hearts of children and adults, also to help unlock their imagination. I find the reward are tremendously satisfying and fulfilling.; [a.] Redwood City, CA

MOORE, MICHELLE
[pen.] Moore, Michelle Marie; [b.] August 19, 1981, Bellevue, WA; [p.] Bonnie Becker, Eugene Moore; [ed.] North Bend Elementary School, Chief Kanim Middle School. I am now in my first year of Mount SI High School; [occ.] I work at Anthony's Pizza; [hon.] 4.0 student for six years, I am now in freshman, Language Arts honors; [oth. writ.] Poems called "All Night I Die," "Face The Consequences"; [pers.] I wrote my first poem at 13 and wish to continue for a long time.; [a.] North Bend, WA

MOORE, PRECIOUS
[b.] March 22, 1979, Hollywood, FL; [p.] Terry J. Moore; [ed.] Currently Attending Colonial High School; [occ.] Part-time Pizza maker; [hon.] Beta Club, High Honors Awards, Honor roll, future Educators of America (F.E.A.); [oth. writ.] Wrote several other poems, but never got around to send them to get published; [a.] Orlando, FL

MOORE, SHARON LEE
[pen.] Shar; [b.] September 22, 1947, Mt. Clemens, MI; [p.] John and Joyce Gusmano, Roger Coppens (Biological Father); [m.] Charles Braden Moore Sr.; [ch.] Heidi, Sherry, Ginger, Jimmy Jr., Amber, Jake, Roger and Trudy; [ed.] St. Mary's Academy - Monroe Michigan, Redford High - Michigan, Miles City College Montana; [occ.] Customer Service Manager (Wal-Mart) Valparaiso, IN; [oth. writ.] I am thinking of possibly writing a book; [pers.] My mother (Jackie) wrote many poems in her youth. Influenced by my Aunt Judy Semenas and Aunt Penny Moross (Andrews) Brothers: Greg Coppens, Kevin Gusmano, Sisters: Trudy Vincke, Judy Plonkey, Rose Gusmano, Poetry is precious to me.; [a.] Portage, IN

MOORE, TIFFANY FAWN
[b.] November 9, 1980, Lawrenceburg, TN; [p.] Gregory W. and Ginger N. Moore; [ed.] Leoma Elementary, Loretto High School; [occ.] Student; [memb.] Jr. Beta Club Drum Major: Loretto High School; [hon.] "Outstanding D.A.R.E. Essay", Leoma Elementary School Jan. 93, Music Award 7th Grade Music Class Certificate of Achievement L.H.S. Band 93-94, Top Ten Elementary School 7th

in class "Directors Award" LHS Band 94-95 "Tennessee River Valley Marching Classic" Superior Drum Major 1995; [oth. writ.] None published

MORALES JR., DANIEL ROMERO
[pen.] D. J. Romales; [b.] March 19, 1975, Douglas, AZ; [p.] Rev. Daniel R. Morales, Maria Morales; [ed.] Ayer Jr./Sr. High School, Oral Roberts University; [occ.] Full-time student, majoring in Chemistry and English Literature; [memb.] National Honor Society (2,3,4), MU Alpha Theta (1,2,3,4), Science Club (2,3,4) O.R.U. Spanish Club, O.R.U. English Club, O.R.U. Hebrew Club; [hon.] Ayer High School Student 1994 Achiever Award, Worcester Telegram and Gazette Visions 2000 Academic Achievement Award Presidential Academic Fitness Award, Middlesex County Bar Association Citizenship Award; [oth. writ.] Essay published by Worcester Telegram and Gazette; [pers.] My duty not be an obligation - but my passion. May honor not be a commendation but my lifestyle. May country not be an artificial creation but my own flesh and blood.; [a.] Douglas, AZ

MORDER, DEBORAH K. TAYLOR
[b.] February 24, 1954, Newton Hamilton, PA; [p.] Robert R. Taylor - Iua I. McCarty; [m.] Governor Walker Sr.; [ch.] Governor Walker Jr., James L. Walker; [ed.] Mount Union Area High School; [occ.] Family Service worker Huntingdon County Head start; [memb.] I am presently enrolled in an Adult Education Program to improve my Basic Skills in English, vocabulary, this Program is Project Reach Remedial Education for the Adults of the County of Huntingdon; [pers.] I would like to thank my brother James for all his help and inspiration and Mrs. Vera Himes for all her help and for sending my poem in.; [a.] Mount Union, PA

MORELLI, ANGELINA
[pen.] Angelina Morelli; [b.] December 9, 1966, Sandusky; [p.] Vincent and Carmella Sharon Sortino; [m.] Tim R. Spencer, September 19, 1994; [ch.] Joseph Gianno, Ryan Angelina; [ed.] Willard H.S., Terra Tech. College, Case Western Reserve University; [occ.] Law Student; [memb.] Phi Kappa Theta Honor Society, Deans List, New Beginnings Center, Young Republicans, National Assoc. of Female Executives; [pers.] Take the bricks that other people throw at you and lay a firm foundation on which to stand; [a.] Sagamore Hills, OH

MORGAN, DWIGHT C.
[b.] August 17, 1975, Kingston, Jamaica; [p.] Andy and Beverley Morgan; [ed.] Jr. at the Univ. of Central Florida and member of Lambda Chi Alpha; [occ.] Full Time student; [memb.] I am a member of Lamda Chi Alpha at the University of Central Florida and was a member of the Naples Youth Soccer Team here in Naples, Florida; [oth. writ.] "The Philosopher" and "The End."; [pers.] I am a Jr. at the University of Central Florida and pursuing a B.S. in Psychology. I would like someday to write my own personal book of poetry or a book on psychology treatments.; [a.] Naples, FL

MORGANTHALER, ADAM
[b.] April 10, 1976, DuQuoin, IL; [p.] Boy Morganthaler, Esther Morganthaler; [m.] Jennifer Morganthaler, September 24, 1994; [ch.] Marshfield High, John A. Logan College; [ed.] Complementary

Evaluator, Blue Cross Blue Shield; [occ.] Richview Church of Christ; [pers.] A poem is a piece of one's personality, which produces powerful penmanship and great pride in the eyes of the printer.; [a.] Marshfield, MO

MORICE, DONNA
[b.] November 2, 1931, St. Louis, MO; [p.] Russel and Myrtle McCoy; [m.] Bill Morice (Deceased), August 8, 1953; [ch.] Dennis Lynn, Nancy Jeanne; [ed.] Elvins High School, Flat River Junior College, Missouri University; [occ.] Retired Teacher; [memb.] First United Methodist Church, Missouri State Teachers Association, Mineral Area Retired Teachers; [pers.] I reflect my inner most feelings about people who have touched my life in special way and about little everyday events that caught my attention.; [a.] Park Hills, MO

MORRILL, ELAINE
[b.] April 18, 1950, Plymouth, NH; [p.] Warner and Audrey Morrill; [m.] Single; [oth. writ.] Several poems, unfortunately unpublished; [pers.] My words come from with-in me!; [a.] Thornton, NH

MORRIS, BRIAN PATRICK
[b.] December 23, 1983, Gallup, NM; [p.] Evelyn and Roger Morris; [ed.] 6th grader at Cathedral School in Gallup, NM; [occ.] Student; [hon.] 3 yrs. Academic Excellence, 3 yrs. science fair winner: Numerous state, national and International Karate Awards. Awards for 6 years of School Perfect Attendance (not one day missed); [oth. writ.] Several poems and short stories; [pers.] "To be the best I can be in whatever I do."; [a.] Gallup, NM

MORRISON, DENNIS MICHAEL
[pen.] Mike; [b.] February 28, 1952, Oakland CA; [p.] George and Agnes Morrison; [m.] Linda Morrison, July 9th 1972; [ch.] Dennis Jr., Angela and Amy; [ed.] Up to 1 yr. of College; [occ.] Owner of a bar in Baypoint Calif.; [hon.] Trophies in Bowling and Softball; [oth. writ.] Mostly poems to the ones he loves; [pers.] Loves to laugh, loves to make people laugh; [a.] Hayward, CA

MORROW, JENNIFER LEE
[b.] September 20, 1969, Dallas, TX; [p.] Sandra Stimson and Jake Morrow; [ed.] Lake Highlands High School, B.a. in Psychology at University of Texas of Dallas - cum laude; [occ.] Graduate student in Counseling at University of North Texas; [hon.] Graduated cum laude from the University of Texas at Dallas, Dean's list; [pers.] I have been greatly influenced by Emily Dickinson. My poems reflect a time in life filled with loss and sadness.; [a.] Dallas, TX

MORSE, FLORENCE M.
[pen.] Leslie Sherill; [b.] February 27, 1916, New Port, RI; [p.] Dennis A. Sullivan, Florence Jackman Sullivan; [m.] William Harold Morse (Deceased), May 5, 1934; [ch.] William H. Morse, Jr.; [ed.] Rogers High, Newport, R.I., University of Rhode Island, Kingston, R.I.; [occ.] Musician, Music Teacher; [oth. writ.] World's Fair Anthology of Verse, 1940, Newspapers, Poetic Voices Of America, 1988; [pers.] I try for simplicity so that anyone may enjoy and understand the thought I am trying to present.

MORTON, ROSEMARY ANDERSON
[b.] February 22, 1948, Richmond, VA; [p.] Laura and James Anderson Sr.; [ch.] Larry, Portia, Cheryl, Randall, Michelle; [ed.] J. Sargeant Reynolds Community College in Richmond, VA; [hon.] Award for a poem previously published; [oth. writ.] A love so true; [a.] Richmond, VA

MOSELEY, KIRA
[b.] November 18, 1982, North Carolina; [p.] Ken and Debbie Moseley; [ed.] Brunswick Academy of Lawrenceville, VA; [occ.] Student; [hon.] Forensics other poetry contests, and other Essay contests; [oth. writ.] "Nature Dances" and "My dad's company is the best."; [pers.] I believe writing poetry or stories should come within you, like your heart. Not what you "think" you should write.; [a.] Emporia, VA

MOSIER, AMBER RAE
[pen.] Amber Rae Mosier; [b.] January 24, 1982, Towanda, PA; [p.] James and Theresa Berry; [ed.] I attend the 8th grade at Wyalusing Valley High School; [occ.] School Student; [memb.] New Albany Meth. Church Wyalusing Valley Junior Chorus; [hon.] Pres. Awards for high Education, received several Citizenship awards; [pers.] I wrote this poem for my history teacher Mr. Cerniglia, who passed away of cancer on September 3, 1995.; [a.] New Albany, PA

MOURAD, ADRIANA
[b.] May 8, 1976, Colombia, South America; [p.] Gloria Gonzalez, Sherif Mourad; [ed.] Nova High, Broward Community College; [occ.] Student, Tutor, Peer Councelor and President, Chairperson; [memb.] Phi Theta Kappa International Honor Society, Inspira International, National Honor Society, Student Government, International Club, National Dean's List,, President's List, Whose who Among American High School Students, Catholic Club, Community Connection; [hon.] Scholar's Award, Certificate of Appreciation for the Saturday Stars Mentor Program, Gold and Silver Cords, Presidential Academic Fitness Award, Miami Herald Article and picture, first place in the Foreign Language Academic Competition; [oth. writ.] Semifinalist in the Literary Magazine Poetry Contest; [pers.] Writing without feeling is merely collection of words.; [a.] Fort Lauderdale, FL

MOWERY, GERALD E.
[b.] March 7, 1927, Buena, WA; [p.] Jennings Bryan Mowery, Opal May Phillips; [ch.] Colleen, Charles, Victoria, Peggy Theresa, Rhonda, Laura; [occ.] Retired Business Owner; [oth. writ.] Over 100 small books on many and varied subjects, but mostly short stories of a philosophy nature, comparing political statements to untruths and unreality, (Which Is pretty easy) Have written and published a book correlating the Electron Volt Values of Sub Atomic Particles to the Atomic mass of Carbon 12, under the equation Illustrating and that many additional Elements Exist within the Current Periodic Table of Elements.; [pers.] Philosophy Statement! There is a direct relationship between the amount of propaganda believed in a poem and intelligence.; [a.] Puyallup, WA

MROHS, JENNIFER MARIE
[pen.] Jennifer; [b.] January 25, 1979, Crisfield, MD; [p.] Steve and Millie Mrohs; [ed.] I am a Junior at

Crisfield High School; [occ.] Lifeguard at Somer Cove Marina, Crisfield, MD; [memb.] Asbury United Methodist Church; [hon.] Editor's Choice Award 1994 for outstanding Achievement in Poetry Certificate in Recognition, Declamation contest Winner 1993; [oth. writ.] In your eyes published in "Songs on the winds" 1995; [pers.] I love to write about the mind and the soul. Inter strength and beauty all about love. I have been influence by romantic poets of today.; [a.] Marion, MD

MUDD, JAMES H.
[pen.] Uncle Herb; [b.] October 30, 1922, Elwood, IN; [p.] Richard C. and Nelia Mary Mudd; [m.] Leo Mae Mudd, October 7, 1954; [ed.] St Joseph's Parochial, Elwood, Indiana; [occ.] Retired; [oth. writ.] Several Poems And One Short Story (all unpublished); [pers.] I am striving to be, in my last few years of life, what I have never been in my past life.; [a.] Stoutland, MO

MUELLER, KATHLEEN
[pen.] Leena Moore; [b.] March 5, 1971, Illinois; [p.] Patrick and Marbeth Dougherty; [m.] John P. Mueller Jr., August 13, 1994; [ed.] Baraboo High, Madison Area Technical College, Assiciate Degree in Photography, CNA and CPR training; [occ.] Certified Nursing Assistant; [memb.] American Heart Association; [pers.] For one to truly be happy they must first look within themselves.; [a.] Portage, WI

MUHAMMAD, PCHERNAVIA
[pen.] P.J.M.; [b.] January 22, 1979, Ogden, UT; [p.] Jamal and Marquitta Muhammad; [ed.] Attending Duncanville High School. I do have plans to go to College. I am 16 years old.; [memb.] I am a member of the Multi-Cultural Association. The French Club. The Book Club.; [hon.] I have received many honorable mention awards for my writings, which I have received blue ribbons red, yellow and white. But my work has never been published before.; [oth. writ.] I have written short story. And a small play for my English Teacher my sophomore year. I have also written year. I have also written several other poems that have not been published.; [pers.] I write my poems on the many things that are happening in my life, and on the many events that are happening in this world. I have been greatly influenced by the many people in my life.; [a.] Dallas, TX

MUHTASIB, YASMINE
[b.] March 23, 1977, Riyadh, Saudi Arabia; [p.] Adnan and Anne Muhtasib; [ed.] Emerson Preparatory School, Washington D.C.; [occ.] Student; [memb.] MYNA (Muslim Youth Of North America); [oth. writ.] School reports!; [pers.] I am working very hard in my senior year. However, I will continue to write down my thoughts - in both English and Arabic.; [a.] College Park, MD

MULLINS, DOROTHY WATERS
[b.] June 6, 1942, Lexington City; [p.] Welton and Lois Cockrell Waters; [m.] John Augustine Mullins, July 5, 1980; [ch.] Kimberly Michelle, Gilbert; [ed.] High School; [occ.] Philips Components (LAB); [memb.] Witten Berg Lutheran Church; [hon.] Peoples Award Philips Components 1984; [pers.] A tribute to my Father on his 85th Birthday March 8th 1995, Loved in his Community as "The Pecan Man" and in memory of as well. Passed away April 6th 1995; [a.] Leesville, SC

MUNFORD, BRENDA G.
[pen.] Twiggy; [b.] January 26, 1942, Ophelia, VA; [p.] Sarah and Raymond Gough; [m.] B.B. Munford, III, October 7, 1983; [ed.] Pan American Bus. School, VCU and U of Rich.; [occ.] Admin. Asst. to federal district judge, Richmond, VA; [memb.] Afton United Methodist Church, United Daughters of the Confederacy; [pers.] I believe poetry should not only be fun to read, but thought provoking as well. Schools especially need to encourage the recitation of and writing of poetry at an early age.; [a.] Richmond, VA

MUNGIN, THEODORE L.
[pen.] Theovale; [b.] July 31, 1961, Philadelphia; [p.] Edward and Brenda Mungin; [m.] Jill M. Mungin, August 23, 1980; [ed.] Plattsburgh Senior High School Graduate; [occ.] Painting Manager at the Handy Man Co. of Delaware Valley Action Builders and Home Remodeling; [oth. writ.] "The Promise", "Quiet Dreams", "Touching you with my eyes" "Woven in a dream" "Recollection"; [pers.] I would like to thank my wife for her loving support and warm encouragement. Also I would like to thank, who have been in my corner, "Thanks 2U2, 2 parts gold." Philosophical Statement, Theo Vale a valley, often coursed by a stream. "Much thanks to a friend who has enabled me to write flowing endless words of love that I must pen."; [a.] Philadelphia, PA

MURCH, RONALD A.
[b.] April 21, 1928, Rockland, ME, [p.] Malcolm S. and Lena E. (Barnes) Murch; [m.] Carol J. (Sylvester) Murch; [ch.] Bruce E. Murch, Miriam R. (Murch) Kezer; [ed.] Bridgton (ME) High School, Aurora (IL) University, B.A. B.Th., Hartford Seminary (CT), University of Massachusetts, M.Ed.; [occ.] Computer Consultant, Financial Officer, Retired Clergyman and Teacher; [oth. writ.] Biography: Neighbor to the Nations, various poems and articles.; [pers.] It si better to give than to receive, but neither can exist without the other, and both have great value.; [a.] Lisbon, ME

MURCHISON, IDA M.
[b.] November 6, Nashville, NC; [p.] Roberta and Fred Freeman; [ed.] Nashville High, Elizabeth City College and Nash Community College in North Carolina; [occ.] Retired; [pers.] I am so thankful to be able to enjoy some of the beauty that God has given to us. When I write poetry, I just let it come alive in my poems.; [a.] Castalia, NC

MURPHY, DAVID H.
[b.] November 26, 1942, New York City, NY; [p.] David and Julia Murphy; [m.] Elaine, August 13, 1988; [ed.] Marist College; [occ.] Team Coordinator of a program for emotionally disturbed teens; [hon.] I Have been honored to be accepted as a co-worker by the Mashonas in Zimbabwe for 17 yrs and here on the Pine Ridge by Lakota people for the past 9 years; [pers.] I have had the priviledge to walk my life in the presence of truly great people. If you know me and read this, please consider it a heart felt thanks; [a.] Pine Ridge, SD

MURRAY, KELLY
[b.] October 24, 1976, Denver, CO; [p.] James Murray Sr., Tyna Murray; [ed.] Cedar Hill High School Sophomore; [occ.] Student; [memb.] Drill Team, Choir; [hon.] Who's Who Among American High School students, 94-95 English Award, ADTS Best Showmanship Award; [pers.] That with God all things are possible and always remember to smile it will help you make it through; [a.] Cedar Hill, TX

MURRAY, NORMA SUSAN
[b.] September 25, 1956, Los Angeles, CA; [p.] Angela and Ralph Montellano; [m.] Keith Murray, July 4, 1986; [ch.] Jeanine Montellano and Sarah Murray; [ed.] Sacred Heart High School, Southland College of Legal Careers, Continuous Seminars related to career enhancement; [occ.] Legal Secretary, Notary Public; [memb.] San Gabriel Valley Legal Secretary Association, National Notary Public Association; [hon.] High Accommodations and Recognitions for jobs well done in Organizing several functions through work in a Social Committee Chairperson capacity. Recognition as the staff artist for intense creativity and appreciation for an abundant flow of ideas.; [oth. writ.] Editor of a Newsletter, Skadden, Arps, Slate, Meagher and Flom (law firm), poems, short stories; [pers.] I believe in the power of POSITIVE ENERGY. I believe it is our mission to generate as much POSITIVITY as we can, any way we can. I bestow through my poetry and writings as much POSITIVITY as I can influence.; [a.] Los Angeles, CA

MURRELL, MARY L. WILLIAMS
[b.] 1911, Hunt County, TX; [p.] J. W. Williams, Kate Dodd Williams; [m.] Milton Jefferson Murrell, 1946; [ed.] R.N. B.A. Degree - Social Studies Public Health Nurse Teaching Certificates in Counseling Alcohol Drugs; [occ.] Retired R.N. Volunteer Service of Civic; [memb.] Life member Delta Sigma Theta Sorority Member. Women in Military Scv. Foundation, Inc. Ft. Worth Water Color Society Top Ladies of Distention St. Eliza Church (Chaplain Afro - Amn -Political Conjurers) outstanding service; [hon.] 50 yrs America Red Cross Nuy Volunteer and Stipend Grunt Tx. State Health Dept Austin, TY Scholarship Mr and Ms A.E. Holand Retd. Mayor Army Nurse Comps will received Meritorious Plaque Pin (Unit 1) Amer. Theater; [a.] Dallas, TX

MURTAGH, KATHLEEN
[b.] July 10, 1981, Rye, NH; [hon.] Won grand prize for Omni Writing Contest; [oth. writ.]; [pers.] This poem was written in direct response to the Oklahoma bombing in 1995.; [a.] Rye, NH

MUSCIANESE, SUZANNE
[b.] May 19, 1975, San Jose, CA; [p.] Paula Marie and Henry Thomas Castro; [ch.] Christopher Lee, Ricky Randol; [ed.] Overfelt High School, Sawyer College; [occ.] Student; [oth. writ.] I have extensive writings that I haven't had published as of to date, September 22, 1995; [pers.] People never regret what they have done as much as they regret what they've never tried.; [a.] San Jose, CA

MYERS, LINDA
[b.] November 17, 1962, East Liverpool, OH; [p.] James Bell, Connie Bell; [m.] Thomas Myers, November 25, 1983; [ed.] Oak Glen High School, West Virginia Northern Community College; [occ.] Receptionist/Secretary for A.E. Petsche Co., Inc.; [memb.] Desoto Christian Church; [oth. writ.] I enjoy writing poems for friends about good times shared; [pers.] I wish to encourage the reader to value the gift of friendship God has given to us.; [a.] Arlington, TX

MYERS, RUTH A.
[pen.] Ruth Ann; [b.] July 10, 1941, Louisville, KY; [p.] Dewey Wible, Ruby Wible; [m.] Divorced; [ch.] Ronald Lewis II (Martha) Sandra Renae Steven Ray (G.C.) Katie Marie, Chelsie Taylor; [ed.] Pennville High School Pennville, IN; [occ.] HHC, Self-Employed Mooreland, IN; [oth. writ.] Family and Friends; [pers.] My inspirations come from God, to express the life of others, along with my feelings to them, in my writings. A great influence to me has been a very special baby and friend Grace Lewellen.; [a.] Mooreland, IN

NANCE, KATHERINE H.
[pen.] Katie; [b.] March 11, 1983, Columbia, SC; [p.] Timothy H. and Rosemary P. Nance; [ed.] 7th Grade, Dent Middle School, Columbia, SC; [occ.] Student; [memb.] Good Shepherd Lutheran Church, Dent Cheerleader, Dent Band; [hon.] Duke TIP Scholar, Beta Club; [a.] Columbia, SC

NAPHTALI, ASHIRAH S.
[pen.] Queen Ashirah; [b.] April 6, 1950, Kingston, Jamaica; [p.] Frederick Solomon Cruise and Theresa T. (Spence) Whitter; [m.] Douglas A. Smith Byroo, June 1, 1978 (div. June 1982); [ch.] Gilah Teshaye Smith Byroo; [ed.] Cert. Med. Ass., N.Y. Sch. of Dental and Med., Assts., Kew Gardens, N.Y., 1995, BA, NYU, 1979, M in Bus. Fin, Hofstra U., 1984, JD, 1983; [occ.] Real estate broker, notary pub. Law asst. Colin A. Moore, Jamaica, N.Y., summer 1983, Michael Laufer, N.Y.C., 1983-85, Reisler and Silverstein, N.Y.C., 1986-87, Barbara Emmanuel and Helen Gregory, Jamaica, 1987-89, Alarid and Naphtali, N.Y.C., 1989-91, pvt. practice Queens, N.Y., 1992-?, cons. NACA, Inc., Jamaica, 1984-89. Sgt. USAF, 1969-74, USAR, 1980-83.; [memb.] Queens Bar Assn., Nat. Bar Assn., Black Entertainment Sports Lawyers Assn., N.Y. Trial Lawyers Assn., N.Y. State Bar Assn., Kiwanis (pres. Cambria Heights, N.Y. chpt. 1994-95).; [pers.] One shall attain spiritual oneness with their higher self and their creator through righteousness; [a.] Saint Laurelton, NY

NEAL, DEMETRIA
[pen.] Meme; [b.] January 22, 1980, Eden, NC; [p.] Robert and Geraldine Neal; [ed.] Currently in Rockingham Senior High School; [memb.] Basketball Team in School, also Softball; [pers.] Go after everything you want in life, because you are the person that have to live it. Then, when you are old you can look on your life and be satisfied or have regrets.; [a.] Eden, NC

NEAL, KELSEY
[pen.] Simple, Simple; [b.] November 30, 1977, Dayton, OH; [p.] Caryle Neal-Zorumski and William E. Zorumski; [ed.] Graduated from Menchville High School, currently at Freshman at Christopher Newport University College; [occ.] Student; [pers.] I wan to dedicate this poem to Lara Fairfield who was my inspiration to begin writing poetry.; [a.] Newport News, VA

NEAL, RACHAEL S.
[b.] December 15, 1979; [p.] James R. Neal, Harriet C. Neal; [ed.] 11th Grade, Rio Americano High School; [memb.] Capital Crew; [hon.] LNRA Outstanding Novice Rower 1995; [pers.] I believe only in being a whole person, being in harmony with oneself, and one's values.; [a.] Fair Oaks, CA

NELLAMS, NICOLA
[pen.] Nicola Nellams; [b.] July 27, 1977, Lake Charles, LA; [p.] Myrtle Benolt and Tim Alford; [ed.] Hackberry High School, Sulphur High School, John Casablancas Modeling and Career Agency (diploma); [occ.] Manager of Taco Bell; [memb.] Hockberry Baptist Church; [hon.] Modeling School Manager of 18 years old; [oth. writ.] Many poems, short stories, article on tor Watch, and art spectrum; [pers.] My life has and always influenced my work. To err is human, but when you hear the eraser out ahead of the pencil, you're over doing it.; [a.] Sulphur, LA

NELSON, ERIN MARIE
[b.] August 31, 1980, Morris, MN; [p.] James Nelson, Angela Nelson; [ed.] Freshman, Alamogordo High School; [memb.] Alamogordo High School Honor Roll, Gold Card Member; [hon.] Mother's Day Poetry Contest, 1994 Mockingbird Society Poetry Contest, Senior Citizen's Essay Contest, Honor Roll Newspaper Editor; [oth. writ.] Numerous newspaper publications, poems, papers essay and stories; [pers.] Always believe in yourself. Never let go of your dreams. To my family thanks for believing in me.; [a.] Alamogordo, NM

NELSON, GRACIE L.
[b.] January 25, 1936, Tampa, FL; [p.] David J. Sr. and Minnie L. McDonald; [m.] Kermit W. (Red) Nelson, April 24, 1970; [ch.] Cheryl, Robin, Leonard, and Kim; [ed.] Elem: Oak Park, Tampa, FL - W.J. Bryan, Plant City, FL, High School: Eagle Lake, FL, Upholstery, Interior Design, Brewster, Tampa FL, Traviss, Lakeland, FL; [occ.] Housewife, Clown, J and K Clowning, Lakeland, FL, Code Inforcement Board, Polk City, FL; [memb.] The Grange, Tops, Polk City, FL, Life and Praise Temple Church, Auburndale, FL, Sang Southern Gospel with "The Florida Singers" out of Lakeland, FL Late 60's and 70's. Now sing part-time with Daugh Cheryl Stephens and my Husband Kermit; [oth. writ.] Many songs unpublished, poem "Mother Natures Work" published, local paper, Plant City Fl at age 14, recently completed poems "Take Me Back Child In Me:" The Old Man, "Ode to the Birth of my First Born."; [pers.] I am a firm believer that our talents are God given, we should make sure they reflect the moral code set forth in the word of God. Morality is never outdated.; [a.] Polk City, FL

NESBIT, HARRY L.
[b.] October 22, 1926, Washington, PA; [p.] Harry and Margaret Nesbit; [ch.] Karen Desai, Cheryl Arce, Valerie Brown; [ed.] Terris Institute, Michigan Waynesburg College, PA; [occ.] Retired History and Geog-Teacher

NEWMAN, MARGARET M.
[pen.] Margaret M. Newman; [b.] December 15, 1947, New Orleans, LA; [p.] Dr. Louis F.D. Marion S. Munro; [m.] Steven B. Newman, June 25, 1983; [ed.] Ph.D University of Florida, M.A., L.S.U., B.S., L.S.U; [occ.] President, Competitive Edge, Communications Training Consultant; [memb.] Alexandria Chamber of Commerce, Arlington Chamber of Commerce, American Society of Training and Development; [hon.] Ph.D., Top Woman Business for 1994, (Federal Transit Administration); [oth. writ.] Best poets of 1994,1995 and 1996, competition among women. (Disserta-

tion); [pers.] Love, service, art and education allow me to appreciate the gift of creativity.; [a.] Arlington, VA

NICHOLS, CARRIE LYNN
[Pen.] Lynn; [b.] December 27, 1970, Georgia; [p.] Carolyn Sanders and Tyrus Scarborough; [m.] Douglas Lee Nichols, May 24, 1991; [ch.] J. Mason Nichols, Andrew Lee Nichols, Matthew Lloyd Nichols; [ed.] Attended Kettering High School 88. Attenden Minac Inc. Health Care Training School. Second in my class, certified nurse; [occ.] Full-time mother of three and wife; [pers.] I need to say thank you to my family. Mom, you are the strongest woman I know. You gave me that strength to write about, you've supported my work when I didn't feel it was any good. Dad, I love you. Doug, my husband, you are my rock I lean on. You've given and been put through so much. I love you forever. Last my children Mason, Andy and Matthew, my boys are my life and without any of you in my life I wouldn't have so much feeling to write of. I love you all and thank you.; [a.] Auburn, KY

NICHOLS, EMILY
[pen.] Emily Nichols; [b.] June 6, 1977, Fairbanks, AK; [p.] Kathy M. Nichols and Fred L. Nichols; [ed.] Austin E. Lathrop High, University of Alaska Fairbanks (UAF); [occ.] Housekeeping - Regency Hotel and PT Sales - Music land; [hon.] The Scholastic Bold Key Award; [oth. writ.] Several personal works and others for classes; [pers.] I over this piece to the wonderful and eye opening influence of Brandon G. and the undying love of Adam Burch to whom I whole heartedly return the sentiment.; [a.] Fairbanks, AK

NICHOLS, TAMELA Y.
[b.] August 28, 1975, Russellville, AR; [p.] Charles Jr. and Mattie Nichols; [ed.] Brazoswood High School, Brazosport College - Associate of Applied Science - Pending 1996 Graduation, Planning to Attend University of Houston Fall '96; [occ.] Office Professional, Freeport, TX; [memb.] Brazosport College in Facility, Maintenance Advisory Committee, Brazosport College Student Senate, Sophomore Vice President, Cast Member in 1994 Martin Luther King Celebration Dreams Production - "Survival"; [hon.] Scholastic Honors - Two Consecutive Semester, nominated for 1995 Distinguished Student of Brazosport College Award; [oth. writ.] None published; [pers.] "O give thanks unto the Lord, for he is good: Because his mercy endureth forever." Psalm 118:1.; [a.] Clute, TX

NIU, JUNE
[pen.] June Niu; [b.] May 6, 1959, Tianjin, China; [p.] Qing Zhen and Lan Ying Xincmomo; [m.] Jin Hua Shi, October 1, 1984; [ch.] Wen-Wen; [ed.] Bachelor of Arts B.A.; [occ.] Travel Agent - China, Hongkong and Orients Tour and Marketing Director of Saint Tours in Sarasota Fl.; [pers.] "Let the world be filled with love" this is my dream and often reflects in my writing. We love and be loved. We shared with people who need love and care. That os a world everybody dreams to live in.; [a.] Sarasota, FL

NOLEN, RUSSELL D.
[pen.] Russell D. Nolen; [b.] October 20, 1959, Little Rock, AR; [p.] Loy Nolen and Joy Richards; [ed.]

Bryant High, Henderson College; [occ.] Disab/ Veteran; [memb.] Sharon Baptist Church, National Rifle Association; [hon.] Captain Varsity Football Squad, 1975 memeber National Honor Society 1974; [oth. writ.] "Stars," "Kissing The Wind," "The Blule Rose,"...; [pers.] What the mind sees, and what the heart believes, can set the spirit free! I hope my poems envoke and instill th virtues of hope, freedom, adventure, and love for one another.; [a.] Benton, AR

NORTON, SARAH NICOLE
[b.] July 6, 1981, Sacramento, CA; [p.] Gary and Helen Gibson; [ed.] Rocklin High School; [occ.] Student; [hon.] 2nd Place in Speech Contest, Academic Achievement in Mathematics, Literary Achievement Award; [oth. writ.] Several unpublished poems and stories; [pers.] Through my writing I try to convey the struggles and triumphs of young adults my age and older, in the last few decades. I have been greatly influenced by V.C. Andrews.; [a.] Kocklin, CA

NOTTINGHAM JR., QUINTON L.
[b.] December 27, 1962, Capeville, VA; [p.] Quiton (Sr.) and Mary Nottingham; [m.] Cheryl Darnell (Carter) Nottingham, October 15, 1983; [ch.] Akeisha Denika, Ishmael Limar; [ed.] Tidewater Community College, Portsmouth, VA, Received a Cerficate in Advance Auto CAD in March, 1993. Received a certificate in Auto CAD I and II December, 1989: Eastern Shore Community College, Melfa, VA. Received a Certificate in Drafting in August, 1986: The Art Institute of Philadelphia, Philadelphia, PA. (1981-1982), Workshops: Annual Advanced Basic Life Training Institute Washington, DC (March 1992, 1993, and 1994), Annual Church Leadership Conference by Dr. Anthony Evans, the Urban Alternative Ministries Dallas, TX (August 1993); [occ.] Engineering Technician II City of Norfolk VA; [hon.] Certificate of Appreciation for naming the Department of Public Works, Information Program (1993), Employee of the Month, Department of Public Works (1992), Employee of the Month, Miller-Stephenson and Associates (1987, 1988); [oth. writ.] An unpublished collection of Christian poems I call "Straight from the Heart."; [pers.] I wish to be a living example of biblical principles. Because of all negative events that occur constantly, showing living and sharing Jesus Christ is the only ray of positive hope.; [a.] Virginia Beach, VA

NOWICKI, JANE M.
[b.] November 21, 1920, Chicago, IL; [p.] Kinga and George Stachura; [m.] Alphonse F. Nowicki, May 12, 1940; [ch.] Marie, Dan, Don, Terry, Mike, Carol; [ed.] Assumption Elementary 8 grades, and Fenger High Chicago, IL; [occ.] Housewife And Home-maker; [memb.] Saint Rose Circle of Saint Francis Catholic Church, Toledo, Ethel grange, was a religious Ed., Teachers for 5th grade for 13 years make Crafts for Bazzaars; [hon.] Won 2nd place for a pome in High School; [pers.] My father wrote poems for personal enjoyment and I do too. I enjoy reading poems at meetings.; [a.] Onalaska, WA

NUSKE, DAVID H.
[pen.] D. H. Nuske; [b.] August 19, 1946, Port Huron, MI; [p.] Vivian Nuske; [ch.] Kelly Marie, Jillanna Alice; [ed.] Port Huron High School, Fort Huron Community College, University of California

San Diego; [occ.] Contract Software Engineer; [memb.] Sierra Club, Couteau Society, Greenpeacc; [pers.] While here on earth, strive to do good and communicate what is good to others. It is our most important gift that we leave behind,; [a.] Kirkland, WA

NUTA, CHRITINA A.
[b.] March 17, 1974, Mohhatten; [p.] Sandram and Dragos A. Nuta; [ed.] Saint Thomas Aquinas College, BS Criminal Justice; [occ.] Legal Assistant; [hon.] Dean's List; [oth. writ.] Have an unpublished book of poetry called "Blinded from the Light Within"; [pers.] If each individual spirit could unite to a share bond of universal thought, feel the connnection of 'MotherEarth' and her world with our-as well as what is unseen, beyond our senses - then the great spitit creation would smile as the sun from within all!; [a.] West Nyack, NY

NZYOKA, CYD WANJIKU
[b.] July 4, 1970, Kenya; [p.] Seth and Margaret Nzyoka; [ed.] MOI University Kenya, Mary Leakey High School; [occ.] Language Teacher Cum Florist; [hon.] Honours Bachelor of Education (in Arts) Literature and English; [oth. writ.] Over 100 poems mainly sentimental poems non has ever been published, P.S. I've never prior opportunity to share my poetry or have any published.; [pers.] real beauty is within 8 counts more than outside beauty and the greatest of all is love. The latter inspired by King Edward of England who abdicate his throne for the woman he loved.; [a.] Nairobi, Kenya

O'CONNOR, ELEANOR ROSE
[b.] October 16, 1984, Grosse Pointe, MI; [p.] Kevin and Elizabeth O'Connor; [ed.] Eastover Elementary School, Bloomfield Hills, MI; [occ.] 5th Grade Student; [oth. writ.] The garden is my first poem. It was written while in 4th grade at Eastover Elementary School Bloomfield Hills, MI.; [a.] Bloomfield Hills, MI

O'CONNOR, ERIN
[pen.] Erin O'Connor; [b.] November 5, 1945, Hollywood, CA; [p.] Dead; [m.] Divorced, December 20, 1968; [ch.] Two sons; [ed.] BA - Sociology/Eng U.C.L.A; [occ.] Massage Therapist; [a.] Los Angeles, CA

O'DONNELL, DIXIE
[pen.] Ella DeLeo; [b.] July 11, 1918, Little Rock, AR; [p.] Martha and Doug O'Donnell; [ed.] I am an 8th grade Student at St. Francis school in Goshen, KY (I wrote the poem as a 13 yrs.. old 7th grader); [occ.] Middle School Student; [hon.] Qualified in 6th grade for Duke University Talent Identification Program, 1994; [oth. writ.] Numerous poems and stories in a personal note book none published.; [pers.] "I guess I tend to find the darker sides of life more attractive than the yellows and oranges." Scott Weiland "Censorship is unamerican."; [a.] Louisville, KY

OCCHIUTO, CHRISTOPHER J.
[b.] June 2, 1966, Dover, NJ; [p.] Ron and Dale Occhiuto; [m.] Maureen Occhiuto, May 16, 1992; [ch.] Rebecca, Josiah, Stacey; [ed.] Lenape Valley High School, Newark School of Fine Art; [occ.] Artist - Welder; [hon.] Numerous Art Awards for Oil and Watercolor Paintings Impressionistic Oils;

[pers.] To give all Glory to our Lord, Jesus Christ. In Splendor, and who no one can hide from.; [a.] Lafayette, NY

ODUM, HARRIETT H.
[pen.] Harriett Hughes Odum; [b.] January 26, 1919, Washington, DC; [p.] William L. and Harriett Morrow hughes; [m.] Leonard E. Odum (Deceased), July 17, 1936; [ch.] Mary Odum Larson, Leonard E. Odum Jr., and Frances Anne Odum; [ed.] High School diploma, Degree in Police Administration from American University (Dean's List) and Adult Oil Painting Classes, Artist James V. Cupoli; [occ.] Met. Police Officer, Retired on Disability Incurred in Performance of Duty; [memb.] Police Association, Washington, DC, Association of Retired Police, Catholic Daughters of America and Michael Feinstein Fan Club; [hon.] Poems published in New Voices in American Poetry, Bi-Centennial Edition of Clover Collection of Verse, Americal Legion Magazines and Memorial Booklets honoring Police Officers who have answered their last call; [oth. writ.] "Poet's Corner" of Police Association Monthly Newspaper, where all of my poetry was published since 1970; [pers.] Love inspires poetry! Good music nourishes the love within us! (Since age 8 have been "rhyming" for all those close to my heart, including nine great grandchildren!); [a.] Washington, DC

OLIVARES, BENJAMIN
[b.] December 15, 1962, Houston, TX; [p.] Abelardo and Floripa Olivares; [ed.] Milby Sr High; [occ.] Carpenter; [oth. writ.] Texas trail ride in song on the wind.; [pers.] I give thanks to God and to a special Lady, Trisha, M. Diaz. Who inspired me to write and holds a special place in my heart. I love you Trisha for always.; [a.] Houston, TX

OLIVEIRA, BRENNA LYNE
[pen.] Smooches; [b.] August 29, 1979, New London, CT; [p.] Paula and Anthony Carnevale; [ed.] Johnston High School; [occ.] Restaurant Kentucky Fried Chicken; [memb.] Teens for Life; [hon.] Honor Roll, Perfect Attendance, Dance Achievement Awards; [oth. writ.] I wrote a song for a band (green day), it will be on one of their next albums. I've also written over 50 other poems and 32 songs for my band.; [pers.] In my poetry I express my feelings, different in style, subject and length. I communicate through these poem sand and only hope for understanding. So, I think I can tale it slow and see where all this hard work brings me?; [a.] Johnston, RJ

OLIVER, BETH
[pen.] Beth Oliver; [b.] December 31, 1971, Memphis; [p.] Phonda and Jerry Oliver; [ed.] Collierville High School - Senior; [occ.] Operator/Cashier at Target Store; [memb.] Shelby County CPR Association; [hon.] Senior Section Leader in Flag Corps at Collierville High School; [oth. writ.] I have been writing since I was five years old. This is the first article to be published.; [pers.] I write about events in my life that also happen to other people. This way they do not feel alone. Writing is my way of expressing both anger and happiness.; [a.] Collierville, TN

OLMSTEAD, NED
[b.] January 24, 1936, Chicago, IL; [p.] Gordon and

Ruth Olmstead; [m.] Mary Faye (Shelton) Olmstead, December 17, 1966; [ch.] Vanessa German, Shawn Olmstead; [ed.] McAlister Grade School, Waukegan, Ill, Waukegan Twp., H.S., Waukegan, Fl., Ringling School of Art, Sarasota, Fla. Engineering; [occ.] Tech - Navy; [memb.] Navfag Eagles Toastmaster Club, Backporch Story Tellers of Charleston; [hon.] A Number Contest Wins in Public Speaking, Many Honors in Art Field Able Toastmaster (atm); [oth. writ.] "The false of Christmas" Natl. L.B. of poetry, items in toast masters magazine, item in "Country" magazine, article accepted for review "chicken soup for the soul."; [pers.] I am an story teller of modern Christian parable for all ages. My stories are written to "Lift Up" the soul and life of my readers and audiences.; [a.] Summerville, SC

OLSEN, SHERRY JANICE
[b.] December 30, 1955, Claresholm, Alberta, Canada (Lived on Farmstead in Stavely, Alberta); [p.] Oswald F. Olsen, Kathleen Iris Olsen; [ch.] Jaimey Dawn, Jennifer Lyndelle; [ed.] Willow Creek Composite HS, Claresholm, Alberta; [occ.] Graduate Program Officer, Faculty of Graduate Studies, The University of Calgary, Calgary, Alberta; [memb.] Epilepsy Assn of Calgary; [hon.] Royal Conservatory of Music of Toronto (Piano) - Grade 8 - Honors, Royal Canadian Legions Essay Award Winner; [oth. writ] Numerous short stories, approx 60 poems; one novel; several articles published in local newspapers.; [pers.] Much of my writing (especially ny poetry) has been inspired by my two daughters and mirrors our passage through the murky waters of Divorce, a kidnapping attempt and a Cult that made even nightmares look good--All of which prove survival is indeed an art form.; [a.] Calgary, Alberta, Canada

OLSON, SHANNON
[pen.] Shanna; [b.] September 27, 1980, Camden, ME; [p.] Sheryl J. Olson; [ed.] I now go to Medomak Valley High School; [occ.] Student 10th Grade; [memb.] Gospel Martial Arts Union; [hon.] High School A/AB Honor Roll, Art Awards; [oth. writ.] A poem read at a funeral - written for my grandmother - I called it "The Rose."; [pers.] The rest is silence. Shakespeare, Hamlet, V,2.; [a.] Waldoboro, ME

ORBECK, ROSEMARIE
[pen.] Rose Orbeck; [b.] March 30, 1970, Chicago, IL; [p.] Nick and Frances Marshall; [m.] Robert Orbeck, July 6, 1975; [ed.] Antioch Community High School, B.S. from Illinois. State University, Currently attending Roosevelt University for a master's Degree in Clinical Psychology; [occ.] Mental Health Professional Outreach Specialist, Allendale Association, Lake Villa, IL, Young Republicans Committee, Volunteer for Students with Disabilities, Child Rights Advocate; [hon.] Illinois State Scholar National Social Science Award all - American College to Scholar, Dean's List too many to List; [pers.] We are all a slave to our senses. Inspired by: Plato - Analogy of the Cave. (From the republic, Book VII).; [a.] Lake Villa, IL

ORR, MAUREEN EMILY
[pen.] Maureen E. Orr; [b.] November 17, 1948, New York City; [p.] Maureen and James Orr; [ed.] George Washington High School, New York City Community College, School of Visual Arts, Hunter

College (currently) Attending Evenings; [occ.] Customer Service Representative, Empire Blue Cross Blue Shield; [memb.] Poetry Society of America Concerned Democratic Coalition Deaf (and Hard of Hearing) Artists of America; [hon.] My watercolor painting "Dancer," an abstract, was exhibited in the Metropolitan Museum of Art in New York City and the Smithsonian Institute of Washington, DC. Several other oil paintings were exhibited in different Universities; [oth. writ.] My poem, "Wounds" was published in the Hunter College's Literary Magazine, The Olive tree Review, My poem, "A Poet's Creation" was published in an anthology, World of Poetry. This was published in California.; [pers.] I have a love of nature and a love of people and I try to express an image sound and emotion through the words of my poetry. I am influenced by the twentieth century free verse American poets.; [a.] New York, NY

OSBORNE, KIM M.
[pen.] Kim M. Osborne; [b.] September 21, 1952, Evansville, IN; [p.] Charlotte and Don Osborne; [ch.] Heather; [ed.] High School; [occ.] Deisel Mechanic; [a.] Evansville, IN

OSBY, LENNE
[pen.] Quarez; [b.] April 9, 1978, Berrien General Hospital; [p.] Ezell Bailey, Carol Bailey; [ed.] I'm a Senior at Eau Claire High School in Eau Claire, Michigan; [occ.] My Future Occupation will to be a Chemical Engineer and Nurse; [memb.] National Honor Society Member of Israel Lite Baptist Church Member of the P.A.C Committee, Representative for Friesen Photography. Vice-President for Student Senate and President of N.H.S. (National Honor Society); [hon.] Honor Roll for Good Grades, Coaches Award for 1994 and 1995 in Softball, Team Leader Award in Volleyball, Varsity Letter in Cheerleading, also in Softball and Article about me in the Herald Pallium for being a Good Kid; [pers.] Always trust and believe in God because with him you never fails.; [a.] Eau Claire, MI

OSCAR, JEFF
[pen.] "El Loco" Oscar; [b.] January 13, 1978, Lawton, OK; [p.] David Cardoza, Janice Cardoza, Jeff Oscar; [ed.] San Jose High Academy 11th Grade, Presently; [occ.] Raging Waters Lifeguard, until September 23 1995; [memb.] Drama Club; [hon.] Several Scouting Awards; [oth. writ.] Several poems, un yet published.; [pers.] My thoughts and feelings pour from my soul, into pools of into onto paper.; [a.] San Jose, CA

OSTROWSKI, JILLIAN
[b.] January 7, 1982, Winfield, IL; [p.] Maynard and Carol Ostrowski; [ed.] 8th Grade Margaret Mead Jr., High School Elk Grove Village, Illinois; [occ.] Student; [memb.] Yearbook Committee, Mead Jr., High Band; [hon.] Northwest Suburban Young Authors Award, Presidential Academic Award, 4 Presidential Fitness Awards; [oth. writ.] Numerous short stories, books, and published poems.; [pers.] I believe that the beauty of nature is the most magnificent thing in the world, but it takes love to uncover that beauty. My advice is to try writing for your own enjoyment, not only as an assignment.; [a.] Elk Grove Village, IL

OTTERNESS, SUSAN ALLEN
[b.] May 8, 1971, Newport News, VA; [p.] Claude and Myrtle Allen; [m.] Tracy L. Otterness, September 17, 1994; [ed.] Bethel High School, Legal Secretary Course - Thomas Nelson Community College; [occ.] Free-lance Writers of Children's Stories; [memb.] Liberty Baptist Church, High School-Newspaper and Year Book Staffs, Keyettes; [oth. writ.] Several articles and poems published in local newspaper, "The Daily Press." Currently seeking to have published two children's stories, "Blossom Opossum" and "Freckle Fairy Fran."; [pers.] This poem was written in memory of my dear friend, Brett Rowland. In his faith I found strength, in his courage I saw grace, and in his death from cancer, I discovered abundant mercy through the Lord above.; [a.] Hampton, VA

OUDBIER, DAVID P.
[b.] November 6, 1974, Grand Rapids, MI; [p.] Tom and Rose Delor; [ed.] Union High School, Currently Enrolled at Sienna Heights College; [memb.] Co-Facilitator of Save (Sienna Against Violent Environment), Residence Hall Council News Editor for school paper, the "Spectra"; [oth. writ.] This is my first nationally published poem. I was published in the yearly school litery journal, "The Eclipse."; [pers.] I wrote the poem "Good-bye Daddy" in memory of my father Darrell R. Oudbier, who died of cancer when I was only ten. This poem is how I remember him and what times were like when we were together.; [a.] Grand Rapids, MI

OUELLETTE, JOE
[pen.] Joe Ouellette; [b.] February 16, 1951, Denver; [occ.] Electronic Tech. Self Employed; [memb.] Atom Electronics; [oth. writ.] Lots of writings of different styles writing is a form of relaxation for me.; [pers.] I enjoy writing hoping to share good thoughts with all comments or remarks. Are always welcome write Joe Ouellette.; [a.] Montrose, CO

OUFRAC, ANNESSA
[b.] December 22, 1980, Baton Rouge, LA; [p.] Kathy and Herman Oufrac; [ed.] 10th Grade in High School, and Maintaining a 4.1 Grade Point Average Central High School; [occ.] School; [memb.] Beta Club, Athletics, such as: Basketball, Valleyball, and Softball, FCA (future Christian Athletes) at Central High School, Top Cats Program at Central High School; [hon.] Beta Club, Scholastic Awards, Athletics, Athletics Include: Valleyball, Basketball, and Softball, I am also a Top Cat; [pers.] I try to do my best in all that I do, and succeed in all ways possible.; [a.] Baton Rorge, LA

OVERFIELD, KENDRA
[b.] March 3, 1980, Grand Haven, MI; [p.] Roger and Linda Overfield; [ed.] Sophomore in High School; [occ.] Student; [oth. writ.] Mix other poems.; [a.] Coopersville, MI

OWENS, LISA
[b.] February 14, 1936, Germany; [p.] Albert Floruss, Emma Floruss; [m.] Frank Owens, October 13, 1979; [ch.] Uwe-Juergen, Karen Christa, Thomas, Dieter, Christa Angela; [ed.] H. S. in Germany, GED in USA currently at College for Associates Degree in Applied Science; [memb.] Cider Painters of America, Wyo. Valley Art League, Miniature Art Society Florida, Northwest High Baud Asso.

Alumni, Luzerne County Election Board; [hon.] Deans List, Art Awards, Best of Show, 1st, 2nd, 3rd Place at County Fairs; [oth. writ.] Unpublished short stories, stories on five senses, how to make herbal Vinegars.; [pers.] Always be true to yourself and see nothing but the good in others.; [a.] Hulock Creek, PA

OWENS, ORA LEE
[b.] March 24, 1942, Michigan; [p.] Jake Smith and Lesester Smith; [m.] Lefate Owens Sr., March 21, 1961; [ch.] Yolanda Lynne, Belinda Faye, Lefate Jr., D. Rolando Miguel and granddaughter Candice; [ed.] Cassopolis High, Washington High, Indiana University; [occ.] Elementary Teacher, Warren Elementary School South Bend Indiana; [memb.] Community Missionary Baptist Church NAACP, National Education Association, Disabled American Veterans auxiliary, Indiana State Teachers Association, NC; [pers.] I strive to reflect the importance of children feeling good about feeling good about themselves in my writing. I have been greatly influenced by children's need for acceptance.; [a.] South Bend, IN

OWENS, JR., WILLIE
[pen.] William Sammuel Owens, Jr.; [b.] September 12, 1945, Pensacola, FL; [p.] Willie, Sr. & Mary (Smith) Owens; [m.] Gladys Marie Owens, September 2, 1972; [ch.] Jhaunee Vashell and Jake Davis; [ed.] George Washington Carver High, Washington/Pensacola Jr. College, University of West Florida (BS); [occ.] Singer/songwriter for SongKrafters 21; [memb.] Mt. Olive Baptist Church, Alpha Phi Alpha, Inc., IMMCP, BMI, NSAI; [hon.] Father of the Year: Mt. Olive Baptist Church, NLP's "Editor's Choice Award (1995), selectee: Best Poems of 1996; [oth. writ.] Several poems published in local newspapers, Contrubutor to the Compilation: When Black Folks Was Colored, Vol II & III, NLP's Songs on the Wind (1995), and the upcoming Best Poems of 1996; [pers.] I am a singer/songwriter, composer/arranger, poet, author, actor, public speaker, speech writer, etc. with but one ambition: to realize the fullest potential of the many gifts GOD has given me.; [a.] Pensacola, FL

OZAN, MAHMUT ESAT
[pen.] Mahmut Esat Ozan; [b.] June 18, 1921, Izmir, Turkey; [p.] Huseyin Avni, Afife; [m.] Ruth S. Ozan, February 23, 1952; [ch.] Deniz, Julide, Kerim; [ed.] Galatasaray French High School in Istanbul, Turkey-Univ. of Istanbul University of Indiana; [occ.] Prof. Emeritus The International Poems written in four different language Studies Department, Miami MDCC - North; [memb.] Florida Foreign Language Association, Co-founder and Past President of F.T.A.A., Florida Turkish American Association Charter, D.C., based English newspaper the Turkish times and the new york based Hurriyet printed in the Turkish Language; [hon.] Galatasaray French High School 50th year graduate Award, The ATAA the Washington, The Assembly of Turkish - American Association's Meritorious Accomplishment Award; [oth. writ.] Towards America (Amerikaya Dogru) a book 1946 Istanbul, Turkey. Poems written in four different languages French-Spanish-English Turkish Bi-monthly articles since 1989 in English Newspaper and Magazine work since 1943.; [pers.] Writing

prose and verse for the pure pleasure of self-satisfaction. If my work evokes some positive feelings in my readers that is an enjoyable plus.; [a.] Miami Lakes, FL

PADILLA, CHRISTINA T.
[b.] November 18, 1975, Weisbaden, Germany; [p.] Manuel and Margaret Padilla; [ed.] Forest Park High, Central Michigan University; [occ.] Student (3 Part Time Jobs); [memb.] Alpha Phi Omega Nat'l Service Fraternity, Phi Eta Sigma Honors Fraternity, St. John's Episcopal Church, Theatre Involvement, CMU, Academic Tutor; [hon.] Dean's List, CMU, Centralis Academic Schoolarship, Outstanding Academic Performance, CMU; [oth. writ.] Poems published in the campus magazine (framework) every semester for two years, articles published in campus newspaper, CM life.; [pers.] I enjoy organizing familiar words to create fresh meanings, and to echo ancient meanings in a new voice.; [a.] Mount Pleasant, MI

PAGANS JR., LONZA RAY
[pen.] Lonza R. "Bo" Pagans; [b.] April 17, 1949, Roanoke, VA; [p.] Anne Marie and Lonza Ray; [m.] Jo K. Nelson; [ch.] Patricia Lynn; [ed.] Ph.D. Candidate the Union Institute, Cincinatti Ohio; [occ.] Licensed Professional Counselor Private Practice; [memb.] Virginia Association of Drug and Alcohol Programs - Executive Board: Mental Health Association of Central Virginia; [hon.] Republican Presidential Legion of Merit: Central Virginia Community Services Board Extraordinary Volunteerism and Leadership Award: Who's Who; [oth. writ.] "Alcoholism and the Elderly" published in Progress Notes "Ways to help battered women stop being abused" New Digest "A journey to the me that I can be a guide to wholeness and a spiritual awakening, fairway.; [pers.] "The proof of our uniqueness lies in the fact that of the millions of people who have ever lived, no one else has our finger prints.; [a.] Lynchburg, VA

PAINE, ROGER DEAN
[b.] July 30, 1912, Palo Alto, CA; [p.] Russell Paine, Marie Spaulding; [m.] Divorced; [ed.] Deanne Skaggs, Debbie Shea, Laura Neal; [occ.] University of California, Berkeley; [memb.] Writer, Retired; [oth. writ.] San Francisco Passage, Skyline San Francisco Poems, 1979-1980 Mutations Short Stories, 1988 Glimpses Sonnets.; [pers.] I think we derive from some geological drift. But are a starstruck species.; [a.] San Leandro, CA

PAKER, AARON
[pen.] Aaron Paker, Hungry Eagle Paker; [b.] September 19, 1975, Winfield, IL; [p.] Phillip Paker, Diane Paker; [ed.] Alt Loma High School, University of Puget Sound; [occ.] Student U.P.S.; [hon.] High School Cum Laude Society, Recipient of Presidential Trustee award; [oth. writ.] Several poems published in high school journal "Inner Visions"; [pers.] Poetry is best when written by the heart instead of the head.; [a.] Rancho Cucamonga, CA

PALANCA, RAMON G.
[b.] June 23, 1928, Manila, Philippines; [p.] Carlos Sr. and Rosa G. Palanca; [m.] Janice Y. Palanca, June 5, 1967; [ch.] Ramon Jr.; [ed.] B.C.S. San Beda College, High Sch. - Ateneo De Mla.; [occ.] Retired; [memb.] Manila Polo Club, Manila Yatch Club,

Wack Wack Golf and Country Club; [oth. writ.] Other poems blending crucible layman's meditation.; [pers.] Feel before you write.

PALCZAK, PEQEEN
[b.] March 19, 1948, Carrollton, KY; [p.] Orlester and Arietta Wood; [m.] Joseph F. Palczak, August 2, 1990; [ch.] Shawne and Spencer (two-sons), Yovanda (one-daughter); [ed.] High School - Tech College - Have Cam Certified Apartment Manager have completed several courses in, and am working with Homeowners Assoc.; [occ.] Property Manager at Forlakeside Village Homeowners Assoc.; [memb.] First Assembly of God Church Apartment Assoc. of Greater Dallas CA. - Community Assoc. Institute; [hon.] Have only received awards from Girl Scouts of America when serving as a Leader/Helper in 1971 or 72 received Honors for 2 years as Property Manager of the Year; [oth. writ.] Have written many Gospel songs, poems and children's short stories in poem form. When I had my own small business, friendship gifts, I wrote and painted - art work gifts, cards, door plagues, etc. and wrote poems for company newsletters.; [pers.] I love lifting up and hopefully inspire cause for reflection that in stills remembering the past and gives hope and laughters to the present and future...to my friends and family, through my writing, paintings, etc.; [a.] Garland, TX

PAMIN, DIANA DOLHANCYK
[pen.] Diana Dolhancyk; [b.] December 13, Cleveland, Ohio; [p.] Peter Dolhancyk, Diana Dribus Dolhancyk; [m.] Leonard Pamin; [ch.] Diana Anne, Louis Peter; [ed.] West Tech High, Titus College of Cosmetology; hobbies, Interior Design, Art, Music, Books; [memb.] Arthritis Foundation, nominated into International Society of Poets. I've sponsored a young girl in INDIA for the past 15 yrs.; [hon.] Awards for outstanding achievement in poetry for "The Parting" in Journey of the Mind, published by the N.L.O.P., for "Stormy" in Songs on the Wind, for "Shadow Side" in At Water's Edge. Received International Poet of Merit Award from International Society of Poets. Nominated Poet of the Year 1995 by I.S.O.P. Accomplishment of Merit Award for Outstanding Literary Achievement, for the poem "Rain," in "Journey To Our Dreams." Published by Creative Arts and Science. Honorable mention for the poem "The View," in Treasured Poems of America, by Sparrowgrass Poetry. Chosen to be in Best Poems of 1996, the poem "Love No More." The poem "The Parting," was in the Sun Star newspaper, along with a picture and write up on the front page.; [pers.] Always give someone a smile, you'll never know whose heart you might lighten.; [a.] North Royalton, OH

PANTALEONE, JOAHNINE
[pen.] Joahnine or Joan Pantaleone; [b.] January 25, 1941, Trenton, NJ; [p.] Mr. and Mrs. Thomas J. Gore; [m.] Mr. Raphael Pantaleone, April 8, 1961; [ch.] Four sons - Edward, Michael, David and Raphael; [ed.] Private School 12 yrs., St. Mary's Grammar and High School Experience of Life's Surprises Joys and Sorrows, Tapestry of Emotions; [occ.] Wife, Mother, Care-Takers, Grandmom - council to many; [memb.] St. Anthony's Church - Pal - Deentown Poetry Club - Past Member of Poetry Club of Trenton; [hon.] Some given during Twelve Years at School, one was a Gold Medal; [oth. writ.] Prose and poetry written for family and friends also

songs co-written with husband.; [pers.] I choose to give hope, inspiration and a smile to others. To make life a little brighter to bring out the best in people through poetry and song.; [a.] Trenton, NJ

PANTANELLI, ELLEN JOY
[pen.] Ellen Joy; [b.] November 6, 1957, Bronx, NY; [p.] Selma and Stanley Riegley; [ch.] Seth Michel and Lia Jean; [ed.] Associates Degree from Nassau Community College, Attended Mineola High School; [occ.] Crisis Intervention Counselor/ Facilitator; [memb.] Host - Student Exchange Program, Women's Center of Greater Danbury Member; [hon.] Dean's List, Phi Theta Kappa; [oth. writ.] Poems "The Personals" published in the volume "Shadows and Light."; [pers.] To my mother with love and appreciation, and to my sister, Barbara... You are truly an inspiration to me.; [a.] Brookfield, CT

PAQUETTE, SUSAN
[b.] May 20, 1959, Lewiston, ME; [p.] Maurice Paquette, Patrica Blais; [ch.] Vicky F. Copeland, Paul S. Copeland, Ginger R.G. Paquette; [ed.] Jay High School, C.N.A. Course at Russel Park Manor; [occ.] Welder at the Largest Shipyard in Maine; [pers.] I feel strongly that all men are created equal and also have the same freedoms of speech and expression. I try to put down in poetry what I see and feel.; [a.] Booth Bau Harbor, ME

PARENDO, JUANITA M.
[b.] August 22, 1942, Minneapolis, MN; [p.] Ray and Doris Howdeshell Peter; [ch.] Eight; [ed.] Graduate of Central High Duluth, MN; [occ.] Grandmother; [oth. writ.] I am now completing my first book of poetry.; [pers.] Writing poetry has been an important part of my life. My poems come from my heart and all the experiences, good and bad that life has given me. I have survival and so can each of you.; [a.] Brooklyn Park, MN

PARIS, KRISTINA
[b.] August 7, 1980, Plainfield, NJ; [p.] Joel and Laurence Paris; [ed.] 10th Grade Student at North Plainfield High School; [a.] North Plainfield, NJ

PARK, SUSANNAH A.
[pen.] S. P. (The Mermaid); [b.] February 21, 1959, Honolulu, HI; [p.] Edward Y. B. Park and Shirley Mae-Samans; [ed.] Castle High/Aiea High, and also, Kyoto Modeling School and Agency Kyoto, Japan; [occ.] Customer Service - Specialist (Dream Occupation: Poet/Songwriter); [memb.] Greenpeace, PETA, and World Wildlife Fund; [hon.] Acceptance to: The Institute of Children's - Literature; [oth. writ.] Essay: "A Piece from the Puzzle in Me." (AT ICL.) (Approx. 300 poems written, - yet to be published.) Goals: To complete manuscript to submit to graphic illusions, on Cape Cod. And to write poetry columns for Cosmopolitan Mag.; [pers.] A born romantic, "Unconditional-love" inspires my writing constantly. There is no limit to the imagination, or realm of fantasy. And, to have the best of both worlds, I live in one/while the other lives in me.; [a.] Wahiawa, HI

PARKER, GAIL C.
[b.] February 7, 1945, Philadelphia; [p.] Claire and J. Gilbert Parker; [ch.] Irish Setter-Renegade and three cats, Shadow, Kelly and Kringle; [ed.] Council Rock

High School, Newtown, PA; [occ.] Writer, Retired early from Prudential Ins. Co., also work part-time as a Receptionist; [memb.] Dog Writers Assoc. of America, Irish Setter Club of America, Anti-Vivisectionist Soc., Dog and Cat Lovers Clubs of America, International Society of Poets, Elmwood Park Zoo, St. Albert the Great Nursing Home Visitation Group (with my dog), Vice Pres. of Lodestar Shelter (A no-kill animal rescue); [hon.] Three "Certificates of Nomination" (top three places only) from the Dog Writers Assoc., a Maxwell (top prize) from the DWAA. An Editors Choice from ISP, and two poems accepted for anthologies by ISP; [oth. writ.] Regular columns in dogsong and Hotline magazines. Articles and poems in Memo, DWAA Newsletter, Dog World, AV Magazine. Irish Edition (newspaper), Texas Dogs, Phila. Daily News, Official Dogs, Anthology of poems pub. in England "His Masters Voice," and various other publications. Besides the written work, I have also had photographs and illustrations published.; [pers.] Loving animals as much as I do, I try to impart that love in my poems and articles. I hope, by my writing, to help people realize that animals are truly special and deserve good compassionate treatment.; [a.] Philadelphia, PA

PARR, CORRIE LEE
[b.] September 29, 1984, Beloit, WI; [p.] Robert C. and Brenda L. Parr; [ed.] 5th Grade at Hackett Elementary; [memb.] 4-H Basketball and Student Council; [a.] Beloit, WI

PARSONS, JOHN THOREN
[b.] October 11, 1913, Detroit, MI; [p.] Carl B. and Edith T. Parsons; [m.] Elizabeth Shaw Parsons, April 20, 1940; [ch.] Carl A., John T. II, Robert S., Grant W., David C., Meredith; [ed.] Grosse Points High (Michigan), Wayne State (1 yr.); [occ.] Authoring my Autobiography; [memb.] Soc. Mtg. Enges (follow and fast direction), Past Memberships: Owner Forestry Assoc., Am. Helecopter Soc., Amer. Foundry men's Soc., Amer. Soc. for Metals; [hon.] Natl. Medal of Technology 1985, National Inventors Hall of Fame. Honorary Dr. of Engineering (Univ. of Mich 1988 Stations Designated once "Father of the Second Industrial Revolution.. Passage from the age Crafts Manager to the age of Erect Science"; [oth. writ.] Misc. Technical Papers Incl. Keynote Paper 5.22. 95 to International Institution of Production Engineering Research (CIRP); [pers.] Technological feasibility doesn't guarantee profitability. The 21st century must be devoted to - expansion of renewable resources and food supply - reduction in consumption of fossil fuels - improve ethical standards every where - expands communication with all the peoples of the earth.; [a.] Traverse City, MI

PATINO-ASTUDILLO, MARIBEL
[pen.] Porcelana; [b.] July 24, 1979, New York; [p.] Julieta Renteria, Edgar Calderon; [ed.] New Town (Still in High School); [occ.] High School Student; [oth. writ.] Many poems for my school yearbooks.; [pers.] Many people are in pain. In my personal experience, that's what mainly my life has been about. So I hope that like me, others could ease there sorrows in my writing.; [a.] Elmhurst, NY

PATRICK, MORGAN
[b.] March 13, 1974; [p.] Simmy Peacock; [ed.] Santa Cruz High School, Currently Enrolled at

N.E.O., A. and M College; [occ.] Salesman at a Record Store called Stick it in your Ear; [oth. writ.] Poem published in local four state area paper.; [pers.] I am oddly influenced by the imagination of a movie director named David Lyncit. Darkness, in a variety of colors, is stapled to my imagination permanery.; [a.] Miami, OK

PAUL, ANGELA ELISE
[b.] August 28, 1976, Burlington, CO; [p.] Gary Paul, Sharon Paul; [ed.] Poteet High School, William Jewell College; [occ.] Student; [memb.] National Forensics League, National Honor Society, Alpha Delta Pi Sorority; [oth. writ.] Several poems included in a person journal.; [pers.] The only knowledge that is true knowledge is what you gain through life experience. Thank you so much to my parents for teaching me about expression.; [a.] Mesquite, TX

PAULHUS, RITA L.
[b.] Woonsocket, RI; [p.] Robert and Jeanne Paulhus; [m.] Divorced; [ch.] David Mencarini; [ed.] BS, Masters Rhode Island College University of RI; [occ.] Teacher Bernon Heights Elementary; [memb.] Woonsocket Teachers Guild, American Heart Assoc., Future Teachers of America National Teachers Assoc.; [hon.] Rhode Island Honor Society Future Teachers of America Award; [oth. writ.] Local newspapers teacher's guild news; [pers.] My writings reflect the memories of experiences that have affected my life.; [a.] Harrisville, RI

PEDERSEN, KURT HAMILTON
[b.] August 9, 1965, Manhatten, NY; [p.] Lee and Barbara Pedersen; [ch.] Luke, Cloe; [ed.] BA in History from the University of North Carolina; [occ.] Freelance Writer; [memb.] E-World; [oth. writ.] Children stories and poetry.; [pers.] I write from experience to express my innermost feelings on a subject hoping to gratify subject hoping to gratify and entertain my readership base.; [a.] Chapel Hill, NC

PEDERSON, NATHAN
[b.] March 18, 1975, Rifle, CO; [p.] Eric Pederson, Andrea Orrison; [ed.] 1-8, St. Stephen's School, 9-10, Denner Academy, 11-12 Glenwood Springs High School, Presently attending College at Colorado Mountain College; [occ.] Bookseller, Andrea's Journeys Bookstore; [hon.] Published several times in High School Newspaper; [oth. writ.] Heart and mind, poet's heart.; [pers.] Poets are masters, not of rhyme or reason, but of the human heart and soul, and of the forces that drive them.; [a.] Carbondale, CO

PEERSON, CLAUDE RANDY
[b.] June 8, 1957, Rodeo, CA; [p.] Don and Dorothy Peerson; [m.] Linda Nunez-Peerson, August 21, 1992; [ch.] Max, Spunky; [pers.] My husband, Randy recently passed away. The last few months have been very difficult for myself, his family, and his friends. I hope in some way with the publication of my husband's thoughts and feelings it will help those of us who love him deal with his death.; [a.] Rodeo, CA

PEGGS, STEPHANIE J.
[b.] January 4, 1980, Chicago, IL; [p.] Nolan Peggs, Patricia Peggs; [ed.] Acaddemy of Our Lady High School; [occ.] Student/Junior; [pers.] I've been

greatly influenced by great poets such as: Maya Angelou and Gwendolyn Brooks. My poems express my feelings, the mood I'm in and Reality.; [a.] Chicago, IL

PEPER, JESSICA
[b.] November 2, 1982, Saint Louis, MO; [p.] Frank and Carol Peper, Laura Douglas; [ed.] K-6 Jefferson Middle School; [occ.] School and Baby Sitting; [hon.] I've been on Honor Roll for 7 years, I've received Citizenship Awards for 5 years, I was Previously in Choir for 2 years; [oth. writ.] I've had other writings displayed, but never published.; [pers.] I am in 7th grade at Jefferson Middle School, and I enjoy writing stories and poems. I was influenced by other poets. I try to make my readers feel what I'm feeling by poetry.; [a.] Hawk Point, MO

PEREIRA, ELENA BRANDAO
[b.] February 7, 1983, Manhasset, NY; [p.] Helena and David Pereira; [ed.] Completed 6th Grade; [occ.] Student; [hon.] Math-A-Thon Honor Award, Presidential Physical Fitness Award and Attended the Intellectually Gifted Program in Grade School; [oth. writ.] "He is Always Watching", "Away in the Night Sky", "Alone," "Awaking of Dusk."; [a.] South Setauket, NY

PETERMAN, VETA
[pen.] Vete; [b.] July 1, 1918, Alabama; [p.] Walter and Nancy Ward; [m.] Frank (Deceased), July 26, 1936; [ch.] Two - Frank and Jimmy; [ed.] High School Early, Childhood Ed., Broward Jr. College; [occ.] Retired; [memb.] St. Ruth Bpt. Church Sunday School Teacher Class No. 7 Pre. of Woman's Mission Society, Sr. Choir Member, Deaconess Vice Chair of Budget Comm.; [hon.] Woman of the Year from the City of Dania 1995, Doctor Martin L. Kings Award 1994, Dania Housing Service. A many others; [oth. writ.] I have a lot of poems. I read in churches, schools and clubs, I only write poems.; [pers.] My mother wrote poems. But something tells me what to write about. I have a strong feeling that it is God guiding me.; [a.] Dania, FL

PETERSON, DOUGLAS N.
[b.] September 10, 1943, Inglewood, CA; [p.] Alive; [m.] Alice N. Peterson, April 19, 1984; [ch.] Lettisia C. Peterson; [ed.] Riverside Polytechnic High School Riverside, California (1961), California State Polytechnic University (1961-63), Architectural Rendering Los Angeles Art Center School (1963-1965), Studied with Paolo Soleri Work Seminar on Cities Arizona State University (1967), Bachelor of Architecture California State Polytechnic University San Luis Obispo, California (1968); [occ.] Architect; [oth. writ.] "Trek to Essence"

PETTENGILL, AMY
[b.] June 11, 1982, Exeter Hospital; [p.] Misty Witham and Alan Pettengill; [ed.] Lamphrey River Elementary and Iber Holmes Gove Middle School; [occ.] Cheerleader for Nor-Rock Vikings Football; [memb.] Nor-Rock Vikings Cheerleading Squad, Softball Team Audioman, Soccer Team Raymond Rockers, Basketball Team Fighting Irish, Volleyball Raymond Rams, Rosie's Dance School; [hon.] 13 Sport trophies, 250 dollars for selling the most raffle tickets, awards for being a secretary, photographer,

and a journalist on the school newspaper staff; [oth. writ] A couple poems in the school newspaper, when I was younger a letter to Santa Claus in the town paper; [pers.] I enjoy writing a lot and hope someday to become a poet or an author ; [a.] Raymond, NH

PHELAN, KRISTEN
[b.] July 3, 1980, Chicago; [p.] Mary Phelan; [ed.] St. Giles (Grammar School) Oak Park River Forest High School; [memb.] St. Giles Youth Group Girls Choir; [oth. writ] Several poems and many short stories.; [a.] Oak Park, IL

PHELPS, CARL A.
[p.] Lloyd and Martha Phelps; [m.] Louise Killey, December 18, 1937, September 18, 1994; [ch.] Lloyd C. Phelps; [ed.] High School; [occ.] Retired - Factory Worker; [oth. writ] Springtime - A dream, seventy-five please Lord, 50 years, alone, for Adam. A friend. Days end.; [pers.] Most of these written after the loss of my son 4/94 and my wife, after being her sole caretaker for 20 years, in 9/94.; [a.] Lareer, MI

PHIFER, LARRY HERBERT
[b.] December 28, 1976, El Paso, TX; [p.] Mr. and Mrs. Herb Phifer Jr.; [ed.] High School Senior 95 and 96; [occ.] Student; [hon.] Outstanding Student Awards, Honor Student, Varsity Football Captain, Various Football Awards Offence and Defense Outstanding Offensive Line Award, 4 years Letterman in Sports; [oth. writ] Poems: "I Contradict and Where Will You Be", "Battle of Glory."; [pers.] "A poet is not made, he is born and love coals his fire."; [a.] El Paso, TX

PHILLIPS, ANNIE KING
[b.] March 2, 1920, Winston-Salem, NC; [p.] Mamie Lawrence King, Willard B. King; [m.] Deceased, July 7, 1955; [ch.] Monica Wilkerson, Dianne Engram; [ed.] B.S. in Education, MA in Education, (NYU) Masters in Public Health Univ. of Michigan; [occ.] Retired - Usual Occupation: Health Adm.; [memb.] Delta Sigma Theta Sorority, Union of Black Episcopalians, Amer. Assoc. of Retired Persons; [hon.] Creative Writing for Seniors Poetry Award: Dance the Mask; [oth. writ] Dance the Mask original poems and Haiku.; [pers.] Poetry is my expression of the beauty in our world - our natural environment and in people met along my journey's path.; [a.] Washington, DC

PHILLIPS, JEANNIE
[b.] July 13, 1961, Marshall, CO; [p.] Gary Thompson and Pattie Brothers; [m.] Robby Phillips, October 4, 1980; [ch.] Madison (daughter), John-Robert (son); [ed.] Gadsden High School attending Gadsden State Community College; [occ.] Homemaker/student; [hon.] "Parent Volunteer of the Year" 1993-94 at Southside Elementary School; [pers.] My personal goal is to: Teach my children a great love for reading and learning that will live in their hearts forever.; [a.] Southside, AL

PHILLIPS, JENNA
[pen.] J. Michelle Phillips; [b.] August 6, 1982, Sonora, CA; [p.] Marl Phillips, Sandy Irwin-Phillips; [ed.] Hazel Fischer Elem., Incline Middle School; [occ.] Student; [memb.] Drama Club, Tahoe Players Association; [hon.] Honor Roll; [oth. writ] "Naomi" a book about Autism.; [a.] Incline Village, NV

PHILLIPS, PATRICIA THOMAS
[pen.] Ann Faith; [b.] May 13, 1964, Lake City, FL; [p.] David Thomas, Sarah Thomas; [m.] Billy Phillips, July 18, 1986; [ch.] Dominique, Anastasia, Lanier; [ed.] Miami Jackson High, University of Florida; [occ.] English Teacher - Eleventh Grade Advanced Placement, African, American History - Coral Gables High; [memb.] Dade County Teachers of English; [hon.] Appreciation for Teaching of Student in the International Baccaulaureate English Program, Teacher of the Year - Coral Gables High 1995-1996; [oth. writ] Poems, short stories, unpublished.; [pers.] I am a strong believer that things may not come when we want them, but G-d plans them right on time. I try to encourage my family and students to be patient and hold on to dreams.; [a.] Miami, FL

PHILLIPS, PAULINE HARDESTY MILLER
[b.] August 19, 1907, Marion Co, WV; [p.] Marion S. and Ora Sadie Hardesty Miller; [m.] George Fred Phillips (deceased), June 29, 1931; [ch.] George Frederick, Jaqueline Jeanne and Mikuel Ann; [ed.] AB Degree in Education; [occ.] Retired Elementary Teacher and Principal; [memb.] First Presbyterian Church, Alpha Delta Kappa, International Honorary Society for Women Educators, Emeritis Club of Fairmont State College - A Church Elder; [hon.] ADK above Previously a Girl Scout Leader of an International Friendship Troop - Unit Leader two Summers at G.S. Camp May Flather in Montgomery Co - Washington DC Area; [oth. writ] Several poems published in local newspaper - also in manor news monthly where I live - Biographies of my two daughters (son deceased).; [pers.] "To thine own self be true," honesty and kindness sees me through. Always be fair.; [a.] Fairmont, WV

PHILPITT, EDWARD T.
[b.] November 15, 1926, Washington, DC; [p.] Richard and Isabel; [ed.] Graduated from Benjamin Franklin Univ., Wash, D.C. (1952); [occ.] Poet and Retired; [memb.] Member of International Society of Poets; [pers.] An empty mind produces nothing but can be used to climate unwanted thoughts. Caring today will produce a better person tomorrow, it's through individual thoughts that we can certain the stardom within.; [a.] Washington, DC

PIA, JOSEPH
[b.] March 17, 1950, Sunbury, PA; [p.] Joe B. Pia, Marian E. Snyder; [ed.] Shikellamy High (Sunbury, PA), Williamsport Area Community College (PA), Academy of Health Sciences (Ft. Sam Houston, San Antonio, TX), US Army Service December 81 - Oct. 89; [occ.] Registered X-ray Technician but working also as convenience store clerk; [memb.] American Registry of Radiologic Technologists, Universal Pantheist Society; [hon.] Army Achievement Medal, Army Good Conduct Medal (2 Awards), Overseas Service Ribbon; [oth. writ] Nothing published or submitted before. This entry was born of personal experience.; [pers.] While faith may be a comforter, fact is a better prescription for living in the real world. The real world is nature of which man is a part. Let us learn, respect for, and live in harmony with nature.; [a.] San Antonio, TX

PICCOLO, PAUL
[b.] December 23, 1921, Brooklyn, NY; [p.] Frank and Natalina Piccolo; [m.] Theresa Piccolo,

September 15, 1946; [ch.] Paul Francis Piccolo; [ed.] Hamilton High, Brooklyn College (Evenings); [occ.] Retired Federal Employee; [memb.] Holy Name Society (Catholic), Veterans Foreign Wars, Benevolent and Protective Order of Elks; [hon.] VFW Award and Plaque Servicing and Counselling WWII, Korean and Vietnam Disabled Veterans and their Families for their VA Benefits - at Office, in Hospitals and in their Homes; [oth. writ] Many poems and many humorous quotations. Never submitted to anyone, never thought my work has good enough for exposure until entering this poetry contest.; [pers.] Was often called upon to write poetry for special occasions for family, co-workers and friends. After heart surgery, and as a hobby, I devoted more time to writing. Influenced by my father (Wrote Poetry in Italian) - I always loved to spread good feeling and humor to others.; [a.] Flushing, NY

PIECIUL, JESSICA LYNN
[b.] August 25, 1983, Springfield, MA; [p.] Richard and Ellen Pieciul; [hon.] Received Medal for the National Language Arts Olympiad; [pers.] I would like to thank all of my past teachers for encouraging me in my writing. Hi, to my parents, my brother Jon, and all my friends.

PIEL, GEORGE
[b.] October 25, 1919, Pittsburgh, PA; [p.] William H. Piel and Alice B. Stewart; [m.] Jean E. Williams, March 13, 1942; [ch.] George Jr., and William R.; [ed.] Schenley High School, Carnegie Tech. Night School, I.C.S. and Realtors Institute; [occ.] Retired Manufacturing Engineer - Realtor; [memb.] Society of Manufacturing Engineers; [hon.] Several Patents on Valves; [oth. writ] Several historical poems (unpublished). Several lyrics for songs. Many technical writings.; [pers.] My writings reflect and are sensitive to the equality of man and the goodness inherent in all persons, when they are given a chance to develop fully.; [a.] Pittsburgh, PA

PINCKNEY, CHRISTINE
[b.] November 6, 1963, Manchester, NH; [p.] Ray and Linda Bilodeau; [m.] Jeffery FeKay; [ch.] Danielle Christine; [ed.] Profile Jr., Sr. High School; [occ.] Housewife and Mother; [oth. writ] Several non-published poems and short stories.; [pers.] I would like to thank my parents for pushing me to publish my work and making it possible for me to leave behind a part of myself to my daughter Danielle, my true love Jeffery, and to all my friends and family. I would also like to thank Brian Pinckney.; [a.] Maitland, FL

PINKERT, PETRYNA K.
[b.] July 4, 1915, Brightstone, Manitoba, Canada; [p.] Stephen and Anna Malyk; [m.] Roland C. Pinkert (deceased), 1952; [ed.] Wayne H.S. (Ashtbula County) OH, 1993, Kent State Univ., Kent OH 1942; [occ.] Retired; [pers.] Former Biology teachers who wishedd to teach all children the beauty of nature. Inspiration mother who always included mixed flowers in her egetable garden for color. Love of poetry: H.S. English Teacher.; [a.] Orlando, FL

PIO, KAREN WALSH
[b.] October 7, 1951, Quincy, MA; [p.] Harald and Norma Walsh; [m.] Rick Pio, September 24, 1977;

[ch.] Devin Walsh Pio, Adrian Mark Pio; [ed.] BA Psychology from UMASS/Amhurst 1973, MSW in Casework from U Connecticut School of Social Work 1975; [occ.] Director of Outpatient Substance Abuse Services at Providence Hospital; [memb.] National Association of Social Work, American Association of Marriage and Family Therapists, Board of Certified Clinical Social Workers, Pioneer Valley Folklore Society, Academy of Certified Social Work; [hon.] Phi Beta Kappa, Alpha Lamda Delta; [oth. writ.] Book reviews for High School and College newspapers, have been writing plays, short stories and poetry since childhood.; [a.] South Hadley, MA

PIPER, ESTELLE
[b.] July 26, 1953, Amarillo, TX; [p.] Harry and Phyllis Sappington; [ed.] San Jose State University, Michigan State University; [occ.] Administrator - Applied Komatsu Technology; [memb.] Actor's Equity; [oth. writ.] "Out of Control" (Stage play.); [pers.] Somewhere between cause and effect, I try to see the difference between desire and love, be it an object, activity or person. Beauty not seen from the heart is not beauty. (Many thanks to David Lober.); [a.] San Jose, CA

PITTMAN II, SAMUEL EDWARD
[b.] March 30, 1981, Houston, TX; [p.] Samuel and Floydie Pittman; [memb.] Goodwill Baptist Church; [hon.] President's Academic Club Award, U.S. Achievement Academy National Award Winner (1994); [oth. writ.] Many unpublished poems that are kept in a binder.; [pers.] "You should always strive to be the best at what you do!"; [a.] College Station, TX

PLANCK, BEV
[b.] June 25, 1938, Petaskey, MI; [p.] Helen and Alfred Heynig; [m.] Roger Planck, April 21, 1956; [ch.] Dian, Terra, Tavi and Anthony; [ed.] Harbor Springs High; [occ.] Homemaker; [memb.] Brigade of Light Church; [oth. writ.] Infinite Horizons (A collection of metaphysical poetry).; [pers.] It is my desire to ease the fear of death and dying through poetry. It is my hope that my poems become the catalyst that enables people to talk about what is yet to come.; [a.] Fort Wayne, IN

PLUMMER, MILTON
[pen.] Mel Palmer; [b.] August 26, 1930, Washington, DC; [p.] Eugene and Arlie Plummer (deceased); [m.] Louise E. Hamilton, August 26, 1990; [ch.] Three, all grown; [ed.] High School, Washington, DC, Armstrong Terrel Junior High; [occ.] Research Clerk at Carlton Computer Support Services, Beltsville, MD; [memb.] US Army (Korea), Community Organization (CIC), DC, Amway Corp., Church of God and Saints of Christ Choir and Chorus; [hon.] US Army: Bronze Star, Three Battle Stars; US Post Office: Superior Accomplishment; Certificate of Award, Community Volunteer Plaque; Interstate Commerce Commission: Sustained Superior Accomplishment Award, DC; [oth. writ.] Poems promoting building fund activities in church, Poetic birthday cards, other random poetry, writing entitled "Life" and one entitled "Unfathomable"; [pers.] I've always has a yearning to engage in what I choose to characterize as `technical writings' borne out of pure desire and enchanted by some training while employed by the Federal Government. This desire has lent itself at times to writing poetry.; [a.] New Carrollton, MD

POCIUS, ETHEL M.
[b.] September 17, 1930, New Jersey; [p.] Alfred and Myrtle Meek; [ch.] Debbie Zaman, Daniel Meek; [ed.] High School Grad., some Computer Training Attending Writer's Digest School by Mail; [occ.] Retired Clerical now poet for Hobby; [memb.] AARP, Diabetes Assoc.; [hon.] From PTA and other Small Town Organizations for poetry I've written; [oth. writ.] Lots of poems a hymn (words and music) a religious choruses.; [pers.] Very strong Christian faith, out going lots of nice friends love to read romances and thrillers, collect cassette tapes from 20's through 60's and collect poetry.; [a.] Baldwin Park, CT

POEHLER, SHELLY
[pen.] Shelly Arlene; [b.] January 20, 1973, Illinois; [pers.] I love words and ideas...they move mountains - they are power... writing is my way of protesting of speaking out...how else will we make a difference...humanity is beautiful - this world is beautiful - it just sometimes needs a push to expand its boarders...imagine if love was tangible - if it dripped from our tongues...that's why I write - to challenge and to create...to create the love and peace that I know is possible...; [a.] Colorado

POLLARD, SUSAN
[b.] May 1, 1958, Philadelphia, PA; [p.] Dr. and Mrs. H. Koren; [m.] Rick Pollard, August 7, 1988; [ed.] B.S. in Special Education from In State University (ISU), M.S. in Counseling from Indiana University (IU) in Indianapolis; [occ.] Mental Health Therapist; [memb.] American Counseling Assoc. (ACA), Assoc. of Specialists in Group Work, IN Mental Health Counselors Assoc., IN Counseling Assoc. (ICA), in Chapter of Prevention of Child Abuse, Children and Adults with Attention Deficit Disorder (CHAAD), Association for Attention Deficit Disorder; [hon.] Graduated Magna Cum Laude from ISU, Dean's List, Academic Scholarships; [pers.] The greatest gifts one human being can give another are hope, love, and acceptance.; [a.] Indianapolis, IN

PORTER, BILL
[b.] September 23, 1948, Silver Spring, Maryland; [p.] William and Patricia Porter; [m.] Janette, December 10, 1976; [ch.] Cindi and Billy; [ed.] Chritopher Columbus High, BS Business Management University of Maryland CLU and CHFC Designation - American College; [occ.] Financial Planner; [memb.] International Association of Financial Planners, Songwriters Club of America; [hon.] Dean's List; [oth. writ.] Have published other poems and songs.; [pers.] If I can be as good a parent as my father and mother, then I will be a great success.; [a.] Miami, FL

POTEETE JR., LEM
[b.] November 19, Byhalia, MS; [p.] Mr. and Mrs. L. E. Poteete; [ed.] Eighth Grade; [oth. writ.] I have written one hundred and three poems so far.

POWELL, ANGELA TAWANNA
[pen.] Angela Powell; [b.] August 6, 1979, Detroit, MI; [p.] Ronald Powell and Annie Williams; [ed.] St. Hilarys Elem, Our Lady of Grace Elem., Cass Technical High School; [memb.] The Democratic Party, Detroit Institute of Art; [hon.] St. Hilary Public Speaking Contest '87, '91, '92 America and Me Contest; [pers.] Poetry is the method I use to express feelings, I can't say vocally.; [a.] Detroit, MI

POWERS, RAMONA BIEGLER
[b.] May 21, 1949, Chicago; [p.] Chester and Betty Lentowski; [m.] Anthony Powers, July 29, 1995; [ch.] Peter and Kevin, Stepchildren, Tim, Katie, Sister - Janice; [ed.] Life is a continuation of learning experiences which will not be complete until I am no longer here at that time I will have truly earned my "Degree in Life"; [occ.] Jill of all trades - I have many, and hopefully many more to come.; [memb.] A lifetime member of the human race. I hope I am worthy of this respectable title; [hon.] I have been Awarded Two cherished Sons, my treasured Nephews and Nieces (the older set and the younger set), and I am honored to have recently become step-mother to my adult step-daughter, step-son and his wife.; [oth. writ.] Many other poems - mostly personal - also a short autobiographical - type story I may attempt to have published someday.; [pers.] I dedicate my poem "A Prelude to New Beginnings," to my old friend, my love, my precious husband Tony, who continually encourages me in all my attempted endeavors. When I was younger, I was very idealistic. Almost everything appeared to be either black or white. In my present stage of existence, gray definitely dominates! I believe it is best to always search for the positive, it makes the difficult times easier to endure, almost every situation. The hardest lesson I have learned is to never say "Never" it backfires!; [a.] Schaumburg, IL

PRESTON, TAMMYE
[b.] April 15, 1964, Georgia Dekalb General, GA; [p.] Rita Braswell, David Braswell; [m.] Charles Preston, October 16, 1991; [ch.] Bridgett Rolader, Perry S. Rolader II; [ed.] Lithonia High School; [occ.] Sr. Health Service, Technician, Georgia Regional Hospital; [pers.] The future lies in our children's hands. Nature is the beauty of life.; [a.] Atlanta, GA

PRICKETT, JOHNNIE M.
[b.] September 22, 1909, Talbot County, GA; [p.] Emmett and Elizabeth Woodall Miller; [m.] Charles Albert Prickett (deceased), December 20, 1948; [ed.] Woodland High School, CBS Business School, Young Harris College, Georgia State University; [occ.] Retired from Social Security Administration, Claims Examiner; [memb.] St. Luke United Methodist Church, DAR, Wynnton Study Club, Tulip Garden Club, Colonial Dames XVII Century; [hon.] Delta Mu Delta, Crimsom Key, shared First Place, Georgia State Graduation, Conference Quiet Disciple; [oth. writ.] Family history articles, special occasion poems.; [pers.] Long fellow's "The Day is Done" expresses the value of poetry in life. My niece says she remembers poems she and I learned as we did household chores 50 years ago. Life is enriched by good literature, including poetry!; [a.] Columbus, GA

PROCOPE, ANDRE L.
[pen.] Andre L. Procope; [b.] September 21, 1928, Nevis-B, WI; [p.] Deceased; [m.] Doreen Procope W.B., July 5, 1990; [ch.] Danielle and Esmond Procope; [ed.] Diploma in Civil Eng. (4 yrs.), B.A. in Criminal Justice Law, Law Student at North Western University - Sacramento - Cal.; [occ.] Semi Retired; [memb.] 100 Black Men N.Y.C., Nevis National Party - a Party Working for Political Change in Government Chamber of Commerce Lydns Club; [hon.] Several Poems Published in Local Newspa-

pers; [oth. writ.] Play-pandemonium in the Spirit World, 400 sonnets/poems, 45 lyrics for hymns, manuscript - the ideal society.; [pers.] I pray daily for the revival of the spirit of mankind. When this is accomplished, we will once again become our brothers keeper instead of just being a good samaritan of convenience.; [a.] Los Angeles, CA

PROSSER, MICHAEL J.
[b.] May 9, 1948, Syracuse, NY; [p.] Palmer Abelbert Prosser, Viola Mary (Clairmont); [ed.] MSLA Univ. So. California, 1981 BA History Calif. State Coll. San Bernardino 1971, AA Riverside Community College; [occ.] Learning Resources Assistant; [memb.] ASDC, Facilitator Patrons 1985 Chapter Riverside, Tutor-Queen of Angels Church Riverside 1985; [oth. writ.] California and the Pacific Plate: A bibliography 1979.; [pers.] To be a light to all people.; [a.] Riverside, CA

QUARTO, TRACY
[b.] December 20, 1978, Queens, NY; [p.] Donna and Tony Quarto; [occ.] Student at Palm Desert High School; [pers.] I was born in Queens, New York. I lived there until I was 13, then my family and I moved to Palm Springs, California. I have a twin sister and a younger sister. I am the oldest.; [a.] Palm Desert, CA

QUICK, KAREN
[pen.] Kacy Cody; [b.] August 5, 1952, Danville, VA; [p.] Everett O. and Etta P. (Deceased) Collins; [m.] James A. Quick; [ch.] Lisa Q. Brown, Tony Quick, (grandchildren) Conner Brown, Skyler and Alex Quick; [ed.] B.S. in Math-Averett College, George Washington High; [memb.] Children's Love Letters, Inc., Contact Ministries, International Pen Friends, Southeast Writers' Association; [hon.] International Essay Award, Alpha Chi Honor Society, College Honor Scholarship, 3 Sustained Incentive Superior Performance Award at I.R.S., Incentive Bonus, Performance Bonus and Savings Commendation as Tax Manager, Publication 3 times in Congressional Record; [oth. writ.] "Tax Simplification - Let's Play Flatball" (published 3 times in Congressional Record); [pers.] I like to read and write about improving communication and enhancing relationships. I treasure those precious intangibles of faith, trust, and respect.; [a.] Kernersville, NC

RACE, JOYCE
[b.] March 27, 1946, St. Peterson, FL; [p.] Roger and Jean Allen; [m.] George Race, September 27, 1981; [ch.] Melvin, Marie, Melinda, Melissa; [ed.] St. Petersburg High, Mesa State College; [occ.] Cashier at Western Implement CO; [oth. writ.] Wrote 1 book of poems for husband never published; [pers.] I say through my poems that I can't say face to face; [a.] Clifton, CO

RADER, JANIE LEIGH
[b.] June 5, 1979, Springfield, MO; [p.] Gary and Sue Rader; [ed.] Currently a Junior at Marshfield High School; [occ.] Student; [memb.] THA, Future Home Makers of America. I play softball for Marshfield High School; [oth. writ.] I had a peom publishedin "Youth" magazine; [pers.] I have found I can express my emotions through poetry.; [a.] Marshfield, MO

RALPH, CHERLYL E.
[b.] June 1, 1948, Canal Zone, Panama; [p.] Altha Seymour - Gib Hockett; [m.] Jon K. Ralph, December 18, 1972; [ch.] Shanteel, Jon E. Cassie; [ed.] GED Diploma; [occ.] School Bus Driver; [oth. writ.] Lady Slipper Scent Children on Probation, Dream Catcher Penelope "The little Country School Bus" Mystic Mystery; [pers.] Though - my education is slight. I've learned to write from my heart, and from the souls of others around me.; [a.] Junction City, OR

RAMET, SABRINA P.
[b.] June 26, 1949, London; [m.] Christine M. Hassenstab, January 1, 1991; [ed.] A.B., Philosophy, Stanford University, 1971, M.A., Internat'l Relations, U of Arkansas, 1974, Ph.D., Political Science, UCLA, 1981; [occ.] Professor, International Studies, University of Washington; [oth. writ.] Author of five books, including Nationalism and Federalism in Yugoslavia 1962-1991, 2nd ed. (1992, Social Currents in Eastern Europe, 2nd ed. (1995), and Balkan Babel, the disintegration of Yugoslavia, 2nd ed, (1996); [pers.] I have been enormously influenced by the philosophies of Immanuel Kant, G.W.F. Hegel, Jean-Paul Sartre, and Martin Heidegger.; [a.] Seattle, WA

RAMIREZ, KATHLEEN L.
[pen.] Kathy Ramirez; [b.] September 5, 1953, Sweethome, OR; [p.] George and Virginia Wilson; [m.] Robert Ramirez, August 31, 1970; [ch.] Robert, Michelle, Christina, Michael; [ed.] Tracy High, James Logan High, Manteca High, San Joaquin Delta College, Stanislaus State University; [occ.] Councilor, Mary Graham Children's Shelter; [memb.] Grace Brethren Ministry Church, Mary Graham Guild, Secretary. I am also on the Employee Recognition Committee at work; [hon.] Dean's List, San Joaquin Delta College; [oth. writ.] Several articles for the Human Service Agency. Newsletter, Daze of our Lives. Had several "Letters to the Editor" published in local newspapers.; [pers.] I feel that writing is an expression of life. Poetry is one way that I voice my feelings and emotions. Edgar Allen Poet and Helen Steiner rice are two of my favorite poets. John Steinbeck, Pearl Buck, and Ray Bradbury are my favorite authors.; [a.] Ripon, CA

RAMOS, ROBYN
[pen.] Marilyn Warhol; [b.] August 16, 1953, California, LA; [p.] Angie P. Martin, Manua L. Ramos; [ch.] Rebecca Thomas (grandson Lorey Ries); [ed.] Crealde Arts and The World and all it holds; [occ.] Writer, photographer poet. Produce the RI Pages is Spirit; [memb.] Community Writers Assoc. of RI; [hon.] Photo "Guardian Angle" of the year. Photo awarded to the Church who had done the most to help the homeless Orl Fl. Documental done one the Homeless 1989; [oth. writ.] Author Publisher "Enchantments" "A Poetry book" "Missives from the Mussed" a monthly column for Spirit of Change in Spirit Magazine. Managing Photo - Editor "City Limits" of Change Mag. Mag. Features Editorials Poems Published; [pers.] The amount of love is good feeling we have at lifes end is equal to amaint of loves good feelings we put out during life; [a.] Cranston, RI

RAMSEY, MORGAN MICHAELA JEANNINE
[pen.] Micki Morgan-Ramsey; [b.] July 11, 1955, Phillipsburg, KS; [p.] Lyle E. Morgan - Lyril J. Morgan; [m.] Bradford L. Ramsey, August 2, 1982; [ch.] Joshua Tyler Ramsey; [ed.] Stockton High School, Stockton, KS., 3 months in Basic Training in Fort McClellan Alabama US Army-served 3 years in Kansas Army National Guard; [occ.] Housewife - Full Time, Mother to my son; [memb.] United Methodist Church; [hon.] Honorable Discharge from the United States Army in 1975. I am a Veteran and to me, that is an honor.; [oth. writ.] None published - I write poems in my spare time, as gifts to friends especially in a time of the loss of a loved one.; [pers.] 14 years ago, I gave birth to a beautiful baby girl who was stillborn. The poem I entered "Silent Tears," was inspired by that tragic event, the poem comes from my heart and soul. Her name was Megan.; [a.] Hugoton, KS

RANDOLPH, KITTY
[b.] June 4, 1948, Newport, WN; [p.] Clair Rex and Eva Rex; [m.] Charles Randolph, June 25 1966; [ch.] Brandy C., Angela L., Stacy J., Davy R., and Krista N.; [ed.] Newport High School North Idaho Junior College; [occ.] Home maker; [memb.] National Honor Society Sanpoint West Athletic Club Southside PTA; [hon.] Newport High School Valedictorian, 1996 National Honor Society Scholarship, Suroptomist girl of the Month, Scholarship, NIJC Dean's List Pocohontus Lodge Degree of ANONA 1st one, State of Washington.; [oth. writ.] Several personal poems for family and friends; [pers.] I have composed several poems to special family members, some comicah, most are very serious and Emotional to convey my true emotions and feelings.; [a.] Sandpoint, ID

RANGEL, JASON
[b.] August 5, 1977, Goshen, IN; [p.] Joe Rangel, Dolores Rangel; [ed.] Wawasee High School, 12th Grade; [occ.] Song Writing, Acoustic's clean up crew at the Papers Inc.; [memb.] Currently playing electric guitar in a working rock band; [hon.] Placed fourth in talent show at Wawasee. Playing Electric Guitar; [oth. writ.] I have written many poems and songs and wish that the world was like art.; [pers.] I feel the rhythm of the world, and hope that other people can voyage in my world by reading my poems.; [a.] Milford, ID

RATHBURN JR., NORMA
[pen.] Jean; [b.] December 23, 1930, Mpls. MN; [p.] Claude and Irene Hoyt; [m.] Robert L. Rathburn (deceased), December 11, 1948; [ch.] Robert Jr., Richard Rodney, Marilyn, Jeunne, Carolyn, Ruth, Randall; [ed.] Dist 1 Menomonie, it is G.E.D. Stout, Wis. Univ.; [occ.] File Clerk, Green Free Financial; [oth. writ.] Life of Abraham Lincoln there is a light - blue.; [pers.] I enjoy writing poetry that reflect on God's goodness to his creation.; [a.] So. St Paul, MN

RAUBUCH, MELISSA A.
[pen.] Melissa; [b.] February 12, 1982, Aberdeen, WA; [p.] Rick and Liz Raubuch; [ed.] Montesano Jr., Sr. High; [occ.] Student 8th Grade; [memb.] Thea Rho Girls Club, JH Newspaper, JH Choir, Cheer-leader, Basketball, Volly\eyball, ASA Softball Band (3 yrs) A-student, in band plays cornet; [hon.] 3-yrs of Young Authors, awards in Baseball, Basketball, Volleyball, 4-yrs in school talent show. Dancing and

Singing, 9-yrs Soccer; [oth. writ.] 12 poems for the Jr. High Newspaper.; [a.] Montesano, WA

RAYL, RITA K
[pen.] Rita K. Rayl; [b.] March 28, 1957, Painesville, OH; [p.] Gene and Corinne Ziegler; [m.] Terrence Rayl, August 6, 1994; [ch.] Devin Corinne; [ed.] Ledgement High School; [occ.] Executive Secretary, Beachwood, Ohio; [oth. writ.] Personal writings, non-published; [pers.] All of my experience in writing has come from personal observations. I have recorded some of my writings into songs.; [a.] Chardon, OH

RAYMOND, BECKY
[b.] June 19, 1979, Concord, NH; [p.] Lyle Raymond, Nancy Raymond; [ed.] Hopkinton High School; [occ.] Student; [memb.] Hopkinton High School Peer Outreach, New Hampshire teen Institute; [pers.] Whenever you see a rainbow, it means that someone you love is smiling. Rainbows are windows into the heavens, and smiles are windows into the soul, so keep love in your heart and smile on your face and you will bring raibows to the lives of the people around you.; [a.] Hopkinton, NH

RAYMOND, JESSICA
[pen.] LaBittle; [b.] February 22, 1981, San Antonio, TX; [p.] Ramona Raymond; [ed.] Olle Middle School - Now attending; [occ.] Full time student, Junior volunteer at Hermann Hospital; [memb.] Junior National Honar Society; [pers.] I feel the truth should always be told and everyone should believe in the unbelievable.; [a.] Houston, TX

READING, SUSAN ISABELLA
[pen.] Allebasi; [b.] March 31, 1954, Mesa, AZ; [p.] Lawrence and Virginia Sheehan; [m.] Joel Dean Readin, April 23, 1971; [ch.] David (16), Stephanie (3), Margaret (10); [ed.] West Phoenix High School; [occ.] I am currently a home-maker; [oth. writ.] I have hundreds of poems and pondering written in the last your which have not been published as yet.; [pers.] My writings are intended to reveal the soft flow and burning passion of eternity - to equip others with knowledge of the Universal Mind - Much of my writing is infuenced by the Universal Mind with the balance reflecting my family and ethereal friends.; [a.] Arizona City, AZ

REASON, SHERRI MORALES
[pen.] Chiquita Reason; [b.] October 24, 1972, Sacramento, CA; [p.] Sharon Hayes Morales (Deceased), Eulalio G. Morales; [m.] Kevin John Reason, July 15, 1995; [ch.] 1 Stepdaughter - Alyssa; [ed.] Vallejo Adult School and National Education Center - Sacramento; [occ.] Phlebotomist Woodland Healthcare - Blevins Medical Group; [hon.] National and Government Phlebotomy Certification; [pers.] With the love of my husband and family and the love of my writing, I have freed myself to learn to live in a word where hardness and cruelty run rampant, a world vanishing in front of my eyes. I've taken myself far away where with pen in hand I've delved into a world of healing.; [a.] West Sacramento, CA

REDDEN, RACHEL
[b.] July 23, 1981, Smith, AL; [p.] Ricky and Holli Redden; [m.] Not married; [ed.] Freshman, Christian Liberty Academy Satellite School; [occ.] Student of Christian Liberty Academy Satellite School; [oth. writ.] I have been writing poems since I was eleven years old; [pers.] I know that my poems are gift to me from God. My only goal is to glorify Him. "I can do all things through Christ which strengthens me." Philippians 4:13; [a.] Smiths, AL

REED, KENNETH
[pen.] Spent Lhange; [b.] January 2, 1975, Arlington, VA; [p.] David and Susan Reed; [ed.] Hyde School, Bath Maine Gettysburg College; [occ.] Inn Keeper; [memb.] Lambda Chi Alpha Fraternity, Circle K Service Club; [hon.] Selected for Who's Who Anonymous High School Students twice, chosen to run in all N.E. Track Championships as a freshmen; [oth. writ.] Self published book of selected poems, novel, on the way; [pers.] It will never be in the way that I wrote them, but always in the way that you read them.; [a.] Bath, ME

REEVES, RONYA L.
[b.] November 5, 1964, Columbus, OH; [p.] Harry and Ilene; [ch.] Brian; [ed.] Penn Hills Sr. High, Forbes Voch. Tech. School; [pers.] I wrote this poem as a x-mas gift for my dad in 1983. I brought tears to his eyes. On June 7, 1995 my dad passed away and he brought tears to my eyes. He always said if I was to touch the stars it would be on his shoulders that I stood.; [a.] Pittsburgh, PA

REGENSBURG, RUTH P.
[b.] September 8, 1930, Princeton, NJ; [p.] Philip J. Golden and Alice M. Fox; [m.] George E. Regensburg, Ed.D., March 26, 1951; [ch.] 3 Daughters, 8 Grandchildren; [ed.] St. Mary's Cathedral H.S., Rider College, School of Business both in Trenton, N.J.; [occ.] Homemaker, Volunteer; [memb.] St. Bridget's R.C. Church, Glassboro, N.J., Legion of Mary; [hon.] Extraordinary Minister of the Eucharist, St. Bridget's Church; [pers.] "Happy Birthday, Mary" is a first attempt at serious writing and was inspired September 8, 1993 as a special gift to the Blessed Virgin Mary on our shared birthday.; [a.] Glassboro, NJ

REICHWEIN, JOHN A.
[pen.] Dusty McKay; [b.] November 1, 1967, Cameron, TX; [p.] Andrew J. Reichwein, Peggy Jones; [ed.] High School Diploma, some college courses; [hon.] Voted Most Friendlist High School, Senior Year; [oth. writ.] Music and poetry currently in the works for future projects.; [pers.] Most of my music and poetry is about politics and God and in that, I try to show how difficult it is for man to live without God.; [a.] Cameron, TX

REIMLER, KARA LEA
[pen.] Kara Lea Reimler; [b.] December 27, 1977, Junction City, KS; [p.] Bill Reimler and Anita Frye; [ed.] High School as of this point.; [occ.] Student; [memb.] Junction City saddle club, 4-H Future Homemakers of America, Alamogordo Rodeo Club, (EKHA) Eastern Kansas Horsemanship Association, super computer challange Team Club; [hon.] None for writing, however I have recieved some for community service, 4-H, Beauty contest titles, spelling bee winner, Presidential honors award, and other.; [oth. writ.] None, that have been recognized in any way.; [pers.] I do not have much strength in subjects such as math and science, so I greatly enjoy writing. When troubles have me a little down, I can escape in my writing. Believe in yourself.; [a.] Alamogordo, NM

RHEM, JOHN WILLIAM
[b.] August 31, 1978, Georgetown, SC; [p.] John S. Rhem Jr., Sandra M. Rhem; [ed.] Georgetown High School, Junior; [occ.] Student; [memb.] Lakewood Baptist Church 2 School Clubs, Bulldogs Against Drugs and Drinking (badd) Fellowship of Christian Students (FCS); [pers.] I enjoy doing what any teenager living in the 90's does. Spending time with friends and preparing for my future. I enjoy computers and writing poems. If you do what you love. Then you'll love what you do! It's the only way!; [a.] Georgetown, SC

RICE, CYNTHIA SAVAGE
[pen.] Cyndi Rice; [b.] February 13, 1953, Washington, DC; [p.] Patricia Sampson, Bill Jones; [m.] David S. Rice, September 4, 1994; [ch.] Hank Savage; [ed.] Gaithersburg High School, Various College courses; [occ.] Sales Manager, Family Counselor; [memb.] Real Estate License, North Florida Association of Blind, Deaf and Multi-Handicapped; [hon.] Dale Carnegie - Humanity Award; [pers.] We each have a responsibility to God to be all that we were created to be in order to enrich the lives of others and bring glory to Him, it's my constant challenge and hope to add value to each person I meet.; [a.] New Port Richey, FL

RICE III, KEVINDEAN D. R.
[b.] January 27, 1961, Long Beach, CA; [p.] Dann Richard, Frances Clair; [hon.] Humor - Too many to list here, then again, not enough, or maybe about, none...; [oth. writ.] Many poems/songs, currently writing a 12 book, short stories, series of children's stories, 2 1/3 stories complete looking for publisher to review them.; [pers.] Age, is nothing but a number, society places upon you, it has nothing to do with your intellect, nor your experiences!; [a.] Long Beach, CA

RICHARDS, MILDRED
[b.] September 29, 1916, Portsmouth, NH; [p.] Hubert Paddock, Mildred Paddock; [m.] Hugh Richards, February 11, 1944; [ch.] David, Thomas, John, Margaret, Beth, Bob; [ed.] American University, B.A. 1938; [occ.] Retired Homemaker; [memb.] Alpha Phi, First Unitarian/Universalist Society of Madison, Dickens Fellowship, Democratic Party; [oth. writ.] Two books of poems: "Twigs" (1992) and "Second Thoughts" (1995) Prose: "For Grandchildren: Stories, Letters, etc." (1994); [pers.] Keep hoping; [a.] Madison, WI

RICHARDSON, ADAM M.
[b.] February 12, 1968, Terre Haute, IN; [p.] Catherine and Richard Walschinski; [ed.] Edgewater High, Orlando, FL; [occ.] Computer Consultant; [memb.] Observer's Club; [oth. writ.] Memories of an Incarnation, the Diaries of Death, Sidewalk Rhapsody, The lyrics of various local bands; [pers.] "To stay in the light we must watch the encroaching darkness. I am merely an observer"; [a.] Altamonte Springs, FL

RICHARDSON, BECKY JOHNSON
[b.] August 11, 1940, Newnan, GA; [p.] Elder Charles I. Johnson (deceased) and Varon Broadwell Johnson; [m.] Divorced; [ch.] Ivy Louise Head, Daughter, born June 14, 1960; [ed.] 1. Sardis High School, Boaz, Alabama, 2. AA Degree from Snead State Junior College, Boaz, Alabama, University of

Alabama, Campus, George Mason University, Fairfax, Virginia, many continuing education courses (CE Credits); [occ.] I retired from IBM (for medical reasons) after 23 years in the publication profession. I just started a small home-based greeting card business, which provides creative opportunities, both artistic and literary, to keep me challenged. I also use my computer to embellish artwork and to visit on the "net."; [memb.] Toastmaster, International (to learn public speaking) Multiple Sclerosis organizations, because I have MS The Association for Retarded Citizens because my daughter is learning disabled. Sigma Tau Delta Sorority (while in college) Drama Club (college); [hon.] National Honor Society (high school) Won High School National Spelling Bee (age 13) and Placed second in my county spelling contest Dean's List several times (college) Several service awards from IBM Won several speaking awards in Toastmasters.; [oth. writ.] Unpublished, until this anthology (ie., except for work at IBM). My greeting card business uses many of my original verses and philosophical thoughts (plus hand-painted original art designs). I maintain an extensive correspondence with work associates, friends, and family.; [pers.] When I need closure to a personal tragedy or trauma, I write poetry that expresses the many emotions I experienced surviving the situation. My favorite one liner is: "Mistakes are wisdom happening"! My daughter inspired it. She needed a positive viewpoint because she was trying but failing at a particular task.; [a.] Marietta, GA

RICHOU, PATSY D.
[b.] March 6, 1941, Sioux City, IA; [p.] Elmer and Darlene Gifford; [m.] John F. Richou, March 12, 1960; [ch.] Kari Sue and Kelly Ann; [ed.] Central High School graduate; [occ.] City Intaker Worker for City of Sioux City; [oth. writ.] Several unpublished poems; [pers.] Patsy passed away June 1, 1995 after a 7 month illness with brain and lung cancer. Her husband John and daughters Kari and Kelly submitted her poem to the National Library of poetry for possible publication in memory of their loving wife and mother.; [a.] Sioux City, IA

RICKMAN, PAUL

RIGGS, STEPHEN
[b.] December 29, 1959, Louisville, KY; [p.] Goerge Riggs and Nancye Inman; [ed.] Atherton High University of Louisville BA in Spanish and Art Photography; [occ.] Spanish/Art teacher Kealing Jr., High Austin TX; [hon.] Dean's Scholar - 4 semesters at University of Louisville. Graduated Cum Laude with BA in Art and Spanish; [oth. writ.] El Salvador - The Savior A book yet to be published which will include my poem among others, mixed with narrative writing; [pers.] Mental and Physical challenges can make life difficult yet can make life difficult yet cann offer opportunities at the sametime. My writing has spring from these chalenges, my greatest writing infuence is Gunter Grass Author of "The Tindrum"; [a.] Austin, TX

RILEY, CHRISTENE WRIGHT
[pen.] Christene Riley; [b.] March 2, 1939, Wilmar, AK; [p.] Cornelious and Charlie, M. Wright; [m.] James D. Riley, May 5, 1956; [ch.] Jimmy, Larry, Donald, Herrie, Tina, Dennis, Christopher, Kevin, and Corey; [ed.] High School, Tech. Class in

Computer; [occ.] Going to School; [memb.] Mt. Tabor M.B. Church , Mt. Senior Choir, Advisory Committee President of P.A.B.; [hon.] Community Service Advance Columnist; [oth. writ.] Columnist for Advance Monticellonian. (Poem) "I Want Turn Back." The Biography of Corcy (song) "You Brought Me From, A Mighty Long Way; [pers.] I've always dreamed of writing and playing the piano that's have been my ambition. I do a little of both; [a.] Wilmar, AR

RILEY, JESSICA
[b.] March 9, 1976, Saratoga Spring; [p.] Stephen and Shelley Riley; [ed.] Saratoga Spring High School, Middlebury College (98); [occ.] Student; [memb.] Northern New York Speedskating Association, Community friends; [hon.] National Honor Society, who's who among High School Students, 1993 Semifinalist Sports Girl of the Year (Teen Magazine), Art award, 12th place finish at '92 and '94 Olympic trials for Speedskating, featured speedskater in Promotional Clairol Commercial during 92 Olympics. Deans List (Middlebury College-freshman year); [pers.] I feel I can only grasp onto life when it is furthest from me because when it's presents, my mind is else where. The main goal of my life is to have fun.; [a.] Saratoga Springs, NY

RILEY, KARENSA
[b.] August 24, 1979, Modesta, CA; [p.] Kolene Deanmore and James Riley; [m.] Nathaniel (Boyfriend); [ed.] I'm a Jr., in High School.; [occ.] Housecleaner, babysitter; [memb.] Magazines, and Music Companies Leukima Association; [hon.] I never really got any honors or awards. But to me to be one of the lucky one's to make it through Leukima, that's for me; [oth. writ.] All my friends are dying devils in disguise; [pers.] If your a person with cancer, you only lose the fight when you give up. But if you keep your faith in God you can make it through any obstacle; [a.] Delhi, CA

RILEY, NANCY M.
[b.] June 30, 1960, Lake Forest, IL; [p.] Nancy B. Riley, (The Late) Fredrick J. Riley; [m.] John S. Gross, November 4, 1988; [ch.] Adam and Natalie; [ed.] BA Regis University, Denver, CO; [occ.] Mom; [memb.] PADs, Dunham Woods Equestrian Center, St. John Nuemann Parish; [hon.] Certificate of Merit for National Achievement in Creative Writing, Scholastic Magazines, Young Idea, Best of Book, Reflections Magazines First Place Awards, Regis University graduated with Honors for my contribu- tions of poetry and short stories; [oth. writ.] Several poems have been published in various publications over the years in addition to the poetry which was awarded honors.; [pers.] The most beautiful poetry seems to flow from the most painful of journeys.; [a.] St. Charles, IL

RINKLE, DANA
[b.] June 5, 1982, Morristown, NJ; [p.] Mike and Deb Rinkle; [ed.] Eastlake School (Grammar School located in Parsippany, NJ) Brooklawn Middle School (also located in Parsippany NJ); [hon.] To be included in the Rainbows End; [pers.] I want to have every person who reads my poem to learn some- thing. Also be inspired, and know my poems come from the heart.; [a.] Parsippany, NJ

RITCHIE, MCKENZIE LYNN
[b.] November 22, 1977, Jackson, MS; [p.] Stephen and Mary Ritchie; [ed.] Lassiter High School - Senior; [occ.] Student - Senior and Lassiter High School; [memb.] Future Business Leader's of America, Key Club, Who's Who in American High School Students, Honor Roll, Lassiter Varsity Cheer Leading, Allegro Vivace Club, Nat'l Fraternity of Student Musicians, Pride; [hon.] 2 years in Who's Who in American High School Students, Recogni- tion for Academic Excellence by the Cobb County Board of Education, Superior Rating in Piano under the Georgia Federation of Music Clubs, Runner-up in Georgia Literary Guild; [pers.] My inspiration comes from everyday life. I try to express, in my writing, the deep pain, sorrow, joy or love that I or another actually feel in their personal life.; [a.] Roswell, GA

RIVERA, CIPRIANO
[pen.] Cip; [b.] January 31, 1984, Fullerton, CA; [p.] Victorino Rivera, Maria Rivera; [ed.] St. Philip Benizi; [occ.] Student; [hon.] Honor Roll; [a.] Fullerton, CA

RIVERA, FLORENCIO E.
[b.] August 3, 1981, Ft. Campbell, KY; [p.] Elias and Solia Rivera; [ed.] Student - J.T. Hutchinson; [memb.] Lubbock Select Soccer Association - Motor 7 Varsity Tennis; [hon.] Letter I in Tennis L.S.A; [pers.] Never give up!; [a.] Lubbock, TX

RIVERA, JOSE ANTONIO
[b.] April 9, 1971, Brooklyn, NY; [p.] Lucrecia Barreda; [m.] Rhea Lorrain Rivera; [ch.] Jose Antonio Rivera II; [ed.] Wilbur L. Cross, Bridgeport, CT., Fairfield Prep., Fairfield, CT., Norwalk Community Technical College, CT., Rochester Institute of Technology, NY; [occ.] Microelectonic Engineering, Development Verification Testing; [memb.] Lambda Alpha Upsilon Fraternity Inc., Society for Hispanic Professional Engineers, Special Olympics Sponsor; [hon.] Tau Alpha P. National Honor Society, SHEP Foundation Scholarship, Dean's List; [oth. writ.] Many poems and a couple of short stories.; [pers.] With this, my first Published Piece, I have achieved what none hope to dream of in the "Bridge-Port-of-Ricans". For J.J. and Michael, one forever in my heart, the other forever on my mind. Peace, to all who love even if they do not understand.; [a.] Rochester, NY

ROBERTS, MARJORIE
[b.] October 17, 1944, Pine Bluff, AR; [p.] Mildred and Lloyd Crawford; [m.] Troy Lee Roberts, March 12, 1995; [ch.] Dasa Miller and Rebecca Roberts; [ed.] High School, some Technical College (shorthand); [occ.] Retired Federal Employee, K-1st Teacher at Christian School; [memb.] International Society of Poetry, Maranatha Baptist Church; [hon.] Several poems published by national Library of Poetry, two poems selected to be read on tapes - the sound of poetry.; [oth. writ.] The Hidden Picture, Christ is everything to me, I want to be a witness, Sunday morning service.; [pers.] I only write what God lays on my heart to write. All my poetry is inspirational.; [a.] White Hall, AR

ROBERTSON, KATHERINE F.
[b.] March 27, 1947, Springfield, MA; [p.] Alberta Langley and Thomas Robertson; [ed.] BA Wells

College, Aurora, NY MSW Simmons College School of Social Work, Boston, MA; [occ.] Clinical Social Worker, Newlife Counseline Center, Waltham MA; [a.] Manchester by The Sea, MA

ROBINSON, BLONDELL CHISOLM
[pen.] B.C. Robinson; [b.] July 25, 1955, Charleston, SC; [p.] Eartha Lee Chisolm, Henry Chisolm; [m.] Ronnie D. Robinson Sr.; [ch.] James, Ronnie Jr., Shirkerah; [ed.] Charles A. Brown High School, Bronx Community College, Winston-Salem State University; [occ.] Self-Employed (Merchandiser); [memb.] National Federation of the Blind Disabled American Veterans, Women's Army Corps Veteran; [hon.] Dean's List, Sigma Tau Delta (Honor Society), Army Commendation Medal, Army Achievement Medal, Good Conduct Medal; [pers.] I have been blessed with the ability to understand human nature. I use my blessings everyday to assist physically, mentally, and elderly people adjust to the ever changing world in which they are surviving.; [a.] Columbia, SC

ROBINSON, CATHERINE DENISE
[pen.] Daven Boon; [b.] April 30, 1961, Orange, TX; [p.] Thomas D. Felder, Bobbie Lee Felder; [m.] Lee A. Robinson, October 12, 1991; [ed.] Concord High, Brandywine Univer; [occ.] Food Service Director; [pers.] I believe feel we all share the same loving concerns for our children. I also believe in instilling positive self esteem and loving thoughts through prayer by searching and Developing not only our minds and bodies but also our spiritual being.; [a.] Kingston, NY

ROBINSON, CHRISTI
[b.] December 6, 1981, Montgomery, AL; [p.] Randell Robinson, Sylvia Robinson; [ed.] Currently on eight-grade student at Greenville Middle School; [memb.] National Junior Honor Society Greenville Middle School Symphonic Band, Greenville Middle School Quiz Bowl Team; [hon.] Duke University Talent Identification Program; [pers.] I believe you can do anything if you truly believe in yourself.; [a.] Greenville, AL

ROBINSON, CLARICE JAMES
[b.] June 20, 1940, Tampa, FL; [p.] Bill and Amanda James; [m.] Dr. Ira C. Robinson, August 11, 1962; [ch.] Ira II, Patricia, Krishwin, Charm; [ed.] B.S. Degree Home Economics, Middleton High - Salutatorian Booker Jr. High; [occ.] Seamstress; [memb.] St. Stephen Catholic Church, Teacher Bible Study; [hon.] Outstanding Parish Member - Blessed Trinity 1992; [oth. writ.] Several poems published in Newspaper, Church Bulletin, Women's Guild; [pers.] God has always walked with me. I write about Him to tell others of his goodness and power. Truly, He is real and able to help all. He has helped me in every possible way. I'm not grateful today.; [a.] Brandon, FL

ROBINSON, JOHN CHRISTOPHER
[pen.] Chris Robinson; [b.] April 20, 1917, Liver Pool, OK; [p.] Joseph H. and Mary Robinson; [m.] Margaret/Nee McClellan, January 2, 1952; [ed.] Parochial Schools/Liver Pool, England, Leicester Tech - UK Raf/Military (Air Force) and British Inst. of Technology; [occ.] Retired 1989, London UK - from Business; [memb.] Assoc/B.I.T London American Society of Cool Engineer - Senior Minister

American Society of MFG Engineers; [hon.] B.I.T London/UK. Selected Assoc. I. Mech. Eng. WW II Air force (RAF) for Service in Middle East, North Africa - and France 1940/1945; [oth. writ.] Machine Tool Sales Catalogs when Copy Writer for US/ Machine Tool "Manufacturer/Incl. Manuals Etc.; [pers.] Established Own Sales Representatives for Machine Tools/Import from UK/Spain and Germany also consultant to British Consulate; [a.] Chicago, IL

ROBINSON, LISHA RACHELLE
[b.] August 10, 1981, Panama, Panama; [p.] Linda and Joseph Robinson; [ed.] Oak Grove Junior High School and Adams Junior High School; [occ.] Going to School; [memb.] PTA; [hon.] Student of the Year in Science, Meric Achievement Award in Math; [pers.] I love writing romantic poems it just gives me an intense feeling that when reading a romance poem you fell there is still romance in the air.; [a.] Tampa, FL

ROBINSON, SHARON
[b.] September 9, 1951, Asheville, NC; [p.] Arnold Robinson, Evelyn Robinson; [m.] Jeffrey Robinson, May 6, 1979; [ch.] Mischelle Miller, Tracie Reynolds, Michael Nix; [ed.] North Buncombe High School, Asheville Buncombe Tech; [occ.] Office Asst., Shell Oil Co., Ft. Lauderdale, FL; [memb.] American Society of Notaries Mystic Stamp Co., My hobby is Stamp Collecting along with writing poetry; [hon.] Special Recognition for Outstanding Performance - Shell Oil Co. Ft. Lauderdale, FL. 1994, Honorable Mention, Photography Contest Asheville, N.C. (Highland Hospital) 1988; [oth. writ.] Unpublished, this is my very first attempt at getting something published, however this poem and one other was read over a local radio station.; [pers.] I am inspired by personal experiences and current events. I try to reflect my innermost feelings and emotions, and hope to touch others and make them see there is good in all people.; [a.] Ft. Lauderdale, FL

ROBINSON, STEVEN CAREY
[b.] July 30, 1964, Kailua, HI; [p.] Wallace S. Robinson, Diane E. Robinson; [m.] Hana Soupova - Robinson, September 9, 1989; [ch.] Wendy Bianca; [ed.] Okanogan H.S., WA, V.S.A.F. Security Police Academy, Washington State Juvenile Security Worker Academy. Currently Planning to attend Vermont College of Norwich University for A B.A. in writing; [occ.] Assistant Director St. Joseph's group Home; [hon.] Editor's choice Award from National Library of Poetry; [oth. writ.] "Take it if I could" in the garden of life, and "A new day is Dawning" in best poems of 1996. Currently writing a children's story called "Who said that?"; [pers.] Life has dealt me a mediocre hand. But, it's up to me to play it like 4 aces, without cheating. If I can achieve this task throughout my life, then I can die a satisfied man.; [a.] Burlington, VT

ROCKER II, JOHN ALBERT
[pen.] Rocky; [b.] June 11, 1957, Charleston, WV; [p.] John and Ann Rocker; [m.] Divorced; [ch.] Maggie Elizabeth Rocker (age 11); [ed.] West virginia Tech West Virginia State College (Business); [occ.] Security Charleston Marriott Hotel; [memb.] Chesapeake Methodist Church, Hospitality Committee (Marriot); [hon.] Tiefel Award (Marriott), Outstanding Hospitality Skills, AAA State

Champion (Football 1974); [pers.] In a world of individuals, we are all interdependent.; [a.] Chesapeake, WV

RODRIGUEZ, JASON
[b.] July 28, 1980, Santa Ana, CA; [p.] Eduardo & Glorya Rodriguez; [ed.] Willow Elementary school, Royal Oak Intermediate, and Charter Oak High School; [occ.] Student; [hon.] 1st Place Essay Award in 4th Grade, 1st Place Essay in 6th Grade, Honor Roll Award in 7th Grade, Citizenship Award in 7th Grade, and Honor Roll Award in 9th Grade.; [oth. writ.] "We Shall Overcome" (short story for 8th Grade U.S. History class), several short stories published in "The Kaleidoscope" Dad's work's [KTI] newspaper), and several poems for the 9th Grade Honors English Class.; [pers.] My ultimate goal through my writing is to procure man's evident struggle in the process of life itself. I have been greatly influenced by minority literature, and its authors.; [a.] Gelndora, CA

ROGERS, KEVIN J.
[b.] January 13, 1962, Brooklyn, NY; [p.] Joseph and Marion Rogers; [ed.] Shenendehowa High School, Siena College, Empire State College; [hon.] Top 1% in S.A.T's and Deans List; [pers.] Kevin is a lyric poet living in upstate New York and presently pursuing a career in law.; [a.] Ballston SPA, NY

ROGERS, NEVA
[pen.] C.J. Rogers; [b.] March 13, 1928, Girard, AL; [p.] Oscar and Vera Jones; [m.] Ralph N. Rogers, June 19, 1950; [ch.] Two, Five Grandchildren; [ed.] High School a few business courses; [occ.] Home Maker; [memb.] Southwest Artist League, Clayton Art Alliance, Church of Christ - National Library of Poetry International Society of Poets Sparrowgrass Poetry Forum; [hon.] Many ribbons in art shows including Best In Show, First Place in oils and water colors given certificate of member of good standing by ISP; [oth. writ.] Children's Stories and short stories as yet unpublished not working at it. Several other poems. Published and unpublished.; [pers.] We can be what we will let ourselves be. We must search the soul for good and remove the dross and then what is right for us and what is good in us can flourish. Love thy God and neighbors; [a.] Fayetteville, GA

ROHM SR., GEORGE A.
[b.] February 4, 1933, Newark, NJ; [p.] Helen and Johnny Rohm; [m.] Donna Dulworth Rohm, July 24, 1952; [ch.] George Jr., Teresa and David Rohm; [ed.] Theodore High School plus 2 yrs college through G.E.D. at University of AL.; [occ.] Aircraft Worker, Teledyne Cont. Mtrs. Mobile, AL; [memb.] Nashville Song Writer Association International, Alabama Songwriters Guild; [oth. writ.] Several songs and poems; [pers.] This work is in memory of all the children killed by the bullet from a street gangs gun. I feel moved and compelled to mention especially, little Stephanie Kurhan, age 3, of L.A., CA. killed September 1995. Another victim of the thunder in the night.; [a .] Mobile, AL

ROOT, EDITH MARIE
[pen.] Edie Root; [b.] March 7, 1961, Norway, ME; [p.] Joseph A. Proctor III, Maria Ezzio Proctor; [m.] Robert L. Root, May 8, 1992; [ch.] Carrie Lee, Robert Lee, II; [ed.] St. John's High School

Darlington, SC; [occ.] Exec. Ass't. to the Sr. Vice President, BCBS of SC; [memb.] South Florence Baptist Church, Florence, SC; [oth. writ.] Numerous poems written for family and friends; [pers.] I hope to be an encourage to anyone who is down-hearted. I try to show my love for Christ and family, so that others might come to know Him.; [a.] Florence, SC

ROOT, JILL COLLEEN
[pen.] Jill Colleen Root; [b.] November 17, 1977, Great Falls, MT; [p.] Mike and Joy Root; [ed.] Custer Country District High School and Anaconda High School Senior in High School. I plan on going into Elementary Education or Music in either Missoula or Bozeman.; [occ.] Student, I work at McDonald's and have for 3 years.; [memb.] I am a member of F.C.A., All State Choir, and Varsity Cheerleading.; [hon.] For the past 2 years, I have been a member of the Montana All State Choir, I was selected as a squad leader of my dance team for 3 years, honor roll Varsity Cheerleading.; [oth. writ.] I have written several other poems, but nothing has been published.; [pers.] Both of my parents are blind, and they are great role models for me. If they can do it, anyone can.; [a.] Anaconda, MT

ROSADO, ELAINE
[b.] November 2, 1980, Chicago, IL; [p.] Sonia Arguelles; [ed.] Nixon Elementary School, Kelvyn Park High School; [occ.] Student; [hon.] Fourteen writing awards, and a JROTC Award for Personal Appearance; [pers.] I dedicate this poem to my family and my JROTC cadets, and also my JROTC Instructor Sgt. Earl Washington who gave me the inspiration to write this poem.; [a.] Chicago, IL

ROSETT, NANCY CARMEN
[pen.] Nancy Rosett; [b.] March 6, 1945, Ironton, MO; [p.] Robert Pettus, Dorris Pettus; [m.] Larry Rosett (Divorced), June 1965; [ch.] Eric Rosett, Renee Rosett; [ed.] Farmington Elementary Farmington, Mo. Sullivan High School Sullivan Mo; [occ.] Volunteer work. (Disabled) Sylvan House.; [oth. writ.] Many of my writings have been destroyed. I write to release my thoughts and feelings. My knowledge of poets is rare.; [pers.] Much of my life has been spent in institutions. I write about my past and people who have passed through the same Turbulence. I would like to read other poets work.; [a.] Saint Louis, MO

ROSS, BARBARA
[b.] April 17, 1932, AR; [ch.] 3; [ed.] Literature and the Arts, Transpersonal Studies, Comparative Religion; [occ.] The Arts; [memb.] Academy of American Poets, Institute and Noetic Sciences; [hon.] Awards in Poetry and Graphic Arts, Academic Honors; [oth. writ.] Essay, Travel Articles; [a.] La Mesa, CA

ROSSMAN, MARY K.
[b.] November 3, 1948, Hillsdale, MI; [p.] Dalton Rossman, Shirley Rossman; [ch.] Abraham Tad; [ed.] Quincy High, Central Technical Institute, Kansas City, MO., Jackson Community College, Jackson, MI; [occ.] Labor, Swift - Eckrich Quincy, Mich; [oth. writ.] Editor, Company Newsletter Free Lance Writer; [pers.] Explore every avenue of life your heart desires.; [a.] Quincy, MI

ROTCHFORD, CATHERINE
[b.] November 11, 1976, Manhasset, NY; [p.] Gil and Carroll Rotchford; [ed.] The Taft School - High

School, Boston College - College; [occ.] Student/ Lifeguard; [hon.] Independent Study Project at Taft; [oth. writ.] Besides school papers, I have not been published; [pers.] Like a child. Like a poem. I wish to live. Speak. Throwing in the trash all those useless words and letters and hours. That don't give. To the hearts within. Ours.; [a.] Oyster Bay, NY

ROTH, ALVIN
[b.] November 27, 1936, NY; [p.] Murray and Eva Roth; [ed.] City College of N.Y. AAS Degree; [occ.] Salesman; [memb.] Country Road Players, (Drama Group), Westbury Players, (Drama Group); [hon.] Former Artistic Director, East Meadow School District; [oth. writ.] Short Plays; [pers.] Whenever I see something beautiful. I try to capture it, by putting it on paper. Maybe someone else will see it, the way I do; [a.] Long Beach, NY

ROTOLO, MARY ELLEN
[b.] December 20, 1960, Hialeah, FL; [ed.] St. Petersburg Junior College Graduate 1991 — Cum Laude with Associate in Science Degree; [occ.] Physical Therapist Assistant; [memb.] American Physical Therapy Assoc. (APTA). Good Samaritan Church. Member of C.H.A.D.D. (Children and Adults with Attention Deficit Disorders).; [oth. writ.] Several poems published in local newspaper and church newsletter, also in 2 previous anthologies; [pers.] I am also a volunteer reading tutor for the Pinellas Country School District.; [a.] Largo, FL

RUCKER, LINDA DIANNE
[pen.] Di Di; [b.] November 29, 1953, Holly Springs, MS; [p.] Purcell and Willie E. Miller; [m.] Charls Rucker, December 25, 1969; [ch.] Charls Rucker, Jessica Campbell; [ed.] High School G.E.D. North West Miss. College; [occ.] DECED - 12-12-1994; [memb.] Reids Gift M.B. Church; [hon.] Every who knew her speaks good of her she always wore a smile she wrote wonderful poems.; [oth. writ.] Poems in local newspaper; [pers.] She raised three children and done all kind of work to help others. She never hurt any if she could not help you she sure did not hurt you.; [a.] Potts Camp, MI

RUEGER, TAMMY
[b.] March 25, 1978, Ashland, WI; [p.] Sandy Kaster, Tim Rueger; [ed.] Sheboygan Lutheran High School; [memb.] Band, Pep Club, Varsity Volleyball, Basketball, and Fastpitch teams, chancel drama, drama; [hon.] 2nd team all conference - fastpitch, Most Improved - Basketball, P.E. award, Band, Drama, and varsity letters in Volleyball, Basketball and Fastpitch; [pers.] The courageous are not the ones who have no fears, but the ones who go forward in spite of them.; [a.] Sheboygan, WI

RUSIECKI, RICHARD M.
[b.] February 7, 1961, Belleville, NJ; [p.] Vincent A. Rusiecke, Loretta Rusiecki; [ed.] Our Lady Of The Valley H.S., Montclair State College; [oth. writ.] Articles published in company Newsletters, several songs requested for publication and performed by local bands.; [a.] Maplewood, NJ

RUSSELL, FRANCES
[pen.] Fran Russell; [b.] November 15, 1942, Bornwell, SC; [p.] James and Bessie Russell; [ch.] Jacqueline, Darryl and Bruce; [ed.] High School Grad, Some College Credits; [occ.] Human Service

Assoc. II; [memb.] Weeping Mary Baptist Church, Parent Aide Association; [pers.] I am raising five grandchildren, then and my job with the elderly of different backgrounds makes my life a mixture of two worlds. It's a book in it's self.; [a.] Hebron, MD

RUSSO, KAREN L.
[b.] February 6, Peekskill, NY; [p.] Lydia R. Pletz, Anthony S. Mazzuca; [ch.] Scott J. Russo; [ed.] Haldane Central, Coldspring, NY High School, currently obtaining Associates Degree - Business Dutchess Community College; [occ.] Training Coordinator - Quality Assurance; [memb.] American Society of Quality Control, American Society for Training and Development, Local Church; [hon.] Dean's List; [a.] Fishkill, NY

RUSSO, MARGARET
[pen.] Margaret Russo; [b.] January 13, 1984, Indianapolis; [p.] Steven and Barbara Russo; [ed.] St. Luke Catholic School and Church (Grade School); [occ.] Student, Sixth Grade; [memb.] Friends of the Ocean (Dolphin Protection), St. Luke Parish, Junior Civic Theatre and CYO Sports League; [hon.] Honor Roll, Service Award, Effort Award, Good Attendance Award, and Citizenship Award; [oth. writ.] None (I have written many poems, and sent them in, but I am unsure if they have been published!); [pers.] If you love something, let it go free. If it is yours, it will come back to you. If it never comes back, it wasn't yours to begin with.

RUSTHOVEN, ANISSA M.
[b.] August 15, 1972, Melrose Park, IL; [ed.] V. J. Andrews High School, Governors State University, Robert Morris College; [occ.] Loan Closing manager, Financial Federal TSB; [pers.] I write what I feel. It comes from the heart. I want my feelings to come alive to my reader.; [a.] Orland Park, IL

RYBA, ANTHONY F.
[pen.] Miles Kramer; [b.] November 12, 1975, Cleveland; [p.] Dale Ryba, Michele Ryba; [ed.] Graduate, Revere High School Freshman - University of Akron; [occ.] Busboy, Papa Joe's; [memb.] Boy Scouts of America, Ohio Rifle Pistol Association, College Republicans; [hon.] Eagle Scout; [oth. writ.] Death of the Vigilante - Short (published in Graphic Noise), The Night's Voice - novel (unpublished at the time of this writing), Waterlight (a self-published comic series); [pers.] To preserve one's principles, is to preserve one's humanity.; [a.] Akron, OH

RYMER, BILL
[pen.] Tiffany; [b.] December 12, 1953; [p.] William and Pauline; [m.] Divorced (6-92), June 1974; [ed.] High School, Electronics School (2), Some College; [occ.] Lab Tech; [memb.] Church; [hon.] National Honor Society in High School, (2) Community Service Awards (From Union Carbide); [oth. writ.] Serval poems Daily Journal for the last 3 years; [pers.] I have a strong religious background that began at age 12 and continues today at age 41. I have worked hard in the church to share the love of Christ to many people. I am also an active supporter for equal rights for the Transgender community, which includes cross-dresses. I have been a cross-dresser all of my life. The rejection that I have receive from this way of life has always put me more in touch with my feelings and God's love for me, and

all of mankind. God has given me a tender spirit to see the hurt that others induces on those who are different, not just Transgender people. Let's be more Christlike in our love toward one another.; [a.] Dunbar, WV

SALAZAR, OMAR E.
[pen.] Mario Swing; [b.] May 20, 1950, Chile; [p.] Ramon Salazar, Idolia Swing; [m.] Bessie, June 17, 1963; [ch.] Sebastian, Pablo, Omar and Gabriela; [ed.] National Institute of Club Catholic University (BS social work) Sause City College and San Jose state (electronics); [occ.] Electronic Technician, Hewlett Packard co, in Roseville, CA; [memb.] Toast masters International; [oth. writ.] "Letters to my children."; [pers.] I admire Pablo Nerude and Gabriela Mistral, two Nobel Laurente poets from my country (child), as well as Manuel Rojas and Isabel Alleude, two great novelists.; [a.] San Jose, CA

SALES, LEONIDES S.
[pen.] Leo; [b.] April 22, 1936, Bacarra Ilocos Norte, Philippines; [p.] Gregorio Albano Sales, Maria S. Sales; [m.] Divorced, March 3, 1955; [ch.] Victor Sales, Glenda Sales, Anthony Sales, Ferdinand Sales, Geraldine Shemoe, Christopher Sales, Lilibeth Sales, Ronald - Reagan Sales; [ed.] High School - Kabankalan Academy. Negros Occidental Philippines Northwestern College, Laoag City, Philippines Bachelor of Science in Commerce, University of the East, Manila, Philippines, Aircraft Ornament repair course, U.S. Army Ordinance Center and School, Aberdeen Proving Ground Maryland 21105 U.S.A., Special Intelligence Operations Course, Philippines; [occ.] Philippines Air Force Armed Forces of the Philippines, Lieutenant Retired 23 years of service. Former Security Aide of President Ferdinand Edralin Marcos of the Philippines; [memb.] American Association of retired persons, May 1986, Filipino American Community of Los Angeles Inc. 1989, 1990, United Bacarreneous of Hawaii Inc. 1992, BNCHS club of Hawaii 1992, Kiss AM fun Club Hawaii 1992, Filipino Californians Senior Citizens Society Inc. 1993, International Circle Inc. 1993 to date; [hon.] The Philippine Republic President trial Unit Citation Badge, Commendation, Official Appreciation, Anti-Dissidence Campaign Ribbon; [oth. writ.] Several articles published "The Youth Grinder" Baccarra Provincial High School Newspaper.; [pers.] To try it to succeed. Be brave in the cause of right, be coward in the cause of wrong. In order to be a leader you must learn to follow. Beyond the clouds the sun still. Beyond the clouds the sun still shining. Smile and the world is your.; [a.] San Francisco, CA

SAMPLES, DARLENE
[b.] February 9, 1973, Toledo, OH; [p.] Delbert and Donna Samples; [ed.] State Line Christian School (Elementary and High), Hyles Anderson College 2 years; [occ.] Waitress; [hon.] High School - Award for Highest Math Scores in my Class Jr. and Sr. Years; [oth. writ.] I hope to have other poems published in the future.; [pers.] Although I am still young, I have seen and experienced many things. By writing, I hope I can help someone who is having a hard time. Life's too short to be too serious!; [a.] Toledo, OH

SAMUEL, JEN
[pen.] J. D. S.; [b.] November 6, 1980, Nashua, NH; [p.] Edward and Sara; [ed.] Currently a freshman in

Avongrove High School, West Grove, PA; [occ.] Teaches piano, babysits, Acting; [memb.] FBLA, High School newspaper, French Lop Club, you through, poetry club, acting club, main line Model; [hon.] 4 High Honor Rolls Award from 8th grade, 4 High Honor Roll Awards from 7th High Honor Awards from 17th, 3 Choir Awards, Best Female Math Student in 8th grade. 400 Reading Club Award for Reading most Books in Grade Mornings and Juice Attendant, Poetry Slam Flinlist, 5 Piano Awards, Student Council Tour Guide, 3 Top 3 Awards for Speed Walking 1st Place Award for Mar Thou, Best Actress Award (2) 3 National Fitness Awards; [oth. writ.] 3 full poetry pockets, several short stories, one poem book, 4 novel finished, school newspaper, poem displayed at loyal book store.; [pers.] I believe in making things happen for yourself, not waiting for them happen. To you I love poetry as well as all writings. Above all else, I believe the truth shall set one free.; [a.] New London, PA

SAMUELSON, SARAH L.
[b.] May 11, 1977, Charleston, SC; [p.] Dr. Dean Samuelson, Gretchen Samuelson; [ed.] Ubangi Academy, Karawa, Zaire; [occ.] Full-time student at Wheaton College; [pers.] Any talent I possess, any inspiration I experience, in fact, my entire being and creative ability is a gift directly from my Lord and savior, Jesus Christ. He is my hope, my joy, and my reason to live. My only goal in life is to love him more each day. He is always with me, and without him I could do nothing.; [a.] Wheaton, IL

SANGUINETI, VITTORIO
[b.] January 25, 1914, Sumy, Russia; [p.] Felice Sanguineti, Maria Vidovich; [m.] Gilda de Sanctis, July 26, 1947; [ch.] Claudia Vittoria, Carla Rumana; [ed.] Ph.D. in Political Science, Majoring in Economics - University of rome, Italy; [occ.] Retired Italian Foreign Service (Trade) formerly Italian Trade Commissioner in Los Angeles; [memb.] International Associate, Stanford Research Institute (SRI); [hon.] 1. Prize of academic Francois (Paris) for poem "Symphonies Behaviours" in French, published in anthology "Poems Francois de poster strangers," 2. Guest Professor of industrial economics at U.C.L.A. Graduate School of Management (3 semesters), 3. Man of the Year for Foreign Trade of the Los Angeles Chamber of Commerce (1973), 4. Knight Commander in the Order to the Merit of the Republic of Italy; [oth. writ.] Contributor to the Italian Quarterly Review "Foreign Affairs" ("Affari Ester"), 1. NATO and Islam, 2. The dilemma of Islam, 3. Turkey and the European Union, 4. The Islamic Ex-Soviet Republic of Central Asia; [pers.] "If you make of revenge and greed the drug-addiction of your life it will destroy it forever."; [a.] Los Angeles, CA

SARVAY, CRYSTAL
[b.] July 12, 1963, Richmond, VA; [p.] Jack and Marie Patterson; [m.] John Sarvay, May 15, 1982; [ch.] Jessica, David and Jordan; [ed.] Hermitage High School, Henrico County/St. Mary's Hospital School of Practical Nursing; [occ.] Pediatric Nurse at Lee Davis Medical Center; [memb.] PTA at Brookland Middle and Maude Trevvett Elementary Schools, Co-leader Girl Scout Troop #680 Team Manager in Richmond Capitals Soccer Instructional League, American Diabetes Assoc.; [oth. writ.]

Several poems and short stories - none submitted for publication.; [pers.] I feel that I am an artist painting a picture with words. The words are brought to life with emotions, and influenced by personal experiences.; [a.] Glen Allen, VA

SAUERS SR., RICHARD A.
[pen.] Richard A. Sauers, Sr.; [b.] April 29, 1950, Baltimore, MD; [p.] Agnes Brown, Ronald Umstead; [m.] Jeanette Hersley, June 21 1925; [ch.] Richard Allen Jr., Jewell Elaine; [ed.] Finish 10th Grade had to quit when I was Young; [occ.] I am on disability do work some at Camp Andrews; [memb.] Prayer partner in Canada for the hurting, Member of Rawlinsville Mennonite Church, Head of Bulletin, Bible Song Leader, and Sunday School Teacher; [hon.] Singing Award at Police Club in Baltimore, MD, Baseball Awards, Diploma for Biblical study's also an Eagle Scout; [oth. writ.] I have several other poems not published yet, I also write articles, none I have published.; [pers.] I am a Christian who see good in everyone, I look at people as Jesus would look at people, as precious as a pearl. I believe all are equal in God's eyes. I also believe love in strongest force to quench evil and hatred.; [a.] Pennsylvania, PA

SAWYER, CAROL
[pen.] C. Metivier; [b.] October 23, 1940, Maracaibo, Ven; [p.] J. H. Sawyer, Aura G. Sawyer; [ed.] Ruston Academy, Reed College New College of California, California Institute of Integral Studies; [occ.] Lead Instructor, New College of CA, S. Francisco, California; [memb.] Institute for Spirituality in Aging, The Nature Conservancy; [oth. writ.] Poetry in Spanish in Buenos Aires, Argentina, Articles for a Natural Health Magazine in Ibiza, Spain, Academic Papers.; [pers.] I am interested in the multifaceted, holographic nature of the human individual as mirror of essential truth.; [a.] San Francisco, CA

SAYLER, RACHEL
[b.] October 9, 1977, Orange Park; [p.] Osbey and Mary, Etta Sayler; [ed.] Trinity Christian Academy from sixth to 12th grade currently a Freshman at the University of North Florida; [occ.] Cashier at the Body Shop (clothing store); [memb.] National Honors Society 4-H for 6 years, Mime Team; [hon.] School Poetry Awards and other Academic Achievement Awards. (4th inn Senior Class); [oth. writ.] "Seek and Ye Shall find" (a poem) published in another anthology book) and articles written for the school newspaper.; [pers.] God has blessed me with a talent for writing. I hope to achieve much more when I have in the future. I would also like to write a book.; [a.] Drs. Inlet, FL

SAZON, BRANDON MICHAEL
[pen.] Bran; [b.] July 7, 1983, New Orleans, LA; [p.] Ms. Angele Maria Sazon; [ed.] 6th Grade student at Edward Hynes Elementary Public School; [occ.] Student; [memb.] Greater St. Stephen's Full Gospel Baptist Church, Hynes Chest Club, Drummer for St. Matthias Catholic Church Choir, Louis Armstrong Manhood Development Program, Chakula cha Jua Theater Company; [hon.] Certificate of Honor from Mayor Sidney Bartholomy; [pers.] I can do anything I put my mind to do with the help of God. Because it was Him that gave me my mind. And I will always use it to do good and help others.; [a.] New Orleans, LA

SCHARICH, LORI
[pen.] Lorily; [b.] August 4, 1961, Colorado Springs, CO; [p.] Boots and Jeannie Smith; [m.] Bill Morris; [ed.] I am attending Emily Griffith School of Opportunity for Cake Decorating; [occ.] Food Service; [memb.] Abate; [oth. writ.] I am very honored that you have chosen my poem and look forward to having my poem in your book to share with others.; [pers.] I enjoy writing poems, I have been writing for 10 years in my spare time. This is the first time I have entered a contest, and first time to have one published I am so excited about it all.; [a.] Colo Broomfield, CO

SCHLICKBERND, STACY
[b.] May 4, 1982, Columbus, NE; [p.] Rich and Karen Schlickbernd; [ed.] Morton Jr. High; [memb.] (past) Student Council President; [oth. writ.] This is my first poem that will be published. I have always enjoyed writing stories and poems, but I have never entered a contest.; [pers.] I would like to thank my 7th grade language arts teacher, Janet Fougeron, for finding my talent. Along with my parents and grandparents for encouraging me all the way through.; [a.] Columbus, NE

SCHLIM, NICOLAS WILLIAM
[b.] May 27, 1977, Denver, CO; [p.] Andrew P. and Carol A. Schlim; [ed.] Pipestone/Jasper High School, currently a Psychology Major at South Dakota State University; [occ.] Student; [oth. writ.] Several other poems none of which are published at the present.; [pers.] For me poetry is like a river it flows from my heart to the paper. So I use it to express myself.; [a.] Pipestone, MN

SCHMIDT, MARY ELLEN
[b.] September 6, 1951, Rhinelander, WI; [p.] Adam Schmidt, Lorene Schmidt; [m.] Michael Jackson, September 25, 1975; [ch.] (Stepchildren) Edward Jackson, Scott Jackson; [ed.] Anderson High, Shasta College; [occ.] Textile Sales Rep; [oth. writ.] Several poems, no publications.; [pers.] To my mother who gave me love and insight.; [a.] Pasadena, CA

SCHMIDT, RAMONA LEE THOMAS
[pen.] Monie; [b.] July 2, 1965, Richmond, VA; [p.] Kathy L. and Wilton A. Thomas; [m.] James I. Schmidt, October 20, 1990; [ch.] Heather Renee and James II; [ed.] Lake Gibson Sr., High Lakeland, Florida, Class of 1983; [occ.] Hobbies Writings and Photography; [memb.] AANR; [hon.] Received "The Editors Choice Award" from the National Library of Poetry on my first entry written. "Believe in Yourself"; [oth. writ.] "Believe in yourself" published in "Between the rain drops," September 1995.; [pers.] Life is like a final exam... there's no time for "re takes" on judgement day!!; [a.] Lando Lakes, FL

SCHRUEDER, JEROD
[b.] May 23, 1967, Milwaukee, WI; [p.] Daniel Schroeder, Joyce Schroeder; [m.] Jennifer Schroeder, April 27, 1996; [ed.] University of Wisconsin - Milwaukee; [occ.] Writer, Poet, Husband; [memb.] Poets of the Great Hunger, Grace Lutheran Church, Sigma Tau Delta; [hon.] Approval from my Mentor; [oth. writ.] The Blue Canory, NSR, Public Administration; [pers.] Look inside of yourself. Write about what is in front of you.; [a.] Milwaukee, WI

SCHUENENANN, KIN
[b.] December 10, 1975, Norfolk, VA; [ed.] Maryville College; [occ.] Student; [memb.] Alpha Psi Omega; [oth. writ.] Unpublished poems, novels short stories, children's stories.; [pers.] Writing should be for the enjoyments of the writer and the reader not for the purpose of analysis.; [a.] Maryville, TN

SCHULERT, VIOLET R.
[b.] November 15, 1963, Lansing, MI; [ch.] Paul; [ed.] BA Moody Bible Institute 87, BA Michigan State University 92; [occ.] Management Sentura Creations; [oth. writ.] Many poems only self published.; [pers.] I write to express my feelings - to describe what it feels like to be an incest/satan is ritual abuse survivor. I would not have survived without God's help.; [a.] Lansing, MI

SCHURADE, RITA MILLER
[b.] February 4, 1942, Oakland, MD; [p.] Hurley and Laretha Miller; [m.] Divorced; [ed.] AA Nursing Certificate FNP; [memb.] American Nurses Assoc.; [hon.] Editors Choice Award International Society of Poets; [oth. writ.] Home Smell the Flowers; [pers.] Like to write poems about nature, outdoors - poems for friends, love, romances.; [a.] Oakland, MD

SCHUYLER, JOAN
[b.] August 7, 1936, Milwaukee, WI; [p.] Earl Kulzick - Claire Kulzick; [m.] Phillip Schuyler, May 7, 1955; [ch.] Robin, Steven, Scott, Renee, Stewart; [ed.] East Troy High School - East Troy, Wi.; [occ.] Domestic Engineer (Housewife); [pers.] My love of life, family and the unknown is in my writing of my poetry.; [a.] Portsmouth, VA

SCOTT, CANDACE WILLRICH
[b.] March 26, 1965, Dallas, TX; [p.] Margie and Late Rev. Theodis Willrich; [m.] Eugene Scott, July 24, 1993; [ed.] B.S. Mathematics, MBA Finance and Info Systems; [occ.] Software Consultant, Strategic Solutions; [memb.] Nat'l Org. of Executive Women, Nat'l Black MBA Assoc.; [hon.] 1993 - 1995 Performance Club, Comshare Inc., 1994 North American Consultant of the Year, Comshare Inc. Who's Who of America; [pers.] Through God all is possible!; [a.] Lewisville, TX

SCOTT, TINA ANN
[b.] January 27, 1981, Saint Mary's; [p.] Shirley and John Scott; [ed.] Freshman at Port High School of Port Washington, Wisconsin; [memb.] To Y.M. Magazine; [oth. writ.] Other poems and short stories.; [pers.] Reach for the unreachable believe in the unbelievable, attain the unattainable and you will obtain all of your dreams.; [a.] Saukville, WI

SCOVELL, GENE R.
[b.] July 20, 1954, Moorpark, CA; [p.] Ralph and Ruth Scovell; [ch.] Alina 16 yrs, Kristen 14 yrs; [pers.] It's quite tragic we live in a world where daily, human life is casually slaughtered while humanity will stop at nothing. To save a species from extinction.; [a.] Paso Robles, CA

SEEGER, TERI LYNN
[pen.] Teri Lynn; [b.] June 23, 1954, Wichita, KS; [p.] Dick and Mary Higgins; [m.] Al Seeger, September 12, 1975; [ch.] Kara, Ryan, Tracy, Adam; [ed.] B.A., Ottawa University, Ottawa, KS, Bishop

Carroll High School, Wichita, KS; [occ.] Pre-school Teacher Assistant, Assistant Director Center for Women; [memb.] Ottawa Bible Church, Kansas for Life, Arts Council; [hon.] Graduated Magna Cum Laude from College; [oth. writ.] Children's books, Christmas plays with accompanying music, life care center for Women Newsletter, Parent Education Program.; [pers.] Most of my early writings were written in response to social or moral issues. More recent writings deal with the heart. Words can be left behind when I'm gone, so I want them to "make a difference."; [a.] Ottawa, KS

SELIKOFF, SCOTT
[b.] April 4, 1980; [p.] Barbara and Mark Selikoff; [ed.] Toms River High School East; [occ.] Student at a High School; [hon.] I have not received any Literary Awards in my Life but I have Won many Awards for Mathematics; [oth. writ.] I have written several poems similar to this one but I have yet to share them with the world.; [pers.] This poem is the piece of poetry I have ever shared with anyone but myself and a few select friends. I would like to add that I wrote this poem at a time when my relationship with a girl whom a cared for greatly was prematurely ending. When I wrote this we were both facing the reality we would not be able to see each other for a very long time if not forever. I would like to delicate this poem to Susan.; [a.] Toms River, NJ

SEWARD, BRADLEY JOHN
[b.] March 15, 1967, Minneapolis, MN; [p.] Louis, Darlene Seward; [ed.] Redlands, High School, Crafton Hills College; [occ.] Screen Writer, Writer, Computer Programmer; [memb.] Muscular Dystrophy Association; [oth. writ.] Several articles printed in sun news paper.; [pers.] Being disabled my parents have always encouraged me to go for my dreams. I believe that no matter what color, race or religion or disabilities one may have you can always fulfill your dreams no matter what you position in life.; [a.] Yucaipa, CA

SEWELL, ELIZABETH GAIL
[pen.] "Quail"; [b.] January 27, 1949, Camden, AK; [p.] Mr. Eugene Ponder and Frances Harrison Ponder; [m.] DPC(SW) Lonnie Clark Sewell, August 7, 1971; [ch.] Daymond Clark and Valeri Lynn Sewell; [ed.] Chidester High School, Southern Ark., University, Southwestern A/G College, North Texas Community College; [occ.] Secretary; [memb.] Christ Chapel Assembly; [hon.] Senior Class Valedictorian, Chi Alpha President; [oth. writ.] Several personal poems including "Seeing Christ through a Christmas Tree."; [pers.] My poems are inspired mostly by my children or other children. I hope to always view life through the eyes of child for such is the kingdom of heaven.; [a.] Woodbridge, VI

SHAFFER, KRYSTAL K.
[pen.] Korin Korbin, Krystal K. L. Shaffer; [b.] June 8, 1962, Peru, IN; [p.] Linda D. Edwards, Donald I. Leffler (Deceased); [ch.] Amber Lynn Shaffer 2 1/2 yrs, adopted; [ed.] Peru High School, International Business College Communications Training: Fast track Assuring Technical Excellence, Basic Voice Communications, T-1 and Data, Fundamentals of Relationship Selling, etc. Altruist, Free Lance Writer, Speaker; [occ.] Altruist, Free lance Writer, Speaker; [memb.] East Side Christian Church Kiwanis, Bd of Dir. Women for Success, Am.

Women's Bowling Congress, IOWIT, SME, Indianapolis Museum of Art, Volunteer: Daysprings Soup Kitchen, RIF Reading is Fundamental, American Cancer Society, Scholarship Judge: International Women's Business Assoc, Circle KAARA, INSRA; [hon.] National Honor Society Who's Who In America, IN State Racquetball Champ 1992 - 1st Place, IN State DB1s RB 1991 - 1st Place President's Circle (World Com) 1988, 1989, 1990, 1991, 1992, 1993, 1994 Award of Excellence 1990 and 1991, Circle of Success 1994; [oth. writ.] Haunted Moon "A Voyage To Remember," IN Corporate America: Successful Selling, Attitude, The Knight in Tarnished Armor, Licence PL8 Language.; [pers.] Good Judgement comes from experience and experience comes from Bad Judgement.; [a.] Fishers, IN

SHAHEEN, BUFFY MARIKO
[b.] April 25, 1977, CA; [p.] James and Mayumi Shaheen; [ed.] Polytechnic High School (Long Beach), Attending University of California at Santa Barbara; [occ.] Student; [memb.] Scarabs Welfare Sorority, Pioneer Project; [hon.] State Farm Foundations Scholarship, Saito Memorial Scholarship; [pers.] Arigato to my grandfather for sharing his memories with me. Thank you, Dr. Shere.; [a.] Long Beach, CA

SHANNON, EMELINE CARETTI
[b.] Page, WV; [p.] Mr. and Mrs. John Caretti; [m.] Harold D. Shannon (Deceased); [ch.] John H. Shannon; [occ.] Retired, 30 yrs. employed in Armstrong County Court House, Treasurers Office, 16 yrs. Deputy Register and Recorder, also appointed by Governor of Penna. to the office of Prothonotary and Clerk of Courts; [oth. writ.] My Poem "Another World and Another Time" dedicated to son John H. Shannon.

SHAW, SERENA
[b.] October 13, 1984, Marlinton, WV; [p.] Kevin and Virginia Shaw; [ed.] 5th Grader at Marlinton Middle School; [occ.] Student

SHELTON, DAVID SCOTT
[b.] March 12, 1964; [p.] David G. Shelton, Sharon Clearwaters; [ed.] Tri-West Hendricks High School; [occ.] Painter/Wallpaper Hanger; [pers.] This poem is a result from my best friend being killed in an auto accident. I hope that it can help heal, or begin the healing process for others as it did for myself when I wrote it.; [a.] Indianapolis, IN

SHELTON, KATHY
[b.] September 1, 1960, Pensacola, FL; [p.] Madelyn Jones; [ch.] Keith, Trisha; [ed.] High School 1978, in College now Calhoun Community College (Nursing Program); [occ.] Pharmacy Technician, Nutritional Home Health; [memb.] Nursing Club; [hon.] Nomination of American Junior College Who's Who (1995); [pers.] It is my hope for each individual to experience their "point of destiny."; [a.] Decatur, AL

SHELTON, RUTHELLEN
[pen.] R'Lee Mayes; [b.] March 18, 1918, Dinuba, CA; [p.] Miles Vernon and Lillie May Lee; [m.] S. Trueman Shelton, April 22, 1939; [ch.] Trueman Leslie Shelton; [ed.] Oakdale U.H. School, CA, Pasadena College, Pasadena, CA; [occ.] Retired Minister and Missionary; [hon.] Distinguished

Service Award for our Life time of Service in the Church as Ministers and Missionaries; [oth. writ.] Poems, articles, stories, published in church periodicals.; [pers.] Because my faith in God has such deep meaning in my life, I enjoy sharing His love and strength with others.; [a.] North Highlands, CA

SHERMAN, DEBORAH
[b.] February 26, 1953; [p.] Loren and Ruth Wicks; [ch.] Jeromy, Justin and Sheila; [ed.] B.A. in Ed, Master's of C and I in Ed. University of MS; [occ.] Teacher, South Panola Schools, Batesville, MS; [hon.] Dean's List; [pers.] I believe poetry is a universal way to communicate. It transcends all prejudice and embraces feelings that are common to all humankind.; [a.] Batesville, MS

SHERROD, MELVIN
[ed.] Beddingfield High School Class of 1982, Wilson, NC; [memb.] USMC, Boot Camp - "H" Company, 3rd BYN, 3048, Series (3048, 3049, 3050, 3051), Parris Island S.C., April 26, 1985, July 19, 1985, School "B" Company Barracks 1642 South MCCES/MCAECC. 29 Palms, CA 3/85 - 11/85 Duty Station HQ Company, 2nd MAR Regt. comm PLT Camp Lejeune December 1, 1985, March 4, 1987; [pers.] I would like to thank the following for their support and friendship Paul Lanceration, Jose Mart, Petter, Denton, James Smith Jr., Joe Fondrecct, James Pendergraft Jr., Jeff Ammons, Mark Schuck, Carmine Santanni, Joey Rosario, Chauva Donnelly, Richard O'Dell Jr., Rodney Jandulman, Richard Christiansen, Gene Mays, Brian Russ, Richard Collins, Tyrone K. Wells, Dave Roberts, John Capps, Robert Wells Russell Doherty, Randy T. Duncan and Kraig McNally.

SHIMOZONO, CATHERINE
[b.] November 9, 1946, Benton Harbor, MI; [p.] Arnold and Mildred Nelson; [m.] Yasuo Richard Shimozono, November 30, 1972; [ed.] A.A. and B.A. in English - Creative Writing, Elementary Teacher with Special Education Credential in Learning Disabilities; [occ.] Teacher; [memb.] South Bay Seventh Day Adventist Church; [hon.] Disabled Students Commissioner (for 2 years) at C.S.U.L.B., Ran a help Center for needy Children for 12 years; [oth. writ.] Hypocrisy's child la book of poems) several children's stories called the "Magic Bed" series.; [pers.] I was totally paralyzed from my neck down from an unknown etiology. Since that time I have learned two things. I your only as disabled as you let the other guy make you, and 2. The average adult human being spends 80 85% of their, time sitting down or laying down - Hey I'm just ahead of them a little.; [a.] Long Beach, CA

SHIREY, WILLIAM L.
[b.] January 24, 1930, Springfield Twp. York County, PA; [p.] Curvin S. Shirey, Mary Floyd Shirey; [m.] Doris M. Walker Shirey, June 11, 1948; [ch.] Cristine Thoman, Roberta Shirey, William S. Shirey, Cathy Kephart, Tamara Stein; [ed.] Shrewsbury High School I.C.S. (Steam Engineering); [occ.] Retired; [pers.] Always do your best.; [a.] Seven Valleys, PA

SHOGREN, MICHAEL
[pen.] Michael Shogren; [b.] September 28, 1947, Wichita, KS; [p.] Tony Shogren, Faye Shogren; [m.]

Deborah (SULLARD) Shogren, July 6, 1973; [ch.] Kristopher Michael, Jillian BreeAnn; [ed.] Wichita High School West, Graduate Friends University, Graduate Studies Kansas State University; [occ.] General Manager, Power Link, Inc. Wichita, Kansas; [memb.] Notre Dame Club of Wichita, St. Josephs Church; [oth. writ.] Several poems in local news letters, letter and essays Wichita Eagle newspaper.; [pers.] Whether we believe it to be divine or not, we are all part of the plan!; [a.] Wichita, KS

SHORTS, LINDA S.
[b.] May 13, 1946, Lancaster, PA; [p.] (The Late) Richard Dehr Hart, Catherine Dusel; [m.] Homer E. Shorts Jr., August 6, 1983; [ch.] Joseph Vidzicki, Phillip Shorts; [ed.] B.S. East Stroudsburg State College, Special Education Certificate Kutztown State College; [occ.] Retired Teacher; [oth. writ.] "The Rainbow and the Dove."; [pers.] My desire is to use any talent or ability God has given me for His honor and glory.; [a.] Mohnton, PA

SHOURDS, TONI ANN GILMORE
[pen.] TAG; [b.] June 6, 1961, Rantoul, IL; [p.] Doward F. and Margie R. Cribb; [m.] Patrick L. Shourds, December 4, 1987; [ch.] Burton, Stephanny, Shauna, Lea, Kasey; [ed.] Dimond High, Anchorage, AK, currently the Institute of Childrens Literature; [occ.] Secretary for Spenard Builders Supply in Anchorage, A.K.; [memb.] Local PTSA Boards; [oth. writ.] Poems published in local newspaper, short stories written for local schools.; [pers.] I would like to touch the lives of many by giving them the openness of me, to make a difference in everyone I meet, and show that one person can make the world a better place.; [a.] Anchorage, AK

SHUBIN, ERLINE E.
[pen.] Erline Shubin; [b.] January 22, 1924, San Benito, TX; [p.] The Rev. Mr. Herman and Mrs. Pauline Atrops; [m.] Andrew J. Shubin, June 20, 1943; [ch.] Linda Diane Johnson, Dr. James A. Shubin, M.D., Christine Louise Reid; [ed.] High School, Home taught music; [occ.] Home maker; [memb.] Zion Lutheran Church, Mo. Synod, Rosemead, Calif. (former organist); [hon.] Honorable Mention for a poem submitted to a local organization; [oth. writ.] Prepare original personal greeting cards with paintings and verse for various occasions.; [pers.] I practice the "Golden Rule", treat others as you would be treated with a sense of humor.; [a.] El Monte, CA

SHUTE, JULIE L.
[b.] May 16, 1979, Fresno, CA; [p.] Annette and Steven Shute; [ed.] I am a Junior at Buchanan High School, and in the future, I plan on attending College; [occ.] High School Student at Buchanan High School in Clovis, CA; [memb.] I am involved in many Co-curricular Activities such as Student Leadership, Rally Club, Fellowship of Christian Athletes, California Scholarship Federation, and the School Softball Team; [hon.] I was a finalist in a group performance for National History Day. I have a Block "B" in Academics, and a Varsity Letter in Softball. I am also a Member of the Championship Team of the Southwest Regional States Softball Tournament; [a.] Clovis, CA

SHUTTS, JASON ALBERT
[b.] October 16, 1985, Norwalk, CT; [p.] Albert and Sally Shutts; [ed.] St. Thomas Choir School NY, NY. The only Boys Shoir School in the U.S.A. Previously attended Darien, CT Public Schools, [occ.] Currently in fifth grade; [memb.] Jr., Sailing Association, Boy Scout's of America, MENSA, Swim Team; [hon.] I consider it a Honor to have been selected to play a lead in Pippin, Chorus in, Fiddler on the Roof, and in the Wizard of oz. all Community Theater Productions; [oth. writ.] Published in school paper. This poem in "The Rainbow's End," written at age 8, is the first published.; [pers.] I am deeply impressed with nature and refer to it in my writings.; [a.] Darien, CT

SIBBERING, ROSEMARY ANDREWS
[pen.] Roe; [b.] August 18, 1964, Bronx, NY; [p.] Margaret and Clifford Andrews; [m.] Edward Sibbering, May 27, 1989; [ed.] Santa Maria Elementary School, St. Raymond's Academy High School, The Wood Secretarial School; [occ.] Office Manager; [oth. writ.] My Christmas Angel, a mother's Day with and mother of the Bride.; [pers.] God's Greatest gift to us is the laughter which releases the beauty held deep in the soul.

SIMIEN, OCTAVIA R.
[pen.] Octavia Ruben Simien; [b.] February 23, 1928, Beaument, TX; [p.] Bud and Emily Ruben; [m.] Joseph Warren Simien, December 26, 1957; [ed.] Diploma in Business BA - MA, Retired School Principal; [occ.] Direct/Teach Reading Tutorial Program/Free Lance Reporter for Catholic Herald; [memb.] The National League of American Pen Women California Writers Club ZICA, The Sacramento Poetry Center; [hon.] Women of the Year 2 Silver Medal (KPC-LA), Parents Club Leadership Award; [oth. writ.] Author Chapbks-"God is able" and my mother Mary." Poetry in Anthologies (2). Free Lance Writer, Articles in Neighbor, Claverite, the Sacto. Observer, Catholic Herald, Modern Maturity.; [pers.] If I can promote some moral and spiritual value/teachings in one person's life, my life will not have been in vain.; [a.] Sacramento, CA

SIMMONS, WILLIAM BRUCE
[b.] October 9, 1949, Silverton, TX; [p.] Orlen and Buell Simmons; [m.] Kathleen J. Simmons, September 12, 1992; [ch.] William Bruce, Carrie Ann, Kelly Lynn, Michelle Marie; [ed.] San Fernando High School, Moorpark College; [occ.] Courier; [memb.] United Auto Workers; [hon.] Honorable Discharge US Army 1967-1974, Honorable Discharge California Air National Guard 1976 Armed Forces Expeditionary Medal "Korea"; [oth. writ.] Made in America, Carousels and Clowns, Lost Children, Escape, and Colorless Rainbows; [pers.] Man should choose his words carefully let not careless thoughts spoken in haste become weapons of the tongue.; [a.] Colorado Springs, CO

SIMMS, A. GAIL
[b.] June 28, 1957, Boston, MA; [m.] Kevin P. Simms, May 22, 1988; [ch.] Lauren Alyse and Kendra Leigh; [ed.] Dorchester High and Hyde Park High, Boston, MA; [occ.] Patient Rep/Financial Screening; [memb.] Damascus SDA Church; [oth. writ.] I have several other unpublished poems.; [pers.] I enjoy writing and reading poetry. I also receive great comfort and pleasure from reading the psalms of the bible.; [a.] Mount Rainier, MD

SIMPSON, TONI L.
[b.] May 8, 1953, Hammond, IN; [p.] Mary Lugo, Antonio Lugo; [m.] Jerald Simpson, February 24, 1995; [ch.] Anthony, Robby, Brandon, Jerame; [ed.] 9th grade; [occ.] Homemaker, Housewife; [hon.] I received an Award for a Poem I sent out 3 or 4 years ago the poem was "My Prayer"; [oth. writ.] My prayer, call on me, "you," without you, Hard to forget, There you are, man and wife.; [a.] Valparaiso, IN

SINGER, SUSAN J.
[ed.] Bachelor of Arts - Creative Writing; [occ.] Human Resources Manager; [memb.] Latin Honor Society, Reading Poetry Outlet, Bard Wire (Reading); [a.] Wyomissing, PA

SINGH, JASMIN
[b.] January 25, 1980, Sacramento; [p.] George and Yolanda Singh; [occ.] Student; [memb.] Ballet Folklorico Juvenile de Woodland; [hon.] N.J. HS, Honor Roll; [oth. writ.] Published once before.; [pers.] This poem is in memory of River Phoenix and Brandon Lee. In losing them I have been able to write many poems. However, no matter how much I write, it can never bring them back.; [a.] Woodland, CA

SITNER, ILENE
[b.] April 28, 1988, Princeton, NJ; [p.] Beth and Robert Sitner; [ed.] 8th grade - Melvin H. Kreps School; [occ.] Student; [hon.] Honor Roll, Dance Trophy; [oth. writ.] Various poems written since Elementary School.; [pers.] I don't like to categorize my poetry because I write about so many different things.; [a.] East Windsor, NJ

SKENE, FLORENCE PETREE
[pen.] "Sissy"; [b.] January 19, 1900, Belgreen, AL; [p.] Walter C. and Elizabeth Foote Petree; [m.] William Hearst Skene; [ch.] Joanne M. Bohman; [occ.] Retired; [oth. writ.] I am currently writing the story of my life.; [pers.] From Micah Chapter 6, verse 8. "What doth the Lord require of thee, but to do justly, and to love mercy, and to walk humbly with thy God?"; [a.] Hagerstown, MD

SKJOLD, CHRISTOPHER JOHN
[b.] July 31, 1971, Hallock, MN; [p.] Stephen and Barbara Skjold; [m.] Anne Elizabeth Skjold, April 29, 1992; [ch.] Brett Christopher Skjold; [ed.] Humboldt - St. Vincent High; [occ.] Military Police, US Army; [oth. writ.] A few poems published in local news papers, and a short narrative.; [pers.] I try to show that love can last and be expressed over the distances of land and time.; [a.] Bejou, MN

SKRZYNECKY, ELIZABETH M.
[b.] December 30, 1979, Pomona, CA; [p.] Nadine and George Skrzynecky; [ed.] Junior, attending Bloomington Christian School, Bloomington, CA; [hon.] Numerous awards for excellence in English and science class. Honor roll. Ranked second place in Sophomore class. Recognized by "Who's Who Among American Advanced High School Students"; [a.] Rialto, CA

SLASTEN, GUENNADI
[pen.] Gene Nicholas Slaston; [b.] May 4, 1957, Kegichevka, Ukraine; [p.] NiKoLai Slasten, Vera Boiko-Slasten; [ch.] Marina Slasten; [ed.] Schwerin Russian Secondary School (Germany), Kishinev State University (Moldavia), Moscow Institute of Information (Russia); [occ.] Construction Worker, Independent Researcher (Interlinguistics); [memb.] The International Society of Poets; [hon.] The International Society of Poets: Nomination as Poet of the Year for 1995, "The International Poet of Merit" Award - 1995, The National Library of Poetry: Editor's Choice Award - 1995.; [oth. writ.] Three dozen poems and songs, including What's the Use of the Sky Lyrics published by The National Library of Poetry in A Moment in Time (ISBN 1-56167-266-1)-1995.; [pers.] My beloved readers, it is high time for you to support the efforts to create a common auxiliary language to be spoken by all and everyone. The science of interlinguistics can help you to communicate with anybody you want.; [a.] Brooklyn, NY

SLOANE, DEBORAH LEE
[pen.] Deborah Lee Sloane; [b.] may 19, 1947, Hartford, CT; [p.] dorothy and John Sloane; [ch.]Benjamin, Jon, Jeffrey, Shannon and Single parent of Brian; [ed.] Early Education inSimsbury, CT (Tobacco Valley), spent 1 year at Vesper George School of Art; [occ.] Currently attending Cape Cod Community College, Studio Art I and Environmental Science, also have small art business and plan on continuing in environmental study; [memb.] Member of the West Yarmouth Congregation Church, Christened First Church of Christ, Cong. Church; [hon.]Numerous dance awards also tailoring awards; [oth. writ.] School newspaper; [pers.] My children are the ones who inspire me the most and thank God for them, and the beautiful earth that our Savior created.; [a.] West Yarmouth, MA

SMITH, CARRIE
[b.] June 20, 1961, Sea, WA; [p.] Gene and Charleen Smith; [ch.] Delmar Dale III and Dierdre Carrie; [occ.] Printer-Production Design - Mother; [oth. writ.] Many poems about a sad marriage - motherhood day care provider and lover of life.; [pers.] Always take time at to stop and observe each management as it's own for most likely that moment is one of a kind.; [a.] Everett, WA

SMITH, JAMES LEE
[pen.] James Lee Smith; [b.] May 8, 1926, Wellington, TX; [p.] Jesse Lee and Stella Mae Smith; [m.] Dorothy L. Smith, June 15, 1990; [ch.] James (5), Dorothy (4); [ed.] High School and 2 yrs. College; [occ.] Retired-State of Texas where I worked for nearly 40 years with the Texas Veterans Commission; [memb.] American Legion - Disabled American Veterans - AMVETS - Church of Christ; [hon.] State and National Awards and Plaques given by Veterans Organizations for Work in Assisting Veterans and their Dependents and Survivors. Local Recognition for Poetry and other Writings for the Church and Local Community; [oth. writ.] Several short stories submitted but none ever published. A number of submittals to magazines, including Reader's Digest, Country, Texas Monthly and Texas Highway Magazine.; [pers.] I like to find and see the good in people, my writings generally reflect this. My short stories have mostly been of the old West, as I favor that particular genre. I like people and enjoy talking with different races and backgrounds, to ask their opinions of life and its meanings. I love my family, and enjoy the company of all children,

grandchildren, and my one great-grandchild.; [a.] New Home Lynn County, TX

SMITH, JOAN W.
[b.] November 12, 1949, Nassawadox, VA; [p.] Alfred & Olive Walters; [m.] Wayne L. Smith, September 14, 1969; [ch.] Cristin Smith; [ed.] Northampton High School graduate; [occ.] Corporate Secretary, Chesapeake Marine Inc., Exmore, VA; [memb.] New Testament Church, Onancock, VA, International Society of Poets 1996/1996; [oth. writ.] Many other unpublished poems; [pers.] I plan to continue to write inspirational poetry as I pursue the opportunity to share my poems with others. I have been greatly influenced by and inspired through the beautiful writing of Helen Steiner Rice.; [a.] (On Virginia's Eastern Shore) Exmore, VA

SMITH, MAE STEVENS
[b.] February 22, 1911, Fulton Chaine, NY; [p.] Charles and Mae Abbeys Stevens; [m.] (The Late) Clinton Smith, December 27, 1959; [ch.] Reed Delano Proper; [ed.] High School and I took Engineering and Quality Control Courses for several Years at a Local College; [occ.] Retired - I was an Air Craft Mechanic for 30 yrs. on Various Instruments, such as Norden Bombsight and Stabilizer - Automatic Pilots Sidewinder Missile and some Aerospace; [hon.] All U.S. Government Projects. I Graduated H.S. in 1929 my College days got delayed for a few Years; [oth. writ.] I have shelves full of notebooks both prose and poetry. I have had occasional letters published on Editorial Pages.; [pers.] It has always been easier for me to express my feelings in writing than vocally.; [a.] Canastota, NY

SMITH, MELANIE L.
[pen.] L. N. Smith and LeEllen Smith; [b.] November 30, 1976, Kettering, OH; [p.] David Smith and Melodee Morgan; [ch.] Isabella River Smith; [ed.] Currently a Film Student at the University of Toledo; [occ.] "Homewrecker"; [hon.] Well, I did Win the "I'm a Kid for COSI" Contest in the 8th Grade; [oth. writ.] Various unpublished poems, short stories and script ideas.; [pers.] This is my first publication, and if is both an honor and a privilege. I want to thank my family and friends, and also say, "I love you," to my daughter, Isabella. Without this sickly dysfunctional group, I'd have nothing to write.; [a.] Toledo, OH

SMITH, MICHAEL
[b.] January 29, 1959, Wichita, KS; [ed.] Wichita South East High School; [occ.] Student; [oth. writ.] Several unpublished fantasy fiction short stories.; [a.] Wichita, KS

SMITH, SHERYL LYNN
[b.] July 24, 1969, Merced, CA; [ed.] California State University at Sacramento; [occ.] Jr. High School Teacher; [pers.] "Searching for Tomorrow" is dedicated to my dear friend, Lt. Mel, who constantly inspires me to search for happiness, within.

SMITH, SHIRLEY
[b.] July 22, 1952, New Orleans, LA; [p.] John and Marie Monk; [ch.] Shannon (25), Sean (24), Peter (10); [ed.] Attending College now some College (completed) Graduated St. Joseph's Academy in Baton Rouge; [occ.] Disabled but studying Business Mgmt.; [memb.] PASS (Grass Roots Organization to

Preneent Instillation of Sludge Sites in our very populated town) St. George and St. Thomas more prayer citation for being member of PASS (People Against Sludge Site) in our town. We defeated placement of Sludge Site there with our Grass Roots Organization; [oth. writ.] I've written petitions, letters for friends and organizations plus my friends love my letters but this is my first published piece. Although I've a bounds full of my works, this is my first submitted piece.; [pers.] My writing is a deep and personal expression of my soul and a soul of inner creed on November 9, 1995.; [a.] Maiden Paper

SMITH, TARA L.
[pen.] Unique Peace; [b.] January 24, 1980; [p.] Willie P. and Mary L. Smith; [ed.] Fort Washington Forest Elem. Gwynn Park Middle School, Oxon Hill High School; [occ.] Student at Oxon Hill High School; [memb.] Faith Temple #2 Baptist Church; [hon.] State of Maryland Citizenship Award, Grand Prize Science fair), Seven (4.0 GPA) Medals, Band Director's Award, all American Scholar Award, US AA Award; [oth. writ.] Unpublished poems, two short stories.; [pers.] I am striving to make most of my poems reflect on nature and its personified relationship with mankind. As I strive to reach my goal, I thank God and my family for being a great influence an me and helping my writing come alive.; [a.] Fort Washington, MA

SMITH, VIRGINIA J. G.
[pen.] V. J. P. Smith; [b.] March 1941, Heber City, UT; [p.] S. Leon and Geneva Nuttall Peterson; [m.] Clyde A. Smith (died January 8, 1988), November 24, 1933; [ch.] Carolyn, A. Leon, Betty Rae, Dennis, Alan, Sandra, Pauline, Sterling, Julie (all married), (59 grandchildren), (30 great grandchildren); [ed.] Hi-School Graduate, Post Grad. Course Past School; [occ.] Homemaker; [memb.] Member of Church of Jesus christ Latter-day-Saints. Member of Bonneville Co. Daughters of Utah Pioneers - Family Pioneers; [hon.] Cub Scout Den Mother award D.U.P. award for 20 yrs. Leadership, Mother of 9 Children and Ancestor of 126 Descendants; [oth. writ.] Many unpublished articles on History, with poems, etc. personal articles and ancestorical and historical articles Diary, letters to public" Member of Historical.; [pers.] I love life and incidents that have been an encourage to me and hope to be such to others. Lives of great men and women can be a reminiscer that we can make our lives...; [a.] Ammour Ben Co, ID

SNARR, MURIEL BETTERIDGE
[b.] April 16, 1916, Grouse Creek, UT; [p.] James W. Betteridge and Emily Ness Betteridge; [m.] Grover Webb Snarr, August 28, 1940; [ch.] Keith, Steven, Gordon, and Norman; [ed.] Graduate of Granite High School Attended Business School; [occ.] Retired; [memb.] Women's Civic Guild: Fine Arts Committee and Program Committee Church of Jesus Christ of LDS: Pres. Relief Society in Murray 2nd and 28th Wards Pres. Primary — Presidency and Teacher in MIA Parent Teacher Association: Health Committee and Welfare Committee; [hon.] Winner in a Commercial Institution Contest A Trophy for Organizing and Editing a Family History Book, Winner of Prizes in a Radio Contest; [oth. writ.] Writings for family and friends.; [pers.] I have an optimistic outlook on life, and I like my writing to

reflect optimistic humor and imagination. I would rather look at the donut than the hole in it.; [a.] Murray, UT

SNEDEKER, HAROLD
[b.] August 12, 1932, Baldwin, NY; [m.] Beverly Snedeker, June 20, 1968; [ed.] 2 yrs College Adelphi, Univ; [occ.] Retired; [memb.] Community Presbyterian Church, L.I.A.A.C. long Island Assoc. for AIDS Care Long Island Council of Churches, Presbytery of L.I.; [hon.] Award for Outstanding Service to the N.Y. State Prof. Photographers, 1st Place in Photo Competition, Recognition for Service to Boy Scouts, of America. Honored for Service to People with A.I.D.S.; [oth. writ.] Short stories - Local Organizations.; [pers.] I write out of my life experiences on my spiritual journey.; [a.] North Babylon, NY

SNYDER, DEBRA L.
[b.] October 25, 1958, Waynesboro, PA; [p.] Marvin Terry and Janice Terry; [m.] Jerry A. Snyder Sr., October 22, 1982; [ch.] Jerry A. Snyder Jr.; [ed.] South View Sr., High; [occ.] Manager, Mini Mart Food Stores; [oth. writ.] Numerous other poems.; [pers.] I write for myself and to show others that no matter how dark it gets, there is always a bright side.; [a.] Gaffney, SC

SOLIS, LAVERNE BORING
[b.] May 3, 1962, Anson, TX; [p.] Elva Mae Boring, Billy George Boring; [m.] David Solis, December 13, 1977; [ch.] Vanessa, Sabring, Patricia, Alesha; [ed.] T.S.T.C., E.M.T.; [occ.] House Wife and Mother; [pers.] I write from my heart. This poem is to my father. If only I could find you.; [a.] Hamlin, TX

SOON, MARY
[pen.] Mare Soon; [b.] May 21, 1954, MI; [m.] Han Soon, August 31, 1991; [ch.] Melissa Davenport, Matthew and Dren Bernard; [oth. writ.] Author of a monthly Newsletter, several unpublished poems and short stories, one poem published locally.; [pers.] We do not all start at the same place. Therefore, it's not how high the mountain you climb, but how deep the hole out of which you crawl. We each define our own success.; [a.] Peoria, IL

SORGE, SARAH
[b.] June 15, 1977, Toledo OH; [p.] Mike and Waneta Sorge; [ed.] Shoreland Elementary School, Jefferson Junior High, Whitmer High School (grad. June, 1995), currently a student at Butler University, Indianapolis, IN; [occ.] College Student (freshman); [memb.] Member of Whitmer High School's National Honor Society, Band Program, and Track Team, current member of the Music Educator's National Conference, Butler University's Symphonic Band, Marching Band, Jordan College Fine Arts, Butler University Crew Team; [hon.] National Honor Society, Music Honorary, Various honor bands, Martin W. Essex School for the gifted, John Philip Sousa Award, high ratings at Solo and Ensemble and indoor drumline competitions, and finalist at regional and Congressional art shows; [pers.] The quality of human life is determined by one's responsibility and effort.; [a.] Toledo, OH

SPARKS, ANNETTE L.
[pen.] Annette L. Sparks; [b.] September 29, 1947,

Opelousas, LA; [p.] Rhinus LeDoux, Irene LeDoux; [m.] Thomas Sparks, July 27, 1982; [ch.] Christopher Sparks, Angela Sparks; [ed.] Reseda High, Pierce Jr. College; [oth. writ.] A collection of poetry unpublished.; [pers.] I've been writing since I was a child. I have always taken a humanitarian approach to my life and my writing.; [a.] West Hills, CA

SPARKS, PATRICK A.
[b.] March 4, 1971, Lexington, KY; [p.] Harrison and Sylvia Sparks; [ed.] High School Graduate College Credits in: Social Psychology, Philosophy, Poetry, Short Story Writing; [occ.] College Student; [memb.] The Crossover Network; [hon.] First Place for Songwriting - City Level in 1989-90-Reflections Contest; [oth. writ.] Theme song for Break-Thru '89 Youth Event, Many poems presented at ASU's Spring '94 ACW Poetry Workshop.; [pers.] Inside my gate a thousand sages do not know me. The beauty of my garden is invisible. Why should one search for the footprints of the patriarchs?; [a.] Lexington, KY

SPENCE, NATASSIA
[b.] April 26, 1971, Dougherty County; [p.] Mr. and Mrs. Earnest Spence; [ed.] Mitchell - Baker High, Albany State College, University of South Carolina; [occ.] Assistant Residence Manager, Albany State College; [memb.] Georgia Press Association, Beulah Baptist Church, National Council for Teachers of English; [hon.] 2nd attendant to Miss ASC 1992-1993, 3rd place winner in Phi Beta Sigma Black History Essay Contest; [oth. writ.] Articles for the Albany Herald and The Tifton Gazette.; [pers.] "I can do all things through Christ who strengthens me."; [a.] Camilla, GA

STAFFORD, DONNIE LEE
[b.] February 11, 1954, Cardwell, MI; [p.] James and Inez Johnson; [ch.] Jaime Lynn Stafford; [ed.] Chaffee High School, Chaffee, Missouri; [memb.] Planetary Society; [pers.] Man has been chosen as caretaker of this planet. That is why we are here. If we neglect our responsibilities to the earth, then it will surely be our down fall.; [a.] Dallastown, PA

STANTON, KIM
[b.] January 3, 1980, Hunt, NY; [p.] Gary and Debbie Stanton; [ed.] Northport High; [hon.] School Papers; [a.] East Northport, NY

STARR, MARY ANN
[pen.] Mary Ann Starr; [b.] July 14, 1978, Fairmont, WV; [p.] John Starr, Rebecca Starr; [ed.] North Marion High School; [occ.] Student; [memb.] Alpha Beta Gamma, Interact, Key Club, Leo Club and College Prep. also Mu Alpha Theta; [hon.] Attended 1995 Rhododendron Girls State, Honor Student, and nominated for the National Youth Leadership Forum of Medicine; [oth. writ.] Several poems published in school newspaper.; [a.] Worthington, WV

STEELE, ANN
[b.] Canada; [p.] Dr. Josephus and Beryl Calarco; [m.] Dr. Peter Steele, December 7, 1985; [ch.] Jasmine and Zachary; [ed.] Brock University (Canada), Walden (U.S.A.); [occ.] Scientist all Children's Hospital, Florida; [memb.] International Academy of Cytology, NSH, FSH, Ducks Unlimited, Canadian Kennel Club; [hon.] International degree P.M.I.A.C., Consultation Requests - National

International, Numerous Speaking/Teaching Engagement; [oth. writ.] Numerous published scientific biomedical articles, numerous children's stories (in preparation).; [pers.] I am very moved by the bravery of the children I see everyday battling life - threatening disease. I am overcome by the bravery of parents helping their children to live, or, if the battle is lost, helping them to to die surrounded by love. These children and their parents are our true American heroes.; [a.] Seminole, FL

STEENBERGEN, ANDREW HENRY
[b.] February 13, 1930, Franklin, NH; [m.] Mary V. Steenbergen, July 6, 1984; [ed.] B.ED - M.ED. Keene State College, Keene, N.H., B.ED - 1960, M.ED - 1970; [occ.] Retired; [memb.] AARP - N.H. Writers and Publishers Project Concord SPCA - Concord, N.H.; [oth. writ.] "Stories and human from Northern New England." "Growing up in Northern New England" - "Cousin Andy Sez:" "Preludes and poetry" and "By the old Harry - and Andy."; [pers.] I write and self publish poetry and humorous short stories based on my life and incidents regarding Northern New Englander's I've known. Enjoy downeast humor, Robert Frost - Robert Service poetry.; [a.] Concord, NH

STEIDLEY, T. W.
[b.] February 12, 1920, Claremore, OK; [p.] Mr. and Mrs. J. D. Steidley; [m.] Ruth Steidley, September 4, 1954; [ch.] 1 son and 1 daughter; [ed.] Some High School and Investing Corespondency Course; [occ.] Retired from American Airlines after 32 1/2 years; [hon.] No honors just a lot of hard work. Oh! There is one honor. I love to honor my Lord and Savior Jesus Christ, and I believe He is coming soon; [oth. writ.] A few poems.; [pers.] Persistence attempt the end, and never stand to doubt, nothing's so hard but search will find it out.; [a.] Chelsea, OK

STENIS, ROWENA S.
[b.] September 27, 1922, Norman, OK; [p.] Matthew Irving and Hazeline Ingram Smith; [m.] Tom B. Stenis, September 22, 1943; [ch.] Melody Phillips, Vaughn Stenis, Bonnie Walvoord, Wayne Stenis; [ed.] Austin High, University of Texas (B. Music) Texas Tech University (M. Educ.); [occ.] Retired Music Teacher; [memb.] Baptist Church, Church Orchestra, Austin Civic Orchestra, Wednesday Morn. Music Club, Mu Phi Epsilon, Grace Notes String Quartet; [hon.] Nat'l Honor Society, Dean's List, Mu Phi Epsilon, Phi Kappa Phi, Poetry chosen for Audio-Taping; [oth. writ.] Poems, many local publications, poems in 4 anthologies, "Reflections, a Book of Poetry" (1994).; [pers.] God loves us, is Maker of all, Master of all and in control. He is good.; [a.] Austin, TX

STEPHENS, DEBRA PATRICIA
[b.] May 13, 1965, Trinidad, WI; [p.] Alfred and Phyllis Stephens; [ed.] Diego Martin Junior Secondary, Trinidad Mucurapo Senior Comprehensive, Trinidad Borough Manhattan Community College, N.Y.; [oth. writ.] Several other poems written and exchanged between my sister and myself for personal pleasure.; [pers.] I migrated to the US more than a decade ago, leaving all immediate family behind. America has been a challenge for me, but I've survived I was inspired to write my poem Ode to Niqel, because though I never knew him, loosing him, hurt just the same...; [a.] Jersey City Heights, NJ

STEPHENS, JOHN M.
[b.] June 29, 1967, Lakewood, CA; [p.] Diane Stephens; [ed.] Woodrow Wilson High School; [memb.] Alcoholics Anonymous; [pers.] I just wish to give away what was so freely given to me.; [a.] Lakewood, CA

STEWART, MANDY
[b.] May 8, 1995, Medina, OH; [p.] Robert Stewart, Donna Stewart; [ed.] Cloverleaf High School Lodi OH; [occ.] Prep Cook at Main street Care in Medina OH; [memb.] I am a Member of SADD at my High School; [oth. writ.] I have wrote several poems that were never published.; [pers.] I just write poems when I'm depressed and it was just a spur of the moment thing. I can't believe something I wrote could go this far, Thank you!!; [a.] Chippewa, OH

STEWART, SHERRY A.
[pen.] Sas; [b.] July 9, 1954, Denver, CO; [p.] Ray N. Hindman, Virginia A. Hindman; [m.] Donald E. Stewart, August 3, 1982; [ch.] Derik Ray Stewart; [ed.] Alameda High, studied at Metropolitan State College, Adult and Continuing Education Center; [occ.] Half-day Secretary, Lakewood High School, Lakewood, Colorado; [memb.] Humane Society of the United States, PETA (People for the Ethical Treatment of Animals); [oth. writ.] Articles for The Rocky Mountain News, poems and short stories for local school newspapers, short story submitted to the Institute of Children's Literature.; [pers.] Fairness and justice for everyone. Environmental issues, political statements as well as a strong sense of right and wrong can be seen in much of my writings and lifestyle. I am greatly influenced by an obscure unrecognized poet of the 20th century, James Douglas Morrison.; [a.] Lakewood, CO

STILL, KEVIN
[pen.] Kevin Still; [b.] September 28, 1977, El Dorado, AR; [p.] Allin Still, Sandra Still; [ed.] El Dorado High School; [occ.] Currently a Student at Ouachita Baptist University in Arkadelphia, AR; [memb.] Immanuel Baptist Church; [oth. writ.] Personal Column in High School Newspaper, Number of Poems Published in Local Publications.; [pers.] If mere words on the lips of God could speak all of creation into being, imagine the revival in our souls that could happen if we simply listened to his every word and recorded the passion of the author of our faith. Bleed me through ink, Lord, and set me free.; [a.] El Dorado, AR

STILLWELL, MEGAN J.
[b.] December 4, 1979, Lebanon, IN; [p.] Ronald and Rowena Osborne; [ed.] I am currently attending San Saba High School, San Saba, TX. I previously attended Boose High School, Lebanon, IN; [memb.] Central Baptist Church Youth Department, Air Force Junior Reserved Officers Training Corps of Abilene High School, Abilene, TX (A.F.J.R.O.T.C.); [hon.] Academic Award in R.O.T.C., promoted to Airmen in R.O.T.C., given Color Guard and Saber Team Recognition; [oth. writ.] "Forgiveness Is Divine," "Young Love" "Yancy" "Cheater," "My Solace," "My Mother" and many, many others.; [pers.] I believe we must learn from our relationships with friends, boy or girl, and draw something from each one to use later in life. No matter how small it may seem, the little somethings may prove useful later on in life.; [a.] San Saba, TX

STINGL, MONIKA
[b.] May 28, 1945, Germany, Kitzingen; [m.] Charles Stingl; [ch.] Katrine - Michelle; [ed.] High School - Germany Australia Naturapathic School - University of Science and Philosophy - College of Life Science; [occ.] Homemaker; [memb.] Poet's Guild; [oth. writ.] "He is with Me" Song on record - American Artists Custom Records "Thoughts!" By Monika Wolter, (Book in process), "Chronicle of a Survivor".; [pers.] My most valuable, cherished accomplishment is finding the courage to transform myself from a "Victim" of sexual child abuse to a "Survivor!" I hope my writings will offer helpful insights to others attempting this Journey thereby creating benefits similar to those that I have been assisted by through the thoughtful words of others.; [a.] Johnson Creek, WI

STOLL, JEREMY
[b.] July 14, 1982, Ypsilanti, MI; [p.] Charles L. Stoll, Anne M. Stoll; [ed.] St. John Elementary School; [pers.] I think R.E.M. Soul Asylum, and The Violent Femmes are the coolest bands in the world. Also, the X-men are awesome. Plus, school is boring and Shakespeare is cool. And I'm 13 yrs. old.; [a.] Willis, MI

STOLL JR., DONALD D.
[b.] March 26, 1966, Lakewood, OH; [p.] Donald D. and Frances J.; [ch.] Ryan D.; [ed.] Lakewood High; [occ.] Office Manager, Nationwide Auto Glass; [pers.] Love is endless when it's given and then returned.; [a.] Lakewood, OH

STORM, JEFFREY
[pen.] That's A.; [ed.] Catholic Punishment, and Public Harassment High, Life is Educational; [occ.] Student; [hon.] Eagle Scout, Emily Dickinson Bronze Award; [oth. writ.] Be Stormfront (unpublished) Be Archives (unpublished).; [pers.] Live, Laugh, Love That's all there is, everything else and just details.

STORY, ELVERA
[ch.] Valerie, Audrey, Jennifer; [occ.] Retired Social Worker; [memb.] Member of Tabernacle Missionary Baptist Church, Dr. Frederick G. Sampson, Pastor; [pers.] My poem is dedicated to my daughters, and their children, whom I love dearly. Each day, I hope to bring some joy to others. If only a kind word or a smile. Perhaps a giggle from someone who has forgotten how to laugh. I wish for world peace. It won't happen overnight. But we start by loving and respecting, ourselves and others. With lots of prayer, and God's blessings, my wish will someday be granted.; [a.] Detroit, MI

STORY, JOHN R.
[b.] February 9, 1959, Greenville, TN; [p.] Peter Dykstra, Marie Dykstra; [m.] Nancy Story, December 1, 1984; [ch.] Ashley, Kelly, Erica; [ed.] Hillsborough Community College, Tampa, FL; [oth. writ.] Several other unpublished poems and thoughts.; [pers.] My writings are aimed at stirring emotions and evoking thoughts about life, death and the world in which we live.; [a.] Tampa, FL

STOVALL, CHARLES
[b.] October 21, 1959, Hazlehurst, MS; [p.] Artice Murray; [m.] Sindy Stovall, April 7, 1979; [ch.] Ta Shara Stovall; [ed.] Crystal Springs High School in Crystal Springs, MS. Hinds Jr., College; [occ.] Tool Room Dept. of CSMI of Hot Springs, AR; [memb.] Pentecostal Assemblies of the World, Bethlehem Temple Church of Hot Springs AR; [hon.] Received Honorable Mentions for a Poem and several Songs from Music City Song Festival of Nashville, TN; [oth. writ.] I am now in the process of writing a book. (You do not have to print this statement in the biography if you wish not to).; [pers.] I thank God for the gift to both write and sing and hope that it can be shared in a positive way throughout the world.; [a.] Hot Springs, AR

STRAWDER, WANDA LITTLE
[pen.] Wanda Little; [b.] November 9, 1938, Lakeland, FL; [p.] Grady and Nina; [m.] Buddie, December 22, 1958; [ch.] Dana, Tonya, Damita, Velvet, Seth; [ed.] High School, G.E.D. some college, in Physiology; [occ.] School Food Service Winn Dixie Cashier; [memb.] School Food Asst.; [hon.] The only Honors are my Children and Grandchildren; [oth. writ.] None in publish. But I have alot that I have finished and have yet to finish. When I retire.; [pers.] I love to write about my poor past childhood and my children and grand children play a large influence in my writings.; [a.] Lakeland, FL

STRAWN, EVELYN L.
[b.] May 5, 1922, Papillion, NE; [ed.] Papillion High, Papillion, Nebraska, attended Nebraska Wesleyan, received Bachelor of Arts, University of Nebraska; [pers.] My poetry is an endeavor, by a great-grandmother, to share her life experiences with her descendants and other persons who may be interested.; [a.] El Paso, TX

STRECKER, SARA
[b.] May 31, 1984, Bristol; [p.] Elaine and Jon Strecker; [ed.] I am in the 6th grade at Highcrest School in Wethersfield, CT; [occ.] Student; [memb.] St. Pauls Lutheran Church, and Depalma's ma's Action Karate; [pers.] When I get out of school I would like to be a paleontologist, study marine no life or write books.; [a.] Wethersfield, CT

STREET, SEMINOLE
[b.] July 11, 1954, Fairhope, AL; [p.] John H. White; [ch.] Jack Wester, Omega Wester, Steven Street, Winston Street; [ed.] Fairhope High School, South Alabama Skill Center; [occ.] Office Administrator (WW II Historical Research); [memb.] Fairhope Church of Christ; [oth. writ.] Fairhope Church of Christ's Bulletin.; [pers.] Omega was killed in 1991. My faith in God, my writing and my friends gave me the strength to cope with my daughter's death. "I can do all things through Christ which strong theneth me." Phil 4:13.; [a.] Fairhope, AL

STRUPP, JANET KAYE
[pen.] Jesse Ryan; [b.] April 19, 1974, Bryan, OH; [p.] Henry and Doris Strupp; [m.] James; [ch.] James, Erik, Jared; [ed.] B.A. in Sociology and Environmental Studies Psy.D. in Clinical Psychology; [occ.] Clinical Psychologist and Art Gallery Director; [memb.] Various Psychological Association, Local, National, and International Animal Groups; [hon.] Scharlarship, Articles and Poetry Published in Newspaper, Doctoral Dissertation Published in "American Psychologist," Poetry Published by the National Library of Poetry; [oth. writ.] Working on writing more poems, children's books, and an Autobiography.; [pers.] A passage from the Tao of pooh - "Within each of us is an owl, a Rabbit, an Eeyore, and a pooh. For too long, we have chosen the way of owl and Rabbit. Now, like eeyore, we complain about the results. But that accomplishes nothing. If we are smart, we will choose the way of pooh. As if from far away, it calls to us with the voice of a child's mind. It may be hard to hear at times, but it is important just the same, because without it, we will never find our way through the forest."; [a.] Dayton, OH

SUSEDIK, KIM
[b.] March 5, 1973, Spokane, WA; [p.] Frank and Debbie Susedik; [ed.] West Valley High, Eastern Washington University; [pers.] I owe my inspiration to good friends, a loving family, and amazing teacher. Special thanks to Mom and Dad, Grama and Grampa, Cindy, Kim, and Mike. And my greatest thanks to Mary Ann Waters - my teacher. I can't say thank you enough.; [a.] Spokane, WA

SUTTERFIELD, DORABETH
[pen.] Dorabeth Dunning Sutterfield; [b.] January 20, 1947, Kokomo, IN; [p.] Roy and Ethel Dunning; [m.] Clifford L. Sutterfield, August 9, 1964; [ch.] Debora, Constance, Edward; [ed.] Pacific High; [occ.] Deputy Clerk, Contra Costa; [oth. writ.] Poems published in newspaper, and in world poetry contest.; [pers.] Praise the Lord always. Call upon his name and he is faithful to answer.; [a.] Antioch, CA

SWAGLER, KATIE
[b.] June 30, 1985, Dearborn, MI; [p.] Linda and Spence; [ed.] 5th Grade, Henry Ford Elementary School Dearborn - MI; [memb.] Dance Class, Ballet, Tap, Jazz, Play Cello School Orchestra, Future Problem Solvers, Computer Club, Gifted and Talented Program; [hon.] Honor Roll, Student of the Month, Science Fair, Young Authors; [a.] Dearborn, MI

SWEENEY, MICHAEL
[b.] November 24, 1981, Jersey City, NJ; [p.] Joseph and Michele Sweeney; [ed.] Currently a Freshman at Dickinson High School in Jersey City NJ

SWIDWA, MARTIN EDWARD
[b.] Grand Rapids, MI; [p.] Edward and Joan Swidwa; [m.] Debra Swidwa, February 24, 1984; [ch.] Phillip (one son), Scott and Chuck (two step-son); [oth. writ.] An extensive and varied body of yet to be published work.; [pers.] Live in the moment and roll with the punches. You cannot change the wind, but you can trim the sails.; [a.] Walker, MI

TABIOS, EILEEN
[b.] 1960, Philippines; [p.] Filamore Tabios Sr., Beatriz Tabios; [ed.] Barnard College, New York University Graduate School of Business; [occ.] Wrestling with a novel; [oth. writ.] Other poems and short stories in a number of literary journals and anthologies.; [pers.] With all due respect to Robert Frost who said, "Writing free verse is like playing tennis with the net down", it's not easy to hit a winning point over the net when there is no net.; [a.] New York City, NY

TALLMAN, EVELYN
[b.] November 13, 1922, South Westerlo, NY; [p.] Mrs. Hazel Mabie; [m.] Deceased, January 23, 1940; [ch.] One; [ed.] Greenville Central High School, National Baking School; [occ.] Retired and write; [memb.] Social Service by Albany County, Social Security Benefits; [hon.] Golden Poetry Gram, World of Poetry; [oth. writ.] International Society of Poets

TANCREDI, DAVID
[pen.] David Tancredi; [b.] October 4, 1956, Detroit, MI; [m.] Roxanne, June 25, 1976; [ch.] Christopher, Joseph, Stephen; [ed.] A.A.S., Law Enforcement Administration, Summa Cum Laude; [occ.] Administrator, Education Field; [hon.] National Recognition for Work in Behavior Management by the United States Department of Labor/Office of Job Corps., Honors Graduate, Summa Cum Laude; [oth. writ.] Co-Author: Technical Assistance Guide - "Behavior Management for the Center Standards Officer and all other staff," Office of Jobcorps, unpublished Children's Stories, Poetry Collection; [pers.] I have been writing since high school, most often poetry, but I have also penned some short stories. A good deal of my writing reflects my experience with our future, our youths.; [a.] Detroit, MI

TANKERSLEY, KRISTY ANN
[b.] January 5, 1984, Watsonville, CA; [p.] Robert Tankersley, Judy Tankersley; [ed.] San Juan Middle School; [occ.] Student; [memb.] Girl Scouts of America; [hon.] 3rd place in San Benito County Science Fair - 1993, 1st place in Judith Whitehead Writing Contest for Fourth Grade 1993, San Juan Elementary School, 1st place over all in Judith Whitehead Writing Contest - 1993, San Juan Elementary School, Honor Roll 4th and 5th grade - 1993, 1994, Principal's Honor Roll 5th and 5th grade - 1994, 1995; [pers.] I think my poem reflects what everyone in the world is wishing for.; [a.] San Juan Bautista, CA

TANZYMORE, SHANE
[pen.] Shayne Tanzymore, Tyggyrr; [b.] October 9, 1973, Baltimore, MD; [p.] Eugene Tanzymore Jr., Harriet Thomas; [ed.] St. Paul's School For Boys, Brooklandville, MD, Bucknell University, Lewisburg, Penna; [occ.] Sales Leader, J. Baker Inc.; [hon.] Nothing of note; [oth. writ.] Several articles for The Bucknellian, The Red Wheelbarrow and The Catalyst.; [pers.] Mothers are the center of the world. From mother I come and to another I will go.; [a.] Lansdowne, PA

TAPP, ROBBRINA
[pen.] Robbi; [b.] August 22, 1979, Vineland, NJ; [p.] Gloria and Robert Tapp; [ed.] Student Hammonton High School; [hon.] 1st place winner for Bookmarker Contest, Hammonton/Atlantic County Library; [a.] Hammonton, NJ

TAYLOR, ANDREA M.
[pen.] Andrea M. Paglia; [b.] July 10, 1950, Chelsea, MA; [p.] Gerald and Gladys Bradley; [m.] Robert W. Taylor; [ch.] The late Terrance R., Andrew D., Victoria A. and Regina M. Paglia; [ed.] Tewksbury Mem H.S., Tewksbury Hospital Sch. Of Nursing; [occ.] "Starving Artist", self employed writer; [memb.] Human Race, Standing is Questionable at times, other Pet Associations; [hon.] "Recognition of Excellence", state of MA Award for Parents Newsletter, The Shawsheen Bridge; [oth. writ.] Where Are We Going? Walk This Way, A Promise To Keep, The Advent of Spring, Most often - The Monthly Bills!; [pers.] To be as good as your word is sometimes at the hands of an editor, but relative to life in context.

TAYLOR, DEBORAH
[pen.] D. L. Taylor; [b.] November 9, 1953, Maryville, IN; [p.] Lawrence and Lelon Justice; [m.] Dwight L. Taylor, October 10, 1981; [ch.] Will, Aimee, Landon; [occ.] Accounting Dept. of Taylor, Turner and Hartsfield; [memb.] First Christian Church of Cumming; [oth. writ.] Several other poems, the majority of which are religious in theme.; [pers.] I strive to reflect the feelings we have deep inside on our lifes, loves and especially our spirituality.; [a.] Cumming, GA

TAYLOR, MARJORIE
[pen.] Marjorie Moss Taylor; [b.] December 26, 1941, Highland Park, MI; [p.] Leona and Taylor Moss; [m.] Robert E. Taylor, March 16, 1958; [ch.] Paul, Diane, Vicky, Roberta; [ed.] High School and the hard knots of life.; [occ.] Free Lance Writer - Window Art; [memb.] U.S. Citizen by birth. The National Poetry Society, The International Poetry Society, Community Volunteer; [hon.] The National Poetry Society Editors Choice - Sound of Poetry, The International Poetry Society; [oth. writ.] Cupids Umbrella, The Birth of a Tree, Winter Tulips Started, maybe 4 lines only, White Capped Mountains; [pers.] I thank the Creator everyday, every way. And when God wills the wind - to steal my hat - it only reminds me, of all the loving second chance.; [a.] Aurora, IL

TAYLOR, MARY ELIZABETH
[b.] May 31, 1985, Everett; [p.] John and Judith Taylor; [ed.] Elementary; [occ.] Student; [a.] Anacortes, WA

TAYLOR, TONYA
[b.] October 1, 1968, Hammond, LA; [p.] Errol and Katie Hano; [m.] Lee A. Taylor, February 15, 1992; [ch.] Kacy Lee Taylor; [ed.] Doyle High, Baton Rouge School of Computers; [occ.] Bus Driver; [memb.] Springville Baptist Church; [hon.] Having been selected for the Rainbows End; [oth. writ.] Numerous poems one of which was published in the church newsletter.; [pers.] I use my inner fears and my Spiritual feelings to express certain thoughts of love and kindness of the world we live in.; [a.] Livingston, LA

TELIKEPALLI, ANIL
[pen.] Anil; [b.] August 4, 1973, Bhimavaram, India; [p.] Ratnavathi and Rahakrishna; [ed.] St. Anthony's High, St. Mary's Jr. College, Osmania University - all in India, University of Kentucky; [occ.] Graduate Student, University of Kentucky, Application Engineer, Xilinnx Inc.; [memb.] Institution of Engineers - India, IEEE, Bay Area Telugu Association; [hon.] National Merit Scholarship, India, Science Talent Search Scholarship - India; [oth. writ.] Poems and short essays in local magazines - as also poems and articles to nurture Telugu (author's mother tongue) among American - born Indians in 'Tana Patrika', started writing poems at 9 years (of age).; [pers.] Most of my poems reflect my thoughts. I admire poets like Tennyson, Wordsworth as also modern poets like Vikram Setti.; [a.] Lexington, KY

TENER, DAVID T.
[b.] October 24, 1955, Las Vegas, NV; [m.] Tammy Tener, June 4, 1994; [ch.] Little David Anthony Tener, Rachel Marie, Valerie Christine, Jasmine Nicole; [ed.] Home Center Manager at (Handy Helper Stores); [oth. writ.] Nothing published but love to write, have many others.; [pers.] I wish to thank my wife and all the love she's given. She truly is my inspiration. I'm a romantic and idealistic person. We all need to look harder at taking time to do our favorite thing, and smell the roses.; [a.] Reno, NV

TERPKO, JOHN E.
[pen.] JT; [b.] August 8, 1960, Jeannette, PA; [p.] John J. Terpko, Donna M. Schultz; [m.] Mary Kathryn McCarthy, April 12, 1996; [occ.] Welfare Caseworker, Reservist, United States Air Force; [memb.] Air Force Sergeants Association, Pennsylvania Social Services Union; [oth. writ.] Various Unpublished Poems; [pers.] Emotion needs not only felt - but, expressed.; [a.] Harrison City, PA

TERRELL, JAMIE LYNNE RHOADS
[pen.] Jamie Lynne Rhoads; [b.] April 25, 1964, Grove City, PA; [p.] John and Carol Filer; [m.] Rick Lee Terrell, May 12, 1988; [ch.] Jessica Lynne, Alexander Jon; [ed.] Grove City High School; [oth. writ.] Many poems and childrens stories, not yet published; [pers.] I strive to educate my children, myself and others through my writing. "I believe poetry are windows to knowledge." I have been greatly encouraged and inspired by my friend "Allison A. Cozzolino Self." "Kimberly D. Rhoads Payne", The Meaning Of "Sister."; [a.] Groton, CT

TERRY, CHRISTINE
[b.] September 27, 1976; [p.] Louis and Patricia Terry; [ed.] I attended High School at West Florence High, my favorite high school of all, and South Florence High; [occ.] I am attempting to become a novelist; [oth. writ.] I have just completed another poem titled "The Mirror World" and I am in the middle of a novel; [pers.] I've come to the conclusion that writing is a method of drawing, by using words and punctuations to paint a picture.; [a.] Florence, SC

TERRY, JESSICA
[pen.] Jessica Terry; [b.] December 7, 1978, Durham, NC; [p.] Al and Mary Terry; [ed.] Hillandale Elementary, Chewning and Stanford Jr. High, presently attending Orange High; [occ.] Student; [memb.] Duke Hospital Junior Volunteer 4 years; [hon.] Durham County, Spring Art exhibit, J.V. cheer leading - certificate of Outstanding Achievement, Volleyball Intramural Tournament-2nd place holder, perfect attendance award 1991, A/B Honor Roll, Good Citizenship award, Outstanding Achievement award in 4 way test Essay Contest; [pers.] Love to model, dance, smile, dress up, date, visit friends, ice skate and just life itself.; [a.] Hillsborough, NC

TERRY, LA VERTA L.
[b.] November 10, 1926, Brazil, IN; [p.] William and Mary Buckner; [m.] Henry David Terry (dec); [ch.]

H. David, Jr., Kay Ellen, Gwen Anne (dec); [ed.] Southern Christian (Miss.) Jr. Coll., Jarvis Christian (Tex), B.A. Sociology Indiana University (Bloomington), Secondary Teaching Certification; [occ.] Retired (Higher Education Administration); [memb.] NAACP, Alpha Kappa Alpha, Inc. First United Methodist Church Liturgical Arts and Membership Committees, Neal-Marshall Alumni Assoc. (Ind Univ.); [hon.] Lifetime membership in MAEDPP, Scholarship in my name, I-MAEDPP, Cite in Congressional Record and read on the floor of Congress by Senator Richard Lugar, Negro History Month Award, and Neal-Marshall Alumni Award, Mid America Educational Opportunity Program Personnel; [oth. writ.] Several unpublished poems; [pers.] I have been greatly inspired by a line from one of my father's poems. "It seems to me that life is just a symphony we live, a consonance of both the sun and rain."; [a.] Bloomington, IN

THOMAS, ARTHUR
[b.] July 27, 1966, Lompoc, CA; [ch.] Avery Gene-Thomas, Amanda Katie; [ed.] Lompoc Senior High - 1994; [occ.] Able-bodied Seaman U.S. Merchant Mariner; [memb.] Honorable Member of the "Too Much Fun Club".; [oth. writ.] "The Waves of Wind" - an un-published short story and other un-published poems.; [pers.] Dedicated in loving memory of my grandfather, Leonard Wellemeyer. A man of wisdom, honesty, knowledge. God be with him.; [a.] Lompoc, CA

THOMAS, ESTHER M.
[b.] October 16, 1945, San Diego, CA; [p.] Merton Alfred Thomas, Nellie Lyda (Von Pilz) Thomas; [ed.] A.A., Grossmont College, 1966, B.A., San Diego State University, 1969, M.A., University of Redlands 1977, Redlands, CA; [occ.] Educator; [memb.] U.S. Senatorial Club, Washington, D.C., 1984, San Diego, Rep. Party, 1995, Mem. Health Articulation Com. Project AIDS, Cajon Valley Union School Distict 1988, Charter Member Marine Corps Museum, San Diego, CA; [hon.] Recipient Outstanding Service Award P.T.A., 1972-1974, Recognized in "Hats Off To Teachers", San Diego Bd. Edn., 1989; [oth. writ.] Songwriter: "Born To Win", "Daniel's Prayer", Ame Record, Hollywood, CA, 1996, "Old Glory", "Never Trouble, Trouble", HillTop Records, Hollywood, CA, 1996, "Clear The Path Lord", "In The Volume Of The Book", "Home Is Where The Heart Is", Hollywood Artists, Hollywood, CA 1996; [a.] Lakeside, CA

THOMAS, PAULA Y.
[b.] November 22, 1967, New Jersey; [p.] Samuel and Shirley McDonald; [m.] Dennis Thomas, April 27, 1991; [ch.] Tracia, Shantell, Cierra, Samantha; [ed.] Peterson Catholic, High School, Katherine Gibbs Business Academy; [occ.] Secretary; [memb.] Mount Zion Baptist Church, Passaic, NJ; [oth. writ.] 1 poem-After the Storm, 1 poem - "Mists of Enchantment"; [pers.] When God gives you a special talent, share it with the world or you'll wake up one day and that talent will be gone. The world is a beautiful place, enjoy it with everything you have and everything you are.; [a.] Peterson, NJ

THOMAS, SHANNON
[b.] July 13, 1975, Janesville, WS; [p.] Pam and Scott Filipek (stepfather), and Gary Thomas; [ed.] 1994 Graduate, Sturgeon Bay H.S., Sturgeon Bay,

Wisc., received Certified Nursing Asst. Certification, July, 1994; [occ.] Certified Nursing Assistant; [memb.] National Registry of Nursing Assistants; [pers.] I live on the Door Peninsula in a small town. My family and friends are nearby. It is here that I write about relationships and how they have personally affected me.; [a.] Sturgeon Bay, WS

THOMPSON, ALICE L.
[pen.] Luka; [b.] January 12, 1943, Mesa, AZ; [oth. writ.] "Meditation On Stations Of The Cross", devotional booklet, articles in local newspapers and church newsletters.; [pers.] I want to return to the universal community of readers and writers. A portion of what they have given me.; [a.] Irving, TX

THOMPSON, BONNIE L.
[pen.] Bonnie L. Thompson; [b.] July 16, 1967, New London, CT; [p.] Mr. and Mrs. Thomas Bump; [oth. writ.] Published in the book Great Poems of Our Time; [pers.] I have been writing since I was a young children and have been greatly influenced by authors such as Walt Whitman and Robert Frost. I believe writing is a positive form of stress relief as well as an emotional and spiritual outlet.; [a.] Plantation, FL

THOMPSON, EILEEN
[b.] August 21, 1957, Pottsville, PA; [p.] Myrtle and Thomas Drobnick; [m.] D. Dave Thompson, June 15, 1994; [ch.] Kim, Michael, Bryan, Son in Law Scott Zimmerman; [occ.] Co-owner of Produce Business - D&A Produce; [memb.] Welcome - United Methodist Church, Landingville, PA; [pers.] First contest ever entered. I like to dabble in all areas of arts and crafts. And am proud to be a part of this publication.; [a.] Orwigsburg, PA

THOMPSON, LORETTA
[b.] December 25, 1937, Wall, SD; [p.] Pearl and Geo Thompson; [ed.] Lenox IA High, NW Missouri State Univ.; [occ.] Training Department Coordinator; [pers.] This poem came to me in the middle of a workday.; [a.] Davenport, IA

THOMPSON, MANDI
[pen.] IviRae; [b.] December 13, 1978, Red Bank, NJ; [p.] Tami Thompson-Ryan; [ed.] South Fork High, Stuart, FL; [occ.] Student; [pers.] I have found poetry, the most beautiful form of communication, to be the only true way I can express my feelings. Laugh or cry, it is all in the way you look at it.; [a.] Palm City, FL

THOMPSON, MATT
[pen.] Young blood; [b.] July 30, 1973; [p.] Margie, Roger; [ed.] Springville High School; [oth. writ.] "Moonlight Passion", "Passion", "Inspire", are a few of my favorite writings I have created; [pers.] I write about my friends around me or about my faith. I am heavily influenced by the music of Michael Sweet.; [a.] Springville, IA

THOMPSON, MELODIE LYNN CLARK
[b.] August 16, 1959, Brockton, MA; [p.] Jack Clark, Ella Clark; [m.] Stanley Thompson, December 20, 1980; [ch.] Rhema Joy, Micah Josiah; [ed.] Peru Central H.S., Wheaton College - B.A. in Education; [occ.] Substitute Teacher, Rhode Island School for the Deaf; [hon.] Newport Writers' Conference Literary Competition, 2nd Place Award; [oth. writ.] Poetry in Newport Life Magazine, essays in local

academic and religious publications; [pers.] Life to me has always been a dance of words and images, a constantly moving, changing picture poem. It is an honor and a blessing from my Heavenly Father each time I have an opportunity to share, through written words, this pulse of my heart.; [a.] Cranston, RI

THOMSEN, LINDA
[pen.] Linda Thomsen; [b.] November 10, 1944, Lima, OH; [p.] Stanley Taylor, Kathryn Taylor; [m.] Alan Thomsen, July 7, 1984; [ch.] Don Kirtland, Mike Kirtland, Kim Thomsen, Tom Thomsen; [ed.] Lima Sr. High, Santa Clara College, San Jose City College; [occ.] Accounting Manager at Pierre Area Chamber of Commerce; [memb.] United Church of Christ Women's Fellowship, Beta Sigma Phi, P.E.D.; [hon.] Dean's List at San Jose City College; [oth. writ.] Several poems for personal cards and letters.; [pers.] Somewhere within me is a poet. A poet whose heart and soul long to reflect a bit of life's beauty to the world.; [a.] Pierre, SD

THURBER, DANIEL M.
[b.] November 25, 1969, Hanover, West Germany; [p.] David Thurber, Sandy Thurber; [ch.] Steven Thurber; [ed.] Southside High School; [pers.] I wrote this poem for a very special person to me, Jana Eisenhut, for no child should be without a mother.; [a.] Fort Wayne, IN

TIKASINGH, JACQLYN SARIKA
[pen.] Jacqui; [b.] May 21, 1995, Trinidad W Indies; [p.] Ruth and Ray Tikasingh, brother-Luke; [ed.] Presently 9th grader-Mast Academy Senior High, (Maritime and Science Technology School), Key Biscayne, Florida., Middle School-John F. Kennedy, NMB, Florida; [occ.] Student; [memb.] National Junior Honor Society, Future Homemakers of America, J.R.O.T.C (United States Coast Guard); [hon.] (USAA) United States achievement academy National English award (1995), (USAA) United States achievement academy all scholar award (1995)., Superior Honor roll award (JFK Middle School), National Junior Honor Society perfect attendance award, Citizenship award, (1st prize) Science Fair award, 6th grade Elem. School); [pers.] I hope to write a book someday that will be published. I dream of being a famous writer.; [a.] North Miami Beach, FL

TIMLEY, EUNICE
[b.] November 4, 1964, Newark, NJ; [p.] Gloria Timley, Charles Timley; [ch.] Vernon Green, Amy Timley; [ed.] Vailsburg High, Rutgers Technical Training; [occ.] Copy Technician; [oth. writ.] I have several other writings but, none published at this time.; [pers.] I strive to reflect the desires, goals, dreams, and tribulations of the everyday people of the world. I have been influenced by great writers such as Dick Gregory, Claude, McCay, Terry McMillian, and James Baldwin. My inspiration however, comes from God.; [a.] Newark, NJ

TITUS, RON
[b.] February 16, 1968, Covina, CA; [p.] Richard E. Titus, Nancy L. Titus; [ed.] B.S. Business Admin., Calif., St. Polytechnic Univ., Pomona; [occ.] Bookkeeper, Mt. San Antonio College, Walnut, CA; [memb.] National Wildlife Federation, Defenders Of Wildlife, Int'l. Society of Poets; [oth. writ.] Castles in the Sky published in Sea of Treasures and

Moonlight Serenade in Best Poems of 1996 from The National Library of Poetry.; [pers.] A hope is for my writings to evoke images that stir the mind and touch the heart.; [a.] Pomona, CA

TJELTA, MARK G.
[b.] July 21, 1960, Storm Lake, IA; [p.] Lars and Fran Tjelta; [m.] Deborah Tjelta, October 7, 1983; [ch.] Zachary Thomas Tjelta; [ed.] Associates Degree - Des Moines Are Community College, Bachelors Degree - Upper Iowa University; [occ.] Project and Account Specialist, The Principal Financial Group; [memb.] Project Management Institute, FLMI Society of Greater Des Moines, Ankeny Evangelical Free Church.; [hon.] Graduated Cum Laude from Upper Iowa University.; [pers.] Instead of asking, "Why me?", ask yourself, "Why NOT me?"; [a.] Ankeny, IA

TODD SR., BILLY J.
[b.] October 29, 1962, Kansas City, MO; [p.] Norma J. and Claudy D. Todd; [m.] Carolyn S. Todd, July 19, 1985; [ch.] Damein, Whitney, Billy J. Todd Sr.; [ed.] Blevins High, Home of the Hornets; [occ.] Potlatch Corp.; [memb.] Masonic Lodge, Ward Chapel Church; [oth. writ.] Several other poems none of which has been published. My own work!; [pers.] My grandmother loved poems. Essie G. Scott, when I am writing sometimes I get a spiritual feeling.

TORRES, CARMEN LOPEZ
[b.] November 8, 1950, San Francisco, CA; [p.] Raul and Virginia Lopez; [m.] Jessie Torres, December 2, 1977; [ch.] Robert and Virginia; [ed.] Mission High, S.F. Calif.; [occ.] Writing, currently working on a second novel; [oth. writ.] Novel "Forever Ours"; [pers.] I hope my poems inspire goodness in Life and Humanity.; [a.] San Lorenzo, CA

TORRES, JOSE A.
[pen.] Jacosta, Jose Maria; [b.] December 13, 1925, Martindale, TX; [ed.] PhD. in Education, Pioneered in ESL—Eng. as a 2nd Language; [occ.] Extraordinary Minister, Archdiocese of San Antonio, Professed in the Secular Franciscan Order.; [hon.] Numerous awards. Also honored by Spanish Government for his writings during HemisFair, re: "The Contributions of Spain to the Development of the Southwest U.S.A."; [oth. writ.] Free lance writer and columnist. Authored several pedagogical books, including Cachito Mio, A to Z Prayers, Accentuating Both Cultures, and others.; [pers.] I try to keep a constant, conscious contact or communion with the Divine presence in my neighbors of the world and in my heart.; [a.] San Antonio, TX

TREPP, ALLEN
[b.] March 14, 1977, Port Huene, ME; [p.] Lorie Elliot, Chuck Trepp; [ed.] H.S. Grad, just starting college; [occ.] Draftsman, Calamforge Corp. CA; [pers.] Up all night drowning in fears, trying to find solutions for problematic tears; [a.] Norco, CA

TRI, KHANH HA
[b.] May 8, 1977, Baclui, Viet Nam; [p.] Huynh, Lang; [ed.] Graduated from Long Beach, Polytechnic High School on June 1995. Currently attending California State University of Long Beach; [occ.] Majoring in Computer Science and minor in Mathematic; [memb.] Love physical activities,

drawings, and both reading and writing poetry. Member of the Vietnamese Club, and Badminton Club; [hon.] Principle Awards, Long Beach Unified School, District Award, High Honor Lamp of Achievement; [pers.] The mind is like the universe. You can travel as far as you and your heart wants.; [a.] Long Beach, CA

TRIMMER, LINDA M.
[b.] January 18, 1949, York, PA; [m.] Mr. Jack D. Trimmer, June 3, 1967; [ch.] Lisa A. Dennis - 26 yrs. old, Donald R. Trimmer - died 18 yrs. old; [ed.] Completed High School, Spring Grove Area High School, Spring Grove, PA 1966; [occ.] Hospitality Aide, Manor Care South Nursing Home; [memb.] 1. "The Compassionate Friends", (for bereaved parents), were chapter leaders for York. 2. Patomic Applachian Trail Club; [hon.] I always got very good grades in school in writing. A's and B's but this is an honor to my children more than prizes. I had 2 poems published in our National Compassionate Friends, Newsletter out of Oak Brook, IL; [oth. writ.] Compiled a booklet on Butterfly Stories that actually happened to bereaved parents and gave them "Hope" for their children in a "New Life". It is called "Flutter-Bys", also poems published in "TCF" Newsletter; [pers.] This poem was written for both my dear children. Life is so precious and so fragile. Give your children all the "Love and Time" you can, for you will never regret time well spent.; [a.] York, PA

TROGDEN, MICKEY C.
[b.] December 10, 1937, Baxter, IA; [p.] Flossie, Loren Gearhart; [m.] Scotty Trogden, May 1, 1965; [ch.] Deborah, Jolene, Sandra, Laurel, Teresa, Casey; [occ.] Housewife; [pers.] This poem is dedicated to my sister Sally, my wonderful family and all those who made my life so rich and full, and thank you God!; [a.] Champaign, IL

TROTTER, DONIQUE KENDRA
[pen.] Doey; [b.] December 28, 1976, New Orleans, LA; [p.] Ms. Esther Trotter; [ed.] Eleanor McMain High School, Xavier University of Louisiana; [occ.] Student, Part-time Photographer at LifeTouch Studios; [memb.] Mu Alpha Theta, Bio-Medical, Honor Corp, Greater Ebenezer B.C. Choir; [hon.] National Dean's List, Bio-Medical SuperStar, National Honor Society, Who's Who Among America H.S. Students (4 yrs.) Young Authors Award; [oth. writ.] Poem published in Gestures, several published and unpublished poems and essays; [pers.] A touch of kindness goes a long way. I'm striving to make things better for Humanity by caring.; [a.] New Orleans, LA

TROYCHAK, STEPHEN
[b.] December 24, 1944, Cleveland, OH; [p.] Stephen and Marion; [m.] Carol; [ch.] Beau, Holly, Bob, Dave; [ed.] MBA, Michigan State University; [occ.] Sales Representative; [memb.] National Eagle Scout Association, Lion's Club; [hon.] Eagle Scout, Full College Scholarship at Michigan State University, Numerous Outstanding Sales Achievement Awards.; [oth. writ.] Poems and games for all occasion; [pers.] You get what you pay for. It take money to make money. You can't do it alone. God above all else.; [a.] Bloomfield Hills, MI

TRUE, VICTORIA
[b.] July 12, 1949, Minneapolis, MN; [p.] father - Pliny, grandmother - Flossy; [ed.] B.F.A. and M.S. from Mankato State University; [occ.] Artist/Writer; [pers.] A poem for Marilyn, unable to walk easily a poem for aunt Vivian, dying of cancer.; [a.] Dickinson, ND

TRUMP, CHARLES S.
[pen.] Steve Trump; [b.] March 2, 1960, Patterson, NJ; [p.] Irene Trump Mongeon; [m.] Zina Lopez-Trump, December 17, 1988; [ch.] Jared and Mariza; [ed.] Dublin High School; [occ.] U.S. Navy; [a.] Manteca, CA

TUGAOEN, JUNALIZA
[pen.] Lisa T.; [b.] February 1, 1982, Honolulu, HI; [p.] Juan And Letida Tugaoen; [ed.] St. Theresa since kindergarten will be attending high school as a freshman 1996-1997; [occ.] Student, a model, and an actress. Also a singer and a typist (for yearbook committee); [memb.] John Robert Powers Model and Talent Agency, Ruth Woodhall Talent Agency, (typist for) year book committee at school; [hon.] 1991 Little Miss Sampaguita 1st princess, 1995 Miss Teen Hawaii Filipina 3rd runner-up; [oth. writ.] Loves writing pomes at home; [pers.] I would like to become a great young well-known poet author. I want to show other teenagers that are a lot of better things to do than getting involved with gangs, drugs, and dropping out of school. To all the female teenagers who are getting pregnant at a very young age, don't waste your life.; [a.] Honolulu, HI

TURNER III, JAMES M.
[pen.] "Duke"; [b.] March 7, 1953, Warren, AK; [p.] James Turner Jr., Crvvisteen Green; [m.] Linda V. Turner, December 30, 1994; [ch.] Criscilla (17), Malaina (18); [ed.] West Division High School, Milwaukee WI. Milwaukee Area Technical College, Milwaukee Stratton Business College, U.C.L.A. Corresondence, Business Science; [occ.] Acquisition Coordinator, Human Services Triangle, Inc. Milwaukee, WI; [memb.] Disabled American Veterans Association (Viet-Nam Veteran 1970-1972 U.S. Marines). ICS, Inventors Organization. Community Activist Crime Prevention, Community Business Counsel Member. Veteran of Foreign Wars Association.; [hon.] Dean's List, Certificate of Wholesales/Retail Completion, MBA, Community Services Awards; [oth. writ.] The Tsuebnam (Man Beast), Horror Story, other poems and short stories, cartoons for children and adults.; [pers.] "Life in 1995", fading corporate profits may `drag' down stocks, afterwards.... your socks, your self esteem, and maybe your lively hood. But never your sense of humor!; [a.] Milwaukee, WI

TURSE, ANDREW
[b.] November 8, 1974, Denville, NJ; [p.] Thomas and Jean Turse; [ed.] Currently attending Rutgers University; [occ.] Student; [memb.] Tau Kappa Epsilon Fraternity; [a.] Denville, NJ

TYLER, THOMAS S.
[b.] April 5, 1964, Cleveland, OH; [p.] Paul and Barbara Tyler; [ch.] Nicolas Tyler; [ed.] Bachelor of Arts in History from Bowling Green State University, Bowling Green State University, Bowling Green, Ohio, Juris Doctor from Cleveland Marshall College of Law; [occ.] Attorney, Defense Logistics

Agency, Cleveland, Ohio; [hon.] Preventive Law Prize Award, American Juris Prudence Awards for High Grades in Torts, Property, Labor Law, English Legal System, Harry S. Blackman Award, Cleveland State Law Review Editor; [pers.] Laugh and the world laughs with you, cry and the world laughs at you - smile and the world wonders what the heck you've been up to.; [a.] Euclid, OH

TYSON, ELANA D.
[b.] November 5, 1960, Chicago, IL; [p.] Mildred Tyson, Armand C. Tyson, Jr.; [ed.] Kenwood Academy, Southern Illinois University, Roosevelt University; [occ.] Secretary, Metropolitan Water Reclamation District of Greater Chicago, Chicago, IL; [oth. writ.] A writing entitled "Spiritually Yours" published in a personal collection by Ms. Roxxy Cooley of Pressed For Time, Inc.; [pers.] I express myself much better in writing, usually having been motivated by events which have occurred in my life, and my own sensitivity towards and empathy for others.; [a.] Chicago, IL

TYSON, WYCLIFFE E.
[pen.] Wycliffe E. Tyson; [b.] January 12, 1953, Nevis, WI; [p.] Samuel Tyson, Margery Tyson; [ed.] Trinity International University Miami, Fl., B. Sci Human Resources Mgmt, Biblical Studies, Miami Dade Community College, Miami Fl., A Sci-District Nutrition Care; [occ.] Student pursuing Dr. Naturepathic, Clayton School of Natural Healing; [memb.] Alabama First United Methodist Church Miami Fl., American Naturepathic Medical Association, International Society of Poets; [hon.] National Defense Medal Honorable Discharge U.S. Navy Viet Nam Veteran; [oth. writ.] Author of good entitled "Messages, Prayers, and Poetry."; [pers.] The stormy fortresses of life can fall, if only you push.; [a.] Miami Beach, FL

ULIASZ, ALAN G.
[b.] July 16, 1962, Meriden, CT; [p.] Kenneth Uliasz, Joanne Uliasz; [m.] Roberta M. Uliasz, June 20, 1987; [ch.] Rebecca Lee, Gregory Alan; [ed.] Glastonbury High; [occ.] Systems Analyst; [pers.] Strive to be your best. Never get too comfortable.; [a.] Meriden, CT

UNDERWOOD, WILLIE BRUCE
[b.] December 26, 1926, Martinsville, VA; [p.] John I. and Mary B. Underwood; [m.] Mildred F. Underwood, February 18, 1954; [ch.] Son Warren, and Daughter Sandra; [ed.] BSEE VPI; [occ.] Retired; [memb.] AARP; [hon.] EKN National Honorary Society for Electrical Engineers.; [oth. writ.] Several poems.; [pers.] This poem is an excerpt from a much longer poem titled, "Garrot Wood". It compares a person's feelings about his surroundings when he is happy and content with his feelings about the same surroundings when he is unhappy and depressed.; [a.] Victoria, VA

UNRUH, BRENT
[b.] June 2, 1959, Greensburg, KS; [ed.] Greensburg High, Dodge City Community College; [occ.] Associated with various jobs in the oil and gas fields of Kansas; [oth. writ.] Many notebooks of philosophical observations, and unfinished, nearly finished, unpublished poetry.; [pers.] To draw poetry out of life in the most supreme, true, accomplished way, whereas to make life more exultant, and

seemingly eternal. The lives and poetry of the biblical, classical, and romantic poet has inspired this duty; [a.] Haviland, KS

USHER, MARCELLA DENISE
[pen.] U'nia Marcella - Denise; [b.] November 13, 1959, Atlanta, GA; [p.] Viola V. Usher, Charles O. Usher; [ed.] Academy of Notre Dame De Namur High School, Marymount University, George Washington University; [occ.] President/Ceo, NIA, Consulting Initiative; [memb.] National Black Women's Health Project, The Capital Area Society for Health Care Planning, and Marketing, The American College of Healthcare Executives, American Hospital Association; [hon.] Phi Theta Kappa, Kappa Delta Phi, Marymount University Baccalaureate Scholarship, Dean's List, George Washington University's HSMP Chairman's List; [pers.] The spirit of the ancestors speak to me guiding and nuturing my creative expressions first planted as a seed of pain and loneliness.; [a.] Clinton, MD

USHER, TROY
[pen.] J.D. Glenn; [b.] May 19, 1972, Cocoa Beach, FL; [p.] Dan Usher, Lourie Usher; [ed.] Waverly - Shell Rock High; [occ.] General Mechanic; [oth. writ.] In process of writing poetry book; [pers.] Silence can sometimes be the greatest sound in the world.; [a.] Waverly, IA

VALDESUSO, JAN
[b.] December 22, 1935, Flomaton, AL; [m.] Roberto; [ch.] Marcia and Louinda; [ed.] X-ray Technician and Decorator degree; [occ.] Housewife retired; [oth. writ.] I have written poems for many years and never submitted any for publication. (This poem was written for my daughters for their graduations. One from college and the other from medical school.); [pers.] I want to be able to evolve in the universe and find the knowledge necessary to create my own reality.

VAN ATTA, MARGARET
[b.] 14, 1919, Indiana; [p.] Frank and Ruby Brown; [m.] Gordon, September 21, 1946; [ch.] Richard, Davies and Darrell; [ed.] Am licenced to teach drama. Studied under Letitia Barnams, School of expression Chgo., Graduated from Bus. College; [occ.] Retired, worked as secretary for many years; [memb.] LWML (Ruth Womens Missionary League), Ladies Guild, also AAL, Received Recognition from the City for my service to the terminally ill.; [hon.] I also was with the Honella Counterbury players for a four years in Chgo before marriage; [oth. writ.] Have written manual poems over the years. But I can only write when the "spirit moves me". Sometimes in a dream. Have only written as a pass time. Was encouraged to send this one in. I was inspired by this verse because when I was growing up money was scare. My father was a hard worker, my mother a homemaker. Being the only girl (I had one brother) my mother told me her problems. I become a very worry-wart. So I realized the value of a dollar at an early age.; [pers.] I come from a talented family my mother was a writers had one book made into a movie. "Over The Hills". It was shamed when I was very young. She had many gifts.; [a.] Andover, NJ

VAN DER SLOOT, DOUGLAS D.
[b.] September 27, 1968, Storm Lake, IA; [p.] Harlen G. Van Der Sloot, Kay Steventon; [ch.] Jonet Marie Van Der Sloot; [ed.] Tombstone High School; [occ.] Land Surveyor; [oth. writ.] None published; [pers.] My goal is to someday write a number one hit. If that never happens, as long as I can reach one person with my writing that is success enough.; [a.] Tucson, AR

VAN HOOSEN, SARAH
[pen.] Sarah Van Hoosen; [b.] April 3, 1981, San Jose; [p.] Gene and Gloria Van Hoosen; [ed.] Currently a freshman in High School; [occ.] Student; [hon.] 1991 1st place young authors 2nd place district wide, 1992 1st place district wide young authors fair, 1994 1st place young authors, 1995 1st place young authors fair, 1995 writer of the month award 1995 excellent author award; [oth. writ.] "The Mice and the Time Machine", Triforce," "Book of poems," and "Book of poems II"; [a.] Escalon, CA

VAN METER, KATHY
[b.] March 7, 1970; [p.] Dayton and Connie Bittinger; [m.] Keith Van Meter, Sr., November 3, 1990; [ch.] Keith Jr. and Kristen Renee; [ed.] Valley High School and the Allegany County Vo-Tech Center; [occ.] Full time mother and wife.; [pers.] My inspiration for writing has come from my son (Keith, Jr.) who's 5 yrs old and my daughter (Kristen) who's 3 years old. Also from my husband and my parents.; [a.] Westernport, MD

VAN NOTE, ROBERTA
[b.] May 5, 1934, Cumberland Co., Il; [p.] Mae Sparks, Jess Lansbery (Deceased); [m.] Don Van Note (Deceased 1994), April 19, 1953; [ch.] Tim, Doris, Tony, Ray and Steve; [ed.] Cumberland Highs School, Ill., Estrella Mountain Comm. College; [occ.] Student - Estrella; [memb.] National Authors Registry; [oth. writ.] Numerous other poems. Several to be published in anthologies in the coming months.; [pers.] I write for people. If someone can smile or feel some encouragement from one of my poems, that makes it more rewarding.; [a.] Phoenix, AZ

VANDERBURG, MANDY
[b.] May 5, 1978, Fullerton, CA; [p.] Lucien and Collene Vanderburg; [ed.] Senior at Katella High School, Anaheim, CA; [occ.] Student; [hon.] Freshman, Student of the Month, History and English, J.V. Basketball's Most Improved Player, Sophomore, Student of the Month, English, J.V. Basketball's M.V.P., Junior Varsity Softball's Most Dedicated Player and All League Honorable Mention Team, Senior, Captain of the Varsity Basketball Team; [oth. writ.] My notebooks poems; [pers.] I relinquish the morbid feelings that completely occupy my body, mind, and soul onto my paper. I was and still am greatly influenced by the words and lyrics of Jim Morrison of THE DOORS and by my best friend, Cynthia Castillo (my partner in crime).; [a.] Anaheim, CA

VANDERWOOD, DEBRAH M.
[b.] November 20, 1950, Ilion, NY; [p.] Frances Benson, Roger Newhouse; [m.] Barry S. Vanderwood, September 7, 1967 (Divorced), Alan R. Piotrowski, October 18, 1975 (Divorced); [ch.] Brandy A. Piotrowski, Dowen-Alan R. Piotrowski,

Christopher M.J. Piotrowski, Grandchild: Dekyse P. Dowen, Son in law: Stephon D. Dowen; [ed.] Utica Free Academy, Pikes Peak Comm. College Peterson Air ForseBase Dental Assistant School College of I.C.S. for Journalism, [occ.] Current writer poet, Songwriter, Prior-Dental Assistant, Preschool Teacher; [memb.] American Redcross, YMCA, P.T.A.; [hon.] Nomination as poet of the year 1995 Certificate of recognition for Preschool teacher, Certificate of recognition from U.S.A.F. Space Command, for Dental Assistant Program, Certificate of recognition from the American Red Cross for the Dental Assistant Program, Certificate of appreciation from Defence Commissary Agency, Pikes Peak Community College for Dental Radiology and Math Science, Health division of Dental Assistant Program, and verification, Certification of degree for Journalism and Short Story Writing from the college of I.C.S.; [oth. writ.] Several poems for Good House Keeping, The National Liberty of Poetry, and Mile High Poetry Society: 1. As Season's Change As We, In A Sea Of Treasures, 2. As Season's Change As We, In a Delicate Balance, 3. Many Years Passed As I waited for You, In the Rainbow's End, 4. Mother's In, The Book of Piera, 5. Grand Parent's, in Ariel, 6. A Poet's Dream, in Ariel, 7. In Passing AS we Meet, In Good House Keeping, 8. Awakened By A Dream, In Good House Keeping; [pers.] As a new poet I hope that poet readers will feel the emotions in my poetry, and I hope to move their emotions with their souls and their lives, as life is poetry I have been greatly influenced by early romantic poets and Emily Dickerson.; [a.] Colorado Springs, CO

VANSICKLE, DANI
[b.] March 1, 1966, Detroit, MI; [p.] Leta and Billie Wall; [m.] David William Vansickle, October 23, 1987; [ch.] Timothy, Samantha, Alexis and Aaron,; [ed.] Lakeshore High School, Macomb Community College; [occ.] Domestic Engineer; [pers.] Don't be so quick to point the finger...Until you have lived within their hand!; [a.] Roseville, MI

VANTREESE, TINA
[b.] July 13, 1978, Winfield, IL; [p.] Dan and Linda Vantreese; [ed.] KD Waldo Jr. High, East Aurora High School; [occ.] Student, Wal-Mart; [memb.] West Chicago Church of Christ; [hon.] History and English awards in junior high several citizenship honors. Volleyball and softball awards in high school; [pers.] Life is a mystery to be lived not a problem to be solved; [a.] Montgomery, IL

VASSALLO, MATTHEW A.
[b.] March 10, 1932, Bronx, NY; [p.] Matthew and Yolana Vassallo; [m.] Janet and Mattick Vassallo, September 14, 1974; [ch.] Madelyon, Mark and Anthony; [ed.] Cardinal Hayes H.S., Broax, Fordham University BA, Bronx, State Univ. of College of Medicine, NC ND, Columbia Univ., School of Public Health, MPH; [occ.] Family Physician; [memb.] N.Y. Academy of Medicine American Public Health Assn.; [pers.] Pour yourself into the work you love and surely honor and glory may follow.; [a.] Garnerville, NY

VELARDO, CATHERINE F.
[pen.] "Terina"; [b.] February 26, 1943, Italy; [p.] Francesco and Guiseppa Cipolla; [m.] Nelson Velardo, May 13, 1984; [ch.] Amon Finocchiaro, Christian Velardo; [ed.] Business Associates Degree,

Data Processing Degree; [occ.] Housewife; [memb.] Daughters of Italy; [hon.] Theater award, Milan Italy, for Theatrical performance, "The Gypsy of Volga"; [oth. writ.] Include a large number of poems and Literary thoughts in Italian and English.; [pers.] Life is a beautiful mystery, intriguing, awesome. Every soul who sojours in our wonderful earth, wishes to leave behind a footprint, a contribution to humanity and the collective soul. To me, besides leaving behind two wonderful children, I also leave a reflection of my spirit, because when I write a poem, I search deep inside my heart and pass on to paper what is eternally written in my soul about my life.; [a.] Longwood, FL

VERMILLION, YVONNE DE LAINE
[pen.] Yvonne De Laine Vermillion; [b.] February 16, 1945, Philadelphia, PA; [p.] Benjamin and Charity De Laine; [m.] LeRoy George Vermillion, August 19, 1982; [ch.] Lisa Renee; [ed.] MA - Univ. of San Francisco (Counseling Psych.); [occ.] Guidance Counselor/Marriage and Family Therapist; [memb.] American Assoc. of Marriage Therapists, Big Brothers/Sisters S.F. Zoological Society; [hon.] Lawnside Scholarship Award, NJ Governors Teachers Award; [oth. writ.] Shadow of the Sun, Here's to Ya; [pers.] My poetry represents the many levels of human experience. It is a challenge and obligation as a human being to change, grow, and learn.; [a.] Pittsgrove, NJ

VICKERS, DAVID PRESTON
[pen.] UD; [b.] July 10, 1971, West Palm Beach, FL; [p.] Sharon W. Vickers; [ed.] A. A. Degree from Palm Beach Community College in Early Childhood Education; [memb.] Life; [oth. Writ.] In Silence, With or Without You, The Battle Within, The Colors of Life, etch. etch. et al.; [pers.] This poem was written for J.M. - The women I now love and always love will love - as both a friend and a lover.; [a.] West Palm Beach, FL

VIGGIANO, NICK
[b.] August 21, 1959, Delaware County, PA; [p.] Nicholas D. Viggiano, Mary Jane Viggiano; [ed.] Archmere Academy, Claymont, Del. Vanous Carses at: Temple University, La Salle University, Villanova University; [occ.] Waiter; [memb.] Amresty International, Greenpeace, Handgin Control; [oth. Writ.] Two Novels Published: "There's A Better Day Ahead", "The Massacre of Innocence"; [pers.] I believe in art and love and that there is a God. I hate the modern world. The book that has influenced me the most is Thoreav's Welden.; [a.] Upper Darby, PA

VINSON, HEATHER KATHARINE
[b.] April 11, 1975, Scituate, MA; [p.] William and Kathryn Vinson; [ed.] Macdonald High School, University of Souther Maine, Boston University; [occ.] Undergrad Student; [memb.] Honors Program, Honors Fraternity Phi Sigma Pi, Dean's List; [oth. writ.] Poems and short stories published in student anthologies; [pers.] I've always tried to communicate the need to create - without fear without end.; [a.] Scarborough, ME

VINSON, LISA MORRISON
[pen.] Neli Morrison; [b.] October 26, 1962, Florence AL; [p.] Robert Clifford and Inez Morrison; [m.] Phillip M. Vinson, December 29, 1979; [ch.]

Jedediah, Liah, Melody; [ed.] West Limestone High School Lester, Alabama; [occ.] Songwriter, Singer of original band, called Heli's Syn; [hon.] Every mother's day I receive my award, "My Mother's Day Card"; [oth. writ.] One of my farovite poems is called, Peace Maker in memory of John Lennon. Poem turned song called Evil's End written on times we live in. Also "A Mama's Dream," memory of my mother; [pers.] Each day reality takes it's toll. My one sactuary I have always found, is when I pick up my pen and paper and open up my heart and soul. Their I find a friend. I have been blessed now with beautiful children, home and my 1st poem published. Soon my first C. Disc will be published. I'll have two dreams come true.; [a.] Pinellas Park, FL

VITALE, JOSEPH M.
[b.] January 24, 1927, New York City; [ch.] A son and three daughters- nine grandchildren; [ed.] B.A. Eng. Lit- Iona College; [occ.] Writer; [oth. writ.] recently completed 'A Return to the Past' - a trilogy of people, places and happenings in Germany during World War II and into the U.S. Occupation.; [pers.] 'Slugger' is my first poem but won't be the last for it opened the door to a new, satisfying and enjoyable experience. My regret is not attempting it before and without the National Library of Poetry's invitation- probably never.; [a.] Bronxville, NY

VOGEL, DEBORAH
[b.] February 16, 1972, Kansas; [pers.] The ocean waters have survived longer than all the animal species on earth. It stands to reason therefore, that the strength and courage needed to endure this single lifetime should be found within its forever changing waters.; [a.] Citrus Heights, CA

VOLZ, EMILY
[b.] August 14, 1901, Brooklyn, NY; [p.] Nora and William Ackerman; [m.] Frederick Volz, December 27, 1924; [ch.] Eleanor and Frederick Jr.; [ed.] Public School in Brooklyn, I could not finish school work as I had to go to work to help pay the bills at home; [occ.] Retired, I worked at the Sperry Airplane Plant in Lake Success on Long Island, NY for years during the world war II. In 1942 I joined the American Hospital Corp under whose direction we drilled and then sold bonds and stamps to do my share in the war effort.; [hon.] Over the years, I have donated more than 24 pints of blood to the american red cross. For these donations I received Silver Pins from their "Gallon Club" of the American Red Cross.; [oth.writ.] Prior to my birthday this yer I wrote: "For my 94th Birthday God kept me living very long, Health and Strength most times were strong. If I see birthday 94 I pray God's blessing for a little more."; [per.] I did celebrate birthday 94 in August 1995 and now I am praying "for a little more!"; [a.] Boynton Beach, FL

VOSBURGH, LISA A.
[b.] February 4, 1964, Sydney, NY; [p.] Robley Evans Vosburgh, Jean M. Hughes; [m.] Cheryl Danekas, February 28, 1991; [ch.] J.C., Emmy, Dax; [occ.] Dispatch Coordinator; [pers.] I do not want what I haven't got.; [a.] Bolingbrook, IL

VOYLES, PAMELA
[b.] February 5, 1965, Corpus Christi, TX; [m.] Robert Voyles, December 27, 1987; [ch.] Katherine Voyles; [ed.] Bachelor of Science; [occ.] Teacher;

[pers.] I wrote this poem for my daughter, Katie.; [a.] Corpus Christi, TX

WADDINGTON, SAMUEL A.
[b.] December 15, 1977, Syracuse, NY; [p.] James and Carolann Kozlowski; [ed.] Currently attending Senior Year at Liverpool High School in Liverpool, New York; [occ.] Student; [memb.] Trinity United Methodist Church, North Area YMCA, Camp Fire Global Adventure Team, Academic Decathelon, Aurora; [hon.] National Merit Scholarship Semi-Finalist, Aurora of C.N.Y. - Young Visual Impaired Person of the Year 1995, O.C.M.T.A. - 1st place Sequential Math II Award - 1993; [oth. writ.] Several poems published in School Literary Magazine; [pers.] The true poet is a dreamer.; [a.] Liverpool, NY

WAGNER, BETH A.
[b.] May 10, 1975, Orlando, FL; [p.] Keith Wagner and Barbara Ridolfo; [ed.] 1993 graduate of Urbana High School, Urbana, Oh.; [occ.] Junior at The Ohio State University, Journalism major; [hon.] Alpha Lambda Delta Honor Society; [oth. writ.] Several articles published in Sidney Daily News, Sidney, OH.; [pers.] Writing allows me to express all of my feelings, emotions and thoughts on paper, sharing them with others if I choose or keeping them in a special place, reflecting on them at another time.; [a.] Columbus, OH

WAGNER, CRYSTAL ARMES
[p.] Glenn and Ruth Armes; [m.] Scott Wagner; [ch.] Steven and Erin Wagner; [ed.] BS and 12 graduate hours from SIV Edwardsville, IL; [memb.] Trinity Lutheran Church, LYR Youth Counselor; [hon.] 3 Certificates of Achievement from US Army Nuclear Biological Chemical Team, Good Conduct Medal, Honorable Discharge; [oth. writ.] 2 Poems in Bereavement Magazine; [a.] Dorsey, IL

WALDON, TAMMARA
[b.] June 26, 1961, Jackson, CA; [p.] Norma Manica; [ch.] Charles, StevieLynn, and Andrew; [ed.] William Daylor High, Cosumnes River College; [pers.] Sometimes life is like a haunting dream... Struggling not to remember, but to be remembered... Dedicated to my family and one special high school teacher, Mitzi Meredith, who believed in me through the struggles of life.; [a.] Elk Grove, CA

WALIGORSKI, ALICIA
[pen.] Katie Waligorski; [b.] June 11, 1979, Centralia, IL; [p.] Katrina and Alexander Waligorski; [ed.] St John the Baptist Elementary, West Frankfort Il. and West Frankfort Community High School; [occ.] Student, Sophomore at West Frankfort Community High School; [memb.] St. John the Baptist Catholic Church; [hon.] The 1994 "Drug Free The Way For Me" essay won 2nd place.; [pers.] Knowledge, understanding and imagination aren't limited by one's age.; [a.] West Frankfort, IL

WALKER III, CURT T.
[b.] December 21, 1966, Sacramento, CA; [p.] Curtis T. Walker and Dianna Nixon; [m.] Linda L. Walker, October 31, 1993; [ch.] Alexander Dionysus; [ed.] Tokay High, Lodi CA, Delta College, Stockton CA; [memb.] DeMolay, Stockton Chapter (1985-1988); [oth. writ.] Waiting in the Wings...; [pers.] Be aware of all things, near and far, from a tiny grain of sand,

to the farthest star. Keep it in perspective, keep it neat, lest ye get a kick in the seat! Be good to yourselves.; [a.] San Francisco, CA

WALKER JR., DON
[b.] March 26, 1952, San Diego, CA; [p.] Donald L Walker Sr. (deceased), Carolyn M. Walker; [m.] Single; [ch.] Angela (deceased), Vickie, David, Brian, Mathew; [ed.] James Madison High School, Houston Baptist University, Howard Payne University; [occ.] Retail Grocery Sales; [memb.] Blood Center, Brazoria County Youth Homes, masonic Lodge 76Z AF-AM.; [hon.] Phi Theta Kappa, Dean's List, Distinguished Service Award; [oth. writ.] Several other poems published; [pers.] Our children are our future. We have been ordained to raise them with Wisdom, Honesty, Integrity, and Spritual Values along with the hope of Everlasting Peace. Let's not fail in this challenge.; [a.] Grand Rapids, MI

WALKER, SILVIA
[b.] Lufkin, TX; [p.] Audrey and Normal Green; [m.] Melvin Eugene Walker; [ch.] Dusty Eugene Walker; [occ.] Manager of Retail Nursery; [hon.] Editors Choice Award '94, Editors Choice Award '95; [oth. writ.] "A Little Treasure", River of Dreams, "Duo of Love", Best Poems of 1995, "School Days", Best Poems of 1996; [a.] Lufkin, TX

WALKER, TERESA
[b.] August 17, 1951, San Diego, CA; [p.] Leslie and Helen Walker; [m.] Ronnie Walker, December 16, 1971; [ch.] Emerson, Choya and Cary; [ed.] High School 1-12; [occ.] Housewife, part time Book-keeper, and in home service worker for elderly; [pers.] Do not fight with questions unanswered so your spirit can see them through; [a.] Guatay, CA

WALLY, ROSEMARY
[pen.] Rebecca Edwards; [b.] November 29, 1974, Pittsburgh, PA; [p.] J. Edward and Theresa R. Wally; [ed.] Shaler Area High School, University of Pittsburgh at Johnstown; [occ.] Student; [a.] Pittsburgh, PA

WALSH, HEATHER
[b.] May 20, 1979, Savannah, GA; [p.] Colette Walsh, Richard Walsh; [ed.] Windsor Forest High School; [occ.] Student; [memb.] Young Life, National Honor Society, Campaigners, Youth Ministries, APLAC, Yearbook Staff, Chorus, Anchor Club, Bible Club, Drama, Ronald McDonald House; [hon.] 1st place Poetry Contest, High Honor Roll, Top Ten in Rank, placed in Spanish Oratorical Contest, National Honor Society, Honor Choir; [oth. writ.] Often, Windy Gap, Semblance is only a Reflection of Realism, The Seed; [pers.] I write for enjoyment. I strive to convey my feelings on paper, so that others can identify with my emotions.; [a.] Savannah, GA

WALSWORTH, MATTHEW
[b.] August 29, 1973, Flint, MI; [p.] William and Marjorie Walsworth; [ed.] Working on a BA in Psychology at the University of Michigan, Flint; [occ.] Respite worker at a Foster Care Agency; [oth. writ.] This is the first time I have ever entered any kind of writing to a contest, so it is the first time I have had anything published.; [pers.] All of my writings are my experiences and my feelings about

everything I encounter in my life. I never try to write, I am usually inspired by an event or experience, and my feelings flow onto the paper.; [a.] Flushing, MI

WANDA, ROBISON SAWHILL
[b.] August 28, 1933, Midway, PA; [p.] Charles W. Sawhill, Stella Rampbell Sawhill; [m.] Thomas J. Robison, October 2, 1953; [ch.] Kim Elaine, Mark Evan; [ed.] Midway High School, El Camino College; [occ.] Sr. Programmer Analyst; [a.] Encinitas, CA

WANG, CHEN
[pen.] Literati Spring; [b.] Qinghai, China; [p.] Yinde Wang, Yilan Lu; [ed.] Eleanor Roosevelt High, University of Md. at College Park; [hon.] 1) National AP Scholar Award, 1993, 2) National AP Scholar Award with Distinction, 1995, 3) National All-Stars of the American Compute Science League (a member), 1992, 4) PG County High School Chess Tournament, 1st place; [oth. writ.] Currently working on a brief/short novel mostly interested in writing poetry and short stories.; [pers.] I can neither play my sorrows off the bow of a violin, nor can I paint my content off the tip of a paint brush. But I can write the entire me off the color of my ink.; [a.] College Park, MD

WANG, DANNY HSIANG-KUO
[b.] April 22, 1971, Tapei, Taiwan; [p.] David T. Wang and Nancy Mo Wang; [ed.] Pinole Valley High School, UC Berkeley - BA: Rhetoric and Economics, UC Berkeley - MA: Education; [occ.] I am currently finishing my MA in Education and student teaching in a 4th/5th grade classroom; [memb.] Northern California Tennis Association; [hon.] Phi Beta Kappa UC Berkeley Alumni Scholar; [pers.] The key to a better future is to invest in our children.; [a.] Oakland, CA

WANTULA, STANLEY
[b.] December 15, 1926, Poland; [p.] Paul Wantula, Karoline Wantula; [m.] Elizabeth Wantula, September 5, 1953; [ch.] Richard Andrew, Irene Renata; [ed.] Baccalaureate - Paris, France, Four Teaching Courses - Columbia University, New York; [occ.] Retired from Lederle - Laboratories, Division of American Cyanamid, worked at Pharmaceutical Control and Pharmaceutical Technical and Training Office, Pearl River, New York (22 years).; [memb.] The Evangelical Lutheran Church of the Good Shepherd; [hon.] Bronze Award 1986 for Innovation (Lied. Lab. Div. of American Cynamid); [oth. writ.] Collection of Poems on Various Themes and for Various Occasions.; [pers.] Through many years of study, of Philosophy and Metaphysics, I am striving to save our Planet for future generations and through Poetry to inspire and enrich peoples life. Performing in the Radio Dramas Presentation on Stage.; [a.] Virginia Beach, VA

WARD, JENNIFER LYN
[b.] April 9, 1975, Colorado Springs; [p.] Vickie Snider, Lance Ward; [m.] Fiance' Scott Ortis; [ed.] Roseburg Senior High School; [hon.] Certificate of honor from Imaginings, publications of Douglas County Schools. Expressions, Poems and Art by Roseburg High School students.; [oth. writ.] Numerous poems published in local art and poetry works. A large gathering of personal writings.;

[pers.] The most important thing for me to do first, is to give thanks to my family. My mom and dad are listed, so I want to acknowledge others. To Chris: "Semper Fi" I miss you and love you. To Grandma and Papa: Thank you for loving me, displaying my work on your walls, and bragging about me at your church. To Scott: 214-"I'm your puppet". To Vic: Thanks for everything you've done for me no matter how big or small I remember, and it's accounted for. And to all of you: Thank you for your never ending love and graciousness. I am blessed for having all of you. I love you very much. I appreciate the support, and all the pushes I received to go toward this dream. All of my writings are based on my experiences, and the feelings I have from them. I believe that if I have not lived it, I cannot put my soul into understanding it, and further more write about it.; [a.] Roseburg, OR

WARREN, SANDRA
[b.] December 31, 1948, Pascagoula, MS; [p.] James and Margaret Owens; [m.] Edward F. Warren, November 20, 1990; [ch.] Vincent Keith Switzer; [ed.] Associate Degree (Nursing), Bachelor of Science (Education), Masters of Science (Counseling Psychology); [occ.] Student/Wife; [memb.] RN, NBCC, Member (First Presbyterian Church - Jackson, MS); [hon.] Who's Who Among American Jr. College Students; [oth. writ.] None published; [pers.] Spontaneous and unpredictable, my poetry has long given me a means to help explain and understand my life.; [a.] Jackson, MS

WASHBURN, LORI ANN
[b.] October 6, 1960, Long Island, NY; [ed.] Shaker High School, Psychic Studies Institute, University of Metaphysics; [occ.] Specialty Cake Designer, Freelance Photographer, President Nelson Network Fan Club; [memb.] President, Nelson Network Fan Club Footlighters Acting Troupe, International Metaphysics Ministry, Capital District Spiritualist Organization; [hon.] Who's Who in Photography, 1991 Ordained, Minister of Metaphysic Ministry, Doctorate in Metaphysical Science; [pers.] Believe in yourself, who you are and what you are inside. Put forth into the Universe only positive emotions and they will return to you. Make the world a better place, one person at a time.; [a.] Latham, NY

WASHINGTON, BOB
[b.] March 21, 1922, New York City, NY; [p.] Robert and Dorthy Washington; [m.] November 2, 1946; [ch.] Howard and Valerie; [ed.] High School (Jamaica High), Officers Candidate School (Infantry Ft. Benning, GA., New York Trade School; [occ.] Retired; [memb.] Kiwanis Club-Wyandanch, NY, St. Croix Players-Community Theatre St. Croix, USVI, American Legion-Lady Lake, Fl, Age On Stage Players-Community Theatre Lady Lake, Fl. (Retired Community); [hon.] Concerned Black Professionals Man of the Year Award...Suffok County, NY 1976-77, Achievement Award-First Black Lt. Governor of Suffolk County, NY...Mayors Committee, Amityville, NY 1972; [oth. writ.] "The Card Game", "The Trial of Dandy Jones Injured Donkey", (or Who Kicked Her Ass), The Blue in "Bea's Flat"; [pers.] I believe in the brotherhood of man under the fatherhood of God..and as a jazz devotee...if the world was a jazz orchestra...the piano would be the symbol and standard bearer...because it takes both the "White Keys and The Black Keys" to make beautiful music...

WATKINS, ELIZABETH THORNTON
[b.] November 4, 1926, Decatur, AL; [p.] Herbert L. and Lorinda F. Thornton; [m.] Hugh A. Watkins, June 29, 1963; [ch.] Alice Lorinda and Reece Thornton Watkins; [ed.] Madison, Ala. High School, Florence State College and Auburn University; [occ.] Retired Vocational Home Economics Teacher; [memb.] Trinity United Methodist Church, Church Women United, Civilian Wives Club, Robinettes Homemakers Club, Society of American Poets, Beta Sigma Phi Sorority, NARFE and AARP.; [hon.] Alpha Delta Kappa, Kappa Delta Pi, Dean's List, Editor's Choice and Humanities Awards for poems in "The Poet's Pen", 1st and 2nd prizes in local "SOAP" Poetry contests, Life Member award United Methodist Women and Valiant Woman Award, Church Women United. Woman of the Year, Beta Sigma Phi; [oth. writ.] Local Newspaper articles, editorials and articles for CWU state and local Newsletters, Poems published in newspapers, "The Poet's Pen," in the Joyce Payne Ministries monthly Newsletters and in Trinity Tidings Church Newsletter which I started and edited for several years.; [pers.] God doesn't give us all our gifts at one time, sometimes they come late in life. I try to give him honor and praise in my poems in gratitude for the gift of poetry he bestowed on me in 1991. I started writing at an Elderhostel in a class taught by Dr. Evelyn Laycock at Hiwassee College in Sweet Water, Tennessee in May, 1991.; [a.] Warner Robins, GA

WATKINS, VERNA M.
[b.] September 22, 1926, Reynolds, IN; [p.] Karl and Edna Ruemler; [m.] Robert E. Watkins, July 6, 1947; [ch.] Andria Louise, Patricia Jean, Linda Marie, William Robert, Phillip Edward; [ed.] Logansport High, Community College; [occ.] Retired; [memb.] Friends of the Library, Good Shepherd Lutheran Church; [pers.] Never being sorry to have lived.; [a.] Meadview, AZ

WATSON, ABBIE LEE
[b.] July 13, 1980, Painsville, OH; [p.] Jim and Donna Watson; [ed.] Perry High School; [memb.] Taca SADD, Spanish Club, Drill Team, Concert Band, Volleyball, Softball, Swim Team, Church Acolyte; [a.] Perry, OH

WATSON, JO DEE
[b.] March 29, 1978, Tipton, IN; [p.] Jim and Judy Watson; [ed.] I will be a 1996 graduate of Tipton High School; [occ.] Student; [memb.] First Baptist Youth Group and Choir, School Choir, Drama Club, Fellowship or Christian Athlete, Students Against Drunk Driving, Tipton Community Theatre, Cadet Teaching; [hon.] Who's Who Among High School Students, Scholarship to National Young Leaders Conference.; [oth. writ.] 1st published poems; [pers.] It's a heart thing. I write to communicate a message.; [a.] Tipton, IN

WATTS, DENISE ELENA
[b.] August 13, 1948, Rhinelander, WI; [p.] Helen Severino Yonker; [m.] L. Adrian Watts, December 23, 1988; [ch.] Dawn Marie, Philip Charles, Anthony (Tony) Raymond, Nikolaus Joseph; [ed.] Glenbard East High School, McHenry Cty. College; [occ.] Owner of Truth Roofing and Gen. Cont. (along with husband); [memb.] Crossroads Church; [pers.] I write about my experiences. All that is close to my heart.; [a.] Wonder Lake, IL

WATTS, FRANK G.
[pen.] Ben Lockhart or Blind Poet of Blendenbough; [b.] March 19, 1921, Sebring, OH; [p.] Rose and John Watts (Deceased); [m.] Betty Watts, September 16, 1950; [ch.] Rosemary and Mark Watts; [ed.] Alliance High, Anderson College, Mt. Union College, Kent State University, Graduate of Anderson College '55, Mount Union College 1 year, Kent State 1 year; [occ.] Retired Special Ed. Teacher; [hon.] Syford Poetry Award 1st Place at Anderson College, 1953, 1954, 1955.. Published 1 book of poems in 1947 with William-Fredrick Press of New York; [oth. writ.] Have several books of poems unpublished such as Slow Fire Mountain along with several other books.; [pers.] The only place my poetry was recognized was in Anderson college by an English Professor, all the books are in boxes, stacked in my garage. Poet's and pigs are recognized after they are dead. We should have creative writers speak in High School and College English Classes.; [a.] Alliance, OH

WAYNE, ALAN
[b.] June 18, 1909, New York City; [p.] Karl Wiesenburg, Martha Horvath; [m.] Muriel Rothstein, August 25, 1934; [ch.] Linda and Susan; [ed.] B.S., M.S. in Ed. AAAS Fellow Grad. work at NYU Columbia U. and 3 Nat. Sci. Foundation Institutes; [occ.] Retired from supervision of Science and Mathematics, NY City; [memb.] American Math. Sos., Math. Assoc. of America, Central Assoc. Sci. and Math., Assoc. of Teachers of Math NYC as well as of NY State, Nat. Council Tchrs, Math., Institute for Retired Professionals; [hon.] Arista, Epsilon Pi Tau, 20-Year Pin from The Cooper Union of NYC; [oth. writ.] Educational: Math., Science Teaching, occasional poems, humor, puzzles (literary and mathematical); [pers.] There is an underlying harmony that enhances literature (poetry), science and mathematics, apart from the qualities that separate them.; [a.] Jamesville, NY

WEAVER-FLOWERS, ALICE MARIE BURAS
[pen.] Alice Marie; [b.] February 8, 1940, Boothville, LA; [p.] John B. and Alice Buras (Deceased); [m.] Jim Weaver, May 23, 1980; [ch.] Timothy Todd, Randy Allen, Brandon Clifford, Grandchildren: Zachary, Amanda, Amber and Alyssa; [ed.] Buras High, ACME Business College; [occ.] CHMP - (Chief Household Managerial Person); [memb.] Freeman Heights Baptist Church; [hon.] American Legion Award, Nat'l Beta Club; [oth. writ.] Several poems and articles published in The Plaquemines Gazette, The Plaquemines Watchman and Featured in Down The Road Magazine - with poems and articles Pamphlet - Listening to GOD; [pers.] I am a passionate writer with ambitions moved by inspirations from an inner spirit. I strive to bring happiness and peace to those who read my words. All of my poems are true stories of my life's experiences and associations.; [a.] Garland, TX

WEAVER, HEATHER SHEA
[b.] February 10, 1976, Birmingham, AL; [p.] Gary and Doris Weaver; [m.] Douglas Beamon (Boy-friend); [ed.] Jefferson Christian Academy, Harding University; [memb.] Member of Roebuck Parkway Church of Christ, Junior Civitan, National Honor Society; [hon.] Who's Who Among American High School Students; [pers.] I write to express my

feelings of life and hope others can benefit from my writings. I would like to say a word of thanks to Douglas for inspiring me to believe in myself.; [a.] Birmingham, AL

WEDEMEYER, DOROTHY
[b.] July 10, 1913, Albany, MO; [p.] David and Elizabeth Roberson; [m.] Alvin Wedemeyer, December 16, 1934; [ch.] Gary A. and D. Elaine; [ed.] High School, Forsyth, Montana; [memb.] United Methodist Church; [pers.] I have no mission, nor any cause, it is my hope that some of the loveliness I see around me is reflected in my lyrics.; [a.] Seattle, WA

WEIDNER, HEATHER
[pen.] Aja; [b.] June 20, 1976, Pittsburgh; [p.] Agnes Weidner, Janet Weidner; [ed.] Mount Alvernia High School, La Roche College; [occ.] Cake Decorator, Giant Eagle Markets and Representative at Solution Marketing; [memb.] Yearbook Staff, Newspaper Staff, Youth Director of North Side Deanery Youth Council; [hon.] Winner of First Diocesan Scholarship in Pittsburgh to attend high school of choice.; [pers.] I have been greatly influenced by Edgar Alan Poe and May Swenson. My poems are a reflection of human emotions and problems faced by everyday people. With each poem I find a greater sense of self.; [a.] Pittsburgh, PA

WEIDNER, JULIE CHRISTINE
[b.] November 4, 1967, Montgomery, AL; [p.] Sara Weidner, Mike Weidner; [ed.] Associate of Arts Degree from Wayne Community College, currently a student at Appalachian State University Boone, N.C.; [occ.] Student at ASU; [memb.] Former Preschool Teacher - after school child care giver, The Word Church, Goldsboro, NC, Adult Student Network at ASU; [hon.] Dean's List at Wayne Community College; [oth. writ.] A few other poems were published in Wayne Community College's Renaissance. Another poem was published in the Adult Student Network's Newsletter at ASU.; [pers.] Take time out to enjoy the simple things in life, a flower, a bird, a tree or just being. Smell the freshness in the air after a Rainstorm and take time out each day to praise God.; [a.] Boone, NC

WEIGEL, DIANA J.
[pen.] Diana Jean; [b.] August 30, 1945, Torrington, Wyoming; [m.] Alvin Weigel, September 10, 1965; [ch.] Shawnalyn Weigel; [ed.] Abraham Lincoln High (Denver, Co), University of Colo. (at Denver, Co., 1 year), Jones Real Estate College, MSEC (Supervisory I - II, Denver, CO.), Jefferson County (WordPerfect I), Disability Awareness (City of Lakewood, CO), Proofreading (City of Lakewood, CO), Productivity Point (WP II, Lotus, Golden, Co.); [occ.] Poet/Writer; [memb.] New Life Christian Church; [hon.] Top Listing Agent Century 21 (October 1981), Commendation (Verification Dept./Cost Efficiency Jan. 1984), Commendation (City of Lkwd, Implement Police Agent New Payroll System, January 1990); [oth. writ.] Rose (1991), Friends (March 28, 1993), Love By The Sea (May 22, 1993), Diana Who (July 10, 1993), Where Am I? (September 8, 1994), Twilight (July 8, 1995), Cool, Cloudy, Grey Day (September 7, 1995); [pers.] Life is a breeze through the trees. It can be a web of lies that seems like truth. Seeking and finding a sometimes painful truth, is better than lies that are devastating.

The peace that comes from truth is eternal.; [a.] Arvada, CO

WEIR, CHERIL DENISE
[pen.] Che-Che; [b.] January 26, 1962, Kingston, Jamaica; [p.] Joyce Weir, Aston Weir; [ch.] Andrew KaVaughn, Evinx Daniel III; [ed.] St. Hugh High - Kingston Jamaica, Miami Lakes Technical; [occ.] Licensed Practical Nurse; [memb.] Local Poetry Clubs; [oth. writ.] Several Poems; [pers.] Writing is one way of fulfilling my humanitarian goals by reflecting on personal feelings and experiences.; [a.] Hollywood, FL

WEISMAN, JUDITH M.
[b.] May 16, 1950, Smithtown, NY; [p.] George and Elizabeth Arns; [m.] John Weisman, December 21, 1968; [ch.] John Jr., George, Jacob, Jadyn, Jenny; [ed.] Smithtown High School, Suffolk Community College; [occ.] Special Education Paraprofessional; [pers.] We must live each day to the fullest and go to sleep each night satisfied that we have done our best. Take each new day as a gift and always give back a part of yourself.; [a.] Smithtown, NY

WELBORN, HUGH
[b.] May 23, 1928, West Haven, CT; [p.] May and Grover Welborn; [m.] Mary Spalding Welborn, May 25, 1985; [ch.] Mark Welborn, Laura Oswald, David Welborn; [ed.] West Haven, Ct, University of Connecticut; [occ.] Copywriter; [memb.] Ratcliffe Hicks Award for Nonfiction Writing; [oth. writ.] The Shaft - an underground Army Newspaper parodying military life, short poems in local newspaper.; [pers.] For me, writing poetry touches feelings and wonders I can reach in no other way.; [a.] Tappan, NV

WELCH, ANNE L.
[b.] November 1, 1949, Gardiner, ME; [p.] Frances Welch, George S. White; [ed.] Halldale High, University of Maine at Farmington; [occ.] Librarian, Maine State Library, Augusta, ME; [memb.] Board of Trustees, Unitarian Universalist Community Church, Maine Writers and Publishers Alliance; [hon.] Dean's List; [pers.] Since I can't do everything, I will do something one thing at a time.; [a.] Hallowell, ME

WELLS, AUSTIN
[b.] Kentucky; [p.] Robert and Patsy Wells; [ed.] High School Diploma, Mapel Wood High School, Hill Wood High School; [occ.] Reelman at Quebecor Printing; [oth. writ.] Just basic poems I have written down in my time.; [pers.] Due to working twelve hour shifts. I have a lot of time to use my brain and think about poems. So I write them down and have a collection of them.; [a.] Nashville, TN

WELTMAN, PETER SPENCER
[b.] June 12, 1986, Detroit, MI; [p.] Robert and Robyn; [ed.] 4th grader at Burton Elementary School; [occ.] Student; [memb.] UID Soccer Team, Tap Dance, and play Guitar; [hon.] Soccer Trophy, Perfect Attendance in school, Award after each school year, I was asked to tap dance at the Ford Headquarters for a holiday show.; [oth. writ.] Reports, Journal Writing, and wrote a song.; [pers.] I decided to put my two grandfathers in my pome because they helped me in different ways, and they are also very special to me. Also Poppa Sam loved to write poems.; [a.] Huntington Woods, MI

WENRICK, MARIE A.
[b.] June 29, 1949, Tulsa, OK; [p.] Mr. and Mrs. E. H. Peters (Father Deceased since 1990); [m.] Tom Wenrick, June 15, 1975; [ch.] David, Rebecca; [ed.] High School graduate, 2 years college - Oklahoma University; [occ.] Home-maker; [memb.] Local Church, Parent-Teacher Fellowship - Daughter's Middle School and "Mom's Club" - Son's University; [oth. writ.] "Graduation" - published 1995 was dedicated to son, David upon his graduation from high school. I have been writing since a young age and kept journals along the way, but "Graduation" was my first submitted work.; [pers.] Someone once asked me why I write. I explained it's something I do because I must. My pen is always unconsciously seeking those for whom it is given. If what I write strikes a chord of resonance within you my own joy is fulfilled.; [a.] Tulsa, OK

WERTH, MEGHAN
[b.] June 4, 1981, Secaucus, NJ; [p.] Kathy and Gary Werth; [ed.] Student at the Academy of the Sacred Heart; [memb.] Member of the School Newspaper and a Cheerleader for Sacred Heart; [hon.] Academic Achievements Honors, Principal's List; [oth. writ.] Several poems and short stories; [pers.] "Always strive for your personal best. You can be what you want in life, and don't let anyone tell you different.";[a.] West New York, NJ

WESTOVER, ROBERT
[b.] October 8, 1936, Independence, MO; [p.] Grace and George Westover; [m.] Mardelle Hudson Westover, August 17, 1957; [ch.] David, Mark, Pamela Joy, Robert Hudson, Daniel and Rebecca Joy; [oth. writ.] Many more poems and a great deal of photography.

WHATLEY, HEATHER
[pen.] Heather Whatley; [b.] May 1, 1982, Mobile, AL; [p.] John and Melissa Whatley; [ed.] Student in Jr. High School (8th Grade); [occ.] Student; [memb.] Poetry Club, T.A.D.A. Club (Teens Against Drugs and Alcohol); [hon.] Science Olympiad Award, Presidential Academic Award, Creativity Award; [oth. writ.] Other poems and short stories that haven't been published, but I intend to and to send to different publishers to have published as a book.; [pers.] If you keep giving up your dreams, and don't set any goals, you'll probably have a dull life, and probably won't enjoy what you do.; [a.] York, SC

WHEELEHON, DONNA M.
[b.] September 15, 1967, California; [p.] Donald D. and Judith A. Wheelehon; [ch.] Wendi M. Wheelehon; [pers.] A special note to my maternal grandmother, Waneta A. Neal: Nana, when I felt loneliest, you were there. When I cried, you wiped the tears. When I needed reassuring, your arms were wide. Nana, thank you, thank you, thank you for taking me inside. I Love You. Donna. To Daniel Pina: Even good things come out of bad times, and we always endure and triumph through them. Thank you for being there when I needed you, and for putting up with me, when even I couldn't. You give me the strength to go forward. Always and forever, Donna.; [a.] Los Angeles, CA

WHEELER, JUSTIN L.
[pen.] Jil Wheeler; [b.] February 25, 1981, Corona,

CA; [p.] Robert T. and Sandra L. Wheeler; [ed.] Currently in 9th Grade at Santiago High School in Corona, CA; [hon.] Outstanding Academic Achievement in Science, President's Education Award for Outstanding Academic Improvement, Principals Honor Roll 1994, 1995; [oth. writ.] (Novel) OCC Oceanic Community Central Santiago High School - Motto, additional poems; [pers.] I write for the entertainment value and hope that my writings have a positive effect. I have been mainly influenced by Stephen King's books.; [a.] Corona, CA

WHITE, ANNA H.
[b.] September 26, 1921, Melrose, MA; [p.] Maud Jacquard (98 yrs. old); [m.] Herbert White (died 9-13-95), January 3, 1943; [ch.] James H. White, Richard A. White, Mary H. Colby; [ed.] H.S. Grad.; [occ.] Homemaker; [memb.] Lifetime V.F.W., Golden Age Club; [hon.] 1988 Senior Volunteer San Diego County 1988, S.D. County Credit Union Special Award; [oth. writ.] 2 poems published in National Library of Poetry Anthology 1993-1994; [pers.] Writing is a great source of relaxation. My poems vary in categories. I write religious, humor, life, family. I am writing my auto biography.; [a.] North Reading, MA

WHITE, JAMES DAVID
[pen.] J. D. White; [b.] July 23, 1938, Hood County, TX; [p.] Gene White, Dorthy White; [m.] Bernice White, May 26, 1966; [ch.] Darla Gale White; [ed.] Grand Burry High School, 11 1/2 years; [occ.] Retired 8-29-95, from Generald Motors Arlington, TX; [memb.] Baptist Church; [oth. writ.] I have none at this time but lots of poems and short stories written up. Just waiting for the chance to have them published for the public. All my friends love to read what I write.; [pers.] I want to share my poems and short stories with the rest of the world, it is fun for me and lots of reading for them. I write four to five each day, it is a perfect way to spend the days away in winter and on rainy days.; [a.] Weatherford, TX

WHITE IV, JAMES LIVINGSTON
[pen.] James Livingston IV; [b.] October 7, 1945, Miami Beach; [p.] James L. White III, Cathryn S. White (Deceased); [m.] Bonnie Monsees White, September 3, 1988; [ed.] Fork Union Military Academy Fork Union, VA 1961 (50 Miles West Richmond, VA), Campbell College, Buis Creek, NC Cape Fear Tech Wilmington, NC.; [occ.] Retired of Disability, Have invention ideas, poems, volunteer work; [memb.] Fork Union, Ciceronean Literary Society, Retan Rifle Drill Team. (In parades, football games.) Sports Club, Officer's Club, Squad Leader (Sgt.) 2nd best drilled squad in entire Cadet Corps. (90 total squads); [hon.] Above medal squad. Electrolux Corps, 1984, Won two (2) Cars, sales of vacuums. Many other prizes Electrolux. Awards, trips, money. (Mutual of New York) Awards Annual Merit Award United Ins. Co. Of America Dean's List tech.; [oth. writ.] Poems about family, Dr.'s, faith in God, even have a politcal poem. Have sayings from grandmother, myself, friends, others, family say I should write a book. Inspirational poems.; [pers.] I have found that I love poetry. (Late in life!) I pray I will be discovered and many will find inspiration, renewed faith to "hand in" and my talent will expand and show mankind the love of God and how worthwhile we are even with a handicap or illness.; [a.] Wilmington, NC

WHITE, RUBY M.
[b.] Cherokee County; [p.] Clara and Vester Taylor; [ch.] Hank Morrow, Patricia Acosta; [ed.] High School; [occ.] Machine Sander Baber Furniture; [mcmb.] Order of the Eastern Star Chapter 15 Andre's N.C.; [oth. writ.] "Speaking of Strange", complied and edited by Joshua P. Warren, my story titled, "Visions" 1994, writings for Wisp Journal, short stories on strange phenomenal; [pers.] I study the Bible, and try to reflect Gods Wisdom into our daily lives, without God I'm nothing, He is my yesterday, my today and all of my tomorrows.

WHITE SR., FLETCHER LEE
[b.] May 15, 1900, Chatham, VA; [p.] Jenny Bates White; [m.] Elizabeth Johnson, August 10, 1919; [ch.] 11; [ed.] Grade School; [occ.] Reeler, Deceased - 1993; [memb.] NAACP; [pers.] "Where ignorance is bliss, tis folly to be wise."; [a.] Cleveland, OH

WHITEHEAD, BRANAN M.
[b.] February 5, 1977, Somerset, KY; [p.] R. Don and Sharon Whitehead; [ed.] Class of 1995 Somerset High School, currently Bachelor of Arts candidate at Northern Kentucky University; [occ.] Theatre major at Northern Kentucky University; [memb.] Northern Kentucky University Theatre Student Union; [hon.] Graduate of 1993 Kentucky Governor's School for the Arts (Drama Class), Turfway Park Starting Gate Scholarship, Undergraduate Academic Housing Scholarship; [pers.] Never forget the immortal words of the man from the refrigerator: "Pray that there's intelligent life somewhere up in space, because there's bugger all down here on Earth."; [a.] Highland Heights, KY

WHITFIELD, PAUL
[b.] March 18, 1972, Boston; [p.] Denise Whitfield; [ed.] Brockton High School and Massasoit Community College; [occ.] Child Care Worker for The Depts of Youth Services; [oth. writ.] Poem published in The Anthology last published by The National Library of Poetry.; [pers.] Don't be afraid to thirst for knowledge, for curiosity may have killed the cat, but satisfaction brought him back.; [a.] Stoughton, MA

WHITLEY, JACLYN
[pen.] Jackie Whitley; [b.] December 19, 1981, Chambersburg; [p.] Robert Whitley and Deborah and Craig Griffin; [ed.] Currently Attending Milford Middle School, 8th grade; [occ.] Student; [hon.] Science Fair "First Place", question was "How can we save the rain forest?"; [pers.] I hope people see the importance of the Rainforest in my writings, "Save The Rain Forest"; [a.] Milford, DE

WIDGREN, RACHEL
[b.] June 13, 1971, Moscow, ID; [p.] John and Charlotte Karling, Diane Boulware; [m.] Christopher Widgren, August 25, 1990; [ch.] Sara Michelle Widgren; [ed.] John R. Rogers High School, Longridge Writers Group; [occ.] Writer, Home-School Teacher; [memb.] Sister City Exchange Representative to Japan 1988; [pers.] This poem is dedicated to the memory of Jordan Teal, 1994.; [a.] Spokane, WA

WILES, FRANCES
[pen.] Frances Wiles; [b.] May 6, 1947, Stokes Co.; [p.] Otlo and Elsie B. Smith; [m.] Desley J. Wiles Jr.,

July 5, 1961; [ch.] Worney J. Wiles, Jeffrey Wiles, Dee J. Wiles; [occ.] Owner and Operator of Flo's Accessories and Gift's, Dobson, NC

WILKES, MARY BETH
[pen.] Chelsea Treverton; [b.] August 6, 1967, Dayton, OH; [p.] Raymond, Judith Otte; [m.] Mikell Wilkes, November 28, 1992; [ch.] Jessica Rae, Kaleb Mikell; [ed.] Currently Attending Florida Metropolitan University, Major: Marketing Management, Dunedin High School graduate; [occ.] Administrative Assistant, Merchandising; [pers.] The pain expressed in this poem is, I hope, more than I ever have to experience again, in my lifetime. I regret my husband's death more than any other regret I may have. However, I know any action possible or impossible, forgivable or not should be taken to free our children from violent homes. This is a circle that must be broken!; [a.] Dunedin, FL

WILLIAMS, ALLEN
[pen.] Allen Williams; [b.] January 29, 1965, Richmond, VA; [p.] John and Gladys Williams; [m.] Debbie Williams, December 16, 1995; [ch.] Rainey Brie-Anne; [ed.] Open door High School, Liberty Univ.; [occ.] Customer Service Rep., John H. Harland Co.; [hon.] Who's Who American High School Students, 2 yrs. H. S. Class President.; [oth. writ.] 1st time; [pers.] I prefer to write on subjects that makes a person think. I like to put people in contact with their emotions.; [a.] Richmond, VA

WILLIAMS, HECTOR J.
[b.] June 24, 1960, Lafayette; [p.] Rena' Williams, Thelma Williams; [m.] Sarah Williams, June 27, 1987; [ch.] Toni Andrea Trent Reginald; [ed.] Lafayette High, Northwestern Unv.; [occ.] Firefighter Engineer Lafayette Fire Dept.; [memb.] International Assoc. of Black Professional Firefighters Laf. Art Assoc. Writers Guild of America; [hon.] Who's Who, National Literary Award; [oth. writ.] Several poems published in local Newspapers, Contributing Writer for Major Newsparper.; [pers.] The basis for my poetry is life in itself, after all life is but poetry in motion; Produced on paper. That of which Document our lives in a Mystical, Simplicity form of Black and White Imagery.; [a.] Lafayette, LA

WILLIAMS, JANINE
[b.] November 23, 1967, Detroit; [p.] Mary Williams, Charles Govan; [ch.] Two; [ed.] Kettering High School, Cosmetology School (IBA), Ross Business Institute; [occ.] Cosmetologist; [hon.] 2nd Place Winner in Hair Contest; [pers.] I enjoy writing, and I've written plenty of poems and lyrics that I haven't published or revealed to anyone (in good taste) to sort of reflect my personality.; [a.] Detroit, MI

WILLIAMS, KEITH R.
[pen.] Ras K. D. C.; [b.] December 10, 1959, Washington, DC; [p.] Barbara A. Williams, Richard Williams; [m.] Marvarene Carnegie-Williams, October 15, 1994; [ch.] Malik Antonio Williams; [ed.] Anacostia Senior High, Georgetown University UBP, Wilber Force University; [occ.] Retail Distributor Washington Hill Rag, Wash., D.C.; [memb.] Rippler Brotherhood, The Artist Elite Inc., Our Lady Queen of Peace Church, Nativity Catholic Church; [hon.] Nominated for Who's Who in the

East, and several Academic Awards; [oth. writ.] Several unpublished books of poetry, "Mental Graffiti", short stories, and novels.; [pers.] I believe poetry is inside everyone. Yet, it must be tapped, the flow will produce visions unimaginable. Why does imagination become reality? Only God knows!; [a.] Landover, MD

WILLIAMS, LENA
[pen.] Lena Williams; [b.] February 25, 1977, Georgia; [p.] May and Kevin Burton; [m.] Chris Babbitt; [ed.] North Hardin High, Murray State University; [occ.] Student majoring in Creative Writing; [oth. writ.] Several poems published and short stories I have also written for the school paper.; [pers.] I use my writing to let my feeling show without anyone getting hurt.; [a.] Murray, KY

WILLIAMS, ROSALIND QUASH
[pen.] R. Q.; [b.] January 21, 1957, Trinidad, WI; [p.] Roy De Suze and Sheila De Suze; [m.] Eyon Williams, September 15, 1994; [ch.] Kisanka, Kleyon and Krystal; [ed.] Holy Faith Convent, Mid-Florida Tech. and Westside Vo-Tech.; [occ.] Clinical Tech.; [memb.] Tangelo Baptist Women's Chior; [pers.] I think mostly of the kids of today day and what I can do to help them.; [a.] Orlando, FL

WILLIAMS, SARA
[b.] July 17, 1980, Tallahassee, FL; [p.] Lavon and Lisa Williams; [ed.] White Sands Elementary, Nuernburg Middle School, Nuernburg High School, Rickards High School; [occ.] High School Student Grade 10; [memb.] Junior Honor Society, Rickards High Marching Band; [a.] Tallahassee, FL

WILLIAMS, TABITHA BERNICE
[b.] February 15, 1981, Forth Worth, TX; [p.] Willie and Frankie Williams; [ed.] Just enter the 9th grade at Green B. Trimble Technical High School; [oth. writ.] I have wrote other poems but I have never enter them in any contest.; [pers.] My poem is about my Grandmother who I loved very much. She passed away in '94.; [a.] Forth Worth, TX

WILLIAMS, WENDY D.
[b.] February 23, 1971, Springfield, MA; [p.] Robert, Barbara Hickey; [m.] Brian Williams, May 27, 1995; [ed.] Graduate from Univ. of Mass., May 1993, Degree: Political Science, Magna Cum Laude; [occ.] Denny's Restaurant; [hon.] Golden Key Honor Society At Univ. Mass., Xeroux Award from Univ. of Rochester High School Award: American Legion Award George E. Russel Award and the Ludlow Legion Post 52 Award; [oth. writ.] Poem written to husband on wedding day.; [a.] Leominster, MA

WILSON, EMMA BERNICE TAYLOR
[pen.] Emma B. Taylor; [b.] March 24, 1922, Laurens, SC; [p.] William Taylor, Rebecca Taylor; [m.] Fletcher Wilson, December 20, 1947; [ch.] Arthur Douglas; [ed.] Graycourt High, Hosp. for joint diseases, New York, NY Nursing; [occ.] Retired Nurse; [memb.] St. Gerard Catholic Church, American Lung Association, National Committee to preserve Social Security and Medicare S.T.E.P. (Service to enhance potential); [oth. writ.] Poetry 127, 4 songs (non published); [pers.] Let there be joy in the foot steps of tomorrow.; [a.] Detroit, MI

WILSON, HELEN MARGARET
[pen.] Helen Margaret Wilson; [b.] October 13, 1916, Woodland, CA; [p.] Deceased; [m.] Twice married (Both Deceased); [ch.] Ken, Judey, Don (killed in car accident); [ed.] Mount Saint Mary's Academy. Being a third-generation Californian and living in this state for 79 years has been quite educational in itself!; [occ.] Retired from Army Corps of Engineers; [memb.] Sacto Poetry Center, Crocker Art Museum, Friends of the Library, Sacto Jazz Society, Sacto Old City Assoc., Downtown Plaza Assoc., Women of the Moose, Retired Senior Volunteer Program, Nat. Assoc. Retired Fed Employees, other writer's and travelers' groups; [hon.] None directly related to writing, Citations for volunteer work; [oth. writ.] Tapestry of Writing I, II, III, Pincusion Poetry (bio-monthly), Birds and Blooms (Reiman Publishers), several chapbooks, in-house newsletters, Sacramento Bee, Grass Valley/ Nevada City Union, part-time columnist, reported; [pers.] I do write seriously at times...but at the retirement centers where I usually read...I'd rather evoke a smile or a chuckle from my fellow elders any time. We have shed tears aplenty in our lives already. I'm smelling roses and picking daisies! I'll be "pushing them up" soon enough!; [a.] Sacramento, CA

WILSON, MATTHEW
[pen.] Matthew Wilson; [b.] March 17, 1984, Ontario, OR; [p.] Dan and Merlene Phillips; [ed.] 6th Grader; [occ.] Student at Renner Middle School; [oth. writ.] Several other untitled poems and short stories.; [a.] Dallas, TX

WINBURNE, LISA FLEMING
[pen.] Lisa D. Winburne; [b.] July 21, 1964, Goliad, TX; [p.] Mary and Roy Winburne; [m.] Micheal J. Fleming, March 2, 1996; [ed.] Coleman High, Angelo State, UT Arlington; [occ.] Admin. Assistant; [oth. writ.] Poems, lyrics and short stories; [pers.] My style was perfected when I studied poetry interpretation at Angelo State and under Mrs. Giles studying the ulter of Shakespeare. My poems reflect the seasons of my life and those people I meet.; [a.] Forth Worth, TX

WINTERS, BETTY J.
[pen.] Winifred; [b.] March 22, Los Angeles, CA; [ch.] 2 sons; [occ.] Housewife; [memb.] Charity Club for Scholarships for High School Students; [oth. writ.] Poem published in the 1995 "The National Library of Poetry" At Water's Edge.; [pers.] My Grandfather wrote poems. He encouraged me to do so when I was a young girl.; [a.] Panorama City, CA

WINTERS, PEGGY J.
[pen.] Peggy Baker Winters; [b.] April 24, 1932, Kingsport, TN; [p.] Joseph B. Baker and Ida Spray Baker; [m.] John W. Winters, May 10, 1952; [ch.] Paula, Geneva, And John B.; [occ.] Homemaker; [memb.] Hillsboro Bible Baptist Church; [oth. writ.] When the shuttle blew up, Family Reunions, Christmas when I awoke.

WINTERS, TERRI L.
[p.] Kenneth Winters, Linda K. Winters; [m.] Greg L. Mullins; [a.] Huntsville, AL

WINTROW, LINDA K.
[b.] February 1, 1950, Columbus, OH; [p.] Mary Schnelle; [ch.] (Grandson) Chad Kelley; [ed.]

Marysville High School, Marysville, OH, Butler Twp., OH Police Academy, American Police Academy; [occ.] 911 Dispatcher, Miami County, OH; [hon.] J. Edgar Hoover Gold Medal for Distinguished Public Service, 1989 Who's Who in American Law Enforcement; [a.] Laura, OH

WOLFE, BARBARA
[b.] May 30, 1939, England; [m.] Landon K. Wolfe; [ch.] Donna Maes and Cathy Knowles; [oth. writ.] Several writings including poems, songs, and a couple of books. One poem published in a Christian Children's Book.; [pers.] This poem is published in memory of its author, Barbara Wolfe. A loving wife, mother and grandmother. A truly inspirational woman now in the arms of the Lord.; [a.] Martinez, CA

WOLFE, MARCUS HAYDEN
[b.] July 31, 1979, Decatur, GA; [p.] Robert L. Wolfe and Hilary H. Wolfe; [ed.] Chattahoochee High School; [occ.] Waiter; [memb.] AA, Atlanta Insight; [hon.] Patchwork Writing Contest, Chattahoochee Poetry Contest, 1st place Patchwork, 3rd place Chattahoochee Poetry; [pers.] Everyday is a miracle so remember to let go and let God because life is a journey, not a destination.; [a.] Roswell, GA

WOOD, NAOMI R.
[pen.] Naomi (Lowry) Wood; [b.] April 26, 1937, Stidham, OK; [p.] Balford and Jewell Lowry; [m.] Gerald L. Wood, May 18, 1956; [ch.] Hollie Ruth - Clayton Ernest, Gerald L. Jr., Penny Sue and Allen Lee; [ed.] Central High School, Tulsa, OK; [occ.] Homemaker, Secretary for our own business; [hon.] Golden Poet Award, 5 yrs. from World of Poetry, 1 silver Poet Award, from World of Poetry, Valedictorian - 8th grade graduating class; [oth. writ.] Several poems, some published in local newspapers, some published in several anthologies by "World of Poetry Press" also 1 Children's Book that I haven't had published yet.; [pers.] I feel that "God" is the author of all my writings. I am only the pen.; [a.] Springtown, TX

WOODEN JR., REV. THOMAS J.
[b.] May 30, 1957, Memphis, TN; [p.] Thomas Sr. and Helen; [ch.] Thomas III Angela; [ed.] B.A., Elementary Education, History; [occ.] Teacher, 3rd Grade, Richmond Public Schools; [memb.] National Education Assn., Virginia Education Assn., Richmond Education Assn., World TaeKwondo Federation; [hon.] 2nd Degree Black Belt, TaeKwondo, Dean's Lost Student, University of Detroit, License Baptist Minister; [oth. writ.] "Ben Tries Out For Baseball." Manuscript Finished, Illustrations being done. This book has not been submitted, as yet, for publication.; [pers.] It should be the goal of every person to give something back to the community from whence they came.; [a.] Richmond, VA

WOODS, RAYMOND D.
[pen.] Ray Woods, Rex T. Slider; [b.] July 7, 1960, New York City; [p.] Harry and Anne Woods; [m.] Elizabeth Woods, September 26, 1986; [ch.] Michelle Orcutt, Kenneth Nathaniel; [ed.] Brentwood H.S. (New York), West Virginia University, where earned a Bachelor of Science in Aerospace Engineering, UCLA, where studied the business of music.; [occ.] Music Producer, and

owner of Independent Record Label Co.; [memb.] Various Music Business Professional Associations, (NARAS, NAS, NAIRD, etc.); [hon.] Commission as an Officer on the United States Air Force (1982), Honorable Discharge as a Captain, USAF in 1987. Supersonic jet solo certificate (1984). Various awards for music and writing over the years.; [oth. writ.] Regular columnist for Pandemonium and Up Front Magazines. Numerous publications as a music journalist. Poems published in a variety of small press outlets. Also a published songwriter.; [pers.] Poetry is one of many creative outlets for me. I am equally inspired by Da Vinci, Thomas Jefferson, Chuck Yeager, Jack Kerouac, Frank Zappa and Peter Gabriel.; [a.] Portland, OR

WOOLSEY, DEBBY
[b.] November 1, 1959, Vandalia, IL; [p.] Fred and Marge Schmitt Sr.; [ch.] Nicole Lynn Woolsey; [ed.] Vandalia High School; [occ.] Press Operator, Crane Packing Vandalia, IL; [memb.] Mother of Dolors Catholic Church; [pers.] I feel we have turned into a society based on sexual attraction. Our relationships need to be based on communication, interests, and true love, love begins from the heart not our sexual organs.; [a.] Vandalia, IL

WOOLSEY, DEBBY
[b.] November 1, 1959, Vandalia, IL; [p.] Fred and Marge Schmitt Sr.; [ch.] Nicole Lynn Woolsey; [ed.] Vandalia Community High School; [occ.] Rubber Press Operator, Crane Packing Vandalia, IL; [memb.] Mother of Dolors Catholic Church; [pers.] This poem was inspired by physical and sexual abuse cases. I would like to thank the Vandalia City Police, Fayette County Sheriff's Dept., Counselor Janet Evans, Dr. Donald Rames, Priest Stephen Sotiroff, favorite singer song writer Marty Stuart. Thanks for your help.; [a.] Vandalia, IL

WORTMAN, BECKY
[b.] January 8, 1980, Comox; [p.] Wayne and Shelly W.; [ed.] grade 9, Lake Trail Junior Secondary School; [oth. writ.] I've had 3 other poems published in a book at Iliad Press, names are "Walking Alone," "In A World That Hates You" and "In A World That Hates Him"; [pers.] I'm 14 years old and my dream is to become a poet. I like to write my poems about my feelings and about other people's feelings.; [a.] Courtneay, Canada

WRIGHT, JACK E.
[pen.] Jack E. Wright; [b.] June 25, 1970, Charleston, SC; [p.] Jack J. Wright and Marylyn Davis; [ed.] Currently Studying English at Thomas Nelson College; [occ.] Catering Mgr. at the Hampton Coliseum; [oth. writ.] Working on a novel and other short stories, and several volumes of painting!; [pers.] In memory and honor of Dill Solomn and for my love. The first one's for you Robin.; [a.] Hampton, VA

WRIGHT, KEVIN BRIAN
[b.] November 3, 1968, New York; [p.] Dorothea and Richard Wright; [m.] Sharyn Lee Wright; [ch.] Alyssa Lauren Wright; [ed.] Whitestone Academy on the Sound, (Art School) Walt Disney; [occ.] Artist (Cartoonist); [oth. writ.] A Devout Request, Benjamin Bugsy Sregel, The Love In Which We Hold, Baby Blue, The Unknown, Shadow Warrior; [pers.] It is the most God for-saken, feeling to

perceive that in the soul's heart is family and my greatest achievement yet. In memory of "Richard J. Wright" for the art of artless art acknowledges no two lives, because it is born of various styles for only you can be strong one "Dad".; [a.] Glendale, NY

WUNSERLIN, MYRTLE L.
[b.] September 24, 1930, Sharp Co., AR; [p.] Pete and Maye Ratliff; [m.] Wade (Deceased), May 12, 1950; [ch.] Cheri, Charles, Paul, Mike, Patty, Teresa; [ed.] High School grad., Graduated with Associate of Arts degree, 1990: Age 60.; [occ.] Retired. Do crafts and painter.; [hon.] Dean's List, President's List, and best of show for my paintings.; [oth. writ.] None published.; [pers.] The qualities I try to live by: Responsibility, perseverance, and goals to strive for.; [a.] Pearcy, AR

WYLLIE, STANLEY CLARKE
[b.] November 19, 1935, Clearwater, FL; [p.] Stanley Clarke and Eugenia Lee (Tison) Wyllie; [m.] Martha Ann Thomason, June 14, 1963; [ch.] Stanley Clarke III, Susan Lynne, Patricia Anne; [ed.] BS Florida Southern College 1958, MS Florida State University 1963; [occ.] Retired Librarian; [memb.] All Saints Anglican Catholic Church, F and AM, IOOF, Ohio Library Association, American Library Association, Mad River Lions, Florida Genealogical Society, Tau Kappa Epsilon, Toastmasters, Omicron Delta Kappa, AARP, Kentucky Colonel, Republican; [hon.] Knight York Cross of Honor, DeMolay Cross of Honor, Grand Cross of Color-Order of Rainbow, Edward M. Selby Award, Florida Southern College Alumni Distinguished Service Award for Outstanding, Service to Humanity, Freedoms Foundation's Georle Washington Medal; [oth. writ.] "Education in Americanism" previous poems published in National High School and National College Anthologies numerous articles in masonic publication, lions and library publications. Book reviewer for several local and national publications; [pers.] Give your best in all areas of your life, using the talents God gives you.; [a.] Riverside, OH

YARBOROUGH, REBECCA LYNN
[pen.] Rebecca Lynn Yarborough; [b.] September 8, 1980, Fayetteville, AR; [p.] Harvey Louis Yarborough, Sabrina Skinner Poe; [ed.] I am in ninth grade attending Gardendale High School; [occ.] Student; [a.] Gardendale, AL

YEOH, KIM HONG
[b.] May 5, 1959, Perak, Malaysia; [p.] Seng Keat Yeoh, Siew Lean Tan; [ed.] SRI Pinang Teachers' Training College, Malaysia, Malayan Teachers' Training College, Malaysia, University of Oklahoma; [occ.] Edu-Care Montessori School Teaching Assistant; [hon.] College of Fine Arts Dean's Honor Roll, President's Honor Roll; [pers.] Poetry is an expression of personal feeling and thoughts that intrinsically serves as reflections to the realization of the true nature of self.; [a.] Norman, OK

YINGLING, HEATHER
[b.] March 28, 1981; [p.] Jerry and Angela Boyette; [ed.] Baker County High School; [occ.] Student; [memb.] FFA, Dance/Drill Team; [pers.] Most of my writings are inspired by my experiences. I express my feelings and situations in my writings.; [a.] Macclenny, FL

YOMOAH, JENNIFER
[b.] May 2, 1981, Accra, Ghana; [p.] Kate Yomoah, Bruno Yomoah; [ed.] Tarsus American School, Tarsus, Turkey (6th and 7th grade), Hebron Academy (8th and 9th grade); [occ.] Student; [hon.] 7th grade Best English Student Award: 1993-94-Tarsus American School, Tarsus, Turkey, English Honors, Hebron Academy 1995-96; [oth. writ.] One poem, "There Will Be A Day", published in Hebron Academy Literary Magazine; [pers.] I my writing I try to express the longings of the human heart.; [a.] Hebron, ME

YOND, AGNES
[pen.] Agnes Yond; [b.] May 22, 1981, West Africa; [p.] Michael and Grace Yond; [ed.] Presently attending Camelback High School; [hon.] Perfect Attendant, Students of Month and Honor Roll; [pers.] One must accept the good and bad of Nature.; [a.] Phoenix, AZ

YONKMAN, FREDRICK A.
[pen.] Frite Yonkman; [b.] August 22, 1930, Holland, MI; [p.] Frite and Janet (Albers); [m.] Divorced; [ch.] Ryan (10), Sara (40), Margriet (38), Nina (35); [sib.] Hope College (Holland, MI) BA (1952) Law School, University of Chicago (1957), Research Society Process Oriented Psychology (Zurich); [ed.] Consultant to Business and Psycho Analyst; [memb.] American Bar Association; [hon.] NCAA Silver Anniversary Award (1977); [oth. writ.] Technical Articles on Law, Psychology and Religion; [pers.] Listen carefully one never really knows many answers.; [a.] New York, NY

YOUNG, JULIUS RAYNARD
[b.] October 17, 1965, Oxford, MS; [p.] Lou Alice and Birk Young (both deceased), Guardian Elizabeth Burnett (Aunt); [m.] Lya Young, November 8, 1994; [ed.] Lafayette High School, The University of Mississippi (BBA/Marketing); [occ.] Restaurant Manager; [oth. writ.] Several poems, two of which were published in a previous poetry contest. I also write songs and record them at home in my four track studio; [pers.] Even though we suffered tragedies and set backs early in life, myself, or none of my six siblings ever gave up. I try to stress in my poetry that although we all suffer tragedies, we must persevere and be industries and we'll be successful.; [a.] Stone Mountain, GA

ZAFUTO, PATRICIA L.
[b.] June 13, 1954, Buffalo, NY; [p.] Hazel and Pasquale Giallella; [m.] Paul R. Zafuto, September 9, 1972; [ch.] Tricia D. Zafuto; [ed.] Lafayette High School; [occ.] Stenographer, City of Buffalo; [pers.] Vacancy: This poem was written for a special friend who took her life in July, 1995 and is greatly loved and missed.; [a.] Buffalo, NY

ZAGIEL, LEYNA
[pen.] Leyna Zagiel; [b.] March 5, 1982, Deptford, NJ; [p.] Donna and John Zagiel; [ed.] St. Margaret's (Grade 8th) School, Woodbury Hgts. NJ; [occ.] Student; [pers.] To all Mr. Einstein and my Mother and Father for all the support over the years!!!; [a.] Deptford, NJ

ZAHODNE, JOHN
[b.] April 21, 1982, Detroit, MI; [p.] Michael & Joanne Zahodne; [ed.] St. Dunstans School, Grade 8,

Schoolcraft College TAG program; [memb.] St. Dunstans Studen Council President, American Student Council Member, Garden City Hockey club, Boy Scouts of America, St. Dunstans Alter Servers, Garden City Athletic Association Member; [hon.] National Geographic Society Award, Knights of Columbus Spelling Bee Champion, Bishop Borgess Scholastic Olympics Champion (Geography), Presidential Fitness Award, Four-Quarter Gold Honor Roll Award; [oth. writ.] Several unpublished poems; [pers.] I write about life's tough times with a hopeful point of view. I also like my writing to suggest that people should try their hardest in everything they do.; [a.] Canton, MI

ZANDER, MARCUS H.
[b.] April 13, 1965, Wilmington, NC; [p.] Elease H. Zander, Horst H. Zander; [ed.] TC Roberson High School; [occ.] Textile; [oth. writ.] No other published working on compiling a book of poetry; [pers.] I use poetry to reflect my feelings and how I see the world around me. My main influence is life and emotions.; [a.] Asheville, NC

ZAREMBA, JASON
[pen.] Jaysunn; [b.] June 9, 1977, Hammond; [p.] Karen and Anthony Zaremba; [ed.] Senior Wheele High school; [occ.] Taco Bell; [hon.] Fourth place in an Anthropology, A Moment in Time; [oth. writ.] Strong in a Moment in Time; [a.] Valparaiso, IN

ZIMMERLE, WALTER M.
[b.] March 23, 1961, Princeton, IN; [p.] Melvin, Eileen Zimmerle; [ed.] Madison High School, Madison, Ohio; [occ.] British Petroleum; [oth. writ.] Manuscript entitled "The Soul Traveler: Outside Looking Out" (unavailable for publication). Several poems and songs lyrics copyrighted under personal logo - "The Obsession For Expression Collection"; [pers.] Favorite poets and lyricists include: Jim Morrison, Bernie Jaupin, Elton John, Neil Young and Edgar Allen Poe. As a published author, I dedicate my poem in this book to all my skeptical friends - Who's laughing now?!; [a.] Madison, OH

ZMITROVICH, BETH
[b.] May 2, 1984, Harrishburg, PA; [p.] Frederick and Bernadette Zmitrovich; [ed.] Currently a student at Hershey Middle School, Hershey, PA; [occ.] Student; [hon.] Hershey Optimist Club Bike Safety Poster, 1st Place, 1993, Falmouth Goat Races 1994, winner trophy and "Prettiest Goat Award" to "Stinky" the goat, trained and raised by Beth, Falmouth Goat Races 1995, 2 winner trophies awarded to "Airplane" the goat, trained and raised by Beth.; [a.] Hummelstown, PA

ZOLL, HENK G.
[b.] January 9, 1935, Ackmaar, The Netherlands; [m.] Elsa, November 2, 1956; [ch.] Marika, Yvonne, Anthony, Daniel; [ed.] In forestry and Agriculture (Holland.) Became an American Citizen in 1962.; [occ.] Professional Land Surveyor with City of Redding since 1967; [oth. writ.] Poems about love and life. Stories in rhyme for retirement, celebrations and others festive occasions; [pers.] We became to America in 1957. Hobbies are: Writing short stories, poetry, watercolors and woodworking.; [a.] Redding, CA

ZUNINO, GIANNA MARIA
[b.] September 26, 1980, Santa Rosa; [p.] Lorenzo Zunino, Cathie Zunino; [ed.] St. Eugene's Elementary School, Ursuline High School; [hon.] Highest Achievements in Literature, Science, Religion, History, Presidential Award for Maintaining above a 3.5 continuously; [pers.] I love to write of lost loves. I hope to continue my education at Ursuline High School and go to College at Harvard or to Davis, I have two sisters; [a.] Santa Rosa, CA

Index
of
Poets

Index

Cannon, Christy   235
Cannon, Kelly   324
Cannon, Sarah   461
Cantori, Maija   435
Capaccio, Dana   14
Capen, Phyllis   118
Capley, Sandy   276
Cappaninee, Gina R.   81
Cappuccino Sr., Anthony J.   511
Carabeo, Stephannie   270
Caras, Jevin W.   397
Carbonell, JWC   107
Cardella, Sandra   277
Carder, Paula B.   102
Cardona, Efrain A.   471
Carey, Lindsey A.   452
Carini, Katherine   182
Carlisle, Alexander Patterson   472
Carmichael, Nancy E.   72
Carnes, Diane W.   533
Carney, Patrick J.   391
Carnley, Jason Sean   500
Carpenter, Austin B.   27
Carpenter, Dani   44
Carpenter, Jennifer M.   418
Carpenter, Linda Jane   171
Carpenter, Mae   431
Carpenter, Nicholas   167
Carr, Dean   449
Carr, Kathleen S.   352
Carr, Marie M.   415
Carr, Patsy   293
Carr, Valerie   92
Carrier, Stacey   222
Carrillo, Sarah   192
Carrington, Kristi   343
Carrizo, Michael A.   339
Carroll, Mary Jane   336
Carruthers, Amy   235
Carson, Curtis J.   477
Carson, John   322
Carson, Mildred M.   356
Carswell, Mary Ann   51
Carswell, Melody A.   413
Cartee, Clifford C.   236
Carter, J. T.   210
Carter, Kristal M.   189
Carter, Shamona Yvonne   206
Carter, Terri S.   94
Carty, Lee   335
Caruolo, Steven P.   213
Carvalho, Juliana   188
Carver, Shirley   91
Casale, Joey Jude   484
Casamassima, Brian   242
Casciato, Jayne   181
Cascino, Melissa   343
Cashell, Deloris E.   403
Casper, Sara   195
Casperson, Charlene   408
Cassel, Barb   248
Cassella, Megan   175
Cassilly, Mary   320
Castaneda, Carmalita Alvina   475
Castanik, Craig   248
Castile, Marjorie M.   184
Castle, Laura   184
Castonguay, Debra   465
Catlin, Frederick B.   40
Cea, Vincent   224
Ceballo, Carmen   405

Cellini, Christian   472
Cellini, Lishele   65
Celso, Erica   256
Cercone, James Anthony   511
Ceresa, Peter A.   230
Cerny, Eve Marie   149
Cerny, Paul   103
Chadwick, Allison   115
Chadwick, Cynthia Leigh   3
Chamberlain, Cathy M.   478
Chambers, Ethel H.   467
Chambers, Kristi   482
Chambley, Joseph P.   307
Chambliss, Tracy   113
Chan, Betsy   247
Chandler, P.   107
Chaney, Catherine   398
Chang, Peicha   112
Chang, Yih-Fian   276
Chapin, Mary Elizabeth   318
Chaplin, William A.   295
Chapman, Adam   247
Chapman, LaWayne   333
Chapman, Sara Rose   212
Chapman, Sarah   209
Chappell, Joy   175
Chapuis, Lisa   356
Charles, Bonnie Atkinson   25
Charlton, Mildred M.   411
Charnesky, Michelle M.   58
Chase Jr., Frank   256
Chatman, Kimberly L.   444
Chavez, Kristy   181
Chavis, Angela Eunice   237
Chavis, Brenda   27
Chedrick, Lee Ann   90
Chen, Catherine   400
Chenette, George   443
Cheser, Jessica Beth   171
Cheslick, Anthony   465
Chiang, Michael   54
Chiari, Phillip Adam   463
Childs, Etta M.   406
Childs, Stephanie Elease   277
Chin, Cynthia Erin   244
Chipman, Mercy   56
Chisambisha, Kasanda D.   397
Chisholm, Ethel Marie   131
Chisolm, Abria L.   242
Chobod, Leslie A.   428
Choi, Min   342
Chow, Jaimee   518
Christenson, Tamra   299
Christian, Judy   439
Christiansen, Yvonne   294
Christianson, Frances M.   524
Christopher, Dolores S.   520
Christopherson, Amber   25
Christopherson, Rachel   219
Chuck, Christopher Tracy   40
Chumly   457
Chung, Satrena   211
Church, Lisa   522
Churchill, Marcia D.   409
Cinelli, Shonda   192
Cisneros, Tomas   292
Claffey, Susan M.   387
Clancy, Joe   373
Clark   102
Clark, Jean   317
Clark, Lisa   164

Clark, Loren D.   182
Clark, Tara D.   118
Clarke, Claudette   243
Clarke, Valeria Lanza   113
Clary, Emmanuel   137
Clauer, Cara Ann   468
Clautice, Edward W.   484
Clawson, Carl H.   4
Clay, Lillian   87
Clay, Mary M.   85
Cleary, Harmony   515
Clelland, Linda K.   165
Clemente, Charity   407
Clendenin, Allisha   156
Clever, Joanna Ella   188
Clifton, Kala R.   409
Clifton, Shirley   216
Clother, Tonya   112
Cluck, Marjorie   439
Coady, Alyssa   471
Cobb, Carol Ann   476
Cobb, E. Marilyn   194
Cobbs, Andre N.   244
Cocherell, Michael J.   380
Cochran, Bessie   30
Coco, Frances   21
Cody, Erin R.   247
Coelho, Amie   245
Coffee, Leona V.   349
Coffin, Kim   166
Coggan, Andrea R.   17
Coggins, Bernadine   148
Cogswell, Laurie M.   74
Cole Jr., Daniel   406
Cole, Juanita M.   369
Cole-Palmer Jr., Rupert   207
Coleman, Alicia Louise   478
Coleman, Elizabeth J.   37
Coleman, Kenneth M.   425
Colgan, Alice   463
Colletti, Tim   453
Collins, Amica   407
Collins, Bobbi   190
Collins, Canadia   480
Collins, Erica K.   464
Collins, Jackie   486
Collins, Janet E.   497
Collins, Marjorie W.   440
Collins, Nicole   185
Collins, Terry Lynn   509
Colón, Lisa Lynn   374
Colton, James H.   495
Combest, Eileen   466
Commers, Paul   208
Commissaris, Lindsay   171
Compton, Phyllis W.   462
Conant-Rusch, June   53
Conaway, William J.   388
Congialdi, Antoinette   463
Conley, Raquel   453
Conner, Clara Jane   406
Conner, Kami   170
Conner, Mary Fox   347
Cook, Christina   156
Cook, Joey N.   81
Cook, Lahoma M.   187
Cook, Richelle   283
Cook, Thomas E.   285
Cook, William A.   199
Cooke, Janette V.   515
Cooke, Patrick M.   211

Coolidge, Frances Dea   155
Coons, Lindsay   353
Cooper, Brenda E.   261
Cooper, Jana Dawn   511
Cooper Jr., Freddie L.   243
Cooper, Kara L.   184
Cooper, Leslie   435
Cooper, Nyanontee E.   451
Cooper, Valerie Ruth   304
Cooper, Wanda   97
Cope, Cindi   124
Copenhaver, Joyce   327
Copenhaver, Rodney   394
Coppler, Cova Moore   22
Corcoran, Christine A.   4
Cordasco, Michelle H.   328
Cordell, Crystal   129
Cordone, Victor E.   193
Corlis, Deborah J.   256
Cormier, Amy   138
Corneille, Susan D.   286
Cornelio III, William A.   395
Cornell, Jennifer   73
Cornett, Mary Galligan   313
Cornish, Paul   190
Cornwell, R. C.   290
Costa, Sandra   195
Cote, Elaine   475
Cotner, Gloria   336
Cottingham, Melissa   190
Courneya, Nicole   411
Couser, Yvette Burnham   202
Cowen, Caroline Louise   151
Cowles, Laurence R.   307
Cox, Andrew J.   246
Cox, Dannie   398
Cox, Helen H.   500
Cox, Kimberlee Bethany   376
Cox, Tara J.   96
Coy-Moultrup, Jennifer   166
Craig, Barbara   466
Craig, Ruby   216
Craig, Sharon   282
Craven, Quintina   92
Craven, Violet   107
Crawford, Wylodine   292
Creach, Mr. Jewel   328
Creamer, Rosalie   282
Crego, Beverly   145
Crider, Kim   356
Crislip, Cindi   476
Croad, Melissa   174
Crockett, Elisabeth   154
Crommett, Ardelle D.   26
Cron, Heather   533
Cronic, David L.   125
Cronin, Therese   191
Cross, Jane Gillespie   491
Crow, E. Anne   96
Crownover, Ethel   521
Crytser, Teresa   453
Cullen, Lisa   450
Culley, Rikki M.   293
Currie, Billy Joe   469
Cvach, Philip E.   93
Cypert-Arnold, Kathleen   353
Czarnecki, Sara   264

D

D. P. F.   224

Filip, Robert E.   195
Finchum, Wendy   454
Findley, Martha   69
Finizio, E. J.   196
Fink, Essie   244
Finke, A. C.   309
Finley, Adam   131
Fiorelli, Linda   410
Fisher, Cary   127
Fisher, Jill L.   349
Fisher, Kevin   434
Fisher, Patrick A.   263
Fisher, Ruth E.   107
Fishman, Julie   430
Fistzgiles, Freda C.   146
Fitzgerald, Andrew   250
Flanders, Charlene S.   400
Fleming, Barbara J.   261
Fleming, Lucindra   181
Fleming, Michael   350
Fletcher, Dawna Holmes   135
Flinchum, Tiffany   455
Flintzer, Albert J.   32
Flipse, Alexander   132
Flores, Rae   454
Florio, Lisa Ann   60
Flynn, A. Benington   396
Flynn, Jamie   519
Flynn, Megan   442
Flynn, Stephanie   442
Foard, Lilia   309
Foat, Emily Fay   33
Focas, Angella A.   12
Foley, Estelle   258
Foltz, Kelly   430
Fontaine, August S.   399
Ford, Adrienne   133
Ford, Jennifer   65
Forehand, Eleanor VanFleet   398
Forest, James J. F.   532
Forester, Terrence Darnell   222
Foster, C. W. Mickey   297
Foster, Jennifer   438
Foster, Shirley   105
Fountain, Kenneth H.   321
Fountain, Wendy   294
Fox, Lois K.   450
Fraites, Roald Constantine   93
Franco, Gerhard Anthony   445
Franklin, Caroline M.   252
Franklin, Mabel E.   370
Franklin, Sandra   110
Frasure, E. P.   99
Frazier, Peggy M.   219
Freckleton, Teresha   291
Fredelake, Genevieve   169
Frederick, Ford   157
Fredricks, Bernadette   486
Freeman, Angela Kaye   153
Freeman, David R.   120
Freeman, Deborah A.   258
Freeman, Hawk   56
Freeman, Rudolph V.   211
Freeze, Evelyn Harmon   177
Fremgen, Frank J.   138
French, Eleanor A.   401
French, Erin   472
Frenzel, Albert   146
Frey, Jennifer   81
Frieben, Kerry   452
Friend, Susan   283

Fries, Richard   103
Fritz, Deborah Marie   144
Frost, Jeff W.   180
Frost Jr., Michael D.   328
Fruehauf, Edna   525
Fry, Dorothy Deuell   513
Fryar, Elaine B.   19
Fugate, Norm   334
Fuhrmann, Norma   88
Fuller, Kimbrely R.   311
Funk, Fred   33
Funkhouser Jr., Charles L.   33
Funkhouser, Shannon   106
Futch, Renee   113
Fye, Patricia   111

G

Gadoury, Gilbert F.   381
Gaeckler, Roger   292
Gagne, Steve   453
Gagnon, Debra   161
Gagnon, Rebecca   192
Gahchan, Elenor   475
Galdi, Antony C.   25
Gale, Bree   120
Gallagher, Craig   136
Gallagher, Linda Sue   172
Gallo, Rosemarie   118
Galvan, Rosie   274
Gamache, Rosalie A.   206
Gambill, Valerie S.   202
Gamble, Paul C.   198
Gamlowski, Bessie N.   407
Gannon, JoAnn   444
Garcia, Christina   5
Garcia, Dana   477
Garcia, Victoria D.   220
Gardner, Adrianna   149
Gardner, Jean   329
Gardner, Rosemary P.   103
Garrett, Eugenia M.   405
Garris Jr., Fred   11
Garrison, Melissa   337
Gartman, Jessica   76
Garver, Gina   81
Garvin, Kelly E.   357
Garwitz, Lawrence D.   451
Garwood, Linda E.   426
Garza, Michael   500
Gaston, Phil   281
Gattuso, Carmen   400
Gauvin, Debbie   239
Gayler, Nancy L.   187
Geanuracos, Christine   24
Geck, Corrine L.   408
Gee, Jason Antone   491
Geiger, Kelvin   444
Geist, Marsha L.   382
George, Michelle Anne   410
George, Carol Wilson   152
Gerardot, Michele   338
Gerber, Robert L.   391
Gerson, Shari   457
Gerulskis, Frank   401
Geurkink, Kate   452
Geyer, Dorothy   492
Ghizali, Atif   242
Giacinto, Mary D.   183
Gianocaro, Michele A.   358
Gibbs, G. Gene   194

Gibbs, Rachel   386
Gibson, Jennifer Lauren   362
Gibson, Marcia   181
Giel, Melinda Leslie   411
Gifford, Sandra K.   302
Gilbert, Jaki M.   511
Gilbreath, Shelia   91
Gilchrest, Winniferd   224
Gillanders, Earl Ross   517
Gilmer, Ruth   279
Gilmore-Shourds, Toni Ann   396
Gingrich, Pamela M.   274
Giriodi, Ethel   236
Girmus, Sylvia   305
Girod, Kendra Jeanne   86
Gisin, Vera L.   201
Gissel, Keith   114
Gjebre, William   228
Glass, Mel   370
Gleason, Reyna   112
Gleason, Sandra   110
Glessman, Dee   251
Gloege, Dayle Susan   132
Glover, Gale   377
Goddard, Linda   318
Godette, Richard A.   305
Goedel , D. C.   385
Goff, Rodger A.   454
Gogerty, J. W.   275
Goh, Jacqueline   510
Goldman, Eleanor   236
Goldman, Martin   378
Goldsbury, Nicole   373
Goldsmith, Serena   232
Golian, Linda Marie   68
Golmon, Frances Walters   404
Gomez, KeriLyn   314
Gonsalves, Ronda Darlene D.   221
Gonzalez, Blanca Estella   126
Gonzalez, Maria   361
Gonzalez, Maria Adorable Theresa   185
Gooch, Christie A.   16
Good, Monroe C.   190
Goode, Alice Louise Jones   120
Goodell, Seth   103
Goodenough, Aimee   139
Goodgame, Lucile H.   366
Gordon, Evelyn Rains   246
Gordon, Ginger   370
Gordon, Kathleen   330
Gordon, Lynne Marie   416
Goreham, Samantha   289
Gorey, Rachael Marie   113
Goshert, Pearl L.   216
Gossett, James A.   528
Gotaas, Julie   343
Gotcher, Tana D.   269
Gouletas, Cassandra   237
Gowdy, Jaime   490
Gower, Bonnie Jean   8
Gower, Cortney   252
Goyette, Moragh   443
Graber, Marina Leigh   319
Grace, Jamie L.   526
Grace, Siobhan   214
Graliker, Mary   411
Gramckow, K. Barnett   112
Grant, Allen   27
Grant, Anthony L.   122
Grass, Paige B.   218
Grasse, Louis   309

Grassl, Mary T.   377
Gray, Charlotte   128
Gray, Debra A.   30
Gray, Ida M.   500
Gray, Mike   415
Gray, William C.   103
Grayson, R. Larry   200
Graziano, H. P.   385
Grebner, Bernice Prill   474
Greco, Margaret   331
Green, Kelli   85
Green, Roy N.   205
Green, Teresa   304
Greenberg, Lisa   322
Greene, Lewis   73
Greene, Susie R.   383
Greene, Tiare   95
Greening, Virginia   293
Greenough, Brian   25
Greenwood, Timothy P.   202
Greer, Judy   316
Gregersen, Lisa   75
Gregory, Nancy   89
Gregory, Rachel   99
Gregory, Sharon A.   198
Gregos, Adele LeBuffe   480
Greuel, Joyce   51
Grewe, Rachel Elizabeth   92
Grice, Kathryn R.   367
Griffel, Scott   223
Griffin, Jessica   374
Griffin, Norma Jean   438
Griffith, Megan   322
Griffith, Staci   273
Griggs, Joanne   314
Grimaldi, Pamela   217
Grimes, Jack   493
Grimes, Sylvia N.   109
Grimm, Barbara J.   127
Grimm, Phyllis   297
Grimsley, Larrie   313
Grindem, Tom   296
Grom, Frank   134
Groman, Janell   491
Groner, Leslie K.   68
Grooms, Angel   23
Grooms, Carolyn   143
Gross, Kenneth   317
Gross, Kim   188
Gross, Laura   527
Grosskopf, Bess   154
Grossman, Ruth   221
Groves, Amber   254
Grubb, Gary M.   363
Gruggett, Jennifer   363
Grusecki, Ryan   98
Guay, Marie C.   188
Gudgel, Brent   240
Gueno, Justine   419
Guernsey, Terry   288
Guffey, Charlene Ann   14
Guild, Theodore F.   283
Gullickson, Margel   330
Gully, Joan Reego   174
Gumbert, Laura   327
Gunby, Laura E.   70
Gunn, Nannette Sexton   411
Gurney, Melinda   307
Gustin, Krissy   312
Guy, Barbara D.   120
Guy, Darlene J.   43

Martin, Bonnie Sherouse   244
Martin, Casey Allen   24
Martin, Chris   33
Martin, Daisy B.   137
Martin, Janet R.   533
Martin, Kris   324
Martin, Lauren   176
Martin, Maria   357
Martin, Monnie   485
Martin, Quentin   114
Martin, Roma   287
Martin-Terry, Wanda J.   224
Martinelli, Lucille   330
Martinez, Bob G.   6
Martinez, Charles   16
Martinez, Ursula   276
Marturano, Susan   460
Martyna, Sharon M.   229
Maser II, Maurice   365
Mason, Edward M.   502
Mason, Patricia A.   266
Masone, Rosanne   110
Massey, Phyllis Johnson   117
Massie, Melissa M.   61
Mastel, Missy Sue   75
Masters, Carol   14
Masters, Gerard G.   330
Matejovitz, Tara Lynn   200
Mathews, Christina   526
Mathews, Kristy   446
Matney, Melissa L.   69
Mattar, Yvonne   108
Matthews, Thomas P.   390
Matthews-Hicks, L. A.   192
Mattson, Christine   255
Mattson, Jennifer   187
Mattson, William C.   287
Maurer, Doreen   498
Mausling, Alen   401
Maxfield, Margaret A.   445
Maxwell, Dorothy R.   498
Maxwell, Katherine   356
May, Bedford D.   466
May, Crystal   145
May, Erin   404
May, Felicity   241
May, Jesse   188
Mayfield, Wilma Gail   267
Maynard, Denise   517
Mayner, Kathy   327
Maynor, Bridget L.   478
Mayo, Catherine   190
Mazella, Julie Ann   446
Mazikoske, Megan   322
Mazzara, Ellen   19
McAdoo, Queen   271
McAllister, Evelyn   10
McBride, Candace   161
McBride, Julie   51
McCain, Kenneth   375
McCall, Delores   35
McCants, Annie M.   10
McCarthy, Elizabeth   514
McCarthy, Lucille C.   87
McCartney, Jennifer   316
McCarty, Kelly   163
McCary, Matthew Charles   47
McCauley, Preston   269
McCay, Michael   329
McClean, Monique   64
McCloud, Trish   193

McClung, Amber   162
McClure, Annie L.   254
McClure, Debi   136
McCollim Jr., Robert J.   278
McConnell, Chrissy   246
McConnell, Ryan M.   457
McCook, Rhonda J.   223
McCormick, Jennifer   171
McCoy, A. Danielle   262
McCoy, Carson E.   257
McCoy, Edmund C.   488
McCoy, Marcus D.   506
McCoy, Muriel   50
McCrary, Julie   430
McCray, Katt   186
McCreery, Kristine K.   177
McCroskey, Theo   205
McCue, Lon Dawson   309
McCullough, Joy   341
McCurley, Harriett   526
McDaniel, William C.   98
McDaniels, Hazel   517
McDeavitt, Patrick   277
McDeed, Kathryn   308
McDermott, Joseph   321
McDonald, Grace   432
McDonnell, Lindsay   179
McDonnell, Mark   52
McDorman, Melissa   190
McDowell, Avice   403
McDowell, Marleene F.   308
McEachern, Shannon   273
McElroy, Becky   464
McElwee, James R.   530
McFeely, Mary   176
McGava, Stacy   455
McGeary, Frank   243
McGee, Amy Lynne   153
McGilvray, Aprile   131
McGinn, Donna M.   504
McGinn, Janet L.   488
McGowan, Les   66
McGrady, Ed   496
McGrath, Judith   51
McGregor, Marion   433
McGuire, Jennifer   177
McGuire, Valerie J. Wiley   275
McHugh, Martha   368
McInerney, Anne   33
McIntire, April   236
McIntire, Mark   178, 411
McIver, Vanessa   394
McKeay, Martin   445
McKenzie, Xanthea   393
McKinney, Ben   255
McKinney, Eleanor V.   157
McKnight, D. Y.   201
McLain, Reta   93
McLaughlin, Delta   530
McLaughlin, Michelle   425
McLemore, William   220
McLester, Carol A.   128
McLochlin, Lynn   171
McMahan, CherylAnn   474
McMahon, Marie M.   347
McMahon, Robert   266
McMenomy, Edward B.   491
McMillin, Janet S.   482
McMorris, Arlene V.   161
McNairy, Harold Gabriel   523
McNeil, Dani   22

McNeill, Rudy   117
McNulty, Lois B.   185
McPheeters, Rex   195
McQueen, Cynthia   18
McRae, Natalie   359
Mead, Kelin J.   163
Meadows, Tara   110
Mealy, Bertha   407
Meché, Daniel E.   125
Mecolick, Sandy   221
Meeink, Susan   112
Meeks, Barbara Jean   160
Mehlberg, Rachel   91
Mehrmann, Michelle   437
Mehta, Dina M.   247
Mehta, Lisa   323
Meier, Angela   21
Meier, Mary D.   70
Meier, Rolf W.   284
Meigs, Cindy   3
Meller, William   306
Mellette, Shirley   394
Mello, Tony   105
Melson, Sadie F.   196
Melton, Rebecca   282
Melville, Anthony   20
Mendenhall, May   359
Mendis, Mary   53
Menides, Laura Jehn   319
Mente, Matthew   417
Mercurio, Cindy   9
Mercurio, Michael N.   80
Merenhole, Marie   315
Merry, Trisha   276
Messinger, Sharlie   228
Messinger, Susan   199
Mestas, Rachael   496
Metters, Shelley   270
Meuer, Norma Shippy   433
Meyer, Christine L.   258
Meyer, Marc   329
Meyer, Melanie Marie   362
Michael, Ted   276
Michel, Olga   423
Michonski, Timothy A.   105
Micklo, Cathleen   153
Miclea, Anamaria   17
MiddleBrooks, Joseph D.   421
Middlemist, Michelle   442
Middleton, Olene   448
Middleton, Ruth   102
Midgette, Vera   100
Migdal, Colleen   237
Migdalski, Wojtek   300
Mihalek, Revina   117
Miles, Deborah S.   408
Miles, Hedy Christine   522
Miles, Nicole   174
Millecam, Jennifer   168
Miller, Alisa Ann   138
Miller, Angelina   257
Miller, Bridget Ann   407
Miller, Carl R.   238
Miller, Debbie   129
Miller, Erin M.   39
Miller, Ernestine   402
Miller, Gloria A.   84
Miller, Jeanette   417
Miller, Jesica   176
Miller, Jessica A.   73
Miller, Joan Y.   337

Miller, Judie L.   325
Miller, Katherine   332
Miller, Melissa A.   59
Miller, Renee M.   99
Miller, Rosemary   229
Miller, Rosemary Shannon   391
Miller, Suzie   529
Miller, Thomas G.   454
Miller, Rev. Titus C.   281
Millias, Teresa   231
Mills, Betty   154
Mills, David   23
Mills, Katie   371
Mills, Mark Spencer   321
Mills, Paul   224
Mills, Robert A.   459
Milner, Edith Faye Wilson   510
Milton, Melanie   333
Mims, Wayne   461
Minano, Janet   508
Mineer, Nancy   419
Miner, Tod K.   275
Minga, Linda   320
Minium, Don W.   483
Miskie, Brianne   4
Mitchell, George   525, 530
Mitchell, Hakima   504
Mitchell, Jean   312
Mitchell, Joanne   426
Mitchell Jr., Arthurlee L.   251
Mitchell, Kelly   314
Mitchell, Marlene L.   372
Mitchell, Romel   387
Mitchell, Sarah   294
Mitcheltree, Leigth   165
Mitchem, Shelby   97
Mizner, Wanda   99
Moehlenpah, Tammy   277
Moeller, Heidi   516
Moeller, Michael R.   311
Mohan, Sherri   520
Molinare, Lisa   169
Mommsen, Laura   177
Mong, Kimberly   321
Montana, Skye   233
Montano, Frances Margaret   404
Montarbo, Joy   397
Montgomery, Lois   166
Montgomery, Melissa C.   166
Montoya, Maria-Elena   164
Moody, Judy   76
Moody, Virginia Blakemore   93
Moon, D. Dragon   115
Mooney, Laura   317
Mooningham, Ellen   402
Moore, Alexandrea   467
Moore, Ashli D.   482
Moore, Bettie Lee   146
Moore, Bridie   239
Moore, Clemis T.   332
Moore, Elnora S.   43
Moore, Eve   474
Moore, Janie M.   504
Moore, Louise   425
Moore, Maronda   174
Moore, Michael J.   324
Moore, Michelle   76
Moore, Precious   291
Moore, Robin A.   203
Moore, Sharon L.   276
Moore, Tiffany   275

Morales Jr., Daniel Romero   34
Morales, Kika   376
Moran, Robert J.   453
Morder, Debbie   119
Morelli, Angelina M.   258
Moreno, Carlos A.   261
Morgan, Charity L.   402
Morgan, Dwight C.   528
Morgan, Patrick   105
Morgan, Petrina   228
Morgan, Sarah Elise   200
Morgan-Ramsey, Micki   176
Morganthaler, Adam   161
Moriarty Jr., Paul J.   298
Morice, Donna M.   520
Morin, Patricia   197
Morrill, Elaine   398
Morris, Brian   6
Morrison, Dennis Michael   513
Morrison, Neli   163
Morrow, Brian R.   474
Morrow, Jennifer Lee   88
Morrow, Natalie   361
Morrow, Nathaniel   428
Morse, Florence   406
Morss-Thomas, Julie A.   55
Morton, J. Michael   430
Moseley, Kira   167
Moseley, Nicole   356
Mosier, Amber   403
Mosior, Toni   456
Moss, Annie Darlene   18
Mossey, K. A.   290
Mourad, Adriana   41
Mowery, Gerald E.   62
Moyer, Tina   218
Mrohs, Jennifer   451
Mudd, James H.   510
Mueller, Kathleen   345
Mueller, Valerie   390
Muhammad, Pchernavia T.   291
Muhtasib, Yasmine   462
Muja, Kathleen A.   179
Mulaosmanovic, Jasmina   484
Mullaney, Abbie   19
Mullar, Betty   254
Mullins, Dorothy W.   16
Mullvain, Richard   114
Muncy, Virginia   110
Munford, Brenda G.   399
Munger, Timothy   115
Mungin, Theodore L.   215
Muntz, Margaret Mills   54
Muntzel, Christiana   129
Murch, Ronald A.   198
Murchison, Ida M.   497
Murdock, Charles W.   16, 494
Murphey, Mary   61
Murphy, David   36
Murphy, Jillian   47
Murphy, Robert W.   98
Murray, Angela   473
Murray, Brad   160
Murray, Kelly   435
Murray, Norma S.   339
Murtagh, Kathleen   308
Musto, Jennifer L.   175
Myatt, Treva   196
Myers, Linda   62
Myers, Ruth A.   92
Myles, Gina D.   49

Mynheir, Sarah   115
Mynster, Louise   55
Myrick, Sharon T.   217
Myszka, Linda   415

N

Nagel, Jennifer Jean   183
Nail, Preston   462
Naivar III, William Joseph   226
Nance, Katie   446
Naphtali, Ashirah S.   479
Narula, Nisha   306
Nassar, Maximilian T.   380
Nation, David   160
Naughton, Heather   487
Neal, Demetria   496
Neal, Kelsey   174
Neal, Rachael S.   105
Nealy, Velma Bailey   96
Nee, P. Vincent   229
Neebling, Marisa Anne   367
Needham, Judith   515
Neely, Tammy   101
Neiffer, Audrey   20
Nellams, Nicola   365
Nelson, Adelle L.   399
Nelson, Eric   137
Nelson, Erin M.   142
Nelson, Gracie L.   416
Nelson, Jarred M.   505
Nelson, Jennifer   363
Nelson, Laurie Gaskell   89
Nelson, Peg   457
Nelson-Kortland, Erik   245
Nesbit, Harry L.   499
Neumann, Gale   363
Nevers, Lilly   342
Nevins, Jennifer   82
Newcombe, Anthony   45
Newharth, Diana   492
Newman, Jennifer (Reddig)   168
Newman, Margaret M.   420
Newman, Meredith   339
Newmyer, Catherine R.   143
Newton-Fox, Sharon   108
Ney, Larry D.   323
Nguyen, Thao Ngoc   106
Nguyen, Thuy   98
Nichols, Carrie   502
Nichols, Emily   21
Nichols, Jane S.   487
Nichols, Jo Lynn   63
Nichols, Matt B.   446
Nichols, Pattie   116
Nichols, Tamela Y.   290
Nickels, Ann E.   35
Nickle, V. Janie   285
Nicol, Henry Joshua   503
Nielsen, Michael P.   54
Nielson, Alyce M.   24
Nielson, M. Edward   111
Nikolla, Rose A.   234
Nikpay, Sayeh   92
Nilles, Laura   84
Nitteberg, Verona   219
Niu, June   358
Nolan, Judy A.   425
Nolen, Russell D.   291
Noll, Lori   180
Nolton, Tiffany   109

Nor, Raneath   291
Nordstrom, Jenny   446
Norman, Gloria-Marie   170
Norris, Scott   462
Northen, Lindsey   427
Norton, Sarah N.   386
Nottingham, Quinton L., Jr.   489
Nowicki, Jane M.   498
Noyce, JoAnn Wright   172
Nuding, Meghan A.   70
Nunez, Cathy   128
Nunley, Sarah Michelle   232
Nuske, D. H.   120
Nuta, Christina A.   13
Nyarko, Stephen   458
Nzyoka, Cyd W.   258

O

O'Brien, Debra K.   406
O'Bryan, Patrick W.   461
O'Byrne, Kim   168
Occhilto, Chris   135
Ochi, Maiko   78
O'Connell, Brian T.   20
O'Connor, Aloysius   489
O'Connor, Eleanor   245
O'Connor, Erin   135
Oden, Renda   285
Odiorne, Maggie   325
O'Donnell, Dixie   521
Odum, Beulah   31
Odum, Harriett H.   315
Ogilvie, Chris   136
O'Hara, John William   331
Ohmes, Donald   483
Oligney, Sandra   195
Olinde, Sarah   296
Olivares, Benjamin   18
Olivarez, Melissa   426
Olive, Mary Allen   354
Oliveira, Brenna Lyne   38
Oliver, Beth   36
Oliver III, Jesse M.   63
Olmstead, Ned   331
Olney, Amy J.   260
Olsen, Connie   246
Olsen, Doreen   487
Olsen, Sherry J.   514
Olson, Gloria   108
Olson, Kelly   88
Olson, Shanna E.   273
Olson, Sherry   278
Olson, Willard J.   456
O'Meara, Dennis   18
O'Neil, Susan   269
O'Quin, Jill   82
Orbeck, Rose   263
O'Reilly, Megan A.   429
Orendorff, Johanna   447
Orme, Della   255
O'Rourke, Sheenagh M.   220
Orr, Maureen Emily   59
Ortiz, Roxanne   116
Orton, Patricia Osborne   208
Osborn, Chadwick D.   251
Osborn, Marisa   314
Osborne, Erin   239
Osborne, Jean   444
Osborne, Kim M.   164
Osborne, Renee Nicole   390

Osby, Lenne   448
Oscar, Jeff   181
Oslund, Pamela S.   96
Ossowski, Stacey   106
Osterberger, Grace   327
Osterman, Donna   531
Ostrowski, Jillian   322
Oudbier, David P.   472
Ouellette, Joe   313
Oufnac, Annessa C.   145
Ouige   264
Overfield, Kendra   361
Owens, Caroline   7
Owens, Catherine A.   474
Owens, Flora   482
Owens, Jean Ann   310
Owens Jr., William Sammuel   281
Owens, Lisa   330
Owens, Ora Lee   357
Owens, S. Krista   392
Ownby, Louise   381
Oxford, Margaret J.   314
Ozan, Mahmut Esat   352

P

Pace, Lu   307
Pacheco, Abril Borrego   470
Packett, Kyle   382
Padgett, Jenny   319
Padgett, Krista   366
Padilla, Christina   26
Pagans, Lonza R.   169
Paine, Roger D.   454
Pajcic, LeAnn   439
Pakstis, Diana Lynn   489
Palanca, Ramon G.   102
Palczak, Pegeen   106
Pall, Charlotte   477
Pallares, Maria-Cristina   56
Palmer, Ann A.   37
Palmer, Heidi   186
Palmer Jr., John   178
Palmer, Stephanie   117
Pangilinan, Jason   189
Panick, Krista   374
Pannell, Perry   223
Pant, Renuka   273
Pantaleone, Joan   324
Pantano, Susan   460
Panza, Michael   47
Panzeter, Barbara Craig   150
Paquette, Susan   290
Paradis, Gilbert   69
Parendo, Juanita M.   318
Parent, Eric   141
Parfitt, Connie   162
Paris, Kristina   365
Park, Susannah A.   278
Parke, Karen   363
Parker, Gail C.   365
Parker, Jennifer   185
Parr, Corrie L.   27
Parrillo, Denise F.   483
Parrish, Melissa Ann   379
Parson, Ella   90
Parson, Nicole   320
Parsons, Brooks   235
Parsons, Darla   33
Parsons, John T.   342
Parsons, Kimberly   435

Shoemaker, Rebecca   384
Shoff, Robert Scott   209
Shogren, Michael R.   343
Shollenberger, Sydni Ann   396
Short, Maryland   173
Shorts, Linda   327
Shoup, Lori   49
Shourds, Alice M.   246
Shryock, Norma E.   368
Shubin, Erline E.   38
Shugar, Elaine S.   152
Shukla, Pooja   307
Shustin, Ilya   514
Shute, Julie   85
Shutts, Jason Albert   369
Siciliano, Lydia C.   412
Siebelts, Frederick W.   403
Siegel, Allison   502
Siegel, Stanley J.   264
Sievers, Dianna   494
Sigler, Michael   182
Sigsworth, Chad W.   466
Sills, LaRose   360
Silva, Lina   336
Silver, Leigh   74
Silver, Loribeth Ann   312
Silverman, Neil   187
Silverwood, Sasha   295
Simien, Octavia Ruben   184
Simmons, John   372
Simmons, William B.   292
Simms, A. Gail   289
Simon, Stephanie   383
Simpson, John T.   360
Simpson, Toni   111
Sinclair, Aimee   119
Singer, Heather   483
Singer, Susan L.   218
Singh, Jasmin   513
Sink, Cassie   243
Sitner, Ilene   497
Skene, Florence P.   469
Skidmore, Sandra K.   97
Skinner, Gwyne   446
Skjold, Christopher J.   481
Skrzynecky, Elizabeth   401
Skutack, Mary Ellen Davis   517
Slappey, Brandy   254
Slasten, Guennadi   173
Slayter, Robert   99
Sloane, Deborah   532
Slominski, Christine   27
Slowik, Joseph   57
Small, Monique   71
Smalley, Sarah   291
Smillie, Justin   518
Smith, Adam   400
Smith, Angela M.   130
Smith, Beva   36
Smith, Bonnie Jayne   407
Smith, Brandy   245
Smith, C. J.   197
Smith, Carrie F.   238
Smith, Christy   239
Smith, Darryl   30
Smith, Dorae   487
Smith, Doris E.   463
Smith, Elizabeth L.   408
Smith, George   506
Smith Sr., J. F.   112
Smith, J. Stephen   388

Smith, James Lee   507
Smith, Jeanne M.   55
Smith, Jo   50
Smith, Joan W.   377
Smith Jr., John F.   368
Smith, June M.   322
Smith, Justin J.   327
Smith, Lottie D.   490
Smith, Mae   78
Smith, Margie D.   310
Smith, Marissa   173
Smith, Mary Farrow   184
Smith, Melanie L.   174
Smith, Michael   373
Smith, Pamela   388
Smith, Patricia   262
Smith, Richard   282
Smith, Samuel M.   383
Smith, Sherri   205
Smith, Sheryl   94
Smith, Shirley   232
Smith, Sonya C.   280
Smith, Staci   301
Smith, Stephen S.   456
Smith, Suzanne L.   300
Smith, Tara   112
Smith, Tim   118
Smith, Wm. Carl   94
Smithers, Sheila   527
Smothers, Kimberly Sheri   428
Snarr, Muriel B.   432
Snedeker, Harold R.   512
Snow, Cleo   257
Snow, Jon   338
Snyder, Debra   143
Snyder, Doris   493
Snyder, Jessica   163
Snyder, Kelly J.   365
Snyder, Mikel C.   421
Sobtzak, Kim   330
Sokolik, Nadine N.   75
Solinsky, Kimberly Ann   69
Solis, Laverne B.   331
Sonderman, Patrick S.   299
Soon, Mary   431
Sorge, Sarah   101
Soth, Angela Michelle   249
Soto, Matthew W.   415
Sowray, Rachel   207
Spain, Greg   65
Spalding, Laura Beth Hunt   89
Sparks, Annette L.   20
Sparks, Reba L.   294
Spear, Helen B.   509
Spear, Jim   168
Spelman, Nathalie   526
Spence, Natassia Sheree   429
Spencer, Geneva   323
Spencer, Jessica   181
Sperry, Marianne   170
Spevak, Janet   501
Spiegel, Tamzen   201
Spitzer, Oly   418
Sponsler, Todd A.   395
Spore, Heather Lea   487
Sprenger, Joanne   311
Springston, Geraldine   341
Sprofera, Summer L.J   216
Spurio, Brick Mengel   18
Spurlock, L. A.   104
Stacy, Marilyn   316

Stadler, Kelle   314
Stamile, Lorri   442
Stamp, John W.   52
Stancil, Catherine L.   243
Stanke, Anita L.   241
Stanley, Lacie   190
Stansbury, Anita   464
Stanton, Sarah   453
Staples, Wendy   104
Stark, Ginger   339
Starr, Mary Ann   71
Staskowski, Maureen   322
Steckmeyer, Erika   139
Steele, Ann Marie   479
Steele, Bessie C.   119
Steen, Jason B.   164
Steenbergen, Andrew Henry   40
Steene, Mary P.   418
Stefanowicz, Jenn   340
Steidley, T. W.   279
Steinbrunner, Lynn   75
Stelljes, Laura   172
Stenis, Rowena   457
Stephens, Cheri   464
Stephens, Christina   499
Stephens, Debra P.   247
Stephens, John M.   310
Stepp, Rachel E.   302
Sternberg, Denise   500
Stevens, Neil   362
Steward, Christine   469
Stewart, Graham H.   173
Stewart, Mandy   351
Stewart, Marge   345
Stewart, Sherry A.   219
Stickler, Eli   484
Stier, Frances   238
Still, Freda B.   22
Still, Kevin A.   176
Stillwell, Megan J   172
Stiner Sr., Edward R.   485
Stingl, Monika   324
Stipp, Linda Denise   179
Stitt, Viona   457
Stoll, Donald   488
Stoll, Jeremy   185
Stone, Angie   134
Stone, Christopher J.   255
Stone, Robin   298
Stone, Rogelio   108
Storey, Melissa   317
Storm, Jeffrey   52
Storti, Franklin William   9
Story, Elvera   127
Story, John R.   428
Story, Stephanie   263
Stouffer, Jenna   359
Stovall, Charles   135
Strain, Edith   490
Stransky, Louise   313
Strawder, Wanda Little   278
Strawn, Evelyn L.   403
Stream, Gray   82
Strecker, Sara   110
Street, Seminole   203
Streich, Brian   25
Strem, George G.   380
Stribling, Susan   279
Strickland, Christy   259
Strickland, Trinicia   94
Strickland, Wanda L.   109

Stringer, Janice   490
Stringham, Dana Marie   260
Struble, Donna J.   524
Struemph, Pam C.   305
Strupp, Janet K.   365
Strzelecki, Ron R.   454
Stuart, Evelyn   31
Stubing, Jeff   344
Stup, J. Jerry   278
Sudo, Rei   277
Sullivan, Brandi   15
Sullivan, Donna   500
Sullivan, Marsha   434
Sullivan, William John   198
Sundararajan, Anuradha   399
Sundell, Carlin   404
Sunyoger, Mary Antoinette Gallo   50
Surprenant, Jeremy   60
Susedik, Kim   309
Sutherland, Debbie   37
Sutterfield, Dorabeth Dunning   520
Sutton, Regan R.   271
Swagler, Katie   55
Swan-Johnson, Anne   15
Swanson, Niel   323
Swartzlander, Bryan   128
Swayne, Kathy   355
Sweeney, Mary L.   353
Sweeney, Michael   335
Sweet-Gross, Lesa   355
Swidwa, Martin   429
Swing, Mario   63
Swoager, Margaret   343
Szentendrei, Lena   352
Szklenski, Betty A.   254

T

Tabajonda, Valerie   303
Tabet-Bresslauer, Erica   249
Tajin, Christo   405
Talbert, Betty K.   398
Tamez, Amanda   121
Tancredi, David   42
Tankersley, Kristy   438
Tanzymore, Shane Perez   215
Tapp, Robbrina   461
Tappert, Corina Ann   239
Tardera, Marilyn   333
Tascione, Loredana N. Palma   47
Tauriainen, Margery   83
Tavella, Katylynne   315
Taylor, Andrea M. Paglia   242
Taylor, Ashley   251
Taylor, Brooke   406
Taylor, Carla   7
Taylor, Casey   28
Taylor, Clare   252
Taylor, Deborah L.   159
Taylor, Jane R.   492
Taylor, Jeff   72
Taylor, Kevin T.   435
Taylor, Marjorie Moss   369
Taylor, Mary   319
Taylor, Mignon   170
Taylor, Robert N.   395
Taylor, Shirley   223
Taylor, Sissy   215
Taylor, Susan   117
Taylor, T. John   393

Taylor, Timothy 97
Taylor, Tonya H. 102
Taylor, Victoria 454
Tekulve, Traci J. 104
Telikepalli, Anil 142
Tembo, Edson P. 487
Tener, David T. 452
Tennison, Josh 347
Terpko, John E. 79
Terrell, Jamie Lynne Rhoads 519
Terronez, Coe 31
Terry, Christina M. 136
Terry, Jessica 450
Terry, Justin 183
Terry, La Verta L. 321
Teufel, Dawn 238
Thimm, Denice 127
Thomas, Arthur 122
Thomas, Carolyn A. 253
Thomas, Dave A. 141
Thomas, Erika 23
Thomas, Esther M. 239
Thomas, Jennifer 79
Thomas, Kathy 170
Thomas, Paula Y. 393
Thomas, Shannon 95
Thompson, Alice L. 398
Thompson, Andrea 249
Thompson, Bonnie L. 464
Thompson, Daniel 464
Thompson, Darlene "Samihah" 151
Thompson, Eileen 132
Thompson, Loretta M. 188
Thompson, Mandi Rae 170
Thompson, Matt 319
Thompson, Melodie Lynn Clark 81
Thompson, Robert W. 389
Thompson, Wanda Marie 264
Thompson-Dalton, Jean M. 363
Thomsen, Linda 419
Thorley, Milon Wayne 314
Thornbrue, Karen 325
Thornhill, Earl 507
Thornhill, Melissa 368
Thorpe, Aaron 10
Thorpe, Linda C. 440
Thurber, Daniel 399
Tiberi, Prim 209
Tikasingh, Jacqlyn 521
Tillar, Haven A. 529
Timko, Kelly 329
Timley, Eunice 404
Timmer, Ellen M. 249
Timon the Bard 532
Tipple, Bob 517
Tipton, Barbara J. 137
Tipton, Erika 126
Tison, Stephanie 92
Titus, Ron 302
Tjelta, Mark G. 371
Todd, Chrystal 244
Todd Sr., Billy J. 31
Todd, Vermeille Davis 207
Toepfer, Deborah S. 154
Tolbert, Mary J. 56
Toler, Pamela Sue 460
Tolle, Elizabeth 133
Tomaro-Chapman, Kathe 56
Tomasi, Autumn 119
Tomei, Elizabeth 40
Tomlinson, Burgess 40

Topham, Theresa J. 113
Torres, Carmen 124
Torres, Jose A. 347
Touch, Bunthay 481
Tous, Manuel J. 421
Tout, Lori Anne 367
Towne, Merrilyn Williams 90
Townsend, Karen 422
Trammell, Shannon 115
Tran, Carole 156
Tranchina, Antoinette Licari 148
Travers, Tricia 116
Travis, Shawn P. 391
Trepp, Allen 39
Treverton, Chelsea 153
Tri, Khanh 354
Trimmer, Linda M. 55
Trogden, Mickey C. 430
Troncale, Ann 470
Trotter, Donique 506
Trotts, Michael A. 436
Troychak, Stephen 393
True, Victoria 290
Trump, Steve 196
Tsoumakas, Amanda Nicole 39
Tucker, Bertha Taylor 488
Tucker, Jessica 166
Tucker, Megan 310
Tucker, Naomi 447
Tucker, Quennie 384
Tugaoen, Junaliza 362
Tullos, Lisa 364
Tunison, Katie 429
Turner, Andrea 472
Turner, Betty 130
Turner, Courtney N. 247
Turner, Harold 492
Turner III, James M. 518
Turner, Joyce 65
Turner, Karen A. 427
Turner, Tami J. 303
Turse, Andrew 151
Tussey, Oliver 422
Tutor, Kathleen 77
Tuttle, Patricia M. 268
Tuttle, Shica 199
Tverberg, Janice 525
TYG 457
Tyler, Douglas M. 490
Tyler, Thomas S. 273
Tyler, Tonia 453
Tyson, Elana D. 130
Tyson, Wycliffe E. 212

U

Ueberholz, Gloria F. 189
Uhley, Carleen O. 253
Uliasz, Alan G. 40
Underwood, Willie Bruce 463
Unger, Gloria 80
Unruh, Brent 135
Untalan, Johanne 330
Unverzagt, Amy 238
Urba, Toni 270
Usher, Marcella D. 58
Usher, Troy 232

V

Valdesuso, Jan 489
Valdez, Karen 309

Valenti, C. J. 265
Valle, Margot 168
Valles, Norma 349
Van Atta, Margaret 323
Van Buskirk, Afton Ruth 251
Van Cleave, Marcia M. 324
Van Der Sloot, Douglas D. 533
Van Dunk, Vi-Anne 265
Van Hoosen, Sarah 113
Van Meter, Kathy 421
Van Note, Roberta 96
Van Scoy, Nicole 178
Van Skiver, Marla Kay 348
VandeGriend-Olsen, Sara J. 108
VandenBerg, Joyce 177
Vanderbeck, Kathleen 52
Vanderburg, Mandy 452
Vanderwood, Deborah M. 477
Vandrick, Scott A. 220
Vangsness, Lisa Lynne 73
VanOcker, Amy 491
VanReed, Cindy 35
VanSickle, Dani 141
Vantreese, Tina 286
Vargo, Cynthia 405
Vasquez, Jessica M. 434
Vasquez, Veronica J. 116
Vasquez, William L. 300
Vassallo, Matthew A. 177
Vassallo, Raven 106
Vassey, Diane 494
Vaughan, Fran C. 18
Vaughan, Rita 488
Vaughan-Scearce, Ruth 192
Vela, Evelyn 136
Velazquez, Samantha M. 109
Velez, Marie-Reine 88
Verch, Joshua 420
Verde, Loretta 334
Vernon, Cassandra 508
Versace, Paula 288
Vetter, Wendy 99
Vickers, Amanda 253
Vickers, David Preston 161
Vickers, Leslie 340
Viggiano, Nick 50
Vincent, Connie 524
Vineyard, Peggy 111
Vinson, Heather 511
Vinson, Norma 334
Vitale, Joseph M. 377
Viviano, Sarah 272
Vogel, Carolyn 488
Vogel, Deborah 3
Voit, Lisa 167, 494
Volz, Emily 27
Vonau Jr., Walt 293
Vorkink, Christy 41
Vosburgh, Lisa A. 427
Voyles, Pamela 210

W

Waddington, Sam 384
Wadenstierna, Becky 503
Wagener, Ruth C. 98
Wagner, Beth A. 235
Wagner, Crystal Armes 8
Wagner, Dan 147
Waikuny, Rosemary 266
Walden, Donnie 521

Waldon, Tammara Kay 198
Waligorski, Alicia 354
Walker, Don 498
Walker III, Curt T. 45
Walker, James Michael 501
Walker, Silvia 204
Walker, Teresa 277
Walker, Tim 221
Wallace, Jean Lewis 324
Wallet, Ericca 147
Wallin, Vernon 269
Wally, Rosemary 231
Walsh, Heather 516
Walsh, Katie 317
Walsworth, Matthew 428
Walter, Eddie 522
Walton, Ruby Foster 202
Wampole, Felicia M. 243
Wampole, Nanette 354
Wang, Chen 38
Wang, Danny H. 141
Wantula, Stanley 211
Ward, David M. 261
Ward, Jennifer 314
Ward, Kristin 310
Warford, Charleen 400
Warner, Shirley Ann 211
Warnock-Root, Sheryl 107
Warren, Dickie W. 493
Warren, Regina 455
Warren, Sandra L. 267
Warren, Tom 214
Warren, Wendell 208
Washburn, Lori A. 346
Washington, Angela R. 521
Washington, Bob 162
Washington, Ceola 19
Washington, Joan Y. 164
Washington, Lisa 83
Waterman, Christy 478
Waters, Andrea 141
Waters, Anna Rose 244
Watkins, Angie 259
Watkins, Elizabeth Thornton 11
Watkins, V. 216
Waton, Richard B. 395
Watson, Abbie L. 27
Watson, JoDee 319
Watson, Melissa 325
Watts, Denise 484
Watts, Kathy 171
Waugh, Fern M. 480
Wayne, Alan 119
Weaver, Alice Marie Buras Flowers 481
Weaver, Heather S. 486
Weaver, Nancy 370
Webb, Alice 44
Webb, Valerie Cara 192
Weber, Jody 380
Weber, Trisha 225
Webster, Diana 253
Weckstrom, Muriel 341
Wedemeyer, Dorothy M. 494
Weece, Karen M. 173
Weeks, Martha L. 77
Weidner, Heather 506
Weidner, Julie 167
Weigel, Diana J. 496, 525
Weinberg, Sylvia Turk 231
Weiner, C. Gassin 305
Weir, Cheril D. 11

Weiser, Michal 67
Weisman, Judith 412
Weismantle, Regina 224
Weisz, Jasmin 512
Weitzel, Tamara E. 300
Welborn, Hugh 484
Welch, Anne L. 141
Welch, Linda 358
Welcher, Cathy J. 405
Weld, Jessica 59
Weldon, Rainbow 194
Weller, Sharon M. 112
Wells, Andrea 5
Wells, Austin R. 148
Wells, C. 193
Wells, D. Q. 234
Wells, Glen 317
Wells, Miles 323
Wells, T. C. 214
Wells, Tameka 92
Weltman, Peter 230
Wendorff, Chris 246
Wenrick, Marie A. 350
Went, Louise 186
Wernimont, Amy 405
Werth, Meghan 436
Wessels, Sharon L. 205
Wesson, C. N. 304
West, April Dawn 476
West, Bill C. 332
West, Thomas 283
Westaby, Eve 259
Westby, Juandah J. 191
Westover, Robert 390
Wetz, Kim 431
Whatley, Heather 494
Wheelehon, Donna Marie 489
Wheeler, Justin 319
Whipple, K. Haley 455
White, Anika 243
White, Anna H. 29
White, Bobi Jo 468
White, Dana 398
White Sr., Fletcher Lee 240
White, James D. 516
White, Lila B. 67
White, Rick 304
White, Ruby M. 100
White, Zaida E. 200
White-Goudas, Dedra A. 204
Whitehead 296
Whitescarver, Wilda N. 108
Whitesel, Lynn 54
Whiteside, Ruth P. 292
Whitley, Jaclyn 486
Whitley, Sandra 117
Whitmire, Larry A. 341
Whitmore, Elyse J. 24
Whitmore, Stephen 461
Whitney, B. Thomas 391
Whitson, J. Lyle 219
Whittaker, Tabatha Lee 231
Whitten, Dimitri 520
Wibracht, Kitty 452
Wicker, Linda 365
Widgren, Rachel S. 101
Widrich, Sarah 199
Wieman, Karen M. 375
Wiener, Florence K. 16
Wiese, Kathryn S. 173
Wiese, Nita L. 324

Wilcox, Chuck 465
Wilcox, Ruth Edwards 102
Wiles, Frances S. 4
Wilhelmi, Misty 187
Wilkerson, Cassie Lynn 34
Wilkey, Tommie Sue 458
Wilkinson, Ellen 520
Williams, Allen W. 470
Williams, Corrinne 260
Williams, Deborah Ann 144
Williams, Florence Vahey 129
Williams, Glenece 56
Williams, Gwin A. 523
Williams, Hector J. 522
Williams I, Bryan 153
Williams, Janine 488
Williams, Keith R. 313
Williams, LaNiece 417
Williams, Laura 526
Williams, Lena 329
Williams, Mary L. 382
Williams, Michelle 317
Williams, Michelle A. 75
Williams, Neta 74
Williams, Sara 100
Williams, Sheila D. 486
Williams, Tabitha 388
Williams, Tara 460
Williams, Wendy 208
Williams-Avila, Linda Carolee 339
Williamson, Sarah 458
Willrich-Scott, Candace 126
Wilson, Donna 513
Wilson, Dorothy 516
Wilson, Eileen D. 140
Wilson, Emma Bernice 137
Wilson, Helen Margaret 493
Wilson, Karen M. 178
Wilson, Katherine E. 83
Wilson, Kristina 186, 417
Wilson, Matthew W. 185
Wilson, Melissa 170
Wilson, Rusty Jay 91
Wilson, Sadie Draper 306
Wilson, Scott 106
Winberg, Benet M. 241
Winburne, Lisa 378
Wincentsen, Dawn M. 408
Winchester, Margaret J. 50
Wineriter, Randall Scott 113
Wingrove, James A. 529
Winn, Dorene 494
Winter, Sarah 105
Winters, Betty J. 498
Winters, Peggy J. 220
Winters, Terri 197
Wintrow, Linda K. 358
Wise, Ruth 115
Witthuhn, Fred 152
Wittrock, Jane M. 488
Wix, Amy N. 398
Wofford, Stacie Lynn 271
Wojda, Joanna 182
Wojewodzki, Christine 251
Wojner, Sarah 114
Wolentarski, Rebecca 394
Wolf, Thomas D. 220
Wolfe, Barbara 482
Wolfe, Marcus 48
Wolfe, Susan 101
Wood, Barbara Eubank 404

Wood, Naomi Lowry 70
Woodall, Jennifer Becker 186
Woodard, Michelle 180
Woodbury, Sandy 266
Wooden Jr., Thomas 461
Woodley, Jennifer 175
Woodlief, Christa 468
Woods, John G. 326
Woods, Ray 213
Woods, Regina 111
Woods, Wendi R. 231
Woods, William R. 394
Woodson, Donald A. 529
Woodward, Evelyn 24
Woodward, Jill 84
Woodward, Lindsay 46
Woody, Jason K. 412
Wooldridge, Jaqueline F. 531
Woolf, Linda L. 441
Woolsey, Debby 480
Woolson, Nancy L. 118
Work, Lynn 325
Worob, Raymond 197
Wortman, Becky 484, 487
Wright, Christina 121
Wright, Jack E. 487
Wright, Kevin Brian 89
Wright, Loraine P. 381
Wright, Sylvia 392
Wright, Todd 222
Wunderlin, Myrtle L. 184
Wygle, Heidi 491
Wykle, Charles R. 240
Wylde, Lisa 180
Wylde, MH 280
Wyllie, Stanley Clarke 101
Wyrick, John 329
Wyrwa, Daisy 406

Y

Yaker, Judith G. 177
Yannayon, Carla 403
Yarber, Lora Renee 84
Yarborough, Rebecca 290
Yarbrough, Patricia A. 110
Yasparro, Rosemary Muntz 226
Yates, Betsi J. 245
Yearout, Michael P. 76
Yeatts, Phyllis D. 460
Yeoh, Kim Hong 176
Yingling, Heather 493
Yocum, Ava 143
Yomoah, Jennifer 449
Yond, Agnes 247
Yonkman, Fred 25
Young, Beverly 141
Young, Joseph H. 171
Young, Julius Raynard 447
Young, William 299
Younger, Melanie 452
Younger, Patrick A. 302
Younker, Barbara L. 21

Z

Zaborsky, Susan M. 97
Zafra, Doris 527
Zafuto, Patricia 293
Zagiel, Leyna Marie 55
Zahn, Allyn Carol 237
Zahodne, John Michael 433

Zander, Marcus H. 171
Zappier, Sheri 266
Zare-Parsi, Moojan 372
Zaremba, Jason 48
Zaspel, Naomi 347
Zavada, Maria 413
Zeigler, Tami 289
Ziavras, Charles E. 150
Zielsdorf, Ad R. 242
Zimmerle, Walter M. 114
Zimmerman, David 467
Zimmerman, Susan J. 205
Ziskie, Shirley 462
Zmitrovich, Beth 403
Zoellick, Erin Michelle 9
Zoll, Henk G. 505
Zuiderveen, Michael 340
Zunino, Gianna N. 88
Zwettler, Brett 131